Warman's ®

Sports
Collectibles

A Value & Identification Guide

Edited by
Tom Mortenson

Published by

**krause
publications**
The World's Largest Hobby & Collectibles Publisher

700 East State St. • Iola, WI 54990-0001
715/445-2214 • FAX: 715/445-4087 • www.krause.com

Please call or write for our free catalog.
Our toll-free number to place an order or obtain a free catalog is 800-258-0929
or please use our regular business telephone: 715-445-2214
for editorial comment and further information.

Library of Congress Catalog Number: 2001-086510
ISBN: 0-87349-247-1

Printed in the United States of America

Acknowledgments

Several individuals have made contributions which have been incorporated into this Warman's book. While all cannot be acknowledged, appreciation is especially extended to David Craft for his valuable contributions to the baseball, basketball, football and hockey sections. Likewise, special thanks are given to Mark Alan Baker for his tireless work in the auto racing, boxing and figure skating sections. Special appreciation is also extended to Ross Forman for his fine contributions to the bowling, soccer and tennis sections.

Other contributors have exhibited a special dedication by creating, revising or verifying listings and technical data, reviewing market listings, loaning items for photography, lending emotional support or assisting in various ways. They include Chris Ambrosius, Kathy Briquelet, Chuck Furjanic, Don Gulbrandsen, Dan Halverson, Cheryl Hayburn, Kris Kandler, Mike Rodell, Kevin Sauter, Duke Tuomi and Gordon Ullom.

●●●

Sources

The following sources have been utilized for information or to help determine prices for this book:

Baker, Mark Allen. *Sports Collectors Digest's All Sport Autograph Guide*, Krause Publications, Iola, Wis., 1994

Baker, Mark Allen. *Sports Collectors Digest's Baseball Autograph Handbook,* Krause Publications, Iola, Wis., second edition, 1991

Baker, Mark Allen. *Sports Collectors Digest's Complete Guide to Boxing Collectibles,* Krause Publications, Iola, Wis., 1995

Bushing, David. *Sports Collectors Digest's Sports Equipment Price Guide,* Krause Publications, Iola, Wis., 1995

Carpentier, John. *Price Guide to Packers Memorabilia*, Krause Publications, Iola, Wis., 1998

Furjanic, Chuck. *Antique Golf Collectibles, A Price and Reference Guide*, Second Edition Krause Publications, Iola, Wis., 1999

Gracia, Oscar. *Collecting Michael Jordan Memorabilia*, Krause Publications, Iola, Wis., 1998

Larsen, Mark K. *Sports Collectors Digest's Complete Guide to Baseball Memorabilia*, third edition, Krause Publications, Iola, Wis., 1996

Larsen, Mark K. *Sports Collectors Digest's Complete Guide to Football, Basketball & Hockey Memorabilia*, Krause Publications, Iola, Wis., 1995

Lemke, Bob. *Standard Catalog of Baseball Cards*, 10th Edition, Krause Publications, Iola, Wis., 2000

Pope, Kristian and Whebbe, Ray, Jr., *Professional Wrestling Collectibles*, Krause Publications, Iola, Wis., 2000

Malloy, Roderick A. *Malloy's Sports Collectibles Value Guide*, Wallace-Homestead Book Co. Radnor, Pa., 1993

Mortenson, Tom. *Standard Catalog of Sports Autographs*, Krause Publications, Iola, Wis., 2000

Mortenson, Tom. *Standard Catalog of Sports Memorabilia*, Krause Publications, Iola, Wis., 1999

Scott, Richard. *The Charlton Standard Catalogue of Hockey Cards*, Ninth Edition, The Charlton Press, St. Catherines, Ontario, Canada, 1999

Warren, Jim; Haynie, Melanie; Shaver, Jerry and Madigan, Dennis. *Tuff Stuff's Baseball Memorabilia Price Guide*, Tuff Stuff Books, Richmond, Va., 1998

Also, back issues of *Sports Collectors Digest*, Internet auctions and numerous sports memorabilia auction company catalogs have been used for reference, identification, checklist compilation and pricing determination.

●●●

Contents

Acknowledgments and Sources..3
Table of Contents...4
Introduction to Sports Collecting..................................6

A
Auto Racing Collectibles
Die-Cast Cars 12
Plastic Model Kits 20
Autographs...22
Cereal Boxes...25

B
Baseball Collectibles
Introduction 26
Cards..28
Hall of Fame Autographs 49
Equipment 65
Bats...68
Stadium Seats..69
Hartland Statues...70
Starting Lineup Figurines..72
Bobbing Head Dolls...81
Yearbooks..84
Media Guides...93
Sports Illustrated Covers......................................104
World Series Programs..110
Movie Posters..113
Games..114
Pennants...118
Cereal Boxes...121
Press Pins and Medallions 125
Rings, Awards, etc...130

Basketball Collectibles
Introduction 131
Cards..133
Hall of Fame Autographs 142
Equipment 149
Starting Lineup Figurines..151
Media Guides...155
Sports Illustrated Covers......................................178
Books..182
Cereal Boxes...184

Bowling Collectibles
Introduction 185

Boxing Collectibles
Introduction 186
Boxing Hall of Fame Collectibles 187
Autographs...188
Programs...194
Posters 196
Ticket Stubs 197

F
Figure Skating Collectibles
Introduction 201
Autographs...202

Football Collectibles

Introduction 203
Cards. 205
Hall of Fame Autographs 217
Equipment 228
Bobbing Head Dolls and Hartland Statues. 230
Starting Lineup Figurines. 232
Yearbooks 238
Media Guides 244
Sports Illustrated Covers 253
Super Bowl Programs. 257
College Bowl Programs 258
Books 261
Super Bowl Ticket Stubs 264
Games. 265
Rings, Awards, etc. 267
Cereal Boxes. 268

G
Golf Collectibles

Introduction 269
Selected Memorabilia. 270
Autographs 272

H
Hockey Collectibles

Introduction 274
Cards. 276
Hall of Fame Autographs 285
Equipment 294
Media Guides 295
Sports Illustrated Covers 302
Books 303
Starting Lineup Figurines. 304
Cereal Boxes. 306

Horse Racing Collectibles

Introduction 307
Programs. 307
Collectible Glasses 310

O
Olympic Collectibles

Introduction 312
Programs. 314
Cereal Boxes. 315

S
Soccer Collectibles

Introduction 316

T
Tennis Collectibles

Introduction 318
Tennis Autographs 319

W
Wrestling Collectibles

Introduction 321
Wrestling Autographs. 324
Wrestling Figurines 328

Glossary of Hobby Terms 338
Sports Addresses. 340
Sports Web sites 343

Introduction to Sports Memorabilia Collecting

Whether it's a Hall of Famer's game-used uniform or one of the exact replica jerseys made by Mitchell and Ness Co. of Philadelphia, memorabilia comes in all different shapes, styles and price ranges.

Whereas owning a souvenir such as a program from a game is a nostalgic reminder of a certain event, owning an item such as a hockey stick that was handled at one time by Gordie Howe puts a collector a little bit closer to a legendary sporting figure.

Some collectors specialize in a favorite player or team, while others collect on a much broader scale such as an entire sport.

Equipment

Equipment collecting spans the gamut of uniforms, gloves, bats, helmets, sticks, skates and game apparel. Your best chance of obtaining game-used items—if you don't get them directly from the player—is to build a base of experienced, trusted collectors.

There are also books and periodicals available from Krause Publications that will give you great tips and pointers on these collectibles. That might be a wise purchase before you head off to buy that Kobe Bryant game-used Los Angeles Lakers jersey.

Uniforms and Jerseys

Although uniforms have become a highly popular collectible in recent years,
pricing is usually predicated on whether the uniform was worn in games and, even more important, who wore it. There is no way to accurately price uniforms in this guide because the team factor is relatively unimportant, although there is generally a premium on uniforms of defunct teams and uniforms that are more colorful.

However, the more famous and popular the player, the higher the value. For example, an authentic jersey worn by Babe Ruth of the New York Yankees in 1930 brought more than $280,000 in an auction in 2000.

Prices like this are beyond the means of most collectors and are the exception rather than the rule. Some modern uniform jerseys sell for less than $100, but in the case of prominent players, the price will always be higher. Because people attach tremendous importance to whether a uniform is game used, some have been artificially aged and others doctored to make the uniform fit the specifications of a particular player during a particular year. Name tags have been changed and recently made patches aged and sewn on the jersey.

Flannel was the material of choice for uniforms until double-knit polyester was introduced in 1970. By 1973, every team in baseball wore uniforms of this material.

Because so many uniforms are not what they appear, be extremely careful before spending thousands of dollars on what could well be a phony.

Baseball Felt Pennant

Pennants

While almost every kid had a felt pennant tacked it up on his bedroom wall, it's unusual to find a vintage pennant in well-preserved, investment grade condition. Most, measuring 12" x 30", have pinholes in them and can be purchased for less than $50.

Today's versions, often available at stadiums and arenas, are made in large quantities, so look for 1950s and before models, and concentrate on pennants for popular
teams, championship teams, teams that no longer exist, or those that commemorate a specific event.

Although it probably isn't going to offer big returns as an investment piece, a pennant can still add a nice decorative touch to any memorabilia display. Some of the more collectible pennants, are those from Championship and All-Star games. Sometimes the names of the players and coaches were printed on the pennant.

Picture pennants are popular because they enable the collector to know the exact year the pennant was produced. The more elaborate a pennant is, the more desirable it becomes.

Some collectors concentrate on collecting only their favorite team. Taking two pennants from the same era, the more colorful one will usually sell more quickly. Other factors, such as a team's popularity, determine value. Pennants from defunct teams, particularly originals from the Brooklyn Dodgers, Milwaukee Braves and Houston Oilers are highly prized.

Pennants were produced before the 20th century. Prior to the 1930s, pennants were issued sporadically, mostly to championship teams. At that time nearly all teams had felt pennants for sale at stadiums. Designs were relatively simple, with little more than the team's name. In the 1940s and 1950s, multi-colored artwork was added, including team logos, stadiums and, often, names of the players. All of these factors add to a pennant's collectibility.

Felt was the principal material used in pennant manufacturing into the 1960s. After that, polyester took over. Although they vary slightly, most pennants today measure 12 inches at the widest point and are approximately 30 inches long.

Bobby Hull Autographed Jersey

Super Bowl XXIII Press Pin

Pins

Press pins, which have been issued since 1911, are distributed to members of the media by the host team for World Series and baseball All-Star games. The lapel pin provides the reporters legitimate access to cover the game.

Generally, the better looking the pin is, and the better condition it is in, the more valuable it will be. Also, because fewer reporters cover the All-Star game, there are fewer of these pins available when compared to World Series pins.

In general, here's a price range for World Series pins for each decade: 1910s ($2,500-$18,000); 1920s ($375-$4,000); 1930s ($225-$5,000); 1940s ($250-$2,400); 1950s ($125-$500); 1960s ($50-$300); 1970s ($50-$375); 1980s ($25-$175); and 1990s ($50-$150).

Super Bowl pins generally range from $1,540 for Super Bowl I to $125 for Super Bowl XXXIII in 1999.

Prior to the 1890s, pinback buttons usually were made of solid brass or silver. The earliest known example is a brass pinback button for the Cincinnati Red Stockings of 1869, America's first professional baseball team. With each package of Cameo Pepsin Gum purchased in 1896, the manufacturer included a pin of baseball's top stars.

American Nut & Chocolate was the first company to issue a set of pins in the 1930s for each of the 16 Major League teams. These lithographs feature different styles on each pin. These pins sell for approximately $15-$20 each, with no premium for any one item.

Tickets and Ticket Stubs

Super Bowl I Ticket

Ticket stubs do not command high prices unless they are from All-Star, playoff, World Series, NBA Finals or Super Bowl games. Tickets from a game where a significant achievement or record occurred are also worth more than a ticket from a regular season game. Special commemorative tickets and unused tickets often are worth a bit more, too.

Publications

Life Magazine from March 6, 1964

Publications encompass all forms of printed works such as scorecards, programs, books, yearbooks, magazines and media guides.

Periodicals often appear after a particularly memorable season. All clubs issue programs or scorecards while yearbooks have been produced by various teams on a sporadic basis. Some teams have replaced a yearbook with an enlarged, fact-filled program that changes several times a year.

Books

Hardbound Collectible Book

Four main factors determine the value of a book: Condition, scarcity, desirability and edition. Condition greatly affects the value — torn pages, coffee stains and general wear and tear all reduce the value. Lack of a dust jacket also drops the book's value. To be worth top dollar, a book should also be a first printing of a first edition. Books that have little or no value to collectors would be those that are discards from libraries.

Autographs add to the book's value. It can be signed by the author or the subject, or both. But a biography of a superstar does not automatically mean that book is valuable. For example, there is no scarce Mickey Mantle biography. But there is a hard to find biography of Rocky Colavito; since it is scarcer, it is more valuable.

There is no guarantee that a book will appreciate dramatically, so the average collector is advised to collect books he enjoys for his own sake. You might consider specializing team, player, genre, topic. You can find books all over at garage sales, card shows, library sales, antiquarian book sales, hobby publications, used book stores and used book dealers.

Media Guides

Sports media guides evolved from large sheets of white or colored paper in varying sizes that were folded in half or thirds and bore the title "roster." Early publications were issued as spring training guides and contained the names of all players invited to training camp. They usually listed the team's schedule of exhibition games and were issued only to members of the press. Because of limited circulation, these items are extremely rare. As collector items, they also have limited appeal because they typically are visually unattractive and contain few photographs other than those used on the covers.

Hockey Media Guide

The Cleveland Indians issued what is generally considered the first authentic press, radio and TV guide in 1948. It is a 55-page guide that contains player biographies and other information on the eventual world champion Indians. The Cincinnati Reds actually issued a comparable piece in 1934 entitled "Press Information, Cincinnati Reds." The inside front piece of the 32-page publication states, "Official Handbook of Information compiled by the Cincinnati Reds Baseball Company" and includes photos of the players as well as front office personnel and Crosley field, home of the Reds. By all standards, this publication would have to rank as the very first press radio guide, while the 1948 Indians' publication would be the first modern press, radio and TV guide.

In recent years, the title "media" guide has been affixed to publications now containing hundreds of pages and issued by the public relations offices of the various Major League teams. Because these media guides are generally not available to the general public, they are increasing in popularity among publications collectors. Some collectors attempt to get guides for every team in both leagues, but the majority concentrate on obtaining only those of their favorite teams.

Although professional teams make their yearbooks available to the general public, some will sell media guides as well.

Team Yearbooks

Basketball Yearbook

Although some exist from the 1940s and earlier, it wasn't until the late 1950s that what we now consider as yearbooks were produced by professional teams on a regular basis. Most yearbooks from the 1960s offer collectors an affordable collectible for less than $100. Those from the 1940s and 1950s can bring top dollar, depending on scarcity and age.

To be classified as a yearbook, generally a publication must have photographs of every player on the 25-man roster, plus biographies and statistics. Media guides, which debuted in the 1940s, were given to radio, television and newspaper beat reporters who covered professional teams during the season. They are designed to provide almost every imaginable kind of biographical and statistical tidbits to the reporters; the reporters quite often were the only source from which collectors could obtain a media guide, but in recent years teams have made copies available to fans.

Boston Braves Public Relations Director Billy Sullivan is generally accepted as the father of the modern baseball yearbook. He published the first one for the Braves in 1946. However, there were many previous attempts at yearbook-type publications, some issued as early as 1880.

Many championship souvenir booklets were issued by various publishers to commemorate pennant-winning seasons. In 1934, the *Detroit Free Press* published a pictorial booklet featuring pictures, biographies and statistics of the 1934 American League champs.

The Chicago Cubs also had a yearbook-type publication as early as 1934. Publication was continuous through 1942, and since the books had photos and stats on the various players, they would certainly be classified as yearbooks. In 1941, the Brooklyn Dodgers came out with *The Dodgers, 1941, Today and Yesterday in Brooklyn Baseball.* After winning the 1941 National League pennant, they reissued it with additional information on the championship season, changed the cover, renamed it *Dodger Victory Book*, and sold it during the 1942 season.

In the late 1940s and early 1950s, some Major League teams began issuing some type of yearbook. In 1952 Jay Publishing Co. began producing *Big League Books*, which became the official yearbook for many baseball teams. Several, including the New York Yankees and Cleveland Indians, continued issuing their own yearbook while allowing Jay to publish *Big League Books* yearbooks for both teams. When there are two for the same year, the official yearbook generally commands a slightly higher price.

Scorecards and Programs

Many fans purchase a souvenir program in which to keep score when they attend a professional game, as reading material, or to have autographed (which increases its value). Unscored programs are preferred, but if the scoring is done neatly the program does have intrinsic value; it provides a history of what happened and can trigger fond memories.

Condition is a key factor in determining a program's value. The nicer it is, the more valuable it will be. In general, football programs from the 1930s are worth approximately $95-$150; those, from 1940-45 are worth $75-$100; those from 1946-50 are worth $50-$75, those from the 1950s are worth $35-$50; those from the 1960s are worth $20-$40; those from the 1970s are worth $7-$10; those from the 1980s are worth $6-$8; and those from the 1990s are worth $6 or less.

In general, NBA programs from the 1960s are $25-$40, while those from the 1970s are $15-$25. Special events bring more. Hockey programs from the 1930s can bring $75-$100, while those from the 1940s can bring $50-$75. Programs from the 1960s can bring $35-$50, while those from the 1970s are worth $25-$35. Programs from the 1980s are up to $30. Regular season programs from before 1900 might bring $700-$900; 1900-1910 will be in the $250-$700 range; 1910-19, $90-$300; 1920-29, $50-$100; 1930-39, $35-$50; 1940-49, $25-$40; 1950-59, $20-$35; 1960-69, $10-$35. Everything after 1970 is usually less than $20.

1934 Detroit Tigers Booklet

1963 NFL Championship Program

The most valuable programs are generally World Series programs, which have been produced since 1903, and Stanley Cup, NBA Finals, and Super Bowl programs. World Series programs, especially from championship teams, are in more demand than those from All-Star games and regular season games. Since 1974, only one program has been produced for the World Series for both teams participating. This holds true for Super Bowl programs. The first two are in great demand.

A plain black-and-white scorecard will pale by comparison to a scorecard featuring an attractive design, color or both.

Historical significance is another consideration. Programs and scorecards from pennant-winning teams command higher prices, as do these items from a team's first year. There always has been added interest in programs from defunct teams.

Schedules

Schedules come in all shapes and sizes. While most collectors associate schedules with the small multiple-folded colorful paper or cardboard items in abundance today, they have been issued in every conceivable form over the years. Pencils, rulers, metal discs, cups and glasses, and postcards are only a few of the unique forms schedules have taken.

Because they are given away by ball clubs, sponsors and other commercial enterprises, the modern schedules are relatively inexpensive. Most are extremely colorful with tremendous eye appeal. A brief letter and a self-addressed stamped envelope sent to any major league team requesting a current schedule would almost always receive a favorable response. Collector

friends in other locales are excellent sources. Wherever you see a large supply, make sure you take some extras to trade with friends in other areas.

Always check the back of the schedule to see if the ad is different. The front is frequently the same, but because different sponsors make them available, they will imprint their message on the back. Particular images on the front of the schedule add to its collectibility. For example, if a club decides to feature a star player, it will have more value than one with a generic image. Schedules featuring stadiums are especially popular, while those showing a new facility in its first year command a premium.

The most valuable modern schedules are those from the first year of a team. A true schedule collector will try to find at least one from each year his favorite team has operated. Other premiums are placed on schedules of pennant-winning and world championship teams.

With everything being relative among schedules of equal value, the most colorful ones with the greatest eye appeal will be selected first. Schedules fit well in protective sleeves, don't take up much space, make a marvelous display, and are among the fastest-growing collectibles.

Team schedules offer collectors an inexpensive alternative to the big ticket items that may anchor a fan's collection. The limits are endless. The easiest way to add to your collection is to contact the professional teams for season ticket information.

Because they are used for advertising purposes, the schedules for each team can have a variety of different sponsors each year. Thus, in addition to being available from the team, they can be found in all sorts of places—restaurants, banks, sporting goods stores, liquor stores, radio stations, motels and hotels, ticket outlets, convenience stores, and kiosks along interstate highways.

Condition plays a factor in a schedule's value. It is more valuable if it isn't damaged, ripped or torn or marked on. Also, schedules for defunct teams carry a slight premium as well, as do those that are scarce localized versions and those featuring team or player photos.

In general, here are values: 1901-1909 ($175); 1910-19 ($125); 1920-29 ($100); 1930-39 ($45); 1940-49 ($35); 1950-59 ($30); 1960-69 ($20); 1970-79 ($15); 1980-1999 ($3).

Championship Events

Championship programs, such as from World's Heavyweight Championship fights and postseason baseball games, have been issued since the 1800s.

Programs pertaining to any of these events command top dollar and are highly desirable among collectors. Pennants, pins, programs, and ticket stubs from these events exist.

World Series

1917 World Series Program

World Series programs were issued by each of the two teams representing their various leagues prior to 1974. After 1974, only one generic program was issued annually. In some cases competing teams added supplemental pages for games played in their home parks, but in many cases the ballpark edition was the same in both parks and also available at newsstands and through mail order. League Championship Series programs prepared exclusively by the competing teams offer original designs and information pertinent to the specific event.

The last time World Series programs were produced by the respective teams was 1973.

The most valuable ticket stubs have seat numbers, which are generally printed in a different color ink in a separate press run. Those without, generally from the 1940s and 1950s, and sold in large blocks, are usually of little or no value because they are artist's proofs. World Series ticket prices vary tremendously and are often determined

A 1950 Pittsburgh Pirates Baseball Schedule.

1946 Boxing Program

by the event itself. For example, a ticket stub from the 1956 World Series would generally run $50. However, a stub from Game 5 at Yankee Stadium, in which Don Larsen pitched the only perfect game in World Series history, commands about $300.

Commemoratives

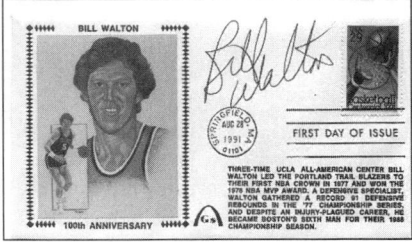

Commemorative Cachet

Commemorative covers and postcards is a category that is ideally suited for sports collecting.

Famous athletic events and individual player accomplishments can be celebrated and remembered long after they occur.

Commemorative covers or cachets usually depict an achievement and often contain a postmark from the nearest U.S. Post Office. Autograph(s) can add extra value and importance to the items. Notable cachet producers include Gateway Stamp Co., Historic Limited Editions Z Silk Cachets, and Wild Horse Cachets.

Also included in this category are Hall of Fame art postcards. Perez-Steele Galleries has issued series of postcards since 1980; generally, these cards range from $5-$15 unsigned, with a few exceptions. Autographed postcards are also more valuable. Goal Line Hall of Fame postcards, which honor pro football's best, are gener-

Goal Line Football HOF Postcard

Highland Mint Medallion

ally $3-$4, with a few exceptions.

Chicagoland Processing Environment offers commemorative limited edition medallions paying tribute to athletes who have set milestones or broken records. Team efforts have also been recognized on the company's one-troy-ounce silver medallions, which are officially licensed by their respective leagues. In general, the medallions will bring $35-$60 each, but sets will bring $125-$150.

Highland Mint offers medallions and cards honoring players from each of the four major sports. The company creates replicas of superstar players' trading cards in bronze, silver and gold varieties.

Determining Pricing

Another determining factor in pricing the memorabilia is how elaborate the item is. For example, take two scorecards from 1890. One containing numerous pages and player profiles would command considerably more than a sheet of folded cardboard. This axiom applies to everything. The more elaborate and attractive the item is, the higher the value.

Pricing is hardly an exact science because many factors are involved. What a dealer pays for an item he intends to resell is very much a determining factor. Location also plays a key role. For example, Boston Celtics memorabilia would command a higher price in New England than it would in another major league market or in a location thousands of miles away. This guide takes that into consideration, as well as placing the same value on similar items from the same era. A premium is placed on items from a particular team's inaugural and championship years. These items usually command a premium of at least 10 percent, and this guide reflects that premium.

All pricing in this book is predicated on the item being in excellent to mint condition. Prices on items in lesser condition should be reduced significantly, as much as 50 percent in some cases. In the case of books, those with dust jackets generally bring twice what those without do. Condition is paramount to an item's value.

Selling Memorabilia

Dealers and collectors are using auctions more frequently to dispose of their collections or particular items. They run auctions in various sports publications such

as *Sports Collectors Digest*, go to sports auction houses or offer items on one of the Internet auction companies, such as eBay. The best way to approach an auction is to determine beforehand the price you are willing to pay and stick to that figure. Although you may not have the winning bid and be able to obtain a particular piece of memorabilia, you'll be a lot more disappointed if you overpay. Be careful, and remember that in virtually every case more than one of a particular item exists.

When offering an item directly to a dealer, realize that his objective is to resell that piece. Therefore, you could usually expect to receive 50 percent, or less, of an item's value. Since the dealer has overhead, he must purchase accordingly in order to make a profit. Don't hesitate to shop around to other dealers or collectors. If you prepare yourself properly, you'll know ahead of time what to expect.

Buying at Auctions

Buying at auctions can be a fun, challenging and interesting way to acquire that treasured sports memorabilia you desire. But if you're not familiar with how auctions are run, you may want to keep a few things in mind. Being informed will allow you to make smarter bids and get more satisfying results.

* Examine the merchandise. Of course, this isn't possible in phone or mail auctions, but when attending an auction in person, arrive early. Examine the items for sale to be sure of their condition. Scout the competition, too. As you attend more auctions, you'll recognize some of the same faces, and get a better handle on what particular people will be bidding on. Likewise, in phone/mail auctions, ask a lot of questions about the items you will be bidding on to avoid future regrets or hassles. Ask for a catalog or photos if available.

* Register early. To avoid tying up bidding lines, register early—even the night before if possible. For phone auctions, don't call at the final hour if you haven't already registered.

* Set a limit for yourself. Before the auction, set a limit on how much you are willing to spend on each item. Allow a little flexibility. It's very easy to get caught up in the excitement of bidding at a live auction and spend more than you intended. You may end up hating the item you won in an auction. Consult a price guide whenever possible.

* Bid wisely. Don't open with an outrageously high bid—if you're the only bidder, you may end up paying too much. But don't open with a laughably low bid either. You may not be taken seriously.

*Honor your bid. If your bid wins, you bought the piece—simple as that, right? It may sound elementary, but too often

auction companies are stiffed by bidders who won't pick up or pay for items. It's a surefire way to ruin future relationships with auction houses.

Avoiding Auction pitfalls

Caveat emptor—Latin for "Let the buyer beware."

That phrase offers good advice for collectors who have never bought items at auction.

Although most people in the auction field are honest, a few unscrupulous people exist in any business.

How do bidders become confident in the items they bid on? Ask questions and read the rules before you bid. Find out about the reputation of the auction company. Does it stand behind its guarantees?

Inexperience Can Be Costly

The biggest problem novice bidders face is paying too much for items due to their lack of experience.

Get to the auction early. Ask questions like, "How does this autograph compare to other signatures of the athlete?"

Look at items carefully, and set a limit of what you're going to pay. The more knowledge you can acquire, the better off you're going to be.

Presale estimates—price ranges of what items are expected to sell for—aren't mandatory but they can be helpful. It gives you a starting point, so you're not starting out too high or too low.

Dealers Face Risks, Too

Bidders are not the only ones who face risks at auctions. Dealers must be wary of people who don't pay—although this doesn't always happen because bidders are usually required to sign contracts called bid sheets that list the amount of the bid. In addition, because many collectors are willing to spend $5-$25 for auction catalogs, dealers believe they are serious bidders.

Some dealers will accept partial payments, but that's not common. In addition, dealers must also take into account the month or two it can take for a check to clear from an absentee bidder.

Some dealers charge buyer's premiums —usually 10-15 percent tacked onto the bid —to help offset the costs of postage, ads, labor and rental space.

Phone Auctions: A Growing Trend

Auctions are generally divided into live or "on premise" auctions, in which bids are made in person, and open or telephone auctions, in which bidders phone or fax in bids.

As busy as people are today, phone auctions seem to be the craze. People can bid from the comfort of their home. The flip side of this is that it's harder to know exactly what you're getting.

Photos and descriptions of items are very important in this kind of auction.

Live Auctions Best for Novices

Going to the auction is the best way to see what's there. Those starting out can see what they're getting and pick up the merchandise on the spot. They can also meet with other collectors and see what kind of interest is out there for specific pieces.

While high-end items tend to get more publicity, auctions also offer better values than many collectors realize. You can find not only rare items at auctions, but some good bargains as well.

While it's true auction prices can sometimes be misleading because some people will bid a lot for an item they really want, auctions, in general, serve as a good frame of reference for people out of touch with current prices.

Look for quality, not just the lowest price. If you're only worried about bidding low, you might not be getting the quality item you want.

If you're going out of town after placing your bid, you might consider making a sealed bid in which you have a range with a maximum limit. Otherwise you might prefer a call back to see how your bid fares to other bidders.

Perhaps the best advice to a new bidder is know the rules and know your options within the rules.

Buying and Selling on the Internet

When you think about it, it almost seems wrong to use the Internet to buy and sell antiques. Most collectors, after all, are attracted to antiques and collectibles for their nostalgic value—reminders of the days when life was easy and people did their chatting in the parlor. But suddenly here we are in the 21st century, and if you're not on the Internet, you might as well be living in a cave. The Internet, sooner than anyone thought, has invaded nearly every aspect of our lives—including our collecting.

Although online auctions are an exhilarating part of the Internet collecting experience, they are certainly not the only thing this new "dot.com" technology has to offer. Collectors online can find collecting clubs, chat with other collectors, research the history of their favorite collectibles, check price guides, view photos, explore new collecting categories, peruse dealers' for sale lists, and more.

Getting Started

The key to navigating around the Internet—whether you're after collectibles or recipes—is to get to the Internet site you're looking for as quickly as possible. If you know the Web site address (that's the string of letters that starts with www. and usually ends with com), there's no problem; simply type it in. But, even if you don't know the address (or if a Web site even exists), there's still no problem—thanks to the magic of search engines. Search engines allow you to type in a key word or phrase (such as "*Sports Illustrated*" or "cereal boxes") and uncover a list of all Web sites dealing with the subject.

There are more than a dozen search engines available to Internet users. Their basic operation is similar, although each operates in its own distinct way that might make some search engines more attractive than others for your particular needs. There are even at least two Internet sites designed to help take the confusion out of selecting a search engine. You'll find them at: www.notess.com and at www.searchenginewatch.com.

Whatever search engine you use, there are some general guidelines to follow:

Refine your search. If you begin your search too broadly (for example, typing in the word "sports"), your search may yield too many sites that are not really what you want. Adding a modifier (such as "sports pennants") targets your search more directly.

Double-check your spelling. This may seem elementary, but a too-hasty keystroke may turn "yearbook" into "yaerbook," which would yield no results and merely be a waste of time.

Use "bookmarks" once you find a site you like. Adding certain sites to your "favorites" list saves time when you want to return to these sites at a later date.

Become familiar with your regular search engine. Each search engine has its own design, layout and search techniques. Get to know the search engine you use and see how well it works for the tasks you generally perform. If one search engine is not satisfactory, try another one.

If you get lost or have a problem, most search engines offer a "Help" or an "Advanced Search" section to guide you along and give you tips for more effective searching.

Take advantage of "links." Most Web sites have "links" to related sites that might also be of interest. Clicking on these "links" often provides more information than the original site.

●●●

Auto Racing Collectibles

1988 MAXX Dale Earnhardt card

If baseball is "Our National Pastime," then auto racing is "Our National Fixation." The sport has grown exponentially over the past few decades and seems boundless in its popularity. This phenomenon has also led to many avenues of marketing including a vast plethora of memorabilia.

Collectors of auto racing memorabilia have numerous options including autographs, plastic model kits, die-cast and trading cards–just to name a few. These collectibles are focused primarily on four segments of the sport: Stock Car (NASCAR Winston Cup/Busch, etc.), drag racing (NHRA Winston), Indy car (CART/IRL) and Formula One. The most popular are stock car collectibles. The organizational chaos in recent years with Indy car has hurt its collectibility, but hopefully not for long. Formula One collectibles have always lagged in the United States primarily due to the lack of exposure of this racing segment. But the negative factors in these two segments have been compensated for by the overwhelming increase in stock car and drag racing collectibles.

Since autographs, plastic model kits, die-cast and cereal boxes are the most popular areas for collectors we will center our attention on these segments.

Die-Cast

One of the most popular areas of racing memorabilia is die-cast models. Die-cast collectors are often die-hard racing fans. Like any area of the hobby, there are those who collect purely for fun and some only for investment. For those who collect only the merchandise of their favorite driver, die-cast can offer an interesting option. From airplanes to panel trucks, die-cast has a fascinating product offering for the racing enthusiast.

It's not unusual for die-cast collectors to purchase more than one of each product—one for fun and one for investment. One can be used to open up, examine or display and the other to preserve in its original state without altering the packaging, which is the preferred method for the investor. Die-cast original packaging is often as important to the value of the collectible as the replica itself. Therefore, if you are collecting die-cast merchandise for investment, preserving the item in its original state is of paramount importance.

Production is always a concern to die-cast collectors, especially when value is the objective. Many collectors prefer limited number or serialized offerings over mass marketed replicas. If you collect memorabilia from only the top 10 racing teams, then limited edition quality products are probably an excellent collecting strategy. With so many products on the market today, accurate production numbers can be a key to value.

In recent years, accuracy in duplication has become a critical factor to the serious collector. From proper color shades to proper decals, all characteristics of a replica are examined for accuracy.

Size

Die-cast collectibles come in many different shapes and sizes, making them a bit confusing for beginning collectors. Once the scales and ratios are understood however, the world of die-cast can become a fascinating element of the hobby. If you can remember studying fractions, such as 1/2, or 1/3, during your math lessons in school, then die-cast scales will be easy to understand. A fraction consists of a numerator (the top number) and a denominator (the bottom number).

So in die-cast the bigger the bottom number gets, the smaller the car. Just as a half is bigger than a quarter, so is a 1/18 die-cast car bigger than a 1/24 or 1/43 scale version.

The intriguing element of die-cast is that scales or ratios actually apply to the real thing. For example, if you were to take a 1/24 die-cast car of the late Dale Earnhardt's (No. 3) Goodwrench Chevrolet Monte Carlo and make it 24 times larger, it would be life-sized.

Typically die-cast manufacturer's use scale sizes of 1/8, 1/24, 1/43, 1/64 and 1/87. Other scales such as 1/16, 1/25, 1/55 and 1/96 can be used, but they are less common.

For years toy manufacturers have produced automotive replicas to a 1/64 scale size. Recognizing this fact, the most common size for racing replicas is 1/64. Many model manufacturers popularized the 1/24 scale and today it is a common size for most die-cast banks. But in the dynamic world of die-cast, what is uncommon today may be typical tomorrow.

Production

Die-cast production varies from manufacturer to manufacturer, with most companies following both competitor and consumer trends. Some companies may produce 10,000 to 15,000 NASCAR transporters, and between 15,000 and 20,000 cars, depending upon scale and driver popularity, while promotional products and limited editions typically have lower production runs of 2,500 to 5,000. Manufacturers can differ dramatically depending upon the type of product release or antici-

Trix Cereal Johnny Lightning
Racing Dreams die-cast car

pated popularity. For example, Racing Champions produced 1/64 scale 1993 Premier Edition Transporters that ranged in production from 1,500 (Sterling Marlin/Raybestos) to 15,000 (Jeff Gordon/DuPont).

Products

Not all die-cast manufacturers keep or release a product checklist to the public, although doing so can only enhance a collector's willingness to buy additional items from a quality manufacturer's product line. White Rose Collectibles of York, Pa., is one example of a company that circulates checklists of their products. Fortunately for collectors, companies that don't produce or circulate checklists are often monitored by many hobby periodicals, thereby bringing the information into collectors' hands.

It is not unusual for die-cast manufacturers to produce a number of versions of a product. For example, Action Racing Collectibles produced three versions of the Dale Earnhardt Winston Select Silver 1/64 car. The Platinum Series version, which comes with a SkyBox trading card, had a production of about 70,000. This product was distributed through the manufacturer's distributors, Chevy dealerships, Earnhardt's racetrack trailers and Action's track trailer. A second version came in a blister pack with black windows added. This version had a production of 20,000 and the same distribution as its predecessor. The final "hood open" version was for the Racing Collectors Club of America (RCCA), a "Club Item" release. This version had a production of 20,000 and was sold to club members or through Action's track trailer.

Variations

A die-cast collectible, like any manufactured product, is subject to a certain amount of variation, whether intended or not by the manufacturer. Typically this variation occurs with the replica – wheels, tires, body style, its detailing – decals, paint, accessories – cards, stands or packaging. For a more detailed understanding of variations contact a local vendor or consult some of the valuable resources serving the hobby.

Pricing

The stock car listings included here are provided as a guide and do not represent an offer to buy or sell on the part of any party. The focus of the listings is stock cars, as they are the most popular element of die-cast. Because of space restrictions, Transporter listings are not included. Within this listing, releases are organized by manufacturer, scale (larger fractions mean bigger pieces), year, car number and driver. For each issue a price range (low to high), average price (Mean Price/Mint Condition) and key releases are provided. As anticipated Winston Cup Champions, Winston Cup rookie standouts, vintage/limited paint schemes, and commemorative issues garner the most interest with die-cast collectors.

Selected Die-Cast Price Guide Stock Cars

1998-99 Action Racing - Collectibles 1:18
Price Range: $50-$180, Average: $120
Key Releases:
3 D. Earnhardt/Bass Pro . . . .$75-$150
3 D. Earnhardt, Jr./AC Delco '99 . . . . .$75-$150
20 T. Stewart/Home Depot . . . .$100-$170
24 J. Gordon/Superman . . . .$80-$150
24 J. Gordon/ NASCAR Racers . . . . .$100-$200
31 D. Earnhardt Jr./ Wrangler . . . .$75-$150

2000 Action Racing - Collectibles 1:18
Price Range: $50-$175 Average: $125
Key Releases:
3 D. Earnhardt/GW Taz No Bull . . . .$100-$175

1993-95 Action Racing - Collectibles 1:24
Price Range: $25-$450, Average: $75
Key Releases:
2 D. Earnhardt/Wrangler '81 Pont . . .$150-$300
2/43 D. Earnhardt/R. Petty 7&7 . . . . .$125-$200
3 D. Earnhardt/Wrangler '81 Pont . . .$150-$275
3 D. Earnhardt/Wrangler '85 MC . . .$150-$300
3 D. Earnhardt/Wrangler '87 MC . . .$250-$450
3/24 D. Earnhardt/J. Gordon BYS . . . .$75-$150
11 B. Elliott/Bud . . . .$100-$175
15 D. Earnhardt/Wrangler '83 T-Bird $200-$325
Comments: These releases have shown significant pricing variations. All Dale Earnhardt releases are highly sought by collectors and have

exhibited substantial price increases.

1996 Action Racing - Collectibles 1:24
Price Range: $25-$300, Average: $60
Key Releases:
3 D. Earnhardt/Olympic, Green bx . .$100-$150
15 D. Earnhardt/Wrangler '82 TB . . . .$75-$150
43 B. Hamilton/5 Car set CW . . . . .$150-$300
Comments: All Dale Earnhardt releases are highly sought by collectors and have exhibited substantial price increases.

1997 Action Racing - Collectibles 1:24
Price Range: $15-$200 Average: $60
Key Releases:
3 D. Earnhardt/Wheaties . . . .$100-$150
3 D. Earnhardt/Wheaties Snap-On . . .$125-$200
14 S. Park/Burger King . . . .$100-$150
24 J. Gordon/DuPont Premier P . . . .$100-$200

1998 Action Racing - Collectibles 1:24
Price Range: $15-$700, Average: $70
Key Releases:
1 D. Waltrip/Pennzoil . . . .$50-$100
1 S. Park/Pennzoil . . . .$50-$100
3 D. Earnhardt/GW Plus Bass Pro . . . .$70-$125
3 D. Earnhardt/GW Plus Gold . . . . . .$400-$700
3 D. Earnhardt, Jr./AC Delco . . . .$150-$250
9 J. Nadeau/Power Puff . . . .$150-$200
12 J. Spencer/Zippo . . . .$100-$175
24 J. Gordon/DuPont Chromalusion . .$75-$125
24 J. Gordon/DuPont Chromalusion MT . . . . . .
. . . .$100-$150
24 J. Gordon/DuPont Mac Tools . . . . .$75-$100
31 D. Earnhardt, Jr./Sikkens Blue . . .$100-$150
31 D. Earnhardt, Jr./Wrangler . . . . . .$150-$200
36 E. Irvan/ M&M's . . . .$100-$125
44 T. Stewart/Shell Small Soldiers . . . .$60-$120

1998 Action Racing - Collectibles/NAPA 1:24
Price Range: $35-$100, Average: $70
Key Releases:
28 B. Baker/ NAPA '80 Olds . . . .$75-$100
Comments: For gold car releases add twice the value.

1999 Action Racing - Collectibles 1:24
Price Range: $25-$400, Average: $70
Key Releases:
3 D. Earnhardt/GW Crash '97 MC . . .$200-$400
3 D. Earnhardt, Jr./Superman . . . . . .$100-$150
8 D. Earnhardt, Jr./Budweiser . . . . . .$100-$125
8 D. Earnhardt, Jr./Bud Track Cars . .$100-$125
17 M. Kenseth/DeWalt . . . .$100-$150
20 T. Stewart/ Home Depot . . . .$150-$250
20 T. Stewart/ Home Depot BW . . . .$150-$200
24 J. Gordon/ Superman . . . .$60-$125
24 J. Gordon/NASCAR Racers . . . . .$70-$125

2000 Action AP 1:24
Price Range: $15-$25, Average: $20

2000 Action Racing - Collectibles 1:24
Price Range: $25-$400, Average: $65
Key Releases:

3 D. Earnhardt/GW Peter Max . . . . . .$100-$150

3 D. Earnhardt/GW Platinum 75th Win . . . .
. . . .$220-$425

3 D. Earnhardt/GW Taz . . . .$100-$225

8 D. Earnahrdt, Jr./Budweiser . . . .$75-$125

18 B. Labonte/IB Frankenstein . . . . . .$75-$125

24 J. Gordon/DuPont Millennium . . . .$70-$125

24 J. Gordon/DuPont Sign . . . .$70-$125

24 J. Gordon/DuPont Peanuts . . . . . .$70-$125

2000 J. Gordon/Action Fantasy Car . .$100-$225

2000 Action/QVC For Race Fans Only 1:24
Price Range: $75-$300, Average: $250
Key Releases:
3 D. Earnhardt/GW Tax Red . . . . . .$200-$300
3 D. Earnhardt/GW 75th Win Platinum . . . .
. . . .$200-$300

1998-99 Action Racing Collectibles 1:32
Price Range: $25-$75, Average: $50
Key Releases:
3 D. Earnhardt, Jr./AC Delco . . . .$40-$75

1993-95 Action Racing Collectibles 1:64
Price Range: $5-$60, Average: $20
Key Releases:
2 D. Earnhardt/Wrangler '81 Pontiac PLS
. . . .$20-$40
3 D. Earnhardt/Wrangler '84 MC PLS .$25-$40
3 D. Earnhardt/GW '88 MC PLS . . . . .$25-$40
6 M. Martin/ Folgers PLS . . . .$30-$60
7 A. Kulwicki/ Army . . . .$25-$50
7 A. Kulwicki/ Hooter's '92 . . . .$20-$40
16 W. Dallenbach/Roush Racing VT . . .$20-$40
24 J. Gordon/ DuPont ACR . . . .$25-$50
24 J. Gordon/ DuPont '94 Lumina PLS .$25-$50

1996 Action Racing Collectibles 1:64
Price Range: $5-$250, Average: $14
Key Releases:
3 D. Earnhardt/Olympic Green Box . . .$15-$30
3 D. Earnhardt/16 car set . . . .$150-$250
5 T. Labonte/Kellogg's Iron Man . . . . .$15-$30
Comments: The alcohol and tobacco related cars are packaged in acrylic, while others are in platinum series blister packs.

1997 Action Racing Collectibles 1:64
Price Range: $3-$60, Average: $10
Key Releases:
3 D. Earnhardt/Wheaties . . . .$15-$30
3 D. Earnhardt/Wheaties HO Sl . . . . . .$20-$50
17 D. Waltrip/ PA 7 car set . . . .$30-$60
23 J. Spencer/Camel . . . .$15-$30
24 J. Gordon/DuPont Premier . . . .$15-$25
24 J. Gordon/Lost World HO Sl . . . . . .$15-$25
27 R. Wallace/MGD '90 GP . . . .$15-$25
Comments: The alcohol and tobacco related cars are packaged in acrylic, while others are in platinum series blister packs.

1998 Action Racing Collectibles 1:64
Price Range: $4-$50, Average: $12
Key Releases:
3 D. Earnhardt, Jr./AC Delco . . . .$15-$25

9 J. Nadeau/Power Puff . . . .$15-$30

24 J. Gordon//DuPont Chromalusion . . .$25-$50

31 D. Earnhardt, Jr./Sikkens . . . .$15-$25

31 D. Earnhardt, Jr./Wrangler . . . .$20-$30

Comments: The alcohol and tobacco related cars are packaged in acrylic, while others are in platinum series blister packs.

1999 Action Racing Collectibles 1:64
Price Range: $4-$40, Average: $12
Key Releases:
20 T. Stewart/Home Depot . . . .$25-$40
27 C. Atwood/Castrol . . . .$15-$30
28/88 K. Irwin/D. Jarrett/ Batman & Joker
. . . .$15-$35
Comments: The alcohol and tobacco related cars are packaged in acrylic, while others are in platinum series blister packs.

2000 Action AP 1:64
Price Range: $3-$8, Average: $7
Key releases: None

2000 Action Racing Collectibles 1:64
Price Range: $5-$30, Average: $12
Key Releases:
3 D. Earnhardt/Taz No Bull . . . .$15-$30
8 D. Earnhardt, Jr./Budweiser . . . .$12-$25
18/20 B. Labonte/T. Stewart P . . . .$10-$20
NNO Armed Forces 5 car set P . . . . . .$15-$30
Comments: The alcohol and tobacco related cars are packaged in acrylic, while others are in platinum series blister packs.

2000 Action Total Concept 1:64
Price Range: $7- $25, Average: $15
Key Releases:
3 D. Earnhardt/GW Peter Max . . . .$10-$25

1995-96 Action Racing Collectibles SuperTrucks 1:64
Price Range: $3-$15, Average: $8
Key Releases:
16 R. Hornaday/Papa John's Pizza . . . . .$10-$15

1993-95 Action/RCCA 1:24
Price Range: $20-$1000, Average: $75
Key Releases:
2/43 D. Earnhardt/R. Petty 7 & 7 . . . .$150-$200
3 D. Earnhardt/Wrangler '84 MC Blue . . . .
. . . .$200-$300
3 D. Earnhardt/Wrangler '84 MC . . .$200-$300
3 D. Earnhardt/Wrangler '87 MC Blue$400-$500
3 D. Earnhardt/GW '88 MC FB . . . .$400-$600
3 D. Earnhardt/GW '94 Lumina . . .$150-$250
3 D. Earnhardt/GW '95 MC . . . . . .$150-$250
3 D. Earnhardt/GW Silver BW . . . .$700-$1000
3 D. Earnhardt/GW Silver RW . . . . .$550-$800
6 M. Martin/Folgers . . . .$250-$400
18 D. Jarrett/Interstate Batteries . . . .$75-$125
23 J. Spencer/Smokin' Joe's . . . .$225-$350
24 J. Gordon/DuPont '95 MC . . . . .$150-$250
30 M. Waltrip/Pennzoil . . . .$60-$100
42 K. Petty/Pumpkin Special . . . . . .$150-$250
51 N. Bonnett/Country Time . . . . . .$125-$200

1999 Action Racing Jeff Gordon car

94 B. Elliot/Thunderbat . . . .$90-$175
Comments: This series has exhibited significant price variations.

1996 Action/RCCA 1:24
Price Range: $25-$250, Average: $65
Key Releases:
5 T. Labonte/Kellogg's Iron Man . . .$100-$175
15 D. Earnhardt/Wrangler '82 T-Bird .$65-$115
27 R. Wallace/Kodiak '89 GP . . . . .$150-$250
43 B. Hamilton/STP 5 car set BW . . .$150-$250

1997 Action/RCCA 1:24
Price Range: $20-$300, Average: $65
Key Releases:
3 D. Earnhardt/Goodwrench . . . .$150-$250
15 D. Earnhardt/ '82 T-Bird . . . .$150-$200
17 D. Waltrip/PA 7 car set . . . .$200-$300
24 J. Gordon/DuPont Premier . . . . . .$100-$175

1997 Action/RCCA Elite 1:24
Price Range: $30-$400, Average: $100
Key Releases:
3 D. Earnhardt/Goodwrench . . . .$250-$400
3 D. Earnhardt/GW Plus . . . .$150-$250
3 D. Earnhardt/Wheaties Gold # . . . .$175-$250
3 D. Earnhardt/Wheaties Pewter # . . .$150-$200
14 S. Park/Burger King . . . .$150-$250
24 J. Gordon/Dupont . . . .$150-$250
24 J. Gordon/Dupont Premier . . . . . .$200-$350
24 J. Gordon/Lost World . . . .$150-$250

1998 Action/RCCA Elite 1:24
Price Range: $40-$450, Average: $150
Key Releases:
1 J. Gordon/Baby Ruth . . . .$150-$200
3 D. Earnhardt/GW Plus Daytona . . .$125-$200
3 D. Earnhardt/AC Delco . . . .$250-$450
5 T. Labonte/Kellogg's Corny . . . . . .$125-$200
12 J. Spencer/Zippo . . . .$200-$350
23 J. Spencer/No Bull . . . .$125-$200
24 J. Gordon/DuPont . . . .$125-$200
24 J. Gordon/DuPont Chromalusion .$150-$300
31 D. Earnhardt, Jr./Sikkens . . . .$150-$250
36 E. Irvan/M&M's . . . .$125-$200
44 T. Stewart/Shell . . . .$150-$225
300 D. Waltrip/Flock Special . . . . . .$125-$200

1999 Action/RCCA Elite 1:24
Price Range: $80-$500, Average: $165
Key Releases:
2 R. Wallace/Harley-Davidson . . . . .$125-$200
3 D. Earnhardt/Wrangler . . . .$125-$200

Johnny Lightning
2000 CBS Sports car

3 D. Earnhardt, Jr./AC Delco ......$125-$250
3 D. Earnhardt, Jr./AC Delco Last Lap$125-$225
3 D. Earnhardt, Jr./Superman ......$125-$225
5 T. Labonte/K-Senitals ....$125-$200
5 T. Labonte/Rice Krispies ....$125-$200
8 D. Earnhardt, Jr./Budweiser .....$125-$200
8 D. Earnhardt, Jr./Budweiser Tracks .$125-$200
17 M. Kenseth/DeWalt Ford ....$125-$225
18 B. Labonte/Interstate Batteries ...$150-$225
19 M. Skinner/Yellow Freight ......$125-$200
20 T. Stewart/Home Depot ....$350-$500
20 T. Stewart/Habitat ....$150-$250
22 W. Burton/Caterpillar ....$125-$225
23 J. Spencer/ No Bull ....$125-$200
24 J. Gordon/Superman ....$125-$225
24 J. Gordon/Pepsi ....$125-$225
27 C. Atwood/Castrol ....$125-$200
31 D. Earnhardt, Jr./Sikkens White ..$125-$250
31 D. Earnhardt, Jr./Wrangler .....$125-$250
33 K. Schrader/Skoal ....$125-$200
33 K. Schrader/Skoal Red ....$125-$200

2000 Action/RCCA Elite 1:24
Price Range: $100-$500, Average: $175
Key Releases:
3 D. Earnhardt/2000 Test Car ......$125-$200
3 D. Earnhardt/GW Taz No Bull ....$150-$300
8 D. Earnhardt, Jr./2000 Test Car ...$150-$250
24 J. Gordon/DuPont Peanuts ......$150-$250
24 J. Gordon/DuPont Winston .....$300-$500

1998 Action/RCCA Gold 1:32
Price Range: $50-$90, Average: $75
Key Releases: None

1991 Action/RCCA Olds Series 1:64
Price Range: $3-$30, Average: $12
Key Releases: None

1991 Action/RCCA T-Bird Series 1:64
Price Range: $3-$40, Average: $16
Key Releases:
15 D. Earnhardt/Wrangler ....$20-$40

1993-95 Action/RCCA 1:64
Price Range: $4-$100, Average: $25
Key Releases:
1 J. Gordon/Baby Ruth REV ....$40-$100
3 D. Earnhardt/GW Silver HO ....$75-$110
6 M. Martin/Folgers P ....$30-$60
6 M. Martin/Strohs Light 2 cars .....$30-$60
42 K. Petty/CL Pumpkin HO ....$35-$60

1996 Action/RCCA 1:64
Price Range: $6-$80, Average: $20

Key Releases:
43 B. Hamilton/STP 5 car set ....$50-$80
Comments: Most hoods open.

1997 Action/RCCA 1:64
Price Range: $6-$80, Average: $20
Key Releases:
3 D. Earnhardt/Wheaties ....$25-$50
17 D. Waltrip/PA 7 car set ....$50-$80
24 J. Gordon/Lost World w/card set ....$30-$50
Comments: All car hoods open.

1998 Action/RCCA 1:64
Price Range: $8-$40, Average: $20
Key Releases:
3 D. Earnhardt/AC Delco ....$30-$45
Comments: All car hoods open.

1999 Action/RCCA 1:64
Price Range: $9-$60, Average: $20
Key Releases:
20 T. Stewart/Home Depot ....$40-$65
Comments: All car hoods open.

2000 Action/RCCA 1:64
Price Range: $8-$40, Average: $20
Key Releases:
3 D. Earnhardt/GW Taz ....$20-$40

1993-98 Ertl 1:18
Price Range: $25-$600, Average: $75
Key Releases:
23 C. Little/John Deere Auto ....$350-$600
24 J. Gordon/DuPont WRC B .....$500-$600
43 B. Hamilton/STP 5-car set .....$125-$250
59 R. Pressley/Alliance ....$250-$325
Comments: Series exhibits significant pricing
variation.

2000 Hot Wheels Crew's Choice 1:24
Price Range: $20-$80, Average: $40
Key Releases:
45 A. Petty/Sprint PCS $85

2000 Hot Wheels Deluxe 1:24
Price Range: $12-$50, Average: $25
Key Releases:
45 A. Petty/Sprint $55

1999 Hot Wheels Track Edition 1:43
Price Range: $7-$15, Average: $15
Key Releases: none
Comments: Release includes a 1:64 car.

1997 Hot Wheels Collector Edition Track
Edition 1:64
Price Range: $5-$250, Average: $20
Key Releases:
44 K. Petty/Hot Wheels white box ...$150-$250

1999 Hot Wheels Collector Edition 1:64
Price Range: $2-$25, Average: $6
Key Releases:
43/44/45 J. Andretti/K. Petty/A. Petty Gen.
......................................$15-$30

43/44/45 J. Andretti/J. Hen./K. Petty/A. Petty 50th
(4 car) ....$15-$30

1999 Hot Wheels Collector Edition Pit Crew
1:64
Price Range: $2-$20, Average: $4
Key Releases:
9 J. Nadeau/Dextor's Lab ....$10-$20
58 R. Craven/Turbine ....$10-$20

1999 Hot Wheels Collector Edition Test Track
1:64
Price Range: $8-$20, Average: $20
Key Releases: None
Comments: Treasure Hunt series limited to
15,000.

1999 Hot Wheels Collector Edition Trading Paint
1:64
Price Range:$8-$20, Average: $2
Key Releases: None
Comments: Treasure Hunt series limited
to 15,000.

2000 Hot Wheels Crew's Choice 1:64
Price Range: $6-$50, Average: $15
Key Releases:
45 A.Petty/PCS ....$25-$50

2000 Hot Wheels Deluxe 1:64
Price Range: $3-$25, Average: $5
Key Releases:
26/44/94 J. Ben./K.Petty/B. Elliott Toy Story 2
..................................$15-$30
45 A. Petty/Sprint PCS ....$15-$25

2000 Hot Wheels Track Edition 1:64
Price Range: $4 - $25, Average: $10
Key Releases:
45 A. Petty/Sprint ....$15-$30

1998 Johnny Lightning Stock Car Legends 1:64
Price Range: $6-$15, Average: $12
Key Releases: None

1990-92 Matchbox White Rose Super Stars 1:64
Price Range: $2-$50, Average: $5
Key Releases:
3 D. Earnhardt/GM BX 90 ....$25-$50
92 NDA/White Rose Coll.BL 92 .....$25-$40

1993 Matchbox White Rose Super Stars 1:64
Price Range: $2-$35, Average: $5
Key Releases:
92 NDA/White Rose Coll.BL 92 .....$20-$35

1994 Matchbox White Rose Super Stars 1:64
Price Range: $2-$25, Average: $5
Key Releases:
43 R. Combs/French's Black Flag BL ..$15-$25
94 NDA/MB WRC ....$15-$25

1995 Matchbox White Rose Super Stars 1:64
Price Range: $3-$30, Average: $5
Key Releases:
3 D. Earnhardt/Gold 7-Time SSA .....$20-$35

1995 Matchbox White Rose SuperTrucks 1:64
Price Range: $3-$5, Average: $5
Key Releases: None

1996 Matchbox White Rose Super Stars 1:64
Price Range: $3-$25, Average: $5
Key Releases:
24 J. Gordon/DuPont SSA . . . .$15-$25

1997 Matchbox White Rose Super Stars 1:64
Price Range: $3-$75, Average: $6
Key Releases:
2 R. Wallace/Miller Lite Bottle . . . .$50-$75
25 R. Craven/Budweiser Bottle . . . .$40-$60
40 R. Gordon/Coors Light Bottle . . . . .$40-$60
75 R. Mast/Remington Shell . . . .$35-$50

1996 Press Pass 1:64
Price Range: $100-$175, Average: $175
Key Releases:
Comments: Includes 1:64 car along with a Burning Rubber II card.

1995-96 Racing Champions 1:18
Price Range: $15-$400, Average: $35
Key Releases:
25 K. Schrader/Bud HO chrome . . . .$200-$400
43 B. Hamilton/STP 5-car set . . . . . .$100-$200

1996 Racing Champions 1:18
Price Range: $25-$60 (Hobby release)
Average: $30
Price Range: $175-$400 (Gold release)
Average: $375

1991-92 Racing Champions 1:24
Price Range: $10-$1,000, Average: $30
Key Releases:
1 J. Gordon/Baby Ruth . . . .$600-$1,000
9 J. Bessey/AC Delco . . . .$400-$600
25 B. Venturini/Rain X . . . .$250-$500
55 T. Musgrave/Jasper . . . .$450-$800
63 C. Bown/Nescafe . . . .$450-$800
Comments: This issue can exhibit significant pricing variations. Packaged in black box.

1993 Racing Champions 1:24
Price Range: $8-$125, Average: $25
Key Releases:
2 D. Allison/True Value IROC . . . .$50-$100
14 T. Labonte/Kellogg's . . . .$75-$100
24 J. Gordon/DuPont . . . .$50-$125
28 D. Allison/Havoline Blk Wht . . . . .$60-$100
48 S. Smith/Ameritron Batt. . . . .$75-$125
59 A. Belmont/FDP Brakes . . . .$60-$100
Comments: Packaged in red box.

1994 Racing Champions 1:24
Price Range: $8-$125, Average: $20
Key Releases:
14 T. Labonte/MW Windows . . . .$75-$100
23 H. Stricklin/Smokin' Joe's . . . .$75-$125
33 B. Labonte/Dentyne . . . .$60-$125
Comments: Packaged in red or black box.

1995 Racing Champions Previews 1:24
Price Range: $10-$40, Average: $20
Key Releases:
98 J. Mayfield/Fingerhut . . . .$25-$40

1995 Racing Champions 1:24
Price Range: $10-$120, Average: $20
Key Releases:
24 J. Gordon/DuPont . . . .$40-$80
24 J. Gordon/DuPont SS . . . .$50-$100
24 J. Gordon/DuPont SS HO . . . .$65-$120
Comments: Packaged in red box.

1996 Racing Champions 1:24
Price Range: $10-$300, Average: $20
Key Releases:
25 K. Schrader/Bud chrome . . . .$150-$300
31 M. Skinner/Realtree HO . . . .$40-$80
43 B. Hamilton/STP 5 car set . . . . . .$60-$100
43 B. Hamilton/STP 5 car TS . . . . . .$75-$150
96 D. Green/Busch chrome . . . .$150-$250

1997 Racing Champions 1:24
Price Range: $10-$100, Average: $16
Key Releases:
9 L. Speed/Univ. of Nebraska . . . .$40-$80
25 R. Craven/Bud Lizard 3 car set . . . .$50-$100
94 B. Elliott/Mac Tonight 3 car set . . .$50-$100

1997 Racing Champions Stock Rods 1:24
Price Range: $10-$40, Average: $20
Key Releases:
10 T. Labonte/Spooky Loops . . . .$25-$45

1998 Racing Champions 1:24
Price Range: $10-$150, Average: $25
Key Releases:
23 J. Spence/No Bull . . . .$100-$150
28 K. Irwin/Havoline Mac Tools . . . .$75-$150
97 C. Little/John Deere P . . . .$75-$100

1998 Racing Champions Reflections of Gold 1:24
Price Range: $12-$75, Average: $25
Key Releases:
6 M. Martin/Valvoline . . . .$30-$75

1998 Racing Champions Stock Rods 1:24
Price Range: $6-$45, Average: $15
Key Releases:
37 B. Elliott/McDonald's Gold . . . . . .$15-$40
48 T. Labonte/Kellogg's Gold . . . .$20-$40
54 B. Elliott/McDonald's Gold . . . . . .$15-$40
58 B. Elliott/McDonald's Gold . . . . . .$15-$40
67 B. Elliott/McDonald's Gold . . . . . .$15-$40

1998 Racing Champions Stock Rods Reflections of Gold 1:24
Price Range: $10-$50, Average: $25
Key Releases:
1 B. Elliott/McDonald's . . . .$20-$50
3 T. Labonte/Kellogg's . . . .$20-$50
5 M. Martin/Valvoline . . . .$20-$50
9 T. Labonte/Kellogg's . . . .$20-$50

1999 Racing Champions 1:24
Price Range: $8-$50, Average: $16,
Key Releases:
45 A. Petty/Spree . . . .$25-$50

1999 Racing Champions Platinum 1:24
Price Range: $15-$75, Average: $40
Key Releases:
5 T. Labonte/Kellogg's . . . .$30-$75
5 M. Martin/Valvoline . . . .$30-$75
94 B. Elliott/Drive Thru . . . .$30-$75

1999 Racing Champions Trackside 1:24
Price Range: $35-$100, Average: $50
Key Releases:
45 A. Petty/Spree . . . .$55-$120

1993 Racing Champions Premier 1:43
Price Range: $10-$75, Average: $20
Key Releases:
7 A. Kulwicki/Hooters BX . . . .$15-$25
98 D. Cope/Bojangles . . . .$40-$75

1994 Racing Champions 1:43
Price Range: $2-25, Average: $5
Key Releases:
24 J. Gordon/DuPont Coke Win . . . . . .$15-$25

1994 Racing Champions Premier 1:43
Price Range: $8-$25, Average: $18
Key Releases: None

1995 Racing Champions Premier 1:43
Price Range: $10-$70, Average: $45
Key Releases:
24 J. Gordon/Brickyard Winner . . . . . .$40-$75

1989 Racing Champions Flat Bottom 1:64
Price Range: $45-$150, Average: $75
Key Releases:
3 D. Earnhardt/Goodwrench . . . .$100-$150

1990 Racing Champions 1:64
Price Range: $15-$150, Average: $50
Key Releases:
3 D. Earnhardt/Goodwrench . . . .$100-$150
14 A.J. Foyt/Buick . . . .$75-$125
16 L. Pearson/Buick White Bump . . . .$75-$125
42 K. Petty/Buick Blue White . . . .$75-$125
42 K. Petty/Lum Blue White . . . .$75-$125

1991 Racing Champions 1:64
Price Range: $2-$150, Average: $10
Key Releases (NASCAR Properties):
3 D. Earnhardt/Lumina . . . .$100-$150
21 N. Bonnett/Old Ford . . . .$50-$100
27 R. Wallace/Pontiac MGD . . . .$50-$100
28 D. Allison/Old Ford . . . .$50-$100
Comments: Three varieties of this release: Earnhardt on the back of the blister pack; NASCAR Properties on the stand; Petty on the back of the blister pack. The NASCAR Properties on the stand variation is the rarest.

1992 Racing Champions 1:64
Price Range: $1-$100, Average: $5
Key Releases:
1 J. Gordon/Baby Ruth . . . .$60-$120

1992 Racing Champions Premier 1:64
Price Range: $5-$40, Average: $25
Key Releases:
3 D. Earnhardt/Goodwrench . . . .$20-$40

1993 Racing Champions 1:64
Price Range: $2-$45, Average: $7
Key Releases:
22 B. Labonte/Maxwell House . . . .$25-$50

1993 Racing Champions Premier 1:64
Price Range: $3-$50, Average: $5
Key Releases:
7 A. Kulwicki/Hooter's . . . .$20-$40
31 N. Bonnett/Mom-n-Pop's . . . .$25-$50

1993 Racing Champions PVC Box 1:64
Price Range: $4-$75, Average: $20
Key Releases:
27 H. Stricklin/McDonald's (250 produced) . . . .
. . . .$25-$50
68 B. Hamilton/Country Time . . . .$40 -$75

1994 Racing Champions 1:64
Price Range: $2-$40, Average: $6
Key Releases:
24 J. Gordon/DuPont . . . .$15-$30
24 J. Gordon/DuPont BYS . . . .$10-$20
33 H. Gant/NS . . . .$20-$40

1994 Racing Champions Hobby 1:64
Price Range: $2-$15, Average: $4
Key Releases:
24 J. Gordon/DuPont . . . .$8-$15
Comments:
Packaged in yellow boxes add $3.

1994 Racing Champions Premier 1:64
Price Range: $3-$50, Average: $10
Key Releases:
7 A. Kulwicki/Army . . . .$15-$30
24 J. Gordon/DuPont . . . .$15-$30
33 B. Labonte/Dentyne . . . .$25-$50

1994 Racing Champions Premier Brickyard 400 1:64
Price Range: $4-$75, Average: $7
Key Releases:
3 D. Earnhardt/Goodwrench . . . .$20-$35
24 J. Gordon/DuPont . . . .$40-$75
Comments: Packaged in purple box.

1994 Racing Champions Previews 1:64
Price Range: $2-$8, Average: $5
Key Releases: None

1995 Racing Champions 1:64
Price Range: $2-$30, Average: $4
Key Releases:
14 T. Labonte/MW Windows . . . .$15-$30
24 J. Gordon/DuPont (all variations) . . .$15-$25

1995 Racing Champions Matched Serial Numbers 1:64
Price Range: $4-$25, Average: $7
Key Releases:
24 J. Gordon/DuPont . . . .$12-$25

1995 Racing Champions Premier 1:64
Price Range: $3-$30, Average: $6
Key Releases:
24 J. Gordon/DuPont . . . .$15-$30
94 B. Elliott/McDonald's . . . .$10-$20

1995 Racing Champions to the Maxx 1:64
Price Range: . . . .$4-$10
Average: $7
Key Releases:
24 J. Gordon/DuPont . . . .$5-$10

1996 Racing Champions Previews 1:64
Price Range: $2-$18, Average: $4
Key Releases:
24 J. Gordon/DuPont . . . .$8-$18

1996 Racing Champions 1:64
Price Range: $2-$100, Average: $7
Key Releases:
43 B. Hamilton/5 car 25th TS . . . .$60-$100
43 B. Hamilton/5 car 25th Ann. . . . . . .$15-$30
43 B. Hamilton/5 car 25th Ann. HO . . .$30-$50
94 B. Elliott/10-time Popular Silver . . .$45-$80

1996 Racing Champions Hobby 1:64
Price Range: $4-$100, Average: $10
Key Releases:
25 K. Schrader/Budweiser Silver . . . . .$50-$100
29 S. Grissom/Cartoon Net. 5-car set . .$25-$50
43 B. Hamilton/STP 5-car set . . . .$30-$60

1996 Racing Champions Silver Chase 1:64
Price Range: $30-$200, Average: $60
Key Releases:
24 J. Gordon/DuPont . . . .$100-$200

1997 Racing Champions 1:64
Price Range: $2-$4, Average: $4
Key Releases:
5 T. Labonte/Kellogg's 2-car set . . . . . .$15-$25
97 NDA/www.racingchamps.com . . . . .$10-$20

1997 Racing Champions Premier w/Medallion 1:64
Price Range: $4-$30, Average: $8
Key Releases:
9 L. Speed/Univ. of Nebraska . . . .$15-$30

1997 Racing Champions Premier w/Medallion/Silver Chase 1:64
Price Range: $40-$150, Average: $80
Key Releases:
5 T. Labonte/Kellogg's . . . .$100-$150

1997 Racing Champions Premier Silver Chase 1:64
Price Range: $30-$125, Average: $50
Key Releases:
5 T. Labonte/Kellogg's . . . .$80-$130

1998 Racing Champions 1:64
Price Range: $2-$50, Average: $4
Key Releases:
6 M. Martin/Kosei . . . .$20-$30
23 J. Spencer/No Bull . . . .$10-$30
23 J. Spencer/No Bull Gold . . . .$10-$30
26 J. Benson/Betty Crocker . . . .$25-$50
40 S. Marlin/Coors Light Gold . . . .$15-$40

1998 Racing Champions Gold w/Medallion 1:64
Price Range: $6-$80, Average: $15
Key Releases:
17 M. Kenseth/Lycos.com . . . .$25-$50
97 C. Little/John Deere P . . . .$40-$80

1998 Racing Champions Signature Series 1:64
Price Range: $2-$6, Average: $6
Key Releases: None

1998 Racing Champions Stock Rods 1:64
Price Range: $2-$20, Average: $6
Key Releases:
79 B. Elliott/McDonald's Gold . . . .$15-$20
87 B. Elliott/McDonald's Gold . . . .$15-$20
96 T. Labonte/Kellogg's Corny Gold . . .$15-$20
112 T. Labonte/Kellogg's Corny Gold . .$15-$20

1998 Racing Champions Toys 'R Us Gold 1:64
Price Range: $2-$15, Average: $6
Key Releases:
1 T. Labonte/Kellogg's (all varieties) . . . .$6-$15
5 M. Martin/Valvoline (all varieties) . . . .$6-$15
94 B. Elliott/McDonald's . . . .$6-$15

1999 Racing Champions 1:64
Price Range: $2-$20, Average: $4
Key Releases:
6 M. Martin/Zerex . . . .$5-$10
45 A. Petty/Spree . . . .$10-$20

1999 Racing Champions Chrome Chase 1:64
Price Range: $6-$20, Average: $13
Key Releases:
6 M. Martin/Zerex . . . .$10-$20
36 E. Irvin/M&Ms . . . .$10-$20
60 M. Martin/Winn Dixie . . . .$10-$20

1999 Racing Champions Chrome Signature Series 1:64
Price Range: $8-$30, Average: $15
Key Releases:
6 M. Martin/Zerex . . . .$15-$30
6 M. Martin/Valvoline . . . .$15-$30
94 B. Elliott/Drive Thru . . . .$15-$30

1999 Racing Champions Gold w/Medallion 1:64
Price Range: $6-$30, Average: $12
Key Releases:
5 T. Labonte/Kellogg's . . . .$15-$30
6 M. Martin/Valvoline . . . .$15-$30
60 M. Martin/Winn Dixie . . . .$15-$30
94 B. Elliott/Drive Thru . . . .$15-$30

1999 Racing Champions Petty Collection 1:64
Price Range: $4-$15, Average: $10
Key Releases:
70 R. Petty/Plymouth Superbird ....$8-$15

1999 Racing Champions Trackside 1:64
Price Range: $15-$50, Average: $25
Key Releases:
45 A. Petty/Spree ....$25-$50

1999 Racing Champions 24K Gold 1:64
Price Range: $8-$30, Average: $15
Key Releases:
5 T. Labonte/Kellogg's ....$15-$30
6 M. Martin/Valvoline ....$15-$30

1997 Revell Club 1:18
Price Range: $70-$200, Average: $150
Key Releases:
5 T. Labonte/Tony the Tiger ....$125-$200

1997 Revell Club 1:18
Price Range: $40-$160, Average: $80
Key Releases:
3 D. Earnhardt/Wheaties ....$100-$150
23 J. Spencer/Camel ....$100-$150
24 J. Gordon/Lost World ....$100-$150

1998 Revell Club 1:18
Price Range: $100-$150, Average: $150
Key Releases:
3 D. Earnhardt Jr./AC Delco ....$200-$300

1998 Revell Club 1:18
Price Range: $40-$200, Average: $110
Key Releases:
31 D. Earnhardt Jr./Wrangler ....$100-$200

1999 Revell Club 1:18
Price Range: $100-$175, Average: $160
Key Releases:
31 D. Earnhardt/Goodwrench ......$100-$175

1999 Revell Club 1:18
Price Range: $50-$175, Average: $115
Key Releases:
20 T. Stewart/Home Depot ....$100-$175

1993-95 Revell Club 1:24
Price Range: $8-$400, Average: $30
Key Releases:
1 J. Gordon/Baby Ruth RCI ....$300-$400
Comments: Increased interest in this release during the past year.

1994 Revell Hobby 1:24
Price Range: $10-$50, Average: $20
Key Releases:
24 J. Gordon/DuPont ....$25-$50

1995 Revell 1:24
Price Range: $10-$50, Average: $20
Key Releases:
24 J. Gordon/DuPont ....$30-$50

Revell Johnny Benson Cheerios

1996 Revell 1:24
Price Range: $12-$50, Average: $20
Key Releases:
24 J. Gordon/DuPont ....$30-$50

1996 Revell Collection 1:24
Price Range: $20-$400, Average: $35
Key Releases:
5 T. Labonte/Honey Crunch ....$250-$400

1997 Revell Club 1:24
Price Range: $50-$350, Average: $95
Key Releases:
5 T. Labonte/Spooky Loops B ......$150-$225
23 J. Spencer/No Bull ....$225-$350

1997 Revell Collection 1:24
Price Range: $25-$350, Average: $50
Key Releases:
5 T. Labonte/Spooky Loops ....$100-$165
23 J. Spencer/No Bull ....$225-$350

1997 Revell Hobby 1:24
Price Range: $15-$75, Average: $35
Key Releases:
5 T. Labonte/Spooky Loops ....$35-$70
18 B. Labonte/Interstate Batteries TMS..$50-$75

1997 Revell Retail 1:24
Price Range: $10-$200, Average: $25
Key Releases:
1 NDA/Mac Tools ....$50-$75
17 D. Waltrip/PA 6 car set ....$130-$210

1998 Revell Club 1:24
Price Range: $60-$250, Average: $120
Key Releases:
1 S. Park/Pennzoil ....$150-$200
3 D. Earnhardt, Jr./AC Delco ......$150-$250
23 J. Spencer/No Bull ....$125-$175
24 J. Gordon/Chromalusion ....$150-$200

1999 Revell Club 1:24
Price Range: $60-$175, Average: $110
Key Releases:
20 T. Stewart/Home Depot ....$100-$175
24 J. Gordon/Superman ....$100-$175

1999 Revell Collection 1:24
Price Range: $40 -$175, Average: $110
Key Releases:
20 T. Stewart/Home Depot ....$100-$175

Revell Goodwrench Dale Earnhardt Sr.

20 T. Stewart/Habitat ....$100-$150
24 J. Gordon/Superman ....$75-$100

2000 Revell Club 1:24
Price Range: $50-$120, Average: $115
Key Releases: None

2000 Revell Collection 1:24
Price Range: $40-$275, Average: $85
Key Releases:
3 D. Earnhardt/Test Car ....$125-$225
8 D. Earnhardt, Jr./Test Car ....$125-$250
24 J. Gordon/Test Car ....$200-$300

1996 Revell Collection 1:64
Price Range: $4-$50, Average: $10
Key Releases:
5 T. Labonte/Honey Crunch ....$30-$50

1997 Revell Collection 1:64
Price Range: $5-$35, Average: $13
Key Releases:
5/18 T. Labonte/2-car tin set ....$20-$35
6/60 M. Martin/Valvoline/WD 2-car tin $20-$35

1997 Revell Hobby 1:64
Price Range: $4-$30, Average: $8
Key Releases:
17 D. Waltrip/Parts America 7-car set ..$15-$30

1997 Revell Retail 1:64
Price Range: $3-$6, Average: $6
Key Releases: None

1998 Revell Collection 1:64
Price Range: $5-$40, Average: $12
Key Releases:
24 J. Gordon/Chromalusion ....$20-$40

1998 Revell Hobby 1:64
Price Range: $4-$20, Average: $10
Key Releases:
3 D. Earnhardt, Jr./AC Delco ....$10-$20

1999 Revell Collection 1:64
Price Range: $8-$40, Average: $15
Key Releases:
20 T. Stewart/Home Depot ....$25-$40
20 T. Stewart/Habitat ....$20-$35

1999 Team Caliber 1:24
Price Range: $35-$250, Average: $75
Key Releases:
12 J. Mayfield/Mobil 1 chrome .....$150-$250

Winner's Circle Lifetime Series Dale Earnhardt Sr. car

2000 Team Caliber Owner Series 1:24
Price Range: $40-$200, Average: $100
Key Releases:
6 M. Martin/Valvoline Gold ......$100-$200
6 M. Martin/Eagle One Gold ......$100-$200
45 A. Petty/Sprint PCS ....$150-$200

2000 Team Caliber Preferred Series 1:24
Price Range: $30-$150, Average: $80
Key Releases:
45 A. Petty/Sprint PCS ....$100-$150

2000 Team Caliber Owner Series 1:64
Price Range: $10-$60, Average: $25
Key Releases:
45 A. Petty/Sprint PCS ....$30-$60

2000 Team Caliber White Knuckle Racing 1:64
Price Range: $4-$20, Average: $10
Key Releases: none

1997 Winner's Circle 1:24
Price Range: $10-$40, Average: $25
Key Releases:
3 D. Earnhardt/Wheaties ....$20-$40
24 J. Gordon/(all varieties) ....$15-$35

1998 Winner's Circle 1:24
Price Range: $10-$40, Average: $25
Key Releases:
3 D. Earnhardt/GW Silver ....$20-$40

1999 Winner's Circle 1:24
Price Range: $10-$40, Average: $25
Key Releases:
3 D. Earnhardt, Jr./AC Delco Superman $25-$50

2000 Winner's Circle 1:24
Price Range: $15-$50, Average: $40
Key Releases:
3 D. Earnhardt/GW Taz ....$25-$50

1999 Winner's Circle 1:43
Price Range: $6-$30, Average: $20
Key Releases:
20 T. Stewart/Home Depot ....$15-$30

1997 Winner's Circle Lifetime Series 1:64
Price Range: $4-$80, Average: $15
Key Releases:
3 D. Earnhardt/SAC Delco '96 MC 2/12 .$40-$80

1998 Winner's Circle 1:64
Price Range: $5-$30, Average: $15

Winner's Circle 2000 Jeff Gordon car

Key Releases:
3/3 D. Earnhardt/GW 25th/Wrangler (2 car)
..............................$15- $30

1998 Winner's Circle Lifetime Series 1:64
Price Range: $5-$30, Average: $15
Key Releases:
16 J. Gordon/'85 Sprint ....$15-$30

1999 Winner's Circle 1:64
Price Range: $2-$30, Average: $12
Key Releases:
3 D. Earnhardt/GW Daytona Win 2/15/98 .....
..............................$15-$30
20 T. Stewart/Home Depot ....$15-$30

1998 Winner's Circle Fantasy Pack 1:64
Price Range: $6-$12, Average: $12
Key Releases: none

1999 Winner's Circle Pit Row 1:64
Price Range: $8-$30, Average: $15
Key Releases:
20 T. Stewart/Home Depot ....$15-$30

Mattel Hurst Hairy Olds model kit

Auto Racing Plastic Model Kits

The model car builders market has grown significantly during the past two decades, so much so that entire publications have been dedicated to the art. From NASCAR Super.Truck model offerings to the latest paint scheme of a NASCAR Winston Cup series driver, hobbyists can totally immerse themselves into the hobby.

Like the collector, plastic kit manufacturers have also evolved, with considerably more attention paid to detailing each model. Correct proportions and crisp, clean molding is now expected by collectors. Any modifications made by NASCAR should be reflected in all updated kits. Cost restrictions or oversights by plastic kit manufacturers often necessitate collectors delving into old kits looking for parts to interchange.

The craving by collectors for exact model kit representation is exemplified most by the after-market for decals. Although plastic kit manufacturers have made considerable strides in trying to improve in every area, it is difficult to keep up with changes in sponsorship. Companies such as UpScale Graphics produce updated decals for collectors to substitute with outdated versions that may be included in some manufacturers' kits. Instruction sheets are included with these decals, and in UpScale's offerings five different angles are

SnapTite Dale Earnhardt Goodwrench Monte Carlo model kit

Chevrolet Camero Pace Car

given of the subject's car. While these sheets give color information as well, they don't give exact decal information for each race, so in some instances a collector will have to know which sticker was used on which car during certain races. If you are a beginning collector, it is also important to note that some manufacturers, such as Monogram, have different skill levels. This company's SnapTite line offers collectors three different skill levels from no glue required to a challenging line for the experienced builder.

And a final note, as you read through the values of the kits provided in this chapter, you may see why it's worthwhile to buy more than one kit. The prices reflected here are for mint condition kits still in original packaging.

Selected Model Kit Price Listings

The manufacturers, scale and model number are listed below. All prices are mint condition kits still in original packaging.

AMT 1/25 Kits

T229 '76 Dodge Dart #43 (R. Petty) . . .$150.00
T373 '73 Chevy Malibu #12 (B. Allison) 135.00
T380 '74 Diehard Chevelle #88 (D. Allison)
. . . . .110.00
T391 '72 Jo Han Rebox #90 . . . . .65.00
T395 '74 Chevelle #28 (G. Johncock) . . .110.00
T421 '73 Coca-Cola Chevy #12 (B. Allison)
. . . . .145.00
T429 '74 Kings Row Chevy #72 (Parsons)125.00
T430 '75 Penske Matador #16 (B. Allison)110.00
T430 '75 Coca-Cola/Penske (B. Allison) .110.00
T443 '75 Chevy Malibu #54 (L. Pond) . .100.00
T565 '76 Penske/Van/Trir #16 (B. Allison)
. . . . .220.00
T569 '76 Dodge/Ford Truck Set #43 (Petty)
. . . . .250.00
1895 '75 Chevy Malibu 30.00
3030 '73 Matador Sportsman #12 (Allison)
. . . . .75.00
3688 '72-'76 Chevelle/Malibu (Generic Kit)
. . . . .70.00
6019 Trailer #9 "Coors" (Elliott - 1/24) . . .50.00
6162 '92 T-Bird #15 "Motorcraft" (Bodine)
. . . . .20.00
6457 '91 T-Bird #22 "Maxwell House" (Marlin)
. . . . .20.00

Mark Martin Valvoline 1/8 car by Ertl

6727 '91 Chevy #4 "Kodiak" (Irvan) 20.00
6728 '90 Pontiac #43 "STP" (Petty) 20.00
6730 '91 T-Bird #15 "Motorcraft" (Shepard)
. . . . .20.00
6731 '90 Olds Cutlass #4 "Kodiak" (Wilson)
. . . . .22.00
6732 '90 Pont #30 "Country Time" (Waltrip)
. . . . .30.00
6733 '90 T-Bird #21 "Citgo" (Bonnett/Jarrett)
. . . . .55.00
6738 '90 Olds #94 "Sunoco" (Marlin) 22.00
6739 '90 T-Bird #7 "Zerex" (Kulwicki) . . .65.00
6740 '91 T-Bird #9 "Coors Light" (Elliott)
. . . . .25.00
6802 'Trailer #4 "Kodak" (Irvan - 1/24) . .45.00
6807 '93 T-Bird #7 "Hooters" (Kulwicki) .35.00
6819 '91 Olds #68 "Country Time" (Hamilton)
. . . . .20.00
6852 '93 Lumina #24 "DuPont" (Gordon)
. . . . .18.00
6892 '93 Pontiac 344 "STP" (Wilson) 13.00
6894 '93 T-Bird #26 "Quaker State" (Bodine)
. . . . .13.00
6961 '90 Pontiac #27 "MGD" (Wallace) . .35.00
6962 '90 T-Bird #9 "Coors" (Elliott) 30.00
8042 '83 T-Bird #21 "Valvoline" (Baker) . .75.00
8043 '83 Chevy #11 "Pepsi" (D. Waltrip) .85.00
8044 '84 Pontiac GP #43 "STP"
(R. Petty) 45.00
8045 '83 Chev. #28 "Hardees" (Yarborough)
. . . . .75.00
8046 '84 T-Bird 315 "Wrangler" (Earnhardt)
. . . . .75.00
8047 '83 Pontiac #7 "7 Eleven" (K.Petty) .85.00
8106 '91 Pontiac #42 "Mello Yello" (K.Petty)
. . . . .17.00
8115 '71 Plym. Roadrunner #43 (Petty) *
re-issue $14.00
8116 '75 Matador #16 "Coca-Cola/AMC"
(Allison) 13.00
8752 '91 Chevy #18 "Interstate Batteries"
(Jarrett) 12.00
8754 '92 T-Bird #66 "Phillips 66" (Little) . .16.00
8756 '92 T-Bird #6 "Valvoline" (Martin) . .22.00
8910 Gift set - 3 piece (Kodak #4, STP #43,
Maxwell House #2) 60.00

AMT 1/32 SNAP KITS

8707 '92 Lumina #4 "Kodak" (Irvan) . . .$14.00
8708 '92 T-Bird #22 "Maxwell House" (Marlin)
. . . . .14.00
8709 '92 Pontiac #43 "STP" (R.Petty) . . .14.00
8712 '93 Pontiac #44 "STP" (Wilson) 9.00
8721 '93 T-Bird #21 "Citgo" (Shepard) 9.00
8722 '92 Lumina #10 "Purolator" (Cope) . .14.00
8723 '93 T-Bird #26 "Quaker State" (Bodine)
. . . . .9.00
8727 '92 Pontiac #42 "Mello Yello" (K.Petty)
. . . . .14.00
8728 '92 Chevy #18 "Interstate Batteries"
(Jarrett) 18.00
8729 '92 T-Bird #6 "Valvoline" (Martin) . .15.00
8730 '92 T-Bird 315 "Motorcraft" (Bodine)
. . . . .14.00
8799 '92 T-Bird 366 "Phillips" (Little) . . .14.00

AMT 1/16 Kits

6717 '85 T-Bird #28 "Hardees" (Yarborough
. . . .$105.00
6718 '85 T-Bird #7 "7 Eleven" (K. Petty)
. . . . .105.00
6741 '85 Grand Prix #43 "STP" (R. Petty)
. . . . .110.00
6746 '85 Pontiac #75 "Nationwise" (Speed)
. . . . .85.00

Jeff Gordon Monte Carlo model car

Johnny Benson Ford Taurus model car

Monogram 1/24 Kits
DA124 '93 T-Bird #28 "Mac Tools" (D. Allison)
. . . .$65.00
EI124 '94 T-Bird #28 "Mac Tools" (Irvan)
. . . . .35.00
HG124 '93 Lumina #7 "Mac Tools" (Gant)
. . . . .35.00
646 '94 T-Bird #21 "Cheerwine" (Shepard)
. . . . .35.00
664 '81-83 Buick Regal (Generic Kit) 22.00
898 '93 Lumina #7 "Mac Tools" (Gant) .85.00
2204 '83 Buick Regal #11 "Mountain Dew"
(Waltrip) .80.00
2205 '82 Buick Regal #1 "UNO" (Baker)
. . . . .105.00
2206 '83 T-Bird #15 "Wrangler" (Earnhardt)
. . . . .90.00
2207 '83 T-Bird #9 "Melling" (Elliott) . . .75.00
2244 '85 T-Bird #9 SH "Coors" (Elliott) .80.00
2244 '84 T-Bird #9 LH "Coors" (Elliott) . .80.00
2244 '84 T-Bird #9 SH "Coors" Winston (Elliott)
. . . . .105.00
2244 '85 T-Bird #9 "Melling Speedway" (Elliott)
. . . . .80.00
2245 '84 Budweiser #11 or #12
(Waltrip/Bonnett) 95.00
2298 '84 Buick GN #22 "Miller" (B. Allison) . . . .
. . . . .80.00
2298 '84 Buick #22 "Miller" Speedway
(B. Allison) 80.00
2299 '84 Chevy #44 "Piedmont"
(T. Labonte) 100.00
2428 '91 Pontiac #42 "Mello Yello"
(K. Petty) 13.00
2430 '91 T-Bird #28 "Havoline"
(D. Allison) 13.00
2431 '91 Buick #12 "Raybestos" (Stricklin)
. . . . .16.00
2432 '91 Olds #75 "Dinner Bell" (Ruttmann)
. . . . .25.00
2440 '93 Lumina #5 "Tide" (Rudd) 25.00
2441 '93 Lumina #24 "DuPont" (Gordon) 17.00
2442 '93 T-Bird #27 "McDonalds" (Stricklin)
. . . . .12.00
2447 '95 Monte Carlo GM Goodwrench
(Earnhardt) 16.00
2448 '95 Monte Carlo Kodak (Marlin) . . .11.50
2449 '94 T-Bird #10 "Tide" (Rudd) 12.00
2450 '94 T-Bird #7 "Exide" (Bodine) 12.00
2451 '94 T-Bird #15 "Quality Care" (Speed)
. . . . .12.00
2465 '95 T-Bird #16 "Family Channel"
(Musgrave) 12.00
2466 '95 T-Bird Stock Car 11.00
2469 '95 McDonald's Thunderbat, (Elliott)
. . . . .13.00
2706 '85 Lumina #3 "Skoal" (Gant) 90.00
2707 '84 Buick #47 "Valvoline" (Bouchard)
. . . . .105.00
2722 '85 Pontiac #43 "STP/CURB" (Petty)
. . . . .100.00

2723 '86 T-Bird #15 "Motorcraft" (Rudd)
. . . . .60.00
2734 '87 Chevy #25 "Folgers" (Richmond)
. . . . .65.00
2754 '87 Olds #29 "Hardee's" (Yarborough)
. . . . .60.00
2755 '87 Chevy #17 "Tide" (Waltrip) 75.00
2779 '87 Olds #83 "Kmart" (Speed) 40.00
2786 '89 Buick 326 "Quaker state" (Rudd)
. . . . .30.00
2787 '89 Pontiac #75 "Valvoline" (Bonnett)
. . . . .80.00
2900 '88 M/C #3 "Goodwrench" (Earnhardt)
. . . . .50.00
2900 '91 M/C #3 "Goodwrench" (Earnhardt) *
re-issue .13.00
2906 '89 Pontiac #42 "Peak" (K.Petty) . . .35.00
2908 '89 T-Bird #7 "Zerex" (Kulwicki) . . .60.00
2914 '90 Pontiac #57 "Heinz"
(Stricklin/Spencer) 30.00
2915 '89 Buick #8, #84, #12 "Miller" 70.00
2916 '89 T-Bird #28 "Havoline" (D. Allison)
. . . . .80.00
2917 '90 Lumina #46 "City Chevy" "Days
of Thunder" 40.00
2920 '90 Lumina #18 "Hardees" "Days
of Thunder" 30.00
2921 '90 Lumina #51 "Mello Yello" "Days
of Thunder" 45.00
2927 '90-'92 Lumina #3 Goodwrench
(Earnhardt) 35.00
2928 '90-'92 T-Bird #6 "Folgers" (Martin)
. . . . .30.00
2930 '90 Pontiac #66 "Tropic Artic" (Trickle)
. . . . .35.00
2932 '90 Pontiac #30 "K.Aid/Country Time"
(Waltrip) 35.00
2939 '91 Pontiac #30 "Pennzoil" (Waltrip) 30.00
2940 '90-'91 Buick #8 "Snickers" (Wilson &
Hillin) 30.00
2941 '91 Lumina #10 "Purolater" (Cope) .30.00
2942 '91 T-Bird #22 "Maxwell House"
(Marlin) .30.00
2949 '91 Lumina #17 "Western Auto" (Waltrip)
. . . . .12.00
2959 '92 T-Bird 36 "Valvoline" (Martin) . .12.00
2960 '92 Pontiac 32 "Pontiac Excitement"
(Wallace) 12.00
2961 '92 T-Bird #21 "Citgo" (Shepard) . .12.00
2973 '94 Pontiac #40 "Dirt Devil" (Wallace)
. . . . .12.00
2974 '94 Lumina #5 "Kellogg" (T. Labonte)
. . . . .12.00
6182 '83-'86 T-Bird (Generic Kit) 60.00
6298 Combo Set #3 "Wrangler" (Earnhardt)
. . . . .30.00
6367 Combo Set #4 "Kodak Film"
(Irvan/Wilson) 25.00
6368 Combo Set "Rookie of the Year"
(Kulwicki/Schrader) 25.00
6389 Combo Set #42/#43 "Racing Pettys"
. . . . .25.00

6391 Combo Set #11 Waltrip "Pepsi & Mt. Dew"
. . . . .25.00
9460 '94 T-Bird #60 "Winn Dixie" (Martin)
. . . . .45.00

Monogram 1/32 Snap Kits
1086 '92 T-Bird #28 "Havoline" (D. Allison)
. . . .$10.00
1087 '92 T-Bird #6 "Valvoline" (Martin) . .10.00
1088 '92 Lumina #3 "Goodwrench" (Earnhardt)
. . . . .25.00
1089 '92 Chevy 312 "Raybestos" (Stricklin)
. . . . .10.00
1090 Race Set #3 "Goodwrench" (Earnhardt)
. . . . .50.00
1091 Race Set #28 "Havoline" (D. Allison)
. . . . .30.00
1094 '93 T-Bird #68 "Country Time" (Hamilton)
. . . . .10.00
1095 '93 T-Bird #26 "Quaker State" (Bodine)
. . . . .20.00
1700 '94 T-Bird #2 "Penske Racing" (Wallace)
. . . . .12.00
1701 '94 McDonald's Thunderbat (Elliott)
. . . . .10.00

MPC 1/25 Kits
681 '76 Malibu #1 "Hawaiian Tropic" . .$95.00
731 '71 "K&K Insurance" (Issac) 240.00
'72 Ford Torino #15 (Issac) 220.00
738 '83 S Stocker Monte Carlo #37 . . . .55.00
845 '82 S Stocker Buick #58 . . . . .55.00
846 '82 S Stocker Grand Prix #20 . . . . .55.00
1701 '71 Daytona Charger #43 (Petty) . .180.00
1702 '71 NASCAR Charger #11 (Baker)
. . . . .180.00
1703 '71 NASCAR Chevelle #56 (Hurtubise)
. . . . .90.00
1704 '71 NASCAR Mercury #21 (D. Allison)
. . . . .150.00
1705 '71 NASCAR Charger #22 (Brooks)
. . . . .180.00
1706 '71 NASCAR GTO #3 (Pearson) . . .140.00
1707 '72 Monte Carlo #11 (Coo Coo Martin)
. . . . .160.00
1708 '73 NASCAR Charger #43 (Petty) . .150.00
1709 '73 Chevy #22 Jr. Johnson (Yarborough)
. . . . .125.00
1710 '73 Ford Torino #25 (Issac) 155.00
1711 '73 NASCAR Charger #71 (Baker)
. . . . 140.00
1712 '77 Chevelle #39 "Pepsi" (Hurtubise)
. . . . .80.00
1713 '78 NASCAR Charger #43 (Petty) .140.00
6365 '85 Chevy #2 "Chattanooga Chew" (Pear-
son) 95.00
6366 '85 Chevy #55 "Copenhagen" (Parsons) . .
100.00
6367 '85 Pontiac #2 "Alugard" (Wallace) 100.00
6368 '85 Chevy #66 "Skoal Bandit" (Parsons)
. . . . .95.00

MPC 1/16 Kits
053 '73 Charger #43 (Petty) $260.00
3055 '73 Charger #71 (Baker) 240.00

Jo Han 1/25 Kits
GC964 '64 Plymouth #43 (Petty) $30.00
GC1470 '70 Superbird #43, #40 (Petty/Hamil-
ton) 30.00
GC1970 '70 Superbird/Plymouth #43 (Petty)
. . . . .30.00
GC2200 '69 Oval Track #22 . . . . .40.00
GC3372 '70 Oval Track #27 . . . . 40.00

Auto Racer Autographs
Active and retired

* - Deceased Driver

J.C. Agajanian *
Cut signature $25
8x10 photo $45

Bobby Allison
Cut signature $11
8x10 photo $19

Davey Allison *
Cut signature $54
8x10 photo $90

Donnie Allison
Cut signature $6
8x10 photo $12

Joe Amato
Cut signature $6
8x10 photo $10

Mario Andretti
Cut signature $21
8x10 photo $35

Michael Andretti
Cut signature $13
8x10 photo $22

Buddy Baker
Cut signature $12
8x10 photo $25

Cannonball Baker *
Cut signature $30
8x10 photo $65

Henry Banks
Cut signature $6
8x10 photo $12

Johnny Benson
Cut signature $13
8x10 photo $20

Joe Bessey
Cut signature $10
8x10 photo $15

Gary Bettenhausen
Cut signature $10
8x10 photo $20

Tony Bettenhausen *
Cut signature $12
8x10 photo $24

Dave Blaney
Cut signature $4
8x10 photo $8

Mike Bliss
Cut signature $4
8x10 photo $8

Brett Bodine
Cut signature $10
8x10 photo $16

Geoff Bodine
Cut signature $13
8x10 photo $21

Todd Bodine
Cut signature $12
8x10 photo $25

Neil Bonnett *
Cut signature $30
8x10 photo $50

Craig Breedlove
Cut signature $15
8x10 photo $25

Jeff Burton
Cut signature $14
8x10 . . . .$24

Ward Burton
Cut signature $14
8x10 . . . .$24

Pancho Carter
Cut signature $8
8x10 photo $17

Eddie Cheever
Cut signature $11
8x10 photo $18

Kevin Cogan
Cut signature $8
8x10 photo $17

Stacy Compton
Cut signature $4
8x10 photo $8

Earl Cooper *
Cut signature $45
8x10 photo $95

Derrick Cope
Cut signature $7
8x10 photo $12

Ricky Craven
Cut signature $6
8x10 photo $10

Wally Dallenbach
Cut signature $15
8 x10 photo $25

Mark Donahue *
Cut signature $55
8x10 photo $110

Mike Dunn
Cut signature $4
8x10 photo $8

Dale Earnhardt, Sr. *
Cut signature . . . .$35-$40
8x10 photo . . . .$85-$100

Dale Earnhardt, Jr.
Cut signature $15
8x10 photo $25

Bill Elliott
Cut signature $20
8x10 photo $30

Teo Fabi
Cut signature $5
8x10 photo $10

Tim Fedewa
Cut signature $15
8x10 photo $25

Adrian Fernandez
Cut signature $14
8x10 photo $22

Harvey Firestone, Jr. *
Cut signature $125
8x10 photo $300

Emerson Fittipaldi
Cut signature $16
8x10 photo $25

A.J. Foyt
Cut signature $15
8x10 photo $25

Dario Francitti
Cut signature $14
8x10 photo $22

Jeff Fuller
Cut signature $15
8x10 photo $25

Harry Gant
Cut signature $15
8x10 photo $27

Don Garlits
Cut signature $5
8x10 photo $15

Scott Goodyear
Cut signature $14
8x10 photo $24

Jeff Gordon
Cut signature $25
8x10 photo $40

Robby Gordon
Cut signature $5
8x10 photo $10

David Green
Cut signature $10
8x10 photo $15

Jeff Green
Cut signature $4
8x10 photo $10

Steve Grissom

Cut signature $5
8x10 photo $8

Roberto Guerrero
Cut signature $12
8x10 photo $24

Dan Gurney
Cut signature $10
8x10 photo $20

Janet Guthrie
Cut signature $5
8x10 photo $10

Dean Hall
Cut signature $5
8x10 photo $8

Bobby Hamilton
Cut signature $10
8x10 photo $15

Jimmy Hensley
Cut signature $10
8x10 photo $15

Damon Hill
Cut signature $14
8x10 photo $22

Graham Hill *
Cut signature $45
8x10 photo $90

Phil Hill
Cut signature $5
8x10 photo $15

Ron Hornaday
Cut signature $4
8x10 photo $8

Ernie Irvan
Cut signature $18
8x10 photo $30

Kenny Irwin *
Cut signature $10
8x10 photo $12

Dale Jarrett

Cut signature $18
8x10 photo $30

Jason Jarrett
Cut signature $12
8x10 photo $25

Ned Jarrett
Cut signature $12
8x10 photo $25

Gordon Johncock
Cut signature $14
8x10 photo $25

Parnelli Jones

Cut signature $13
8x10 photo $25

Steve Kinser
Cut signature $4
8x10 photo $8

Steve Knapp

Cut signature $14
8x10 photo $22

Benny Parsons
Cut signature $10
8x10 photo $15

Matt Kenseth
Cut signature $10
8x10 photo $15

Alan Kulwicki *
Cut signature $50
8x10 photo $90

Bobby Labonte
Cut signature $14
8x10 photo $24

Terry Labonte
Cut signature $16
8x10 photo $27

Randy LaJoie
Cut signature $10
8x10 photo $15

Buddy Lazier
Cut signature $5
8x10 photo $10

Joe Leonard
Cut signature $5
8x10 photo $10

Kevin Lepage
Cut signature $10
8x10 photo $15

Chad Little
Cut signature $10
8x10 photo $15

Arie Luyendyk
Cut signature $12
8x10 photo $20

Jimmy Makar
Cut signature $10
8x10 photo $15

Nigel Mansell
Cut signature $20
8x10 photo $25

Dave Marcis
Cut signature $12
8x10 photo $15

Sterling Marlin

Cut signature $13
8x10 photo $20

Mark Martin
Cut signature $18
8x10 photo $30

Rick Mast
Cut signature $4
8x10 photo $8

Jeremy Mayfield
Cut signature $14
8x10 photo $24

Rex Mays *
Cut signature $140
8x10 photo $275

Roger McCluskey
Cut signature $8
8x10 photo $18

Mike McLaughlin
Cut signature $10
8x10 photo $15

Rick Mears
Cut signature $16
8x10 photo $27

Juan Montoya
Cut signature $15
8x10 photo $25

Ralph Moody Jr.
Cut signature $8
8x10 photo $15

Rob Moroso *
Cut signature $15
8x10 photo $25

Sterling Moss
Cut signature $20
8x10 photo $25

Ted Musgrave
Cut signature $14
8x10 photo $25

Jerry Nadeau
Cut signature $10
8x10 photo $15

Joe Nemechek
Cut signature $10
8x10 photo $15

Barney Oldfield *
Cut signature $165
8x10 photo $350

Danny Ongais
Cut signature $5
8x10 photo $10

Steve Park
Cut signature $12
8x10 photo $15

Todd Parrot

Cut signature $12
8x10 photo $24

Benny Parsons
Cut signature $12
8x10 photo $24

Johnny Parsons *
Cut signature $22
8x10 photo $45

Phil Parsons
Cut signature $12
8x10 photo $18

David Pearson
Cut signature $8
8x10 photo $12

Roger Penske
Cut signature $20
8x10 photo $25

Andy Petree
Cut signature $8
8x10 photo $15

Adam Petty *
Cut signature $20
8x10 photo $30

Kyle Petty
Cut signature $17
8x10 photo $21

Lee Petty*
Cut signature $20
8x10 photo $65

Richard Petty

Cut signature $20
8x10 photo $35

Alan Prost
Cut signature $5
8x10 photo $11

Scott Pruett
Cut signature $5
8x10 photo $8

Bobby Rahal
Cut signature $15
8x10 photo $25

Peter Revson *
Cut signature $45
8x10 photo $90

Eddie Rickenbacker *
Cut signature $125
8x10 photo $300

Tim Richmond *
Cut signature $12
8x10 photo $24
Floyd Roberts *

Cut signature $55
8x10 photo $140

Kenny Roberts
Cut signature $5
8x10 photo $10

Ricky Rudd
Cut signature $11
8x10 photo $19

Johnny Rutherford

Cut signature $12
8x10 photo $20

Elliot Sadler
Cut signature $8
8x10 photo $15

Elton Sawyer
Cut signature $10
8x10 photo $15

Ken Schrader
Cut signature $12
8x10 photo $19

Carroll Shelby
Cut signature $5
8x10 photo $12

Morgan Shepherd
Cut signature $10
8x10 photo $15

Mike Skinner
Cut signature $10
8x10 photo $14

Tom Sneva
Cut signature $13
8x10 photo $21

Lake Speed
Cut signature $4
8x10 photo $8

Jimmy Spencer
Cut signature $12
8x10 photo $20

Lyn St. James
Cut signature $6
8x10 photo $12

Jackie Stewart
Cut signature $12
8x10 photo $20

Tony Stewart
Cut signature $13
8x10 photo $22

Hut Strickland
Cut signature $10
8x10 photo $17
Danny Sullivan
Cut signature $16

8x10 photo $24

Mickey Thompson*
Cut signature $55
8x10 photo $110

Dick Trickle
Cut signature $14
8x10 photo $22

Al Unser
Cut signature $12
8x10 photo $20

Al Unser, Jr.
Cut signature $14
8x10 photo $25

Bobby Unser
Cut signature $10
8x10 photo $20

Jimmy Vasser
Cut signature $12
8x10 photo $20

Jacques Villeneuve
Cut signature $10
8x10 photo $20

Kenny Wallace
Cut signature $13
8x10 photo $21

Rusty Wallace
Cut signature $19
8x10 photo $32

Darrell Waltrip
Cut signature $17
8x10 photo $27

Michael Waltrip
Cut signature $10
8x10 photo $15

Roger Ward
Cut signature $20
8x10 photo $50

A.J. Watson
Cut signature $5
8x10 photo $10

Gar Wood *
Cut signature $25
8x10 photo $50

Cale Yarborough
Cut signature $14
8x10 photo $22

Lee Roy Yarborough
Cut signature $8
8x10 photo $16

Smokey Yunick
Cut signature $5
8x10 photo $10

Auto Racing Cereal Boxes
Cheerios
1998 Johnny Benson $7

Kellogg's Corn Flakes
1992 Richard Petty $30
1992 G. Sacks/H. Hyde 30
1992 Corn Flakes car #41 30
1993 Terry Labonte holding helmet 30
1993 Corn Flakes Car #14 30
1994 #5 car bursting through 25
1994 #5 car with pit crew (18/24) 30
1994 Dale Earnhardt '93 Champ 40
1994 Terry Labonte eating cereal 25
1995 Terry Labonte/D. Waltrip 15
1995 #5 car at finish line 15
1995 "Corney" in uniform 8
1995 Dale Earnhardt '94 Champ 20
1995 D. Earnhardt 7-Time Champ (20) 20
1995 Terry Labonte w/Wilks trophy 15
1996 Terry Labonte Ironman 15
1996 Terry Labonte Ironman #5 car 15
1996 Terry Labonte/R. Petty 20
1996 Jeff Gordon '95 WC Champ 25
1997 Terry Labonte Sam Bass art 15

1997 Terry Labonte/Jeff Gordon 20
1997 Top-Four drivers 25
1997 Terry Labonte HC pack w/car 15
1998 Labonte/R. Byron 8
1998 NASCAR 50th Anniversary 5
1998 Terry Labonte car cut-out 8

Kellogg's Frosted Flakes
1994 Tony Tiger in NASCAR uniform $10
1995 Bill Elliott 15
1995 Bill Elliott w/Tony the Tiger 10
1996 Dale Earnhardt w/Tony (15 oz.) 15
1997 Terry Labonte w/Tony the Tiger 12

Kellogg's Frosted Mini-Wheats
1933 Jeff Gordon (Sam Bass art) $30
1994 Jeff Gordon .25
1995 Earnhardt/Gordon (red) 20
1995 Earnhardt/Gordon (org.) 20
1995 Earnhardt/Gordon (48) 20
1995 Jeff Gordon/#24 car at Indy 18
1995 Jeff Gordon Brickyard 400 18
1996 Jeff Gordon '95 Champ (red) 20
1996 Jeff Gordon '95 Champ (org.) 20
1996 MBNA car .15

1997 Top-Four drivers 20
1997 Jeff Gordon in helmet (19) 15
1997 Jeff Gordon in helmet (48) 20
1997 Terry Labonte/Jeff Gordon 18
1997 Dale Earnhardt in helmet 20
1998 Jeff Gordon '97 WC Champ 15
1999 Jeff Gordon '98 NASCAR Champ 8

Kellogg's Raisin Bran
1993 Terry Labonte on back $40
1994 Bill Elliott/Joe Gibbs 15
1996 Darrell/Michael Waltrip 15
1997 Top-Four drivers 20
1997 Dale/Ned Jarrett 15
1997 Terry Labonte/G. DeHart 15
1997 Dale Jarrett wearing helmet 15

General Mills
Wheaties
1997 Dale Earnhardt (Al) $15
1998 A. Zanardi/J. Vasser 6
1998 Richard Petty Leg. 5
1998 Richard Petty Leg. (CWR) 5
1998 Richard Petty Leg. (HW) 5
1999 Target/Ganassi 3-Time Champs 5

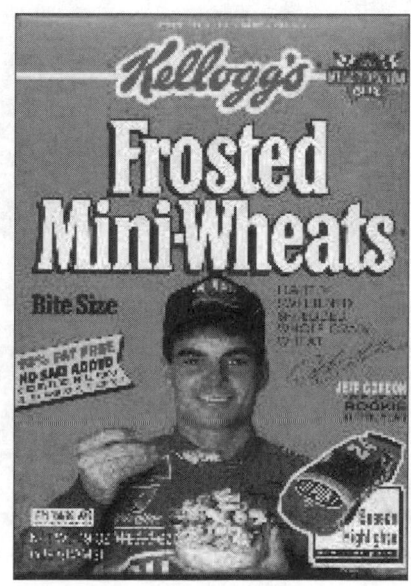

Baseball Collectibles

The National Pastime is the national passion when it comes to collecting. It seems that, on any given weekend in any U.S. city, a baseball card show is always under way.

And, as any collector–from rookie to veteran–will tell you, these shows spotlight everything from vintage baseball cards from the late 19th and early 20th centuries to the latest 400-card sets hot off the presses; from board games and plastic figurines to game-used equipment and uniforms; from autographed balls, bats and 8x10 glossies to World Series pins originally distributed to writers and broadcasters who cover the Fall Classic.

In other words, in the collector's pursuit of baseball memorabilia, like the trajectory of a Mark McGwire home run, the sky's the limit. Collectors search for what they want at these card shows, at their local hobby shops and other retailers, on the Internet, and in the classified sections or the full-page ads in various hobby publications.

Newcomers to the hobby may feel overwhelmed at first. Why? Baseball card price guides feature thousands of different sets. Dealers at major shows display a dazzling array of collectibles. Newspaper and magazine stories note the staggering sums of money paid for rare items.

Where and how does one start?

To begin with, baseball collectibles enjoy a history nearly as rich as the one the game itself celebrates. Knowing a little about that history will give the newcomer a greater appreciation for the fun and satisfaction that lie ahead and spark some interest in specific collectibles. At the heart of this hobby's history is the baseball card.

Trade 'Em If You Got 'Em

Baseball cards in one form or another have been with us since the 1870s. Those early novelties, printed on heavy cardboard and often the size of postcards, as well as the smaller varieties of cards issued in their wake, bear little resemblance to the high-tech, full-color cards made by today's card companies. But together, those early cards form a cornerstone of the hobby known as collecting baseball memorabilia.

The popularity of baseball cards really hit its stride in the late 1880s. That's when U.S. tobacco companies began packaging small baseball cards (1fi" by 2fi," for example) as premiums with their packs of cigarettes. Depending on the company and the series, these player depictions could be photographs, line drawings or some variation on the printing process such as color lithographs or sepia tone.

The two most prominent corporate names from that period of "smokes and cards" were Allen & Ginter and Goodwin & Company. They issued baseball cards that remain among the most popular (if priciest) collectibles on the market today. One such series, packaged with the latter's Old Judge brand of cigarettes, featured more than 600 players that included stars not only from the National League, but stars from the American Association, the International League, the Pacific Coast League, the Western League and even the Players League (which took the field for one season, 1890).

Ironically, the merger of several smaller tobacco firms to become the American Tobacco Company nearly sounded the death knell of baseball card inserts in the late 1800s. Less competition for the tobacco consumer's dollar convinced the corporate giant there was little need to package such premiums with its products.

But in the early 1900s, Turkish tobacco firms began enjoying success in overseas markets. They even wisely allowed their Stateside distributors to insert baseball cards with packs of Turkish cigarettes sold in the United States. U.S. firms met the competition head on, once again issuing "tobacco cards" with their home-grown products. Only America's entry into World War I, when paper and printing materials were reserved for the war effort, ended the boom.

Tobacco companies generally eased themselves out of the baseball card market after the Great War. However, candy and chewing gum companies, which in the early 1900s began distributing baseball cards with their confections to attract younger buyers, picked up the slack. And, as the growing popularity of baseball cards in the 20th century mirrored the fans' insatiable appetite for the game itself, more and more companies issued their own sets.

Over the years, names such as Goudey, Bowman, Leaf, Topps, Fleer, Donruss, Upper Deck, Pinnacle, Score and many others became synonymous with the sports card craze that continues to flourish. Cards have been packaged with hot dogs, magazines, books, toys, breakfast cereals, videos–you name it–and they have been packaged simply by themselves. Card designs have run the gamut from so-so to the spectacu-

An assortment of items honoring the career of baseball great Ted Williams.

lar, from retro to gimmicky to gaudy to simple and straightforward.

The current market is filled with major sets, regional sets, team-issued sets and more. There have been sets spotlighting big-league umpires, minor league teams and the legends of the Negro Leagues. If you desire selection, have you ever come to the right hobby.

May I Have Your Autograph?

Baseball cards are still the backbone of the hobby, but many kinds of memorabilia await the collector.

A long-time favorite is the autographed baseball. It wasn't invented by Babe Ruth in the 1920s, it just seems that way because of old newsreel footage and still shots that show him surrounded by kids.

Programs, scorecards and player photos also lend themselves well to player signatures. It's always more fun if you can obtain those signatures in person from the player at the ballpark before the game or at hobby shows that host guest athletes for autograph sessions.

Just remember to be polite to the signer and courteous to your fellow collectors seeking the player's autograph.

You can also obtain signed items from reputable dealers at those shows or through the mail. Check out the ads in the popular hobby publications to see who's selling what. Compare dealer prices and stated conditions of the merchandise.

If you have Internet access, that's another way to search for the collectibles you desire—some dealers now maintain their own Web sites.

Other Fields, Other Dreams

Make plans to attend a major hobby show in your area. It is there where you will experience firsthand the three key ingredients that make collecting baseball "stuff" so much fun, so fascinating, so rewarding.

Thousands of other men, women and children who share your interest in collecting and your love of the game will be there. Want to break the ice? Simply start a conversation about some aspect of baseball. You'll soon find that your fellow collectors possess varying degrees of knowledge about baseball memorabilia and the game's history, but you are never among strangers at a hobby show. Enthusiasm for collecting is contagious.

Dealers will gladly provide you with the facts and background on the items they sell so that you can make informed purchases. Simply ask them.

And finally, you will discover an amazing treasure trove of baseball memorabilia. Think you'll see nothing but a huge expanse of baseball cards when you enter the room? Then consider these baseball collectibles,

Baseball signed by the 1946 Yankees.

nearly all of which you will likely see being offered for sale at major card shows:

● Board games
● Plastic figurines (including Hartland and Starting Lineup)
● Posters, pocket schedules and press guides
● Vintage periodicals (*The Sporting News, Baseball Digest, Sport, Sports Illustrated* and others)
● World Series programs, tickets and scorecards
● Team publications
● Prerecorded videotapes highlighting the accomplishments of specific players, teams or eras
● Toys (coin banks and bobbin' head dolls, for example)
● Uniforms and equipment (always among the more expensive collectibles at any show, but fascinating to study and admire even if you're "only looking")
● Vintage pennants (perhaps those of the Washington Senators, St. Louis Browns or Seattle Pilots)
● Autographed baseballs and bats
● Specially designed plaques sporting signed baseballs
● Framed and matted photos of historic deeds or memorable plays involving the legends of the game

What's great about collecting baseball memorabilia (or any sport's memorabilia) is the freedom of choice. It's not a matter of right or wrong. You can go after the same kind of item–felt pennants, for example– and build an impressive collection over a period of years.

If cards are your passion, you may decide to limit your collection to team sets–that is, the cards of all the players representing a given team in a regular annual set from any of the major card companies.

Or you can be a truly casual collector and obtain "a little of this and a little of that." A couple of World Series highlights videos here, an out-of-print hardcover biog-

raphy of Willie Mays there, and, for good measure, the rookie cards of your favorite current players. Voila! You have acquired a small but interesting assortment of baseball collectibles. It's unique and it's yours. It will doubtless lead to future acquisitions. So have fun.

Oh, and take all the time you need. Savor the effort you make to search for the item or items you wish to add to your collection. Part of the joy in collecting baseball memorabilia is that individual tastes and timetables rule.

To Market We Go

Today's market for baseball memorabilia is as wide open as home plate umpire Eric Gregg's strike zone in Game 5 of the 1997 NLCS. And with so many baseball card sets, subsets, update sets and limited-issue sets dotting the landscape, collectors are turning to some of the other aforementioned items as a way to stay active in the hobby. Still, cards remain the staple of the hobby.

With that in mind, here are some of the popular baseball collectibles to consider:

● McFarlane Toys' 2000 Big League Challenge baseball figurines: Series I features Barry Bonds, Chipper Jones, Mark McGwire, Manny Ramirez, Alex Rodriguez and Sammy Sosa, plus a Ramirez/McGwire two-figure set produced exclusively for Babbage's software stores. These figurines boast superb coloring and detailing, right down to the dirt on the uniforms.

● Insert cards: Numerous choices here, including the Alex Rodriguez 1994 No. 415 autograph card in the 1997 SP Vintage Autographs set; the various insert cards containing actual swatches of a player's uniform, chips from a player's bat, or even dirt taken from the batter's box or pitcher's mound; and, from the "If one is good, two are better" philosophy, a jersey swatch and a signature from 2000 World Series MVP, Derek Jeter.

● Items relating to this year's Hall of Fame inductees (watch the asking prices of their items soar).

● Items relating to "The Splendid Splinter," Hall of Famer Ted Williams.

● Vintage cards ranging from tobacco cards to virtually any cards dealing with legendary Yankees heroes Lou Gehrig, Babe Ruth and Mickey Mantle.

● Items relating to active players expected to make the Hall of Fame in the not-too-distant future, including Greg Maddux, Roger Clemens, Barry Bonds, Tony Gwynn and Mark McGwire.

Embrace the abundance of baseball artifacts and collectibles out there, don't be overwhelmed by it. Just remember that you decide what's right for you.

Selected Baseball Cards
(1948-1989)

1948 BOWMAN

		NM
Complete Set (48):		$3400.00
Common Player (1-36):		20.00
Common Player (37-48):		32.00

		NM
3	Ralph Kiner	135.00
4	Johnny Mize	95.00
5	Bob Feller	220.00
6	Yogi Berra	425.00
8	Phil Rizzuto	250.00
18	Warren Spahn	250.00
36	Stan Musial	775.00
38	Red Schoendienst	120.00

1948-49 LEAF

JOE DI MAGGIO

		NM
Complete Set (98):		24000.00
Common Player:		25.00
Common Short-print:		200.00
Album:		900.00

		NM
1	Joe DiMaggio	2100.00
3	Babe Ruth	2000.00
4	Stan Musial	700.00
5	Virgil Trucks	275.00
8	Satchel Paige	2400.00
11	Phil Rizzuto	225.00
13	Casimer Michaels	200.00
19	John Wyrostek	200.00
20	Hank Sauer	250.00
30	Bill Goodman	200.00
32	Warren Spahn	250.00
33	Harry Lowrey	200.00
36	Al Zarilla	200.00
43	Eddie Stevens	200.00
45	Ken Keltner	200.00
48	Johnny Schmitz	200.00

51	Alvin Dark	275.00
54	Bobby Adams	200.00
55	Tommy Henrich	300.00
62	Eddie Joost	200.00
63	Barney McCosky	200.00
66	Orval Grove	200.00
68	Ed Miller	200.00
70	Honus Wagner	265.00
75	Dom DiMaggio	450.00
76	Ted Williams	750.00
78	Walter Evers	200.00
79	Jackie Robinson	750.00
81	George Kurowski	200.00
85	Dave Philley	250.00
88	Frank Gustine	200.00
91	Ralph Kiner	175.00
93	Bob Feller	1250.00
98	Hal Newhouser	550.00
102a	Gene Hermanski	2100.00
104	Edward Stewart	200.00
108	Matthew Batts	200.00
113	Emil Leonard	200.00
120	George Kell	500.00
121	John Pesky	300.00
123	Clifford Fannin	200.00
127	Enos Slaughter	725.00
129	Kirby Higbe	200.00
131	Sid Gordon	200.00
133	Tommy Holmes	275.00
136b	Cliff Aberson	300.00
137	Harry Walker	200.00
138	Larry Doby	525.00
142	Danny Murtaugh	275.00
143	Dick Sisler	200.00
144	Bob Dillinger	200.00
146	Harold Reiser	450.00
149	Henry Majeski	200.00
153	Floyd Baker	200.00
158	Harry Brecheen	275.00
160	Bob Scheffing	250.00
161	Vernon Stephens	275.00
163	Freddy Hutchinson	275.00
165	Dale Mitchell	275.00
158	Phil Cavarretta	300.00

1949 BOWMAN

		NM
Complete Set (240):		11000.00
Common Player (1-144):		15.00
Common Player (145-240)		45.00

		NM
1	Vernon Bickford	125.00
24	Stan Musial	500.00
27	Bob Feller	165.00
33	Warren Spahn	145.00
36	Pee Wee Reese	150.00
46	Robin Roberts	200.00
50	Jackie Robinson	800.00

60	Yogi Berra	265.00
84	Roy Campanella	850.00
98a	Phil Rizzuto	125.00
98b	Phil Rizzuto	250.00
100	Gil Hodges	250.00
175	Luke Appling	135.00
214	Richie Ashburn	550.00
224	Satchel Paige	950.00
226	Duke Snider	850.00
233	Larry Doby	200.00
238	Bob Lemon	200.00

1950 BOWMAN

		NM
Complete Set (252):		7000.00
Common Player (1-72):		35.00
Common Player (73-252):		15.00

		NM
1	Mel Parnell	125.00
6	Bob Feller	160.00
11	Phil Rizzuto	200.00
19	Warren Spahn	200.00
21	Pee Wee Reese	195.00
22	Jackie Robinson	625.00
23	Don Newcombe	115.00
32	Robin Roberts	135.00
33	Ralph Kiner	80.00
35	Enos Slaughter	90.00
39	Larry Doby	125.00
46	Yogi Berra	350.00
62	Ted Kluszewski	85.00
75	Roy Campanella	275.00
77	Duke Snider	235.00
84	Richie Ashburn	100.00
98	Ted Williams	700.00
112	Gil Hodges	90.00
139	Johnny Mize	75.00
217	Casey Stengel	100.00

1951 BOWMAN

ENOS SLAUGHTER

			NM
Complete Set (324):			18000.00
Common Player (1-36):			17.50
Common Player (37-252):			14.00
Common Player (253-324):			40.00

			NM
1	Whitey Ford		795.00
2	Yogi Berra		300.00
3	Robin Roberts		80.00
7	Gil Hodges		70.00
10	Red Schoendienst		55.00
26	Phil Rizzuto		115.00
30	Bob Feller		125.00
31	Roy Campanella		210.00
32	Duke Snider		210.00
46	George Kell		50.00
80	Pee Wee Reese		125.00
122	Joe Garagiola		80.00
134	Warren Spahn		125.00
151	Larry Doby		80.00
165	Ted Williams		625.00
181	Casey Stengel		70.00
186	Richie Ashburn		90.00
198	Monte Irvin		75.00
232	Nellie Fox		175.00
233	Leo Durocher		55.00
253	Mickey Mantle		5500.00
254	Jackie Jensen		90.00
260	Carl Erskine		95.00
275	Bucky Harris		55.00
282	Frank Frisch		60.00
290	Bill Dickey		90.00
291	Tommy Henrich		50.00
295	Al Lopez		65.00
305	Willy Mays		2500.00
308	Jim Piersall		90.00
312	Gene Mauch		50.00
317	Smoky Burgess		70.00
323	Joe Adcock		70.00
324	Johnny Pramesa		85.00

1951 TOPPS BLUE BACKS

			NM
Complete Set (32):			1600.00
Common Player:			30.00

			NM
3	Richie Ashburn		110.00
6	Red Schoendienst		85.00
30	Enos Slaughter		75.00
37	Bobby Doerr		75.00
50	Johnny Mize		95.00

1951 TOPPS RED BACKS

			NM
Complete Set (32):			830.00
Common Player:			10.00

			NM
1	Yogi Berra		90.00
5	Phil Rizzuto		45.00
22	Bob Feller		50.00
30	Warren Spahn		50.00
31	Gil Hodges		40.00
36a	Gus Zernial		35.00
38	Duke Snider		65.00
50	Monte Irvin		45.00
52a	Tommy Holmes		35.00

1952 BOWMAN

			NM
Complete Set (252):			9000.00
Common Player (1-216):			12.00
Common Player (217-252):			32.00

			NM
1	Yogi Berra		550.00
4	Robin Roberts		60.00
5	Minnie Minoso		115.00
8	Pee Wee Reese		95.00
11	Ralph Kiner		50.00
21	Nellie Fox		65.00
23	Bob Lemon		50.00
27	Joe Garagiola		40.00
30	Red Schoendienst		45.00
33	Gil McDougald		60.00
43	Bob Feller		100.00
44	Roy Campanella		200.00
52	Phil Rizzuto		130.00
53	Richie Ashburn		75.00

			NM
75	George Kell		40.00
80	Gil Hodges		65.00
101	Mickey Mantle		2200.00
115	Larry Doby		45.00
116	Duke Snider		210.00
142	Early Wynn		50.00
145	Johnny Mize		45.00
156	Warren Spahn		125.00
162	Monte Irvin		42.00
196	Stan Musial		500.00
217	Casey Stengel		120.00
218	Willie Mays		1100.00
232	Enos Slaughter		80.00
240	Billy Loes		42.00
244	Lew Burdette		42.00
252	Frank Crosetti		75.00

1952 TOPPS

			NM
Complete Set (407):			55000.00
Common Player (1-80):			40.00
Common Player (81-250):			30.00
Common Player (251-310):			40.00
Common Player (311-407):			220.00

			NM
1	Andy Pafko		3500.00
2	Pete Runnels		125.00
11	Phil Rizzuto		225.00
20	Billy Loes		85.00
22	Dom DiMaggio		75.00
29	Ted Kluszewski		80.00
31	Gus Zernial		80.00
33	Warren Spahn		250.00
36	Gil Hodges		140.00
37	Duke Snider		250.00
48a	Joe Page		1100.00
48b	Joe Page		70.00
49a	Johnny Sain		1100.00
49b	Johnny Sain		75.00
57	Ed Lopat		80.00
59	Robin Roberts		125.00
65	Enos Slaughter		125.00
66	Preacher Roe		80.00
67	Allie Reynolds		70.00
88	Bob Feller		175.00
91	Red Schoendienst		90.00
129	Johnny Mize		100.00
175	Billy Martin		275.00
191	Yogi Berra		550.00
195	Minnie Minoso		125.00
218	Richie Ashburn		150.00
227	Joe Garagiola		80.00
243	Larry Doby		70.00
246	George Kell		80.00

250	Carl Erskine	70.00
261	Willie Mays	2000.00
268	Bob Lemon	125.00
274	Ralph Branca	80.00
277	Early Wynn	135.00
311	Mickey Mantle	15000.00
312	Jackie Robinson	1800.00
313	Bobby Thomson	300.00
314	Roy Campanella	1750.00
315	Leo Durocher	400.00
316	Davey Williams	250.00
317	Connie Marrero	220.00
318	Hal Gregg	220.00
319	Al Walker	220.00
320	John Rutherford	260.00
321	Joe Black	275.00
322	Randy Johnson	220.00
323	Bubba Church	220.00
324	Warren Hacker	220.00
325	Bill Serena	220.00
326	George Shuba	250.00
327	Archie Wilson	220.00
328	Bob Borkowski	220.00
329	Ike Delock	220.00
330	Turk Lown	220.00
331	Tom Morgan	220.00
332	Tony Bartirome	220.00
333	Pee Wee Reese	1500.00
334	Wilmer Mizell	245.00
335	Ted Lepcio	220.00
336	Dave Koslo	220.00
337	Jim Hearn	220.00
338	Sal Yvars	220.00
339	Russ Meyer	220.00
340	Bob Hooper	220.00
341	Hal Jeffcoat	220.00
342	Clem Labine	275.00
343	Dick Gernert	220.00
344	Ewell Blackwell	220.00
345	Sam White	220.00
346	George Spencer	220.00
347	Joe Adcock	260.00
348	Bob Kelly	220.00
349	Bob Cain	220.00
350	Cal Abrams	220.00
351	Al Dark	220.00
352	Karl Drews	220.00
353	Bob Del Greco	220.00
354	Fred Hatfield	220.00
355	Bobby Morgan	240.00
356	Toby Alwell	220.00
357	Smoky Burgess	245.00
358	John Kucab	220.00
359	Dee Fondy	220.00
360	George Crowe	220.00
361	Bill Posedel	220.00
362	Ken Heintzelman	220.00
363	Dick Rozek	220.00
364	Clyde Sukeforth	220.00
365	Cookie Lavagetto	240.00
366	Dave Madison	220.00
367	Bob Thorpe	220.00
368	Ed Wright	220.00
369	Dick Groat	360.00
370	Billy Hoeft	220.00
371	Bob Hofman	220.00
372	Gil McDougald	350.00
373	Jim Turner	275.00
374	Al Benton	220.00
375	Jack Merton	220.00
376	Faye Throneberry	220.00

377	Chuck Dressen	300.00
378	Les Fusselman	220.00
379	Joe Rossi	220.00
380	Clem Koshorek	220.00
381	Milton Stock	220.00
382	Sam Jones	220.00
383	Del Wilber	220.00
384	Frank Crosetti	325.00
385	Herman Franks	220.00
386	Eddie Yuhas	220.00
387	Billy Meyer	220.00
388	Bob Chipman	220.00
389	Ben Wade	220.00
390	Rocky Nelson	260.00
391	Ben Chapman	220.00
392	Hoyt Wilhelm	675.00
393	Ebba St. Claire	220.00
394	Billy Herman	300.00
395	Jake Pitler	220.00
396	Dick Williams	300.00
397	Forrest Main	220.00
398	Hal Rice	220.00
399	Jim Fridley	220.00
400	Bill Dickey	650.00
401	Bob Schultz	220.00
402	Earl Harrist	220.00
403	Bill Miller	220.00
404	Dick Brodowski	220.00
405	Eddie Pellagrinni	220.00
406	Joe Nuxhall	350.00
407	Eddie Mathews	4500.00

1953 BOWMAN (Color)

		NM
Complete Set (160):		11000.00
Common Player (1-112):		27.50
Common Player (113-128):		55.00
Common Player (129-160):		50.00

		NM
1	Davey Williams	85.00
9	Phil Rizzuto	170.00
10	Richie Ashburn	135.00
18	Nellie Fox	75.00
32	Stan Musial	650.00
33	Pee Wee Reese	675.00
40	Larry Doby	75.00
44	Bauer, Berra, Mantle	550.00
46	Roy Campanella	275.00
59	Mickey Mantle	2400.00
65	Robin Roberts	125.00
80	Ralph Kiner	90.00
92	Gil Hodges	175.00
93	Billy Martin, Phil Rizzuto	275.00
97	Eddie Mathews	250.00

99	Warren Spahn	200.00
114	Bob Feller	275.00
117	Duke Snider	450.00
118	Billy Martin	175.00
121	Yogi Berra	600.00
146	Early Wynn	110.00
153	Whitey Ford	425.00

1953 BOWMAN (Black & White)

		NM
Complete Set (64):		2500.00
Common Player:		35.00

		NM
1	Gus Bell	90.00
15	Johnny Mize	115.00
27	Bob Lemon	110.00
28	Hoyt Wilhelm	135.00
39	Casey Stengel	300.00

1953 TOPPS

PEE WEE REESE
shortstop BROOKLYN DODGERS

		NM
Complete Set (280):		9500.00
Common Player (1-220):		20.00
Common Player (221-280):		40.00
Short-print Player (221-280):		80.00

		NM
1	Jackie Robinson	600.00
10	Smoky Burgess	55.00
27	Roy Campanella	175.00
37	Eddie Mathews	125.00
41	Enos Slaughter	90.00
54	Bob Feller	90.00
61	Early Wynn	110.00
76	Pee Wee Reese	140.00
77	Johnny Mize	55.00
78	Red Schoendienst	55.00
81	Joe Black	75.00

82	Mickey Mantle	2600.00
86	Billy Martin	100.00
104	Yogi Berra	225.00
114	Phil Rizzuto	125.00
147	Warren Spahn	150.00
149	Dom DiMaggio	50.00
151	Hoyt Wilhelm	60.00
191	Ralph Kiner	80.00
207	Whitey Ford	150.00
220	Satchel Paige	400.00
221	Bob Millikan	90.00
222	Vic Janowicz	50.00
223	John O'Brien	50.00
224	Lou Sleater	50.00
225	Bobby Shantz	90.00
226	Ed Erautt	90.00
227	Morris Martin	50.00
228	Hal Newhauser	130.00
229	Rocky Krsnich	90.00
230	Johnny Lindell	50.00
231	Solly Hemus	50.00
232	Dick Kokos	90.00
233	Al Aber	90.00
234	Ray Murray	50.00
235	John Hetki	50.00
236	Harry Perkowski	50.00
237	Clarence Podbielan	50.00
238	Cal Hogue	50.00
239	Jim Delsing	90.00
240	Freddie Marsh	50.00
241	Al Sima	50.00
242	Charlie Silvera	120.00
243	Carlos Bernier	50.00
244	Willie Mays	2400.00
245	Bill Norman	90.00
246	Roy Face	85.00
247	Mike Sandlock	50.00
248	Gene Stephens	50.00
249	Ed O'Brien	90.00
250	Bob Wilson	90.00
251	Sid Hudson	90.00
252	Henry Foiles	90.00
254	Preacher Roe	90.00
255	Dixie Howell	90.00
256	Les Peden	90.00
257	Bob Boyd	90.00
258	Jim Gilliam	235.00
259	Ray McMillan	50.00
260	Sam Calderone	90.00
262	Bob Oldis	90.00
263	Johnny Podres	250.00
264	Gene Wooding	55.00
265	Jackie Jensen	110.00
266	Bob Cain	90.00
269	Duane Pillette	90.00
270	Vern Stephens	90.00
272	Bill Antonello	90.00
273	Harvey Haddix	110.00
274	John Riddle	90.00
276	Ken Raffensberger	90.00
277	Don Lund	90.00
278	Willie Miranda	90.00
279	Joe Coleman	50.00
280	Milt Boling	400.00

1954 BOWMAN

	NM
Complete Set (224):	4200.00
Common Player (1-128):	8.00
Common Player (129-224):	10.00

		NM
1	Phil Rizzuto	120.00
15	Richie Ashburn	60.00
23	Harvey Kuenn	30.00
33b	Vic Raschi	30.00
45	Ralph Kiner	30.00
50	George Kell	30.00
58	Pee Wee Reese	65.00
62	Enos Slaughter	40.00
64	Eddie Mathews	52.50
65	Mickey Mantle	1000.00
66a	Ted Williams	3500.00
66b	Jimmy Piersall	70.00
84	Larry Doby	30.00
89	Willie Mays	350.00
90	Roy Campanella	150.00
95	Robin Roberts	50.00
101	Don Larsen	48.00
132	Bob Feller	75.00
138a	Gil Hodges	65.00
138b	Gil Hodges	65.00
145a	Billy Martin	45.00
145b	Billy Martin	45.00
161	Yogi Berra	125.00
163a	Dave Philley	30.00
164	Early Wynn	45.00
170	Duke Snider	150.00
177	Whitey Ford	90.00
196	Bob Lemon	35.00
210	Jimmy Piersall	30.00

1954 TOPPS

	NM
Complete Set (250):	6000.00
Common Player (1-50):	15.00
Common Player (51-75):	24.00
Common Player (76-250):	15.00

		NM
1	Ted Williams	800.00
10	Jackie Robinson	225.00
13	Billy Martin	50.00
17	Phil Rizzuto	60.00
20	Warren Spahn	65.00
30	Eddie Mathews	70.00
32	Duke Snider	150.00
37	Whitey Ford	80.00
45	Richie Ashburn	65.00
50	Yogi Berra	175.00
70	Larry Doby	65.00
90	Willie Mays	400.00
94	Ernie Banks	700.00
102	Gil Hodges	70.00
128	Hank Aaron	1200.00
132	Tom Lasorda	145.00
201	Al Kaline	550.00
239	Bill Skowron	85.00
250	Ted Williams	750.00

1955 BOWMAN

	NM
Complete Set (320):	4250.00
Common Players (1-224):	8.00
Common Players (225-320):	16.00

		NM
1	Hoyt Wilhelm	100.00
10	Phil Rizzuto	65.00
22	Roy Campanella	120.00
23	Al Kaline	145.00
33	Nellie Fox	35.00
37	Pee Wee Reese	60.00
59	Whitey Ford	65.00
68	Elston Howard	82.00
103	Eddie Mathews	45.00
132b	Harvey Kuenn	35.00
134	Bob Feller	65.00
158	Gil Hodges	45.00
168	Yogi Berra	95.00
179	Hank Aaron	200.00
184	Willie Mays	190.00
202	Mickey Mantle	800.00
242	Ernie Banks	300.00
265	Al Barlick	65.00
267	George Honochick	60.00
283	Nestor Chytak	50.00
303	Jocko Conlan	75.00
308	Al Lopez	42.00
315	Cal Hubbard	65.00
320	George Susce, Jr.	45.00

1955 TOPPS

		NM
Complete Set (210):		6000.00
Common Player (1-150):		12.00
Common Player (151-160)		20.00
Common Player (161-210)		30.00

			NM
1	Dusty Rhodes		75.00
2	Ted Williams		400.00
4	Al Kaline		165.00
28	Ernie Banks		175.00
31	Warren Spahn		75.00
47	Hank Aaron		290.00
50	Jackie Robinson		245.00
123	Sandy Koufax		675.00
124	Harmon Killebrew		225.00
125	Ken Boyer		60.00
152	Harry Agganis		60.00
155	Eddie Mathews		85.00
164	Roberto Clemente		1750.00
187	Gil Hodges		130.00
189	Phil Rizzuto		125.00
194	Willie Mays		425.00
198	Yogi Berra		175.00
210	Duke Snider		375.00

1956 TOPPS

		NM
Complete Set (340):		5750.00
Common Players (1-100):		8.00
Common Players (101-180):		9.00
Common Players (181-260):		12.00
Common Players (261-340):		9.00

			NM
1	William Harridge		90.00
5	Ted Williams		325.00
10	Warren Spahn		70.00

11a	Cubs Team	75.00
15	Ernie Banks	80.00
20	Al Kaline	100.00
30	Jackie Robinson	175.00
31	Hank Aaron	235.00
33	Roberto Clemente	300.00
79	Sandy Koufax	250.00
85a	Indians Team	75.00
90a	Redlegs Team	80.00
95a	Braves Team	75.00
100a	Orioles Team	75.00
101	Roy Campanella	135.00
110	Yogi Berra	125.00
113	Phil Rizzuto	80.00
130	Willie Mays	275.00
135	Mickey Mantle	1100.00
150	Duke Snider	115.00
164	Harmon Killebrew	90.00
200	Bob Feller	100.00
226	Giants Team	70.00
240	Whitey Ford	110.00
251	Yankees Team	200.00
260	Pee Wee Reese	100.00
292	Luis Aparicio	120.00
-	Checklist 1/3	235.00
-	Checklist 2/4	275.00

1957 TOPPS

		NM
Complete Set (407):		6300.00
Common Player (1-88):		8.00
Common Player (89-264):		7.00
Common Player (265-352):		17.00
Common Player (353-407):		7.00

			NM
1	Ted Williams		450.00
2	Yogi Berra		115.00
10	Willie Mays		195.00
18	Don Drysdale		175.00
20	Hank Aaron		190.00
24	Bill Mazeroski		60.00
25	Whitey Ford		70.00
30	Pee Wee Reese		60.00
35	Frank Robinson		180.00
55	Ernie Banks		100.00
76	Roberto Clemente		265.00
90	Warren Spahn		60.00
95	Mickey Mantle		900.00
97	Yankees Team		72.00
125	Al Kaline		90.00
170	Duke Snider		100.00
210	Roy Campanella		100.00
212	Rocky Colavito		125.00
286	Bobby Richardson		110.00

302	Sandy Koufax	275.00
312	Tony Kubek	65.00
317	Giants Team	60.00
322	Redlegs Team	60.00
324	Dodgers Team	100.00
328	Brooks Robinson	350.00
338	Jim Bunning	120.00
400	Dodgers' Sluggers	200.00
407	M. Mantle, Y. Berra	375.00
-	Checklist Series 1-2	250.00
-	Checklist Series 1-2	250.00
-	Checklist Series 2-3	275.00
-	Checklist Series 2-3	275.00
-	Checklist Series 3-4	600.00
-	Checklist Series 3-4	600.00
-	Checklist Series 4-5	900.00
-	Checklist Series 4-5	900.00
-	Contest July 19	60.00

1958 TOPPS

		NM
Complete Set (495):		4500.00
Common Player (1-110):		11.00
Common Player (111-474):		7.50
All-Stars (475-495):		10.00

			NM
1	Ted Williams		400.00
2A	Bob Lemon		25.00
2B	Bob Lemon (YT)		50.00
5	Willie Mays		200.00
19	Giants Team		30.00
20B	Gil McDougald (YL)		35.00
25	Don Drysdale		65.00
30A	Hank Aaron		200.00
30B	Hank Aaron (YL)		425.00
42	John Roseboro (R)		20.00
44	Senators Team		20.00
47	Roger Maris (R)		440.00
52A	Roberto Clemente		250.00
52B	Roberto Clemente (YT)		450.00
70A	Al Kaline		80.00
70B	Al Kaline (YL)		165.00
71	Dodgers Team		50.00
85A	Luis Aparicio		30.00
85B	Luis Aparicio (YT)		65.00
88	Duke Snider		65.00
90	Robin Roberts		30.00
100A	Early Wynn		25.00
100B	Early Wynn (YT)		55.00
101A	Bobby Richardson		25.00
101B	Bobby Richardson (YL)		60.00
115	Jim Bunning		30.00
142	Enos Slaughter		20.00
150	Mickey Mantle		825.00
162	Gil Hodges		26.00
175	Marv Throneberry (R)		10.00
187	Sandy Koufax		200.00

230	Richie Ashburn	.30.00
238	Bill Mazeroski	.20.00
246	Yankees Team	.80.00
270	Warren Spahn	.50.00
271	Billy Martin	.15.00
275	Elston Howard	.15.00
285	Frank Robinson	.100.00
288	Harmon Killebrew	.75.00
296	Ryne Duren (R)	.15.00
304	Kaline/Kuenn	.20.00
307	Brooks Robinson	.100.00
310	Ernie Banks	.100.00
314	Snider/Alston	.25.00
320	Whitey Ford	.45.00
321	Kluszewski/Williams	.60.00
324	Hoyt Wilhelm	.15.00
343	Orlando Cepeda (R)	.100.00
350	Ken Boyer	.15.00
351	Aaron/Mathews	.35.00
368	Rocky Colavito	.45.00
370	Yogi Berra	.80.00
375	Pee Wee Reese	.50.00
377B	Braves Team (num)	.80.00
393	Tony Kubek	.20.00
397B	Tigers Team (num)	.85.00
400	Nellie Fox	.20.00
408B	Orioles Team (num)	.85.00
418	Mantle/Aaron	.250.00
420	Vada Pinson (R)	.35.00
429B	Redlegs Team (num)	.85.00
433A	Pancho Herrera (err)	.600.00
436	Mays/Snider	.70.00
440	Eddie Mathews	.30.00
464	Curt Flood (R)	.30.00
475	Haney/Stengel (AS/Mgr.)	.20.00
476	Stan Musial (AS, TP)	.40.00
480	Eddie Mathews (AS)	.15.00
482	Ernie Banks (AS)	.30.00
483	Luis Aparicio (AS)	.15.00
484	Frank Robinson (AS)	.25.00
485	Ted Williams (AS)	.120.00
486	Willie Mays (AS)	.50.00
487	Mickey Mantle (AS, TP)	.180.00
488	Hank Aaron (AS)	.50.00
494	Warren Spahn (AS)	.20.00
495	Herb Score (AS)	.15.00

1959 TOPPS

		NM
Complete Set (572):		.5250.00
Common Player (1-110):		.6.00
Common Player (111-506):		.4.00
Common Player (507-572):		.15.00

		NM
1	Ford Frick (Com.)	.50.00
8	Phillies Team	.60.00
10	Mickey Mantle	.550.00
20	Duke Snider	.45.00
30	Nelson Fox	.3000
34	Kaline/Maxwell	.15.00
35	Ted Kluszewski	.15.00
40A	Warren Spahn (err)	.60.00
40B	Warren Spahn (err)	.100.00
40C	Warren Spahn (cor)	.50.00
48	Orioles Team	.20.00
50	Willie Mays	.130.00
69	Giants Team	.20.00
76	Bobby Richardson	.20.00
94	White Sox Team	.30.00
102	Felipe Alou (R)	.35.00
147	Banks/Long/Moryn	.20.00
149	Jim Bunning	.20.00
150	Stan Musial	.125.00
155	Enos Slaughter	.15.00
163	Sandy Koufax	.140.00
180	Yogi Berra	.65.00
202	Roger Maris	.110.00
212	Aaron/Mathews	.70.00
237	McDougald/Turley/Richardson	.15.00
260	Early Wynn	.15.00
262	Podres/Drysdale/Labine	.15.00
270	Gil Hodges	.25.00
295	Billy Martin	.10.00
300	Richie Ashburn	.25.00
310	Luis Aparicio	.15.00
316B	Ralph Lumenti (no opt.)	.75.00
317	Ashburn/Mays	.65.00
321B	Giallmbdo. (no opt.)	.75.00
322B	Harry Hanebrink (no TR)	.70.00
336B	Billy Loes (no TR)	.75.00
338	Sparky Anderson (R)	.75.00
340	Hoyt Wilhelm	.15.00
350	Ernie Banks	.70.00
352	Robin Roberts	.15.00
359	Bill White (R)	.22.00
360	Al Kaline	.60.00
362B	D. Nichols (no opt.)	.75.00
380	Hank Aaron	.125.00
387	Don Drysdale	.40.00
390	Orlando Cepeda	.25.00
408	Aparicio/Fox	.20.00
420	Rocky Colavito	.30.00
430	Whitey Ford	.40.00
435	Frank Robinson	.45.00
439	Brooks Robinson	.45.00
450	Eddie Mathews	.25.00
457	Dodgers Team	.25.00
461	Mantle Hits 42nd HR	.150.00
463	Kaline Young Champ	.15.00
464	Mays' Series Catch	.35.00
466	Aaron's Series HR	.30.00
468	Snider's Victory	.15.00
469	Banks Wins MVP	.15.00
470	Musial's 3000th Hit	.20.00
478	Roberto Clemente	.225.00
480	Red Schoendienst	.15.00
509	Norm Cash (R)	.60.00
510	Yankees Team	.125.00
514	Bob Gibson (R)	.250.00
515	Harmon Killebrew	.120.00
518	Mike Cuellar (R)	.30.00
528	Pirates Team	.55.00
542	Jim Perry (R)	.25.00
543	Clemente/Skinner/Virdon	.150.00

550	Roy Campanella	.160.00
552	Casey Stengel (AS, Mgr)	.35.00
356	Nellie Fox (AS)	.35.00
559	Ernie Banks (AS)	.60.00
560	Luis Aparicio (AS)	.30.00
561	Hank Aaron (AS)	.115.00
562	Al Kaline (AS)	.60.00
563	Willie Mays (AS)	.115.00
564	Mickey Mantle (AS)	.300.00
571	Warren Spahn (AS)	.35.00
572	Billy Pierce (AS)	.25.00

1960 LEAF

BROOKS ROBINSON
INFIELDER—BALTIMORE ORIOLES

		NM
Complete Set (144):		.1250.00
Common Player (1-72):		.4.00
Common Player (73-144):		.15.00

		NM
27	Brooks Robinson	.50.00
37	Duke Snider	.50.00
58b	Hal Smith	.65.00
58c	Hal Smith	.65.00
125	Sparky Anderson	.80.00
128	Orlando Cepeda	.65.00
144	Jim Bunning	.80.00

1960 TOPPS

DUKE SNIDER OUTFIELD
LOS ANGELES DODGERS

		NM
Complete Set (572):		.3500.00
Common Players (1-440):		.3.50
Common Players (441-506):		.6.00
Common Players (507-572):		.4.00

		NM
1	Early Wynn	.30.00
7	Mays/Rigney	.20.00
10	Ernie Banks	.45.00
18	Dodgers Team	.35.00

28	Brooks Robinson	45.00
34	Sparky Anderson	20.00
35	Whitey Ford	40.00
50	Al Kaline	45.00
72	Tigers Team	15.00
73	Bob Gibson	45.00
100	Nellie Fox	15.00
132	Frank Howard (R)	20.00
136	Jim Kaat (R)	40.00
148	Carl Yastrzemski (R)	140.00
160	Boyer/Mantle	130.00
173	Billy Martin	15.00
200	Willie Mays	100.00
210	Harmon Killebrew	25.00
212	Walter Alston (Mgr)	15.00
227	Casey Stengel (Mgr)	15.00
230	Buhl/Burdette/Spahn	10.00
240	Luis Aparicio	15.00
260	Colavito/Francona	10.00
264	Robin Roberts	10.00
295	Gil Hodges	15.00
300	Hank Aaron	100.00
305	Richie Ashburn	30.00
316	Willie McCovey (R)	110.00
327	Roberto Clemente	200.00
332	Yankees Team	50.00
335	Red Schoendienst	10.00
343	Sandy Koufax	140.00
350	Mickey Mantle	450.00
366	Dallas Green (R)	8.00
388	Roger Maris	120.00
388	WS Game 4 (Hodges)	10.00
389	WS Game 5 (Aparicio)	10.00
395	Hoyt Wilhelm	10.00
400	Rocky Colavito	15.00
405	Bobby Richardson	15.00
420	Eddie Mathews	25.00
445	Warren Spahn	40.00
448	Jim Gentile (R)	15.00
450	Orlando Cepeda	20.00
475	Don Drysdale	40.00
480	Yogi Berra	70.00
484	Pirates Team	30.00
490	Frank Robinson	45.00
493	Duke Snider	45.00
502	Jim Bunning	15.00
509	Tommy Davis (R)	30.00
513	Cubs Team	30.00
537	Red Sox Team	30.00
554	Willie McCovey (AS)	45.00
558	Eddie Mathews (AS)	30.00
560	Ernie Banks (AS)	60.00
561	Al Kaline (AS)	60.00
563	Mickey Mantle (AS)	120.00
564	Willie Mays (AS)	90.00
566	Hank Aaron (AS)	100.00
570	Don Drysdale (AS)	30.00
572	John Antonelli (AS)	30.00

1961 TOPPS

	NM
Complete Set (589):	4000.00
Common Player (1-370):	2.50
Common Player (371-446):	3.00
Common Player (447-522):	5.00
Common Player (522-589):	24.00

		NM
1	Dick Groat	30.00
2	Roger Maris	175.00
10	Brooks Robinson	35.00

20	Robin Roberts	10.00
25	Pinson/Robinson/Bell	10.00
35	Ron Santo (R)	55.00
41	Mays/Clemente (LL)	25.00
43	Banks/Aaron/Mathews (LL)	25.00
44	Mantle/Maris/Colavito (LL)	120.00
49	Drysdale/Koufax (LL)	15.00
80	Harmon Killebrew	20.00
88	Richie Ashburn	10.00
120	Eddie Mathews	25.00
141	Billy Williams (R)	60.00
150	Willie Mays	100.00
160	Whitey Ford	36.00
180	Bobby Richardson	10.00
200	Warren Spahn	30.00
207	Koufax/Podres	25.00
211	Bob Gibson	35.00
228	Yankees Team	50.00
260	Don Drysdale	30.00
273A	Checklist 4	15.00
287	Carl Yastrzemski	50.00
290	Stan Musial	100.00
300	Mickey Mantle	450.00
307	WS Game 2 (Mantle)	85.00
311	WS Game 6 (Ford)	15.00
312	WS Game 7 (Mazeroski)	20.00
313	WS Summary	15.00
327	Matty Alou (R)	10.00
330	Rocky Colavito	15.00
344	Sandy Koufax	100.00
350	Ernie Banks	40.00
360	Frank Robinson	40.00
361B	Checklist	515.00
371	Bill Skowron (SP)	50.00
388	Roberto Clemente	150.00
401	Ruth Hits 60th HR	40.00
402	Larsen's Per. Game	20.00
405	Gehrig Benched	75.00
406	Mantle's 565 HR	75.00
408	Mathewson's 267 Ks	20.00
415	Hank Aaron	100.00
416	Dick Howser (R)	10.00
417	Juan Marichal (R)	115.00
425	Yogi Berra	70.00
426	Braves Team (#463)	10.00
429	Al Kaline	40.00
430	Bill Mazeroski (SP)	50.00
435	Orlando Cepeda	15.00
436	Jim Maloney (R)	15.00
437A	Checklist 6 (err)	10.00
437B	Checklist 6 (cor)	10.00
440	Luis Aparicio	15.00
443	Duke Snider	40.00
455	Early Wynn	15.00
460	Gil Hodges	15.00
471	Phil Rizzuto (MVP)	15.00

472	Yogi Berra (MVP)	55.00
475	Mickey Mantle (MVP)	200.00
478	Roger Maris (MVP)	50.00
480	Roy Campanella (MVP)	35.00
482	Willie Mays (MVP)	45.00
484	Hank Aaron (MVP)	45.00
485	Ernie Banks (MVP)	30.00
490	Jim Bunning	15.00
506	Willie Davis (R)	15.00
516	Checklist 7	10.00
517	Willie McCovey	45.00
525	Ron Perranoski (R)	35.00
541	Roland Sheldon (R)	35.00
542	Twins Team	60.00
545	Hoyt Wilhelm	50.00
554	Pirates Team	65.00
559	Jim Gentile	50.00
563	Bob Cerv	40.00
565	Felipe Alou	45.00
568	Bill Skowron (AS)	35.00
570	Nellie Fox (AS)	50.00
571	Bill Mazeroski (AS)	35.00
572	Brooks Robinson (AS)	80.00
573	Ken Boyer (AS)	35.00
575	Ernie Banks (AS)	90.00
576	Roger Maris (AS)	175.00
577	Hank Aaron (AS)	170.00
578	Mickey Mantle (AS)	450.00
579	Willie Mays (AS)	175.00
580	Al Kaline (AS)	90.00
581	Frank Robinson (AS)	85.00
588	Whitey Ford (AS)	85.00
589	Warren Spahn (AS)	100.00

1962 TOPPS

	NM
Complete Set (598):	5500.00
Common Player (1-370):	3.75
Common Player (371-446):	4.50
Common Player (447-522):	8.00
Common Player (523-598):	15.00

		NM
1	Roger Maris	160.00
5	Sandy Koufax	110.00
10	Roberto Clemente	140.00
18	M. Mantle, Willie Mays	150.00
50	Stan Musial	70.00
53	A.L. HR Leaders	80.00
139a	Hal Reniff	55.00
199	Gaylord Perry	70.00
200	Mickey Mantle	400.00
251	Yankees Team	55.00
300	Willie Mays	100.00

318	Mickey Mantle	120.00
320	Hank Aaron	95.00
360	Yogi Berra	70.00
387	Lou Brock	110.00
394	Hank Aaron	40.00
395	Willie Mays	40.00
401	R. Maris, O. Cepeda	50.00
425	Carl Yastrzemski	90.00
458b	Bob Buhl	40.00
462b	Willie Tasby	45.00
471	Mickey Mantle	145.00
500	Duke Snider	40.00
530	Bob Gibson	110.00
537	Indians Team	42.00
544	Willie McCovey	125.00
552	Cubs Team	45.00
575	Red Schoendienst	40.00
584	Twins Team	45.00
591	Rookie Parade Pitchers	60.00
592	Rookie Parade Pitchers	70.00
594	Bob Uecker	60.00
595	Rookie Parade Infielders	42.00
596	Rookie Parade Infielders	65.00
597	Rookie Parade Infielders	42.00
598	Rookie Parade Outfielders	75.00

1963 FLEER

CARL YASTRZEMSKI
Boston Red Sox—Outfield

	NM
Complete Set (67):	1500.00
Common Player:	11.00

		NM
4	Brooks Robinson	80.00
5	Willie Mays	175.00
8	Carl Yastrzemski	75.00
41	Don Drysdale	55.00
42	Sandy Koufax	165.00
43	Maury Wills	95.00
45	Warren Spahn	55.00
46	Joe Adcock	160.00
56	Robert Clemente	175.00
61	Bob Gibson	55.00
-	Checklist	500.00

1963 TOPPS

	NM
Complete Set (576):	4500.00
Common Player (1-283):	3.00
Common Player (284-446):	4.00
Common Player (447-552):	16.00
Common Player (553-576):	11.00

		NM
1	Musial/Aaron (LL)	40.00
2	Mantle/Runnels (LL)	40.00

MICKEY MANTLE
N. Y. YANKEES   OF

3	Mays/Aaron/Banks (LL)	30.00
4	Killebrew/Maris/Colavito (LL)	15.00
5	Koufax/Drysdale/Gibson LL)	20.00
9	Drysdale/Koufax/Gibson (LL)	15.00
18	Burgess/Clemente/Skinner	60.00
25	Al Kaline	32.00
54A	Dave DeBusschere (R, 62)	15.00
68	Hodges/Snider	15.00
108	Hoyt Wilhelm	10.00
115	Carl Yastrzemski	40.00
120	Roger Maris	50.00
125	Robin Roberts	10.00
126	Bob Uecker	15.00
135	Richie Ashburn	15.00
138	Mays/Musial	50.00
144	WS Game 3 (Maris)	10.00
169	Gaylord Perry	22.00
173	Mantle/Richardson/Tresh	175.00
200	Mickey Mantle	550.00
205	Luis Aparicio	15.00
210	Sandy Koufax	150.00
228	Oliva/Kranepool (R)	40.00
233	Casey Stengel (Mgr)	15.00
240	Rocky Colavito	15.00
242	Aaron/Banks	50.00
245	Gil Hodges	20.00
247	Yankees Team	35.00
250	Stan Musial	120.00
275	Eddie Mathews	20.00
288	White Sox Team	10.00
300	Willie Mays	125.00
312	Colt .45s Team	20.00
320	Warren Spahn	35.00
337	Dodgers Team	20.00
340	Yogi Berra	65.00
345	Brooks Robinson	50.00
353	Billy Williams	25.00
360	Don Drysdale	40.00
377	Orioles Team	10.00
380	Ernie Banks	70.00
390	Hank Aaron	130.00
397	A's Team	10.00
398	Boog Powell	25.00
400	Frank Robinson	40.00
412	Drysdale/Koufax/Podres	38.00
415	Bob Gibson	50.00
417	Giants Team	10.00
431B	Checklist	620.00
440	Juan Marichal	30.00
446	Whitey Ford	40.00
451	Indians Team	35.00
466	Bill Freehan (R, SP)	55.00
470	Tom Tresh (SP)	60.00
472	Lou Brock	100.00
473	Mets Team	90.00
490	Willie McCovey	125.00

500	Killebrew, H. (SP)	135.00
503	Braves Team	35.00
509A	Checklist	720.00
509B	Checklist 7	20.00
524	Cardinals Team	25.00
537	Pete Rose (R)	750.00
540	Roberto Clemente	350.00
544	Rusty Staub (R)	40.00
550	Duke Snider	70.00
552	Tigers Team	40.00
553	Willie Stargell (R)	125.00
562	Dave McNally (R)	20.00

1964 TOPPS

PIRATES
BOB CLEMENTE   outfield

	NM
Complete Set (587):	2550.00
Common Player (1-196):	2.00
Common Player (197-370):	3.00
Common Player (371-522):	7.00
Common Player (523-587):	12.50

		NM
1	Koufax/Friend (LL)	25.00
3	Koufax/Marichal/Spahn (LL)	15.00
5	Drysdale/Koufax (LL)	15.00
7	Aaron/Clemente (LL)	15.00
8	Kaline/Yastrzemski (LL)	10.00
9	Aaron/Mays/McCovey (LL)	25.00
11	Aaron/Boyer/White (LL)	10.00
21	Yogi Berra (Mgr)	30.00
29	Lou Brock	35.00
35	Eddie Mathews	20.00
38	Jim Wynn (R)	10.00
50	Mickey Mantle	300.00
55	Ernie Banks	35.00
81	Fox/Killebrew	10.00
116	Tony Oliva	10.00
120	Don Drysdale	20.00
125	Pete Rose	125.00
128	Mickey Lolich (R)	20.00
136	WS Game 1 (Koufax)	15.00
146	Tommy John (R)	25.00
150	Willie Mays	85.00
155	Duke Snider	25.00
167	Lou Piniella (R)	35.00
175	Billy Williams	10.00
177	Harmon Killebrew	20.00
192	Schilling/Yastrzemski	15.00
200	Sandy Koufax	90.00
205	Nellie Fox	10.00
210	Carl Yastrzemski	35.00
225	Roger Maris	55.00
230	Brooks Robinson	40.00
243	Richie Allen (R)	30.00
244	Tony LaRussa (R)	30.00

250	Al Kaline	40.00
260	Frank Robinson	40.00
262	Mike Shannon (R)	10.00
265	Jim Bunning	10.00
267	Wilbur Wood (R)	7.00
280	Juan Marichal	15.00
285	Robin Roberts	15.00
287	Tony Conigliaro (R)	45.00
300	Hank Aaron	90.00
306	Cepeda/Mays	35.00
320	Rocky Colavito	10.00
324	Casey Stengel (Mgr)	15.00
331	Kaline/Mantle/Maris	175.00
337	Jeff Torborg (R)	7.50
342	Willie Stargell	25.00
350	Willie McCovey	20.00
368	Don Buford (R)	7.00
380	Whitey Ford	35.00
400	Warren Spahn	35.00
419	Ken Harrelson (R)	10.00
423	Aaron/Mays	120.00
433	Yankees Team	30.00
438	Checklist 6	10.00
440	Roberto Clemente	235.00
460	Bob Gibson	40.00
468	Gaylord Perry	35.00
471	Gates Brown (R)	10.00
476	Rico Carty (R)	10.00
509	Gene Alley (R)	10.00
512	Willie Horton (R)	15.00
517A	Checklist 7 (err)	25.00
517B	Checklist 7 (cor)	15.00
541	Phil Niekro (R)	100.00
543	Bob Uecker	35.00
550	Ken Hubbs	30.00
579	Red Sox Team	25.00

1965 TOPPS

	NM
Complete Set (598):	3000.00
Common Players (1-283):	2.00
Common Players (284-370):	3.00
Common Players (371-598):	5.00

		NM
1	Oliva/ Robinson (LL)	20.00
2	Aaron/Clemente (LL)	25.00
3	Killebrew/Mantle (LL)	40.00
4	Mays/ Williams/Cepeda (LL)	15.00
5	Killebrew/Mantle/Robinson (LL)	40.00
6	Boyer/Mays/Santo (LL)	10.00
8	Drysdale/Koufax (LL)	20.00
15	Robin Roberts	10.00
16	Joe Morgan (R, DP)	65.00

50	Juan Marichal	10.00
55	Tony Conigliaro	10.00
74	Rico Petrocelli (R)	10.00
120	Frank Robinson	30.00
130	Al Kaline	30.00
134	WS Game 3 (Mantle)	65.00
138	WS Game 7 (Gibson)	10.00
145	Luis Tiant (R)	25.00
150	Brooks Robinson	30.00
155	Roger Maris	50.00
160	Roberto Clemente	160.00
170	Hank Aaron	80.00
176	Willie McCovey	20.00
187	Casey Stengel (Mgr)	15.00
193	Gaylord Perry	15.00
205	Warren Spahn	30.00
207	Pete Rose	150.00
208	Tommy John	10.00
220	Billy Williams	10.00
236	Denny McLain (R)	25.00
250	Willie Mays	90.00
260	Don Drysdale	20.00
266	Bert Campaneris (R)	10.00
276	Hoyt Wilhelm	10.00
282	Masanori Murakami (R)	30.00
300	Sandy Koufax	120.00
308	Cleon Jones (R)	8.00
320	Bob Gibson	35.00
330	Whitey Ford	30.00
340	Tony Oliva	15.00
350	Mickey Mantle	550.00
361	Checklist 5	10.00
377	Willie Stargell	25.00
385	Carl Yastrzemski	70.00
400	Harmon Killebrew	35.00
443	Checklist 6	10.00
460	Richie Allen	35.00
461	Carroll/Niekro (R)	45.00
470	Yogi Berra (Co.)	50.00
473	Blair/Johnson (R)	10.00
477	Steve Carlton (R)	225.00
485	Nellie Fox	15.00
500	Eddie Mathews	30.00
508	Checklist 7	10.00
510	Ernie Banks	75.00
513	Yankees Team	45.00
519	Bob Uecker	25.00
526	Jim Hunter (R, SP)	80.00
527	Jeff Torborg (SP)	15.00
533	McGraw/Swoboda (R, SP)	25.00
540	Lou Brock (SP)	50.00
549	Glenn Beckert (R, SP)	15.00
550	Mel Stottlemyre (R, SP)	30.00
551	Mets Team (SP)	30.00
356	Red Schoendienst (Mgr. SP)	20.00
560	Boog Powell (SP)	20.00
372	Orioles Team (SP)	25.00
573	Jim Lonborg (R, SP)	20.00
581	Tony Perez (R, SP)	90.00
598	Al Downing, (R, SP)	20.00

1966 TOPPS

	NM
Complete Set (598):	2750.00
Common Player (1-109):	1.50
Common Player (110-283):	2.00
Common Player (284-370):	2.50
Common Player (371-446):	5.00
Common Player (447-522):	8.00
Common Player (523-598):	12.50

		NM
1	Willie Mays	125.00
24	Don Kessinger (R)	5.00
28	Phil Niekro	20.00
30	Pete Rose (DP)	40.00
36	Jim Hunter (DP)	20.00
50	Mickey Mantle (DP)	200.00
62B	Merritt Ranew (sold)	30.00
70	Carl Yastrzemski	30.00
72	Tony Perez	25.00
80	Richie Allen	5.00
91A	Bob Uecker (traded)	10.00
91B	Bob Uecker (no trade)	35.00
92	Yankees Team	15.00
99	Clendenon/Stargell	5.00
100	Sandy Koufax	75.00
101A	Checklist 2 (err)	15.00
101B	Checklist 2 (cor)	10.00
103B	Dick Groat (no trade)	30.00
104B	Johnson, (no trade)	30.00
110	Ernie Banks	30.00
120	Harmon Killebrew	15.00
125	Lou Brock	15.00
126	Jim Palmer (R)	100.00
150	Rocky Colavito	6.00
160	Whitey Ford	15.00
195	Joe Morgan	15.00
200	Eddie Mathews	10.00
215	Aaron/Clemente/Mays (LL)	45.00
217	Mays/McCovey/Williams (LL)	20.00
219	Mays/Robinson (LL)	10.00
221	Koufax/Marichal (LL)	10.00
223	Drysdale/Koufax (LL)	10.00
225	Gibson/Koufax (LL)	10.00
234	Roy White (R)	8.00
254	Fergie Jenkins (R)	80.00
255	Willie Stargell	15.00
288	Don Sutton (R)	60.00
300	Roberto Clemente	160.00
310	Frank Robinson	35.00
320	Bob Gibson	25.00
363	Checklist 5	10.00
365	Roger Maris	45.00
379	Cardinals Team	10.00
380	Tony Conigliaro	10.00
390	Brooks Robinson	35.00
404	Pirates Team	10.00
410	Al Kaline	35.00
420	Juan Marichal	12.00
424	May/Osteen (R)	10.00
426	White Sox Team	10.00
430	Don Drysdale	20.00
435	Jim Bunning	10.00
444	Checklist 6	10.00
445	Jim Kaat	10.00

469 Bobby Murcer (R) 30.00
500 Hank Aaron 120.00
517A Checklist 715.00
517B Checklist 715.00
526 Twins Team (SP) 90.00
530 Robin Roberts 50.00
535 Willie Davis (SP) 40.00
540 Denny McLain (SP) 70.00
547 Horace Clarke (R, SP) 35.00
550 Willie McCovey (SP) 90.00
558 George Scott (R) 20.00
565 Jim Piersall (SP) 30.00
580 Billy Williams (SP) 60.00
583 Tigers Team (SP) 115.00
590 Bill Skowron (SP) 30.00
591 Grant Jackson (R, SP) 35.00
598 Gaylord Perry (SP) 175.00

1967 TOPPS

		NM
Complete Set (609):	. . . .	.3600.00
Common Player (1-370):	. . . .	.1.50
Common Player (371-457):	. . . .	.3.00
Common Player (458-533):	. . . .	.5.00
Common Player (534-609):	. . . .	.12.00

			NM
1	Bauer/Robinson/Robinson	. . . .	.20.00
5	Whitey Ford	. . . .	.20.00
20	Orlando Cepeda	. . . .	.6.00
26A	Bob Priddy (no trade)	. . . .	.25.00
30	Al Kaline (DP)	. . . .	.15.00
33	Sal Bando (R)	. . . .	.5.00
42	Mets Team	. . . .	.6.00
45	Roger Maris	. . . .	.50.00
50	Tony Oliva	. . . .	.5.00
55	Don Drysdale	. . . .	.15.00
60	Luis Aparicio	. . . .	.5.00
63	Brock/Flood	. . . .	.7.00
86A	McCormick (no trd)	. . . .	.25.00
100	Frank Robinson (DP)	. . . .	.15.00
103	Checklist 2 (Mantle)	. . . .	.15.00
131	Yankees Team	. . . .	.10.00
140	Willie Stargell	. . . .	.15.00
146	Steve Carlton	. . . .	.70.00
150	Mickey Mantle	. . . . .300.00
152	WS Game 2 (Palmer)	. . . .	.7.00
166	Eddie Mathews	. . . .	.15.00
191B	Checklist 3 (Mays)	. . . .	.10.00
200	Willie Mays	. . . .	.90.00
210	Bob Gibson	. . . .	.20.00
215	Ernie Banks	. . . .	.20.00
216	Cash/Kaline	. . . .	.10.00
234	Koufax/Marichal (LL)	. . . .	.15.00
236	Gibson/Koufax/Marichal/Perry (LL)	.25.00

238 Bunning/Koufax (LL) 10.00
239 Kaline/Oliva/Robinson (LL) 10.00
241 Killebrew/Powell/Robinson (LL) . . .10.00
242 Aaron/Allen/Clemente (LL) 20.00
243 Killebrew/Powell/Robinson (LL) . . .10.00
244 Aaron/Allen/Mays (LL) 20.00
250 Hank Aaron 75.00
280 Tony Conigliaro 10.00
285 Lou Brock 20.00
314 Reggie Smith (R) 8.00
315 Billy Williams 10.00
320 Gaylord Perry 10.00
333 Fergie Jenkins 20.00
337 Joe Morgan 15.00
355 Carl Yastrzemski 30.00
361 Checklist 5 (Clemente) 10.00
369 Jim Hunter 15.00
400 Roberto Clemente (DP) 90.00
417A Bob Bruce (err, DP) 25.00
423 Mays/McCovey (DP) 25.00
430 Pete Rose 75.00
445 Don Sutton 25.00
456 Phil Niekro 15.00
460 Harmon Killebrew 50.00
475 Jim Palmer 70.00
476 Tony Perez (SP) 65.00
477 Braves Team 15.00
480 Willie McCovey 35.00
481 Leo Durocher (Mgr) 15.00
485 Tim McCarver 15.00
492 Pirates Team 15.00
500 Juan Marichal 20.00
503 Dodgers Team 15.00
516 Giants Team 15.00
531 Checklist 7 (Robinson) 10.00
536 Joe Niekro (R) 35.00
540 Norm Cash 30.00
544 Indians Team 30.00
553 Mike Hegan (R) 25.00
558 Mark Belanger (R) 45.00
560 Jim Bunning 65.00
569 Rod Carew (DP) 175.00
570 Maury Wills 85.00
573 White Sox Team 30.00
580 Rocky Colavito 85.00
581 Tom Seaver (R) 600.00
587 Shaw/Sutherland (R) 20.00
600 Brooks Robinson 260.00
604 Red Sox Team 110.00
605 Mike Shannon 45.00
607 Mickey Stanley 30.00
609 Tommy John 65.00

1968 TOPPS

		NM
Complete Set (598):	. . . .	.2750.00
Common Player (1-457):	. . . .	.1.50
Common Player (458-533):	. . . .	.3.00
Common Player (534-598):	. . . .	.3.50

			NM
1	Alou/Clemente (LL)	. . . .	.30.00
2	Kaline/Robinson/Yaz (LL)	. . . . . .	.15.00
3	Aaron/Cepeda/Clemente (LL)	. . . .	.15.00
4	Killebrew/Robinson/Yaz (LL)	. . . .	.10.00
5	Aaron/McCovey/Santo (LL)	. . . .	.10.00
6	Howard/Killebrew/Yaz (LL)	. . . .	.7.00
16	Lou Piniella	. . . .	.6.00
20	Brooks Robinson	. . . .	.25.00
27	Gil Hodges (Mgr)	. . . .	.7.00
37	Billy Williams	. . . .	.9.00

40	Denny McLain	. . . .	.7.00
45	Tom Seaver	. . . .	.50.00
59B	Ed Brinkman (YT)	. . . .	.40.00
50	Willie Mays	. . . .	.70.00
58	Eddie Mathews	. . . .	.10.00
66B	Casey Cox (YT)	. . . .	.85.00
72	Tommy John	. . . .	.5.00
80	Rod Carew	. . . .	.50.00
85	Gaylord Perry	. . . .	.7.00
86	Willie Stargell	. . . .	.10.00
99	Rocky Colavito	. . . .	.6.00
100	Bob Gibson	. . . .	.25.00
103	Don Sutton	. . . .	.8.00
110	Hank Aaron	. . . .	.60.00
130	Tony Perez	. . . .	.10.00
140	Tony Conigliaro	. . . .	.7.00
144	Joe Morgan	. . . .	.10.00
145	Don Drysdale	. . . .	.10.00
150	Roberto Clemente	. . . .	.80.00
151	WS Game 1 (Brock)	. . . .	.9.00
152	WS Game 2 (Yaz)	. . . .	.9.00
154	WS Game 4 (Gibson)	. . . .	.7.00
177	Ryan/Koosman (R)	. . . . .700.00
192A	Checklist 3 (Yaz)	. . . .	.7.00
192B	Checklist 3 (Yaz)	. . . .	.7.00
200	Orlando Cepeda	. . . .	.5.00
201	Mike Marshall (R)	. . . .	.4.00
205	Juan Marichal	. . . .	.8.00
215	Jim Bunning	. . . .	.5.00
220	Harmon Killebrew	. . . .	.15.00
230	Pete Rose	. . . .	.40.00
235	Ron Santo	. . . .	.5.00
240	Al Kaline	. . . .	.25.00
247	Johnny Bench (R)	. . . . .125.00
250	Carl Yastrzemski	. . . .	.25.00
251	Manny Sanguillen (R)	. . . .	.5.00
256	Norm Cash	. . . .	.5.00
257	Phil Niekro	. . . .	.7.00
280	Mickey Mantle	. . . . .250.00
290	Willie McCovey	. . . .	.11.00
310	Luis Aparicio	. . . .	.5.00
330	Roger Maris	. . . .	.40.00
350	Hoyt Wilhelm	. . . .	.7.00
355	Ernie Banks	. . . .	.25.00
361	Harmon Killebrew (AS)	. . . .	.7.00
363	Rod Carew (AS)	. . . .	.7.00
364	Joe Morgan (AS)	. . . .	.7.00
365	Brooks Robinson (AS)	. . . .	.8.00
369	Carl Yastrzemski (AS)	. . . .	.8.00
370	Hank Aaron (AS)	. . . .	.16.00
372	Lou Brock (AS)	. . . .	.8.00
373	Frank Robinson (AS)	. . . .	.8.00
374	Roberto Clemente (AS)	. . . . . .	.25.00
378	Bob Gibson (AS)	. . . .	.8.00
384	Hal McRae (R)	. . . .	.7.00
385	Jim Hunter	. . . .	.12.00

400B	Mike McCormick (WT)	.125.00
408	Steve Carlton	.30.00
410	Fergie Jenkins	.10.00
414	Mickey Lolich	.5.00
454A	Checklist 6 (Robsn)	.7.00
454B	Checklist 6 (Robsn)	.7.00
460	Jim Lonborg	.5.00
470	Bill Freehan	.5.00
477	Phillies Team	.6.00
480	Cardenas/Clemente/Oliva	.50.00
490	Killebrew/Mantle/Mays	.175.00
500	Frank Robinson	.28.00
518A	Checklist 7 (Boyer)	.10.00
518B	Checklist 7 (Boyer)	.10.00
520	Lou Brock	.20.00
528	Tigers Team	.60.00
530	Robinson/Robinson	.35.00
571	Tony LaRussa	.10.00
575	Jim Palmer	.30.00
579	Larry Hisle (R)	.7.00

1969 TOPPS

	NM
Complete Set (664):	.2000.00
Common Player (1-218):	.1.50
Common Player (219-327):	.2.50
Common Player (328-512):	.1.50
Common Player (513-588):	.2.50
Common Player (589-664):	.3.00

		NM
1	Cater/Oliva/Yaz (LL)	.10.00
2	Alou/Alou/Rose (LL)	.6.00
4	McCovey/Santo/Williams (LL)	.5.00
6	Allen/Banks/McCovey (LL)	.5.00
10	Gibson/Jenkins/Marichal (LL)	.6.00
20	Ernie Banks	.20.00
35	Joe Morgan	.9.00
47B	Paul Popovich (emblem)	.20.00
49B	Jones/Rodriguez (R, cor)	.20.00
50	Roberto Clemente	.50.00
77B	Ron Perranoski (no emb.)	.20.00
82	Al Oliver (R)	.15.00
85	Lou Brock	.15.00
95	Johnny Bench	.50.00
99A	Nettles (R, no loop)	.20.00
99B	Nettles (R, loop)	.18.00
100	Hank Aaron	.50.00
107B	Checklist 2 (Gibson, cor)	.7.00
120	Pete Rose	.25.00
130	Carl Yastrzemski	.15.00
150	Denny McLain	.5.00
151B	Clay Dalrymple (Phillies)	.10.00
162	WS Game 1 (Gibson)	.7.00

164	WS Game 3 (McCarver)	.6.00
165	WS Game 4 (Brock)	.7.00
166	WS Game 5 (Kaline)	.7.00
168	WS Game 7 (Gibson)	.7.00
190	Willie Mays	.40.00
200	Bob Gibson	.15.00
208B	Donn Clendenon (Expos)	.10.00
235	Jim Hunter	.9.00
237	Bobby Cox (R)	.7.50
244	Ray Fosse, R (R)	.5.00
250	Frank Robinson	.30.00
255	Steve Carlton	.35.00
260	Reggie Jackson (R)	.275.00
295	Tony Perez	.12.00
304	Cito Gaston (R)	.10.00
311	Sparky Lyle (R)	.12.00
370	Juan Marichal	.8.00
375	Harmon Killebrew	.16.00
394	Lou Piniella	.5.00
400	Don Drysdale	.15.00
410	Al Kaline	.15.00
412	Checklist 5 (Mantle)	.15.00
416	Willie McCovey (AS)	.6.00
419	Rod Carew (AS)	.8.00
421	Brooks Robinson (AS)	.7.00
424	Pete Rose (AS)	.15.00
425	Carl Yastrzemski (AS)	.10.00
428	Lou Brock (AS)	.6.00
430	Johnny Bench (AS)	.10.00
432	Bob Gibson (AS)	.6.00
440A	Willie McCovey	.15.00
440B	Willie McCovey (WL)	.90.00
450	Billy Williams	.6.00
470B	Mel Stottlemyre (WL)	.25.00
4768	Ken Brett (R, WL)	.25.00
480	Tom Seaver	.75.00
485A	Gaylord Perry	.10.00
485B	Gaylord Perry (WL)	.75.00
500A	Mickey Mantle	.350.00
500B	Mickey Mantle (WL)	.1000.00
504	Checklist 6 (Robinson)	.7.00
510	Rod Carew	.35.00
516	Earl Weaver (R. Mgr)	.16.00
533	Nolan Ryan	.450.00
539	Epstein/Williams	.8.00
545	Willie Stargell	.15.00
550	Brooks Robinson	.25.00
560	Luis Tiant	.5.00
562	Bob Watson (R)	.6.00
564	Gil Hodges (Mgr)	.10.00
565	Hoyt Wilhelm	.6.00
570	Ron Santo	.6.00
572	Marichal/McCovey	.15.00
573	Jim Palmer	.30.00
582B	Checklist 7 (Oliva)	.7.00
587	Joe Rudi (R)	.5.50
597	Rollie Fingers (R)	.40.00
601	Tug McGraw (SP)	.7.00
630	Bobby Bonds (R)	.35.00
640	Fergie Jenkins	.20.00
650	Ted Williams (Mgr)	.15.00
653	Aurelio Rodriguez (R)	.5.00

1970 TOPPS

	MT
Complete Set (720):	.1350.00
Common Player (1-372):	.1.00
Common Player (373-546):	.1.25
Common Player (547-633):	.3.50
Common Player (634-720):	.7.50

		NM
1	Mets Team	.15.00
10	Carl Yastrzemski	.15.00
61	Clemente/Rose (LL)	.15.00
140	Reggie Jackson	.50.00
189	Thurman Munson (R)	.50.00
195	NLCS Game 1 (Seaver)	.10.00
197	NLCS Game 3 (Ryan)	.25.00
198	NLCS Summary (Ryan)	.10.00
210	Juan Marichal	.6.00
211	Ted Williams (Mgr)	.10.00
220	Steve Carlton	.10.00
230	Brooks Robinson	.10.00
290	Rod Carew	.20.00
300	Tom Seaver	.35.00
350	Roberto Clemente	.70.00
449	Jim Palmer	.10.00
450	Willie McCovey (AS)	.6.00
458	Pete Rose (AS)	.10.00
459	Reggie Jackson (AS)	.10.00
461	Carl Yastrzemski (AS)	.10.00
462	Hank Aaron (AS)	.15.00
464	Johnny Bench (AS)	.10.00
470	Willie Stargell	.10.00
500	Hank Aaron	.55.00
502	Rollie Fingers	.10.00
530	Bob Gibson	.15.00
565	Jim Hunter	.10.00
580	Pete Rose	.50.00
600	Willie Mays	.70.00
621	Darrell Evans (R)	.10.00
622	Don Sutton	.10.00
630	Ernie Banks	.50.00
640	Al Kaline	.50.00
654	Oscar Gamble (R)	.10.00
660	Johnny Bench	.90.00
700	Frank Robinson	.50.00
712	Nolan Ryan	.375.00
713	Pilots Team	.25.00
720	Rick Reichardt	.15.00

1971 TOPPS

	NM
Complete Set (752):	.1950.00
Common Player (1-393):	.1.50
Common Player (394-523):	.2.00
Common Player (524-643):	.3.50
Common Player (644-752):	.6.00

		NM
1	Orioles Team	.15.00
5	Thuman Munson	.20.00
14	Dave Concepcion (R)	.15.00
20	Reggie Jackson	.25.00
55	Steve Carlton	.15.00

100	Pete Rose	.35.00
117	Ted Simmons (R)	.10.00
160	Tom Seaver	.20.00
180	Al Kaline	.20.00
210	Rod Carew	.20.00
250	Johnny Bench	.15.00
300	Brooks Robinson	.15.00
341	Steve Garvey (R)	.25.00
380	Ted Williams (Mgr)	.10.00
400	Hank Aaron	.40.00
450	Bob Gibson	.15.00
513	Nolan Ryan	.250.00
525	Ernie Banks	.50.00
530	Carl Yastrzemski	.30.00
550	Harmon Killebrew	.25.00
570	Jim Palmer	.25.00
580	Tony Perez	.15.00
600	Willie Mays	.80.00
619B	Checklist 6 (cor)	.10.00
625	Lou Brock	.25.00
630	Roberto Clemente	.100.00
640	Frank Robinson	.35.00
648	Jon Matlack (R, SP)	.20.00
649	Sparky Lyle (SP)	.15.00
650	Richie Allen (SP)	.35.00
665	Ron Swoboda (SP)	.15.00
688	Anderson (Mgr, SP)	.40.00
698	Brewers Team (SP)	.20.00
700	Boog Powell (SP)	.20.00
709	Baker/Baylor (R, SP)	.80.00
722	Astros Team (SP)	.20.00
740	Luis Aparicio (SP)	.20.00
750	Denny McLain (SP)	.20.00

1972 TOPPS

	NM
Complete Set (787):	.1650.00
Common Player (1-132):	..75
Common Player (133-263):	.1.25
Common Player (264-394):	.1.50

Common Player (395-525):		.1.75
Common Player (526-656):		.2.50
Common Player (657-787):		.10.00

		NM
1	Pirates Team	.6.00
18B	Juan Pizarro (green)	.5.00
29B	Bill Bonham (green)	.5.00
33	Billy Martin (Mgr)	.4.00
37	Carl Yastrzemski	.10.00
38	Carl Yastrzemski (IA)	.5.00
45B	Glenn Beckert (green)	.5.00
49	Willie Mays	.20.00
50	Willie Mays (IA)	.10.00
51	Harmon Killebrew	.6.00
79	Fisk/Cooper (R)	.70.00
80	Tony Perez	.4.00
87	Aaron/Stargell (LL)	.3.00
88	Killebrew/Robinson (LL)	.3.00
89	Aaron/Stargell (LL)	.3.00
93	Carlton/Jenkins/Seaver (LL)	.3.00
95	Jenkins/Seaver (LL)	.3.00
100	Frank Robinson	.6.00
117B	Cleo James (green)	.5.00
130	Bob Gibson	.7.00
132	Joe Morgan	.5.00
142	Chris Chambliss (R)	.5.00
147	Dave Kingman (R)	.5.00
198	Charlie Hough (R)	.5.00
200	Lou Brock	.6.00
226	WS Game 4 (Clemente)	.6.00
241	Rollie Fingers	.5.00
270	Jim Palmer	.8.00
280	Willie McCovey	.6.00
285	Gaylord Perry	.5.00
299	Hank Aaron	.40.00
300	Hank Aaron (IA)	.20.00
309	Roberto Clemente	.40.00
310	Roberto Clemente (IA)	.25.00
330	Jim Hunter	.4.00
420	Steve Carlton	.15.00
433	Johnny Bench	.25.00
434	Johnny Bench (IA)	.10.00
435	Reggie Jackson	.25.00
436	Reggie Jackson (IA)	.10.00
441	Thurman Munson	.15.00
442	Thurman Munson (IA)	.7.00
445	Tom Seaver	.25.00
446	Tom Seaver (IA)	.12.00
447	Willie Stargell	.6.00
474	Oates/Baylor (R)	.15.00
510	Ted Williams (Mgr)	.10.00
539	Terry Forster (R)	.5.00
550	Brooks Robinson	.20.00
559	Pete Rose	.40.00
560	Pete Rose (IA)	.20.00
567	Juan Marichal	.10.00
579	Doyle Alexander (R)	.5.00
595	Nolan Ryan	.200.00
600	Al Kaline	.25.00
604A	Checklist 6	.8.00
604B	Checklist 6	.8.00
668	Rangers Team	.20.00
686	Steve Garvey	.45.00
695	Rod Carew	.65.00
696	Rod Carew (IA)	.35.00
741	Hutton/Millner/Miller (R)	.10.00
751	Steve Carlton (TR)	.50.00
752	Joe Morgan (TR)	.40.00
754	Frank Robinson (TR)	.40.00
761	Oglivie/Cey(R)	.20.00
778	Rick Dempsey (R)	.15.00

1973 TOPPS

	NM
Complete Set (660):	.1000.00
Common Player (1-264):	..40
Common Player (265-396):	..60
Common Player (397-528):	..90
Common Player (529-660):	.2.50

		NM
1	Aaron/Ruth/Mays	.40.00
31	Buddy Bell (R)	.3.00
50	Roberto Clemente	.60.00
61	Williams/Carew (LL)	.3.00
62	Bench/Allen (LL)	.2.00
63	Bench/Allen (LL)	.2.00
64	Brock/Campaneris (LL)	.2.00
65	Carlton/Tiant (LL)	.2.00
66	Carlton/Perry/Wood (LL)	.2.00
67	Carlton/Ryan (LL)	.25.00
90	Brooks Robinson	.8.00
100	Hank Aaron	.30.00
130	Pete Rose	.20.00
142	Thurman Munson	.6.00
160	Jim Palmer	.6.00
165	Luis Aparicio	.3.00
170	Harmon Killebrew	.5.00
174	Rich Gossage (R)	.6.00
175	Frank Robinson	.6.00
180	Fergie Jenkins	.4.00
190	Bob Gibson	.6.00
193	Carlton Fisk	.8.00
200	Billy Williams	.3.50
213	Steve Garvey	.6.00
220	Nolan Ryan	.75.00
230	Joe Morgan	.6.00
235	Jim Hunter	.3.00
245	Carl Yastrzemski	.10.00
255	Reggie Jackson	.15.00
257A	Yogi Berra (Mgr)	.2.50
257B	Yogi Berra (Mgr)	.4.00
275	Tony Perez	.3.00
280	Al Kaline	.6.00
300	Steve Carlton	.8.00
305	Willie Mays	.35.00
320	Lou Brock	.5.00
330	Rod Carew	.7.00
350	Tom Seaver	.10.00
370	Willie Stargell	.5.00
380	Johnny Bench	.8.00
400	Gaylord Perry	.4.00
410	Willie McCovey	.5.00
449B	Aspromonte (Mgr., Spahn)	.3.50
471	Ty Cobb (ATL)	.7.00
471	Lou Gehrig (ATL)	.10.00

473	Hank Aaron (ATL)	10.00
474	Babe Ruth (ATL)	15.00
475	Ty Cobb (ATL)	6.00
480	Juan Marichal	4.00
497B	Red Schoendienst (Mgr)	3.00
498	Graig Nettles	3.00
503	Phil Niekro, P.	4.00
517B	Bill Virdon, B. (Mgr)	3.00
556	Yankees Team	10.00
588	Checklist 5	20.00
605	Enos Cabell (R)	5.00
606	Gary Matthews (R)	5.00
608	Busby/Medich (R)	5.00
609	Davey Lopes (R)	5.00
610	Charlie Hough (R)	5.00
613	Bob Boone (R)	25.00
614	Bumbry/Evans (R)	25.00
615	Schmidt/Cey (R)	250.00

1974 TOPPS

PHIL NIEKRO BRAVES

	NM
Complete Set (660):	500.00
Common Player:	.30

		NM
1	Hank Aaron	40.00
7	Jim Hunter	3.00
10	Johnny Bench	10.00
20	Nolan Ryan	75.00
35	Gaylord Perry	3.00
40	Jim Palmer	7.00
50	Rod Carew	5.00
55	Frank Robinson	5.00
60	Lou Brock	5.00
80	Tom Seaver	10.00
85	Joe Morgan	6.00
87	Fergie Jenkins	3.00
95	Steve Carlton	6.00
100	Willie Stargell	4.00
105	Carlton Fisk	10.00
110	Billy Williams	3.00
130	Reggie Jackson	15.00
160	Brooks Robinson	6.00
173B	Randy Jones (R, Wash.)	8.00
187	Don Baylor	2.00
201	Carew/Rose (LL)	5.00
202	Jackson/Stargell (LL)	4.50
203	Jackson/Stargell (LL)	4.50
206	Palmer/Seaver (LL)	4.00
207	Ryan/Seaver (LL)	20.00
212	Rollie Fingers	2.50
215	Al Kaline	5.50
226B	Padres Team (Wash.)	8.00
230	Tony Perez	3.00

250A	McCovey, W. (SD)	5.00
250B	McCovey (Wash.)	25.00
252	Dave Parker (R)	10.00
280	Carl Yastrzemski	7.00
283	Mike Schmidt	40.00
300	Pete Rose	15.00
309B	Dave Roberts (Wash.)	8.00
330	Juan Marichal	2.50
331	Fisk/Bench (AS)	6.00
332	Allen/Aaron (AS)	4.00
333	Carew/Morgan (AS)	3.00
338	Jackson/Williams (AS)	4.00
340	Thurman Munson	7.00
350	Bob Gibson	5.00
364B	Cito Gaston (Wash.)	10.00
387B	Rich Morales (Wash.)	8.00
400	Harmon Killebrew	5.00
456	Dave Winfield (R)	50.00
470	ALCS (Jackson)	5.00
473	WS Game 2 (Mays)	6.00
477	WS Game 6 (Jackson)	5.00
575	Steve Garvey	5.00
598	Ken Griffey (R)	15.00
599B	Dan Freisleben (R, SD)	3.00
599C	Dan Freisleben (R, SD)	5.00
600	Bill Madlock (R)	4.00
601	Downing/McBride (R)	4.00
604	Thornton/White (R)	5.00
605	Frank Tanana (R)	4.00
654A	Jesus Alou (err)	6.00

Traded

Complete Set (44):	8.00
Common Player:	.15
330T Juan Marichal	1.50

1975 TOPPS

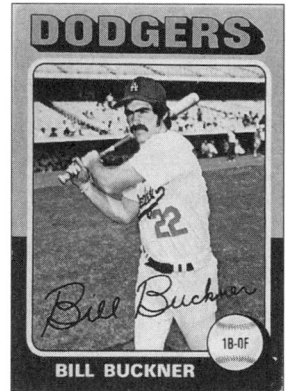

DODGERS BILL BUCKNER

	NM
Complete Set (660):	600.00
Common Player (1-132):	.35
Common Player (133-660):	.30
Mini Stars: 1x to 1.5x	
Mini Rookies: 1x	.40

		NM
1	Hank Aaron (HL)	30.00
2	Lou Brock (HL)	3.00
3	Bob Gibson (HL)	3.00
4	Al Kaline (HL)	4.00
5	Nolan Ryan (HL)	30.00
7	Bosman/Busby/Ryan (HL)	10.00
20	Thurman Munson	6.00
21	Rollie Fingers	3.00

29	Dave Parker	4.00
50	Brooks Robinson	6.00
60	Fergie Jenkins	3.00
61	Dave Winfield	40.00
70	Mike Schmidt	50.00
80	Carlton Fisk	10.00
100	Willie Stargell	3.00
140	Steve Garvey	6.00
150	Bob Gibson	5.00
180	Joe Morgan	6.00
185	Steve Carlton	6.00
189	Berra/Campanella (MVP)	3.00
192	Berra/Mays (MVP)	3.00
193	Berra/Camnla (MVP)	3.00
194	Mantle/Newcombe (MVP)	20.00
195	Mantle/Aaron (MVP)	30.00
200	Mantle/Wills (MVP)	20.00
204	Clemente/Robinson (MVP)	5.00
211	Jackson/Rose (MVP)	5.50
220	Don Sutton	3.00
223	Robin Yount (R)	50.00
228	George Brett (R)	95.00
230	Jim Hunter	3.00
260	Johnny Bench	15.00
280	Carl Yastrzemski	6.00
284	Ken Griffey	4.50
300	Reggie Jackson	15.00
307	Allen/Schmidt (LL)	3.00
312	Ryan/Carlton (LL)	15.00
320	Pete Rose	20.00
335	Jim Palmer	7.00
370	Tom Seaver	10.00
450	Willie McCovey	4.00
461	WS Game 1 (Jackson)	3.00
500	Nolan Ryan	65.00
531	Reds Team (Anderson)	3.00
540	Lou Brock	5.00
545	Billy Williams	3.00
580	Frank Robinson	5.00
600	Rod Carew	5.00
616	Jim Rice (R)	10.00
617	DeCinces/Trillo (R)	2.00
620	Gary Carter (R)	20.00
622	Fred Lynn (R)	7.00
623	Hernandez/Garner (R)	7.00
640	Harmon Killebrew	5.00
660	Hank Aaron	20.00

1976 TOPPS

TUG McGRAW PHILLIES

	NM
Complete Set (660):	275.00
Common Player:	.30
Wax Box:	850.00

		NM
1	Hank Aaron (RB)	15.00
5	Tom Seaver (RB)	4.00
10	Lou Brock	4.50
19	George Brett	60.00
55	Gaylord Perry	2.50
95	Brooks Robinson	5.00
98	Dennis Eckersley (R)	35.00
100	Jim Hunter	2.50
104	Reds Team (Anderson)	2.00
128	Ken Griffey	2.00
150	Steve Garvey	4.00
160	Dave Winfield	20.00
192	Carew/Munson (LL)	2.50
193	Kingman/Schmidt (LL)	2.50
194	Reggie Jackson (LL)	2.50
202	Eckersley/Hunter/Palmer (LL)	4.00
230	Carl Yastrzemski	6.00
240	Pete Rose	15.00
250	Fergie Jenkins	2.00
270	Willie Stargell	3.00
300	Johnny Bench	7.00
316	Robin Yount	30.00
325	Tony Perez	2.00
330	Nolan Ryan	70.00
340	Jim Rice	4.00
341	Lou Gehrig (AS)	10.00
342	Rogers Hornsby (AS)	3.00
344	Honus Wagner (AS)	3.50
345	Babe Ruth (AS)	10.00
346	Ty Cobb (AS)	7.00
347	Ted Williams (AS)	10.00
349	Walter Johnson (AS)	2.00
355	Steve Carlton	6.00
365	Carlton Fisk	8.00
400	Rod Carew	5.00
405	Rollie Fingers	2.50
420	Joe Morgan	5.00
441	Gary Carter	7.00
450	Jim Palmer	5.00
480	Mike Schmidt	20.00
500	Reggie Jackson	10.00
520	Willie McCovey	3.50
525	Billy Williams	2.50
550	Hank Aaron	20.00
592	Willie Randolph (R)	5.00
599	Ron Guidry (R)	7.00
600	Tom Seaver	7.00
650	Thurman Munson	5.00

Traded

Complete Set (44):		10.00
Common Player:		.25
250T	Fergie Jenkins	3.00

1977 TOPPS

		NM
Complete Set (660):		250.00
Common Player:		.20
Wax Box:		450.00

		NM
1	Brett/Madlock (LL)	6.00
6	Ryan/Seaver (LL)	15.00
10	Reggie Jackson	10.00
60	Jim Rice	3.00
70	Johnny Bench	6.00
100	Joe Morgan	4.00
110	Steve Carlton	4.00
120	Rod Carew	4.00

140	Mike Schmidt	10.00
144	Bruce Sutter (R)	2.00
150	Tom Seaver	6.00
170	Thurman Munson	4.00
231	George Brett (RB)	10.00
234	Nolan Ryan (RB)	15.00
265	Mark Fidrych (R)	3.00
280	Jim Hunter	2.00
285	Brooks Robinson	4.00
355	Lou Brock	3.00
359	Willie Randolph	2.00
387	Yankees Team (Martin)	2.00
390	Dave Winfield	10.00
400	Steve Garvey	2.50
430	Fergie Jenkins	2.00
450	Pete Rose	10.00
460	Willie Stargell	2.00
473	Andre Dawson (R)	25.00
476	Dale Murphy (R)	18.00
480	Carl Yastrzemski	5.00
488	Clark/Mazzilli (R)	4.00
491	Dennis Martinez (R)	4.00
525	Dennis Eckersley	5.00
547	Willie McCovey	3.00
580	George Brett	35.00
600	Jim Palmer	3.00
631	Brett Brothers	7.00
635	Robin Yount	20.00
640	Carlton Fisk	5.00
650	Nolan Ryan	35.00

1978 TOPPS

ANDY ETCHEBARREN

		NM
Complete Set (726):		150.00
Common Player:		.20
Wax Box:		400.00

		NM
1	Lou Brock (RB)	2.50
3	Willie McCovey (RB)	1.50

4	Brooks Robinson (RB)	1.50
5	Pete Rose (RB)	3.00
6	Nolan Ryan (RB)	15.00
7	Reggie Jackson (RB)	3.00
20	Pete Rose (DP)	4.50
34	Willie McCovey	2.00
36	Eddie Murray (R)	35.00
40	Carl Yastrzemski	4.00
60	Thurman Munson	3.50
72	Andre Dawson	10.00
100	George Brett	20.00
119	Dennis Martinez	2.00
120	Gary Carter	2.50
122	Dennis Eckersley	3.50
160	Jim Palmer	3.00
170	Lou Brock	3.00
173	Robin Yount	10.00
200	Reggie Jackson	7.00
205	Carlton/Palmer (LL)	1.50
206	Niekro/Ryan (DP, LL)	4.00
270	Carlton Fisk	3.00
282	Yankees Team	2.00
300	Joe Morgan	3.00
350	Steve Garvey	1.50
360	Mike Schmidt	10.00
400	Nolan Ryan	35.00
413	World Series (Jackson)	2.50
450	Tom Seaver	3.50
460	Jim Hunter	1.50
510	Willie Stargell	1.50
530	Dave Winfield	10.00
540	Steve Carlton	2.50
580	Rod Carew	2.50
670	Jim Rice	2.00
674	Ray Knight (R)	2.00
700	Johnny Bench	4.00
703	Jack Morris (R, DP)	5.00
704	Lou Whitaker (R)	15.00
707	Molitor/Trammell (R)	40.00
708	Murphy/Parrish (R)	6.00

1979 TOPPS

TED SIMMONS C
CARDINALS

		NM
Complete Set (726):		125.00
Common Player:		.15
Wax Box:		250.00

		NM
1	Carew/Parker (LL)	2.00
6	Richard/Ryan (LL)	5.00
24	Paul Molitor	15.00
25	Steve Carlton	2.00
30	Dave Winfield	7.00
39	Dale Murphy	3.00

55	Willie Stargell	2.00
95	Robin Yount	10.00
100	Tom Seaver (DP)	2.00
115	Nolan Ryan	15.00
116	Ozzie Smith (R)	50.00
123	Lou Whitaker	5.00
200	Johnny Bench (DP)	2.00
204	Pete Rose (RB)	2.00
212	Carney Lansford (R)	2.00
215	Willie McCovey	2.00
300	Rod Carew	2.00
310	Thurman Munson	2.00
320	Carl Yastrzemski	3.00
330	George Brett	10.00
340	Jim Palmer	2.00
348	Andre Dawson	6.00
358	Alan Trammell	8.00
369A	Bump Wills (err)	2.50
369B	Bump Wills (cor)	2.50
400	Jim Rice	1.50
417	Johnson/Ryan (ATL, DP)	4.00
610	Mike Schmidt	7.00
640	Eddie Murray	15.00
650	Pete Rose	5.00
665	Lou Brock	2.00
680	Carlton Fisk	2.50
700	Reggie Jackson (DP)	2.00

1980 TOPPS

	MT
Complete Set (726):	175.00
Common Player:	.12
Wax Box:	200.00

		MT
4	Pete Rose	2.00
40	Carlton Fisk	3.00
100	Johnny Bench	3.00
160	Tony Perez	2.00
206	J. R. Richard/Nolan Ryan	3.00
210	Steve Carlton	2.00
230	Dave Winfield	4.00
265	Robin Yount	5.00
270	Mike Schmidt	4.00
274	Dale Murphy	2.00
335	Willie McCovey	2.00
387b	Fred Stanley	3.00
393	Ozzie Smith	12.00
406	Paul Molitor	6.00
450	George Brett	9.00
482	Rickey Henderson	30.00
500	Tom Seaver	3.00
540	Pete Rose	9.00
544	Rick Sutcliffe	2.00
580	Nolan Ryan	12.50
590	Jim Palmer	2.00

600	Reggie Jackson	6.00
610	Willie Stargell	2.00
650	Joe Morgan	2.00
700	Rod Carew	2.00
720	Carl Yastrzemski	3.00

1981 DONRUSS

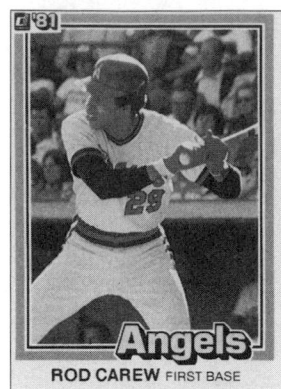

	MT
Complete Set (605):	45.00
Complete Set, Uncut Sheets (5):	75.00
Common Player:	.08
Wax Box:	70.00
Eight-card promo sheet:	20.00

		MT
1	Ozzie Smith	4.00
11	Mike Schmidt	3.00
100	George Brett	6.00
112	Eddie Murray	4.00
119	Rickey Henderson	4.00
131a	Pete Rose	2.50
203	Paul Molitor	3.00
228	Reggie Jackson	2.50
251	Pete Rose	2.50
260	Nolan Ryan	8.00
323	Robin Yount	4.00
348	Reggie Jackson	2.50
371	Pete Rose	2.50
468	Reggie Jackson	2.50
491	George Brett	3.00
538	Tim Raines	6.00
569	Danny Ainge	4.00

1981 FLEER

	MT
Complete Set (660):	50.00
Common Player:	.08
Wax Box:	60.00

	MT
6c	Steve Carlton	3.00
28a	George Brett	4.00
57	Nolan Ryan	8.00
79a	Reggie Jackson	4.00
87a	Graig Nettles	10.00
184	Eddie Murray	3.00
346	Harold Baines	4.00
351	Rickey Henderson	6.00
418	Dan Ainge	5.00
481	Kirk Gibson	3.00
488	Ozzie Smith	3.00
511	Robin Yount	3.00
515	Paul Molitor	3.00
574	Rickey Henderson	7.00
655	George Brett	4.00

(The first column entries are: 6c, 28a, 57, 79a, 87a, 184, 346, 351, 418, 481, 488, 511, 515, 574, 655)

1981 TOPPS

	MT
Complete Set (726):	50.00
Common Player:	.10
Wax Box:	90.00

		MT
100	Rod Carew	2.00
110	Carl Yastrzemski	2.00
180	Pete Rose	3.00
220	Tom Seaver	2.00
240	Nolan Ryan	12.00
254	Ozzie Smith	7.50
261	Rickey Henderson	7.00
300	Paul Molitor	5.00
302	M. Scioscia, F. Valenzuela	2.00
315	Kirk Gibson	3.00
347	Harold Baines	8.00
370	Dave Winfield	4.00
400	Reggie Jackson	2.00
479	Tim Raines	4.00
490	Eddie Murray	5.00
515	Robin Yount	4.00
540	Mike Schmidt	4.00
600	Johnny Bench	3.00
630	Steve Carlton	2.00
700	George Brett	6.00

Traded

	MT
Complete Set (132):	30.00
Common Player:	.20

816	Tim Raines	12.00
855	Dave Winfield	12.00

1982 DONRUSS

	MT
Complete Set (660):	85.00
Common Player:	.08

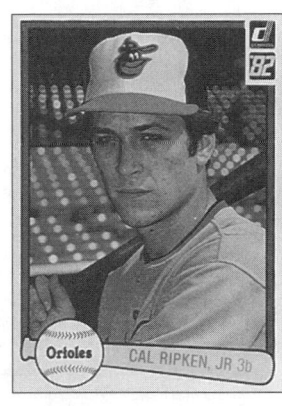

Babe Ruth Puzzle: 3.00
Wax Box: 120.00

		MT
1	Pete Rose	3.00
13	Nolan Ryan	4.00
31	Dave Winfield	2.00
34	George Brett	3.00
78	Paul Molitor	2.50
94	Ozzie Smith	2.50
113	Rickey Henderson	2.00
168	Pete Rose	2.50
252	Lee Smith	8.00
275	Brett Butler	2.00
294	Mike Schmidt	2.25
405	Cal Ripken, Jr.	50.00
410	Dave Stewart	2.50
419	Nolan Ryan	9.00
483	Eddie Murray	2.00
510	Robin Yount	2.50
535	Reggie Jackson	2.00
557	Kent Hrbek	2.00
575	R. Jackson/D. Winfield	2.00

1982 FLEER

		MT
Complete Set (6560):		60.00
Common Player:		.08
Wax Box:		110.00

		MT
24	Dave Stewart	2.00
39	Reggie Jackson	1.50
56	Dave Winfield	2.00
92	Rickey Henderson	2.50
148	Paul Molitor	3.00
155	Robin Yount	3.00
174	Eddie Murray	3.00
176	Cal Ripken, Jr.	50.00

		MT
229	Nolan Ryan	9.00
256	Pete Rose	2.50
258	Mike Schmidt	3.00
405	George Brett	4.00
438a	Al Hrabosky	16.00
576a	John Littlefield	200.00
582	Ozzie Smith	3.00
603a	Lee Smith	8.00
603b	Lee Smith	8.00
640	Pete Rose, Pete Rose, Jr.	2.00
643	Rickey Henderson	1.50
646a	R. Jackson, D. Winfield	2.00
646b	R. Jackson, D. Winfield	2.00

1982 TOPPS

		MT
Complete Set (792):		100.00
Common Player:		.10
Wax Box:		225.00

		MT
5	Nolan Ryan	3.00
21	Cal Ripken, Jr.	60.00
90	Nolan Ryan	12.00
95	Ozzie Smith	3.00
100	Mike Schmidt	3.00
171	Chili Davis	3.00
191	Tim Wallach	2.50
195	Paul Molitor	4.00
200	George Brett	5.00
201	George Brett	2.50
213	Dave Stewart	4.00
300	Reggie Jackson	3.00
342a	George Foster	2.50
383a	Pascual Perez	8.00
390	Eddie Murray	4.00
435	Robin Yount	3.50
452	Lee Smith	8.00
502	Brett Butler	2.00
600	Dave Winfield	2.50
610	Rickey Henderson	3.50
766	Kent/Hrbek	2.00
780	Pete Rose	3.00

Traded

		MT
Complete Set (132)		250.00
Common Player:		.20

		MT
47T	Reggie Jackson	12.00
98T	Cal Ripken, Jr.	200.00
109T	Ozzie Smith	25.00

1983 DONRUSS

		MT
Complete Set (660):		90.00
Common Player:		.08

Ty Cobb Puzzle: .3.00
Wax Box: 180.00

		MT
11	Rickey Henderson	2.00
35	Rickey Henderson	2.50
42	Pete Rose	2.50
118	Nolan Ryan	8.00
120	Ozzie Smith	2.00
169	Mike Schmidt	2.50
258	Robin Yount	2.50
277	Ryne Sandberg	14.00
279	Cal Ripken Jr.	16.00
338	George Brett	3.00
405	Eddie Murray	2.50
525	Julio Franco	4.00
586	Wade Boggs	15.00
598	Tony Gwynn	30.00
639a	Ron Jackson	6.00

1983 FLEER

		MT
Complete Set (792):		100.00
Common Player:		.08
Wax Box:		180.00

		MT
15	Willie McGee	1.50
22	Ozzie Smith	2.50
40	Paul Molitor	2.50
51	Robin Yount	2.50
67	Eddie Murray	2.50
70	Cal Ripken Jr.	15.00
108	George Brett	3.50
171	Pete Rose	3.00
173	Mike Schmidt	2.50
179	Wade Boggs	17.50
360	Tony Gwynn	25.00
398	Dave Winfield	2.00

463 Nolan Ryan .8.00
507 Ryne Sandberg 15.00
519 Rickey Henderson 2.50

1983 TOPPS

		MT
Complete Set (132):	. . . .	125.00
Common Player:	. . . .	.08
Wax Box:	. . . .	225.00

49	Willie McGee	. . . .	1.50
60	Johnny Bench	. . . .	1.50
83	Ryne Sandberg	. . . .	27.50
100	Pete Rose	. . . .	3.00
101	Pete Rose	. . . .	2.00
163	Cal Ripken Jr.	. . . .	15.00
180	Rickey Henderson	. . . .	3.00
300	Mike Schmidt	. . . .	3.50
350	Robin Yount	. . . .	3.00
360	Nolan Ryan	. . . .	12.00
361	Nolan Ryan	. . . .	5.00
482	Tony Gwynn	. . . .	60.00
498	Wade Boggs	. . . .	30.00
500	Reggie Jackson	. . . .	2.00
530	Eddie Murray	. . . .	3.00
540	Ozzie Smith	. . . .	3.00
580	Tom Seaver	. . . .	1.50
586	Frank Viola	. . . .	1.50
600	George Brett	. . . .	4.00
630	Paul Molitor	. . . .	3.00
699	Lee Smith	. . . .	1.50
770	Dave Winfield	. . . .	2.50

Traded

Complete Set (132):	. . . .	25.00
Common Player:	. . . .	.10

101T	Tom Seaver	. . . .	7.50
108T	Darryl Strawberry	. . . .	10.00

1984 DONRUSS

	MT
Complete Set (660):	. . . .	180.00
Common Player:	. . . .	.15

Duke Snider Puzzle:	. . . .	3.50
Wax Box:	. . . .	300.00

		MT
A	Rollie Fingers, G. Perry	. . . .	5.00
B	J. Bench/C. Yastrzemski	. . . .	8.00
1a	Robin Yount	. . . .	3.00
1b	Robin Yount	. . . .	5.00
22b	Eddie Murray	. . . .	4.00
23a	Mike Schmidt	. . . .	4.00

26a	Wade Boggs	. . . .	3.00
32	Tony Fernandez	. . . .	3.00
41	Joe Carter	. . . .	40.00
47	Eddie Murray	. . . .	8.00
48	Robin Yount	. . . .	6.00
51	Dave Winfield	. . . .	6.00
53	George Brett	. . . .	12.00
54	Rickey Henderson	. . . .	5.00
57	Reggie Jackson	. . . .	6.00
59	Ozzie Smith	. . . .	6.00
60	Nolan Ryan	. . . .	30.00
61	Pete Rose	. . . .	8.00
68	Darryl Strawberry	. . . .	10.00
106	Cal Ripken, Jr.	. . . .	30.00
107	Paul Molitor	. . . .	8.00
111	Steve Carlton	. . . .	5.00
116	Tom Seaver	. . . .	5.00
151	Wade Boggs	. . . .	12.00
183	Mike Schmidt	. . . .	12.00
248	Don Mattingly	. . . .	55.00
302	Carlton Fisk	. . . .	4.00
311	Ryne Sandberg	. . . .	18.00
324	Rony Gwynn	. . . .	20.00
352	Rod Carew	. . . .	4.00
576	Jim Palmer	. . . .	3.00

1984 FLEER

		MT
Complete Set (660):	. . . .	75.00
Common Player:	. . . .	.08
Wax Box:	. . . .	150.00

		MT
14	Eddie Murray	. . . .	4.00
17	Cal Ripken, Jr.	. . . .	12.50
25	Steve Carlton	. . . .	3.50
46	Pete Rose	. . . .	7.50
48	Mike Schmidt	. . . .	8.00
131	Don Mattingly	. . . .	30.00
143	Dave Winfield	. . . .	3.00
207	Paul Molitor	. . . .	4.00
219	Robin Yount	. . . .	4.00
239	Nolan Ryan	. . . .	17.50
301	Tony Gwynn	. . . .	12.00
336	Ozzie Smith	. . . .	4.00
339	Andy Van Slyke	. . . .	2.00
344	George Brett	. . . .	7.50
392	Wade Boggs	. . . .	4.00
447	Rickey Henderson	. . . .	3.00
504	Ryne Sandberg	. . . .	8.00
520	Reggie Jackson	. . . .	1.50
595	Tom Seaver	. . . .	1.50
599	Darryl Strawberry	. . . .	7.50

Update

Complete Set (132):	. . . .	400.00
Common Player:	. . . .	.25

27	Roger Clemens	. . . .	240.00
34	Dennis Eckersley	. . . .	10.00
43	Dwight Gooden	. . . .	10.00
61	Jimmy Key	. . . .	8.00
70	Mark Langston	. . . .	8.00
93	Kirby Puckett	. . . .	150.00
99	Jose Rijo	. . . .	10.00
102	Pete Rose	. . . .	15.00
103	Bret Saberhagen	. . . .	15.00
106	Tom Seaver	. . . .	15.00

1984 TOPPS

		MT
Complete Set (792):	. . . .	40.00
Common Player:	. . . .	.08
Wax Box:	. . . .	75.00

		MT
8	Don Mattingly	. . . .	10.00
10	Robin Yount	. . . .	2.00
30	Wade Boggs	. . . .	4.00
60	Paul Molitor	. . . .	2.00
100	Reggie Jackson	. . . .	1.50
130	Ozzie Smith	. . . .	2.00
182	Darryl Strawberry	. . . .	1.50
230	Rickey Henderson	. . . .	1.75
240	Eddie Murray	. . . .	1.50
251	Tony Gwynn	. . . .	6.00
300	Pete Rose	. . . .	2.00
400	Cal Ripken, Jr.	. . . .	2.00
460	Dave Winfield	. . . .	1.50
470	Nolan Ryan	. . . .	7.00
490	Cal Ripken, Jr.	. . . .	7.00
500	George Brett	. . . .	2.00
596	Ryne Sandberg	. . . .	4.00
700	Mike Schmidt	. . . .	2.00

Traded

Complete Set (132):	. . . .	35.00
Common Player:	. . . .	.25

34T	Dennis Eckersley	4.00
42T	Dwight Gooden	4.00
62T	Jimmy Key	3.00
70T	Mark Langston	3.00
82T	Joe Morgan	3.00
84T	Phil Niekro	3.00
103T	Pete Rose	8.00
104T	Bret Saberhagen	6.00
108T	Tom Seaver	6.00

1985 DONRUSS

	MT
Complete Set (660):	110.00
Common Player:	10
Lou Gehrig Puzzle:	3.00
Wax Box:	215.00

		MT
1	Ryne Sandberg	2.60
7	Don Mattingly	3.50
14	Cal Ripken, Jr.	8.00
25	Tony Gwynn	3.00
47	Eddie Murray	2.50
48	Robin Yount	2.50
53	George Brett	4.00
59	Ozzie Smith	2.50
60	Nolan Ryan	10.00
61	Mike Schmidt	4.00
63	Tony Gwynn	7.50
67	Ryne Sandberg	6.00
169	Cal Ripken, Jr.	10.00
172	Wade Boggs	3.00
176	Rickey Henderson	2.00
254	Pete Rose	2.50
273	Roger Clemens	50.00
295	Don Mattingly	6.00
369	Paul Molitor	3.00
424a	Tom Seaver	2.00
424b	Tom Seaver	30.00
438	Kirby Puckett	30.00
534a	Jeff Pendleton	3.00
534b	Terry Pendleton	12.00
581	Orel Hershiser	3.50
616	Joe Carter	4.00
641	Pete Rose	2.00
651a	Two for the Title	4.00
651b	Two for the Title	6.00

1985 FLEER

	MT
Complete Set (660):	110.00
Common Player:	06
Wax Box:	275.00

		MT
34	Tony Gwynn	6.00
65	Ryne Sandberg	5.00
110	Jimmy Key	2.00
133	Don Mattingly	9.00
146	Dave Winfield	3.00
151	Wade Boggs	4.50
155	Roger Clemens	50.00
184	Eddie Murray	2.50
187	Cal Ripken, Jr.	10.00
199	George Brett	4.50
212	Bret Saberhagen	2.00
236	Terry Pendleton	2.00
240	Ozzie Smith	3.00
246	Steve Carlton	1.50
265	Mike Schmidt	5.00
286	Kirby Puckett	30.00
297	Rod Carew	1.50
303	Reggie Jackson	2.00
359	Nolan Ryan	10.00
371	Orel Hershiser	3.50
425	Rickey Henderson	3.00
443	Joe Carter	4.00
492	Mark Langston	1.50
533	Eric Davis	2.50
550	Pete Rose	3.00
588	Paul Molitor	3.00
601	Robin Yount	3.00
626	Cal Ripken, Jr.	4.00
627	Mike Schmidt	1.50
630	R. Sandberg/Mike Schmidt	2.00
641	Cal Ripken, Jr., & Sr.	4.00
649	S. Dunston/Bill Hatcher	2.00

Update

	MT
Complete Set (132):	12.00
Common Player:	10

33	Darren Daulton	3.00
51	Rickey Henderson	3.00

1985 TOPPS

	MT
Complete Set (792):	240.00
Complete Set, Uncut Sheets (6):	450.00
Common Player:	05
Wax Box:	375.00

		MT
7	Nolan Ryan	1.50
30	Cal Ripken, Jr.	4.00
100	George Brett	2.00
181	Roger Clemens	25.00
350	Wade Boggs	1.50
401	Mark McGwire	175.00
460	Ryne Sandberg	2.50

493	Orel Hershiser	1.50
500	Mike Schmidt	1.50
536	Kirby Puckett	7.00
660	Tony Gwynn	3.00
665	Don Mattingly	3.00
694	Joe Carter	3.00
704	Cal Ripken, Jr.	2.00
760	Nolan Ryan	5.00

Traded

	MT
Complete Set (132):	8.00
Common Player:	10
49 Rickey Henderson	2.00

1986 DONRUSS

	MT
Complete Set (660):	60.00
Complete Factory Set (660):	75.00
Common Player:	08
Hank Aaron Puzzle:	5.00
Wax Box:	120.00

		MT
28	Fred McGriff	6.00
33a	Andres Galarraga	10.00
33b	Andres Galarraga	10.00
37	Paul O'Neill	6.00
39	Jose Canseco	40.00
48	Robin Yount	1.75
53	George Brett	2.00
59	Ozzie Smith	2.00
61	Mike Schmidt	2.00
62	Pete Rose	2.00
67	Ryne Sandberg	2.00
72	Kirby Puckett	6.00
88	Eddie Murray	1.50
112	Tony Gwynn	3.50
124	Paul Molitor	2.00
172	Roger Clemens	5.00
173	Don Mattingly	4.00

210	Cal Ripken, Jr.	5.00
258	Nolan Ryan	6.00
371	Wade Boggs	1.50
477	Darren Daulton	1.50
482	Len Dykstra	1.50
512	Cecil Fielder	3.00
609b	Tom Seaver	3.00
653	King of Kings Pete Rose	2.50

Rookies

		MT
Comp. Unopened Set (56):		30.00
Complete Opened Set (56):		20.00
Common Player:		.10

7	Andres Galarraga	3.00
11	Barry Bonds	20.00
22	Jose Canseco	8.00
32	Will Clark	4.00

1986 FLEER

JACK MORRIS
PITCHER

		MT
Complete Set (660):		40.00
Factory Set (660):		50.00
Common Player:		.08
Wax Box:		100.00

		MT
5	George Brett	2.25
46	Ozzie Smith	2.00
78	Len Dykstra	2.00
109	Don Mattingly	3.00
282	Eddie Murray	1.50
284	Cal Ripken, Jr.	8.00
310	Nolan Ryan	8.00
323	Tony Gwynn	4.00
341	Wade Boggs	2.00
345	Roger Clemens	7.00
378	Ryne Sandberg	3.00
401	Kirby Puckett	6.00
438	Darren Daulton	2.50
450	Mike Schmidt	1.50
495	Paul Molitor	2.00
506	Robin Yount	2.00
646	Paul O'Neill	5.00
647	Andres Galarraga	6.00
649	Jose Canseco	20.00
653	Cecil Fielder, Cory Snyder	1.50

Update

Complete Set (132):		25.00
Common Player:		.08

14	Barry Bonds	20.00
20	Jose Canseco	6.00
25	Will Clark	3.00
44	Andres Galarraga	5.00

1986 TOPPS

	MT
Complete Set (792):	25.00
Common Player:	.05
Wax Box:	30.00

		MT
100	Nolan Ryan	2.00
329	Kirby Puckett	2.00
340	Cal Ripken, Jr.	2.00
661	Roger Clemens	4.00

Traded

JOSE CANSECO

Complete Set (132):		20.00
Common Player:		.10

11T	Barry Bonds	15.00
20T	Jose Canseco	6.00
24T	Will Clark	2.00
40T	Andres Galarraga	3.00

1987 DONRUSS

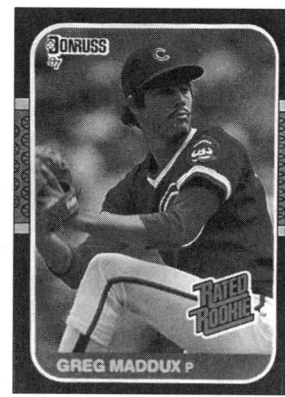

GREG MADDUX P

		MT
Complete Set (660):		60.00
Common Player:		.05

Roberto Clemente Puzzle:		9.00
Wax Box:		55.00

		MT
35	Bo Jackson	2.00
36	Greg Maddux	20.00
43	Rafael Palmeiro	8.00
46	Mark McGwire	30.00
66	Will Clark	2.00
89	Cal Ripken, Jr.	2.50
97	Jose Canseco	2.00
138	Nolan Ryan	2.50
361	Barry Bonds	10.00

492	Barry Larkin	2.00
502	David Cone	2.50
627	Kevin Brown	4.00

Rookies

Comp. Unopened Set (56):		35.00
Complete Set (56):		30.00
Common Player:		.05

1	Mark McGwire	20.00
47	Rafael Palmeiro	5.00
52	Greg Maddux	12.00

1987 FLEER

Barry Bonds
OUTFIELD

FLEER

	MT
Complete Set (660):	50.00
Factory Set (672):	60.00
Common Player:	.06
Wax Box:	110.00

		MT
29	Wade Boggs	1.50
32	Roger Clemens	3.50
67	Nolan Ryan	4.00
104	Don Mattingly	2.25
204	Barry Larkin	5.00
269	Will Clark	3.00
366	George Brett	2.00
369	Bo Jackson	3.00
389	Jose Canseco	3.00
416	Tony Gwynn	2.50
478	Cal Ripken, Jr.	4.00
549	Kirby Puckett	2.50
604	Barry Bonds	35.00

Update

Complete Set (132):		30.00
Common Player:		.08

68	Greg Maddux	10.00
76	Mark McGwire	20.00
129	Matt Williams	3.00

1987 TOPPS

	MT
Complete Set (792):	12.00
Common Player:	.05
Wax Box:	15.00

		MT
320	Barry Bonds	1.50
366	Mark McGwire	5.00
620	Jose Canseco	1.00
634	Rafael Palmeiro	1.50

Traded

Complete Set (132):		8.00
Common Player:		.08

24	Dave Cone	1.00
70	Greg Maddux	5.00
129	Matt Williams	1.50

1988 DONRUSS

Darryl Strawberry OF

	MT
Complete Factory Set, Sealed (660):	15.00
Complete Set (660):	12.00
Common Player:	.05
Stan Musial Puzzle:	1.00
Wax Box:	9.00

		MT
34	Roberto Alomar	1.50
256	Mark McGwire	1.50
539	Greg Maddux	1.00

Rookies

Complete Set (56):	10.00
Common Player:	.10

1	Mark Grace	2.00
26	David Wells	1.50
35	Roberto Alomar	5.00

1988 FLEER

	MT
Complete Set (660):	15.00
Common Player:	.06
Wax Box:	25.00

		MT
101	Matt Williams	1.50
286	Mark McGwire	4.00
322	Barry Bonds	1.00
349	Roger Clemens	1.00
378	Edgar Martinez	1.50
423	Greg Maddux	2.00
425a	Keith Moreland	3.00

441	Ken Caminiti	1.50
455	Nolan Ryan	1.50
462a	Jerry Browne	2.50
538	Ron Gant	2.50
539	Tom Glavine	3.00
570	Cal Ripken, Jr.	1.50
624	Canseco, Mark McGwire	2.00
629	Mark McGwire	2.00
633	Mark McGwire	1.00
641	Mark Grace	3.00

Update

Complete Set (132):	10.00
Common Player:	.06

69	David Wells	1.50
74	John Smoltz	2.00
77	Mark Grace	1.50
89	Craig Biggio	2.50
122	Roberto Alomar	5.00

1988 SCORE

RAFAEL PALMEIRO OF

	MT
Complete Set (660):	15.00
Common Player:	.05
Wax Box:	10.00

		MT
5	Mark McGwire	1.50
164	Ken Caminiti	.75
638	Tom Glavine	.75
648	Mark McGwire	.75
659	Mark McGwire	.75

Traded/Rookie

Complete Set (110):	50.00
Common Player:	.20

70	Brady Anderson	4.00
80	Mark Grace	8.00
95	Jay Buhner	4.00

97	Al Leiter	2.50
013	Craig Biggio	15.00
105	Roberto Alomar	20.00

1988 TOPPS

DON MATTINGLY

	MT
Complete Set (792):	15.00
Common Player:	.05
Wax Box:	8.00

		MT
3a	Mark McGwire	1.00
250	Nolan Ryan	.75
361	Greg Maddux	1.00
372	Matt Williams	.75
580	Mark McGwire	1.50
759	J. Canseco, M. McGwire	.75
779	Tom Glavine	.75

Traded

Complete Set (132):	12.00
Common Player:	.05

4	Roberto Alomar	3.00
5	Brady Anderson	1.00
21	Jay Buhner	1.00
42	Mark Grace	3.00
66	Tino Martinez	3.00
124	Robin Ventura	4.00
128	David Wells	1.00

1989 BOWMAN

	MT
Complete Set (484):	30.00
Common Player:	.05
Wax Box:	50.00

9	Cal Ripken, Jr.	.75
197	Mark McGwire	1.50
220	Ken Griffey, Jr.	20.00
225	Nolan Ryan	.75
259	Ken Griffey	1.00

1989 DONRUSS

	MT
Factory Set, Unopened (660):	40.00
Complete Set (660):	25.00
Common Player:	.05
Warren Spahn Puzzle:	1.00
Wax Box:	25.00

		MT
31	Gary Sheffield	1.00
33	Ken Griffey, Jr.	18.00
42	Randy Johnson	2.50

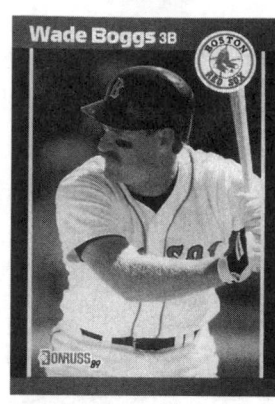

51	Cal Ripken, Jr.	.75
95	Mark McGwire	1.00
154	Nolan Ryan	.75
373	Greg Maddux	.75
634	Dante Bichette	.75
645	Curt Schilling	.75
642	John Smoltz	.75

Rookies

Comp. Unopened Set (56):	30.00
Complete Set (56):	24.00
Common Player:	.10

3	Ken Griffey, Jr.	25.00
29	Dante Bichette	1.50
43	Randy Johnson	6.00

1989 FLEER

	MT
Fact. Set, Unopened (660):	35.00
Complete Set (660):	30.00
Common Player:	.05
Wax Box:	30.00

		MT
17	Mark McGwire	1.00
130a	Tom Brookens	2.00
132a	Mike Health	2.00
173a	Jeff Treadway	15.00
196	Gary Sheffield	1.50
368	Nolan Ryan	.75
381	Randy Johnson	2.50
440a	Manny Trillo	1.50
548	Ken Griffey, Jr.	20.00
616a	Bill Ripken	8.00
616b	Bill Ripken	8.00
616d	Bill Ripken	30.00
617	Cal Ripken, Jr.	.75
634	J. Canseco M. McGwire	.75

Update

	MT
Complete Set (132)	8.00
Common Player:	.06

25	Joey (Albert) Belle	3.00
41	Greg Vaughn	1.50
53	Deion Sanders	.75
59	Randy Johnson	3.00
67	Nolan Ryan	1.00

1989 SCORE

	MT
Complete Set (660):	10.00
Common Player:	.05
Wax Box:	9.00

		MT
3	Mark McGwire	1.50
75a	George Brett	1.00
350a	Roger Clemens	2.00
625	Gary Sheffield	1.00
630	Sandy Alomar	.75
645	Randy Johnson	3.00
654a	Wade Boggs	2.00

Traded

	MT
Complete Set (110):	50.00
Common Player:	.06

2	Nolan Ryan	2.00
77	Randy Johnson	6.00
100	Ken Griffey, Jr.	40.00
106	Albert Belle	6.00

1989 TOPPS

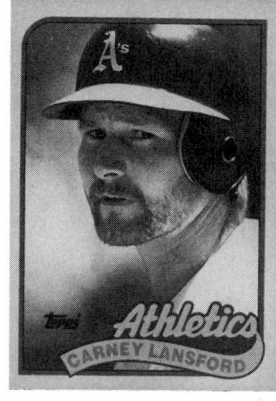

	MT
Complete Set (792):	10.00
Factory Set (792):	14.00
Common Player:	.05
Wax Box:	9.00

		MT
49	Craig Biggio	.60
70	Mark McGwire	1.50

250	Cal Ripken, Jr.	.60
343	Gary Sheffield	1.50
530	Nolan Ryan	.75
605a	Bob Welch	1.00
647	Randy Johnson	2.00
764	Robin Ventura	.75

Traded

Complete Set (132):	30.00
Common Player:	.05

41T	Ken Griffey, Jr.	25.00
57T	Randy Johnson	3.00
106T	Nolan Ryan	1.50
110T	Deion Sanders	.75

1989 UPPER DECK

Ken Griffey Jr.

	MT
Complete Set (800):	220.00
Unopened Fact. Set (800):	250.00
Complete Low Set (700):	210.00
Complete High Set (100):	15.00
Common Player:	.10
Low Wax Box:	360.00
High Wax Box:	250.00

		MT
1	Ken Griffey, Jr.	160.00
5	Sandy Alomar, Jr.	1.50
13a	Gary Sheffield	6.00
13b	Gary Sheffield	6.00
17	John Smoltz	.75
24	Dante Bichette	2.00
25	Randy Johnson	15.00
120	Ryne Sandberg	1.00
141	Ken Caminiti	1.00
145	Nolan Ryan	3.00
195	Roger Clemens	2.00
200	Don Mattingly	1.50
215	George Brett	1.50
235	Rafael Palmeiro	1.00
241	Greg Maddux	3.00
265	Ozzie Smith	1.00
273	Craig Biggio	4.00
300	Mark McGwire	5.00
357a	Dale Murphy	20.00
360	Tom Glavine	2.00
371	Jose Canseco	1.00
376	Kirby Puckett	1,00
384	Tony Gwynn	1.50
406	Mike Schmidt	1.50
440	Barry Bonds	1.50
467	Cal Ripken, Jr.	3.00
471	Roberto Alomar	1.50
742	Steve Finley	1.50
752	Kevin Brown	2.00
772	Rafael Palmeiro	1.00
774	Nolan Ryan	3.00
787	Omar Vizquel	3.00

Baseball
Hall of Fame Autographs
(with year inducted into Hall of Fame)

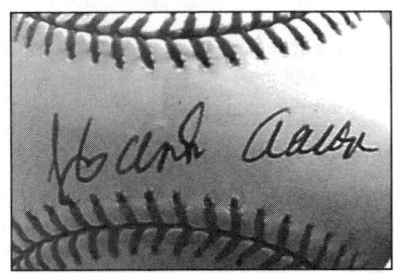

Hank Aaron (1934-)1982
Cut signature $15
Single-signature ball $50
3x5 index card . . . .$20-$25
Photograph/baseball card . . . .$30-$40
HOF plaque postcard . . . . . .$20-$30
Perez-Steele postcards $30

Grover Cleveland Alexander
                     (1887-1950) 1938
Cut signature $500
Single-signature baseball $5,000
3x5 index card . . . .$450-$700
Photograph/baseball card $900
HOF plaque postcard $1,000
Perez-Steele postcards . . . .Impossible

Walter Alston (1911-1984) 1983
Cut signature $35
Single-signature baseball $700
3x5 index card . . . .$40-$50
Photograph/baseball card $300
HOF plaque postcard . . . . . .$85-$150
Perez-Steele postcards . . . .$750-$800

Sparky Anderson (1934-) 2000
Cut signature $8
Single-signature baseball $35
3x5 index card $10
Photograph/baseball card . . . .$20-$25
HOF plaque postcard $15
Perez-Steele postcards $20

Cap Anson (1852-1922) 1939
Cut signature $1,500
Single-sign. baseball $17,000
3x5 index card $2,000
Photograph/baseball card $3,500
HOF plaque postcard . . . .Impossible
Perez-Steele postcards . . .Impossible

Luis Aparicio (1934-) 1984
Cut signature $8
Single-signature baseball $25
3x5 index card $10
Photograph/baseball card $20
HOF plaque postcard $15
Perez-Steele postcards $20

Luke Appling (1907-1991) 1964
Cut signature $10
Single-signature baseball $75
3x5 index card $15
Photograph/baseball card $35
HOF plaque postcard $20
Perez-Steele postcards $40

Richie Ashburn (1927-1997) 1995
Cut signature $8
Single-signature baseball $40
3x5 index card $10
Photograph/baseball card $25
HOF plaque postcard $75
Perez-Steele postcards $100

Earl Averill (1902-1983) 1975
Cut signature $25
Single-signature baseball . .$450-$500
3x5 index card $40
Photograph/baseball card $150
HOF plaque postcard $35
Perez-Steele postcards . . . .$450-$550

Frank Baker (1886-1963) 1955
Cut signature $150
Single-signature baseball $3,600
3x5 index card . . . .$300-$350
Photograph/baseball card $800
HOF plaque postcard $700
Perez-Steele postcards . . . .Impossible

Dave Bancroft (1891-1972) 1971
Cut signature $50
Single-signature baseball $2,800
3x5 index card $75
Photograph/baseball card $250
HOF plaque postcard $600
Perez-Steele postcards . . . .Impossible

Ernie Banks (1931-) 1977
Cut signature $10
Single-signature baseball $45
3x5 index card $15
Photograph/baseball card $35
HOF plaque postcard . . . . . .$15-$25
Perez-Steele postcards . . . . .$30-$35

Al Barlick (1915-1995) 1989
Cut signature $10
Single-signature baseball $50
3x5 index card . . . .$8-$10
Photograph/baseball card $25
HOF plaque postcard . . . . . .$15-$20
Perez-Steele postcards $25

Edward Barrow (1868-1953) 1953
Cut signature $75
Single-signature baseball $3,300
3x5 index card $160
Photograph/baseball card $400
HOF plaque postcard . . . .Impossible
Perez-Steele postcards . . . .Impossible

Jake Beckley (1867-1918) 1971
Cut signature ....$1,200-$1,300
Single-signature baseball
.................$4,800-$5,500
3x5 index card $1,700
Photograph/baseball card $3,500
HOF plaque postcard ....Impossible
Perez-Steele postcards ....Impossible

Cool Papa Bell (1903-1991) 1974
Cut signature $20
Single-signature baseball $350
3x5 index card $35
Photograph/baseball card $150
HOF plaque postcard $35
Perez-Steele postcards ......$45-$70

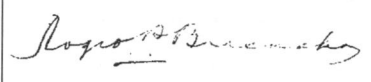

Johnny Bench (1947-) 1989
Cut signature $10
Single-signature baseball ....$35-$40
3x5 index card $15
Photograph/baseball card ....$30-$35
HOF plaque postcard ....$25-$35
Perez-Steele postcards ......$35-$40

Chief Bender (1883-1954) 1953
Cut signature $100
Single-signature baseball$2,000-$3,500
3x5 index card $250
Photograph/baseball card ..$450-$500
HOF plaque postcard $1,200
Perez-Steele postcards ....Impossible

Yogi Berra (1925-) 1972
Cut signature $8
Single-signature baseball ....$30-$35
3x5 index card $12
Photograph/baseball card ....$20-$25
HOF plaque postcard ......$20-$25
Perez-Steele postcards ......$25-$30

Jim Bottomley (1900-1959) 1974
Cut signature $150
Single-signature baseball $3,000
3x5 index card $300
Photograph/baseball card $400
HOF plaque postcard ....Impossible
Perez-Steele postcards ....Impossible

Lou Boudreau (1917-) 1970
Cut signature $8

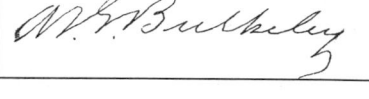

Single-signature baseball $30
3x5 index card $10
Photograph/baseball card .....$12-$15
HOF plaque postcard ....$10-$15
Perez-Steele postcards ......$15-$25

Roger Bresnahan (1879-1944) 1945
Cut signature $500
Single-signature baseball $6,000
3x5 index card $650
Photograph/baseball card $1,200
HOF plaque postcard .....Impossible
Perez-Steele postcards ....Impossible

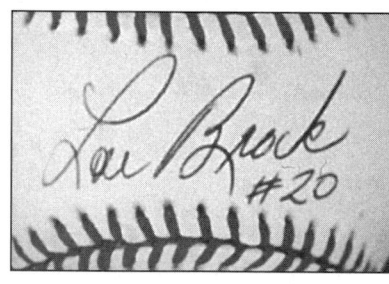

George Brett (1953-) 1999
Cut signature $10
Single-signature baseball ....$55-$60
3x5 index card $15
Photograph/baseball card $40
HOF plaque postcard $25
Perez-Steele postcards $40

Lou Brock (1939-) 1985
Cut signature ....$5-$8
Single-signature baseball ....$30-$35
3x5 index card ....$10-$12
Photograph/baseball card $20
HOF plaque postcard $15
Perez-Steele postcards $25

Dan Brouthers (1858-1932) 1945
Cut signature $1,250
Single-signature baseball
.................$15,000-$20,000

3x5 index card $1,700
Photograph/baseball card $5,000
HOF plaque postcard ....Impossible
Perez-Steele postcards ....Impossible

Mordecai Brown (1876-1948) 1949
Cut signature ....$250-$300
Single-signature baseball
.................$3,000-$5,500
3x5 index card ....$350-$500
Photograph/baseball card $900
HOF plaque postcard ....Impossible
Perez-Steele postcards ....Impossible

Morgan Bulkeley (1837-1922) 1937
Cut signature ....$800-$1,450
Single-signature baseball $6,000
3x5 index card $1,200
Photograph/baseball card $4,000
HOF plaque postcard ....Impossible
Perez-Steele postcards ....Impossible

Jim Bunning (1931-) 1996
Cut signature ....$5-$7
Single-signature baseball $35
3x5 index card $10
Photograph/baseball card $20
HOF plaque postcard $35
Perez-Steele postcards $30

Jesse Burkett (1868-1953) 1946
Cut signature $450
Single-signature baseball $5,500
3x5 index card $600
Photograph/baseball card $1,000
HOF plaque postcard $1,500
Perez-Steele postcards ....Impossible

Roy Campanella (1921-1993) 1969
Cut signature ....$350-$400
Single-signature baseball $3,500
3x5 index card $500
Photograph/baseball card $800
HOF plaque postcard $325
Perez-Steele postcards ...$200-$250

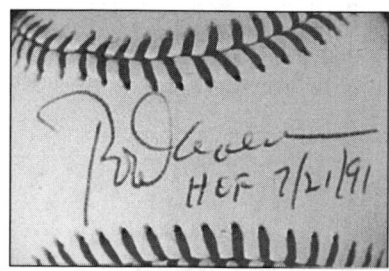

Rod Carew (1945-) 1991
Cut signature $8
Single-signature baseball ...$30-$40

3x5 index card . . . . $7-$9
Photograph/baseball card $20
HOF plaque postcard $20
Perez-Steele postcards $25

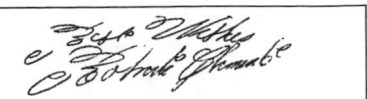

Max Carey (1890-1976) 1961
Cut signature $30
Single-signature baseball $750
3x5 index card $40
Photograph/baseball card $125
HOF plaque postcard $95
Perez-Steele postcards . . . . Impossible

Steve Carlton (1944-) 1994
Cut signature $8
Single-signature baseball . . . . $25-$30
3x5 index card $10
Photograph/baseball card . . . . $20-$25
HOF plaque postcard $35
Perez-Steele postcards $30

Alexander Cartwright (1820-1892) 1938
Cut signature $1,500
Single-signature baseball . . . Unknown
3x5 index card $1,750
Photograph/baseball card $3,500
HOF plaque postcard . . . . Impossible
Perez-Steele postcards . . . . Impossible

Orlando Cepeda (1937-) 1999
Cut signature $7
Single-signature baseball $35
3x5 index card $10
Photograph/baseball card $25
HOF plaque postcard $25
Perez-Steele postcards $30

Henry Chadwick (1824-1908) 1938
Cut signature . . . . $1,000-$1,500
Single-signature baseball . . . Unknown
3x5 index card $1,200
Photograph/baseball card $3,200
HOF plaque postcard . . . . Impossible

Perez-Steele postcards . . . . Impossible
Frank Chance (1877-1924) 1946
Cut signature . . . . $600-$750
Single-signature baseball
. . . . $5,500-$7,000
3x5 index card $750
Photograph/baseball card $2,000
HOF plaque postcard . . . . Impossible
Perez-Steele postcards . . . . Impossible

Happy Chandler (1898-1991) 1982
Cut signature $10
Single-signature baseball $100
3x5 index card $15
Photograph/baseball card $50
HOF plaque postcard $25
Perez-Steele postcards $40

Oscar Charleston (1896-1954) 1976
Cut signature $600
Single-signature baseball $7,000
3x5 index card . . . . $1,000-$1,750
Photograph/baseball card $3,000
HOF plaque postcard . . . . Impossible
Perez-Steele postcards . . . . Impossible

Jack Chesbro (1874-1931) 1946
Cut signature . . . . $600-$1,150
Single-signature baseball .$10,000-$20,000
3x5 index card $750
Photograph/baseball card . .$2,000-$2,750
HOF plaque postcard . . . . Impossible
Perez-Steele postcards . . . . Impossible

Nestor Chylak (1922-1982) 1999
Cut signature . . . . $200-$250
Single-signature baseball .$800-$1,000
3x5 index card . . . . $250-$300
Photograph/baseball card . .$300-$350
HOF plaque postcard . . . . Impossible
Perez-Steele postcards . . . . Impossible

Fred Clarke (1872-1960) 1945
Cut signature $100
Single-signature baseball$1,500-$3,000
3x5 index card $200
Photograph/baseball card $400
HOF plaque postcard . . . . $400-$500
Perez-Steele postcards . . . . Impossible

John Clarkson (1861-1909) 1963
Cut signature . . . . $1,200-$1,845
Single-signature baseball . . . Unknown
3x5 index card $2,000
Photograph/baseball card $2,500
HOF plaque postcard . . . . Impossible
Perez-Steele postcards . . . . Impossible

Roberto Clemente (1934-1972) 1973
Cut signature . . . . $300-$350

Single-signature baseball$2,000-$4,000
3x5 index card $400
Photograph/baseball card . .$350-$600
HOF plaque postcard . . . . Impossible
Perez-Steele postcards . . . . Impossible

Ty Cobb (1886-1961) 1936
Cut signature . . . . $500-$600
Single-signature baseball$2,750-$3,000
3x5 index card $700
Photograph/baseball card $1,200
HOF plaque postcard $1,000
Perez-Steele postcards . . . . Impossible

Mickey Cochrane (1903-1962) 1947
Cut signature $150
Single-signature baseball .$750-$2,000
3x5 index card . . . . $200-$250
Photograph/baseball card $350
HOF plaque postcard $500
Perez-Steele postcards . . . . Impossible

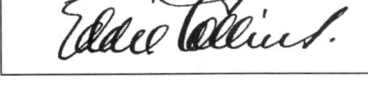

Eddie Collins (1887-1951) 1939
Cut signature $100
Single-signature baseball$2,250-$5,000
3x5 index card . . . . $175-$225
Photograph/baseball card $400
HOF plaque postcard $550
Perez-Steele postcards . . . . Impossible

Jimmy Collins (1870-1943) 1945
Cut signature . . . . $500-$750
Single-signature baseball $6,000
3x5 index card . . . . $700-$950
Photograph/baseball card $1,500
HOF plaque postcard . . . . Impossible
Perez-Steele postcards . . . . Impossible

Earle Combs (1899-1976) 1970
Cut signature . . . . $15-$17
Single-signature baseball
. . . . $500-$2,000

3x5 index card $40
Photograph/baseball card $350
HOF plaque postcard $100
Perez-Steele postcards . . . .Impossible

Charles Comiskey (1859-1931) 1939
Cut signature . . . .$350-$375
Single-signature baseball$4,500-$8,000
3x5 index card . . . .$450-$500
Photograph/baseball card $1,200
HOF plaque postcard . . . . .Impossible
Perez-Steele postcards . . . .Impossible

Jocko Conlan (1899-1989) 1974
Cut signature $10
Single-signature baseball . .$100-$125
3x5 index card . . . .$15-$20
Photograph/baseball card $35
HOF plaque postcard . . . .$15-$20
Perez-Steele postcards . . . . .$60-$500

Thomas Connolly (1870-1963) 1953
Cut signature $275
Single-signature baseball . .$2,345-$7,000
3x5 index card . . . .$250-$350
Photograph/baseball card $900
HOF plaque postcard . .$1,000-$1,200
Perez-Steele postcards . . . .Impossible

Roger Connor (1857-1931) 1976
Cut signature . . . .$1,000-$1,185
Single-signature baseball$5,600-$8,000
3x5 index card $1,700
Photograph/baseball card $2,500
HOF plaque postcard . . . . .Impossible
Perez-Steele postcards . . . .Impossible

Stan Coveleski (1889-1984) 1969
Cut signature $20
Single-signature baseball $450
3x5 index card . . . .$35-$40
Photograph/baseball card $150
HOF plaque postcard $30
Perez-Steele postcards . . . .$325-$400

Sam Crawford (1880-1968) 1957
Cut signature . . . .$75-$100
Single-signature baseball$1,900-$2,500
3x5 index card $125
Photograph/baseball card $250
HOF plaque postcard . . . .$250-$400
Perez-Steele postcards . . . .Impossible

Joe Cronin (1906-1984) 1956
Cut signature $20
Single-signature baseball . .$225-$500
3x5 index card $25
Photograph/baseball card $100
HOF plaque postcard . . . . . .$35-$50
Perez-Steele postcards . . . .$700-$750

Candy Cummings (1848-1924) 1939
Cut signature . . . .$1,500-$1,750
Single-signature baseball . .Unknown
3x5 index card $1,700
Photograph/baseball card $4,500
HOF plaque postcard . . . .Impossible
Perez-Steele postcards . . . .Impossible

Ki Ki Cuyler (1899-1950) 1968
Cut signature $150
Single-signature baseball
. . . .$1,500-$3,500
3x5 index card $175
Photograph/baseball card . .$400-$425
HOF plaque postcard . . . .Impossible
Perez-Steele postcards . . . .Impossible

Ray Dandridge (1913-1994) 1987
Cut signature . . . .$15-$20
Single-signature baseball . . .$40-$50
3x5 index card $25
Photograph/baseball card . .$25-$30
HOF plaque postcard . . . . . .$15-$25
Perez-Steele postcards . . . . .$15-$25

George Davis (1870-1940) 1998
Cut signature . . . . .Unknown
Single-signature baseball . .Unknown
3x5 index card . . . . .Unknown
Photograph/baseball card . . .Unknown
HOF plaque postcard . . . .Impossible
Perez-Steele postcards . . . .Impossible

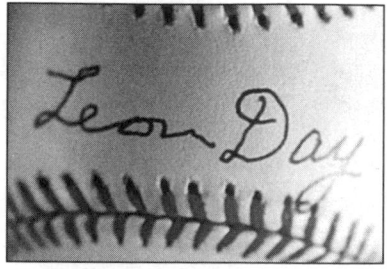

Leon Day (1916-1995) 1995
Cut signature $20
Single-signature baseball . . .$75-$100
3x5 index card $25
Photograph/baseball card . . . .$30-$40
HOF plaque postcard . . . . .Impossible
Perez-Steele postcards . . . .Impossible

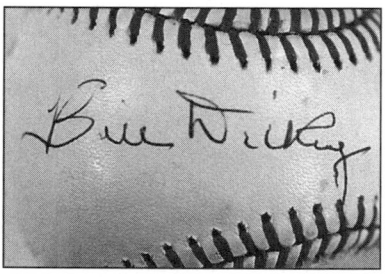

Dizzy Dean (1911-1974) 1953
Cut signature . . . .$75-$80
Single-signature baseball . .$675-$800
3x5 index card . . . .$90-$100
Photograph/baseball card . .$250-$350
HOF plaque postcard . .$125-$150
Perez-Steele postcards . . . .Impossible

Ed Delahanty (1867-1903) 1945
Cut signature $1,500
Single-signature baseball . .Unknown
3x5 index card $2,000
Photograph/baseball card $4,000
HOF plaque postcard . . . .Impossible
Perez-Steele postcards . . . .Impossible

Bill Dickey (1907-1993) 1954
Cut signature $15
Single-signature baseball . .$150-$200
3x5 index card $20
Photograph/baseball card $50
HOF plaque postcard . . . . . .$35-$45
Perez-Steele postcards . . . . . .$45-$80

Martin DiHigo (1905-1971) 1977
Cut signature . . . .$650-$675
Single-signature baseball $4,000
3x5 index card . . . .$800-$1,000
Photograph/baseball card
. . . .$1,500-$2,000
HOF plaque postcard . . . .Impossible
Perez-Steele postcards . . . .Impossible

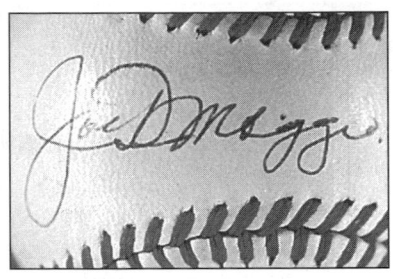

Joe DiMaggio (1914-1999) 1955
Cut signature . . . .$30-$35
Single-signature baseball . .$300-$350
3x5 index card $60
Photograph/baseball card . .$150-$200
HOF plaque postcard . . . . .$175-$200
Perez-Steele postcards . . . .$300-$350

Larry Doby (1924-) 1998
Cut signature . . . .$7-$10
Single-signature baseball . . . .$30-$35
3x5 Index card . . . .$10-$12
Photograph/baseball card $20
HOF plaque postcard $15
Perez-Steele postcards . . . . . .$15-$20

Bobby Doerr (1918-) 1986
Cut signature . . . .$5-$7
Single-signature baseball $25
3x5 index card . . . .$3-$7
Photograph/baseball card . . . .$10-$13
HOF plaque postcard . . . .$6-$10
Perez-Steele postcards . . . . . .$15-$20

Don Drysdale (1936-1993) 1984
Cut signature . . . .$25-$30
Single-signature baseball . .$125-$150
3x5 index card . . . .$30-$35
Photograph/baseball card . . . .$75-$90
HOF plaque postcard $35
Perez-Steele postcards $40

Hugh Duffy (1866-1954) 1945
Cut signature . . . .$300-$350
Single-signature baseball$2,200-$3,500
3x5 index card . . . .$350-$450
Photograph/baseball card . .$600-$750
HOF plaque postcard $900
Perez-Steele postcards . . . .Impossible

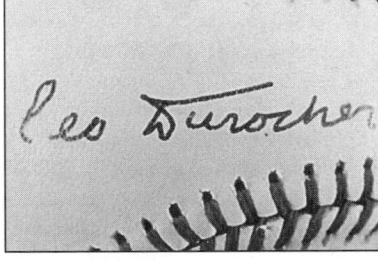

Leo Durocher (1905-1991) 1994
Cut signature . . . .$15-$20
Single-signature baseball . . . .$65-$90
3x5 index card $25
Photograph/baseball card $40
HOF plaque postcard . . . .Impossible
Perez-Steele postcards . . . .Impossible

Billy Evans (1864-1956) 1973
Cut signature $225
Single-signature baseball
. . . .$2,000-$4,000
3x5 index card . . . .$300-$350
Photograph/baseball card . .$500-$525
HOF plaque postcard . . . .Impossible
Perez-Steele postcards . . . .Impossible

Johnny Evers (1881-1947) 1946
Cut signature $300
Single-signature baseball$3,500-$6,000
3x5 index card $400
Photograph/baseball card$1,000-$1,200
HOF plaque postcard $1,100
Perez-Steele postcards . . . .Impossible

Buck Ewing (1859-1906) 1939
Cut signature $1,000
Single-signature baseball $3,000
3x5 index card $2,400
Photograph/baseball card
. . . .$2,500-$4,000
HOF plaque postcard . . . .Impossible
Perez-Steele postcards . . . .Impossible

Red Faber (1888-1976) 1964
Cut signature $15
Single-signature baseball .$450-$1,800
3x5 index card . . . .$35-$45
Photograph/baseball card . . .$75-$100
HOF plaque postcard $85
Perez-Steele postcards . . . .Impossible

Bob Feller (1918-) 1962
Cut signature $5
Single-signature baseball . . . .$20-$25
3x5 index card . . . .$7-$10
Photograph/baseball card . . . .$10-$12
HOF plaque postcard . . . . . .$20-$25
Perez-Steele postcards . . . . . .$15-$35

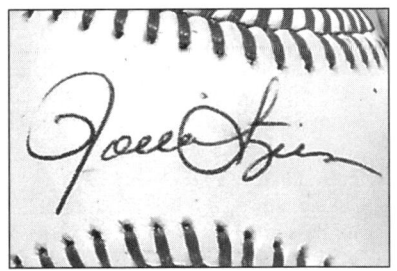

Rick Ferrell (1905-1995) 1984
Cut signature . . . .$6-$8
Single-signature baseball . . .$70-$80
3x5 index card $9
Photograph/baseball card $25
HOF plaque postcard $25
Perez-Steele postcards . . . . . .$30-$35

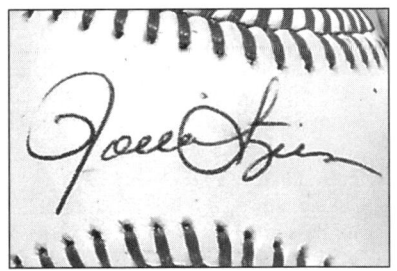

Rollie Fingers (1946-) 1992
Cut signature . . . .$5-$7
Single-signature baseball . . . .$25-$30
3x5 index card . . . .$8-$12
Photograph/baseball card $25
HOF plaque postcard $10
Perez-Steele postcards $25

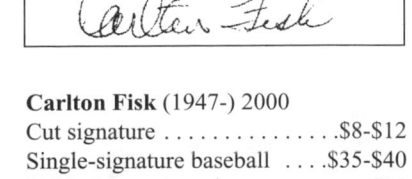

Carlton Fisk (1947-) 2000
Cut signature . . . .$8-$12
Single-signature baseball . . . .$35-$40
3x5 index card $10
Photograph/baseball card $25
HOF plaque postcard . . . . . .$15-$20
Perez-Steele postcards $25

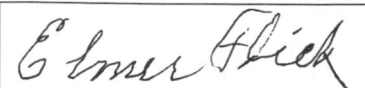

Elmer Flick (1876-1971) 1963
Cut signature . . . .$45-$50
Single-signature baseball
. . . .$2,200-$2,500
3x5 index card . . . .$50-$60
Photograph baseball card . .$175-$250
HOF plaque postcard . . . . .$300-$450
Perez-Steele postcards . . . .Impossible

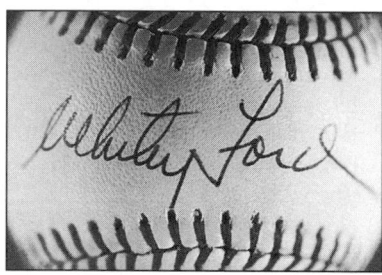

Whitey Ford (1926-) 1974
Cut signature . . . .$8-$10
Single-signature baseball $30
3x5 index card . . . .$10-$12
Photograph/baseball card $20
HOF plaque postcard . . . . . .$12-$20
Perez-Steele postcards . . . . . .$20-$30

Bill Foster (1904-1978) 1995
Cut signature $2,000
Single-signature baseball
. . . .$5,000-$7500
3x5 index card $3,000
Photograph/baseball card . . .Unknown
HOF plaque postcard . . . . .Impossible
Perez-Steele postcards . . . .Impossible

Rube Foster (1878-1930) 1981
Cut signature $2,000
Single-signature baseball $13,000
3x5 index card $3,800
Photograph/baseball card . .$3,150-$5,500
HOF plaque postcard . . . . .Impossible
Perez-Steele postcards . . . .Impossible

Nellie Fox (1927-1975) 1997
Cut signature . . . .$150-$200
Single-signature baseball
. . . .$1,000-$1,500
3x5 index card $250
Photograph/baseball card . .$350-$400
HOF plaque postcard . . . . .Impossible
Perez-Steele postcard . . . .Impossible

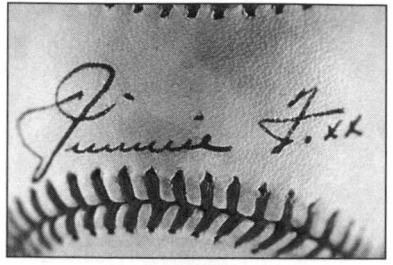

Jimmie Foxx (1907-1967) 1951
Cut signature . . . .$200-$250
Single-signature baseball $3,000
3x5 index card . . . .$300-$350
Photograph/baseball card . .$500-$900
HOF plaque postcard $550
Perez-Steele postcards . . . .Impossible

Ford Frick (1894-1978) 1970
Cut signature . . . .$25-$30
Single-signature baseball . . .$300-$800
3x5 index card . . . .$40-$50
Photograph/baseball card . .$75-$100
HOF plaque postcard $125
Perez-Steele postcards . . . .Impossible

Frankie Frisch (1898-1973) 1947
Cut signature . . . .$50-$75
Single-signature baseball
. . . .$1,700-$1,800
3x5 index card . . . .$75-$90
Photograph/baseball card . .$100-$150
HOF plaque postcard . . . . .$100-$150
Perez-Steele postcards . . . .Impossible

Pud Galvin (1855-1902) 1965
Cut signature $1,300
Single-signature baseball
. . . .$10,000-$12,000
3x5 index card $2,500
Photograph/baseball card $3,000
HOF plaque postcard . . . . .Impossible
Perez-Steele postcards . . . .Impossible

Lou Gehrig (1903-1941) 1939
Cut signature $650
Single-signature baseball
. . . .$5,000-$7,000
3x5 index card $800
Photograph/baseball card
. . . .$2,000-$4,000
HOF plaque postcard . . . . . .Unknown
Perez-Steele postcards . . . .Impossible

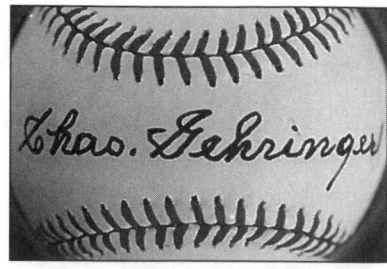

Charlie Gehringer (1903-1993) 1949
Cut signature . . . .$20-$25
Single-signature baseball . .$150-$200
3x5 index card $35
Photograph/baseball card . . .$85-$100
HOF plaque postcard . . . . . .$35-$40
Perez-Steele postcards . . . . . .$45-$65

Bob Gibson (1935-) 1972
Cut signature . . . .$8-$10
Single-signature baseball . . . .$25-$30
3x5 index card $12
Photograph/baseball card . . . .$20-$25
HOF plaque postcard . . . . . .$15-$20
Perez-Steele postcards $20

Josh Gibson (1911-1947) 1972
Cut signature . . . .$700-$950
Single-signature baseball
. . . .$4,500-$6,500
3x5 index card $800
Photograph/baseball card
. . . .$1,200-$1,700
HOF plaque postcard . . . . .Impossible
Perez-Steele postcards . . . .Impossible

Warren Giles (1896-1979) 1979
Cut signature $20
Single-signature baseball .$250-$1,000
3x5 index card . . . .$35-$45
Photograph/baseball card . . .$75-$125
HOF plaque postcard . . . . .Impossible
Perez-Steele postcards . . . .Impossible

Lefty Gomez (1908-1989) 1972
Cut signature . . . .$15-$20
Single-signature baseball . .$150-$200
3x5 index card . . . .$20-$25
Photograph/baseball card . . . .$35-$45
HOF plaque postcard . . . . . .$20-$25
Perez-Steele postcards . . . . . .$40-$65

Goose Goslin (1900-1971) 1968
Cut signature . . . .$70-$75
Single-signature baseball
. . . .$800-$2,700

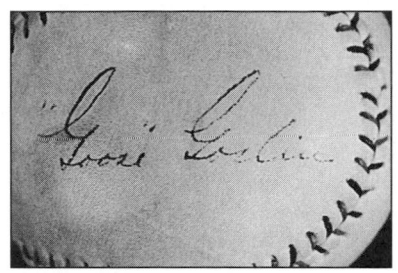

3x5 index card . . . .$75-$100
Photograph/baseball card $300
HOF plaque postcard . . . .$700-$3,000
Perez-Steele postcards . . . .Impossible

Jesse Haines (1893-1978) 1970
Cut signature . . . .$30-$35
Single-signature baseball . .$300-$950
3x5 index card . . . .$20-$40
Photograph/baseball card . .$75-$125
HOF plaque postcard $75
Perez-Steele postcards . . . .Impossible

Billy Hamilton (1866-1940) 1961
Cut signature . . . .$500-$1,500
Single-signature baseball . .$4,250-$5,500
3x5 index card $750
Photograph/baseball card . .$2,150-$2,500
HOF plaque postcard . . . . .Impossible
Perez-Steele postcards . . . .Impossible

Ned Hanlon (1857-1937) 1996
Cut signature . . . . Unknown
Single-signature baseball . . .Unknown
3x5 index card . . . . .Unknown
Photograph/baseball card . . .Unknown
HOF plaque postcard . . . .Impossible
Perez-Steele postcards . . . .Impossible

Will Harridge (1883-1971) 1972
Cut signature . . . .$85-$90
Single-signature baseball . .$875-$2,500
3x5 index card $125
Photograph/baseball card . .$225-$300
HOF plaque postcard . . . . .Impossible
Perez-Steele postcards . . . .Impossible

Bucky Harris (1896-1977) 1975
Cut signature . . . .$25-$30
Single-signature baseball . .$450-$1,200
3x5 index card $40
Photograph/baseball card $200
HOF plaque postcard . . . .$150-$200
Perez-Steele postcards . . . .Impossible

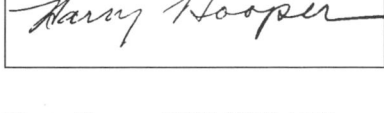

3x5 index card . . . .$300-$350
Photograph/baseball card . .$475-$500
HOF plaque postcard . . . . .Impossible
Perez-Steele postcards . . . .Impossible

Billy Herman (1909-1992) 1975
Cut signature $8
Single-signature baseball . .$90-$100
3x5 index card $12
Photograph/baseball card $60
HOF plaque postcard $20
Perez-Steele postcards . . . . .$25-$30

Harry Hooper (1887-1974) 1971
Cut signature . . . .$25-$30
Single-signature baseball .$450-$1,200
3x5 index card $35
Photograph/baseball card . .$80-$150
HOF plaque postcard $115
Perez-Steele postcards . . . .Impossible

Hank Greenberg (1911-1986) 1956
Cut signature . . . .$20-$30
Single-signature baseball . .$500-$700
3x5 index card . . . .$35-$75
Photograph/baseball card . . .$75-$100
HOF plaque postcard . . . .$50-$75
Perez-Steele postcards . . . .$300-$325

Clark Griffith (1869-1955) 1946
Cut signature . . . .$130-$135
Single-signature baseball$1,000-$2,200
3x5 index card . . . .$150-$175
Photograph/baseball card $350
HOF plaque postcard $600
Perez-Steele postcards . . . .Impossible

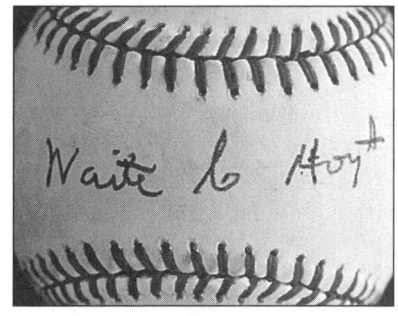

Rogers Hornsby (1896-1963) 1942
Cut signature . . . .$250-$300
Single-signature baseball $2,500
3x5 index card $300
Photograph/baseball card . .$500-$700
HOF plaque postcard $650
Perez-Steele postcards . . . .Impossible

Burleigh Grimes (1893-1985) 1964
Cut signature $20
Single-signature baseball . . .$90-$200
3x5 index card . . . .$20-$25
Photograph/baseball card . . . .$50-$60
HOF plaque postcard . . . .$25-$30
Perez-Steele postcards . . . .$150-$200

Gabby Hartnett (1900-1972) 1955
Cut signature . . . .$40-$50
Single-signature baseball$1,000-$2,000
3x5 index card . . . .$60-$75
Photograph/baseball card . .$200-$250
HOF plaque postcard . . . . .$200-$325
Perez-Steele postcards . . . .Impossible

Lefty Grove (1900-1975) 1947
Cut signature $75
Single-signature baseball
. . . .$1,200-$1,300
3x5 index card $100
Photograph/baseball card $200
HOF plaque postcard . . . . .$150-$175
Perez-Steele postcards . . . .Impossible

Waite Hoyt (1899-1984) 1969
Cut signature . . . .$30-$40
Single-signature baseball . .$175-$450
3x5 index card $45
Photograph/baseball card . . . .$50-$80
HOF plaque postcard . . . . . .$30-$35
Perez-Steele postcards . . . .$450-$550

Chick Hafey (1903-1973) 1971
Cut signature . . . .$40-$45
Single-signature baseball .$425-$1,500
3x5 index card $50
Photograph/baseball card . . .$75-$175
HOF plaque postcard $600
Perez-Steele postcards . . . .Impossible

Harry Heilmann (1894-1951) 1952
Cut signature . . . .$175-$250
Single-signature baseball$2,000-$2,500

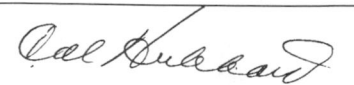

Cal Hubbard (1900-1977) 1976
Cut signature . . . .$30-$35
Single-signature baseball .$500-$1,000
3x5 index card $40
Photograph/baseball card . .$175-$250
HOF plaque postcard $500
Perez-Steele postcards . . . .Impossible

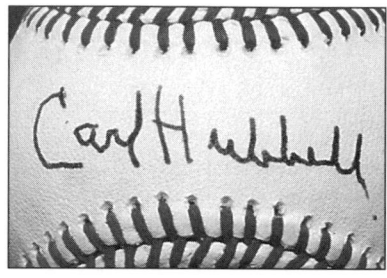

Carl Hubbell (1903-1988) 1947
Cut signature . . . .$15-$20
Single-signature baseball . .$160-$175
3x5 index card $25
Photograph/baseball card . . . .$30-$35
HOF plaque postcard . . . .$35-$40
Perez-Steele postcards . . . . . .$60-$80

Miller Huggins (1879-1929) 1964
Cut signature . . . .$700-$750
Single-signature baseball$4,500-$6,000
3x5 index card $1,000
Photograph/baseball card $1,500
HOF plaque postcard . . . . .Impossible
Perez-Steele postcards . . . .Impossible

William Hulbert (1832-1882) 1995
Cut signature - letter $8000
Single-signature baseball . . .Unknown
3x5 index card . . . . .Unknown
Photograph/baseball card . . .Unknown
HOF plaque postcard . . . . .Impossible
Perez-Steele postcards . . . .Impossible

Catfish Hunter (1946-1999) 1987
Cut signature $8
Single-signature baseball . . . .$50-$60
3x5 index card $10
Photograph/baseball card $35
HOF plaque postcard $15
Perez-Steele postcards . . . . . .$20-$25

Monte Irvin (1911-) 1973
Cut signature . . . .$5-$8
Single-signature baseball . . . .$20-$25
3x5 index card $10
Photograph/baseball card . . . .$15-$20
HOF plaque postcard . . . .$10-$15
Perez-Steele postcards . . . . . .$20-$25

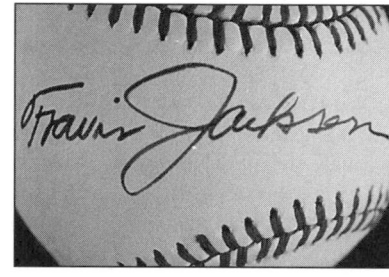

Reggie Jackson (1946-) 1993
Cut signature $15
Single-signature baseball . . . .$60-$65
3x5 index card $20
Photograph/baseball card . . . .$40-$50
HOF plaque postcard $65
Perez-Steele postcards $60

Travis Jackson (1903-1987) 1982
Cut signature $15
Single-signature baseball $350
3x5 index card $25
Photograph/baseball card $80
HOF plaque postcard $40
Perez-Steele postcards . . . . . .$75-$80

Fergie Jenkins (1943-) 1991
Cut signature . . . .$3-$5
Single-signature baseball . . . .$22-$28
3x5 index card $7
Photograph/baseball card . . . .$12-$15
HOF plaque postcard . . . . . .$10-$15
Perez-Steele postcards . . . . . .$10-$15

Hugh Jennings (1869-1928) 1945
Cut signature . . . .$500-$825
Single-signature baseball . .$4,750-$6,000
3x5 index card $900
Photograph/baseball card$1,000-$1,500
HOF plaque postcard . . . . .Impossible
Perez-Steele postcards . . . .Impossible

Ban Johnson (1864-1931) 1937
Cut signature $200
Single-signature baseball
. . . .$2,700-$3,500

3x5 index card $250
Photograph/baseball card . .$500-$550
HOF plaque postcard . . . . .Impossible
Perez-Steele postcards . . . .Impossible

Judy Johnson (1900-1989) 1975
Cut signature . . . .$10-$15
Single-signature baseball . . .$75-$200
3x5 index card . . . .$15-$20
Photograph/baseball card . . . .$30-$60
HOF plaque postcard $25
Perez-Steele postcards . . . . . .$80-$90

Walter Johnson (1887-1946) 1946
Cut signature . . . .$600-$650
Single-signature baseball $5,000
3x5 index card $750
Photograph/baseball card$1,200-$1,400
HOF plaque postcard . . . . . .Unknown
Perez-Steele postcards . . . .Impossible

Addie Joss (1880-1911) 1978
Cut signature $1,500
Single-signature baseball .$7,500-$10,000
3x5 index card $2,500
Photograph/baseball card$3,900-$4,000
HOF plaque postcard . . . . .Impossible
Perez-Steele postcards . . . .Impossible

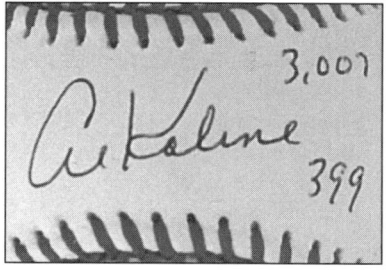

Al Kaline (1934-) 1980
Cut signature . . . .$5-$7
Single-signature baseball . . . .$25-$30
3x5 index card . . . .$8-$10
Photograph/baseball card $15
HOF plaque postcard . . . . . .$12-$15
Perez-Steele postcards . . . . . .$20-$25

Tim Keefe (1857-1933) 1964
Cut signature . . . .$600-$1,500
Single-signature baseball $7,000
3x5 index card $800
Photograph/baseball card $2,000
HOF plaque postcard . . . . .Impossible
Perez-Steele postcards . . . .Impossible

Wee Willie Keeler (1872-1923) 1939
Cut signature . . . .$1,000-$1,400
Single-signature baseball $8,000
3x5 index card $2,000
Photograph/baseball card
. . . .$3,000-$3,250
HOF plaque postcard . . . . .Impossible
Perez-Steele postcards . . . .Impossible

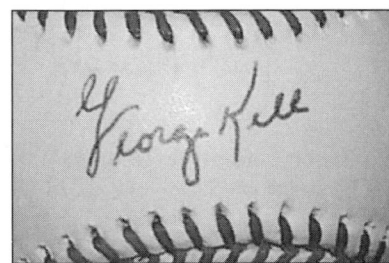

George Kell (1922-) 1883
Cut signature . . . .$5-$7
Single-signature baseball . . . .$20-$24
3x5 index card $7
Photograph/baseball card . . . .$10-$12
HOF plaque postcard . . . .$6-$10
Perez-Steele postcards . . . . .$10-$15

Joe Kelley (1871-1943) 1971
Cut signature . . . .$800-$1,100
Single-signature baseball$7,300-$8,000
3x5 index card $1,000
Photograph/baseball card$1,500-$2,250
HOF plaque postcard . . . . .Impossible
Perez-Steele postcards . . . .Impossible

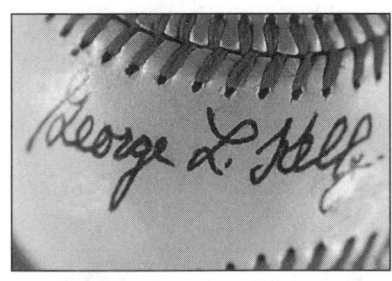

George Kelly (1895-1984) 1973
Cut signature . . . .$7-$8
Single-signature baseball $350
3x5 index card $15
Photograph/baseball card . . . .$50-$75
HOF plaque postcard $30
Perez-Steele postcards . . . .$300-$325

Mike Kelly (1857-1894) 1945
Cut signature $2,000
Single-signature baseball $7,000
3x5 index card $3,500
Photograph/baseball card $5,000
HOF plaque postcard . . . . .Impossible
Perez-Steele postcards . . . .Impossible

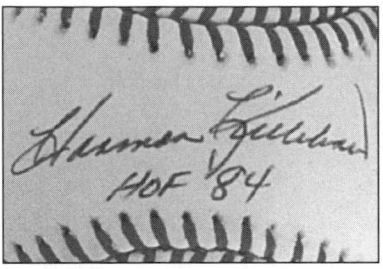

Harmon Killebrew (1936-) 1984
Cut signature $8
Single-signature baseball . . . .$30-$35
3x5 index card $10
Photograph/baseball card $25
HOF plaque postcard $25
Perez-Steele postcards $35

Ralph Kiner (1922-) 1975
Cut signature $8
Single-signature baseball $25
3x5 index card $10
Photograph/baseball card $20
HOF plaque postcard . . . . . .$15-$20
Perez-Steele postcards . . . . .$20-$25

Chuck Klein (1904-1958) 1980
Cut signature $200
Single-signature baseball$1,500-$3,000
3x5 index card $300
Photograph/baseball card . .$400-$500
HOF plaque postcard . . . . .Impossible
Perez-Steele postcards . . . .Impossible

Bill Klem (1874-1951) 1953
Cut signature . . . .$230-$400
Single-signature baseball$2,750-$3,500
3x5 index card $600
Photograph/baseball card . .$900-$1,200
HOF plaque postcard . . . . .Impossible
Perez-Steele postcards . . . .Impossible

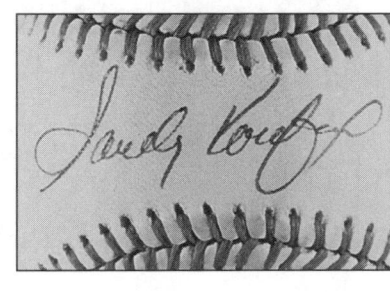

Sandy Koufax (1935-) 1971
Cut signature $10
Single-signature baseball . . . .$65-$70
3x5 index card $15
Photograph/baseball card . . . .$45-$50
HOF plaque postcard $30
Perez-Steele postcards . . . . .$35-$70

Nap Lajoie (1875-1959) 1937
Cut signature $250
Single-signature baseball
. . . .$4,500-$4,950
3x5 index card $350
Photograph/baseball card .$900-$1,000
HOF plaque postcard $750
Perez-Steele postcards . . . .Impossible

Kenesaw Landis (1866-1944) 1944
Cut signature . . . .$475-$500
Single-signature baseball $3,500
3x5 index card $600
Photograph/baseball card . .$750-$900
HOF plaque postcard . . . . .Impossible
Perez-Steele postcards . . . .Impossible

Tommy Lasorda (1927-) 1997
Cut signature $8
Single-signature baseball $30
3x5 index card . . . .$8-$10
Photograph/baseball card $25
HOF plaque postcard $15
Perez-Steele postcards . . . . .$10-$25

Tony Lazzeri (1903-1946) 1991
Cut signature $275
Single-signature baseball$2,500-$4,000
3x5 index card $450
Photograph/baseball card . .$500-$700
HOF plaque postcard . . . . .Impossible
Perez-Steele postcards . . . .Impossible

Bob Lemon (1920-2000) 1976
Cut signature . . . .$7-$9
Single-signature baseball $30
3x5 index card $10
Photograph/baseball card . . . .$25-$30
HOF plaque postcard . . . . . .$10-$15
Perez-Steele postcards . . . . .$15-$20

Buck Leonard (1907-1997) 1972
Cut signature $10
Single-signature baseball . . . .$40-$50
3x5 index card . . . .$12-$15
Photograph/baseball card . . . .$25-$35
HOF plaque postcard $15
Perez-Steele postcards . . . . .$25-$30

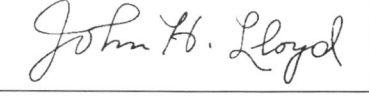

Freddie Lindstrom (1905-1981) 1976
Cut signature . . . .$12-$15
Single-signature baseball . .$200-$700
3x5 index card $20
Photograph/baseball card . . .$75-$100
HOF plaque postcard $40
Perez-Steele postcards . . . .Impossible

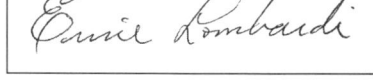

John Lloyd (1884-1964) 1977
Cut signature $700
Single-signature baseball
. . . .$5,600-$7,000
3x5 index card $750
Photograph/baseball card
. . . .$1,200-$2,500
HOF plaque postcard . . . . .Impossible
Perez-Steele postcards . . . .Impossible

Ernie Lombardi (1908-1977) 1986
Cut signature . . . .$35-$50
Single-signature baseball .$525-$1,200
3x5 index card . . . .$50-$60
Photograph/baseball card . .$225-$300
HOF plaque postcard . . . . .Impossible
Perez-Steele postcards . . . .Impossible

Al Lopez (1908-) 1977
Cut signature $15
Single-signature baseball . . . .$75-$85
3x5 index card $20
Photograph/baseball card . . . .$50-$60
HOF plaque postcard $45
Perez-Steele postcards . . . . . .$50-$75

Ted Lyons (1900-1986) 1955
Cut signature . . . .$8-$12
Single-signature baseball . .$125-$225
3x5 index card $15
Photograph/baseball card . . . .$45-$75
HOF plaque postcard . . . . . .$30-$35
Perez-Steele postcards . . . .$200-$250

Connie Mack (1862-1956) 1937
Cut signature $300
Single-signature baseball $1,000
3x5 index card $350
Photograph/baseball card . .$400-$450
HOF plaque postcard $600
Perez-Steele postcards . . .Impossible

Larry MacPhail (1890-1975) 1978
Cut signature $60
Single-signature baseball .$785-$1,700
3x5 index card $175
Photograph/baseball card . .$300-$400
HOF plaque postcard . . . . .Impossible
Perez-Steele postcards . . . .Impossible

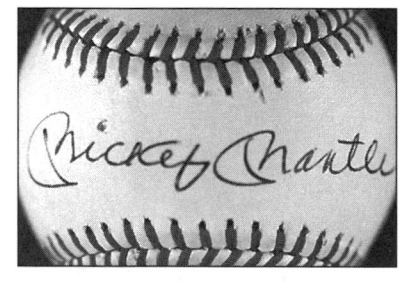

Lee MacPhail (1917-) 1998
Cut signature $6
Single-signature baseball $20
3x5 index card $8
Photograph . . . .$12-$15
HOF plaque postcard $12
Perez-Steele postcard $20

Mickey Mantle (1931-1995) 1974
Cut signature $70
Single-signature baseball . .$175-$250
3x5 index card . . . .$75-$100
Photograph/baseball card $125
HOF plaque postcard $155
Perez-Steele postcards . . . .$200-$250

Heinie Manush (1901-1971) 1964
Cut signature . . . .$25-$40
Single-signature baseball . .$1,500-$2,200
3x5 index card $60
Photograph/baseball card . .$200-$300
HOF plaque postcard . . . . . .$250-$300
Perez-Steele postcards . . . .Impossible

Rabbit Maranville (1891-1954) 1954
Cut signature . . . .$140-$150
Single-signature baseball
. . . .$1,600-$2,000
3x5 index card $250
Photograph/baseball card . .$350-$425
HOF plaque postcard . . . .Impossible
Perez-Steele postcards . . . .Impossible

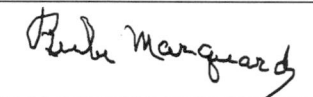

Juan Marichal (1938-) 1983
Cut signature . . . .$6-$8
Single-signature baseball $25
3x5 index card $10
Photograph/baseball card . . . .$15-$18
HOF plaque postcard $12
Perez-Steele postcards . . . . . .$10-$20

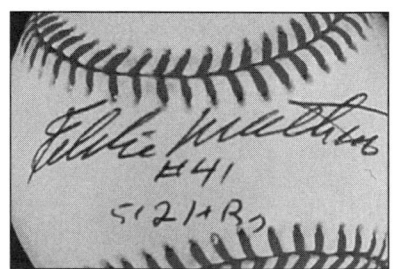

Rube Marquard (1889-1980) 1971
Cut signature . . . .$10-$15
Single-signature baseball . .$450-$700
3x5 index card $20
Photograph/baseball card . .$100-$150
HOF plaque postcard $45
Perez-Steele postcards . . . .Impossible

Eddie Mathews (1931-2001) 1978
Cut signature $10
Single-signature baseball . . . .$25-$38
3x5 index card . . . .$10-$12
Photograph/baseball card . . . .$25-$30
HOF plaque postcard $15
Perez-Steele postcards . . . . . .$20-$25

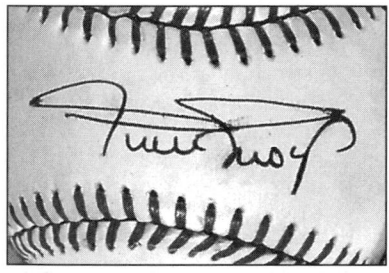

Christy Mathewson (1880-1925) 1936
Cut signature $1,200
Single-sign. baseball .$11,500-$13,000
3x5 index card $1,400
Photograph/baseball card .$2,900-$3,000
HOF plaque postcard . . . .Impossible
Perez-Steele postcards . . . .Impossible

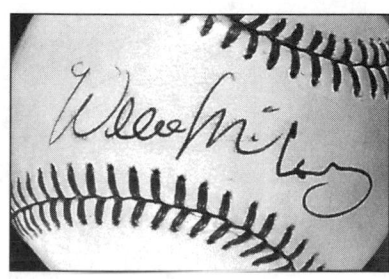

Willie Mays (1931-) 1979
Cut signature $15
Single-signature baseball . . . .$45-$50
3x5 index card $20
Photograph/baseball card . . .$25-$35
HOF plaque postcard $30
Perez-Steele postcards . . . . . .$35-$65

Joe McCarthy (1887-1978) 1957
Cut signature . . . .$25-$35
Single-signature baseball .$650-$1,000
3x5 index card $40
Photograph/baseball card . .$100-$150
HOF plaque postcard . . . .$50-$80
Perez-Steele postcards . . . .Impossible

Tom McCarthy (1864-1922) 1946
Cut signature . . . .$1,500-$1,675
Single-signature baseball
. . . .$4,000-$4,250
3x5 index card $2,000
Photograph/baseball card$4,000-$4,250
HOF plaque postcard . . . .Impossible
Perez-Steele postcards . . . .Impossible

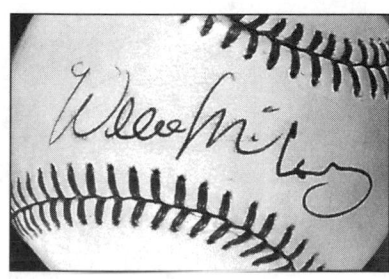

Willie McCovey (1938-) 1986
Cut signature . . . .$4-$5
Single-signature baseball $30

3x5 index card $8
Photograph/baseball card . . . .$20-$25
HOF plaque postcard $12
Perez-Steele postcards . . . . .$10-$25

Joe McGinnity (1871-1929) 1946
Cut signature . . . .$800-$1,250
Single-signature baseball
. . . .$5,000-$9,000
3x5 index card $1,500
Photograph/baseball card$4,000-$5,000
HOF plaque postcard . . . .Impossible
Perez-Steele postcards . . . .Impossible

Bill McGowan (1871-1954) 1992
Cut signature $300
Single-signature baseball $5,000
3x5 index card $400
Photograph/baseball card $2,000
HOF plaque postcard . . . .Impossible
Perez-Steele postcards . . . .Impossible

John McGraw (1873-1934) 1937
Cut signature . . . .$450-$500
Single-signature baseball
. . . .$3,500-$6,000
3x5 index card $650
Photograph/baseball card$1,250-$1,500
HOF plaque postcard . . . .Impossible
Perez-Steele postcards . . . .Impossible

Bid McPhee (1859-1943) 2000
Cut signature . . . .$75-$100
Single-signature baseball
. . . .$2,000-$2,500
3x5 index card $150
Photograph/baseball card . .$350-$400
HOF plaque postcard . . . .Impossible
Perez-Steele postcards . . . .Impossible

Bill McKechnie (1886-1965) 1962
Cut signature . . . .$60-$75
Single-signature baseball
. . . .$1,500-$2,000
3x5 index card $150
Photograph/baseball card . .$300-$350
HOF plaque postcard $300
Perez-Steele postcards . . . .Impossible

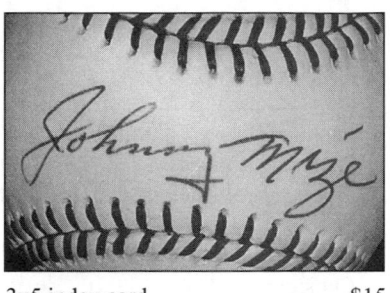

Ducky Medwick (1911-1975) 1968
Cut signature . . . .$20-$25
Single-signature baseball .$500-$1,700
3x5 index card $45
Photograph/baseball card . .$150-$200
HOF plaque postcard $125
Perez-Steele postcards . . . .Impossible

Johnny Mize (1913-1993) 1981
Cut signature $10
Single-signature baseball . . .$75-$100

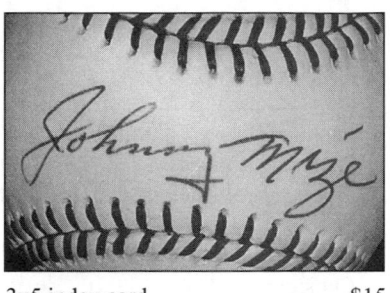

3x5 index card $15
Photograph/baseball card . . . .$30-$35
HOF plaque postcard $25
Perez-Steele postcards $40

Joe Morgan (1943-) 1990
Cut signature . . . .$8-$10
Single-signature baseball . . .$25-$30
3x5 index card . . . .$10-$12
Photograph/baseball card . . .$20-$30
HOF plaque postcard . . . . . .$15-$20
Perez-Steele postcards . . . . .$20-$25

Stan Musial (1920-) 1969
Cut signature . . . .$10-$12
Single-signature baseball $50
3x5 index card $15
Photograph/baseball card . . . .$30-$35
HOF plaque postcard $25
Perez-Steele postcards . . . . . .$30-$80

Hal Newhouser (1921-1998) 1992
Cut signature . . . .$3-$5
Single-signature baseball . . . .$22-$27
3x5 index card $7
Photograph/baseball card $12
HOF plaque postcard $8
Perez-Steele postcards . . . . . .$15-$20

Kid Nichols (1869-1953) 1949
Cut signature . . . .$150-$200
Single-signature baseball . .$3,200-$4,000
3x5 index card $300

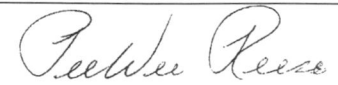

Photograph/baseball card . . .$475-$500
HOF plaque postcard $1,000
Perez-Steele postcards . . . .Impossible

Phil Niekro (1939-) 1997
Cut signature $7
Single-signature baseball $25
3x5 index card $10
Photograph/baseball card . . . .$15-$20
HOF plaque postcard $15
Perez-Steele postcards $20

James O'Rourke (1852-1919) 1945
Cut signature . . . . $1,500-$1,750
Single-signature baseball
. . . .$5,200-$10,000
3x5 index card $2,500
Photograph/baseball card$3,500-$3,700
HOF plaque postcard . . . .Impossible
Perez-Steele postcards . . . .Impossible

Mel Ott (1909-1958) 1951
Cut signature . . . .$200-$300
Single-signature baseball
. . . .$2,500-$3,500
3x5 index card $300
Photograph/baseball card . .$500-$725
HOF plaque postcard $650
Perez-Steele postcards . . . .Impossible

Satchel Paige (1906-1982) 1971
Cut signature . . . .$35-$45
Single-signature baseball . .$900-$990
3x5 index card . . . .$80-$125
Photograph/baseball card . .$200-$235
HOF plaque postcard $140
Perez-Steele postcards $3,500

Jim Palmer (1945-) 1990
Cut signature $7
Single-signature baseball . . . .$25-$30
3x5 index card $10
Photograph/baseball card . . . .$15-$20
HOF plaque postcard . . . . . .$12-$20
Perez-Steele postcards . . . . .$15-$25

Herb Pennock (1894-1948) 1948
Cut signature $175
Single-signature baseball
. . . .$1,625-$2,500
3x5 index card $200
Photograph/baseball card $350
HOF plaque postcard . . . .Impossible
Perez-Steele postcards . . . .Impossible

Gaylord Perry (1938-) 1991
Cut signature . . . .$5-$7
Single-signature baseball . . . .$20-$25
3x5 index card $10
Photograph/baseball card . . . .$15-$20
HOF plaque postcard $10
Perez-Steele postcards $15

Tony Perez (1943-) 2000
Cut signature $7
Single-signature baseball . . . .$25-$30
3x5 index card $10
Photograph/baseball card . . . .$15-$20
HOF plaque postcard $15
Perez-Steele postcards $20

Ed Plank (1875-1926) 1946
Cut signature . . . . $1,500-$1,775
Single-signature baseball $8,000
3x5 index card $2,200
Photograph/baseball card
. . . .$3,200-$3,500
HOF plaque postcard . . . .Impossible
Perez-Steele postcards . . . .Impossible

Charles Radbourne (1854-1897) 1948
Cut signature . . . . $1,425-$2,000
Single-signature baseball $7,500
3x5 index card $2,500
Photograph/baseball card
. . . .$3,200-$3,500
HOF plaque postcard . . . .Impossible
Perez-Steele postcards . . . .Impossible

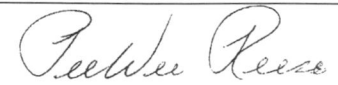

Pee Wee Reese (1918-1999) 1984
Cut signature $10
Single-signature baseball $75
3x5 index card $15
Photograph/baseball card . . . .$45-$50
HOF plaque postcard . . . .$40-$45
Perez-Steele postcards . . . . . .$55-$60

Sam Rice (1890-1974) 1963
Cut signature . . . .$25-$50
Single-signature baseball .$625-$1,500
3x5 index card $60
Photograph/baseball card . .$125-$150
HOF plaque postcard . . . .$100-$135
Perez-Steele postcards . . . .Impossible

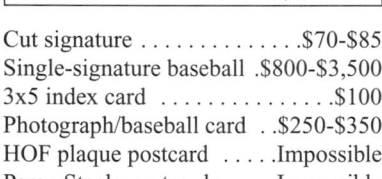

Branch Rickey (1881-1965) 1967
Cut signature . . . .$175-$225
Single-signature baseball
. . . .$1,100-$2,500
3x5 index card $300
Photograph/baseball card . .$525-$750
HOF plaque postcard . . . .Impossible
Perez-Steele postcards . . . .Impossible

Eppa Rixey (1891-1963) 1963

Cut signature . . . .$70-$85
Single-signature baseball .$800-$3,500
3x5 index card $100
Photograph/baseball card . .$250-$350
HOF plaque postcard . . . .Impossible
Perez-Steele postcards . . . .Impossible

Phil Rizzuto (1918-) 1994
Cut signature . . . .$5-$7
Single-signature baseball $25
3x5 index card $10
Photograph/baseball card . . . .$12-$18
HOF plaque postcard $12
Perez-Steele postcards $35

Robin Roberts (1926-) 1976
Cut signature . . . .$5-$7
Single-signature baseball $25
3x5 index card $10
Photograph/baseball card $15
HOF plaque postcard $10
Perez-Steele postcards . . . . . .$15-$20

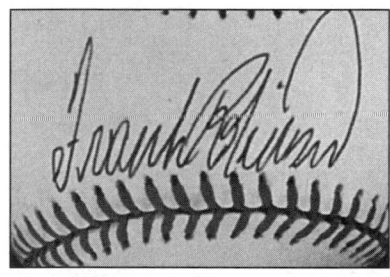

Brooks Robinson (1937-) 1983
Cut signature . . . .$5-$7
Single-signature baseball . . . .$25-$30
3x5 index card $10
Photograph/baseball card . . . .$15-$20
HOF plaque postcard $10
Perez-Steele postcards . . . . . .$12-$20

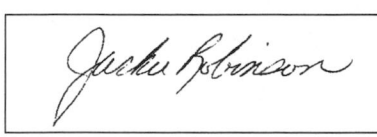

Frank Robinson (1935-) 1982
Cut signature . . . .$4-$5
Single-signature baseball $30
3x5 index card $8
Photograph/baseball card $20
HOF plaque postcard . . . .$12-$20
Perez-Steele postcards $25

Jackie Robinson (1919-1972) 1962
Cut signature . . . .$400-$450
Single-signature baseball $3,000
3x5 index card $500
Photograph/baseball card . .$750-$800
HOF plaque postcard . . . . .$750-$800
Perez-Steele postcards . . . .Impossible

Wilbert Robinson (1863-1934) 1945
Cut signature . . . .$700-$750
Single-signature baseball
. . . .$4,225-$6,000
3x5 index card $750
Photograph/baseball card $2,000
HOF plaque postcard . . . .Impossible
Perez-Steele postcards . . . .Impossible

Joe Rogan (1889-1967) 1998
Cut signature $2,500
Single-signature baseball $10,000
3x5 index card $2,500
Photograph $3,000
HOF plaque postcard . . . .Impossible
Perez-Steele postcards . . . .Impossible

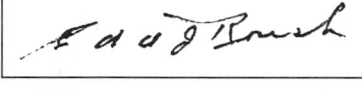

Edd Roush (1893-1988) 1962
Cut signature . . . .$9-$12
Single-signature baseball . . .$80-$160
3x5 index card $10
Photograph/baseball card . . . .$45-$75
HOF plaque postcard . . . . . .$30-$80
Perez-Steele postcards . . . . . .$65-$80

Red Ruffing (1904-1986) 1967
Cut signature . . . .$20-$35
Single-signature baseball . .$195-$500
3x5 index card $40
Photograph/baseball card . .$70-$125
HOF plaque postcard $100
Perez-Steele postcards . . . .$350-$400

Amos Rusie (1871-1942) 1977
Cut signature . . . .$700-$1,100
Single-signature baseball . .$5,000-$6,500
3x5 index card $750
Photograph/baseball card . .$2,000-$2,300
HOF plaque postcard . . . .Impossible
Perez-Steele postcards . . . .Impossible

Babe Ruth (1895-1948) 1936
Cut signature $1,000
Single-signature baseball . .$4,500-$5,500
3x5 index card $1,500
Photograph/baseball card . .$2,500-$3,000
HOF plaque postcard $4,500
Perez-Steele postcards . . . .Impossible

Nolan Ryan (1947-) 1999
Cut signature . . . .$10-$12
Single-signature baseball . . . .$55-$60
3x5 index card $15
Photograph/baseball card . . . .$40-$45
HOF plaque postcard . . . . . .$40-$50
Perez-Steele postcards . . . . . .$50-$65

Ray Schalk (1892-1970) 1955
Cut signature . . . .$35-$45
Single-signature baseball . .$600-$1,700
3x5 index card . . . .$75-$85
Photograph/baseball card . .$225-$350
HOF plaque postcard . . . . .$300-$450
Perez-Steele postcards . . . .Impossible

Mike Schmidt (1949-) 1995
Cut signature . . . .$8-$10
Single-signature baseball . . . .$40-$60
3x5 index card $15
Photograph/baseball card . . . .$35-$55
HOF plaque postcard $40
Perez-Steele postcards $35

Red Schoendienst (1923-) 1989
Cut signature . . . .$5-$7
Single-signature baseball $25
3x5 index card $10

Photograph/baseball card ....$15-$20
HOF plaque postcard $15
Perez-Steele postcards ......$15-$20

Frank Selee (1859-1909) 1999
Cut signature $550
Single-signature baseball $850
3x5 index card $600
Photograph/baseball card ..$700-$800
HOF plaque postcard ....Impossible
Perez-Steele postcards ...Impossible

Tom Seaver (1944-) 1992
Cut signature ....$7-$10
Single-signature baseball ....$40-$45
3x5 index card $15
Photograph/baseball card $35
HOF plaque postcard $30
Perez-Steele postcards ......$35-$40

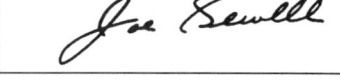

Joe Sewell (1898-1990) 1977
Cut signature ....$8-$10
Single-signature baseball ..$80-$125
3x5 index card $12
Photograph/baseball card ....$30-$35
HOF plaque postcard $20
Perez-Steele postcards ......$35-$60

Al Simmons (1902-1956) 1953
Cut signature ....$90-$180
Single-signature baseball .$950-$2,800
3x5 index card ....$225-$325
Photograph/baseball card $500
HOF plaque postcard $800
Perez-Steele postcards ....Impossible

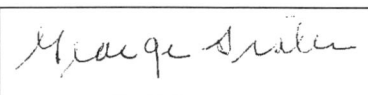

George Sisler (1893-1973) 1939
Cut signature ....$25-$40
Single-signature baseball .$550-$1,200

3x5 index card ....$50-$60
Photograph/baseball card ..$135-$175
HOF plaque postcard $125
Perez-Steele postcards ....Impossible

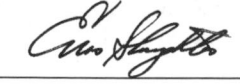

Enos Slaughter (1916-) 1985
Cut signature $5
Single-signature baseball ....$20-$25
3x5 index card $7
Photograph/baseball card ....$12-$15
HOF plaque postcard ....$8-$10
Perez-Steele postcards ......$12-$20

Duke Snider (1926-) 1980
Cut signature ....$5-$8
Single-signature baseball ....$25-$30
3x5 index card $10
Photograph/baseball card ....$20-$25
HOF plaque postcard ......$15-$20
Perez-Steele postcards ......$15-$25

Warren Spahn (1921-) 1973
Cut signature ....$5-$8
Single-signature baseball ....$20-$25
3x5 index card $10
Photograph/baseball card ....$15-$20
HOF plaque postcard $10
Perez-Steele postcards ......$20-$30

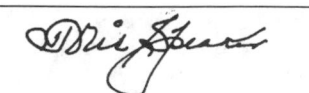

Al Spalding (1850-1915) 1939
Cut signature ....$750-$1,250
Single-signature baseball $12,000
3x5 index card $1,750
Photograph/baseball card
 ....$1,800-$2,200
HOF plaque postcard ....Impossible
Perez-Steele postcards ....Impossible

Tris Speaker (1888-1958) 1937
Cut signature ....$125-$200
Single-signature baseball
 ....$2,900-$3,000
3x5 index card ....$225-$275
Photograph/baseball card ..$500-$700

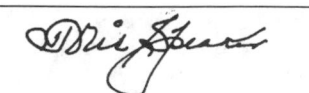

HOF plaque postcard $600
Perez-Steele postcards ....Impossible

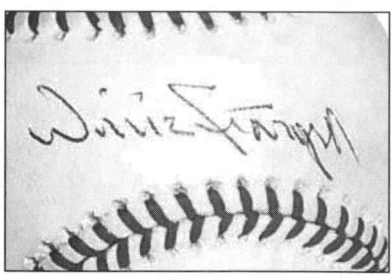

Willie Stargell (1940-2001) 1988
Cut signature ....$5-$8
Single-signature baseball ....$25-$30
3x5 index card $10
Photograph/baseball card ....$15-$20
HOF plaque postcard $10
Perez-Steele postcards ......$12-$20

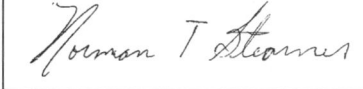

Turkey Stearn (1901-1979) 2000
Cut signature $250
Single-signature baseball ..$400-$500
3x5 index card $300
Photograph/baseball card $700
HOF plaque postcard .....Impossible
Perez-Steele postcards ...Impossible

Casey Stengel (1890-1975) 1966
Cut signature ....$20-$40
Single-signature baseball .$480-$1,000
3x5 index card ....$90-$100
Photograph/baseball card $150
HOF plaque postcard $100
Perez-Steele postcards ...Impossible0

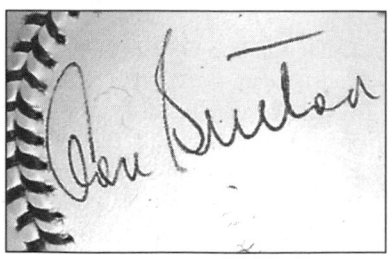

Don Sutton (1945-) 1998
Cut signature . . . .$5-$8
Single-signature baseball $25
3x5 index card $10
Photograph/baseball card . . . .$15-$20
HOF plaque postcard . . . . . . $12-$20
Perez-Steele postcards . . . . . .$20-$25

Bill Terry (1898-1989) 1954
Cut signature $15
Single-signature baseball . .$160-$175
3x5 index card $20
Photograph/baseball card . . . .$45-$50
HOF plaque postcard . . . . . . $25-$30
Perez-Steele postcards . . . . .$65-$80

Sam Thompson (1860-1922) 1974
Cut signature . . . .$1,200-$2,125
Single-signature baseball $10,000
3x5 index card $3,250
Photograph/baseball card $6,000
HOF plaque postcard . . . . .Impossible
Perez-Steele postcards . . . .Impossible

Joe Tinker (1880-1948) 1946
Cut signature . . . .$300-$350
Single-signature baseball $6,000
3x5 index card . . . .$375-$400
Photograph/baseball card .$900-$1,200
HOF plaque postcard $1,000
Perez-Steele postcards . . . .Impossible

Pie Traynor (1899-1972) 1948
Cut signature . . . .$50-$100
Single-signature baseball
. . . .$1,175-$1,200
3x5 index card . . . .$125-$175
Photograph/baseball card $300
HOF plaque postcard $450
Perez-Steele postcards . . . .Impossible

Dazzy Vance (1891-1961) 1955
Cut signature . . . .$70-$200
Single-signature baseball
. . . .$1,500-$3,200

3x5 index card . . . .$250-$300
Photograph/baseball card . .$650-$750
HOF plaque postcard $600
Perez-Steele postcards . . . .Impossible

Arky Vaughan (1912-1952) 1985
Cut signature . . . .$150-$175
Single-signature baseball
. . . .$1,525-$3,500
3x5 index card $250
Photograph/baseball card . .$500-$650
HOF plaque postcard . . . .Impossible
Perez-Steele postcards . . . .Impossible

William Veeck (1914-1986) 1991
Cut signature . . . .$15-$45
Single-signature baseball .$550-$2,000
3x5 index card $75
Photograph/baseball card . .$250-$325
HOF plaque postcard . . . .Impossible
Perez-Steele postcards . . . .Impossible

Rube Waddell (1876-1914) 1946
Cut signature . . . .$1,000-$1,400
Single-signature baseball $12,500
3x5 index card $1,500
Photograph/baseball card $4,500
HOF plaque postcard . . . .Impossible
Perez-Steele postcards . . . .Impossible

Honus Wagner (1874-1955) 1936
Cut signature . . . .$275-$300
Single-signature baseball $4,000
3x5 index card $350
Photograph/baseball card . .$800-$850
HOF plaque postcard $1,200
Perez-Steele postcards . . . .Impossible

Bobby Wallace (1873-1960) 1953
Cut signature . . . .$175-$225
Single-signature baseball
. . . .$3,000-$4,500
3x5 index card $300
Photograph/baseball card . .$625-$700
HOF plaque postcard $800
Perez-Steele postcards . . . .Impossible

Ed Walsh (1881-1959) 1946
Cut signature . . . .$125-$150
Single-signature baseball$2,725-$3,600
3x5 index card $200
Photograph/baseball card . .$350-$400
HOF plaque postcard $350
Perez-Steele postcards . . .Impossible

Lloyd Waner (1906-1982) 1967
Cut signature . . . .$15-$20
Single-signature baseball $500
3x5 index card $25
Photograph/baseball card $150
HOF plaque postcard $30
Perez-Steele postcards $3,500

Paul Waner (1903-1965) 1952
Cut signature . . . .$50-$100
Single-signature baseball
. . . .$2,300-$2,500
3x5 index card $125
Photograph/baseball card . .$200-$300
HOF plaque postcard $350
Perez-Steele postcards . . . .Impossible

Monte Ward (1860-1925) 1964
Cut signature . . . .$1,000-$1,450
Single-signature baseball $12,000
3x5 index card $1,500
Photograph/baseball card
. . . .$3,000-$3,250
HOF plaque postcard . . . .Impossible
Perez-Steele postcards . . . .Impossible

Earl Weaver (1930-) 1996
Cut signature . . . .$5-$7
Single-signature baseball $25
3x5 index card $10
Photograph/baseball card $15
HOF plaque/postcard $10
Perez-Steele postcards $15

George Weiss (1895-1972) 1971
Cut signature . . . .$40-$45
Single-signature baseball .$675-$3,500
3x5 index card . . . .$75-$100
Photograph/baseball card . .$250-$300
HOF plaque postcard . . . . . .Unknown
Perez-Steele postcards . . . .Impossible

Mickey Welch (1859-1941) 1973
Cut signature . . . .$1,700-$2,000
Single-signature baseball
. . . .$5,800-$8,500
3x5 index card $2,750
Photograph/baseball card $4,000
HOF plaque postcard . . . .Impossible
Perez-Steele postcards . . . .Impossible

Willie Wells (1905-1989) 1997
Cut signature . . . .$10-$12
Single-signature baseball $35
3x5 index card $15
Photograph $30
HOF plaque postcard . . . . .Impossible
Perez-Steele postcards . . . .Impossible

Zack Wheat (1888-1972) 1959
Cut signature . . . .$20-$50
Single-signature baseball .$975-$1,600
3x5 index card $80
Photograph/baseball card . .$175-$200
HOF plaque postcard . . . .$200-$350
Perez-Steele postcards . . . .Impossible

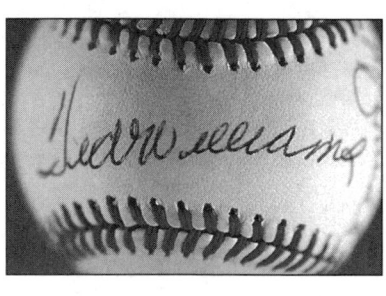

Hoyt Wilhelm (1923-) 1985
Cut signature $5
Single-signature baseball $20
3x5 index card $8
Photograph/baseball card . . . .$12-$16
HOF plaque postcard . . . . . .$10-$15
Perez-Steele postcards $15

Billy Williams (1938-) 1987
Cut signature . . . .$5-$7
Single-signature baseball $25
3x5 index card $10
Photograph/baseball card . . . .$15-$20
HOF plaque postcard $10
Perez-Steele postcards . . . . . .$12-$20

Smoky Joe Williams (1885-1946) 1999
Cut signature . . . .$400-$450
Single-signature baseball . .$600-$800
3x5 index card $450
Photograph/baseball card . .$500-$600
HOF plaque postcard . . . .Impossible
Perez-Steele postcards . . . .Impossible

Ted Williams (1918-) 1966
Cut signature $40
Single-signature baseball . .$275-$300
3x5 index card $60
Photograph/baseball card $150
HOF plaque postcard $275
Perez-Steele postcards . . . .$250-$300

Vic Willis (1876-1947) 1995
Cut signature $1,500
Single-signature baseball . . .Unknown
3x5 index card $425
Photograph/baseball card $750
HOF plaque postcard . . . .Impossible
Perez-Steele postcards . . . .Impossible

Hack Wilson (1900-1948) 1979
Cut signature . . . .$235-$300
Single-signature baseball
. . . .$2,400-$3,000
3x5 index card $450
Photograph/baseball card . .$675-$800
HOF plaque postcard . . . .Impossible
Perez-Steele postcards . . . .Impossible

George Wright (1847-1937) 1937
Cut signature . . . .$800-$900
Single-signature baseball
. . . .$5,725-$8,500
3x5 index card $1,200
Photograph/baseball card $2,750
HOF plaque postcard . . . .Impossible
Perez-Steele postcards . . . .Impossible

Harry Wright (1835-1895) 1953
Cut signature . . . .$1,200-$1,600
Single-signature baseball $5,000
3x5 index card $2,000
Photograph/baseball card $3,500
HOF plaque postcard . . . .Impossible
Perez-Steele postcards . . . .Impossible

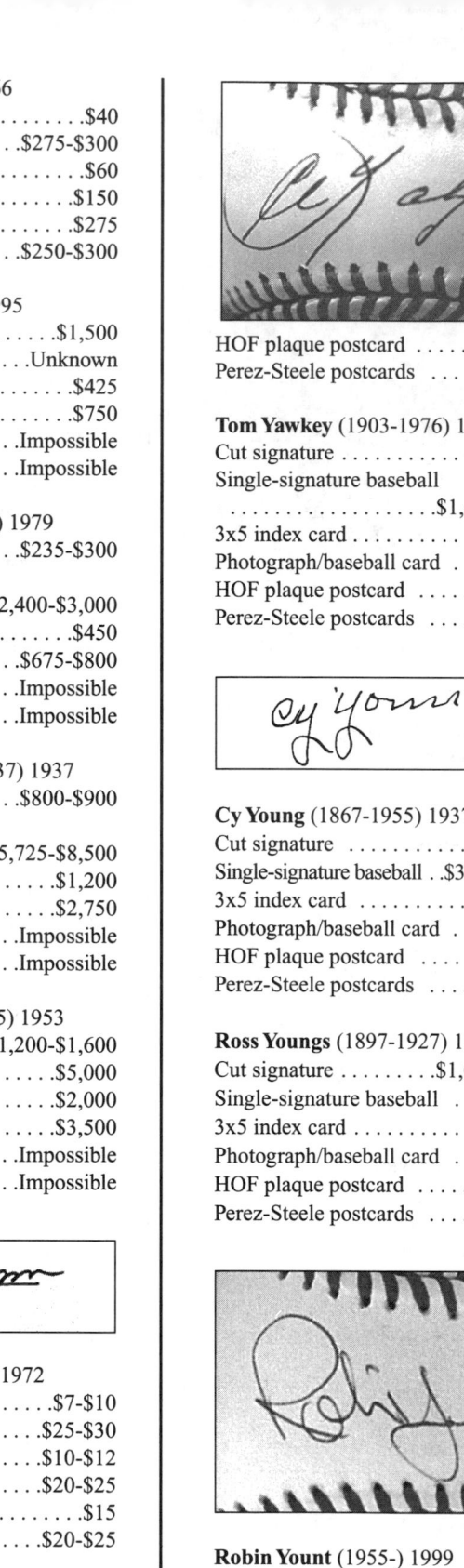

Early Wynn (1920-1999) 1972
Cut signature . . . .$7-$10
Single-signature baseball . . . .$25-$30
3x5 index card . . . .$10-$12
Photograph/baseball card . . . .$20-$25
HOF plaque postcard $15
Perez-Steele postcards . . . . . .$20-$25

Carl Yastrzemski (1939-) 1989
Cut signature . . . .$8-$10
Single-signature baseball . . . .$35-$45
3x5 index card $15
Photograph/baseball card $30

HOF plaque postcard $20
Perez-Steele postcards . . . . .$20-$30

Tom Yawkey (1903-1976) 1980
Cut signature . . . .$70-$100
Single-signature baseball
. . . .$1,050-$2,000
3x5 index card . . . .$125-$175
Photograph/baseball card . .$325-$400
HOF plaque postcard . . . .Impossible
Perez-Steele postcards . . . .Impossible

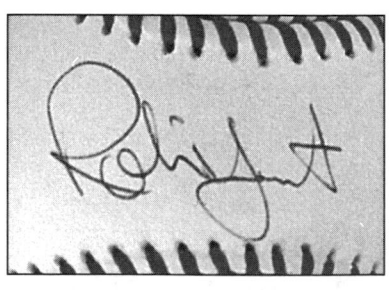

Cy Young (1867-1955) 1937
Cut signature $300
Single-signature baseball . .$3,400-$3,500
3x5 index card $350
Photograph/baseball card . .$700-$825
HOF plaque postcard $1,000
Perez-Steele postcards . . . .Impossible

Ross Youngs (1897-1927) 1972
Cut signature . . . .$1,000-$1,150
Single-signature baseball $7,000
3x5 index card $1,500
Photograph/baseball card $2,500
HOF plaque postcard . . . .Impossible
Perez-Steele postcards . . . .Impossible

Robin Yount (1955-) 1999
Cut signature $8
Single-signature baseball . . .$25-$30
3x5 index card $15
HOF plaque postcard $20
Perez-Steele postcards . . . . .$20-$25

Baseball Equipment

All listed equipment values are for game-used equipment only. The only exception is the "player endorsed baseball glove" section. Many variables are involved in pricing equipment, including player popularity, condition, scarcity, year the item is from, provenance and whether or not it was a home or road jersey. The prices listed below are merely a starting point.

Hall of Fame Players

Player	Bat	Cap	Jersey
Hank Aaron	$2,500	$1,500	$32,000
Grover Alexander	14,000	4,000	90,000
Cap Anson	5,750	2,500	55,000
Luis Aparicio	900	350	11,500
Luke Appling	1,450	700	16,000
Richie Ashburn	800	325	11,000
Earl Averill	1,350	900	13,750
Frank Baker	4,000	2,000	45,000
Dave Bancroft	2,000	1,350	23,000
Ernie Banks	2,000	900	25,000
Jake Beckley	2,000	1,600	20,000
Johnny Bench	1,050	300	15,000
Chief Bender	1,800	1,400	19,500
Yogi Berra	7,500	3,750	24,000
Jim Bottomley	1,800	900	14,500
Lou Boudreau	2,000	950	19,000
Roger Bresnahan	9,500	4,000	70,000
George Brett	600	400	8,500
Lou Brock	475	300	9,000
Dan Brouthers	3,250	1,450	25,000
Mordecai Brown	2,000	1,800	30,000
Jim Bunning	350	300	5,250
Jesse Burkett	2,500	1,600	20,000
Roy Campanella	4,000	1,200	30,000
Rod Carew	800	500	5,500
Max Carey	2,500	1,600	20,000
Steve Carlton	350	250	6,000
Orlando Cepeda	550	450	9,400
Frank Chance	3,000	2,000	30,000
Jack Chesbro	2,500	2,000	32,000
Fred Clarke	2,000	1,400	20,000
John Clarkson	2,000	1,600	20,000
Roberto Clemente	5,000	2,500	65,000
Ty Cobb	16,500	9,000	170,000
Mickey Cochrane	6,000	3,500	40,000
Eddie Collins	3,000	1500	30,000
Jimmy Collins	2,000	1,600	20,000
Earle Combs	2,450	1,750	26,000
Roger Connor	2,000	1,250	18,000
Stan Coveleski	2,000	1,250	19,000
Sam Crawford	2,250	1,450	24,000
Joe Cronin	2,750	1,550	34,500
Kiki Cuyler	2,750	2,100	30,000
Dizzy Dean	2,500	2,000	36,000
Ed Delahanty	2,200	1,500	22,000
Joe DiMaggio	8,000	5,000	130,000
Bill Dickey	9,000	4,000	45,000
Larry Doby	500	250	9,000
Bobby Doerr	750	300	9,500
Don Drysdale	400	350	12,000
Hugh Duffy	2,250	2,000	24,000
Johnny Evers	2,000	1,600	22,000
Buck Ewing	3,500	2,500	35,500
Red Faber	2,000	1,200	17,000
Bob Feller	3,000	1,500	30,000
Rick Ferrell	1,500	900	15,500
Rollie Fingers	400	250	9,000

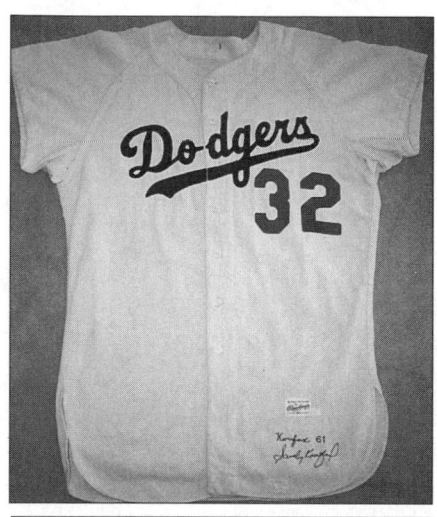

Sandy Koufax game-used jersey.

	Bat	Cap	Jersey
Carlton Fisk	500	375	7,500
Elmer Flick	2,000	1,200	20,000
Whitey Ford	2,500	1,250	36,000
Jimmie Foxx	9,000	2,500	80,000
Frankie Frisch	2,750	2,000	38,000
Pud Galvin	2,000	2,000	30,000
Lou Gehrig	20,000	20,000	250,000
Charlie Gehringer	2,000	1,500	30,000
Bob Gibson	600	500	12,000
Lefty Gomez	1,500	900	23,000
Goose Goslin	1,800	1,200	24,000
Hank Greenberg	3,500	2,500	50,000
Burleigh Grimes	1,800	1,000	27,000
Lefty Grove	2,800	1,500	36,000
Chick Hafey	1,500	1,600	20,000
Jesse Haines	1,500	1,500	20,000
Billy Hamilton	1,800	1,500	22,000
Gabby Hartnett	3,500	2,500	40,000
Harry Heilmann	1,500	1,400	20,000
Billy Herman	1,600	1,500	24,000
Harry Hooper	1,500	1,400	16,000
Rogers Hornsby	5,500	3,000	85,000
Waite Hoyt	1,500	1,200	20,000
Carl Hubbell	1,500	750	20,000
Catfish Hunter	600	500	15,000
Monte Irvin	550	400	6,500
Reggie Jackson	950	600	20,500
Travis Jackson	1,400	1,000	15,000
Fergie Jenkins	450	300	12,500
Hugh Jennings	1,500	1,000	24,000
Walter Johnson	9,000	3,500	90,000
Addie Joss	1,400	1,200	19,000
Al Kaline	1,750	700	20,000
Tim Keefe	1,500	750	20,000
Willie Keeler	2,000	1,750	35,000
George Kell	1,000	900	17,000
Joe Kelley	2,000	1,500	24,000
George Kelly	2,200	1,600	32,000
King Kelly	1,800	1,500	18,500
Harmon Killebrew	1,250	650	27,000
Ralph Kiner	1,400	600	25,000
Chuck Klein	1,500	1,200	20,000
Sandy Koufax	2,250	1,500	36,000
Nap Lajoie	2,500	1,700	40,000
Tony Lazzeri	1,750	1,300	18,500
Bob Lemon	600	300	12,500
Fred Lindstrom	1,500	1,400	20,000
Ernie Lombardi	2,500	1,200	30,000
Ted Lyons	1,750	1,400	20,000
Mickey Mantle	9,000	5,500	140,000
Heinie Manush	2,000	1,500	34,000
Rabbit Maranville	2,200	1,600	34,500

	Bat	Cap	Jersey
Juan Marichal	750	350	12,500
Rube Marquard	1,500	1,200	20,000
Eddie Mathews	2,100	1,000	28,000
Christy Mathewson	9,250	3,000	90,000
Willie Mays	3,500	1,400	40,000
Bill Mazeroski	800	375	12,000
Tommy McCarthy	1,500	1,200	20,000
Willie McCovey	950	500	22,000
Joe McGinnity	1,750	1,500	35,000
Ducky Medwick	1,950	1,750	36,000
Johnny Mize	1,750	1,500	20,000
Joe Morgan	800	400	12,500
Stan Musial	3,000	1,750	45,000
Kid Nichols	2,250	2,000	30,000
Phil Niekro	450	300	9,000
Jim O'Rourke	2,750	2,000	30,000
Mel Ott	4,000	2,750	50,000
Satchel Paige	2,500	1,200	35,000
Jim Palmer	800	425	12,500
Herb Pennock	1,900	1,400	30,000
Tony Perez	750	375	7,250
Gaylord Perry	350	275	6,500
Eddie Plank	3,000	1,250	74,500
Kirby Puckett	550	325	7,000
Old Hoss Radbourn	2,500	1,750	45,000
Pee Wee Reese	1,000	800	16,000
Sam Rice	1,500	1,000	20,000
Eppa Rixey	1,600	1,250	24,500
Phil Rizzuto	900	450	11,000
Robin Roberts	500	325	10,500
Brooks Robinson	450	300	9,500
Frank Robinson	900	400	25,000
Jackie Robinson	9,500	3,500	125,000
Edd Roush	1,500	1,100	20,000
Red Ruffing	1,750	1,400	22,000
Amos Rusie	1,250	1,200	21,000
Babe Ruth	23,000	15,000	200,000
Nolan Ryan	900	600	13,000
Ray Schalk	3,250	2,750	40,000
Mike Schmidt	1,000	700	14,250
Red Schoendienst	850	325	16,500
Tom Seaver	750	600	18,500
Joe Sewell	950	750	12,000
Al Simmons	2,000	1,400	28,000
George Sisler	2,150	1,800	38,000
Enos Slaughter	1,250	950	16,500
Duke Snider	2,750	1,750	30,000
Warren Spahn	2,000	1,800	38,500
Tris Speaker	2,500	2,500	40,000
Willie Stargell	1,000	500	9,500
Casey Stengel	1,900	1,250	25,000
Don Sutton	350	300	6,500
Bill Terry	1,500	1,200	24,000
Sam Thompson	1,400	1,000	20,000
Joe Tinker	2,250	1,500	25,500
Pie Traynor	1,500	1,200	24,500
Dazzy Vance	1,400	1,000	22,500
Arky Vaughan	1,550	1,250	20,000
Rube Waddell	1,900	1,450	38,000
Honus Wagner	7,000	5,000	120,000
Bobby Wallace	1,400	1,000	15,000
Ed Walsh	1,750	1,200	22,500
Lloyd Waner	1,750	1,200	27,000
Paul Waner	2,400	1,700	31,500
John M. Ward	1,400	1,150	12,500
Mickey Welch	1,250	1,000	20,000
Zack Wheat	2,200	1,900	30,000
Hoyt Wilhelm	650	325	9,500
Billy Williams	750	450	11,000
Ted Williams	3,500	1,850	85,000
Hack Wilson	1,950	1,450	30,000
Dave Winfield	575	325	5,000
Early Wynn	550	375	7,250
Carl Yastrzemski	950	450	9,500

Player	Bat	Cap	Jersey
Cy Young	12,000	4,000	140,000
Ross Youngs	1,400	1,200	17,000
Robin Yount	550	450	7,500

Inactive Players

Player	Bat	Cap	Jersey
Dick Allen	425	325	2,800
Hank Bauer	450	375	5,250
George Bell	200	175	1,075
Albert Belle	300	265	1,375
Bert Blyleven	125	250	2,300
Wade Boggs	400	350	3,250
Bobby Bonds	325	290	1,050
Jim Bouton	150	140	1,950
Ken Boyer	685	480	3,875
Ralph Branca	325	300	2,250
Lew Burdette	365	360	3,850
Brett Butler	270	250	1,225
Gary Carter	350	275	2,500
Joe Carter	325	260	2,400
Norm Cash	575	465	6,875
Ron Cey	325	285	3,400
Jack Clark	250	175	925
Will Clark	350	275	2,250
Rocky Colavito	725	490	7,500
Vince Coleman	200	155	1,325
Dave Concepcion	385	365	2,375
Alvin Dark	450	400	4,850
Andre Dawson	400	385	3,650
Len Dykstra	225	160	1,425
Dennis Eckersley	250	255	4,250
Carl Erskine	485	400	5,900
Dwight Evans	525	455	2,350
Cecil Fielder	300	225	1,750
Curt Flood	590	485	4,825
Carl Furillo	650	575	5,750
Steve Garvey	320	270	2,000
Kirk Gibson	300	260	1,625
Goose Gossage	225	245	2,100
Ken Griffey, Sr.	290	285	2,500
Dick Groat	275	270	4,725
Ron Guidry	225	265	1,500
Orel Hershiser	150	190	975
Gil Hodges	850	425	7,250
Elston Howard	425	325	5,875
Frank Howard	375	290	1,825
Kent Hrbek	200	150	1,000
Jackie Jensen	550	485	4,825
Howard Johnson	200	185	850
Ted Kluszewski	575	390	9,850
Roger Maris	1,500	650	22,000
Billy Martin	925	375	8,200
Don Mattingly	800	350	6,250
Willie McGee	175	100	1,250
Paul Molitor	325	290	5,125
Jack Morris	125	400	1,475
Thurman Munson	750	600	14,500
Bobby Murcer	275	200	1,250
Dale Murphy	250	100	2,700
Eddie Murray	450	300	5,750
Graig Nettles	225	220	1,750
Tony Oliva	325	290	2,650
Dave Parker	225	200	1,450
Terry Pendleton	125	95	900
Jimmy Piersall	400	300	2,675
Phil Plantier	175	150	850
Boog Powell	195	160	1,300
Tim Raines	210	190	950
Willie Randolph	150	170	875
Jeff Reardon	120	90	750
Bobby Richardson	350	300	2,750
Pete Rose	1,200	700	19,500
Al Rosen	350	195	1,750
Ryne Sandberg	550	350	3,750
Ron Santo	475	370	4,500
Moose Skowron	550	400	4,600
Lee Smith	125	100	1,250
Ozzie Smith	220	180	1,450
Rusty Staub	300	275	1,150
Dave Stewart	250	250	1,300
Joe Torre	450	375	4,325
Alan Trammell	230	195	1,250
Bob Uecker	500	440	4,600
Fernando Valenzuela	150	125	1,500
Andy Van Slyke	225	260	1,325
Frank Viola	125	160	1,275
Bob Welch	125	150	1,250
Lou Whitaker	225	265	1,350
Bill White	300	275	3,250
Maury Wills	475	450	3,500

Active Players

Player	Bat	Cap	Jersey
Roberto Alomar	225	200	950
Moises Alou	220	190	900
Jeff Bagwell	325	275	1,425
Kevin Appier	150	125	500
Harold Baines	175	165	975
Jay Bell	175	150	1,100
Andy Benes	175	150	625
Craig Biggio	185	165	650
Barry Bonds	375	350	3,750
Ellis Burks	185	165	975
Jeromy Burnitz	250	225	1,250
Jose Canseco	375	300	2,500
Roger Cedeno	165	150	600
Jeff Cirillo	225	200	1,200
Roger Clemens	NA	400	4,600
David Cone	175	150	1,550
Johnny Damon	200	175	750
Carlos Delgado	250	225	1,250
Shawon Dunston	175	150	800
Jim Edmonds	240	210	1,100
Darin Erstad	200	180	1,000
Cliff Floyd	195	175	900
John Franco	190	160	775
Travis Fryman	200	160	800
Nomar Garciaparra	325	290	2,500
Jason Giambi	240	210	1,100
Tom Glavine	175	155	1,325
Juan Gonzalez	285	260	2,300
Luis Gonzalez	200	175	950
Dwight Gooden	225	200	1,200
Mark Grace	280	250	1,225
Shawn Green	260	220	2,300
Ben Grieve	275	225	2,500
Ken Griffey, Jr.	750	600	9,500
Marquis Grissom	175	145	625
Vladamir Guerrero	300	260	1,280
Tony Gwynn	450	350	4,000
Mike Hampton	175	150	975
Pete Harnisch	125	140	775
Todd Helton	175	150	975
Rickey Henderson	550	400	3,500
Todd Hundley	150	140	875
Geoff Jenkins	225	185	1,200
Derek Jeter	450	400	4,500
Randy Johnson	300	275	3,000
Andruw Jones	325	300	3,200
Chipper Jones	350	325	3,500
David Justice	275	225	2,800
Jason Kendall	200	175	1,000
Jeff Kent	225	200	1,300
Ryan Klesko	185	155	975
Chuck Knoblauch	170	155	1,050
Ray Lankford	175	155	850
Barry Larkin	225	190	1,450
Greg Maddux	225	250	2,225
Edgar Martinez	225	200	950
Pedro Martinez	300	275	2,000
Ramon Martinez	125	165	1,300
Tino Martinez	165	145	765
Fred McGriff	225	165	1,250
Mark McGwire	575	465	6,800
Orlando Merced	145	140	550
Mike Mussina	NA	150	1,250
John Olerud	150	145	975
Rafael Palmeiro	200	175	1,200
Mike Piazza	400	360	2,200
Manny Ramirez	375	350	2,000
Cal Ripken	600	550	5,600
Alex Rodriguez	450	400	3,400
Ivan Rodriguez	65	50	225
Tim Salmon	200	175	950
Richie Sexson	190	165	850
Gary Sheffield	200	175	950
Curt Schilling	140	160	1,200
John Smoltz	135	155	1,175
Sammy Sosa	450	400	3,750
Frank Thomas	400	375	3,250
Greg Vaughn	260	245	1,425
Mo Vaughn	375	260	2,300
Robin Ventura	200	175	1,400
Larry Walker	275	250	1,350
Matt Williams	225	200	1,300
Kerry Wood	160	140	1,300
Todd Zeile	200	175	1,000

A Frank Thomas game-used and autographed Chicago White Sox cap.

Player Endorsed Baseball Gloves
*Not Game-used

Player	Glove	Value
Hank Aaron	MacGregor Special 715 fielder's glove	275
Max Alvis	Wilson Fieldmaster fielder's glove	65
Richie Ashburn	MacGregor fielder's glove	100
Glenn Beckert	Wilson fielder's glove	80
Gus Bell	MacGregor fielder's glove	100
Johnny Bench	Rawlings catcher's mitt	100
Yogi Berra	Franklin C655 catcher's mitt	165
Johnny Blanchard	Rawlings catcher's mitt	110
Lyman Bostock	Regent fielder's glove	115
Ken Boyer	Rawlings fielder's glove	125
Harry Brecheen	Wilson A2944 fielder's glove	150
Jim Bunning	GRCH fielder's glove	145
Smokey Burgess	J.C. Higgins catcher's mitt	115
Roy Campanella	Wilson catcher's mitt	170
Andy Carey	Rawlings fielder's glove	90

Gil Hodges model Sonnett mitt.

Phil Rizzuto model glove for left-handers.

Roberto Clemente	JC Higgins #1633 fielder's glove	225
Joe Collins	OK J700 three-finger first baseman's mitt	115
Ripper Collins	Goldsmith two-finger first baseman's mitt	180
Del Crandall	Franklin catcher's mitt	170
Al Dark	Spalding fielder's glove	90
Jim Davenport	Wilson fielder's glove	80
Spud Davis	Wilson #500 catcher's mitt	120
Bill Dickey	Hawthorne catcher's mitt	350
Bill Dickey	Wilson catcher's mitt	225
Joe DiMaggio	Professional Model F16	750
Joe DiMaggio	Reach fielder's glove	900
Joe DiMaggio	Unknown Mfg. fielder's glove	400
Vince DiMaggio	Hutch fielder's glove	175
Bobby Doerr	MacGregor fielder's glove	125
Bobby Doerr	OK SF fielder's glove	135
Leo Durocher	MacGregor GI 30 fielder's glove	175
Johnny Edwards	MacGregor catcher's mitt	80
Ron Fairly	Spalding 42-486 first base man's glove	95
Bob Feller	J.C. Higgins fielder's glove	225
Bob Feller	Starline fielder's glove	200
Lew Fonseca	Wards Marathon fielder's glove	250
Whitey Ford	Spalding fielder's glove	110
Bill Freehan	Wilson catcher's mitt	95
Frankie Frisch	Spalding fielder's glove	330
Joe Gordon	Marathon fielder's glove	110
Joe Gordon	Wards 60-1205 fielder's glove	125
Joe Gordon	Wilson fielder's glove	105
Joe Gordon	Wilson fielder's glove	90
Mudcat Grant	Rawlings fielder's glove	95
Frank Gustine	Reach Co. four-finger fielder's glove	120
Gabby Hartnett	1911 patent catcher's mitt	300
Hassell, Buddy	Processed leather two-finger first baseman's glove	140
Billy Herman	Hutch 40 fielder's glove	125
Billy Herman	J.C. Higgins fielder's glove	190
Pinky Higgins	Spalding 1939-40 fielder's glove	120
Pinky Higgins	Spalding #273 fielder's glove	130
Ken Holtzman	Rawlings Japan Mfg. fielder's glove	80
Johnny Hopp	Wilson fielder's glove	85

Rogers Hornsby	Wilson fielder's glove	450
Frank House	J.C. Higgins catcher's mitt	105
Larry Jackson	Rawlings fielder's glove	70
Jackie Jensen	Buts 3F9 fielder's glove	100
Jackie Jensen	MacGregor fielder's glove	55
George Kell	Wilson A2020 fielder's glove	90
George Kell	Wilson A2932 fielder's glove	120
Ken Keltner	Rawlings KR fielder's glove	115
Ralph Kiner	SNNT fielder's glove	120
Harvey Kuenn	Wilson "Ball Hawk" fielder's glove	110
Harvey Kuenn	Wilson fielder's glove	90
Don Larsen	Spalding No Hitter model fielder's glove	115
Bob Lemon	A.H.I. Brand fielder's glove	95
Billy Loes	Nokono Pro Line FG scarce	120
Johnny Logan	Franklin fielder's glove	80
Johnny Logan	Franklin 119 fielder's glove	100
Jerry Lumpe	Spalding fielder's glove	55
Mickey Mantle	Rawlings Triple Crown Winner fielder's glove	235
Mickey Mantle	Rawlings #MM4 FG	225
Mickey Mantle	Rawlings FG later issue	200
Roger Maris	Spalding fielder's glove	155
Billy Martin	Wilson fielder's glove	120
Billy Martin	Wilson four-finger fielder's glove	125
Gil McDougald	MacGregor fielder's glove	95
Joe Medwick	Marathon Sporting Goods fielder's glove	125
Roman Mejias	Spalding fielder's glove	70
Johnny Mize	Firestone Olympians two-finger first baseman's glove	175
Johnny Mize	O.K. MFG Co. "The Snapper" first baseman's mitt	125
Joe Morgan	MacGregor fielder's glove	75
Stan Musial	Franklin fielder's glove	195
Hal Newhouser	Sonnet fielder's glove	110
Mel Ott	Goldsmith fielder's glove	340
Mickey Owen	Rawlings catcher's mitt	100
Monte Pearson	Marathon fielder's glove	105
Johnny Pesky	Rawlings G490 fielder's glove	105
Jimmy Piersall	SNNT JP64 fielder's glove	95
Vada Pinson	Spalding lst baseman's mitt	90
Pee Wee Reese	Denkert fielder's glove	150
Pete Reiser	MacGregor fielder's glove	105
Pete Reiser	OK 758 fielder's glove	105
Bobby Richardson	Denkert fielder's glove	85
Robin Roberts	MacGregor fielder's glove	90
Jackie Robinson	CPRO Japanese Mfg. fielder's glove	125
Schoolby Rowe	Reach fielder's glove	410
Joe Rudi	Rawlings fingerhole fielder's glove	70
Red Schoendienst	MacGregor fielder's glove	95
Tom Seaver	Rawlings fielder's glove	95
Roy Sievers	Rawlings fielder's glove	105
Curt Simmons	MacGregor fielder's glove	90
Bob Skinner	Rawlings "The Trapper" first baseman's mitt	110
Duke Snider	Yale F600 fielder's glove	145
Willie Stargell	Rawlings 626 first baseman's mitt	85
Snuffy Stirnweiss	Spalding #193 fielder's glove	105
Bobby Thomson	MacGregor fielder's glove	95
Hank Thompson	Dekert fielder's glove	105
Frank Torre	MacGregor "Trapper" three-finger first baseman's mitt	95
Pie Traynor	J.C. Higgins fielder's glove	170

Harry Walker	J.C. Higgins fielder's glove	85
Early Wynn	Wilson fielder's glove	90
Carl Yastrzemski	Spalding fielder's glove	120
Pep Young	Hutch 42 fielder's glove	125
Cy Young	Hutch fielder's glove	650

Team Jersey Values

Team	Flannel	Knit
American League		
Baltimore Orioles	2,600	.400
Boston Red Sox	2,000	.450
California Angels	1,900	.400
Chicago White Sox	2,000	.450
Cleveland Indians	2,000	.450
Detroit Tigers	2,200	.550
Kansas City Royals	1,700	.300
New York Yankees	3,500	.800
Oakland A's	1,950	.450
Seattle Mariners	N/A	.400
Tampa Bay Rays	N/A	.400
Texas Rangers	2,000	.450
Toronto Blue Jays	N/A	.400

Note: No flannel listings are entered for Seattle or Toronto, as neither team played during the flannel era. Texas only used flannels for spring training of their first year (1972). The Texas flannels are extremely rare, and are actually re-lettered Washington Senators jerseys.

National League

Team	Flannel	Knit
Arizona Diamondbacks	N/A	.450
Atlanta Braves	2,200	.475
Chicago Cubs	2,200	.475
Cincinnati Reds	2,400	.450
Colorado Rockies	N/A	.425
Florida Marlins	N/A	.400
Houston Astros	2,750	.500
L. A. Dodgers	2,800	.550
Milwaukee Brewers	2,750	.500
Montreal Expos	2,450	.425
New York Mets	3,000	.550
Philadelphia Phillies	2,450	.450
Pittsburgh Pirates	2,250	.425
St. Louis Cardinals	2,650	.450
San Diego Padres	2,250	.425
San Francisco Giants	2,550	.475

Note: Generally, a defunct team flannel will be valued at $2,000, or higher. The Los Angeles Angels jersey is an exception to this general rule, as the style of the jersey did not change when the team changed from LA to California.

●●●

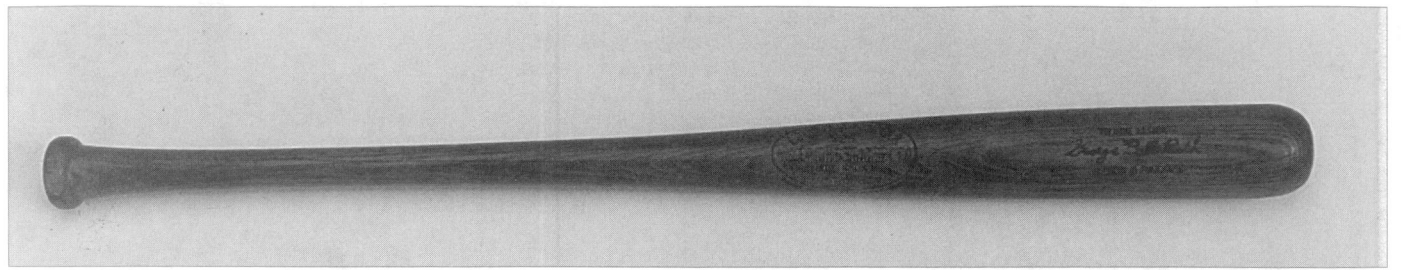

A game-used Babe Ruth personal model bat.

Baseball Bats

There are basically four categories of baseball bats which collectors pursue. They are:

1) Authentic cracked vs. uncracked, but game-used bat. The player has actually used the bat in a game; it shows wear and tear from use, including scuffs, dents, tape, filing of the handle, uniform numbers on the handles, use of pine tar, hollowed ends and cracks. The value of a bat decreases according to the size of the crack.

This bat is made to a player's specifications, with his name and signature on it, or it could be a bat ordered by the team, with the team name branded into it. Pitchers and coaches generally use these bats. Coaches' bats may carry the player's name, but are not necessarily made according to the specifics he used as an active player.

2) Authentic bats, made to the players' specifications, but which have not been used in a game. It's possible the player didn't even own the bat, which could have been ordered by the team for promotions or giveaways, or made for other businesses for resale. These bats are often used for autographing.

3) Retail or store model bats, which are purchased in sporting goods stores. They are not made according to the player's specifications, but often carry his name as an endorsement. Vintage model bats of stars before the 1950s generally sell well. Naive collectors can end up purchasing these bats for $100 to $200, thinking they are game-used bats when they aren't.

Store models can be distinguished from game-used bats because the knobs carry inch markings, a single-digit number or both initials of the player whose name is on the barrel. Also, if the bat number in the brand oval is followed by any letters, probably player initials, it's likely the bat is a store model.

4) Commemoratives: These bats are made to recognize a particular person, place or event in baseball history, such as a World Series or Hall of Fame induction. These customized bats, generally more desirable than store models, are often created for display purposes and are suitable for autographing, which makes them more valuable. Black Sharpie pens work best.

Many collectors have their commemorative bats signed by the players involved.

The complexities of bat markings will not be delved into, but some general guidelines follow:

Baseball's rules limit the length of bats to 42 inches long and 2fl inches wide. Generally, bats weigh between 30-50 ounces.

These are the most common bat brands used by major leaguers:

1) **Hillerich & Bradsby**: This company has undergone several name modifications from 1884 until 1979, when its bats became more commonly known as Louisville Sluggers, H&B's most popular style. Since 1945, H&B has labeled bats with player initials and a model number on the knob, which is an identifying number for each individual style. In 1976, those numbers were moved to the barrel of the bat. If the player is contracted with the manufacturer, his name is burned into the bat barrel in autograph form. If he isn't, his name is in block letters.

Hillerich & Bradsby adopted the slogan Powerized in 1932 and began putting model numbers—which have one letter and at least one number—on the knob in 1944. Those numbers were removed beginning in 1976 and then placed on the barrel. The H&B logo was dropped in 1979, with Louisville Slugger becoming the brand label.

2) **A.G. Spalding & Bros**. bats, used primarily before the turn of the century.

3) **A.J. Reach** bats, which were prominent at the beginning of the century.

4) **Rawlings**, which labels its bats as Adirondacks. They feature a single-colored ring around the neck and a diamond-shaped trademark.

5) **Worth**, which entered the market in the 1970s and offers its Tennessee Thumper bats.

6) **Cooper** bats, produced in Canada since 1986.

7) **Mizuno** bats, made in Japan.

It is very difficult to verify a bat actually used by a player in a major-league game. (Was it scuffed at a softball game last week? Did the player himself use it, or did one of his teammates? Was it used only in batting practice? Often, players themselves cannot remember which stick they used.)

If you invest in one of these bats, deal only with a dealer who is an expert in the area and insist on written documentation. Reliable dealers usually get these items from unimpeachable sources—the player's attorney or agent, a family member, the clubhouse attendant or a batboy.

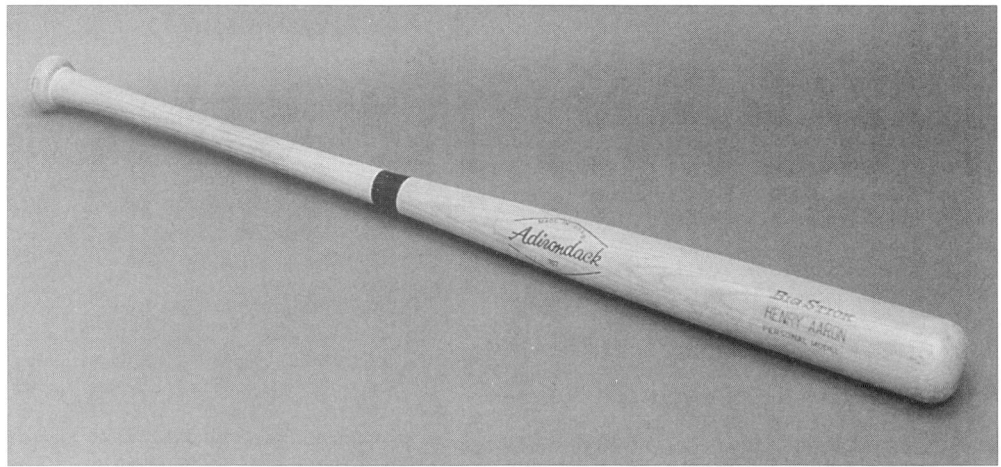

A game-used Hank Aaron Adirondack Big Stick personal model bat from the 1969 season.

●●●

Stadium Seats

As it is with most collectibles, the value of stadium seats is often subject to their condition. However, condition is subjective to begin with. Pricing for stadium seats is not an exact science. Replacement parts, such as slats or broken/welded cast iron standards, will obviously lessen the value. Also, the debate rages as to whether repainting the seat diminishes its value.

Listed below is a guide to the values for regular and figural versions of some of the most popular stadium seats. Prices are for unrestored seats with paint in good shape, with minimal or no rust on the metal parts.

Ballpark	Reg. Seat	Fig. Seat
Braves Field	$800	$1,800
Cleveland Stadium	$250	N/A
Comiskey Park	$275	$475
Milwaukee County Stadium	$250	N/A
Crosley Field	$500	$1,800
Ebbets Field	$1,200	N/A
Fenway Park	$850	N/A
Forbes Field	$750	N/A
Fulton County (wood)	$250	N/A
Griffith Stadium	$450	N/A
Polo Grounds	$500	$2,200
Shibe Park	$350	N/A
Sportsman's Park	$650	N/A
Tiger Stadium	$400	$1,200
Wrigley Field	$600	N/A
Yankee Stadium	$800	N/A

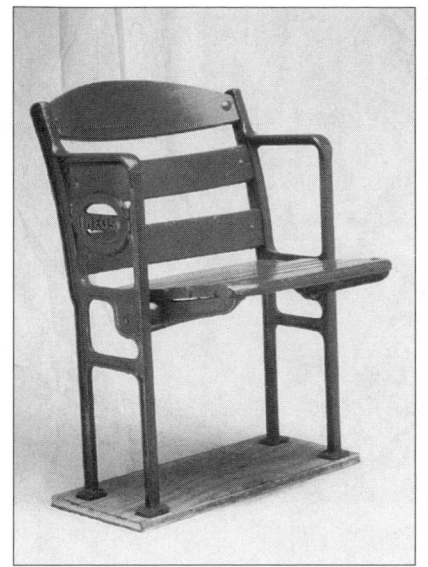

Crosley Field seat

Polo Grounds seat

Wrigley Field seat

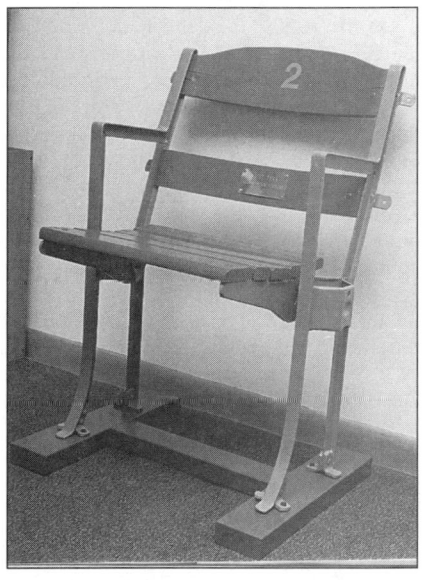

Shibe Park seat

Tiger Stadium box seat

Yankee Stadium seat

Dick Groat Hartland statue with original box and tag

Original Hank Aaron statue

Hartland Plastics and USA Hartland Statues

In the 1950s, Hartland Plastics of Hartland, Wis., manufactured a variety of products for different industries. Point-of-purchase items for breweries, display cases for Timex, boat seat covers for Sears, religious figurines and western toy statues were made.

In 1958, Hartland introduced a series of baseball players. The figurines were approximately 8" high and were made from acetate plastic and painted with acetate-based paint. The first group of players introduced were Hank Aaron, Eddie Mathews, Warren Spahn, Mickey Mantle and Babe Ruth. They retailed for $1.98. They were meant to be toys.

In 1959, the company produced 5,000 figurines each of Baltimore Colts quarterback Johnny Unitas and Los Angeles Rams running back Jon Arnett.

Hartland produced 28 additional football players. At the time, there were 14 teams in the NFL. Hartland made a running back and a lineman for each team, with 5,000 of each manufactured between 1959 and 1963.

The 5" Batboy was originally titled the "Little Leaguer." However, the Little League Baseball Association of America complained about the use of the name. As a result, more than 40,000 statues were destroyed out of the 50,000 made to that point. The statue was renamed the "Batboy." The 4" Minor Leaguer was created and used for trophy tops and cake decorations.

Included with each player, except Roger Maris, was a circular red tag with white lettering with the player's facsimile autograph and nickname. The tags have a string that is used to hang the tag around the neck of the figurine.

Some of the figurines were produced from reground plastic, causing them to yellow in various degrees. Generally, the brighter the white portions of the uniforms, the more valuable the statues are for collectors.

Eleven figurines are known to have been made with magnets glued to the bottom of each foot or base (Minor Leaguer) and a small black metal plate that would serve as the base. They also had a small hole in one corner for fitting a nail or screw through to fasten the plate to another surface.

Steven Manufacturing Co. of Hermann, Mo., purchased many of the original Hartland molds in 1978. It was later discovered that the original baseball molds, that were thought destroyed, were among the items purchased.

The end of an era occurred on June 30, 1978. Hartland Plastics closed its doors for good. From 1963 to 1978 the company had been sold to many conglomerates. It was even owned by its employees at one point.

In 1987, Bill Alley, a Dallas lawyer, became interested in the Hartland sports figurines. Alley secured the rights to produce a commemorative series of the original 18 ballplayers.

In 1990, Hartland created six new statues: Roberto Clemente, Lou Gehrig, Dizzy Dean, Whitey Ford, Bob Feller and Ty Cobb and a two-figure set known as "The Confrontation."

Production was reported to be 10,000 of each. Actual production of each is believed to be: 25th Anniversary Players 6,000; Clemente and Ford 10,000; Gehrig and Dean 500; Cobb 45; Feller 25; and "The Confrontation" 20, Batboy and Minor Leaguer 2,500. The Batboy was originally offered free as a bonus to anyone who ordered a complete set of the 25th Anniversary.

While on a business trip in March 1991, in New York, Alley mysteriously disappeared. During the following months the company virtually halted its production of figurines. Rumor has it that the rarity of the boxes used for "The Confrontation" was created by non-payment to the vendor that produced the boxes. It is believed all boxes were destroyed; however, an employee managed to hide 10 boxes from destruction and these are the only boxes known to exist for "The Confrontation." "The Confrontation" is a manager and an umpire squared off at one another. The umpire was

"Safe at Second"

Batboy

produced first and he was available as a singular statue. The managers are used to complete Confrontation sets.

In 1992, Alley's wife sold the company to family friend Bill Dunlap, who formed USA Hartland, Inc. The company accepted advance orders for Nolan Ryan, Cy Young and Honus Wagner. USA Hartland was then purchased by Steven Manufacturing and moved to Hermann, Mo. The "Missouri" Hartlands were packaged in a gray box.

Alley eventually turned up in Virginia, using a different name.

A total of 15,000 "Safe at Second" sets were produced from an original Hartland mold that had been on the drawing table but was never produced. It contains a second baseman, umpire and runner sliding on a base.

USA Hartland also acquired an NFL license and offered a commemorative Unitas figurine as well as the other 14 original generic football players. Only the Unitas figure was released.

The Ryan figure was offered in two forms, a home white and road gray uniform. The gray-uniformed Ryan was sold through Target stores in an open front display box in select states. Production is believed to be 5,500 gray road uniforms and 4,500 home uniforms.

A Carl Yastrzemski statue was in production in July, 1993, when a flood destroyed the Steven factory that was located on the banks of a river. The Yastrzemski is boxed in a Ryan open front display box and has a production of approximately 400.

In 1994, Hartland closed its doors again. However, in late 2000, it was announced that the Hartland name would be revived again. Entrepreneur Ken Movald, of Hermann, Mo., who at one time worked with Dunlap, and Joe Sterkx have obtained the rights to the Hartland name and will be seeking licensing to produce more Hartland statues. It appears the Hartland saga will live on.

Nolan Ryan, Honus Wagner and Cy Young 1993 Hartlands

Original 1960 Hartland Baseball

Hank Aaron	$300.00
Luis Aparicio	300.00
Ernie Banks	350.00
Yogi Berra	250.00
Rocky Colavito	900.00
Don Drysdale	450.00
Nellie Fox	300.00
Dick Groat	1,500.00
Harmon Killebrew	500.00
Mickey Mantle	350.00
Roger Maris	450.00
Eddie Mathews	225.00
Willie Mays	300.00
Stan Musial	300.00
Babe Ruth	300.00
Duke Snider	500.00
Warren Spahn	225.00
Ted Williams	300.00
Batboy	175.00
Minor Leaguer	125.00

1990 25th Commemorative Baseball

Hank Aaron	$80.00
Luis Aparicio	50.00
Ernie Banks	60.00
Yogi Berra	80.00
Rocky Colavito	60.00
Don Drysdale	60.00
Nellie Fox	50.00
Dick Groat	60.00
Harmon Killebrew	65.00
Mickey Mantle	120.00
Roger Maris	80.00
Eddie Mathews	75.00
Willie Mays	80.00
Stan Musial	60.00
Babe Ruth	60.00
Duke Snider	60.00
Warren Spahn	50.00
Ted Williams	120.00

Hartland "Dallas"

Roberto Clemente	$100.00
Ty Cobb	700.00
Dizzy Dean	200.00
Bob Feller	750.00
Whitey Ford	100.00
Lou Gehrig	375.00
Umpire	75.00
"The Confrontation"	750.00

1993 Baseball

Roberto Clemente	$40.00
Whitey Ford	40.00
Nolan Ryan (home)	45.00
Nolan Ryan (away)	45.00
Honus Wagner	40.00
Carl Yastrzemski	40.00
Cy Young	40.00
"Safe at Second"	40.00

1990 Babe Ruth

1993 Whitey Ford

Baseball
Starting Lineup Figurines

In 1986, Pat McInally, a Harvard graduate and 10-year veteran of the Cincinnati Bengals, was in the process of moving his family from Cincinnati to the West Coast. Preparations included selling his condominium, and the prospective buyer was a newly-hired Kenner executive.

McInally was the author of a syndicated newspaper column called "Pat Answers For Kids." The Kenner executive was in the business of developing toys for those very readers. It was suggested that McInally come up with some ideas for Kenner.

A field trip to a toy store was suggested to provide some inspiration. McInally and his wife journeyed across the Ohio River to wander the aisles of one of the major toy store chains. What they found in abundant quantity were "heroes" based upon fictional characters. The question that occurred to them both was, why not make toys of real world heroes such as sports stars, who were demonstrating their prowess in sports?

Nothing further happened until McInally moved to California, but Kenner kept in touch. Finally, arrangements were made for him to return to Cincinnati and make a presentation of his idea to the company.

On his way to the meeting, he made a brief detour to a local store to pick up a pack of baseball cards to supplement his presentation. Grabbing one of Kenner's current action figures, McInally had the "total" package for his proposal. The reaction was overwhelming. Two hours of discussion ended with only one potential snag: How to get the licensing rights? McInally thought he could help with that, as well.

On the following Monday, a trip to New York to obtain licensing rights with the major sports leagues took place. McInally proved to be the key to success there as well. At NFL Properties, they met with John Flood. Flood had been a fullback at Harvard during McInally's tenure there. After a bit of reminiscing about college, the attendees sat down and negotiated an arrangement. The next stop was MLB Properties. Once again, McInally's college and professional background proved to be a key element in getting the ball rolling. The MLB Properties' legal counsel was Ed Durso, a former running back for the Bengals, and Rick White, head of the division was an alumnus of Chapman College in McInally's California neighborhood. The next morning, they visited NBA offices. The merit of the proposal and the prospect of a line featuring the full gamut of major league sports was impossible to reject. By the end of that week, commitments were in hand and Starting Lineup figurines became a reality.

Starting Lineups were owned and produced by Hasbro Toy Co. Hasbro obtained Tonka (which owned Kenner) in May 1990. The product development responsibility did not change, however. The Kenner logo appeared on the product through 1997 and was changed to the Hasbro logo in 1998. Previous to Tonka owning Kenner, Kenner had been a part of Kenner Parker Toys. And prior to that, it was a part of the General Mills fun group.

In January of 2001, Hasbro announced that it was discontinuing its entire line of figurines following the release of its 2001 baseball product lines.

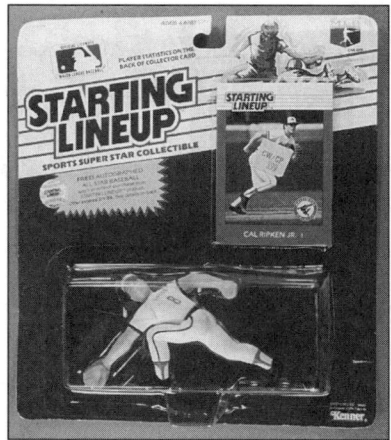

1988 Baseball

Complete Set (124):	$3,000.00
Collector Stand:	$30.00
Autographed Baseball:	$30.00
Alan Ashby	$25.00
Harold Baines	15.00
Kevin Bass	15.00
Steve Bedrosian	16.00
Buddy Bell	25.00
George Bell	14.00
Mike Boddicker	25.00
Wade Boggs	30.00
Barry Bonds	100.00
Bobby Bonilla	20.00
Sid Bream	15.00
George Brett	70.00
Chris Brown	14.00
Tom Brunansky	25.00
Ellis Burks	40.00
Jose Canseco	40.00
Gary Carter	20.00
Joe Carter	40.00
Jack Clark	18.00
Will Clark	30.00
Roger Clemens	50.00
Vince Coleman	15.00
Kal Daniels	15.00
Alvin Davis	15.00
Eric Davis	15.00
Glen Davis	15.00
Jody Davis	15.00
Andre Dawson	25.00
Rob Deer	15.00
Brian Downing	14.00
Mike Dunne	14.00

Shawon Dunston	20.00
Leon Durham	14.00
Len Dykstra	30.00
Dwight Evans	20.00
Carlton Fisk	70.00
John Franco	20.00
Julio Franco	20.00
Gary Gaetti	15.00
Dwight Gooden	14.00
Ken Griffey Sr.	25.00
Pedro Guerrero	12.00
Ozzie Guillen	20.00
Tony Gwynn	150.00
Mel Hall	15.00
Billy Hatcher	16.00
Von Hayes	20.00
Rickey Henderson	30.00
Keith Hernandez	16.00
Willie Hernandez	16.00
Tom Herr	16.00
Ted Higuera	16.00
Charlie Hough	20.00
Kent Hrbek	16.00
Pete Incaviglia	16.00
Howard Johnson	20.00
Wally Joyner	26.00
Terry Kennedy	15.00
John Kruk	30.00
Mark Langston	30.00
Carney Lansford	25.00
Jeffrey Leonard	14.00
Fred Lynn	20.00
Candy Maldonado	16.00
Mike Marshall	16.00
Don Mattingly	35.00
Willie McGee	18.00
Mark McGwire	120.00
Kevin McReynolds	15.00
Paul Molitor	50.00
Donnie Moore	20.00
Jack Morris	25.00
Dale Murphy	14.00
Eddie Murray	90.00
Matt Nokes	15.00
Pete O'Brien	15.00
Ken Oberkfell	15.00
Dave Parker	25.00
Larry Parrish	15.00
Ken Phelps	15.00
Jim Presley	15.00
Kirby Puckett	80.00
Dan Quisenberry	20.00
Tim Raines	15.00
Willie Randolph	16.00
Shane Rawley	16.00
Jeff Reardon	25.00
Gary Redus	15.00
Rick Reuschel	15.00
Jim Rice	25.00
Dave Righetti	16.00
Cal Ripken, Jr.	300.00
Pete Rose	70.00
Nolan Ryan	300.00
Bret Saberhagen	20.00
Juan Samuel	15.00
Ryne Sandberg	70.00
Benito Santiago	18.00
Steve Sax	14.00
Mike Schmidt	60.00
Mike Scott	12.00
Kevin Seitzer	14.00
Ruben Sierra	25.00
Ozzie Smith	80.00
Zane Smith	14.00
Cory Snyder	14.00
Darryl Strawberry	12.00
Franklin Stubbs	14.00
B.J. Surhoff	20.00
Rick Sutcliffe	16.00

Pat Tabler 14.00
Danny Tartabull 18.00
Alan Trammell 20.00
Fernando Valenzuela 12.00
Andy Van Slyke 25.00
Frank Viola 20.00
Ozzie Virgil 14.00
Greg Walker 14.00
Lou Whitaker 25.00
Devon White 28.00
Dave Winfield 50.00
Mike Witt 12.00
Todd Worrell 20.00
Robin Yount 80.00

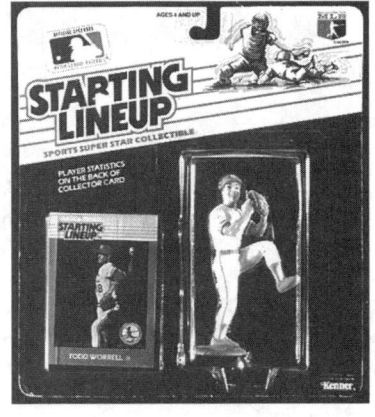

1989 Baseball

Complete Set (168): $4,500.00
Counter Display: 300.00

Roberto Alomar *450.00*
Brady Anderson *150.00*
Harold Baines 15.00
Marty Barrett *15.00*
Kevin Bass 12.00
Steve Bedrosian 12.00
George Bell 12.00
Damon Berryhill *14.00*
Wade Boggs 25.00
Barry Bonds 90.00
Bobby Bonilla 18.00
Phil Bradley *20.00*
Glenn Braggs *15.00*
Mickey Brantley *15.00*
George Brett 75.00
Tom Brookens *14.00*
Tom Brunansky 14.00
Steve Buechele *16.00*
Ellis Burks 16.00
Brett Butler *20.00*
Ivan Calderon *18.00*
Jose Canseco 18.00
Gary Carter 18.00
Joe Carter 20.00
Will Clark 25.00
Roger Clemens 30.00
Vince Coleman 12.00
David Cone *40.00*
Kal Daniels 15.00
Alvin Davis 16.00
Chili Davis *12.00*
Eric Davis 125.00
Glenn Davis 12.00
Mark Davis *20.00*
Andre Dawson 20.00
Rob Deer 12.00
Bo Diaz *15.00*
Bill Doran *20.00*
Doug Drabek *30.00*
Shawon Dunston 20.00

Len Dykstra 30.00
Dennis Eckersley *90.00*
Kevin Elster *14.00*
Scott Fletcher *12.00*
John Franco 12.00
Gary Gaetti 14.00
Ron Gant *200.00*
Kirk Gibson *14.00*
Dan Gladden *15.00*
Dwight Gooden 12.00
Mark Grace *35.00*
Mike Greenwell *12.00*
Mark Gubicza *12.00*
Pedro Guerrero 12.00
Ozzie Guillen 25.00
Tony Gwynn 350.00
Albert Hall *15.00*
Mell Hall 12.00
Billy Hatcher 12.00
Von Hayes 12.00
Rickey Henderson 20.00
Mike Henneman *12.00*
Keith Hernandez 12.00
Orel Hershiser *20.00*
Ted Higuera 20.00
Jack Howell *100.00*
Kent Hrbek 12.00
Pete Incaviglia 12.00
Bo Jackson *20.00*
Danny Jackson *12.00*
Brook Jacoby *12.00*
Chris James *12.00*
Dion James *15.00*
Gregg Jefferies *45.00*
Doug Jones *15.00*
Wally Joyner 14.00
John Kruk 35.00
Mark Langston 25.00
Carney Lansford 20.00
Barry Larkin *70.00*
Tim Laudner *20.00*
Mike LaValliere *12.00*
Al Leiter *18.00*
Chet Lemon *15.00*
Jose Lind *20.00*
Greg Maddux *375.00*
Candy Maldonado 12.00
Mike Marshall 12.00
Don Mattingly 25.00
Willie McGee 15.00
Mark McGwire 100.00
Kevin McReynolds 18.00
Kevin Mitchell *20.00*
Paul Molitor 45.00
Jack Morris 25.00
Dale Murphy 12.00
Randy Myers *20.00*
Matt Nokes 12.00
Mike Pagliarulo *12.00*
Dave Parker 20.00
Dan Pasqua *16.00*
Tony Pena *20.00*
Terry Pendleton *25.00*
Melido Perez *20.00*
Gerald Perry *15.00*
Dan Plesac *12.00*
Kirby Puckett 60.00
Rey Quinones *20.00*
Tim Raines 12.00
Johnny Ray *100.00*
Jeff Reardon 40.00
Harold Reynolds *20.00*
Jim Rice 18.00
Dave Righetti 18.00
Cal Ripken, Jr. 375.00
Jeff Russell *20.00*
Bret Saberhagen 18.00
Chris Sabo *18.00*
Luis Salazar *15.00*

Juan Samuel 12.00
Ryne Sandberg 50.00
Benito Santiago 20.00
Mike Schmidt 60.00
Dick Schofield *100.00*
Mike Scioscia *25.00*
Mike Scott 10.00
Kevin Seitzer 12.00
Larry Sheets *15.00*
John Shelby *12.00*
Ruben Sierra 25.00
Don Slaught *12.00*
Dave Smith *12.00*
Lee Smith *75.00*
Ozzie Smith 50.00
Zane Smith 12.00
Cory Snyder 12.00
Pete Stanicek *12.00*
Terry Steinbach *20.00*
Dave Stewart *25.00*
Kurt Stillwell *10.00*
Darryl Strawberry 12.00
B.J. Surhoff 20.00
Rick Sutcliffe 15.00
Bruce Sutter *30.00*
Greg Swindell *20.00*
Pat Tabler 12.00
Danny Tartabull 12.00
Bobby Thigpen *30.00*
Milt Thompson *20.00*
Robby Thompson *15.00*
Alan Trammell 15.00
Jeff Treadway *30.00*
Jose Uribe *12.00*
Fernado Valenzuela 12.00
Andy Van Slyke 15.00
Frank Viola 12.00
Bob Walk *12.00*
Greg Walker 15.00
Walt Weiss *30.00*
Bob Welch 25.00
Lou Whitaker 25.00
Devon White 125.00
Dave Winfield 25.00
Mike Witt 100.00
Todd Worrell 15.00
Marvell Wynne *25.00*
Gerald Young *15.00*
Robin Yount 75.00

1989 Baseball Greats

Complete Set (10): $400.00
Set Price Incudes Ruth, Gehrig Gray/White
Version Only.

Aaron, Mathews $40.00
Banks, Williams 40.00
Bench, Rose 50.00
Clemente, Stargell 45.00

Drysdale, Jackson 50.00
Mantle, DiMaggio 80.00
Mays, McCovey 40.00
Stan Musial, Gehrig white 35.00
Ruth gray, Gehrig white 35.00
Ruth white, Gehrig gray 40.00
Ruth white, Gehrig white 60.00
Yastrzemski, Aaron 75.00

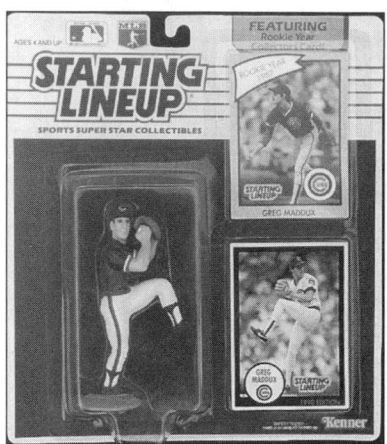

1990 Baseball

Complete Set (85): $1,600.00

Allan Anderson *12.00*
Wally Backman *15.00*
Jeff Ballard *12.00*
Jesse Barfield *12.00*
Steve Bedrosian 12.00
Todd Benzinger *12.00*
Damon Berryhill 12.00
Wade Boggs .25.00
Barry Bonds .70.00
Bobby Bonilla 15.00
Chris Bosio *15.00*
Ellis Burks 15.00
Jose Canseco 14.00
Will Clark (batting) 20.00
Will Clark (power) 22.00
Roger Clemens 25.00
Vince Coleman 12.00
Ron Darling *12.00*
Eric Davis 12.00
Andre Dawson 20.00
Rob Dibble *14.00*
Len Dykstra .20.00
Dennis Eckersley 50.00
Nick Esasky *25.00*
Gary Gaetti .12.00
Andres Galarraga *30.00*
Kirk Gibson .12.00
Dwight Gooden 12.00
Mark Grace (power) 20.00
Mike Greenwell 12.00
Ken Griffey Jr. *125.00*
Pedro Guerrero 12.00
Von Hayes *10.00*
Dave Henderson *12.00*
Rickey Henderson 15.00
Tom Herr 10.00
Orel Hershiser 18.00
Kent Hrbek .10.00
Gregg Jefferies 14.00
Howard Johnson 12.00
Ricky Jordan *12.00*
Roberto Kelly *15.00*
Barry Larkin 40.00
Greg Maddux 500.00
Joe Magrane *12.00*
Don Mattingly 18.00
Don Mattingly (power) 25.00

Fred McGriff *60.00*
Mark McGwire 40.00
Kevin McReynolds 10.00
Kevin Mitchell 12.00
Paul Molitor .30.00
Eddie Murray 150.00
Matt Nokes .12.00
Paul O'Neill *25.00*
Jose Oquendo *14.00*
Gary Pettis *20.00*
Kirby Puckett 40.00
Willie Randolph 12.00
Jody Reed *12.00*
Rick Reuschel 12.00
Dave Righetti 12.00
Cal Ripken, Jr. 175.00
Nolan Ryan .55.00
Chris Sabo 12.00
Juan Samuel 12.00
Ryne Sandberg 35.00
Steve Sax 10.00
Mike Scott 10.00
Gary Sheffield *35.00*
John Smiley *12.00*
Ozzie Smith .35.00
Dave Stewart 15.00
Darryl Strawberry (batting) 10.00
Darryl Strawberry 15.00
Rick Sutcliffe 12.00
Mickey Tettleton *18.00*
Alan Trammell 12.00
Andy Van Slyke 16.00
Frank Viola .12.00
Lou Whitaker 12.00
Mitch Williams 15.00
Dave Winfield 40.00
Robin Yount .70.00

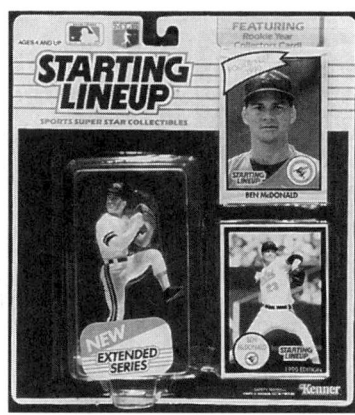

1990 Baseball Extended

Complete Set (7): $200.00

Jim Abbott *20.00*
Sandy Alomar *12.00*
Joe Carter 35.00
Ken Griffey Jr. Jump *125.00*
Bo Jackson 12.00
Ben McDonald *20.00*
Jerome Walton *10.00*

1991 Baseball

Complete Set (46): $400.00

Send away Card Poster: 15.00
Jim Abbottt 12.00
Sandy Alomar Jr. 10.00
Jack Armstrong *10.00*
Barry Bonds .40.00
Bobby Bonilla 15.00
Tom Browning *10.00*

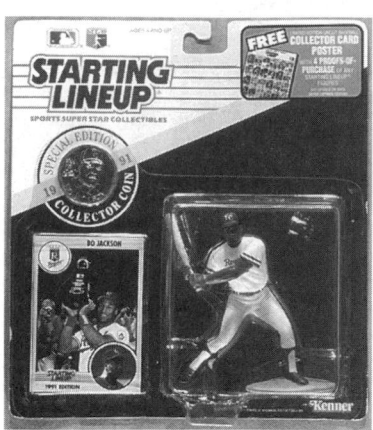

Jose Canseco 10.00
Will Clark 12.00
Eric Davis 10.00
Andre Dawson 16.00
Delino DeShields *15.00*
Doug Drabek 12.00
Shawon Dunston 10.00
Len Dykstra .14.00
Cecil Fielder *15.00*
John Franco .10.00
Dwight Gooden 12.00
Mark Grace .12.00
Ken Griffey Jr. (batting) 25.00
Kelly Gruber *20.00*
Ozzie Guillen 10.00
Rickey Henderson 10.00
Bo Jackson (Royals) 10.00
Gregg Jefferies 10.00
Howard Johnson 10.00
Robert Kelly 10.00
Barry Larkin 15.00
Kevin Maas *10.00*
Dave Magadan *10.00*
Ramon Martinez *14.00*
Don Mattingly 15.00
Ben McDonald 12.00
Mark McGwire 25.00
Kevin Mitchell 10.00
Kirby Puckett 25.00
Nolan Ryan .50.00
Chris Sabo 10.00
Ryne Sandberg 25.00
Benito Santiago 10.00
Steve Sax 10.00
Dave Stewart 10.00
Darryl Strawberry (Mets) 10.00
Alan Trammell 10.00
Frank Viola .10.00
Matt Williams *35.00*
Todd Zeile *15.00*

1991 Baseball Extended

Complete Set (10): $175.00

George Bell 10.00
Vince Coleman 10.00
Glenn Davis 10.00
Kcn Griffey Jr. (Run) 30.00
Ken Griffey Sr. 20.00
Bo Jackson (W.S.) 15.00
David Justice *35.00*
Tim Raines 12.00
Nolan Ryan 45.00
Darryl Strawberry (L.A.) 10.00

1991 Baseball Headline Collection

Complete Set (7): $200.00

Jose Canseco .20.00
Will Clark 25.00
Ken Griffey Jr. 50.00
Rickey Henderson 20.00
Bo Jackson 15.00
Don Mattingly .40.00
Nolan Ryan 60.00

1992 Baseball

Complete Set (37): $400.00

Give Away Poster: 15.00
Roberto Alomar 20.00
George Bell 10.00
Albert Belle *50.00*
Craig Biggio *12.00*
Barry Bonds 25.00
Ivan Calderon .10.00
Jose Canseco .10.00
Will Clark 15.00
Roger Clemens 15.00
Rob Dibble 10.00
Scott Erickson *10.00*
Cecil Fielder 12.00
Chuck Finley *10.00*
Tom Glavine *35.00*
Juan Gonzalez 40.00
Ken Griffey Jr. (regular) 25.00
Ken Griffey Jr. (spring) 30.00
Tony Gwynn 25.00
Dave Henderson 10.00
Rickey Henderson 10.00
Bo Jackson (regular) 10.00
Bo Jackson (spring) 10.00
Howard Johnson 10.00
Felix Jose *10.00*
Dave Justice 18.00
Kevin Maas 10.00
Ramon Martinez 12.00
Fred McGriff 20.00
Brian McRae *10.00*
Cal Ripken, Jr. 75.00
Nolan Ryan 35.00
Chris Sabo 10.00
Ryne Sandberg 16.00
Ruben Sierra 10.00
Darryl Strawberry 10.00
Frank Thomas (fielding) *45.00*
Matt Williams .15.00

1992 Baseball Extended

Complete Set (9): $175.00

Steve Avery *15.00*
Bobby Bonilla .10.00
Eric Davis 10.00
Kirby Puckett .30.00
Bret Saberhagen 10.00
Tom Seaver *35.00*
Danny Tartabull 10.00
Frank Thomas (Bat) *60.00*
Todd Van Poppel *10.00*

1992 Baseball Headline Collection

Complete Set (7): $150.00

George Brett 40.00
Cecil Fielder 15.00
Ken Griffey Jr. 30.00
Rickey Henderson 15.00
Bo Jackson 15.00
Nolan Ryan 40.00
Ryne Sandberg 35.00

1993 Baseball

Complete Set (38): $450.00

Roberto Alomar 15.00
Carlos Baerga *16.00*
Jeff Bagwell *50.00*
Barry Bonds (Pirates) 25.00
Kevin Brown *10.00*
Jose Canseco .12.00
Will Clark 10.00
Roger Clemens 10.00
David Cone 10.00
Travis Fryman *10.00*
Tom Glavine 20.00
Juan Gonzalez 20.00
Ken Griffey Jr. 20.00
Marquis Grissom *10.00*
Juan Guzman *10.00*
Eric Karros *15.00*
Roberto Kelly .10.00
John Kruk 10.00
Ray Lankford *14.00*
Barry Larkin 12.00
Shane Mack *10.00*
Jack McDowell *10.00*
Fred McGriff 12.00
Mark McGwire 20.00
Mike Mussina *25.00*
Dean Palmer *12.00*
Terry Pendleton 10.00
Kirby Puckett .15.00
Cal Ripken, Jr. 35.00
Bip Roberts *10.00*
Nolan Ryan 30.00
Ryne Sandberg 15.00
Gary Sheffield .14.00
John Smoltz *60.00*
Frank Thomas .20.00
Andy Van Slyke 10.00
Robin Ventura *12.00*
Larry Walker *25.00*

1993 Baseball Extended

Complete Set (7): $375.00

Barry Bonds 25.00
Carlton Fisk 30.00
Bo Jackson 10.00
Greg Maddux .150.00

David Nied *12.00*
Nolan Ryan 160.00
Benito Santiago 10.00

1993 Baseball Headline Collection

Complete Set (8): $180.00

Jim Abbott 15.00
Roberto Alomar 18.00
Tom Glavine 18.00
Mark McGwire 25.00
Cal Ripken 50.00
Nolan Ryan 50.00
Deion Sanders 20.00
Frank Thomas .30.00

1993 Baseball Stadium Stars

Complete Set (6): $175.00

Roger Clemens 25.00
Cecil Fielder 20.00
Ken Griffey Jr. 45.00
Nolan Ryan 45.00
Ryne Sandberg 30.00
Frank Thomas .50.00

1994 Baseball

Complete Set (57): $450.00

Kevin Appier *10.00*
Steve Avery 10.00
Carlos Baerga .10.00
Jeff Bagwell 20.00
Derek Bell *10.00*
Jay Bell *12.00*
Albert Belle 16.00
Wade Boggs 10.00
Barry Bonds 12.00
John Burkett *10.00*
Joe Carter 10.00
Roger Clemens 12.00
David Cone 10.00
Chad Curtis *10.00*
Darren Daulton *14.00*
Delino DeShields 10.00
Alex Fernandez *14.00*
Cecil Fielder 10.00
Andres Galarraga 12.00
Mark Grace 10.00
Tommy Greene *8.00*
Ken Griffey Jr. 20.00
Brian Harper *10.00*
Bryan Harvey *10.00*
Charlie Hayes *10.00*
Chris Hoiles *12.00*
Dave Hollins *10.00*
Gregg Jefferies *10.00*
Randy Johnson *25.00*
David Justice .12.00

Eric Karros .10.00
Jimmy Key *12.00*
Darryl Kile *10.00*
Chuck Knoblauch *20.00*
Mark Langston 10.00
Don Mattingly 15.00
Orlando Merced *10.00*
Paul Molitor 12.00
Mike Mussina 12.00
John Olerud *14.00*
Tony Phillips *10.00*
Mike Piazza *50.00*
Jose Rijo 10.00
Cal Ripken Jr. 30.00
Ivan Rodriguez *18.00*
Tim Salmon *15.00*
Ryne Sandberg *20.00*
Curt Schilling 15.00
Gary Sheffield 10.00
J.T. Snow *15.00*
Frank Thomas 18.00
Robby Thompson 10.00
Greg Vaughn *15.00*
Mo Vaughn 20.00
Robin Ventura 10.00
Matt Williams 12.00
Dave Winfield 12.00

1994 Baseball
Cooperstown Collection

Complete Set (8): $130.00

Ty Cobb 15.00
Lou Gehrig 15.00
Reggie Jackson 35.00
Willie Mays 15.00
Jackie Robinson (42) 18.00
Jackie Robinson (44) 550.00
Babe Ruth .15.00
Honus Wagner 35.00
Cy Young .15.00

1994 Baseball Extended

Complete Set (8): $150.00

Steve Carlton *30.00*
Will Clark .12.00
Lenny Dykstra 12.00
Juan Gonzalez 30.00
Kenny Lofton 50.00
Fred McGriff 15.00
Rafael Palmeiro *18.00*
Gary Sheffield (power) 12.00

1994 Baseball Stadium Stars

Complete Set (8): $200.00

Barry Bonds 25.00
Will Clark .25.00
Dennis Eckersley 25.00
Tom Glavine 25.00
Juan Gonzalez 25.00
Bo Jackson 50.00
Kirby Puckett 25.00
Deion Sanders 40.00

1995 Baseball

Complete Set (58): $500.00

Jim Abbott 10.00
Moises Alou *14.00*
Carlos Baerga 10.00
Jeff Bagwell 12.00
Albert Belle 14.00
Geronimo Berroa *12.00*
Dante Bichette 20.00
Barry Bonds 12.00
Jay Buhner *15.00*
Jose Canseco 10.00

Chuck Carr *10.00*
Joe Carter .10.00
Andujar Cedeno *10.00*
Will Clark .10.00
Roger Clemens 10.00
Jeff Conine *10.00*
Scott Cooper *10.00*
Darren Daulton 10.00
Carlos Delgado *14.00*
Cecil Fielder 10.00
Cliff Floyd *10.00*
Julio Franco 10.00
Juan Gonzalez 12.00
Ken Griffey, Jr. 20.00
Tony Gwynn 16.00
Bob Hamelin 10.00
Jeffrey Hammonds *12.00*
Randy Johnson 15.00
Jeff Kent *14.00*
Jeff King *12.00*
Ryan Klesko 40.00
Chuck Knoblauch 12.00
John Kruk .10.00
Ray Lankford 10.00
Barry Larkin 12.00
Javier Lopez *40.00*
Al Martin *10.00*
Brian McRae 10.00
Paul Molitor 10.00
Raul Mondesi *30.00*
Mike Mussina 10.00
Troy Neel *10.00*
David Nilsson *12.00*
John Olerud 10.00
Paul O'Neill 20.00
Mike Piazza 20.00
Kirby Puckett 14.00
Cal Ripken, Jr. 30.00
Tim Salmon 10.00
Reggie Sanders *12.00*
Sammy Sosa *40.00*
Mickey Tettleton 10.00
Frank Thomas 15.00
Andy Van Slyke 10.00
Mo Vaughn 10.00
Rick Wilkins *10.00*
Matt Williams 10.00

1995 Baseball Cooperstown Collection

Complete Set (10): $125.00

Rod Carew 13.00
Dizzy Dean 13.00
Don Drysdale 13.00
Bob Feller .13.00
Whitey Ford 13.00
Bob Gibson 13.00
Harmon Killebrew 25.00
Eddie Mathews 25.00
Satchel Paige 13.00
Babe Ruth .20.00

1995 Baseball Extended

Complete Set (9): $300.00

Jose Canseco 12.00
Rusty Greer *14.00*
Kenny Lofton 50.00
Tom Pagnozzi *10.00*
Mike Piazza (hitting) 25.00
Manny Ramirez *55.00*
Cal Ripken, Jr. 75.00
Alex Rodriguez *110.00*
Mike Schmidt 15.00

1995 Baseball Stadium Stars

Complete Set (9): $250.00

Darren Daulton 30.00
Lenny Dykstra 25.00

Ken Griffey Jr. 30.00
Randy Johnson 45.00
Dave Justice 25.00
Greg Maddux 50.00
Mark McGwire 40.00
Frank Thomas 30.00
Mo Vaughn 25.00

1996 Baseball

Complete Set (52): $550.00

Roberto Alomar 10.00
Jeff Bagwell 12.00
Albert Belle 15.00
Craig Biggio 10.00
Barry Bonds 12.00
Ricky Bones *10.00*
Rico Brogna *10.00*
Ken Caminiti *16.00*
Vinny Castilla *10.00*
Will Clark .10.00
David Cone 10.00
Wil Cordero 10.00
Marty Cordova *12.00*
Shawon Dunston 8.00
Lenny Dykstra 8.00
Jim Edmonds *10.00*
Jim Eisenreich *8.00*
Gary Gaetti 8.00
Ron Gant .10.00
Ken Griffey Jr. 20.00
Marquis Grissom 10.00
Ozzie Guillen 8.00
Brian Hunter *10.00*
Derek Jeter *80.00*
Charles Johnson *12.00*
Chipper Jones *150.00*
Greg Maddux 35.00
Jeff Manto *10.00*
Edgar Martinez *12.00*
Fred McGriff 10.00
Mark McGwire 20.00
Raul Mondesi 12.00
Eddie Murray 12.00
Hideo Nomo (WHI) *30.00*
Hideo Nomo (GR) *30.00*
Paul O'Neill 10.00
Mike Piazza 15.00
Kirby Puckett 10.00
Cal Ripken, Jr. 30.00
Ivan Rodriguez 10.00
Deion Sanders 10.00
Ozzie Smith 12.00
Sammy Sosa 20.00
Terry Steinbach 10.00
Frank Thomas 20.00
Jim Thome *30.00*
Ryan Thompson *10.00*
John Valentin *10.00*
Mo Vaughn 10.00
Larry Walker 14.00
Rondell White *12.00*
Matt Williams 10.00

1996 Baseball
Cooperstown Collection

Complete Set (10): $125.00
Set price does not include the Ashburn.

Hank Aaron 20.00
Grover Alexander 12.00
Richie Ashburn 20.00
Roberto Clemente 15.00
Jimmie Foxx 12.00
Hank Greenberg 12.00
Rogers Hornsby 12.00
Joe Morgan 12.00
Mel Ott 12.00

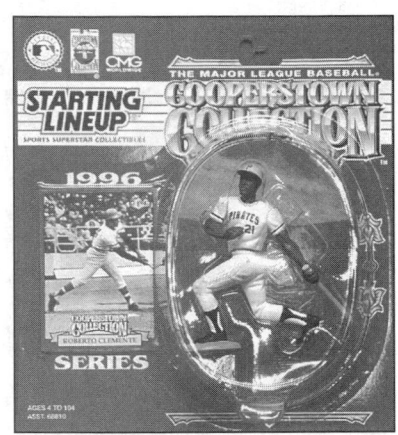

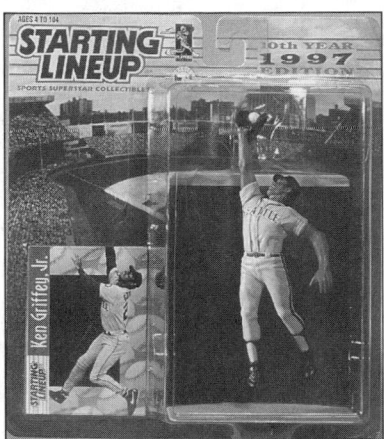

Walter Johnson 10.00
Dotty Kamenshek 15.00
Mickey Mantle 35.00
Brooks Robinson 10.00
Jackie Robinson 60.00
Duke Snider 10.00
Hoyt Wilhelm 10.00
Carl Yastrzemski 10.00

Robin Roberts 12.00
Jackie Robinson 15.00

1996 Baseball Cooperstown Collection 12" Figures

Complete Set (6): $130.00

Ty Cobb 25.00
Lou Gehrig 25.00
Babe Ruth .25.00
Babe Ruth .25.00
Honus Wagner 25.00
Cy Young .25.00

1996 Baseball Extended

Complete Set (16): $220.00

Moises Alou 12.00
Garret Anderson *12.00*
Carlos Baerga 10.00
Dante Bichette 12.00
Joe Carter .10.00
Jeff Conine 10.00
Chad Curtis 10.00
Juan Gonzalez 15.00
Eric Karros 10.00
Ken Griffey Jr. 30.00
Dave Justice 15.00
Barry Larkin 12.00
Don Mattingly 20.00
Hal Morris *10.00*
Denny Neagle 15.00
Rafael Palmeiro 14.00

1996 Baseball Stadium Stars

Complete Set (11): $275.00

Albert Belle 30.00
Jay Buhner 25.00
Jose Canseco 25.00
Darren Daulton 25.00
Mark Grace 25.00
Chuck Knoblauch 25.00
Javy Lopez 30.00
Mike Piazza 30.00
Cal Ripken Jr. 50.00
Robin Ventura 25.00
Matt Williams 25.00

1997 Baseball

Complete Set (48): $700.00

Roberto Alomar 12.00
Brady Anderson 25.00
Jeff Bagwell 12.00
Derek Bell .12.00
Albert Belle 12.00
Dante Bichette 12.00
Barry Bonds 12.00
Scott Brosius *12.00*
Ellis Burks 14.00

Roger Clemens 14.00
Johnny Damon *12.00*
Steve Finley *14.00*
Tom Glavine 15.00
Rusty Greer 12.00
Ken Griffey Jr. 16.00
Todd Hundley *20.00*
Jason Isringhausen *12.00*
John Jaha *10.00*
Randy Johnson 15.00
Chipper Jones 40.00
Brian Jordan 15.00
Wally Joyner 10.00
Jason Kendall *14.00*
Ryan Klesko *15.00*
Javier Lopez 15.00
Tino Martinez *30.00*
Brian McRae 10.00
Jose Mesa *10.00*
Paul Molitor 12.00
Raul Mondesi 12.00
Hideo Nomo 20.00
Rey Ordonez *18.00*
Chan Ho Park *15.00*
Mike Piazza 14.00
Manny Ramirez 20.00
Cal Ripken Jr. 16.00
Alex Rodriguez 30.00
Henry Rodriguez *14.00*
Ivan Rodriguez 12.00
Ryne Sandberg 12.00
Reggie Sanders 10.00
John Smoltz 25.00
J.T. Snow .10.00
Frank Thomas 14.00
Ismael Valdes *15.00*
Devon White 10.00
Bernie Williams *25.00*
Matt Williams 10.00

1997 Baseball Classic Doubles

Complete Set (10): $260.00

Hank Aaron, Jackie Robinson 25.00
Barry Bonds, Bobby Bonds 25.00
Don Drysdale, Hideo Nomo 25.00
Griffey Sr., Griffey Jr. 40.00
Randy Johnson, Nolan Ryan 35.00
Greg Maddux, Cy Young 40.00
Mantle, Maris 45.00
Maris, McGwire 30.00
Ripken Jr., Robinson 35.00
Babe Ruth, F. Thomas 35.00

1997 Baseball Cooperstown Collection

Complete Set (11): $125.00

Johnny Bench 10.00
Rollie Fingers 10.00
Josh Gibson 10.00

1997 Baseball Cooperstown Stadium Stars

Complete Set (7): $175.00

Hank Aaron 25.00
Fergie Jenkins 25.00
Al Kaline 25.00
Mickey Mantle 50.00
Babe Ruth .40.00
Mike Schmidt 25.00
Carl Yastrzemski 25.00

1997 Baseball Extended

Complete Set (14): $200.00

Albert Belle 12.00
Rickey Bottalico 12.00
Ken Caminiti 12.00
Tony Clark 20.00
Roger Clemens 15.00
Dennis Eckersley 12.00
Derek Jeter 18.00
Andruw Jones 30.00
Mark McGwire 25.00
Mike Mussina 15.00
Andy Pettitte 20.00
Alex Rodriguez 20.00
Deion Sanders 12.00
Matt Williams 12.00

1997 Baseball Freeze Frames

Complete Set (6): $200.00

Dante Bichette 25.00
Juan Gonzalez 30.00
Ken Griffey Jr. 50.00
Chipper Jones 50.00
Mike Piazza 40.00
Frank Thomas 40.00

1997 Baseball 12" Figures

Complete Set (4): $150.00

Ken Griffey Jr. 50.00
Greg Maddux 40.00
Mike Piazza 40.00
Cal Ripken Jr. 40.00

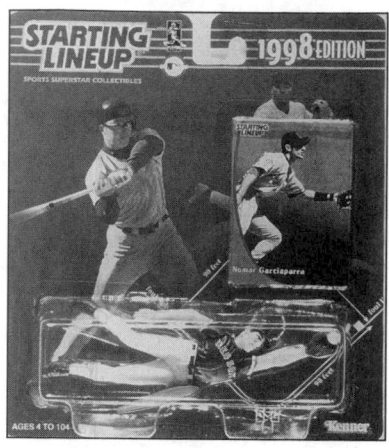

1998 Baseball

Complete Set (40): $450.00

Albert Belle 10.00
Craig Biggio 10.00
Barry Bonds 10.00
Kevin Brown 8.00
Jose Canseco 8.00
Will Clark 8.00
Darin Erstad *20.00*
Andres Galarraga 8.00
Nomar Garciaparra *40.00*
Tom Glavine 8.00
Juan Gonzalez 10.00
Mark Grace 8.00
Mark Grace (Special) 12.00
Ken Griffey Jr. 20.00
Mark Grudzielanek *12.00*
Tony Gwynn 12.00
Bobby Higginson *12.00*
Glenallen Hill *10.00*
Derek Jeter 14.00
Chipper Jones 18.00
David Justice 10.00
Chuck Knoblauch 10.00
Ray Lankford 8.00
Barry Larkin 8.00
Mickey Morandini *8.00*
Marc Newfield *8.00*
Hideo Nomo 12.00
Rafael Palmeiro 8.00
Mike Piazza 12.00
Cal Ripken, Jr. 18.00
Mariano Rivera *20.00*
Alex Rodriguez 18.00
Deion Sanders 8.00
Gary Sheffield 8.00
Ed Sprague *8.00*
Frank Thomas 14.00
Jim Thome 10.00
Mo Vaughn 10.00
Larry Walker 10.00
Bernie Williams 8.00

1998 Cooperstown Collection

Complete Set (11): $100.00

Yogi Berra.........................10.00
Lou Brock..........................10.00
Roy Campanella.....................10.00
Roberto Clemente...................15.00
Buck Leonard.......................10.00
Phil Niekro........................10.00
Jim Palmer 12.00
Frank Robinson 12.00
Tom Seaver 12.00
Warren Spahn 10.00
Tris Speaker 10.00

1998 Baseball Stadium Stars

Complete Set (7): $150.00

Albert Belle 25.00
Ken Griffey Jr. 30.00
Mike Piazza 25.00
Cal Ripken Jr. 30.00
Ivan Rodriguez 25.00
John Smoltz 25.00
Bernie Williams 25.00

1998 Baseball Classic Doubles

Complete Set (10): $200.00

Belle, Thomas 25.00
Bench, Morgan 25.00
Berra, Munson 25.00
Canseco, McGwire 50.00
Jackson, Hunter 25.00
Jeter, Ordonez 25.00
A. Rodriguez, Griffey 30.00
Piazza, I. Rodriguez, ...25.00

Ruth, Maris 25.00
Ryan, Johnson 25.00

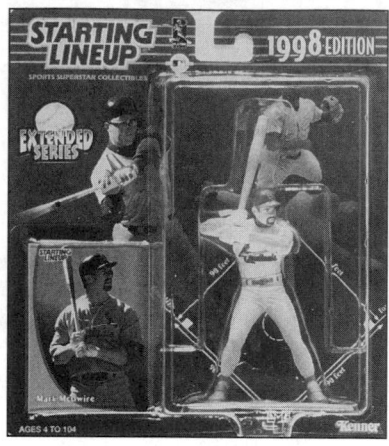

1998 Baseball Extended Series

Complete Set (14): $300.00

Sandy Alomar 15.00
Moises Alou 20.00
Jay Bell 15.00
Jim Edmonds 15.00
Ken Griffey Jr. 20.00
Hideki Irabu 25.00
Greg Maddux 25.00
Fred McGriff 15.00
Mark McGwire 125.00
Dean Palmer 15.00
Scott Rolen 30.00
Sammy Sosa 85.00
Larry Walker 15.00
Tony Womack 15.00

1998 Baseball Toys R Us Freeze Frame

Complete Set (6): $140.00

Jeff Bagwell 20.00
Barry Bonds 20.00
Derek Jeter 25.00
Greg Maddux 35.00
Cal Ripken, Jr. 35.00
Alex Rodriguez 30.00

1998 12" Baseball Figures

Complete Set (4): $100.00

Derek Jeter 30.00
Chipper Jones 30.00
Hideo Nomo 25.00
Alex Rodriguez 30.00

1999 Baseball

Complete Set (38): $400.00

Edgardo Alfonzo *15.00*
Wilson Alvarez *10.00*
Jeff Bagwell 10.00
David Cone 12.00
Jose Cruz Jr. *20.00*
Darin Erstad 15.00
Vinny Castilla 12.00
Tony Clark 10.00
Roger Clemens 14.00
Nomar Garciaparra
(regular) 18.00
(FanFest) 20.00

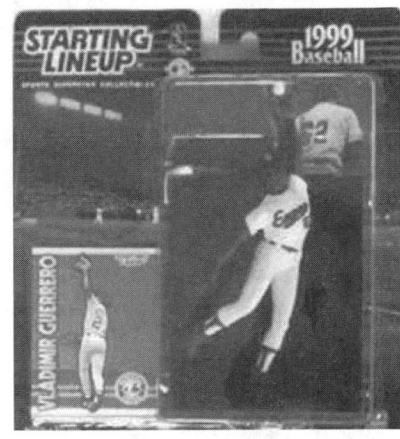

Juan Gonzalez 10.00
Ken Griffey Jr. 15.00
Vladimir Guerrero *65.00*
Jose Guillen *10.00*
Tony Gwynn 12.00
Livan Hernandez *10.00*
Derek Jeter 12.00
Randy Johnson 14.00
Chipper Jones 15.00
Travis Lee *12.00*
Kenny Lofton 10.00
Pedro Martinez 55.00
Tino Martinez 12.00
Mark McGwire
(regular) 35.00
(Wal-Mart) 25.00
Denny Neagle 10.00
Chan Ho Park 12.00
Mike Piazza 15.00
Brad Radke 10.00
Manny Ramirez 10.00
Edgar Renteria *12.00*
Cal Ripken 15.00
Scott Rolen 15.00
Alex Rodriguez 12.00
Ivan Rodriguez 10.00
Sammy Sosa
(regular) 20.00
(Wal-Mart) 20.00
Omar Vizquel *20.00*
Larry Walker 14.00
Kerry Wood *18.00*

1999 Baseball Extended Series

Complete Set (10): $120.00

Kevin Brown 10.00
Sean Casey *35.00*
J.D. Drew *20.00*
Nomar Garciaparra 15.00
Ben Grieve 15.00
Greg Maddux 12.00
Mo Vaughn 10.00
David Wells 15.00
Bernie Williams 10.00
Jaret Wright 10.00

1999 Baseball 12" Figures

Complete Set (6): $125.00

Roger Clemens 25.00
Nomar Garciaparra 25.00
Ken Griffey Jr. 25.00
Tony Gwynn 25.00
Mark McGwire 40.00
Sammy Sosa 25.00

1999 Baseball Classic Doubles

Complete Set (12): $200.00

Sandy Alomar 20.00
Darin Erstad 18.00
Nomar Garciaparra 35.00
Ken Griffey Jr. 30.00
Derek Jeter 30.00
Javier Lopez 20.00
Greg Maddux 25.00
Mark McGwire 35.00
M. McGwire/R. Maris 35.00
Raul Mondesi 20.00
Alex Rodriguez 30.00
S. Sosa/R. Maris .35.00

1999 Baseball Cooperstown

Complete Set (7): $75.00

George Brett 16.00
Pepper Davis 10.00
Bob Gibson 10.00
Juan Marichal 10.00
Nolan Ryan 20.00
Earl Weaver 12.00
Ted Williams 16.00

1999 Baseball One-on-One

Complete Set (5): $90.00

S. Alomar/K. Griffey 30.00
J. Kendall/R. Ordonez 20.00
N. Garciaparra/J. Edmonds 25.00
C. Jones/L. Walker 22.00
C. Ripken/K. Lofton 20.00

1999 Baseball Sport Star

Complete Set (2): $40.00

Mark McGwire 35.00
Sammy Sosa 30.00

1999 Baseball Stadium Stars

Complete Set (9): $200.00

Roger Clemens 20.00
Nomar Garciaparra 25.00
Derek Jeter 25.00
Chipper Jones 25.00
Kenny Lofton 25.00
Mark McGwire
(regular) 35.00
(Wal-Mart) 25.00
Alex Rodriguez 25.00
Sosa, Sammy (Wal-Mart) 25.00

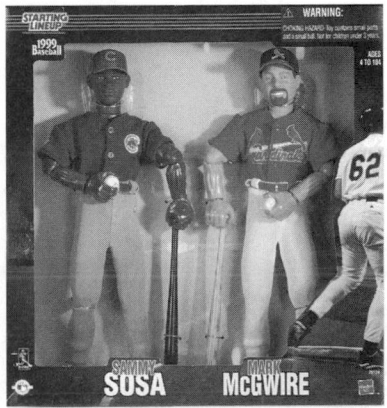

1999 Baseball 12" Internet Special

M. McGwire/S. Sosa $50.00

2000 Baseball

Complete Set (29): $275.00

Roberto Alomar .12.00
Barry Bonds 10.00
Bret Boone *8.00*
Jose Canseco 10.00
Roger Clemens 10.00
J.D. Drew 10.00
Nomar Garciaparra 10.00
Troy Glaus *15.00*
Shawn Green *20.00*
Ken Griffey Jr. 15.00
Vladimir Guerrero 18.00
Todd Helton *30.00*
Orlando Hernandez *15.00*
Trevor Hoffman *10.00*
Derek Jeter 12.00
Randy Johnson 8.00
Barry Larkin 8.00
Greg Maddux 10.00
Pedro Martinez 15.00
Mark McGwire
(regular with shin guard) 25.00
(regular w/o shin guard) 20.00

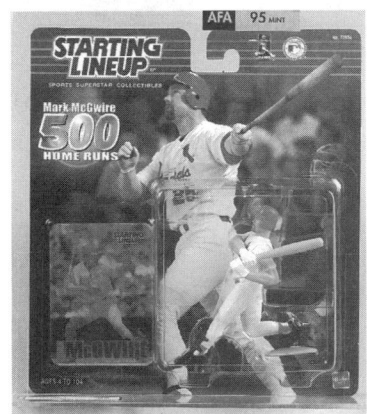

(500 HR Wal-Mart Exclusive) 20.00
Mike Piazza 12.00
Shane Reynolds *10.00*
Cal Ripken, Jr. 10.00
Curt Schilling 10.00
Aaron Sele *12.00*
Sammy Sosa 15.00
Matt Stairs *10.00*
Robin Ventura 10.00
Bernie Williams 10.00

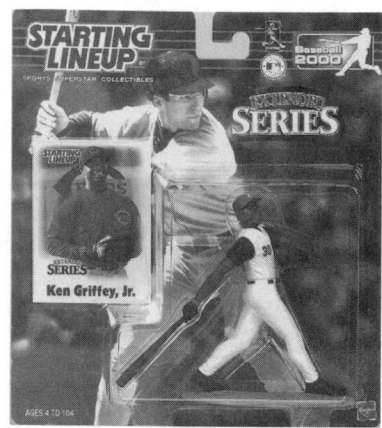

2000 Baseball Extended

Complete Set (9): $100.00

Roger Cedeno	*........10.00*
Ken Griffey Jr.	........20.00
Tony Gwynn	........10.00
Mike Hampton	*........12.00*
Chipper Jones	........15.00
Kevin Millwood	*........15.00*
Cal Ripken Jr.	........14.00
Alex Rodriguez	........12.00
Scott Williamson	*........12.00*

2000 Baseball All-Century

Complete Set (10): $65.00

Hank Aaron	........8.00
Johnny Bench	........8.00
Lou Gehrig	........10.00

Mickey Mantle	........10.00
Christy Mathewson	........15.00
Jackie Robinson	........10.00
Babe Ruth	........12.00
Mike Schmidt	........8.00
Honus Wagner	........10.00
Cy Young	........8.00

2000 Baseball Classic Doubles

Complete Set (5): $120.00

D. Jeter/M. Piazza	........25.00
R. Clemens/C. Schilling	........25.00
J. Thome/S. Casey	........25.00
P. Martinez/J. Smoltz	........25.00
C. Ripken/C. Jones	........25.00

2000 Baseball Elite

Complete Set (6): $90.00

Ken Griffey Jr.	........18.00
Derek Jeter	........20.00
Greg Maddux	........15.00
Mark McGwire	........18.00
Mike Piazza	........18.00
Sammy Sosa	........18.00

2001 Baseball

Complete Set (21)
Rick Ankiel (R)
Barry Bonds
Pat Burrell (R)
Rafael Furcal (R)
Nomar Garciaparra
Jason Giambi (R)
Shawn Green

Ken Griffey Jr.
Vladimir Guerrero
Todd Helton
Derek Jeter
Randy Johnson
Chipper Jones
Pedro Martinez
Mark McGwire
Magglio Ordonez (R)
Mike Piazza
Pokey Reese (R)
Cal Ripken Jr.
Ivan Rodriguez
Sammy Sosa

Insert Figures

Bobby Abreu (R)
Brian Giles (R)
Andruw Jones
Preston Wilson (R)

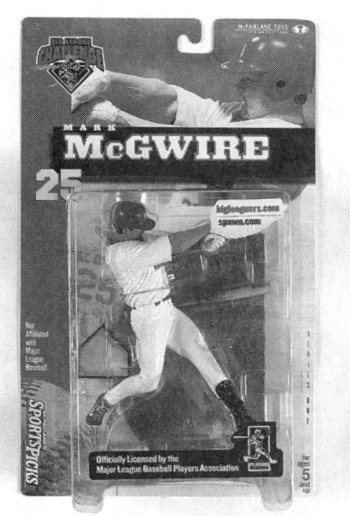

McFarlane Baseball Figurines

2000-01 Series I
Complete Set (6): $100.00

Barry Bonds	........20.00
Chipper Jones	........20.00
Mark McGwire	........25.00
Manny Ramirez	........20.00
Alex Rodriguez	........20.00
Sammy Sosa	........25.00

Baseball Bobbin' Head Dolls

Although bobbin' head dolls didn't necessarily garner much respect when they first came over from Japan in 1960, today people are shaking their heads over how much those $2.95 dolls have appreciated in value.

Over the years, the supply has decreased; the bobbers were not built to last, a factor that contributes to their values. It's rare when a now-scarce bobbing head doll does not have a small crack or paint chip in it.

The dolls were originally sold at Major League ball parks and through mail orders.

They can be found today, if a collector is patient and persistent. Thorough perusal of a hobby publication such as *Sports Collectors Digest* may turn up a doll or two, especially in auctions or classified ads. Card shows, garage sales, flea markets and antique shops are also good places to find these dolls.

Options to pursue in collecting bobbers would be by base color, by team, or by head type, which is either a mascot or boy's head.

The heads, attached by the neck with a spring to the body, bob, or nod, up and down at the slightest vibration. They were originally produced by Lego (a Swiss firm) and imported exclusively by Sports Specialties of Los Angeles. Many gold-based dolls still have stickers on the base that read "Sports Specialties 10203 Santa Monica Blvd. Los Angeles Calif. 67." The 67 represented a postal code.

Generally, eight categories, based on the doll's base color, are used when listing baseball bobbin' head dolls. They are: 1) Square colored bases, 1960-61; 2) Square white bases, 1961-62; 3) Caricatures, 1961-62; 4) White round miniatures, 1961-62; 5) Round green bases, 1962-64; 6) Green round bases, black players, 1962-64; 7) Round gold bases, 1965-72; and 8) others.

1960-61 Baseball
Square Colored Bases 1960-61

These were the first bobbin' head dolls ever made. Every baseball franchise from 1960-61 is represented, including the expansion teams of the Minnesota Twins, New York Mets, Houston Colts and Los Angeles Angels. The Twins dolls apparently were produced in great abundance. Four teams from the Minor League Pacific Coast League were also created.

	MT
Complete Set (18):	.$4,000.00
Baltimore Orioles	.190.00
Boston Red Sox	.400.00
Chicago Cubs	.250.00
Cincinnati Reds	.450.00
Detroit Tigers	.250.00
Houston Colts	.200.00
Los Angeles Angels	.100.00
Los Angeles Dodgers	.150.00
Minnesota Twins	.90.00
New York Mets	.290.00
New York Yankees	.160.00
Pittsburgh Pirates	.180.00
San Francisco Giants	.150.00
Washington Senators	.1,400.00
Hawaii	.200.00
Portland Beavers	.180.00
Seattle	.350.00
Tacoma Giants	.225.00

1961-62 Baseball Caricatures
Clemente, Mantle, Maris, Mays

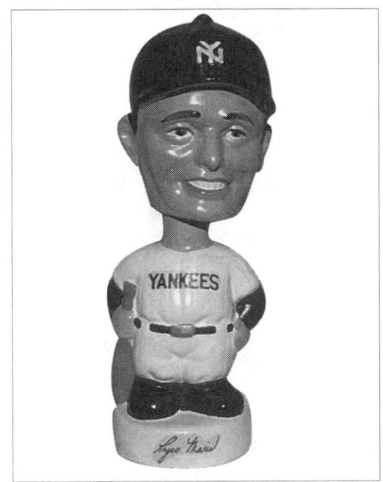

Roger Maris

Four dolls, fairly accurate and pretty realistic in likeness, were made of individual players – Roberto Clemente, Mickey Mantle, Roger Maris and Willie Mays. Both round and square white bases were made, with the player's facsimile autograph on the front of the base. All dolls are extremely rare and very much sought after.

A) Clemente is the rarest of all the caricatures. He wasn't the most popular player of that time, but his doll is the most expensive of all dolls to locate. Only a few surface every year. No box was made with this doll, and there was no miniature made for Clemente. This 7" doll commands a hefty price of $1,200-$1,850; perhaps as few as 40 exist in any condition.

B) Mantle is not the rarest doll but is certainly the most popular. It has an embossed

Mickey Mantle

"N.Y." or "Yankees" decal on the chest. The doll was originally issued with a box, which is worth $50-$150. The Mantle is worth $550-$800 and can often be found at most major card shows. A miniature Mantle was also made and is very difficult to find. An embossed "N.Y." or "Yankees" decal is on the chest. The mini Mantle is worth $800-$1,100.

C) Maris is rarer than Mantle, due to far less distribution than Mantle. It also includes an original box, worth $50-$150, with color pictures of the doll/player on it. An embossed "N.Y." or "Yankees" decal is on the chest. Maris is worth $475-$650. A miniature Maris was also made and is very difficult to locate. It's worth between $800-$1000.

D) Mays is the most common of the caricatures but is found in two variations, made with either a bat or ball. A "dark variation" (the skin tone is darker) of the two types is far more difficult to find. Its value is $300-$450. The "light variation" (with a lighter skin tone) has Oriental-like eyes. This is the most common of the types and is worth between $225-$275.

	MT
Complete Set (7):	.$4,200.00
Roberto Clemente	.1,850.00
Mickey Mantle	.800.00
Mickey Mantle (mini)	.1,950.00
Roger Maris	.500.00
Roger Maris (mini)	.800.00
Willie Mays (dark)	.500.00
Willie Mays (light)	.400.00

1961-62 Baseball
Square White Bases 1961-62

This series, the most difficult to complete, features 22 dolls, including the Anaheim (California) Angels and Houston Colts. The dolls in this series are perhaps the most beautiful and most desirable of all dolls. They are colorfully hand-painted, with embossed team logos on the uniform's chest.

Nine teams are represented with figural head mascots: Chicago Cubs, Cub head; Detroit Tigers, Tiger head; Cincinnati Reds, ball head; Cleveland Indians, "Wahoo" Indian head; Milwaukee Braves, Braves Indian head; Pittsburgh Pirates, Pirate head; Houston Colts, boy head with ten-gallon hat; Baltimore Orioles, Oriole bird head; and St. Louis Cardinals, Cardinal bird head.

This series is most difficult to find, especially the figurals and bobbers for the Chicago White Sox, New York Mets, Minnesota Twins, San Francisco Giants and defunct teams of the Milwaukee Braves, Los Angeles Angels, Washington Senators, Houston Colts and Kansas City A's. The Colt 45's in a blue uniform is super rare.

	MT
Complete Set (22):	.$8,800.00
Anaheim Angels	.500.00
Baltimore Orioles	.500.00
Boston Red Sox	.475.00
Chicago Cubs	.700.00
Chicago White Sox	.275.00
Cincinnati Reds	.500.00
Cleveland Indians	.600.00
Detroit Tigers	.550.00
Houston Colts	.350.00
Houston Colts (blue)	.1,000.00
Kansas City A's	.325.00
Los Angeles Angels	.175.00
Los Angeles Dodgers	.150.00
Milwaukee Braves	.700.00
Minnesota Twins	.650.00
New York Mets	.325.00

New York Yankees	225.00
Philadelphia Phillies	175.00
Pittsburgh Pirates	1,000.00
St. Louis Cardinals	300.00
San Francisco Giants	250.00

1961-62 Miniatures Baseball

White round miniatures were intended to sit on car dashes. These dolls are extremely fragile, especially near the neck. They are about 4" tall.

There are 10 National League and 10 American League dolls. None appear to be more rare than the others.

They were boxed individually or were packaged by a league, 10 to a large box.

A few variations exist; dolls hold either a bat or ball. Reportedly some mavericks with green bases also exist. Some team decals come in script and block.

	MT
Complete Set (21):	$6,200.00
Baltimore Orioles	450.00
Boston Red Sox	350.00
Chicago Cubs	450.00
Chicago White Sox	375.00
Cincinnati Reds	500.00
Cleveland Indians	700.00
Detroit Tigers	275.00
Houston Colts	275.00
Kansas City A's	250.00
Los Angeles Angels	175.00
Los Angeles Dodgers	150.00
Milwaukee Braves	400.00
Minneapolis Twins	400.00
Minnesota Twins	225.00
New York Mets	325.00
New York Yankees	325.00
Philadelphia Phillies	225.00
Pittsburgh Pirates	600.00
St. Louis Cardinals	750.00
San Francisco Giants	325.00
Washington Senators	325.00

1962-64 "Green" Baseball

The green round series continued with the same teams as the white base series but reduced the number of variations on curls. One major change featured the Houston Colts doll, which was made with a pistol, not a bat, in its hand. This doll is one of the more popular green base bobbers. Most dolls were made with decals, not embossed team logos.

	MT
Complete Set (21):	$3,400.00
Baltimore Orioles	225.00
Boston Red Sox red	100.00

Boston Red Sox blue	125.00
Chicago Cubs	300.00
Chicago White Sox	100.00
Cincinnati Reds	125.00
Cleveland Indians	150.00
Detroit Tigers	125.00
Kansas City A's	200.00
Los Angeles Angels	150.00
Los Angeles Dodgers	100.00
Milwaukee Braves	200.00
Minnesota Twins	100.00
New York Mets	125.00
New York Yankees	150.00
Philadelphia Phillies	100.00
Pittsburgh Pirates	175.00
St. Louis Cardinals	150.00
San Francisco Giants	100.00
Washington Senators	200.00

1962-64 "Black" Baseball

This series, featuring black players on green round bases, is an offshoot of the green series. It is by far the most difficult and rarest series to complete. There are no mascots in the series, but the Houston Colts is different; it has a cowboy hat. Each black, boyish face is not simply a white face painted black; these bobbers have distinctive features, including larger eyes, thicker redder lips and curly hair. All dolls are extremely rare.

	MT
Complete Set (19):	$14,000.00
Baltimore Orioles	900.00
Boston Red Sox	1,200.00
Chicago Cubs	600.00
Chicago White Sox	950.00
Cincinnati Reds	950.00
Cleveland Indians	1,600.00
Detroit Tigers	700.00
Houston Colts	1,800.00
Kansas City A's	1,000.00
Los Angeles Angels	1,400.00
Los Angeles Dodgers	1,100.00
Milwaukee Braves	1,100.00
Minnesota Twins	400.00
New York Mets	1,300.00
New York Yankees	1,000.00
Philadelphia Phillies	600.00
Pittsburgh Pirates	500.00
St. Louis Cardinals	900.00
San Francisco Giants	500.00

1965-72 Baseball
Round Gold Bases

This set is the easiest and most reasonable to obtain. Most dolls are abundant and common. The series, which contains the largest number of

dolls, is the last series of Japanese-made dolls. It includes teams that moved and expansion teams. The rarest, most expensive doll in the series, is the Seattle Pilot, made for a team which existed only one year. The Kansas City A's is also popular and scarce because it is one of few to have a uniform entirely in its team colors—green jersey and gold pants. The new Oakland A's issue, in a white uniform, is also quite rare. But an A's doll with a yellow uniform also exists; it is exceedingly common. Two Astros dolls—a plain white uniform with blue trim and hat, or the famous "shooting star" insignia with orange hat—exist. The Padres, Cubs and Kansas City A's are tricky, but popular, as are the figurals. This series marked the end of the Japanese era of bobbers; companies in Hong Kong, Korea and Taiwan attempted to revive them with plastic, but they were not well distributed. From 1983 to the present, Taiwan-made dolls brought back the nationwide ballpark/mail-order concept.

	MT
Complete Set (28):	$2,800.00
Atlanta Braves	100.00
Baltimore Orioles	100.00
Boston Red Sox	125.00
California Angels	100.00
Chicago Cubs	150.00
Chicago White Sox	75.00
Cincinnati Reds	150.00
Cleveland Indians	150.00
Detroit Tigers	150.00
Houston Astros	100.00
Kansas City Royals	125.00
Los Angeles Angels	100.00
Los Angeles Dodgers	100.00
Milwaukee Brewers	75.00
Minnesota Twins	125.00
Montreal Expos	75.00
New York Mets	100.00
New York Yankees	125.00
Oakland A's (yellow)	50.00
Oakland A's (white)	175.00
Philadelphia Phillies	75.00
St. Louis Cardinals	125.00
San Diego Padres	125.00
San Francisco Giants	100.00
Seattle Pilots	350.00
Texas Rangers	125.00
Washington Senators	225.00

1975 Hank Aaron caricature

Other Baseball Bobbin' Heads

A) Little League baseball boy, early 1960s. This features a boy sitting on half a baseball. The ball

Lady Met

is a bank. It's rare, and worth around $100-$150.

B) Weirdoes Los Angeles Dodgers, early 1960s. The dolls on these white bases feature silly expressions. The dolls are holding various items, and wearing uniforms with fractions as numbers. They go for $150 and up.

C) Pitcher/Catcher/Umpire set, early 1960s. They are extremely rare and feature blinking eyes, freckles and feet bases. The players sell for about $100 each; the umpire is worth $150-$200.

D) Umpires, early 1960s. Several variations exist, including a square base with a scowling umpire holding a mask and broom in each hand. Another umpire has a boyish grin and is wearing a curved hat. The last is a Little League miniature on a green round base. These dolls are highly desirable, worth at least $100.

E) Green square bases, rounded corners, 1962. These are similar to the white bases, but it's doubtful there is a complete set. Dolls for the Tigers, Red Sox, Twins and Senators are known to exist, but all dolls are rare and demand prices between whites and greens.

F) Cleveland Indians, miniature boy's head, late 1960s, Japanese. These 4½-inch dolls are rare, worth between $50-$70, and were evidently given away at ballparks with a purchase.

G) Mr. and Mrs. Met gold round base, 1969. These beautiful, extremely rare dolls were made to commemorate the Mets participation in the World Series. Mr. and Mrs. (more expensive) were made. The doll features a ball-head logo/mascot, with legs crossed, leaning on a bat. It's valued at $250-$325. One (of two varieties) is a bank with a coin slot on the back.

H) Gold square bases, early 1970s. All dolls feature boys' heads. The Houston Astros "shooting star" (worth $500) and the Kansas City A's green jersey/gold pants ($450) are extremely rare, but the most popular.

I) Series of plastic dolls, mid-1970s, with boxes. These dolls were never too popular, hence are worth $5-$10.

J) Plastic Henry Aaron caricature, with box, 1975. This doll, worth up to $35, is quite common.

K) Modern heavy ceramics, by Twins Enterprises, 1983-84. The 1983 series came with a ball; the 1984 set had bats. All dolls were boxed. The dolls, made in Taiwan, have round green bases which are thicker and heavier than the 1960s Japanese dolls. Eight dolls are mascots. The dolls are in the $10-$15 range.

L) Modern heavy ceramic, Twins Enterprises, 1988-89. These dolls, also made in Taiwan, have new designs for the eight mascots and are larger than the 1983-84 versions. They sell for between $5-$10.

M) Modern porcelain, Sports, Accessories & Memorabilia Inc., 1993-present. Each doll is hand-painted and resembles the player whose name is painted on the base of the eight-inch statue. Issue prices were $40 each, with 3,000 made for each player.

SAM Bobbin' Heads

Sports, Accessories & Memorabilia (SAM) of Menlo Park, Calif., has been producing hand-painted, ceramic bobbin' head dolls and figurines of professional athletes and entertainment stars since 1992.

Beginning with four Major League Baseball players (Ruth, Seaver, Griffey and Ryan) the company has expanded its line to more than 150 bobbin' head dolls. Each doll is licensed by one or more of the following: the professional sports leagues, sanctioning bodies or the athlete and/or his representatives.

Roberto Alomar	$50.00
Luis Aparicio	50.00
Ernie Banks	50.00
Johnny Bench	55.00
Yogi Berra	60.00
George Brett	55.00
Rod Carew	50.00
Steve Carlton	50.00
Gary Carter	50.00
Roger Clemens	60.00
Roberto Clemente	150.00
Ty Cobb	60.00
Leon Day – Newark Eagles	50.00
Don Drysdale	50.00
Rollie Fingers – A's	60.00
Rollie Fingers – Brewers	50.00
Whitey Ford	60.00
Lou Gehrig	60.00
Bob Gibson	48.95
Ken Griffey Jr.-white	65.00
Ken Griffey Jr.-teal	65.00
Ken Griffey Jr.-grey	80.00
Tony Gwynn	48.95
Martinez Jackson – Eagles	65.00
Reggie Jackson	65.00
Derek Jeter	50.00
Chipper Jones	50.00

Michael Jordan – Barons	200.00
Mickey Mantle	100.00
Roger Maris	60.00
Willie Mays	60.00
Mark McGwire	65.00
Joe Morgan	55.00
Eddie Murray	48.95
Stan Musial	48.95
Hideo Nomo	48.95
Satchel Paige – K.C. Monarchs	65.00
Jim Palmer	48.95
Tony Perez	55.00
Gaylord Perry	48.95
Mike Piazza	48.95
Kirby Puckett	55.00
Cal Ripken Jr.-white	60.00
Cal Ripken Jr.-grey	60.00
Cal Ripken Jr.-black	60.00
Alex Rodriguez	48.95
Brooks Robinson	48.95
Pete Rose	60.00
Babe Ruth	60.00
Nolan Ryan	80.00
Nolan Ryan set of five (Mets, Angels, Astros, Rangers)	200.00
Mike Schmidt	$48.95
Tom Seaver	48.95
Duke Snider	48.95
Willie Stargell	48.95
Frank Thomas-1994	300.00
Frank Thomas-1998	48.95
Larry Walker	48.95
Ted Williams	100.00
Carl Yastrzemski	100.00
All-Star Team-set of 2	80.00

500 Home Run Club

Hank Aaron	$70.00
Ernie Banks	70.00
Reggie Jackson	85.00
Willie Mays	70.00
Eddie Murray	70.00
Mike Schmidt	70.00
Ted Williams	70.00

MLB Mascots

Atlanta Braves	$38.95
Baltimore Orioles	48.95
Chicago Cubs	48.95
Cincinnati Reds	48.95
Cleveland Indians	48.95
Detroit Tigers	48.95
Pittsburgh Pirates	48.95
St. Louis Cardinals	48.95

Four different versions of the Nolan Ryan bobbin' head by SAM.

Baseball Yearbooks

Although some exist from the 1940s (and earlier), it wasn't until the 1950s that what we now generally consider as yearbooks were produced by professional teams on a regular basis. The main problem in creating a yearbook checklist is that there is not a general consensus as to whether a certain publication should be considered a yearbook or something else; many teams have labeled their publications with a variety of other names—magazines, roster books, photo albums and sketch books.

Early New York Yankees yearbooks can be confusing to collectors because a company called *Jay Publishing* produced unofficial yearbooks in the 1950s and '60s.

To be classified as a yearbook, generally a publication must at the very least have photographs of every player on the 25-man roster, plus biographies and player statistics. If, however, a publication has photos, stats and biographies, but is labeled as a media guide, scorecard or program, then it's obviously something other than a yearbook.

Most yearbooks from the 1960s offer collectors an affordable alternative for under $100. Those from the 1940s and 1950s bring the top dollars, depending on scarcity and age, while those that are autographed are even more valuable. Yearbooks should be stored in plastic holders and be kept out of direct sunlight.

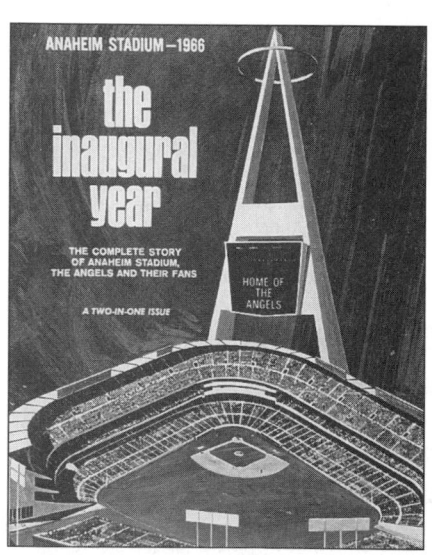

Angels

Los Angeles Angels:
1961 . . . . .None issued
1962 Angels baby with cake . . . .$85-$100
1963 Rocket, Chavez Ravine . . . . . .$35-$50
1964 Angels in action . . . .$25-$35
1965 Angels in action . . . .$25-$35
California Angels:
1966 Anaheim Stadium . . . .$50-$65
1967 All About the Angels, with logo $12-$15
1968-1982 . . . . .None issued

1983 Lynn, Carew, Jackson, others . . . .$8-$12
1984 Anaheim Stadium . . . .$5-$10
1985 25th Anniversary, Angel greats . .$7-$10
1986-1991 . . . . None issued
1992 Abbott, Langston, Harvey, Finley . . .$12
1993 Nolan Ryan $12
1994 Tim Salmon $8
1995-1997 . . . . .None issued

Anaheim Angels:
1998-1999 . . . . .None issued
2000 40th Anniv./Players in action $10

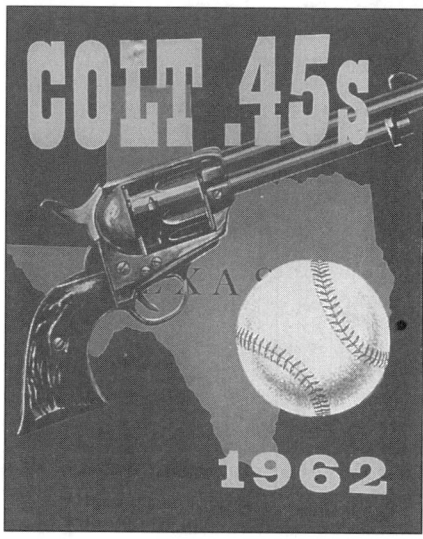

Astros

Houston Colt 45s:
1962 Baseball/ pistol/ Texas map $150
1963 . . . . .None issued
1964 Colt .45s logo $125

Houston Astros:
1965 Inside the Astrodome $100
1966 Astrodome $75
1967 . . . . None issued
1968 . . . .$45
1969-1971 . . . . None issued
1972 . . . .$25
1973-1976 . . . . None issued
1977 Photo album $20
1978 Photo album $20
1979 Photo album $20

1980-1981 . . . . None issued
1982 Nolan Ryan . . . .$12-$15
1983-1991 . . . . None issued
1992 Luis Gonzalez $12
1993 Photo album $12
1994 New logo, Bagwell, others $10
1995-1998 . . . . .None issued

Athletics

Philadelphia Athletics:
1949 Connie Mack . . . .$60-$125
1950 Connie Mack Golden Jubilee . . . .$60-$125
1951 Team mascot (elephant) . . . . . .$60-$125
1952 Team mascot (elephant) . . . . . .$60-$125
1953 Elephant pitching baseball $20
1954 Play at first base $75

Kansas City Athletics:
1955 A's batter ripping through map
. . . .$100-$150
1956 Elephant mascot . . . .$100-$150
1957 Kansas City Municipal Stadium
. . . .$100-$150
1958 Play at first $125
1959 Kansas City Municipal Stadium . . .$125
1960 Baseball wearing Athletics hat $125
1961 Pitcher and baseball $125
1962 A's players in action $125
1963 Play at home plate . . . .$25-$40
1964 Player making a catch . . . .$25-$40
1965 A's donkey/ Finley flag . . . .$25-$45

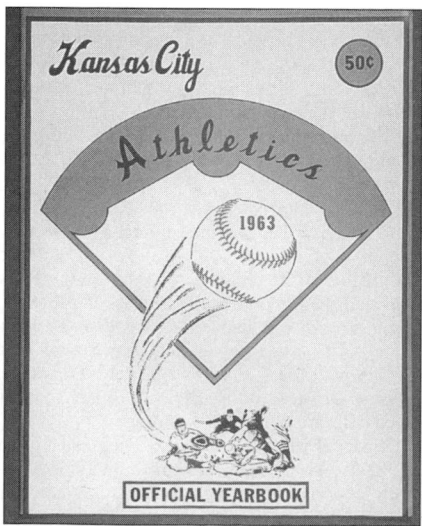

1966 . . . .$65
1967 Athletics pitcher $40

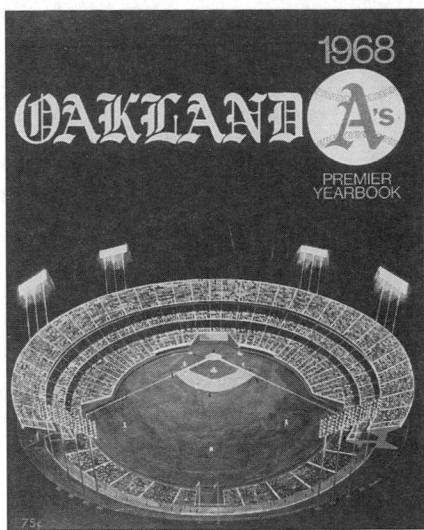

Oakland Athletics:
1968 Oakland Coliseum . . . .$45-$75
1969 Connie Mack . . . .$25-$35
1970 Monday/ Odom/ Jackson/ others $25
1971 Sal Bando/ Bert Campaneris . . . . .$15-$25
1972 Dick Williams/ Vida Blue . . . . .$15-$22
1973 Rudi/ Fingers/ Williams/ Hunter . . .$20
1974 One More in '74/ two trophies . . .$15-$20
1975 Keep it Alive in '75 . . . .$20
1976 Bicentennial celebration $15
1977 A's logo/ arch of baseballs . . . . . .$7-$9
1978 . . . . None issued
1979 The Swingin' A's, with logo $20
1980-1981 . . . . None issued
1982 Billy Ball baseball . . . .$5-$10
1983 A's baseball card collage $15
1984-1999 . . . . None issued
2000 Giambi, Tejeda, Foxx, others $12

Blue Jays

1977 The First Year, fans . . . .$15-$20
1978 . . . . None issued
1979 Rico Carty $9
1980 Rico Carty, Roy Howell $15
1981 Ernie Whitt, Jim Clancy $15
1982 Martinez, Moseby, Whitt $15
1983 Blue Jays baseball $15

1984 Exhibition Stadium $15
1985 Logo and year $15
1986 American League baseball, bat $15
1987 Barfield, Clancy, Whitt $15
1988 Blue Jays player batting $15
1989 Fred McGriff $15
1990 George Bell $15
1991 Player drawing $15
1992 Roberto Alomar $15
1993 Trophy $15
1994 Carter/Molitor/White others $12
1995 Logo and baseball $10
1996 20th Anniv. All-Time greats $10
1997 Roger Clemens $10
1998 R. Clemens, C. Delgado $10
1999 Shawn Green $10
2000 . . . .$9

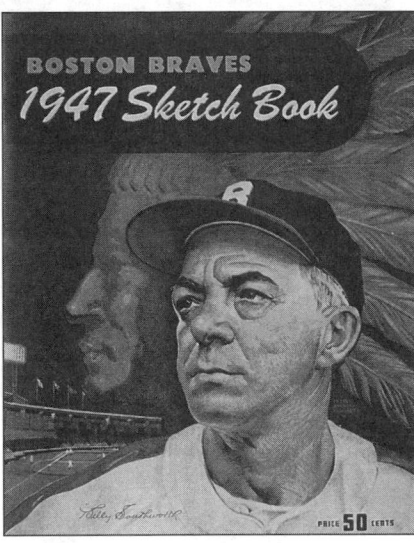

Braves

Boston Braves:
1946 Billy Southworth $300
1947 Billy Southworth . . . .$150-$165
1948-1949 . . . . None issued
1950 Smiling Brave $150
1951 Baseball diamond and ball $125
1952 Braves players talking $125

Milwaukee Braves:
1953 Runner sliding into home . . . . .$150-$175
1954 To the People of Milwaukee . . . .$75-$100

1955 Fans and stadium . . . .$50-$60
1956 Cartoon of Braves fans . . . .$100-$125
1957 Braves logo in crystal ball . . .$100-$125
1958 Brave raising World Series pennant
. . . .$100-$125
1959 Brave in hot-air balloon . . . . . .$65-$70
1960 Brave with two baseball bats $60
1961 Braves player, other N.L. players . . . .$40-$65
1962 Braves logo . . . .$45-$50
1963 Braves player/other N.L. players $40
1964 Aaron/ Mathews/Torre/Spahn . . . . .$40-$60
1965 Bobby Bragan/Felipe Alou $40

Atlanta Braves:

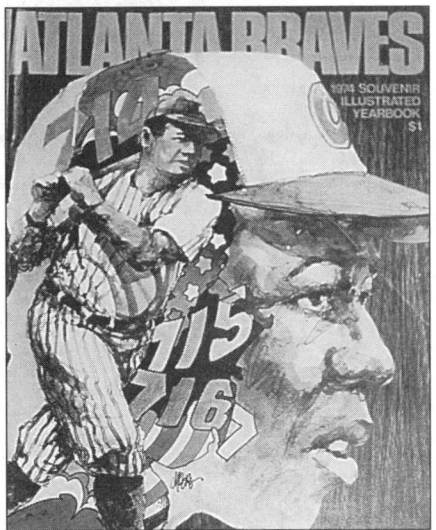

1966 Aaron/ Mathews/ others . . . .$25-$50
1967 Play at home plate . . . .$10-$30
1968 Play at second base . . . .$10-$25
1969 Braves infielder . . . .$15-$25
1970 Braves in action $20
1971 Hank Aaron/Babe Ruth . . . .$7-$9
1972 Five Braves . . . .$5-$9
1973 Braves pitcher $20
1974 Hank Aaron/Babe Ruth $20
1975 Four Braves $15
1976 Niekro/ Cepeda/ Aaron/ others $15
1977 Former Braves/ Hank Aaron $10
1978 Spahn/ Niekro/ Burdette $10
1979 Garber stops Rose's streak . . . . .$12-$15
1980 Bob Horner/ Bobby Cox $15
1981 D. Murphy/ B. Horner/ others $15
1982 Spahn/ Horner/ Aaron/ others . .$12-$15
1983 Phil Niekro in an Uncle Sam outfit $10
1984 Horner/ Murphy/Aaron $10
1985 Aaron/ Murphy/20th Anniversary $10
1986 Dale Murphy/Chuck Tanner $12
1987 Dale Murphy $12
1988 Braves Illustrated $10
1989 .None issued
1990 25 years in Atlanta $12
1991 .None issued
1992 N.L. Champions $12
1993 . . . . None issued
1994 B. Cox/G. Maddux/others $7
1995-1999 . . . . .None Issued
1998 Collage of players $10

Brewers

Seattle Pilots:
1969 Pilot logos, 10 pictures $150

Milwaukee Brewers:
1970 Brewers hitter . . . .$50-$75
1971-1978 . . . . None issued

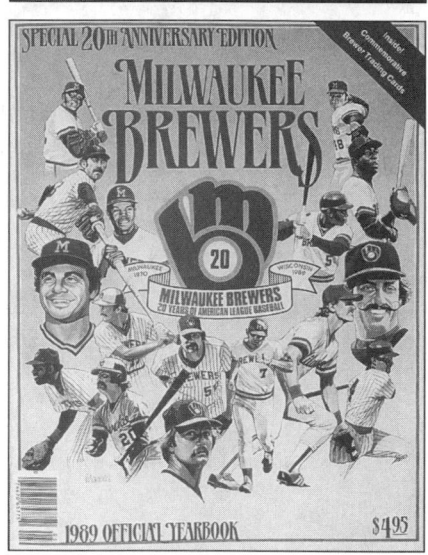

1962 Stan Musial and his milestone
. . . .$40-$60
1963 Musial slides into second . . . . .$35-$50
1964 Groat/Boyer/Javier/White . . . .$35-$50
1965 Bob Gibson $35
1966 New Busch Stadium photo $65
1967 World Champs . . . .$50-$75
1968 Busch Stadium $45
1969 Brock/ Flood/Gibson/others $30
1970 Five Cardinal drawings . . . .$12-$15
1971 Brock/ Torre/Gibson/others . . . .$12-$15
1972 Cardinals fielder $25
1973 Cardinals batter . . . .$15-$20
1974 Simmons/Torre $15
1975 Brock/Gibson, others $20
1976 Centennial yearbook $20
1977 Lou Brock/Ty Cobb . . . .$12-$15
1978 . . . . None issued
1979 St. Louis city skyline $12
1980 Simmons/Hernandez $10
1981-1987 . . . . None issued
1988 Wraparound team photo $12
1989 Coleman, Worrell . . . .$7-$12
1990 Herzog/Busch Stadium $10
1991 Lee Smith $12
1992 Moore/Slaughter/Musial/others $12
1993 Ozzie Smith $12
1995 K. Hill/S. Cooper/D. Jackson/T. Henke . . .$10
1996-98 . . . . .None issued
1999 Mark McGwire $10
2000 Greatest Moments in Cards history . .$10

Cubs

1934 Wraparound batting scene . . . . .$200-$275
1939 Players records $200
1941 Players history/record book . . .$175-$250
1942 Roster/record book . . . .$150-$200
1948 Logo and blue 1948 . . . .$100-$150
1949 Logo and blue 1949 . . . .$35-$50
1950 Hat and red 1950 . . . .$35-$50
1951 Ball in center of red glove $60
1952 Logo/ year in red and blue . . . .$50-$70
1953 Cubs logo $50
1954 Name and year $50
1955 Name and year $50
1956 Name and year . . . .$75-$100
1957 Head with Cubs hat $125
1958-1984 . . . . None issued
1985 Wrigley photo . . . .$5-$8
1986 70th Anniversary/R. Sandberg . . . .$5-$7
1987 Billy Williams/Ryne Sandberg . .$7-$8
1988 Andre Dawson . . . .$7-$9

1989 Wrigley Field Diamond Anniv. $12
1990 Photo of six bats $12
1991 Ryne Sandberg $12
1992 Scoreboard/celebration $12
1993 Mark Grace $12
1994 Moments from 1984 season $10
1995 Wrigley Field $10
1996-1999 . . . . .None issued

Devil Rays

1998 . . . . .None issued
1999 Celebration at home plate $10

Diamondbacks

1998 Two hardbound books $10

Dodgers

Brooklyn Dodgers:
1947 League Champs $100
1948 . . . . None issued
1949 League Champs $250
1950 Artwork of a fielder . . . .$175-$200
1951 The Bum picking daisy petals $125
1952 The Bum holding a sign $125
1953 The Bum holding a bat $125
1954 The Bum with saw, hammer $125
1955 The Bum reaching for a star $300
1956 The Bum holding #6 . . . .$50-$125
1957 The Bum holding pennants . . . . .$125-$150

Los Angeles Dodgers:
1958 Autographed team baseball . .$150-$175
1959 Play at second base . . . .$75-$135

1979 Larry Hisle . . . .$5-$9
1980 Gorman Thomas . . . .$5-$9
1981 Molitor/ Fingers/Yount/ others . . .$5-$9
1982 Crowd celebrating $12
1983 Robin Yount and fans $10
1984 County Stadium . . . .$5-$9
1985 George Bamberger and fans . . . . .$5-$9
1986 Brewers locker room . . . .$5-$9
1987 Brewers baseball cards . . . .$5-$9
1988 Paul Molitor hologram $10
1989 Brewer greats/ Hank Aaron $12
1990 Brewers logo/ Milwaukee skyline . . .$10
1991 Paul Molitor $12
1992 Molitor/ Yount/ Gantner $12
1993 . . . . None issued
1994 New Brewer uniforms $7
1995 . . . . .None issued
1996 John Jaha $8
1997-2000 . . . . .None issued

Cardinals

1951 Cardinal in bottom right $250
1952 Cardinal and soldier $125
1953 Stan Musial . . . .$125-$175
1954 Red Schoendienst $100
1955 Cardinal pitcher gets the sign $75
1956 Cardinal pitcher gets the sign $75
1957 Cardinal circles the bases . . . .$40-$50
1958 Cardinal circles the bases $50
1959 Stan Musial $55
1960 Cardinal catches a ball $40
1961 C. Simmons/ Sadecki, others $40

1960 Dodger stadium drawing $50
1961 Artwork of Dodger Stadium $50
1962 Map of area around Stadium . . . .$15-$20
1963 Maury Wills $50
1964 World Champions banner $30
1965 Dodger Stadium $35
1966 Walter Alston . . . .$20-$25
1967 Dodger juggling crowns . . . . .$10-$20
1968 Drysdale/Koufax/others . . . .$10-$20
1969 Baseballs centennial logo . . . .$10-$20
1970 Dodgers and Mets mascots . . . .$10-$20
1971 10th Anniversary of stadium . . .$10-$20
1972 Dodger Stadium . . . .$10-$20
1973 Maury Wills/Walter Alston . . . .$15-$25
1974 Jimmy Wynn . . . .$10-$20
1975 Steve Garvey/N.L. Champions
. . . .$12-$18
1976 Davey Lopes . . . .$12-$18
1977 20th Anniversary, players $10
1978 Lasorda/Garvey/Cey/others . . . .$12-$15
1979 Tommy Lasorda . . . .$10-$12
1980 Dodgers baseball cards $10
1981 Dusty Baker, Steve Garvey . . . .$10-$12
1982 World Series trophy . . . .$8-$12
1983 25th Anniversary in Los Angeles . . .$10
1984 A Winning Tradition/Lasorda . . .$7-$10
1985 Russell/ Valenzuela/Garvey . . . . .$9-$10
1986 Guerrero/ Hershiser/Marshall . .$7-$10
1987 24 previous Los Angeles yearbooks
. . . .$7-$10
1988 Blueprint for Success . . . .$8-$9
1989 World Series trophy . . . .$6-$10
1990 Dodger greats painting . . . .$6-$10
1991 Dodgers Field of Dreams . . . .$5-$7
1992 Dodger greats . . . .$5-$7
1993 Hershiser, Lasorda/collage $8
1994 Team photo, uniform background $8
1995 Dodger rookies of the year $8
1996 Nomo/Piazza/Mondesi/Karros $8
1997 Jackie Robinson patch, photo $10
1998 Art collage of 40 Year Anniversary $10
1999 Drysdale/Campanella uniform patches .$10
2000 Photos inside number 2000 . . . .$12

Expos

1969 Larry Jaster $35-50
1970 Expos equipment and fan . . . .$25-$35
1971 Fan with Expos pennant . . . . . .$25-$35
1972 Four different covers, each . . . .$25-$35
1973-81 . . . . None issued
1982 Expos celebration, All-Star logo $10
1983 Dawson, Carter, Oliver, others . . .$7-$12

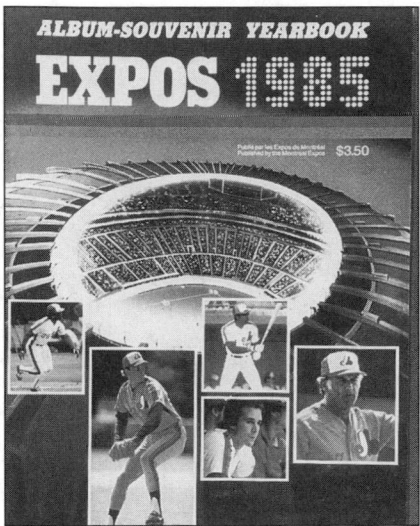

1984 Raines/Rose/Dawson/others . . . .$8-$12
1985 Wallach/Raines/Dawson/others $10
1986 Baseball in hand $8
1987-91 . . . . None issued
1992 Gary Carter $10
1993-2000 . . . . None issued

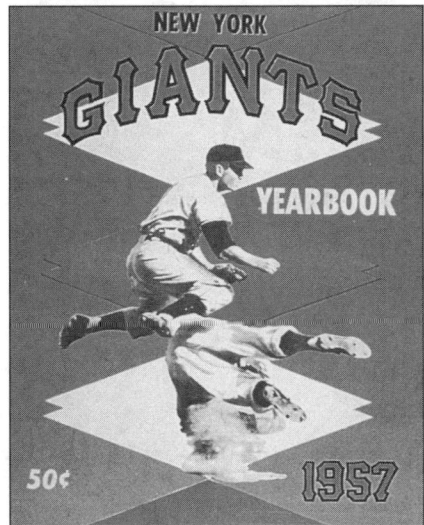

Giants

New York Giants:
1947 First Year . . . .$150-$165
1948-1950 . . . . None issued
1951 Logo/art of leaping player $125
1952 Durocher and Giant $85
1953 Polo Grounds photo $85
1954 Giant cutting a 1951 book $85
1955 Giant holding other mascots $125
1956 Giants cap . . . .$75-$85
1957 Photo of play at second . . . . . .$85-$100

San Francisco Giants:
1958 Giant with a load of books $250
1959 Photo of a play at third . . . . . .$75-$100
1960 Al Dark/ play at first $50
1961 Giants hat $50
1962 N.L. Champs $50
1963 Trolley car w/Giants pennant . . . . .$30-$40
1964 Child looking at Candlestick $30
1965 Painting of a play at second $30
1966 W. Mays with S.F. baseball . . . .$30-$50
1967 Willie Mays, Juan Marichal $40
1968 Willie Mays $25

1969 Mays/Bonds/McCovey $30
1970 Photos of Mays/McCovey . . . . .$20-$25
1971 Willie McCovey . . . .$15-$20
1972 Willie Mays sliding into third . .$10-$15
1973 Marichal/Bonds/Speier . . . .$10-$15
1974 Young Giants '74 . . . .$10
1975 Gary Matthews/Mike Caldwell $12
1976 Giants memorabilia $15
1977-1979 . . . . None issued
1980 Giant batter $9
1981 Frank Robinson $10
1982 Silver Anniversary yearbook . . . .$8-$10
1983 Frank Robinson . . . .$7-$9
1984 Giants All-Star memorabilia . . . . .$7-$9
1985 Horizontal, A History of... . . . . . .$5-$7
1986-1991 . . . . None issued
1992 Will Clark $12
1993 . . . . None issued
1994 Willie Mays $10
1995 Matt Williams/Barry Bonds $10
1996 W. Mays/Bonds/ W. McCovey/
J. Marichal/G. Perry/R. Beck $10
1997 . . . . None issued
1998 Brian Johnson $9
1999 Farewell to 3Com Park $9
2000 Pac Bell Park $9

Indians

1948 World Champs . . . .$100-$125
1949 Logo wearing crown . . . .$40-$85
1950 Fans entering stadium . . . .$40-$75
1951 50th Anniversary with logo . . . .$60-$75

1952 Chain with Indians logo $60
1953 Umpire yelling "Play ball" . . . .$65-$95
1954 Lemon/Wynn/Doby/Rosen $100
1955 Indian wearing crown . . . . . .$75-$100
1956 Indian mascot $75
1957 Indian mascot . . . .$75-$125
1958 Herb Score $250
1959 Indians logo . . . .$125-$175
1960 Jim Perry, Indians pitcher $100
1961 Sketch book $100
1962 Team photo $75
1963 Sketch book $100
1964 Indian sliding into home $75
1965 Past and present uniforms $65
1966 Sam McDowell . . . .$50-$65
1967 Picture set . . . .$50-$65
1968 Baseball and year . . . .$25-$40
1969 Runner sliding into base $20
1970 Sam McDowell $25
1971 Indians in action $15
1972 Indians in action . . . .$7-$9
1973 Jim Perry, others $15
1974-1983 . . . . None issued
1984 Franco/Sutcliffe/others . . . .$5-$6
1985-1988 . . . . None issued
1989 Autographed team ball $10
1990 90th Anniversary in Cleveland $10
1991 Score/Alomar/Chambliss $10
1992 Alomar, Hargrove $12
1993 . . . . None issued
1994 Hardcover, Jacobs Field $15
1995 Jacobs Field, Belle, Baerga, others $10
1996 A.L. Championship artwork $10
1997 All-Star logo/Cleveland skyline $10
1998 Championship celebration $10
1999 M. Ramirez/M. Hargrove, others $9

Mariners

1978-1984 . . . . None issued
1985 Davis/ Beattie/Langston $10
1986-1993 . . . . None issued
1994 Griffey/Martinez/others $5
1995-1998 . . . . None issued
1999 K. Griffey Jr./A. Rodriguez $9

Marlins

1993 Marlins hitter/pitcher/catcher $10
1994 B. Harvey/R. Lachemann/others $8
1995 -1996 . . . . .None issued
1997 G. Sheffield/J. Conine/others $7

1998 World Series ring $7
1999 A. Fernandez/Old-Time players $6
2000 Player photo collage $10

Mets

1962 First year . . . .$300-$350
1963 Mr. Met leaning on bat . . . . .$125-$150
1964 Cartoon . . . .$75-$100
1965 Cartoon/Shea Stadium . . . .$50-$60
1966 "Go-Go-Go" Mets banner $50
1967 Cartoon . . . .$50-$75
1968 Gil Hodges $45
1969 Koosman/Grote/Seaver . . . . .$100-$125
1970 Film strips/World Series celebration
. . . .$35
1971 Play at the plate . . . .$35-$50
1972 Harrelson/McGraw/Seaver $15
1973 All-Star gallery w/Mays/Seaver/others
. . . .$15-$35
1974 N.L. Champions pennant $15
1975 Tom Seaver . . . .$15-$25
1976 Mr. Met . . . .$15-$20
1977 Jerry Koosman . . . .$10-$15
1978 Play at home plate . . . .$6-$10
1979 Mets logo . . . .$10-$15
1980 Mazzilli with fan/others $30
1981 Joe Torre/All-Time Mets $15
1982 G. Foster/G. Bamberger . . . . . .$12-$15
1983 Foster/M. Wilson/Seaver $20
1984 Orosco/Hernandez/Strawberry . $15-$20

1985 Hernandez/Gooden/D. Johnson $15
1986 25th Anniversary logo $20
1987 World Champions logo . . . . . .$10-$15
1988 Strawberry/Gooden/Johnson/others
. . . .$15
1989 Strawberry/Gooden/Carter/others
. . . .$15
1990 Mets starting pitchers $15
1991 Shea Stadium $10
1992 Bonilla/Saberhagen/Murray/Torborg
. . . .$15
1993 30 years at Shea $15
1994 25th Anniv. of 1969 Championship . . .$10
1995 Logo on bats $10
1996 T. Hundley/Everett/others $10
1997 Motion card of Hundley swing $10
1998 Player celebration photo $10
1999 Piazza/R. Henderson, others $10
2000 Piazza/Hampton, others $10

Orioles

St. Louis Browns:

1944 . . . .$275
1945 . . . .$250
1946 . . . .$250
1947 . . . .$225
1948 . . . .$200
1949 . . . .$200
1950 Browns sketchbook $200
1951 Browns logo $200
1952 Logo on Browns sketchbook $300
1953 . . . .$150

Baltimore Orioles:

1954 Orioles mascot in spotlight $250
1955 Oriole mascot batting $150
1956 Oriole mascot on deck $125
1957 Oriole mascot pitching $125
1958 Oriole mascot riding a rocket $125
1959 Oriole mascot with report . . .$100-$125
1960 Oriole mascot sitting on eggs $100
1961 Oriole mascot hitting opponent $75
1962 Jim Gentile $75
1963 Brooks Robinson $75
1964 Orioles catcher $75
1965 B. Robinson, Bauer, Bunker $75
1966 Robinsons/Blefary/Powell $50
1967 Frank Robinson and fans $50
1968 Brooks and Frank Robinson $25
1969 Dave McNally $25
1970 Boog Powell . . . .$20-$35
1971 B. Robinson/Palmer/others . . . .$15-$25

1972 Palmer/McNally/Cuellar $15
1973 Orioles player . . . .$12-$15
1974 Orioles jukebox . . . .$10-$12
1975- 1979 . . . . None issued
1980 Orioles mascot . . . .$10-$12
1981 Orioles players . . . .$8-$10
1982 Frank Robinson/Earl Weaver $15
1983 Brooks Robinson . . . .$9-$10
1984 30th Anniversary in Baltimore . . . .$10-$12
1985 . . . . None issued
1986 Robinsons/Ripken/Murray $10
1987-1992 . . . . None issued
1993 Camden Yards $10
1994 40th Anniversary Issue $10
1995-1997 .None issued
1998 Cal Ripken, Jr./Brady Anderson $8
1999 . . . . .None issued

Padres
1969 Jack Murphy Stadium $75
1970-1978 . . . . None issued
1979 Dave Winfield . . . .$5-$6
1980 Dave Winfield . . . .$6-$7
1981 . . . . None issued
1982 Dick Williams . . . .$7-$12
1983 Dick Williams/Steve Garvey . . . .$7-$12
1984 Templeton/Williams/Garvey $12
1985 Padres hat/N.L. Championship ring .$12
1986 Padres memorabilia $10

1987-1991 . . . . None issued
1992 Fernandez/Gwynn/Santiago $10
1993 25th Anniversary $10
1994-1998 . . . . .None issued
1999 Yearbook/Media guide $10

Phillies
1949 Batting scene . . . .$175-$250
1950 Phillie and sheet music $150
1951 Six player drawings $400
1952 Color stadium photo . . . . . .$100-$125
1953 Phillie batter . . . .$35-$75
1954 Smiling Phillie (head only) $100
1955 Phillie pitcher . . . .$75-$100
1956 R. Roberts/ R. Ashburn $150
1957 Ball wearing a Phillies hat . . . .$50-$100
1958 Hat on pinstriped background . .$75-$80
1959 Five balls, one with a logo . . . . .$50-$75
1960 New faces of 1960/11 photos $75
1961 First edition $150
1961 Second edition $150
1962 Four balls and logo . . . .$60-$75
1963 Bat, ball and logo $75
1964 First or second edition $75
1964 Third edition, Bunning/others $75
1965 Richie Allen/Jim Bunning $45
1966 Stadium photo $45
1967 Child eating a hot dog $45
1968 Phillies ballplayers . . . .$35-$45
1969 Connie Mack Stadium . . . .$35-$45
1970 Veterans Stadium in tree bark . . . .$20-$40
1971 Veterans Stadium drawing $45
1972 Stadium/fans and players $30
1973 12 drawings, with Carlton $45
1974 12 drawings, with Carlton/Bowa $20
1975 Schmidt/Carlton . . . .$20-$30
1976 Drawings with Schmidt/Carlton
. . . .$12-$15
1977 Larry Bowa . . . .$12-$15
1978 Schmidt/Carlton/photos . . . .$7-$9
1979 Schmidt/Rose/Carlton . . . .$7-$9
1980 Schmidt/Rose/Carlton $30
1981 World Series ring photo $30
1982 Schmidt/Rose/Carlton $10
1983 Centennial celebration . . . .$9-$12
1984 Schmidt/Carlton/20 others . . . . . .$6-$7
1985 Schmidt/Carlton/Samuel/Hayes . .$7-$10
1986 Mike Schmidt at bat . . . .$10-$12
1987 Schmidt/ Samuel, others $10
1988 Veterans Stadium photo $10
1989 Jordan/ V. Hayes/ Schmidt $10
1990 Photo of John Kruk's equipment $10

1991 Veterans Stadium $10
1992 Kruk/Dykstra/Daulton/others $10
1993 Kruk/Dykstra/Daulton/others $10
1994 1993 N.L. Championship ring $8
1995 L. Dykstra/D. Hollins/others $8
1996 Montage of action photos $8
1997 Curt Schilling $8
1998 S. Rolen/C. Jefferies/others $7
1999 C. Schilling/S. Rolen/others $7

Pirates
1951 Forbes Field photo $250
1952 Pirate with sword and pistol $125
1953 Buc youngster in sailboat $100
1954 Honus Wagner statue . . . .$100-$175
1955 Pirate batter - "It's a hit!" $100
1956 Pirate swinging at 1956 ball $100
1957 Pirate winding up . . . .$85-$100
1958 Pirate head between two bats $65
1959 Pirate with Pa Pitt $50
1960 Pirate in sailboat $50
1961 Pirate on a treasure chest $35
1962 Ball wearing bandana and cap . .$35-$50
1963 Pirate batter . . . .$35-$50
1964 Pirate sliding into third $15
1965 Mgr. Harry Walker and coaches $25
1966 Wraparound Forbes Field photo $25
1967 Clemente/Mazeroski/others $25
1968 Clemente/Stargell/others $25
1969 Wraparound Forbes Field photo $25
1970 Three Rivers Stadium $75
1971 Three Rivers Stadium $75
1972 Clemente/Stargell/others $20
1973 Clemente/Stargell/others $20
1974 Stargell, Parker, others $12
1975 Historical photos . . . .$5-$6
1976 Yosemite Sam cartoon . . . .$5-$6
1977 Pirate baseball cards . . . .$6-$7
1978 Tanner/Candelaria/others . . . .$5-$6
1979 Dave Parker $20
1980 The Family of Stars . . . .$5-$6
1981 Lacy/Rhoden/Madlock/others $10
1982 Stargell/Madlock/others $10
1983 Chuck Tanner . . . .$6-$7
1984 Madlock/Pena/Ray/others . . . .$5-$6
1985 Painting of Mazs '60 homer . . . . .$5-$9
1986 Leland/Pena/Ray/M. Brown . . . .$7-$12
1987 Centennial yearbook . . . .$7-$12
1988 Bonds/ Bonilla/ Van Slyke/others
. . . .$7-$12
1989 Photo of official N.L. balls . . . .$7-$12
1990 Van Slyke bat/Leyland uniform $10

1991 Pirates greats $10
1992 Locker room/uniforms $10
1993 Jay Bell $10
1994 J. Leyland/O. Merced/others $9
1995 25th Anniversary of stadium $9
1996-99 .None issued
2000 Three Rivers Stadium/Clemente/etc. .$10

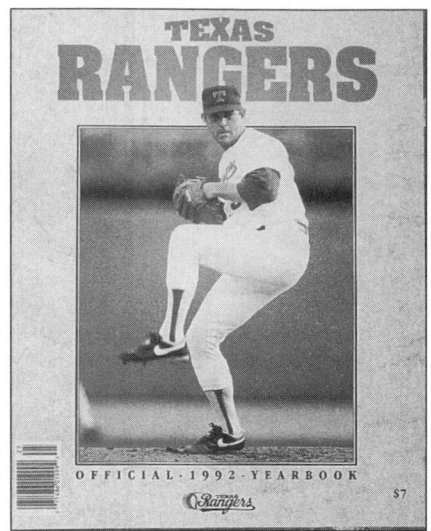

Rangers

1972-1975 . . . . None issued
1976 Rangers cowgirl on horse . . . . .$15-$25
1977 Autographed Rangers ball . . . . . .$7-$15
1978 Squared photo collage $12
1979 Jenkins/Oliver/others . . . .$5-$9
1980 Arlington Stadium $15
1981 Rangers hitter . . . .$5-$9
1982 Rangers baseball . . . .$10-$12
1983 . . . . None issued
1984 George Wright . . . .$10-$12
1985 Pete O'Brien/equipment $10
1986-1987 . . . . None issued
1988 Ruben Sierra $10
1989 . . . . None issued
1990 Rangers helmet rack . . . .$6-$8
1991 20 Years in Texas $10
1992 Nolan Ryan $12
1993 Arlington Stadium tribute $10
1994 Ballpark at Arlington $8
1995 Will Clark artwork $8
1996 Nolan Ryan $10
1997 25th Anniv. logo/Gonzalez/others $8
1998 J. Gonzalez/I. Rodriguez $8
1999 Nolan Ryan $8
2000 I. Rodriguez/R. Palmeiro $8

Nationals/Senators

1947 "Photo Book," W. Johnson . . .$250-$400
1948 . . . . None issued
1949 . . . .$150-$350
1950 . . . .$125-$300
1951 . . . . None issued
1952 Nationals batter $100
1953 Capitol building and baseball $25
1954 Bob Porterfield/Mickey Vernon $75
1955 National with four bats $75
1956 Clark C. Griffith memorial $100
1957 Senators pitcher . . . .$75-$100
1958 Roy Sievers $100
1959 100 Years of Baseball art $50
1960 Harmon Killebrew $65
Franchise becomes Minnesota Twins.

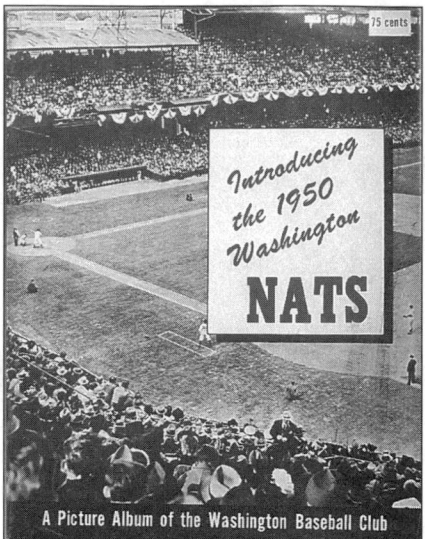

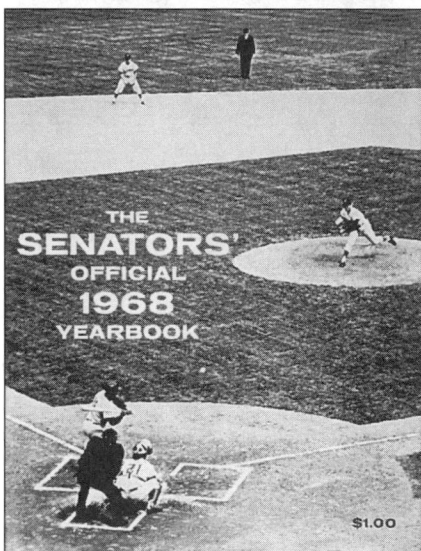

As expansion team Washington Senators.
1961 A Team is Born . . . .$100-$150
1962 Washington Stadium $75
1963 Red cover with dedication . . . . .$30-$45
1964 Off the Floor in '64 . . . .$15
1965 Frank Howard signing autograph . . .$25
1966 Senators in action $20
1967 Capitol and Washington Monument
. . . .$25-$30
1968 Pitcher delivering . . . .$15-$20
1969 Ted Williams . . . .$20-$30
1970-1971 . . . . None issued
Becomes Texas Rangers.

Reds

1948 Ewell Blackwell/Ray Lamanno $150
1949 Bucky Walters/Harry Gumbert $200
1950 . . . . None issued
1951 75th Anniversary of N.L. . . . .$100-$125
1952 Crosley Field . . . .$100-$125
1953 Reds mascot leaning on bat $75
1954 Reds mascot swinging bat $75
1955 Reds mascot rising on bat $75
1956 Reds mascot swinging bat $75
1957 Reds mascot in space ship . . . . .$60-$75
1958 Reds mascot in orbit . . . .$40-$50
1959 Vander Meer/Lombardi/others $50
1960 Reds mascot/Goodman/Rixey $30
1961 Reds mascot running after ball $40

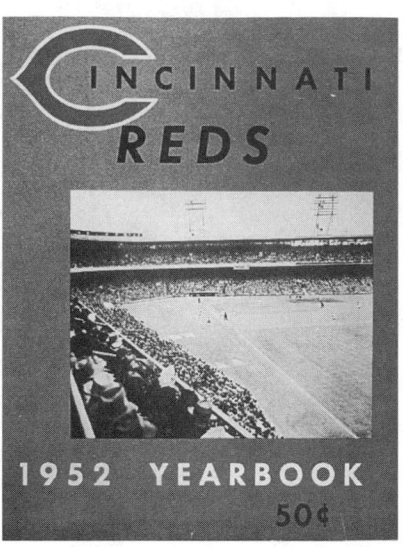

1962 Reds mascot raising pennant $40
1963 Reds mascot yelling "Charge" $65
1964 Reds mascot in action . . . .$30-$40
1965 Reds mascot making catch . . . .$30-$40
1966 Reds mascot reaching for ball $30
1967 Reds mascot/Crosley Field $30
1968 Autographed team baseball . . . .$15-$25
1969 Perez, Rose, Bench, others . . . .$15-$25
1970 Johnny Bench $25
1971 Rose/ Bench/Anderson, others $15
1972 Bench/ Perez/other film strips $15
1973 Morgan/Bench/others $10
1974 Pete Rose sliding into home $20
1975 Joe Morgan $30
1976 Morgan/Rose/Perez $10
1977 Morgan/Bench/Foster/others $12
1978 Pete Rose $10
1979 Bench/ Perez/Griffey/Foster $10
1980 Reds equipment $8
1981 Riverfront Stadium and baseball $8
1982 Binoculars on stadium seat $8
1983 Red player signing autographs $8
1984 Bats and baseball equipment $8
1985 Pete Rose/Ty Cobb . . . .$8-$10
1986 . . . . None issued
1987 Rose/Parker/E. Davis/others $12
1988 All-Star Game logo $10
1989 Baseball with Reds logo $10
1990 Red player with fans $10
1991 World Series trophy $10
1992 Equipment collage $10
1993 Barry Larkin's jersey $10
1994 Reds pinstriped cap $8
1995 Big Red Machine commemorative . . .$8
1996 Marge Schott and Schottzie $7
1997 J. Brantley/B. Larkin $8
1998 . . . . .None issued
1999 Reds cartoon mascot $8
2000 Ken Griffey Jr. $8

Red Sox

1951 Fenway Park $250
1952 Red Sox sliding into home $150
1953-1954 . . . . .None issued
1955 Red Sox fielder . . . .$115-$125
1956 Red Sox owners $75
1957 Fenway Park . . . .$75-$125
1958 Red Sox signing autograph $65
1959 Red Sox pitcher $65
1960 Gary Geiger $65
1961 Red Sox batter $65
1962 Carl Yastrzemski $65
1963 Johnny Pesky/Play at third base $50

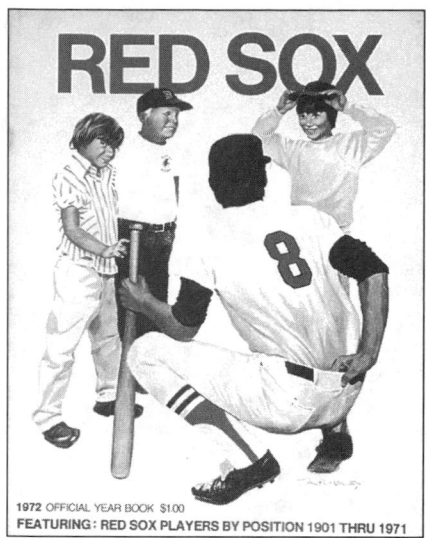

1972 OFFICIAL YEAR BOOK $1.00
FEATURING: RED SOX PLAYERS BY POSITION 1901 THRU 1971

1964 Fenway Park at night $50
1965 Dick Radatz . . . .$40-$45
1966 Fenway Park . . . .$35-$45
1967 Scott/ T. Conigliaro/ Yastrzemski . . . .$50-$75
1968 Yastrzemski/ Lonborg/D. Williams $40
1969 Fenway Park $40
1970 Lyle/Petrocelli/ Yastrzemski $40
1971 Scott/Yastrzemski/Petrocelli . . .$12-$15
1972 Carl Yastrzemski and fans . . . . . .$7-$12
1973 Carlton Fisk and fans $25
1974 C. Fisk/with T. Munson $10
1975 Foxx/Williams/Yastrzemski/Fisk . . .$10
1976 Fred Lynn $10
1977 Carl Yastrzemski . . . .$10-$15
1978 Jim Rice/Carl Yastrzemski . . . . .$12-$15
1979 Jim Rice $10
1980 Fred Lynn $8
1981 Rice/ Yastrzemski/Eckersley $10
1982 Yastrzemski/Evans/Rice/Lansford $10
1983 Carl Yastrzemski $10
1984 Jim Rice $7
1985 Tony Armas $6
1986 Wade Boggs $8
1987 R. Clemens and Fenway Park . . . .$7-$9
1988 Wade Boggs/Roger Clemens . . . .$7-$9
1989 Dwight Evans $10
1990 Mike Greenwell/Ellis Burks $10
1991 Pena/Clemens/Burks $10
1992 Clemens/Reardon/Viola $12
1993 Roger Clemens $10
1994-1998 . . . .$10
1999 Garciaparra/P. Martinez, others $9
2000 Garciaparra/P. Martinez $9

Rockies
1993 Hologram of Rockies emblem $10
1994-1999 . . . . .None issued

Royals
1969 Pitcher inside large R $25
1970 Piniella/Otis/others $10
1971 Piniella/Otis/others $10
1972 Catchers mitt with face $10
1973 Mayberry/ Splittorff/ others $10
1974 Otis, Mayberry, Splittorff $10
1975 Killebrew/McRae/Mayberry $15
1976-77 . . . . None issued
1978 Fans, Royals pitcher $12
1979 American League players $12
1981 Photo of A. L. Champions $12
1982 Royals action photos $12
1983 Bronze Royals statue . . . .$7-$10
1984 Royals jacket and equipment . . . .$7-$10

1989 Kansas City Royals Yearbook

1985 Division championship celebration
. . . .$10-$12
1986 Hand wearing World Series ring . .$5-$10
1987 Royals championship pennants . . .$5-$8
1988 Fireworks over Royals Stadium $10
1989 Royals' player locker $10
1990 Royals in action $10
1991 Scoreboard replay $10
1992 Newspaper format $10
1993 Memorabilia collage $10
1994 Caricatures of players $9
1995 Organization of year trophy $7
1996 Players celebrating $7
1997 25th anniv. of Kauffman Stadium $7
1998 Autographed baseballs $6
1999 George Brett in tuxedo $7
2000 Artwork of players in action $6

Detroit Tigers — Official 1958 YEAR BOOK 50¢ — Records and Pictures of All Tiger Players

Tigers
1934 Batter and Mascot head $1,000
1935-1938 . . . . .None issued
1939 "100 Years of Detroit baseball" $750
1940-1954 . . . . .None issued
1955 Catcher drawing $300
1956 . . . . None issued
1957 Tiger sliding into home . . . . .$150-$175
1958 Tiger Hall of Famers, with Cobb . . .$150
1959 Tiger batting and logo $150
1960 Tiger Stadium $100
1961 Tiger head and five baseballs . . . .$50-$100
1962 Tiger head and nine players . . .$75-$100

1963 Tiger head $100
1964 Tiger head $65
1965 Bill Freehan $65
1966 Willie Horton $65
1967 Denny McLain $45
1968 Al Kaline . . . .$40-$60
1969 World Series trophy $45
1970 Tiger hat/bats/baseballs $10
1971 Billy Martin/Kaline/Horton $20
1972 Mickey Lolich $10
1973 Tiger infielder in action $10
1974 Tiger sliding into home $10
1975 Ron LeFlore . . . .$12-$15
1976 75th Anniversary $15
1977 Fidrych/Staub/LeFlore . . . .$10-$12
1978 . . . .$8-$12
1979 A. Trammell/ L. Whitaker . . . . . .$8-$12
1980 Trammell/Whitaker/Morris/others
. . . .$8-$15
1981 Trammell/Whitaker/Morris/others
. . . .$7-$15
1982 Clubhouse photo with Gibson $12
1983 H. Greenberg/C. Gehringer $8
1984 Morris/Whitaker/Trammell/others
. . . .$10-$12
1985 World Championship trophy $8
1986 Sparky Anderson $10
1987 Tiger on top of baseball $8
1988 Tiger face, Eye of the Tiger $8
1989 Intend-a-Pennant $10
1990 Roaring into the '90s Tiger $8
1991 Whitaker/Trammell/Fielder/others . .$12
1992 Anderson/ Stengel $10
1993-1999 . . . . None issued

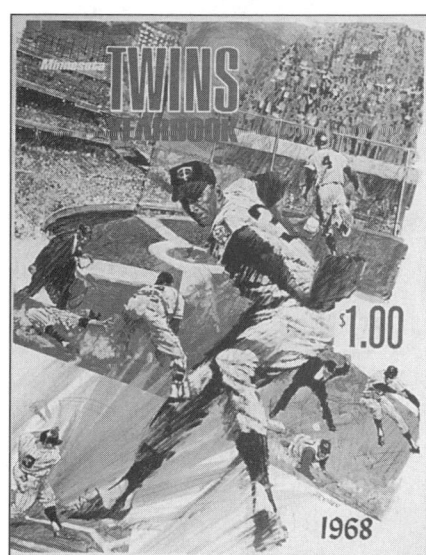

Minnesota TWINS YEARBOOK $1.00 1968

Twins
1961 Twins batters . . . .$125-$175
1962 Metropolitan Stadium $100
1963 Harmon Killebrew . . . .$75-$100
1964 Gloved hand and baseball $50
1965 Autographed Twins ball . . . . . .$40-$60
1966 Tony Oliva,/A.L. Champions $45
1967 Killebrew/Kaat/Oliva . . . .$25-$35
1968 Jim Kaat/Harmon Killebrew . . .$15-$25
1969 Killebrew/Carew/Oliva/others $20
1970 Rod Carew $20
1971 Carew/Killebrew/Oliva/others $20
1972 Tony Oliva, Harmon Killebrew $15
1973 Frank Quilici $15
1974 Rod Carew . . . .$20-$25
1975 Rod Carew $15

1976 Rod Carew $25
1977 Past Twins yearbooks $10
1978 Rod Carew $12
1979 Twins batting helmet $10
1980 Twins baseball cards $10
1981 20th Anniversary/Rod Carew . . .$8-$12
1982 Metrodome $8
1983-1984 . . . . None issued
1985 Yearbook/scorecard . . . .$6-$10
1986 25th Anniversary celebration . . . .$7-$10
1987 Twins uniforms $10
1988 World Champions celebration . . .$8-$10
1989 Viola/Puckett/Gaetti/Reardon $10
1990 Carew/Puckett/Oliva $10
1991 Uniform collage . . . .$5-$7
1992 World Series trophy $10
1993 . . . . None issued
1994 Twins greats/Killebrew/others $9
1996 Puckett, Molitor, others $7
1997 . . . . .None issued
1998 Molitor/Steinbach/others $9
1999 M. Lawton/R. Coomer/others $8
2000 40th Season/collage of all-time stars .$8

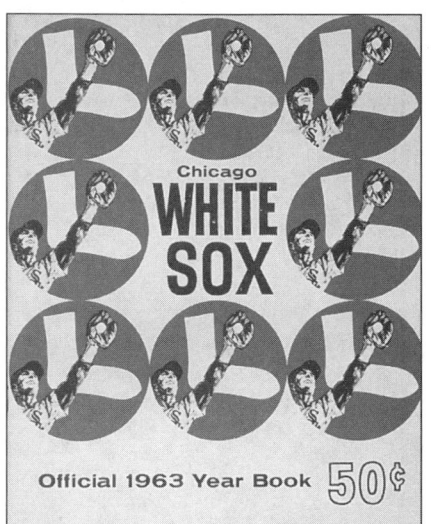

White Sox
1951 . . . .$250
1952 White Sox and year $150
1953 Comiskey Park $125
1954 White Sox batter $100
1955 White Sox batter $75
1956 White Sox sliding into home $75

1957 White Sox fielder . . . .$70-$75
1958 White Sox batter . . . .$60-$65
1959 White Sox mascot with hat $125
1960 White Sox fielding . . . .$50-$65
1961 White Sox pitching $50
1962 White Sox batting $35
1963 White Sox fielding . . . .$15-$25
1964 Fireworks at Comiskey Park . . .$30-$40
1965 White Sox uniform #80 . . . .$25-$35
1966 White Sox batter swinging $35
1967 White Sox in action $20
1968 White Sox batter at plate $20
1969 Tommy John $20
1970 White Sox in action $40
1971-1981 . . . . None issued
1982 LaRussa/Luzinski/Fisk $10
1983 All-Star Game with Fisk/others $10
1984 Hoyt/LaRussa/Kittle/Luzinski $10
1985 . . . . None issued
1986 Walker/Guillen/J. Davis/Baines $12
1987 . . . . None issued
1988 White Sox memorabilia $10
1989 . . . . None issued
1990 Comiskey Park . . . .$5-$6
1991 Comiskey Park $5
1992 Good Guys Wear Black $7
1993 Cooperstown Collection $7
1994 Frank Thomas $8
1995 1917 Championship team $8
1996 F. Thomas/R. Ventura, others $8
1997 F. Thomas/A. Belle $8
1998 Belle, Thomas/Manuel/others $7
2000 Player collage $7

Yankees
1950 Yankees emblem/pennants $300
1951 Balls on shelf . . . .$175-$250
1952 Yankee Stadium/action . . . . .$150-$200
1953 Yankees infielder $150
1954 Yankee with World Series bats $150
1955 Yankee player body $250
1956 Yankee sliding into home $250
1957 Bobby Richardson $250
1958 Yankee Stadium $150
1959 Yankee Stadium . . . .$125-$150
1960 Yankee Stadium, players . . . .$100-$125
1961 Yankee Stadium sketch $150
1962 Yankee Stadium sketch $75
1963 Yankee holding three bats $65
1964 Yogi Berra, Ralph Houk $65
1965 Photo inside Yankee Stadium $65
1966 Two autographed balls $50
1967 Mickey Mantle drawing $50
1968 Mantle/Stottlemyre/others $25

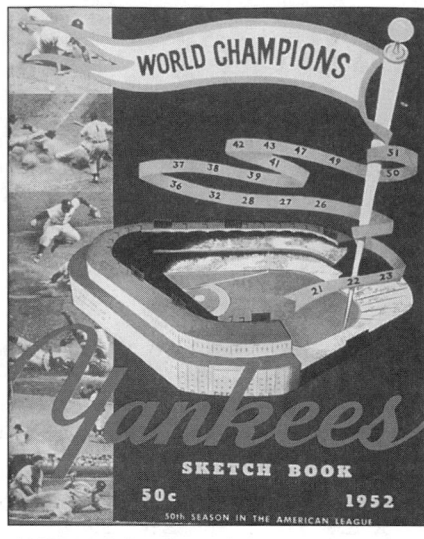

1969 Mantle/Stottlemyre/others $50
1970 Murcer/Stottlemyre/others $75
1971 Murcer/White/others $10
1972 Murcer/White/Stottlemyre $20
1973 Ruth/DiMaggio/Mantle/Gehrig $20
1974 B. Murcer/ T. Munson $20
1975 25th Annual w/past yearbooks $15
1976 Yankees Stadium $25
1977 Chris Chambliss $12
1978 World Series trophy $15
1979 World Series celebration . . . . . .$10-$15
1980 Yankee Stadium $8
1981 Yankees Big Apple $15
1982 Winfield/Guidry/Gossage/others $8
1983 Billy Martin $7
1984 Yankee greats $15
1985 Maris/Mantle/Ruth/Gehrig $8
1986 Yankees MVPs $6
1987 Gehrig/Mattingly/Mantle $10
1988 Mattingly/Clark/Randolph . . . . .$10-$15
1989 Yankees memorabilia $10
1990 Don Mattingly $12
1991 Pitcher vs. batter $10
1992 Don Mattingly $12
1993 Team photo $10
1994 125th Anniv. logo/Yankee greats $12
1995 Babe Ruth $12
1996 Mickey Mantle $12
1997 Championship ring $12
1998 Yankee Stadium at 75 years $12
1999 Players celebrating $10
2000 M. Rivera/J. Girardi, celebrating $10

Baseball Media Guides

Angels

Los Angeles Angels:
1961 Player emerging from baseball $75
1962 Baby with Angels logo $75
1963 Angels logo/Rigney/Haney $75
1964 Angels in action $75
1965 Dean Chance/Cy Young Award $40

California Angels:
1966 Anaheim Stadium $75
1967 League logos and Anaheim $40
1968 Anaheim Stadium and logo $30
1969 New look, A.L. West $30
1970 Press box and player . . . .$12-$15
1971 Four Angels in California . . . .$12-$15
1972 Del Rice . . . .$10-$12
1973 Nolan Ryan $20
1974 Anaheim Stadium $10
1975 Dick Williams $10
1976 Angels baseball cards $10
1977 Frank Tanana $12
1978 Tanana/Ryan/Rudi $15
1979 Anaheim Stadium . . . .$10-$12
1980 Don Baylor $7
1981 Angels equipment $6
1982 Angels logo $7
1983 Angels in action/R. Jackson $8
1984 Angels celebrating/R. Jackson $7
1985 . . . .$6
1986 DeCinces/Schofield/Downing $6
1987 Donnie Moore $6
1988 Wally Joyner/Brian Downing $10
1989 All-Star Game logo $10
1990 Angels stars/Joyner/Finley $10
1991 Pitcher in action $10
1992 Bryan Harvey $10
1993 Old Angels uniforms $10
1994 Tim Salmon $7
1995 Anaheim Stadium $6
1996 Anderson/Edmonds/Salmon $6

Anaheim Angels:
1997 New Anaheim Angels logo $6
1998 Edison Int'l. Field of Anaheim $6
1999 Gene Autry $7
2000 . . . .$6

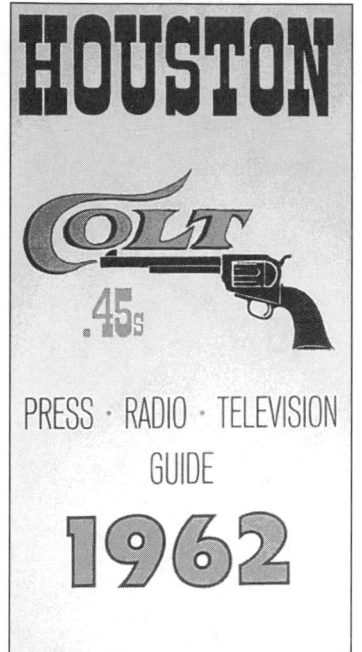

Astros

Houston Colt 45s:
1962 45s logo $150
1963 45s logo $100
1964 Player art $100

Houston Astros:
1965 New logo $75
1966 Catcher's mask $75
1967 Astroturf $50
1968 Astrodome art $40
1969 Baseball Anniversary $30
1970 Team roster $20
1971 Locker-room scene $20
1972 Ball/bat as pool cue $20
1973 Zodiac signs $15
1974 Big orange $10
1975 Equipment . . . .$8-$10
1976 Bicentennial logo . . . .$8-$10
1977 Player art . . . .$6-$7
1978 Art . . . .$6-$7
1979 Art . . . .$6-$7

1980 Baseball scene $6
1981 Team logo $6
1982 20th Anniversary in Houston . . . . . .$5-$6
1983 Nolan Ryan . . . .$5-$6
1984 Equipment . . . .$5-$6
1985 Jersey . . . .$4-$6
1986 Memorabilia $10
1987 Mike Scott/Hal Lanier $10
1988 Bill Doran $10
1989 Glenn Davis $10
1990 Team logo $10
1991 Helmet/bat/ball $10
1992 Craig Biggio/Pete Harnisch $10
1993 Luis Gonzalez/Jeff Bagwell $10
1994 Cap $9
1995 Jeff Bagwell $9
1996 Craig Biggio $9
1997 Bell/Biggio/Bagwell $9
1998 Biggio/Bagwell/Hampton celebrating $10
1999 35 Great Years patch $10
2000 J. Bagwell/C. Biggio $10

Athletics

Philadelphia Athletics
1928 Roster sheet $125
1929 Roster sheet $125
1930 Roster sheet (elephant) . . . .$75-$100
1931 Roster sheet (elephant) . . . .$75-$100
1932 Roster booklet (elephant) $125
1933 Roster booklet (elephant) $100
1934 Roster booklet (elephant) $100
1935 Roster booklet (elephant) $100
1936 Team mascot (elephant) . . . . . .$55-$75
1937 Team mascot (elephant) . . . . . .$50-$75
1938 Team mascot (elephant) . . . . . .$50-$75
1939 A's and elephant . . . .$50-$75
1940 Pennant and elephant . . . .$45-$75
1941 A's and baseball . . . .$45-$75
1942 . . . .$40-$45
1943 Team mascot with flag . . . .$40-$60
1944 Team mascot with flag . . . .$40-$60
1945 . . . .$40-$60
1946 Connie Mack . . . .$45-$60
1947 . . . .$35-$60
1948 Baseball and elephant . . . .$35-$60
1949 . . . .$60-$100
1950 Connie Mack . . . .$60-$100
1951 . . . .$60-$100
1952 Team mascot (elephant) . . . . . .$60-$100
1953 . . . .$60-$100
1954 Eddie Joost . . . .$60-$100

Kansas City Athletics:

1955 K.C. Municipal Stadium $75
1956 Elephant logo $75
1957 Elephant logo $75
1958 Elephant logo $75
1959 A's baseball $75
1960 Baseball and A's hat $75
1961 K.C. Municipal Stadium $75
1962 . . . .$75
1963 Player sliding/baseball $75
1964 1964 and A's logo $75
1965 1965 and A's logo $30
1966 1966 and A's logo $30
1967 1967 and A's logo $30

Oakland Athletics:

1968 Oakland Stadium/ball/logo $25
1969 Bando/Campaneris/Hunter $20
1970 Player at bat $20
1971 A's logo and 1971 . . . .$15
1972 A's logo and 1972 . . . .$15
1973 A's logo and 1973 . . . .$15
1974 A's logo and 1974 . . . .$15
1975 A's logo and 1975 . . . .$15
1976 A's logo and 1976 . . . .$8-$10
1977 A's logo and 1977 . . . .$7-$10
1978 A's logo and 1978 . . . .$7-$10
1979 A's logo and 1979 . . . .$6-$10
1980 A's logo and 1980 . . . .$6
1981 Billy Ball baseball . . . .$6-$7
1982 Running spikes $6
1983 A's jukebox $6
1984 Oakland sportswriters $6
1985 Athletics memorabilia $6
1986 . . . .$10
1987 All-Time Athletics team $10
1988 Batter hitting $10
1989 Canseco, Eckersley, Weiss $10
1990 World Series trophy $10
1991 Team memorabilia $10
1992 25th Anniversary/A's greats $10
1993 Dennis Eckersley $10
1994 Players $7
1995 A's logo $7
1996 Baseballs spelling out "A's" $7
1997 Mark McGwire swinging $9
1998 Action at second base $7
1999 Ben Grieve artwork $7
2000 . . . .$7

Blue Jays

1977 Toronto Exhibition Stadium $45
1978 Blue Jays pitcher $15
1979 Blue Jays in action $15
1980 Alfredo Griffin $10
1981 Blue Jays equipment $10
1982 Blue Jays in action/Bobby Cox $10
1983 Blue Jays equipment and hat $10
1984 Blue Jays in action $10
1985 Blue Jays logo $10
1986 Blue Jays 10th anniversary $10
1987 Bell, Barfield/Fernandez $10
1988 George Bell $10
1989 Blue Jays stars/McGriff $12
1990 Blue Jays/McGriff/Gruber $12
1991 Dave Stieb $10
1992 Roberto Alomar $12
1993 World Series trophy $10
1994 World Championship rings $7
1995 Blue Jays logo $7
1996 Joe Carter/Blue Jays logo $7
1997 Pat Henten holding Cy Young Award . . .$7
1998 Roger Clemens $7
1999 Carlos Delgado $7
2000 . . . .$7

Braves

Boston Braves:

1927 Roster sheet $125
1928 Roster sheet $100
1929 Roster sheet $100
1930 Roster sheet $100
1931 Roster booklet/Indian head $100
1932 Roster booklet/Indian head $100
1933 Roster booklet/Indian head $100
1934 Roster booklet/Indian head $100
1935 Roster booklet/Indian head $100
1936 Roster booklet $75
1937 Roster booklet $75
1938 Roster booklet/Bees Baseball $75
1939 Roster booklet $75
1940 Roster booklet/Casey Stengel $75
1941 Roster booklet/Casey Stengel $60
1942 Roster booklet/Indian head . . . . .$45-$60
1943 Roster booklet/Indian head . . . . .$40-$60
1944 Booklet/bat/flag/airplane . . . . . .$40-$60
1945 Roster booklet/Indian head . . . . .$40-$60
1946 Booklet/Billy Southworth . . . . . .$40-$60

1947 Booklet/Billy Southworth . . . . .$60-$100
1948 Roster booklet/Bob Elliott . . . . .$60-$100
1949 Booklet/ Billy Southworth . . . . .$50-$100
1950 Roster booklet/Braves logo . . . .$50-$100
1951 Roster booklet . . . .$50-$100
1952 Booklet/ baseball/Indian head . . . .$50-$100

Milwaukee Braves:

1953 State of Florida $125
1954 . . . .$125
1955 . . . .$125
1956 . . . .$125
1957 . . . .$100
1958 . . . .$100
1959 . . . .$100
1960 Pennant and Indian head $75
1961 Pennant and Indian head $75
1962 Pennant and Indian head $75
1963 Pennant and Indian head $75
1964 Aaron/Alou/Mathews/Spahn $75
1965 Felipe Alou/Bobby Bragan $75

Atlanta Braves:

1966 Player hitting $40
1967 Felipe Alou $40
1968 Hands gripping bat $30
1969 Players in action $30
1970 Hank Aaron $20
1971 Foot sliding into base $20
1972 Players in action . . . .$12-$15
1973 Players in action . . . .$12-$15
1974 Players in action $10
1975 Knit baseballs $10
1976 Dave Bristol . . . .$8-$10
1977 Braves hat . . . .$8-$10
1978 Atlanta-Fulton Co. Stadium $10
1979 Phil Niekro/All-Stars . . . .$10-$12
1980 Baseball and stadium $8
1981 Bob Horner/Dale Murphy . . . .$6-$8
1982 Joe Torre $6
1983 Bedrosian/Murphy/ Niekro/ Torre . . . .$6-$7
1984 Braves logo $6
1985 Dale Murph/Bruce Sutter . . . .$6-$7
1986 Bobby Cox/Chuck Tanner $6
1987 Braves uniform . . . .$5-$6
1988 Dale Murphy $8
1989 Gant/Glavine/Perry/Smith/Thomas . . .$10
1990 25th Anniversary logo $10
1991 Ron Gant/Dave Justice $10
1992 Greg Olson/John Smoltz $10

1993 N.L. Champions $10
1994 Maddux/McGriff/Glavine/Justice $7
1995 30th Season in Atlanta $7
1996 World Series Trophy $7
1997 Maddux/Smoltz/Glavine/jerseys $6
1998 Bobby Cox $5
1999 Hank Aaron, Home Run #715 . . . .$6
2000 . . . .$6

LOG BOOK, 1970

Press - Radio - TV Guide

Brewers

Seattle Pilots:
1969 Pilots logo . . . .$100-$125
1970 Pilots logo $100

Milwaukee Brewers
1971 Newspaper clipping . . . .$30-$40
1972 State of Wisconsin $10
1973 Del Crandall/George Scott $12
1974 Team mascot $10
1975 Team mascot . . . .$8-$10
1976 Baseball glove . . . .$8-$10

1977 Robin Yount $15
1978 Larry Hisle $10
1979 George Bamberger $10
1980 Cooper/Lezcano/Thomas $6
1981 Cooper/Oglivie/Yount . . . .$6-$8
1982 Rollie Fingers . . . .$7-$8
1983 Kuenn/Vuckovich/Yount . . . .$6-$8
1984 County Stadium $6
1985 Brewers uniform, #85 . . . .$6
1986 Brewers pitcher in action $6
1987 Ted Higuera $6
1988 Player running $6
1989 20th anniversary logo $10
1990 Player running $10
1991 Team logo $10
1992 Phil Garner $10
1993 Pat Listach $10
1994 New uniforms/25th Anniv. logo $7
1995 Bob Uecker with huge bat $8
1996 Outline of new Miller Park $6
1997 Jose Valentin $6
1998 Brewers logo $6
1999 . . . .$6

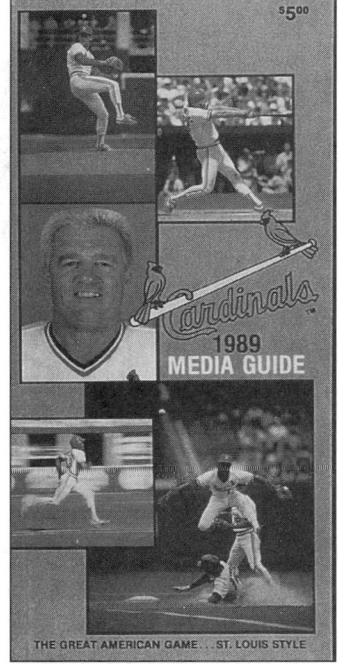

Cardinals

1926 Roster sheet $200
1927 Roster sheet $125
1928 Roster sheet $125
1929 Roster sheet $100
1930 Logo and 1930, sheet $115
1931 Roster sheet $115
1932 Logo and 1932/booklet $125
1933 Logo and 1933/booklet $125
1934 Logo and 1934/booklet $115
1935 Logo and 1935/booklet $100
1936 Logo and 1936/booklet $75
1937 Logo and 1937/booklet . . . .$50-$75
1938 Roster booklet . . . .$50-$75
1939 Name and year/booklet . . . .$50-$75
1940 Logo and 1940/booklet . . . .$45-$75
1941 Logo and 1941/booklet . . . .$45-$60
1942 Logo, Statue of Liberty . . . .$45-$65
1943 Flag and logo/booklet . . . .$40-$70
1944 Victory V and logo/booklet . . . . .$40-$70
1945 Logo and 1945/booklet . . . .$40-$60
1946 Roster booklet . . . .$35-$70
1947 Team logo, booklet . . . .$35-$60
1948 Logo and baseball/booklet . . . . . .$35-$60
1949 Logo and baseball/booklet . . . . . .$30-$60
1950 Baseball and players $150

1951 25th Anniv. of World Champs $125
1952 Team logo $125
1953 It's the Cardinals $125
1954 Team logo $125
1955 Team logo $125
1956 Team logo $100
1957 Team logo $100
1958 Team mascot $75
1959 Stan Musial $100
1960 Team mascot $75
1961 Broglio/ McDaniel/Sadecki/Simmons . . .$75
1962 Stan Musial $75
1963 Player in action $60
1964 Boyer/Groat/Javier/White $60
1965 Team logo $60
1966 Busch Stadium/team logo $60
1967 Busch Stadium $60
1968 World Series trophy $45
1969 Bob Gibson $45
1970 Joe Torre $20
1971 Bob Gibson/Joe Torre $25
1972 Red Schoendienst/Joe Torre $20
1973 Brock/Gibson/Simmons/Torre $20
1974 Cardinals uniform and hat . . . . . .$10-$15
1975 Lou Brock and team logo . . . . . .$10-$15
1976 Busch Stadium . . . .$10-$15
1977 Lou Brock/Vern Rapp . . . .$6-$7
1978 Cardinals equipment . . . .$6-$7
1979 St. Louis Arch $6
1980 Keith Hernandez . . . .$6-$8
1981 Whitey Herzog . . . .$6-$8
1982 Whitey Herzog $7
1983 World Series celebration $6
1984 Player running . . . .$5-$6
1985 Busch Stadium/St. Louis Arch $10
1986 Coleman/Herzog/McGee $10
1987 Whitey Herzog/former managers $10
1988 N.L. Champions celebrate $10
1989 Action photos/Whitey Herzog $10
1990 Team logo $8
1991 Joe Torre $10
1992 Todd Zeile $10
1993 Team logo $10
1994 Bats/home plate $7
1995 Cardinals Mascot $6
1996 Tony La Russa $6
1997 Busch Stadium $6
1998 Mark McGwire $8
1999 . . . .$7
2000 Cardinals jerseys $7

Cubs

1927 The year, booklet $175
1928 The year, booklet $150
1929 The year, booklet $150
1930 The year, booklet $100
1931 Rogers Hornsby, booklet $100
1932 Rogers Hornsby, booklet $125
1933 Team mascot, booklet $100
1934 Team mascot, booklet $100
1935 Team mascot, booklet $115
1936 Team mascot, booklet $75
1937 Team mascot throwing/booklet $75
1938 Team mascot hitting/booklet $85
1939 Mascot with pennant/booklet $65
1940 Roster booklet $65
1941 Jimmy Wilson, booklet $65
1942 Roster booklet $65
1943 Roster booklet $65
1944 Roster booklet $65
1945 Roster booklet $75
1946 Charlie Grimm, booklet $65
1947 Team mascot, booklet $65
1948 Roster booklet $100
1949 Roster booklet $100
1950 Roster booklet $100
1951 Roster booklet $100
1952 . . . .$100
1953 . . . .$100

CHICAGO CUBS

1941 PLAYER ROSTER

1954 . . . .$75
1955 . . . .$75
1956 . . . .$75
1957 . . . .$75
1958 Team logo $75
1959 Team logo $75
1960 Team logo $50
1961 Team logo $50
1962 Team logo $50
1963 Team logo $50
1964 Team logo $50
1965 Team logo $50
1966 Team logo $30
1967 Team logo $30
1968 Team logo $30
1969 Team logo $30
1970 Team logo . . . .$15-$20
1971 Team logo . . . .$15-$20
1972 Team logo $15
1973 Team logo . . . .$10-$15
1974 Team logo $10
1975 Team logo . . . .$8-$10
1976 Team logo . . . .$8-$10
1977 Team logo . . . .$7-$10
1978 Team logo . . . .$7-$10
1979 Team logo . . . .$6-$10
1980 Team logo . . . .$6-$7
1981 Team logo . . . .$6-$7
1982 Team logo . . . .$5-$7
1983 Wrigley Field, celebration . . . .$5-$7
1984 Autographed baseballs $6
1985 Frey, Green, Sandberg, Sutcliffe . . .$10
1986 Cubs second baseman (Sandberg) $12
1987 Billy Williams $10
1988 Andre Dawson $10
1989 Wrigley Field $10
1990 Wrigley Field $10
1991 Ryne Sandberg $12
1992 Wrigley Field $10
1993 Wrigley Field $10
1994 Grace/Sandberg/Sosa $7
1995 Collage $5
1996 Brian McRae $5
1997 Sammy Sosa $6
1998 Ball exploding through stat sheet $7
1999 Sammy Sosa, Kerry Wood $7
2000 Cubs greats $7

Devil Rays
1998 Artwork inside outline of Devil Ray $10
1999 . . . .
2000 . . . .

Diamondbacks
1998 Mountain background, jersey no. 98 . . .$8
1999 Interior of Bank One Ballpark $7
2000 . . . .$7

Dodgers
Brooklyn Dodgers:
1927 Roster sheet $125
1928 Name and 1928/booklet $150
1929 Name and 1929/booklet $100
1930 Name and 1930/booklet $100
1931 Name and 1931/booklet $100
1932 Name and 1932/booklet $100
1933 Logo and 1933/booklet $100
1934 Logo and 1934/booklet $100
1935 Logo and 1935/booklet $100
1936 Logo and 1936/booklet . . . .$55-$75
1937 Logo and 1937/booklet . . . .$55-$75
1938 Logo and 1938/booklet . . . .$50-$75
1939 100th anniversary logo . . . .$50-$75
1940 50th anniversary in Brooklyn . . . .$45-$75
1941 Team airplane $85
1942 V logo . . . .$45-$65
1943 Roster booklet . . . .$40-$65
1944 Roster booklet . . . .$40-$65
1945 Roster booklet . . . .$40-$65
1946 Roster booklet . . . .$35-$65
1947 Roster booklet . . . .$35-$70
1948 Roster booklet . . . .$35-$65
1949 Roster booklet $150
1950 The Bum $125
1951 The Bum $125
1952 . . . .$125
1953 The Bum $125
1954 . . . .$125
1955 Walter Alston $125
1956 Walter Alston $100
1957 Walter Alston $100

Los Angeles Dodgers
1958 Walter Alston $75
1959 L.A. Coliseum $75
1960 Dodger Stadium drawing $30
1961 Dodger Stadium $30
1962 Cartoon and airplane $50
1963 T. Davis/Drysdale/Koufax/Wills $50
1964 Players celebrating $40
1965 Championship pennants $40
1966 Mascot climbing mountains $40
1967 Mascot juggling crowns $40
1968 Walter Alston $30
1969 100th anniversary $30
1970 W. Davis/ Osteen/ Singer/ Sizemore $30
1971 Dodgers in action $20
1972 Dodgers in action $20
1973 Dodgers in action $10
1974 Dodgers in action $10
1975 Steve Garvey $12
1976 Buckner/ Cey/ Garvey/ Lopes/ Sutton $14
1977 Tom Lasorda . . . .$9-$12
1978 Baker/ Cey/ Garvey/ Smith . . . .$9-$14
1979 Dodger Stadium $6
1980 Team logo $6
1981 1980 highlights $7
1982 World Series trophy/Howe/Yeager $8
1983 Sax, Guerrero, Valenzuela $8
1984 Fireworks over Dodger Stadium . . . .$5-$6
1985 Bill Russell . . . .$6-$7
1986 Player swinging bat . . . .$4-$6
1987 Dodger Stadium $10
1988 Baseballs $10
1989 World Series trophy $10
1990 100th anniversary caps and pins $10
1991 Name and 1991 . . . .$10
1992 Team stadium $10
1993 Eric Karros $10
1994 M. Piazza/E. Karros $7
1995 Dodger Stadium $6
1996 Karros/Piazza/Mondesi/Nomo $6
1997 Rookies of the Year $6
1998 40th year anniversary logo $6
1999 Davey Johnson $6
2000 Memorabilia $6

Expos
1969 Team logo $75
1970 Jarry Park $40
1971 Baseball $20
1972 Action photos, Jarry Park $20
1973 Montreal photos . . . .$10-$12
1974 Gene Mauch $20
1975 Players in action . . . .$8-$10
1976 Players in action . . . .$8-$10

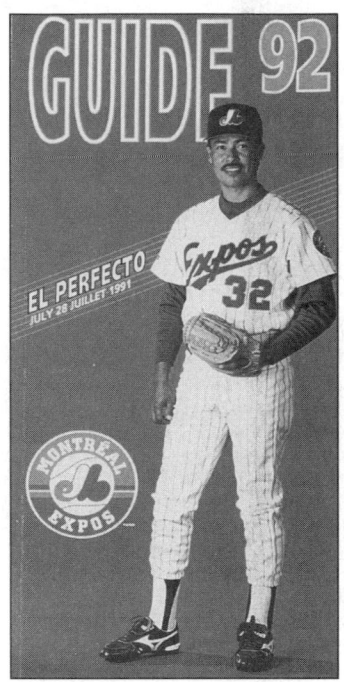

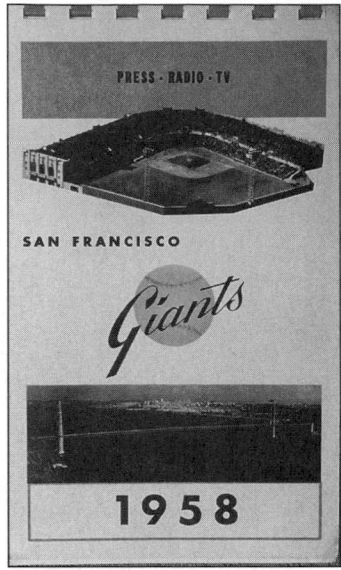

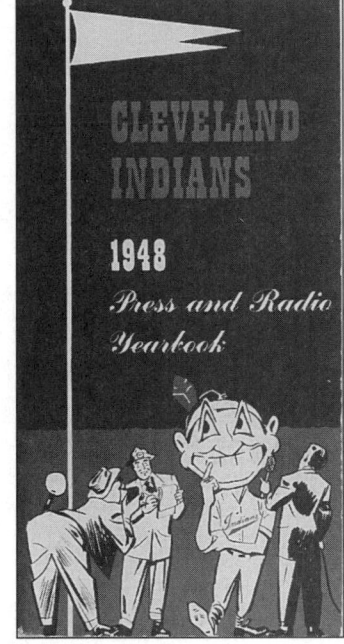

1977 Cash/McEnaney/Perez/D. Williams $6
1978 Gary Carter/Andre Dawson $10
1979 Team logo $6
1980 Locker with uniform $6
1981 Pennant $6
1982 Players in action $6
1983 Hands holding a bat $6
1984 Team hats $6
1985 Olympic Stadium with dome $6
1986 Baseball and team logo $6
1987 Olympic Stadium with dome $10
1988 20th anniversary bat $10
1989 Hands giving high-five $10
1990 Team logo $10
1991 Team logo $10
1992 Dennis Martinez $10
1993 25th anniversary $10
1994 New Expos logo $7
1995 Felipe Alou $5
1996 Autographed ball $5
1997 Baseball scene $5
1998 30 years anniversary logo $6
1999 . . . .$6
2000 Vladimir Guerrero $6

Giants

New York Giants:
1927 Name and 1927/booklet $150
1928 Name and 1928/booklet $100
1929 Name and 1929/booklet $100
1930 Name and 1930/booklet $100
1931 Name and 1931/booklet $100
1932 Name and 1932/booklet $100
1933 Name and 1933/booklet $125
1934 Name and 1934/booklet . . . .$60-$100
1935 Name and 1935/booklet . . . .$60-$100
1936 Name and 1936 . . . .$55-$85
1937 Name and 1937 . . . .$55-$85
1938 Name and 1938 . . . .$50-$75
1939 New York World's Fair . . . .$50-$75
1940 Name and 1940 . . . .$45-$75
1941 Name and 1941 . . . .$45-$60
1942 Name and 1942 . . . .$45-$60
1943 Name and 1943 . . . .$40-$60
1944 Name and 1944 . . . .$40-$60
1945 Name and 1945 . . . .$40-$60
1946 Name and 1946 . . . .$150
1947 Baseball with 1947 . . . .$150
1948 Baseball with 1948 . . . .$150
1949 Baseball with 1949 . . . .$150

1950 Polo Grounds $125
1951 Team logo $125
1952 Leo Durocher, a Giant $125
1953 Polo Grounds $125
1954 Team logo $125
1955 The Giant $125
1956 Team hat $125
1957 Team hat $125

San Francisco Giants:
1958 Candlestick Park drawing $150
1959 Players in action $100
1960 Team logo $80
1961 Giants in action $80
1962 Players in action $70
1963 Candlestick Park $70
1964 Candlestick Park $70
1965 Candlestick Park $70
1966 Baseball and team logo $65
1967 Team logo $45
1968 Team logo $45
1969 Team logo $45
1970 Willie Mays/Willie McCovey $25
1971 Year of the Fox $20
1972 Best in the West $20
1973 Candlestick Park $15
1974 Matthews, Bryant, Bonds $15
1975 Team logo $15
1976 Team logo . . . .$8-$10
1977 Joe Altobelli/John Montefusco . . . . .$7-$10
1978 Players in action $6
1979 Blue/Clark/Giants management $6
1980 On deck circle with team logo $6
1981 Golden Gate Bridge $6
1982 25th anniversary in city $6
1983 Team logo $6
1984 Team logo $6
1985 Team logo $6
1986 Team logo $6
1987 Team logo $6
1988 Team logo $10
1989 Team logo $10
1990 Team logo $10
1991 Team logo $10
1992 Team uniform $10
1993 Team logo $10
1994 Dusty Baker $7
1995 B. Bonds/M. Williams $6
1996 B. Bonds/M. Williams $6
1997 40 years in San Francisco $6
1998 J. T. Snow/B. Mueller/B. Johnson $6
1999 "Tell it Goodbye" (Candlestick)" $6
2000 Pacific Bell Park $12

Indians
1927 Roster sheet $125
1928 Roster sheet $100
1929 Roster sheet $100
1930 Roster sheet $100
1931 Roster sheet $100
1932 Roster booklet $100
1933 Roster booklet $100
1934 Roster booklet $100
1935 Roster booklet $100
1936 Chief and 1936/booklet . . . .$55-$75
1937 Chief and 1937/booklet . . . .$50-$75
1938 Chief and 1938/booklet . . . .$50-$75
1939 Chief and 1939/booklet . . . .$50-$75
1940 Chief and 1940/booklet . . . .$50-$75
1941 Chief and 1941/booklet . . . .$50-$60
1942 Lou Boudreau/booklet . . . .$55-$60
1943 Lou Boudreau/booklet . . . .$50-$60
1944 Mascot and year/booklet . . . .$40-$60
1945 Mascot and year/booklet . . . .$40-$60
1946 Lou Boudreau/booklet . . . .$45-$60
1947 Team mascot/booklet . . . .$35-$60
1948 Team mascot with media . . . . .$100-$150
1949 Team mascot $100
1950 Team mascot at bat $100
1951 Team mascot $100
1952 Garcia/Wynn/Lemon/Feller $100
1953 Press box and media $100
1954 Al Rosen $100
1955 Mascot $100
1956 Mascot $100
1957 Kirby Farrell $75
1958 Bobby Bragan, Frank Lane $75
1959 Rocky Colavito $75
1960 Tito Francona $75
1961 Jim Perry $75
1962 Team mascot $75
1963 Team uniform #20 . . . .$75
1964 Team mascot $75
1965 Team mascot $35
1966 Baseball with feather $35
1967 Cleveland Stadium $30
1968 Autographed baseball $30
1969 100th anniversary, mascot $30
1970 Team mascot $20
1971 Team hat, feather $20
1972 Players in action $20
1973 Team logo $10
1974 Team logo $10
1975 Frank Robinson . . . .$8-$10
1976 Baseball with feather . . . .$8-$10

1977 Player hitting . . . .$6-$7
1978 Baseball/logo/glove . . . .$6-$7
1979 Team logo . . . .$6-$7
1980 Fireworks over stadium . . . .$6-$7
1981 Team logo . . . .$6-$7
1982 Cleveland Stadium . . . .$5-$7
1983 Team logo . . . .$5-$7
1984 Team memorabilia . . . .$5-$6
1985 Bert Blyleven/Andre Thornton $7
1986 Past team uniforms . . . .$4-$6
1987 Joe Carter $7
1988 Indians uniform #88 . . . .$6
1989 Candiotti/Farrell/Jones/Swindell $10
1990 90 Years of Cleveland baseball $10
1991 Jacoby/Jones/Alomar $10
1992 60 years at Cleveland Stadium $10
1993 Memorabilia collage $10
1994 A. Belle/C. Baerga/K. Lofton $7
1995 Jacobs Field at night $7
1996 Player celebration $7
1997 Cleveland city outline $7
1998 Player celebration collage $7
1999 M. Hargrove/Thome/others $6
2000 . . . .$6

1986 MEDIA GUIDE

Mariners

1977 Kingdome $30
1978 Baseball with team logo $10
1979 Kingdome $10
1980 Mariners equipment $6
1981 Maury Wills $7
1982 Team logo $6
1983 Gaylord Perry/team equipment $8
1984 Team logo $6
1985 Beattie/Davis/Henderson/Langston $7
1986 Team memorabilia $6
1987 Team logo $6
1988 Team bat $10
1989 Kingdome/baseball/logo $10
1990 A.L. baseballs/team logo $10
1991 Highlights $10
1992 Team logo $10
1993 Team logo/Kingdome $10
1994 Mariners cap $7
1995 Mariners logo $5
1996 A.L. West Championship $6
1997 Griffey Jr./A. Rodriguez $7
1998 Griffey Jr. holding trophy $7

1999 Logo/grass background $7
2000 Rodriguez/Sasaki/others $7

Marlins

1993 Logo/player $20
1994 Mascot $10
1995 Logo $15
1996 Mascot $10
1997 Logo $10
1998 Players celebrating/trophy $6
1999 A. Fernandez/others $6
2000 . . . .$6

Mets

1962 First year $500
1963 Mr. Met/Stadium $150
1964 Shea Stadium $100
1965 Mr. Met $100
1966 Mass media $100

1967 Donald Grant/George Weiss $100
1968 Gil Hodges/crowd shot $100
1969 Gil Hodges $100
1970 World Series ticket/action photos $75
1971 Scoreboard $50
1972 Tom Seaver $50
1973 Yogi Berra and pennant $50
1974 N.L. Champs flag $50
1975 Mets general managers $20
1976 Joe Frazier $20
1977 Mets uniform #77 . . . .$20
1978 Team logo/hat/glove $20
1979 Willie Mays $15
1980 Team logo $15
1981 New York City/baseball $15
1982 George Bamberger locker $15
1983 Tom Seaver/others $15
1984 Davey Johnson $15
1985 Tom Seaver/Mets stars $15
1986 R. Craig/Gooden/Shea Stadium $15
1987 World Series ring $15
1988 Shea 25th anniversary $15
1989 Frank Cashen/Howard Johnson $15
1990 Howard Johnson $15
1991 Bud Harrelson $15
1992 Bonilla/Murray/Saberhagen/Torborg $15
1993 Team uniform #93 . . . .$15
1994 Dwight Gooden $7
1995 Shea Stadium $7
1996 Organization of the Year Trophy $6
1997 Hundley/Franco/Gilkey $6
1998 Valentine/Ordone/others $6
1999 Piazza/Henderson/Ventura/others $6
2000 . . . .$8

Orioles

St. Louis Browns

1927 Name and 1927/booklet $150
1928 Name and 1928/booklet $125
1929 Roster booklet $125
1930 Roster booklet $125
1931 Sportsmans Park/booklet $125
1932 Sportsmans Park/booklet . . . . . .$70-$100
1933 Sportsmans Park/booklet . . . . . .$70-$100
1934 Roster booklet . . . .$65-$100
1935 Roster booklet . . . .$65-$100
1936 Rogers Hornsby/booklet . . . .$75-$80

1937 Team logo, booklet . . . . $60-$75
1938 Roster booklet . . . . $60-$75
1939 Roster booklet . . . . $60-$75
1940 Fred Haney/booklet . . . . $55-$75
1941 Statue and 1941/booklet . . . . $55-$60
1942 Roster booklet . . . . $55-$60
1943 Team logo/booklet . . . . $50-$60
1944 Roster booklet . . . . $70-$150
1945 . . . . $150
1946 Team logo/booklet $150
1947 Baseball/logo $150
1948 Meet the Brownies $150
1949 . . . . $150
1950 Team logo $150
1951 Team logo $150
1952 Team mascot $150
1953 Team mascot $150

Baltimore Orioles

1954 Team mascot $125
1955 Team mascot $100
1956 Team mascot $100
1957 Team mascot $100
1958 Team mascot $100
1959 Team mascot $100
1960 Team mascot $75
1961 Team mascot $75
1962 Team mascot $75
1963 Team mascot $75
1964 Team mascot $75
1965 Hank Bauer $40
1966 Team mascot $40
1967 Dave McNally/Brooks Robinson $50
1968 Memorial Stadium $40
1969 View from press box $30
1970 Orioles dugout $25
1971 World Series celebration $20
1972 Team mascot with pennants $15
1973 Player face drawing $10
1974 Orioles award winners $10
1975 Players in action $10
1976 Team logo $10
1977 Palmer/L. May/Belanger $15
1978 Earl Weaver . . . . $10-$12
1979 25th anniversary hats $10
1980 Players celebrating $6
1981 Orioles locker room $6
1982 Team logo and mascot $6
1983 Frank and Brooks Robinson $8
1984 World Series celebration $6
1985 Bumbry, Palmer, Singleton $7
1986 Eddie Murray, Cal Ripken $8
1987 Cal Ripken Sr. $6
1988 Team logo $10
1989 New team uniforms $10
1990 1989 highlights $10
1991 Team stadium drawing $10
1992 Team stadium $10
1993 Team stadium $10
1994 150 Years of Baseball $7
1995 Cal Ripken Jr. $20
1996 Davey Johnson $6
1997 Cartoon $6
1998 . . . . $6
1999 . . . . $6
2000 . . . . $6

Padres

1969 Preston Gomez, stadium $75
1970 Jack Murphy Stadium $15
1971 Jack Murphy Stadium $15
1972 Padres vs. Dodgers/July 3, 1971 . . . . $15
1973 Nate Colbert $15
1974 Player hitting $10
1975 Players in action $8
1976 Randy Jones $8
1977 Randy Jones/Butch Metzger $7
1978 Batter, pitcher in action $6

1993 MEDIA GUIDE

1979 Roger Craig, Padres stars $6
1980 Jerry Coleman/Dave Winfield $8
1981 Frank Howard/stadium $7
1982 Dick Williams $6
1983 Padres memorabilia $6
1984 Team logo/Ray Kroc memorabilia $10
1985 N.L. Champions trophy $10
1986 Team logo $10
1987 Larry Bowa $10
1988 Tony Gwynn/Benito Santiago $10
1989 Team logo/stadium $10
1990 Players in action $10
1991 Padres uniform/ball/glove $10
1992 All-Star Game $10
1993 Gary Sheffield/Fred McGriff $10
1994 San Diego $7
1995 Gwynn/Caminiti/Finley $7
1996 Tony Gwynn $7
1997 Pitchers $7
1998 Padres players in the community $10
1999 . . . . $7
2000 . . . . $7

Phillies

1927 Roster sheet $125
1928 Roster sheet $100
1929 Roster sheet $100
1930 Team logo, sheet . . . . $75-$100
1931 Roster sheet . . . . $70-$100
1932 Team logo/booklet . . . . $65-$125
1933 Phillies golden anniversary . . . . $60-$100
1934 Team logo/booklet . . . . $60-$100
1935 Team logo/booklet . . . . $55-$100
1936 Team logo/booklet . . . . $55-$75
1937 Team logo/booklet . . . . $50-$75
1938 Roster booklet . . . . $50-$75
1939 Roster booklet . . . . $50-$75
1940 Roster booklet . . . . $45-$75
1941 Player hitting/booklet . . . . $45-$60
1942 Soldier with crossed bats . . . . $45-$60
1943 Roster booklet . . . . $40-$60
1944 Roster booklet . . . . $40-$60
1945 Roster booklet . . . . $40-$60
1946 Logo/Shibe Park/booklet . . . . $35-$60
1947 Logo/Shibe Park/booklet . . . . $35-$60
1948 Logo/Shibe Park/booklet . . . . $35-$60
1949 Roster booklet . . . . $30-$70
1950 . . . . $150

1992 MEDIA GUIDE

1951 . . . . $30-$50
1952 Shibe Park . . . . $25-$50
1953 Player hitting . . . . $25-$50
1954 Robin Roberts . . . . $35-$50
1955 Get Set To Go In '55 . . . . $20-$50
1956 Crowd photo . . . . $20-$40
1957 Crowd photo . . . . $20-$40
1958 Crowd photo . . . . $20-$40
1959 Team logo . . . . $20-$40
1960 Team logo . . . . $20-$40
1961 Team logo . . . . $15-$40
1962 . . . . $15-$20
1963 . . . . $15-$20
1964 Team hat $150
1965 Team hat $100
1966 Team hat $100
1967 Team hat $75
1968 Team hat $75
1969 Team hat $50
1970 Phillies P $50
1971 Frank Luchessi $35
1972 Team logo $35
1973 Steve Carlton/Cy Young Award $25
1974 Players in action $20
1975 Players in action $20
1976 Players in action $15
1977 Division champs pennant $15
1978 Fireworks over stadium $15
1979 Team logo $15
1980 Team logo/baseball $10
1981 World Series trophy $10
1982 Basket of baseballs $10
1983 100th anniversary logo $10
1984 N.L. Championship trophy $10
1985 Hands holding bat $10
1986 Home plate with team logo $10
1987 Mike Schmidt, trophies $15
1988 Steve Bedrosian, Mike Schmidt $15
1989 Nick Leyva/Lee Thomas $15
1990 Ashburn/Carlton/Roberts/Schmidt $15
1991 Catcher's mask, baseball $15
1992 Memorabilia collage $15
1993 Phillies league leaders $15
1994 Jim Fregosi $7
1995 Silver Anniversary of stadium logo $6
1996 All-Star Game logo $6
1997 Terry Francona $6
1998 Scott Rolen/Curt Schilling $6

1999 ....$6
2000 ....$6

Pirates

1927 Roster sheet $175
1928 Roster sheet $100
1929 Roster sheet $125

1930 Pirate and 1930, sheet $100
1931 Pirate and 1931, sheet $100
1932 Pirate and 1932, booklet $125
1933 Pirate and 1933, booklet ......$60-$100
1934 Pirate and 1934, booklet ......$60-$100
1935 Pirate and 1935, booklet ......$55-$100
1936 Pirate and 1936 ....$55-$75
1937 Pirate and 1937 ....$50-$75
1938 Pirate and 1938 ....$50-$75
1939 100th anniversary, Pirate ......$50-$75
1940 Pirate and 1940 ....$45-$75
1941 Pirate and 1941 ....$45-$60
1942 Pirate, Remember Pearl Harbor .....$45-$60
1943 Pirate, Buy War Bonds, Stamps .....$40-$60
1944 Pirate and 1944 ....$40-$60
1945 Pirate and 1945 ....$40-$60
1946 Pirate, Buy Victory Bonds ....$35-$60
1947 Billy Herman ....$40-$60
1948 William Meyer ....$40-$60
1949 40th anniversary ....$30-$60
1950 Baseballs ....$30-$50
1951 Logo and 1951 ....$125
1952 Baseball and 1952 ....$125
1953 Fred Haney $125
1954 Honus Wagner statue $125
1955 Baseball diamond and 1955 ....$125
1956 Pirate cartoon $125
1957 Pirate cartoon $100
1958 Danny Murtaugh $100
1959 Pirate cartoon $100
1960 Pirate cartoon $75
1961 Pirate cartoon $75
1962 Pitcher $75
1963 Baseballs $75
1964 Logo and 1964 ....$60
1965 Harry Walker $60
1966 Pirate cartoon $60
1967 Pirate cartoon $45
1968 Larry Shepard and coaches $45
1969 100th anniversary, Forbes $30

1970 Three Rivers Stadium model $30
1971 Danny Murtaugh $25
1972 World Series celebration $25
1973 Clemente memorial $35
1974 Three Rivers Stadium $10
1975 Championship Stars, logo $10
1976 Rennie Stennett $10
1977 Players in action $6
1978 Three Pirates $6
1979 Team uniform $10
1980 Willie Stargell $9
1981 Team logo $6
1982 Team hat $6
1983 Team logo $6
1984 Bill Madlock $6
1985 Tony Pena $6
1986 Three Rivers Stadium $10
1987 100th anniversary logo $10
1988 Pirates memorabilia $10
1989 Bonilla/LaValliere/Van Slyke $10
1990 Bonds/Bonilla/Drabek/Van Slyke $10
1991 N.L. Champions/logo $10
1992 Doug Drabek/Don Slaught $10
1993 Jim Leyland $10
1994 Three Rivers Stadium $7
1995 Artwork of pirates $6
1996 Cap $6
1997 Uniforms/caps/logos $6
1998 Previous Pirates media guides $6
1999 Three bats $6
2000 ....$6

Rangers

1972 Team logo $30
1973 Burke/Herzog/Short $20
1974 Billy Martin $15

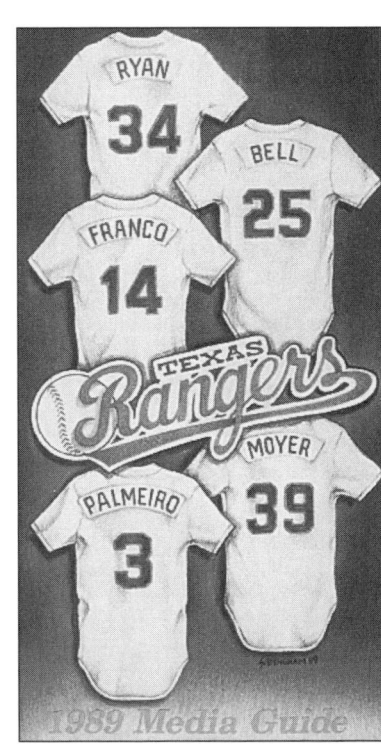

1975 Hargrove, Jenkins, Martin $15
1976 Toby Harrah, old-timers $6
1977 Team equipment/hat $6
1978 Billy Hunter $6
1979 Baseball and 1979 ....$6
1980 Rangers catcher $6
1981 Fireworks over scoreboard $6
1982 Baseball with logo $6
1983 Baseball glove $6
1984 Buddy Bell/others $6
1985 Team hat $6

1986 Arlington Stadium $6
1987 Bobby Valentine $10
1988 Team logo and baseball $10
1989 Rangers uniforms $10
1990 Home plate with team logo $10
1991 Nolan Ryan $15
1992 Julio Franco $10
1993 Arlington Stadium $10
1994 Jersey $7
1995 Ballpark at Arlington $5
1996 Ballpark at Arlington $5
1997 Juan Gonzalez $6
1998 Ivan Rodriguez $6
1999 J. Gonzalez/multiple A.L. MVP winners ...$6
2000 Painting of Pudge Rodriguez $6

Reds

1927 Roster sheet $125
1928 Roster sheet $100
1929 Roster sheet $100

1930 Team logo/sheet ....$65-$100
1931 Team logo/sheet ....$60-$100
1932 Team logo/booklet ....$60-$100
1933 Roster booklet ....$60-$100
1934 Cincinnati Reds/booklet ....$55-$100
1935 Team logo/booklet ....$55-$100
1936 Team logo/booklet ....$55-$75
1937 Team logo/booklet ....$50-$75
1938 Bill McKechnie/booklet ....$50-$75
1939 1869 Reds ....$50-$85
1940 Team logo ....$45-$85
1941 Baseball, champions pennant $125
1942 Team logo/eagle $125
1943 Team logo/eagle $125
1944 Team logo/hitter $125
1945 Baseball/eagle $125
1946 Catcher and batter $125
1947 Baseball and eagle $125
1948 Team logo/batter $125
1949 City, team logo $125
1950 Cartoon sportswriter $100
1951 75th anniversary logo $100
1952 Team logo/eagle $100
1953 ....$100
1954 ....$100
1955 Team mascot $100
1956 Birdie Tebbetts $100

1957 Schedule $100
1958 Team mascot batting $100
1959 Mayo Smith $100
1960 Fred Hutchinson $75
1961 Fred Hutchinson/Bill DeWitt $75
1962 Team mascot $75
1963 Team mascot $75
1964 Team mascot $75
1965 Team mascot $75
1966 Team mascot $75
1967 . . . .$75
1968 . . . .$40
1969 100th anniversary logo $40
1970 N.L. hats $30
1971 . . . .$30
1972 Baseball field $20
1973 Sparky Anderson $20
1974 Jack Billingham/Don Gullett $15
1975 Johnny Bench $15
1976 Joe Morgan/MVP Trophy $20
1977 Johnny Bench $20
1978 George Foster $15
1979 John McNamara $15
1980 Riverfront Stadium $8
1981 Players in action $8
1982 Team uniform $8
1983 Russ Nixon $8
1984 Team logo $8
1985 Riverfront Stadium $8
1986 Pete Rose $10
1987 N.L. logos $8
1988 All-Star Game logo $8
1989 Autographed bats $8
1990 Lou Piniella $10
1991 World Series trophy $10
1992 Equipment $10
1993 Reds locker $10
1994 Team logo $7
1995 Riverfront Stadium $5
1996 Knight/Morris/Boone $5
1997 Larkin/Sanders/Boone $5
1998 Reds logo on uniform/cap $5
1999 "Cincinnati" on uniform $5
2000 . . . .$6

Red Sox

1927 Roster sheet $125
1928 Roster sheet $100
1929 Roster sheet $100
1930 Roster sheet $100
1931 Roster sheet $100
1932 Roster sheet $100
1933 Roster sheet $100
1934 Roster booklet $150
1935 Roster booklet $100
1936 Roster booklet $75
1937 Roster booklet $75
1938 Roster booklet $75
1939 Jimmie Foxx/ booklet . . . .$65-$70
1940 Team logo, booklet . . . .$45-$65
1941 Fenway Park, booklet . . . .$45-$60
1942 Baseball bats &1942/ booklet . . . . .$45-$60
1943 Tufts College batting cage . . . .$40-$60
1944 Roster booklet . . . .$40-$60
1945 Name and 1945/ booklet . . . . . .$40-$60
1946 Player in action . . . .$35-$70
1947 World Series pennant/ booklet . . . . .$35-$60
1948 Joe McCarthy, booklet . . . .$45-$60
1949 Roster booklet . . . .$30-$60
1950 Team mascot . . . .$30-$50
1951 Old-timer, current player $125
1952 Fenway Park $125
1953 Team logo $125
1954 Team logo $125
1955 Team logo $125
1956 Name and 1956 . . . .$125
1957 Player in action $125
1958 Red Sox media $100
1959 Player in mirror $100

1960 Player on horse $100
1961 Baseball glove, ball $100
1962 Carl Yastrzemski, others $125
1963 Johnny Pesky $75
1964 Team logo $75
1965 Team logo $75
1966 Showerhead/team logo $40
1967 Team logo $40
1968 A.L. Championship pennant $40
1969 100th anniversary $40
1970 Fenway Park $20
1971 Red Sox stars $20
1972 Cheering fan $10
1973 Player in action $10
1974 Darrell Johnson $10
1975 Fenway Park $10
1976 A.L. Championship pennant $10
1977 Don Zimmer $10
1978 Carl Yastrzemski, Jim Rice $15
1979 Jim Rice $12
1980 Carl Yastrzemski $12
1981 Ralph Houk $6
1982 Ralph Houk and players $6
1983 Dwight Evans, Bob Stanley $6
1984 Wade Boggs, Jim Rice $8
1985 Tony Armas $6
1986 Boggs, Boyd, Buckner, Gedman $8
1987 Roger Clemens, John McNamara $6
1988 Dwight Evans, Roger Clemens $8
1989 Joe Morgan $10
1990 Fenway Park $10
1991 Ellis Burks, Tony Pena $10
1992 Roger Clemens, Butch Hobson $10
1993 Red Sox baseball $10
1994 Mo Vaughn $7
1995 Team logos $5
1996 Mo Vaughn $5
1997 Mo Vaughn $5
1998 Nomar Garciaparra $6
1999 N. Garciaparra, P. Martinez $6
2000 . . . .$6

Rockies

1993 Silhouette $20
1994 Coors Field $10
1995 Coors Field $15
1996 Coors Field $6
1997 Baseball scenes $6

1998 All-Star Game logo/stars $6
1999 Coors Field/baseballs $6
2000 . . . .$6

Royals

1969 Team logo $60
1970 Player hitting $20
1971 Team bat rack $20

1972 Royals Stadium $15
1973 Players in action $15
1974 Royals Stadium $15
1975 Player hitting $15
1976 Whitey Herzog $10
1977 Players in action $6
1978 Players hitting, pitching $6
1979 1976-1978 A.L. West Champions $6

1980 Team logo, scoreboard $6
1981 Players in action, logo $6
1982 Team logo, pitcher $6
1983 Statue of hitter $6
1984 George Brett and fans $8
1985 Scoreboard (A.L. West Champions) $6
1986 World Series trophy $6
1987 Players in action $6
1988 Fireworks over scoreboard $10
1989 Team equipment $10
1990 Players in action $10
1991 George Brett $12
1992 Equipment $10
1993 25th anniversary $10
1994 K. Appier/J. Montgomery/G. Gagne . . .$7
1995 Magazine covers $7
1996 Player photo collage $6
1997 25th Anniv. of Kaufman Stadium $6
1998 Royals logo on wood background $6
1999 George Brett, Baseball HOF $7
2000 . . . .$6

Senators

1928 Roster sheet $125
1929 Roster sheet $100
1930 Roster sheet $100
1931 Roster sheet $100
1932 Roster booklet $100
1933 Roster booklet $100
1933 Capitol and 1933, booklet . . . . .$80-$115
1934 Capitol and 1934, booklet . . . . .$80-$100
1935 Capitol and 1935, booklet . . . . .$75-$100
1936 Capitol and 1936 . . . .$75
1937 Capitol and 1937 . . . .$75
1938 Capitol and 1938 . . . .$70-$75
1939 Capitol and 1939 . . . .$70-$75
1940 Capitol and 1940 . . . .$70-$75
1941 Capitol and 1941 . . . .$60-$65
1942 Capitol and 1942 . . . .$60-$65
1943 Capitol and 1943 . . . .$60-$65
1944 Capitol and 1944 . . . .$60
1945 Capitol and 1945 . . . .$60
1946 Capitol and 1946 . . . .$60
1947 Capitol and 1947 . . . .$55-$60
1948 Capitol and 1948 . . . .$55-$60
1949 Capitol and 1949 . . . .$55-$60
1950 Capitol and 1950 . . . .$50
1951 Capitol and 1951 . . . .$50
1952 Capitol and 1952 . . . .$50
1953 Capitol, bat, baseball . . . .$45-$50
1954 Capitol, bat, baseball . . . .$45-$50
1955 Capitol, bat, baseball . . . .$45-$50
1956 Sportswriter $40
1957 Team mascot pitching $40
1958 Golden anniversary of BBWAA $40
1959 Mascot blowing out candles . . . . .$35-$40
1960 Home run celebration $75

Becomes Minnesota Twins

1961 Doherty, Quesada, Vernon $75
1962 Stadium and team logo $75
1963 Stadium and team logo $75
1964 Stadium and team logo $60
1965 Stadium and team logo $35
1966 Stadium and team logo $25
1967 Pitcher and baseball $25
1968 Batter and baseball $25
1969 Frank Howard $25
1970 Bob Short, Ted Williams $25
1971 Stadium and team logo $25

Becomes Texas Rangers

Tigers Media Guides

1927 Roster sheet $125
1928 Roster sheet $100
1929 Roster sheet $100
1930 Roster sheet $100
1931 Roster booklet $100
1932 Roster booklet $100

[1992 Press Guide illustration]

1933 Tiger head and 1933, booklet . . . . . .$60-$100
1934 Tiger head and 1934, booklet . . . . . .$55-$110
1935 Tiger head and 1935, booklet . . . . . .$55-$115
1936 Tiger head and 1936 . . . .$55-$75
1937 . . . .$50-$75
1938 Tiger head and 1938 . . . .$50-$75
1939 Tiger head and 1939 . . . .$50-$75
1940 . . . .$45-$85
1941 Briggs Stadium . . . .$45-$60
1942 Flag over Briggs Stadium . . . .$45-$60
1943 Tiger head and 1943 . . . .$40-$60
1944 Tiger head and 1944 . . . .$40-$60
1945 Tiger head and 1945 . . . .$40-$70
1946 Tiger head and 1946 . . . .$35-$60
1947 Tiger head and 1947 . . . .$35-$60
1948 Tiger head and 1948 . . . .$150
1949 Tiger head and 1949 . . . .$150
1950 Tiger head and 1950 . . . .$150
1951 Tiger head and 1951 . . . .$150
1952 Tiger head and 1952 . . . .$150
1953 Tiger head and 1953 . . . .$150
1954 Tiger head and 1954 . . . .$100
1955 Tiger head and 1955 . . . .$100
1956 Ray Boone, Al Kaline $100
1957 Frank Lary $100
1958 Jim Bunning $100
1959 Tiger head and 1959 . . . .$100
1960 Tiger head and 1960 . . . .$75
1961 Tiger Stadium $75
1962 Players and team logo $75
1963 Team logo $75
1964 Team logo $50
1965 Team logo $40
1966 Team mascot and 1966 . . . .$40
1967 Team mascot and 1967 . . . .$40
1968 Team mascot and 1968 . . . .$40
1969 Team mascot $30
1970 Team mascot fielding $20
1971 Team mascot throwing $15
1972 Team mascot fielding $10
1973 Team mascot fielding $10
1974 Team mascot sliding $10
1975 Team mascot in field $10
1976 Team mascot pitching $10
1977 Team mascot catching $10
1978 Team mascot hitting $10
1979 Team logo and 1979 . . . .$10
1980 Team mascot in action $6
1981 Tiger jumping $6

1982 Team logo $6
1983 Greenberg and Gehringer uniforms $6
1984 Team mascot boxing $6
1985 World Series trophy, logo $6
1986 Team mascot in stadium $6
1987 Baseball and Tiger $6
1988 . . . .$6
1989 The Press Guide and logo $10
1990 Uniform D $10
1991 And Once Again $10
1992 Alan Trammell, Lou Whitaker $10
1993 Tiger greats $10
1994 Team logo $9
1995 Baseballs $8
1996 Buddy Bell $8
1997 Stripes $8
1998 J. Thompson, B. Higginson, T. Clark . . .$8
1999 Tiger Stadium at night $8
2000 . . . .$8

Twins

1961 Metropolitan Stadium drawing $150
1962 Metropolitan Stadium $75
1963 Player hitting $75

1964 Baseball and 1964 . . . .$75
1965 All-Star Game hosts $40
1966 Player fielding $40
1967 Twins uniform $30
1968 Pitcher throwing $30
1969 Metropolitan Stadium $25
1970 Rod Carew, Twins stars $25
1971 Jim Perry $25
1972 Minnesota media $25
1973 Rod Carew $25
1974 Baseballs $10
1975 Rod Carew, Ty Cobb $15
1976 R. Carew/ H. Killebrew/ others $15
1977 Old press guide covers $10
1978 Rod Carew $10
1979 Metropolitan Stadium $6
1980 Twins baseball cards $6
1981 Twins bats, hats, uniforms $6
1982 Metrodome $6
1983 Kent Hrbek $7
1984 Twins uniforms $6
1985 All-Star Game logo $6
1986 25th anniversary logo $6
1987 Gary Gaetti, Kirby Puckett $8

1988 World Series trophy $10
1989 Kirby Puckett, Frank Viola $10
1990 Carew, Oliva, Puckett $10
1991 Drawings of Carew, Killebrew $10
1992 Celebration, World Series trophy $10
1993 Kirby Puckett $10
1994 Autographs $7
1995 Bat/glove/uniform $6
1996 Rookies of the Year $5
1997 Team logo $5
1998 Paul Molitor $5
1999 Tom Kelly, others $5
2000 . . . .$5

White Sox

1927 Roster sheet $125
1928 Roster sheet $100
1929 Roster sheet $100
1930 Roster sheet $100
1931 Roster sheet $100
1932 Roster sheet $100
1933 Name and 1933, sheet . . . .$60-$100
1934 Name and 1934, booklet . . . . . .$55-$100
1935 Name and 1935, booklet . . . . . .$55-$100
1936 Name and 1936, booklet . . . .$55-$75
1937 Name and 1937, booklet . . . .$50-$75
1938 Name and 1938, booklet . . . .$50-$75
1939 Name and 1939, booklet . . . .$50-$75
1940 Name and 1940, booklet . . . .$45-$75
1941 Ted Lyons, booklet . . . .$50-$60
1942 Jimmy Dykes, booklet . . . .$45-$60
1943 Buy More War Bonds, booklet . . . .$40-$60
1944 Back the Attack, booklet . . . .$40-$60
1945 Roster booklet . . . .$40-$60
1946 Name and 1946, booklet . . . .$35-$60
1947 Ted Lyons, booklet $100
1948 Team mascot and 1948, booklet $100
1949 Team logo and 1949, booklet $100
1950 Luke Appling $100
1951 Paul Richards $100
1952 Carrasquel, Fox, Minoso, Rogovin $100
1953 Player in action $100
1954 Team mascot $100
1955 Team mascot $100
1956 Team mascot $100

1957 Team mascot $90
1958 Team mascot $90
1959 Team mascot $90
1960 Team mascot $75
1961 Name and 1961 . . . .$75
1962 Player in action $75
1963 Player in action $75
1964 Player in action $75
1965 Pitcher throwing $40
1966 Batter hitting $30
1967 Player in action $25
1968 Hitter up to bat $25
1969 Batter hitting $25
1970 Fielder in action $10
1971 Chuck Tanner $10
1972 Player in action $10
1973 Allen, Tanner, Wood $10
1974 Team logo $10
1975 A.L. 75th anniversary $6
1976 Team logo $6
1977 Team logo $6
1978 Team logo, hitter $6
1979 Don Kessinger $6
1980 Fans in crowd $6
1981 Pitcher in action $6
1982 Team logo $6
1983 Sportswriter equipment $6
1984 Scoreboard, A.L. West Champs $6
1985 Comiskey Park $6
1986 Aparicio, Appling, Guillen $7
1987 New White Sox uniform #87 . . . .$6
1988 Player in action $6
1989 Former White Sox stars $6
1990 Comiskey Park 80 years $10
1991 Catcher's mask, uniform, bat $10
1992 Team logo $10
1993 Team logo $10
1994 Lamont/Thomas/McDowell $7
1995 Comiskey Park $6
1996 Thomas/Guillen/Fernandez $6
1997 Frank Thomas hitting $6
1998 Jerry Manuel $6
1999 . . . .$6
2000 . . . .$7

Yankees

1927 Roster sheet . . . .$150-$175
1928 Roster sheet $150
1929 Roster sheet $150
1930 Roster sheet $150
1931 Roster sheet $150
1932 Roster booklet $200
1933 Roster booklet $100
1934 Roster booklet $100
1935 Roster booklet $100
1936 Joe McCarthy, booklet . . . .$70-$100
1937 Joe McCarthy, booklet . . . . . .$65-$100
1938 Joe McCarthy, booklet . . . . . .$65-$100
1939 Joe McCarthy, booklet . . . . . .$65-$100
1940 Joe McCarthy, booklet . . . .$60-$75
1941 Joe McCarthy, booklet . . . .$60-$65
1942 Joe McCarthy . . . .$60-$65
1943 . . . .$45-$65
1944 . . . .$45-$60
1945 Victory V and 1945 . . . .$40-$60
1946 Team logo and 1946 . . . .$40-$60
1947 Team logo and 1947 . . . .$35-$65
1948 Team logo and 1948 . . . .$35-$60
1949 Team logo and 1949 . . . .$30-$65
1950 Team logo and 1950 . . . .$150
1951 Team logo and 1950 . . . .$150
1952 Team logo and 1952 . . . .$150
1953 Team logo and 1953 . . . .$150
1954 Team logo and 1954 . . . .$150
1955 Team logo and 1955 . . . .$150
1956 Team logo and 1956 . . . .$150
1957 Team logo and 1957 . . . .$150
1958 Team logo and 1958 . . . .$150
1959 Team logo and 1959 . . . .$150
1960 Yankee Stadium $100
1961 Team logo and 1961 . . . .$100
1962 Team logo and 1962 . . . .$100
1963 Team logo and 1963 . . . .$100
1964 Yogi Berra and logo $75
1965 Team logo $40
1966 Yankee Stadium and logo $40
1967 Team logo and hitter $40
1968 Yankee Stadium $40
1969 Yankee glove and hat $40
1970 Mel Stottlemyre $25
1971 Logo and players in action $20
1972 Bobby Murcer, Roy White $20
1973 Yankee Stadium $20
1974 Whitey Ford, Mickey Mantle $25
1975 Bobby Bonds, Catfish Hunter $20
1976 Yankee Stadium $20
1977 Chris Chambliss, Thurman Munson $25
1978 Reggie Jackson, Babe Ruth $25
1979 Goose Gossage, Thurman Munson $20
1980 Dick Howser, Gene Michael $15
1981 Team logo $20
1982 Team logo $5
1983 Billy Martin with umpire $8
1984 Righetti, Yankee no-hitters $6
1985 Don Mattingly $7
1986 Guidry/ Henderson/ Mattingly/ Niekro $7
1987 Lou Piniella and team $15
1988 Team logo $15
1989 Dallas Green $15
1990 Baseball bat and ball $15
1991 Maas/ Mattingly/ Meulens/ Sax $15
1992 A tradition of great moments $15
1993 Collage $10
1994 Players $10
1995 Babe Ruth's 100th birthday $12
1996 Memorabilia $10
1997 Players $10
1998 Yankee Stadium at 75 Years $13
1999 . . . .$12
2000 . . . .$12

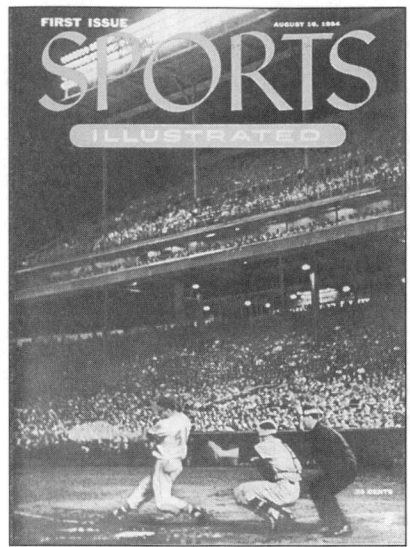

August 16, 1954

Sports Illustrated Baseball Covers

The premiere issue of publishing mogul Henry Luce Booth's weekly *Sports Illustrated* with Eddie Mathews pictured on the cover is a favorite of collectors. That issue, and the second issue (picturing a golf bag) as well (which is even more valuable), includes fold-out pages of 1954 Topps baseball cards printed on thin paper stock.

Since then, *SI* has been recognized as a leading name in sports publishing.

The attractive cover photos are generally what drive the collectibility of *SI*s. A popular athlete's first appearance on a cover is also desirable.

Autographed covers are also popular. Generally, prices for autographed issues are worth the price of the magazine, plus the value of the athlete's signature on an 8x10 photo.

August 1, 1955

May 14, 1956

Date	Cover Subject	VG	EX	NM
	1954			
08/16	Eddie Mathews	$125	$190	$300
	1955			
04/18	Al Rosen	50	75	100
04/11	Durocher/Mays	75	100	125
05/30	Herb Score	6	12	20
06/27	Duke Snider	30	50	75
07/11	Yogi Berra	15	25	50
08/01	Ted Williams	50	75	100
08/22	Don Newcombe	6	12	20
09/26	Walter Alston	8	15	25
12/26	Jim Swink	4	6	10
	1956			
01/02	Johnny Podres	$15	$25	$35
03/05	Stan Musial	20	30	50
04/09	Special Baseball Issue	5	10	15
04/23	Billy Martin	15	25	35
05/14	A. Kaline/H. Kuenn	12	22	40
06/18	Mickey Mantle	90	140	200
06/25	Warren Spahn	15	25	35
07/09	All-Star Game	10	20	30

June 18, 1956

July 16, 1956

Date	Cover Subject	VG	EX	NM
07/16	Reds' Musclemen	25	35	60
07/30	Joe Adcock	5	10	15
09/10	Whitey Ford	20	30	50
10/01	M. Mantle: World Series	50	75	100
	1957			
03/04	Mantle: Spring Training	50	75	100
04/15	Spring Baseball	10	20	30
04/22	Wally Moon	5	10	15
05/13	Billy Pierce	5	10	15
06/03	Clem Labine	5	10	15
07/08	T. Williams/S. Musial	50	75	100
07/22	Hank Bauer	5	10	15
09/09	Roy McMillan	5	10	15
09/30	World Series Issue	8	15	25
11/04	Bobby Cox	4	6	10
12/23	Stan Musial	12	22	40
	1958			
03/03	Yankee Spring Training	6	12	20
03/17	Sal Maglie	5	10	15
03/31	Roy Sievers	5	10	15
04/14	Baseball Special	5	10	15
04/21	Del Crandall	5	10	15

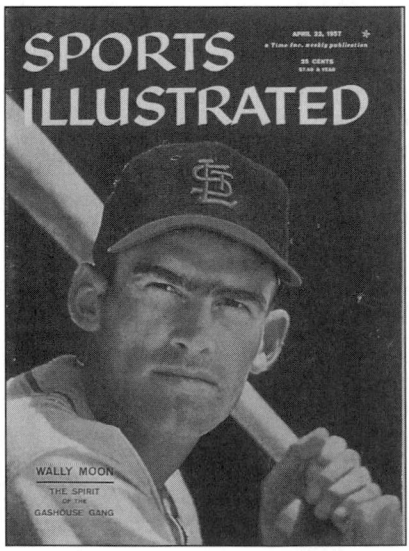

April 22, 1957

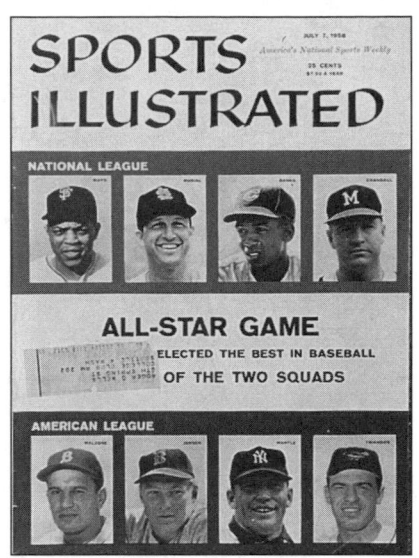

July 7, 1958

June 3, 1963

October 16, 1967

Date	Cover Subject	VG	EX	NM
05/05	Gil McDougald	5	10	15
05/19	Richie Ashburn	5	10	15
06/02	Eddie Mathews	9	20	35
06/23	Jackie Jensen	5	10	15
07/07	All Stars Mays/Mantle	12	22	40
07/28	Frank Thomas	5	10	15
09/29	World Series	5	10	15

1959
03/02	Casey Stengel	10	20	30
04/13	Willie Mays	20	30	50
05/04	Bob Turley	5	10	15
08/10	L. Aparicio/ N. Fox	20	30	50
09/28	Chicago White Sox	5	10	15

1960
03/07	Spring Training	5	10	15
04/11	Baseball Annual	5	10	15
06/06	Red Schoendienst	6	12	20
07/04	Comiskey Park Fireworks	5	10	15
07/18	Candlestick Park	4	6	10
08/08	Dick Groat	6	12	20
10/10	Vernon Law	4	6	10

1961
03/06	Spring Training/Reds	5	10	15
04/10	Baseball Issue	5	10	15
05/15	Cookie Lavagetto	4	7	12
06/26	W. Mays/E. Broglio	6	12	20
07/31	Split-Second Baseball	4	7	12
08/14	Murray Rose, Mays	5	10	20
10/02	Roger Maris	12	22	40
10/09	Joey Jay	4	7	12

1962
03/05	Casey Stengel	10	20	30
04/09	Frank Lary	4	7	12
04/30	Luis Aparicio	8	15	25
06/04	Willie Mays	11	21	35
07/02	Mickey Mantle	55	80	125
07/30	Ken Boyer	6	12	20
08/20	Don Drysdale	10	20	30
10/01	World Series	6	12	20

1963
03/04	Sandy Koufax	14	23	45
04/08	Harmon Killebrew	10	20	30
04/29	Art Mahaffey	4	7	12

06/24	Roy Face	4	7	12
07/22	Dick Groat	5	10	15
09/30	Whitey Ford	8	15	25

1964
03/02	Y. Berra/C. Stengel	10	20	30
04/13	Sandy Koufax	10	20	30
05/11	Al Kaline	6	12	20
05/25	Frank Howard	4	7	12
07/06	Alvin Dark	4	7	12
08/10	Johnny Callison	4	6	10
08/31	Brooks Robinson	6	12	20

1965
03/01	J. Bunning/B. Belinsky	5	10	15
04/19	Baseball 1965	5	10	15
05/17	Bill Veeck	4	7	12
06/21	Mickey Mantle	12	22	40
07/05	Bill Talbert	3	5	8
07/12	Maury Wills	5	10	15
08/09	Juan Marichal	6	12	20
08/23	Tony Oliva	5	10	15
10/04	Zoilo Versalles	4	7	12
12/20	Sandy Koufax	8	15	25

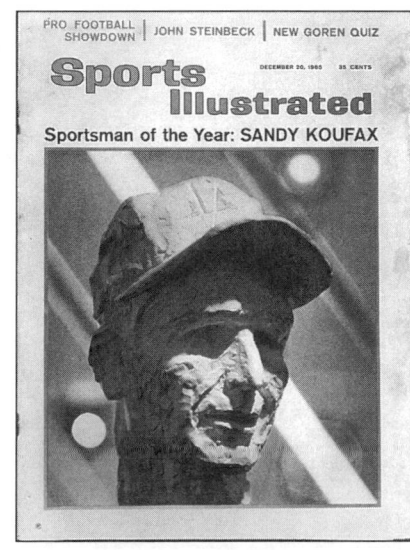

December 20, 1965

1966
02/28	L. Durocher/E. Stanky	5	10	15
04/18	Dick Groat	5	10	15
05/23	Sam McDowell	4	7	12
07/11	Andy Etchebarren	4	6	10
09/26	Gaylord Perry	5	10	15
10/10	Brooks/ F. Robinson	8	15	25

1967
04/17	Maury Wills	5	10	15
05/08	Mickey Mantle	9	22	35
05/15	Koufax/Drysdale/Wills	10	20	30
06/05	Al Kaline	5	10	15
07/03	Roberto Clemente	10	20	30
07/31	The Spitball	4	6	10
08/21	Carl Yastrzemski	6	12	20
09/04	Tim McCarver	4	7	12
10/16	Lou Brock	6	12	20
12/25	Carl Yastrzemski	6	12	20

1968
03/11	Johnny Bench	8	12	25
04/15	Lou Brock	5	10	15
05/06	Ron Swoboda	4	6	10
05/27	Pete Rose	8	12	25
06/17	Don Drysdale	6	12	20
07/08	Ted Williams	10	20	30

May 27, 1968

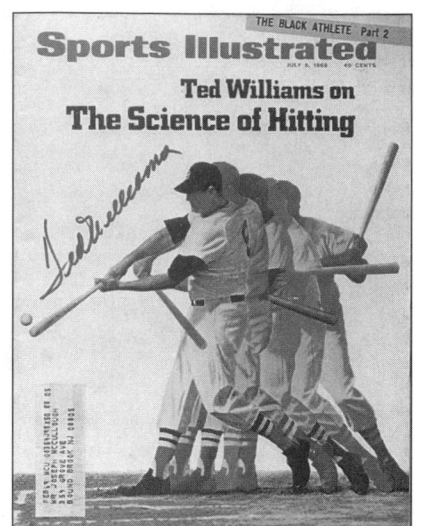

July 8, 1968

October 18, 1971

June 12, 1972

Date	Cover Subject	VG	EX	NM
07/29	Denny McLain	5	10	15
08/19	Curt Flood	5	10	15
09/02	Ken Harrelson	3	5	8
09/23	D. McLain/ A. Kaline	5	10	15
10/07	St. Louis Cardinals	5	10	15

1969

03/17	Ted Williams	8	15	25
05/19	Walter Alston	6	12	20
06/30	Ron Santo	5	10	15
07/07	Reggie Jackson	8	12	25
07/21	Billy Martin	5	10	15
08/18	Hank Aaron	8	12	25
09/08	P. Rose/E. Banks	6	12	20
10/06	Frank Robinson	5	10	15
10/20	Brooks Robinson	5	10	15
12/22	Tom Seaver	10	20	30

1970

02/23	Denny McLain	4	6	10
03/23	Dick Allen	4	6	10
04/13	Jerry Koosman	4	7	12
05/25	Hank Aaron	4	7	12
06/22	Tony Conigliaro	4	7	12
07/13	Johnny Bench	4	7	12
07/27	Willie Mays	4	7	12

09/07	Bud Harrelson	3	5	8
09/28	L. Durocher/D. Murtaugh	3	5	8
10/19	Brooks Robinson	4	6	10

1971

03/22	Wes Parker	2	4	7
04/12	Boog Powell	3	5	8
05/03	D. Duncan /J. Fregosi	3	5	8
05/31	Vida Blue	3	5	8
06/21	Jerry Grote	3	5	8
07/05	Alex Johnson	2	4	7
08/02	Willie Stargell	3	5	8
08/30	Ferguson Jenkins	3	5	8
09/27	Maury Wills	3	5	8
10/18	Frank Robinson	3	5	8

1972

03/13	Johnny Bench	3	5	8
03/27	Vida Blue	2	4	7
04/10	Joe Torre	4	6	10
05/01	Willie Davis	2	4	7
05/22	Willie Mays	4	6	10
06/12	Dick Allen	3	5	8
07/03	Steve Blass	2	4	7
08/21	Sparky Lyle	3	5	8
09/25	Carlton Fisk	3	5	8
10/23	Catfish Hunter	3	5	8

1973

03/12	Bill Melton	3	5	8
04/09	Steve Carlton	3	6	10
04/30	Chris Speier	3	5	8
06/04	Wilbur Wood	3	5	8
07/30	Carlton Fisk	4	6	10
08/20	Dodgers/ Russell/ Osteen	4	6	10
09/24	Danny Murtaugh	3	5	8
10/22	Bert Campaneris	3	5	8

1974

03/18	Babe Ruth	4	6	10
04/08	Pete Rose	4	6	10
04/15	Hank Aaron	6	12	20
05/27	Jim Wynn	2	4	7
06/17	Reggie Jackson	4	6	10
07/01	Rod Carew	3	5	8
07/22	Lou Brock	3	5	8
08/12	Mike Marshall	2	4	7
10/07	Catfish Hunter	3	5	8
10/21	A's/ Dodgers	3	5	8

1975

03/03	Reds Spring Training	4	6	10
04/07	Steve Garvey	3	5	8

December 22, 1969

July 13, 1970

April 15, 1974

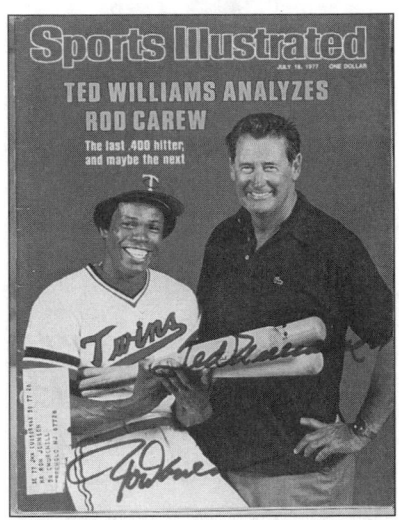

July 18, 1977

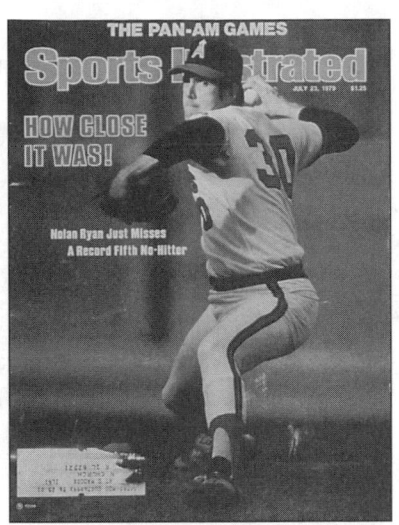

July 23, 1979

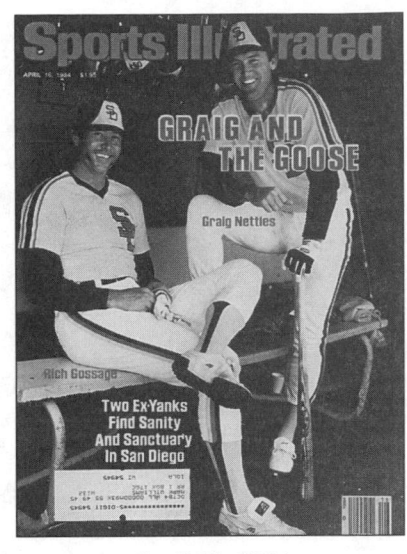

April 16, 1984

Date	Cover Subject	VG	EX	NM
05/26	Jimmy Wynn	2	4	7
06/02	Billy Martin	3	5	8
06/16	Nolan Ryan	4	7	12
07/07	Fred Lynn	3	5	8
07/21	T. Seaver /J.Palmer	4	6	10
08/11	Baseball Boom	3	5	8
10/06	Reggie Jackson	4	6	10
10/20	J. Bench/L. Tiant	4	6	10
11/03	J. Bench/W.McEnaney	3	5	8
12/22	Pete Rose	4	6	10

1976

Date	Cover Subject	VG	EX	NM
03/15	Bill Veeck	2	4	7
04/12	Joe Morgan	3	5	8
05/03	Mike Schmidt	3	5	8
05/31	C. Fisk/L. Piniella	3	5	8
06/21	George Brett	4	6	10
07/12	Randy Jones	2	4	7
08/30	Reggie Jackson	4	6	10
11/01	Johnny Bench	4	6	10

1977

Date	Cover Subject	VG	EX	NM
03/14	Tommy Lasorda	3	5	8
03/28	Bump Wills	2	4	7
04/11	Joe Rudi	3	5	8
05/02	Reggie Jackson	4	6	10
05/30	Dave Parker	3	5	8

Date	Cover Subject	VG	EX	NM
06/06	Mark Fidrych	3	5	8
06/27	Tom Seaver	4	6	10
07/04	Ted Turner	2	4	7
07/18	R. Carew/ T. Williams	4	6	10
08/15	Sadaharu Oh	3	5	8
08/29	Greg Luzinski	2	4	7
10/24	World Series	3	4	7

1978

Date	Cover Subject	VG	EX	NM
03/20	Clint Hurdle	2	4	7
04/10	R. Carew/G. Foster	3	5	8
04/24	Mark Fidrych	3	5	8
07/31	Billy Martin	3	5	8
08/07	Pete Rose's Streak	4	6	10
10/23	Lee Lacy/Brian Doyle	2	4	7

1979

Date	Cover Subject	VG	EX	NM
03/05	Spring Training	3	5	8
04/09	J. Rice/D. Parker	3	5	8
04/30	George Bamberger	2	4	7
05/28	Pete Rose: Phillies	3	5	8
06/18	Earl Weaver	3	5	8
07/23	Nolan Ryan	4	7	12
08/13	Silver Anniversary	4	6	10
08/27	BB'S Golden Oldies	4	6	10
10/22	D. DeCinces/P. Garner	2	4	7
12/24	Stargell/Bradshaw	3	5	8

1980

Date	Cover Subject	VG	EX	NM
03/24	Kirk Gibson	$3	$5	$8
04/07	Keith Hernandez	3	5	8
06/09	Darryl Porter	2	4	7
07/21	Steve Carlton	3	5	8
08/04	Reggie Jackson	4	6	10
08/18	J.R. Richard	2	4	7
08/25	Baltimore Orioles	3	5	8
10/06	Gary Carter	2	4	7
10/27	Schmidt/Porter	3	5	8

1981

Date	Cover Subject	VG	EX	NM
01/05	Dave Winfield	$3	$5	$8
03/02	J.R. Richard	2	4	7
03/16	Rollie Fingers	3	5	8
04/13	G. Brett/M. Schmidt	4	6	10
04/27	Oakland's 5 Aces	2	4	7
05/18	Fernando Valenzuela	3	5	8
06/08	Greg Luzinski	2	4	7
06/22	Strike	1	3	6
07/27	Tom Seaver	3	5	8
08/10	Brett/Schmidt	3	5	8
08/17	Gary Carter	2	4	7
10/26	Graig Nettles	2	4	7
11/02	World Series	2	4	7

July 31, 1978

October 17, 1988

March 25, 1985

May 6, 1985

May 12, 1986

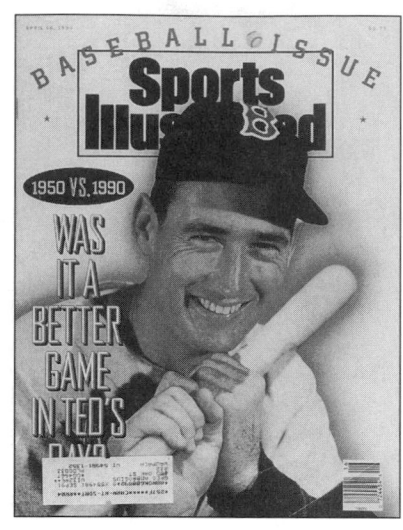

April 16, 1990

1982

Date	Cover Subject	VG	EX	NM
03/15	Reggie Jackson	3	5	8
04/12	Steve Garvey	3	5	8
05/17	Gaylord Perry	2	4	7
07/05	Kent Hrbek	2	4	7
07/19	Rose/Yaz	3	5	8
08/09	Dale Murphy	3	5	8
09/06	Rickey Henderson	3	5	8
10/11	Robin Yount	4	6	10
10/25	Yount/Smith	3	5	8

1983

Date	Cover Subject	VG	EX	NM
03/14	Rose/Morgan/Perez	4	6	10
04/04	Gary Carter	2	4	7
04/18	Tom Seaver	3	5	8
04/25	Steve Garvey	3	5	8
06/13	Rod Carew	3	5	8
07/04	Dale Murphy	3	5	8
07/18	A. Dawson/D. Stieb	3	5	8
10/03	Steve Carlton	3	5	8
10/24	Rick Dempsey	2	4	7

1984

Date	Cover Subject	VG	EX	NM
03/12	George Brett	3	5	8
04/02	Yogi Berra	3	5	8
04/16	Gossage/Nettles	3	5	8

Date	Cover Subject	VG	EX	NM
04/23	Darryl Strawberry	3	5	8
05/28	Alan Trammell	3	5	8
06/11	Leon Durham	2	4	7
08/27	Pete Rose	3	5	8
09/24	Gooden/Sutcliffe	3	5	8
10/22	Alan Trammell	2	4	7

1985

Date	Cover Subject	VG	EX	NM
03/04	Schmidt/Millionaires	3	5	8
03/18	Fred Lynn	2	4	7
03/25	Mantle/Mays/Ueberroth	5	10	15
04/15	Dwight Gooden	3	5	8
05/06	Billy Martin	3	5	8
07/08	Fernando Valenzuela	3	5	8
08/05	Pedro Guerrero	2	4	7
08/19	Pete Rose	3	5	8
09/02	Dwight Gooden	3	5	8
09/23	Ozzie Smith	3	5	8
10/28	Ozzie Smith	3	5	8
11/04	K.C. Royals	2	4	7
12/09	Kirk Gibson	2	4	7

1986

Date	Cover Subject	VG	EX	NM
04/14	Wade Boggs	3	5	8
05/12	Roger Clemens	4	6	10
07/14	Bo Jackson	3	5	8
07/28	Rickey Henderson	3	5	8
08/04	Oil Can Boyd	2	4	7

Date	Cover Subject	VG	EX	NM
08/25	Ron Darling	2	4	7
10/06	Darryl Strawberry	3	5	8
10/20	DeCinces/Grich	2	4	7
10/27	Rice/Carter	2	4	7
11/03	Ray Knight	2	4	7

1987

Date	Cover Subject	VG	EX	NM
03/09	Ripken Family	3	5	8
03/16	Gary McLain	1	3	6
04/06	Carter/Snyder: BB Issue	3	5	8
04/27	Rob Deer	2	4	7
05/11	Reggie Jackson	4	6	10
07/06	One Day in Baseball	2	4	7
07/13	Strawberry/Mattingly	4	6	10
07/20	Andre Dawson	3	5	8
08/17	Alan Trammell	2	4	7
09/28	Ozzie Smith	3	5	8
10/05	Lloyd Moseby	2	4	7
10/19	Twins/World Series	3	5	8
10/26	Dan Gladden	2	4	7
11/02	Minnesota Twins	3	5	8

1988

Date	Cover Subject	VG	EX	NM
03/07	Kirk Gibson	2	4	7
03/14	Pam Postema	1	3	6
04/04	M.McGwire/W. Clark	4	6	10

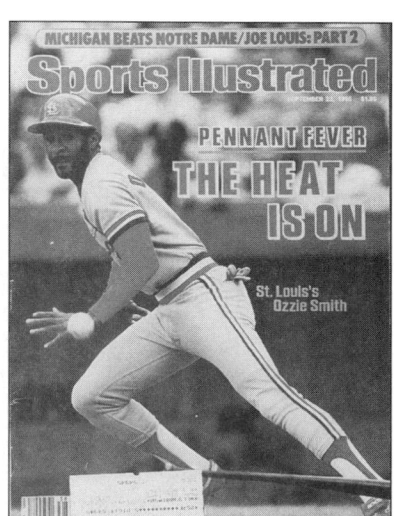

September 23, 1985

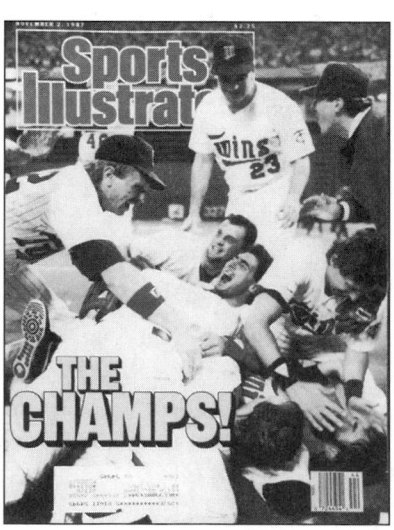

November 2, 1987

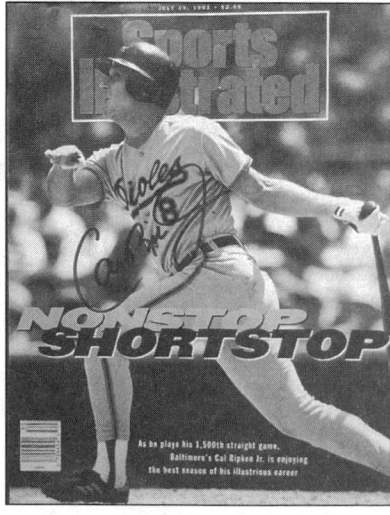

July 29, 1991

March 14, 1994

Date	Cover Subject	VG	EX	NM
05/02	Billy Ripken	2	4	7
05/09	Pete Rose: Super Red	3	5	8
07/11	Darryl Strawberry	3	5	8
07/18	Casey at the Bat	2	4	7
09/26	Dwight Evans	2	4	7
10/17	Jose Canseco	3	5	8
10/31	Orel Hershiser	2	4	7
12/19	Orel Hershiser	2	4	7

1989

Date	Cover Subject	VG	EX	NM
03/06	Wade Boggs	3	5	8
04/03	Pete Rose: BB Issue	4	6	10
05/01	Nolan Ryan: Texas Heat	5	10	15
06/12	Bo Jackson	3	5	8
07/03	Pete Rose	3	5	8
07/10	Rick Rueschel	2	4	7
07/24	Gregg Jefferies	2	4	7
10/16	Rickey Henderson	3	5	8
10/30	Earthquake	1	3	6

1990

Date	Cover Subject	VG	EX	NM
03/12	Tony LaRussa	-	2	5
04/16	Ted Williams	2	4	7
05/07	Ken Griffey, Jr.	5	8	15
05/28	Will Clark	-	2	5
06/04	Len Dykstra	-	2	5
07/09	Darryl Strawberry	-	2	5

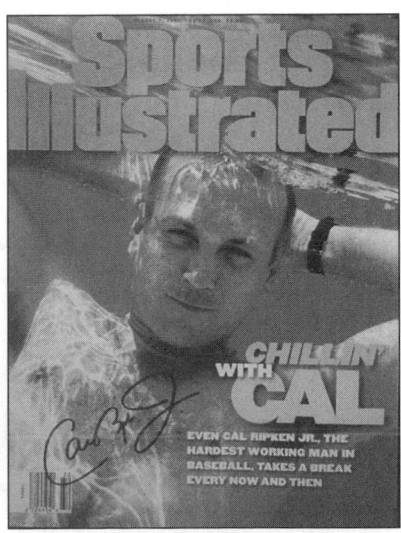

August 7, 1995

Date	Cover Subject	VG	EX	NM
07/23	Minor League Baseball	1	3	6
08/13	Autographs	1	3	6
08/20	Jose Canseco	1	3	6
10/01	Bobby Bonilla	1	3	6
10/22	Dennis Eckersley	1	3	6
10/29	Chris Sabo	2	4	7

1991

Date	Cover Subject	VG	EX	NM
03/04	Darryl Strawberry	-	2	5
04/15	N. Ryan: Baseball '91	3	5	8
05/13	Roger Clemens	4	7	7
05/27	M. Mantle/R. Maris	4	6	10
07/01	Orel Hershiser	-	3	5
07/29	Cal Ripken Jr.	5	10	15
09/30	Ramon Martinez	1	3	6
10/21	Kirby Puckett	3	5	8
10/28	Twins /Braves Series	2	4	7
11/04	Twins Win Series	3	5	8

1992

Date	Cover Subject	VG	EX	NM
03/16	Ryne Sandberg	4	7	12
04/06	K. Puckett: Baseball '92	2	4	7
04/27	Deion Sanders	1	3	6
05/04	Barry Bonds	3	5	8
05/18	Baseball '92	-	3	5
06/01	Mark McGwire	3	5	8
10/05	George Brett	1	3	6
10/19	Dave Winfield	1	3	6
10/26	R. Alomar/J. Smoltz	2	4	7
Fall Sp	Willie Mays	2	4	7
11/02	Toronto Blue Jays	2	4	7

1993

Date	Cover Subject	VG	EX	NM
03/01	George Steinbrenner	-	2	5
03/22	Dwight Gooden	1	3	6
04/05	David Cone	1	3	6
05/03	Joe DiMaggio	4	6	10
05/24	Barry Bonds	1	3	6
07/19	B. Gibson/ D. McLain	1	3	6

1994

Date	Cover Subject	VG	EX	NM
04/04	K. Griffey/M. Piazza	3	5	8
04/18	Mickey Mantle	4	6	10
05/23	Braves vs. Mets	1	3	6
06/06	Ken Griffey Jr.	-	6	10
07/18	Mussina/ McDonald	1	3	6
08/08	Frank Thomas	2	4	7
08/15	Ed Mathews: 40th Anniv.	3	5	8
08/22	Baseball Strike	-	2	5

1995

Date	Cover Subject	VG	EX	NM
02/27	Gooden/Strawberry	1	3	6
03/20	Michael Jordan	4	7	12
03/27	Michael Jordan	4	7	12
05/01	Cal Ripken Jr.	3	5	8
07/10	Hideo Nomo	1	3	6
08/07	Cal Ripken Jr.	3	5	8
08/14	Greg Maddux	2	4	7
08/21	Mickey Mantle	4	6	10
09/11	Cal Ripken Jr.	3	5	8
10/02	Mo Vaughn	1	3	6
10/16	Ken Griffey Jr.	1	3	6
10/30	Bo Jackson	1	3	6
11/07	Greg Maddux	1	3	6
12/18	Cal Ripken Jr.	3	5	8

1996

Date	Cover Subject	VG	EX	NM
03/18	Jay Buhner	1	3	6
04/01	Manny Ramirez	2	4	7
05/06	Albert Belle	-	2	5
05/20	Marge Schott	-	2	5
07/08	Alex Rodriguez	4	6	10
08/19	Al Simmons	1	3	6
10/14	Roberto Alomar	1	3	6
10/21	Derek Jeter	3	5	8

August 24, 1998

Date	Cover Subject	VG	EX	NM
11/04	Joe Girardi	-	2	5
11/25	Ted Williams	2	4	7
-	Special: Champion Yanks	4	6	10

1997

Date	Cover Subject	VG	EX	NM
03/31	Randy Johnson	-	2	5
08/11	Pudge Rodriguez	1	3	6
11/03	Edgar Renteria	1	3	6

1998

Date	Cover Subject	VG	EX	NM
04/20	Pedro Martinez	1	3	6
05/25	Mike Piazza	1	3	6
06/20	Sammy Sosa	4	6	10
07/06	Alex Rodriguez	3	5	8
08/03	Mark McGwire	4	7	12
08/24	Babe Ruth	2	4	7
09/07	McGwire & Son	4	7	12
09/14	McGwire: "The Record"	4	7	12
09/14	SI Extra Edition Mark McGwire "62!"	4	7	12
09/21	Sammy Sosa	4	6	10
010/05	Mark McGwire	4	7	12
10/07	Special Comm. Ed. McGwire/Sosa	5	10	15
10/12	Greg Vaughn	1	3	6
10/19	"Kill the Umps"	-	2	5
11/02	Yankees celebration	2	4	7

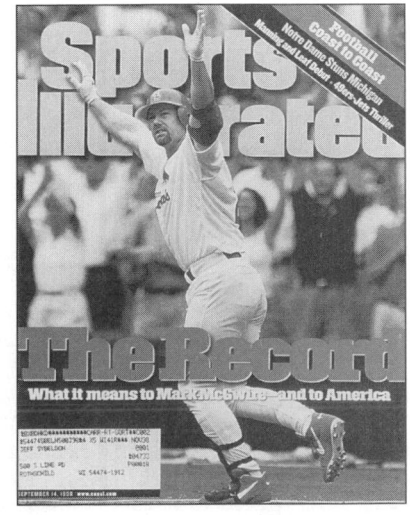

September 14, 1998

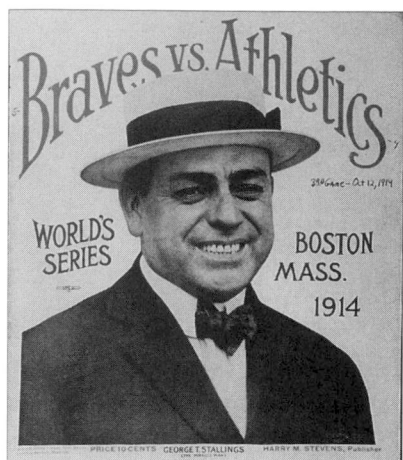

∫1914 World Series Program

World Series Programs

World Series programs have been produced since 1903 when Boston (A.L.) defeated Pittsburgh (N.L.) five games to three. Programs have been produced and saved as souvenirs each year since with the exception of 1904 (when John J. McGraw refused to allow his New York Giants to play an "inferior" team from the American League) and 1994 (MLB strike season).

In general, World Series programs, especially from championship teams, are in more demand than those from All-Star games and regular season games.

Since 1974, only one program has been produced for the World Series for both American and National League teams.

Like any other collectible, the better the condition, the more valuable the program. Programs that are unscored, not torn or faded and containing the original inserts, are more valuable.

1917 World Series Program

Year	Team	Price
1903	Pittsburgh	$15,000/$30,000
1903	Boston	$15,000/$30,000
1905	Philadelphia	$7,000/$16,000
1905	New York Giants	$7,000/$10,000
1906	Chicago Cubs	$7,000/$10,000
1906	Chicago White Sox	$7,000/$7,500
1907	Detroit	$10,000/$14,000
1907	Chicago Cubs	$7,000/$10,000
1908	Detroit	$8,000/$12,000
1908	Chicago Cubs	$8,000/$12,500
1909	Detroit	$8,000/$10,000
1909	Pittsburgh	$6,000/$10,000
1910	Chicago Cubs	$5,000/$7,500
1910	Philadelphia A's	$5,000/$10,000
1911	Philadelphia A's	$5,000/$6,000
1911	New York Giants	$3,000/$4,000
1912	New York Giants	$2,000/$4,000
1912	Boston Red Sox	$1,500/$3,000
1913	New York Giants	$2,000/$3,500
1913	Philadelphia A's	$2,000/$4,500
1914	Boston Braves	$3,000/$5,000
1914	Philadelphia	$2,000/$3,500
1915	Philadelphia A's	$2,500/$3,500
1915	Boston Red Sox	$2,000/$3,500
1916	Brooklyn	$2,000/$5,000

1926 World Series Program

Year	Team	Price
1916	Boston Red Sox	$2,000/$4,000
1917	New York Giants	$1,500/$3,500
1917	Chicago White Sox	$3,500/$5,000
1918	Boston Red Sox	$5,000/$10,000
1918	Chicago Cubs	$3,000/$5,000
1919	Cincinnati	$2,500/$4,000
1919	Chicago White Sox	$5,000/$9,000
1920	Brooklyn	$2,000/$5,000
1920	Cleveland	$3,000/$7,000
1921	New York Yankees	$1,500/$3,000
1921	New York Giants	$1,500/$3,000
1922	New York Yankees	$1,500/$2,500
1922	New York Giants	$1,500/$2,500
1923	New York Yankees	$1,500/$4,000
1923	New York Giants	$1,500/$3,500
1924	New York Giants	$1,500/$3,000
1924	Washington	$1,000/$2,000
1925	Pittsburgh	$3,000/$5,000
1925	Washington	$500/$1,000
1926	St. Louis Cardinals	$1,000/$2,000
1926	New York Yankees	$700/$1,500
1927	Pittsburgh	$2,000/$5,000
1927	New York Yankees	$2,000/$3,000
1928	St. Louis Cardinals	$1,000/$1,500

1927 World Series Program

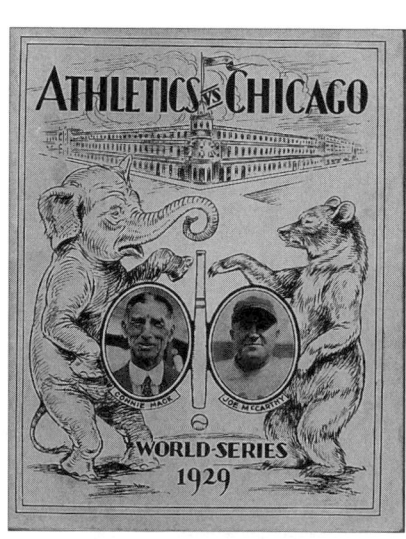

1929 World Series Program

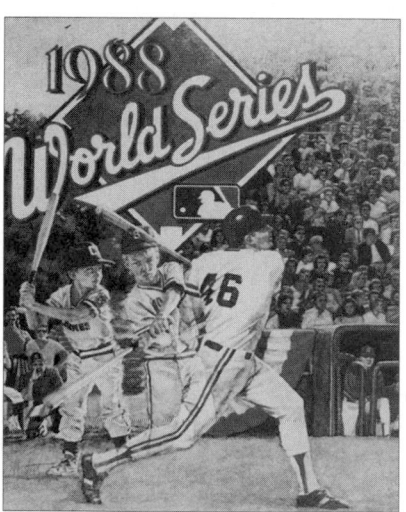

1931 World Series Program

1933 World Series Program

1942 World Series Program

1957 World Series Program

Year	Team	Price
1928	New York Yankees	$1,500/$2,750
1929	Chicago Cubs	$500/$1,000
1929	Philadelphia A's	$1,000/$1,500
1930	St. Louis Cardinals	$400/$750
1930	Philadelphia A's	$500/$1,000
1931	St. Louis Cardinals	$350/$750
1931	Philadelphia A's	$450/$750
1932	Chicago Cubs	$700/$1,000
1932	New York Yankees	$750/$1,250
1933	New York Giants	$700/$1,000
1933	Washington	$550/$700
1934	St. Louis Cardinals	$350/$600
1934	Detroit	$450/$600
1935	Chicago Cubs	$350/$500
1935	Detroit	$500/$700
1936	New York Giants	$200/$400
1936	New York Yankees	$375/$400
1937	New York Giants	$275/$350
1937	New York Yankees	$250/$375
1938	Chicago Cubs	$250/$350
1938	New York Yankees	$200/$400
1939	Cincinnati Reds	$275/$350
1939	New York Yankees	$300/$350

Year	Team	Price
1940	Cincinnati	$300/$350
1940	Detroit	$250/$325
1941	Brooklyn	$200/$400
1941	New York Yankees	$125/$250
1942	St. Louis Cardinals	$125/$250
1942	New York Yankees	$125/$250
1943	St. Louis Cardinals	$200/$250
1943	New York Yankees	$200/$250
1944	St. Louis Cardinals	$175/$250
1944	St. Louis Browns	$200/$350
1945	Chicago Cubs	$150/$200
1945	Detroit	$225/$350
1946	St. Louis Cardinals	$175/$200
1946	Boston Red Sox	$175/$225
1947	Brooklyn	$250/$300
1947	New York Yankees	$175/$250
1948	Boston Braves	$150/$175
1948	Cleveland	$100/$175
1949	Brooklyn	$200/$250
1949	New York Yankees	$175/$200
1950	Philadelphia Phillies	$125/$200
1950	New York Yankees	$150/$225
1951	New York Giants	$150/$225
1951	New York Yankees	$150/$225

Year	Team	Price
1952	Brooklyn	$200/$275
1952	New York Yankees	$150/$200
1953	Brooklyn	$225/$325
1953	New York Yankees	$150/$200
1954	New York Giants	$200/$250
1954	Cleveland	$125/$200
1955	Brooklyn	$250/$300
1955	New York Yankees	$150/$225
1956	Brooklyn	$175/$300
1956	New York Yankees	$125/$200
1957	Milwaukee	$100/$175
1957	New York Yankees	$100/$175
1958	Milwaukee	$100/$175
1958	New York Yankees	$100/$175
1959	Los Angeles	$75/$125
1959	Chicago White Sox	$150/$200
1960	Pittsburgh	$100/$125
1960	New York Yankees	$75/$100
1961	Cincinnati	$100/$125
1961	New York Yankees	$100/$150
1962	San Francisco	$150/$225
1962	New York Yankees	$75/$100
1963	Los Angeles	$60/$75
1963	New York Yankees	$60/$75

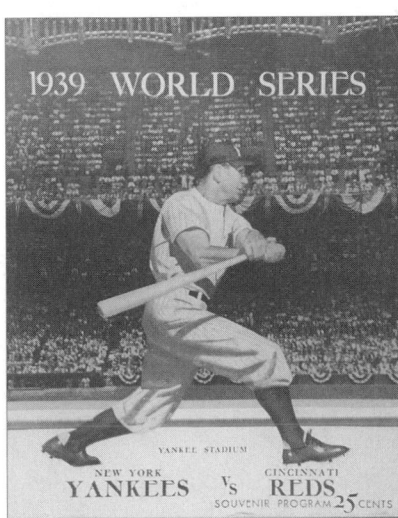

1939 World Series Program

1950 World Series Program

1956 World Series Program

1969 World Series Program

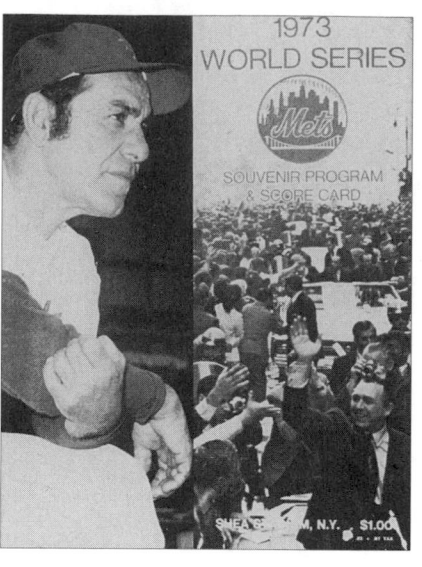

1973 World Series Program

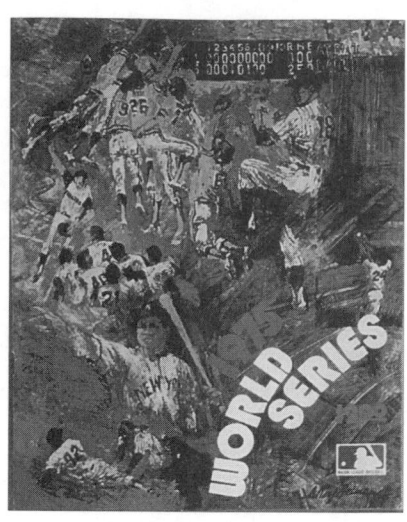

1975 World Series Program

Year	Team	Price
1964	St. Louis	$100/$125
1964	New York Yankees	$60/$75
1965	Los Angeles	$30/$40
1965	Minnesota	$75/$100
1966	Los Angeles	$40/$50
1966	Baltimore	$85/$125
1967	St. Louis	$100/$125
1967	Boston	$100/$125
1968	St. Louis	$100/$125
1968	Detroit	$125/$225
1969	New York Mets	$125/$150
1969	Baltimore	$50/$75
1970	Cincinnati	$50/$75
1970	Baltimore	$25/$55
1971	Pittsburgh	$75/$100
1971	Baltimore	$40/$50
1972	Cincinnati	$50/$75
1972	Oakland	$60/$75
1973	New York Mets	$20/$60
1973	Oakland	$60/$75
1974	Oakland/Los Angeles	$15/$35
1975	Cincinnati/Boston	$25/$50
1976	Cincinnati/N.Y. Yankees	$15/$30

Year	Team	Price
1977	N.Y. Yankees/Los Angeles	$10/$25
1978	N.Y. Yankees/Los Angeles	$10/$20
1979	Pittsburgh/Baltimore	$10/$15
1980	Philadelphia/Kansas City	$10/$15
1981	Los Angeles/N.Y. Yankees	$12/$18
1982	St. Louis/Milwaukee	$15
1983	Philadelphia/Baltimore	$15
1984	Detroit/San Diego	$10
1985	Kansas City/St. Louis	$10
1986	New York Mets/Boston	$10
1987	Minnesota/St. Louis	$10
1988	Los Angeles/Oakland	$10
1989	Oakland/San Francisco	$10
1990	Cincinnati/Oakland	$10
1991	Minnesota/Atlanta	$10
1992	Atlanta/Toronto	$10
1993	Toronto/Philadelphia	$10
1995	Atlanta/Cleveland	$10
1996	N.Y. Yankees/Atlanta	$10
1997	Florida/Cleveland	$10
1998	N.Y. Yankees/San Diego	$10
1999	N.Y. Yankees/Atlanta	$10
2000	N.Y. Yankees/N.Y. Mets	$10

1987 World Series Program

1965 World Series Program

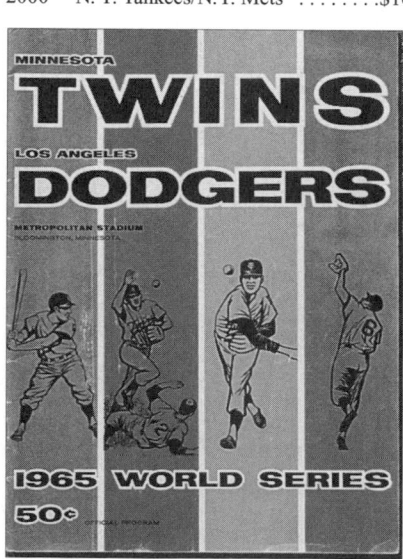

1965 World Series Program

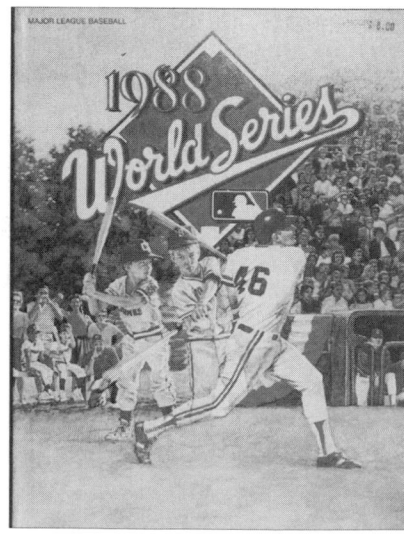

1988 World Series Program

Poster from the 1948 motion picture starring William Bendix, "The Babe Ruth Story."

Baseball Movie Posters

Interest in movie posters continues to increase every day, with the potential to grow even more. Posters, in general, have caught the eye of top auction houses.

In the general hobby, some posters from the 1950s, '60s and '70s are upwards of $500 in value. But there are 27x41 sports posters from the 1970s and later that are valued at less than $100.

Movie Poster Definitions

The first step of any movie poster collector is to understand the descriptions and variations of poster types and sizes.

One Sheet 27" x 41" H: This is the standard movie poster and the one form most familiar to the general public. A one-

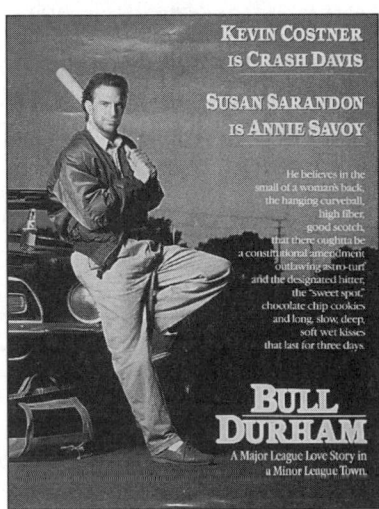

Poster from the 1988 movie starring Kevin Costner, "Bull Durham."

sheet is produced for every film, but this is not so for many other poster types. The first one sheets were produced around 1910 and since then have been printed using a variety of methods. Confusing to many collectors are the different styles that can be produced for a single motion picture.

Half Sheet 28" x 22" H: This type of poster is printed on a heavier stock. After 1960, fewer of this style poster were produced. They typically command 35 percent of the value of a one sheet.

Window Card 14" x 22" H: This is a heavy cardboard poster that was easy to display in a variety of locations, most of which were not the theater. A 4-inch blank border appeared at the top of the poster and was used by the theater to print show dates and locations. This type of poster typically commands 15 percent of the one-sheet value.

Insert 14" x 36" H: A tall and thin poster was printed on a variety of paper stocks. Earlier (pre-1960) inserts tend to be heavier. Inserts typically are priced the same as a half sheet, with the exception of those produced after 1960. Post-1960 inserts can command prices equal to one-sheet posters.

Six Sheet Various Sizes: A three to four section poster was often used for the creation of billboards. This type of poster is generally found after 1950. For a popular motion picture such as "The Natural," a six sheet can command upwards of twice the price of a one sheet. A lesser known film may not even reach full one-sheet value.

Three Sheet 41" x 81" H: A two to three section poster can command upwards of 150 percent of a one-sheet value.

Lobby Cards 14" x 11" H: A card set was usually produced in sets of eight; this may vary. A complete set of 8, 10 or 12 cards can bring upwards of 75 percent of a one-sheet value. There are different types of lobby cards in a set. The first card is often referred to as the title card and is most desirable among collectors. In some cases it may be worth 25 percent of the entire set. The rest are scene cards that vary in value.

Posters are packaged in two forms, folded or rolled. Rolled is preferred by collectors because the process avoids creases and preserves condition. The condition of a movie poster is one of the key factors in determining its value.

Prices listed are for selected one-sheet baseball movie posters in excellent condition.

Year	Movie	Price
1951	Angels in the Outfield	$100
1994	Angels in the Outfield (Remake)	$10
1992	The Babe	$20
1948	The Babe Ruth Story	$500
1976	The Bad News Bears	$60
1977	Bad News Bears Break Training	$45
1978	Bad News Bears Go To Japan	$40
1973	Bang the Drum Slowly	$100
1953	Big Leaguer	$150
1976	Bingo Long Traveling All-Stars and Motor Kings	$120

Poster from the 1962 motion picture with Mickey Mantle and Roger Maris, "Safe at Home."

Year	Movie	Price
1985	Brewster's Millions	$25
1988	Bull Durham	$90
1919	The Busher	$150
1994	Cobb	$40
1958	Damn Yankees	$300
1934	Death on the Diamond	$350
1988	Eight Men Out	$150
1996	The Fan	$90
1957	Fear Strikes Out	$150
1989	Field of Dreams	$120
1998	For the Love of the Game	$20
1949	It Happens Every Spring	$100
1950	The Jackie Robinson Story	$350
1992	A League of their Own	$35
1994	Little Big League	$10
1989	Major League I	$15
1994	Major League II	$10
1998	Major League III: Back to the Minors	$10
1938	Manhattan Merry-Go Round	$400
1984	The Natural	$50
2000	Perfect Game	$20
1952	The Pride of St. Louis	$450
1942	Pride of the Yankees	$500
1954	Roogie's Bump	$350
1993	Rookie of the Year	$10
1962	Safe At Home	$400
1993	The Sandlot	$25
1994	The Scout	$15
1985	The Slugger's Wife	$30
1949	The Stratton Story	$350
1949	Take Me Out to the Ballgame	$200

Poster from the 1942 motion picture, "Pride of the Yankees."

Base Ball by J. H. Singer Co.

Baseball Games

Generally, player- or team-related games are in greater demand than generic games, while board games are more valuable than card games. Game values are also determined in part by age (older is more valuable); company (Milton Bradley and Parker Bros. are two of the top); graphics/illustrations (those with higher quality of lithography and highly-detailed, colorful illustrations, especially on the box, are more valuable); box and board style (wooden boxes are more valuable than heavy cardboard; metal games are more valuable than cardboard ones); theme; the region in which the item is being sold; rarity; implements (game parts): and completeness (missing game cards or integral parts may drop a value by 50 percent). The American Game Collectors Association has archives of game instructions and can supply copies by contacting AGCA, 49 Brooks Ave., Lewiston, Maine 04240.

The game recognized as the first professional baseball game, The New Parlor Game of Baseball, was produced in 1869. Published by M.B. Sumner, the game included team rosters and lineup cards.

The first data-enhanced game based on player statistics appeared in 1950, when APBA Game Co. of Lancaster, Pa., created a dice and card game. The company produces new player game cards annually. The first game to be endorsed by a player —the Rube Walker & Harry Davis Baseball Game—was produced in 1905 by Champion Athletics. Since that time, several athletes have loaned their names to games—Hank Aaron, Bob Feller, Lou Gehrig, Walter Johnson, Mickey Mantle, Christy Mathewson, Willie Mays, Babe Ruth and Carl Yastrzemski, to name a few.

Generally, player- or team-related games are in greater demand than generic games. Condition is also a big factor in determining game values. Look for games which are in Very Good or Excellent condition — those which are not faded, water stained, covered with soot or mildew, and have all the parts and instructions

The best places to find games are at game conventions, collectibles shows, antique shops, flea markets, and through auction houses and hobby publications,

such as Krause Publications' *Toy Shop* and *Warman's Today's Collector* publications. When buying sight-unseen through the mail, however, get a detailed description about condition and inquire if the seller has a return policy if the material is not satisfactory.

Many games are repairable, but that's best left to an archivist or other professional who can clean your game using special materials such as acid-free glue and paper. Rubber cement thinner can be used to remove price stickers or tape on the outside box cover on games that are taped shut. Mildew can be cleaned with a bathroom mildew remover and a damp sponge, but test a small area first.

Games should be kept out of extremely cold or hot temperatures and places with wide temperature fluctuations. Direct sunlight, spotlights and other bright lights should be avoided, too, to prevent fading. Damp areas can cause mildew buildup, so a dehumidifier is recommended. Also, although stacking is not suggested, if you are going to stack your games, do so by cross-stacking them, alternating them vertically and horizontally, so that the weight of the games on top do not crush those underneath.

Note: Because so few exist in that condition, games from 1844-1945 are virtually impossible to find in mint condition. Prices fluctuate, too, oftentimes based on auction fever, which tends to drive prices up. Remember, value is what someone is willing to pay, not necessarily the selling price.

Selected Baseball Games

ABC Baseball Game, 1910s ......$430-$715
Action Baseball, Pressman, 1965 ....$35-$75
Alexander's Baseball Game, 1930s, .$245-$400
All Pro Baseball, Ideal, 1950 ....$45-$110
All-Star Baseball Game, Whitman, 1935
...........................$100-$165
All-Star Baseball, Cadaco-Ellis, 1959-60
...........................$40-$90
All-Star Baseball Game, Cadaco-Ellis, 1962
...........................$15-$40
All-Star Baseball, Cadaco, 1989 .....$12-$30
All-Star Electric Baseball & Football, Harett-Gilmar, 1955 ....$35-$90
All-Time Greats Baseball Game, Midwest Research, 1971 ....$15-$35
Alpha Baseball Game, Redlich Mfg. Co., 1930s
...........................$110-$275
APBA Baseball Master Game, APBA, 1975
...........................$35-$90

Alpha Baseball Game

All-Star Baseball by Cadaco

ASG Baseball, 3M, 1989 ....$12-$30
ASG Major League, Baseball, Gerney Games, 1973 ....$55-$135
Atkins Real Baseball, Atkins & Co., 1915
...........................$450-$750
Autograph Baseball Game, F.J. Raff, 1948
...........................$110-$275
Auto-Play Baseball Game, Auto-Play Games Co., 1911 ....$425-$700
Aydelott's Parlor Baseball, Aydelott's Base Ball Card Co., 1910 ....$195-$325
Babe Ruth Baseball Game, 1933 ..$640-$1075
Babe Ruth National Game of Baseball, Keiter-Fry Mfg. Co., 1929 ....$550-$910
Babe Ruth's Baseball Game, Milton Bradley, 1936 ....$200-$500
Babe Ruth's Official Baseball Game, Toy Town Corp., 1940s ....$430-$715
Ballplayer's Baseball Game, Jon Weber, 1955
...........................$30-$75
Bambino, Johnson Store Equipment Co., 1933
...........................$295-$490
Bambino Baseball Game, Mansfield-Zesiger Mfg. Co., 1946 ....$145-$250
Base-Ball Game of 1886, McLoughlin Bros., 1886 ....$750-$1300
Baseball, George Parker, 1885 .....$700-$1000
Baseball, George B. Doan & Co., 1920
...........................$70-$100
Baseball, J. Ottman Litho Co., 1915 .$140-$200
Baseball Game, All-Fair, 1930 .....$100-$125
Baseball, All-Fair, 1946 ....$30-$60
Baseball, Milton Bradley, 1940s ......$35-$50
Baseball, Samuel Lowe Co., 1942 .....$15-$25
Baseball, Football & Checkers, Parker Bros., 1957 ....$35-$90
Baseball & Checkers, Milton Bradley, 1910s
...........................$75-$150
Baseball Card All-Star Game, Captoys, 1987
...........................$6-$15
Baseball Card Game, Ed-U-Cards, 1950s
...........................$20-$50
Baseball Challenge, Tri-Valley Games, 1980
...........................$15-$35
Baseball Dominoes, Evans, 1910 ....$250-$400
Baseball Game, Brinkman Engineering, 1925
...........................$95-$135
Baseball Game, Corey Games, 1943 ..$70-$100

Game of Base-Ball

Babe Ruth's BaseBall Game by Milton Bradley from 1936.

Baseball Game, Parker Bros., 1949 . . . .$10-$25

Baseball Game, Parker Bros.,1950 . . . .$10-$22

The Baseball Game, Horatio, 1988 . . . .$12-$30

Baseball Game & G-Man Target Game, Marks Bros., 1940 . . . .$100-$165

Baseball's Greatest Moments, Ashburn, Ind., . . . 1979 . . . .$5-$12

Baseballitis Card Game, Baseballitis Card Co., 1909 . . . .$125-$205

Baseball Knapp Electro Game Set, Knapp, 1929 . . . .$125-$175

Baseball Mania The Board Game, Baseball Mania, 1993 . . . .$14-$30

Baseball Strategy, Avalon Hill, 1973 . . .$10-$20

Baseball Wizard Game, Morehouse Mfg., 1916 . . . .$265-$450

Base Hit, Games Inc.,1944 . . . .$55-$90

Bases Full Hand Skill Game, 1930 . . . .$45-$70

Batter-Rou Baseball Game, Memphis Plastic, 1950s . . . .$100-$250

Batter-Up Card Game, Ed-U-Cards, 1949 . . . .$25-$60

Batter Up, M. Hopper, 1946 . . . .$30-$75

Bee Gee Baseball Dart Target, Bee Gee, 1935 . . . .$70-$115

Bible Baseball, Standard Publishing Co., 1950 . . . .$10-$25

Big League Baseball Card Game, Whitman Publishing, 1933 . . . .$35-$60

Big League Baseball Game, J. Chein & Co. 1930s . . . .$42-$60

Big League Baseball Game, A.E. Gustafson 1938 . . . .$85-$125

Big League Baseball, Saalfield, 1959 .$55-$135

Big League Baseball Game, 3M Corp., 1966 . . . .$55-$135

Big League Baseball, 3M Corp., 1971 .$14-$30

Big Six: Christy Mathewson Indoor Baseball Game, Piroxloid Products Corp., 1922 . . . .$775-$1300

Big 6 Sports Games, Gardner & Co., 1950s . . . .$175-$450

Bob Feller's Big League Baseball, Saalfield Artcraft, 1950 . . . .$75-$250

Bobby Shantz's Baseball Game, Realistic Games, 1954 . . . .$80-$225

Boston Baseball Game, Boston Game Co., 1906 . . . .$495-$825

Boston Red Sox Game, Ed-U-Cards, 1964 . . . .$55-$135

Broadcast Baseball, J. Pressman & Co., 1938-40 . . . .$70-$100

Carl Hubbell Mechanical Baseball, Gotham, 1950 . . . .$100-$300

Carl Yastrzemski's Action Baseball, Pressman, 1962 . . . .$90-$195

Casey on the Mound, Kamm Games Inc., 1947 . . . .$190-$275

Challenge the Yankees, Hasbro, 1960s . . . .$125-$325

Challenge the Yankees Baseball Game by Hasbro.

The Champion Game of Base Ball, Schultz 1889 . . . .$4100-$6800

The Champion Base Ball Game, New York Game Co., 1913 . . . .$140-$200

The Champion Game of Baseball, Proctor Amusement Co., 1890s . . . .$60-$100

Championship Baseball, Championship Games Inc., 1966 . . . .$10-$30

Championship Baseball, Milton Bradley, 1984 . . . .$18-$40

Championship Base Ball Parlor Game Grebnelle Novelty Co., 1914 . . . .$1050-$1750

Charlie Brown's All Star Baseball Game, Parker Bros., 1965 . . . .$35-$90

Chicago Game Series Base Ball, George Doan Co., 1890s . . . .$1175-$1950

Classic Major League Baseball Classic green, 1987 . . . .$115-$250

Classic Major League Baseball, Classic, yellow update, 1987 . . . .$18-$40

Classic Major League Baseball, Classic red, 1988 . . . .$7.50-$15

Classic Major League Baseball, Classic blue, 1988 . . . .$10-$20

Classic Major League Baseball, Classic, 1989 . . . .$18-$40

Classic Major League Baseball, Classic travel orange, 1989, ...$10-$20

Classic Major League Baseball, Classic, 1989 . . . .$7.50-$15

Classic Major League Baseball, Classic, 1990 . . . .$7.50-$15

Classic Major League Baseball, Classic, 1990 . . . .$6-$13

Classic Major League Baseball, Classic 1990 . . . .$7.50-$15

Classic Major League Baseball, Classic, 1991 . . . .$6-$14

College Base Ball Game, Parker Bros., 1898 . . . .$350-$900

Computer Baseball, Epoch Playtime, 1966 . . . .$25-$65

Danny McFayden's Stove League Baseball Game, National Games Co., 1927 . . . .$295-$490

Dennis The Menace Baseball Game, 1960 . . . .$20-$70

National League Ball game by Yankee Novelty Co.

The Diamond Game of Base Ball, McLoughlin Bros., 1894 . . . .$1275-$2150

DiceBall, Ray-Fair Co., 1938 . . . . . .$90-$145

DiceBall, Intellijedx, 1993 . . . .$12-$25

The Dicex Baseball Game, Chester S. Howland, 1925 . . . .$195-$325

Double Game Board, Parker Bros., 1926 . . . .$165-$275

Double Header Baseball, Redlich Mfg. Co., 1935 . . . .$145-$250

Durgin's New BaseBall Game, Durgin & Palmer, 1885 . . . .$425-$700

Earl Gillespie Baseball Game, Wei-gill Inc., 1961 . . . .$25-$65

Ebbets Field Pro Baseball Game, Montminy Games, LLC, 1998 . . . .$10-$12

Egerton R. Williams Baseball Game, The Hatch Co., 1886 . . . .$2500-$5000

Electric Baseball, Einson-Freeman Publishing Corp., 1935 . . . .$35-$60

Electric Baseball, Jim Prentice, 1940s . .$55-$80

Electric Baseball, Jim Prentice, 1950s . .$30-$65

Electric Magnetic Baseball, 1900 . . .$175-$295

Ethan Allen's All-Star Baseball, Cadaco Ltd., 1941 . . . .$60-$150

Ethan Allen's All-Star Baseball Game, Cadaco-Ellis, 1942 . . . .$60-$150

Ethan Allen's All-Star Baseball Game, Cadaco-Ellis, 1946 . . . .$28-$60

Ethan Allen's All-Star Baseball Game, Cadaco-Ellis, 1955 . . . .$22-$50

Extra Innings, J. Kavanaugh, 1975 . . . .$15-$35

Fan-I-Tis, C.W. Marsh, 1913 . . . .$110-$180

Follow The Stars Watts Indoor Baseball League, H. Allan Watts, 1922 . . . .$225-$375

Fortune Telling & Baseball Game, 1889 . . . .$85-$140

Game of Base Ball, J.H. Singer, 1888 . . . .$325-$550

Game of Baseball, Milton Bradley, 1910 . . . .$100-$150

Game of Baseball, Milton Bradley, 1925 . . . .$42-$60

Game of Baseball, Canada Games Co., 1925 . . . .$210-$300

Game of Batter Up, Fenner Game Co., ...1908 . . . .$100-$165

George Brett's 9th-Inning Baseball Game, Brett Ball, 1981 . . . .$16-$40

Get The Balls Baseball Game, 1930 . . .$20-$30

Gil Hodges Pennant Fever, Research Games, 1970 . . . .$65-$150

Golden Trivia Game, Western Pub., 1984 . . . .$6-$15

Gonfalon Scientific Baseball, General Specialties Corp., 1930 . . . .$110-$180

Goose Goslin's Scientific Baseball Game Wheeler Toy Co., 1935 . . . .$250-$400

Graham McNamee Radio Scoreboard World Series Baseball Game, Radio Sports Inc., 1937 . . . .$250-$400

Grand Slam, Sming Game Co.,1979 . . . .$14-$30

Graphic BaseBall, North Western, 1930s . . . .$165-$275

The Great American Baseball Game, William Dapping, 1906 . . . .$145-$250

The Great American Game, Frantz Toys, 1925 . . . .$110-$180

The Great American Game of Baseball, Pittsburgh Brewing Co., 1907 . . . .$145-$250

The Great American Game of Baseball, Hustler Toy Co., 1923 . . . .$105-$175

Great American Game of Pocket Baseball, Neddy Pocket Game Co., 1910 . . . .$140-$200

Great Mails Baseball Card Game, Walter Mails Baseball Game Co., 1919 ......$2475-$4100

Great Pennant Races, Great Pennant Races 1980 ....$14-$28

Grebnelle Championship Base Ball Parlor Game, Grebnelle Novelty Co., 1914 ......$150-$250

Hank Aaron Baseball Game, Ideal, 1973 ....$50-$125

Hank Aaron's Eye Ball Game, 1960s .$85-$215

Hank Bauer's "Be A Manager", Bamo Enterprises, 1953 ....$75-$175

Hatfield's Parlor Base-Ball Game, Hatfield Co., 1914 ....$140-$200

Hening's In-Door Game of Professional Baseball, Inventor's Co., 1889 ....$525-$875

Home Baseball Game, McLaughlin Bros., 1900 ....$900-$1700

Home Baseball Game, McLaughlin Bros., 1910 ....$775-$1100

Home Baseball Game, Rosebud Art. Co., 1936 ....$100-$150

Home Diamond The Great Baseball Game, Phillips Co., 1913 ....$175-$295

Home Run King, Selrite Products Inc., 1930s ....$275-$450

Home Run With Bases Loaded, T.V. Morrison 1935 ....$205-$350

Home Team Baseball Game, Ben Dickenson, 1917 ....$140-$200

Home Team Baseball Game, Ben Dickenson/Selchow & Righter, 1918 $140-$200

Home Team Baseball Game, Selchow & Righter, 1957 ....$35-$90

Home Team Baseball Game, Selchow & Righter, 1964 ....$14-$30

Houston Astros Baseball Challenge Game Croque Ltd., 1980 ....$15-$35

In-Door Baseball, E. Bommer Foundation, 1926 ....$100-$180

Inside Base Ball Game, Popular Games Co., 1913 ....$300-$500

Jackie Robinson Baseball Game, Gotham Pressed Steel Corp., 1948 ....$425-$725

Jacmar Big League Electric Baseball, Jacmar, 1952 ....$100-$250

JDK Baseball, JDK Baseball, 1982 ....$10-$25

Jim Thome's Pro Baseball Game, Montminy Games LLC, 1998 ....$10-$12

Joe "Ducky" Medwick's Big Leaguer Baseball Game, Johnson-Breier Co., 1939 ....$125-$200

Jose Canseco's Perfect Baseball Game, Perfect Game Co., 1991 ....$8-$20

Junior Baseball Game, Benjamin-Seller Mfg. Co., 1913 ....$100-$165

Kellogg's Baseball Game, Kellogg's, 1936 ....$21-$30

KSP Baseball, Koch Sports Products, 1983 ....$15-$35

Las Vegas Baseball, Samar Enterprises, 1987 ....$8-$20

Lawson's Patent Base Ball Playing Cards, T.H. Lawson & Co., 1884 ....$350-$700

League Parlor BaseBall, Bliss, 1880s ....$1050-$1750

League Parlor BaseBall, R. Bliss Mfg., 1889s ....$600-$1000

Leslie's Base Ball Game, Perfection Novelty & Advertising Co., 1909 ....$145-$250

Lew Fonseca The Carrom BaseBall Game, Carrom Co., 1930s ....$525-$875

LF Baseball, Len Feder, 1980 ....$12-$30

Line Drive, Lord & Freber Inc., 1953 .$60-$125

Little League Baseball Game, Standard Toycraft Inc., 1950s ....$25-$70

LongBall, Ashburn Industries, 1975 ...$30-$75

Look All-Star Baseball Game, Progressive Research, 1960 ....$35-$90

Lou Gehrig's Official Play Ball, Christy Walsh, . 1930s ....$525-$875

Lucky 7th BaseBall Game, All-American Games Co., 1937 ....$55-$90

"Mac" Baseball Game, McDowell Mfg. Co., 1930s ....$145-$250

Main Street BaseBall, Main Street Toy Co., 1989 ....$20-$55

Major League Ball, National Game Makers, 1921 ....$325-$550

Major League Indoor Base Ball, Philadelphia Game Mfg. Co., 1913 ....$650-$1000

The Major League BaseBall Game, 1910 ....$85-$145

Major Legue BaseBall, Negamco, 1959 ....$12-$25

Major League BaseBall Magnetic Dart Game, Pressman, 1958 ....$55-$135

Major League Indoor BaseBall Game, Philadelphia Game Mfg. Co., 1912 .....$4200-$6000

Manage Your Own Team, Warren, 1950s ....$55-$135

Mather's Parlor Base Ball Game, Mathers, .1908 ....$350-$500

Mickey Mantle's Baseball Action Game, Kohner Bros., 1960s ....$50-$175

Mickey Mantle's Big League Baseball, Gardner & Co., 1962 ....$125-$325

Mickey Mouse Baseball, Post Cereal, 1936 ....$55-$90

Montreal Expos Super Baseball, Super Sports Games, 1979 ....$7.50-$15

MVP Baseball The Sports Card Game, Ideal , 1989 ....$8-$20

National American Base Ball Game, Parker Bros., 1910 ....$110-$180

The National Base Ball Game, National Baseball Playing, 1913 ....$700-$1200

The National Game of Base Ball, McLoughlin 1901 ....$500-$875

The National Game, National Game Co., 1889 ....$875-$1450

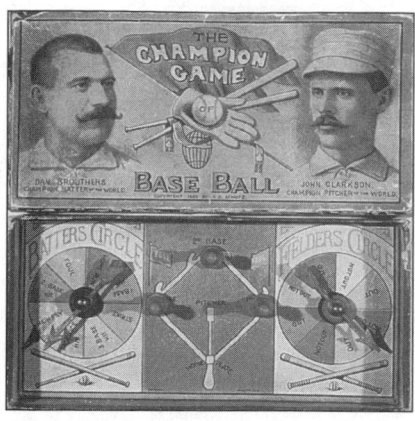

∫The Champion Game of Base Ball by A. S. Schutz from 1889.

National League Ball Game, Yankee Novelty Co., 1890 ....$350-$575

NBC Baseball Game of the Week, Hasbro, 1969 ....$25-65

New Baseball Game, Clark & Martin, 1885 ....$165-$275

The New Parlor Game Baseball, M.B. Summer, 1869 ....$7000-$10,000

New York Recorder Newspaper Supplement Baseball Game, 1896 ....$430-$715

Official Baseball Game, Milton Bradley, 1965 ....$175-450

Official Baseball Game, Milton Bradley, 1953 ....$100-$250

Official Baseball Game, Milton Bradley, 1970 ....$55-$125

Official Denny McLain Magnetik Game, Gotham, 1968 ....$115-$295

Official Dizzy and Daffy Dean Nok-Out Baseball Game, Nok-Out Manufacturing Co., 1930 ....$350-$575

Our National Ball Game, McGill & DeLany, 1887 ....$425-$650

Our No. 7 Baseball Game Puzzle, Satisfactory Co.,1910 ....$110-$180

Ozark Ike's Complete 3 Game Set, Builtrite, 1956 ....$55-$135

Parlor Baseball, E.B. Pierce, 1878 .$1750-$2900

Parlor Base Ball, American Parlor Base Ball Co., 1903 ....$165-$250

Parlor BaseBall Game Chicago vs. Boston, 1880s ....$2100-$3000

Parker Bros. Baseball Game, Parker Bros., 1950 ....$45-$110

Pat Moran's Own Baseball Game, Smith, Kline & French, 1919 ....$325-$550

Pee-Wee (Pee Wee Reese Marble Game)Pee Wee Enterprises, 1956 ....$175-$450

Peg Base Ball, Parker Bros., 1908 ...$105-$175

Pennant Chasers Baseball Game, Craig Hopkins, 1946 ....$25-$70

Pennant Drive, Accu-Stat Game Co., 1980 ....$8-$20

Pennant Puzzle, L.W. Harding, 1909 .$250-$400

Pennant Winner Wolverine Supply & Manufacturing Co., 1939 ....$175-$295

The Philadelphia Inquirer Baseball Game *Philadelphia Inquirer*, 1896 ......$145-$250

Photo-Electric Baseball, Cadaco-Ellis, 1951 ... .$55-$135

Pinch Hitter, J&S Corp., 1938 ......$110-$180

Play Ball, National Game Co., 1920 .$145-$250

Pocket Baseball, Toy Creations, 1940 .$15-$25

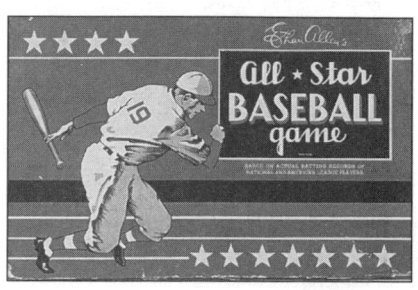

Ethan Allen's Baseball Game

Major League Indoor Base Ball

Mickey Mantle's Baseball Game

Pocket Edition Major League Baseball Game, Anderson, 1943 ....$85-$140
Polar Ball Baseball, Bowline Game Co., 1940 ....$90-$145
Poosh-em-up Slugger, Bagatelle, North Western Products, 1946 ....$30-$105
Popular Indoor Baseball Game, Egerton R. Williams, 1896 ....$500-$850
Pro Baseball, 1940s ....$70-$115
Pro Baseball Card Game, Just Games, 1980s ....$6-$60
Pursue the Pennant, Pursue the Pennant, 1984 ....$25-$60
Psychic Base Ball Game, Psychic Baseball Corp., 1927 ....$60-$150
Psychic Base Ball Game, Parker Bros., 1935 ....$175-$295
Radio Baseball, Toy Creations, 1939 . .$50-$125
Real Action Baseball Games, Real-Action Games, 1966 ....$20-$50
Real Baseball Card Game, National Baseball, 1900 ....$110-$275
Realistic Baseball Realistic Game & Toy Co., 1925 ....$205-$350
Red Barber's Big League Baseball Game, G&R Anthony Inc., 1950s ....$350-$900
Replay Series Baseball, Bond Sports Ent., 1983 ....$6-$15
Robin Roberts Sports Club Baseball Game, Dexter Wayne, 1960 ....$100-$250
Roger Maris' Action Baseball, Pressman Toy Co., 1962 ....$50-$175
Roll-O Junior Baseball Game, Roll-O Mfg., 1922 ....$325-$550
Roulette Base Ball Game, W. Bartholomae, 1929 ....$115-$195
Rube Bressler's Baseball Game, Ray B. Bressler, 1936 ....$130-$215
Rube Waddell & Harry Davis Baseball Game, Inventors and Investors Corp., 1905 $875-$1450
St. Louis Cardinals Baseball Card Game, Ed-U-Cards, 1964 ....$35-$85
Sandlot Slugger, 1960s ....$35-$90
Say Hey! Willie Mays Baseball Game, Toy Development Co., 1954 ....$200-$525
Scott's Baseball Card Game, Scott's BaseBall Cards, 1989 ....$12-$30
Skor-It Bagatelle, Northwestern Products, 1930s ....$145-$250
Slide Kelly! Baseball Game, B.E. Ruth Co. 1936 ....$70-$115
Slugger Baseball Game, Marks Bros.,1930 ....$110-$180

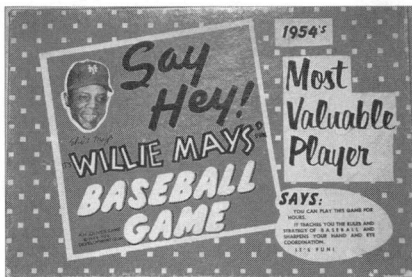

Say Hey! Willie Mays Baseball by Centennial Games.

Snappet Catch Game with Harmon Killebrew, Killebrew Inc., 1960 ....$55-$135
Spin Cycle Baseball, Pressman, 1965 . .$25-$65
Sporting News BaseBall, Mundo Games, 1986 ....$8-$20
Sport-O-Rama Pin-Bo, 1950s ....$35-$90
A Sports Illustrated Game Baseball, Time Inc., 1975 ....$25-$65
Sports Illustrated Baseball, *Sports Illustrated* 1972 ....$25-$65
Sports Illustrated Pennant Race Avalon Hill-*Sports Illustrated*, 1982 ....$7.50-$15
Star Baseball Game, W.P. Ulrich, 1941 ....$70-$115
Statis Pro Baseball, Avalon Hill, 1979 . .$17-$40
Strategy Manager Baseball, McGuffin-Ramsey, 1967 ....$20-$50
Strat-O-Matic Baseball, Strat-O-Matic, 1961 ....$100-$250
Strat-O-Matic Baseball, Strat-O-Matic, 1969 ....$10-$25
Strike-Like, Saxon Toy Corp., 1940's . .$55-$90
Strike-Out, All-Fair Inc., 1920s .....$175-$295
Strike 3 by Carl Hubbell, Tone Products Corp., 1946 ....$275-$725
Superstar Baseball, Sports Illustrated, 1966 ....$30-$75
Superstar Baseball, *Sports Illustrated-Time* Inc., 1974 ....$12-$25
Swat Baseball, Milton Bradley, 1948 ..$20-$50
Tiddle Flip Baseball, Modern Craft Ind., 1949 ....$20-$50
Time Travel Baseball, Time Travel, 1979 $8-$18
Tom Seaver Game Action Baseball, Pressman Toy Co., 1969 ....$50-$175
Toto The New Game BaseBall, Toto Sales Co., 1925 ....$55-$90
Triple Play, National Games Inc., 1930s ....$12-$20
Tru-Action Electric Baseball Game, Tudor, 1955 ....$25-$80
Ty Cobb's Own Game of Baseball, National Novelty Co., 1924 ....$350-$650
U-Bat-It, Schultz III Star Co., 1920s . .$70-$115
Ultimate Sports Trivia, Ram Games, 1992 ....$17-$35
Uncle Sam's Base Ball, J.C. Bell, 1890 ....$525-$875
Wachter's Parlor Base Ball, Wachter, 1888 ....$145-$250
Walter Johnson Baseball Game, Walter Johnson Baseball Game, 1920s .....$125-$250
Walter Johnson Baseball Game, Walter Johnson Baseball Game, 1930s ....$195-$325
Waner's Baseball Game, Waner's BaseBall Inc., 1939 ....$350-$575
Whirly Bird Play Catch, Game Innovation Industries, 1958 ....$20-$50

Slide Kelly! game by B.E. Ruth Co., from 1936

Whiz BaseBall, Electric Game Co., 1945 ....$42-$60
Wil-Croft Baseball, Wil-Croft, 1971 . . .$10-$25
William's Popular Indoor Baseball, Hatch Co., 1889 ....$700-$1175
Willie Mays Push Button Baseball, Eldon Champion, 1965 ....$175-$450
Willie Mays "Say Hey" Baseball, Centennial Games, 1958 ....$190-$450
Win A Card Trading Game, Milton Bradley, 1965 ....$350-$900
Winko Baseball, Milton Bradley, 1945 .$45-$70
Wiry Dan's Electric Baseball Game, Harrett-Gilmore, 1950 ....$15-$65
World's Championship Baseball, Champion Amusement Co., 1910 ....$175-$295
World's Championship Baseball Game, Beacon Hudson Co., 1930s ....$100-$150
World's Greatest Baseball Game, J. Woodlock, 1977 ....$30-$80
World Series Baseball Game, Radio Sports, 1940s ....$205-$350
World Series Big League Baseball Game, E.S. Lowe, 1945 ....$115-$150
World Series Parlor Baseball, Clifton E. Hooper, 1916 ....$150-$250
"You're Out" Baseball Game, Corey Games,1941 ....$85-$140
Zimmer BaseBall Game, McLoughlin Bros., 1885 ....$1300-$2150

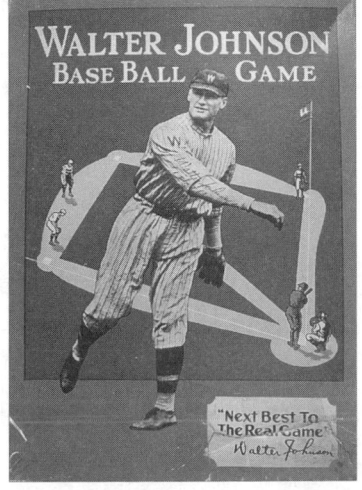

Walter Johnson Base Ball Game.

Baseball Pennants

Since almost every kid who had a felt pennant tacked it up on his bedroom wall, it's unusual to find a vintage pennant in well-preserved, investment-grade condition. Most, measuring 12x30, have pin holes in them and can be purchased for less than $50. Today's versions, often available at stadiums and arenas, are made in large quantities, so look for 1950s and before models, and concentrate on pennants for popular teams, championship teams, teams that no longer exist, or those that commemorate a specific event. Some places to find pennants would be at larger card shows or through sports memorabilia auctions. Sometimes a pennant or two will turn up in an antique shop, too. Although it probably isn't going to offer big returns as an investment piece, a pennant can still add a nice decorative touch to any memorabilia display.

Selected Pennants

1920s Cleveland Indians, red with white letters $135
1930s Boston Braves, batting scene, red $125
1934-35 Detroit Tigers pennant winners, black-and-white on orange $375
1935 Detroit Tigers World Champs scroll pennant, orange on black $350
Early-1940s Boston Red Sox, large baseball over the stadium, gray and red $100
Early-1940s Brooklyn Dodgers, batter and catcher, white on red $285
Early-1940s Brooklyn Dodgers, Brooklyn Dodgers: Our Champs, white on purple . . . $395
Mid-1940s Boston Red Sox, batter hitting pitched ball, white on red $135
Late-1940s Brooklyn Dodgers, shows catcher and batter from backside, white on blue . . . $175
Late-1940s New York Yankees, player sliding into tag, white on blue $95
Late-1940s Philadelphia Phillies signature pennant with names and numbers, Fightin' Phillies, white and red $195
Late-1940s St. Louis Cardinals, two birds on a bat, red, yellow and white on red $65
Late-1940s St. Louis Browns, player making a catch, orange on blue $175
1940s Boston Red Sox, runner sliding into base, white on red $145
1940s Brooklyn Dodgers, player sliding into tag, blue on white $150
1940s Chicago Cubs, large C in Chicago, white on blue $110
1940s Chicago Cubs, player sliding into a tag, black on orange $95
1940s Chicago White Sox, infield play in progress, white on dark blue $125
1940s Cincinnati Reds, Cincinnati in Gothic letters, white and red $150
1940s Cleveland Indians, Indian with full head-dress, white on red $80
1940s Detroit Tigers, black tiger head on orange $85
1940s New York Giants, batter, catcher and umpire, white and blue $125
1948 Cleveland Indians American League Champs/World Series, multi-color on dark red $195
Early-1950s Brooklyn Dodgers, red, white and blue $295
Early-1950s Philadelphia A's, white on blue . $85
Mid-1950s Chicago Cubs Wrigley Field, Cub playing with a ball, white on blue $75
Mid-1950s Baltimore Orioles, bird on a baseball, white and pink on red $100
Mid-1950s New York Yankees, Uncle Sam, multi-color on blue $125
Late-1950s Baltimore Orioles, bird pitching over Memorial Stadium $95
Late-1950s San Francisco Giants, mascot on the bridge, white, gray and pink and green $85
1950s Chicago Cubs, two cubs standing, white and peach on blue $55
1950s Chicago White Sox, winged foot, white and yellow on blue $75
1950s Detroit Tigers, Tiger head inside Tiger Stadium $60
1950s New York Giants, orange and white on black $60
1950s New York Yankees, Yankees logo, red and blue on white $95
1950s Philadelphia Phillies, Go Phillies Go with batting scene $60
1950s Philadelphia Phillies, elephant with a ball in its trunk, white and blue $125
1950s-60s Pittsburgh Pirates, black with Pirate head with a sword in his mouth $90
1950 Philadelphia Phillies, Fightin' Phillies, with tag scene and players' names and numbers around it, white on red $165
1950 New York Yankees American League Champs, player sliding into a tag $125
1950 New York Yankees American League Champions, Bronx Bombers batter, white on blue $375
1954 New York Giants World Series $125
1955 Brooklyn Dodgers National League Champs, scroll, Bum, multi-color on blue $475
1957 Milwaukee Braves World Champions, names of players, white and purple $250
1958 Milwaukee Braves National League Champs, Indian dancing, player names, white and red $110

1942 St. Louis Cardinals World Series pennant

Boston Red Sox pennant

1957 Milwaukee Braves pennant

1958 Milwaukee Braves 1958 National League Champs scroll pennant $100

1959 Chicago White Sox American League Champs, white on blue $125

Early-1960s Chicago Cubs, Wrigley Field, multi-color on blue $55

Early-1960s Houston Colt 45s, blue and orange on white $65

Early-1960s New York Mets, skyline, team logo, blue and white on dark blue $85

Mid-1960s San Francisco Giants, SF in block, Giants logo, bat, black on orange $65

Late-1960s Baltimore Orioles, bird on top of an O, bat and glove, black on orange $65

Late-1960s New York Mets, shows Shea, Mr. Met and Liberty on blue $45

Late-1960s Washington Senators, white on red $60

1960s Atlanta Braves, multi-color on navy . .$35

1960s Pittsburgh Pirates, multi-color on black $40

1960s St. Louis Cardinals, multi-color on red $40

1960s San Francisco Giants, play at the plate, black on orange $85

1960s Washington Senators, pitcher and capital, red, white and blue $75

1960 Pittsburgh Pirates 1960 National League Champions, pirate holding a sword $135

1960 St. Louis Browns, shows batter, white on brown $55

1961 Cincinnati Reds picture pennant $135

1961 Cincinnati Reds National League Champions, players' names, red and blue on white .$110

1961 New York Yankees picture pennant . .$250

1962 Dodger Stadium grand opening, blue and red vertical pennant $75

1963 New York Mets black-and-white picture pennant $155

1964 Philadelphia Phillies picture pennant . .$85

1965 Houston Colt .45s/Houston Astrodome, double-sided pennant $150

1965 World Series Los Angeles Dodgers vs. Minnesota Twins, multi-color on blue felt $85

1966 Baltimore Orioles team picture pennant $100

1966 Chicago White Sox team picture pennant, red and blue on white $110

1966 New York Mets team picture pennant $135

1966 World Series Los Angeles Dodgers vs. Baltimore Orioles, bird over Dodger Stadium $65

1966-67 California Angels, Anaheim Stadium $55

1967 Boston Red Sox vs. St. Louis Cardinals World Series at Fenway Park, black and red on white $125

1967 St. Louis Cardinals National League Champions $40

1968 Chicago White Sox picture pennant . . .$85

1968 Detroit Tigers American League Champions, black and orange on white $85

1968 St. Louis Cardinals National League Champions/World Series, white and pink on red . .$65

1969 Baltimore Orioles World Series picture pennant $110

1969 Boston Red Sox picture pennant $55

1969 Cincinnati Reds picture pennant $95

1969 Houston Astros $20

1969 Kansas City Royals $40

1969 Montreal Expos $35

1969 Mickey Mantle Day at Yankee Stadium $55

1969 New York Mets World Champions, orange on blue $95

1969 Seattle Pilots, MLB logo, Seattle in script, multi-colored on red $185

1969-71 Washington Senators, red and blue on white $75

Early-1970s Chicago White Sox, batter on sock in red circle $45

Early-1970s Cleveland Indians, Chief Wahoo with bat and ball $45

Early-1970s Minnesota Twins, TC in dot over in Minnesota, white on blue $35

1970s Baltimore Orioles $10

1970s Houston Astros $10

1970s Milwaukee Brewers $10

1970s St. Louis Cardinals $10

1970s San Diego Padres, crossed bats with Padre, white on brown $55

1970s San Francisco Giants $10

1970 Baltimore Orioles team picture, orange and black on white $75

1970 Baltimore Orioles picture pennant . . .$125

1970 Milwaukee Brewers, barrel man swinging a bat, gold on blue $55

1971 Pittsburgh Pirates color team photo pennant $95

1971 Pittsburgh Pirates National League Champs scroll, black and gold on white $60

1972 All-Star Game in Atlanta, red and blue on white $55

1973 Boston Red Sox Fenway Park, white and green on red $75

1973 Chicago White Sox American League Western Division Champions $10

1973 New York Mets World Champs signature pennant $45

1973 New York Mets You Gotta Believe, Mets #1 Again, 1973 Champions, blue on white $75

1973 New York Mets Eastern Division Champs scroll pennant, white and orange on blue . . .$65

1973 Oakland A's American League Champs scroll pennant $45

1974 Cincinnati Reds picture pennant $95

1974 Hank Aaron Home Run King, dated April 8, 1974 . . . .$45

1974 Los Angeles Dodgers World Series signature pennant $50

1960 Pittsburgh Pirates N.L. Championship pennant

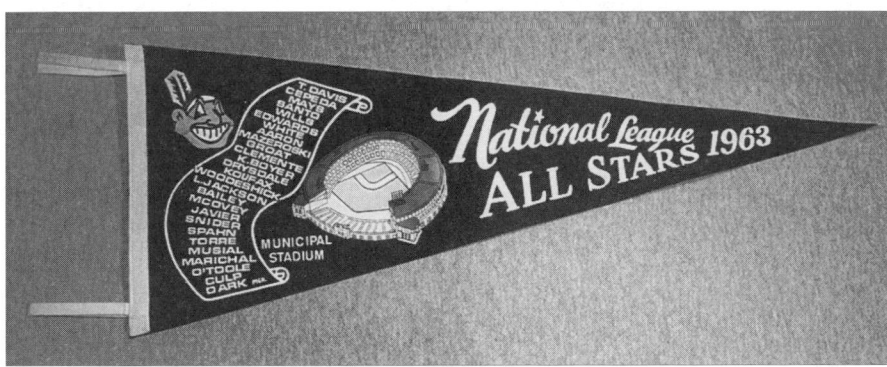

1963 National League All-Stars pennant

1969 New York Yankees Mickey Mantle Day Pennant

1975 Boston Red Sox World Series signature pennant $55
1975 Boston Red Sox World Champions phantom $25
1975 Boston Red Sox American League Champions scroll pennant $50
1975 Cincinnati Reds picture pennant $65
1975 Cincinnati Reds World Champs signature pennant $65
1976 Cincinnati Reds World Champs trophy $45
1977 New York Yankees picture pennant . . .$55
1977 All-Star Game at Yankee Stadium $30
1977 Los Angeles Dodgers National League Champs scroll pennant, blue on white $50
1978 Do it Pete! Do it Pete! for Rose's hitting streak, 7/25/78 at Shea Stadium $55
1979 Baltimore Orioles American League Champions signature pennant $45
1979 California Angels American League West Champions scroll pennant $65

1979 Philadelphia Phillies picture pennant, black-and-white $75
1979 Pittsburgh Pirates World Champions scroll pennant $45
1980 Kansas City World Series scroll pennant, blue and gold on white $45
1980 New York Yankees $10
1980 New York Yankees American League Eastern Division Champs, blue and red on white $35
1980 Philadelphia Phillies World Champions scroll pennant, We're #1 . . . .$45
1981 All-Star Game in Cleveland, Chief Wahoo on a star $45
1981 New York Yankees American League Champions scroll pennant $45
1982 Milwaukee Brewers American League Eastern Division Champs, blue and gold on white $40
1983 50th All-Star Game at Comiskey Park .$10
1983 Carl Yastrzemski retirement day pennant $55

1983 Baltimore Orioles World Champions, scroll pennant, black and orange on white $45
1983 Philadelphia Phillies National League Champs, maroon, blue and red on white $40
1984 Chicago Cubs World Series $20
1984 Detroit Tigers World Champions scroll pennant, blue and orange on black $55
1984 Kansas City Royals American League Western Division Champions, scroll $35
1984 San Diego Padres National League Western Division Champions $10
1985 Kansas City Royals American League Western Division Champions, scroll $35
1985 Los Angeles Dodgers National League Western Division Champions $10
1986 Boston Red Sox American League Eastern Division Champions $10
1986 Boston Red Sox World Series $10
1986 New York Mets World Champs signature pennant $35
1986 New York Yankees color team picture .$35
1987 Minnesota Twins World Series $10
1988 All-Star Game in Cincinnati $10
1989 Chicago Cubs N.L. East Champs $10
1993 Florida Marlins Opening Day $20
1994 All-Star Game in Pittsburgh $10

1950s Chicago Cubs pennant

Chicago White Sox pennant

1940s Brooklyn Dodgers pennant

1950 American Nut & Chocolate Pennants

Although there is nothing on these small (1⅞ by 4) felt pennants to identify the issuer, surviving ads show that the American Nut & Chocolate Co. of Boston sold them as a set of 22 for 50 cents. The pennants of American League players are printed in blue on white, while National Leaguers are printed in red on white. The pennants feature crude line-art drawings of players on the left, along with a facsimile autograph. The pennants carry an *American Card Catalog* designation of F510. The complete set of 22 pennants is worth $350 in Near Mint condition.

Ewell Blackwell $15
Harry Brecheen $15
Phil Cavarretta $15
Bobby Doerr $17.50
Bob Elliott $15
Boo Ferriss $15
Joe Gordon $15
Tommy Holmes $15
Charles Keller $15
Ken Keltner $15
Whitey Kurowski $15
Ralph Kiner $20
Johnny Pesky $15
Pee Wee Reese $35
Phil Rizzuto $30
Johnny Sain $17.50
Enos Slaughter $17.50
Warren Spahn $30
Vern Stephens $15
Earl Torgeson $15
Dizzy Trout $15
Ted Williams $70

Baseball Cereal Boxes

Cheerios
1998 Marlins '97 WS Champs (HN) $8

General Mills Grand Slam Baseball
1998 McGwire/Thomas/Piazza $7

Kellogg's Corn Flakes

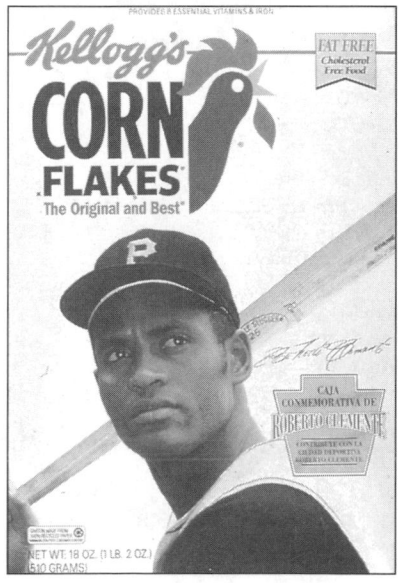

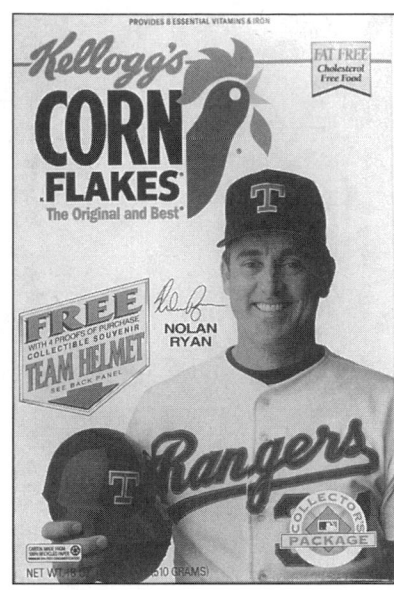

1970 Willie Mays $50
1983 San Diego Chicken 25
1983 Mike Reilly (umpire) 20
1983 Fernando Valenzuela 40
1991 Hank Aaron 40
1991 Ernie Banks 25
1991 Yogi Berra 25
1991 Lou Brock 25
1991 Steve Carlton 25
1991 Bob Gibson 25
1991 Aaron/Berra/Mays/Spahn 30
1992 Mike Schmidt 30
1993 Roberto Clemente (Spanish) 35
1933 Nolan Ryan 20
1933 Nolan Ryan farewell 30
1994 Roberto Clemente batting 30
1994 Roberto Clemente bat (Spanish) 40

Kellogg's Corn Pops
1993 Tom Seaver $20

Kellogg's Frosted Flakes

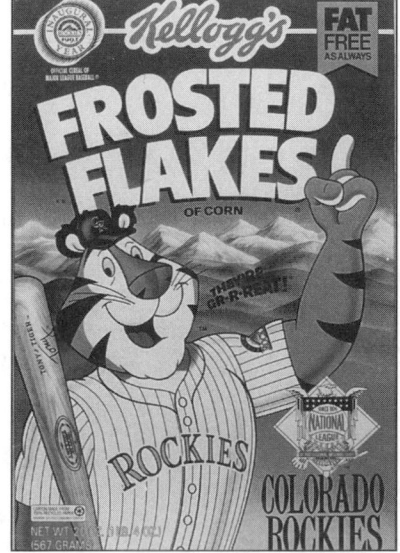

1991 Atlanta Braves NL Champs $30
1991 Braves WS (phantom) 75
1991 Twins WS Champs 35

1992 Blue Jays Champs (*Canada) 35
1992 Braves NL Champs 35
1992 St. Louis Cardinals 35
1993 Ken Griffey, Jr. (20/25) 20
1993 Florida Marlins Inaugural 18
1993 Colorado Rockies Inaugural 18
1995 Carlos Baerga (Spanish) 15
1995 Colorado Rockies (Spanish) 15

Frosted Mini-Wheats
1995 Reggie Jackson (20) $25

Kellogg's Froot Loops
1983 Reggie Jackson/ Robin Yount/ Fernando
Valenzuela $20

Post
Post Alpha-Bits
Canadian
1994 Joe Carter $20

Post 40% Bran Flakes
1960s Baseball cards on back . . . .$50-$100

Post Grape Nuts
1960s Baseball cards on back . . . .$50-$100

Post Grape Nut Flakes
1959 Warren Spahn $45

Post Honeycomb
1993 Barry Bonds, Ken Griffey, Jr. $15
1994 Mattingly/ Gonzalez/ Bonds/ Thomas/
Olerud/ Bonilla .20

Post Sugar Crisp
1955 Ted Williams $50
1960s Baseball cards on back 50
1994 Mattingly/Gonzalez, Bonds, Thomas,
Olerud, Bonilla 15

Post Raisin Bran
1960s Baseball Cards on back . . . . . .$50-$100

Post Sugar Crisp
Canadian
1994 Joe Carter $20
1995 Devon White 15
1997 Moises Alou 15

Post Toasties
1960s Baseball cards on back ..... $50-$100

Ralston
Cookie Crisp
1981 Jim Palmer $12
1984 Dale Murphy .... .10

Ralston
Donkey Kong
1983 Jim Palmer $12

General Mills
Wheaties
1935
Fancy Frame with Script Signature
Jack Armstrong $20
Wally Berger .... .20
Tommy Bridges .... .20
Mickey Cochrane .... .175
James "Rip" Collins .... .20
Dizzy Dean .... .55
Paul Dean .... .22
William Delaney .... .20
Jimmie Foxx .... .50
Frank Frisch .... .37
Lou Gehrig .... .225
Goose Goslin .... .30
Lefty Grove .... .45
Carl Hubbell .... .35
Travis Jackson .... .30
"Chuck" Klein .... .30
Gus Mancuso .... .20
"Pepper" Martin .... .20
Joe Medwick .... .35
Melvin Ott .... .50
Harold Schumacher .... .20
Al Simmons .... .30
"Jo Jo" White .... .20

1936
Fancy Frame with Printed Name and Data
Earl Averill $30
Mickey Cochrane .... .40
"Jimmie" Foxx .... .45
Lou Gehrig .... .225
Hank Greenberg .... .40
"Gabby" Hartnett .... .30
Carl Hubbell .... .35
"Pepper" Martin .... .17

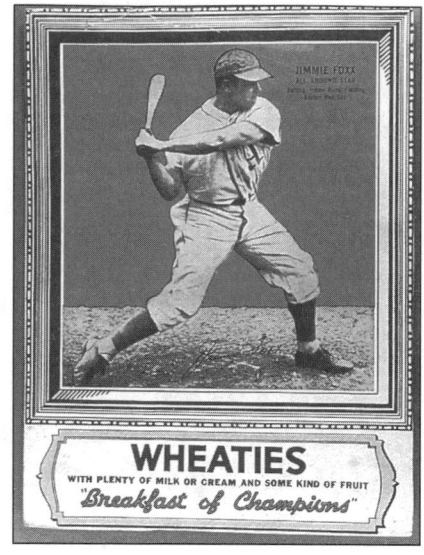

Van L. Mungo .... .20
"Buck" Newsom .... .20
"Arky" Vaughan .... .30
Jimmy Wilson .... .20

1936
How to Play Winning Baseball
Lefty Gomez $35
Billy Herman .... .30
Luke Appling .... .35
Jimmie Foxx .... .45
Joe Medwick .... .35
Charlie Gehringer .... .35
Mel Ott .... .45
Odell Hale .... .20
Bill Dickey .... .50
"Lefty" Grove .... .50
Carl Hubbell .... .40
Earl Averill .... .35

1936
Thin Orange Border/Figures In Border
Curt Davis $20
Lou Gehrig .... .250
Charlie Gehringer .... .40
Lefty Grove .... .40
Rollie Hemsley .... .20
Billy Herman .... .30
Joe Medwick .... .30
Mel Ott .... .45
Schoolboy Rowe .... .20
Arky Vaughan .... .30
Joe Vosmik .... .20
Lon Warneke .... .20

1937
Color Series
Zeke Bonura $20
Tom Bridges .... .20
Harland Clift .... .20
KiKi Cuyler .... .30
Joe DiMaggio .... .225
Robert Feller .... .75
Lefty Grove .... .50
Billy Herman .... .30
Carl Hubbell .... .35
Buck Jordan .... .20
"Pepper" Martin .... .20
Wally Moses .... .20
Van L. Mungo .... .20

Cecil Travis .... .20
Arky Vaughan .... .30

1937
How to Star In Baseball
Bill Dickey $50
Red Ruffing .... .30
Zeke Bonura .... .20
Charlie Gehringer .... .35
"Arky" Vaughan .... .20
Carl Hubbell .... .35
John Lewis .... .20
Heinie Manush .... .30
Lefty Grove .... .40
Billy Herman .... .30
Joe DiMaggio .... .225
Joe Medwick .... .30

1937
Small Panels with
Orange Background Series
Zeke Bonura $40
Tom Bridges .... .40
Dolph Camilli .... .40
Frank Demaree .... .40
Joe DiMaggio .... .250
Billy Herman .... .70
Carl Hubbell .... .75
Ernie Lombardi .... .55
"Pepper" Martin .... .40
Jo Jo Moore .... .40
Van L. Mungo .... .40
Mel Ott .... .75
Raymond Radcliff .... .40
Cecil Travis .... .40
Harold Trosky .... .40
Arky Vaughan .... .55

1937
Speckled Orange, White and Blue Series
Luke Appling $30
Earl Averill .... .30
Joe DiMaggio .... .175
Robert Feller .... .75
Charles Gehringer .... .40
Lefty Grove .... .45
Carl Hubbell .... .45
Joe Medwick .... .35

1937
29 Series
"Zeke" Bonura $20
Cecil Travis .... .20
Frank Demaree .... .20
Jo Jo Moore .... .20
Ernie Lombardi .... .30
John "Pepper" Martin .... .25
Harold Trosky .... .20
Raymond Radcliff .... .20
Joe DiMaggio .... .225
Tom Bridges .... .20
Van L. Mungo .... .20
"Arky" Vaughan .... .30
Arnold Statz .... .150
Fred Muller .... .150
Gene Lillard .... .150

1938
Biggest Thrills In Baseball
Bob Feller $75
Cecil Travis .... .20

Joe Medwick 35
Gerald Walker 20
Carl Hubbell 35
Bob Johnson 20
Beau Bell 20
Ernie Lombardi .30
Lefty Grove 40
Lou Fette 20
Joe DiMaggio 250
Pinky Whitney 20
Dizzy Dean 55
Charlie Gehringer 40
Paul Waner 30
Dolph Camilli 20

1938
Dress Clothes or Civilian Series

Lou Fette $20
Jimmie Foxx 40
Charlie Gehringer 35
Lefty Grove 35
Hank Greenberg 35
Ernie Lombardi .30
Joe Medwick 35
Lon Warneke 20

1938
Small Panels with Orange, Blue
and White Background

Zeke Bonura $40
Joe DiMaggio 250
Charley Gehringer 80
Hank Greenberg 80
Lefty Grove 60
Carl Hubbell 60
John "Buddy" Lewis 40
Heinie Manush .60
Joe Medwick 60
Arky Vaughan 60

1939
100 Years of Baseball

Design of First Diamond $20
Gets News of Nomination on Field 20
Crowd Boos First Baseball Glove 20
Curve Ball Just an Illusion. 20
Fencer's Mask Is Pattern 20
Baseball Gets "All Dressed Up" 20
Modern Bludgeon Enters Game 20
"Casey at the Bat" 20

1939
Personal Pointers Series

Ernie Lombardi $30
Johnny Allen 20
Lefty Gomez 35
Bill Lee 20
Jimmie Foxx 45
Joe Medwick 35
Hank Greenberg 35
Mel Ott 50
Arky Vaughan .30

1940
Champs of the U.S.A.

Bob Feller
Lynn Patrick
Charles "Red" Ruffing $50
Leo Durocher
Lynn Patrick
Charles "Red' Ruffing 45
Joe DiMaggio
John Duge
Hank Greenberg 150
Joe DiMaggio
Mel Ott
Ellsworth Vines 150
Bernie Bierman
Bill Dickey
Jimmie Foxx 40
Morris Arnovich
Capt. R.L. Baker
Earl "Dutch" Clark 20
"Matty" Bell
Ab Jenkins
Joe Medwick 20
Ralph Guldahl
John Mize
Davey O'Brien .20
Ralph Guldahl
Gabby Hartnett
Davey O'Brien .20
Bob Feller
John Mize
Rudy York 45
Joe Cronin
Hank Greenberg
Byron Nelson 20
Ernie Lombardi
Jack Manders
George Myers .20
Bob Bartlett
Capt. R.C. Hanson
Terrell Jacobs .20
Lowell "Red" Dawson
Billy Herman
Adele Inge 20
Dolph Camilli
Antoinette Concello
Wallace Wade .20
Luke Appling
Stanley Hack
Hugh McManus 20
Felix Adler
Hal Trosky
Mabel Vinson .20

1941
Champs of the U.S.A.

Felix Adler
Jimmie Foxx
Capt. R.G. Hanson $45

Bernie Bierman
Bob Feller
Jessie McLeod .45
Lowell "Red" Dawson
Hank Greenberg
J.W. Stoker 35
Antoinette Concello
Joe DiMaggio
Byron Nelson. .125
Capt. R.L. Baker
Frank "Buck" McCormick
Harold "Pee Wee" Reese 45
Harry Danning
Barney McCosky
Bucky Walters .20
William Robbins
Gene Sarazan
Gerald "Gee" Walker 20
Joe "Flash" Gordon
Stan Hack
George Myers .20

1951

Bob Feller (Baseball) $100
John Lujack (Football) 60
George Mikan (Basketball) 100
Stan Musial (Baseball) 150
Sam Snead (Golfer) 40
Ted Williams (Baseball) 150

1952

Larry "Yogi" Berra $40
Roy Campanella 40
Bob Feller 30
George Kell 12
Ralph Kiner 20
Bob Lemon 20
Stan Musial 50
Phil Rizzuto 25
Elwin "Preacher" Roe 10
Ted Williams 75

Wheaties

1964 Tom Tresh $50
1985 Pete Rose (8 oz.) 45
1985 Pete Rose (12/18 oz.) 40
1987 Minnesota Twins WS Champs R 15
1989 Johnny Bench HOF R 40
1990 Jim Palmer HOF R 40
1990 Cincinnati Reds R 25

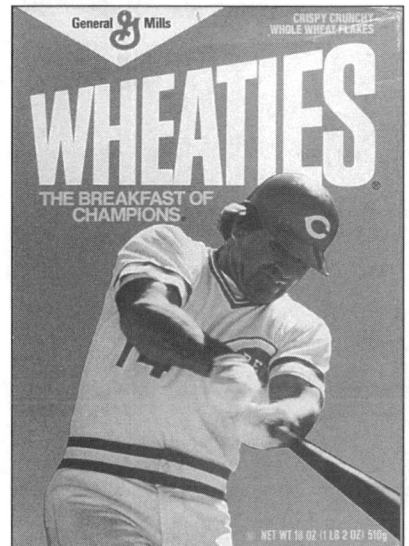

1991 Rod Carew R 125
1991 Twins WS Champ (.75 oz) R 100
1991 Twins WS Champs R 30
1993 Lou Gehrig 10
1993 Willie Mays 10
1993 Babe Ruth 10
1995 Cal Ripken no O's logo R 25
1995 Cal Ripken w/O's logo 10
1995 Braves WS Champs R 18
1995 Indians AL Champs R 18
1996 Ken Griffey, Jr. (HF) 5
1996 Ken Griffey, Jr. (HF 14.75 oz.) 8
1996 Griffey, Jr. gold emb. (HF) 10
1996 Ken Griffey, Jr. (HF) 15
1996 Kirby Puckett R 20
1996 Braves NL Champs R 12
1996 Cards Champs (phantom) 75
1996 Negro Leagues (75th Anniversary) 10
1996 Yankees AL Champs R 12
1997 Jackie Robinson (Al) 7
1997 Mariners '97 WD champs 20
1997 Cone/Maddux/Nomo 6
1997 Bonds/Griffey/Gwynn 8
1997 Piazza/Ripken/Sandberg 8
1997 Bonds/Griffey/C. Jones 8
1997 Griffey/Ripken/Thomas 8
1998 R. Clemens (Canada) (MFW) 10
1998 McGwire/Griffey/T. Martinez 15
1998 A. Rod/Maddux/Garciaparra (HF) 8

1998 Arizona Diamondbacks 10
1998 Mark McGwire/70HR 6
1998 Yankees WS Champs 15
1998 Nolan Ryan Leg. 5
1998 Nolan Ryan Leg. (CWR) 5
1998 Nolan Ryan Leg. (HW) 5
1999 Joe Torre/Yankees WS 10

Wheaties
75 Years of Champions
1999 L. Gehrig/W. Payton/C. Evert/etc. $10

Additional Cereal Boxes
Famous Fixins
1999 Cal's Classic O's $10
1999 Slammin' Sammy's Frosted Flakes . .$10

General Mills Corp.
1998 Major League Grand Slams (McGwire, F. Thomas, Piazza) $10

Famous Fixins
1999
Slammin' Sammy's (Sosa) Frosted Flakes . .$10
Cal's (Ripken) Classic O's 10
A-Rod's (Alex Rodriguez) 40/40 Crunch . . .10
Barry Bonds MVP Crunch 10
(Derek) Jeter's Frosted Flakes 10

Houston's Triple Play (Jeff Bagwell, Craig Biggio and Ken Caminiti) 10
Amazing Mets Frosted Flakes 10

Global Sports & Promotions
1999
Albert Belle's Slugger Cereal $10
Roberto Clemente 10

1960 Post Cereal box back

General Mills Corp.
1960 Post Cereal Box Backs

These cards were issued on the backs of Grape Nuts cereal and measure an oversized 7-by-8fl. The nine cards in the set include five baseball players, two football players (Johnny Unitas and Frank Gifford) and two basketball players (Bob Pettit and Bob Cousy). The full-color photos were placed on a color background and bordered by a wood frame design. The cards covered the entire back of the cereal box and were blank-backed. Card fronts also include the player's name and team and a facsimile autograph. A panel on the side of the box contains player biographical information. A scarce set, the cards are very difficult to obtain in Mint condition. A Mint condition set of all nine is worth $4,500.

Bob Cousy $450
Don Drysdale 400
Frank Gifford 350
Al Kaline 450
Harmon Killebrew .300
Eddie Mathews 300
Mickey Mantle .1,500
Bob Pettit 400
Johnny Unitas 400

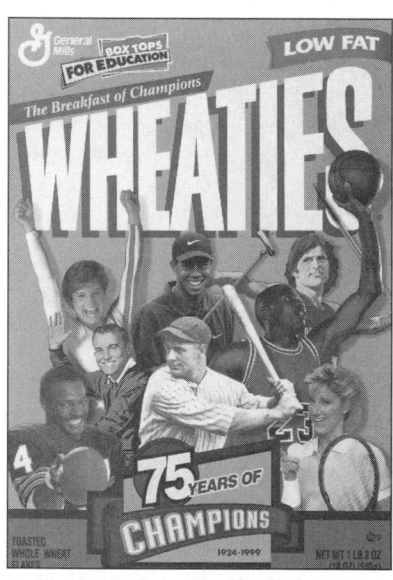

Press Pins and Medallions

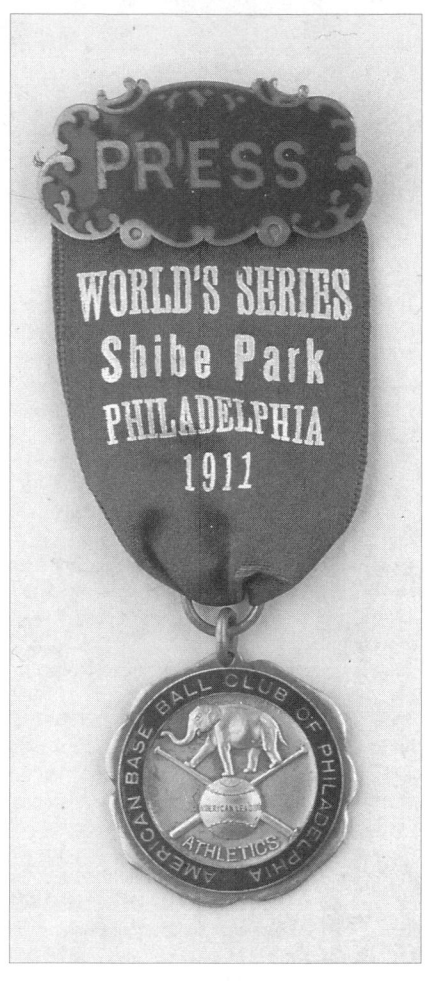

1911 World Series medallion

1912 World Series medallion

World Series Pins

1911 Philadelphia Athletics: Allen A. Kerr; brooch; blue . . . .$13,850-$18,000
1912 New York Giants: Whitehead & Hoag; brooch; blue . . . .$6,500-$12,500
1912 Boston Red Sox: Unknown; threaded post; red . . . .$3,500-$5,000
1913 New York Giants: Whitehead & Hoag; threaded post; blue . . . .$5,000-$10,000
1913 Philadelphia Athletics: J.E. Caldwell; brooch; blue/green . . . .$6,000-$6,500
1914 Boston Braves: Bent & Bush; threaded post; blue . . . .$5,000-$5,500
1914 Philadelphia Athletics: J.E. Caldwell; brooch; blue/white/green . . . .$6,500-$11,000
1915 Philadelphia Phillies: J.E. Caldwell; brooch; red . . . .$6,000-$11,000
1915 Boston Red Sox: Bent & Bush; threaded post; gold . . . .$4,000-$5,500
1916 Brooklyn Dodgers: Dieges & Clust; threaded post; blue/white . . . .$4,000-$4,400
1916 Boston Red Sox: Bent & Bush; threaded post; red/blue . . . .$4,000-$5,000
1917 New York Giants: Unknown; brooch; gold . . . .$4,500-$7,000
1917 Chicago White Sox, with banner: Greenduck; threaded post; blue . . . . . .$4,000-$9,500
1918 Boston Red Sox: Bent & Bush; threaded post; gold . . . .$3,000-$5,500
1919 Cincinnati Reds: Gustave Fox; threaded post; gold . . . .$2,500-$4,750
1919 Chicago White Sox, with banner: Greenduck; threaded post; gold . . . .$5,000-$12,000
1920 Brooklyn Dodgers: Unknown; threaded post; red . . . .$2,500-$3,000
1920 Cleveland Indians, enamel: Unknown; threaded post; green/white . . . . . .$1,500-$3,000
1920 Cleveland Indians celluloid button: Unknown; safety brooch; black/white . . .$2,500-$3,500
1921 New York Yankees/Giants: Whitehead & Hoag; brooch; bluc/whitc . . . .$2,000-$2,500
1922 New York Yankees/Giants: Whitehead & Hoag; brooch; blue/white . . . .$3,000-$4,000
1923 New York Yankees: Dieges & Clust; threaded post; red/white/blue . . . .$2,300-$3,800
1924 New York Giants: Dieges & Clust; threaded post; blue . . . .$845-$1,500
1924 Washington Senators: Dieges & Clust; threaded post; red/white/blue . . . . .$1,000-$1,500
1925 Pittsburgh Pirates: Whitehead & Hoag; threaded post; black/white . . . . . .$1,500-$2,500
1925 Washington Senators: Dieges & Clust; threaded post; blue . . . .$1,375-$2,000
1926 St. Louis Cardinals: Unknown; threaded post; red . . . .$1,300-$2,400
1926 New York Yankees: Dieges & Clust; threaded post; red/white/blue . . . .$1,200-$1,500
1927 Pittsburgh Pirates: Whitehead & Hoag; threaded post; black/white . . . . . .$1,100-$2,000
1927 New York Yankees: Dieges & Clust; threaded post; red/white/blue . . . .$2,000-$2,300
1928 St. Louis Cardinals: St. Louis Button; threaded post; red/white/blue . . . . . .$875-$1,200
1928 New York Yankees: Dieges & Clust; threaded post; red/white/blue . . . .$1,850-$2,400
1929 Chicago Cubs: Hipp & Coburn; threaded post; red/white/blue . . . .$1,500-$2,350
1929 Philadelphia Athletics: Unknown; threaded post; blue/white . . . .$375-$800
1930 St. Louis Cardinals: St. Louis Button; threaded post; red/white/blue . . . . . .$500-$1,000
1930 Philadelphia Athletics: Unknown; threaded post; blue/white . . . .$3,000-$5,000

1915 World Series medallion

1931 St. Louis Cardinals: St. Louis Button; threaded post; red/white/blue . . . .$650-$900
1931 Philadelphia Athletics: Unknown; threaded post; blue/white . . . .$1,300-$1,500
1932 Chicago Cubs: Dieges & Clust; threaded post; black/white . . . .$1,900-$2,200
1932 New York Yankees: Dieges & Clust; threaded post; gold . . . .$1,000-$1,200
1933 New York Giants: Dieges & Clust; threaded post; red/green/blue . . . .$235-$700
1933 Washington Senators: Dieges & Clust; threaded post; gold . . . .$700-$950
1934 St. Louis Cardinals: St. Louis Button; threaded post; red/white . . . .$650-$800
1934 Detroit Tigers: Dieges & Clust; threaded post; black/white . . . .$600-$750
1935 Chicago Cubs: S.D. Childs; brooch; red/white/blue . . . .$2,200-$3,000
1935 Detroit Tigers: Unknown; threaded post; black . . . .$600-$800
1936 New York Giants: Dieges & Clust; threaded post; black/white/orange . . . .$275-$400

1916 World Series pin

1923 World Series pin

1939 World Series pin

1948 World Series pin

1936 New York Yankees: Dieges & Clust; threaded post; red/white/blue ....$550-$800
1937 New York Giants: Dieges & Clust; threaded post; black/orange ....$225-$350
1937 New York Yankees: Dieges & Clust; threaded post; red/white/blue ....$450-$600
1938 Chicago Cubs: Lambert Bros.; brooch; red/white/blue ....$1,400-$2,250
1938 New York Yankees: Dieges & Clust; threaded post; red/white/blue ....$475-$750
1939 Cincinnati Reds: Bastian Bros.; threaded post, brooch; red/white/blue ....$275-$425
1939 New York Yankees: Dieges & Clust; threaded post; red/white/blue ....$400-$750
1940 Cincinnati Reds: Bastian Bros.; threaded post, brooch; red/white/blue ....$425-$475
1940 Detroit Tigers: Unknown; threaded post; gold $475-$650
1941 Brooklyn Dodgers: Dieges & Clust; threaded post; red/white/blue ....$450-$725
1941 New York Yankees: Dieges & Clust; threaded post; red/white/blue ....$275-$475
1942 St. Louis Cardinals: St. Louis button; safety brooch; red/white/black ....$2,000-$2,400
1942 New York Yankees: Dieges & Clust; threaded post, brooch; silver ....$275-$400
1943 St. Louis: St. Louis button; safety brooch; red/black/white ....$1,000-$2,000
1943 New York Yankees: Dieges & Clust; threaded post, brooch; silver ....$300-$500
1944 St. Louis Cardinals: St. Louis button; threaded post ....$450-$575
1944 St. Louis Browns: St. Louis button; threaded post ....$500-$575
1945 Chicago Cubs: Unknown; threaded post; red/white/blue ....$400-$550
1945 Detroit Tigers: Unknown; threaded post; red/blue ....$425-$575
1946 St. Louis Cardinals: St. Louis button; threaded post; red/white/silver ....$350-$500

1946 Boston Red Sox: Balfour; threaded post; red/white ....$300-$575
1947 Brooklyn Dodgers: Dieges & Clust; threaded post, brooch; blue ....$400-$800
1947 New York Yankees: Dieges & Clust; threaded post; red/white/blue ....$500-$600
1948 Boston Braves: Balfour; threaded post; red/white/copper ....$400-$475
1948 Cleveland Indians: Balfour; threaded post; red/white/black ....$250-$400
1949 Brooklyn Dodgers: Dieges & Clust; threaded post, brooch; blue ....$350-$400
1949 New York Yankees: Dieges & Clust; threaded post, brooch red/white/blue ....$300-$400
1950 Philadelphia Phillies: Martin; needle post; red/silver ....$250-$350
1950 New York Yankees: Dieges and Clust; threaded post, brooch red/white/blue ...$250-$375
1951 New York Giants: Dieges & Clust; threaded post; black/white ....$150-$175
1951 New York Yankees: Dieges & Clust; threaded post, brooch; red/white/blue ....$125-$175
1952 Brooklyn Dodgers: Dieges & Clust; threaded post, brooch; red/blue ....$300-$400
1952 New York Yankees: Balfour; threaded post, brooch; red/white/blue ....$200-$300
1953 Brooklyn Dodgers: Dieges & Clust; threaded post, brooch; white/blue ....$275-$350
1953 New York Yankees: Balfour; threaded post and brooch; red/white/blue ....$250-$325
1954 New York Giants: Dieges and Clust; threaded post; black/white ....$150-$200
1954 Cleveland Indians: Balfour; threaded post; red/white/blue/black ....$250-$300
1955 Brooklyn Dodgers: Dieges & Clust; threaded post, brooch; silver/white/blue ....$400-$500
1955 New York Yankees: Balfour; threaded post, brooch; red/white/blue ....$125-$275
1956 Brooklyn Dodgers: Dieges & Clust; clasps; silver/white/blue ....$500-$750

1956 New York Yankees: Balfour; threaded post, brooch; red/white/blue ....$200-$300
1957 Milwaukee Braves: Balfour; threaded post; copper/red ....$150-$200
1957 New York Yankees: Balfour; threaded post, brooch red/white/blue ....$150-$200
1958 Milwaukee Braves: Balfour; threaded post; black/white ....$200-$275
1958 New York Yankees: Balfour; threaded post, brooch, white/blue ....$175-$200
1959 Los Angeles Dodgers: Balfour; threaded post, charm, brooch; white/blue ....$125-$250
1959 Chicago White Sox: Balfour; threaded post, brooch; blue/green ....$175-$275
1960 Pittsburgh Pirates: Josten; threaded post; black/white ....$175-$250
1960 New York Yankees: Balfour; threaded post, brooch white/blue ....$100-$150
1961 Cincinnati Reds: Balfour; threaded post, charm; red/white/blue ....$100-$175
1961 New York Yankees: Balfour; threaded post, brooch; red/white/blue ....$125-$225
1962 San Francisco Giants: Balfour; threaded post; white ....$200-$275
1962 New York Yankees: Balfour; threaded post, brooch; red/white/blue ....$100-$150
1963 Los Angeles Dodgers: Balfour; threaded post; blue ....$125-$150
1963 New York Yankees: Balfour; needle post, brooch; red/white/blue ....$100-$175
1964 St. Louis Cardinals: Josten; threaded post, brooch; red ....$125-$200
1964 New York Yankees: Balfour; needle post, red/white/blue ....$175-$200
1965 Los Angeles Dodgers: Balfour; needle post, charm; blue ....$50-$150
1965 Minnesota Twins: Balfour; needle post, red/white/blue ....$50-$125
1966 Los Angeles Dodgers: Balfour; needle post, charm; blue ....$50-$150

1932 World Series pin

1941 World Series pin

1954 World Series pin

1963 World Series pin

1966 Baltimore Orioles: Balfour; needle post, clasp, charm, brooch; black/white/orange ....$175-$200
1967 St. Louis Cardinals: Balfour; needle post, charms; red/white/black ....$75-$100
1967 Boston Red Sox: Balfour; needle post, charm; red/white/blue ....$150-$200
1968 St. Louis Cardinals: Balfour; needle post, charms; red/white/black ....$75-$125
1968 Detroit Tigers: Balfour; needle post, charms; blue ....$125-$200
1969 New York Mets: Balfour; needle post, charm; blue/orange ....$200-$300
1969 Baltimore Orioles: Balfour; needle post, charms, clasp, brooch; black/white/orange ....$150-$200
1970 Cincinnati Reds: G.B. Miller; needle post, charms; red/white/black ...$125-$150
1970 Baltimore Orioles: Jenkins; needle post, clasp, charm, brooch; black/white/orange ....$100-$150
1971 Pittsburgh Pirates: Balfour; needle post; black ....$75-$150
1971 Baltimore Orioles: Balfour; needle post, clasp, brooch; black/white/orange ....$100-$150
1972 Cincinnati Reds: Balfour; needle post, charm; red/white ....$100-$150
1972 Oakland A's: Balfour; needle post, charm; green/white ....$125-$250
1973 New York Mets: Balfour; needle post, charm; orange/blue ....$125-$150
1973 Oakland A's: Josten; needle post, charms; green/white ....$200-$275
1974 Los Angeles Dodgers: Balfour; needle post, charms; blue ....$125-$150
1974 Oakland As: Josten; needle post; green/white ....$300-$375
1975 Cincinnati Reds: Balfour; needle post, charms; red ....$100-$200

1952 World Series pin

1966 World Series pin

1975 Boston Red Sox: Balfour; needle post, charms; red/white ....$125-$200
1976 Cincinnati Reds: Balfour; needle post, charms; red ....$125-$175
1976 New York Yankees: Balfour; needle post; red/white/blue ....$125-$175
1977 Los Angeles Dodgers: Balfour; needle post, charms; red/white/blue ....$125-$150
1977 New York Yankees: Balfour; needle post, charms; blue ....$75-$125
1978 Los Angeles Dodgers: Balfour; needle post, charms; blue/white ....$75-$100
1978 New York Yankees: Balfour; needle post, charms; red/white/blue ....$50-$125
1979 Pittsburgh Pirates: Balfour; needle post; gold ....$50-$125
1979 Baltimore Orioles: Balfour; needle post, clasp, charm, brooch; white/black/orange .....$50-$100
1980 Philadelphia Phillies: Balfour; needle post; gold ....$50-$75
1980 Kansas City Royals: Green Co.; needle post, charms; blue/white ....$50-$175
1981 Los Angeles Dodgers: Balfour; needle post, charms; red/white/blue ....$50-$100
1981 New York Yankees: Balfour; needle post; blue ....$75-$100
1982 St. Louis Cardinals: Balfour; needle post, charms; red ....$50-$75
1982 Milwaukee Brewers: Balfour; needle post, charms; blue ....$50-$100
1983 Philadelphia Phillies: Balfour; needle post, charms; red/white/green ....$40-$75
1983 Baltimore Orioles: Balfour; needle post, charm, brooch; orange/white/black .....$65-$100
1984 San Diego Padres: Balfour; needle post, charms; brown/white ....$25-$75
1984 Detroit Tigers: Balfour; needle post, charms; blue ....$45-$75

1986 World Series pin

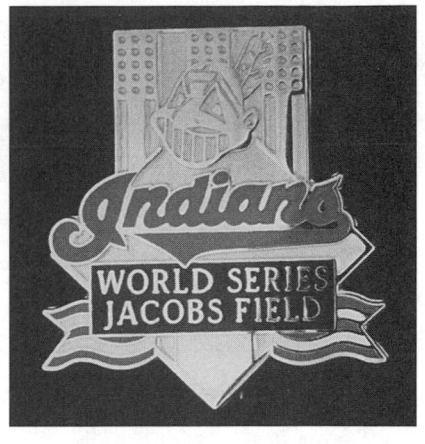

1995 World Series pin

1985 Kansas City Royals: Green Co.; needle post, charms; blue/white ....$75-$100
1985 St. Louis Cardinals: Balfour; needle post, charms; red/black ....$75-$100
1986 New York Mets: Balfour; needle post, charms; blue/orange ....$100-$135
1986 Boston Red Sox: Balfour; needle post, charms; red/white/blue ....$75-$125
1987 St. Louis Cardinals: Balfour; needle post, charms; red/white/gold ....$100-$125
1987 Minnesota Twins: Josten; needle post, charms; gold ....$75-$125
1988 Oakland A's ....$60-$75
1988 Los Angeles Dodgers ....$50-$75
1989 San Francisco Giants ....$75-$100
1989 Oakland A's ....$75-$100
1990 Cincinnati Reds ....$125-$150
1990 Oakland A's ....$75-$100
1991 Atlanta Braves ....$60-$100
1991 Minnesota Twins ....$60-$100
1992 Atlanta Braves ....$100-$125
1992 Toronto Blue Jays ....$125-$150
1993 Philadelphia Phillies .....$50-$100
1993 Toronto Blue Jays ....$125-$150
1995 Atlanta Braves ....$100-$150
1995 Cleveland Indians ....$100-$150

Phantom Press Pins

1938 Pittsburgh Pirates: Whitehead & Hoag; threaded post; red/white/black ......$500-$1,000
1944 Detroit Tigers: Unknown; threaded post; red/white/blue ....$375-$500
1945 St. Louis Cardinals: St. Louis Button; threaded post; red/white ....$475-$600
1946 Brooklyn Dodgers: Dieges & Clust; threaded post, brooch ....$125-$275
1948 Boston Red Sox: Balfour; threaded post; red/white/blue ....$1,200-$1,800
1948 New York Yankees: Dieges & Clust, threaded post; red/white/blue ....$1,600-$1,800
1949 St. Louis Cardinals: Unknown; threaded post; red/white/black ....$450-$725
1949 Boston Red Sox: Balfour; threaded post; red/white/blue ....$950-$1,400
1950 Brooklyn Dodgers: Balfour; threaded post; red/white/blue ....$1,600-$2,400
1951 Cleveland Indians: Balfour; threaded post; red/white/black ....$1,200-$1,750
1951 Brooklyn Dodgers: Dieges & Clust; threaded post, brooch; red/white/blue ...$125-$400
1952 New York Giants: Dieges & Clust; threaded post, brooch; white/black ....$275-$350
1955 Chicago White Sox: Unknown; threaded post; red/white/blue ....$800-$1,400

1951 World Series phantom

1955 Cleveland Indians: Balfour; threaded post; red/white/blue/black ....$600-$800
1956 Milwaukee Braves: Balfour; threaded post; red/copper ....$100-$150
1959 San Francisco Giants: Balfour; threaded post; white/black ....$550-$800
1959 Milwaukee Braves: Balfour; threaded post, charm; red/copper ....$400-$500
1960 Chicago White Sox: Balfour; threaded post; red/white ....$1,200-$1,600
1960 Baltimore Orioles: Balfour; threaded post; red/green/black ....$800-$1,250
1963 St. Louis Cardinals: Josten; threaded post; red ....$75-$150
1964 Philadelphia Phillies: Martin; needle post; red/blue ....$15-$30
1964 Chicago White Sox: Balfour; needle post; red/white/blue ....$800-$1,100
1964 Baltimore Orioles: Balfour; needle post; orange/white/black ....$625-$850
1964 Cincinnati Reds: Balfour; needle post, brooch; red/white/black ....$200-$250
1965 San Francisco Giants: Balfour; threaded post; white/black ....$125-$150
1966 Pittsburgh Pirates: Balfour; needle post; black ....$375-$450
1966 San Francisco Giants: Balfour; threaded post; white/black ....$950-$1,200
1967 Minnesota Twins: Balfour; needle post; red/white/blue ....$50-$60
1967 Chicago White Sox: Balfour; needle post; red/white/blue ....$75-$100
1969 San Francisco Giants: Balfour; needle post; white/black ....$100-$150
1969 Atlanta Braves: Josten; needle post and charm; blue ....$45-$75
1969 Minnesota Twins: Balfour; needle post; red/white/blue ....$75-$150
1970 California Angels: Balfour; needle post; red/white/blue ....$450-$500
1970 Chicago Cubs: Balfour; needle post; blue/white ....$450-$500

1959 World Series phantom

1971 San Francisco Giants: Balfour; needle post; black ....$125-$150
1971 Oakland A's (smaller pin): Unknown; needle post; green/white ....$100-$150
1971 Oakland A's (larger pin): Balfour; needle post, charm; green/white ....$650-$750
1972 Chicago White Sox: Balfour; needle post; red/white/blue ....$875-$1,000
1972 Pittsburgh Pirates: Balfour; needle post; no color ....$600-$750
1974 Texas Rangers: Balfour; needle post; red/white/blue/gold ....$400-$550
1975 Oakland A's: Josten; needle post; green/white $300-$450
1976 Philadelphia Phillies: Balfour; needle post; no color ....$35-$75
1977 Boston Red Sox: Balfour; needle post, charm; red/blue ....$50-$75
1978 San Francisco Giants: Balfour; needle post; black/orange ....$30-$50
1978 Cincinnati Reds: Balfour; needle post, charm; red ....$75-$100
1978 Milwaukee Brewers ....$50-$75
1979 Montreal Expos: Balfour; needle post; no color ....$50-$75
1979 California Angels: Balfour; needle post; red/white/blue ....$200-$250
1979 Houston Astros: Balfour; needle post; white/blue ....$850-$900
1980 Houston Astros: Balfour; needle post, charm; blue/orange ....$150-$200
1981 Oakland A's: Balfour; needle post, charm; green ....$55-$85
1981 Chicago Cubs: Balfour; needle post; red/white/blue ....$175-$200
1981 Philadelphia Phillies: Balfour; needle post; red/white ....$45-$75
1982 Los Angeles Dodgers: Balfour; needle post, charm; red/white/blue ....$125-$150
1983 Milwaukee Brewers: Balfour; needle post; white/black ....$200-$250
1983 Chicago White Sox: Balfour; needle post; red/blue ....$40-$50
1983 Pittsburgh Pirates: Balfour; needle post; black ....$200-$275
1984 Chicago Cubs: Balfour; needle post, charm; red/black ....$125-$200
1985 Toronto Blue Jays: Balfour; needle post, charm; red/white/blue ....$200-$250
1986 California Angels: Gem Peddler; needle post, charm; no color ....$175-$200
1986 Houston Astros: Balfour; needle post, charm; red/blue ....$75-$150
1987 Detroit Tigers: Balfour; needle post; blue/white/gold ....$125-$175
1987 New York Yankees: Balfour; threaded post; blue/white/gold ....$175-$200
1987 New York Mets: Balfour; needle post; orange/black/white/gold ....$200-$225
1987 San Francisco Giants: Balfour; needle post; black/white/gold ....$75-$100
1987 Boston Red Sox ....$150-$175
1988 Boston Red Sox ....$75-$100
1990 Pittsburgh Pirates ....$300-$350
1990 Boston Red Sox ....$60-$75

All-Star Pins

1938 Cincinnati: Bastian Brothers; safety pin; red/white/blue ....$7,000-$8,000
1941 Detroit: Dodge; threaded post; blue ....$2,200-$2,500
1943 Philadelphia: Unknown; threaded post; silver ....$1,200-$1,500

1946 All-Star Game pin

1946 Boston: Balfour; threaded post; red ....$575-$1,000
1947 Chicago: Unknown; threaded post; red/white/blue ....$1,100-$1,850
1948 St. Louis: St. Louis Button; threaded post; brown/white ....$650-$2,250
1949 Brooklyn: Balfour; threaded post, brooch; blue ....$325-$400
1950 Chicago: Balfour; threaded post, brooch; red/white ....$150-$325
1951 Detroit: Unknown; threaded post, brooch; red/white/blue ....$250-$375
1952 Philadelphia: Martin; needle post; red/white/blue ....$175-$400
1953 Cincinnati: Robbins; threaded post; red/white/black ....$225-$375
1954 Cleveland: Balfour; threaded post; red/white/black ....$250-$375
1955 Milwaukee: Balfour; brooch; gold ....$175-$350
1956 Washington: Balfour; threaded post, clasp; red/white/blue ....$225-$350
1957 St. Louis: Balfour; threaded post, brooch; black/red ....$300-$350
1958 Baltimore: Balfour; threaded post, charm; black/white/orange ....$400-$650
1959 Los Angeles: Balfour; threaded post, brooch; blue/white ....$100-$150
1959 Pittsburgh: Balfour; threaded post; red/white/black ....$225-$400
1960 Kansas City: Balfour; threaded post; red ....$200-$325
1960 New York Yankees: Balfour; threaded post; red/white/blue ....$200-$400
1961 Boston: Balfour; needle post; red/white/blue ....$400-$500
1961 San Francisco: Balfour; threaded post; white ....$475-$600
1962 Chicago: Balfour; needle post; red/white/blue ....$250-$350

1947 All-Star Game pin

1948 All-Star Game pin

1962 Washington: Balfour; threaded post, clasp; white/blue ....$200-$250
1963 Cleveland: Balfour; threaded post; red/white/blue/black ....$75-$150
1964 New York (Shea Stadium): Balfour; needle post, charm; blue/orange ....$200-$250
1965 Minnesota: Balfour; needle post; red/white/blue ....$100-$175
1966 St. Louis: Balfour; needle post; red .$35-$80
1967 California: Balfour; needle post, charm; blue/white ....$50-$150
1968 Houston: Balfour; needle post, charm; blue/white ....$100-$125
1969 Washington: Balfour; needle post, clasp; blue $75-$150
1970 Cincinnati: Balfour; needle post, charm; red/white/black ....$75-$100
1971 Detroit: Balfour; needle post, charms; red/white/blue ....$100-$175
1972 Atlanta: Balfour; needle post, charm; red/blue ....$75-$125
1973 Kansas City: Balfour; needle post, charm; blue ....$75-$150
1974 Pittsburgh: Balfour; needle post; gold ....$175-$275
1975 Milwaukee: Unknown; brooch; gold . ...$50-$100
1976 Philadelphia: Balfour; needle post; gold ....$50-$75
1977 New York Yankees: Balfour; pin ..$100-$125
1977 New York: Balfour; charm; gold ....$30-$50
1978 San Diego: Balfour; needle post, charm, brooch; brown/blue ....$40-$80
1979 Seattle: Balfour; needle post, charm, brooch; blue/white ....$30-$60

1949 All-Star Game pin

1956 All-Star Game pin

1980 Los Angeles: Balfour; needle post, charm; gold ....$30-$60
1981 Cleveland: Balfour; needle post, charm; red/white/blue ....$25-$50
1982 Montreal: Balfour; needle post, straight pin; gold ....$60-$75
1983 Chicago: Balfour; needle post, charms; red/blue ....$25-$50
1984 San Francisco: Balfour; needle post, charm; orange/black/white ....$20-$35
1985 Minnesota: Peter David; needle post, charms; red/white/blue ....$20-$25
1986 Houston: Balfour; needle post, charms; red/white/blue/silver ....$65-$125
1987 Oakland: Josten; needle post; copper ....$75-$90
1988 Cincinnati: Josten; needle post; red/white/blue/silver ....$75-$100
1989 California ....$55-$75
1990 Chicago ....$125-$150
1991 Toronto ....$100-$125
1992 San Diego ....$20-$100
1993 Baltimore ....$100-$150
1994 Pittsburgh ....$125-$150
1995 Texas ....$50-$100
1996 Philadelphia ....$50-$100
1997 Cleveland ....$50-$100
1998 Denver ....$50-$100
1999 Boston ....$100-$150
2000 Atlanta ....$75-$100

Hall of Fame Press Pins

1983 Hall of Fame pin

1982: Balfour; charms and standard needle post: Hank Aaron, Happy Chandler, Travis Jackson, Frank Robinson ....$400-$700
1983: Balfour; charms and standard needle post: Walter Alston, George Kell, Juan Marichal, Brooks Robinson ....$400-$525
1984: Balfour; charms and standard needle post: Luis Aparicio, Don Drysdale, Harmon Killebrew, Rick Ferrell, Pee Wee Reese ....$225-$375
1985: Balfour; charms and standard needle post: Lou Brock, Enos Slaughter, Arky Vaughan, Hoyt Wilhelm ....$250-$350
1986: Balfour; charms and standard needle post: Bobby Doerr, Ernie Lombardi, Willie McCovey .. ..$225-$350
1987: Balfour; charms and standard needle post: Ray Dandridge, Jim Hunter, Billy Williams ....$500-$650
1988: Balfour; charms and standard needle post: Willie Stargell ....$500-$650
1989: Al Barlick, Johnny Bench, Red Schoendienst, Carl Yastrzemski ....$500-$650
1989: 50th Anniversary Medallion: Al Barlick, Johnny Bench, Red Schoendienst, Carl Yastrzemski ....$650-$700
1990: Joe Morgan, Jim Palmer ......$450-$650
1990: (1936 inductees) Ty Cobb, Walter Johnson, Christy Mathewson, Babe Ruth, Honus Wagne $750
1991: Rod Carew, Fergie Jenkins, Gaylord Perry, Tony Lazzeri, Bill Veeck ....$375-$575
1991: (1937 inductees) Morgan Bulkeley, Ban Johnson, Nap Lajoie, Connie Mack, John McGraw, Tris Speaker, George Wright, Cy Young $700
1992: Rollie Fingers, Bill McGowan, Hal Newhouser, Tom Seaver $400
1992: (1938 inductees) Grover Cleveland Alexander, Alexander Cartwright, Henry Chadwick .$375
1992: (1955 inductees) Frank Baker, Joe DiMaggio, Gabby Hartnett, Ted Lyons, Ray Schalk, Dazzy Vance $495
1993: Reggie Jackson $450
1993: (1939 inductees) Charles Comiskey, Buck Ewing, Cap Anson, Candy Cummings, Eddie Collins $400
1993: (1939 inductees) Charles Radbourne, George Sisler, Al Spalding, Lou Gehrig, Wee Willie Keeler $500
1994: Steve Carlton, Leo Durocher, Phil Rizzuto ....$425-$450
1994: (1942 inductee) Rogers Hornsby $375
1994: (1966 inductees) Casey Stengel, Ted Williams $375
1995: Richie Ashburn, Leon Day, William Hulbert, Mike Schmidt, Vic Willis $375
1995: (1944 inductee) Kenesaw Mountain Landis $375
1995: (1969 inductees) Roy Campanella, Stan Coveleski, Waite Hoyt, Stan Musial $375
1996: Jim Bunning, Earl Weaver, Ned Hanlon, B. Foster $375
1996: (1974 inductees) Cool Papa Bell, Jim Bottomley, Jocko Conlan, Whitey Ford, Mickey Mantle, Sam Thompson $375
1997: Tommy Lasorda, Phil Niekro, Nellie Fox, Willie Wells $350
1997: (1962 inductees) Bob Feller, Bill McKechnie, Jackie Robinson, Edd Roush $350
1997: (1962 inductees) Yogi Berra, Josh Gibson, Lefty Gomez, Will Harridge, Sandy Koufax, Buck Leonard, Early Wynn, Ross Youngs $350

*1988 L. A. Dodgers
World Championship ring*

Awards/Rings/Trophies

Although each player, coach, front office worker and team dignitary receives one, less than 100 rings are made for each championship team. This makes them quite rare and more valuable compared to other memorabilia.

Jostens, of Minneapolis, Minn., has created many of the rings designed for championship teams. Each year the designs have become more expensive and complex; as more gold and diamonds are added to the design, the ring's value on the gold and precious gem market increases, too.

It generally takes four to six weeks to design a ring. The teams often request special design elements or graphics, words or logos. The sides (the shank) often feature a year, a message, symbol, team/league logo or game score. Most of the rings are made of gold and contain diamonds, but some contain other stones, either natural or synthetic, in the team's colors.

Most of the championship rings which are listed for sale in advertisements are marked "salesman's sample." These rings have a serial number inside the band and were not created for a player, but rather for a salesman to market and advertise the rings. Instead of real diamonds, they generally contain a diamond look-alike, called cubic zirconia.

Rings are also created for players entering their respective sport's Hall of Fame. Balfour, of Attleboro, Mass., has created the majority of these rings.

The best places to find rings are at memorabilia shows in larger cities, or for sale through auctions. Another alternative is to scan ads in pages of various hobby publications. Although they are generally on the high end of the monetary scale, rings offer a lasting memory from a championship season.

Selected Rings/Pendants

George Brett Silver Gillette special award trophy for being the leading vote-getter for the 1981 All-Star Game, signed $3,250
Cito Gaston's San Diego Padres Baseball Writers Association MVP Award $895

Jostens National League Player of the Week presentation watch with box $295
100th anniversary of baseball commemorative watch, the face depicts a red, white and blue 100th anniversary baseball player logo, with baseball bats as hour hands, plus a black leather band and gold encasement $125
Babe Ruth wristwatch, working $595
Elroy Face Dapper Dan Award for outstanding contribution to baseball, sterling silver award $1,650
Mickey Mantle New York Yankees World Series Championship ring, salesman's sample $7,000
New York Yankees World Champs ladies watch, 14k with diamonds $895
Mickey Mantle/Roger Maris All-Star kids watch, with new band $145
New York Yankees 14k World Series ring, vs. the Pittsburgh Pirates $4,950
St. Louis Cardinals 14k World Series ring, white gold championship ring, vs. the New York Yankees $2,995
Sporting News/Rawlings Gold Glove Award, presented to California Angels shortstop Jim Fregosi, shows his model glove, flanked by two gold baseballs, on a base with his picture $3,995
Harmon Killebrew watch, Swiss-made, face features Killebrew photo with a facsimile autograph against a green baseball diamond background, includes a black imitation leather band $295
Nolan Ryan New York Mets 10k World Series ring, salesman's sample $2,850
Baltimore Orioles World Series championship ring, Frank Robinson salesman's sample $1,795
Pittsburgh Pirates 10k World Series ring, vs. the Baltimore Orioles, salesman's sample $3,500
Oakland A's 10k World Series ring, Charles Finley salesman's sample, vs. the Los Angeles Dodgers $2,750
Rawlings Mitsui Japanese Central Gold Glove Award, just like an American version, presented to Clete Boyer $3,495
Cincinnati Reds 10k World Series ring, Joe Morgan salesman's sample white gold championship ring, vs. the Boston Red Sox . .$3,150
All-Star Game 10k yellow-gold ring, for the game in New York, belonged to a Yankee executive $2,250

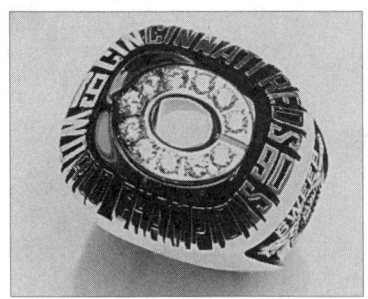

*1990 Cincinnati Reds
Championship ring.*

*1993 Phillies N.L.
Championship ring.*

Los Angeles Dodgers 14k World Series ring, vs. the New York Yankees, salesman's sample $3,500
New York Yankees 10k World Series ring, Reggie Jackson salesman's sample . . .$3,500
George Brett June 1979 Player of the Month Award $1,750
Philadelphia Phillies World Series ring, Pete Rose salesman's sample, vs. the Kansas City Royals $2,100
Los Angeles Dodgers World Series trophy, presented to Danny Goodman $3,850
Manny Mota presentation award/plaque, Los Angeles Dodgers 1981 World Champions and 145 Pinch Hits Major League Record . .$695
Bob Boone Eraser Mate 1982 Best Defensive Catcher Award, with a large lucite baseball diamond with an engraved colored plaque $995
All-Star Game ring, for the game in San Francisco, with original presentation box . .$1,250
Kansas City Royals 10k World Series Champions pendant with diamonds $2,000
Kansas City Royals 10k World Series ring, George Brett salesman's sample $3,695
Kansas City Royals World Series trophy, sample, autographed by Bret Saberhagen $1,750
Boston Red Sox World Series ring, with presentation box, vs. the New York Mets $2,850
Minnesota Twins World Series ring, Frank Viola, vs. the St. Louis Cardinals $2,100
Los Angeles Dodgers World Championship 10k pendant, vs. the Oakland As $1,500
San Francisco Giants National League Champions ring, 14k gold plated, Will Clark salesman's sample $2,250
Oakland A's World Series ring, vs. the Cincinnati Reds, salesman's sample $3,500
Cincinnati Reds World Series ring, vs. the Oakland A's, salesman's sample $4,500
Atlanta Braves 10k World Series ring, yellow-gold salesman's sample, vs. the Minnesota Twins $3,500
Roberto Alomar World Series MVP trophy, has his name engraved on the front, includes two press pins attached to the base of the award $6,000
All-Star Game ring, in Baltimore, made for a non-player $395
Philadelphia Phillies National League Champs 10k gold ring, Lenny Dykstra salesman's sample $2,395
All-Star Game ring, in Texas, made for a front office executive $995

Basketball Collectibles

Lakers center George Mikan always stepped onto a basketball court to help his team win a game. He had no idea his name would years later be associated with trading cards and other basketball memorabilia.

But the 1948 rookie card of Mikan, the first of the National Basketball Association's great centers, is today considered one of the cornerstones of the hobby. That hobby now encompasses nearly 2,000 card sets as well as game-worn jerseys; autographed basketballs; home videos and DVDs highlighting the game's history; toy action figures of some of today's stars and many, many more collectibles celebrating the pro game.

Like the NBA itself, the basketball collectibles market has experienced peaks and valleys over the years. Both pro hoops and the hobby are enjoying relative prosperity as we enter a new millennium.

Mikan is now enshrined in the Basketball Hall of Fame. The incomparable Michael Jordan is retired and will one day join Mikan in the Hall of Fame. Does that mean there's nothing worth collecting? No way. The pro game today is filled with exciting new stars, colorful coaches and stirring rivalries. Likewise, the basketball collectibles market is filled with a tremendous variety of vintage memorabilia, eye-pleasing cards and inventive new collectibles, and they're all being pursued by a growing collector base that bodes well for the hobby's future.

Hoops Hallmarks
(Collectively Speaking)

Collectibles associated with pro basketball lack the long history enjoyed by those associated with big-league baseball and pro football in large part because the NBA just turned 50 a few years ago. Yet the unquestioned popularity of the NBA has sparked a growing interest in NBA collectibles. Basketball memorabilia, like that of the three other major team sports, is rooted in its trading cards.

Hobbyists generally consider the 1948 Bowman set of 72 cards the first major basketball collectible available on a mass scale. It's the one that contains the Mikan rookie card. Devoted solely to the game of basketball, the set remains a building block of the hobby.

That year also marked the issue of basketball cards by Topps and Kelloggs, though in both instances the cards were part of multisport sets.

Like other sports cards in their infancy, those focusing on pro hoops were packaged with gum, candy, meat, bread, cereal and other foods. Most of those early sets are extremely rare. Basketball cards have also been inserted into periodicals, packaged with toys and games, and sold over the Internet.

Following the 1948 Bowmans, the hobby's next truly major issue was the 80-card set released by Topps in 1957-58. That set featured the rookie cards of eventual Hall of Famers Bob Cousy, Bob Pettit and Bill Russell.

Fleer is credited with issuing the hobby's third major basketball set. Its 66-card set in 1961-62 contained the rookie cards of three more eventual HOFers—Wilt Chamberlain, Oscar Robertson and Jerry West.

Despite these efforts, overall weak public response to basketball cards resulted in no new major sets hitting the market until the late 1960s and early 1970s, when Topps again hoped to entice the masses to buy its "BK" cards. Otherwise, the decade of the 1960s was marked by a number of regional sets most often issued as premiums with various kinds of snack foods.

Public response to the return of Topps basketball sets was strong enough that the company continued to issue them through the early 1980s. That's when the basketball card market crashed like a backboard's fiberglass after a booming slam dunk. Topps dropped its NBA line.

In its wake, Star, Fleer, SkyBox, Star Pics, Hoops, Upper Deck and several other companies (including Topps, yet again) have added much to the hobby through their innovative design features, brilliant color and superb photography, highly prized subsets and cleverly marketed inserts that range from autographed cards to cards packaged with swatches of game jerseys.

1948 Bowman George Mikan card.

Michael Jordan poster

The only downside to all this was that many of the sets from the early 1990s, though beautifully rendered from a design standpoint and highly popular with collectors, were overproduced. The values of some of those card sets have not risen appreciably since they came out.

Still, such stiff competition for the hobbyist's dollar has led to some spectacular cards in recent years. Stop in at your local card and hobby shop and plan to attend a sports memorabilia show in your area to see what awaits you.

Other Hits From 3-Point Range

Basketball, as with the other major team sports, will likely remain a haven for card collectors. After all, card sets are mass produced and distributed and therefore more reasonably priced and easier to come by than, say, team-autographed basketballs or game jerseys. But other kinds of basketball collectibles have found their hobby niche.

Perhaps the second-most popular basketball collectible is the player autograph. Collectors will enhance their enjoyment of owning a player's signature if they get it in person, well before game time. Be polite. Have your pen or fine-point marker ready. It's best not to ask the player to sign multiple items. After all, other collectors want their opportunity to get the player's signature, plus the player will have a limited time to sign requests before his presence in the locker room is required.

Hobby shows are another major source for player autographs. Guest signers will be facing time limitations (or, sometimes, a limit on the number of

items they and the show promoter have agreed upon prior to the event). Buy your ticket in advance of the show. Get there early. Be patient and courteous in line. Offer a friendly greeting to the player but don't gush over him. A player's reactions to the collectors in front of you will clue you in to his mood and how best to approach him.

Autographs can also be obtained through the mail, either by sending your request in care of his team—which is the usual method—or, directly to his home, which some players view as an invasion of their privacy. It's your call. What you send is also your call. The preferred method is to send flat, less expensive items such as a player photo, a magazine with the player featured on the front cover, a trading card of the player or even a blank note card.

Always include a self-addressed, stamped envelope or clasp envelope (or bubble-pack mailer or easy-seal carton if the item isn't flat) for the player to use to return your item. In a cover letter, keep your autograph request short, personable and polite. You'll need to specify if the item is to be personalized, dated, etc.

Pro basketball players are no different from athletes in other sports when it comes to signing their autographs. They are leery of people who ask them to sign more than one or two items because there's a strong likelihood that those extra autographs will

be sold at a later time. Many longtime collectors who acquire autographs through the mail will send an extra item for the player to keep. It's no guarantee the player will sign more than one item for you, but it's a tactic you might wish to consider.

Current Cager Collectibles

The current market for basketball collectibles is as wide open as your down-court teammate on a fast break.

In addition to the latest hot card sets, keep an eye out for NBA stars featured in Starting Lineup figurines. The original, complete set of 88 basketball stars, released in 1988, is now valued at more than $4,000. Even the values of subsequent major sets are often in the $500 range.

A brand new NBA collectible to look for in 2001 is Upper Deck's bobbin' head dolls series called Playmakers. Your local hobby shops, retail toy departments and hobby shows are your best bets for finding these 7-inch-high gems that sport incredible detail in the facial expressions. The first series features eight current stars (Kobe Bryant, Vince Carter, Tim Duncan, Kevin Garnett, Grant Hill, Allen Iverson, Shaquille O'Neal and Latrell Sprewell) and one retired legend, Larry Bird. Upper Deck has indicated it will produce a second series in the fall of 2001 and a third set sometime in 2002.

Visit your local hobby shop to begin your odyssey through the wonderful world of basketball collectibles. Then plan to attend a major memorabilia show in your area. There's no time like the present to be part of the fun.

Michael Jordan's game-used shoes.

●●●

Selected Basketball Cards
(1948-1989)

1948 BOWMAN

		NM
Complete Set (72):		$8300.00
Common Player (1-36):		50.00
Common Player (37-72)		100.00

		NM
1	Ernie Calverley	220.00
9	Andy Philip	140.00
10	Bob Davies	150.00
32	Red Holzman	425.00
34	Joe Fulks	425.00
37	Don (Swede) Carlson	100.00
38	Buddy Jeanette	140.00
39	Ray Kuka	100.00
40	Stan Masek	100.00
41	Basketball Play	100.00
42	George Nostrand	100.00
43	Chuck Halbert	100.00
44	Arnie Johnson	100.00
45	Bob Doll	100.00
46	Horace McKinney	140.00
47	Basketball Play	100.00
48	Ed Sadowski	100.00
49	Bob Kinney	100.00
50	Charles (Hawk) Black	100.00
51	Jack Dwan	100.00
52	Cornelius Simmons	100.00
53	Basketball Play	100.00
54	Bud Palmer	140.00
55	Max Zashlotsky	300.00
56	Lee Roy Robbins	100.00
57	Arthur Spector	100.00
58	Arnie Risen	140.00
59	Basketball Play	100.00
60	Ariel Maughan	100.00
61	Dick O'Keefe	100.00
62	Herman Schaefer	100.00
63	John Mahnken	100.00
64	Tommy Byrnes	100.00
65	Basketball Play	100.00
66	Jim Pollard	400.00
67	Lee Mogus	100.00
68	Lee Knorek	100.00
69	George Mikan	4500.00
70	Walter Budko	100.00
71	Basketball Play	100.00
72	Carl Braun	500.00

1957-58 Topps

		NM
Complete Set (80):		5500.00
Common Player:		35.00
Common Player (DP):		25.00

		NM
1	Nat Clifton	250.00
2	George Yardley	50.00
3	Neil Johnston	50.00
5	Bill Sharman	170.00
10	Paul Arizin	100.00
12	Slater Martin	50.00
13	Dolph Schayes	125.00
15	Frank Ramsey	75.00
16	Dick McGuire	50.00
17	Bob Cousy	525.00
19	Tom Heinsohn	300.00
24	Bob Pettit	200.00
26	Gene Shue	65.00
27	Ed Macauley	75.00
28	Vern Mikkelsen	75.00
29	Willie Naulls	60.00
32	John Kerr	150.00
33	Larry Costello	50.00
37	Cliff Hagen	120.00
39	Jim Loscutoff	50.00
42	Maurice Stokes	120.00
43	Rod Hundley	120.00
44	Tom Gola	75.00
48	Lennie Rosenbluth	50.00
51	Frank Selvy	50.00
59	Al Bianchi	75.00
71	Jack Twyman	100.00
73	Jim Paxson	50.00
75	Andy Phillip	50.00
77	Bill Russell	2000.00
78	Clyde Lovellette	100.00
80	Dick Schnittker	100.00

1960-61 FLEER

		NM
Complete Set (66):		4500.00
Common Player (1-66):		20.00

		NM
1	Al Attles	100.00
2	Paul Arizin	40.00
3	Elgin Baylor	325.00
4	Walt Bellamy	50.00
8	Wilt Chamberlain	1300.00
10	Bob Cousy	230.00
14	Tom Gola	40.00
16	Hal Greer	75.00
17	Richie Guerin	40.00
18	Cliff Hagan	40.00
22	K. C. Jones	100.00
23	Sam Jones	100.00
25	John Kerr	40.00
29	Clyde Lovellette	45.00
34	Bob Pettit	75.00
35	Frank Ramsey	40.00
36	Oscar Robertson	500.00
38	Bill Russell	500.00
39	Dolph Schayes	45.00
42	Jack Twyman	40.00
43	Jerry West	700.00
44	Len Wilkens	140.00
46	Elgin Baylor	125.00
47	Wilt Chamberlain	400.00
49	Bob Cousy	100.00
54	Tom Heinsohn	40.00
59	Bob Pettit	40.00
61	Oscar Robertson	160.00
62	Bill Russell	240.00
66	Jerry West	280.00

1969-70 TOPPS

		NM
Complete Set (99):		1750.00
Common Player:		4.00

		NM
1	Wilt Chamberlain	190.00
2	Gail Goodrich	30.00
3	Cazzie Russell	15.00
10	Nate Thurmond	30.00
12	Gus Johnson	15.00
15	Connie Hawkins	45.00
20	John Havlicek	175.00
25	Kareem Abdul-Jabbar	550.00

35	Elgin Baylor	.50.00
40	Billy Cunningham	.50.00
43	Bill Bradley	.160.00
44	Len Wilkens	.35.00
45	Jerry Lucas	.40.00
50	Oscar Robertson	.70.00
55	Dave Bing	.40.00
56	Wes Unseld	.42.00
60	Willis Reed	.50.00
61	Paul Silas	.15.00
65	Lou Hudson	.22.00
75	Elvin Hayes	.60.00
78	Bob Love	.30.00
80	Earl Monroe	.40.00
82	Don Nelson	.35.00
85	Dave DeBusschere	.45.00
90	Jerry West	.100.00
91	Chet Walker	.15.00
98	Walt Frazier	.60.00
99	Checklist	.300.00

1970-71 TOPPS

	NM
Complete Set (175):	.1150.00
Common Player (1-110):	.2.50
Common Player (111-175):	.3.00

		NM
1	NBA Scoring Leaders	.35.00
2	NBA Scoring	.35.00
4	NBA FT Pct. Leaders	.9.00
5	NBA Rebound Leaders	.25.00
7	Bill Bradley	.45.00
10	John Havlicek	.70.00
13	Pat Riley	.60.00
20	Earl Monroe	.13.00
24	Checklist 1-110	.40.00
46	Jerry Lucas	.13.00
47	Don Chaney	.9.00
50	Wilt Chamberlain	.90.00
63	Bob Dandridge	.9.00
65	Elgin Baylor	.30.00
70	Elvin Hayes	.30.00
72	Wes Unseld	.11.00
75	Lew Alcindor	.110.00
80	Len Wilkens	.20.00
84	Bob Love	.8.00
86	Don Nelson	.18.00
90	Nate Thurmond	.9.00
93	Gail Goodrich	.8.00

95	Cazzie Russell	.10.00
97	Norm Van Lier	.15.00
100	Oscar Robertson	.38.00
101	Checklist 111-175	.25.00
106	Walt Frazier	.14.00
107	Jerry West	.28.00
108	Bill Cunningham	.10.00
110	Willis Reed	.10.00
112	John Havlicek	.30.00
113	Elgin Baylor	.15.00
114	Oscar Robertson	.25.00
170	Walt Frazier	.30.00
123	Pete Maravich	.275.00
124	Matt Guokas	.10.00
125	Dave Bing	.10.00
130	Connie Hawkins	.15.00
135	Dave DeBusschere	.15.00
137	Calvin Murphy	.40.00
140	Billy Cunningham	.15.00
143	Jo Jo White	.20.00
148	Jerry Sloan	.15.00
150	Willis Reed	.18.00
160	Jerry West	.55.00
165	Clem Haskins	.8.00
167	Rod Thorn	.9.00
171	Playoff Game 4 Jerry West	.15.00
172	Playoff Game 5 Bill Bradley	.15.00
173	Playoff Game 6 Wilt Chamberlain	.16.00
174	Playoff Game 7 W. Frazier	.9.00
175	Champs Knicks	.22.00

1971-72 TOPPS

	NM
Complete Set (233):	.800.00
Common Player:	.1.50

		NM
1	Oscar Robertson	.40.00
2	Bill Bradley	.40.00
10	Elgin Baylor	.25.00
20	Spencer Haywood	.9.00
29	Nate Archibald	.25.00
30	Willis Reed	.9.00
35	John Havlicek	.35.00
47	Dave Cowens	.50.00
50	Jerry West	.40.00
55	Pete Maravich	.60.00
63	Bob Lanier	.40.00
65	Walt Frazier	.16.00
70	Wilt Chamberlain	.50.00
78	Dave Bing	.7.00
79	Billy Cunningham	.8.00
80	Len Wilkens	.10.00
81	Jerry Lucas	.7.00
91	Rudy Tomjanovich	.25.00

100	Kareem Abdul-Jabbar	.50.00
105	Connie Hawkins	.8.00
107	Dave DeBusschere	.8.00
114	Don Nelson	.7.00
120	Elvin Hayes	.12.00
121	Gail Goodrich	.8.00
130	Earl Monroe	.10.00
133	NBA Playoffs Game 1 Lew Alcindor	.10.00
139	NBA Scoring Average Leaders Lew Alcindor, John Havlicek, Elvin Hayes	.15.00
140	NBA Field Goal % Leaders Johnny Green, Lew Alcindor, Wilt Chamberlain	.12.00
142	NBA Rebound Leaders Wilt Chamberlain, Elvin Hayes, Lew Alcindor	.20.00
144	NBA Checklist 1-144	.10.00
145	ABA Checklist 145-233	.10.00
152	Larry Brown	.25.00
165	Zelmo Beaty	.7.00
170	Rick Barry	.55.00
181	Doug Moe	.8.00
190	Charlie Scott	.8.00
195	Mel Daniels	.8.00
200	Dan Issel	.40.00
213	Rick Mount	.7.50
224	Louie Dampier	.7.00

1972-73 TOPPS

	NM
Complete Set (264):	.750.00
Common Player:	.1.00

		NM
1	Wilt Chamberlain	.40.00
5	Pete Maravich	.35.00
7	Dave Cowens	.15.00
20	Sidney Wicks	.10.00
25	Oscar Robinson	.20.00
32	Phil Jackson	.50.00
44	Rick Barry	.17.00
60	Walt Frazier	.10.00
73	Earl Monroe	.7.00
75	Jerry West	.22.00
80	Bob Lanier	.12.00
90	Austin Carr	.7.00
100	Kareem Abdul-Jabbar	.32.00
103	Rudy Tomjanovich	.9.00
110	John Havlicek	.27.00
115	Nate Archibald	.8.00
122	Bill Bradley	.20.00
129	Willie Reed	.9.00
144	Pat Riley	.14.00
150	Elvin Hayes	.12.00
158	NBA Playoffs Game 5 Jerry West	.7.00
159	NBA Champs - Lakers Wilt Chamberlain	.8.00

160	Checklist 1-176 ....15.00	
161	John Havlicek 14.00	
163	Kareem Abdul-Jabbar 30.00	
164	Jerry West 16.00	
168	Wilt Chamberlain 20.00	

171 NBA Scoring Leaders Kareem Abdul-Jabbar, J. Havlicek, Nate Archibald 10.00
172 NBA Scoring Average Leaders K. Abdul-Jabbar, Nate Archibald, John Havlicek ...10.00
173 NBA FG Pct. Leaders W. Chamberlain, K. Abdul-Jabbar, Walt Bellamy 10.0
175 NBA Rebound Leaders W. Chamberlain, K. Abdul-Jabbar, Wes Unseld 12.00

180	Artis Gilmore 20.00	
183	George McGinnis 15.00	
195	Julius Erving 280.00	
215	Billy Cunningham 7.00	
230	Dan Issel 16.00	
250	Rich Barry 10.00	
255	Julius Erving 65.00	

263 ABA Rebound Leaders A. Gilmore, Julius Erving, Mel Daniels 20.00

1973-74 TOPPS

		NM
1	Nate Archibald 8.00	
10	Walt Frazier 6.00	
20	John Havlicek 15.00	
21	Pat Riley 5.00	
30	Dave DeBusschere 6.00	
40	Dave Cowens 6.00	
43	Connie Hawkins 4.00	
48	Henry Bibby 4.50	
50	Kareem Abdul-Jabbar 25.00	
53	Kevin Porter 5.00	

54 NBA Western semi-finals
Wilt Chamberlain 6.00

70	Oscar Robertson 15.00	
71	Phil Jackson 10.00	
80	Wilt Chamberlain 22.00	
82	Bill Bradley 14.00	
90	Rick Barry 10.00	
95	Elvin Hayes 8.00	
100	Jerry West 22.00	
105	Willis Reed 6.00	
110	Bob Lanier 7.00	
121	Checklist 1-176 ....12.00	
126	Paul Westphal 25.00	
130	Pete Maravich 30.00	
135	Bob McAdoo 28.00	
142	Earl Monroe 5.00	
145	Rudy Tomjanovich 8.00	

153 NBA Scoring Leaders Nate Archibald, K. Abdul-Jabbar, Spencer Haywood 5.00
154 NBA Scoring Average Leaders Nate Archibald, K. Abdul-Jabbar, Spencer Haywood 5.00

155 NBA FG Pct. Leaders Wilt Chamberlain, Matt Guokas, Kareem Abdul-Jabbar 8.00
157 NBA Rebound Leaders Wilt Chamberlain, N. Thurmond, Dave Cowens 6.00

176	Wes Unseld 5.00	
200	Bill Cunningham 5.00	
210	Dan Issel 6.00	

234 ABA Scoring Average Leaders Julius Erving, George McGinnis, Dan Issel 7.00

240	Julius Erving 60.00	
242	ABA Checklist 177-264 ....10.00	
250	Artis Gilmore 6.00	

1974-75 TOPPS

	NM
Complete Set (264): 340.00	
Common Player: 50	
NBA Team Leaders: 1.00	
ABA Team Leaders: 75	
NBA League Leaders: 1.00	
ABA League Leaders: 1.25	
NBA Playoffs: 1.00	
ABA Playoffs: 1.25	

		NM
1	Kareem Abdul-Jabbar 35.00	
10	Pete Maravich 20.00	
25	Earl Monroe 5.00	
28	Rudy Tomjanovich 6.00	
30	Elvin Hayes 8.00	
31	Pat Riley 7.50	
39	Bill Walton 65.00	
50	Rick Barry 8.00	
55	Oscar Robertson 13.00	
64	Paul Westphal 5.00	
80	Bob McAdoo 7.00	

91 Milwaukee Bucks team Karrem Abdul-Jabbar, O. Robertson 7.50
93 New York Knicks team W. Frazier, B. Bradley, D. DeBusschere 5.00

100	John Havlicek 10.00	
113	Bill Bradley 10.00	
129	Doug Collins 14.00	
131	Bob Lanier 5.00	
132	Phil Jackson 5.00	
141	NBA Checklist 1-176 ....8.00	

144 NBA Scoring Leaders Bob McAdoo, K. Abdul-Jabbar, P. Maravich 6.00
145 NBA Scoring Average Leaders Bob McAdoo, Pete Maravich, Kareem Abdul-Jabbar 5.00

150	Walt Frazier 6.50	
155	Dave Owens 7.00	
176	Jerry West 20.00	
187	Caldwell Jones 5.00	

190-	Dan Issel 5.50	
196	George Gervin 50.00	
200	Julius Erving 55.00	
203	ABA Cl 177-264 ....8.00	

207 ABA Scoring Average Leaders Julius Erving, George McGinnis, Dan Issel 7.00
221 Carolina Cougars team Billy Cunningham, Mack Calvin, Tom Owens, Joe Caldwell ...5.00
226 New York Mets team Erving, John Roche, Larry Kenon 8.00

249	ABA Championship J. Erving 7.00	
250	Wilt Chamberlain 30.00	
257	George Karl 5.00	

1975-76 TOPPS

	NM
Complete Set (330): 475.00	
Common Player: 50	
NBA Leaders: 1.00	
NBA Playoffs: 1.00	
ABA Leaders: 1.25	
ABA Playoffs: 1.25	
ADA Team Leaders: 1.25	
NBA Team Leaders: 1.00	

	NM

1 NBA Scoring Average Leaders Bob McAdoo, Rick Barry, Kareem Abdul-Jabbar 10.00

10	Bob McAdoo 5.00	
37	Bill Bradley 9.50	
50	Jamal Wilkes 10.00	
55	Walt Frazier 7.00	
60	Elvin Hayes 7.00	
61	Checklist 1-110 ....8.00	
70	Rudy Tomjanovich 7.00	
71	Pat Riley 8.00	
73	Earl Monroe 6.00	
75	Pete Maravich 25.00	
77	Bill Walton 20.00	
80	John Havlicek 10.00	
100	Rick Barry 7.00	
111	Phil Jackson 5.00	

126 Milwaukee Bucks team Kareem Abdul-Jabbar, Mickey Davis 5.00
127 New Orleans Jazz team Pete Maravich, Stu Lantz, E.C. Coleman 5.00

148	Doug Collins 5.00	
170	Dave Cowens 7.00	
181	Checklist 111-220 ....7.00	
186	Paul Westphal 6.00	
219	Seattle Super Sonics chklist 6.00	

221 ABA Scoring Average Leaders George McGinnis, Julius Erving, Ron Boone 6.00
222 ABA 2 pt FG pct Leaders Artis Gilmore, Bobby Jones, Moses Malone 6.00

228	Billy Knight	.5.00
233	George Gervin	.14.00
250	Artis Gilmore	.5.00
252	Marvin Barnes	.6.00
254	Moses Malone	.50.00
257	Checklist 221-330	.7.00
259	Len Elmore	.5.00
260	Dan Issel	.6.00
282	New York Nets teams Julius Erving, John Williamson	.6.00
286	Utah Stars team Ron Boone, Moses Malone, Al Smith	.5.00
298	Bobby Jones	.13.00
300	Julius Erving	.50.00
302	Maurice Lucas	.7.00

JAMES SILAS · G

1976-77 TOPPS

		NM
Complete Set (144):		.350.00
Common Player:		.1.00
All-Stars (126-135):		.1.50

		NM
1	Julius Erving	.70.00
25	Artis Gilmore	.6.00
30	Dave Cowens	.9.00
38	Doug Collins	.6.00
43	Bill Bradley	.14.00
48	Checklist	.25.00
50	Rick Barry	.9.00
55	Paul Westphal	.9.00
57	Bill Walton	.25.00
60	Pete Maravich	.40.00
64	Walt Frazier	.6.00
66	Rudy Tomjanovich	.5.00
68	George Gervin	.15.00
69	Gus Williams	.6.00
75	Alvan Adams	.5.00
77	Phil Jackson	.10.00
90	John Havlicek	.15.00
93	Billy Cunningham	.5.00
94	Dan Issel	.6.50
100	Kareem Abdul-Jabbar	.40.00
101	Moses Malone	.25.00
110	David Thompson	.40.00
120	Elvin Hayes	.6.00
126	Kareem Abdul-Jabbar	.18.00
127	Julius Erving	.25.00
130	Pete Maravich	.20.00
131	Dave Cowens	.5.00
132	Rick Barry	.5.00
140	Bob McAdoo	.6.00

143	Lloyd Free	.8.00
144	Bobby Jones	.6.00

JUNIOR BRIDGEMAN

1977-78 TOPPS

		NM
Complete Set (132):		.100.00
Common Player:		.25

		NM
1	Kareem Abdul-Jabbar	.18.00
20	Pete Maravich	.10.00
40	Elvin Hayes	.4.00
56	Adrian Dantley	.7.00
70	John Havlicek	.7.00
73	George Gervin	.6.00
100	Julius Erving	.20.00
111	Robert Parish	.35.00
120	Bill Walton	.10.00
124	Moses Malone	.10.00
129	Walt Frazier	.4.00
132	Darryl Dawkins	.9.00

WASHINGTON BULLETS — ELVIN HAYES — FWD

1978-79 TOPPS

		NM
Complete Set (132):		.80.00
Common Player:		.25

		NM
1	Bill Walton	.12.00
10	Walter Davis	.5.00
20	George Gervin	.4.00
27	James Edwards	.3.00
38	Moses Malone	.6.50
45	Earl Monroe	.3.00
60	Rick Barry	.3.00

63	Norm Nixon	.3.00
75	Bernard King	.9.00
78	Dennis Johnson	.7.00
80	Pete Maravich	.10.00
83	Walt Frazier	.3.00
86	Robert Parish	.7.00
110	Kareem Abdul-Jabbar	.8.00
126	Marques Johnson	.3.50
130	Julius Erving	.12.00
132	Adrian Dantley	.3.50

Mychal Thompson CTR-FWD BLAZERS

1979-80 TOPPS

		NM
Complete Set (132):		.80.00
Common Player:		.20

		NM
1	George Gervin	.3.00
5	Dave Cowens	.2.00
6	Dennis Johnson	.2.00
8	Earl Monroe	.2.00
10	Kareem Abdul-Jabbar	.8.00
14	Bernard King	.2.00
20	Julius Erving	.14.00
31	Alex English	.8.00
44	Reggie Theus	.3.00
45	Bill Walton	.4.00
50	David Thompson	.2.00
60	Pete Maravich	.6.00
63	Mychal Thompson	.4.00
90	Elvin Hayes	.3.00
93	Robert Parish	.4.00
100	Moses Malone	.4.00
101	Checklist	.2.00
108	Phil Ford	.3.00
120	Rick Barry	.2.25

1980-81 TOPPS

		NM
Complete Set (176):		.550.00
Common Player:		.25
Wax Box:		.825.00

		NM
1	Dan Roundfield- 3(AS), Julius Erving -181, Ron Brewer -258 (SD)	.6.00
6	Larry Bird -34, Erving -174 (TL), Magic Johnson -139	.450.00
8	P. Maravich - 38, Lloyd Free - 264 (SD), D. Johnson - 194	.3.00
26	R. Parish - 97, L. Robinson - 187 (TL), Dwight Jones - 46	.3.00
44	Kareem Abdul-Jabbar - 135, David Thompson - 79, Brian Taylor - 216 (TL)	.5.00

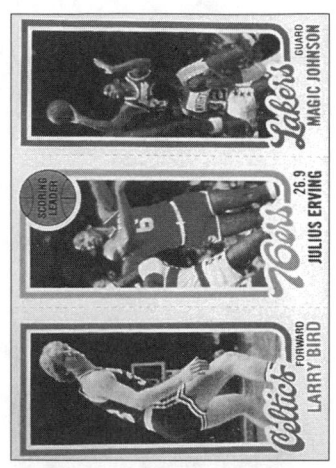

45   Michael Cooper - 137, Moses Malone -103
(TL), George Johnson - 148 . . . . .3.00
48   M. Johnson - 143 (TL), L. Bird - 30 (TL),
J. Sikma -232 . . . . .20.00
49   J. Bridgeman -146, L. Bird - 31 (TL), R.
Brewer -198 . . . . .20.00
52   S. Moncrief - 151, L. Shelton - 260 (SD),
Paul Silas - 220 . . . . .4.00
60   B. Cartwright - 166, K. Porter - 244 (TL),
Armond Hill - 25 .3.00
66   M. Cheeks - 178, Magic Johnson - 18 (AS)
Ron Boone - 237 .20.00
94   L. Bird - 34, Bill Cartwright -164 (TL),
John Drew - 23 . . . . .60.00
98   Scott May - 47, Larry Bird - 30 (TL), Jack
Sikma - 232 . . . . .20.00
111   J. Long - 88, Magic Johnson - 18 (AS),
Ron Boone -237 .15.00
114   R. Parish - 97, M. Malone - 103 (TL), G.
Johnson - 148 . . . . .4.00
130   S. Wedman - 131, K. Porter - 244 (TL),
Armond Hill - 25 .3.00
131   K. Abdul-Jabbar - 132 (TL), R. Parish - 93
(TL), T. Burleson - 126 . . . . .3.00
132   Kareem Abdul-Jabbar - 125, John Shumate
- 253 (SD), Larry Demic -167 . . . . .5.00
137   J. Bridgeman -146, J. Erving - 1 (AS), R.
Sobers - 49 . . . . .3.00
140   S. Moncrief - 151, K. Abdul-Jabbar - 133
(TL), Mike Gale - 207 . . . . .6.00
142   W. Lucas - 158, J. Erving - 262 (SD),
Abdul Jeelani - 62 . . . . .3.00
146   Jan Van Breda Kolff - 162, Julius Erving -
174 (TL), Magic Johnson - 139 . . . . .50.00
148   Bill Cartwright - 166, Eddie Johnson - 13
(AS), D. Collins - 179 . . . . .3.00
154   M. Cheeks - 178, G. Gervin - 11 (AS), J.
Chones - 136 . . . . .5.00
165   Fred Brown - 228, Larry Bird - 31 (TL),
Ron Brewer - 198 . . . . .20.00
176   E. Hayes - 157 (SD), J. Erving - 181, Ron
Brewer - 258 (SD) 7.50

1981-82 TOPPS

		MT
Complete Set (198):		.80.00
Common Player:		..15
Wax Box:		.325.00

#		MT
1	Larry Bird	.27.00
6	Robert Parish	.2.00
20	Kareem Abdul-Jabbar	.5.00
21	Magic Johnson	.15.00
30	Julius Erving	.5.00

45   Celtics team Larry Bird, Nate Archibald
. . . . .2.50
58   Knicks team Bill Cartwright, Michael Ray
Richardson 2.00
75   Kevin McHale 27.00
101   Larry Bird 12.00
104   Julius Erving 4.00
106   Robert Parish 2.00
74   Bill Laimbeer 3.50
68   Alex English 2.00
106   Kareem Abdul-Jabbar 2.50

109   Magic Johnson 12.00

1983-84 STAR

	MT
Complete Bag Set (276):	.1800.00
Comp. Bag 76ers (12):	.125.00
Comp. Bag Lakers (13):	.200.00
Comp. Bag Celtics (12):	.500.00
Comp. Bag Bucks: (11):	.60.00
Comp. Bag Mavs (12):	.500.00
Comp. Bag Knicks (12):	.30.00
Comp. Bag Rockets (12):	.20.00
Comp. Bag Pistons (12):	.150.00
Comp. Bag Blazers (12):	.225.00
Comp. Bag Suns (12):	.60.00
Comp. Bag Clippers (12):	.70.00
Comp. Bag Jazz (12):	.25.00
Comp. Bag Nets (12):	.25.00
Comp. Bag Pacers (12):	.20.00
Comp. Bag Bulls (12):	.25.00
Comp. Bag Nuggets (12):	.30.00
Comp. Bag Sonics (11):	.45.00
Comp. Bag Bullets (12):	.25.00
Comp. Bag Kings (12):	.25.00
Comp. Bag Cavs (13):	.20.00
Comp. Bag Spurs (11):	.30.00

	MT
Comp. Bag Warriors (11):	.20.00
Comp. Bag Hawks (14):	.200.00
Common 76ers SP:	.4.00
Common Lakers SP:	.4.00
Common Celtics SP:	.8.00
Common Bucks SP:	.4.00
Common Mavs SP:	.20.00
Common Player:	.2.00
Minor Stars:	.4.00

		MT
1	Julius Erving	.75.00
2	Maurice Cheeks	.10.00
6	Bobby Jones	.10.00
7	Moses Malone	.20.00
10	Sedale Threatt	.10.00
11	Andrew Toney	.10.00
13	Magic Johnson	.95.00
14	Kareem Abdul-Jabbar	.40.00
15	Michael Cooper	.10.00
18	Bob McAdoo	.10.00
21	Kurt Rambis	.12.00
22	Byron Scott	.20.00
23	James Worthy	.55.00
25	Larry Bird	.325.00
27	Danny Ainge	.55.00
32	Dennis Johnson	.18.00
33	Cedric Maxwell	.10.00
34	Kevin McHale	.45.00
35	Robert Parish	.40.00
38	Sidney Moncrief	.15.00
39	Nate Archibald	.15.00
44	Marques Johnson	.10.00
45	Bob Lanier	.15.00
46	Mark Aguirre	.29.00
50	Rolando Blackman	.29.00
52	Brad Davis	.30.00
53	Dale Ellis	.45.00
54	Bill Garnett	.20.00
55	Derek Harper	.60.00
56	Kurt Nimphius	.20.00
57	Jim Spanarkel	.20.00
58	Elston Turner	.20.00
59	Jay Vincent	.30.00
60	Mark West	.20.00
61	Bernard King	.10.00
76	Elvin Hayes	.10.00
94	Isiah Thomas	.120.00
100	Clyde Drexler	.200.00
115	Larry Nance	.20.00
120	Paul Westfield	.10.00
121	Bill Walton	.18.00
123	Terry Cummings	.15.00
130	Ricky Pierce	.10.00
145	Buck Williams	.20.00
186	Alex English	.10.00
189	Dan Issel	.10.00
195	Tom Chambers	.17.00
212	Jeff Malone	.12.00
241	George Gervin	.15.00
250	John Paxson	.12.00
263	Dominique Wilkins	.140.00
271	Doc Rivers	.20.00

1984 STAR DENVER POLICE ALL-STAR GAME

	NM
Complete Set (34):	$170.00
Commons:	.2.00
Unlisted Stars:	.2.50-5.00

#	Player	NM
1	Checklist	.7.00
2	Larry Bird	.45.00

#	Player	NM
4	Julius Erving	15.00
7.	Kevin McHale	8.00
9	Robert Parish	6.00
11	Isiah Thomas	8.00
14	Kareem Abdul-Jabbar	13.00
19	George Gervin	8.00
21	Magic Johnson	28.00
27	Clyde Drexler	25.00
28	Julius Erving	15.00
33	Dominique Wilkins	17.00

1984 STAR AWARDS BANQUET

	NM
Complete Set (24):	$65.00
Commons:	2.00
Unlisted Stars	2.50-3.00

#	Player	NM
5	Kevin McHale	5.00
6	Magic Johnson	12.00
8	Larry Bird (MVP)	20.00
10	Statistical Leaders	9.00
11	Statistical Leaders II	6.00
12	Isiah Thomas	5.00
15	Larry Bird	20.00
17	Magic Johnson	12.00
21	Kareem Abdul-Jabbar	9.00
24	All-NBA Team	12.00

1984 STAR LARRY BIRD

	NM
Complete Set (18):	$75.00
Singles:	5.00

1984 STAR CELTICS CHAMPS

	NM
Complete Set (25):	$250.00
Commons:	3.00
Unlisted Stars	3.50-7.00

#	Player	NM
1	Checklist	10.00
4	Larry Bird	38.00
5	Magic Johnson	20.00
7	Larry Bird	38.00
8	Jabbar/McHale	10.00
10	Magic Johnson	20.00
11	Magic/Bird	65.00
12	Worthy/Ainge	10.00
14	Larry Bird	40.00
15	Pat Riley	8.00
16	Kareem Abdul-Jabbar	8.00
18	Kareem Abdul-Jabbar	8.00
20	Kareem Abdul-Jabbar	8.00
23	Auerbach, R.	10.00
24	Larry Bird (MVP)	38.00
25	Road to the Title	14.00

MOSES MALONE
Center-Philadelphia 76ers

1984-85 STAR

	MT
Complete Bag Set (288):	5000.00
Comp. Bag Celtics (12):	260.00
Comp. Bag Clippers (12):	25.00
Comp. Bag Knicks (13):	20.00
Comp. Bag Suns (14):	25.00
Comp. Bag Pacers (12):	50.00
Comp. Bag Spurs (12):	30.00
Comp. Bag Hawks (12):	85.00
Comp. Bag Nets (13):	20.00
Comp. Bag Bulls (12):	3000.00
Comp. Bag Sonics (12):	20.00
Comp. Bag Bucks (12):	25.00
Comp. Bag Nuggets (12):	25.00
Comp. Bag Warriors (12):	20.00
Comp. Bag Blazers (11):	125.00
Comp. Bag Lakers (13):	170.00
Comp. Bag Bullets (10):	20.00
Comp. Bag Oly/Spec (14):	900.00
Comp. Bag 76ers (12):	250.00
Comp. Bag Cavs (12):	20.00
Comp. Bag Jazz (12):	220.00
Comp. Bag Rockets (13):	350.00
Comp. Bag Mavs (11):	50.00
Comp. Bag Pistons (9):	55.00
Comp. Bag Kings (11):	30.00
Common Pacers SP:	4.00
Common Player:	2.00
Minor Stars:	4.00

		MT
1	Larry Bird	160.00
2	Danny Ainge	14.00
9	Kevin McHale	15.00
10	Robert Parish	12.00
12	Larry Bird	80.00
22	Bill Walton	18.00
47	Larry Nance	10.00
67	George Gervin	12.00
76	Dominique Wilkins	60.00
101	Michael Jordan	2800.00
142	Dan Issel	10.00
165	Clyde Drexler	75.00
172	Magic Johnson	90.00
173	Kareem Abdul-Jabbar	50.00
184	James Worthy	14.00
195	Michael Jordan (Oly)	100.00
201	Moses Malone	15.00
202	Charles Barkley	200.00-
204	Julius Erving	35.00
235	John Stockton	200.00
237	Hakeem Olajuwon	335.00
238	Craig Ehlo	15.00
257	Sam Perkins	18.00
261	Isiah Thomas	45.00
278	Otis Thorpe	15.00
281	Julius Erving	20.00
282	Kareem Abdul-Jabbar	15.00
287	Isiah Thomas	20.00
288	Michael Jordan Spec	425.00

1984-85 STAR ARENA

Comp. Set w/Lanier (49):	600.00
Complete Set (48):	300.00
Complete Bag Celts (9):	100.00

1A	Larry Bird	50.00
9A	Champions	30.00
Complete Bag Lakers (10):		90.00
1C	Kareem Abdul-Jabbar	20.00
3C	Magic Johnson	40.00
9C	Kareem Abdul-Jabbar, Magic Johnson	30.00

10C	Kareem Abdul-Jabbar	15.00
Complete Bag Bucks (8):		25.00
6D	Bob Lanier	300.00
Complete Bag 76ers (10):		50.00
1E	Julius Eving	25.00

Court Kings

UTAH
1989-90 Season

JOHN STOCKTON

1984-85 STAR COURT KINGS

Complete Set (50):	450.00
Common Player:	2.00

1	Kareem Abdul-Jabbar	15.00
4	Julius Erving	15.00
12	Dominique Wilkins	15.00
15	Magic Johnson	25.00
18	Larry Bird	38.00
26	Michael Jordan	190.00
30	Isiah Thomas	15.00
41	Charles Barkley	45.00
42	Kevin McHale	10.00
47	Akeem Olajuwon	40.00

1984-85 STAR JULIUS ERVING

	NM
Complete Set (18):	$75.00
Singles	5.00

CLYDE DREXLER
Forward — Portland Trailblazers

1984-85 STAR MR. Z'S BLAZERS

	NM
Complete Set (5):	$290.00

#	Player	NM
1	Carr, K.	25.00
2	Drexler, C.	125.00
3	Norris, A.	60.00
4	Thompson, M.	32.00
5	Valentine, D.	32.00

1985 STAR KAREEM ABDUL-JABBAR

	NM
Complete Set (18):	$50.00
Singles:	4.00

1985 STAR CRUNCH 'N MUNCH

Complete Set (11):	$425.00
Common Player:	2.00

#	Player	
1	All-Star	5.00
2	Larry Bird	95.00
3	Julius Erving	25.00
4	Michael Jordan	275.00
7	Kareem Abdul-Jabbar	20.00
10	Magic Johnson	65.00

1985 STAR GATORADE SLAM DUNK

Complete Set (9):	$250.00
Common Player:	2.50

#	Player	
4	Clyde Drexler	30.00
5	Julius Erving	25.00
7	Michael Jordan	235.00
8	Dominique Wilkins	20.00
(XX)	Charles Barkley	90.00

1985 STAR LAST 11 R.O.Y.

Complete Set (11):	$285.00
Common Player:	2.50

#	Player	
1	Michael Jordan	225.00
6	Larry Bird	90.00

1985 STAR SLAM DUNK

Complete Set (10):	$250.00
Common Player:	2.00

#	Player	
2	Clyde Drexler	25.00
3	Julius Erving	20.00
5	Michael Jordan	190.00
8	Dominique Wilkins	12.00

1985 STAR COACHES

	NM
Complete Set (10):	$25.00
Commons:	2.00
Unlisted Stars	2.50-3.00

#	Player	NM
No #	Don Nelson	4.00
No #	Jack Ramsey	4.00
No #	Pat Riley	8.00
No #	Len Wilkens	6.00

1985 STAR MILWAUKEE CARD NIGHT

	NM
Complete Set (12):	$25.00
Complete Set (13):	75.00

Commons:	2.00
Unlisted Stars	2.50-3.00

#	Player	NM
1	Don Nelson	4.00
3	Terry Cummings	4.00
10	L. Micheaux	50.00
12	Sidney Moncrief	5.00

1985 STAR SCHICK LEGENDS

	NM
Complete Set (25):	$70.00
Commons	2.00
Unlisted Stars	2.50-7.00

#	Player	NM
7	Bob Cousy	12.00
12	John Havlicek	15.00
18	Pete Maravich	25.00
21	Oscar Robertson	9.00

1985-86 STAR

	MT
Complete Bag Set (172):	1500.00
Comp. Bag 76ers (9):	110.00
Comp. Bag Pistons (8):	45.00
Comp. Bag Rockets (8):	120.00
Comp. Bag Lakers (8):	250.00
Comp. Bag Suns (8):	24.00
Comp. Bag Hawks (8):	70.00
Comp. Bag Nuggets (8):	18.00
Comp. Bag Nets (8):	18.00
Comp. Bag Sonics (8):	18.00
Comp. Bag Kings (7):	18.00
Comp. Bag Pacers (7):	18.00
Comp. Bag Clippers (7):	18.00
Comp. Bag Celtics (8):	130.00
Comp. Bag Blazers (7):	100.00
Comp. Bag Bullets (7):	18.00
Comp. Bag Bulls (7):	900.00
Comp. Bag Bucks (7):	20.00
Comp. Bag Warriors (7):	18.00
Comp. Bag Jazz (7):	110.00
Comp. Bag Spurs (7):	18.00
Comp. Bag Cavs (7):	18.00
Comp. Bag Mavs (7):	20.00
Comp. Bag Knicks (7):	185.00
Common Lakers SP:	5.00
Common Player:	2.00
Minor Stars:	4.00

#	Player	MT
2	Charles Barkley	80.00
3	Julius Erving	30.00
6	Moses Malone	10.00
10	Isiah Thomas	30.00
18	Hakeem Olajuwon	85.00
26	Kareem Abdul-Jabbar	40.00
27	Michael Cooper	10.00
28	Magic Johnson	120.00
33	James Worthy	15.00
42	Dominique Wilkins	35.00
48	Kevin Willis	18.00
95	Larry Bird	80.00
96	Danny Ainge	12.00
98	Kevin McHale	12.00
99	Robert Parish	10.00
101	Bill Walton	15.00
106	Clyde Drexler	70.00
117	Michael Jordan	850.00
121	George Gervin	15.00
144	John Stockton	85.00
166	Patrick Ewing	170.00

1985-86 STAR ALL-ROOKIE TEAM

Complete Set (11):	$500.00
Common Player:	4.00

#	Player	
1	Hakeem Olajuwon	70.00
2	Michael Jordan	300.00
3	Charles Barkley	60.00
8	John Stockton	60.00

1985-86 STAR FRANZ BLAZERS

	NM
Complete Set (13):	$60.00
Commons:	2.00
Unlisted Stars	8.00-12.00

#	Player	NM
5	Clyde Drexler	35.00

1985-86 STAR LAKERS CHAMPS

	NM
Complete Set (18):	$100.00
Commons:	2.50
Unlisted Stars	3.00-4.00

#	Player	NM
1	'85 Champs-Jabbar	10.00
2	Bird, L.	25.00
6	McHale, K.	6.00
7	Johnson, M.	18.00
8	Abdul-Jabbar (MVP)	9.00
9	Bird, L.	25.00
10	Abdul-Jabbar, L.	9.00
12	Riley, P.	7.00
14	Johnson, M.	18.00
18	Champs/Reagan	30.00

1986 STAR BEST OF THE BEST

	NM
Complete Set (15):	.$165.00
Commons:	.3.00
Unlisted Stars	.10.00-18.00

#	Player	NM
3	Larry Bird	.35.00
8	Magic Johnson	.30.00
9	Michael Jordan	.100.00
11	Hakeem Olajuwon	.20.00

1986 STAR BEST OF THE NEW/OLD

	NM
Complete Set (8):	.$600.00
Best of the New (4):	.250.00
Best of the Old (40):	.350.00

#	Player	NM
No #	P. Ewing (New)	.20.00
No #	M. Jordan (New)	.165.00
No #	H. Olajuwon (New)	.35.00
No #	R. Sampson (New)	.8.00
No #	K. Abdul-Jabbar (Old)	.120.00
No #	J. Erving (Old)	.120.00
No #	G. Gervin (Old)	.75.00
No #	B. Walton (Old)	.75.00

1986-87 FLEER

	MT
Complete Set (132):	.$2000.00
Common Player:	.2.00
Minor Stars:	.3.00
Pack (13):	.450.00
Box (36):	.14,500.00

		MT
1	Kareem Abdul-Jabbar	.10.00
4	Danny Ainge	.8.00
7	Charles Barkley	.85.00
9	Larry Bird	.45.00
26	Clyde Drexler	.70.00
27	Joe Dumars	.30.00
31	Julius Erving	.16.00
32	Patrick Ewing	.60.00
53	Magic Johnson	.30.00
57	Michael Jordan	.1600.00
68	Karl Malone	.25.00
77	Chris Mullin	.25.00
81	Charles Oakley	.8.00
82	Hakeem Olajuwon	.100.00
91	Doc Rivers	.7.00
99	Byron Scott	.6.00
109	Isiah Thomas	.30.00
120	Spud Webb	.6.00
121	Dominique Wilkins	.25.00
123	Buck Williams	.6.00
131	James Worthy	.12.00
132	Checklist	.10.00

Stickers

Complete Set (11):	.$450.00
Common Player:	.2.00

1	Larry Bird	.17.00
5	Julius Erving	.6.00
7	Magic Johnson	.12.00
8	Michael Jordan	.400.00
9	Hakeem Olajuwon	.20.00

1987-88 FLEER

	MT
Complete Set (132)	.350.00
Common Player:	.1.00
Minor Stars:	.2.00
Wax Box:	.1200.00

		MT
1	Kareem Abdul-Jabbar	.7.00
9	Charles Barkley	.25.00
11	Larry Bird	.30.00
30	Clyde Drexler	.15.00
31	Joe Dumars	.7.00
35	Julius Erving	.10.00
37	Patrick Ewing	.15.00
42	A. C. Green	.6.00
49	Ron Harper	.8.00
56	Magic Johnson	.20.00
59	Miachael Jordan	.250.00
68	Karl Malone	.15.00
80	Hakeem Olajuwon	.20.00
97	Detlef Schrempf	.12.00
106	Isiah Thomas	.8.00
109	Otis Thorpe	.6.00
118	Dominique Wilkins	.6.00

Stickers

Complete Set (11):	.$150.00
Common Player:	.1.00

1	Magic Johnson	.7.00
2	Michael Jordan	.125.00
4	Larry Bird	.8.00

1988-89 FLEER

	MT
Complete Set (132):	.$225.00
Common Player:	.25
Minor Stars:	.50
Wax Box:	.600.00

		MT
9	Larry Bird	.10.00
16	Horace Grant	.8.00
17	Michael Jordan	.90.00
20	Scottie Pippen	.50.00
43	Dennis Rodman	.25.00
53	Hakeem Olajuwon	.8.00
57	Reggie Miller	.35.00
67	Magic Johnson	.8.00
85	Charles Barkley	.6.00
114	Karl Malone	.4.00
115	John Stockton	.25.00
120	Michael Jordan	.20.00
124	Larry Bird	.4.00
126	Hakeem Olajuwon	.4.00
127	John Stockton	.5.00
129	Charles Barkley	.4.00

Stickers

Complete Set (11): $65.00
Common Player: 50

2	Larry Bird	. . . . .4.00
6	Magic Johnson	. . . . .3.00
7	Michael Jordan	. . . . .50.00

1988 FOURNIER NBA ESTRELLAS

Complete Set (33): $65.00
Common Player: 25

1	Larry Bird	. . . . .5.00
4	Magic Johnson	. . . . .4.00
16	Karl Malone	. . . . .4.00

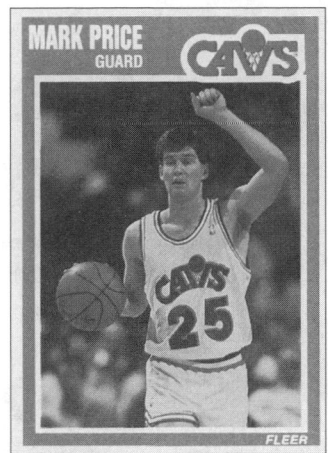

22	Michael Jordan	. . . . .25.00
32	John Stockton	. . . . .4.00
xx	Jordan "Rules"	. . . . .25.00

1989-90 FLEER

Complete Set (168): $40.00
Common Player 10
Minor Stars: 20
Wax Box: 75.00

			MT
8	Larry Bird	. . . .	.3.00
10	Reggie Lewis	. . . .	.1.00
15	Rex Chapman	. . . .	.1.00
20	Horace Grant	. . . .	.1.50
21	Michael Jordan	. . . .	35.00
23	Scottie Pippen	. . . .	.4.00
49	Dennis Rodman	. . . .	.3.00
56	Mitch Richmond	. . . .	.5.00
61	Hakeem Olajuwon	. . . .	.2.00
65	Reggie Miller	. . . .	.2.00
68	Rik Smits	. . . .	.1.50
71	Danny Manning	. . . .	.1.00
77	Magic Johnson	. . . .	.2.00
100	Patrick Ewing	. . . .	.1.00
104	Rod Strickland	. . . .	.2.50
113	Charles Barkley	. . . .	.2.00
117	Hersey Hawkins	. . . .	.1.00
121	Jeff Hornacek	. . . .	.1.00
123	Kevin Johnson	. . . .	.1.50
124	Dan Majerle	. . . .	.1.00
128	Clyde Drexler	. . . .	.1.50
155	Karl Malone	. . . .	.1.00
156	John Stockton	. . . .	.2.00

Stickers

Complete Set (11): $45.00
Common Player: 20

3	Michael Jordan	. . . . .40.00
5	Magic Johnson	. . . . .1.00
10	Larry Bird	. . . . .1.50

1989-90 HOOPS

	MT
Complete Set (352):	.$25.00
Complete Series 1 (300):	.20.00
Complete Series 2 (52):	.5.00
Common Player:	.05
Common Player (SP):	.15
Minor Stars:	.10
Minor Stars: (SP):	.25
Series 1 Wax Box:	.40.00
Series 2 Wax Box:	.15.00

			MT
21	Michael Jordan	. . . .	.1.50
35	Kevin Johnson	. . . .	..75
37	Rik Smits	. . . .	..75
138	David Robinson	. . . .	.10.00
150	Larry Bird	. . . .	.1.00
200	Michael Jordan	. . . .	.3.00
211	Dennis Rodman	. . . .	.1.25
244	Scottie Pippen	. . . .	.1.00
249	Scott Skiles	. . . .	..75
260	Mitch Richmond	. . . .	.3.00
310	David Robinson	. . . .	.2.00
353	Pistons Champions	. . . .	.4.00

Basketball Autographs
Hall of Famers

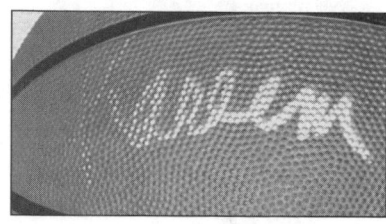

Kareem Abdul-Jabbar (Lew Alcindor)
(1947-) 1995
Basketball $150
Cut signature $15
3x5 index card $25
8x10 photograph . . . .$30-$40

Nate Archibald (1948-) 1991
Basketball . . . .$90-$110
Cut signature $6
3x5 index card $10
8x10 photograph . . . .$15-$20

Paul Arizin (1928-) 1977
Basketball $100
Cut signature $5
3x5 index card $10
8x10 photograph $30

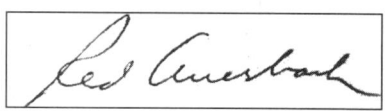

Red Auerbach (1917-) 1968
Basketball . . . .$150-$175
Cut signature . . . .$8-$10
3x5 index card $12
8x10 photograph . . . .$25-$30

Thomas Barlow (1896-1983) 1980
Basketball $100
Cut signature $5
3x5 index card $8
8x10 photograph $35

Rick Barry (1944-) 1987
Basketball $125
Cut signature . . . .$7-$10

3x5 index card $12
8x10 photograph $20

Elgin Baylor (1934-) 1976
Basketball $150
Cut signature . . . .$7-$10
3x5 index card . . . .$12-$15
8x10 photograph $20

John Beckman (1895-1968) 1972
Basketball $100
Cut signature $4
3x5 index card $10
8x10 photograph $40

Clair Bee (1896-1983) 1967
Basketball $100
Cut signature $5
3x5 index card $10
8x10 photograph $40

Walt Bellamy (1939-) 1992
Basketball . . . .$75-$100
Cut signature $5
3x5 index card $10
8x10 photograph . . . .$15-$20

Danny Biasone (19??-1992) 2000
Basketball $100
Cut signature $6
3x5 index card $8
8x10 photograph . . . .$20-$25

Sergei Belov (1944-) 1992
Basketball . . . .$75-$100
Cut signature $5
3x5 index card . . . .$6-$8
8x10 photograph . . . .$15-$17

Dave Bing (1943-) 1990
Basketball . . . .$100-$110
Cut signature . . . .$4-$5
3x5 index card $10
8x10 photograph . . . .$15-$18

Larry Bird (1956-) 1998
Basketball $200
Cut Signature . . . .$15-$20
3x5 index card $20
8x10 photograph $50

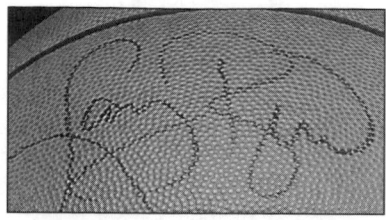

Carol Blazejowski (1956-) 1994
Basketball . . . .$75-$100
Cut signature $5
3x5 index card . . . .$6-$7
8x10 photograph . . . .$15-$17

Ernest Blood (1872-1955) 1960
Basketball $110
Cut signature $8
3x5 index card $10
8x10 photograph . . . .$25-$30

Bennie Borgmann (1899-1978) 1961
Basketball $100
Cut signature $4
3x5 index card $8
8x10 photograph $40

Bill Bradley (1943-) 1982
Basketball . . . .$125-$150
Cut signature . . . .$8-$12
3x5 index card $15
8x10 photograph . . . .$30-$35

Joseph Brennan (1900-1989) 1974
Basketball $100
Cut signature $5
3x5 index card $10
8x10 photograph $35

Lou Carnesseca (1925-) 1991
Basketball $100
Cut signature $7
3x5 index card $10
8x10 photograph . . . .$12-$16

Alfred Cervi (1917-) 1984
Basketball $100
Cut signature . . . .$4-$6
3x5 index card $10
8x10 photograph . . . .$12-$14

Wilt Chamberlain (1936-1999) 1978
Basketball . . . .$250-$300
Cut signature $20
3x5 index card $40
8x10 photograph . . . .$75-$100

Jody Conradt (1941-) 1998
Basketball . . . .$75-$100
Cut signature $5
3x5 index card $7
8x10 photograph . . . .$12-$15

Charles Cooper (1926-1984) 1976
Basketball $100
Cut signature $15
3x5 index card $17
8x10 photograph $35

Bob Cousy (1928-) 1970
Basketball $150
Cut signature . . . .$9-$10
3x5 index card $25
8x10 photograph . . . .$25-$30

Dave Cowens (1948-) 1991
Basketball . . . .$100-$125
Cut signature . . . .$6-$7
3x5 index card $7
8x10 photograph $30

Billy Cunningham (1943-) 1986
Basketball $110
Cut signature . . . .$6-$7
3x5 index card $9
8x10 photograph . . . .$15-$17

Chuck Daly (1930-) 1994
Basketball $100
Cut signature $5
3x5 index card $7
8x10 photograph . . . .$15-$18

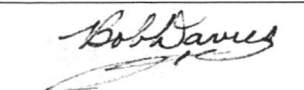

Robert Davies (1920-1990) 1969
Basketball $100
Cut signature $20
3x5 index card $25
8x10 photograph $45

Forrest DeBernardi (1899-1970) 1961
Basketball $100
Cut signature $15
3x5 index card $18
8x10 photograph $35

Dave DeBusschere (1940-) 1982
Basketball . . . .$125-$150
Cut signature . . . .$5-$6
3x5 index card $8
8x10 photograph . . . .$15-$20

Henry Dehnert (1898-1979) 1968
Basketball $100
Cut signature $7
3x5 index card $9
8x10 photograph . . . .$12-$17

Antonio Diaz-Miguel (1933-2000) 1997
Basketball $100
Cut signature . . . .$5-$6
3x5 index card $8
8x10 photograph . . . .$15-$20

Anne Donovan (1961-) 1995
Basketball $75-100
Cut signature . . . .$5-$6
3x5 index card $8
8x10 photograph . . . .$15-$20

Wayne Embry (1937-) 1999
Basketball . . . .$80-$100
Cut signature $6
3x5 index card $10
8x10 photograph . . . .$15-$18

Paul Endacott (1902-1977) 1971
Basketball $100
Cut signature $6
3x5 index card $10
8x10 photograph . . . .$12-$17

Alex English (1954-) 1997
Basketball $125
Cut signature . . . .$8-$10
3x5 index card $20
8x10 photo $35

Julius Erving (1950-) 1992
Basketball . . . .$175-$225
Cut signature $15
3x5 index card $25
8x10 photograph $30

Bud Foster (1906-1996) 1964
Basketball $125
Cut signature $30
3x5 index card $35
8x10 photograph $50

Walt Frazier (1945-) 1987
Basketball . . . .$100-$125
Cut signature $15
3x5 index card $20
8x10 photograph $20

Marty Friedman (1889-1986) 1971
Basketball $100
Cut signature $15
3x5 index card $20
8x10 photograph $40

Joe Fulks (1921-1976) 1977
Basketball $125
Cut signature $20
3x5 index card $25
8x10 photograph $50

Clarence Gaines (1923-) 1981
Basketball $100
Cut signature . . . .$7-$9
3x5 index card $15
8x10 photograph $20

Laddie Gale (1917-1996) 1976
Basketball $100
Cut signature $7
3x5 index card $12
8x10 photograph $15

Harry Gallatin (1927-) 1990
Basketball $110
Cut signature . . . .$6-$8
3x5 index card $15
8x10 photograph . . . .$15-$18

William Gates (1917-1999) 1988
Basketball $125
Cut signature . . . .$8-$10
3x5 index card $12
8x10 photograph . . . .$20-$25

George Gervin (1952-) 1996
Basketball . . . .$110-$120
Cut signature $6
3x5 index card $10
8x10 photograph . . . .$20-$25

Tom Gola (1933-) 1975
Basketball . . . .$90-$100
Cut signature $5
3x5 index card $8
8x10 photograph . . . .$15-$18

Alexsandr Gomelsky (1928-) 1995
Basketball . . . .$75-$100
Cut signature $5
3x5 index card $7
8x10 photograph . . . .$15-$17

Gail Goodrich (1943-) 1996
Basketball . . . .$100-$110
Cut signature . . . .$6-$8
3x5 index card $10
8x10 photograph . . . .$15-$20

Edward Gottlieb (1898-1979) 1972
Basketball $110
Cut signature $8
3x5 index card $10
8x10 photograph . . . .$25-$30

Hal Greer (1936-) 1981
Basketball $120
Cut signature $4
3x5 index card . . . .$3-$6
8x10 photograph . . . .$17-$22

Robert Gruenig (1913-1958) 1963
Basketball $125
Cut signature . . . .$10-$15
3x5 index card $12
8x10 photograph . . . .$25-$35

Cliff Hagan (1931-) 1977
Basketball $125
Cut signature . . . .$4-$7
3x5 index card $6
8x10 photograph $20

Alex Hannum (1923-) 1998
Basketball . . . .$75-$100
Cut signature $5
3x5 index card $6
8x10 photograph . . . .$15-$17

Victor Hanson (1903-1982) 1960
Basketball $125
Cut signature . . . .$10-$14
3x5 index card $15
8x10 photograph $40

Lusia Harris-Stewart (1955-) 1992
Basketball . . . .$75-$100
Cut signature $5
3x5 index card . . . .$6-$7
8x10 photograph . . . .$15-$17

Marv Harshman (1917-) 1985
Basketball . . . .$75-$100
Cut signature . . . .$5-$6
3x5 index card . . . .$7-$8
8x10 photograph . . . .$15-$17

Don Haskins (1930-) 1997
Basketball . . . .$75-$100
Cut signature $5
3x5 index card . . . .$6-$7
8x10 photograph . . . .$15-$17

John Havlicek (1940-) 1983
Basketball . . . .$150-$160
Cut signature $10
3x5 index card $15
8x10 photograph $25

Connie Hawkins (1942-) 1991
Basketball $125
Cut signature $8
3x5 index card $10
8x10 photograph $22

Elvin Hayes (1945-) 1990
Basketball $125
Cut signature $8
3x5 index card $12
8x10 photograph $17

Marques Haynes (1926-) 1998
Basketball $120
Cut signature $7
3x5 index card $10
8x10 photograph $20

Tommy Heinsohn (1934-) 1985
Basketball $125
Cut signature $6
3x5 index card $8
8x10 photograph $17

Nat Holman (1896-1995) 1964
Basketball $150
Cut signature $15
3x5 index card $20
8x10 photograph $100

Red Holzman (1920-1998) 1985
Basketball $125
Cut signature . . . .$8-$10
3x5 index card $15
8x10 photograph . . . .$22-$27

Robert Houbregs (1932-) 1986
Basketball $110
Cut signature . . . .$5-$7
3x5 index card $10
8x10 photograph $15

Bailey Howell (1937-) 1997
Basketball $100
Cut signature` . . . .$6-$8
3x5 index card $10
8x10 photo . . . .$15-$20

Chuck Hyatt (1908-1978) 1959
Basketball $100
Cut signature $5
3x5 index card $10
8x10 photograph $25

Henry Iba (1904-1993) 1968
Basketball $150
Cut signature $10
3x5 index card $15
8x10 photograph $30

Edward "Ned" Irish (1905-1982) 1964
Basketball ....$100-$110
Cut signature $8
3x5 index card $10
8x10 photograph ....$25-$30

Dan Issel (1948-) 1992
Basketball $115
Cut signature $7
3x5 index card $12
8x10 photograph $15

Buddy Jeannette (1917-1998) 1994
Basketball $110
Cut signature ....$4-$7
3x5 index card $9
8x10 photograph ....$15-$17

William Johnson (1911-1980) 1976
Basketball $125
Cut signature $5
3x5 index card $10
8x10 photograph $30

Neil Johnston (1929-1978) 1989
Basketball $110
Cut signature $10
3x5 index card $15
8x10 photograph $35

K.C. Jones (1932-) 1988
Basketball $100
Cut signature $6
3x5 index card $8
8x10 photograph $15

Sam Jones (1933-) 1983
Basketball $120
Cut signature ....$6-$7

3x5 index card $8
8x10 photograph $20

Bobby Knight (1931-) 1990
Basketball $100
Cut signature $10
3x5 index card $12
8x10 photograph $15

Edward Krause (1913-1942) 1975
Basketball $110
Cut signature $5
3x5 index card $10
8x10 photograph $20

John Kundla (1916-) 1995
Basketball ....$75-$100
Cut signature $5
3x5 index card ....$6-$7
8x10 photograph ....$15-$17

Bob Kurland (1924-) 1961
Basketball $110
Cut signature $5
3x5 index card $10
8x10 photograph ....$15-$20

Bob Lanier (1948-) 1992
Basketball $100
Cut signature $7
3x5 index card $10
8x10 photograph $15

Joe Lapchick (1900-1970) 1966
Basketball $150
Cut signature $10
3x5 index card $15
8x10 photograph $35

Nancy Lieberman-Cline (1958-) 1996
Basketball ....$75-$100
Cut signature $5
3x5 index card ....$7-$8
8x10 photograph ....$15-$17

Clyde Lovellette (1929-) 1987
Basketball $110
Cut signature ....$4-$7
3x5 index card $9
8x10 photograph ....$15-$17

Jerry Lucas (1940-) 1979
Basketball $125
Cut signature $5
3x5 index card $10
8x10 photograph ....$15-$20

Hank Luisetti (1916-) 1959
Basketball $125
Cut signature $7
3x5 index card $12
8x10 photograph ....$15-$25

Ed Macauley (1928-) 1960
Basketball $150
Cut signature $15
3x5 index card $20
8x10 photograph $30

Pete Maravich (1947-1988) 1987
Basketball ....$500-$600
Cut signature $10
3x5 index card $15
8x10 photograph ....$225-$250

Slater Martin (1925-) 1981
Basketball $130
Cut signature ....$4-$6
3x5 index card $9
8x10 photograph $17

Bob McAdoo (1961-) 2000
Basketball . . . .$100-$110
Cut signature . . . .$6-$8
3x5 index card $9
8x10 photograph . . . .$20-$25

John McLendon (1915-1999) 1979
Basketball $100
Cut signature $7
3x5 index card $10
8x10 photograph $20

Branch McCracken (1908-1970) 1960
Basketball $100
Cut signature $7
3x5 index card $10
8x10 photograph $20

Jack McCracken (1911-1958) 1962
Basketball $100
Cut signature $7
3x5 index card $10
8x10 photograph $20

Bobby McDermott (1914-) 1987
Basketball $110
Cut signature . . . .$6-$7
3x5 index card $14
8x10 photograph . . . .$15-$20

Al McGuire (1928-2001) 1991
Basketball . . . .$100-$150
Cut signature $7
3x5 index card $15
8x10 photograph $20

Dick McGuire (1926-) 1992
Basketball . . . .$75-$100
Cut signature $5
3x5 index card $10
8x10 photograph $20

Frank McGuire (1916-1994) 1976
Basketball $110
Cut signature $7
3x5 index card $9
8x10 photograph . . . .$16-$18

Kevin McHale (1957-) 1999
Basketball $110
Cut signature $8
3x5 index card $10
8x10 photograph . . . .$18-$20

John McLendon (1915-1999) 1979
Basketball $100
Cut signature . . . .$6-$7

3x5 index card . . . .$8-$9
8x10 photograph . . . .$17-$20

Walter Meanwell (1884-1953) 1959
Basketball $110
Cut signature $8
3x5 index card $10
8x10 photograph . . . .$20-$25

Ray Meyer (1913-) 1978
Basketball $125
Cut signature $15
3x5 index card $20
8x10 photograph $30

Ann Meyers (1955-) 1993
Basketball . . . .$90-$100
Cut signature $5
3x5 index card $6
8x10 photograph . . . .$15-$20

George Mikan (1924-) 1959
Basketball $125
Cut signature $7
3x5 index card $10
8x10 photograph . . . .$20-$25

Vern Mikkelsen (1928-) 1995
Basketball $110
Cut signature $6
3x5 index card $9
8x10 photograph $20

Cheryl Miller (1964-) 1995
Basketball $100
Cut signature $6
3x5 index card $8
8x10 photograph . . . .$20-$25

William Mokray (1907-1974) 1965
Basketball $100
Cut signature $10
3x5 index card $15
8x10 photograph $35

Billie Moore (1943-) 1999
Basketball . . . .$75-$100
Cut signature $5
3x5 index card . . . .$6-$7
8x10 photograph . . . .$15-$17

Earl Monroe (1944-) 1989
Basketball $125
Cut signature . . . .$8-$10
3x5 index card $12
8x10 photograph . . . .$20-$25

Calvin Murphy (1948-) 1992
Basketball $100
Cut signature $6
3x5 index card $8
8x10 photograph $15

Charles Murphy (1907-1992) 1960
Basketball $100
Cut signature . . . .$7-$10
3x5 index card $12
8x10 photograph . . . .$15-$20

James Naismith (1861-1939) 1959
Basketball $1,000
Cut signature $200
3x5 index card $300
8x10 photograph $500

C. M. Newton (1931-) 2000
Basketball $100
Cut signature $6
3x5 index card $8
8x10 photograph . . . .$15-$17

Aleksandar Nikolic (1924-2000) 1998
Basketball $100
Cut signature $8
3x5 index card $10
8x10 photograph . . . .$20-$25

Larry O'Brien (1917-1990) 1990
Basketball $125
Cut signature $25
3x5 index card $15
8x10 photograph $65

Harlan Page (1887-1965) 1962
Basketball $100
Cut signature $5
3x5 index card $10
8x10 photograph $20

Bob Pettit (1932-) 1970
Basketball $150
Cut signature $10
3x5 index card $15
8x10 photograph . . . .$20-$25

Andy Phillip (1922-) 1961
Basketball $100
Cut signature . . . .$5-$7
3x5 index card $7
8x10 photograph . . . .$15-$16

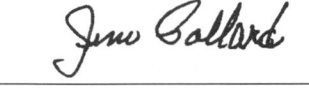

Maurice Podoloff (1890-1985) 1973
Basketball $100
Cut signature $5
3x5 index card $7
8x10 photograph $20

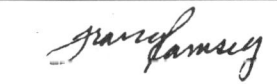

Jim Pollard (1922-1993) 1977
Basketball $100
Cut signature $5
3x5 index card $10
8x10 photograph $15

Frank Ramsey (1931-) 1981
Basketball $100
Cut signature . . . .$6-$7
3x5 index card $10
8x10 photograph $15

Jack Ramsey (1925-) 1991
Basketball $125
Cut signature $7
3x5 index card $10
8x10 photograph $20

Willis Reed (1942-) 1981
Basketball $100
Cut signature $9
3x5 index card $12
8x10 photograph $20

Arnie Risen (1924-) 1998
Basketball $110
Cut Signature $10

3x5 index card $12
8x10 photograph . . . .$20-$25

Oscar Robertson (1938-) 1979
Basketball $125
Cut signature $8
3x5 index card $10
8x10 photograph . . . .$25-$35

John Roosma (1900-1983) 1961
Basketball $100
Cut signature $5
3x5 index card $10
8x10 photograph $15

Adolph Rupp (1901-1977) 1968
Basketball $120
Cut signature $10
3x5 index card $15
8x10 photograph $50

Bill Russell (1934-) 1974
Basketball $350
Cut signature $25
3x5 index card $30
8x10 photograph $160

John Russell (1902-1973) 1974
Basketball $150
Cut signature $20
3x5 index card $25
8x10 photograph $45

Abe Saperstein (1901-1966) 1970
Basketball $150
Cut signature $10
3x5 index card $20
8x10 photograph $75

Dolph Schayes (1928-) 1972
Basketball $125
Cut signature $10
3x5 index card $15
8x10 photograph . . . .$15-$20

Ernest Schmidt (1911-1986) 1973
Basketball $110
Cut signature $7
3x5 index card $12
8x10 photograph . . . .$20-$30

John Schommer (1884-1960) 1959
Basketball $100
Cut signature $5
3x5 index card $10
8x10 photograph $15

Barney Sedran (1891-1964) 1962
Basketball $100
Cut signature $5
3x5 index card $7
8x10 photograph $15

Bill Sharman (1926-) 1975
Basketball $100
Cut signature $5
3x5 index card $7
8x10 photograph $20

Dean Smith (1931-) 1982
Basketball $100
Cut signature . . . .$15-$18
3x5 index card $20
8x10 photograph . . . .$25-$35

Amos Alonzo Stagg (1862-1965) 1959
Basketball . . . .$150-$175
Cut signature . . . .$8-$10
3x5 index card $20
8x10 photograph $30

Christian Steinmetz (1887-1963) 1961
Basketball $110
Cut signature $8
3x5 index card $12
8x10 photograph . . . .$20-$30

Earl Strom (1927-1994) 1995
Basketball . . . .$75-$100
Cut signature . . . .$6-$7

3x5 index card . . . .$8-$10
8x10 photograph . . . .$17-$20

Pat Summitt (1952-) 2000
Basketball . . . .$75-$100
Cut signature . . . .$5-$6
3x5 index card . . . .$7-$8
8x10 photograph . . . .$15-$17

Isiah Thomas (1961-) 2000
Basketball $125
Cut signature $10
3x5 index card $12
8x10 photograph . . . .$25-$30

David Thompson (1954-) 1996
Basketball $110
Cut signature . . . .$5-$8
3x5 index card $7
8x10 photograph . . . .$20-$25

John Thompson (1906-1990) 1962
Basketball $100
Cut signature $8
3x5 index card $10
8x10 photograph $30

John R. Thompson (1941-) 1999
Basketball $100
Cut signature $7
3x5 index card $9
8x10 photograph $25

Nate Thurmond (1941-) 1984
Basketball $115
Cut signature . . . .$6-$8
3x5 index card $12
8x10 photograph . . . .$15-$20

Arthur Trester (1878-1944) 1995
Basketball $125
Cut signature . . . .$12-$14
3x5 index card . . . .$15-$20
8x10 photograph $40

Jack Twyman (1934-) 1982
Basketball $125
Cut signature . . . .$6-$9
3x5 index card . . . .$9-$10
8x10 photograph . . . .$15-$18

Wes Unseld (1946-) 1987
Basketball $110
Cut signature . . . .$6-$10
3x5 index card $9
8x10 photograph . . . .$15-$20

Robert Vandivier (1903-1993) 1974
Basketball $100
Cut signature $5
3x5 index card $7
8x10 photograph $25

Edward Wachter (1883-1966) 1961
Basketball $100
Cut signature $6
3x5 index card $8
8x10 photograph $35

Margaret Wade (1912-1995) 1985
Basketball . . . .$75-$100
Cut signature $5
3x5 index card $7
8x10 photograph . . . .$15-$17

Bill Walton (1952-) 1992
Basketball $125
Cut signature $6
3x5 index card $10
8x10 photograph . . . .$20-$25

David Walsh (1889-1975) 1961
Basketball $125
Cut signature $10
3x5 index card $15
8x10 photograph . . . .$30-$40

Robert Wanzer (1921-) 1986
Basketball $125
Cut signature . . . .$5-$6
3x5 index card $10
8x10 photograph . . . .$16-$17

Stanley Watts (1911-2000) 1986
Basketball . . . .$75-$100
Cut signature . . . .$5-$6
3x5 index card . . . .$7-$8
8x10 photograph . . . .$15-$20

Clifford Wells (1896-1977) 1972
Basketball $100
Cut signature $8
3x5 index card $10
8x10 photograph . . . .$20-$25

Jerry West (1938-) 1979
Basketball $150
Cut signature $7
3x5 index card $10
8x10 photograph . . . .$25-$30

Lenny Wilkens (1937-) 1988 and 1998
Basketball $100
Cut signature . . . .$6-$10
3x5 index card $20
8x10 photograph . . . .$12-$15

John Wooden (1910-) 1972
Basketball $115
Cut signature . . . .$8-$10
3x5 index card $15
8x10 photograph . . . .$15-$20

Morgan Wootten (1931-) 2000
Basketball $100
Cut signature $6
3x5 index card . . . .$7-$8
8x10 photograph . . . .$15-$17

George Yardley (1928-) 1996
Basketball $110
Cut signature $10
3x5 signature $15
8x10 photograph . . . .$20-$25

Fred Zollner (1901-1982) 1999
Basketball $250
Cut signature $45
3x5 signature $50
8x10 photograph $100

Basketball Equipment

All listed equipment values are for game-used equipment only. Many variables are involved in pricing equipment, including player popularity, condition, scarcity, year the item is from, provenance and whether or not it was a home or road jersey. The prices listed below are merely a starting point.

Hall of Fame Players

Player	Sneakers	Jersey
Kareem Abdul-Jabbar	.$3,500	.$14,750
Nate Archibald	2,500	9,250
Paul Arizin	2,000	5,000
Rick Barry	2,100	5,250
Elgin Baylor	2,500	12,500
Walt Bellamy	1,000	4,000
Dave Bing	1,750	4,250
Larry Bird	3,000	6,750
Bernie Borgmann	2,500	5,750
Bill Bradley	3,000	7,250
Alfred Cervi	2,750	7,500
Wilt Chamberlain	5,000	26,000
Charles Cooper	2,500	5,000
Bob Cousy	4,750	14,750
Dave Cowens	1,100	4,500
Billy Cunningham	1,750	6,500
Robert Davies	2,500	5,750
Dave DeBusschere	2,250	5,500
Henry Dehnert	3,000	7,000
Wayne Embry	2,000	5,000
Paul Endacott	3,000	7000
Alex English	1,250	2,250
Julius Erving	3,250	9,500
Bud Foster	3,000	5,750
Walt Frazier	2,750	6,750
Marty Friedman	3,000	6,250
Joe Fulks	3,000	7,750
Laddie Gale	2,750	4,500
Harry Gallatin	2,750	4,750
William Gates	2,500	5,700
George Gervin	1,900	4,100
Tom Gola	2,500	5,750
Gail Goodrich	1,500	1,375
Hal Greer	2,500	6,750
Robert Gruenig	3,500	8,750
Cliff Hagan	3,000	7,250
Victor Hanson	3,500	8,750
John Havlicek	2,750	9,000
Connie Hawkins	2,000	4,250
Elvin Hayes	1,750	4,000
Tommy Heinsohn	3,200	8,250
Nat Holman	3,500	8,750
Robert Houbregs	3,000	8,000
Bailey Howell	2,000	4,500
Chuck Hyatt	3,750	9,750
Dan Issel	1,250	4,275
Buddy Jeannette	2,500	5,500
William Johnson	2,250	4,500
Neil Johnston	2,000	5,250
K. C. Jones	3,250	8,500
Sam Jones	3,000	7,500
Edward Krause	2,250	4,500
Bob Kurland	3,750	8,250

Larry Bird game-used jersey

Bob Lanier	1,750	5,750
Joe Lapchick	3,750	8,750
Clyde Lovellette	1,750	4,500
Jerry Lucas	2,000	5,500
Hank Luisetti	1,500	8,500
Ed Macauley	3,750	8,500
Pete Maravich	2,750	9,000
Slater Martin	2,000	5,250
Bob McAdoo	1,500	4,275
Dick McGuire	2,000	5,500
Branch McCracken	3,500	8,250
Jack McCracken	3,500	8,250
Bobby McDermott	2,000	4,750
Kevin McHale	1,000	4,000
George Mikan	9,000	24,000
Earl Monroe	2,750	5,500
Calvin Murphy	1,750	6,500
Charles Murphy	3,250	8,000
Harlan Page	2,750	6,750
Bob Pettit	3,250	8,000
Andy Phillip	3,000	7,500
Jim Pollard	2,000	4,500
Frank Ramsey	2,500	4,750
Willis Reed	2,150	6,750
Oscar Robertson	3,250	12,250
John Roosma	2,750	6,250
Bill Russell	3,200	11,800
Dolph Schayes	2,700	6,250
Ernest Schmidt	2,750	6,000
Barney Sedran	2,500	4,750
Bill Sharman	3,250	8,500
Christian Steinmetz	3,200	8,000
David Thompson	1,200	3,275
John (Cat) Thompson	1,000	7,500
Nate Thurmond	1,750	4,900
Jack Twyman	1,750	4,900
Wes Unseld	1,650	4,250
Robert Vandivier	2,500	5,250
Edward Wachter	3,500	6,500
Bill Walton	2,250	7,500

Robert Wanzer	1,800	4,750
Jerry West	2,000	6,500
Lenny Wilkens	1,750	5,250
John Wooden	7,000	14,500
George Yardley	3,000	7,500

Inactive Players

Player	Sneakers	Jersey
Alvan Adams	$200	$300
Rick Adelman	225	375
Mark Aguirre	200	300
Danny Ainge	175	275
Lucius Allen	175	275
B. J. Armstrong	175	275
Al Attles	250	375
Thurl Bailey	175	225
Charles Barkley	650	2,750
Dick Barnett	200	400
Zelmo Beatty	200	325
Henry Bibby	200	300
Manute Bol	325	825
Carl Braun	225	375
Fred Brown	200	300
Larry Brown	325	425
Quinn Buckner	225	325
Austin Carr	225	375
Bill Cartwright	195	350
Don Chaney	225	325
Maurice Cheeks	175	225
Phil Chenier	200	300
Nat Clifton	225	375
Doug Collins	225	325
Terry Cummings	175	250
Louie Dampier	200	200
Bob Dandridge	250	350
Adrian Dantley	275	375
Brad Daugherty	200	350
Walter Davis	275	325
Darryl Dawkins	350	600
Clyde Drexler	625	1,875
Joe Dumars	250	450
Mike Dunleavy	350	550
Chris Ford	250	350
World B. Free	250	375
Artis Gilmore	325	675
Matt Goukas	200	400
Harvey Grant	195	325
Happy Hairston	325	550
Clem Haskins	200	300
Spencer Haywood	375	625
Walt Hazzard	225	375
Craig Hodges	200	350
Lou Hudson	225	395
Rod Hundley	360	675
Phil Jackson	375	680
Dennis Johnson	350	475
Gus Johnson	325	425
Kevin Johnson	325	575
Magic Johnson	3,500	9,500
Marques Johnson	325	475
Bobby Jones	325	475
Caldwell Jones	200	300
Wali Jones	275	375
Michael Jordan	6,250	24,000
Bernard King	300	500

Player	Sneakers	Jersey
Mitch Kupchak	.200	.325
Player	**Sneakers**	**Jersey**
Bill Laimbeer	.225	.375
Reggie Lewis	.600	2,500
Bob Love	.350	.600
John Lucas	.225	.450
Maurice Lucas	.200	.300
Jeff Malone	.175	.225
Moses Malone	.450	1,000
Cedric Maxwell	.200	.300
Cornbread Maxwell	.175	.275
Xavier McDaniel	.175	.275
George McGinnis	.200	.300
Sidney Moncrief	.225	.425
Don Nelson	.350	.750
Norm Nixon	.225	.375
Ken Norman	.175	.225
Robert Parish	.375	.950
Jim Paxson	.200	.300
John Paxson	.175	.275
Chuck Person	.250	.400
Kevin Porter	.200	.300
Pat Riley	.425	.950
Doc Rivers	.200	.350
Alvin Robertson	.175	.225
Dennis Rodman	.500	1,750
Byron Scott	.200	.325
Dennis Scott	.200	.350
Jack Sikma	.225	.375
Paul Silas	.225	.375
Scott Skiles	.175	.250
Jerry Sloan	.200	.325
Reggie Theus	.225	.350
Wayman Tisdale	.175	.225
Rudy Tomjanovich	.250	.450
Fat Lever	.175	.225
Norm Van Lier	.300	.500
Chet Walker	.250	.425
Slick Watts	.250	.400
Spud Webb	.250	.450
Bob Weiss	.200	.300
Paul Westphal	.200	.300
Jo Jo White	.325	.575
Sidney Wicks	.225	.325
James Wilkes	.275	.375
Dominique Wilkins	.575	1,450
Buck Williams	.200	.275
Gus Williams	.200	.300
Willie Wise	.200	.300
James Worthy	.475	1,100
Max Zaslofsky	.200	.300

Active Players

Player	Sneakers	Jersey
Shareef Abdur-Rahim	$150	$300
Ray Allen	.250	.375
Derek Anderson	.225	.350
Kenny Anderson	.225	.350
Nick Anderson	.225	.350
Ron Artest	.225	.350
Stacey Augmon	.200	.300
Vin Baker	.225	.350
Rolando Blackman	.175	.275
Mookie Blaylock	.200	.300
Elton Brand	.375	.575
Terrell Brandon	.175	.250

Tim Duncan game-used jersey

	Sneakers	Jersey
Kobe Bryant	.800	2,500
Marcus Camby	.350	.500
Elden Campbell	.175	.250
Vince Carter	.700	2,200
Sam Cassell	.250	.375
Cedric Ceballos	.175	.225
Rex Chapman	.175	.225
Calbert Cheaney	.175	.225
Mateen Cleaves	.225	.375
Derrick Coleman	.300	.550
Michael Curry	.175	.225
Vlade Divac	.175	.225
Sherman Douglas	.175	.225
Tim Duncan	.450	.800
Sean Elliott	.195	.275
Laphonso Ellis	.175	.225
Patrick Ewing	.650	1,875
Danny Ferry	.175	.225
Michael Finley	.275	.400
Steve Francis	.250	.375
Rick Fox	.220	.350
Kevin Garnett	.700	2,200
Chris Gatling	.175	.225
Kendall Gill	.175	.225
Brian Grant	.175	.225
Horace Grant	.175	.225
A. C. Green	.175	.250
Anfernee Hardaway	.350	.900
Tim Hardaway	.325	.575
Derek Harper	.200	.275
Ron Harper	.225	.375
Grant Hill	.500	.850
Juwan Howard	.200	.325
Allen Iverson	.575	1,000
Mark Jackson	.250	.385
Antawan Jamison	.275	.400
Larry Johnson	.320	.550
Popeye Jones	.200	.300
Shawn Kemp	.350	.595
Jerome Kersey	.175	.275

	Sneakers	Jersey
Jason Kidd	.400	.950
Toni Kukoc	.225	.350
Christian Laettner	.250	.425
Grant Long	.225	.350
Mark Macon	.175	.225
Dan Majerle	.275	.375
Karl Malone	.525	.975
Danny Manning	.220	.325
Stephon Marbury	.325	.550
Donyell Marshall	.300	.450
Kenyon Martin	.275	.425
Jamal Mashburn	.300	.500
Anthony Mason	.275	.400
Antonio McDyess	.325	.500
Tracy McGrady	.275	.400
Ron Mercer	.250	.375
Chris Mihm	.300	.500
Reggie Miller	.400	.925
Eric Montross	.250	.395
Alonzo Mourning	.450	1,100
Chris Mullin	.325	.575
Dikembe Mutombo	.250	.450
Johnny Newman	.225	.375
Charles Oakley	.175	.325
Lamar Odom	.225	.375
Hakeem Olajuwon	.675	1,750
Shaquille O'Neal	1,200	6,500
Billy Owens	.225	.375
Cherokee Parks	.250	.375
Gary Payton	.175	.275
Sam Perkins	.225	.375
Paul Pierce	.300	.500
Scottie Pippen	.550	.875
Terry Porter	.175	.275
Theo Ratliff	.200	.300
J. R. Reid	.175	.225
Glen Rice	.175	.275
Quentin Richardson	.250	.385
Mitch Richmond	.250	.425
Isaiah Rider	.300	.500
David Robinson	.650	1,600
Glenn Robinson	.375	.625
Jalen Rose	.250	.375
Michael Ruffin	.250	.385
Detlef Schrempf	.175	.375
Rony Seikaly	.200	.300
Joe Smith	.275	.475
Steve Smith	.225	.375
Latrell Sprewell	.275	.500
Jerry Stackhouse	.265	.475
John Starks	.225	.325
John Stockton	.425	.925
Rod Strickland	.250	.400
Wally Szczerbiak	.325	.550
Tim Thomas	.225	.375
Otis Thorpe	.250	.385
Nick Van Exel	.275	.425
Keith Van Horn	.225	.375
Loy Vaught	.225	.375
Rasheed Wallace	.325	.550
Charlie Ward	.250	.385
Chris Webber	.400	.700
Jason Williams	.270	.500
Kevin Willis	.225	.375

●●●

Basketball
Starting Lineup Figurines

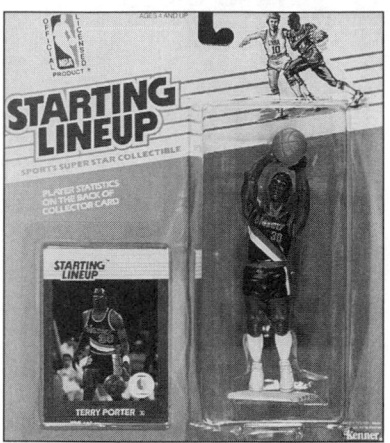

1988 Basketball

Complete Set (85):	.$4,500.00
Collector Stand:	.45.00
Kareem Abdul-Jabbar	.50.00
Michael Adams	.35.00
Mark Aguirre	.40.00
Danny Ainge	.50.00
Thurl Bailey	.250.00
Charles Barkley	.80.00
Walter Berry	.35.00
Larry Bird	.80.00
Rolando Blackman	.45.00
Michael Cage	.35.00
Joe Barry Carroll	.35.00
Tom Chambers	.35.00
Maurice Cheeks	.35.00
Michael Cooper	.50.00
Terry Cummings	.35.00
Adrian Dantley	.120.00
Brad Daugherty	.40.00
Johnny Dawkins	.35.00
Clyde Drexler	.100.00
Mark Eaton	.275.00
Dale Ellis	.40.00
Alex English	.40.00
Patrick Ewing	.50.00
Sleepy Floyd	.35.00
Winston Garland	.35.00
Armon Gilliam	.40.00
Mike Gminski	.35.00
David Greenwood	.35.00
Derek Harper	.40.00
Ron Harper	.40.00
Rod Higgins	.35.00
Dennis Hopson	.35.00
Jeff Hornacek	.50.00
Mark Jackson	.40.00
Dennis Johnson	.50.00
Eddie Johnson	.40.00
Magic Johnson	.75.00
Steve Johnson	.35.00
Vinnie Johnson	.130.00
Michael Jordan	.100.00
Bernard King	.35.00
Bill Laimbeer	.125.00
Lafayette Lever	.35.00
Jeff Malone	.35.00
Karl Malone	.750.00
Moses Malone	.70.00
Danny Manning	.40.00
Rodney McCray	.40.00
Xavier McDaniel	.35.00
Kevin McHale	.50.00
Derrick McKey	.40.00
Reggie Miller	.200.00

Sidney Moncrief	.35.00
Chris Mullin	.50.00
Hakeem Olajuwon	.75.00
Robert Parish	.40.00
John Paxson	.40.00
Sam Perkins	.35.00
Chuck Person	.35.00
Scottie Pippen	.125.00
Terry Porter	.45.00
Paul Pressey	.35.00
Mark Price	.125.00
Doc Rivers	.35.00
Alvin Robertson	.35.00
Cliff Robinson	.35.00
Ralph Sampson	.35.00
Danny Schayes	.50.00
Jack Sikma	.35.00
Kenny Smith	.40.00
Steve Stipanovich	.35.00
John Stockton	.450.00
Isiah Thomas	.40.00
Lasalle Thompson	.35.00
Otis Thorpe	.40.00
Wayman Tisdale	.35.00
Kiki Vandeweghe	.35.00
Spud Webb	.40.00
Dominique Wilkins	.40.00
Gerald Wilkins	.35.00
Buck Williams	.35.00
John Williams	.35.00
Reggie Williams	.35.00
Kevin Willis	.40.00
James Worthy	.40.00

1988-89 Basketball
Slam Dunk Red Box

Complete Set (6):	.$700.00
Larry Bird	.175.00
Patrick Ewing	.100.00
Magic Johnson	.175.00
Michael Jordan	.250.00
Isiah Thomas	.70.00
Dominique Wilkins	.70.00

1988-89 Basketball
Slam Dunk White Box

Complete Set (6):	.$325.00
Larry Bird	.100.00
Patrick Ewing	.50.00
Magic Johnson	.100.00
Michael Jordan	.150.00
Isiah Thomas	.40.00
Dominique Wilkins	.40.00

1989 Basketball

Complete Set (5):	.$100.00
Rex Chapman	*.30.00*

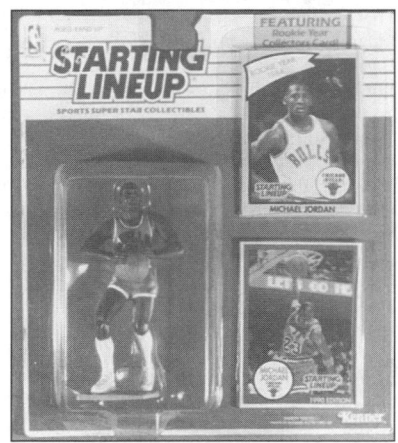

1990 Basketball

Complete Set (17):	.$525.00
Charles Barkley	.70.00
Larry Bird	.60.00
Tom Chambers	.15.00
Clyde Drexler	.50.00
Joe Dumars	*.20.00*
Patrick Ewing	.35.00
Magic Johnson	.45.00
Michael Jordan	.125.00
Karl Malone	.60.00
Chris Mullin	.20.00
David Robinson	*.40.00*
Byron Scott	*.15.00*
John Stockton	.60.00
Isiah Thomas	.20.00
Spud Webb	.15.00
Dominique Wilkins	.25.00
James Worthy	.15.00

1991 Basketball

Complete Set (16):	.$500.00
Charles Barkley	.90.00
Larry Bird	.50.00
Derrick Coleman	*.30.00*
Clyde Drexler	.30.00
Joe Dumars	.15.00
Patrick Ewing	.25.00
Kevin Johnson	*.20.00*
Magic Johnson	.35.00
Michael Jordan (dunk)	.120.00
Michael Jordan (jump)	.120.00
Reggie Lewis	*.25.00*
David Robinson	.15.00
Dennis Rodman	*.80.00*
Isiah Thomas	.15.00
Spud Webb	.15.00
Dominique Wilkins	.30.00

1992 Basketball

Complete Set (29):	.$700.00
Set price does not include Magic yellow.	
Charles Barkley	.50.00
Larry Bird	.45.00
Manute Bol	*.10.00*
Dee Brown	*.12.00*
Derrick Coleman	.12.00
Vlade Divac	*.15.00*
Clyde Drexler	.20.00
Joe Dumars	.10.00

At top right of 1990 column (before Complete Set):

Dell Curry	*.20.00*
Ron Harper	.25.00
Larry Nance	*.20.00*
Kelly Tripucka	*.20.00*

Patrick Ewing	.25.00
Tim Hardaway	*.30.00*
Kevin Johnson	.15.00
Larry Johnson	*.30.00*
Magic Johnson (purple)	.60.00
Magic Johnson (yellow)	.475.00
Michael Jordan (regular)	.120.00
Michael Jordan (warm ups)	.120.00
Dan Majerle	*.15.00*
Karl Malone	.20.00
Reggie Miller	.40.00
Chris Mullin	.15.00
Dikembe Mutombo	*.20.00*
Hakeem Olajuwon	.35.00
John Paxson	.15.00
Scottie Pippen	.25.00
Mark Price	.15.00
David Robinson (regular)	.20.00
David Robinson (warm ups)	.20.00
Dennis Rodman	.50.00
John Stockton	.25.00
Isiah Thomas	.12.00

1992 Basketball Headline Collection

Complete Set (8):	.$400.00
Charles Barkley	.70.00
Larry Bird	.70.00
Patrick Ewing	.35.00
Magic Johnson	.70.00
Michael Jordan	.125.00
Dikembe Mutombo	.20.00
Scottie Pippen	.50.00
David Robinson	.25.00

1992 Basketball Olympic

Complete Set (10):	.$125.00
Charles Barkley	.15.00
Larry Bird	.20.00
Patrick Ewing	.8.00
Magic Johnson	.20.00
Michael Jordan	.40.00
Karl Malone	.10.00

Chris Mullin	.7.00
Scottie Pippen	.12.00
David Robinson	.10.00
John Stockton	.10.00

1993 Basketball

Complete Set (29)	.$625.00
Kenny Anderson	*.20.00*
Stacey Augmon	*.14.00*
Charles Barkley	.25.00
Brad Daugherty	.14.00
Todd Day	*.15.00*
Clyde Drexler	.20.00
Sean Elliott	*.16.00*
Patrick Ewing	.25.00
Horace Grant	*.20.00*
Tom Gugliotta	.40.00
Tim Hardaway	.20.00
Larry Johnson	.15.00
Michael Jordan	.200.00
Shawn Kemp	*.35.00*
Christian Laettner	*.35.00*
Dan Majerle	.14.00
Karl Malone	.20.00
Alonzo Mourning	*.60.00*
Dikembe Mutombo	.14.00
Shaquille O'Neal	*.70.00*
Scottie Pippen	.30.00
Terry Porter	.12.00
Mark Price	*.12.00*
Glen Rice	*.25.00*
Mitch Richmond	*.25.00*
David Robinson	.15.00
Detlef Schrempf	*.15.00*
John Stockton	.20.00
Dominique Wilkins	.15.00

1994 Basketball

Complete Set (26):	.$400.00
(Set price does not include Rodman red)	
B. J. Armstrong	*.10.00*
Stacey Augmon	.10.00
Charles Barkley	.20.00
Shawn Bradley	*.12.00*
Calbert Cheaney	.12.00
Derrick Coleman	.10.00
Sean Elliott	.10.00
LaPhonso Ellis	*.12.00*
Patrick Ewing	.12.00
Anfernee Hardaway	*.80.00*
Jim Jackson	*.14.00*
Larry Johnson	.10.00
Shawn Kemp	.18.00
Karl Malone	.15.00
Jamal Mashburn	*.14.00*
Harold Miner	.12.00
Alonzo Mourning	.12.00
Chris Mullin	.10.00
Hakeem Olajuwon	.20.00
Shaquille O'Neal	.35.00
Scottie Pippen	.20.00
David Robinson	.12.00
Dennis Rodman - (blond)	.45.00
Dennis Rodman - (red)	.120.00
Latrell Sprewell	*.20.00*
Chris Webber	*.25.00*
Dominique Wilkins	.10.00

1995 Basketball

Complete Set (31):	.$450.00
Charles Barkley	.20.00
Muggsy Bogues	*.12.00*
Patrick Ewing	.12.00
Horace Grant (blue)	.20.00
Horace Grant (black)	.30.00
Anfernee Hardaway	.40.00
Grant Hill	*.20.00*
Grant Hill (ROY sticker)	*.20.00*
Jeff Hornacek	.10.00
Jim Jackson	.10.00
Shawn Kemp	.15.00
Jason Kidd	*.40.00*
Toni Kukoc	*.20.00*
Dan Majerle	.12.00
Karl Malone	.15.00
Reggie Miller	.16.00
Eric Montross	*.12.00*
Alonzo Mourning	.12.00
Hakeem Olajuwon	.15.00
Shaquille O'Neal	.30.00
Robert Pack	*.10.00*
Scottie Pippen	.20.00
Mark Price	.10.00
Clifford Robinson	*.12.00*
David Robinson	.12.00
Glenn Robinson	*.25.00*
Steve Smith	*.15.00*
Latrell Sprewell	.12.00
John Starks	*.15.00*
Nick Van Exel	*.25.00*
Clarence Weatherspoon	*.15.00*
Chris Webber	.15.00
Dominique Wilkins	.10.00

1996 Basketball

Complete Set (34):	.$525.00
(Set price only includes Grant Hill and Dennis Rodman green.)	
Vin Baker	.25.00
Charles Barkley	.14.00
Clyde Drexler	.14.00
Sean Elliott	.10.00
Patrick Ewing	.12.00

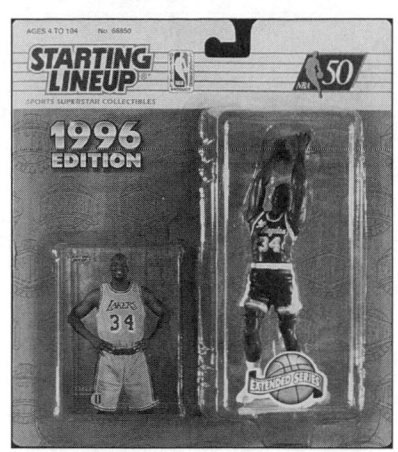

Kevin Garnett *75.00*
Anfernee Hardaway 20.00
Grant Hill 20.00
Grant Hill special 30.00
Tyrone Hill *12.00*
Juwan Howard *30.00*
Larry Johnson 15.00
Eddie Jones *30.00*
Jason Kidd 20.00
Karl Malone .15.00
Jamal Mashburn 12.00
Antonio McDyess *25.00*
Reggie Miller 15.00
Alonzo Mourning 12.00
Hakeem Olajuwon 15.00
Shaquille O'Neal 20.00
Gary Payton *30.00*
Scottie Pippen 15.00
Dino Radja *10.00*
Bryant Reeves 18.00
Pooh Richardson *12.00*
Mitch Richmond 12.00
Cliff Robinson 10.00
David Robinson 12.00
Glenn Robinson 14.00
Dennis Rodman (green) 40.00
Dennis Rodman (yellow) 40.00
Dennis Rodman (orange) 40.00
Joe Smith *15.00*
Rik Smits 15.00
Jerry Stackhouse *15.00*
Damon Stoudamire *15.00*

1996-97 Asian Basketball

Complete Set (13): $525.00
Charles Barkley 25.00
Sean Elliott 10.00
Anfernee Hardaway 35.00
Grant Hill 35.00
Larry Johnson 12.00
Magic Johnson 325.00
Eddie Jones 30.00
Reggie Miller 15.00
Hakeem Olajuwon 20.00
Shaquille O'Neal 30.00
Scottie Pippen 20.00
Dennis Rodman (green) 40.00
Dennis Rodman (yellow) 40.00

1996 Basketball DreamTeam III

Complete Set (2): $60.00
Five player boxes: 30.00

1996-97 Basketball Extended

Complete Set (8): $200.00
Charles Barkley 20.00

Kobe Bryant 100.00
Grant Hill 30.00
Allen Iverson *50.00*
Larry Johnson 15.00
Dikembe Mutombo 15.00
Shaquille O'Neal 30.00
Damon Stoudamire 20.00

1997 Basketball

Complete Set (39): $500.00
Shareef Abdur-Rahim 25.00
Ray Allen 18.00
Kenny Anderson 10.00
Vin Baker 10.00
Charles Barkley 10.00
Terrell Brandon 18.00
Marcus Camby 18.00
Vlade Divac .10.00
Patrick Ewing 10.00
Michael Finley 18.00
Kevin Garnett 20.00
Horace Grant 10.00
Tim Hardaway 10.00
Grant Hill 15.00
Allan Houston 15.00
Juwan Howard 12.00
Allen Iverson 15.00
Mark Jackson 10.00
Shawn Kemp 12.00
Jason Kidd 15.00
Kerry Kittles .20.00
Stephon Marbury 30.00
Reggie Miller 10.00
Alonzo Mourning 10.00
Hakeem Olajuwon 12.00
Shaquille O'Neal 15.00
Gary Payton .15.00
Scottie Pippen 15.00
Mitch Richmond 10.00
David Robinson 12.00
Dennis Rodman 25.00
Steve Smith .10.00
Latrell Sprewell 12.00
Damon Stoudamire 10.00
John Stockton 12.00
Loy Vaught 10.00
Nick Van Exel 10.00
Antoine Walker 50.00
Chris Webber 12.00

1997-98 Basketball Extended

Complete Set (8): $150.00
Clyde Drexler 10.00
Tim Duncan .50.00

Anfernee Hardaway 12.00
Eddie Jones 15.00
Luc Longley .12.00
Anthony Mason 10.00
Antonio McDyess 10.00
Keith Van Horn 45.00

1997 Basketball Classic Doubles

Complete Set (7): $170.00
L. Bird, K. McHale 30.00
W. Chamberlain, B. Russell 30.00
J. Dumars, G. HIll 35.00
P. Ewing, W. Reed 25.00
O'Neal, Abdul-Jabbar 35.00
B. Russell, H. Olajuwon 30.00
J. Stockton, K. Malone 30.00

1997 Basketball 14" Figures

Complete Set (5): $180.00
Charles Barkley 40.00
Grant Hill 50.00
Shawn Kemp 40.00
Shaquille O'Neal 40.00
Dennis Rodman 45.00

1997 Basketball Backboard Kings

Complete Set (6): $150.00
Charles Barkley 25.00
Grant Hill 30.00
Karl Malone .25.00
Shaquille O'Neal 25.00
Scottie Pippen 25.00
Damon Stoudamire 25.00

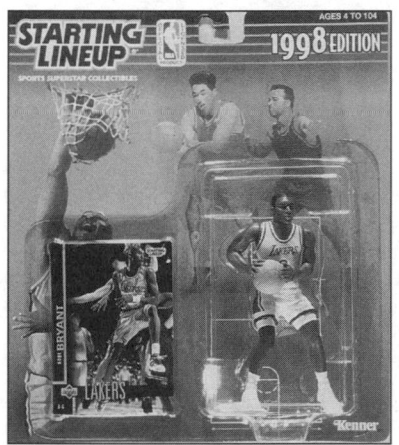

1998 Basketball

Complete Set (16) $150.00
Vin Baker 10.00
Terrell Brandon 10.00
Kobe Bryant .25.00
Patrick Ewing 10.00
Kevin Garnett 15.00
Grant Hill 12.00
Allen Iverson 24.00
Magic Johnson 15.00
Shawn Kemp 10.00
Jason Kidd 10.00
Karl Malone .12.00
Stephon Marbury 12.00
Alonzo Mourning 10.00
Shaquille O'Neal 15.00
Dennis Rodman 12.00
Rik Smits 8.00

1998 Basketball 12" Figures

Complete Set (5)	$90.00
Tim Duncan	30.00
Kevin Garnett	24.00
Juwan Howard	15.00
Allen Iverson	24.00
Glen Rice	20.00

1998 Collegiate Basketball

Complete Set (9)	$120.00
Kareem Abdul-Jabbar	10.00
Larry Bird	15.00
Patrick Ewing	10.00
Juwan Howard	10.00
Allen Iverson	20.00
Magic Johnson	12.00
Jason Kidd	10.00
Bill Russell	10.00
Sheryl Swoopes	12.00

2000 Basketball NCAA March Madness

Complete Set (6)	$35.00
David Robinson	8.00
Jerry Stackhouse	8.00
Sheryl Swoopes	8.00
Isiah Thomas	8.00
Bill Walton	8.00
James Worthy	8.00

Basketball
Bobbin' Head Dolls

Basketball had the fewest amount of bobbers released. Two teams exist for 1962; three are represented in 1967, with two teams also represented by a black-faced doll. In the late 1960s and early 1970s, an offshoot version of the bobbers was produced. These dolls, called "Little Dribblers," had the head and body as one piece. A ball, underneath the player's hand, is connected to the back of the base by a flat band of metal. If the ball is touched, it bobs up and down, creating an illusion that the doll is dribbling the ball.

1962 Bobbers

1) Los Angeles Lakers	$425
2) New York Knicks	.450

1967 Bobbers

1) Los Angeles Lakers	$35-$60
2) Los Angeles Lakers (black)	150-300
3) San Diego Rockets	150-275
4) Seattle Sonics	125-325
5) Seattle Sonics (black)	175-350

Michael Jordan by SAM

Little Dribblers

1) Baltimore Bullets	$175-$300
2) Chicago Bulls	$100-$150
3) Detroit Pistons	$110-$130
4) Milwaukee Bucks	$60-$80
5) New York Knicks	$15-$30
6) Philadelphia 76ers	$100

SAM Bobbin' Head
Dolls

Sports, Accessories & Memorabilia (SAM) of Menlo Park, Calif., has been producing hand-painted, ceramic bobbin' head dolls and figurines of professional athletes and entertainment stars since 1992.

Larry Bird (white)	$65.00
Larry Bird (green)	65.00
Michael Jordan (red)	150.00
Michael Jordan (white)	150.00
David Robinson (white)	60.00
David Robinson (black)	60.00
Dennis Rodman (red)	48.95
Dennis Rodman (green)	48.95

Four different New York Knicks bobbers.

Basketball Media Guides

Atlanta Hawks

1968-69 Team mascot $75
1969-70 Lou Hudson $25
1970-71 Atlanta skyline, team art $20
1971-72 Richie Guerin, Hawks bench $20
1972-73 Team logo $20
1973-74 Overhead shot of Omni court $20
1974-75 Lou Hudson $20
1975-76 Tom Van Ardsdale $20
1976-77 John Drew $15
1977-78 Team logo, artwork $15
1978-79 Team logo, newspaper clips $15
1979-80 H. Brown, J. Drew, A. Hill $8
1980-81 Dan Roundfield vs. Abdul-Jabbar $8
1981-82 Action artwork $8
1982-83 Dan Roundfield $8
1983-84 Action artwork $8
1984-85 Dominique Wilkins $8
1985-86 Dominique Wilkins $7.50
1986-87 Dominique Wilkins $7.50
1987-88 Dominique Wilkins $7.50
1988-89 Dominique Wilkins $7
1989-90 M. Malone, D. Rivers, D. Wilkins . .$6
1990-91 "Let's Run One" $5
1991-92 Bob Weiss $5
1992-93 Dominique Wilkins, Doc Rivers $5
1993-94 "Atlanta Hawks Media Guide" $5
1994-95 L. Wilkins, Red Auerbach $8
1995-96 Lenny Wilkins $6
1996-97 D. Mutombo $6
1997-98 D. Mutombo, C. Laettner, others . . .$6
1998-99 D. Mutombo, others $6

Boston Celtics

1951-52 Folder report with plain brown cover
. . . .$125-$150
1952-53 . . . .$25-$40
1953-54 . . . .$25-$40
1954-55 Player photos . . . .$50-$75
1955-56 Bob Cousy . . . .$55-$80
1956-57 Player photos . . . .$50-$75
1957-58 Player photos . . . .$45-$70
1958-59 Frank Ramsey . . . .$40-$65
1959-60 Gene Conley . . . .$35-$50
1960-61 Boston Garden . . . .$30-$45
1961-62 Red Auerbach, five starters . . . . . .$40-$60
1962-63 Bob Cousy . . . .$40-$60
1963-64 Tom Heinsohn . . . .$35-$50
1964-65 Boston Garden . . . .$15-$25
1965-66 . . . .$20-$30
1966-67 Bill Russell . . . .$25-$45

1967-68 John Havlicek . . . .$45-$60
1968-69 Red Auerbach, Bill Russell $60
1969-70 Team mascot $45
1970-71 D. Cowens, D. Nelson, J. J. White,
   others $45
1971-72 D. Cowens, J. Havlicek, J. J. White $45
1972-73 Dave Cowens, John Havlicek $45
1973-74 Dave Cowens, John Havlicek,
   Jo Jo White $35
1974-75 John Havlicek, Paul Silas $30
1975-76 Dave Cowens, John Havlicek $30
1976-77 Championship trophy $25
1977-78 John Havlicek $20
1978-79 Dave Cowens $20
1979-80 Larry Bird, M.L. Carr $20
1980-81 R. Auerbach, L. Bird, B. Fitch $15
1981-82 Championship banner, trophy $15
1982-83 Team art, Larry Bird $15
1983-84 Celtics vs. Atlanta Hawks $15
1984-85 Championship trophy $15
1985-86 Larry Bird $20
1986-87 Larry Bird photos $15
1987-88 Larry Bird, four other starters $15
1988-89 Historical team photos $15
1989-90 Red Auerbach $15
1990-91 Team artwork $15
1991-92 McHale, Bird, Parrish, C. Ford $10
1992-93 Cartoon figures of Bird, others $10
1993-94 Cartoon mascot, crowd photo $10
1994-95 Cartoon mascot, parquet floor $10
1995-96 Fleet Center $8
1996-97 Photos of Celtics greats $8
1997-98 R. Pitino, R. Auerbach $8
1998-99 Rick Pitino $8

Charlotte Hornets

1988-89 David Stern, G. Shinn, Hornets uniform
. . . .$25
1989-90 NBA attendance, championship banner
. . . .$10
1990-91 Gene Little photos $8
1991-92 Larry Johnson $5
1992-93 Larry Johnson photos $5
1993-94 Alonzo Mourning $5
1994-95 Muggsey Bogues, Del Curry $8
1995-96 L. Johnson, A. Mourning $6
1996-97 Dave Cowans $6
1997-98 A. Mason, G. Rice, D. Cowans $6
1998-99 Hornets starting five $6

Chicago Bulls

1966-67 Team logo $50
1967-68 Team logo $45

1968-69 Team logo $35
1969-70 Team logo $25
1970-71 Team logo $20
1971-72 Team logo $20
1972-73 Chet Walker $20
1973-74 Chet Walker $20
1974-75 Team logo, action photos $20
1975-76 Team logo, Jerry Sloan $15
1976-77 Team artwork $15
1977-78 Action photos $15
1978-79 Artis Gilmore $15
1979-80 Artis Gilmore, Jerry Sloan $10
1980-81 Reggie Theus $10
1981-82 A. Gilmore, D. Greenwood $10
1982-83 Rod Thorn, Paul Westhead $10
1983-84 Kevin Loughery $10
1984-85 M. Jordan, O. Woolridge $10
1985-86 S. Albeck, M. Jordan, O. Woolridge . . .$35
1986-87 Michael Jordan $35
1987-88 Michael Jordan, action photos,
   All-Star Game logo $35
1988-89 B. Cartwright, H. Grant, M. Jordan . . .$25
1989-90 Bulls comics $15
1990-91 25th Anniversary artwork $15
1991-92 . . . .$15
1992-93 Bulls back-to-back $15
1993-94 Players entrance to stadium $12
1994-95 Aerial photo of United Center $12
1995-96 30th Anniversary logo $10
1996-97 NBA 50th anniversary $15
1997-98 Hand with five rings $10
1998-99 Championship trophy $6

Cleveland Cavaliers

1970-71 Team logo, year $50
1971-72 Team logo, year $25
1972-73 Team logo, year $25
1973-74 Cavalier artwork $15
1974-75 Team logo, artwork $15
1975-76 Cleveland Coliseum $10
1976-77 Team photo $10
1977-78 Team logo, mascot $10
1978-79 C'mon Cavaliers $10
1979-80 A New Era...Cavaliers II $10
1980-81 Team action photos $10
1981-82 Mike Mitchell artwork $10
1982-83 Ron Brewer, city skyline $10
1983-84 New team logo $6
1984-85 15th season Cavs basketball cards $6
1985-86 Team artwork $6
1986-87 Lenny Wilkens $8
1987-88 B. Daugherty, R. Harper, Hot Rod
   Williams $8
1988-89 Cavaliers vs. Chicago Bulls $8
1989-90 20th season, L. Wilkens, action
   photos $8
1990-91 Team uniform, action photos $8
1991-92 Cavs tickets $8
1992-93 Players celebrating $8
1993-94 Tickets/The Coliseum $8
1994-95 Gund Arena $7
1995-96 Interior photo of Gund Arena $7
1996-97 All-Star action photos $7
1997-98 Shawn Kemp $7
1998-99 B. Knight, C. Henderson, others . . .$7

Dallas Mavericks

1980-81 Dallas Mavericks uniform $15
1981-82 Dallas Reunion Arena $8
1982-83 Dick Motta $8
1983-84 Mark Aguirre $8
1984-85 Rolando Blackmon $8
1985-86 Mavericks in action artwork $10
1986-87 Derek Harper $10
1987-88 J. Donaldson, J. MacLeod, team logo . . .$10
1988-89 Roy Tarpley $10
1989-90 Brad Davis, 10th Anniversary $10
1990-91 R. Blackman, D. Harper, F. Lever $10
1991-92 D. Harper, R. Blackman $8
1992-93 Doug Smith $8
1993-94 Jim Jackson $8
1994-95 J. Kidd/J. Mashburn/J. Jackson $8
1995-96 J. Kidd/J. Mashburn/J. Jackson $8
1996-97 D. Harper/J. Kidd/others $8
1997-98 Michael Finley $8
1998-99 Michael Finley $8

Denver Nuggets

Denver Rockets
1968-69 . . . .$45
1969-70 Nuggets artwork $35
1970-71 . . . .$35
1971-72 Ralph Simpson $35
1972-73 Alex Hannum $35
1973-74 Team photo $35
Denver Nuggets
1974-75 L. Brown, M. Calvin, C. Scheer . . .$20
1975-76 D. Issel, D. Moe, C. Scheer, D. Thompson
   . . . .$20
1976-77 Nuggets in action artwork $20
1977-78 Team logo, year $15
1978-79 Team mascot $15
1979-80 David Thompson $8
1980-81 Dan Issel $8
1981-82 A. English, D. Issel, D. Thompson $8
1982-83 Team logo $8
1983-84 10th Anniversary photos $6
1984-85 Nugget in action artwork $6
1985-86 Alex English, Calvin Natt $8
1986-87 Alex English, team logo $8
1987-88 A. English, F. Lever, C. Natt $8
1988-89 A. English, F. Lever, D. Moe $8
1989-90 Alex English, city skyline $8
1990-91 Bernie Bickerstaff, Carl Scheer $8
1991-92 NBA Basketball in gift box $5
1992-93 Dan Issel $5
1993-94 Nuggets logo $8
1994-95 Get in the Game $8
1995-96 Bernie Bickerstaff $6

1996-97 LaPhonso Ellis/Bryant Stith $6
1997-98 Bill Hanzlik $6
1998-99 Denver greats, D. Thompson, etc. $7

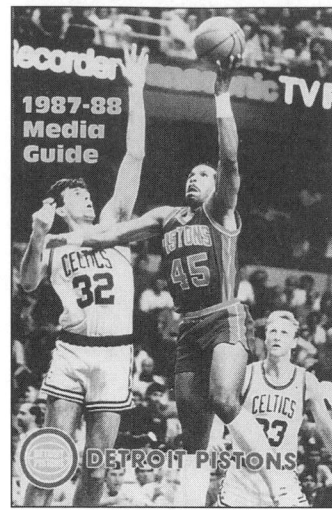

Detroit Pistons

1958-59 . . . .$100-$125
1960-61 . . . .$60-$75
1961-62 . . . .$50-$60
1962-63 . . . .$50-$60
1963-64 . . . .$45-$55
1964-65 . . . .$45-$55
1965-66 . . . .$45-$55
1967-68 . . . .$65
1969-70 Happy Hairston $40
1970-71 . . . .$30
1971-72 . . . .$25
1972-73 Earl Lloyd $20
1973-74 . . . .$20
1974-75 Team logo $15
1975-76 Pistons in action artwork, logo $10
1976-77 L. Douglas, E. Money, K. Porter, C. Rowe
   . . . .$10
1977-78 Pistons in action artwork $10
1978-79 Pistons in action artwork $10
1979-80 Silverdome, team logo $10
1980-81 Player completing tip in $10
1981-82 Kent Benson, Isiah Thomas $10
1982-83 . . . .$8
1983-84 Isiah Thomas, Kelly Tripucka $8
1984-85 Isiah Thomas $8
1985-86 Bill Laimbeer, Isiah Thomas $8
1986-87 Isiah Thomas $8
1987-88 Adrian Dantley $8

1988-89 The Palace $8
1989-90 Championship celebration $6
1990-91 J. Dumars, I. Thomas, trophies $6
1991-92 J,. Dumars, I. Thomas $6
1992-93 Chuck Daly $8
1993-94 Basketball with blue seams $8
1994-95 B. Laimbeer, J. Dumars, T. Mills,
  I. Thomas $8
1995-96 Joe Dumars illustration $8
1996-97 Grant Hill $8
1997-98 J. Dumars, G. Hill $8
1998-99 Hour glass with "bad boys" and
  current players $8

Golden State Warriors

San Francisco Warriors
1962-63 . . . .$50
1963-64 . . . .$25
1964-65 . . . .$20
1965-66 . . . .$75
1966-67 . . . .$35
1967-68 . . . .$50
1968-69 Team logo $40
1969-70 Nate Thurmond $40
1970-71 Nate Thurmond $30
Golden State Warriors
1971-72 Al Attles $20
1972-73 Nate Thurmond $15
1973-74 Nate Thurmond $15
1974-75 Warriors artwork $15
1975-76 NBA Championship trophy $15
1976-77 Al Attles $15
1977-78 Warriors in action artwork $15
1978-79 Warriors in action $10
1979-80 Team logos $8
1980-81 Team logo $8
1981-82 Al Attles $8
1982-83 Basketball $8
1983-84 Still the Best Game in Town $8
1984-85 Warriors in action artwork $8
1985-86 Sleepy Floyd, C. Mullin, P. Short . . .$8
1986-87 The New Warriors $8
1987-88 Larry Smith $8
1988-89 Ralph Sampson $8
1989-90 Chris Mullin $8
1990-91 Warriors in action artwork $8
1991-92 Action artwork $5
1992-93 Notebooks, calculator $5
1993-94 Card game with player cards $5
1994-95 Cartoon of players using elevator $8
1995-96 Artwork of jerseys on wash line $6
1996-97 50th anniv. art of Warriors greats . . .$6
1997-98 P. J. Carlisimo, lightning bolt $6
1998-99 Photo of warmup jersey $6

Houston Rockets

San Diego Rockets
1967-68 Team logo, basketball $35
1968-69 Team logo $35
1969-70 Elvin Hayes $25
1970-71 Elvin Hayes $20
Houston Rockets
1971-72 Rockets in action artwork $20
1972-73 Rockets in action artwork $20
1973-74 M. Newlin, R. Tomjanovich $10
1974-75 Rudy Tomjanovich $10
1975-76 Mike Newlin $10
1976-77 Calvin Murphy, Tom Nissalke $10
1977-78 John Lucas, R. Tomjanovich $10
1978-79 R. Barry, M. Malone, R. Tomjanovich . .$10
1979-80 Moses Malone $10
1980-81 Rockets in action artwork $10
1981-82 Moses Malone $10
1982-83 Elvin Hayes $10
1983-84 Ralph Sampson $10
1984-85 B. Fitch, H. Olajuwon, R. Sampson . . .
. . . .$10
1985-86 R. McCray, H. Olajuwon, R. Sampson . .$10
1986-87 H. Olajuwon, R. Reid, R. Sampson $10
1987-88 Hakeem Olajuwon $10
1988-89 D. Chaney, R. Tomjanovich $10
1989-90 E. Floyd, H. Olajuwon, O. Thorpe $10
1990-91 20th Anniversary logo $10
1991-92 Rockets on a basketball $8
1992-93 Rockets on a basketball $8
1993-94 Rockets memorabilia $10
1994-95 . . . .$8
1994-95 Players, fans celebrating $8
1995-96 H. Olajuwon, C. Drexler $8
1996-97 Olajuwon, Drexler, Barkley $8
1997-98 Olajuwon, Drexler, Barkley $8
1998-99 Hakeem Olajuwon photos $8

Indiana Pacers

1968-69 Mel Daniels $30
1969-70 Mel Daniels $25
1970-71 Roger Brown $20
1971-72 Bob Leonard cartoon $20
1972-73 M. Daniels, B. Leonard, G. McGinnis . . .$20
1973-74 Three ABA trophies $20
1974-75 Market Square Arena $15
1975-76 Team logo $10
1976-77 Billy Knight $10
1977-78 Bob Leonard, team logo $10
1978-79 Market Square Arena $10
1979-80 Team logo $8
1980-81 Year of Excitement $8

1981-82 Jack McKinney $8
1982-83 Herb Williams $8
1983-84 Indianapolis artwork $8
1984-85 "Pacer Pride" basketball $8
1985-86 Uniform, ball, sneaker artwork $8
1986-87 Herb Williams $8
1987-88 Jack Ramsey, player artwork $8
1988-89 Steve Stipanovich $8
1989-90 Reggie Miller $8
1990-91 Pacers in action artwork $8
1991-92 D. Schrempf/R. Miller/C. Person . . .$8
1992-93 D. Davis/R. Smits/R. Miller $8
1993-94 Larry Brown $8
1994-95 Larry Brown/Reggie Miller $8
1995-96 Rik Smits $7
1996-97 Dale Davis/Antonio Davis $7
1997-98 Larry Bird "Back Home Again" $8
1998-99 L. Bird, R. Miller, others $8

Los Angeles Clippers

Buffalo Braves
1970-71 Team logo $20
1971-72 Team logo $20
1972-73 Elmore Smith vs. W. Chamberlain $20
1973-74 Team action photo $20
1974-75 Buffalo Braves vs. K. C. Kings . . .$20
1975-76 Braves in action $15
1976-77 Team action photos $15
1977-78 Buffalo skyline $15
San Diego Clippers
1978-79 Randy Smith $10
1979-80 Bill Walton $8
1980-81 Paul Silas $8

1981-82 Freeman Williams $8
1982-83 Tom Chambers $8
1983-84 Terry Cummings $8
1988-89 Team logo $20
1989-90 Rory Sparrow with a fan $12
1990-91 House with basketball in driveway $12
1991-92 Clippers on blue background $10
1992-93 Newspaper clippings $10
1993-94 10 year anniversary logo $8
1994-95 Diagram of basketball court $8
1995-96 Bill Fitch, player huddle $7
1996-97 Clippers logo $7
1997-98 Coach's clipboard $7
1998-99 Montage of player photos $6

Los Angeles Lakers

1960-61 Name, year artwork . . . .$75-$125
1966-67 Team logo $50
1967-68 Team logo, year $45
1968-69 Elgin Baylor, Wilt Chamberlain . . .$45
1969-70 . . . .$35
1970-71 . . . .$35
1971-72 . . . .$35
1972-73 Championship trophy $30
1973-74 Gail Goodrich $30
1974-75 Gail Goodrich $30
1975-76 Kareem Abdul-Jabbar $25
1976-77 Jerry West $20
1977-78 Laker cheerleader in uniform #1 . . . .$20
1978-79 Kareem Abdul-Jabbar $20
1979-80 K. Abdul-Jabbar, M. Johnson $20
1980-81 K. Abdul-Jabbar, M. Johnson $20
1981-82 The Forum, artwork $12
1982-83 K. Abdul-Jabbar, M. Johnson, N. Nixon
. . . .$12
1983-84 The Forum $12
1984-85 Kareem Abdul-Jabbar $12
1985-86 K. Abdul-Jabbar, championship
    trophy $12
1986-87 Chick Hearn $12
1987-88 K. Abdul-Jabbar, M. Johnson, J. Worthy,
    trophy $12
1988-89 K. Abdul-Jabbar uniform, locker $12
1989-90 Magic Johnson $12
1990-91 M. Johnson, S. Perkins, J. Worthy $12
1991-92 M. Johnson, J. Worthy $10
1992-93 Magic Johnson photos $10
1993-94 Caricatures of J. West, others $10
1994-95 Magic Johnson, others $10
1995-96 D. Harris, N. Van Exel, others $8
1996-97 S. O'Neal with jerseys $9
1997-98 S. O'Neal, N. Van Exel, E. Jones . . .$8
1998-99 Shaq dunking $7

Miami Heat

1993-94 Art of generic player $9
1994-95 Art of three generic players $8
1995-96 P. Riley, P. J. Brow, H. Mine, G. Rice $8
1996-97 P. Riley, A. Mourning, others $7
1997-98 A. Mourning, J. Mashburn, others $7
1998-99 P. Riley, A. Mourning, T. Hardaway $7

Milwaukee Bucks

1968-69 Bucks vs. Royals, W. Embry $30
1969-70 Team logo $25
1970-71 Kareem Abdul-Jabbar $25
1971-72 Kareem Abdul-Jabbar $25
1972-73 Kareem Abdul-Jabbar $25
1973-74 Lucius Allen $20
1974-75 K. Abdul-Jabbar, city skyline $20
1975-76 Bucks vs. Chicago Bulls action . . .$15
1976-77 Gary Brokaw $15
1977-78 Brian Winters $15
1978-79 Marques Johnson artwork $15
1979-80 Five starters artwork $8
1980-81 Team artwork $8
1981-82 Sidney Moncrief $8
1982-83 Bucks artwork $8
1983-84 M. Johnson, S. Moncrief, D. Nelson . . .$6
1984-85 Sidney Moncrief $6
1985-86 Paul Pressey $8
1986-87 Sidney Moncrief, city skyline $8
1987-88 20th anniversary artwork $8
1988-89 Bucks vs. Houston Rockets $8
1989-90 Del Harris $8
1990-91 Action photos $8

1991-92 D. Harris/ seven players $8
1992-93 M. Dunleavy/M. Malone $8
1993-94 T. Day/B. Edwards/F. Brickowski $8
1994-95 G. Robinson/V. Baker hologram inset . . .$8
1995-96 V. Baker/G. Robinson $8
1996-97 G. Robinson/Vin Baker $8
1997-98 Art of Bucks all-time greats $8
1998-99 George Karl $8

Minnesota Timberwolves

1989-90 Team logo $12
1990-91 Timberwolves basketball $12
1991-92 Ball going through a hoop $10
1992-93 Closeup of a Wolf's head $10
1993-94 Wolf howling at moon $8
1994-95 Wolf on basketball court $8
1995-96 Trees with wolf in background $7
1996-97 Kevin Garnett $7
1997-98 K. Garnett, T. Gugliotta, S. Marbury $7
1998-99 Team logo on white background $7

New Jersey Nets

New York Nets
1968-69 Nets in action . . . .$15-$25
1969-70 . . . .$10-$20
1970-71 Nets player in action . . . .$7-$10
1971-72 Rick Barry, others . . . .$8-$12
1972-73 Eastern Div. Playoff Champions $30
1973-74 Julius Erving $30
1974-75 Dave DeBusschere, Rowe $20
1975-76 Julius Erving $20
1976-77 Julius Erving $15

New Jersey Nets

1977-78 State of New Jersey, artwork $15
1978-79 Jordan, B. King, J. Williamson $15
1979-80 The Excitement is Building $10
1980-81 Up & Coming $10
1981-82 A New Era logo $10
1982-83 Darryl Dawkins, Mike Gminski ...$6
1983-84 Nets in action artwork $6
1984-85 Darryl Dawkins $6
1985-86 Buck Williams $10
1986-87 Mike Gminski $10
1987-88 M. Gminski, B. Williams, O. Woolridge
....$10
1988-89 Donaldson, Reed, B. Williams $10
1989-90 Roy Hinson $10
1990-91 Nets in action artwork $8
1991-92 D. Coleman/M. Blaylock/others ..$8
1992-93 Chuck Daly $8
1993-94 Derrick Coleman $8
1994-95 Kenny Anderson $8
1995-96 A. Gilliam/P.J. Brown $7
1996-97 J. Calipari/S. Bradley/others $7
1997-98 S. Cassell/C. Gatling/others $7
1998-99 Road jersey No. 98 ....$7

New York Knicks

1956-57 ....$95
1957-58 ....$95
1958-59 ....$75
1959-60 ....$75
1960-61 ....$75
1961-62 ....$75
1962-63 ....$65
1963-64 ....$65
1964-65 ....$35
1965-66 ....$35
1966-67 Cartoon player $35
1967-68 ....$45
1968-69 ....$45
1969-70 D. DeBusschere, W. Reed $45
1970-71 ....$40
1971-72 Reed, DeBusschere, Frazier $25
1972-73 ....$25
1973-74 Championship trophy $30
1974-75 Bill Bradley uniform $20
1975-76 ....$15
1976-77 Earl Monroe $15
1977-78 Willis Reed $15
1978-79 Earl Monroe, Marvin Webster $10
1979-80 Bill Cartwright $10
1980-81 B. Cartwright, R. Holzman, J. ....
    Richardson $10

1981-82 City skyline $10
1982-83 Hubie Brown $10
1983-84 Knicks in action $10
1984-85 Action artwork $10
1985-86 B. Cartwright, P. Ewing, B. King,
    others $10
1986-87 Uniforms, locker $10
1987-88 Al Bianchi, Rick Pitino $10
1988-89 P. Ewing, M. Jackson, C. Oakley ...$10
1989-90 P. Ewing, M. Jackson, S. Jackson $10
1990-91 Patrick Ewing art $10
1991-92 P. Riley, R. Holtzman $8
1992-93 Logo, newspaper headlines $8
1993-94 Patrick Ewing $8
1994-95 Ewing, Oakley, Starks $9
1995-96 Don Nelson, P. Ewing, others $7
1996-97 Golden Anniversary logo $7
1997-98 Knicks all-time greats $7
1998-99 Red Holtzman $7

Orlando Magic

1989-90 Magic artwork $20
1990-91 Matt Goukas $15
1991-92 S. Skiles/D. Scott/N. Anderson $10
1992-93 Shaquille O'Neal $10
1993-94 Shaquille O'Neal dunking $10
1994-95 H. Grant/A.Hardaway/S. O'Neal/
    D. Scott/N. Anderson $10
1995-96 B. Hill/Hardaway/Shaq/others $9
1996-97 Hill/Hardaway/Anderson/Grant $9
1997-98 C. Daly/A. Hardaway/J. Erving $9
1998-99 10th anniversary logo/Rich Devos/
    Pat Williams/others $8

Philadelphia 76ers

1966-67 ....$45
1967-68 W. Chamberlain, B. Cunningham $45
1968-69 Hal Greer $45
1969-70 Billy Cunningham, Hal Greer ...$35
1970-71 Team pictures artwork $20
1971-72 Team mascot $20
1972-73 J. Block, B. Bridges, F. Carter ...$20
1973-74 Gene Shue $20
1974-75 Billy Cunningham, Gene Shue $15
1975-76 H. Catchings, B. Cunningham,
    G. McGinnis $15
1976-77 Doug Collins, George McGinnis $15
1977-78 Julius Erving $15
1978-79 D. Collins, J. Erving, B. Jones ...$15
1979-80 Julius Erving $15
1980-81 76ers basketball $15
1981-82 Julius Erving, trophies $15
1982-83 Julius Erving $15

1983-84 Julius Erving, Moses Malone $10
1984-85 Julius Erving $10
1985-86 Moses Malone $10
1986-87 Charles Barkley $10
1987-88 M. Cheeks, 25th Anniversary $10
1988-89 C. Barkley, M. Cheeks $10
1989-90 Charles Barkley $10
1990-91 Charles Barkley $10
1991-92 Jim Lynam, C. Barkley, H. Hawkins ..$10
1992-93 Hersey Hawkins $10
1993-94 ....$10
1994-95 76er greats, J. Erving, etc. $10
1995-96 Huge basketball, "It's Real" $8
1996-97 A. Iverson, Stackhouse, others $8
1997-98 Larry Brown $7
1998-99 76er greats, A. Iverson, T. Ratliff ...$7

Phoenix Suns

1968-69 Team logo, year $35
1969-70 Team logo, year $35
1970-71 Team logo, year $20
1971-72 Connie Hawkins $20
1972-73 Suns in action $20
1973-74 Charlie Scott, Neil Walk $15
1974-75 Team logo, year $15
1975-76 Team logo, year $15
1976-77 Alvan Adams $10
1977-78 Paul Westphal $10
1978-79 W. Davis, R. Lee, P. Westphal $10
1979-80 John MacLeod $10
1980-81 Alvan Adams $8
1981-82 Computer graphics picture $8
1982-83 Basketball $6

1983-84 Larry Nance $6
1984-85 Walter Davis $6
1985-86 Catch our Fire, team logo $8
1986-87 Suns artwork $10
1987-88 Suns basketball $10
1988-89 T. Chambers, J. Hornacek, others $10
1989-90 T. Chambers, C. Fitzsimmons,
  K. Johnson $10
1990-91 Suns basketball $10
1991-92 . . . .$10
1992-93 25th Anniversary, action photos . . .$10
1993-94 C. Barkley, downtown Phoenix . . .$10
1994-95 "Playing with Fire" $10
1995-96 . . . .$8
1996-97 A. C. Green, M. Finley, others $8
1997-98 . . . .$8
1998-99 Outstretched arms at tipoff $8

Portland Trailblazers

1970-71 Rick Adelman $25
1971-72 Geoff Petrie $25
1972-73 Sidney Wicks $20
1973-74 Jack McCloskey $20
1974-75 Bill Walton $20
1975-76 Lenny Steele $15
1976-77 Bill Walton $15
1977-78 Bill Walton, NBA Champs $15
1978-79 Maurice Lucas $10
1979-80 Jack Ramsey, Bill Walton $10

1980-81 Billy Bates $10
1981-82 Jim Paxson $10
1982-83 Mychal Thompson $10
1983-84 Calvin Natt $10
1984-85 Sam Bowie, Kiki Vandeweghe $10
1985-86 Clyde Drexler $10
1986-87 Kiki Vandeweghe $10
1987-88 Steve Johnson $10
1988-89 Kevin Duckworth $10
1989-90 Rick Adelman, 20th anniversary $10
1990-91 Western Conference Champs $10
1991-92 Clyde Drexler $8
1992-93 C. Drexler, others $8
1993-94 Harry Glickman $8
1994-95 Trailblazers memorabilia $8
1995-96 Rose Garden Arena $6
1996-97 Arvydas Sabonis $6
1997-98 Kelvin Cato $6
1998-99 Caracatures of R. Wallace, others $6

Sacramento Kings

Cincinnati Royals
1957-58 World wearing a Royals crown $100
1958-59 Basketball wearing Royals crown $100
1959-60 Basketball wearing Royals crown $75
1960-61 Team mascot cartoon $75
1961-62 Team mascot, snake charmer $75
1962-63 Team mascot, with briefcase $75
1963-64 . . . .$75
1964-65 . . . .$75
1965-66 . . . .$75
1966-67 . . . .$75
1967-68 Ed Tucker art $75
1968-69 O. Robertson, W. Chamberlain $75
1969-70 Bob Cousy $75
1970-71 N. Archibald, T. Van Ardsdale, N. Van Lier
. . . .$25
1971-72 Royals patch $25
Kansas City-Omaha Kings
1972-73 Team logo $35
1973-74 Nate Archibald, Bob Cousy $25
1974-75 Phil Johnson, artwork $20
Kansas City Kings
1975-76 Nate Archibald, Phil Johnson $15
1976-77 Five starters $15
1977-78 L. Allen, O. Birdsong, T. Burleson $10
1978-79 Team logo $10
1979-80 Team logo, player $8

1980-81 Scott Wedman, Reggie King $8
1981-82 Phil Ford $8
1982-83 Axelson, Fitzsimmons, scoreboard $6
1983-84 Team logo $6
1984-85 Team photo $6
Sacramento Kings
1985-86 Team logo $6
1986-87 Kings fans in crowd $8
1987-88 We're Building Together $8
1988-89 Kenny Smith $8
1989-90 D. Ainge, R. McCray, W. Tisdale . . .$8
1990-91 A. Bonner, L. Simmons, others $8
1991-92 W. Tisdale, dance team $8
1992-93 Spud Webb, Mitch Richmond $8
1993-94 Basketball background, players $8
1994-95 Mitch Richmond $8
1995-96 Gary St. Jean, players $7
1996-97 Mitch Richmond $7
1997-98 Eddie Jordan $7
1998-99 Rick Adelman, player photos $7

San Antonio Spurs

1973-74 Hemisfair Arena $20
1974-75 Team logo $15
1975-76 G. Gervin, J. Silas, others $15
1976-77 James Silas $10
1977-78 George Gervin $10
1978-79 Billy Paultz $10
1979-80 Team logo $10
1980-81 Stan Albeck $8
1981-82 George Gervin, Bruise Brothers $8
1982-83 G. Gervin, A. Gilmore, M. Mitchell . .$6
1983-84 Artis Gilmore $6
1984-85 Cotton Fitzsimmons $6
1985-86 Mike Mitchell $8
1986-87 Alvin Robertson $8
1987-88 Johnny Moore, Alvin Robertson . . .$8
1988-89 Larry Brown $8
1989-90 T. Cummings, S. Elliott, D. Robinson . . .$10
1990-91 David Robinson $8
1991-92 David Robinson $8
1992-93 20th Anniversary flag $8
1993-94 Alamodome $8
1994-95 B. Hill, D. Robinson, others $8
1995-96 David Robinson $7
1996-97 D. Robinson dunking $7
1997-98 T. Duncan, D. Robinson, G. Gervin . . .$7
1998-99 T. Duncan, D. Robinson, A. Johnson . . .$7

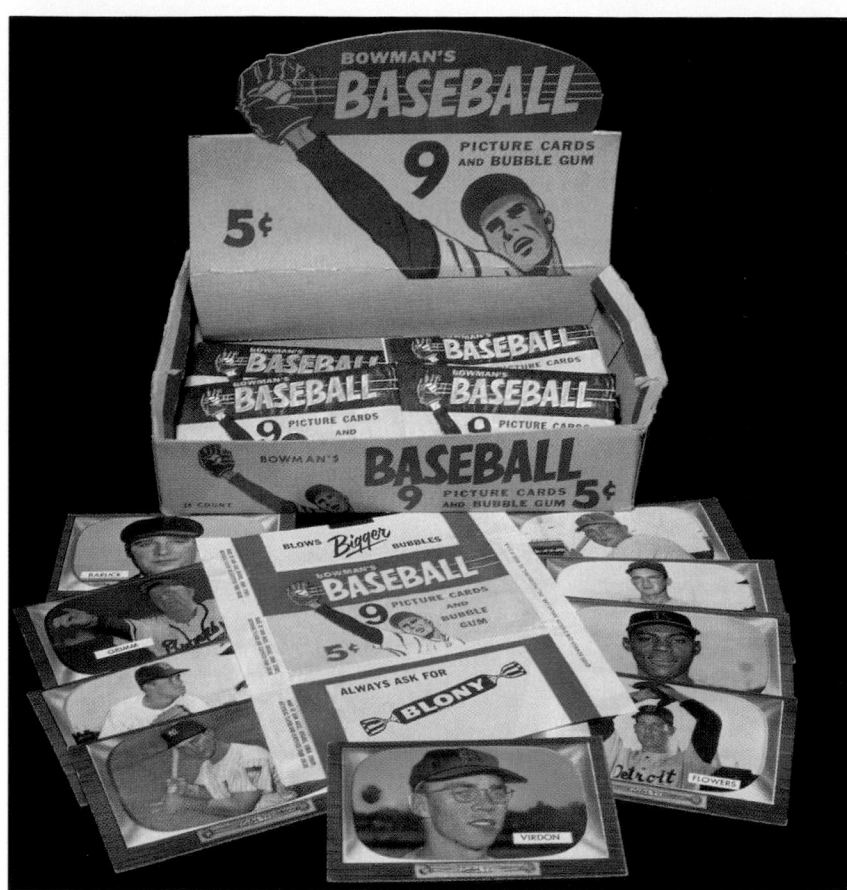

Rare 1909-11 T-206 tobacco card of baseball great Honus Wagner ($2,200,000).

Partially opened box of 1955 Bowman (color TV design) baseball cards ($4,250 for a complete set).

E145 1914 Cracker Jack card (No. 30) of baseball immortal Ty Cobb ($6,000-$8,000).

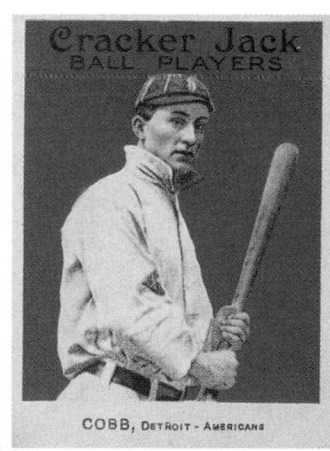

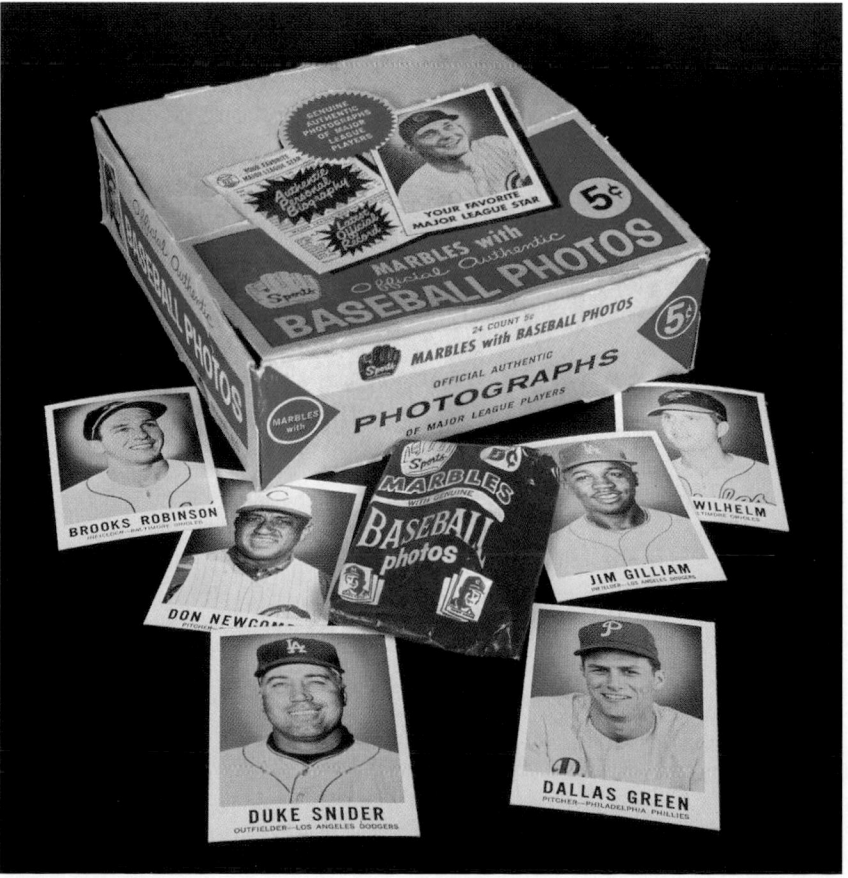

Partially opened box of 1960 Leaf black and white baseball cards that were packaged with marbles ($1,250 for complete set).

Program from 1927 World Series between the New York Yankees and Pittsburgh Pirates ($2,000-$5,000).

Uncut sheet of 1953 Topps first series baseball cards ($4,000-$6,000).

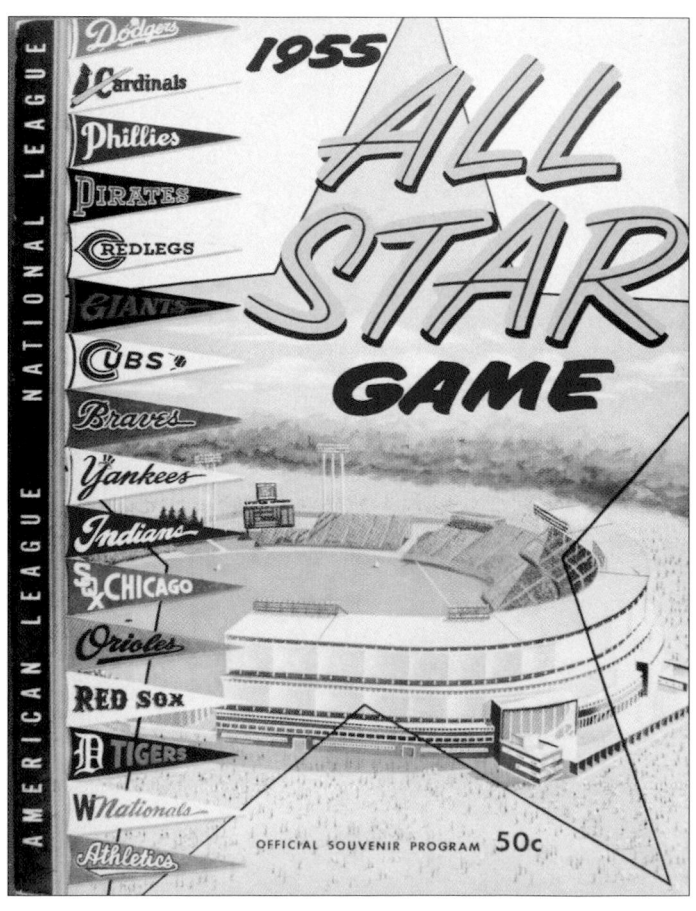

*Aug. 1, 1949 unsigned **Life** magazine picturing baseball great Joe DiMaggio on the cover ($150-$175).*

Baseball All-Star Game program played at Milwaukee County Stadium in 1955 ($125-$175).

1999 Rawlings game-used black fielder's glove autographed by Alex Rodriguez ($1,500-$2,000).

Los Angeles Dodgers baseball cap signed on the brim by Hall of Famer Sandy Koufax ($150-$200).

1957 Tim McAuliffe Inc., Boston Red Sox home flannel game-used and autographed jersey by Hall of Famer Ted Williams ($30,000-$40,000).

1964 Auravision 6 ¾ x 6 ¾-inch laminated record picturing Roger Maris with facsimile signature ($25-$30).

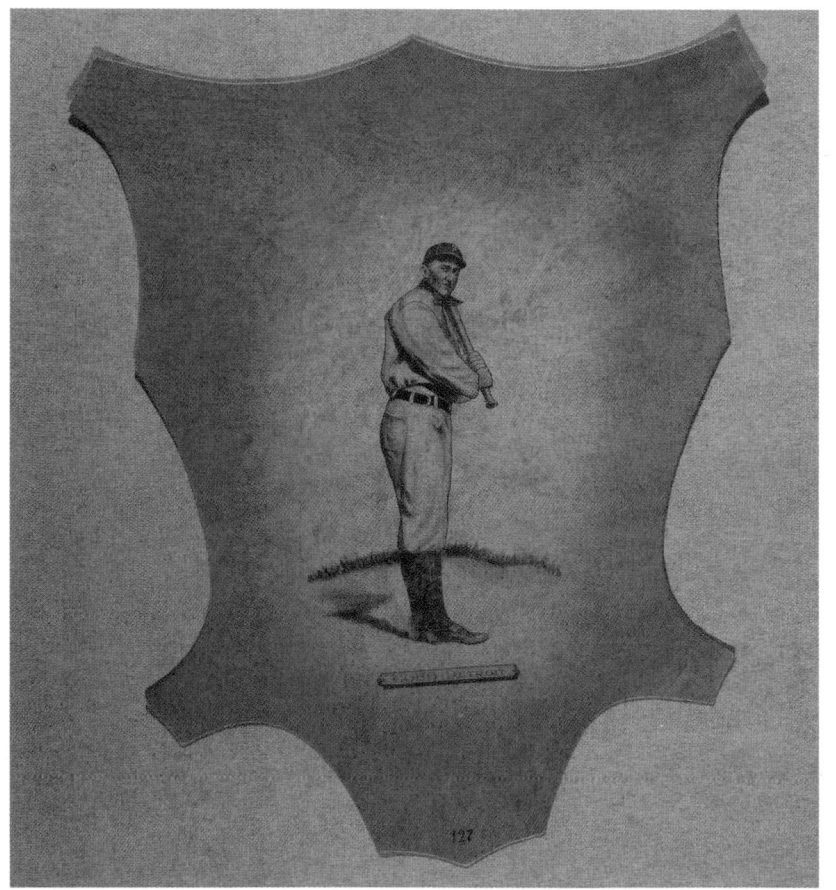

Press brooches (with medallions) from the 1911 ($18,000) and 1912 ($12,500) World Series.

1912 L1 10 x 12-inch "leather" Helmar Tobacco Co., premium featuring Ty Cobb ($11,000).

Lobby card from the 1953 motion picture "The Kid From Left Field" starring Dan Dailey and Anne Bancroft ($100-$150).

1916 Ferguson Bakery BF2 8 ½ -inch felt pennant featuring "Shoeless" Joe Jackson ($1,350).

1914 B18 5 ¼-inch square tobacco Blanket featuring Washington Senators' pitching great Walter Johnson ($400).

Original 1960 Dick Groat Hartland Statue complete with box and tag ($1,500-$2,000).

1961-62 Roger Maris Bobbin' Head Doll complete with original box ($500-$750).

1956 bronze-colored 3-inch Big League Star Statues of Stan Musial ($250) and Mickey Mantle ($800), complete with packaging.

Original 1930s Old Gold Cigarettes 38 x 50-inch metal advertising sign featuring American baseball icon Babe Ruth. ($500-$700). Reproductions of this sign were made in the early 1990s.

Original 30 x 20-inch Ted's Creamy Root Beer heavy cardboard counter display sign picturing Ted Williams ($1,500-$2,000).

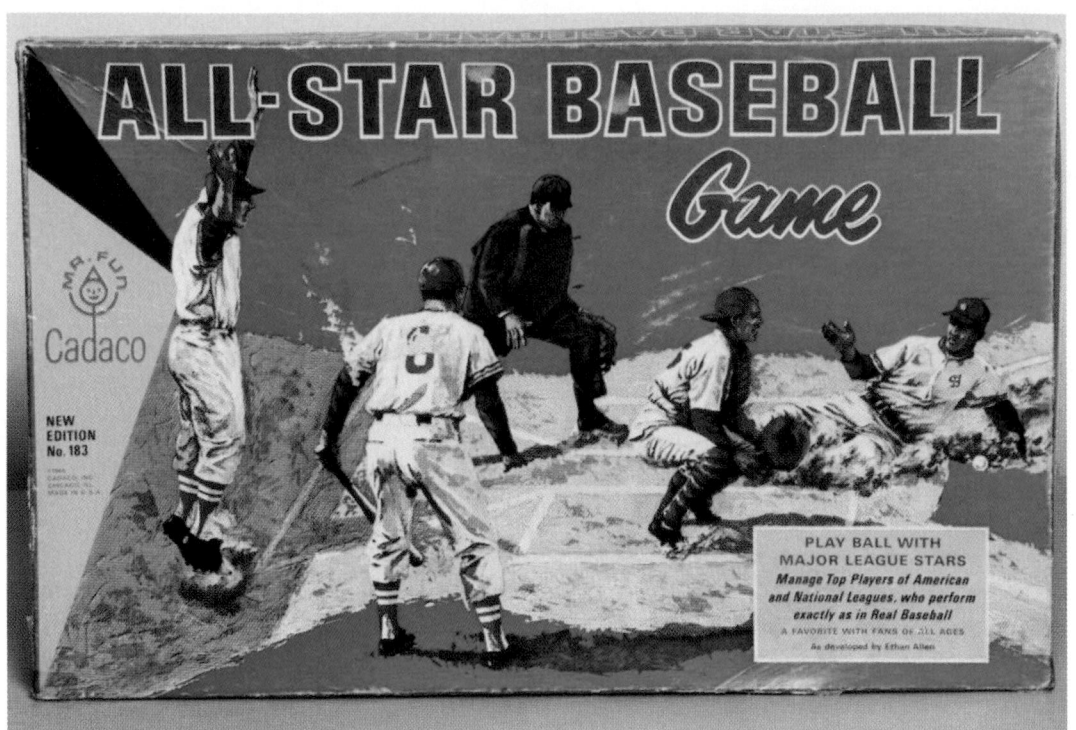

*1959-60 Cadaco
All-Star Baseball Game
($50-$90).*

*1951 (2 ½ x 3 ¼-inch) Wheaties Box
picturing Stan Musial ($95-$100).*

*1980s Seagrams 16 x 20 framed
mirror picturing Babe Ruth. Mirror
is from a series created by
Connecticut artist Clifford Spohn
($100-$125).*

Helmet signed by members of Super Bowl XXIV Champion San Francisco 49ers ($800-$900).

Rawlings (circa. 1960s) high top football cleats with original box ($150-$200).

Dallas Cowboys replica Wilson jersey autographed by Pro Football Hall of Famer Roger Staubach ($450).

1960 Green Bay Packers yearbook picturing Paul Hornung and Jerry Kramer on the cover ($300).

Program from Super Bowl XXVII held Jan. 31, 1993 in Pasadena, Calif., between the Dallas Cowboys and Buffalo Bills ($15-$25.)

1996 Edition Brett Favre Starting Lineup figurine ($15-$25.)

GTE seat cushion from Super Bowl XXIX held Jan. 29, 1995 in Miami, Fla., between the San Francisco 49ers and San Diego Chargers ($20-$25).

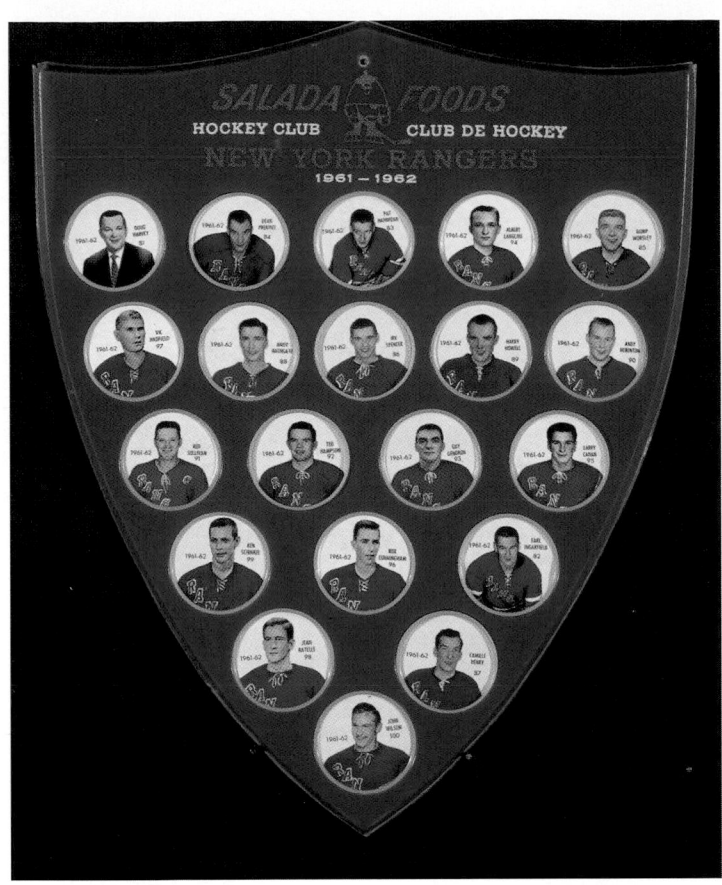

1913 American Tobacco Co., 7 ¼-inch "A Fan For A Fan" picturing Christy Mathewson ($2,750).

Salada Foods coins of the 1961-62 New York Rangers in plastic shield ($75-$80).

1959-60 Topps card of hockey great Gordie Howe ($450).

1963-64 Montreal Canadiens media guide   ($45-$50).

Electric figural 12-inch bronze-finish clock of heavyweight boxing champion Joe Louis ($150-$200).

1965 Great Moments in Sport, Jack Dempsey vs. Louis Firpo model kit ($90-$100).

Uncut sheet of 1951 Topps boxing cards ($300-$350).

Everlast boxing glove signed by former heavyweight champions Muhammad Ali, Joe Frazier and Ken Norton ($350-$400).

Everlast boxing trunks signed by Muhammad Ali ($400-$450).

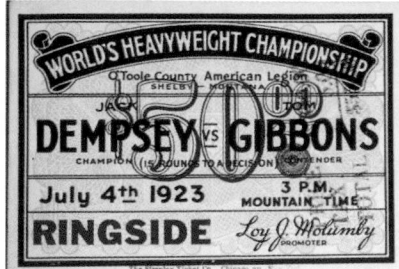

Ticket stub from July 4, 1923 heavyweight championship boxing bout between Jack Dempsey and Tom Gibbons ($175-$200).

Program from June 22, 1938 heavyweight championship boxing bout between Joe Louis and Max Schmeling ($425).

8 x 10 color photograph autographed by auto racing legend A.J. Foyt ($25-$30).

1997 Masters Tiger Woods Grand Slam Ventures Collection card ($1,500-$2,000).

Weekly program for Aug. 4-10, 1936 Olympic Games in Berlin, Germany. Includes official Olympic program. ($150-$200).

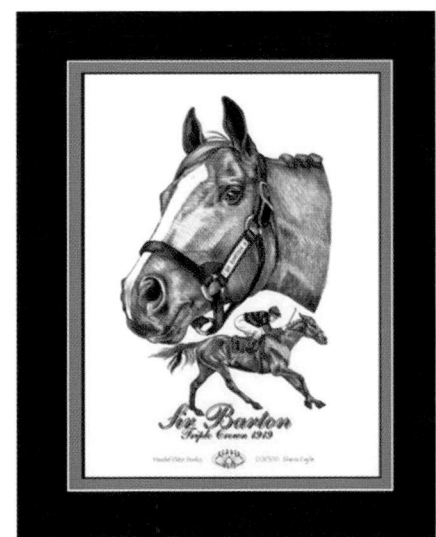

Matted art lithograph of Sir Barton, winner of 1919 Triple Crown ($60-$80).

1999 Coca-Cola bottles of auto racers Bobby Labonte and Dale Earnhardt ($5-$8 per bottle).

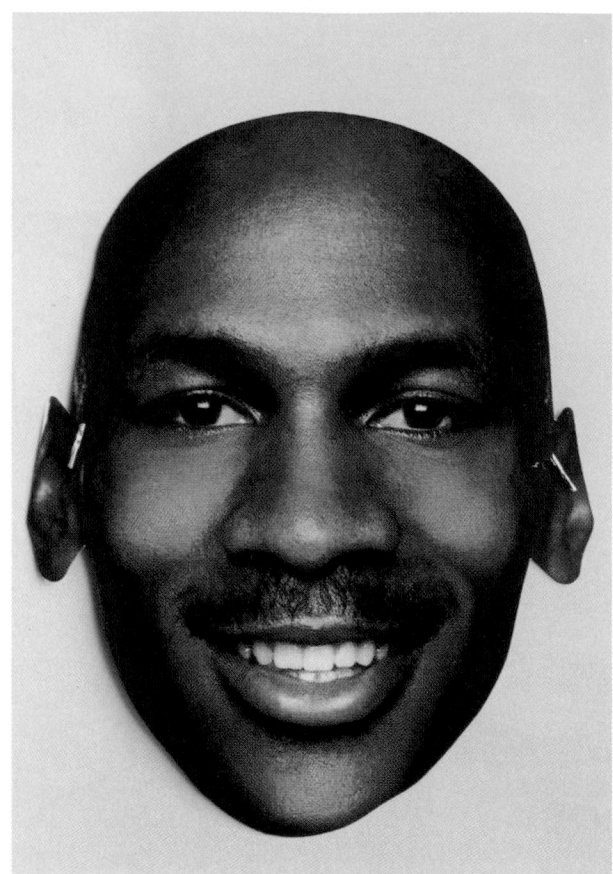

Front and back of 1993 Michael Jordan cardboard mask sponsored by Chicagoland Chevrolet Dealers and Michael Jordan's Restaurant ($12-$20).

1948 Bowman card of Basketball Hall of Famer George Mikan ($4,500).

Seattle Supersonics (cont.)

1977-78 Great Stuff! $10
1978-79 John Johnson, Jack Sikma $10
1979-80 Dennis Johnson $8
1980-81 Lonnie Shelton $8
1981-82 Jack Sikma $8
1982-83 Gus Williams $6
1983-84 Fred Brown $6
1984-85 Team logo $6
1985-86 Sonics artwork $10
1986-87 T. Chambers, X. McDaniel $10
1987-88 Bernie Bickerstaff $10
1988-89 Sonics equipment, locker $10
1989-90 Derrick McKey $7
1990-91 K. C. Jones $7
1991-92 25th Anniv. logo, Sonics greats $7
1992-93 Basketball $7
1993-94 Shawn Kemp, Gary Payton $6
1994-95 Shawn Kemp $6
1995 96 Team logo $6
1996-97 Gary Payton $6
1997-98 Gary Payton $6
1998-99 Logo, artwork $6

Toronto Raptors

1995-96 Raptors logo $8
1996-97 Collage, Damon Stoudamire $7
1997-98 D. Stoudamire, M. Camby, others $7
1998-99 Player, crystal ball, new arena $7

Utah Jazz

New Orleans Jazz
1974-75 New Orleans scene, logo $20
1975-76 . . . .$20
1976-77 Pete Maravich $15
1977-78 . . . .$10
1978-79 P. Maravich, L. Robinson $10
Utah Jazz
1979-80 Salt Palace $8
1980-81 Adrian Dantley, Tom Nissalke $8
1981-82 Adrian Dantley $8
1982-83 A. Dantley, D. Griffith, F. Layden . .$8
1983-84 Mark Eaton, Rickey Green $6
1984-85 A Winning Combination $6
1985-86 T. Bailey, K. Malone, J. Stockton . .$10
1986-87 Mark Eaton $10
1987-88 T. Bailey, M. Eaton, K. Malone . . .$10
1988-89 Karl Malone, 10th Anniversary . . .$10
1989 90 Team logo $10
1990-91 Jerry Sloan photos $10
1991-92 Player and arena caricatures $8
1992-93 Jazz memorabilia $8
1993-94 Basketball and logo $8
1994-95 Basketball going through hoop $8
1995-96 Player's arm, "I Love Basketball" . . .$7
1996-97 Logo, "I Love Basketball" $7
1997-98 J. Stockton, K. Malone, J. Hornacek $7
1998-99 Jazz logo, Silver Anniversary logo $7

Vancouver Grizzlies

1995-96 Shadow figure, basketball court . . .$8
1996-97 G. Anthony, B. Reeves $7
1997-98 B. Reeves, R. Rogers, others $7
1998-99 B. Reeves, Abdur-Rahim, M. Smith . . .$7

Washington Wizards

Baltimore Bullets
1964-65 Gus Johnson $40
1965-66 Media equipment $35
1966-67 Media equipment $35
1967-68 20th Anniversary of basketball in
  Baltimore $35
1968-69 Bullets in action $35
1969-70 E. Monroe, G. Shue, W. Unseld . . .$30
1970-71 Wes Unseld $30
1971-72 Team artwork $20
1972-73 Bullets in action $20
Capital Bullets
1973-74 K. C. Jones, five starters $20
Washington Bullets
1974-75 Elvin Hayes $15
1975-76 P. Chenier, E. Hayes, W. Unseld $15
1976-77 Dick Motta $10
1977-78 E. Hayes, M. Kupchak, W. Unseld, ...
  others $10
1978-79 The Fat Lady Sang, NBA Champs $10
1979-80 Championship trophy $8
1980-81 E. Hayes, K. Porter, G. Shue, W. Unseld . .$8
1981-82 Action photos $8
1982-83 G. Ballard, J. Lucas, J. Ruland $8
1983-84 Rick Mahorn, Jeff Ruland $8
1984-85 G. Ballard, R. Mahorn, J. Ruland . .$8
1985-86 Action artwork $8
1986-87 Moses Malone $8
1987-88 M. Malone, Washington Monument $8
1988-89 Wes Unseld $8
1989-90 T. Hammonds, B. King, W. Unseld . . .$8
1990-91 T. Hammonds, B. King, W. Unseld $8
1991-92 Bernard King $8
1992-93 Harvey Grant/Purvis Ellison $8
1993-94 Puzzle w/R. Chapman, others $8
1994-95 Illustration of uniforms $8
1995-96 Montage of players $7
1996-97 Montage of players $7
Washington Wizards
1997-98 MCI Center and game ticket $7
1998-99 Mitch Richmond $7

Sports Illustrated Basketball Covers

1954
l2/20/54 Ken Sears, Santa Clara . .$15-$20

1956
01/09/56 Bob Cousy, Celtics (FC) $45

1957
01/21/57 Johnny Lee, Yale $10
02/18/57 Jim Krebs, SMU $10
12/09/57 College Basketball Preview .$20

1958
01/20/58 George Dempsey/Neil Johnston, Warriors $10
12/08/58 College Basketball Preview .$20

1959
12/07/59 College Basketball Preview
. . . .$15-$20

1960
01/11/60 Jerry Lucas, Ohio State . .$15-$20
12/12/60 College Basketball Preview
. . . .$15-$20

1961
01/16/61 Bob Cousy, Celtics $25
03/27/61 John Havlicek, Jerry Lucas Ohio State . . . .$10-$15
10/30/61 Wilt Chamberlain, Dick McGuire. $35
01/08/62 Jerry Lucas, Ohio State (SOY) . . . .$20-$25
03/19/62 UCLA vs. USC $15
12/10/62 Cotton Nash, Kentucky $15

1963
03/18/63 Larry Singleton, Cincinnati
. . . .$15-$20
10/28/63 Art Heyman, Jerry Lucas
. . . .$12-$15
12/09/63 Frank Ramsey, Celtics $15

1964
03/30/64 Walt Hazzard, UCLA . . .$10-$15
10/26/64 Tommy Heinsohn, Celtics . . .$20
12/07/64 Bill Bradley, Princeton $40

1965
02/08/65 Jerry West, Lakers . . . . .$25-$30
03/29/65 Gail Goodrich, UCLA . .$15-$20
04/12/65 Wilt Chamberlain, Warriors
. . . .$25-$30
10/25/65 Bill Russell, Celtics (FC) . .$25
12/06/65 UCLA Basketball . . . . . .$15-$20
01124/66 George Peeples, Iowa $10
02/14/66 Rick Mount, top high school player . . . .$12-$17
03/07/66 Adolph Rupp, Kentucky $15-$20
03/28/66 Texas Western wins NCAA tide
. . . .$25

October 25, 1965

05/09/66 John Havlicek, Celtics (FC)
. . . .$25-$30
10/24/66 Elgin Baylor, Lakers $20
12/05/66 Lew Alcindor, UCLA (FC) . .$35

1967
02/13/67 Rick Barry, Warriors $15
02/27167 Walters/Thomforde, Princeton $8
04/03/67 Lew Alcindor, UCLA $25
04/24/67 Rick Barry, Warriors (FC)
. . . .$12-$15
10/23/67 Pro Basketball Preview $12
12/04/67 12-foot basket $10
01/29/68 Lew Alcindor vs. Elvin Hayes
. . . .$20-$25
03/04/68 Pete Maravich, LSU . . . .$45-$55
03/18/68 Bill Bradley, Knicks . . . .$20-$30
04/01/68 UCLA vs. Houston . . . .$15-$20
04/29/68 Elgin Baylor/Jerry West, Lakers
. . . .$12-$15
11/04/68 Earl Monroe, Bullets . . .$10-$15
12/2368 Bill Russell, Celtics (SOY) . . .$20

November 4, 1968

December 23, 1968

1969
01/27/69 Wilt Chamberlain, Lakers . . .$15
02/10/69 Bud Ogden, Santa Clara $6
02/24/69 Knicks vs. Philadelphia $8
03/24/69 Richie Guerin, Jeff Mullins . . .$7
03/31/69 Lew Alcindor, UCLA $15
04/28/69 Bill Russell, Celtics $12
05/12/69 John Havlicek, Celtics $12
08/04/69 Bill Russell, Celtics $9
10/27/69 Lew Alcindor, Bucks . . .$15-$20
12/01/69 Pete Maravich, LSU . . . .$30-$35
12/08/69 Walt Frazier, Knicks $15

1970
01/26/70 Bob Cousy, Royals . . . . .$15-$17
02/16/70 Tom McMillen, top prep star .$12
03/09/70 Lew Alcindor, Bucks $15
03/16/70 Collins, Issel, Lanier, Vallely .$7
03/30/70 UCLA wins NCAA Championship 10
04/27/70 Lew Alcindor, Willis Reed . .$12
05/18/70 Dave DeBusschere, Knicks . .$15
08/24/70 Rick Barry, Squires . . . . .$8-$10

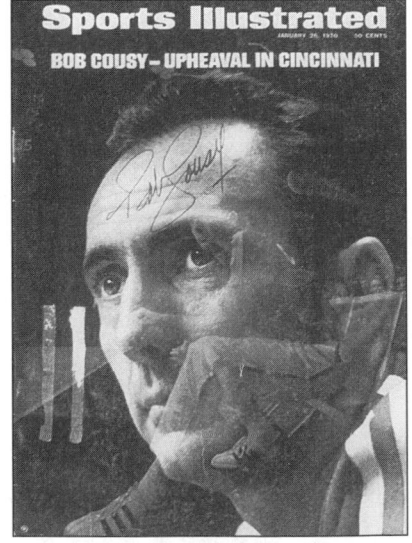

January 26, 1970

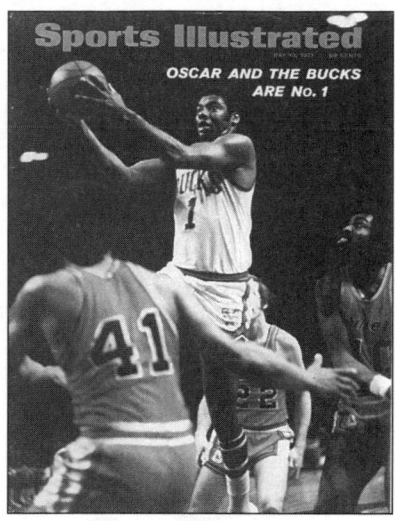

May 10, 1971

10/26/70 Oscar Robertson $10
11/16/70 Calvin Murphy, Rockets $10
11/30/70 Sidney Wicks, UCLA $10

1971
01/04/71John Roche, South Carolina . . .$8
02/08/71 Lew Alcindor, Willis Reed . .$12
04/05/71 Steve Patterson, UCLA $7
04/19/71 Willis Reed, Lew Alcindor . .$10
05/10/71 Oscar Robertson, Bucks $10
08/09/71 Mike Peterson, Kansas high
school $7
10/25/71 Gus Johnson, Dave DeBusschere
. . . .$10
11/29/71 Tom Burleson, North Carolina
State. $8-12
12/13/71 Gail Goodrich, Lakers . .$10-12
02/07/72 Dave Cowens, Walt Frazier . .$10
02/21/72 Allie McGuire, Marquette $6
03/06/72 Bill Walton, UCLA (FC) $10-12
03/20/72 NCAA Championship $8
04/03/72 Bill Walton, UCLA $12
04/24/72 Lew Alcindor, Bucks $8-10
05/15/72 Wilt Chamberlain, Lakers . . .$12
10/16/72 Wilt Chamberlain, Lakers
. . . .$12-15

December 10, 1973

October 14, 1974

11/13/72 John-Havlicek, Celtics $12
11/27/72 Walter Luckett, Ohio $10
12/11/72 Campy Russell, Michigan $7
12/25/72 John Wooden/B.J. King
(SOY) $15

1973
01/15/73 Doug Collins, Illinois State . . .$8
02/05/73 Bill Walton, UCLA $8
02/19/73 Kareem Abdul-Jabbar, Bucks
. . . .$7-$9
03/26/73 Bill Walton, UCLA $8
04/16/73 Earl Monroe, Knicks . . . .$8-$10
05/07/73 Jerry West, Walt Frazier .$12-$15
10/15/73 Nate Archibald, Kings $10
11/12/73 Pete Maravich, Hawks . .$12-$15
11/26/73 David Thompson, N.C. State .$10
12/10/73 Len Elmore, Bill Walton $8

1974
01/14/74 Julius Erving, Nets (FC) $25
02/18/74 John Havlicek, Celtics $12
02/25/74 Bill Walton, UCLA $10
03/25/74 Tom Burleson, Bill Walton . .$10
04/01/74 UCLA vs. N.C. State $12

October 25, 1976

March 31, 1975

05/20/74 John Havlicek, Celtics . .$10-12
10/14/74 Bill Walton, Kareem
Abdul-Jabbar $8
12/02/74 College Basketball Preview .$10
12/16/74 Rick Barry, Warriors $10

1975
02/03/75 John Laskowski, Indiana $8
02/17/75 Dave Meyers, UCLA $6
03/17/75 Phil Ford, North Carolina $7
03/31/75 Mike Flynn, Kentucky $6
04/28/74 Garfield Heard, Braves $6
10/27/75 George McGinnis, 76ers $10
12/01/75 Kent Benson, Indiana $8
02/09/76 Ernie Grunfield/Bernard King,
Tennessee . . . .$8-$10
03/08/76 Bob McAdoo, Braves $7
02/39/76 Kent Benson, Indians $6
04/05/76 Scott May, Indiana $6
05/17/76 Julius Erving, Nets $15
06/07/76 Alvan Adams, Dave Cowens
. . . .$8-$10
10/25/76 Dave Cowens, Julius Erving
. . . .$12-$15
11/15/76 David Thompson, Nuggets
. . . .$8-$10
11/29/76 Rickey Green, Michigan $10
12/13/76 Bill Walton, Trailblazers $10

1977
01/31/77 Bill Cartwright, San Francisco $8
02/14/77BB Kareem Abdul-Jabbar, Lakers
. . . .$8
03/21/77 George McGinnis, 76ers $7
04/04/77 Butch Lee, Marquette $8
04/25/77 Sidney Wicks, Celtics $8
05/23/77 Bill Walton, Kareem
Abdul-Jabbar $12
06/13/77 Bill Walton, Trailblazers $7
10/31/77 Maurice Lucas, Trailblazers
. . . .$8-10
11/28/77 Larry Bird, Indiana State (FC)
. . . .$35-$50
02/13/78 Sidney Moncrief, Arkansas$8-$10
02/20/78 Walter Davis, Suns . . . . . .$8-$10
03/13/78 Gene Banks, Duke $6

May 5, 1980

04/03/78 Goose Gives, Duke $8
05/08/78 Elvin Hayes, Bullets . . . . . $5-$7
05/22/78 Marvin Webster, Sonics $6
08/21/78 Bill Walton, Trailblazers $6
10/16/78 Marvin Webster, Knicks $8
11/27/78 Magic Johnson, Michigan State (FC) . . . . $40-$50

1979
01/22/79 Ohio State vs. Illinois $6
02/19/79 Moses Malone, Rockets (FC) $10
03/12/79 Dudley Bradley, North Carolina $7
03/26/79 Larry Bird, Indiana State $25
04/02/79 Magic Johnson, Michigan State $30
05/07/79 Elvin Hayes, Bullets $7
06/11/79 Gus Williams, Sonics $6
10/15/79 Bill Walton, Clippers . . . . .$6-$8
11/19/79 Magic Johnson, Lakers $20
12/17/79 Ralph Sampson, Virginia $6

1980
03/17/80 Albert King, Maryland $6
03/31/80 Darrell Griffith, Louisville . . . .$5-$7

November 28, 1983

04/28/80 Larry Bird, Julius Erving . . . .$15-$20
05/05/80 Kareem Abdul-Jabbar, Lakers . . . .$7-$5
05/26/80 Magic Johnson, Lakers $15
10/20/80 Paul Westphal, Sonics $12
12/01/80 College Basketball Preview . .$8
12/15/80 Lloyd Free, Warriors $5

1981
01/26/81 Bobby Knight, Indiana $7
02/16/81 Boston College point shaving .$5
03/09/81 Magic Johnson, Lakers $10
03/23/81 Rolando Blackman, Kansas State $4
03/30/81 Ralph Sampson, Virginia $5
04/06/81 Isiah Thomas, Indiana (FC) . .$10
05/11/81 Kevin McHale (FC), Maurice Cheeks $10
11/09/81 Larry Bird, Celtics $20
11/30/81 Dean Smith, North Carolina .$10

1982
02/22/82 Sidney Moncrief, Bucks $8
03/22/82 Patrick Ewing, Georgetown (FC) $10
03/29/82 Sam Perkins, North Carolina . . . .$10-$15
04/05/82CBBJames Worthy, North Carolina . . . .$10-$6
05/03/82 Moses Malone, Jack Sikma . . .$6
05/24/82 Michael Cooper/Magic Johnson, Lakers $12
05/31/82 Julius Erving, 76ers $15
11/01/82 Moses Malone, 76ers $7
12/20/82 Ralph Sampson, Virginia $7

1983
02/21/83 Terry Cummings, Clippers . . .$8
02/28/83 Julius Erving, 76ers $15
03/21/83 Billy Goodwin, St. John's $5
04/11/83 N.C. State wins NCAA title . .$5
05/02/83 Larry Bird, Celtics $15
05/09/83 Kareem Abdul-Jabbar, Lakers $10

June 22, 1987

06/06/83 Moses Malone, 76ers $8
10/31/83 Ralph Sampson, Houston $5
11/28/83 Michael Jordan (FC) Sam Perkins, North Carolina . . . .$40-$50
12/05/83 Sam Bowie, Kentucky $5
03/05/84 Magic Johnson, Lakers .$10-$15
03/19/84 Patrick Ewing, Georgetown . .$8
03/25/84 Sam Perkins, North Carolina $12
04/09/84 Michael Graham, Georgetown $5
05/07/84 Bernard King, Knicks $7
06/04/84 Magic Johnson, Lakers .$10-$12
07/23/84 Michael Jordan, Olympic team . . . .$35-$40
11/26/84 Patrick Ewing, John Thompson, Ronald Reagan $6
12/10/84 Michael Jordan, Bulls .$25-$35

1985
02/04/85 Walter Berry, St. John's $7
04/01/85 Patrick Ewing, Dwayne McClain, Chris Mullin $7
04/08/85 Ed Pinckney, Villanova $7
05/13/85 Magic Johnson, Lakers $15
05/20/85 Patrick Ewing, Knicks $8
06/10/85 Kareem Abdul-Jabbar, Lakers .$6
06/17/85 Kareem Abdul-Jabbar, Lakers $6
11/18/85 Dale Brown, LSU $5
12/23/85 BB Kareem Abdul-Jabbar, Lakers (SOY) $10

1986
02/17/86 Danny Manning, Kansas $9
03/03/86 Larry Bird, Celtics . . . . .$15-$20
03/17/86 Mark Alarie, Duke $5
03/31/86 NCAA Final Four $7
04/07/86 Pervis Ellison, Louisville $5
04/28/86 Dominique Wilkins, Hawks . . . .$7-$10
05/19/86 James Worthy, Lakers $8
05/26/86 Hakeem Olajuwon, Rockets (FC) $8
06/09/86 Larry Bird, Celtics $15
06/16/86 Kevin McHale, Celtics $7
06/30/86 Len Bias, Maryland $5
11/17/86 Michael Jordan, Bulls $20

March 11, 1991

1987

02/23/87 Magic Johnson, Lakers . . .$6-$9
03/02/87 J.R. Reid, North Carolina . .$7-$8
03/16/87 Gary McLain, Villanova . . . .$3-$4
03/23/87 Bobby Knight, Indiana $7
05/04/87 Julius Erving, 76ers . . . . .$7-$10
05/18/87 Isiah Thomas, Pistons . . . .$5-$6
06/08/87 Larry Bird, Celtics . . . . .$8-$12
06/15/87 Los Angeles Lakers vs. Boston
Celtics $10
06/22/87 Kareem Abdul-Jabbar, Lakers
. . . .$10
12/28/87-01/04/88 Michael Jordan, Bulls
. . . .$15-$20

1988

02/22/88 Wilt Chamberlain, Bill Russell
. . . .$6-7
03/21/88 Larry Bird, Celtics $10
03/28/88 Mark Macon, Temple $5
04/11/88 Danny Manning, Kansas $5
04/18/88 Los Angeles Lakers . . . . . .$7-$9
05/16/88 Michael Jordan, Bulls $10
05/23/88 Magic Johnson, Karl Malone $10
06/27/88 Magic Johnson, Bill Laimbeer
. . . .$7-$8
08/22/88 Wayne Gretzky, Magic Johnson
. . . .$10-$15
11/07/88 Karl Malone, Jazz (FC) . . .$7-$8

1989

01/23/89 Kareem Abdul-Jabbar . . . .$6-$7
02/13/89 Patrick Ewing, Knicks . . . .$6-$7
02/20/89 Chris Jackson, LSU . . . . . .$4-$6
03/13/89 Michael Jordan, Bulls . .$12-$15
04/10/89 Glen Rice/Rumeal Robinson,
Michigan . . . .$4-$6
05/15/89 Michael Jordan, Chicago $10-$12
05/29/89 Kentucky Wildcats on probation
. . . .$3-$4
06/05/89 James Worthy, Lakers . . . .$5-$6
08/14/89 Michael Jordan, Bulls . .$10-$12
11/20/89 Rumeal Robinson, Michigan
. . . .$5-$6
12/11/89 Larry Bird, Celtics . . . . .$10-$12
12/18/89 Gretzky, Magic Johnson,
Montana $15

1990

01/29/90 David Robinson, Spurs $10
03/05/90 Gary Payton, Oregon State
. . . .$3-$4
03/26/90 Bo Kimble, Loyola-Marymount
. . . .$3-$4
04/02/90 UNLV Runnin' Rebels . . . .$4-$6
04/09/90 UNLV wins NCAA title . . . .$4-$6
05/21/90 Michael Jordan, Bulls $12
06/11/90 Isiah Thomas, Pistons . . . .$5-$6
11/05/90 Bill Laimbeer, Pistons . . . .$4-$5
11/19/90 Stacey Augmon/Larry Johnson,
UNLV . . . .$6-$7
12/03/90 Magic Johnson, Lakers . . .$5-$6
12/17/90 Michael Jordan, Bulls . .$10-$15

1991

01/21/91 Shaquille O'Neal, LSU (FC) .$15
02/11/91 Robert Parish, Celtics $5
02/18/9 Dream Team (Malone, Barkley,
Ewing, M. Johnson, Jordan) $15
04/01/91 Mark Randall, Kansas $4
04/08/91 Grant Hill, Duke $7

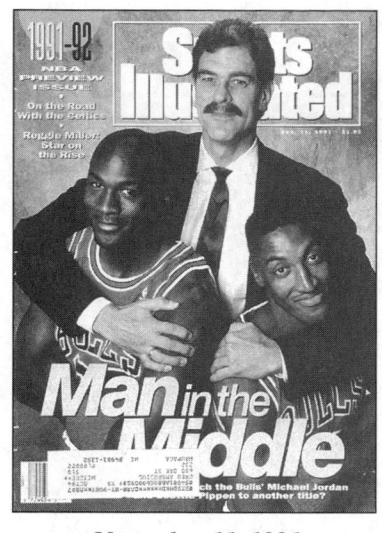

November 11, 1991

06/03/91 Michael Jordan, Bulls $15
06/10/91 Michael Jordan, Magic Johnson
. . . .$15
06/17/91 Michael Jordan, Bulls $15
11/11/91 Phil Jackson, Michael Jordan,
Scottie Pippen $12
11/18/91 Magic Johnson, Lakers $9
11/25/91 CBB Christian Laettner, Duke .$6
12/23/91 Michael Jordan (SOY) $15

1992

02/10/92 Patrick Ewing, Knicks $3
03/23/92 Larry Bird, Celtics $6
04/13/92 Bobby Hurley, Duke $6
05/11/92 Clyde Drexler, Michael Jordan
. . . .$12
05/25/92 Patrick Ewing, Michael Jordan
. . . .$6
06/15/91 Michael Jordan, Bulls $9
06/22/92 Michael Jordan, Bulls $9
11/09/92 Charles Barkley, Suns $5
11/30/92 Shaquille O'Neal, Magic $8
12/14/92 Larry Bird, Magic Johnson . . .$9

1993

01/11/93 Jim Valvano, NC State $3
03/08/93 Brian Reese, North Carolina . .$3
03/29/93 Bobby Hurley, Jason Kidd . . .$4
04/12/93 Eric Montross, North Carolina $3
05/17/93 Hakeem Olajuwon, Rockets . .$4
05/31/93 Bill Cartwright, Patrick Ewing $3
06/07/93 Michael Jordan $5
06/21/93 Charles Barkley, Michael Jordan
. . . .$10
06/28/93 Michael Jordan/Scottie Pippen,
Bulls $10
08/09/93 Reggie Lewis, Celtics $3
10/18/93 Michael Jordan, Bulls $10
11/08/93 Alonzo Mourning, Bill Russell
. . . .$3
12/13/93 Damon Bailey, Indiana $3
03/07/94 David Robinson, Spurs $5
03/28/94 Boston College vs.
North Carolina $4
04/11/94 Corliss Williamson, Arkansas .$3
05/02/94 Gary Payton, Supersonics $4
05/30/94 John Starks, Knicks $4
06/20/94 Patrick Ewing $5
11/07/94 Charles Barkley, Suns $5
11/28/94 Felipe Lopez, St. John's $4

1995

01/30/95 Derrick Coleman $5
02/13/95 Penny Hardaway $6
03/06/95 Jerry Stackhouse $6
03/20/95 Michael Jordan, Bulls . . .$12
03/27/95 Michael Jordan, Bulls . . .$12
04/03/95 Arkansas Basketball $5
05/08/95 Vlade Divac $3
05/22/95 Michael Jordan, Shaquille O'Neal
. . . .$10
05/29/95 Dennis Rodman $6
06/19/95 Clyde Drexler $4
10/23/95 Michael Jordan, Dennis Rodman .
. . . .$8
12/11/95 Pat Riley $4
12/25/95 Shaquille O'Neal, Magic $6

1996

02/12/96 Magic Johnson, Lakers $7
02/26/96 Rick Pittino $5
03/04/96 Dennis Rodman $6
04/08/96 Antoine Walker $5
04/29/96 David Robinson, Spurs $6
05/27/96 Phil Jackson, Michael Jordan $10
06/03/96 Michael Jordan, Bulls $12

1997

02/10/97 Terrell Brandon $5
03/24/97 Kansas Sweet 16 . . . .$5
04/07/97 Miles Simon $5
06/09/97 Michael Jordan, Bulls $12
06/23/97 Michael Jordan, Bulls $12
10/27/97 Larry Bird $7
11/10/97 Grant Hill, Pistons $7
12/15/97 Latrell Sprewell $6

1998

02/16/98 Michael Jordan, Bulls $12
03/02/98 Pat Summitt, Tennessee $5
04/06/98 Kentucky Wildcats $5
04/27/98 Kobe Bryant, Lakers $8
06/01/98 John Stockton, Jazz $6
06/08/98 Michael Jordan, Scottie Pippen
. . . .$10
06/15/98 Michael Jordan, Bulls $12
06/22/98 Michael Jordan "The Shot" . .$12

April 7, 1997

Basketball Books

Selected Hard covers

Against the World, by Kerry Eggers and Dwight Jaynes (1993), HC, recaps the Portland Trailblazer's 1991-92 season $12.50

A Season Inside: One Year in College Basketball, by John Feinstein, HC 462 pages, with dust jacket $9.95

A Season On The Brink: A Year with Bob Knight and the Indiana Hoosiers, by John Feinstein (1986), HC 311 pages, with dust jacket . . .$8.95

A View From Above, by Wilt Chamberlain (1991), HC 290 pages, with dust jacket of Chamberlain, autographed $30

A View From the Bench, Red Holzman with Leonard Lewin (1980), HC 288 pages, with dust jacket $25

A View From the Rim: Willis Reed on basketball, by Willis Reed and Phil Pepe (1971), HC 208 pages $20

Bill Bradley: One to Remember, by Halter (1975), HC, with dust jacket $35

Bill Walton, Nothing But Net, by Bill Walton with Gene Wojciechowski (1994), HC 257 pages, with dust jacket $23

Bird: The Making of An American Sports Legend, by Lee Daniel Levine (1988), HC, 342 pages
. . . .$35

The Cockroach Basketball League, by Charles Rosen (1992), HC $18

Cousy on the Celtic Mystique, by Bob Cousy with Bob Ryan (1988), HC 202 pages $20

Drive, the Story of My Life, Larry Bird with Bob Ryan (1989), HC 260 pages, with dust jacket$25

Forty-Eight Minutes, A Night in the Life of the NBA, by Bob Ryan and Terry Pluto (1987), 356 pages $20

Foul! The Connie Hawkins Story, by David Wolf (1972), HC 400 pages, with dust jacket $35

The Franchise, by Cameron Stauth (1990), HC 365 pages, with dust jacket $19.95

George McGinnis: Basketball Superstar, by James Haskins, HC 128 pages, with dust jacket
. . . .$8

Giant Steps, by Kareem Abdul-Jabbar and Peter Knobler (1983), HC 324 pages, with dust jacket
. . . .$18

Go Up For Glory, by Bill Russell and William McSweeney (1966), HC 224 pages $25

Hang Time, Days & Dreams with Michael Jordan, by Bob Greene (1992), HC 406 pages, with dust jacket $30

Heir to a Dream, by Pete Maravich and Darrel Campbell (1987), HC, 234 pages $30

Holzman's Basketball: Winning Strategy and Tactics, by Red Holzman (1973), HC 242 pages, with dust jacket $16.95

Hondo, Celtic Man In Motion, by Bob Ryan (1977), HC, biography of John Havlicek, autographed $40

In the Land of the Giants, My Life in Basketball, by Tyrone "Muggsy" Bogues and David Levine (1994), HC 233 pages, with dust jacket $20

The Jordan Rules, by Sam Smith (1992), HC 333 pages, with dust jacket $20

John Wooden: They Call Me Coach, by Jack Tobin (1973), HC 190 pages, with dust jacket
. . . .$45

Kareem, by Kareem Abdul-Jabbar with Mignon McCrthy (1990), HC, 233 pages, with dust jacket
. . . .$12

The Killer Instinct, by Bob Cousy with Jim Devaney (1975), HC 212 pages, with dust jacket
. . . .$35

Krazy about the Knicks, by Marv Albert (1971), HC, with dust jacket $35

The Last Loud Roar - Bob Cousy with Ed Linn (1964), HC 271 pages, with dust jacket $45

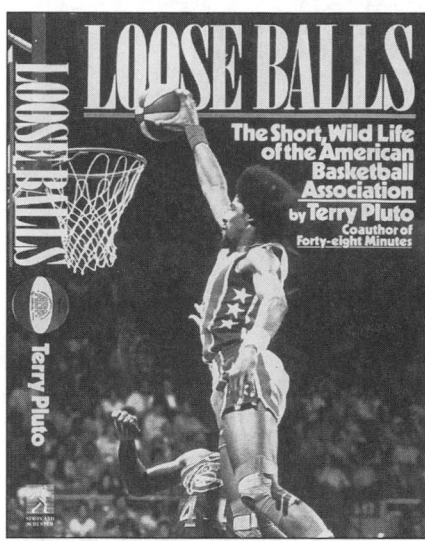

Willis Reed, The Knicks Take Charge Man, by Larry Fox (1970), HC, with dust jacket $30
Wilt, by Wilt Chamberlain and David Shaw (1973), HC 310 pages $35
The Winner Within, A Life Plan for Team Players, by Pat Riley (1993), HC 272 pages, with dust jacket $30

Selected Soft covers

Basketball Stars of 1970, by Lou Sabin (1970), SC, Lew Alcindor cover $10
Basketball Stars of 1975, by Hal Bock and Ben Olan (1974), SC $6
Big A: The Story of Lew Alcindor, by Joel Cohen (1971), SC $12
John Wooden: They Call Me Coach, by Jack Tobin (1972), SC $6
Loose Balls, by Terry Pluto (1990), SC, traces the history of the ABA, Julius Erving cover $15
Michael Jordan/Magic Johnson, by Richard Brenner (1989), SC $6
Pete Maravich: Basketball Magician, by Lou Sabin (1973), SC $10
Pro Basketball 1976-77, by Ballantine (1976), SC, Jo Jo White cover $7
Red Auerbach, Basketball: For the Player, the Fan, and the Coach (1953) SC $20
Second Wind, by Bill Russell (1991), SC ...$10
Shaq!, by Bill Dunn (1993), SC, reviews Shaquille O'Neal's rookie season, done by the staff at the *Orlando Sentinel* newspaper $10
Wilt Chamberlain, by George Sullivan (1967) $6

Life on the Run, by Bill Bradley (1976), HC 229 pages, with dust jacket $25
Loose Balls, by Terry Pluto (1990), HC 450 pages, traces the history of the ABA, Julius Erving cover $25
Magic's Touch, by Earvin "Magic" Johnson Jr. and Roy S. Johnson, HC 236 pages $20
Mr. Basketball, by George Mikan and Bill Carlson (1951), HC, inscribed inside $65
Mr. Clutch: The Jerry West story, by Jerry West and Bill Libby (1969), HC 238 pages, with dust jacket $35
My Life, by Earvin "Magic" Johnson with William Novak (1992), HC 331 pages $10
Obsession - Timberwolves Stalk the NBA, by Bill Heller (1989), HC, traces startup of the Minnesota Timberwolves basketball team ..$10
One Basketball and Glory, by Newt Oliver (1969), HC, the Bevo Francis story $15
The Open Man: A championship diary, by Dave DeBusschere with Paul Zimmerman and Dick Schaap (1970), HC 267 pages, with dust jacket $25
Pistol Pete Maravich, the making of a basketball star, by Bill Gutman (1972), HC 192 pages .$25
Rebound: K. C. Jones Autobiography, by Jack Warner (1986), HC 190 pages, with dust jacket of K. C. Jones $15
Red on Red, Red Holzman and Harvey Frommer (1987), HC 206 pages, with dust jacket $18

Second Wind, the Memoirs of an opinionated man, by Bill Russell with Taylor Branch (1979), HC 265 pages $25
Shaq Attaq!, by Shaquille O'Neal with Jack McCallum (1993), HC, with dust jacket .$12.50
Show Time - Inside the Lakers' Breakthrough Season, by Pat Riley (1988), HC 259 pages, with dust jacket $22
Stand Tall, the Lew Alcindor Story, by Phil Pepe (1970), HC 206 pages, with dust jacket $25
Tall Tales - Glory Years of the NBA, by Terry Pluto (1992), HC 397 pages, with dust jacket $25
24 Seconds to Shoot: Informal History of the NBA, by Leonard Koppett (1968), HC, with dust jacket $35
Unfinished Business, by Jack McCallum (1992), HC, recaps the 1990-91 Celtics season $20
The View From Section III, by Mike Shatzkin (1970), HC , with dust jacket, recaps the Knicks' 1969-70 season $35
Vitale, by Dick Vitale (1988), HC 334 pages, with dust jacket $10
Walt Frazier: One Magic Season and a Basketball Life, by Walt Frazier and Neil Offen (1988), HC 259 pages, with dust jacket $15
The Walton Gang, by Bill Libby (1974), HC 288 pages, with dust jacket $12.95

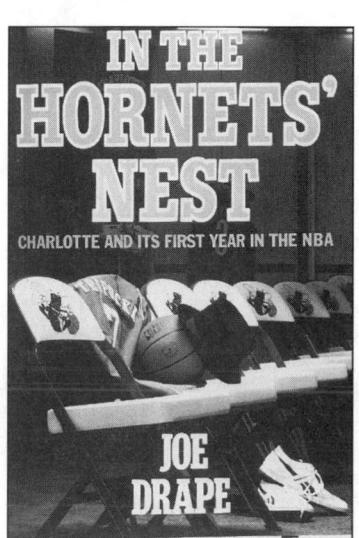

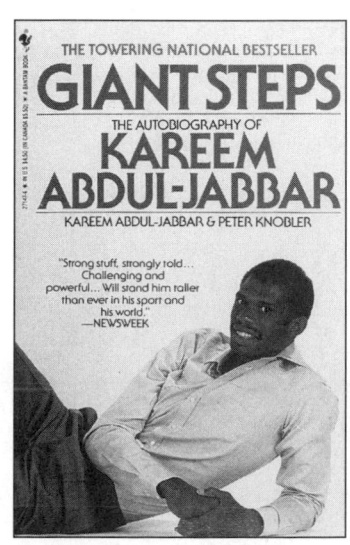

Basketball Cereal Boxes

Famous Fixins
2000 Zo's O's $6
2000 Slam Duncan's 6

Kellogg's Chocos
European
1996 M. Jordan Space Jam (Germany) $30
1996 H. Olajuwon (Germany) 15
1997 M. Jordan Space Jam (Germany) 30

Kellogg's Corn Flakes
1992 Larry Bird $30
1992 David Robinson 25
1992 Bird/Malone/Mullin/Rob/Stockton (2) 20

Kellogg's Corn Pops
1997 Penny Hardaway 10

Kellogg's Corn Pops
Canadian
1997 Awesome Rookies $15
1997 Defensive Dynamos 15
1997 Legendary Leaders 15
1997 Scoring Machines 15

Kellogg's Frosted Flakes
1998 Grant Hill/Sheryl Swoops $10

Kellogg's Frosted Flakes
Canadian
1994 Vancouver Grizzlies $18
1994 Toronto Raptors 18
1996 Hakeem Olajuwon 20
1996 Bryant Reeves 15
1996 Damon Stoudamire 18

Kellogg's
Frosted Mini-Wheats
1992 Larry Bird $30
1992 Karl Malone 25
1992 Chris Mullin 20
1992 David Robinson 20
1992 John Stockton 25
1995 Grant Hill ROY (20/24) 20
1995 Grant Hill dunking (16/19) 20
1996 Damon Stoudamire ROY (Canada) . . .20

Kellogg's Frosties
European
1996 M. Jordan Space Jam (Germany) $30
1996 Hakeem Olajuwon (France) 15

1996 Hakeem Olajuwon (Germany) 15
1997 M. Jordan Space Jam (Germany) 30
1997 Scottie Pippen (France) 15

Kellogg's Honey Nut Loops
European
1996 M. Jordan Space Jam (Germany) $30
1996 Hakeem Olajuwon (Germany) 15

Kellogg's Raisin Bran
1992 Bird/Mal/Mull/Robinson/Stockton $30
1992 Bird/Pippen/Hakeem college cards 20
1992 David Robinson college card 20
1992 Scottie Pippen/David Robinson 20

Kellogg's Rice Krispies
1998 Grant Hill $9

Kellogg's Special K
1997 Comets '97 WNBA Champs $10
1998 Comets '98 WNBA Champs 10
1999 Comets '99 WNBA Champs 6

PLB Sports Promotions
2000 Brian Grant's Monsta O's $8

Post
1994 Olajuwon, Ewing, Pippen, L. Johnson
(Honeycomb) $15
1995 Ewing/Mourning/Kemp (Honeycomb) 15
1996 Olympic Dream Team (Honeycomb) 20
1997 Penny Hardaway (FSW) 6
1997 Penny Hardaway (Honeycomb) 6
1998 Penny Hardaway (Waffle Crisp) 6
1998 Penny Hardaway (Golden Crisp) 6
1998 Penny Hardaway (Honey-Nut) 6

General Mills

Wheaties
1951
George Mikan $100

Wheaties
1988 LA Lakers (24 oz.) (R) $50
1988 LA Lakers (18) (R) 45
1988 Detroit Pistons (han.) (R) 35
1989 Detroit Pistons (R) 40
1991 Chicago Bulls (.75 oz.) (R) 25
1991 Chicago Bulls (18) (R) 35
1992 Clyde Drexler (R) 35
1992 Chicago Bulls (R) 30
1992 Chicago Bulls (.75 oz.) (R) 25
1993 Larry Bird (.75 oz.) (R) 40

1993 Larry Bird (18) (R) 25
1993 Chicago Bulls (R) 30
1994 Harlem Globetrotters (R) 12
1995 Boston Garden w/Auerbach, etc. (R) 18
1996 Chicago Bulls R 20
1996 NCAA Final Four (HF 30) (R) 15
1998 Larry Bird Pacers (R) 12
1998 Larry Bird Boston (R) 12

Wheaties
Michael Jordan
1988 First Edition (12/18 oz.) $100
1988 Pouring ($5 video rebate) 50
1988 Eating cereal (12) 45
1989 Eating cereal (18) 30
1989 Cham. Trad. Cont. 45
1989 Green/post/video offer (18) 50
1989 Blue/post/video offer (18) 50
1989 Purple/post/video offer (18) 50
1989 Story/video offer (8/12/18) 25
1989 Story part 2 (18) 40
1990 Pouring cereal (12) 35
1990 Pouring cereal (18) 40
1990 Chan. Trad. Cont. (12) 45
1990 Blue w/poster; also 43A 50
1990 Green w/poster, also 43B 50
1990 Purple w/poster, also 43C 50
1991 Eating cereal (.75 oz) 10
1991 Sweatsuit w/bag (12) 40
1991 Eating cereal (18) 25
1991 Pouring cereal (18) 25
1991 Air Jordan Calendar 30
1991 Shoot Hoops w/Jordan 40
1991 Sweatsuit w/bag 20
1992 Super single (1) 10
1992 Super single (1.5) 10
1992 Air Jordan 75
1992 Cards Isiah Thomas (18) 20
1992 Cards: Jordan (18) 30
1992 Cards: L. Bird/D. Rodman (18) 25
1992 Cards: Scottie Pippen (18) 20
1992 Cards: Charles Barkley (18) 20
1992 Cards: Karl Malone (18) 20
1992 Cards: Patrick Ewing (18) 20
1992 Cards: David Robinson (18) 20
1993 Silver commemorative 20
1993 Silver com. Can. Bilingual 40
1993 Shoot Hoops w/game 25
1993 Playing golf (18) 30
1995 "He's Back" (18) 20
1995 Video game offer (HG 18) 20
1996 Space Jam (CW) 8

(R) = Regionally Distributed Box

Bowling Collectibles

The exact origin of bowling is unknown, other than the knowledge that the sport is one of the most popular worldwide. The sport is either old, older or really, really old. Regardless, that means there are many, many opportunities for bowling collectors.

You see, a British anthropologist, Sir Flinders Petrie, discovered in the 1930s a collection of objects in a child's grave in Egypt that appeared to him to be used for a crude form of bowling. If he was correct, then bowling traces its ancestry to 3200 BC. Meanwhile, a German historian, William Pehle, says bowling began in his native country in 300 AD.

Jump forward a bit to, oh, 1366 England. King Edward III was in charge then and, reportedly, outlawed bowling to keep his troops focused on archery practice. Later, bowling was definitely popular during the reign of Henry VIII. There were, also at this time, several variations of "pin games," and also games in which a ball was thrown at objects other than pins.

English, Dutch and German settlers all imported their own version of bowling to America. The earliest mention of it in serious American literature is by Washington Irving, when Rip Van Winkle awakens to the sound of "crashing ninepins."

The first permanent American bowling location probably was for lawn bowling, in New York's Battery area. Today's financial district is still called Bowling Green. How else has bowling evolved in America? Let's see:

In 1841, Connecticut law made it illegal to maintain "any ninepin lanes," due to the gambling association. Nonetheless, the sport survived.

Bowling really picked up in such states as Ohio and Illinois by the late-1880s. Interestingly, ball weights and pin dimensions varied by regions.

In 1895, the American Bowling Congress (strictly for men) was founded in New York. Shortly thereafter, standardization was established and major competitions were held.

In 1917, the Women's International Congress was born in St. Louis and a tournament formed the Women's National Bowling Association.

In 1905, the first rubber ball, the Evertrue, was introduced, replacing lignum vitae, a very hard wood. Less than 10 years later, the Brunswick Corporation promoted the Mineralite ball, touting its "mysterious rubber compound."

In 1951, the first commercial installation for Gottfried Schmidt's automatic pinspotter was made in Michigan. A year later, production model pinspotters were introduced, thus eliminating "pinboys."

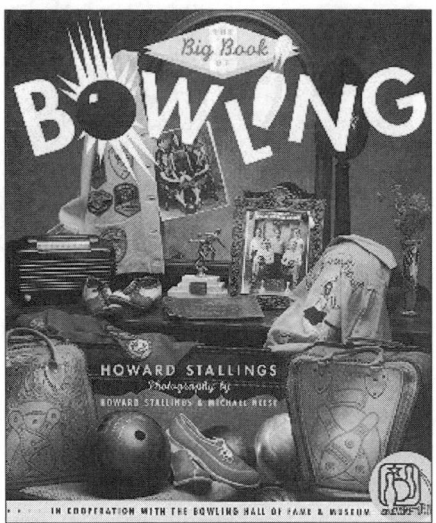

*Howard Stalling's **Big Book of Bowling** was published in cooperation with The Bowling Hall of Fame and Museum in St. Louis.*

Bowling hit the television airwaves in the 1950s. NBC's broadcast of "Championship Bowling" was the first network coverage of bowling. It was followed by such shows as Make That Spare, Celebrity Bowling and Bowling For Dollars. In 1961, ABC became the first network to telecast competition of the PBA, founded by Eddie Elias.

In 2001, more than 100 million people enjoy bowling in about 100 countries worldwide.

What does that mean for collectors and collectibles?

Lots, literally.

As with other sports, any member of the PBA Hall of Fame, especially those who were inducted for performance (as opposed to meritorious or veterans), is sought-after by collectors. They include: Earl Anthony (elected 1981), Mike Aulby (1996), Buzz Fazio (1976), George Pappas (1986),

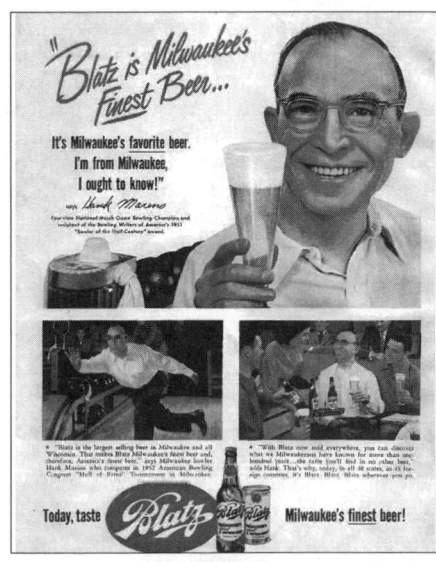

1952 Blatz Beer magazine ad featuring bowler Hank Marino

Carmen Salvino (1975), Dick Weber (1975) and Wayne Zahn (1981), among others. Those Hall of Famers of note for Meritorious Service include Elias (1976), Frank Esposito (1975), Dick Evans (1986), Steve Nagy (1977), Jack Reichert (1992), Chris Schenkel (1976) and more. Members of the Hall of Fame from the Veterans Selection include such notables as Glenn Allison (1984), Joe Joseph (1985), Mike McGrath (1988) and Bob Strampe (1987).

There are other bowling-related Halls of Fame that also offer collecting opportunities (can you say, autograph?). Let's see, there's the World Bowling Writers Hall of Fame, with its international members including Les Zikes (U.S., 2000) and Arne Stroem (Norway, 1994). There are the Women's International Bowling Congress Hall of Fame, the American Bowling Congress Hall of Fame and, of course, the Professional Women's Bowling Association Hall of Fame. Plus, there's the Bowling Proprietors Association of America "Victor Lerner Memorial Award."

On the trading card front, Kingpins produced a set in the 1990s and though it never took off with collectors, select cards are sought after. Norm Duke, for instance, sells for about $3. Earl Anthony goes for about $4. The set is great for bowlers and card collectors. It was released in 1990 and licensed by the PBA. Other collectors, meanwhile, go for the women on cards. The 1991 Premier Set of the Ladies Pro Bowling cards has 64 cards and includes such LPBA names as Robin Ramero, Nikki Guanulias, Tish Johnson and others.

For old-time bowling fans, cards can be the thing, too. There is a 14-card Original set, dating back to 1928 and representing such countries as Spain, New Zealand and France, among others.

No collector (or player) can be without any number of bowling books on the market, such as *From Gutterballs to Strikes: Correcting 101 Common Bowling Errors*, written by Mike Durbin, Dan Herbst and Dan Herbs.

Match-used pins, though hard to obtain at times, are a unique collectible, especially when signed by the bowler who scored well against them. Just imagine that Mike Aulby rolls a 300 game, and you've got a pin from that game. That's smart collecting.

No bowling memorabilia collection would—or could—be complete without a few bowling shirts, those loud-as-can-be, tacky-as-can-be, over-sized shirts for play. At least that was the case in years past, and on the amateur scene. Today's bowling shirts are more conservative, but collectible nonetheless. But wouldn't you rather have a XXXL, super-stained, sweat-covered shirt instead? Thought so.

•••

Boxing Collectibles

Bare-knuckle fighting was a sport about 6,000 years ago in what is now known as Ethiopia. From there it spread to ancient Egypt and eventually throughout the Mediterranean area. Ancient Crete also had a boxing-like sport, which probably developed independently, about 1,500 B.C.

Pugilism wasn't added to the ancient Olympic program until 688 B.C. Some sort of fighting had become established among the Greeks before that time. In one form of Greek boxing, two opponents simply sat on stones facing and pounded away at one another until one of them was knocked out.

Boxing in the Olympics wasn't nearly as brutal, but there were no breaks in the action. Fighters wore leather thongs, originally to protect their hands and wrists.

The Romans added iron or brass studs, creating the cestus, which could be deadly. They went even farther, developing a cruel, spur-like instrument of bronze, called the myrmex ("limb piercer"). Boxing in the Roman Empire was not so much a sport as a bloody amusement for spectators, like the gladiator contests, with slaves pitted against one another in battles to the death.

With the spread of Christianity, pugilism in any form evidently disappeared from Europe completely. It resurfaced in England in the late 17th century. A London newspaper referred to a bout in 1681, and the Royal Theatre in London was the site of regularly scheduled matches in 1698.

The sport at that time was actually a mixture of wrestling and boxing. Although hitting with fists was emphasized, a boxer could grab and throw his opponent, then jump on him and hit him while he was down.

James Figg, who opened a boxing academy in London in 1719, introduced a measure of skill to the sport. Figg was an expert fencer as well as a boxer, and his academy was patterned after the fencing academies of the period. He taught parrying and counter-punching, just as fencing masters taught parries to their students.

Figg won great publicity for his academy by challenging all comers to bouts of boxing or cudgeling. He never lost, and was generally considered champion of Great Britain until he retired in 1730.

His success inspired the establishment of several other boxing academies in London, and the fact that he was a fencer also gave the sport some prestige. A number of "gentlemen" took up boxing as a pastime. They also became enthusiastic fans at prize fights.

One of Figg's pupils, Jack Broughton, became known as the "father of English boxing." Broughton, generally acknowledged as champion from 1729 to 1750, taught boxing and operated an arena in London. In 1743, he drew up the first formal rules for the sport.

Ring Classics record

Under Broughton's rules, there was a 3-foot square in the center of the ring. When a fighter was knocked down, his handlers had 30 seconds to get him into position on one side of the square, facing his opponent. In effect, this marked the first division of a bout into rounds, since each knockdown ended fighting for at least 30 seconds. Although wrestling holds were permitted, a boxer was not allowed to grab his opponent below the waist.

Broughton also invented the first boxing gloves, to protect the hands and face from blows. However, they were used only in practice, not in actual bouts.

Unlike baseball, basketball, football or hockey, the sport of boxing has had the ability to influence forces far beyond the ring.

Two individuals, Max Schmeling and Joe Louis, emerged at the dawn of World War II, with Adolph Hitler at the helm in Germany and the Depression firmly entrenched in the United States. Unlikely as it seemed, these two boxers would represent an entire culture. Max Schmeling, a German fighter, represented the Aryan race and was a symbol for Nazi fascism, while Joe Louis, an American fighter, the son of a poor black American sharecropper, represented democratic ideals.

After Schmeling knocked out Louis in their first fight on June 19, 1936, the German press called it, "another example of Aryan superiority, both physically as well as intellectually." Within a day after the victory, Schmeling, who had been offered free passage aboard the Hindenberg, was dining with the Nazi dictator and watching unedited footage of the fight. The Nazi myth of supremacy was soon shattered, however, during the 1936 Olympics, primarily by a black American sprinter named Jesse Owens. To regain their lost credibility, additional physical contests needed to be staged or at least condoned.

On June 22, 1938, Schmeling returned to America for a rematch with Louis and a shot at the heavyweight championship of the world. Schmeling stood not as an individual on that day, but for an entire race. As information was just beginning to filter to the American public about some of the Nazi atrocities in Europe, hatred was starting to show its ugly signs. Amid considerable thrown debris, it took 20 policemen to escort the German into the ring at Yankee Stadium. Louis entered the ring, not as an individual, or black American, but as a symbol for all under democratic rule. After two minutes and four seconds of the first round, the fight was over. Louis had upheld American honor and allowed all to embrace his victory. Hitler, after learning of the defeat, was furious; this time there would be no Hindenberg or parade awaiting Schmeling in his homeland. Instead the great fighter would return home aboard ship, after spending two weeks in an American hospital nursing his fight wounds.

The fight was so significant that some Jews in Nazi concentration camps viewed the outcome as an example that they could overcome their painful hardships; they now had proof that the Germans could be defeated.

We collect to preserve a moment, to remind us that it is the human spirit and the willingness to succeed, despite all adversity, that guides us throughout our lives. Our artifacts speak without words, as no words could define them. For those who lived these events, a simple glance at a boxing ticket from the 1938 Schmeling-Louis bout can send shivers up their spine. After all, who can accurately describe the challenges faced by both of these great fighters?

Each boxing artifact becomes a reflection of its time. Although we can not stop its deterioration, we can try to preserve its relevance. Through it we can share an association with the subject—it is for our benefit. As we stare at our autographed Willie Pep or Jake LaMotta boxing glove, we remember gathering around our black-and-white television set and watching "Friday Night Fights." We recall the fierce battles between Pep and Saddler, and between Robinson and LaMotta. We remember vividly staring at the television screen, wondering how a human being could endure so much physical pain, and the guts it must have taken to step into the ring against any of these outstanding fighters. We remember our fathers giving us boxing lessons between rounds, or telling us their favorite fight stories before we went to bed late Friday night. Through an autographed boxing glove we are assured that these vivid memories will never end, rekindled by a glance to the shelf where it remains transfixed in time.

By collecting boxing memorabilia, we experience through association the triumphs of our subjects. It is our nature to want to share in the successes of others. The smart collector remembers that a boxer, too, is only human, and that one's own accomplishments, gained outside of a boxing ring, are equally as rewarding. And although they often go unrecognized, they are equally as significant.

●●●

Boxing Collectibles

On June 8, 1989 the International Boxing Hall of Fame was officially opened in Canastota, N.Y. It marked the first time that a legitimate and permanent shrine was created for the sport. The popularity of boxing's premier sanctuary has led to the production of many outstanding collectibles including, programs, philatelic souvenirs, press kits, press pins and equipment.

International Boxing Hall of Fame Collectibles & Commemoratives

Induction Programs *

1990 Flip Amato First Printing – 500	.$30
Second Printing – 500	$25
1991 Wayne Prokopiak 1000 copies	$20
1992 Wayne Prokopiak 1500 copies	$15
1993 Wayne Prokopiak 1500 copies	$10
1994 Wayne Prokopiak 1500 copies	$10
1995 Wayne Prokopiak 1500 copies	$10
1996 Wayne Prokopiak 1200 copies	$12
1997 Richard Slone 1800 copies	$10
1998 Richard Slone 1400 copies	$10
1999 Richard Slone 1400 copies	$10
2000 Richard Slone 1400 copies	$10

* Adding the autographs of all the living inductees on the front of these programs has become very popular with collectors. Naturally such additions can increase the value of the program. Collectors can consult the autograph section with regard to the addition of a fighter's name to a program. The initial cost of the program was $5 per copy, followed by an increase in cost to $10 in 1998.

Philatelic Souvenirs

1990 Induction Day Folder Interior lists names of 1990 inductees $15
Same as above with cancellation $20
1990 Induction Day Envelope Exterior depicts ticket & Queensberry $10
Same as above with cancellation $15
1991 Induction Day Folder Interior lists names of 1991 inductees $9
Same as above with cancellation $10
1991 Induction Day Envelope Exterior lists names of 1991 inductees $8
Same as above with cancellation $9
Induction Day Philatelic Souvenir Folder, single-fold, 500 copies $8
1992 Induction Day Envelope Exterior pictures two fighters $4.50
Same as above with cancellation ...$5.50
1993 Induction Day Envelope Exterior pictures two fighters $4
Same as above with cancellation $5
Joe Louis Commemorative Envelope, business size with cancellation and Joe Louis stamp, limited to 750 copies $10
1994 Induction Day Envelope Exterior lists names of 1994 inductees $4
Same as above with cancellation $5
Induction Day Philatelic Souvenir Folder, single-fold, 500 copies $5

1995 Induction Day Envelope Exterior lists names of 1995 inductees $4
Same as above with cancellation $5
Aaron Pryor Celebrity Weekend $5
1996 Induction Day Envelope Exterior lists names of 1996 inductees $4
Same as above with cancellation $5
1997 Induction Day Envelope Exterior lists names of 1997 inductees $4
Same as above with cancellation $5
1998 Induction Day Envelope Exterior lists names of 1998 inductees $4
Same as above with cancellation $5
1999 Induction Day Envelope Exterior lists names of 1999 inductees $4
Same as above with cancellation $5
2000 Induction Day Envelope Exterior lists names of 2000 inductees $4
Same as above with cancellation $5

Commemorative Series

1995 #1 Jack Dempsey Series of 100, sold out $15
1996 #2 Joe Louis/Max Schmeling Series of 100, sold out $15
1997 #3 Robinson/Basilio Series of 250, sold out $12
1997 #4 Hagler/Leonard Series of 250 ....$10
1998 #5 Holmes/Norton Series of 200 ....$10
1998 #6 Foster/Tiger Series of 200 ...$10
1998 #7 Rocky Marciano Series of 100 ....$13
1999 #8 Basilio/Fullmer Series of 150 .$10
1999 #9 Pep/Saddler Series of 150 ....$10
1999 #10 Tenth Anniversary Series of 250 ....$10
2000 #11 Hagler/Hearns Series of 150 ....$10
2000 #12 Patterson/Johanssen Series of 150 ....$10

Press Pins & Kit

Beginning in 1995 the museum included a single press pin and bound booklet as part of every press kit. The pins, each individually numbered, and booklets have become extremely popular with boxing collectors because of their limited distribution. In fact, the pins are harder to find than those issued by the Baseball Hall of Fame. The bound official press kit/booklet includes condensed and comprehensive biographies of all the inductees for that specific year along with an updated list of members. Each booklet is typically 16 pages and its inclusion with the corresponding press pin can add $25 to the price listed below.

1995 Red & Gold (First year of issue) $225
1996 Blue & Silver $200
1997 Green & silver (First year living inductees names added) $175
1998 Black & Gold (Hard to find in mint condition – pin chipped easily) $150
1999 Blue & Silver (Tenth Anniversary) $150
2000 Violet & S Gold Error Pin ...$150

Equipment

Autographed Gloves

Michael Moorer Limited to 50 gloves (94) Dated 1994 as Champ. $75
Basilio & DeMarco Limited to 25 gloves (94) Com. 1955 Title bouts $55
Michael & Leon Spinks Limited to 50 gloves (94) Heavyweight Champs ...$100
Marvin Hagler Limited to 200 gloves (93) Dated June 13, 1993 ....$110
Pep & Saddler Limited to 10 gloves (93) $150
Riddick Bowe Limited to 50 gloves (93) Signed on 26th B-day $100
Ray Mancini Limited to 50 gloves (94) $70

Induction Gloves

1990 Limited to 12 gloves, Signed by living members who attend Induction weekend, also signed, numbered, and dated by IBHOF director inside of each glove. (14 sigs.) $1,000
1991 Limited to 12 gloves, Signed by living members who attend Induction weekend, also signed, numbered, and dated by IBHOF director inside of each glove. (8 sigs.) $750
1992 Limited to 12 gloves, Signed by living members who attend Induction weekend, also signed, numbered, and dated by IBHOF director inside of each glove. (6 sigs.) $425
1993 Limited to 12 gloves, Signed by living members who attend Induction weekend, also signed, numbered, and dated by IBHOF director inside of each glove. (6 sigs.) $400
1994 Limited to 12 gloves, Signed by living members who attend Induction weekend, also signed, numbered, and dated by IBHOF director inside of each glove. (4 sigs.) $400
1995 Limited to 12 gloves, Signed by living members who attend Induction weekend, also signed, numbered, and dated by IBHOF director inside of each glove. (4 sigs.) $375
1996 Limited to 12 gloves, Signed by living members who attend induction weekend, also signed, numbered, and dated by IBHOF director inside of each glove. (4 sigs.) $375
1997 Limited to 12 gloves, Signed by living members who attend Induction weekend, also signed, numbered, and dated by IBHOF director inside of each glove. (3 sigs.) $350
1998 Limited to 12 gloves, Signed by living members who attend Induction weekend, also signed, numbered, and dated by IBHOF director inside of each glove. (3 sigs.) $350
1999 Limited to 12 gloves, Signed by living members who attend Induction weekend, also signed, numbered, and dated by IBHOF director inside of each glove. (6 sigs.) $350
2000 Limited to 12 gloves, Signed by living members who attend Induction weekend, also signed, numbered, and dated by IBHOF director inside of each glove. (43 sigs.) $350

Boxing Autographs

Charles Adkins
Cut Signature $5
Photo $19
Glove $45

Virgil Akins
Cut Signature $15
Photo $35
Glove $145

Muhammad Ali
Cut Signature $25
Photo . . . .$75-$100
Glove . . . .$150-$200
(as Cassius Clay)
Cut Signature . . . .$125-$175
Photo . . . .$350-$400
Glove . . . .$(varies)

Lou Ambers *
Cut Signature $20
Photo $40
Glove $150

Fred Apostoli *
Cut Signature $35
Photo $90
Glove $390

Art Aragon
Cut Signature $5
Photo $10
Glove $45

Alexis Arguello
Cut Signature $7
Photo $15
Glove $65

Henry Armstrong *
Cut Signature $75
Photo $175
Glove $755

Abe Attell *
Cut Signature $60
Photo $160
Glove $690

Buddy Baer *
Cut Signature $12
Photo $40
Glove $175

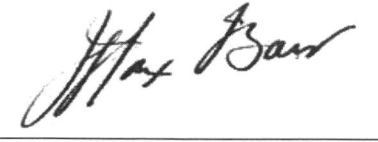

Max Baer *
Cut Signature $110
Photo $300
Glove $1,250

Carmen Basilio
Cut Signature $8
Photo $15
Glove $65

Nino Benvenuti
Cut Signature $15
Photo $65
Glove $265

Kid Berg *
Cut Signature $25
Photo $60
Glove $260

Paul Berlenbach *
Cut Signature $30
Photo $60
Glove $270

Melio Bettina *
Cut Signature $8
Photo $20
Glove $85

Riddick Bowe
Cut Signature $8
Photo . . . .$15-$20
Glove $90

James J. Braddock *
Cut Signature $65
Photo $250
Glove $1,200

Mark Breland
Cut Signature $6
Photo $15
Glove $60

Teddy Brenner
Cut Signature $5
Photo $20
Glove $40

Joe Brown
Cut Signature $6
Photo $15
Glove $60

Frank Bruno
Cut Signature $5
Photo $10
Glove $40

Ken Buchanan
Cut Signature $6
Photo $17
Glove $60

Tommy Burns *
Cut Signature $275
Photo $750
Glove $2,500

Mushy Callahan
Cut Signature $12
Photo $25
Glove $100

Hector Camacho
Cut Signature $10
Photo $20
Glove $65

Tony Canzoneri *
Cut Signature $60
Photo $130
Glove $570

Michael Carbajal
Cut Signature $7
Photo $15
Glove $75

Primo Carnera *
Cut Signature $225
Photo $500
Glove $2,150

Georges Carpentier *
Cut Signature $110
Photo $225
Glove $975

Jimmy Carter *
Cut Signature $12
Photo $25
Glove $100

Rubin "Hurricane" Carter
Cut Signature $10
Photo . . . .$15-$20
Glove . . . .$50-$60

Rocky Castellani
Cut Signature $5
Photo $15
Glove $60

Marcel Cerdan *
Cut Signature $280
Photo $775
Glove $3,200

Bobby Chacon
Cut Signature $10
Photo $20
Glove $85

Jeff Chandler
Cut Signature $5
Photo $10
Glove $40

Ezzard Charles *
Cut Signature $110
Photo $225
Glove $975

Julio Cesar Chavez
Cut Signature $12
Photo $32
Glove $125

George Chuvalo
Cut Signature $5
Photo $10
Glove $40

Gil Clancy
Cut Signature $5
Photo $10
Glove $40

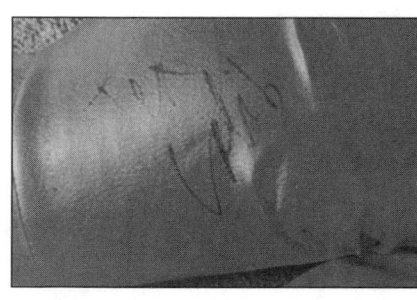

Randal "Tex" Cobb
Cut Signature $8
Photo $15
Glove $50

Gerrie Coetzee
Cut Signature $5
Photo $10
Glove $40

Curtis Cokes
Cut Signature $4
Photo $8
Glove $35

Billy Conn *
Cut Signature $20
Photo $65
Glove $260

Gerry Cooney
Cut Signature $5
Photo $10
Glove $40

James J. Corbett *
Cut Signature $400
Photo $800
Glove $3,500

Johnny Coulon *
Cut Signature $45
Photo $100
Glove $425

Bobby Czyz
Cut Signature $5
Photo $10
Glove $45

Chuck Davey
Cut Signature $4
Photo $8
Glove $35

Oscar De La Hoya
Cut Signature $15
Photo $35
Glove $125

Paddy DeMarco
Cut Signature $6
Photo $13
Glove $50

Tony DeMarco
Cut Signature $6
Photo $13
Glove $50

Jack Dempsey
Cut Signature $75
Photo $165
Glove $730

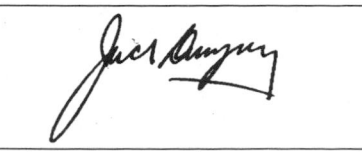

Michael Dokes
Cut Signature $5
Photo $13
Glove $50

Angelo Dundee
Cut Signature $6
Photo $12
Glove $50

Chris Dundee
Cut Signature $15
Photo $40
Glove $100

Johnny Dundee *
Cut Signature $45
Photo $100
Glove $400

Don Dunphy
Cut Signature $5
Photo $20
Glove $50

Roberto Duran
Cut Signature $15
Photo $35
Glove $125

Flash Elorde
Cut Signature $25
Photo $55
Glove $240

Jimmy Ellis
Cut Signature $5
Photo $10
Glove $40

Alfredo Escalera
Cut Signature $6
Photo $14
Glove $55

Johnny Famechon
Cut Signature $6
Photo $14
Glove $55

Tommy Farr
Cut Signature $25
Photo $60
Glove $250

Jeff Fenech
Cut Signature $8
Photo $17
Glove $70

Jackie Fields
Cut Signature $8
Photo $14
Glove $50

Bob Fitzsimmons *
Cut Signature $2,200
Photo $6,000
Glove $13,000

Nat Fleischer
Cut Signature $15
Photo $30
Glove $120

George Foreman
Cut Signature $10
Photo $20
Glove $80

Bob Foster
Cut Signature $8
Photo $15
Glove $65

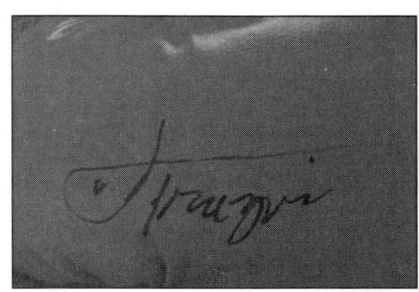

Joe Frazier
Cut Signature $9
Photo $20
Glove $85

Gene Fullmer
Cut Signature $8
Photo $15
Glove $65

Charlie Fusari
Cut Signature $5
Photo $10
Glove $40

Eddie Futch
Cut Signature $8
Photo $15
Glove $65

Tony Galento
Cut Signature $45
Photo $95
Glove $390

Ceferino Garcia
Cut Signature $5
Photo $10
Glove $40

Kid Gavilan
Cut Signature $12
Photo $25
Glove $90

Joey Giambra
Cut Signature $5
Photo $10
Glove $40

Joey Giardello
Cut Signature $6
Photo $15
Glove $65

Abe Goldstein *
Cut Signature $45
Photo $90
Glove $390

Wilfredo Gomez
Cut Signature $10
Photo $20
Glove $75

Rocky Graziano *
Cut Signature $30
Photo $55
Glove $240

Emile Griffith
Cut Signature $6
Photo $15
Glove $45

Marvin Hagler
Cut Signature $12
Photo $30
Glove $100

Marvin Hart *
Cut Signature $800
Photo $1,700
Glove $7,325

Thomas Hearns
Cut Signature $10
Photo $30
Glove $95

Larry Holmes
Cut Signature $11
Photo $25
Glove $65

Evander Holyfield
Cut Signature $20
Photo $40
Glove $80

Al Hostak
Cut Signature $15
Photo $30
Glove $125

Beau Jack *
Cut Signature $10
Photo $30
Glove $70

James J. Jeffries *
Cut Signature $370
Photo $750
Glove $3,225

Lew Jenkins
Cut Signature $5
Photo $10
Glove $40

Eder Jofre
Cut Signature $10
Photo $22
Glove $70

Ingemar Johansson
Cut Signature $15
Photo $30
Glove $110

Harold Johnson
Cut Signature $8
Photo $15
Glove $50

Jack Johnson *
Cut Signature $775
Photo $1,400
Glove $6,100

Ralph Jones
Cut Signature $7
Photo $20
Glove $55

Roy Jones
Cut Signature $8
Photo $20
Glove $80

Jack Kearns
Cut Signature $30
Photo $60
Glove $250

Don King
Cut Signature $5
Photo $10
Glove $40

Fidel LaBarba
Cut Signature $10
Photo $20
Glove $75

Jake LaMotta
Cut Signature $12
Photo $20
Glove $75

Roland Lastarza
Cut Signature $5
Photo $10
Glove $40

Benny Leonard *
Cut Signature $40
Photo $100
Glove $450

Sugar Ray Leonard
Cut Signature $20
Photo $35
Glove $150

Gus Lesnevich
Cut Signature $25
Photo $50
Glove $215

John Henry Lewis *
Cut Signature $65
Photo $160
Glove $690

Lennox Lewis
Cut Signature $10
Photo $30
Glove $110

Sonny Liston *
Cut Signature $250
Photo $750
Glove $3,250

Danny Lopez
Cut Signature $5
Photo $10
Glove $40

Tommy Loughran *
Cut Signature $35
Photo $80
Glove $345

Joe Louis *
Cut Signature $175
Photo $325
Glove $1,400

Ray Mancini
Cut Signature $10
Photo $24
Glove $80

Sammy Mandell
Cut Signature $10
Photo $20
Glove $85

Rocky Marciano *
Cut Signature $300
Photo $700
Glove $2,100

Buster Mathis, Sr.*
Cut Signature $15
Photo . . . .$25-$30
Glove $90

Joey Maxim
Cut Signature $8
Photo $20
Glove $75

Jimmy McLarnin
Cut Signature $15
Photo $30
Glove $100

Ray Mercer
Cut Signature $7
Photo $15
Glove $60

Freddie Mills
Cut Signature $20
Photo $50
Glove $215

Charles Mitchell
Cut Signature $20
Photo $50
Glove $215

Carlos Monzon *
Cut Signature $40
Photo $110
Glove $260

Archie Moore *
Cut Signature $9
Photo $20
Glove $90

Michael Moorer
Cut Signature $10
Photo $20
Glove $70

Tommy Morrison
Cut Signature $10
Photo $25
Glove $75

Eddie M. Muhammad
Cut Signature $5
Photo $13
Glove $55

Matthew S. Muhammad
Cut Signature $5
Photo $13
Glove $55

Jose Napoles
Cut Signature $11
Photo $25
Glove $75

Battling Nelson *
Cut Signature $80
Photo $175
Glove $760

Terry Norris
Cut Signature $7
Photo $15
Glove $60

Ken Norton
Cut Signature $10
Photo $25
Glove $75

Lou Nova
Cut Signature $5
Photo $10
Glove $45

Ruben Olivares
Cut Signature $8
Photo $18
Glove $60

Carl Olson
Cut Signature $7
Photo $15
Glove $60

Carlos Ortiz
Cut Signature $7
Photo $16
Glove $55

Carlos Palmino
Cut Signature $5
Photo $10
Glove $45

Bob Montgomery
Cut Signature $6
Photo $13
Glove $55

Billy Papke *
Cut Signature $245
Photo $500
Glove $2,150

Willie Pastrano
Cut Signature $5
Photo $10
Glove $45

Floyd Patterson
Cut Signature $10
Photo $20
Glove $85

Eusebio Pedroza
Cut Signature $5
Photo $10
Glove $40

Willie Pep
Cut Signature $6
Photo $15
Glove $60

Aaron Pryor
Cut Signature $5
Photo $15
Glove $55

Dwight Qawi
Cut Signature $5
Photo $10
Glove $40

Jerry Quarry *
Cut Signature $9
Photo $20
Glove $75

Sugar Ramos
Cut Signature $7
Photo $18
Glove $70

Tex Rickard *
Cut Signature $170
Photo $360
Glove $1,600

Eddie Risko
Cut Signature $10
Photo $25
Glove $85

Willie Ritchie *
Cut Signature $20
Photo $40
Glove $170

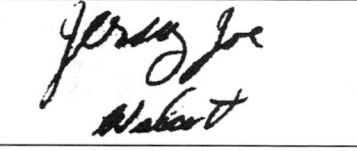

Sugar Ray Robinson *
Cut Signature ....$50-$60
Photo ....$175-$200
Glove ....$750-$1,000

Louis Rodriguez
Cut Signature $10
Photo $25
Glove $100

Edwin Rosario
Cut Signature $7
Photo $18
Glove $60

Maxie Rosenbloom *
Cut Signature $40
Photo $80
Glove $350

Barney Ross *
Cut Signature $40
Photo $80
Glove $350

Sandy Saddler
Cut Signature $10
Photo $28
Glove $80

Johnny Saxton
Cut Signature $8
Photo $19
Glove $80

Max Schmeling *
Cut Signature $20
Photo $40
Glove $175

Marty Servo
Cut Signature $5
Photo $10
Glove $40

Jack Sharkey *
Cut Signature $75
Photo $150
Glove $600

Ernie Shavers
Cut Signature $6
Photo $15
Glove $50

Leon Spinks
Cut Signature $7
Photo $15
Glove ....$65-$70

Michael Spinks
Cut Signature $10
Photo $25
Glove $75

John L. Sullivan *
Cut Signature $500
Photo $950
Glove $4,100

John Tate
Cut Signature $8
Photo $18
Glove $65

Ernie Terrell
Cut Signature $6
Photo $13
Glove $55

Pinklon Thomas
Cut Signature $6
Photo $13
Glove $55

Dick Tiger *
Cut Signature $75
Photo $200
Glove $850

Gene Tunney *
Cut Signature $80
Photo $180
Glove $775

Randy Turpin *
Cut Signature $110
Photo $175
Glove $800

Mike Tyson
Cut Signature $30
Photo $75
Glove $150

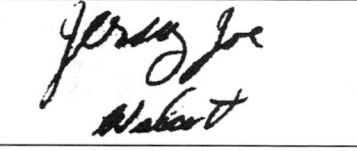

Jersey Joe Walcott *
Cut Signature $25
Photo $95
Glove $275

Mickey Walker *
Cut Signature $50
Photo $160
Glove $650

Mike Weaver
Cut Signature $5
Photo $10
Glove $45

Sweet Pea Whitaker
Cut Signature $5
Photo $9
Glove $40

Jess Willard *
Cut Signature $220
Photo $450
Glove $2,000

Cleveland Williams
Cut Signature $6
Photo $13
Glove $50

Ike Williams *
Cut Signature $12
Photo $25
Glove $125

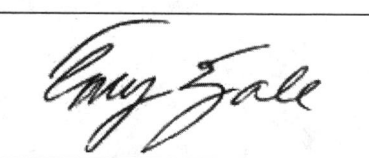

Tony Zale *
Cut Signature $9
Photo $18
Glove $65

Alfonso Zamora
Cut Signature $5
Photo $12
Glove $50

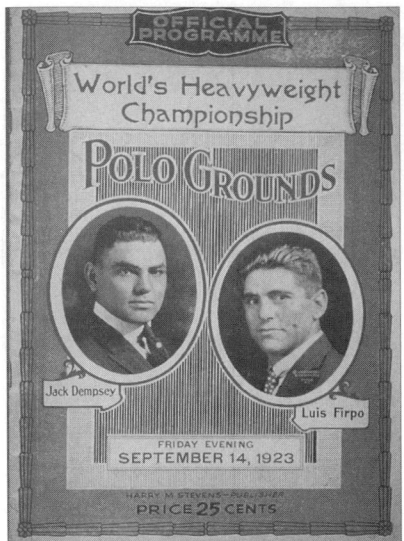

September 14, 1923 Program

July 21, 1927 Program

June 22, 1938 Program

Boxing Programs

Programs are used as a simple vehicle to convey information. When they are read they can enhance the reader's enjoyment of the sporting event. They were created first and foremost for this reason, but over time have also become a profitable source of revenue for their creators. The artwork of a particular era, the significance of the event and the available printing technology, are all reflected in the design of the program.

Early boxing programs were often nothing more than a simple one-sheet broadside. Boxing programs were originally not designed to last, but rather to be used at the event and discarded.

Heavyweight championship bouts were usually more elaborate than those of non-title bouts or different class championships.

Fight promoters now realize that the demand for programs exceeds that prepared for the fight site. Therefore, additional programs are commonly printed and sold.

Selected Heavyweight Bouts

Date	Opponents	Price
07/04/19	Dempsey vs. Willard	$1,500
09/06/20	Dempsey vs. B. Miske	1,250
12/14/20	Dempsey vs. Brennan	1,250
07/02/21	Dempsey vs. Carpentier	1,200
07/04/23	Dempsey vs. Gibbons	1,100
09/14/23	Dempsey vs. Firpo	1,000
09/23/26	Tunney vs. Dempsey	1,500
07/21/27	Dempsey vs. Sharkey	1,000
09/22/27	Tunney vs. Dempsey	1,500
07/26/28	Tunney vs. Heaney	350
06/12/30	Schmeling vs. Sharkey	400
07/03/31	Schmeling vs. Stribling	350
06/21/32	Sharkey vs. Schmeling	350
09/26/32	Schmeling vs. Walker	375
06/25/35	Louis vs. Carnera	500
09/24/35	Louis vs. Baer	475
06/19/36	Schmeling vs. Louis	425
08/18/36	Louis vs. Sharkey	400
06/22/37	Louis vs. Braddock	500

06/22/38	Louis vs. Schmeling	425
07/13/39	Conn vs. J. Bettina	275
09/25/39	Conn vs. J. Bettina	250
11/17/39	Conn vs. Lesnevich	250
06/05/40	Conn vs. Lesnevich	250
05/23/41	Louis vs. Baer	375
06/18/41	Louis vs. Conn	375
01/09/42	Louis vs. Baer	350
06/19/46	J. Louis vs. Conn	300
12/05/47	Louis vs. Walcott	265
06/25/48	Louis vs. J. Walcott	250
06/22/49	Charles vs. Walcott	75
09/27/50	Charles vs. Louis	100
03/07/51	Charles vs. Walcott	50
07/18/51	Walcott vs. Charles	50
10/26/51	Marciano vs. Louis	250
06/05/52	Walcott vs. Charles	50
09/23/52	Marciano vs. Walcott	200
05/15/53	Marciano vs. Walcott	100
06/17/54	Marciano vs. Charles	100
09/17/54	Marciano vs. Charles	100
05/16/55	Marciano vs. Cockell	100
09/21/55	Marciano vs. Moore	100

August 18, 1936 Program

June 19, 1946 Program

July 28, 1952 Program

September 20, 1955 Program

Date	Opponents	Price
11/30/56	Patterson vs. Moore	$100
06/26/59	Johansson vs. Patterson	80
06/20/60	Patterson vs. Johansson	75
03/13/61	Patterson vs.Johansson	75
09/25/62	Liston vs. Patterson	80
11/15/62	Clay vs. Moore	250
07/22/63	Liston vs. Patterson	110
02/25/64	Clay vs. Liston	200
05/25/65	Ali vs. Liston	100
11/22/65	Ali vs. Patterson	75
03/04/68	Frazier vs. Mathis	35
11/28/70	Frazier vs. Foster	50
03/08/71	Frazier vs. Ali	75
09/20/72	Ali vs. Patterson	65
11/21/72	Ali vs. Foster	50
01/22/73	Foreman vs. Frazier	65
03/31/73	Norton vs. Ali	60
09/01/73	Foreman vs. Roman	40
09/10/73	Ali vs. Norton	50
01/28/74	Ali vs. Frazier	65
03/26/74	Foreman vs. Norton	50
10/30/74	Ali vs. Foreman	45

Feb. 25, 1964 Program

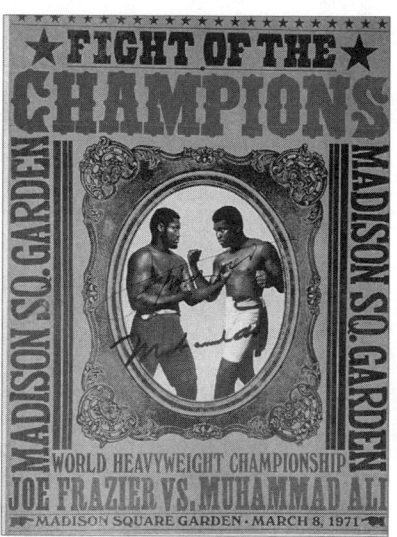

March 8, 1971 Program

10/01/75	Ali vs. Frazier	50
09/15/76	Foreman vs. Frazier	40
09/28/76	Ali vs. Norton	35
09/29/77	Ali vs. Shavers	45
02/15/78	Spinks vs. Ali	45
06/09/78	Holmes vs. Norton	20
09/15/78	Ali vs.L.Spinks	40
10/02/80	Holmes vs. Ali	30
06/12/81	L. Holmes vs. L. Spinks	15
06/11/82	Holmes vs. Cooney	35
05/20/83	Holmes vs. Witherspoon	25
09/21/85	M. Spinks vs. Holmes	15
04/19/86	M. Spinks vs. Holmes	10
11/22/86	Tyson vs. Berbick	45
03/07/87	Tyson vs. Bonecrusher Smith	30
05/30/87	Tyson vs. Thomas	25
05/30/87	Tucker vs. Douglas	25
08/01/87	Tyson vs. Tucker	30
10/16/87	Tyson vs. Biggs	20
01/22/88	Tyson vs. Holmes	25
03/20/88	Tyson vs. Tubbs	25
06/27/88	Tyson vs. Spinks	25
02/25/89	Tyson vs. Bruno	40

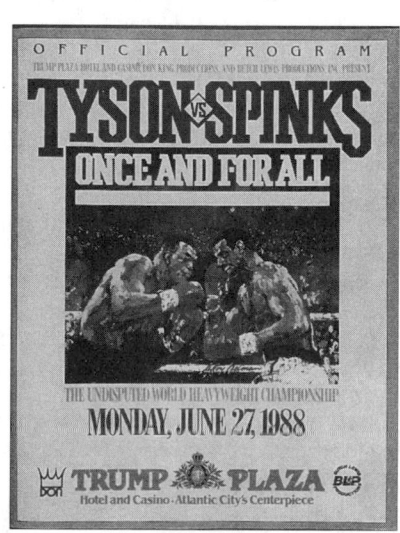

June 27, 1988 Program

June 7, 1993 Program

07/21/89	Tyson vs. C. Williams	15
01/15/90	Forman vs. Cooney	20
02/10/90	Douglas vs. Tyson	25
10/25/90	Holyfield vs. Douglas	20
03/18/91	Tyson vs. Ruddock	20
04/19/91	Holyfield vs. Foreman	15
06/28/91	Tyson vs. Ruddock	15
10/18/91	Mercer vs. Morrison	8
11/23/91	Holyfield vs. Cooper	8
02/07/92	Holmes vs. Mercer	8
05/15/92	Moorer vs. Cooper	8
06/19/92	Holyfield vs. Holmes	8
07/18/92	Bowe vs. Coetzer	10
07/28/92	Dokes vs. Ferguson	8
10/31/92	Lewis vs. Ruddock	10
11/13/92	Bowe vs. Holyfield	10
06/07/93	Morrison vs. Foreman	12
04/22/94	Holyfield vs. Moorer	10
09/24/94	L. Lewis vs. McCall	8
11/05/94	Foreman vs. Moorer	10
11//09/96	Tyson vs. Holyfield	15
06/28/97	Holyfield vs. Tyson	20
03/14/99	Holyfield vs. L. Lewis	12

April 22, 1994 Program

June 22, 1938 poster

Boxing Posters

Much of boxing's rich history is preserved on vintage boxing posters. For many, these posters are the only visual link to the past, as many early fights were not recorded on film. Understandably, collecting fight, and also film, posters has become extremely popular. Pre-1940s fight posters are desirable to collectors, but are scarce on the market. Additionally, these vintage posters in top condition usually command a significant price. The high cost and limited availability of vintage posters force most boxing collectors to begin their collection with posters issued during the 1940s and 1950s.

Selected Heavyweight Bouts

Date	Opponents	Value
07/04/19	J. Dempsey vs. J. Willard	$750
09/06/20	J. Dempsey vs. B. Miske	600
12/14/20	J. Dempsey vs. B. Brennan	750
07/02/21	J. Dempsey vs. G. Carpentier	600
07/04/23	J. Dempsey vs. T. Gibbons	500
09/14/23	J. Dempsey vs. L. Firpo	500
09/23/26	G. Tunney vs. J. Dempsey	750
07/21/27	J. Dempsey vs. J. Sharkey	500
09/22/27	G. Tunney vs. J. Dempsey	700
07/26/28	G. Tunney vs. T. Heeney	350
06/12/30	M. Schmeling vs. J. Sharley	450
07/03/31	M. Schmeling vs. Y. Stribling	250
06/21/32	J. Sharkey vs. M. Schmeling	250
09/26/32	M. Schmeling vs. Walker	325
06/25/35	J. Louis vs. P. Carnera	400
09/24/35	J. Louis vs. M. Baer	350
06/19/36	M. Schmeling vs. J. Louis	325
08/18/36	J. Louis vs. J. Sharkey	300
06/22/37	J. Louis vs. J. Braddock	450
06/22/38	J. Louis vs. M. Schmeling	325
07/13/39	B. Conn vs. J. Bettina	200

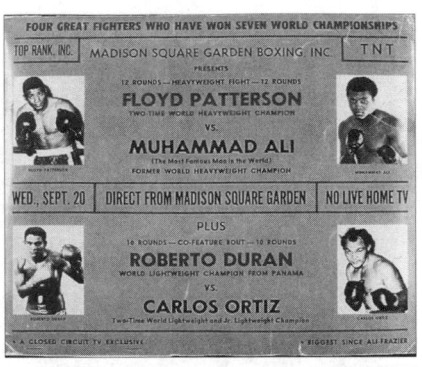

September 20, 1972 poster

Date	Opponents	Value
09/25/39	B. Conn vs. J. Bettina	150
11/17/39	B. Conn vs. G. Lesnevich	150
06/05/40	B. Conn vs. G. Lesnevich	150
05/23/41	J. Louis vs. B. Baer	350
06/18/41	J. Louis vs. B. Conn	250
01/09/42	J. Louis vs. B. Baer	150
06/19/46	J. Louis vs. B. Conn	100
12/05/47	J. Louis vs. J. Walcott	165
06/25/48	J. Louis vs. J. Walcott	150
06/22/49	E. Charles vs. J. Walcott	75
09/27/50	E. Charles vs. J. Louis	100
03/07/51	E. Charles vs. J. Walcott	75
07/18/51	J. Walcott vs. E. Charles	75
10/26/51	R. Marciano vs. J. Louis	250
06/05/52	J. Walcott vs. E. Charles	75
09/23/52	R. Marciano vs. J. Walcott	225
05/15/53	R. Marciano vs. J. Walcott	150
06/17/54	R. Marciano vs. E. Charles	150
09/17/54	R. Marciano vs. E. Charles	150
05/16/55	R. Marciano vs. D. Cockell	150
09/21/55	R. Marciano vs. A. Moore	150
11/30/56	F. Patterson vs. A. Moore	150
06/26/59	I. Johansson vs. F. Patterson	100
06/20/60	F. Patterson vs. I. Johansson	75
03/13/61	F. Patterson vs. I. Johansson	75
09/25/62	S. Liston vs. F. Patterson	85
11/15/62	C. Clay vs. A. Moore	475
07/22/63	S. Liston vs. F. Patterson	125
02/25/64	C. Clay vs. S. Liston	250
05/25/65	M. Ali vs. S. Liston	125
11/22/65	M. Ali vs. F. Patterson	110
04/04/68	J. Frazier vs. B. Mathis	45
11/28/70	J. Frazier vs. B. Foster	50
03/08/71	J. Frazier vs. M. Ali	100
09/20/72	M. Ali vs. F. Patterson	90
11/21/72	M. Ali vs. B. Foster	70
01/22/73	G. Foreman vs. J. Frazier	65
03/31/73	K. Norton vs. M. Ali	90
09/01/73	G. Foreman vs. J. Roman	40
09/10/73	M. Ali vs. K. Norton	75
01/28/74	M. Ali vs. J. Frazier	95
03/26/74	G. Foreman vs. K. Norton	50
10/30/74	M. Ali vs. G. Foreman	95
09/30/75	M. Ali vs. J. Frazier	100
06/15/76	G. Foreman vs. J. Frazier	50
09/28/76	M. Ali vs. K. Norton	75
09/29/77	M. Ali vs. E. Shavers	70
02/15/78	L. Spinks vs. M. Ali	75
06/09/78	L. Holmes vs. K. Norton	40
09/15/78	M. Ali vs. L. Spinks	70
10/02/80	L. Holmes vs. M. Ali	60

Date	Opponents	Value
06/12/81	L. Holmes vs. L. Spinks	35
06/11/82	L. Holmes vs. G. Cooney	35
05/20/83	L. Holmes vs. T. Witherspoon	40
09/21/85	M. Spinks vs. L. Holmes	35
04/19/86	M. Spinks vs. L. Holmes	30
11/22/86	M. Tyson vs. T. Berbick	85
03/07/87	M. Tyson vs. Bonecrusher Smith	50
05/30/87	M. Tyson vs. Pinklon Thomas	50
05/30/87	T. Tucker vs. B. Douglas	30
08/01/87	M. Tyson vs. T. Tucker	50
10/16/87	M. Tyson vs. T. Biggs	40
01/22/88	M. Tyson vs. L. Holmes	50
03/20/88	M. Tyson vs. T. Tubbs	45
06/27/88	M. Tyson vs. M. Spinks	50
02/25/89	M. Tyson vs. F. Bruno	40
07/21/89	M. Tyson vs. C. Williams	40
02/10/90	B. Douglas vs. M. Tyson	75
10/25/90	E. Holyfield vs. B. Douglas	35
03/18/91	M. Tyson vs. R. Ruddock	35
04/19/91	E. Holyfield vs. G. Foreman	35
06/28/91	M. Tyson vs. R. Ruddock	30
10/18/91	R. Mercer vs. T. Morrison	20
11/23/91	E. Holyfield vs. B. Cooper	25
02/07/92	L. Holmes vs. R. Mercer	20
05/15/92	M. Moorer vs. B. Cooper	15
06/19/92	E. Holyfield vs. L. Holmes	30
07/18/92	R. Bowe vs. P. Coetzer	30
01/31/92	L. Lewis vs. R. Ruddock	25
10/31/92	L. Lewis vs. R. Ruddock	10
11/13/92	R. Bowe vs. E. Holyfield	30
02/06/93	R. Bowe vs. M. Dokes	15
06/07/93	T. Morrison vs. G. Foreman	15
11/05/94	G. Foreman vs. M. Moorer	12
11/09/96	M. Tyson vs. E. Holyfield	15
06/28/97	E. Holyfield vs. M. Tyson	15
03/14/99	E Holyfield and L. Lewis (draw)	15

This special poster, entitled, "Champions Forever," pictures Ken Norton, George Foreman, Larry Holmes, Joe Frazier and Muhammad Ali. It goes for about $350-$400 when signed by all fighters.

Boxing Tickets

Boxing is one of the most ancient of all sports. Formal matches have been traced to the Twenty-third Olympiad held near Athens in 688 B.C. As it grew in popularity, admission requirements to major events became necessary. When and where these requirements first included a ticket, or a remuneration to associated individuals, in any shape or form, is not known. There is not an overabundance of boxing tickets available to collectors for fights held prior to 1900.

A popular starting point for many serious collectors of boxing tickets has been the James J. Corbett versus John L. Sullivan Heavyweight Championship fight of Sept. 7, 1892. It was one of boxing's great bouts. The 10,000 fans who witnessed the fight paid $15 for a ticket. Upon entering the arena, the ticket was punched, leaving three small holes on a now "used" ticket. In spite of his loss, Sullivan was arguably the most beloved sporting figure of the 19th century. Many of those who attended the fight honorably adhered their used ticket into a scrapbook or set it aside for safekeeping. The popularity of the fighters, the admission fee—considered exorbitant at the time—and the importance of the event contributed significantly to the survival of some fine examples of this ticket. Collectors have also found an aesthetic appeal to

Ticket stub from the May 18, 1900 McCoy/Creedon bout.

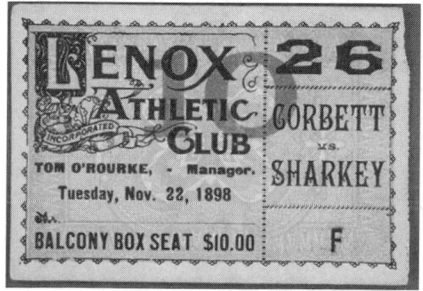

Stub from the November 22, 1898 Corbett/Sharkey bout.

Ticket from May 4, 1900 Smith/Walcott bout.

the ticket's design—exemplary artwork from this era. Purchasing an excellent example of this ticket today can cost collectors around $2,000.

Ticket Forms And Types

Boxing tickets are typically found in three forms: full boxing ticket, boxing ticket without stub and ticket stub. Full boxing tickets are preferred by collectors because they are usually unaltered. A ticket in this state is assumed to be unused. Since most individuals who purchase admission tickets generally attend the fight, altered boxing tickets are the most common form found by collectors.

Altered tickets are commonly differentiated from unused by the lack of a ticket portion, such as a stub. The stub, which is usually smaller than the main portion of the ticket, normally detaches at the perforation or perforation line. Boxing ticket stubs often have little aesthetic appeal and in many cases even fail to include the fighters' names. It is the main portion of the ticket that fascinates collectors most. This section usually has an attractive design, the fighters' names or perhaps a photograph, and venue information.

Illustrated tickets, or tickets that include photos of the fighters, have greater aesthetic appeal, but not necessarily more value. Placing photographic images of the

fighters on tickets, usually just a portrait, became popular during the end of the first decade of the 1900s. Some early examples of this technique include the Johnson versus Jeffries heavyweight championship ticket (1910) and the Jim Flynn versus Jack Johnson world championship ticket (1912).

Older tickets were often "hole punched" during admittance into the arena. This practice remained common into the 1930s, despite the inclusion of a stub into the ticket's design. Improved perforation equipment eventually made it easier for ticket takers to remove the stubs rather than punch the tickets. Punch size, design and placement can vary. For example, tickets used for the Johnny Dundee versus Benny Leonard fight were punched with a star shape. Tickets used for the Patterson versus Harris fight (8/18/58) had a stub removed and were punched with a variety of shapes (round and "E").

*Prices listed are for full tickets unless noted.

Selected Boxing Tickets
1884
Kilrain vs. Cleary Ticket Stub, VG $700
1890
Corbett vs. McCaffrey, EX $5,500
1892
Sullivan vs. Corbett VG $1,875
Dixon vs. Skelly, 9/6, rare, VG $1,000

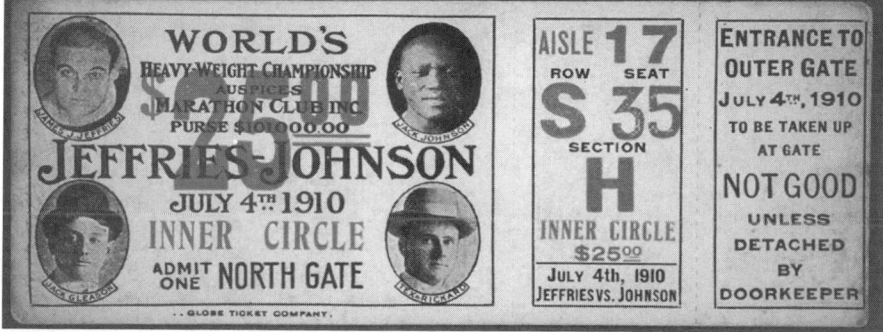

Ticket from July 4, 1910 Jim Jeffries/Jack Johnson bout.

1897

Mysterious Billy Smith, from Tuxedo Athletic
Club $550

Sullivan vs. Kaigh, VG $625

1902

Corbett vs. McGovern, Fair $450

Erne vs. Gans Ticket Stub, G, minor creases
. . . .$400

Ryan vs. Carter, EX $950

1904

Britt vs. Corbett Ticket Stub, minor creases, G
. . . .$400

Ryan vs. O'Brien, EX $975

Ryan vs. Root EX $975

1907

Gans vs. Britt II Ticket Stub, VG $375

1909

Nelson vs. Hyland, EX $680

Johnson vs. O'Brien, Ticket Stub, (Fighters'
names do not appear.), G $125

Attell vs. Weeks, Ticket Stub, VG $295

1910

Jeffries vs. Johnson, EX $950

Nelson vs. Moran, Ticket Stub, EX $400

1912

Flynn vs. Johnson, rare, EX $950

1913

Burns vs. McCarthy, rare, EX $1,150

Ritchie vs. Rivers, rare, EX $750

1919

Leonard vs. Dundee, EX $180

Leonard vs. White, EX $180

Willard vs. Dempsey, NM $325

Unused, set of 5, printer's proofs $450

1921

Dempsey vs. Carpentier, Ticket without stub, EX
. . . .$100

1922

Leonard vs. White, NM $125

1923

Criqui vs. Dundee, EX $150

NM $175

Dempsey vs. Firpo Ticket Stub, G, ...$175

(Fighters not named). $60

Dempsey vs. Gibbons, EX $175

Kilbane vs. Criqui, EX $140

Wilde vs. Villa, NM $150

1924

Carpentier vs. Gibbons, NM $175

Firpo vs. Wills Stub, EX $60

1925

McTigue vs. Berlenbach, G $125

Berlenbach vs. Delaney II, VG, postponed until
Dec. $140

Walker vs. Shade, NM $250

1926

Carpentier vs. Loughran, Ticket without stub,
NM $125

Flowers vs. Walker, Ticket without stub, VG
. . . .$115

1927

Sharkey vs. Maloney, NM $225

Dempsey vs. Sharkey, Ticket Stub, G $55

Dempsey vs. Tunney, EX $200

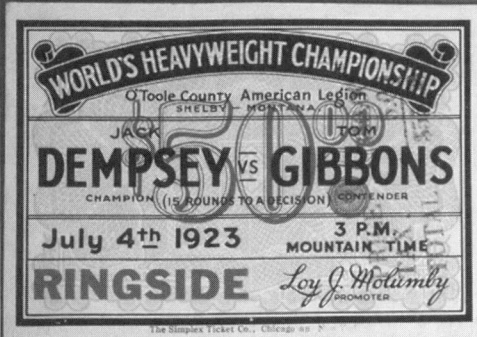

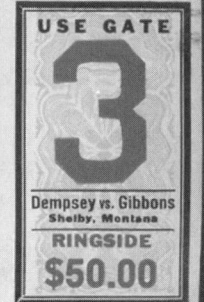

Ticket from July 4, 1923 Jack Dempsey/Tom Gibbons bout.

1929

Fields vs. Dundee, VG $125

Loughran vs. Braddock, NM $265

Schmeling vs. Uzcudo, (Paolino on ticket -
boxer's first name), EX $185

Sharkey vs. Loughran I, NM $230

Singer vs. Chocolate, NM $150

EX, punched $125

1930

Carnera vs. Christner, EX $195

Carnera vs. Godfrey, Ticket (with detached stub),
EX $190

Chocolate vs. Berg, EX $135

Mandell vs. Singer, EX $110

Sharkey vs. Campolo, NM $210

Singer vs. McLarnin, NM $95

1931

Canzoneri vs. Berg, EX $200

VG $175

Jack Dempsey . . . ."All Star Fight Card," 11/18,
. . . . .NM
$115

Schmeling vs. Stribling, VG $185

1932

Canzoneri vs. Petrolle, G $110

Dempsey vs. Wine Ticket Stub, EX $120

Schaaf vs. Gross, NM $100

McLarnin vs. Brouillard Boxing Ticket, EX
. . . .$60

1933

Corbett vs. McLarnin, NM $115

1934

Baer vs. Carnera Ticket Stub, (Fighters are not
named), EX $55

Ticket without stub, EX $90

Rodak vs. Chocolate, NM, postponed $85

Rosenbloom vs. Knight, NM $95

1935

Baer vs. Willis, Exhibition, EX $155

Baer vs. Braddock Ticket Stub, VG $80

Canzoneri vs. Klick, EX $150

NM $175

Jack Dempsey "Boxing Show," 6/17, NM
. . . .$95

Louis vs. Baer, EX $375

Louis vs. Levinsky, EX $325

Louis vs. Ramage, EX $150

1936

Louis vs. Sharkey, NM $300

Schmeling vs. Joe Louis I Ticket Stub, (Fighters
are not named.), EX $55

EX, printer's proofs $365

1937

Baer vs. Farr Ticket Stub, NM $75

Baer vs. Foord Ticket Stub, VG $60

Carnival of Champions Ambers/Montanez,
Ross/Garcia, NM $135

Louis vs. Farr, NM $290

Steele vs. Overlin, EX $70

Steele vs. Williams, NM $115

Braddock vs. Louis, EX $300

Ticket Stub $65

Galento vs. Nova, VG $100

1938

Ambers vs. Armstrong, EX $135

Farr vs. Nova, M $110

Galento vs. Lewis, 7/13, EX $130

Galento vs. Thomas, VG $145

1939

Ambers vs. Arizmendi, NM $100

Apostoli vs. Conn, NM $135

Archibald vs. Jeffra, NM $120

Archibald vs. Rodak, NM $120

Ticket from June 19, 1946 Joe Louis/Billy Conn bout.

Armstrong vs. Fontaine, NM $165

Baer vs. Nova "Dressing Room Pass," NM

. . . .$100

Conn vs. Lesnevich, NM $135

Escobar vs. Morgan, NM $110

Galento vs. Bresica, NM $80

Louis vs. Lewis, VG $245

Mann vs. Knox, NM $75

1940

Ambers vs. Jenkins, EX $140

VG $100

Archibald vs. Jeffra, NM $115

Armstrong vs. Montanez, NM $145

Armstrong vs. Zivic, NM, 10/4, Sugar Ray

Robinson Pro Debut $155

Angott vs. Day, NM $60

Conn vs. Pastor, "Working Press," EX $145

NM $150

Conn vs. Savoid, EX $150

Hostak vs. Zale, NM $140

Garcia vs. Armstrong, EX $110

Garcia vs. Belloise, VG $60

Jenkins vs. Armstrong, "Club Official," NM .

. . . .$140

Jenkins vs. Lello, EX $95

Louis vs. Godoy, EX, printer's proofs $250

Mann vs. Baer, EX $100

1941

Baer vs. Louis, EX, printer's proofs $120

Jenkins vs. Tribuani, NM $110

Jenkins vs. Cochrane, EX $115

Louis vs. Conn I, NM $275

Louis vs. Nova, NM $250

Soose vs. Vigh, EX $85

Zivic vs. Davis, NM, proofs $90

1942

Angott vs. Montgomery, EX $115

Louis vs. Conn, NM, postponed, 10/12 . .$125

Overlin vs. Apostoli, NM $110

Salica vs. Ortiz Boxing Ticket, NM $80

1943

Pep vs. Angott, "Working Press," EX $135

1944

Armstrong vs. Davis, NM $130

Montgomery vs. Jack, EX $115

1946

Louis vs. Conn II, NM $265

Louis vs. Mauriello, NM $190

Robinson vs. Sebastian, EX $175

Servo vs. Robinson, NM, fight postponed .$240

1947

Graziano vs. Zale, Ticket without stub, EX

. . . .$105

1948

Graziano vs. Zale, NM $210

Louis vs. Foxworth, Ticket Stub, EX $85

Williams vs. Flores, Robinson/Gavilan, G

. . . .$125

1949

Charles vs. Valentino, Ticket without stub, NM

. . . .$85

Charles vs. Walcott "Official Pass," VG

. . . .$60

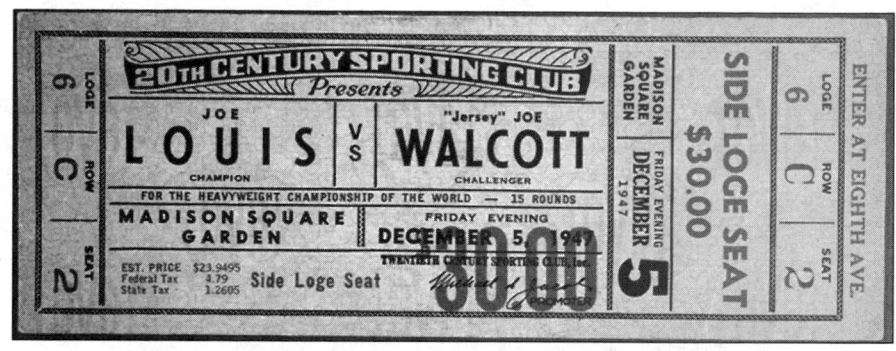

Ticket from December 5, 1947 Joe Louis/Jersey Joe Walcott bout.

LaMotta vs. Cerdan, "Photographer," NM .

. . . .$160

Graziano vs. Fusari, NM $130

"Dressing Room Pass" $55

1950

Graziano vs. Curcio, NM $150

LaMotta vs. Mitri, NM $135

Louis vs. Charles, NM $240

Pep vs. Famechon, EX $105

Pep vs. Saddler, NM $150

1951

Charles vs. Maxim, scarce, EX $210

Louis vs. Marciano, postponed for two weeks,

11/11, MT $275

Pep vs. Saddler, NM $120

Turpin vs. Robinson, EX $135

1952

Gavilan vs. Dykes, NM $120

Graziano vs. Davey, Ticket without stub, EX

. . . .$85

Marciano vs. Mathews, NM $260

Maxim vs. Moore, NM $100

Robinson vs. Maxim $130

EX, printer's proof $150

Walcott vs. Charles, "Dressing Room Pass," EX

. . . .$135

Walcott vs. Marciano "Dressing Room Pass,"

NM $150

EX $295

Ticket Stub, EX $45

1953

Gavilan vs. Bratton. Ticket without stub, NM

. . . .$60

Gavilan vs. Davey, Ticket without stub, EX .

. . . .$70

Marciano vs. Lastarza, NM $100

Marciano vs. Walcott II, NM $90

1956

Basilio vs. Saxton, 3/14 . . . .$110

Charles vs. Richardson, Ticket without stub, NM

. . . .$60

Saxton vs. Basillo, NM, 9/12 . . . .$125

1957

Gavilan vs. Martinez, NM $110

1958

Max Baer Television Show Full Ticket, NM .$40

Robinson vs. Basilio Full Closed-Circuit Ticket,

NM $65

EX $185

Napoles vs. Cobblah, G $35

1959

Aikins vs. Jordan, NM $60

Basilio vs. Fullmer, Ticket VG $70

Patterson vs. London, NM $185

1960

Tournament of Champions Press Pass, Golden

Gloves, Cassius Clay, 3/2 . . . .$260

U.S. Olympic Amateur Finals, 5/8 Cassius Clay,

small size (1.25"x4"), EX $400

Fullmer vs. Robinson Boxing Ticket without

stub, M $100

Paret vs. Thompson, NM $135

Johansson vs. Patterson II Ticket Stub, EX*

. . . .$65

1961

Liston vs. Westphal, NM $185

Patterson vs. McNeeley, NM, postponed three

weeks $120

Pender vs. Downes $95

1962

Clay vs. Lavorante Ticket Stub, EX $220

VG $400

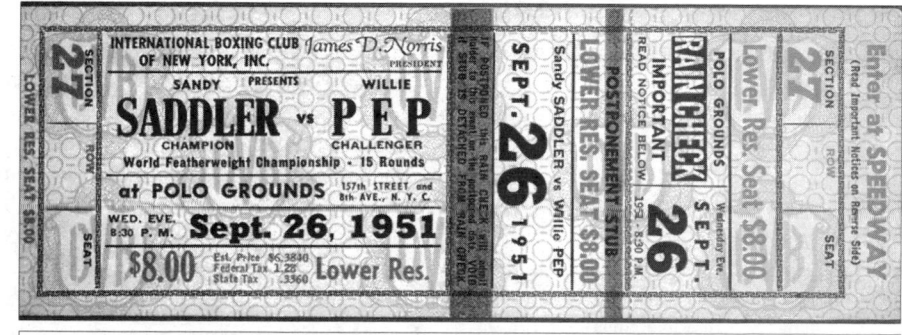

Ticket from September 26, 1951 Sandy Saddler/Willie Pep bout.

Gavilan vs. Dykes, NM $95
Patterson vs. Liston I, G $125

1963

Clay vs. Cooper, Ticket without stub, NM
. . . .$310
Liston vs. Patterson, M $120
4/4, postponed $50
Liston vs. Patterson II, EX $195

1964

Joe Frazier vs. Buster Mathis, Sr.,
Griffith/Benvenuti, EX $90
Griffith vs. Charnley, Ticket without stub, EX
. . . .$35
Griffith vs. Rodriguez, NM $60
"Dressing Room Pass," EX $25
Liston vs. Clay . . ."Interview Room" Pass, 2/25,
NM $235
Full Ticket, 11/16 "Dressing Room," post-
poned, NM $235
Full Ticket, 11/16 "Weigh-in," postponed, NM
. . . .$235
Patterson vs. Powell, NM $170

1965

Clay vs.Patterson Interview Area Pass, scarce,
NM $205
Perkins vs. Hernandez, Ticket, EX $35

1966

Ali vs. Cooper II Boxing Ticket without stub,
NM $110
NM $220
Weigh-in, EX $120
Ali vs. Terrell, NM, fight postponed $100
Ali vs. C. Williams .Boxing Ticket without stub,
EX $105
"Working Press Pass," NM $160
"Dressing Room Pass," VG $115
Burruni vs. McGowan . . .Boxing Ticket without
stub, G $35
Giardello vs. White, NM $100
Griffith vs. Archer, NM $110
Tiger vs. Griffith, EX, "Press" $60
Torres vs. Thornton, "Employee," EX $70

1967

Ali vs. Terrell Boxing Ticket without stub, EX
. . . .$115
"Pre-fight Pass," EX $145
"Clubhouse Pass," NM $145
"Working Press Pass," EX $145
Benvenuti vs. Griffith II, VG $120
Patterson vs. Johnson, EX $40
Quarry vs. Patterson, NM $155

1969

Castillo vs. Jangalay Ticket without stub, VG
. . . .$25
Ellis vs. Cooper, NM, postponed $130
Napoles vs. Cokes Ticket without stub, G . .$30
Olivares vs. Castillio I, Ticket, EX $35

1970

Louis vs. Charles, NM $275

1971

Ali vs. Ellis Closed-Circuit Ticket, NM $20
Ali vs. Mathis, Sr. Closed-Circuit Ticket, EX
. . . .$35

Ali vs. Shavers, NM $160
EX $125
Backus vs. Napoles Ticket without stub, VG
. . . .$60
Frazier vs. Ali I, Closed-Circuit Ticket $25

1972

Foster vs. Finnegan, Ticket without stub, EX
. . . .$40
Foster vs. Rondon, NM $105
Monzon vs. Briscoe, EX $125

1973

Ali vs. Norton, "Dressing Room" $125
Otero vs. Buchanan, NM $50
Ali Exhibition, 10/24, NM $365

1974

Quarry vs. Frazier, NM $145

1975

Ali vs. Wepner Circuit Boxing Ticket, EX .$105
"Press," NM $185
Ali vs. Lyle, EX $520
Ali vs. Frazier NM $120
Frazier vs. Ellis . . . .Boxing Ticket without stub,
NM $100

1976

Boxing Writers Assoc., EX $15
Foreman vs. Frazier II, Full Closed-Circuit
Ticket, NM $25

1977

Ali vs. Evangelista, Ticket without stub, NM
. . . .$310
"Dressing Room" $160
"Working Press" $160
Ali vs. Shavers, EX $105
NM $150

1978

L. Spinks vs. Ali, NM $550
"Press Ringside," Full Boxing Pass, autographed
by Ali $475
Galindez vs. Lopez, NM $105
Holmes vs. Shaver, NM $150
Holmes Exhibition, NM $110

1979

Ali vs. Alzado, EX $350
Holmes vs. Weaver, NM $215
Benitez vs. Leonard Boxing Ticket without stub,
EX $35
Leonard vs. Marcotte, (Marcotte not named),
NM $100
Lopez vs. Ayala, NM $50

1980

Antuofermo vs. Minter Partial Ticket, VG . .$40
Leonard vs. Duran, Ticket Stub VG $150
Tate vs. Weaver, NM $120
Hearns vs. Cuevas Ticket without stub, NM
. . . .$70
Holmes vs. Ali, NM $125
Watt vs. O'Grady, NM $45

1981

Chandler vs. Lujan, NM $15
Cooney vs. Norton, EX $60
Duran vs. Minchillo, NM $100

Hearns vs. Shields "Official's Pass," NM . . .$20
Holmes vs. Berbick, NM $100
Holyfield vs. Edleon, NM $100

1982

Holmes vs. Cooney, "Complimentary, no refund,"
NM $60
Mancini vs. Kim, NM $125
Benitez vs. Duran, NM $110
Witherspoon vs. Snipes, NM $50

1983

Hagler vs. Duran Boxing Ticket without stub,
NM $45
Hagler vs. Scypion, EX $130
Hagler vs. Mamby, EX $32
Holmes vs. M. Frazier, NM $200

1984

Witherspoon vs. Thomas, EX $100
Hearns vs. Duran, NM $90
Ticket without stub, NM $40

1985

Hagler vs. Hearns, NM $110
Holmes vs. Bey, NM $100

1986

Berbick vs. Tyson Full Ticket Stub, NM . . .$200
Hagler vs. Mugabi Hearns/Shuler , NM . . .$125
Full Closed-Circuit Ticket, NM $35
M. Spinks vs. Holmes II, VG $65

1987

Hagler vs. Leonard, NM $135
Hearns vs. Andries"Ref's Pass," NM $60
Hearns vs. Roldan, NM $60
Holyfield vs. Ocasio, NM $65
Tyson vs. Biggs, NM $120

1988

Hearns vs. Barkley, NM $75
Foreman vs. Qwai, NM $90
Holyfield vs. DeLeon, NM $90
Leonard vs. LaLonde, NM $90
Tyson vs. Michael Spinks, NM $145
"Press Pass," coated, NM $40
Full Closed-Circuit Ticket, NM $15
Tyson vs. Holmes, NM $140

1989

Chavez vs. Fuentes, NM $60
Dokes vs. Holyfield, NM $100
B. Mitchell vs. I. Mitchell, NM $25

1990

Foreman vs. Cooney, NM $110
Douglas vs. Holyfield, NM $115

1991

Brown vs. McGrits, NM $45
Holmes vs. Anderson, NM $45
Tyson vs. Ruddock, NM $200
Tyson vs. Ruddock II, NM $135

1992

Bowe vs. Coetzer, NM $65
Czyz vs. Lalonde, NM $35
Holyfield vs. Bowe, NM $75

●●●

Figure Skating

Figure skating traces its roots practically back to the origins of human beings. To cross frozen lakes and streams, early humans tied animal bones to their feet and glided through the winter months. Eventually, iron and steel blades replaced the bones and a rough means of travel was transformed into recreation. Skating remained popular among all social classes, but as a competitive sport, only the extremely well-to-do could afford to participate.

Since 1908, figure skating championships have taken place within the scope of Olympic Games. In those days, there were no independent Winter Olympic Games. In the early 1920s, the IOC (International Olympic Committee) permitted future organizers of Olympic Games to hold a week of winter sports. Such a week was held within the scope of the VIII Olympic Games (took place in Paris) 1924 in Chamonix/FRA for the first time. As a result of the success of the first "International Week of Winter Sports," the IOC decided in 1925 to hold independent Winter Olympic Games in the future. In 1926, the week of winter sports of 1924 was belatedly recognized as the first Winter Olympic Games.

Dance became a Olympic competition in 1976.

While there is certainly a substantial viewers market for figure skating, such is not the case for related memorabilia. The only exception is autographs of those key contributors to the sport. Granted, an occasional event-used costume or pair of skates

*March 2, 1992 issue of **Sports Illustrated** picturing Kristi Yamaguchi*

Poster picturing Tara Lipinski

may appear in the market but seldom does it create overwhelming interest.

Collecting options in this area include autographs, event advertising, event ticket stubs, event related merchandising, programs and related Olympic items. The most popular area of figure skating collecting is autographs.

Autographs

Tenley Albright
Cut signature $10
8 x 10 photo $20

Scott Allen
Cut signature $5
8 x 10 photo $15

Oksana Baiul
Cut signature $5
8 x 10 photo $12

Denise Biellmann
Cut signature $7
8 x 10 photo $14

Nicole Bobek
Cut signature $5
8 x 10 photo $10

Brian Boitano
Cut signature $10
8 x 10 photo $20

Christopher Bowman
Cut signature $7
8 x 10 photo $15

Kurt Browning
Cut signature $10
8 x 10 photo $20

Petra Burka
Cut signature $6
8 x 10 photo $12

Gundi Busch
Cut signature $10
8 x 10 photo $20

Richard Button
Cut signature $5
8 x 10 photo $15

Maria Butyrskaya
Cut signature $5
8 x 10 photo $10

Alain Calmat
Cut signature $7
8 x 10 photo $14

Tiffany Chin
Cut signature $5
8 x 10 photo $10

Robin Cousins
Cut signature $5
8 x 10 photo $10

John Curry
Cut signature $6
8 x 10 photo $12

Emmerich Danzer
Cut signature $10
8 x 10 photo $20

Scott Davis
Cut signature $5
8 x 10 photo $10

Dianne de Leeuw
Cut signature $5
8 x 10 photo $10

Sjoukje Dijkstra
Cut signature $10
8 x 10 photo $20

Jacqueline du Bief
Cut signature $10
8 x 10 photo $25

Todd Eldredge
Cut signature $5
8 x 10 photo $10

Christine Errath
Cut signature $6
8 x 10 photo $12

Aleksandr Fadeev
Cut signature $7
8 x 10 photo $15

Peggy Fleming
Cut signature $10
8 x 10 photo $20

Linda Fratianne
Cut signature $6
8 x 10 photo $12

Rudy Galindo
Cut signature $5
8 x 10 photo $10

8 x 10 Photo of Peggy Fleming

Dorothy Hamill
Cut signature $10
8 x 10 photo $20

Scott Hamilton
Cut signature $10
8 x 10 photo $20

Lorraine Hanlon
Cut signature $6
8 x 10 photo $12

Tonya Harding
Cut signature $2
8 x 10 photo $5

Carol Heiss
Cut signature $10
8 x 10 photo $20

Sonja Henie
Cut signature $35
8 x 10 photo $65

Jan Hoffman
Cut signature $6
8 x 10 photo $12

Monty Hoyt
Cut signature $5
8 x 10 photo $10

Don Jackson
Cut signature $6
8 x 10 photo $12

Dave Jenkins
Cut signature $7
8 x 10 photo $15

Hayes Jenkins
Cut signature $8
8 x 10 photo $16

Nancy Kerrigan
Cut signature $5
8 x 10 photo $15

Vladimir Kovalev
Cut signature $6
8 x 10 photo $13

Terry Kubicka
Cut signature $6
8 x 10 photo $12

Michelle Kwan
Cut signature $5
8 x 10 photo $12

Tara Lapinski
Cut signature $6
8 x 10 photo $15

Tommy Litz
Cut signature $6
8 x 10 photo $14

Bradley Lord
Cut signature $6
8 x 10 photo $15

Chen Lu
Cut signature $7
8 x 10 photo $14

Janet Lynn
Cut signature $5
8 x 10 photo $15

Karen Magnussen
Cut signature $5
8 x 10 photo $10

Gordon McKellen, Jr.
Cut signature $6
8 x 10 photo $15

Don McPherson
Cut signature $6
8 x 10 photo $12

Midori Ito
Cut signature $6
8 x 10 photo $12

Ondrej Nepela
Cut signature $8
8 x 10 photo $18

Brian Orser
Cut signature $5
8 x 10 photo $10

Laurence Owen
Cut signature $6
8 x 10 photo $15

John Misha Petkevich
Cut signature $6
8 x 10 photo $12

Anett Potzsch
Cut signature $7
8 x 10 photo $14

Barbara Roles Pursley
Cut signature $6
8 x 10 photo $12

Manfred Schnelldorfer
Cut signature $7
8 x 10 photo $14

Beatrix Schuba
Cut signature $6
8 x 10 photo $15

Gabriele Seyfert
Cut signature $6
8 x 10 photo $15

Ken Shelly
Cut signature $6
8 x 10 photo $12

Elvis Stojko
Cut signature $6
8 x 10 photo $15

Rosalynn Sumners
Cut signature $5
8 x 10 photo $12

Debbie Thomas
Cut signature $5
8 x 10 photo $15

Charles Tickner
Cut signature $7
8 x 10 photo $15

Jill Trenary
Cut signature $6
8 x 10 photo $12

Gary Visconti
Cut signature $7
8 x 10 photo $15

Sergi Volkov
Cut signature $6
8 x 10 photo $14

Michael Weiss
Cut signature $5
8 x 10 photo $10

Katarina Witt
Cut signature $7
8 x 10 photo $15

Tim Wood
Cut signature $7
8 x 10 photo $15

Alexi Yagudin
Cut signature $7
8 x 10 photo $15

Kristi Yamaguchi
Cut Signature $7
8 x 10 photo $15

Football Collectibles

Football memorabilia always seemed to be facing third and long when it came to collector interest, but in recent years the hobby has gone deep for gridiron goodies.

It's gone deep for trading cards, deep for autographs, deep for nearly everything associated with pro football. Gone are the days when football card sets looked like an afterthought by the card companies. Now it's a matter of which stunning new set most collectors will go wild for. And if you're talking about autographs, big-name players —from those enshrined in the Pro Football Hall of Fame in Canton, Ohio, to the current crop of exciting rookies—are huge draws at hobby shows.

It's fairly simple. The growth in popularity of football collectibles has paralleled the growth in popularity of the National Football League, particularly in the past three decades.

Knowing a little about the history of football collectibles will help you gain a greater appreciation of this remarkable turnaround for football collectibles. As with baseball, basketball and hockey, the heart and soul of football memorabilia is the trading card.

From Humble Beginnings to a Battle Royal

Young baby boomers in post-World War II America generally looked to Bowman for their football cards. Leaf in the late 1940s and Topps by the early 1950s also issued football card sets.

Prior to that period of national economic boom, very few trading cards—and even fewer sets—focusing on football players had been issued.

Topps bought out Bowman in the mid-'50s and continued to issue sets spotlighting the NFL until 1961-63, which also included players from the fledgling American Football League. Topps then issued sets from 1964-1967 that concentrated solely on the AFL. Since then, however, the veteran card company has issued a major football card set every year. (In the mid 1980s, Topps even issued a set of the United States Football League and did an XFL set in 2001.)

Resembling a pro wrestling free-for-all more than a duel between fierce foes in the NFL playoffs, a growing number of manufacturers joined the fray by the early 1990s. Action Packed, Collector's Edge, Fleer, Pacific, Pro Set, Score, SkyBox, Upper Deck, Wild Card and several other companies engaged Topps in a lively battle for the collector's loyalty. Still more companies introduced their sets throughout the 1990s. Competition was tough, and some of these names were eliminated from contention within a few years of their debuts.

The market has settled down of late. However, those companies still in the game continue to introduce all kinds of special sets (some of them plainly geared toward collectors with deeper pockets).

Happily, this is also an era of creativity behind today's football cards. While the traditional card stock variety still rules, companies have issued card sets printed on leather, metal and plastic. Special inserts have included cards packaged with swatches of jerseys, cards autographed by highly publicized rookies and even newly created cards depicting Pro Football Hall of Famers. Colors are more vibrant. Computer graphics offer exciting new ways to frame the player photo. It's a great time to be a collector.

Football cards continue to delight NFL fans worldwide with their innovations. So, even if the Super Bowl turns out to be a dud in any given year, the cards that celebrate that season's players will likely retain their sheen.

Do the Players Go in the Wrong Direction When the Field Vibrates?

There are football games that allow you to play football games.

Say what?

Let's put it another way: A popular collectible among football fans is the board game. More than 100 different games have been identified and catalogued, some more than 100 years old.

And if rolling the dice or turning over a card to determine the outcome of your last play from scrimmage doesn't excite you, how about plugging that cord into the wall outlet and watching 22 miniature football players move haphazardly across a metal playing field that vibrates (and hums) when you flip a switch? Those silly electric football games that parents gave to their kids at Christmas time are now a very collectible commodity.

The value of a football game (the toy kind) depends on several factors, including its scarcity, age and condition.

Many games fall into the affordable category of $10 and up; many more will run you several hundred dollars. (And a select few are in the "$1,000" category, but they spotlight collegiate rivalries such as Princeton-Yale or Harvard-Yale of the 1890s.)

1954 NFL Championship Program

There's just no stopping the genre. APBA, which for decades has been manufacturing a popular baseball simulation board game, released its National Football League Game and its Pro Bowl Edition in the fall of 2000.

And if it isn't a visual account of pro football that you seek, how about an oral account? Everything from the actual play-by-play highlights of specific games (the legendary 1958 Colts-Giants Championship Game is an obvious choice) to instructional records such as "Paul Warfield's How to Catch a Pass," released in 1972, can be found if you patiently search for them. Although new memorabilia in this category may well be unearthed over time, currently there is a relatively small number of NFL recordings on the market, and they run from $10 to about $100. That combination makes them an intriguing item to fans pursuing an unusual collectible.

Super Bowl programs and their next of kin, the NFL and AFL Championship Game

programs, are among the priciest individual collectibles on the market but they also happen to boast some of the most dynamic and memorable artwork in all of sports. You can find the more recent programs (any of the Super Bowl programs from the 1990s, for example) for about $15 apiece. But the further back you go, the more you'll have to pay for such programs as the 1971 Colts-Cowboys Super Bowl program ($300 and up) or the 1962 Oilers-Texans AFL Championship Game program (a cool $700).

Collectibles in the New Millennium: A Pigskin Preview

The current market for football collectibles is as wide open as a speedy receiver whose defender slipped to the turf 20 yards back.

That means there's so much to choose from that it's impossible to offer a comprehensive listing. So here is just a sampling of what you can look for in the next few years:

● New releases from the tandem of NFL Films and USA Home Entertainment, including Super Bowl XXXV, on home VHS-format video and probably an enhanced version (additional sound bites, interview clips, etc.) on the DVD format. Last year's three-tape home video titled Matchup of the Millennium (which magically created "dream games" between four legendary NFL dynasties in a mythic battle for the coveted title of "Team of the Ages") was an instant classic.

● Figurines of NFL players. Little kids enjoy playing with them, but these figurines —which continue to improve in the realism department—have had the biggest impact on the collectibles market. Serious collectors sometimes behave like gleeful children when they finally locate that elusive linebacker figurine.

● Autographs of players certain to make the Pro Football Hall of Fame in the very near future, including field captains Dan Marino and John Elway.

● Trading card sets that contain special inserts such as autographed rookie cards and cards packaged with swatches of game jerseys from high-profile players.

Newcomers to the world of football collectibles should keep in mind that their local hobby shop and respected periodicals such as the weekly *Sports Collectors Digest* will be their best sources for the latest news and opinions about cards and other football memorabilia.

You can spend a little or a lot. Either way, it's a fascinating, wholesome and fun hobby.

●●●

A football autographed by John Elway

Selected Football Cards
(1935-1989)

1935 NATIONAL CHICLE
Complete Set (36): $17500.00
Common Player (1-24): 110.00
Common Player (25-36): 375.00

1	Earl "Dutch" Clark	950.00
9	Knute Rockne	3000.00
34	Bronko Nagurski	6500.00
36	Bernie Masterson	1300.00

1948 BOWMAN
NM
Complete Set (108): 6000.00
Common Player: 20.00
SP Cards: .50.00

NM
1	Joe Tereshinski	150.00
3	John Lujack	320.00
6	Paul Briggs	100.00
7	Steve Van Buren	150.00
9	Nolan Luhn	100.00
12	Charlie Conerly	320.00
15	Gil Bouley	100.00
17	Charlie Trippi	100.00
18	Vince Banonis	100.00
21	Bill Chipley	100.00
22	Sammy Baugh	425.00
24	John Koniszewski	100.00
26	Bob Waterfield	200.00
27	Tony Compagno	100.00
30	Vic Lindskog	100.00
33	Fred Gehrke	100.00
36	Bulldog Turner	250.00
39	Russ Thomas	100.00
42	Wat Stickle	100.00
45	Jay Rhodemyre	100.00

48	Mal Kutner	100.00
51	Gerald Cowhig	100.00
54	John Sanchez	100.00
57	John Badaczewski	100.00
60	Elbert Nickel	125.00
61	Alex Wojciechowicz	75.00
63	Pete Pihos	220.00
66	Cecil Souders	100.00
69	Frank Minni	100.00
72	Ted Fritsch, Sr.	100.00
75	Dante Mangani	100.00
78	Joe Scott	100.00
80	Bill Dudley	100.00
81	Marshall Goldberg	100.00
84	Harold Crisler	100.00
87	Dan Sandifer	100.00
90	Bill Garnass	100.00
93	Vic Sears	100.00
95	George McAfee	100.00
96	Ralph Heywood	100.00
99	Harry Gilmer	160.00
102	Bud Angsman	100.00
105	Bob Cifers	100.00
107	Sid Luckman	220.00
108	Buford Ray	350.00
-	Album	450.00

1948 LEAF
NM
Complete Set (98): 5800.00
Common Player (1-49): 20.00
Common Player (50-98): 100.00

NM
1	Sid Luckman	300.00
4	Doak Walker	125.00
6	Bobby Layne	300.00
13	Johnny Lujack	125.00
22	Steve Van Buren	140.00
26	Bob Waterfield	200.00
34	Sammy Baugh	425.00
52	Leo Nomellini	250.00
53	Charlie Conerly	250.00
54	Chuck Bednarik	400.00
73	Jackie Jensen	300.00
91	Leon Hart	175.00
98	Al DiMarco	175.00

1949 LEAF
NM
Complete Set (49): 2000.00
Common Player: 25.00

NM
1	Bob Hendren	75.00
15	Sid Luckman	100.00

26	Sammy Baugh	250.00
49	Charlie Conerly	80.00
56	John Lujack	80.00
67	Bobby Layne	140.00
79	Steve Van Buren	80.00
89	Bob Waterfield	90.00
134	Chuck Bednarik	100.00
150	Bulldog Turner	125.00

1950 BOWMAN
NM
Complete Set (144): 4250.00
Common Player: 20.00

NM
1	Doak Walker	175.00
5	Y.A. Tittle	300.00
6	Lou Groza	180.00
9	Tony Canadeo	55.00
15	Tank Younger	50.00
16	Glenn Davis	130.00
17	Bob Waterfield	75.00
23	Steve Van Buren	60.00
26	John Lujack	60.00
27	Sid Luckman	80.00
35	Joe Perry	160.00
37	Bobby Layne	190.00
43	Marion Motley	130.00
45	Otto Graham	450.00
51	Tom Fears	80.00
52	Elroy Hirsch	150.00
78	Dante Lavelli	80.00
100	Sammy Baugh	200.00
103	Charlie Conerly	60.00
107	Leo Nomellini	60.00
123	Buddy Young	50.00
132	Chuck Bednarik	75.00

1950 TOPPS FELT BACKS
Complete Set (100): 4800.00
Common Player: 40.00

Jackie Jensen		125.00
Charlie Justice		100.00
Leo Nomellini		140.00
Joe Paterno		375.00
Ernie Stautner		135.00
Doak Walker		150.00

1951 BOWMAN

	NM
Complete Set (144):	3500.00
Common Player:	18.00

		NM
1	Weldon Humble	60.00
2	Otto Graham	150.00
4	Norm Van Brocklin	250.00
10	Steve Van Buren	60.00
12	Chuck Bednarik	60.00
15	John Lujack	50.00
20	Tom Landry	500.00
25	Doak Walker	50.00
32	Y.A. Tittle	120.00
34	Sammy Baugh	150.00
40	Bob Waterfield	60.00
42	Glenn Davis	50.00
56	Charlie Conerly	50.00
75	Lou Groza	70.00
76	Elroy Hirsch	60.00
91	Emlen Tunnell	100.00
96	Ernie Stautner	70.00
102	Bobby Layne	120.00
105	Joe Perry	60.00
109	Marion Motley	50.00
140	Leo Nomellini	50.00
144	Bill Dudley	75.00

1951 TOPPS

	NM
Complete Set (75):	1000.00
Common Player:	16.00

		NM
2	Bill Wade	45.00
4	Babe Parilli	35.00
10	Vic Janowicz	100.00
19	Marion Campbell	32.00
30	Bert Rechichar	32.00
48	George Young	40.00

1952 BOWMAN
LARGE

	NM
Complete Set (144):	12000.00
Common Player (1-72):	25.00
Common Player (73-144)	35.00

		NM
1	Norm Van Brocklin	425.00
2	Otto Graham	275.00
3	Doak Walker	75.00
9	Joe Spencer	75.00
10	Chuck Bednarik	175.00
14	Paul Brown	225.00
16	Frank Gifford	475.00
17	Y.A. Tittle	175.00
18	Charlie Justice	150.00
19	George Connor	125.00
23	Gino Marchetti	200.00
27	Bob Miller	285.00
28	Kyle Rote	140.00
29	Hugh McElhenny	200.00
30	Sammy Baugh	350.00
36	John Lee Hancock	350.00
37	Elroy Hirsch	150.00
45	Steve Van Buren	225.00
46	Art Donovan	350.00
48	George Halas	275.00
54	Glen Christian	75.00
55	Andy Davis	75.00
63	Charlie Conerly	475.00
64	Howard Hartley	75.00
72	John Schweder	500.
73	Vitamin Smith	150.00
78	Bobby Layne	225.00
81	John Kastan	150.00
82	Harry Minarik	130.00
83	Joe Perry	80.00
85	Andy Robustelli	175.00
90	Thomas Johnson	150.00
91	Leon Heath	100.00
92	Pete Pihos	75.00
99	Joe Stydahar	575.00
100	Dick Alban	150.00
105	Lou Groza	100.00
108	Hubert Johnston	625.00
109	Volney Quinlan	100.00
117	Jim O'Donahue	150.00
118	Darrell Hogan	100.00
126	Steve Romanik	300.00
127	Ollie Matson	300.00
128	Dante Lavelli	75.00
129	Jack Christiansen	150.00
135	Gene Ronzani	625.00
136	Bert Rechichar	100.00
137	Bob Waterfield	120.00
140	Yale Lary	150.00
142	Tom Landry	600.00
144	Jim Lansford	2800.00

1952 BOWMAN
SMALL

	NM
Complete Set (144):	5000.00
Common Player (1-72):	20.00
Common Player (73-144):	25.00

		NM
1	Norm Van Brocklin	200.00
2	Otto Graham	125.00
10	Chuck Bednarik	60.00
14	Paul Brown	125.00
16	Frank Gifford	325.00
17	Y.A. Tittle	80.00
23	Gino Marchetti	100.00
28	Kyle Rote	50.00
29	Hugh McElhenny	125.00
30	Sammy Baugh	200.00
37	Elroy Hirsch	50.00
45	Steve Van Buren	45.00
46	Art Donovan	150.00
48	George Halas	150.00
63	Charlie Conerly	50.00
78	Bobby Layne	90.00
83	Joe Perry	60.00
85	Andy Robustelli	100.00
105	Lou Groza	50.00
125	Leo Nomellini	50.00
127	Ollie Matson	120.00
129	Jack Christiansen	75.00
137	Bob Waterfield	60.00
140	Yale Lary	80.00
142	Tom Landry	300.00
144	Jim Lansford	125.00

1953 BOWMAN

	NM
Complete Set (96):	3200.00
Common Player:	25.00
SP Cards:	40.00

		NM
1	Eddie LeBaron	100.00
6	Doak Walker	50.00
9	Marion Motley	50.00
11	Norm Van Brocklin	80.00
20	Charlie Conerly	50.00
21	Bobby Layne	100.00
22	Elroy Hirsch	60.00
24	Chuck Bednarik	60.00
26	Otto Graham	135.00
32	Hugh McElhenny	60.00
43	Frank Gifford	350.00
53	Emlen Tunnell	100.00
56	Y.A. Tittle	100.00
62	Ray Renfro	50.00

95	Lou Groza	100.00
96	William Cross	75.00

1954 BOWMAN

	NM
Complete Set (128):	1600.00
Common Player (1-64):	6.00
Common Player (65-96):	25.00
Common Player (97-128):	6.00

		NM
4	Doug Atkins	45.00
8	Norm Van Brocklin	45.00
23	George Blanda	180.00
40	Otto Graham	75.00
42	Y.A. Tittle	50.00
53	Bobby Layne	50.00
55	Frank Gifford	100.00
76	Leo Nomellini	50.00
85	Lou Creekmur	50.00
97	Tom Finnin	50.00
128	John Lattner	75.00

1955 BOWMAN

	NM
Complete Set (160):	1500.00
Common Player (1-64):	4.50
Common Player (65-160):	6.00

		NM
1	Doak Walker	50.00
2	Mike McCormack	30.00
7	Frank Gifford	75.00
8	Alan Ameche	30.00
14	Len Ford	30.00
16	Charlie Conerly	25.00

25	Ollie Matson	25.00
32	Norm Van Brocklin	35.00
37	Lou Groza	24.00
42	John Henry Johnson	40.00
44	Joe Perry	25.00
52	Pat Summerall	55.00
62	George Blanda	70.00
70	Jim Ringo	35.00
71	Bobby Layne	60.00
72	Y.A. Tittle	60.00
75	Hugh McElhenny	20.00
101	Bob St. Clair	35.00
119	Frank Gatski	28.00
121	Andy Robustelli	20.00
133	Vic Janowicz	20.00
134	Ernie Stautner	20.00
136	Emlen Tunnell	20.00
152	Tom Landry	175.00
158	Chuck Bednarik	25.00
160	L.G. Dupre	30.00

1955 TOPPS ALL-AMERICAN

	NM
Complete Set (100):	3500.00
Common Player:	15.00
SP Cards:	17.50

		NM
1	Herman Hickman	90.00
6	Niles Kinnick	70.00
9	Tom Hamilton	35.00
10	Bill Dudley	30.00
11	Bobby Dodd	35.00
12	Otto Graham	175.00

15	Ed Kaw	35.00
16	Knute Rockne	325.00
18	Pudge Heffelfinger	35.00
20	Sammy Baugh	200.00
21	Whizzer White	70.00
21a	Whizzer White	70.00
24	Ken Strong	30.00
25	Casimir Myslinski	35.00
26	Larry Kelley	35.00
27	Red Grange	350.00
28	Mel Hein	40.00
29	Leo Nomellini	50.00
35	Tom Harmon	50.00
36	Turk Edwards	40.00
37	Jim Thorpe	375.00
38	Amos Alonzo Stagg	60.00
41	Joseph Alexander	35.00
42	J. Edward Tryon	35.00
51	Duane Purvis	35.00
52	John Lujack	50.00
54	Edwin Dooley	35.00
55	Frank Merritt	35.00
56	Ernie Nevers	50.00
57	Vic Hanson	35.00
59	Doc Blanchard	45.00
61	Charles Brickley	35.00
63	Charlie Justice	30.00
65	Joe Donchess	35.00
68	Four Horsemen	475.00
77	Bowden Wyatt	35.00
83	Ted Coy	35.00
84	Ace Parker	40.00
85	Sid Luckman	85.00
86	Albie Booth	35.00
87	Adolph Schultz	35.00
93	Willie Heston	35.00
94	Joe Bernard	35.00
95	Red Cagle	35.00
96	Bill Hollenbeck	35.00
97	Don Hutson	225.00
98	Beattie Feathers	75.00
99	Don Witmire	35.00
100	Wilbur "Fats" Henry	150.00

1956 TOPPS

	NM
Complete Set (120):	1500.00
Common Player:	5.00
SP Cards:	30.00
Team Cards:	17.00
Checklist:	375.00

		NM
1	Jack Carson	75.00
11	George Blanda	50.00
13	Vic Janowicz	40.00
22	Chicago Cardinals	100.00
41	Roosevelt Brown	40.00
44	Joe Schmidt	45.00
47	Bill George	35.00
49	Eddie LeBaron	40.00
53	Frank Gifford	60.00
58	Ollie Matson	75.00
60	Lenny Moore	85.00
61	Washington Redskins	85.00
86	Y.A. Tittle	40.00
116	Bobby Layne	40.00
120	Billy Vessels	35.00

1957 TOPPS

		NM
Complete Set (155):		2400.00
Common Player (1-88):		4.50
Common Player (89-154):		6.50
Checklist:		700.00

		NM
1	Eddie LeBaron	30.00
22	Norm Van Brocklin	25.00
26	Ollie Matson	16.00
28	Lou Groza	20.00
30	Y.A. Tittle	32.50
31	George Blanda	45.00
32	Bobby Layne	30.00
46	Elroy Hirsch	20.00
49	Chuck Bednarik	15.00
58a	Willard Sherman	150.00
65	Art Donovan	20.00
85	Dick Lane	40.00
88	Frank Gifford	85.00
92	Ernie Stautner	15.00
94	Raymond Berry	125.00
95	Hugh McElhenny	25.00
104	Earl Morrall	50.00
106	Jack Christiansen	15.00
109	Charley Conerly	25.00
119	Bart Starr	400.00
128	Joe Perry	25.00
138	Johnny Unitas	450.00
147	Len Ford	15.00
151	Paul Hornung	400.00
154	Fred Morrison	40.00

1958 TOPPS

		NM
Complete Set (132):		1300.00
Common Player:		3.75

		NM
2	Bobby Layne	25.00
10	Lenny Moore	15.00
22	Johnny Unitas	115.00
35	Chuck Bednarik	15.00
52	Lou Groza	15.00
62	Jim Brown	400.00
66	Bart Starr	95.00
73	Frank Gifford	50.00
84	Charley Conerly	15.00
86	Y.A. Tittle	30.00
90	Sonny Jurgensen	100.00
106	Art Donovan	15.00
120	Raymond Berry	30.00
122	Hugh McElhenny	15.00
127	Ollie Matson	15.00
129	George Blanda	35.00

		NM
132	Don Bosseler	16.00

1959 TOPPS

		NM
Complete Set (176):		1000.00
Common Player (1-88):		2.50
Common Player (89-176):		2.00
Team Cards:		5.00

		NM
1	Johnny Unitas	100.00

		NM
4	Max McGee	20.00
10	Jim Brown	125.00
20	Frank Gifford	30.00
23	Bart Starr	55.00
40	Bobby Layne	25.00
51	Sam Huff	40.00
55	Raymond Berry	15.00
60	Lou Groza	15.00
82	Paul Hornung	60.00
103	Alex Karras	40.00
116	Jerry Kramer	25.00
130	Y.A. Tittle	25.00
132	Jim Parker	20.00
140	Bobby Mitchell	35.00
155	Jim Taylor	17.00

1960 FLEER

		NM
Complete Set (132):		750.00
Common Player:		3.00

		NM
1	Harvey White	20.00
7	Sid Gillman	15.00
20	Sammy Baugh	40.00
58	George Blanda	40.00
66	Billy Cannon	16.00
73	Abner Haynes	16.00
76	Paul Lowe	15.00
116	Hank Stram	45.00
118	Ron Mix	35.00
124	Jack Kemp	350.00
128	Paul Maguire	16.00
132	Ron Beagle	16.00

1960 TOPPS

		NM
Complete Set (132):		.625.00
Common Player:		.1.75
Team Cards:		.5.00

		NM
1	Johnny Unitas	.80.00
23	Jim Brown	.85.00
51	Bart Starr	.40.00
54	Paul Hornung	.35.00
56	Forrest Gregg	.28.00
74	Frank Gifford	.45.00
80	Sam Huff	.15.00
93	Bobby Layne	.23.00
113	Y.A. Tittle	.22.00
132	Washington Redskins	.25.00

JIM OTTO
CENTER • OAKLAND RAIDERS

1961 FLEER

		NM
Complete Set (220):		.1600.00
Common Player (1-132):		.3.50
Common Player (133-220):		.5.50

		NM
11	Jim Brown	.130.00
30	John Unitas	.70.00
41	Don Meredith	.140.00
59	John Brodie	.50.00
88	Bart Starr	.50.00
89	Jim Taylor	.30.00
90	Paul Hornung	.45.00
117	Bobby Layne	.25.00
155	Jack Kemp	.230.00
160	Paul Maguire	.125.00
162	Ron Mix	.16.00
166	George Blanda	.45.00
188	Tom Flores	.35.00
197	Jim Otto	.60.00
215	Don Maynard	.90.00
220	Sid Youngelman	.22.00

1961 TOPPS

		NM
Complete Set (198):		.1100.00
Common Player:		.2.00

		NM
1	Johnny Unitas	.90.00
35	Alex Karras	.20.00

DON MAYNARD
FLANKER-BACK OR END • NEW YORK TITANS

39	Bart Starr	.40.00
40	Paul Hornung	.28.00
41	Jim Taylor	.24.00
45	Henry Jordan	.15.00
57	25-TD Passes Johnny Unitas	.15.00
58	Y.A. Tittle	.22.00
59	John Brodie	.40.00
67	Checklist	.50.00
71	Jim Brown	.85.00
77	Jim Brown IA	.35.00
95	Sonny Jurgensen	.20.00
104	Bobby Layne	.20.00
122	Checklist	.35.00
145	George Blanda	.26.00
150	Don Maynard	.50.00
166	Jack Kemp	.150.00
182	Jim Otto	.40.00
186	Tom Flores	.25.00
198	Checklist	.90.00

JACK KEMP
QUARTERBACK
SAN DIEGO CHARGERS

1962 FLEER

		NM
Complete Set (88):		.800.00
Common Player:		.6.00

		NM
1	Billy Lott	15.00
3	Gino Cappelletti	.17.00
46	George Blanda	.55.00
48	Charlie Hennigan	.16.00
59	Don Maynard	.35.00
72	Jim Otto	.25.00
74	Fred Williamson	.20.00
79	Jack Kemp	.250.00
86	Ernie Ladd	.30.00

88
Ron

DON MEREDITH
DALLAS COWBOYS
QUARTERBACK

Nery 15.00

1962 TOPPS

		NM
Complete Set (176):		.1700.00
Common Player:		.3.50
SP Cards:		.7.50

		NM
1	Johnny Unitas	.125.00
5	Raymond Berry	.20.00
17	Mike Ditka	.225.00
28	Jim Brown	.126.00
36	Ernie Davis	.110.00
39	Don Meredith	.80.00
58	Alex Karras	.15.00
62	Detroit Lions Team	.15.00
63	Bart Starr	.70.00
64	Paul Hornung	.50.00
66	Jim Taylor	.30.00
68	Jim Ringo	.15.00
69	Fuzzy Thurston	.15.00
75	Green Bay Packers	.20.00
76	Checklist	.80.00
79	Ollie Matson	.20.00
88	Roman Gabriel	.50.00
89	Los Angeles Rams	.15.00
90	Fran Tarkenton	.200.00
92	Hugh McElhenny	.20.00
101	Minnesota Vikings Team	.20.00
102	Y.A. Tittle	.30.00
104	Frank Gifford	.40.00
110	Sam Huff	.20.00
115	Sonny Jurgensen	.20.00
127	Bobby Layne	.25.00
134	Ernie Stautner	.15.00
151	Bill Kilmer	.25.00
152	John Brodie	.15.00
164	Norm Snead	.30.00

1963 FLEER

		NM
Complete Set (88):		.1990.00
Common Player:		.8.00
Checklist		.350.00

		NM
1	Larry Garron	.17.00
6	Charles Long	.180.00
10	Nick Buoniconti	.75.00
15	Don Maynard	.45.00
23	Cookie Gilchrist	.40.00
24	Jack Kemp	.250.00
36	George Blanda	.55.00

47	Len Dawson	250.00
57	Clem Daniels	15.00
62	Jim Otto	30.00
64	Bob Dougherty	230.00
70	Keith Lincoln	25.00
72	Lance Alworth	250.00
73	Ron Mix	22.00
76	Ernie Ladd	15.00
88	Bud McFadin	16.00

1963 TOPPS

		NM
Complete Set (170):		1300.00
Common Player:		2.00

		NM
1	Johnny Unitas	100.00
14	Jim Brown	200.00
19	Lou Groza	17.00
44	Deacon Jones	50.00
49	Y.A. Tittle	40.00
62	Mike Ditka	60.00
74	Don Meredith	50.00
82	Bob Lilly	125.00
84	Dallas Cowboys	16.00
85	Checklist	25.00
86	Bart Starr	40.00
87	Jim Taylor	16.00
95	Willie Wood	27.00
96	Ray Nitschke	80.00
98	Fran Tarkenton	50.00
107	Jim Marshall	25.00
110	Sonny Jurgensen	22.00

155	Larry Wilson	25.00
170	Checklist	60.00

1964 PHILADELPHIA

		NM
Complete Set (198):		876.00
Common Player:		1.75

		NM
1	Raymond Berry	20.00
3	John Mackey	25.00
12	Johnny Unitas	40.00
14	Don Shula	25.00
17	Mike Ditka	32.00
30	Jim Brown	65.00
48	Bob Lilly	40.00
51	Don Meredith	35.00
71	Herb Adderley	30.00
72	Willie Davis	30.00
74	Paul Hornung	25.00
79	Bart Starr	40.00
80	Jim Taylor	15.00
84	Vince Lombardi	24.00
91	Merlin Olsen	50.00
109	Fran Tarkenton	30.00
117	Frank Gifford	45.00
124	Y.A. Tittle	20.00
161	Jim Johnson	15.00
186	Sonny Jurgensen	18.00

1964 TOPPS

		NM
Complete Set (176):		1500.00
Common Player:		3.00
SP Cards:		6.00

		NM
1	Tommy Addison	30.00
29	Cookie Gilchrist	15.00
30	Jack Kemp	200.00
31	Daryle Lamonica	60.00
65	Denver Broncos Team	17.00
68	George Blanda	60.00
82	Checklist	50.00
90	Bobby Bell	35.00
92	Buck Buchanan	35.00
96	Len Dawson	75.00
121	Don Maynard	30.00
125	Matt Snell	15.00

139	Tom Flores	15.00
148	Jim Otto	25.00
155	Lance Alworth	40.00
159	John Hadl	35.00
168	Ron Mix	15.00
176	Checklist	150.00

1965 PHILADELPHIA

		NM
Complete Set (198):		775.00
Common Player:		1.50

		NM
12	Johnny Unitas	35.00
19	Mike Ditka	25.00
31	Jim Brown	60.00
41	Paul Warfield	75.00
47	Bob Lilly	20.00
50	Don Meredith	25.00
53	Mel Renfro	30.00
76	Paul Hornung	25.00
79	Ray Nitschke	15.00
91	Bart Starr	25.00
94	Merlin Olsen	17.00
105	Carl Eller	26.00
110	Fran Tarkenton	30.00
188	Sonny Jurgensen	15.00
189	Paul Krause	16.00
195	Charley Taylor	60.00
197	Checklist 1	20.00
198	Checklist 2	35.00

1965 TOPPS

		NM
Complete Set (176):		3800.00
Common Player:		6.50
SP Cards:		11.50

		NM
1	Tommy Addison	35.00
3	Nick Buoniconti	24.00
5	Gino Cappelletti	20.00
35	Jack Kemp	300.00
36	Daryle Lamonica	40.00
37	Paul Maguire	20.00
46	Willie Brown	65.00
51	Cookie Gilchrist	25.00
65	Lionel Taylor	20.00
69	George Blanda	90.00
87	Checklist 1-88	145.00
90	Pete Beathard	22.00
91	Bobby Bell	25.00
94	Buck Buchanan	25.00
99	Len Dawson	80.00
116	Winston Hill	20.00
117	John Huarte	30.00
121	Don Maynard	35.00
122	Joe Namath	1650.00
127	Matt Snell	25.00
133	Fred Biletnikoff	200.00
134	Billy Cannon	20.00
137	Ben Davidson	50.00
139	Tom Flores	27.00
145	Jim Otto	25.00
152	Fred Williamson	20.00
155	Lance Alworth	65.00
161	John Hadl	28.00
164	Ernie Ladd	20.00
165	Keith Lincoln	20.00
166	Paul Lowe	20.00
168	Ron Mix	20.00
176	Checklist 89-176	200.00

1966 PHILADELPHIA

		NM
Complete Set (198):		875.00
Common Player:		1.50

		NM
24	Johnny Unitas	30.00
31	Dick Butkus	185.00

		NM
32	Mike Ditka	25.00
38	Gale Sayers	210.00
39	Gale Sayers	25.00
41	Jim Brown	55.00
58	Bob Hayes	25.00
60	Bob Lilly	15.00
61	Don Meredith	25.00
88	Bart Starr	25.00
114	Fran Tarkenton	20.00
194	Charley Taylor	18.00
197	Checklist 1	15.00
198	Checklist 2	40.00

1966 TOPPS

		NM
Complete Set (132):		1300.00
Common Player:		4.00

		NM
1	Tom Addison	20.00
15	Funny Ring CL	275.00
26	Jack Kemp	170.00
48	George Blanda	40.00
61	Checklist	40.00
67	Len Dawson	35.00
75	Otis Taylor	17.00
95	Don Maynard	25.00
96	Joe Namath	340.00
104	Fred Biletnikoff	50.00
115	Jim Otto	15.00
119	Lance Alworth	30.00
132	Checklist	90.00

1967 PHILADELPHIA

		NM
Complete Set (198):		650.00
Common Player:		1.50

		NM
7	Tommy Nobis	16.00
23	Johnny Unitas	30.00
28	Dick Butkus	60.00
29	Mike Ditka	25.00
35	Gale Sayers	75.00
43	Leroy Kelly	30.00
46	Paul Warfield	20.00
54	Lee Roy Jordan	22.00
57	Don Meredith	20.00
58	Dan Reeves	33.00
82	Bart Starr	20.00
106	Fran Tarkenton	20.00
123	Paul Hornung	18.00
165	Jackie Smith	15.00
197	Checklist 1	18.00
198	Checklist 2	35.00

1967 TOPPS

		NM
Complete Set (132):		650.00
Common Player:		2.50

		NM
24	Jack Kemp	100.00
59	Checklist	40.00
61	Len Dawson	20.00
82	Wahoo McDaniel	30.00
97	Don Maynard	20.00
98	Joe Namath	185.00
106	Fred Biletnikoff	30.00
123	Lance Alworth	25.00
132	Checklist	60.00

1968 TOPPS

		NM
Complete Set (219):		575.00
Common Player (1-131):		.80
Common Player (132-219):		1.50

		NM
1	Bart Starr	35.00
25	Don Meredith	21.00
55	Checklist	15.00
65	Joe Namath	80.00
75	Gale Sayers	50.00
100	Johnny Unitas	25.00

160	Bob Griese	12.00
200	Bart Starr	22.00
245	Joe Greene	50.00
250	Joe Namath	50.00
260	O.J. Simpson	25.00

127	Dick Butkus	36.00
142	George Blanda	23.00
149	Jack Kemp	60.00
161	Fran Tarkenton	20.00
162	Mike Ditka	25.00
173	Floyd Little	20.00
196	Bob Griese	85.00

		NM
1	Len Dawson	15.00
10	Bob Griese	15.00
30	Bart Starr	20.00
59	Alan Page	40.00
70	Gale Sayers	35.00
75	Lem Barney	15.00
80	Fran Tarkenton	20.00
90	O.J. Simpson	80.00
114	Bubba Smith	25.00
150	Joe Namath	50.00
162	Larry Csonka	25.00
180	Johnny Unitas	22.00
247	Fred Dryer	15.00

1969 TOPPS

	NM
Complete Set (263):	550.00
Common Player (1-132):	1.00
Common Player (133-263):	1.15

		NM
25	Johnny Unitas	25.00
26	Brian Piccolo	75.00
51	Gale Sayers	50.00
75	Don Meredith	20.00
100	Joe Namath	80.00
120	Larry Csonka	80.00
132	Checklist 133-263	15.00
139	Dick Butkus	25.00
150	Fran Tarkenton	20.
161	Bob Griese	30.00
215	Bart Starr	25.00
232	George Blanda	20.00

1970 TOPPS

	NM
Complete Set (263):	450.00
Common Player (1-132):	50
Common Player (133-263):	75

1971 TOPPS

	NM
Complete Set (263):	500.00
Common Players (1-132):	50
Common Player (133-263):	75

		NM
1	Johnny Unitas	30.00
3	Marty Schottenheimer	20.00
25	Dick Butkus	20.00
39	George Blanda	15.00
45	Larry Csonka	12.00
113	Ken Houston	20.00
114	Willie Lanier	20.00
120	Fran Tarkenton	30.00
150	Gale Sayers	30.00
156	Terry Bradshaw	175.00

1972 TOPPS

	NM
Complete Set (351):	2300.00
Common Player (1-132):	50
Common Players (133-263):	75
Common Player (264-351):	20.00

		NM
13	John Riggins	32.00
55	Archie Manning	15.00
65	Jim Plunkett	15.00
93	Ted Hendricks	20.00
100	Joe Namath	35.00
101	L.C. Greenwood	20.00
110	Gale Sayers	22.00
120	Terry Bradshaw	15.00
122	Roger Staubach	20.00
150	Terry Bradshaw	45.00
160	O.J. Simpson	15.00
165	Johnny Unitas	20.00
200	Roger Staubach	160.00
225	Fran Tarkenton	16.00
230	Joe Greene	17.00
240	Larry Little	17.00
244	Charlie Joiner	25.00
264	Charlie Sanders	22.00
265	Ron Yary	27.50
266	Rayfield Wright	20.00
267	Larry Little	40.00
268	John Niland	20.00
269	Forrest Blue	20.00
270	Otis Taylor	20.00
271	Paul Warfield	60.00
272	Bob Griese	75.00
273	John Brockington	20.00
274	Floyd Little	27.00
275	Garo Yepremian	30.00
276	Jerrel Wilson	20.00
277	Carl Eller	30.00
278	Bubba Smith	40.00
279	Alan Page	40.00
280	Bob Lilly	45.00
281	Ted Hendricks	45.00
282	Dave Wilcox	20.00
283	Willie Lanier	27.50

284	Jim Johnson	20.00
295	Willie Brown	27.50
286	Bill Bradley	20.00
287	Ken Houston	27.50
288	Mel Farr	20.00
289	Kermit Alexander	20.00
290	John Gilliam	25.00
291	Steve Spurrier	140.00
292	Walter Johnson	20.00
293	Jack Pardee	20.00
294	Checklist 264-351	80.00
295	Winston Hill	20.00
296	Hugo Hollas	20.00
297	Ray May	25.00
298	Jim Bakken	20.00
299	Larry Carwell	20.00
300	Alan Page	50.00
301	Walt Garrison	25.00
302	Mike Lucci	20.00
303	Nemiah Wilson	20.00
304	Carroll Dale	20.00
305	Jim Kanicki	20.00
306	Preston Pearson	25.00
307	Lemar Parrish	20.00
308	Earl Morrall	22.00
309	Tommy Nobis	25.00
310	Rich Jackson	20.00
311	Doug Cunningham	20.00
312	Jim Marsalis	20.00
313	Jim Beirne	20.00
314	Tom McNeill	20.00
315	Milt Morin	20.00
316	Rayfield Wright	24.00
317	Jerry LeVias	20.00
318	Travis Williams	27.50
319	Edgar Chandler	20.00
320	Bob Wallace	20.00
321	Delles Howell	20.00
322	Emerson Boozer	20.00
323	George Atkinson	22.00
324	Mike Montler	20.00
325	Randy Johnson	20.00
326	Mike Curtis	20.00
327	Miller Farr	20.00
328	Horst Muhlmann	20.00
329	John Niland	25.00
330	Andy Russell	20.00
331	Mercury Morris	35.00
332	Jim Johnson	20.00
333	Jerrel Wilson	20.00
334	Charley Taylor	40.00
335	Dick LeBeau	20.00
336	Jim Marshall	25.00
337	Tom Mack	25.00
338	Steve Spurrier	60.00
339	Floyd Little	25.00
340	Len Dawson	40.00
341	Dick Butkus	70.00
342	Larry Brown	27.50
343	Joe Namath	335.00
344	Jim Turner	20.00
345	Doug Cunningham	20.00
346	Edd Hargett	20.00
347	Steve Owens	21.00
348	George Blanda	45.00
349	Ed Podolak	20.00
350	Rich Jackson	20.00
351	Ken Willard	35.00

1973 TOPPS

	NM
Complete Set (528):	425.00
Common Player:	40

		NM
15	Terry Bradshaw	25.00
34	Ken Anderson	20.00
60	Frank Tarkenton	15.00
77	Art Shell	20.00
89	Franco Harris	50.00
115	Jack Ham	25.00
322	Dan Dierdorf	20.00
341	Jim Langer	13.00
343	Jack Youngblood	15.00
400	Joe Namath	30.00
455	Johnny Unitas	18.00
475	Roger Staubach	40.00
487	Ken Stabler	60.00
500	O.J. Simpson	15.00

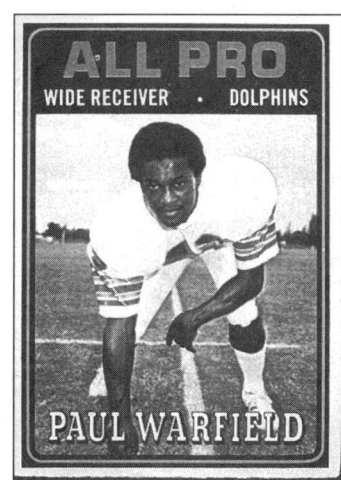

1974 TOPPS

	NM
Complete Set (528):	325.00
Common Player:	35

		NM
1	O.J. Simpson	20.00
105	Ahmad Rashad	15.00
121	Harold Carmichael	15.00
129	Fran Tarkenton	10.00
130	O.J. Simpson	15.00

150	Johnny Unitas	16.00
219	Ray Guy	10.00
220	Franco Harris	20.00
383	John Hannah	15.00
451	Ken Stabler	20.00
470	Terry Bradshaw	20.00
500	Roger Staubach	28.00

1975 TOPPS

	NM
Complete Set (528):	325.00
Common Player:	30

		NM
12	Mel Blount	25.00
39	Rocky Bleier	15.00
65	Drew Pearson	12.00
145	Roger Staubach	25.00
282	Lynn Swann	45.00
300	Franco Harris	12.00
355	O.J. Simpson	7.00
367	Dan Fouts	50.00
380	Ken Stabler	14.00
400	Fran Tarkenton	8.50
4116	Joe Theismann	25.00
459	Lynn Swann	7.00
461	Terry Bradshaw	15.00
500	O.J. Simpson	12.00
524	Cliff Branch	10.00

1976 TOPPS

	NM
Complete Set (528):	350.00
Common Player:	25
Team Cards:	1.25

		NM
75	Terry Bradshaw	14.00
128	Dan Fouts	10.00
140	Lynn Swann	15.00
148	Walter Payton	200.00
158	Randy White	25.00
220	Jack Lambert	28.00
300	O.J. Simpson	10.00
376	Steve Grogan	8.00
395	Roger Staubach	15.00
415	Ken Stabler	8.00
427	Ed "Too Tall" Jones	20.00

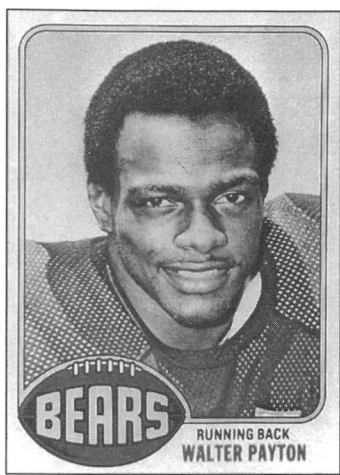

365	Ken Stabler	.6.00
400	O.J. Simpson	.5.00
443	Steve Largent	.15.00
499	Dan Fouts	.5.00

1979 TOPPS

		NM
Complete Set (528):		.140.00
Common Player:		..15

		NM
1	Passing Leaders Roger Staubach, Terry Bradshaw	.5.00
3	Rushing Leaders Walter Payton, Earl Campbell	.7.00
160	Tony Dorsett	.8.00
198	Steve Largent	.8.00
308	Ozzie Newsome	.15.00
310	James Lofton	.15.00
331	Record: Campbell	.5.50
390	Earl Campbell	.30.00
400	Roger Staubach	.8.00
480	Walter Payton	.12.00
500	Terry Bradshaw	.5.50

1980 TOPPS

		NM
Complete Set (528):		.65.00
Common Player:		..08

		NM
160	Walter Payton	.8.00
170	Ottis Anderson	.5.00
225	Phil Simms	.15.00

1981 TOPPS

		NM
Complete Set (528):		.250.00
Common Player:		..08
Wax Box:		.400.00

		MT
55	Phil Simms	.5.00
150	Kellen Winslow	.10.00
194	Art Monk	.12.00
216	Joe Montana	.175.00
316	Dan Hampton	.4.00
400	Walter Payton	.4.50
422	Dwight Clark	.4.00
430	James Lofton	.3.50
435	Ozzie Newsome	.3.00
524	Kellen Winslow	.3.00

1977 TOPPS

		NM
Complete Set (528):		.230.00
Common Player:		..20

		NM
3	Rushing Leaders: Walter Payton, O.J. Simpson	.9.00
29	Lee Roy Selmon	.17.00
45	Roger Staubach	.10.00
99	Mike Webster	.8.00
110	Ken Stabler	.8.00
146	Harry Carson	.7.00
177	Steve Largent	.50.00
195	Lynn Swann	.10.00
245	Terry Bradshaw	.7.00
342	Randy White	.7.00
360	Walter Payton	.35.00
400	Fran Tarkenton	.6.00
480	Jack Lambert	.7.00

1978 TOPPS

		NM
Complete Set (528):		.140.00
Common Player:		..15

		NM
3	Walter Payton	.6.00
65	Terry Bradshaw	.6.00
200	Walter Payton	.20.00
290	Roger Staubach	.8.00
315	Tony Dorsett	.35.00
320	John Stallworth	.20.00

1982 TOPPS

		MT
Complete Set (528):		.90.00
Common Player:		..05
Wax Box:		.150.00

		MT
51	Anthony Munoz	.7.00
241	Kennen Winslow	.2.00
257	Joe Montana, Ken Anderson	.2.00
302	Walter Payton	.4.00
303	Walter Payton IA	.2.00
379	Drew Hill	.2.00
434	Lawrence Taylor	.30.00
435	Lawrence Taylor IA	.10.00
486	Ronnie Lott	.15.00
487	Ronnie Lott IA	.6.00
488	Joe Montana	.30.00
489	Joe Montana IA	.10.00
515	Art Monk	.4.00

1983 TOPPS

		MT
Complete Set (396):		.50.00
Common Player:		..05
Wax Box:		.50.00

		MT
4	Joe Montana	.2.00
33	Jim McMahon	.3.00
36	Walter Payton	.2.00
38	Mike Singletary	.7.00
133	Lawrence Taylor	.5.00

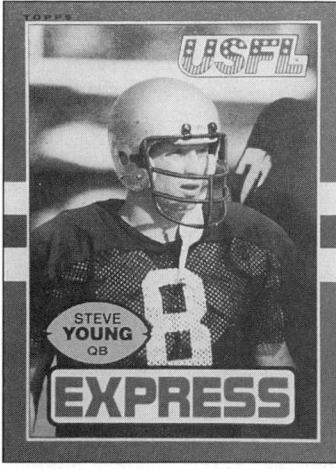

168	Ronnie Lott	3.00
169	Joe Montana	7.00
293	Marcus Allen	2.00
294	Marcus Allen	25.00
298	Todd Christensen	2.00

52	Steve Young	250.00
58	Reggie White	100.00
59	Anthony Carter	15.00
62	Bobby Hebert	10.00
74	Herschel Walker	25.00

		MT
14	William Fuller	6.00
19	Sam Mills	8.00
45	Jim Kelly	40.00
49	Gary Clark	15.00
65	Steve Young	80.00
75	Reggie White	30.00
80	Doug Flutie	70.00
86	Herschel Walker	6.00

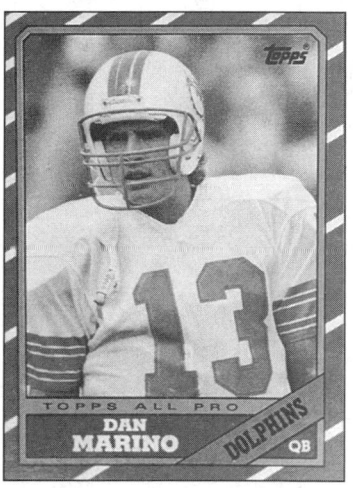

1984 TOPPS

	MT
Complete Set (396):	230.00
Common Player:	.05
Wax Box:	500.00

		MT
63	John Elway	125.00
98	Marcus Allen	4.00
111	Howie Long	6.00
123	Dan Marino	140.00
124	Dan Marino IR	15.00
202	Passing Leaders: Dan Marino, Steve Bartkowski	4.00
280	Eric Dickerson	7.00
353	Roger Craig	5.00
358	Joe Montana	9.00
359	Joe Montana IR	4.00

1984 TOPPS USFL

	MT
Complete Set (132):	375.00
Common Player:	1.50

		MT
36	Jim Kelly	100.00
38	Ricky Sanders	10.00

1985 TOPPS

	MT
Complete Set (396):	80.00
Common Player:	.05
Wax Box:	125.00

		MT
4	Dan Marino RB	8.00
24	Richard Dent	4.00
80	Henry Ellard	5.00
157	Joe Montana	7.00
192	Passing Leaders: Joe Montana, Dan Marino	13.00
207	Darryl Talley	2.00
238	John Elway	15.00
251	Warren Moon	20.00
282	Marcus Allen	2.00
292	Howie Long	2.00
314	Dan Marino	30.00
325	Irving Fryar	4.00

1985 TOPPS USFL

	MT
Complete Set (132):	175.00
Common Player:	.35

1986 TOPPS

	MT
Complete Set (396):	180.00
Common Player:	.05
Wax Box:	425.00

		MT
11	Walter Payton	2.00
34	Irving Fryar	1.50
44	Miami Dolphins Team Dan Marino	2.00
45	Dan Marino	15.00
112	John Elway	7.00
119	Karl Mecklenburg	2.50
156	Joe Montana	6.00
161	Jerry Rice	120.00
176	Gary Clark	2.00
187	Bernie Kosar	2.00
255	Boomer Esiason	4.00
275	Reggie White	12.00
297	Anthony Carter	2.00
350	Warren Moon	4.00
357	Ray Childress	1.50

374	Steve Young	35.00
388	Andre Reed	5.00
389	Bruce Smith	5.00

1987 TOPPS

	MT
Complete Set (396):	45.00
Common Player:	05
Wax Box:	60.00

		MT
6	Dan Marino	2.00
31	John Elway	4.00
45	Doug Flutie	12.00
112	Joe Montana	4.00
115	Jerry Rice	10.00
125	Charles Haley	3.00
145	Jim Everett	3.00
233	Dan Marino	8.00
264	Herschel Walker	2.50
296	Randall Cunningham	18.00
301	Reggie White	3.00
307	Warren Moon	2.25
347	Leslie O'Neal	2.00
362	Jim Kelly	6.00
378	Brooks	2.00
384	Steve Young	5.00

1000 Yard Club

	MT
Complete Set (24):	4.50
Common Player:	15

1	Eric Dickerson	75
2	Jerry Rice	75
7	Walter Payton	90
18	Steve Largent	60

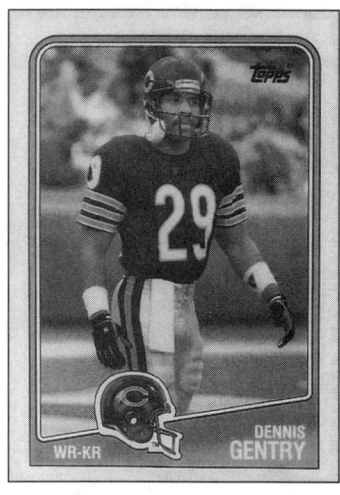

1988 TOPPS

	MT
Complete Set (396):	12.00
Common Player:	05
Wax Box:	10.00

		MT
38	Joe Montana	1.50
39	Steve Young	1.00
43	Jerry Rice	2.00
190	Dan Marino	1.50
221	Jim Kelly	1.00
230	Cornelius Bennett	1.00
300	Kevin Greene	1.00

327	Bo Jackson	2.00
352	Vinny Testaverde	4.00

1000 Yard Club

Complete Set (28):	4.50
Common Player:	10

2	Eric Dickerson	75
4	Jerry Rice	75
14	Steve Largent	75
15	Herschel Walker	75

1989 PRO SET

	MT
Complete Set (561):	30.00
Complete Series 1 (440):	8.00
Complete Series 2 (100):	20.00
Complete Series 3 (21):	2.00
Common Player:	03
Minor Stars:	10
Series 1 Wax Box:	10.00
Series 2 Wax Box:	20.00

		MT
32	Thurman Thomas	1.50
47	William Perry ERR	3.00
89	Michael Irvin	1.50
100	John Elway DRAFT	4.00
100a	John Elway TRADE	2.00
159	Chris Chandler	2.00
183	Tim Brown	1.50
220	Dan Marino	2.00
314	Cris Carter	2.50
381	Joe Montana	1.50
383	Jerry Rice	1.50
388	Steve Young	1.00
404	Curt Warner	1.00
486	Deion Sanders	2.00
490	Troy Aikman	3.00
494	Barry Sanders	15.00
497	Andre Rison	1.00
498	Derrick Thomas	1.00
535	Gizmo Williams	10.00
550	Sterling Sharpe	1.00

1989 SCORE

	MT
Complete Set (330):	240.00
Complete Factory Set (330):	250.00
Common Player:	10

Minor Stars:		20
Wax Box:		500.00

		MT
1	Joe Montana	3.00
11	Bubby Brister	8.00
13	Dan Marino	4.00
18	Michael Irvin	5.00
27	Chris Chandler	6.00
72	Cris Carter	25.00
78	Rod Woodson	4.00
86	Tim Brown	8.00
167	Chris Spielman	3.00
191	Quinn Early	2.00
200	Steve Beuerlein	5.00
211	Thurman Thomas	8.00
212	Steve Young	2.00
221	Jerry Rice	3.00
243	Doug Flutie	2.00
246	Deion Sanders	20.00
257	Barry Sanders	165.00
258	Derrick Thomas	4.00
259	Eric Metcalf	2.00
270	Troy Aikman	40.00
272	Andre Rison	5.00
275	Joe Montana, Jerry Rice	2.00
279	Joe Montana, Jerry Rice	2.00
305	Tim Brown ERR	2.00
305a	Tim Brown COR	2.00
328	Tim Brown	2.00

1989 SCORE SUPPLEMENTAL

Complete Set (110):	10.00
Common Player:	05
Minor Stars:	10

333	Sterling Sharpe	4.00
339	John Elway	3.00
384	Bo Jackson	1.50
407	Neil Smith	2.50

1989 TOPPS

	MT
Complete Set (396):	15.00
Common Player:	05
Wax Box:	10.00

		MT
7	Jerry Rice	1.25
12	Joe Montana	1.50
13	John Taylor	1.00
45	Thurman Thomas	2.00
121	Cris Carter	2.00
148	Michael Dean Perry	1.00
209	Chris Chandler	2.00
265	Tim Brown	1.50
270	Steve Beuerlein	1.00
293	Dan Marino	2.00
313	Anthony Miller	1.00
379	Sterling Sharpe	1.50
383	Michael Irvin	1.50

1000 Yard Club

Complete Set (24):	4.00
Common Player:	10

1	Eric Dickerson	60
2	Herschel Walker	60
5	Jerry Rice	60

Football Autographs
Pro Football Hall of Famers

Herb Adderley (1939-) 1980
Football . . . .$75-$85
Cut signature . . . .$3-$7
Goal Line art $15
3x5 index card . . . .$5-$9
8x10 photograph . . . .$15-$20
Mini helmet $40

Lance Alworth (1940-) 1978
Football . . . .$75-$100
Cut signature . . . .$8-$10
Goal Line art $25
3x5 index card . . . .$7-$10
8x10 photograph $20
Mini helmet $50

Doug Atkins (1930-) 1982
Football . . . .$75-$85
Cut signature . . . .$2-$6
Goal Line art $15
3x5 index card . . . .$5-$9
8x10 photograph . . . .$15-$20
Mini helmet $40

Morris "Red" Badgro (1902-1998) 1981
Football . . . .$75-$100
Cut signature . . . .$3-$5
Goal Line art $30
3x5 index card . . . .$5-$8
8x10 photograph . . . .$18-$20
Mini helmet $45

Lem Barney (1945-) 1992
Football . . . .$85-$100
Cut signature . . . .$4-$5
Goal Line art $15
3x5 index card $7
8x10 photograph . . . .$12-$18
Mini helmet $40

Cliff Battles (1910-1981) 1968
Football . . . . .Unknown
Cut signature . . . .$40-$65
Goal Line art . . . . .Impossible
3x5 index card . . . .$40-$50
8x10 photograph . . . .$100-$200
Mini helmet . . . . .Impossible

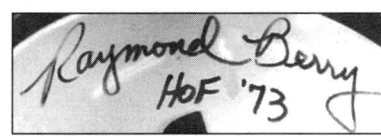

Sammy Baugh (1914-) 1963
Football . . . .$250-$300
Cut signature . . . .$10-$15

Goal Line art $60
3x5 index card . . . .$20-$25
8x10 photograph $35-50
Mini helmet $75

Chuck Bednarik (1925-) 1967
Football . . . .$75-$100
Cut signature . . . .$3-$5
Goal Line art $20
3x5 index card . . . .$5-$8
8x10 photograph . . . .$12-$20
Mini helmet $40

Bert Bell (1895-1959) 1963
Football . . . . .Unknown
Cut signature $100
Goal Line art . . . . .Impossible
3x5 index card $150
8x10 photograph $400
Mini helmet . . . . .Impossible

Bobby Bell (1940-) 1983
Football . . . .$75-$100
Cut signature . . . .$4-$6
Goal Line art $20
3x5 index card . . . .$7-$12
8x10 photograph . . . .$15-$20
Mini helmet $40

Raymond Berry (1933-) 1973
Football . . . .$75-$100
Cut signature $10
Goal Line art $20
3x5 index card . . . .$5-$7
8x10 photograph . . . .$15-$18
Mini helmet $40

Charles Bidwill (1895-1947) 1967
Football . . . . .Unknown
Cut signature $150
Goal Line art . . . . .Impossible
3x5 index card $450
8x10 photograph $750
Mini helmet . . . . .Impossible

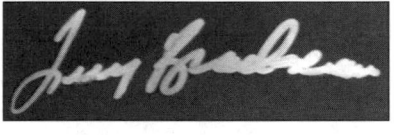

Fred Biletnikoff (1943-) 1988
Football . . . .$80-$100
Cut signature . . . .$6-$10
Goal Line art $20

3x5 index card . . . .$6-$9
8x10 photograph . . . .$20-$25
Mini helmet $40

George Blanda (1927-) 1981
Football . . . .$100-$125
Cut signature . . . .$5-$10
Goal Line art $50
3x5 index card . . . .$8-$11
8x10 photograph $25
Mini helmet $40

Mel Blount (1948-) 1989
Football $75
Cut signature . . . .$3-$6
Goal Line art $15
3x5 index card . . . .$5-$9
8x10 photograph $20
Mini helmet $50

Terry Bradshaw (1948-) 1989
Football $150
Cut signature . . . .$7-$10
Goal Line art $25
3x5 index card $10
8x10 photograph $30
Mini helmet $125

Jim Brown (1936-) 1971
Football $150
Cut signature . . . .$7-$10
Goal Line art $25
3x5 index card $12
8x10 photograph . . . .$25-$35
Mini helmet $100

Paul Brown (1908-1991) 1967
Football . . . .$150-$250
Cut signature . . . .$10-$15
Goal Line art $50
3x5 index card . . . .$18-$25
8x10 photograph $75
Mini helmet . . . . .Impossible

Roosevelt Brown (1932-) 1975
Football $75
Cut signature ....$5-$10
Goal Line art $15
3x5 index card $7
8x10 photograph $20
Mini helmet $40

Willie Brown (1940-) 1984
Football $75
Cut signature ....$3-$6
Goal Line art $20
3x5 index card ....$5-$6
8x10 photograph ....$15-$20
Mini helmet $40

Buck Buchanan (1940-1992) 1990
Football ....$150-$200
Cut signature ....$7-$8
Goal Line art $50
3x5 index card $15
8x10 photograph ....$40-$60
Mini helmet ....Impossible

Dick Butkus (1942-) 1979
Football ....$125-$150
Cut signature $10
Goal Line art $25
3x5 index card ....$8-$12
8x10 photograph $25
Mini helmet $50

Earl Campbell (1955-) 1991
Football ....$100-$125
Cut signature ....$10-$12
Goal Line art $15
3x5 index card ....$5-$10
8x10 photograph $20
Mini helmet $50

Tony Canadeo (1919-) 1974
Football $75
Cut signature ....$3-$4
Goal Line art $20
3x5 index card $5
8x10 photograph $20
Mini helmet $40

Joe Carr (1880-1939) 1963
Football ....Unknown
Cut signature $500
Goal Line art ....Impossible

3x5 index card $700
8x10 photograph $1,000
Mini helmet ....Impossible

Guy Chamberlin (1894-1967) 1965
Football ....Unknown
Cut signature $60
Goal Line art ....Impossible
3x5 index card $75
8x10 photograph $150
Mini helmet ....Impossible

Jack Christiansen (1928-1986) 1970
Football ....Unknown
Cut signature $15
Goal Line art ....Impossible
3x5 index card $40
8x10 photograph ....$100-$150
Mini helmet ....Impossible

Dutch Clark (1906-1978) 1963
Football ....Unknown
Cut signature $15
Goal Line art ....Impossible
3x5 index card $40
8x10 photograph $100
Mini helmet ....Impossible

George Connor (1925-) 1975
Football $75
Cut signature ....$3-$6
Goal Line art $25
3x5 index card $5
8x10 photograph $15
Mini helmet $40

Jimmy Conzelman (1898-1970) 1964
Football ....Unknown
Cut signature $75
Goal Line art ....Impossible
3x5 index card $100
8x10 photograph $350
Mini helmet ....Impossible

Lou Creekmur (1927-) 1996
Football $80
Cut signature $6
Goal Line art $15
3x5 index card $6
8x10 photograph $15
Mini helmet $40

Larry Csonka (1946-) 1987
Football ....$75-$125
Cut signature $6
Goal Line art $35
3x5 index card ....$7-$10

8x10 photograph $20
Mini helmet $60

Al Davis (1929-) 1992
Football $125
Cut signature $10
Goal Line art ....$75-$100
3x5 index card $20
8x10 photograph ....$35-$50
Mini helmet $50

Willie Davis (1934-) 1981
Football $75
Cut signature ....$3-$7
Goal Line art $15
3x5 index card ....$6-$7
8x10 photograph ....$15-$20
Mini helmet $40

Len Dawson (1935-) 1987
Football $125
Cut signature ....$5-$8

Goal Line art $25
3x5 index card ....$7-$8
8x10 photograph $25
Mini helmet $50

Eric Dickerson (1960-) 1999
Football $90
Cut signature $5
Goal Line art $16
3x5 index card $5
8x10 photograph ....$20-$25
Mini helmet $50

Dan Dierdorf (1949-) 1996

Football $80
Cut signature $5
Goal Line art $15
3x5 index card $5
8x10 photograph $15
Mini helmet $40

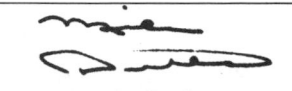

Mike Ditka (1939-) 1988
Football . . . .$100-$150
Cut signature . . . .$10-$12
Goal Line art $20
3x5 index card . . . .$7-$10
8x10 photograph . . . .$20-$30
Mini helmet $50

Art Donovan (1925-) 1968
Football $75
Cut signature . . . .$3-$7
Goal Line art $20
3x5 index card $5
8x10 photograph $20
Mini helmet $40

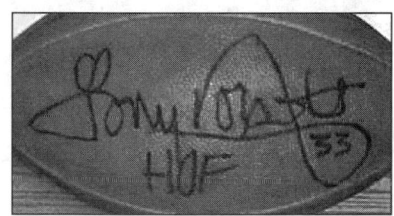

Tony Dorsett (1954-) 1994
Football . . . .$125-$150
Cut signature $3
Goal Line art $40
3x5 index card $5
8x10 photograph $25
Mini helmet $60

Paddy Driscoll (1896-1968) 1965
Football . . . . .Unknown
Cut signature $100
Goal Line art . . . . .Impossible
3x5 index card $200
8x10 photograph . . . .$250-$350
Mini helmet . . . . .Impossible

Bill Dudley (1921-) 1966
Football $75
Cut signature . . . .$5-$6
Goal Line art $15
3x5 index card . . . .$5-$7
8x10 photograph $15
Mini helmet $40

Turk Edwards (1907-1973) 1969
Football . . . . .Unknown
Cut signature $80

Goal Line art . . . . .Impossible
3x5 index card $125
8x10 photograph $300
Mini helmet . . . . .Impossible

Weeb Ewbank (1907-1998) 1978
Football $75
Cut signature . . . .$3-$6
Goal Line art $15
3x5 index card . . . .$7-$10
8x10 photograph $20
Mini helmet $45

Tom Fears (1923-2000) 1970
Football $85
Cut signature . . . .$3-$7
Goal Line art $15
3x5 index card . . . .$5-$9
8x10 photograph $15
Mini helmet $45

Jim Finks (1904-1994) 1995
Football $150
Cut signature $5
Goal Line art . . . . .Impossible
3x5 index card $10
8x10 photograph $30
Mini helmet . . . . .Unknown

Ray Flaherty (1904-1994) 1976
Football $150
Cut signature $5
Goal Line art $40
3x5 index card $10
8x10 photograph $25
Mini helmet . . . . .Unknown

Len Ford (1926-1972) 1976
Football . . . . .Unknown
Cut signature . . . .$25-$30
Goal Line art . . . . .Impossible
3x5 index card $50
8x10 photograph $200
Mini helmet . . . . .Impossible

Dan Fortmann (1916-1995) 1985
Football . . . . .Unknown
Cut signature $20
Goal Line art . . . . .Impossible
3x5 index card $25
8x10 photograph . . . .$50-$75
Mini helmet . . . . .Unknown

Dan Fouts (1951-) 1993
Football $100
Cut signature $4
Goal Line art $25
3x5 index card $7
8x10 photograph $35
Mini helmet $50

Frank Gatski (1922-) 1985
Football $75
Cut signature $3
Goal Line art $15
3x5 index card $3
8x10 photograph . . . .$15-$20
Mini helmet $40

Bill George (1930-1982) 1974
Football . . . . .Unknown
Cut signature . . . .$40-$50
Goal Line art . . . . .Impossible
3x5 index card $75
8x10 photograph $250
Mini helmet . . . . .Impossible

Joe Gibbs (1940-) 1996
Football . . . .$100-$125
Cut signature . . . .$6-$7
Goal Line art $15
3x5 index card . . . .$7-$10
8x10 photograph $25
Mini helmet $40

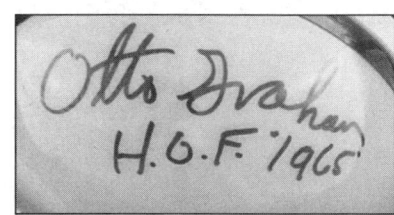

Frank Gifford (1930-) 1977
Football . . . .$100-$150
Cut signature . . . .$6-$7
Goal Line art $35
3x5 index card . . . .$10-$15
8x10 photograph $35
Mini helmet $45

Sid Gillman (1911-) 1983
Football $75
Cut signature . . . .$3-$6
Goal Line art $15
3x5 index card $6
8x10 photograph $20
Mini helmet $45

Otto Graham (1921-) 1965
Football . . . .$125-$150
Cut signature . . . .$7-$9
Goal Line art $20
3x5 index card . . . .$5-$8
8x10 photograph $20
Mini helmet . . . . .Impossible

Red Grange (1903-1991) 1963
Football . . . .$475-$600
Cut signature $35

Goal Line art $200
3x5 index card $25
8x10 photograph $125
Mini helmet . . . . .Impossible

Bud Grant (1927-) 1994
Football $85
Cut signature $3
Goal Line art $30
3x5 index $5
8x10 photograph $25
Mini helmet $40

Joe Greene (1946-) 1987
Football . . . .$75-$125
Cut signature $3
Goal Line art $25
3x5 index card $7
8x10 photograph $35
Mini helmet $45

Forrest Gregg (1933-) 1977
Football $75
Cut signature . . . .$7-$9
Goal Line art $20
3x5 index card $6
8x10 photograph $15
Mini helmet $40

Bob Griese (1945-) 1990
Football $125
Cut signature . . . .$4-$6
Goal Line art $30
3x5 index card $7
8x10 photograph $20
Mini helmet $45

Lou Groza (1924-2000) 1974
Football $100
Cut signature . . . .$3-$6
Goal Line art $15
3x5 index card $6

8x10 photograph . . . .$15-$20
Mini helmet $40

Joe Guyon (1892-1971) 1966
Football . . . . .Unknown
Cut signature $35
Goal Line art . . . . .Impossible
3x5 index card $75
8x10 photograph $300
Mini helmet . . . . .Impossible

George Halas (1895-1983) 1963
Football . . . .$250-$300
Cut signature . . . .$20-$25
Goal Line art . . . . .Impossible
3x5 index card $50
8x10 photograph . . . .$175-$250
Mini helmet . . . . .Impossible

Jack Ham (1948-) 1988
Football . . . .$75-$100
Cut signature $3
Goal Line art $15
3x5 index card . . . .$7-$10
8x10 photograph . . . .$15-$20
Mini helmet $45

John Hannah (1951-) 1991
Football $75
Cut signature . . . .$3-$6
Goal Line art $20
3x5 index card . . . .$5-$8
8x10 photograph $20
Mini helmet $40

Franco Harris (1950-) 1990
Football $125
Cut signature . . . .$10-$12
Goal Line art $40
3x5 index card $8
8x10 photograph $25
Mini helmet $90

Mike Haynes (1953-) 1997
Football $75
Cut signature $7
Goal Line Art $15
3x5 index card $7
8x10 photograph . . . .$15-$18
Mini helmet $40

Ed Healey (1894-1978) 1964
Football $150
Cut signature $60
Goal Line art . . . . .Impossible
3x5 index card . . . .$50-$75
8x10 photograph $250
Mini helmet . . . . .Impossible

Mel Hein (1909-1992) 1963
Football $175
Cut signature . . . .$10-$15
Goal Line art . . . . .Impossible
3x5 index card . . . .$12-$15
8x10 photograph . . . .$40-$60
Mini helmet . . . . .Unknown

Ted Hendricks (1947-) 1990
Football $75
Cut signature . . . .$3-$6
Goal Line art $20
3x5 index card $6
8x10 photograph . . . .$15-$20
Mini helmet $40

Pete Henry (1897-1952) 1963
Football . . . . .Unknown
Cut signature $50
Goal Line art . . . . .Impossible
3x5 index card $75
8x10 photograph $275
Mini helmet . . . . .Impossible

Arnie Herber (1910-1969) 1966
Football . . . . .Unknown
Cut signature $75
Goal Line art . . . . .Impossible
3x5 index card $125
8x10 photograph . . . .$400-$500
Mini helmet . . . . .Impossible

Bill Hewitt (1909-1947) 1971
Football . . . . .Unknown
Cut signature $100
Goal Line art . . . . .Impossible
3x5 index card $200
8x10 photograph $600
Mini helmet . . . . .Impossible

Clarke Hinkle (1909-1988) 1964
Football $200
Cut signature $10
Goal Line art . . . . .Impossible
3x5 index card $30
8x10 photograph $50
Mini helmet . . . . .Impossible

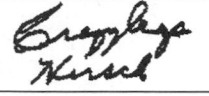

Elroy Hirsch (1923-) 1968
Football $125
Cut signature $5
Goal Line art $15
3x5 index card $8
8x10 photograph $20
Mini helmet $50

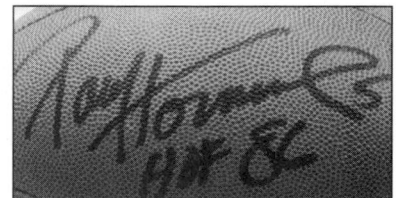

Paul Hornung (1935-) 1986
Football $125
Cut signature . . . .$5-$10
Goal Line art $30
3x5 index card $8
8x10 photograph . . . .$20-$25
Mini helmet $50

Ken Houston (1944-) 1986
Football $75
Cut signature . . . .$7-$10
Goal Line art $15
3x5 index card $6
8x10 photograph . . . .$15-$20
Mini helmet $40

Cal Hubbard (1900-1977) 1963
Football . . . . .Unknown
Cut signature $25
Goal Line art . . . . .Impossible
3x5 index card $50
8x10 photograph . . . .$200-$250
Mini helmet . . . . .Impossible

Sam Huff (1934-) 1982
Football $100
Cut signature $3

Goal Line art $20
3x5 index card $6
8x10 photograph $25
Mini helmet $45

Lamar Hunt (1932-) 1972
Football $75
Cut signature . . . .$6-$8
Goal Line art $15
3x5 index card $8
8x10 photograph $20
Mini helmet $40

Don Hutson (1913-1997) 1963
Football $75
Cut signature . . . .$8-$10
Goal Line art $40
3x5 index card $10
8x10 photograph . . . .$25-$35
Mini helmet $60

Jimmy Johnson (1938-) 1994
Football $75
Cut signature $3
Goal Line art $20
3x5 index card $5
8x10 photograph $20
Mini helmet $40

John Henry Johnson (1929-) 1987
Football $75
Cut signature . . . .$6-$7
Goal Line art $20
3x5 index card . . . .$6-$8
8x10 photograph $15
Mini helmet . . . .$

Charlie Joiner (1947-) 1996
Football . . . .$75-$80
Cut signature $5
Goal Line art $15
3x5 index card $5
8x10 photograph . . . .$15-$18
Mini helmet $40

Deacon Jones (1938-) 1980
Football $100
Cut signature $3
Goal Line art $15
3x5 index card $7
8x10 photograph $15
Mini helmet $45

Stan Jones (1931-) 1991
Football $75
Cut signature . . . .$5-$6
Goal Line art $15
3x5 index card $6
8x10 photograph . . . .$12-$15
Mini helmet $40

Henry Jordan (1935-1976) 1995
Football . . . . .Unknown
Cut signature $50

Goal Line art . . . . .Impossible
3x5 index card $100
8x10 photograph $175
Mini helmet . . . . .Impossible

Sonny Jurgensen (1934-) 1983
Football $125
Cut signature $5
Goal Line art . . . .$25-$30
3x5 index card $5
8x10 photograph $20
Mini helmet $50

Leroy Kelly (1942-) 1994
Football $100
Cut signature $3
Goal Line art $15
3x5 index card $5
8x10 photograph $15
Mini helmet $40

Walt Kiesling (1903-1962) 1966
Football . . . . .Unknown
Cut signature $75
Goal Line art . . . . .Impossible
3x5 index card $150
8x10 photograph . . . .$100-$200
Mini helmet . . . . .Impossible

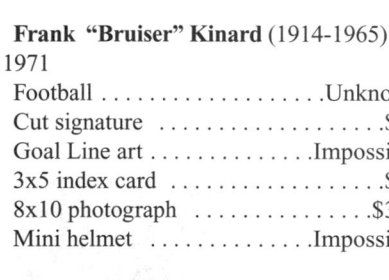

Frank "Bruiser" Kinard (1914-1965) 1971
Football . . . . .Unknown
Cut signature $50
Goal Line art . . . . .Impossible
3x5 index card $75
8x10 photograph $300
Mini helmet . . . . .Impossible

Paul Krause (1942-) 1998
Football $75
Cut signature $5
Goal Line art $15
3x5 index card $5
8x10 photograph . . . .$15-$18
Mini helmet $40

Curly Lambeau (1898-1965) 1963
Football . . . . .Unknown
Cut signature $125
Goal Line art . . . . .Impossible
3x5 index card $200

8x10 photograph . . . .$300-$400
Mini helmet . . . . .Impossible

Jack Lambert (1952-) 1990
Football $150
Cut signature $3
Goal Line art $30
3x5 index card $6
8x10 photograph . . . .$22-$25
Mini helmet $60

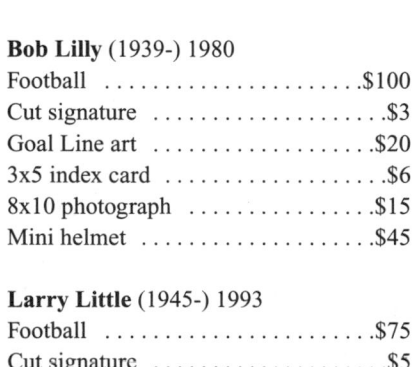

Tom Landry (1924-2000) 1990
Football $125
Cut signature $5
Goal Line art $25
3x5 index card $7
8x10 photograph . . . .$25-$35
Mini helmet $50

Dick Lane (1928-) 1974
Football $75
Cut signature $3
Goal Line art $15
3x5 index card $6
8x10 photograph $15
Mini helmet $40

Jim Langer (1948-) 1987
Football . . . .$75-$100
Cut signature . . . .$5-$8
Goal Line art $15
3x5 index card . . . .$6-$8
8x10 photograph $15
Mini helmet $40

Willie Lanier (1945-) 1986
Football $75
Cut signature $3
Goal Line art $15
3x5 index card $6
8x10 photograph $15
Mini helmet $40

Steve Largent (1954-) 1995
Football $125
Cut signature $4
Goal Line art $15
3x5 index card $8
8x10 photograph $20
Mini helmet $45

Yale Lary (1930-) 1979
Football $75
Cut signature $3
Goal Line art $15
3x5 index card $5
8x10 photograph $15
Mini helmet $40

Dante Lavelli (1923-) 1975
Football $75
Cut signature $3
Goal Line art $15
3x5 index card $6
8x10 photograph $15
Mini helmet $40

Bobby Layne (1926-1986) 1967
Football . . . .$400-$500
Cut signature $15
Goal Line art . . . . .Impossible
3x5 index card $35
8x10 photograph . . . .$65-$85
Mini helmet . . . . .Impossible

Tuffy Leemans (1912-1979) 1978
Football . . . . .Unknown
Cut signature $75
Goal Line art . . . . .Impossible
3x5 index card $125
8x10 photograph $200
Mini helmet . . . . .Impossible

Bob Lilly (1939-) 1980
Football $100
Cut signature $3
Goal Line art $20
3x5 index card $6
8x10 photograph $15
Mini helmet $45

Larry Little (1945-) 1993
Football $75
Cut signature $5
Goal Line art $15
3x5 index card $5
8x10 photograph $15
Mini helmet $40

Vince Lombardi (1913-1970) 1971
Football . . . .$1,500-$1,750
Cut signature . . . .$75-$100
Goal Line art . . . . .Impossible
3x5 index card $150
8x10 photograph . . . .$400-$500
Mini helmet . . . . .Impossible

Howie Long (1960-) 2000
Football $125
Cut signature $8
Goal Line art $18
3x5 index card $10
8x10 photograph $20
Mini helmet $40

Ronnie Lott (1959-) 2000
Football $100
Cut signature . . . .$5-$7
Goal Line art $15
3x5 index card $8
8x10 photograph $15
Mini helmet $40

Sid Luckman (1916-1998) 1965
Football $125
Cut signature $3
Goal Line art $30
3x5 index card $6
8x10 photograph . . . .$17-$20
Mini helmet $45

Link Lyman (1898-1972) 1964
Football . . . . .Unknown
Cut signature $75
Goal Line art . . . . .Impossible
3x5 index card $100
8x10 photograph $200
Mini helmet . . . . .Impossible

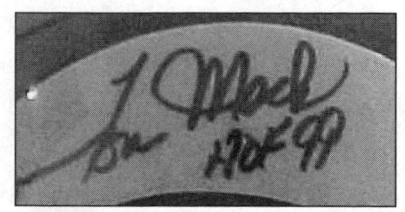

Tom Mack (1943-) 1999
Football $75
Cut signature $4
Goal Line art $15
3x5 index card $4
8x10 photograph . . . .$14-$17
Mini helmet $40

John Mackey (1941-) 1992
Football $75
Cut signature $3
Goal Line art $15
3x5 index card $6
8x10 photograph $15
Mini helmet $40

Tim Mara (1887-1959) 1963
Football . . . . .Unknown
Cut signature $200
Goal Line art . . . . .Impossible
3x5 index card $300
8x10 photograph $700
Mini helmet . . . . .Impossible

Wellington Mara (1916-) 1997
Football $70
Cut signature $3
Goal Line art $14
3x5 index card $3
8x10 photograph $14
Mini helmet $40

Gino Marchetti (1927-) 1972
Football $75
Cut signature $3
Goal Line art $15
3x5 index card $5
8x10 photograph $15
Mini helmet $40

George Marshall (1887-1969) 1963
Football . . . . .Unknown
Cut signature $125
Goal Line art . . . . .Impossible
3x5 index card $200
8x10 photograph $400
Mini helmet . . . . .Impossible

Ollie Matson (1930-) 1972
Football $75
Cut signature $3
Goal Line art $20

3x5 index card $6
8x10 photograph $15
Mini helmet $40

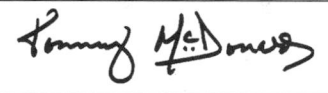

Don Maynard (1935-) 1987
Football $100
Cut signature . . . .$3-$7
Goal Line art $20
3x5 index card $6
8x10 photograph $15
Mini helmet $45

George McAfee (1918-) 1966
Football $75
Cut signature $7
Goal Line art $15
3x5 index card $5
8x10 photograph $15
Mini helmet $40

Mike McCormack (1930-) 1984
Football $75
Cut signature . . . .$3-$5
Goal Line art $15
3x5 index card $5
8x10 photograph $15
Mini helmet $40

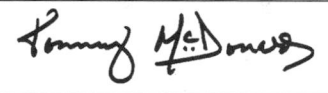

Tommy McDonald (1934-) 1998
Football $70
Cut signature $6
Goal Line art $15
3x5 index card $6
8x10 photograph . . . .$15-$19
Mini helmet $40

Hugh McElhenny (1928-) 1970
Football $100
Cut signature $10
Goal Line art $20
3x5 index card . . . .$10-$13
8x10 photograph $25
Mini helmet $40

John McNally (1903-1985) 1963
Football $500
Cut signature $25
Goal Line art . . . . .Impossible
3x5 index card $50
8x10 photograph . . . .$100-$150
Mini helmet . . . . .Impossible

Mike Michalske (1903-1983) 1964
Football $400
Cut signature $20
Goal Line art . . . . .Impossible
3x5 index card $40
8x10 photograph . . . .$150-$200
Mini helmet . . . . .Impossible

Wayne Millner (1913-1976) 1968
Football . . . . .Unknown
Cut signature $75
Goal Line art . . . . .Impossible
3x5 index card $100
8x10 photograph $300
Mini helmet . . . . .Impossible

Bobby Mitchell (1935-) 1983
Football $75
Cut signature $3
Goal Line art $20
3x5 index card $5
8x10 photograph . . . .$15-$20
Mini helmet $40

Ron Mix (1938-) 1979
Football $75
Cut signature . . . .$5-$6
Goal Line art $20
3x5 index card $6
8x10 photograph $15
Mini helmet $40

Lenny Moore (1933-) 1975
Football $75
Cut signature . . . .$6-$7
Goal Line art $20
3x5 index card . . . .$6-$9
8x10 photograph $15
Mini helmet $40

Joe Montana (1956-) 2000
Football $250
Cut signature $40
Goal Line art $65
3x5 index card $45
8x10 photograph $75
Mini helmet $100

Marion Motley (1920-1999) 1968
Football $75
Cut signature . . . .$3-$8
Goal Line art $15
3x5 index card . . . .$6-$10
8x10 photograph $15
Mini helmet $40

Anthony Munoz (1958-) 1998
Football $80
Cut signature $8
Goal Line art $16
3x5 index card $8
8x10 . . . .$18-$20
Mini helmet $40

George Musso (1910-2000) 1982
Football $75
Cut signature . . . .$3-$5
Goal Line art $15
3x5 index card $5
8x10 photograph $15
Mini helmet $40

Bronko Nagurski (1908-1990) 1963
Football $350
Cut signature $25
Goal Line art . . . . .Impossible
3x5 index card . . . .$35-$50
8x10 photograph . . . .$100-$150
Mini helmet . . . . .Impossible

Joe Namath (1943-) 1985
Football $150
Cut signature . . . .$10-$12
Goal Line art $60
3x5 index card . . . .$20-$30
8x10 photograph $40
Mini helmet $150

Earle "Greasy" Neale (1891-1973) 1969
Football . . . . .Unknown
Cut signature . . . .$50-$75
Goal Line art . . . . .Impossible
3x5 index card $100
8x10 photograph $300
Mini helmet . . . . .Impossible

Ernie Nevers (1903-1976) 1963
Football . . . . .Unknown
Cut signature $50
Goal Line art . . . . .Impossible

3x5 index card $80
8x10 photograph . . . .$150-$250
Mini helmet . . . . .Impossible

Ozzie Newsome (1956-) 1999
Football $75
Cut signature $5
Goal Line art $20
3x5 index card $6
8x10 photograph . . . .$15-$20
Mini helmet $40

Ray Nitschke (1936-1998) 1978
Football $100
Cut signature . . . .$3-$6
Goal Line art $25
3x5 index card $6
8x10 photograph $20
Mini helmet $60

Chuck Noll (1932-) 1993
Football $75
Cut signature $3
Goal Line art $15
3x5 index card $6
8x10 photograph $15
Mini helmet $40

Leo Nomellini (1924-) 1969
Football $75
Cut signature . . . .$3-$10
Goal Line art $20
3x5 index card $6
8x10 photograph . . . .$15-$20
Mini helmet $40

Merlin Olsen (1940-) 1982
Football . . . .$75-$100
Cut signature . . . .$5-$7
Goal Line art $20
3x5 index card $10
8x10 photograph . . . .$25-$30
Mini helmet $45

Jim Otto (1938-) 1980
Football $75
Cut signature . . . .$3-$6

Goal Line art $20
3x5 index card $6
8x10 photograph $15
Mini helmet $40

Steve Owen (1898-1964) 1966
Football . . . . .Unknown
Cut signature $200
Goal Line art . . . . .Impossible
3x5 index card $400
8x10 photograph $750
Mini helmet . . . . .Impossible

Alan Page (1945-) 1988
Football . . . .$75-$100
Cut signature $3
Goal Line art $15
3x5 index card $6
8x10 photograph $15
Mini helmet $40

Ace Parker (1912-) 1972
Football $75
Cut signature $3
Goal Line art $15
3x5 index card $6
8x10 photograph $15
Mini helmet $40

Jim Parker (1934-) 1973
Football $75
Cut signature $3
Goal Line art $15
3x5 index card $5
8x10 photograph $15
Mini helmet $40

Walter Payton (1954-1999) 1993
Football $150
Cut signature . . . .$6-$8
Goal Line art . . . .$30-$35
3x5 index card . . . .$8-$10
8x10 photograph . . . .$25-$30
Mini helmet $150

Joe Perry (1927-) 1969
Football $100
Cut signature . . . .$3-$8
Goal Line art $25
3x5 index card . . . .$7-$8
8x10 photograph $20
Mini helmet $40

Pete Pihos (1923-) 1970
Football $75
Cut signature $3

Goal Line art $15
3x5 index card $6
8x10 photograph $15
Mini helmet $40

Hugh Ray (1884-1956)1966
Football . . . . .Unknown
Cut signature $200
Goal Line art . . . . .Impossible
3x5 index card . . . .$350-$400
8x10 photograph $750
Mini helmet . . . . .Impossible

Dan Reeves (1912-1971) 1967
Football . . . . .Unknown
Cut signature . . . .$50-$75
Goal Line art . . . . .Impossible
3x5 index card $100
8x10 photograph . . . .$300-$400
Mini helmet . . . . .Impossible

Mel Renfro (1941-) 1996
Football $75
Cut signature $5
Goal Line art $15
3x5 index card $5
8x10 photograph $17
Mini helmet $40

John Riggins (1949-) 1992
Football $125
Cut signature . . . .$5-$6
Goal Line art $25
3x5 index card $8
8x10 photograph $50
Mini helmet $60

Jim Ringo (1931-) 1981
Football $75
Cut signature . . . .$3-$5
Goal Line art $20
3x5 index card $15
8x10 photograph $15
Mini helmet $40

Andy Robustelli (1925-) 1971
Football $100
Cut signature $3
Goal Line art $15
3x5 index card $6
8x10 photograph $15
Mini helmet $40

Art Rooney (1901-1988) 1964
Football $300
Cut signature . . . .$7-$10
Goal Line art . . . . .Impossible
3x5 index card $25
8x10 photograph . . . .$75-$125
Mini helmet . . . . .Impossible

Dan Rooney (1932-) 2000
Football $75
Cut signature $3
Goal Line art $15
3x5 index card $6
8x10 photograph $15
Mini helmet $40

Pete Rozelle (1926-1996) 1985
Football $125
Cut signature . . . .$7-$10
Goal Line art $40
3x5 index card $15
8x10 photograph $30
Mini helmet $60

Bob St. Clair (1931-) 1990
Football $75
Cut signature . . . .$3-$6
Goal Line art $30
3x5 index card $6
8x10 photograph $15
Mini helmet $40

Gale Sayers (1943-) 1977
Football $125
Cut signature . . . .$4-$7
Goal Line art $30
3x5 index card . . . .$7-$10
8x10 photograph $20
Mini helmet $50

Joe Schmidt (1932-) 1973
Football $75
Cut signature $3
Goal Line art $15
3x5 index card . . . .$6-$9
8x10 photograph $15
Mini helmet $40

Tex Schramm (1920-) 1991
Football $75
Cut signature . . . .$3-$6

Goal Line art $15
3x5 index card . . . .$6-$9
8x10 photograph $15
Mini helmet $40

Lee Roy Selmon (1954-) 1995
Football . . . .$70-$85
Cut signature $3
Goal Line art $16
3x5 index card $5
8x10 photograph . . . .$19-$21
Mini helmet $40

Billy Shaw (1938-) 1999
Football $70
Cut signature $3
Goal Line art $14
3x5 index card $3
8x10 photograph $15
Mini helmet $40

Art Shell (1946-) 1989
Football . . . .$75-$100
Cut signature $4
Goal Line art $15
3x5 index card $6
8x10 photograph $15
Mini helmet $40

Don Shula (1930-) 1997
Football . . . .$85-$100
Cut signature $6
Goal Line art $20
3x5 index card $8
8x10 photograph . . . .$20-$25
Mini helmet $75

O.J. Simpson (1947-) 1985
Football $250
Cut signature $25
Goal Line art . . . . .Impossible
3x5 index card $35
8x10 photograph . . . .$60-$75
Mini helmet $75

Mike Singletary (1958-) 1998
Football $100
Cut signature $7
Goal Line art $25
3x5 index card $7
8x10 photograph $20
Mini helmet $45

Jackie Smith (1940-) 1994
Football $75
Cut signature $3
Goal Line art $15
3x5 index card $5
8x10 photograph $15
Mini helmet $40

Bart Starr (1934-) 1977
Football . . . .$100-$125
Cut signature $4
Goal Line art $30
3x5 index card $8
8x10 photograph $25
Mini helmet $60

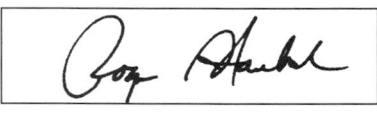

Roger Staubach (1942-) 1985
Football $150
Cut signature . . . .$5-$7
Goal Line art $40
3x5 index card $8
8x10 photograph . . . .$25-$40
Mini helmet $60

Ernie Stautner (1925-) 1969
Football $75
Cut signature $4
Goal Line art $15
3x5 index card $7
8x10 photograph $20
Mini helmet $40

Jan Stenerud (1942-) 1991
Football $75
Cut signature . . . .$3-$5
Goal Line art $15
3x5 index card $6
8x10 photograph $15
Mini helmet $40

Dwight Stephenson (1957-) 1998
Football $70
Cut signature $3
Goal Line art $14
3x5 index card $3
8x10 photograph $16
Mini helmet $40

Ken Strong (1906-1979) 1967
Football . . . . .Unknown
Cut signature $40
Goal Line art . . . . .Impossible
3x5 index card $60
8x10 photograph $200
Mini helmet . . . . .Impossible

Joe Stydahar (1912-1977) 1967
Football . . . . .Unknown
Cut signature $40
Goal Line art . . . . .Impossible
3x5 index card $60
8x10 photograph $25
Mini helmet . . . . .Impossible

Fran Tarkenton (1940-) 1986
Football $150
Cut signature . . . .$5-$10
Goal Line art $40
3x5 index card $10
8x10 photograph . . . .$25-$30
Mini helmet $55

Charley Taylor (1941-) 1984
Football $75
Cut signature $4
Goal Line art $20
3x5 index card $6
8x10 photograph $15
Mini helmet $40

Jim Taylor (1935-) 1976
Football $75
Cut signature $4
Goal Line art $20
3x5 index card $5
8x10 photograph $15
Mini helmet $45

Lawrence Taylor (1959-) 1999
Football . . . .$80-$90
Cut signature . . . .$6-$8
Goal Line art $25
3x5 index card $7

8x10 photograph . . . .$20-$25
Mini helmet $60

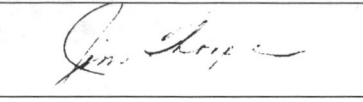

Jim Thorpe (1888-1953) 1963
Football $6,000
Cut signature $500
Goal Line art . . . . .Impossible
3x5 index card $700
8x10 photograph $1,500
Mini helmet . . . . .Impossible

Y.A. Tittle (1926-) 1971
Football $100
Cut signature $4
Goal Line art $25
3x5 index card $6
8x10 photograph $25
Mini helmet $45

George Trafton (1896-1971) 1964
Football . . . . .Unknown
Cut signature $75
Goal Line art . . . . .Impossible
3x5 index card $125
8x10 photograph $250
Mini helmet . . . . .Impossible

Charley Trippi (1922-) 1968
Football $75
Cut signature $3
Goal Line art $15
3x5 index card $6
8x10 photograph . . . .$18-$20
Mini helmet $40

Emlen Tunnell (1925-1975) 1967
Football . . . . .Unknown
Cut signature $40
Goal Line art . . . . .Impossible
3x5 index card $75
8x10 photograph $200
Mini helmet . . . . .Impossible

Bulldog Turner (1919-1998) 1966
Football $100
Cut signature $4
Goal Line art $25

3x5 index card $7
8x10 photograph $20
Mini helmet $45

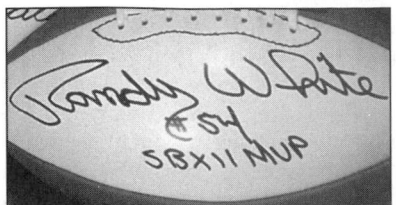

Johnny Unitas (1933-) 1979
Football $150
Cut signature . . . .$5-$10
Goal Line art . . . . .Impossible
3x5 index card $8
8x10 photograph $20
Mini helmet $70

Gene Upshaw (1945-) 1987
Football $75
Cut signature . . . .$3-$7
Goal Line art $15
3x5 index card $6
8x10 photograph $15
Mini helmet $40

Norm Van Brocklin (1926-1983) 1971
Football $350
Cut signature $40
Goal Line art . . . . .Impossible
3x5 index card $75
8x10 photograph . . . .$200-$225
Mini helmet . . . . .Impossible

Steve Van Buren (1920-) 1965
Football $75
Cut signature $3
Goal Line art $20
3x5 index card $5
8x10 photograph $15
Mini helmet $40

Doak Walker (1927-1998) 1986
Football $100
Cut signature $3

Goal Line art $25
3x5 index card $5
8x10 photograph $20
Mini helmet $45

Bill Walsh (1931-) 1993
Football $125
Cut signature $5
Goal Line art $50
3x5 index card $10
8x10 photograph $25
Mini helmet $45

Paul Warfield (1942-) 1983
Football $75
Cut signature $3
Goal Line art $15
3x5 index card $6
8x10 photograph . . . .$15-$20
Mini helmet $40

Bob Waterfield (1920-1983) 1965
Football $350
Cut signature . . . .$30-$40
Goal Line art . . . . .Impossible
3x5 index card $75
8x10 photograph . . . .$175-$250
Mini helmet . . . . .Impossible

Mike Webster (1952-) 1997
Football $75
Cut signature $4
Goal Line art $15
3x5 index card $4
8x10 photograph . . . .$15-$20
Mini helmet $40

Arnie Weinmeister (1923-2000) 1984
Football $75
Cut signature $3
Goal Line art $15
3x5 index card $5
8x10 photograph $15
Mini helmet $40

Randy White (1953-) 1994
Football $75
Cut signature $4
Goal Line art $15
3x5 index card $4
8x10 photograph . . . .$16-$18
Mini helmet $45

Dave Wilcox (1942-) 2000
Football $75
Cut signature $4
Goal Line art $15
3x5 index card $4
8x10 photograph . . . .$16-$18
Mini helmet $40

Bill Willis (1921-) 1977
Football $75
Cut signature $3
Goal Line art $20
3x5 index card $6
8x10 photograph $15
Mini helmet $40

Larry Wilson (1938-) 1978
Football $75
Cut signature $3
Goal Line art $15
3x5 index card $6
8x10 photograph $15
Mini helmet $40

Kellen Winslow (1957-) 1995
Football $100
Cut signature $3
Goal Line art $15
3x5 index card $5
8x10 photograph $15
Mini helmet $40

Alex Wojciechowicz (1915-1992) .1968
Football $200
Cut signature $8
Goal Line art $150
3x5 index card $10
8x10 photograph . . . .$35-$50
Mini helmet . . . . .Unknown

Willie Wood (1936-) 1989
Football $75
Cut signature $3
Goal Line art $15
3x5 index card $5
8x10 photograph $15
Mini helmet $40

Football Equipment

All listed equipment values are for game-used equipment only. Many variables are involved in pricing equipment, including player popularity, condition, scarcity, year the item is from, provenance and whether or not it was a home or road jersey. The prices listed below are merely a starting point.

Hall of Fame Players

Player	Spikes	Helmet	Jersey
Herb Adderley	200	2,000	1,900
Lance Alworth	200	2,250	2,000
Doug Atkins	200	1,950	1,900
Cliff Battles	225	4,750	4,500
Sammy Baugh	825	30,000	28,000
Chuck Bednarik	275	8,000	6,750
Bobby Bell	200	1,975	1,900
Raymond Berry	250	4,500	4,300
Fred Biletnikoff	175	1,725	1,650
George Blanda	225	7,750	6,500
Mel Blount	175	1,700	1,600
Terry Bradshaw	225	8,000	6,750
Jim Brown	400	10,000	8,250
Roosevelt Brown	200	1,975	1,900
Willie Brown	200	1,950	1,875
Buck Buchanan	200	2,000	1,925
Nick Buoniconti	175	1,725	1,650
Dick Butkus	325	4,250	4,000
Earl Campbell	185	1,850	1,800
Tony Canadeo	200	4,500	3,750
Jack Christiansen	225	4,250	4,000
George Connor	200	1,925	1,650
Larry Csonka	180	1,875	1,800
Willie Davis	195	1,850	1,800
Len Dawson	225	2,250	2,000
Eric Dickerson	200	2,150	2,100
Mike Ditka	200	2,000	1,900
Art Donovan	200	2,500	2,250
Tony Dorsett	200	2,500	2,250
Bill Dudley	225	4,250	4,000
Turk Edwards	225	4,000	2,900
Tom Fears	225	4,000	2,750
Len Ford	200	1,950	1,900
Danny Fortmann	250	4,500	4,250
Frank Gatski	185	1,850	1,800
Bill George	225	2,750	2,500
Frank Gifford	375	10,750	10,500
Otto Graham	400	12,250	12,000
Red Grange	500	24,000	12,500
Joe Greene	180	1,850	1,775
Forrest Gregg	185	1,875	1,725
Bob Griese	190	1,950	1,825
Lou Groza	200	2,500	2,400
Jack Ham	165	1,675	1,550
John Hannah	175	1,650	1,500
Franco Harris	190	2,000	1,850
Arnie Herber	400	12,000	10,000
Bill Hewitt	225	4,000	2,950
Clarke Hinkle	450	14,000	12,000
Elroy Hirsch	325	10,400	10,200
Paul Hornung	200	2,250	2,000
Ken Houston	195	1,950	1,900

Earl Campbell Houston Oilers helmet

Player	Spikes	Helmet	Jersey
Sam Huff	200	2,250	2,000
Don Hutson	550	24,500	20,000
Jimmy Johnson	300	6,000	5,500
John H. Johnson	195	1,950	1,875
Deacon Jones	200	1,850	1,775
Stan Jones	190	1,875	1,800
Henry Jordan	200	2,000	1,850
Sonny Jurgensen	225	2,500	2,250
Leroy Kelly	200	2,000	1,850
Bruiser Kinard	250	2,750	2,500
Paul Krause	175	1,750	1,650
Jack Lambert	175	1,750	1,700
Tom Landry	300	8,500	8,250
Dick Lane	195	1,975	1,925
Jim Langer	185	1,800	1,750
Willie Lanier	185	1,850	1,775
Steve Largent	200	2,150	2,000
Yale Lary	185	1,825	1,750
Dante Lavelli	195	1,975	1,900
Bobby Layne	350	14,250	14,000
Tuffy Leemans	185	1,950	1,900
Bob Lilly	180	1,850	1,800
Howie Long	175	2,200	2,000
Ronnie Lott	175	2,100	1,950
Sid Luckman	275	8,000	6,800
Link Lyman	325	NA	16,000
Tom Mack	175	2,100	1,900
Gino Marchetti	200	2,250	2,000
Ollie Matson	200	2,250	2,000
Don Maynard	190	1,950	1,900
George McAfee	225	6,000	4,800
Mike McCormack	195	1,975	1,900
Tommy McDonald	175	2,000	1,850
Hugh McElhenny	225	4,750	4,600
Mike Michalske	400	NA	16,000
Wayne Milner	250	6,000	4,850
Bobby Mitchell	195	1,900	1,850
Ron Mix	190	1,875	1,800
Joe Montana	3,250	6,500	6,250
Lenny Moore	200	2,000	1,850
Marion Motley	225	4,250	4,000
Mike Munchak	175	1,800	1,700
Anthony Munoz	195	2,000	1,900
George Musso	195	1,950	1,900
Bronko Nagurski	2,500	40,000	38,000
Joe Namath	400	11,000	8,500
Ernie Nevers	1,250	NA	30,000
Ozzie Newsome	195	2,100	1,950
Ray Nitschke	350	3,500	3,250
Leo Nomellini	225	2,800	2,500
Merlin Olsen	200	2,500	2,350

Player	Spikes	Helmet	Jersey
Jim Otto	200	2,250	2,000
Steve Owen	750	NA	18,000
Alan Page	190	1,900	1,850
Ace Parker	225	2,500	2,250
Jim Parker	200	2,250	2,000
Walter Payton	750	12,000	10,500
Joe Perry	250	4,000	2,750
Pete Pihos	200	2,250	2,000
Mel Renfro	200	2,000	1,900
Jim Ringo	195	1,950	1,875
Andy Robustelli	225	2,500	2,250
Bob St. Clair	190	1,900	1,800
Gale Sayers	300	11,000	10,000
Joe Schmidt	225	2,400	2,200
Lee Roy Selmon	195	1,900	1,800
Billy Shaw	225	1,950	1,750
Art Shell	225	1,900	1,850
O.J. Simpson	300	4,000	3,750
Mike Singletary	200	2,250	2,000
Jackie Slater	175	1,750	1,650
Jackie Smith	175	1,800	1,700
Bart Starr	300	11,750	10,500
Roger Staubach	275	6,500	6,250
Ernie Stautner	250	4,000	2,750
Jan Stenerud	180	1,800	1,700
Dwight Stephenson	175	1,750	1,650
Ken Strong	225	2,500	2,250
Joe Stydahar	225	2,500	2,250
Lynn Swann	200	2,750	2,500
Fran Tarkenton	250	4,500	4,000
Charley Taylor	190	1,900	1,825
Jim Taylor	200	2,250	2,000
Lawrence Taylor	250	2,300	2,200
Jim Thorpe	2,500	NA	40,000
Y.A. Tittle	300	8,750	8,500
George Trafton	350	19,000	18,500
Charlie Trippi	275	7,000	6,500
Emlen Tunnell	275	6,750	6,250
Bulldog Turner	300	10,500	10,000
Johnny Unitas	300	12,750	12,500
Gene Upshaw	190	1,900	1,825
Norm Van Brocklin	250	8,500	8,250
Steve Van Buren	225	2,750	2,500
Doak Walker	225	2,900	2,825
Paul Warfield	190	1,950	1,875
Bob Waterfield	375	20,000	19,750
Mike Webster	195	1,900	1,800
Arnie Weinmeister	190	1,975	1,900
Randy White	190	1,900	1,800
Dave Wilcox	175	1,800	1,650
Bill Willis	195	1,950	1,875
Larry Wilson	190	1,925	1,850
Kellen Winslow	195	2,000	1,900
Alex Wojciechowicz	250	4,000	3,800
Willie Wood	190	1,950	2,875
Ron Yary	210	2,300	2,000
Jack Youngblood	200	2,250	2,100

Inactive Players

Player	Spikes	Helmet	Jersey
Marcus Allen	200	1,250	1,100
Flipper Anderson	150	425	325
Neal Anderson	180	850	750
Ottis Anderson	160	550	400
Steve Atwater	150	600	475
Johnny Bailey	145	450	325

Dan Marino game-used helmet

Player	Spikes	Helmet	Jersey
Troy Aikman	370	4,300	4,200
Jerry Ball	135	1,650	1,550
Fred Barnett	140	1,675	1,575
Nick Bell	145	1,200	1,000
Cornelius Bennett	160	1,800	1,675
Rod Bernstine	140	1,375	1,300
Eric Bieniemy	140	1,400	1,325
Brian Blades	150	1,500	1,375
James Brooks	150	1,450	1,350
Steve Broussard	140	1,425	1,325
Jerome Brown	140	1,375	1,325
Jarrod Bunch	140	1,425	1,300
Marion Butts	145	1,500	1,450
Keith Byars	140	1,400	1,325
Mark Carrier	145	1,650	1,575
Wesley Carroll	140	1,375	1,300
Anthony Carter	145	1,425	1,350
Dexter Carter	140	1,450	1,350
Mark Clayton	140	1,450	1,375
Reggie Cobb	140	1,500	1,450
Roger Craig	175	1,900	1,800
Mike Croel	145	1,475	1,400
Richard Dent	185	1,625	1,475
John Elway	1,500	6,250	5,750
Ricky Ervins	150	1,700	1,625
Boomer Esiason	175	1,575	1,475
Jim Everett	175	1,750	1,600
Derrick Fanner	140	1,350	1,250
Willie Gault	145	1,500	1,375
Derrick Fenner	1 40	1,350	1,250
Willie Gault	145	1,500	1,375
Eric Green	145	1,475	1,425
Gaston Green	140	1,475	1,400
Harold Green	140	1,475	1,425
Rodney Hampton	160	1,575	1,450
Alvin Harper	145	1,550	1,500
Michael Haynes	140	1,450	1,400
Bobby Hebert	160	1,500	1,450
Craig Heyward	150	1,525	1,475
Randall Hill	140	1,425	1,350
Dalton Hilliard	140	1,400	1,350
Jeff Hostetler	165	1,550	1,475
Bobby Humphrey	140	1,400	1,325
Michael Irvin	245	2,800	2,725
Bo Jackson	375	3,250	3,000
Haywood Jeffires	140	1,425	1,325
Johnson Johnny	140	1,400	1,325
Seth Joyner	140	1,375	1,300
Napoleon Kaufman	220	2,000	1,850
Jim Kelly	235	2,650	2,550
Bernie Kosar	215	1,900	1,800
Greg Lewis	140	1,400	1,300
James Lofton	195	1,950	1,850
Don Majkowski	145	1,450	1,325
Dan Marino	750	6,400	6,250
Dan McGwire	50	800	750
Jim McMahon	185	1,950	1,850
Dave Meggett	145	1,475	1,350
Chris Miller	150	1,525	1,450
Art Monk	275	3,000	2,850
Warren Moon	185	2,800	2,675
Browning Nagle	150	1,450	1,350
Christian Okoye	145	1,425	1,325
William Perry	200	1,800	1,700
Mike Pritchard	145	1,450	1,375
Ricky Proehl	140	1,375	1,300
Leonard Russell	150	1,475	1,400
Barry Sanders	400	4,750	4,500
Sterling Sharpe	175	2,450	2,375
Clyde Simmons	140	1,375	1,300
Phil Simms	205	2,100	2,000
Bruce Smith	160	1,800	1,675
Robert Smith	250	2,225	2,100
Chris Spielman	140	1,350	1,275
John Stallworth	195	1,950	1,900
John Stephens	140	1,350	1,300
John Taylor	185	1,850	1,750
Blair Thomas	150	1,450	1,350
Derrick Thomas	275	1,800	1,700
Thurman Thomas	375	2,900	2,800
Al Toon	145	1,425	1,325
Herschel Walker	165	1,750	1,675
Steve Walsh	150	1,400	1,350
Andre Ware	145	1,425	1,350
Reggie White	460	4,750	4,650
Harvey Williams	150	1,550	1,475
John L. Williams	140	1,350	1,275
Barry Word	145	1,475	1,425
Alexander Wright	145	1,475	1,400
Steve Young	300	4,850	4,750
Chris Zorich	140	1,350	1,300

Active Players

Player	Spikes	Helmet	Jersey
Mike Alstott	240	2,300	2,150
Champ Bailey	180	1,300	1,350
Ronde Barber	185	1,200	1,000
Tiki Barber	195	1,300	1,100
Charlie Batch	150	1,500	1,400
Jerome Bettis	190	2,000	1,900
Drew Bledsoe	250	2,750	2,500
Aaron Brooks	165	1,600	1,400
Tim Brown	200	2,000	1,950
Isaac Bruce	225	2,100	2,000
Mark Brunell	250	2,250	2,100
Cris Carter	275	2,750	2,600
Wayne Chrebet	190	1,900	1,800
Kerry Collins	175	1,500	1,400
Tim Couch	225	2,200	2,150
Daunte Culpepper	240	2,400	2,300
Randall Cunningham	225	2,250	2,150
Terrell Davis	250	2,600	2,500
Ron Dayne	185	2,000	1,900
Brett Favre	450	4,200	3,950
Marshall Faulk	325	2,900	2,750
Doug Flutie	275	2,200	2,000
Antonio Freeman	225	2,100	1,900
Joey Galloway	200	1,850	1,700
Eddie George	275	2,300	2,200
Jeff George	175	1,600	1,500
Tony Gonzalez	215	1,800	1,700
Ahman Green	170	1,500	1,400
Brian Griese	190	1,900	1,800
Jim Harbaugh	155	1,550	1,450
Garrison Hearst	200	1,900	1,800
Ike Hilliard	140	1,450	1,350
Torry Holt	190	1,800	1,750
Raghib Ismail	170	1,700	1,550
Edgerrin James	275	2,300	2,100
Brad Johnson	200	2,000	1,900
Keyshawn Johnson	240	2,300	2,200
Jevon Kearse	225	2,100	1,900
Ryan Leaf	150	1,200	1,000
Peyton Manning	300	2,800	2,600
Curtis Martin	200	1,900	1,800
Russell Maryland	140	1,425	1,350
O.J. McDuffie	210	1,950	1,850
Donovan McNabb	225	2,100	2,000
Steve McNair	210	1,900	1,750
Cade McNown	185	1,600	1,450
Eric Metcalf	140	1,375	1,250
Herman Moore	220	2,200	2,175
Rob Moore	200	1,850	1,750
Randy Moss	300	2,800	2,700
Terrell Owens	190	1,900	1,800
Jake Plummer	180	1,700	1,500
Jerry Rice	450	4,400	4,250
Andre Rison	160	1,700	1,650
Willie Roaf	150	1,600	1,450
Warren Sapp	265	2,600	2,400
Deion Sanders	300	3,000	2,800
Darnay Scott	200	1,850	1,700
Junior Seau	240	2,250	2,150
Shannon Sharpe	190	1,750	1,600
Akili Smith	235	1,950	1,800
Emmitt Smith	300	2,950	2,800
J.J. Stokes	160	1,650	1,500
Eric Swann	140	1,350	1,275
Fred Taylor	225	2,000	1,850
Vinny Testaverde	190	1,975	1,800
Ricky Watters	200	2,000	1,900
Ricky Williams	250	2,300	2,100
Charles Woodson	215	1,950	1,750

Jerry Rice game-used jersey

Football Bobbin' Head Dolls

Made in Japan from around 1960-70, there are 10 NFL categories known, due to the variations in the dolls. All are boy heads; no mascots were made. Black players exist in the gold round base series dated 1962. There were also college bobbin' head dolls made from 1962-68.

NFL wood base (1961-62)

All of these dolls, the first NFL dolls to be made, have square bases.

Team	Base Color	Value
1) Baltimore Colts	Blue	$90-$100
2) Chicago Bears	Black	$95-$105
3) Cleveland Browns	Brown	$140-$150
4) Dallas Cowboys	Blue	$160-$170
5) Detroit Lions	Silver	$60-$70
6) Green Bay Packers	Green	$100-$125
7) Los Angeles Rams	Black	$95-$125
8) Minnesota Vikings	Purple	$120-$130
9) New York Giants	Blue/Red	$130-$140
10) Philadelphia Eagles	Green	$80-$90
11) Pittsburgh Steelers	Gold	$150-$175
12) St. Louis Cardinals	Red	$50-$60
13) San Francisco 49ers	Red	$60-$70
14) Washington Redskins	Maroon	$160-$180

NFL square or round ceramic bases (1961-62)

If "NFL" is embossed on the base, add $10-$15 to basic prices. The team names are embossed on the chest; bases are various colors.

Team	Base color	Value
1) Baltimore Colts	Blue	$50-$90
2) Chicago Bears	Black	$55-$95
3) Cleveland Browns	Brown	$80-$110
4) Dallas Cowboys	Blue	$120-$140
5) Detroit Lions	Silver	$40-$80
6) Green Bay Packers	Green	$100-$175
7) Los Angeles Rams	Black	$55-$95
8) Minnesota Vikings	Purple	$65-$105
9) New York Giants	Blue/Red	$85-$125
10) Philadelphia Eagles	Green	$60-$90
11) Philadelphia Eagles	Green 1960 Champions"	$125-$185
12) Pittsburgh Steelers	Gold	$100-$175
13) St. Louis Cardinals	Red	$50-$90
14) San Francisco 49ers	Red	$65-$105
15) Washington Redskins	Maroon	$85-$125

NFL "Toes Up," vertical ball, square bases (1962)

The team name is embossed on the chest; the city name is on the base.

Team	Value
1) Baltimore Colts	$450-$600
2) Chicago Bears	$350-$550
3) Cleveland Browns	$350-$550
4) Dallas Cowboys	$350-$600
5) Detroit Lions	$350-$550
6) Green Bay Packers	$350-$550
7) Los Angeles Rams	$350-$550
8) Minnesota Vikings	$350-$550
9) New York Giants	$300-$500
10) Philadelphia Eagles	$500-$700
11) Pittsburgh Steelers	$500-$700
12) St. Louis Cardinals	$300-$500
13) Washington Redskins	$400-$600

NFL "00" series, gold round bases (1966-68)

"00" is on the player's back and on the sleeves, too.

Team	Value
1) Atlanta Falcons	$50-$80
2) Baltimore Colts	$70-$130
3) Chicago Bears	$60-$120
4) Cleveland Browns	$100-$225
5) Dallas Cowboys	$90-$200
6) Detroit Lions	$60-$90
7) Green Bay Packers	$90-$175
8) Los Angeles Rams	$60-$125
9) Minnesota Vikings	$75-$180
10) New Orleans Saints	$40-$75
11) New York Giants	$70-$130
12) Philadelphia Eagles	$70-$130
13) Pittsburgh Steelers	$90-$150
14) St. Louis Cardinals	$40-$75
15) San Francisco 49ers	$100-$220
16) Washington Redskins	$110-$225

Merger series, gold round bases, modern NFL decals

Some teams appear in home/away uniforms.

Team	Value
1) Atlanta Falcons	$50-$90
2) Baltimore Colts	$60-$130
3) Buffalo Bills	$100-$175
4) Chicago Bears	$50-$90
5) Cincinnati Bengals	$30-$70
6) Cleveland Browns	$90-$150
7) Dallas Cowboys	$95-$160
8) Denver Broncos	$90-$150
9) Detroit Lions	$30-$60
10) Green Bay Packers	$90-$190
11) Houston Oilers	$30-$70
12) Kansas City Chiefs	$30-$70
13) Los Angeles Rams	$40-$90
14) Miami Dolphins	$100-$175
15) Minnesota Vikings	$100-$185
16) New England Patriots	$60-$110
17) New Orleans Saints	$40-$80
18) New York Giants	$40-$80
19) New York Jets	$60-$125
20) Oakland Raiders	$80-$100
21) Philadelphia Eagles	$90-$125
22) Pittsburgh Steelers	$85-$170
23) St. Louis Cardinals	$30-$70
24) San Diego Chargers	$50-$90
25) San Francisco 49ers	$100-$175
26) Washington Redskins	$125-$200

AFL, various colored square and round bases (1961-62)

Enlarged shoulder pads, team name on the chest, some with baggy pants, toes up, and wood bases.

Team	Value
1) Boston Patriots	$300-$600
2) Buffalo Bills	$235-$550
3) Dallas Texans	$350-$800
4) Denver Broncos	$300-$650
5) Houston Oilers	$300-$650
6) Los Angeles Chargers	$500-$600
7) New York Titans	$450-$1,000
8) Oakland Raiders (patch over eye)	$400-$750

AFL gold round bases, "ear pads" on helmet

Team names on chest, cities on base, AFL decals.

Team	Value
1) Boston Patriots	$200-$500
2) Buffalo Bills	$250-$555
3) Denver Broncos	$325-$700
4) Houston Oilers	$250-$600
5) Kansas City Chiefs	$325-$500
6) New York Jets	$250-$600
7) Oakland Raiders	$300-$750
8) San Diego Chargers	$220-$450

AFL decals, gold round bases (1966-67)

Team	Value
1) Boston Patriots	$100-$180
2) Buffalo Bills	$150-$225
3) Denver Broncos	$75-$100
4) Houston Oilers	$75-$100
5) Kansas City Chiefs	$75-$150
6) New York Jets	$80-$160
7) Oakland Raiders	$125-$180
8) San Diego Chargers	$70-$120

Black players, gold round bases, toes up, vertical ball (1962)

The team name is embossed on the chest, with the city name on the base. All teams were represented, using NFL decals. These are extremely rare and are generally pursued by advanced collectors. Values are double the high range of category III bobbers.

NFL boy and girl kissing dolls, gold round bases (1962)

The team name is embossed on the chest, while the city name is on the base. Each team is represented; the pair was boxed together. The player has a magnet inside the cheek. These are slightly bigger than their 4.5" miniature baseball bobber counterparts. Values are similar to the price ranges for category III statues.

SAM Bobbin' Heads

Dan Marino by SAM

Sports, Accessories & Memorabilia (SAM) of Menlo Park, Calif., produced hand-painted, ceramic bobbin' head dolls and figurines of professional athletes and entertainment stars beginning in 1992.

Troy Aikman-white	$60.00
Troy Aikman-blue	55.00
Drew Bledsoe	48.95
Terry Bradshaw	90.00
Randall Cunningham	48.95
Dan Dierdorf	110.00
John Elway	55.00
Marshall Faulk	48.95
Brett Favre-green	85.00
Brett Favre-SE green	48.95
Brett Favre-SE white	48.95
Bob Griese	48.95
Ronnie Lott-49ers	48.95
Ronnie Lott-Raiders	48.95
Ronnie Lott-Jets	48.95
Dan Marino-white	90.00
Dan Marino-teal	65.00
Rick Mirer-Seahawks	48.95
Art Monk	65.00
Joe Montana-Chiefs	80.00
Joe Montana-49ers, red	80.00
Joe Montana-49ers, white	48.95
Brian Piccolo	48.95
Jerry Rice-red	150.00
Jerry Rice-white	48.95
Barry Sanders-white	175.00
Barry Sanders-blue	48.95
Gale Sayers	48.95
Emmitt Smith-white	65.00
Emmitt Smith-blue	50.00
Roger Staubach	55.00
Lawrence Taylor	70.00
Steve Young	55.00

1995 NFL

Atlanta Falcons	$50.00
Arizona Cardinals	50.00
Baltimore Ravens	50.00
Buffalo Bills	50.00
Carolina Panthers	50.00
Chicago Bears	60.00
Cincinnati Bengals	50.00
Dallas Cowboys	100.00
Denver Broncos	100.00
Detroit Lions	50.00
Green Bay Packers	100.00
Indianapolis Colts	50.00
Jacksonville Jaguars	50.00
Kansas City Chiefs	60.00
Miami Dolphins	60.00
Minnesota Vikings	50.00
New England Patriots	60.00
New York Giants	80.00
New York Jets	50.00
New Orleans Saints	50.00
Oakland Raiders	65.00
Philadelphia Eagles	60.00
Pittsburgh Steelers	75.00
St. Louis Rams	50.00
San Diego Chargers	50.00
San Francisco 49ers	100.00
Seattle Seahawks	50.00
Tampa Bay Buccaneers	60.00
Tennessee Oilers	50.00
Washington Redskins	75.00

Green Bay Lineman (original)

Hartland Plastics and USA Hartland

In 1959, Hartland Plastics Co. of Hartland, Wis., produced 5,000 figurines each of Baltimore Colts quarterback Johnny Unitas and Los Angeles Rams running back Jon Arnett.

Hartland produced 28 additional football players. At the time, there were 14 teams in the NFL. Hartland made a running back and a lineman for each team, with 5,000 of each manufactured between 1959 and 1963.

They were sold in a plain white cardboard box with blue and red ink printing, sketches and logos. The front panel tore away to reveal a cello panel through which the figure could be seen. The top flap of the box was then stamped with a black label indicating RUNNING BACK or LINEMAN.

In 1959, LSU won the NCAA football championship and in 1961, their star running back, Billy Cannon won the Heisman Trophy. In 1962, Hartland used the running back mold and created the LSU running back. The university ordered 10,000 figures that were sold out by the end of the first semester.

Jon Arnett (original)

In 1993, Steven Manufacturing Co. of Hermann, Mo., which took over USA Hartland, was granted an NFL license and offered a commemorative Johnny Unitas figurine.

1959-63 Hartland Plastics

	Lineman	Running back
Baltimore Colts	$225.00	$250.00
Chicago Bears	200.00	225.00
Cleveland Browns	225.00	250.00
Dallas Cowboys	525.00	550.00
Detroit Lions	200.00	225.00
Green Bay Packers	200.00	225.00
Los Angeles Rams	225.00	250.00
Minnesota Vikings	200.00	225.00
New York Giants	200.00	225.00
Philadelphia Eagles	225.00	250.00
Pittsburgh Steelers	250.00	275.00
San Francisco 49ers	250.00	275.00
St. Louis Cardinals	225.00	250.00
Washington Redskins	500.00	550.00

LSU Running Back	500.00
Jon Arnett	175.00
Johnny Unitas	250.00

1993 "Missouri" Hartland

Johnny Unitas	50.00

Johnny Unitas ("Missouri")

Football Starting Lineup Figurines

Starting Lineup figurines were originally known as Kenner Starting Lineup figurines. They were produced by toy giant Hasbro Toy Co. Hasbro obtained Tonka (which owned Kenner) in May of 1990. The product development responsibility did not change, however. The Kenner logo appeared on the product through 1997 and was changed to the Hasbro logo in 1998. Previous to Tonka owning Kenner, Kenner had been a part of Kenner Parker Toys. And prior to that, it was a part of the General Mills fun group.

In January of 2001, Hasbro announced that it was discontinuing its entire line of figurines following the release of its 2001 baseball product lines.

1988 Football

Complete Set (137):	$8,000.00
Collector Stand:	30.00
Marcus Allen	80.00
Neal Anderson	35.00
Chip Banks	75.00
Mark Bavaro	45.00
Cornelius Bennett	140.00
Albert Bentley	35.00
Duane Bickett	60.00
Todd Blackledge	45.00
Brian Bosworth	35.00
Brian Brennan	40.00
Bill Brooks	45.00
James Brooks	50.00
Eddie Brown	50.00
Joey Browner	45.00
Aundray Bruce	45.00
Chris Burkett	125.00
Keith Byars	35.00
Scott Campbell	35.00
Carlos Carson	35.00
Harry Carson	35.00
Anthony Carter	80.00
Gerald Carter	40.00
Michael Carter	70.00
Tony Casillas	40.00
Jeff Chadwick	35.00
Deron Cherry	45.00
Ray Childress	70.00
Todd Christensen	80.00
Gary Clark	60.00
Mark Clayton	75.00
Cris Collinsworth	90.00
Doug Cosbie	80.00
Roger Craig	45.00
Randall Cunningham	50.00
Jeff Davis	35.00
Ken Davis	80.00
Richard Dent	40.00
Eric Dickerson	80.00
Floyd Dixon	35.00
Tony Dorsett	280.00
Mark Duper	60.00
Tony Eason	45.00
Carl Ekern	40.00
Henry Ellard	45.00
John Elway	200.00
Phillip Epps	35.00
Boomer Esiason	70.00
Jim Everett	45.00
Brent Fullwood	40.00

Mark Gastineau	35.00
Willie Gault	110.00
Bob Golic	35.00
Jerry Gray	35.00
Darrell Green	80.00
Jacob Green	40.00
Roy Green	40.00
Steve Grogan	45.00
Ronnie Harmon	120.00
Bobby Hebert	40.00
Alonzo Highsmith	35.00
Drew Hill	35.00
Earnest Jackson	35.00
Rickey Jackson	40.00
Vance Johnson	40.00
Ed Jones	120.00
James Jones	35.00
Rod Jones	35.00
Rulon Jones	35.00
Steve Jordan	40.00
E.J. Junior	35.00
Jim Kelly	225.00
Bill Kenney	35.00
Bernie Kosar	35.00
Tommy Kramer	40.00
Dave Krieg	75.00
Tim Krumrie	70.00
Mark Lee	45.00
Ronnie Lippett	35.00
Louis Lipps	35.00
Neil Lomax	35.00
Chuck Long	35.00
Howie Long	100.00
Ronnie Lott	130.00
Kevin Mack	35.00
Mark Malone	75.00
Dexter Manley	35.00
Dan Marino	300.00
Eric Martin	35.00
Rueben Mayes	35.00
Jim McMahon	35.00
Freeman McNeil	35.00
Karl Mecklenburg	45.00
Mike Merriweather	35.00
Stump Mitchell	35.00
Art Monk	275.00
Joe Montana	250.00
Warren Moon	100.00
Stanley Morgan	35.00
Joe Morris	35.00
Darrin Nelson	35.00
Ozzie Newsome	45.00
Ken O'Brien	35.00
John Offerdahl	60.00
Christian Okoye	40.00
Mike Quick	35.00
Jerry Rice	350.00
Gerald Riggs	35.00
Reggie Rogers	40.00
Mike Rozier	35.00
Jay Schroeder	40.00
Mickey Shuler	40.00
Phil Simms	40.00
Mike Singletary	45.00
Bill Ray Smith	125.00
Bruce Smith	150.00
J.T. Smith	35.00
Troy Stradford	40.00
Lawrence Taylor	70.00
Vinnie Testaverde	60.00
Andre Tippett	35.00
Anthony Toney	35.00
Al Toon	35.00
Jack Trudeau	35.00
Herschel Walker	35.00
Curt Warner	35.00
Dave Waymer	35.00
Charles White	35.00
Danny White	85.00

Randy White	150.00
Reggie White	100.00
James Wilder	35.00
Doug Williams	35.00
Marc Wilson	150.00
Sammy Winder	35.00
Kellen Winslow	325.00
Rod Woodson	300.00
Randy Wright	50.00

1989 Football

Complete Set (122):	$6,500.00
(Set price does not include O'Brien error.)	
Marcus Allen	40.00
Neal Anderson	30.00
Carl Banks	*35.00*
Bill Bates	*250.00*
Mark Bavaro	35.00
Cornelius Bennett	65.00
Duane Bickett	45.00
Bennie Blades	*60.00*
Bubby Brister	*30.00*
Bill Brooks	*35.00*
James Brooks	30.00
Eddie Brown	30.00
Jerome Brown	*225.00*
Tim Brown	*80.00*
Joey Browner	30.00
Kelvin Bryant	*30.00*
Jim Burt	*45.00*
Keith Byars	40.00
Dave Cadigan	*65.00*
Anthony Carter	30.00
Michael Carter	40.00
Chris Chandler	*30.00*
Gary Clark	40.00
Shane Conlan	*100.00*
Jimbo Covert	65.00
Roger Craig	30.00
Randall Cunningham	30.00
Richard Dent	30.00
Hanford Dixon	*45.00*
Chris Doleman	*35.00*
Tony Dorsett	130.00
Dave Duerson	*35.00*
John Elway	125.00
Boomer Esiason	30.00
Jim Everett	30.00
Thomas Everett	*30.00*
Sean Farrell	*45.00*
Bill Fralic	*90.00*
Irving Fryar	*100.00*
David Fulcher	*45.00*
Ernest Givins	*30.00*
Alex Gordon	*30.00*
Charles Haley	*175.00*
Bobby Hebert	30.00
Johnny Hector	*30.00*
Drew Hill	40.00
Dalton Hilliard	*30.00*
Bryan Hinkle	*90.00*
Michael Irvin	*125.00*
Keith Jackson	40.00
Garry James	*30.00*
Sean Jones	*40.00*
Jim Kelly	200.00
Joe Kelly	*30.00*
Bernie Kosar	30.00
Tim Krumrie	45.00
Louis Lipps	40.00
Eugene Lockhart	*60.00*
James Lofton	*75.00*
Neil Lomax	30.00
Chuck Long	30.00
Howie Long	50.00
Ronnie Lott	90.00
Kevin Mack	30.00
Pete Mandley	*30.00*

Dexter Manley 30.00
Charles Mann 40.00
Lionel Manuel 30.00
Dan Marino 275.00
Leonard Mashall 40.00
Eric Martin .30.00
Rueben Mayes 30.00
Vann McElroy 35.00
Dennis McKinnon 30.00
Jim McMahon 30.00
Steve McMichael 50.00
Erik McMillan 30.00
Freeman McNeil 30.00
Keith Millard 40.00
Chris Miller 30.00
Frank Minnifield 40.00
Art Monk 80.00
Joe Montana 130.00
Warren Moon 60.00
Joe Morris 30.00
Anthony Munoz 150.00
Ricky Nattiel 30.00
Darrin Nelson 30.00
Danny Noonan 60.00
Ken O'Brien 30.00
Ken O'Brien error 75.00
Steve Pelluer 60.00
Mike Quick .30.00
Andre Reed 125.00
Jerry Rice 60.00
Mike Rozier 30.00
Jay Schroeder 30.00
John Settle 30.00
Mickey Shuler 30.00
Phil Simms .30.00
Mike Singletary 30.00
Webster Slaughter 30.00
Bruce Smith 150.00
Chris Spielman 200.00
John Stephens 30.00
Kelly Stouffer 30.00
Pat Swilling 40.00
Lawrence Taylor 50.00
Vinny Testaverde 40.00
Thurman Thomas 175.00
Andre Tippett 30.00
Anthony Toney 30.00
Al Toon 30.00
Garin Veris 60.00
Herschel Walker 30.00
Curt Warner 30.00
Reggie White 50.00
Doug Williams 30.00
John Williams 40.00
Wade Wilson 30.00
Ickey Woods 30.00
Rod Woodson 225.00
Steve Young 375.00

1989 Football Helmets

Complete Set (4): $275.00

1990 Football

Complete Set (66): $2,000.00
Set price does not include home uniforms.
Troy Aikman 60.00
Neal Anderson (blue) 15.00
Neal Anderson (white) 15.00
Mark Bavaro 20.00
Steve Beuerlein 18.00
Bubby Brister 15.00
James Brooks 15.00
Tim Brown .40.00
Cris Carter 150.00
Roger Craig (red) 18.00
Roger Craig (white) 18.00
Randall Cunningham 15.00

Hart Lee Dykes 15.00
John Elway (orange) 50.00
John Elway (white) 50.00
Boomer Esiason (black) 20.00
Boomer Esiason (white) 20.00
Jim Everett .15.00
Simon Fletcher 20.00
Doug Flutie 140.00
Dennis Gentry 15.00
Dan Hampton 30.00
Jim Harbaugh 60.00
Rodney Holman 15.00
Bobby Humphries 15.00
Michael Irvin 70.00
Bo Jackson 15.00
Keith Jackson 20.00
Vance Johnson 15.00
Jim Kelly 25.00
Bernie Kosar (brown) 20.00
Bernie Kosar (white) 20.00
Louis Lipps .15.00
Don Majkowski 15.00
Charles Mann 15.00
Lionel Manuel 15.00
Dan Marino 200.00
Tim McGee 15.00
David Meggett 15.00
Mike Merriweather 15.00
Eric Metcalf 25.00
Keith Millard 15.00
Joe Montana (red) 60.00
Joe Montana (white) 60.00
Warren Moon 30.00
Christian Okoye 15.00
Tom Rathman 25.00
Andre Reed 25.00
Gerald Riggs 15.00
Mark Rypien 15.00
Barry Sanders 120.00
Deion Sanders 60.00
Rickey Sanders 15.00
Clyde Simmons 20.00
Phil Simms .15.00
Mike Singletary (blue) 15.00
Mike Singletary (white) 15.00
Webster Slaughter 15.00
Bruce Smith 25.00
John Stephens 15.00
John Taylor 25.00
Thurman Thomas 40.00
Mike Tomczak 15.00
Greg Townsend 15.00
Odessa Turner 15.00
Herschel Walker 15.00
Steve Walsh 18.00
Reggie White (green) 30.00
Reggie White (white) 30.00
Wade Wilson 15.00
Ickey Woods 15.00
Donnell Woolford 20.00
Tim Worley 20.00
Felix Wright 15.00

1991 Football

Complete Set (26): $550.00
Troy Aikman 95.00
Flipper Anderson 15.00
Neal Andrson 15.00
James Brooks 15.00
Eddie Brown 15.00
Mark Carrier 15.00
Boomer Esiason 15.00
James Francis 20.00
Jeff George 20.00
Rodney Hampton 20.00
Jim Harbaugh 30.00
Jeff Hostetler 25.00
Bobby Humphrey 15.00

Don Majkowski 10.00
Dan Marino 120.00
David Meggett 15.00
Joe Montana 35.00
Warren Moon 25.00
Christian Okoye 10.00
Jerry Rice 30.00
Andre Rison 20.00
Barry Sanders 40.00
Phil Simms .15.00
Emmitt Smith 225.00
Thurman Thomas 25.00
Herschel Walker 15.00

1991 Football Headline Collection

Complete Set (6): $200.00
John Elway .50.00
Boomer Esiason 20.00
Dan Marino 85.00
Joe Montana 40.00
Jerry Rice 30.00
Barry Sanders 40.00

1992 Football

Complete Set (26): $425.00
Troy Aikman 30.00
Earnest Byner 10.00
Randall Cunningham 12.00
Rodney Hampton 12.00
Bobby Hebert 10.00
Jeff Hostetler 20.00
Michael Irvin 20.00
Bo Jackson .12.00
Haywood Jeffires 12.00
Seth Joyner 12.00
Jim Kelly 15.00
Ronnie Lott 25.00
Dan Marino 100.00
Joe Montana 40.00
Warren Moon 15.00
Rob Moore 10.00
Jerry Rice 30.00
Andre Rison 12.00
Mark Rypien 10.00
Barry Sanders 30.00
Deion Sanders 20.00
Emmitt Smith 50.00
Pat Swilling 12.00
Derrick Thomas 25.00
Thurman Thomas 15.00
Steve Young 55.00

1992 Football Headline Collection

Complete Set (6): $125.00
Joe Montana 25.00
Warren Moon 16.00
Mark Rypien 12.00
Barry Sanders 30.00

Emmitt Smith .45.00
Thurman Thomas 18.00

1993 Football

Complete Set (27): $325.00
Troy Aikman .20.00
Cornelius Bennett 10.00
Randall Cunningham 10.00
Chris Doleman 10.00
John Elway 40.00
Barry Foster *10.00*
Michael Irvin .15.00
Rickey Jackson 10.00
Cortez Kennedy *12.00*
David Klingler *12.00*
Chip Lohmiller *14.00*
Russell Maryland *12.00*
Anthony Miller 12.00
Chris Miller 10.00
Joe Montana 45.00
Warren Moon (blue) 20.00
Warren Moon (white) 20.00
Andre Reed 10.00
Barry Sanders .30.00
Deion Sanders 14.00
Junior Seau *12.00*
Sterling Sharpe *20.00*
Emmitt Smith .25.00
Neil Smith *10.00*
Pete Stoyanovich *15.00*
Ricky Watters *20.00*
Rod Woodson .15.00
Steve Young 30.00

1994 Football

Complete Set (32): $525.00
Troy Aikman .20.00
Jerome Bettis *30.00*
Drew Bledsoe *75.00*
Randall Cunningham 10.00
Boomer Esiason 10.00
Brett Favre *130.00*
Barry Foster 10.00
Rodney Hampton 10.00
Ronnie Harmon 20.00
Garrison Hearst *15.00*
Raghib Ismail *15.00*
Brent Jones *15.00*
Cortez Kennedy 10.00
Nick Lowery *14.00*
Dan Marino 35.00
Eric Metcalf 15.00
Rick Mirer *15.00*
Joe Montana 35.00
Ken Norton *15.00*
Jerry Rice 20.00
Andre Risen 10.00
Barry Sanders .30.00
Deion Sanders 15.00
Junior Seau 10.00
Phil Simms 10.00
Emmitt Smith .25.00
Lawrence Taylor 15.00
Chris Warren *15.00*
Lorenzo White *10.00*
Reggie White .20.00
Rod Woodson .10.00
Steve Young 25.00

1995 Football

Complete Set (33): $400.00
Troy Aikman .20.00
Jerome Bettis .15.00
Drew Bledsoe .25.00
Steve Christie *12.00*
Ben Coates *18.00*

Randall Cunningham 10.00
Willie Davis *10.00*
Jim Everett 10.00
Marshall Faulk *30.00*
Brett Favre 45.00
Irving Fryar 15.00
Jeff George 20.00
Stan Humphries *12.00*
Michael Irvin .12.00
Johnny Johnson *10.00*
Seth Joyner 10.00
Greg Lloyd *12.00*
Dan Marino 35.00
Terry McDaniel *12.00*
Natrone Means 25.00
Scott Mitchell *14.00*
Joe Montana 70.00
Warren Moon .12.00
Hardy Nickerson *12.00*
Michael Dean Perry *12.00*
Jerry Rice 15.00
Barry Sanders .25.00
Deion Sanders 15.00
Shannon Sharpe *18.00*
Emmitt Smith .20.00
Dan Wilkinson *12.00*
Steve Young 15.00
Chris Zorich *12.00*

1996 Football

Complete Set (38): $450.00
Troy Aikman .15.00
Troy Aikman (Albertson) 25.00
Troy Aikman (Blue Star) 225.00
Terry Allen *20.00*
Steve Beuerlein 12.00
Jeff Blake *15.00*
Drew Bledsoe .15.00
Steve Bono *10.00*

Kyle Brady *10.00*
Robert Brooks *25.00*
Dave Brown *10.00*
Isaac Bruce *20.00*
Mark Brunell *40.00*
Mark Carrier *10.00*
Cris Carter 12.00
Kerry Collins *30.00*
John Elway 20.00
Marshall Faulk 14.00
Brett Favre (Shopko) 45.00
Joey Galloway *20.00*
Kevin Greene *12.00*
Dan Marino 25.00
Steve McNair *25.00*
Eric Metcalf 12.00
Jay Novacek *14.00*
Bryce Paup 12.00
Carl Pickens *20.00*
Frank Reich *12.00*
Errict Rhett *15.00*
Jerry Rice 15.00
Rashaan Salaam *15.00*
Barry Sanders .35.00
Deion Sanders 15.00
Junior Seau 12.00
Emmitt Smith .30.00
Chris Spielman 15.00
Kordell Stewart *60.00*
Ricky Watters .15.00
Reggie White .16.00
Harvey Williams *14.00*
Steve Young 14.00

1997 Football

Complete Set (43): $550.00
Karim Abdul-Jabbar *25.00*
Troy Aikman .15.00
Jamal Anderson *12.00*
Jerome Bettis .15.00
Jeff Blake 10.00
Drew Bledsoe .15.00
Terry Bradshaw (Hill's) 30.00
Mark Brunell .20.00
Dale Carter *10.00*
Larry Centers *10.00*
Mark Chmura .15.00
Kerry Collins .15.00
Brian Cox *10.00*
Terrell Davis 10.00
Quinn Early *10.00*
John Elway 15.00
Brett Favre 25.00
Eddie George *35.00*
Jeff George 10.00
Elvis Grbac *12.00*
Kevin Greene .10.00
Marvin Harrison *15.00*
Jim Harbaugh .10.00
Brad Johnson *15.00*
Keyshawn Johnson *12.00*
Daryl Johnston 12.00
Dan Marino 16.00
Curtis Martin *45.00*
Tony Martin *12.00*
Herman Moore 20.00
Jerry Rice 15.00
Willie Roaf *10.00*
Deion Sanders 14.00
Bruce Smith 10.00
Emmitt Smith .20.00
Emmitt Smith Alb. 25.00
Phillipi Sparks *10.00*
Kordell Stewart 25.00
Vinny Testaverde 10.00
Eric Turner *10.00*
Chris Warren .10.00
Rickey Watters 10.00

Michael Westbrook 15.00
Reggie White 14.00
Steve Young 14.00

1997 Football Classic Doubles

Complete Set (9): $225.00
F. Biletnikoff, T. Brown 35.00
T. Dorsett, E. Smith 25.00
B. Favre, B. Starr 25.00
B. Favre, B. Starr 25.00
D. Marino, B. Griese 25.00
J. Montana, D. Clark 25.00
J. Montana, J. Rice 40.00
W. Payton, B. Sanders 100.00
R. Staubach, T. Aikman 25.00

1997 Football Gridiron Greats

Complete Set (9): $250.00
Brett Favre 40.00
Kevin Greene 25.00
Dan Marino 35.00
Joe Montana 30.00
Jerry Rice 30.00
Deion Sanders 40.00
Emmitt Smith 35.00
Thurman Thomas 30.00
Ricky Watters 30.00

1997 Football Heisman Contenders

Complete Set (9): $120.00
Tony Dorsett 15.00
Doug Flutie 15.00
Eddie George 25.00
Archie Griffin 15.00
Bo Jackson 12.00
Steve Owens 12.00
Johnny Rodgers 12.00
Barry Sanders 30.00
Danny Wuerffel 15.00

1998 Football

Complete Set (42) $450.00
Troy Aikman 15.00
Terry Allen 10.00
Jerome Bettis 15.00
Drew Bledsoe 15.00
Tony Boselli 10.00
Derrick Brooks 10.00
Mark Brunell 15.00
Kerry Collins 10.00
Terrell Davis 25.00
Trent Dilfer 20.00
Corey Dillon 30.00
John Elway 15.00

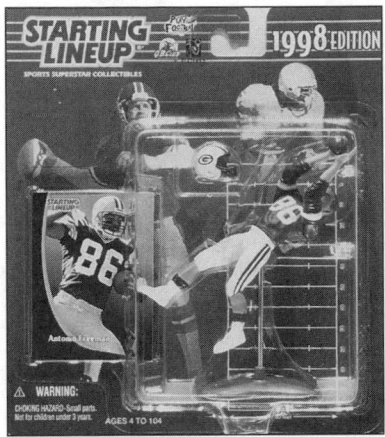

Brett Favre 20.00
Antonio Freeman 20.00
Gus Frerotte 12.00
Joey Galloway 12.00
Eddie George 15.00
Terry Glenn 15.00
Elvis Grbac 10.00
Raymont Harris 12.00
Bobby Hoying 12.00
Carnell Lake 12.00
Lamar Lathon 20.00
Dan Marino 15.00
Randall McDaniel 12.00
Chester McGlockton 12.00
Scott Mitchell 10.00
Adrian Murrell 20.00
Nate Newton 12.00
Jonathan Ogden 12.00
Orlando Pace 12.00
Carl Pickens 10.00
Jerry Rice 15.00
Simeon Rice 12.00
Barry Sanders Special 20.00
Deion Sanders 12.00
Antowain Smith 25.00
Emmitt Smith 15.00
Kordell Stewart Special 20.00
Dana Stubblefield 15.00
Vinny Testaverde 10.00
Tyrone Wheatley 12.00
Reggie White 12.00
Steve Young 12.00

1998 Gridiron Greats

Complete Set (7) $150.00
Troy Aikman 25.00
Drew Bledsoe 25.00
Mark Brunell 25.00
John Elway 30.00
Barry Sanders 30.00
Junior Seau 20.00
Steve Young 25.00

1998 Football Classic Doubles

Complete Set (8) $170.00
Aikman, Smith 30.00
Allen, Garrett 25.00
Elway, Marino 35.00
Namath, Maynard 25.00
Rice, Young 30.00
Sanders, Adderley 25.00
Seau, Butkus 25.00
Tittle, Huff 25.00

1998 Quarterback Club Classic Doubles

Complete Set (6) $150.00
Drew Bledsoe 30.00
John Elway 30.00
Jim Harbaugh 20.00
Dan Marino 35.00
Emmitt Smith 35.00
Steve Young 30.00

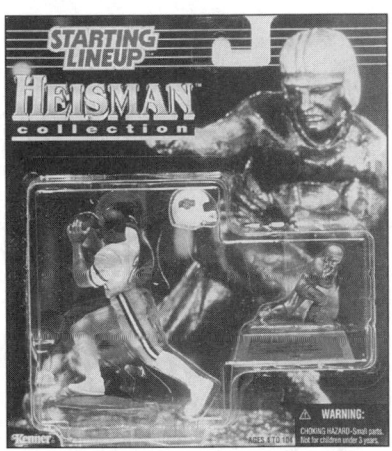

1998 Heisman Collection

Complete Set (10) $100.00
Marcus Allen 12.00
Earl Campbell 12.00
John Cappelletti 10.00
Glenn Davis 10.00
Paul Hornung 12.00
Desmond Howard 10.00
Rashaan Salaam 10.00
Roger Staubach 12.00
Herschel Walker 10.00
Charles Woodson 20.00

1998 Pro Football Hall of Fame Legends

Complete Set (11) $100.00
Dick Butkus 10.00
Gale Sayers 10.00
Bob Lilly .10.00
Larry Csonka 12.00
Y.A. Tittle 10.00
Bart Starr 12.00
Vince Lombardi 15.00
Gene Upshaw 10.00
Deacon Jones 10.00
Joe Greene 12.00
Ray Nitschke 12.00

1998 12" Starting Lineup Football

Complete Set (5)	.$140.00
Drew Bledsoe	.30.00
John Elway	.30.00
Brett Favre	.45.00
Dan Marino	.40.00
Jerry Rice	.30.00

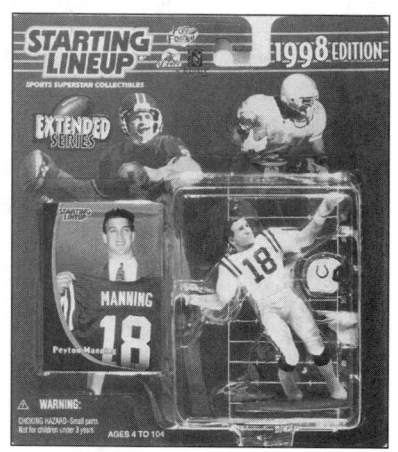

1998 Football Extended Series

Complete Set (10)	.$180.00
Mike Alstott	.20.00
Terrell Davis	.25.00
Jim Harbaugh	.10.00
Ryan Leaf	.25.00
Peyton Manning	.50.00
Curtis Martin	.20.00
Steve McNair	.15.00
Deion Sanders	.12.00
Shannon Sharpe	.15.00
Charles Woodson	.25.00

1999 Football

Complete Set (34)	.$500.00
Troy Aikman	.10.00
Drew Bledsoe	.10.00
Mark Brunell	.12.00
Chris Chandler	.12.00
Wayne Chrebet	*.12.00*
Randall Cunningham	.12.00
Terrell Davis	.15.00
Dermontti Dawson	*.20.00*
Corey Dillon	.10.00
Warrick Dunn	*.15.00*

John Elway	.12.00
Curtis Enis	*.18.00*
Brett Favre	.10.00
Doug Flutie	.14.00
Eddie George	.15.00
Kaufman Napoleon	*.15.00*
Jim Kelly (Ames)	.20.00
Ryan Leaf	.8.00
Dorsey Levens	*.15.00*
Peyton Manning	.20.00
Dan Marino	.12.00
Curtis Martin	.12.00
Randy Moss	*.65.00*
Jake Plummer	*.20.00*
Jerry Rice	.10.00
Andre Rison	.10.00
Barry Sanders	
(regular)	.12.00
(Meijers)	.16.00
Warren Sapp	*.25.00*
Emmitt Smith	.10.00
Jimmy Smith	*.14.00*
Neil Smith	.10.00
Robert Smith	*.20.00*
R. Staubach (Albertson's)	.20.00
Kordell Stewart	.10.00
Eric Swann	*.12.00*
Zach Thomas	*.40.00*
Ricky Watters	.10.00
Steve Young	.10.00

Extended

Complete Set (8)	.$120.00
Jamal Anderson	.12.00
Charlie Batch	*.15.00*
Tim Couch	*.30.00*
Ed McCaffery	*.15.00*
Donovan McNabb	*.18.00*
John Randle	*.15.00*
Fred Taylor	*.20.00*
Ricky Williams	*.20.00*

1999 Football 12" Figures

Complete Set (5)	.$125.00
Terrell Davis	.30.00
Brett Favre	.25.00
Barry Sanders	.30.00
Kordell Stewart	.25.00
Steve Young	.25.00

1999 Football Classic Doubles

Complete Set (10)	.$150.00
M. Alstott/W. Dunn	.15.00
E. Campbell/E. George	.15.00
C. Carter/R. Moss	.35.00
J. Elway/ T. Davis	.20.00
F. Harris/J. Bettis	.15.00
J. Lambert/J. Ham	.18.00
A. Manning/P. Manning	.30.00
A. Munoz /B. Esiason	.15.00
K. Stabler/D. Casper	.15.00
J. Unitas /R. Berry	.15.00

QB Club

Complete Set (5)	.$75.00
Troy Aikman	.18.00
Terrell Davis	.20.00
Brett Favre	.18.00
Jake Plummer	.18.00
Kordell Stewart	.18.00

1999 Football Heroes of the Gridiron

Complete Set (9)	.$100.00
Charlie Batch	.15.00
Mark Brunell	.15.00
Ernie Davis	.10.00
Warrick Dunn	.10.00
Curtis Martin	.10.00
Randy Moss	.35.00
Jim Plunkett	.10.00
Charlie Ward	.10.00
Ricky Williams	.20.00

1999 Football Gridiron Greats

Complete Set (8)	.$110.00
Dick Butkus	.15.00
Terrell Davis	.20.00
Warrick Dunn	.16.00
Eddie George	.20.00
Dan Marino	.18.00
Curtis Martin	.15.00
Barry Sanders	.15.00
Kordell Stewart	.15.00

2000 Football

Complete Set (40)	.$600.00
Troy Aikman	.8.00
Mike Alstott	.10.00
Jesse Armstead	*.15.00*
Champ Bailey	*.18.00*
Drew Bledsoe	.9.00
Tony Brackens	*.12.00*
Mark Brunell	.8.00
Tim Couch	
(Regular)	.12.00
(Ames Exclusive)	.15.00
Daunte Culpepper	*.70.00*
Stephen Davis	*.15.00*
Terrell Davis	.10.00
John Elway	.12.00
Brett Favre	.10.00
Doug Flutie	.10.00
Antonio Freeman	.10.00
Tony Gonzalez	*.20.00*
Brian Griese	*.13.00*
Torry Holt	*.30.00*
Edgerrin James	*.35.00*
Brad Johnson	.10.00
Keyshawn Johnson (Jets uniform)	.12.00
(Buccaneers uniform)	.15.00
Shaun King	*.30.00*
Jon Kitna	*.15.00*
Peyton Manning	.14.00

Dan Marino 15.00
Steve McNair 12.00
Joe Montana 15.00
Randy Moss 15.00
Ozzie Newsome 15.00
Jim Otto *15.00*
Terrell Owens *12.00*
Jake Plummer 10.00
Takeo Spikes *12.00*
Fred Taylor 10.00
Vinny Testaverde 10.00
Kurt Warner
(old uniform) 40.00
(new uniform) 40.00
(Wal-Mart Exclusive) 25.00
Ricky Williams
(old uniform) 12.00
(new uniform) 12.00

Extended

Complete Set (10) $140.00
Shawn Alexander *12.00*
Isaac Bruce 12.00
Cris Carter 10.00

Ron Dayne *25.00*
Marvin Harrison 18.00
Jevon Kearse *20.00*
Jason Sehorn *18.00*
Shawn Springs *12.00*
Peter Warrick
(white uniform) 20.00
(black uniform) 15.00

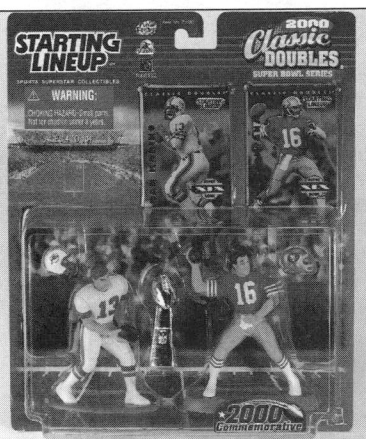

2000 Football Classic Doubles

Complete Set (7) $100.00
T. Aikman/J. Kelly 18.00
T. Davis/ J. Anderson 15.00
J. Elway/B. Favre 18.00
B. Favre/D. Bledsoe 15.00
E. George/M. Faulk 25.00
J. Montana/D. Marino 35.00
P. Simms/Elway J. 18.00
P. Manning college/pro (Wilk's) 25.00

2000 Football Elite

Complete Set (6) $80.00
Terrell Davis 15.00

Brett Favre 15.00
Peyton Manning 25.00
Joe Montana 30.00
Randy Moss 20.00
Emmitt Smith 18.00

2000 Football Hobby Set

Complete Set (9) $85.00
Troy Aikman 8.00
Terrell Davis 9.00
Marshall Faulk 14.00
Peyton Manning 14.00
Randy Moss 14.00
Jake Plummer 8.00
Akili Smith *18.00*
Ricky Williams 10.00
Darren Woodson *12.00*

2000 Football Wheaties

Complete Set (5) $70.00
John Elway 20.00
Brett Favre 18.00
Dan Marino 18.00
Jerry Rice 15.00
Steve Young 15.00

Football Yearbooks

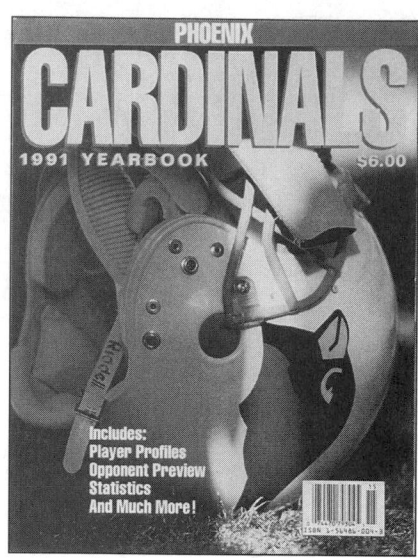

Arizona Cardinals

St. Louis Cardinals

1967 Team photo $35
1968 Team photo $35
1969 . . . . $35
1976 . . . . $15

Phoenix Cardinals

1988 . . . . $6
1989 Team helmet in the desert $6
1990 . . . . $6
1991 Team helmet $6
1992 Closeup of player holding football $6
1993 M. Bankston, R. Davis, M. Jones,
  K. Rucker, E. Swann $6

Become Arizona Cardinals

1994 Buddy Ryan, generic player $6
1995 . . . . $6
1996 . . . . $6
1997 . . . . $6
1998 . . . . $6
1999 Jake Plummer, others $6

Atlanta Falcons

1966 Team logo and 1966 . . . . $45
1967 Team logo and 1967 . . . . $35
1968 Team logo and 1967 . . . . $30

1969 Team logo and 1969 . . . . $25
1970 . . . . $25
1971 . . . . $25
1972 Bob Berry, others $20
1973 Dave Hampton, team helmet $20
1974 Tommy Nobis $20
1975 . . . . $15
1976 Steve Bartkowski, others $15
1977 . . . . $15
1992 Exterior of Georgia Dome $8
1993 Georgia Dome field $8
1995 J. George, B. Emanuel $8
1997 T. Hall, M. Andersen, others $8
1998 M. Andersen/J. Tuggle/C. Chandler $8
1999 . . . . $8
2000 . . . . $8

Buffalo Bills

1965 Bills vs. Chiefs in action $35
1968 J. Kemp, B. Byrd, P. Maguire $45
1969 Gary McDermott $45
1971 O. J. Simpson $40
1972 O. J. Simpson $40
1984 Joe Ferguson $20
1989 Team logo, Bills in action $6
1990 Bills red helmet $6
1991 Helmet, AFC Championship trophy . . . $6
1992 Bills flag flying at Rich Stadium $6
1993 View inside Rich Stadium $6
1994 Bills memorabilia $6
1995 Bills logo, several players $6
1996 Helmet, 3 Pro Bowl players $6
1997 B. Smith tackling Broncos runner $6
1998 W. Phillips, T. Washington, others $6
1999 . . . . $6
2000 E. Moulds, others $6

Carolina Panthers

1995 K. Collins, S. Mills, D. Capers $8

Chicago Bears

1952 Growling bear $40
1955 Rams players tackling a Bear $35
1956 Kicker and holder $35
1960 Artwork of player, bear $25
1964 Helmet $20
1983 Helmet $12
1986 Locker with Super Bowl Trophy $10
1987 Helmet, reflection of city skyline $12

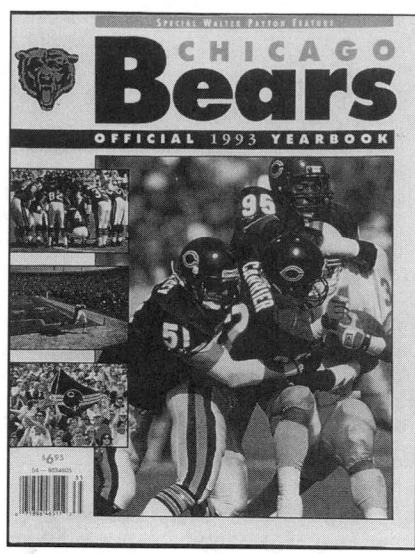

1988 Huge red bear looking over huddle . . . $10
1989 Player introductions, helmet $8
1990 Bears defense vs. Packers $8
1991 . . . . $8
1992 N. Anderson, W. Perry, T. Armstrong $8
1993 M. Carrier, R. Dent, J. Morrissey $8
1994 Bears memorabilia $8
1995 Flag, A. Spellman, C. Zorich, others . . . $8
1996 . . . . $8
1997 . . . . $8
1998 . . . . $8
1999 D. Jauron, G. Halas, others $9
2000 D Jauron, group celebrations $9

Cincinnati Bengals

1999 Players as construction workers $9
2000 . . . . $9

Cleveland Browns

1987 Bernie Kosar $8
1988 B. Kosar, E. Byner $8
1989 Bernie Kosar $8
1990 Langhorne, Slaughter $8
1991 . . . . $8
1992 Artwork of hand and helmet $8
1993 Clay Matthews $8
1994 Eric Metcalf $6

1995 Pepper Johnson $6
Become Baltimore Ravens
Cleveland Browns (Expansion Team)
1999 Inaugural Year $8

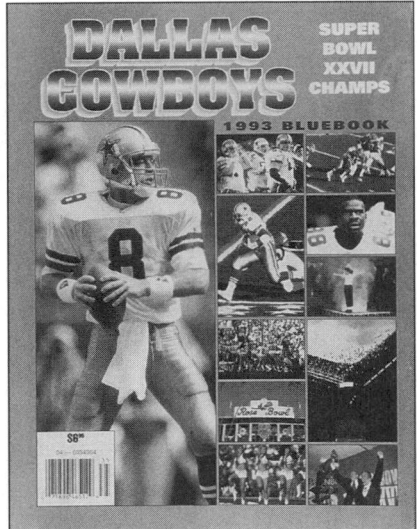

Dallas Cowboys

1967 Don Meredith $45
1968 Bob Hayes $40
1969 Bob Lilly $40
1970 Calvin Hill $30
1971 Walt Garrison $30
1972 Roger Staubach $30
1973 Tom Landry $25
1980 T. Landry, T. Dorsett, cheerleaders $20
1982 Danny White $15
1992 Cowboys greats, "Return to Glory" . . .$10
1993 Troy Aikman, Super Bowl photos $10
1994 Four Super Bowl trophies, helmet . . .$10
1995 Collage with Aikman, Haley, others $10
1996 Five Super Bowl Trophies, helmet $10
1997 T. Aikman, E. Smith $10
1998 Collage with D. Sanders, others $10

Denver Broncos

1974 The Making of a Contender $20
1978 Craig Morton $10
1986 Louis Wright $7

1987 John Elway $7
1988 . . . .$7
1989 . . . .$7
1991 Fireworks over stadium $7
1992 Broncos defense in action $7
1993 John Elway $8
1994 John Elway $8
1995 John Elway $8
1996 . . . .$8
1997 Broncos helmet, Elway Tribute $8
1998 . . . .$9
1999 Shanahan, Sharpe, T. Davis, Elway $9

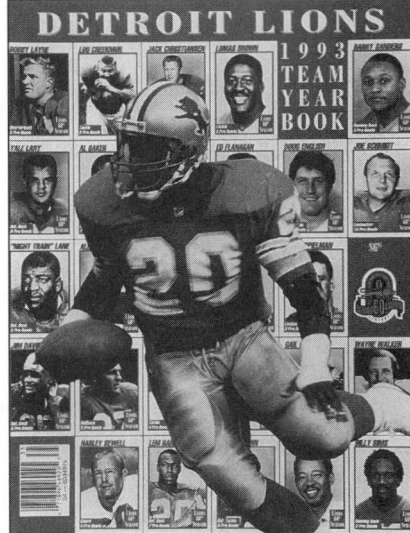

Detroit Lions

1984 . . . .$10
1985 Player No. 35 . . . .$10
1991 Barry Sanders $10
1992 . . . .$10
1993 Barry Sanders and others $10
1994 Barry Sanders $10
1995 Barry Sanders $10
1996 Barry Sanders $8
1997 B. Sanders, H. Moore, K. Glover $8
1998 . . . .$8
1999 Barry Sanders in action $8

1961 YEARBOOK

Green Bay Packers

1960 Paul Hornung, Jerry Kramer $300
1961 Forrest Gregg $250
1962 Vince Lombardi $200
1963 Jim Taylor $150
1964 Bart Starr $125
1965 Curly Lambeau, Vince Lombardi . . .$125
1966 Willie Davis $100
1967 Packers vs. Kansas City Chiefs $100
1968 Ray Nitschke $75
1969 Donny Anderson $40
1970 Travis Williams $35
1971 Dan Devine $35
1972 John Brockington $30
1973 Chester Marcol, Ron Widby $30
1974 Jerry Tagge $25
1975 Bart Starr $30
1976 Fred Carr $20
1977 Lynn Dickey $20
1978 Johnnie Gray $15
1979 T. Middleton, D. Whitehurst $10
1980 Rich Wingo $10
1981 Gerry Ellis, Eddie Lee Ivery $10
1982 John Jefferson, James Lofton $15
1983 Mike Douglass $10
1984 25th Anniversary, Forrest Gregg $12
1985 Paul Coffmann $9
1986 Randy Scott $6
1987 Randy Wright $6
1988 Lindy Infante $6
1989 Tim Harris $6
1990 Don Majkowski $6
1991 Sterling Sharpe $7
1992 Mike Holmgren $6
1993 Brett Favre $8
1994 Reggie White $8
1995 Edgar Bennett $7
1996 Brett Favre $9
1997 Super Bowl XXXI trophy $8
1998 Antonio Freeman/Robert Brooks $8
1999 B. Favre/R. Rhodes/others $8
2000 . . . .$8

Indianapolis Colts

Baltimore Colts
1953 10th Anniversary helmet $60
1958 Memorial Stadium $45
1959 . . . .$45

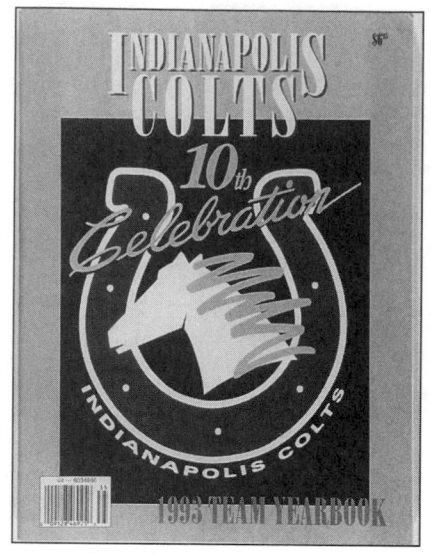

1960 . . . .$40
1961 Weeb Eubank, Colts sideline $40
1962 Team helmet $40
1963 . . . .$35
1964 Johnny Unitas $35
1978 Bert Jones $10
1980 Bert Jones, other $10
Indianapolis Colts
1988 Eric Dickerson $8
1989 . . . .$8
1991 Jack Herrod $8
1992 Q. Coryatt, S. Emtman, T. Marchibroda . . .$8
1993 10th Celebration logo $8
1994 . . . .$8
1995 . . . .$8
1996 . . . .$8
1997 . . . .$8
1998 . . . .$8

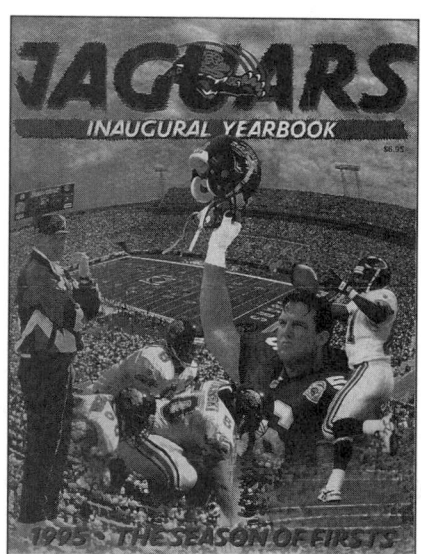

Jacksonville Jaguars
1995 T. Coughlin/M. Brunell/W. Moore/J. Lageman $10
1996 T. Coughlin/K. Hardy/M. Brunell $10
1997 M. Brunell/K. Hardy $10
1998 M. Brunell/T. Boselli/J. Smith/M.
  Hollis/B. Barker $10

Kansas City Chiefs
1968 . . . .$40
1969 . . . .$40
1970 Hank Stram $35
1971 H. Stram, L. Dawson, others $35
1972 Ed Podolak $20
1990 Silver Anniversary Season $10
1994 Joe Montana $10

1996 Neil Smith $8
1997 . . . .$8
1999 Tony Gonzalez $8
2000 . . . .$8

Miami Dolphins
1984 Topps card collage $25
1985 Dan Marino $20
1986 Dolphins helmet, jacket $15
1987 . . . .$10
1988 Dan Marino $10
1990 Silver Anniv. Season $20
1993 J.B. Brown, B. Cox, D. Griggs,
  J. Offerdahl, L. Oliver, T. Vincent $8
1994 Dan Marino $8
1995 Team photo $8
1996 . . . .$8
1997 . . . .$8
1998 . . . .$9

Minnesota Vikings
1961 Vikings cartoon and referee $55
1975 . . . .$15
1976 Viking artwork $15
1991 . . . .$8
1992 D. Green, R. McDaniel, others $8
1993 Artwork by Allen J. Peterson $8
1994 . . . .$8
1995 Cris Carter $8
1996 . . . .$8
1997 Brad Johnson $8
1998 John Randle $8
1999 Cris Carter $8

New England Patriots
Boston Patriots
1964 Cartoon $40
1965 Gino Cappelletti, Babe Parilli $35
1966 J.D. Garrett, Jim Nance $35
1967 Jim Nance $35
New England Patriots
1978 . . . .$13
1979 Sam Cunningham artwork, others $10
1980 Rod Shoate $13
1981 Vagas Ferguson $10
1985 Tony Eason, Craig James, others $6
1986 . . . .$7

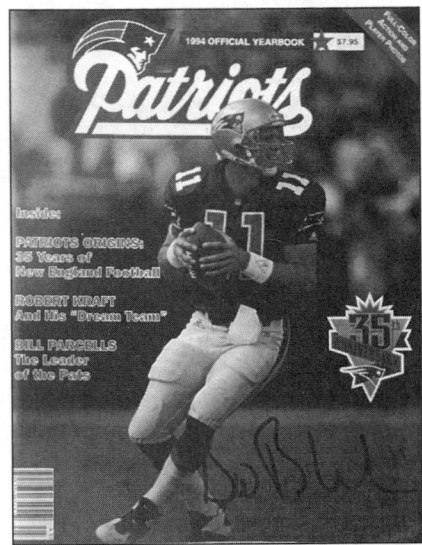

1987 . . . .$6
1988 Player pileup $6
1989 Defense vs. Bills $6
1991 . . . .$6
1992 View of Stadium during a game $6
1993 Bledsoe, Parcells, others $6
1994 Drew Bledsoe $8
1995 Parcells, Bledsoe, Coates $8
1996 . . . .$8
1997 D. Bledsoe, T. Glenn $8
1998 C. Slade, T. Johnson, W. McGinist $8
1999 Drew Bledsoe, Patriots greats $8

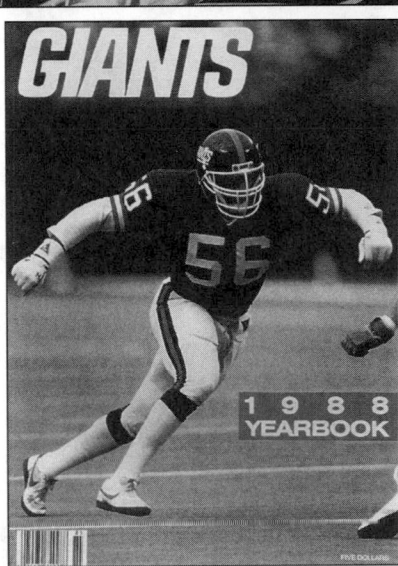

New Orleans Saints
1968 Dan Abramowicz $25
1988 Helmet, musical instuments $8
1991 25th Anniversary $8
1992 Bobby Hebert $8
1993 Saints defense making tackle $8
1994 . . . .$8
1995 . . . .$8
1996 . . . .$8
1997 Mike Ditka $8
1998 Mike Ditka $8

New York Giants
1963 Y. A. Tittle $95
1964 Y.A. Tittle, Alex Webster $40

1965 Giants offensive line $40
1966 Tucker Frederickson $40
1967 Giants vs. St. Louis Cardinals $35
1968 Fran Tarkenton $30
1969 Fran Tarkenton $30
1970 Joe Morrison $30
1971 Giants defense vs. Rams $10
1974 . . . .$25
1975 . . . .$20
1976 John Mendenhall $20
1985 . . . .$10
1986 Phil Simms $10
1987 Lombardi Trophy, helmet $10
1988 Lawrence Taylor $10
1989 M. Bavaro, C. Banks $10
1990 Lawrence Taylor in action $10
1991 Ottis Anderson $10
1992 Leonard Marshall $8
1993 Phil Simms $8
1994 70th Anniversary artwork $8
1995 Player looking through helmet $8
1996 Championship anniversary art $8
1997 Giants helmet and footballs $8
1998 . . . .$8
1999 75th Anniversary, helmets $8
2000 Fassel, K. Collins, others $9

New York Jets
1960 . . . .$80
1961 Titans AFL $70

1962 . . . .$60
1963 . . . .$60
1964 L. Grantham, W. McDaniel, M. Snell $60
1965 Matt Snell $60
1966 Joe Namath $60
1967 Jets vs. Chargers $35
1968 Emerson Boozer, Joe Namath $35
1969 Joe Namath $75
1970 Don Maynard $20
1971 Action photo vs. Giants $15
1972 Joe Namath/John Riggins $15
1973 Artwork collage $15
1974 Charles Winner, Joe Namath $15
1975 Jets in action artwork $15
1976 . . . .$15
1977 Greg Buttle, Clark Gaines, Richard Todd/
others $15
1978 Richard Todd/others $15
1979 Richard Todd/others $15
1980 R. Todd, Statue of Liberty $15
1981 F. McNeil, B. Harper, M. Powell $15
1982 J. Klecko, M. Gastineau $15
1983 Freeman McNeil artwork $15
1984 Helmet, Silver Anniversary $12
1985 Namath, McNeil, Gastineau $12
1986 O'Brien, McNeil, others $10
1987 D. Maynard, others $10
1988 Snapshots on jersey background $10
1989 Al Toon, others $10

1990 B. Coslett, Toon, others $10
1991 B.Thomas, Namath, Boozer, others $8
1992 Jets soaring over stadium $8
1993 Player #93 holding helmet $8
1994 J. Johnson, B. Washington $8
1995 Mo Lewis $8
1996 . . . .$8
1997 B. Parcells, A, Murrrell, W. Chrebet . . .$8
1998 . . . .$8
1999 Bill Parcells, others $8
2000 V. Testaverde, W. Chrebet, others $8

Oakland Raiders

Oakland Raiders
1968 Raider ballcarrier $25
Los Angeles Raiders
1982 Raider player on the sidelines $8
1983 Raiders in action $8
1984 Super Bowl XVIII ring $8
1985 Helmet, three Super Bowl trophies $8
1986 Team logo $6
1987 Matt Millen $6
1988 Van McElroy $6
1989 Team helmet $6
1990 Team helmet $6
1991 . . . .$6
1992 "Tradition of Greatness" $6
1993 . . . .$6
1994 . . . .$6
Oakland Raiders
1995 Super Bowl trophies $6
1996 Trophies, Raiders helmet $6
1997 . . . .$6
1998 . . . .$6

Philadelphia Eagles

1972 Eagles vs. Dallas Cowboys $25
1973 Eagles vs. Kansas City Chiefs $20
1974 H. Carmichael, R. Gabriel $20
1975 Eagles in action $20
1976 Dick Vermiel $20
1977 . . . .$20
1978 . . . .$20
1979 "Winners" $20
1980 "The Eagles have Arrived" $15
1981 NFC Champions ring $10
1982 Eagles memorabilia $10
1983 H. Carmichael, W. Montgomery $10

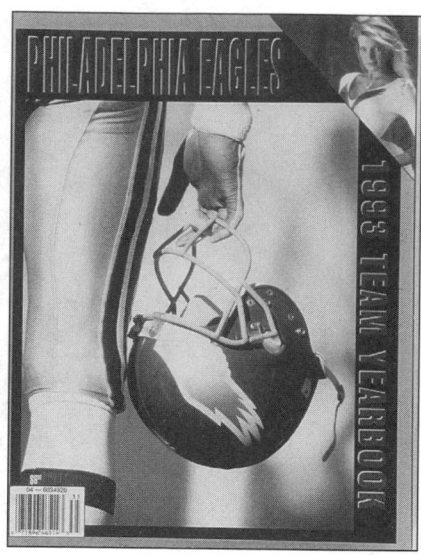

1984 Ron Jaworski $10
1985 . . . .$10
1986 Mike Quick $10
1987 Reggie White $10
1988 Mike Quick $10
1989 William Frizzell, others $10
1990 Randall Cunningham $10
1991 Player raising football over head $8
1992 Eagles on defense $8
1993 Player holding a helmet at his side $8
1994 Four Eagle defenders $8
1995 Ricky Watters $7
1996 Eagles defense in action $7
1997 Ray Rhodes/Irving Fryar $7
1998 Bobby Hoying/Tommy McDonald $7

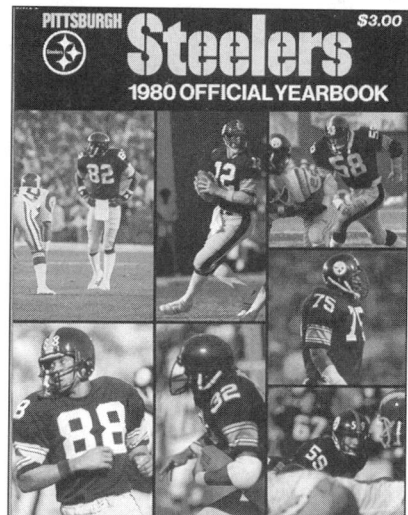

Pittsburgh Steelers

1978 Super Bowl trophies $10
1979 T. Bradshaw, J. Greene $10
1980 T. Bradshaw, others $10
1990 B. Brister, L. Lipps, R. Woodson, others . . .$8
1991 Team helmet $8
1992 Steelers greats $8
1993 Bill Cowher, action scenes $8
1994 Night scene of city, helmet $8
1995 N. O'Donnell, B. Cowher, others $8
1996 Bill Cowher holding trophy $8
1997 Team helmet $8
1998 Crowded stadium during game $8

1999 J. Bettis, K. Stewart, others $8
2000 Steelers memories $8

St. Louis Rams

Los Angeles Rams
1958 Cartoon running back $40
1959 Cartoon mascot on a ram $40
1960 Cartoon ram, helmet $35
1961 Cartoon ram $35
1962 Jon Arnett $35
1963 Dick Bass $35
1983 Rams offense $10
1984 Quarterback taking snap $10
1985 Football cards of Rams greats $10
1987 Ram's head, helmet $10
1988 Rams '88 with action photos inside . . .$10
1989 10th Anniversary in Anaheim $10
1990 Newspaper headlines $8
1991 . . . .$8
1992 . . . .$8
1993 . . . .$8
1994 Jerome Bettis $5
St. Louis Rams
1995 Bern Bostek $8
1999 Trent Green $8
2000 C. Warner, M. Faulk $8

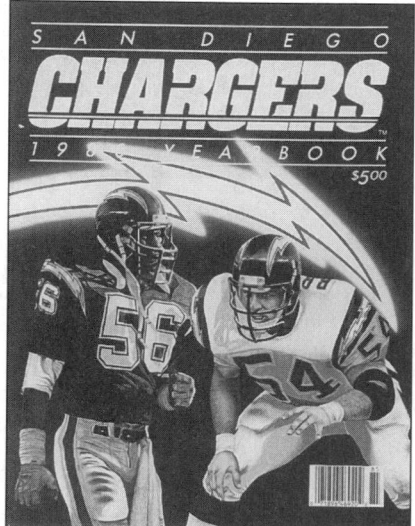

San Diego Chargers

1984 Dan Fouts $15
1988 Player artwork $10

1989 Chargers helmet $10
1991 Football flying over stadium $8
1992 Marion Butts $8
1993 B. Ross, J. Seau, R. Harmon, others $8
1994 Junior Seau in action $8
1995 AFC Championship ring $8
1996 . . . .$8
1997 . . . .$8
1998 Ryan Leaf, J. Seau, others $8

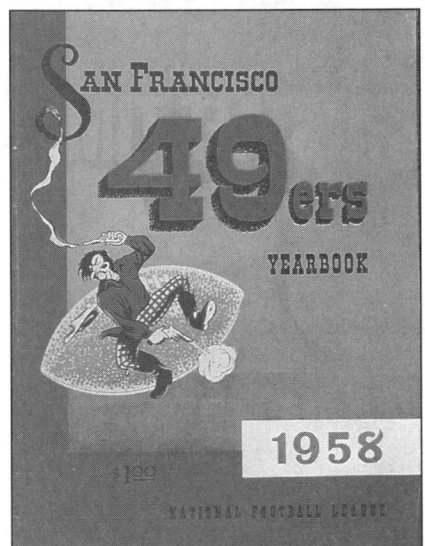

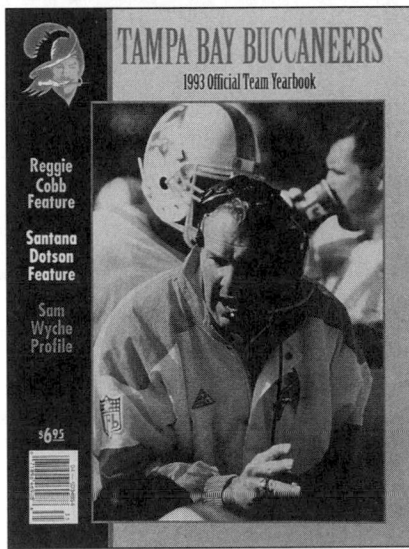

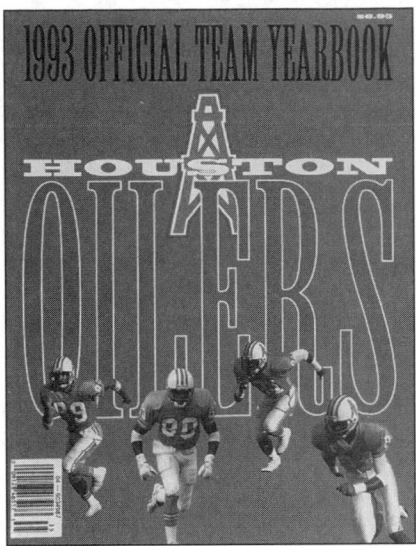

1995 Graphics generic player photo $8
Become Tennessee Oilers
1998 Eddie George/Steve McNair $8
Become Tennesee Titans

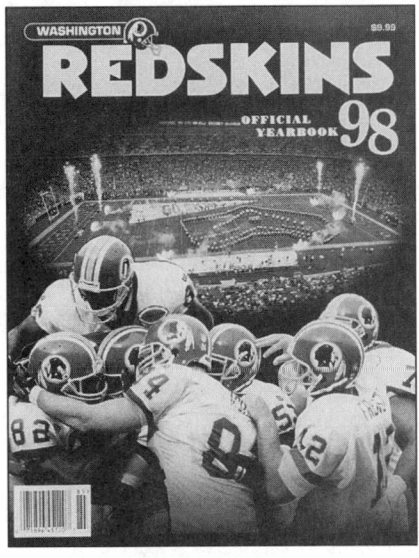

San Francisco 49ers
1958 Team mascot shooting guns $50
1963 John Brodie $40
1982 . . . .$20
1983 . . . .$15
1984 B. Walsh, J.. Montana, others $15
1985 Bill Walsh, Super Bowl celebration . . .$10
1986 Joe Montana $15
1987 J. Montana, R. Francis $15
1988 Red Porsche Golden Gate Bridge $9
1989 Three Super Bowl trophies $9
1990 Super Bowl trophies $9
1991 Winning Tradition Continues $9
1992 J. Montana, J. Rice $9
1993 Steve Young $9
1994 Jerry Rice $8
1995 Five Time World Champions $8
1996 50th Anniversary $8
1997 New Era Begins $8
1998 Rice/J.J. Stokes/T. Owens $8

Seattle Seahawks
1976 Team helmet, NFL pennants $25
1987 E. Robinson, others $10
1988 Team helmet $8
1989 Team helmet $8
1993 Defense gang tackling a Falcon $8
1994 Rick Mirer $8
1997 Defensive pileup $8
1998 Warren Moon $8
1999 . . . .$8

Tampa Bay Buccaneers
1992 Center snapping ball to quarterback . . .$8
1993 Sam Wyche $8
1994 . . . .$6
1995 . . . .$6
1996 . . . .$6
1997 . . . .$6
1998 T. Dilfer, H. Nickerson $6
1999 M. Alstott, R. Brooks $10
2000 . . . .$8

Tennessee Titans
Houston Oilers
1965 Oilers vs. San Diego Chargers $40
1968 . . . .$30
1970 . . . .$30
1990 . . . .$8
1991 Warren Moon $8
1992 Jack Pardee $8
1993 C. Duncan, E. Givens, H. Jeffires,
  W. Slaughter $8
1994 Ray Childress $8

Washington Redskins
1973 George Allen, Chris Hanburger $25
1974 George Allen, others $20
1976 Redskins' field goal attempt $20
1977 . . . .$20
1986 50th Anniversary logo $10
1987 Doug Williams $10
1988 Super Bowl action photos $10
1989 K. Bryant, M. Rypien, R. Sanders/
  D. Williams $8
1990 Art Monk, others $8
1991 Game action $8
1992 A. Monk, R. Grimm, J. Jacoby, others . . .$8
1993 Redskins defense $8
1994 Norv Turner, Heath Schuler $7
1995 B. Mitchell, H. Schuler $7
1996 Norv Turner, player collage $7
1997 . . . .$7
1998 Players celebrating marching band $7

Football Media Guides
Arizona Cardinals

Chicago Cardinals

1947 Team logo and 1947	$50
1948 Team logo and 1948	$50
1949 Team logo and 1949	$50
1950 Team logo and 1950	$40
1951 Team logo and 1951	$40
1952 Team logo and 1952	$40
1953 Team logo and 1953	$40
1954 Team logo and 1954	$40
1955 Team logo and 1955	$40
1956 Team logo and 1956	$40
1957 Team logo and 1957	$40
1958 Team logo and 1958	$40
1959 Team logo and 1959	$40

St. Louis Cardinals

1960 Team mascot and 1960	$27
1961 Team mascot and 1961	$27
1962 Team mascot and 1962	$27
1963 Charley Johnson, Wally Lemm	$27
1964 Bobby Joe Conrad	$27
1965 Jim Bakken	$27
1966 Busch Stadium	$27
1967 Larry Wilson	$27
1968 Jim Hart, Johnny Roland	$27
1969 Dave Williams	$27
1970 Cardinals in action	$13
1971 Team helmets	$13
1972 Team helmet, St. Louis Arch	$13
1973 Jim Bakken	$15
1974 Busch Stadium	$13
1975 D. Coryell/ J. Hart/ T. Metcalf	$13
1976 Jim Hart	$15
1977 Cardinals vs. Dallas Cowboys	$13
1978 St. Louis Cardinals greats	$13
1979 Cardinals in action	$13
1980 Cardinals in action	$6
1981 Cardinals in action	$6
1982 Stump Mitchell	$6
1983 Team helmets	$6
1984 25th Anniversary in St. Louis	$6
1985 Team mascot, St. Louis Arch	$6
1986 Gene Stallings	$6
1987 Cardinals uniform #87	$6

Phoenix Cardinals

1988 N. Lomax, V. Sikahema, L. Sharpe, others	$6
1989 Cardinals in the desert	$6
1990 Cardinals defense	$6
1991 Timm Rosenbach, Ken Harvey	$6

1992 Greg Davis, Rich Camarillo	$6
1993 Eric Swann, others	$6

Arizona Cardinals

1994 Art of Buddy Ryan	$6
1995 Eric Hill, fireworks	$6
1996 V. Tobin, A. Williams, R. Moore	$6
1997 Lomas Brown	$6
1998 Collage of Cardinals history	$6

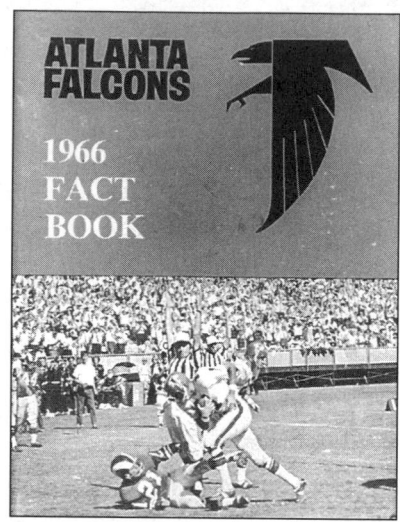

Atlanta Falcons

1966 Randy Johnson	$27
1967 Team helmet	$27
1968 R. Johnson, B. Lothridge, T. Nobis, others	$27
1969 Four Falcons linemen	$27
1970 Falcons in action	$19
1971 Falcon in action	$16
1972 Bob Berry	$16
1973 Team logos	$16
1974 Bob Lee, offensive line	$13
1975 Marion Campbell	$13
1976 Jim Mitchell	$13
1977 Steve Bartkowski	$13
1978 The new training complex	$13
1979 Falcons defensive line	$12
1980 Falcons in action	$10
1981 Falcons offensive	$9
1982 Three Falcons in action	$9
1983 Team helmet, city skyline	$9
1984 W. Andrews, B. Curry, B. Johnson	$9
1985 S. Bailey, R. Bryan, G. Riggs	$9
1986 Team helmet and falcon	$6
1987 Falcons media equipment	$6
1988 Putting it All Together	$6
1989 Chris Miller	$6
1990 25th Anniversary logo	$6
1991 Falcons helmet	$6
1992 Georgia Dome	$6
1993 Falcon	$6
1994 Falcon	$5
1995 Football cards of eight players	$5
1996 Jessie Tuggle	$5
1997 Dan Reeves	$5
1998 Falcons helmet	$6

Baltimore Ravens

1996 Painting of bird	$7
1997 Logo, Memorial Stadium	$6
1998 Logo, artwork of new stadium	$6

Buffalo Bills

1960 Team logo and 1960	$27
1961 Team mascot and 1961	$27

1962 Team mascot and 1962	$27
1963 Team mascot and 1963	$27
1964 Team logo and 1964	$27
1965 Team logo and 1965	$27
1966 Team picture	$27
1967 Bills in action	$27
1968 Bills in action	$27
1969 John Rauch	$27
1970 O.J. Simpson	$30
1971 Dennis Shaw	$16
1972 Dennis Shaw, O.J. Simpson	$20
1973 Bills Stadium	$16
1974 O.J. Simpson	$20
1975 Tony Greene	$13
1976 Team helmet	$13
1977 Team logo	$13
1978 Chuck Knox	$13
1979 20th Anniversary photos	$13
1980 J. Butler, J. Ferguson, J. Haslett	$9
1981 Joe Cribbs, Eastern Division Championship celebration	$9
1982 Team helmet	$9
1983 Buffalo	$9
1984 25th Anniversary logo	$9
1985 Past and present team helmets	$9
1986 Scott Norwood	$6
1987 Team helmet	$6
1988 C. Bennett, J. Kelly, B. Smith, others	$7
1989 Scott Norwood, others	$6
1990 Team helmet and uniform	$6
1991 Bills helmet	$6
1992 M. Levy/T. Thomas/J. Kelly	$6
1993 Bills helmet	$6
1994 35 year logo	$6
1995 J. Kelly/others	$6
1996 Marv Levy	$6
1997 Thurman Thomas	$6
1998 Bills lineman	$6

Carolina Panthers

1995 Inaugural painting of #95	$8
1996 Artwork of panther sculpture	$6
1997 Artwork of Sam Mills	$6
1998 Panther logo on raised format	$6

Chicago Bears

1934 Name and 1934	$70
1935 Beattie Feathers	$70
1936 Jack Manders	$70

1937	$70
1938	$70
1939	$70
1940	$50
1941 Bears in action	$50
1942 Bears in action	$50
1943 Bears in action	$50
1944 George Wilson	$50
1945 Team picture	$50
1946 Name and 1946	$50
1947 Bear sprawled over football	$50
1948 Team mascot	$50
1949 Team mascot	$50
1950 Team mascot	$40
1951 Team mascot	$40
1952 Team mascot	$40
1953 Team mascot	$40
1954 Name and 1954	$40
1955 Bears in action	$40
1956 Bears in action	$40
1957 Bears in action	$40
1958 Team mascot	$40
1959 Team picture	$40
1960 Team mascot	$27
1961 Team mascot	$27
1962 Bears in action	$27
1963 Team mascot and 1963	$27
1964 World Champions banner	$27
1965 Bears in action	$27
1966 Bears action photos	$27
1967 Bears in action	$27
1968 Team helmet and 1968	$27
1969 Golden Anniversary helmets	$27
1970 Helmet and 1970	$13
1971 Helmet and 1971	$13
1972 Helmet and 1972	$13
1973 Abe Gibron	$13
1974 Helmet and 1974	$13
1975 Doug Buffone	$13
1976 Helmet and 1976	$13
1977 Jack Pardee	$13
1978 Team logo and 1978	$13
1979 Bears in action	$13
1980 George Halas	$7
1981 Home of the Bears	$7
1982 Mike Ditka	$7
1983 Mike Ditka, George Halas	$7
1984 Walter Payton	$9
1985 Bears in action	$7
1986 Bears in action	$7
1987 R. Grange, B. Nagurski, W. Payton, G. Sayers	$7

1994 MEDIA GUIDE

1988 Team helmet	$7
1989 Bears equipment	$6
1990 Team helmet	$6
1991 B. George/D. Butkus/M. Singletary	$6
1992 Nine photos of Mike Ditka	$6
1993 M. McCaskey, D. Wannstedt	$6
1994 Memorabilia	$6
1995 Helmet, hands holding up sign	$6
1996 Bears defense in action	$6
1997 Halas Hall, R. Harris, R. Salaam	$6
1998 Curtis Conway	$6

1990 Media Guide

Cincinnati Bengals

1968 Paul Brown	$27
1969 Riverfront Stadium	$27
1970 Date Book and Media Guide, 1970	$13
1971 Date Book and Media Guide, 1971	$13
1972 Date Book and Media Guide, 1972	$13
1973 Date Book and Media Guide, 1973	$13
1974 Artwork of player over stadium	$13
1975 Bengals in action	$13
1976 Ken Anderson	$15
1977 Riverfront Stadium	$13
1978 Riverfront Stadium	$13
1979 Team helmets	$13
1980 Tiger, Bengals in action	$7
1981 New uniform	$7
1982 K. Anderson/ B. Bush/ D. Lapham/Tiger	$7
1983 Team helmet	$7
1984 Ken Anderson	$7
1985 Cris Collinsworth	$7
1986 Boomer Esiason	$7
1987 J. Brooks/ E. Brown/ B. Esiason, others	$7
1988 Tiger	$6
1989 Tiger	$6
1990 Tiger	$6
1991 Drawing of Tiger	$6
1992 Tiger artwork, 25th Anniversary	$6
1993 Bengal Tiger	$6
1994 Bengals helmet	$6
1995 Orange and black swirl	$6
1996 J. Blake, C. Pickens high fiving	$6
1997 Tiger	$6
1998 Tiger	$6

Cleveland Browns

1949 Team mascot	$50
1950 Cleveland Stadium and crowd	$50

1989 CLEVELAND BROWNS FAN AND MEDIA GUIDE

1951 Name and 1951	$50
1952 Paul Brown	$50
1953 Cartoon Brown	$45
1954 Media equipment	$45
1955 Cartoon reporter	$45
1956 Cartoon reporter	$45
1957 Coach and player	$40
1958 Browns in action	$40
1959 Browns in action	$40
1960 Team mascot and helmet	$27
1961 Team mascot and helmet	$27
1962 Jim Brown	$30
1963 Jim Brown	$30
1964 Jim Brown	$30
1965 Team helmet	$27
1966 Action pictures	$27
1967 Leroy Kelly	$27
1968 Team helmet	$27
1969 Team helmet	$27
1970 Team helmet	$13
1971 Team helmet	$13
1972 Team helmet	$13
1973 Team helmet	$13
1974 Team helmet	$13
1975 Team helmet	$13
1976 Team helmet	$13
1977 Team helmet	$13
1978 Team helmet	$13
1979 Browns in action	$13
1980 Sam Rutigliano	$6
1981 Brian Sipe	$7
1982 Team helmet and Cleveland	$6
1983 Browns defense in action	$6
1984 Ozzie Newsome	$8
1985 C. Matthews, M. Schottenheimer	$6
1986 Earnest Byner, Kevin Mack	$6
1987 Bernie Kosar	$6
1988 Earnest Byner, Bernie Kosar	$6
1989 Bernie Kosar	$6
1990 R. Langhorne/ W. Slaughter	$6
1991 Fireworks exploding over goalpost	$6
1992 Player's arm and helmet	$6
1993 Entrance to training facility	$6
1994 75th NFL logo on pigskin	$6
1995 "Browns" on white background	$6

Become Baltimore Ravens

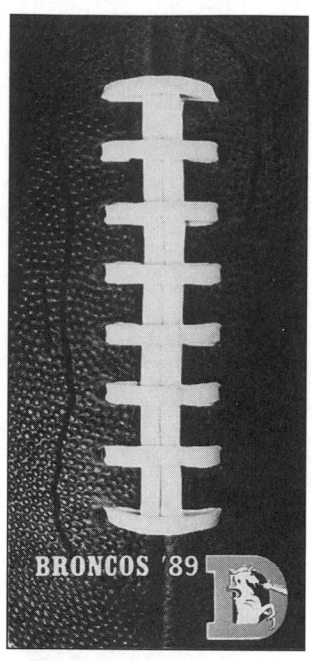

Dallas Cowboys

1960 Team mascot $27
1961 L.G. Dupre $27
1962 Players in uniforms 19, 62 . . . .$27
1963 Bill Howton $27
1964 Team helmet $27
1965 Bob Lilly $27
1966 Bob Hayes $27
1967 Don Meredith $27
1968 Don Perkins $27
1969 Tom Landry $27
1970 Calvin Hill $17
1971 Texas Stadium $13
1972 T. Landry/ Murchison/ T.Schram/ trophy
. . . .$13
1973 Mel Renfro $13
1974 Cornell Green $13
1975 Roger Staubach $15
1976 Cliff Harris $13
1977 Drew Pearson $13
1978 H. Martin, R. White, two trophies $13
1979 20th Anniversary $13
1980 Tony Dorsett $10
1981 Randy White $9
1982 Tom Landry $8
1983 Texas Stadium, Cowboys star $7
1984 25th Anniversary logo $7
1985 Randy White $7
1986 Tony Dorsett, Tom Landry $7
1987 Tony Dorsett, Herschel Walker $6
1988 Cowboys star $6
1989 Jimmy Johnson, Jimmy Jones $6
1990 Eugene Lockhart $6
1991 Troy Aikman $6
1992 Emmitt Smith $6
1993 J. Johnson, Aikman, J. Jones, K, Norton $6
1994 Four Super Bowl trophies $6
1995 Troy Aikman $6
1996 Five Super Bowl rings $6
1997 Darren Woodson $6
1998 Cowboys helmet $6

Denver Broncos

1960 None issued
1961 Empty Denver Bears stadium $27
1962 Cartoon quarterback throwing $27
1963 Team mascot $27
1964 Lionel Taylor $27
1965 Team mascot $27
1966 Lionel Taylor $27
1967 Lou Saban $27
1968 Team helmet $27

1969 Team mascot $27
1970 Mike Haffner $13
1971 R. Jackson, F. Little, L. Saban $15
1972 Floyd Little, John Ralston $15
1973 Offensive huddle $15
1974 Team helmet, huddle $13
1975 Otis Armstrong $13
1976 Riley Odoms $15
1977 Orange Crush defense $13
1978 Mile High Stadium $13
1979 Team helmet $13
1980 Team helmet $7
1981 Broncos uniform #81 . . . .$7
1982 Dan Reeves $7
1983 Broncos in action $7
1984 John Elway $8
1985 Bronco silhouette $7
1986 Broncos in action $6
1987 John Elway $7
1988 Karl Mecklenburg $6
1989 Football stitching $6
1990 Team headquarters $6
1991 Defense on line of scrimmage $6
1992 Torso of player No. 92 . . . .$6
1993 John Elway $6
1994 35th Anniversary art $6
1995 Mike Shanahan $6
1996 Elway, Zimmerman celebrating $6
1997 Broncos new logo $6
1998 Elway lifting Lombardi trophy $6

Detroit Lions

1946 Team mascot $50
1947 Name and 1947 . . . .$50
1948 Bo McMillin $50
1949 a: Lions mascot (40 pgs.) $50
       b: Bo McMillin (20 pgs.) $40
1950 Name and 1950 . . . .$40
1951 a: Doak Walker (48 pgs.) $40
       b: Lions mascot (48 pgs.) $40
1952 Name and 1952 . . . .$40
1953 Mascot, World Champions pennant $40
1954 Mascot, World Champions pennant $40
1955 Mascot, W. Division Champs banner $40
1956 Briggs Stadium $40
1957 Lions in action $40
1958 Team picture $40
1959 Name and 1959 . . . .$40
1960 Lions in action $27

1961 Jim Gibbons $27
1962 Briggs Stadium $27
1963 Lions mascot $27
1964 Player in action $27
1965 Team helmet $27
1966 Players with uniform #s 19, 66 . . . .$27
1967 Team logo $27
1968 Lions in action $27
1969 Lions in action $27
1970 Lions in action $13
1971 Team helmet $13
1972 Team logo $13
1973 Team logo $13
1974 Team logo $13
1975 Lions in action $13
1976 Team helmet $13
1977 Lions in action $13
1978 Lions in action $13
1979 Monte Clark, Gary Danielson $10
1980 Lions in action $10
1981 Billy Sims $10
1982 Lions in action $6
1983 50th Anniversary logo $6
1984 Team helmet $6
1985 James Jones $6
1986 Ford, Rogers, Thomas, helmet $6
1987 Lion $6
1988 Lion $6
1989 Wayne Fontes $6
1990 J. Ball, E. Murray, B. Sanders, C. Spielman .
. . . .$7
1991 Barry Sanders $6
1992 Barry Sanders $6
1993 Lions memorabilia $6
1994 C. Spielman, J. Hanson, B. Sanders $6
1995 Barry Sanders $6
1996 Six player photos $6
1997 B. Sanders, H. Moore $6
1998 Actual wild lion $6

Green Bay Packers

1947 C. Lambeau, Championship teams $50
1948 Curly Lambeau $50
1949 Home of the Packers $50
1950 Name and 1950 . . . .$40
1951 State of Wisconsin $40
1952 State of Wisconsin $40
1953 Name and 1953 . . . .$40
1954 Name and 1954 . . . .$40
1955 State of Wisconsin $40
1956 State of Wisconsin $40
1957 Green Bay Stadium $40

1958 Green Bay Stadium $40
1959 Vince Lombardi and Stadium $45
1960 Packers in action $27
1961 West Division Champs 1960 . . . .$27
1962 Football in hand $27
1963 World Champions $27
1964 Team logo $27
1965 Jim Taylor $30
1966 Bart Starr $27
1967 Elijah Pitts $27
1968 Willie Davis $30
1969 Donny Anderson $25
1970 Packers in action $20
1971 Packers training $20
1972 John Brockington $25
1973 Packers defense $20
1974 John Brockington $25
1975 Bart Starr $17
1976 Dave Hanner, Bart Starr $17
1977 Lynn Dickey $13
1978 Packers entering the field $13
1979 Bart Starr, Vince Lombardi $15
1980 Packers celebrating $6
1981 Mike Douglass $6
1982 Jan Stenerud $8
1983 Larry McCarren $6
1984 Forrest Gregg $6
1985 Lynn Dickey $7
1986 Packers defense vs.Dolphins $6
1987 Mark Lee $6
1988 Lindy Infante $6
1989 Lindy Infante $6
1990 Tim Harris $6
1991 Sterling Sharpe $6
1992 Mike Holmgren $6
1993 Brett Favre $6
1994 LeRoy Butler $6
1995 Ken Ruettgers $6
1996 Reggie White $7
1997 Three Lombardi Trophies $7
1998 Brett Favre $7

Indianapolis Colts

Baltimore Colts
1950 Team logo $40
1951 $40
1952 $40
1953 Team mascot $40
1954 Team mascot $40
1955 Team mascot $40
1956 Team mascot $40
1957 Team logo $40
1958 Memorial Stadium $40

1959 Team logo $40
1960 World Champions pennants $27
1961 Team helmet, logo $27
1962 Team helmet, logo $27
1963 Colts in action $27
1964 Offensive huddle $27
1965 Colts offense $27
1966 Colts cheerleaders $27
1967 Kickoff formation $27
1968 Johnny Unitas $35
1969 Colts sideline $27
1970 Colts offense $13
1971 Super Bowl Trophy $13
1972 The Baltimore Colts $13
1973 Ted Hendricks $15
1974 Colt in action $13
1975 Lydell Mitchell $13
1976 Bert Jones $13
1977 Bert Jones $13
1978 Bert Jones, Colts in action $13
1979 Team helmet $13
1980 Team helmet $8
1981 Team helmet $8
1982 Championship pennants $8
1983 Mike Pagel $8
Indianapolis Colts
1984 Colts in action $6
1985 Team helmet, Hoosierdome $6

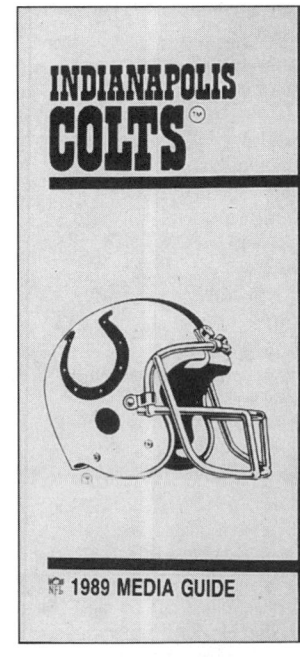

1986 Team helmet, NFL flag $6
1987 Team helmet $6
1988 Team helmet $6
1989 Team helmet $6
1990 Team helmet $6
1991 Aerial photo of RCA Dome $6
1992 Ted Marchibroda $6
1993 10th Anniversary logo $6
1994 Colts logo on splashy background $6
1995 Colts helmet inside Indiana map $5
1996 Colts helmet $5
1997 Robert Irsay, individual action photos $5
1998 Indiana outline over cityscape $5

Jacksonville Jaguars

1995 Jaguar $6
1996 M. Brunell/Jaguars $6
1997 Tom Coughlin $6
1998 Helmet/Jaguar silhouette $8

Kansas City Chiefs

1960 . . . .$27
1961 Little cowboy shooting $27
1962 . . . . .None issued
1963 L. Dawson, C. McClinton, H. Stram $30
1964 Curtis McClinton $27
1965 L. Dawson, J. Mays, H. Stram $30
1966 Chiefs in action $27
1967 L. Hunt, H. Stram, AFL Trophy $27
1968 Chiefs in action $27
1969 Willie Lanier $30
1970 Hank Stram, Chiefs celebrating $13
1971 Ed Podolak $13
1972 Arrowhead Stadium $13
1973 L. Dawson, O. Taylor, H. Stram $15
1974 Chiefs in action $13
1975 Team helmet $13
1976 Helmet, action photos $13
1977 Mike Livingston, Paul Wiggin $13
1978 Team helmet and football $13
1979 Chiefs on offense $13
1980 Marv Levy, Chiefs in action $6
1981 Gary Barbaro, Art Still, J. T. Smith $6
1982 Joe Delaney, Jack Rudnay $6
1983 Carlos Carson, John Mackovic $6
1984 25th Anniversary logo $6
1985 John Mackovic, team helmet $6
1986 Stephone Paige $6

1987 L. Burruss, D. Cherry, A. Lewis/K. Ross

. . . .$6
1988 A. Lewis, N. Lowery, P. Palmer $6
1989 C. Peterson, Marty Schottenheimer $6
1990 Center gripping the ball $6
1991 Player photo from waist down $6
1992 Arm raising Chiefs helmet $6
1993 Football bursting through paper $6
1994 Stone arrowheads $6
1995 Stadium photo from end zone $6
1996 Players at line of scrimmage $6
1997 Fans with arms raised $6
1998 Player's back wearing Chiefs jacket $6

Miami Dolphins

1966 George Wilson $27
1967 Dolphins helmet $27
1968 Orange Bowl $27
1969 J. Clancy, B. Griese, K. Noonan $27
1970 Team logo and 1970 . . . .$13
1971 B. Griese, D. Shula, P. Warfield, others . . .$15
1972 Garo Yepremian $13
1973 Super Bowl trophy $13

1974 Helmet and Super Bowl trophies $13
1975 Bob Griese, Don Shula $15
1976 B. Kuechenberg, J. Langer, B. Malone $13
1977 Bob Griese $15
1978 Nat Moore $13
1979 Delvin Williams $13
1980 Vern DenHerder $6
1981 David Woodley $6
1982 Tony Nathan $6
1983 Andra Franklin $6
1984 Dan Marino $10
1985 Clayton/Duper/Marino $8
1986 Joe Robbie, Dwight Stephenson $6
1987 Don Shula $6
1988 Dan Marino $8
1989 Team logo $6
1990 25th Anniversary logo $6
1991 John Offerdahl $6
1992 Mark Clayton, Mark Duper $6
1993 D. Shula/D. Marino/others $6
1994 Don Shula celebrating $6
1995 Dan Marino/Bryan Cox $6
1996 Dan Marino, Jimmy Johnson $6
1997 J. Johnson/D.Marino/others $6
1998 J. Johnson/D. Marino/others $6

Minnesota Vikings

1961 Team logo $27
1962 Team logo $27
1963 Team logo $27
1964 Team logo $27
1965 Team logo $27
1966 Fran Tarkenton $30
1967 Vikings in action $27
1968 Joe Kapp $27
1969 Bud Grant $27
1970 Fred Cox $13
1971 Jim Marshall $15
1972 Alan Page $15
1973 Fan in Viking costume $13
1974 Players during National Anthem $13
1975 Fans cheering $13
1976 Fran Tarkenton $15
1977 Team logo $13
1978 Chuck Foreman $13
1979 Ahmad Rashad $15
1980 Vikings new offices, stadium $6
1981 T. Kramer, A. Rashad, S. White $8
1982 Vikings in action $6
1983 M. Blair, Johnson, D. Martin, S. Studwell . .$6
1984 Les Steckel $6

1985 25th Anniversary logo $6
1986 Jerry Burns $6
1987 Tommy Kramer, others $6
1988 J. Browner, C. Doleman, K. Millard, others

. . . .$6
1989 Tim Irwin, others $6
1990 30th Anniversary logo $6
1991 Photo of HHH Dome and Skyline $6
1992 D. Green, R. McDaniel, others $6
1993 Team action photo $6
1994 Cris Carter $6
1995 Warren Moon $6
1996 R. McDaniel being congratulated $6
1997 Warren Moon $6
1998 Cris Carter/Jake Reed $6

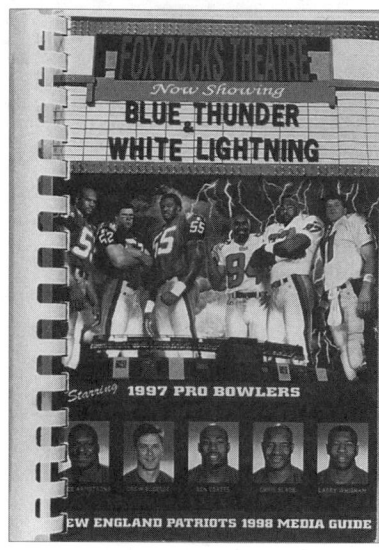

New England Patriots
Boston Patriots

1960 . . . . .None issued
1961 . . . . .None issued
1962 . . . . .None issued
1963 Cartoon Patriot, reporters $27
1964 Patriots helmet $27
1965 Gino Cappelletti, Babe April $30
1966 Nick Buoniconti $30
1967 Jim Nance $27
1968 Team logo $27
1969 Clive Rush $27
1970 Patriots action photos $13
New England Patriots
1971 Foxboro Stadium $13
1972 J. Adams, J. Plunkett, R. Vataha $13
1973 Patriots coaching staff $13
1974 Patriots action photos $13
1975 Patriots fans $13
1976 Patriots of 76 . . . .$13
1977 Chuck Fairbanks $13
1978 Patriot Superhero cartoon $13
1979 Patriots in action $13
1980 Stanley Morgan $10
1981 Ron Erhardt, action photos $6
1982 Ron Meyer $6
1983 Boston sites $6
1984 Steve Grogan $6
1985 Patriots helmet $6
1986 Andre Tippett $6
1987 Stanley Morgan $6
1988 Raymond Clayborn $6
1989 Patriots in action $6
1990 Rod Rust $6
1991 Helmet $6

1992 Patriots logo $6
1993 Helmet $6
1994 Patriots greats/S. Grogan/others $6
1995 D. Bledsoe/B. Coates/B. Armstrong $6
1996 B. Coates/C. Martin/B. Armstrong $6
1997 AFC Championship Trophy $6
1998 Patriots' 1997 Pro Bowl Players $6

New Orleans Saints

1967 Player in action $27
1968 Band playing in the stadium $27
1969 Saints defense $27
1970 Dan Abramowicz $13
1971 Tom Dempsey 63-yard field goal $15
1972 J. Kupp, A. Manning, J. Strong $13
1973 Bob Pollard $13
1974 Saints defense $13
1975 Saints in action $13
1976 Hank Stram $13
1977 C. Muncie, H. Stram, Superdome $13
1978 Superdome $13
1979 Joe Federspiel, Dick Nolan $13
1980 Saints helmet, uniform $6
1981 Archie Manning, Bum Phillips $7
1982 George Rogers $6
1983 Team logo $6
1984 Bum Phillips $6
1985 Team helmet and Louisiana $6
1986 Team logo, helmet, uniform $6
1987 R. Jackson, R. Mayes, J. Mora $6
1988 Team helmet $6
1989 Team helmet $6
1990 Dalton Hilliard $6
1991 25th anniversary logo $6
1992 Superdome crowd $6
1993 J. Mora, helmet, referee, musician $6
1994 Art of QB, Mardi Gras joker $6
1995 Saints player artwork $6
1996 Saints 30 seasons logo $6
1997 M. Ditka, W. Roaf, W. Martin $6
1998 M. Ditka, W. Roaf, W. Martin $6

New York Giants

1945 Ward Cuff $50
1946 Giants in action $50
1947 Giants in action $50
1948 Team logo $50
1949 1925 Giants $50
1950 Polo Grounds $40
1951 Polo Grounds $40
1952 Radio microphone $40
1953 Steve Owens, others $40
1954 Team logo $40

1955 Team logo $40
1956 Team logo $40
1957 Team logo $40
1958 Team logo $40
1959 Team logo $40
1960 Team logo and 1960 . . . .$27
1961 Team logo and 1961 . . . .$27
1962 Team logo and 1962 . . . .$27
1963 Team logo and 1963 . . . .$27
1964 Team logo and 1964 . . . .$27
1965 Team logo and 1965 . . . .$27
1966 Team mascot and 1966 . . . .$27
1967 Team helmet and 1967 . . . .$27
1968 Team helmet and 1968 . . . .$27
1969 Team helmet and 1969 . . . .$27
1970 Team helmet and 1970 . . . .$13
1971 Team helmet and 1971 . . . .$13
1972 Team helmet and 1972 . . . .$13
1973 Team helmet and 1973 . . . .$13
1974 Team logo $13
1975 Team helmet $13
1976 Giants Stadium construction $13
1977 Giants Stadium opening day $13
1978 Giants offensive line $13
1979 Harry Carson $13
1980 H. Carson, P. Simms, L. Taylor $15
1981 Phil Simms, offensive line $6
1982 Harry Carson, Lawrence Taylor $8
1983 H. Carson, P. Simms, L. Taylor, others $8
1984 Giants greats $6
1985 H. Carson, P. Simms, L. Taylor, others $8
1986 H. Carson, P. Simms, L. Taylor, others $8
1987 Phil Simms, Super Bowl tickets $6
1988 G. Banks, L. Marshall, L. Taylor $7
1989 Giants Stadium, previous homesites $6
1990 M. Bavarro, P. Simms, L. Taylor $6
1991 Team helmet w/two SB trophies $6
1992 Team helmet on footballs $6
1993 Giants logo on red border $6
1994 Giants 70th Anniversary logo $6
1995 20 years at Giants Stadium $6
1996 Line of scrimmage faded out $6
1997 Giants helmet $6
1998 New York Giants on blue background $6

New York Jets

1960 . . . . .None issued
1961 . . . . .None issued
1962 . . . . .None issued

1963 Artwork of player #37 . . . .$27
1964 Team logo and 1964 . . . .$27
1965 Team logo and 1965 . . . .$27
1966 Team logo and 1966 . . . .$27
1967 Team logo and 1967 . . . .$27
1968 Team logo and 1967 . . . .$27
1969 Team logo and 1969 . . . .$27
1970 Team logo and 1970 . . . .$13
1971 Team logo and 1971 . . . .$13
1972 Team logo and 1972 . . . .$13
1973 Team logo and 1973 . . . .$13
1974 Team logo and 1974 . . . .$13
1975 Team logo and 1975 . . . .$13
1976 Team logo and 1976 . . . .$13
1977 Team logo and 1977 . . . .$13
1978 Team helmet and logo $13
1979 Jets defensive line $13
1980 M. Powell/ R. Todd/Statue of Liberty $6
1981 Bruce Harper/ Marvin Powell $6
1982 Mark Gastineau, others $6
1983 Freeman McNeil, others $6
1984 25th Anniversary logo $6
1985 M. Gastineau/ F. McNeil/J. Namath $8
1986 M. Gastineau/ J. Klecko/F. McNeil $6
1987 D. Maynard, M. Shuler, A. Toon $6
1988 Al Toon $6
1989 E. McMillan, M. Shuler, A. Toon $6
1990 Bruce Coslet, Dick Steinberg $6
1991 Bandaged arm holding helmet $6
1992 Art of jets flying over stadium $6
1993 Jets helmet, 25th Anniv. logo $6
1994 Helmet and NFL 75th Anniv. logo $6
1995 New York Jets repeated across cover $6
1996 Helmet, stars in background $6
1997 Photo of stadium at Meadowlands $6
1998 Jets original logo $6

Oakland Raiders

Oakland Raiders
1960 . . . . .None issued
1961 Team mascot $27
1962 . . . . .None issued
1963 Bo Roberson $27
1964 Raiders helmet $27
1965 Oakland-Alameda Co. Stadium $27
1966 Raiders helmet $27
1967 Player in action $27
1968 AFL Champions ring $27
1969 Dan Birdwell $27
1970 Raiders offensive huddle $19

1971 Raiders offense, Daryle Lamonica $16
1972 Team logo and 1972 .... $13
1973 Raiders in action $13
1974 Pre-game huddle $13
1975 Raiders action photos $13
1976 Raider player on the sidelines $13
1977 Super Bowl XI ring $13
1976 Dave Casper in action $13
1979 20th Anniversary memorabilia $13
1980 Raiders third decade $10
1981 Super Bowl XV ring $7
Los Angeles Raiders
1982 Raider player on the sidelines $6
1983 Raiders in action $6
1984 Super Bowl XVIII ring $6
1985 Helmet, three Super Bowl trophies $6
1986 Team logo $6
1987 Matt Millen $6
1988 Van McElroy $6
1989 Team helmet $6
1990 Team helmet $6
1991 Raiders offense $6
1992 Black background, logo $6
1993 Logo on back of generic player $6
1994 Helmet, 3 trophies, 35th Anniv. $6
Oakland Raiders
1995 Metallic background, logo $6
1996 Super Bowl trophies, helmet $6
1997 Super Bowl rings $6
1998 "Team of Decades" in silver $6

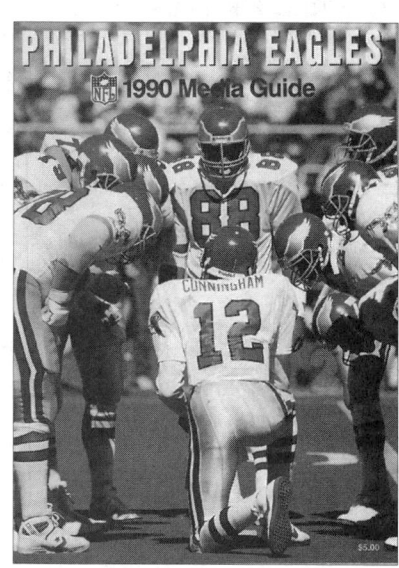

Philadelphia Eagles
1947 Season schedule $50
1948 Photo of 1947 team $50
1949 Earle Neale $50
1950 Steve Van Buren $40
1951 Eagle $40
1952 Eagles in action $40
1953 Jim Trimble $40
1954 Eagle $40
1955 Eagle $40
1956 Hugh Devore $40
1957 25th Anniversary eagle $40
1958 L. Buck Shaw $40
1959 Eagle, Franklin Field $40
1960 Franklin Field $27
1961 Eagle wearing a crown $27
1962 Baby eagle hatching from ball $27
1963 Eagle and goalposts $27
1964 Franklin Field $27
1965 Norm Snead in action $27

1966 Tim Brown $27
1967 Harold Wells $27
1968 Norm Snead, offensive line $27
1969 Apollo XI logo $27
1970 Zodiac symbols $13
1971 Eagles history $13
1972 Eddie Khayat $13
1973 Bradley, R. Gabriel, McCormack $13
1974 H. Carmichael, R. Gabriel, others $13
1975 Eagles in action $13
1976 Dick Vermiel $13
1977 Dick Vermiel, action photos $13
1978 Harold Carmichael $13
1979 H. Carmichael/ W. Montqomery $13
1980 Dick Vermiel and coaches $6
1981 Team helmet $6
1982 50th Anniversary logo $6
1983 Marion Campbell $6
1984 Mike Quick $6
1985 Norman Braman $6
1986 Buddy Ryan $6
1987 Reggie White $8
1988 Mike Quick $6
1989 Randall Cunningham $7
1990 R. Cunningham/ offensive huddle $7
1991 Rich Kotite $6
1992 Eagles defense/Jerome Brown $6
1993 Eagles helmet $6
1994 Jeffrey Lurie $6
1995 Jeffrey Lurie, Ray Rhodes $6
1996 Eagles helmet $6
1997 Eagles helmet $6
1998 Closeup of Eagles logo on jersey $6

Pittsburgh Steelers
1947 Name and 1947 .... $50
1948 Cartoon reporters $50
1949 Cartoon reporters $50
1950 Cartoon reporters $40
1951 John P. Michelosen $40
1952 Cartoon steelworker $40
1953 Steeler kicker $40
1954 City of Pittsburgh $40
1955 Steelers in action $40
1956 Steelers in action $40
1957 Brovelli, Elbert Nickel $40
1958 Steelers in action $40
1959 Team mascot and logo $40

1960 Steelers in action $27
1961 Team helmet $27
1962 Steelers uniform $27
1963 Steelers helmet and 1963 .... $27
1964 Steelers helmet and 1964 .... $27
1965 City of Pittsburgh $27
1966 City of Pittsburgh $27
1967 Steelers in action $27
1968 Team helmet $27
1969 Three Rivers Stadium $27
1970 Steelers in action $13
1971 Black and yellow stripes $13
1972 Team helmet $13
1973 Joe Greene $15
1974 Team helmet $13
1975 T. Bradshaw/ R. Bleier/F. Harris $15
1976 Team helmet $13
1977 Team helmet $13
1978 Team helmet $13
1979 Team helmet $13
1980 Steelers 1980 football $6
1981 Football $6
1982 50th Anniversary logo $6
1983 Team helmet $6
1984 Franco Harris $8
1985 Team helmet $6
1986 Team helmet $6
1987 Team helmet $6
1988 Chuck Noll $6
1989 Team helmet, Pittsburgh $6
1990 Steelers '90 logo $6
1991 Helmet, stadium in background $6
1992 60 seasons anniversary logo $6
1993 Steelers logo on helmet $6
1994 Helmet $6
1995 Logo and 1995 .... $6
1996 Logo and 1996 .... $6
1997 Helmets $6
1998 Logo and 1998 .... $6

San Diego Chargers
Los Angeles Chargers
1960 Team logo and 1960 .... $27

San Diego Chargers
1961 Team logo and 1961 .... $27
1962 Team logo and 1962 .... $27
1963 Team logo and 1963 .... $27
1964 Team logo and 1964 .... $27
1965 Team mascot and 1965 .... $27
1966 Chargers in action $27
1967 Jack Murphy Stadium $27
1968 Chargers in action $27
1969 John Hadl, offensive line $27
1970 Lance Alworth $15
1971 Chargers in action $13
1972 John Hadl $13
1973 Dennis Partee $13
1974 New Chargers uniform $13
1975 Don Woods $13
1976 Dan Fouts $13
1977 Dan Fouts $13
1978 Joe Washington $13
1979 Chargers in action $13
1980 Chargers in action $6
1981 Greg McCrary, Cliff McGee $6
1982 Team airplanes $6
1983 Team helmet $6
1984 25th Anniversary logo $6
1985 Dan Fouts, Charlie Joiner $8
1986 Lionel James, others celebrating $6
1987 Team helmet $6
1988 Team logo $6
1989 Chargers in action $6

1990 A. Miller, L. O'Neal, L. Williams $6
1991 Chargers logo $6
1992 Nate Lewis $6
1993 Snapshots of crowd $6
1994 Junior Seau, fans $6
1995 AFC Championship ring, David Griggs $6
1996 Rodney Culver $6
1997 T. Martin, J. Seau, K. Gilbride, others $6
1998 R. Leaf/P. Tagliabue/J. Seau/others $6

San Francisco 49ers
1950 Three cartoon reporters $40
1951 Team mascot $40
1952 Three team mascots $40
1953 Team mascot $40
1954 Team mascot $40
1955 Action shot and team mascot $40
1956 Team mascot $40
1957 Three team mascots $40
1958 Prospector firing revolvers $40
1959 Team mascot $40
1960 Red Hickey $27
1961 Team mascot $27
1962 Team mascot $27
1963 Team mascot $27
1964 Team mascot $27
1965 Team mascot $27
1966 Team mascot $27
1967 49ers in action $27
1968 Player on the sideline $27
1969 John Brodie, Gary Lewis $27
1970 Frankie Albert, John Brodie $13
1971 Candlestick Park $13
1972 Team helmet, Candlestick Park $13
1973 Dick Nolan $13
1974 Team helmet, Golden Gate Bridge $13
1975 Footballs/team helmet $13
1976 Monte Clark $13
1977 E. DeBartolo, K. Meyer, J. Thomas $13
1978 Golden Gate Bridge $13
1979 O.J. Simpson $20
1980 John Ayers, Paul Hofer $6
1981 Joe Montana, Fred Solomon $8
1982 The Catch, Super Bowl trophy $6
1983 Ronnie Lott $6
1984 Hand holding helmet $6
1985 Randy Cross, Wendell Tyler $6
1986 40th Anniversary logo $6
1987 Joe Montana $8
1988 Tom Rathman $6
1989 Joe Montana, Jerry Rice $8
1990 Roger Craig $6
1991 Jerry Rice $6

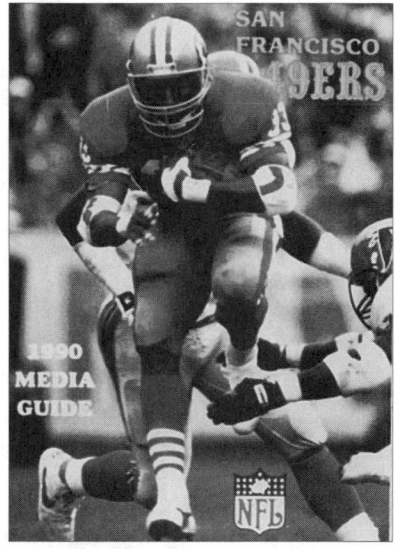

1992 Joe Montana $6
1993 Steve Young $6
1994 Jerry Rice $5
1995 Super Bowl trophies and ring $5
1996 50th anniversary/memorabilia collage $5
1997 Steve Mariucci $5
1998 B. Young/M. Hanks/T.McDonald/K, Norton $5

Seattle Seahawks
1976 Team helmet $15
1977 S. Niehaus, J. Patera, J. Zorn $13
1978 Sherman Smith $13
1979 Steve Largent, Jim Zorn $13
1980 Jack Patera $6
1981 Steve Largent, seahawk $8
1982 Steve Largent $8
1983 Chuck Knox, Kingdome $6
1984 Chuck Knox $6
1985 Players entering the field $6
1986 Steve Largent in action $8
1987 Referee signaling a TD $6
1988 Ron Heller, Johnny Holloway $6
1989 D. Krieg, S. Largent, J. L. Williams $6
1990 Uniform #90, equipment $6
1991 Seahawks helmet $6

1992 Tom Flores $6
1993 Cortez Kennedy $6
1994 Eugene Robinson $6
1995 D. Erickson/C. Warren/B. Blades $6
1996 C. KennedyC. Warren/T. Wooden $6
1997 C. Kennedy/M. Sinclair $6
1998 W. Moon/M. Sinclair/W.Williams $6

St. Louis Rams
Los Angeles Rams
1945 Bob Waterfield $50
1946 Bob Waterfield in punting pose $50
1947 Bob Waterfield $50
1948 Goat mascot $50
1949 Team logo and 1949 ....$50
1950 Team logo and 1950 ....$40
1951 Team logo and 1951 ....$40
1952 Team logo and 1952 ....$40
1953 Team logo and 1953 ....$40
1954 Team logo and 1954 ....$40
1955 Team logo and 1955 ....$40
1956 Team logo and 1956 ....$40
1957 Team logo and 1957 ....$40
1958 Team logo and 1958 ....$40
1959 Team logo and 1959 ....$40
1960 Team logo and 1960 ....$27
1961 Team logo and 1961 ....$27
1962 Team logo and 1962 ....$27
1963 Team logo and 1963 ....$27
1964 Team logo and 1964 ....$27
1965 Team logo and 1965 ....$27
1966 Team logo and 1966 ....$27
1967 Team logo and 1967 ....$27
1968 Team logo and 1968 ....$27
1969 Team logo and 1969 ....$27
1970 Team logo and 1970 ....$13
1971 Team logo and 1971 ....$13
1972 Team logo and 1972 ....$13
1973 Rams in action $13
1974 Team helmet $13
1975 Team helmet $13
1976 Team helmet $13
1977 Team helmet $13
1978 Old and new helmets $13
1979 Carroll Rosenbloom $13
1980 Rams in action $13
1981 Ram wearing uniform No. 81 ....$13
1982 Los Angeles sites $7
1983 Team helmet $6
1984 Players entering field $6
1985 40th Anniversary logo $6

1986 Eric Dickerson $7
1987 Three legs $6
1988 Rams in action $6
1989 Team helmet, equipment $6
1990 Ram wearing uniform No. 90 ....$6
1991 Ram wearing uniform No. 91 ....$6
1992 Coach with yell horns and players $6
1993 Players showing biceps $6
1994 Group clasping hands $6
Become St. Louis Rams
1995 Newspaper heralds return to NFL $6
1996 Rams goat inside helmets $6
1997 Dick Vermeil with players $6
1998 Isaac Bruce $6

Tampa Bay Buccaneers

1976 Team helmets $15
1977 Dave Pear, Lee Roy Selmon $15
1978 John McKay $13
1979 Team helmet, John McKay $13
1980 Jimmy Giles, fans celebrating $6
1981 John McKay $6
1982 Hugh Culverhouse, John McKay $6
1983 Buccaneers in action $6
1984 H. Green, J. McKay, L.R. Selmon $8
1985 Leeman Bennett, James Wilder $6
1986 Buccaneers in action $6
1987 Ray Perkins $6
1988 Ray Perkins, Vinny Testaverde $6
1989 Buccaneers in action $6
1990 Mark Carrier $6
1991 Richard Williamson $6
1992 Sam Wyche $6
1993 Two players celebrating $6
1994 John McKay, Sam Wyche $6
1995 LeRoy Selmon, H. Nickerson $6
1996 Tony Dungy/players celebrating $6
1997 Helmet on black background $6
1998 Raymond James Stadium $6

Tennesee Titans

Houston Oilers
1960 None issued
1961 Team mascot $27
1962 Ed Husmann, Ivy, Al Jamison $27
1963 Oilers in action $27
1964 Sammy Baugh, Oilers in action $27

1965 Team helmets $27
1966 O. Burrell, W.K. Hicks, B. Talamini $27
1967 Logo $27
1968 Astrodome $27
1969 Astrodome $27
1970 Oilers artwork $16
1971 Oilers sculpture $16
1972 Team helmet $16
1973 Team helmet $16
1974 Sid Gillman, Oilers in action $15
1975 Oilers in action $13
1976 Cheering fans $13
1977 Team logo $13
1978 Oilers in action $13
1979 20th Anniversary, Oilers in action $10
1980 Bum Phillips $10
1981 Oiler in action $6
1982 Team helmets $6
1983 Team helmet $6
1984 Silver Annniversary logo,. montage $6
1985 W. Moon, M. Munchak, D. Steinkuhler $8
1986 Artwork of group of players $6
1987 R. Childress, E. Givins, J. Grimsley, D. Hill .$6
1988 Team helmet, field $6
1989 Team helmet $6
1990 E. Givins/ D. Hill/ W. Moon $6
1991 Warren Moon $6
1992 Jack Pardee $6
1993 Bruce Matthews/Mike Munchak $6
1994 Player collage $6
1995 Oilers helmet and Texas flag $6
1996 Collage of team history $6
Become Tennessee Oilers
1997 Player collage/Oilers logo $6
1998 Steve McNair/Eddie George $6

Become Tennessee Titans

Washington Redskins

1946 Redskins head logo $50
1947 Name, Indian mascot $50
1948 Indian mascot and 1948 ....$50
1949 Indian mascot and 1949 ....$50
1950 Indian mascot and 1950 ....$40
1951 Indian mascot and 1951 ....$40

Pro Bowl cornerbacks Darrell Green and Cris Dishman

1952 Indian mascot and 1952 ....$40
1953 Indian mascot and 1953 ....$40
1954 Indian mascot and 1954 ....$40
1955 Redskins in action $40
1956 Redskins in action $40
1957 Redskins in action $40
1958 Year and 1958 ....$40
1959 Team helmet, pennant $40
1960 Football and 1960 ....$27
1961 Silver Anniversary $27
1962 Football $27
1963 Capitol building $27
1964 Tomahawk and drum $27
1965 Team helmet $27
1966 Tepee, D.C. Stadium $27
1967 Tepee, D.C. Stadium $27
1968 Tepee, D.C. Stadium $27
1969 Tepee, D.C. Stadium $27
1970 Tepee, D.C. Stadium $13
1971 Tepee, D.C. Stadium $13
1972 Team helmet $13
1973 Team logo, D.C. sites $13
1974 Team helmet, Capitol $13
1975 Pregame huddle $13
1976 Team logo, George Allen $13
1977 Redskins in action $13
1978 Mark Moseley $13
1979 Indian, Redskins in action $13
1980 Team helmet $6
1981 Team logo $6
1982 Redskins and helmet $6
1983 Helmet, Super Bowl trophy $8
1984 Joe Theismann $7
1985 John Riggins, Joe Theismann $8
1986 50th Anniversary logo $6
1987 Gary Clark, Art Monk $8
1988 Super Bowl XXII ring $8
1989 Art Monk in action $8
1990 Charles Mann $6
1991 Darrell Green $6
1992 Art Monk catching a pass $6
1993 Jim Lachey $6
1994 Previous press guides $6
1995 Redskins Pro Bowlers $6
1996 Brian Mitchell/Redskins Stadium $6
1997 Terry Allen $6
1998 Darrell Green, Cris Dishman $6

September 28, 1954

Sports Illustrated Football Covers

1954

09/28/54 Calvin Jones, Iowa $15
11/10/54 Oklahoma Sooners $15
11/22/54 Y.A. Tittle, 49ers (FC) . . . .$35-$40

1955

09/12/55 Bud Wilkinson, Oklahoma $20
10/03/55 Doak Walker, Lions $30
10/24/55 Howard Cassidy, Ohio State $25
11/07/55 Bob Pellegrini, Maryland $12
11/28/55 Don Holleder, Army $15
12/26/55 Jim Swink, Texas Christian . . .$12-$14

1956

09/24/56 College Football Preview . . . . .$10-$15
10/08/56 Paul Brown, George Ratterman $20
10/29/56 P. Hornung, Notre Dame
(FC) . . . .$30-$35
11/05/56 Yale vs. Dartmouth $8
10/12/56 Tom Maentz/Ron Kramer, Michigan
. . . .$10
11/26/56 USC vs. UCLA $10
12/03/56 Chuck Conerly, Giants . . . . . .$15-$20

1957

09/23/57 College Football Preview $15
10/07/57 Ollie Matson, Cardinals $12
11/04/57 Bobby Cox, Minnesota $20
11/18/57 Oklahoma Sooners $10

1958

09/22/58 College Football Preview $12
10/27/58 Chick Zimmerman, Syracuse $10
11/24/58 Dawkins/Walters/Anderson, Army .$15

1959

09/21/59 College Football Preview $17
10/05/59 Johnny Unitas, Colts (FC) . . . .$30-$35
10/26/59 George Izo, Notre Dame $12
11/09/59 College Football Preview $12

1960

09/19/60 College Football Preview $12
09/26/60 Jim Brown, Browns $35
10/03/60 Bob Schloredt, Washington $17

10/24/60 Violence in Pro Football $10
11/28/60 Joe Bellino, Navy . . . .$7-$10
12/19/60 Norm Van Brocklin, Eagles $20

1961

09/18/61 College Football Preview . . . . .$12-$15
09/25/61 Bart Starr, Packers (FC) $25
10/16/61 Terry Baker, Oregon State . . . .$12-$15
10/23/61 Jon Amett/Roy Hord, Rams $15
11/20/61 Y.A. Tittle, Giants . . . .$20-$25
11/27/61 Jimmy Saxton, Texas . . . .$10-$15
12/01/61 Dan Currie, Packers . . . .$8-$12

1962

09/10/62 Jim Taylor, Packers (FC) $20
09/24/62 College Football Preview $17
10/08/62 Tommy McDonald, Eagles $15
10/15/62 Sonny Gibbs, TCU $15
10/29/62 Fran Tarkenton, Vikings (FC) $25
11/19/62 Nick Pietrosante, Lions . . . .$8-$12
11/26/62 Paul Dietzel, Army . . . .$4-$7
12/17/62 Frank Gifford, Giants . . . .$20-$25

1963

01/07/63 Terry Baker, Oregon State (SOY) . .$17
05/20/63 Paul Hornung, Packers . . . .$20-$25
09/09/63 Pro Football Preview $17
09/23/63 George Mira, Miami $12
10/14/63 Ronnie Bull, Bears . . . .$8-$12
10/21/63 Duke Carlisle, Texas . . . .$6-$8
11/04/63 Jack Cvercko, Northwestern $6
11/11/63 Violence in Pro Football . . . .$4-$6
11/25/63 Willie Galimore, Bears . . . .$8-$12
12/02/63 Roger Staubach, Navy (FC) . . .$35-$45
12/16/63 Paul Lowe/Tobin Rote, Chargers
. . . .$10-$15

1964

01/06/64 Pete Rozelle, (SOY) $20
08/17/64 Don Trull, Oilers $12
09/07/64 Pro Football Preview $20
09/21/64 College Football Preview $15
09/28/64 Tommy Mason, Vikings . . . .$8-$12
10/12/64 Dick Butkus, Illinois (FC) . . . .$25-$30
11/02/64 John Huarte, Notre Dame $12
11/30/64 Alex Karras, Lions . . . .$10-$15
12/14/64 Charley Johnson, Cardinals $17

1965

01/04/65 Frank Ryan, Browns $20
01/11/65 Ernie Koy, Texas $10
07/19/65 Joe Namath, Jets (FC) . . . .$25-$30
08/16/65 Y.A. Tittle, Giants $20
09/13/65 Fran Tarkenton, Vikings $25
09/20/65 Frank Solich, Nebraska . . . .$10-$12
09/27/65 Frank Ryan, Browns . . . .$10-$12
10/11/65 Ken Willard, 49ers $10
10/18/65 Tommy Nobis, Texas $12
11/01/65 S. Randle/C. Johnson, Cardinals . . .$10
11/08/65 Harry Jones, Arkansas $12
11/29/65 Dennis Gaubatz, Colts $8
12/13/65 Lance Alworth, Chargers . . . . .$20-$25

1966

01/03/66 College Bowl Games $12
01/10/66 Jim Taylor, Packers 25
07/25/66 O. Graham/E. B. Williams, Browns
. . . .$12
08/09/66 Frank Emanuel, Dolphins . . . . .$8-$10
08/15/66 Bear Bryant, Alabama (FC) $25
08/22/66 Hornung/Taylor, Packers . . . . .$25-$30

January 22, 1968

09/12/66 Paul Bukich/Gale Sayers, Bears . . .$25
09/19/66 Gary Beban, UCLA . . . .$10-$12
10/03/66 Roman Gabriel, Rams $12
10/17/66 Joe Namath, Jets $30
10/31/66 Bart Starr, Packers $25
11/07/66 Terry Hanratty, Notre Dame . .$10-$15
11/21/66 Ross Fichtner, Browns $8
11/28/26 Notre Dame vs. Michigan State . . .$20
12/12/66 Jim Nance, Patriots $8

1967

01/09/67 Bart Starr, Packers . . . .$25-$30
01/23/67 Max McGee, Packers . . . .$35-$40
07/17/67 Fran Tarkenton, Giants $20
08/14/67 J. Taylor/G.Cuozzo, Saints . . . . .$8-$10
09/11/67 Terry Hanratty, Notre Dame . . . .$8-$10
09/18/67 Tommy Mason, Rams . . . .$12-$15
10/09/67 Texas vs. USC $8
10/16/67 Mike Phipps, Purdue $8
10/30/67 Tennessee vs. Alabama $15
11/06/67 Dan Reeves, Cowboys . . . .$15-$20
11/20/67 Gary Beban, O.J. Simpson (FC) . . .$25
11/27/67 Jim Hart, Cardinals . . . .$8-$12
12/18/67 Roman Gabriel, Rams . . . .$8-$12

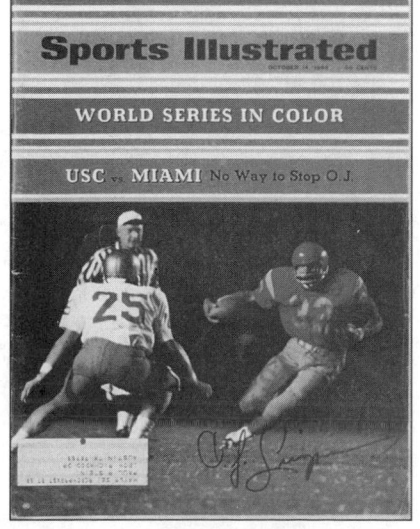

October 14, 1968

December 9, 1968

1968

01/08/68	H. Dixon, C. Mercein . . . .$10-$12
01/22/68	V.Lombardi, Packers (FC) . . . .$30-$35
07/15/68	Ray Nitschke, Packers $12
08/12/68	Paul Brown, Bengals $8
09/09/68	College Football Preview 12
09/16/68	Don Meredith, Cowboys $12
10/14/68	O.J. Simpson, USC 15
10/28/68	Bob Brown/F. Gregg, Packers $10
11/11/68	Bruce Jankowski, Ohio State $7
11/25/68	Earl Morral, Colts $10
12/09/68	Joe Namath, Jets $20
12/16/68	Colts vs. Packers . . . .$8-$10

1969

01/06/69	Tom Matte, Colts . . . .$8-$12
01/20/69	Joe Namath, Jets $50
03/03/69	V. Lombardi, Redskins . . . .$8-$12
06/16/69	Joe Namath, Jets $15
07/14/69	O.J. Simpson, Bills $15
07/29/69	V. Lombardi, S. Jurgensen . . . . .$8-$12
08/11/69	Joe Namath, Jets $15
08/25/69	O.J. Simpson, Bills $20
09/15/69	Ohio State Buckeyes $10
09/22/69	Jim Turner, Jets $10
09/29/69	Jimmy Jones, USC $8

September 29, 1969

November 24, 1969

10/13/69	Bruce Kemp, Georgia . . . .$6-$8
11/03/69	Minnesota Vikings defense $10
11/10/69	Steve Owens, Oklahoma $7
11/24/69	Len Dawson, Chiefs . . . .$10-$12

1970

01/05/70	Dave Osborn, Vikings . . . .$6-$8
01/19/70	Len Dawson, Chiefs . . . .$20-$25
02/09/70	Terry Bradshaw, Louisiana Tech . . .$15
07/20/70	Joe Kapp, Vikings $8
08/10/70	Mike Garrett, Chiefs . . . .$7-$9
08/17/70	Joe Namath, Jets . . . .$10-$15
08/31/70	Les Shy, Cowboys $8
09/14/70	A. Manning,Mississippi $15
09/02/70	Dick Butkus, Bears $20
10/05/70	Colorado vs. Penn State $10
10/12/70	Alex Karras, Lions . . . .$10-$12
11/09/70	Tatum, Theismann, Worster . . . .$8-$12
11/23/70	George Blanda, Raiders . . . . . .$10-$15
12/07/70	Roman Gabriel, Ram . . . .$8-$12
12/14/70	Steve Worster, Texas $8

1971

01/11/71	Joe Theismann, Notre Dame $10
01/18/71	Craig Morton, Cowboys $10
01/25/71	Jim O'Brien, Jets . . . .$15-$20
01/15/71	Jim Plunkett, Standford $10
05/17/71	James McAlister, UCLA . . . .$5-$8
07/19/71	George Blanda, Raiders . . . . . .$12-$15
08/16/71	Calvin Hill, Cowboys $8
09/13/71	Tommy Caanova, LSU . . . . . .$10-$12
09/20/71	John Brodie, 49ers $12
10/04/71	Sonny Sixkiller, Washington . . .$6-$10
10/11/71	Mean Joe Greene, Steelers $10
11/01/71	Ed Marinaro, Dolphins $10
11/08/71	Norm Bulaich, Colts . . . .$4-$7
11/22/71	Oklahoma vs. Nebraska $10
12/06/71	Johnny Musso, Alabama $7

1972

01/03/72	Garo Yepremian, Dolphins $10
01/10/72	Nebraska Orange Bowl victory $8
01/24/72	Duane Thomas, Cowboys $20
07/10/72	Johnny Unitas, Colts $18
07/24/72	Tommy Prothro, Rams $8
08/07/72	Larry Csonka/Jim Kiick, Dolphins .$12
09/11/72	Bob Dvaney, Nebraska $8
09/18/72	Walt Garrison, Cowboys . . . . .$12-$15

10/02/72	Greg Pruitt, Oklahoma $6
10/09/72	Joe Namath, Jets . . . .$12-$15
10/30/72	Dave and Don Buckey, Ohio State
	. . . .$4-$6
11/06/72	Larry Brown, Redskins $7
11/20/72	Terry Davis, Alabama . . . .$4-$6
12/04/72	Steve Spurrier. 40ers . . . .$8-$12
12/18/72	Lee Roy Jordan, Cowboys $10

1973

01/08/73	Mercury Morris, Dolphins . . . . .$8-$10
01/22/73	Bob Griese, Miami . . . .$15-$20
08/06/73	John Matusazak, Houston . . . . . .$4-$8
08/27/73	Duane Thomas, Redskins $8
09/10/73	Texas football $10
09/17/73	Csonka/Griese, Dolphins . . . . .$12-$15
10/01/73	Anthony Davis, USC $8
10/08/73	Fran Tarkenton, Vikings $10
10/29/73	O.J. Simpson, Bills $15
11/05/73	Anthony Davis, USAC $8
12/03/73	Bear Bryant, Alabama . . . .$7-$10
12/17/73	Marv Hubbard, Raiders . . . .$6-$8

1974

01/07/74	Fran Tarkenton, Vikings . . . . . .$8-$12
01/21/74	Larry Csonka, Dolphins . . . . . .$15-$20
04/29/74	Bruce Hardy, Utah $6
07/29/74	Terry Bradshaw, Steelers . . . . .$8-$12
08/05/74	Pro Football Strike . . . .$4-$6
09/09/74	Archie Griffin, Ohio State $10
09/16/74	O.J. Simpson, Bills $15
09/23/74	Joe Gilliam, Steelers . . . .$6-$8
09/30/74	Tom Clemens, Notre Dame . . . . .$5-$7
11/04/74	Oklahoma Football . . . .$6-$8
11/18/74	Woody Green, Chiefs $6
12/09/74	Anthony Davis, USC . . . .$6-$10

1975

01/06/75	Franco Harris, Steelers (FC) . .$10-$12
01/20/75	Terry Bradshaw, Steelers $15
06/09/75	Rocky Bleier, Steelers $8
07/28/75	Csonka/Kiick/Warfield, WFL $12
08/25/75	Bart Starr, Packers $15
09/08/75	College Football Preview . . . . . .$8-$10
09/22/75	Mean Joe Greene, Steelers $8-10
09/29/75	D.Devine/R. Slager, Notre Dame . . .$7
11/10/75	Fran Tarkenton, Vikings . . . . . .$8-$12
11/24/75	Chuck Muncie, California $7
12/08/75	Bubba Bean, Texas A&M $6

1976

01/05/76	Preston Pearson, Cowboys $10
01/12/76	Franco Harris, Steelers $10
01/26/76	Lynn Swann, Steelers . . . .$15-$20
08/16/76	Calvin Hill, Redskins $6
08/23/76	Steve Spurrier, Buccaneers $10
09/06/76	Rick Leach, Michigan $8
09/13/76	Bert Jones, Colts $10
10/04/76	Mark Manges, Maryland . . . .$4-$6
10/18/76	Chuck Foreman, Vikings . . . .$6-$8
11/08/76	Tony Dorsett, Pitt $8
11/22/76	Walter Payton, Bears . . . .$15-$20
12/06/76	Rocky Bleier, Steelers $7

1977

01/03/77	Clarence Davis, Raiders . . . .$8-$10
01/10/77	Tony Dorsett, Pitt $15
01/17/77	Ken Stabler, Raiders . . . .$15-$18
07/25/77	Conrad Dobler, Cardinals . . . . . .$4-$6
09/05/77	Ross Browner, Notre Dame $8
09/19/77	Kenny Stabler, Raiders $15

10/03/77 Billy Sims, Oklahoma $7
10/16/77 Rubin Carter, Broncos $5
11/07/77 Semi-Tough, the movie . . . .$4-$6
11/21/77 AFC/NFC rivalry . . . .$5-$7
12/05/77 Earl Campbell, Texas $6

1978

01/02/78 Mark Van Eeghen, Raiders . . . . .$6-$8
01/09/78 Terry Eurick, Notre Dame . . . . .$6-$8
01/23/78 H.Martin/R. White, Cowboys $12
08/14/78 Brutality in Football $4
09/04/78 R. Staubach, Cowboys . . . .$12-$15
09/11/78 Lou Holtz, Arkansas $10
01/02/78 Charles White, USC . . . .$5-$7
10/09/78 Terry Bradshaw, Steelers . . . . . .$7-$8
11/13/78 Chuck Fusina, Penn State $6
11/20/78 Rick Berns, Nebraska $6
12/04/78 Earl Campbell, Houston . . . .$5-$7

1979

01/08/79 Alabama vs. Penn State . . . . . .$12-$15
01/15/79 Terry Bradshaw, Steelers $15
01/29/79 Rocky Bleier, Steelers $12
08/06/79 Ken Stabler, Raiders $8
08/20/79 John Jefferson, San Diego . . . . .$5-$7
09/03/79 Earl Campbell, Houston . . . . . .$8-$10
09/10/79 Billy Sims, Charles White $7
09/24/79 Vagus Ferguson, Notre Dame $6
10/01/79 Dewey Selmon, Tampa Bay $6
11/05/79 Franco Harris, Steelers $8
11/12/79 Heismann candidates $6
11/26/79 Art Schlichter, Ohio State . . . . .$4-$6
12/24/79 Terry Bradshaw, (SOY) $10

1980

01/07/80 Rickey Bell, Buccaneers . . . .$5-$7
01/14/80 L.C. Greenwood, Steelers . . . . . .$6-$7
01/28/80 John Stallworth, Steelers $15
09/01/80 Hugh Green, Pitt $7
09/08/80 Pro Football Preview $8
09/22/80 Billy Sims, Lions $4
11/10/80 L.C. Greenwood, Steelers . . . . . .$6-$7
11/17/80 Herschel Walker, Georgia (FC) . .$5-$7
12/08/80 Vince Ferragamo, Rams $8

1981

01/12/81 Chuck Muncie, San Diego . . . . .$4-$6
01/19/81 Mark Van Eeghen, Raiders $6
02/02/81 Rod Martin, Raiders $10

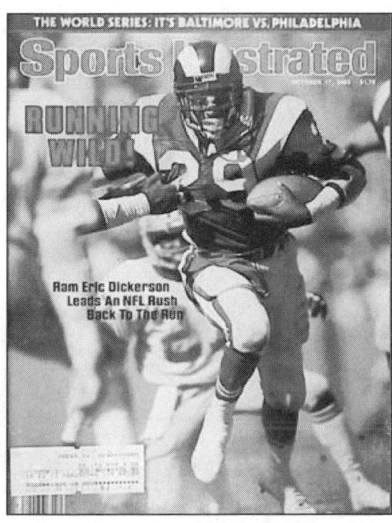

October 17, 1983

07/20/81 Vince Ferragamo, Alouettes $7
08/03/81 John Hannah, Patriots $5
08/24/81 Wendell Tyler, Rams $5
08/31/81 Herschel Walker, Georgia . . . .$8-$10
09/07/81 Jim Plunkett, Raiders . . . .$8-$10
10/05/81 Marcus Allen, USC (FC) $6
10/19/81 Texas vs. Oklahoma . . . .$4-$6
11/23/81 Bear Bryant, Alabama $6
12/07/81 Tony Dorsett, Cowboys $7
12/14/81 Cris Collinsworth, Bengals $7
12/21/81 Earl Cooper, 49ers $8

1982

01/11/82 Perry Tuttle, Clemson $5
01/17/82 Dwight Clark, 49ers . . . .$25-$30
01/25/82 Joe Montana, 49ers (FC) $25
02/01/82 Earl Cooper, 49ers $10
03/01/82 Herschel Walker, Georgia . . . . . .$5-$7
04/26/82 Renaldo Nehemiah, 49ers $5
05/10/82 Georgia Frontiere/B.Jones, Rams . .$5
08/16/82 Walter Payton, Bears (FC) . . . . .$8-$10
08/23/82 Franco Harris, Steelers . . . .$6-$8
08/30/82 Tom Cousineau, Browns $5
09/13/82 Wayne Peace, Florida $5
09/27/82 NFL Strike $5
10/04/82 Todd Blackledge, Penn State $5
11/08/82 John Elway, Stanford (FC) $15
12/06/82 Redskins vs. Eagles $5
12/13/82 Marcus Allen, Raiders $7

1983

01/10/83 Greg Garrity, Penn State $6
01/17/83 Chuck Muncie, Chargers $7
01/24/83 Andra Franklin, Dolphins $6
01/31/83 Darryl Grant, Redskins $6
02/07/83 John Riggins, Redskins (FC) . . .$8-$10
03/07/83 Herschel Walker, Generals $7
06/20/83 Marcus Dupree, Oklahoma $6
08/01/83 Richard Todd, Jets $6
08/15/83 John Elway, Broncos . . . .$8-$10
08/29/83 Tony Dorsett, Cowboys $8
09/05/83 Mike Rozier, Nebraska $7
09/26/83 Doug Flutie, Boston College $5
10/10/83 Joe Washington, Redskins $5
10/17/83 Eric Dickerson, Rams $8
11/14/83 Dan Marino, Dolphins $15
12/12/83 Jim Brown, Raiders $5
12/19/83 John Riggins, Redskins $5

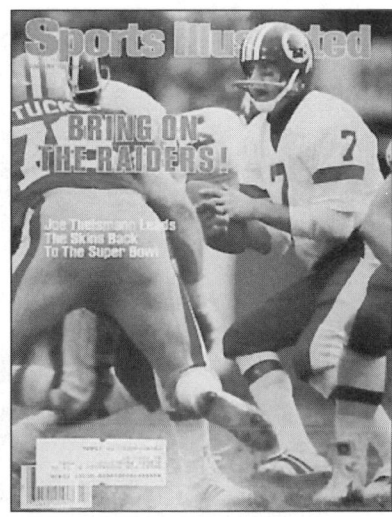

January 16, 1984

December 8, 1986

1984

01/09/84 Keith Griffin, Miami $6
01/16/84 Joe Theismann, Redskins $7
01/30/84 Jack Squirek, Redskins . . . .$8-$10
07/30/84 Jack Lambert, Steelers $7
09/03/84 J. Theismann, Redskins $7
09/10/84 Dolphins vs. Washington $5
10/01/84 Jeff Smith, Nebraska $4
10/08/84 Sammy Winder, Broncos $5
10/15/84 Walter Payton, Bears . . . .$10-$15
11/05/84 Gerry Faust, Notre Dame $7
11/12/84 Troubles in the NFL $5
11/19/84 Mark Duper, Dolphins $5
12/03/84 Doug Flutie, Boston College $5
12/17/84 Eric Dickerson, Rams $7
01/07/85 Walter Abercrombie, Steelers $6
01/14/85 Dan Marino, Dolphins . . . .$12-$15
01/21/85 Dan Marino, Joe Montana . . . .$12-$15
01/28/85 Roger Craig, 49ers $12
02/25/85 Doug Flutie, Generals $6
07/22/85 Howie Long, Raiders $6
08/12/85 Tony Dorsett, Cowboys $8
08/26/85 Bernie Kosar, Browns $7
10/07/85 Tony Robinson, Tennessee $5
10/14/85 Eddie Robinson, Grambling $5
10/21/85 Jim McMahon, Bears $7
11/11/85 Florida vs. Penn State $6
11/25/85 Danny White, Cowboys . . . .$6-$8
12/02/85 Heismann Trophy candidates $15
12/16/85 Marcus Allen, Raiders $7

1986

01/13/86 Craig James, Patriots $6
01/20/86 Jim McMahon vs. Packers $8
01/27/86 Mike Singletary, Bears $7
02/03/86 Bears vs. Patriots $8
07/21/86 "Too Tall" Jones, William Perry $5
08/18/86 Herschel Walker, Cowboys $7
09/22/86 Michigan vs. Notre Dame $7
09/29/86 M. Gastineau, L. Taylor . . . .$6-$8
10/13/86 NFL Injuries $4
11/24/86 Vinny Testaverde, Miami . . . . . .$6-$7
12/08/86 Walter Payton, Bears $8
12/15/86 Mark Bavarro, Giants $8
12/22/86 Joe Paterno, Penn State (SOY) $7

1987

01/05/87 Brian Bosworth, Oklahoma . . . . .$3-$7
01/12/87 Ozzie Newsome, Browns . . . . . .$4-$7

01/19/87	Rich Karlis, Broncos	$4-$7
01/26/87	Lawrence Taylor, Giants	$8-$10
02/02/87	Phil Simms, Giants	$7-$10
08/03/87	Vinny Testaverde, Bucanneers	$5
08/24/87	Jim McMahon, Bears	$5
08/31/87	Tim Brown, Notre Dame	$3-$5
09/21/87	John Elway, Broncos	$5-$6
10/12/87	Steve Walsh, Miami	$4-$5
11/09/87	Eric Dickerson, Colts	$7
11/16/87	Rotnei Anderson, Oklahoma	$4
11/23/87	Oklahoma vs. Nebraska	$5
12/14/87	Bo Jackson, Raiders	$6-$8

1988

01/11/88	Miami vs. Oklahoma	$5-$7
01/25/88	John Elway, Broncos	$5-$7
02/08/88	Doug Williams, Redskins	$7-$9
08/01/88	Tony Dorsett, Broncos	$4-$5
08/29/88	Bernie Kosar, Browns	$5-$7
09/05/88	Florida Gators football	$4-$6
09/12/88	Jim McMahon, Bears	$5-$6
10/24/88	Tony Rice, Notre Dame	$5-$8
11/14/88	Tom Landry, Chuck Noll	$7-$8
11/21/88	Saints vs. Rams	$4-$5
11/28/88	Rodney Peete, USC	$4
12/05/88	Tony Rice, Notre Dame	$5

1989

01/09/89	Tony Rice, Notre Dame	$5
01/16/89	Ickey Woods, Bengals	$4-$5
01/30/89	Jerry Rice, 49ers (FC)	$9-$12
02/27/89	Charles Thompson, Oklahoma	$6
03/20/89	Jimmy Johnson, Cowboys	$5-$7
04/24/89	T. Mandarich, Michigan State	$4-$5
08/07/89	Boomer Esiason, Bengals	$4-$5
08/21/89	Troy Aikman, Cowboys (FC)	$5-$10
09/04/89	College Football Preview	$4-$5
09/11/89	R. Cunningham, Eagles	$4-$8
09/25/89	Raghib Ismail, Notre Dame	$5
10/02/89	Joe Montana, 49ers	$6-$10
10/23/89	Herschel Walker, Vikings	$4-$5
11/06/89	Deion Sanders, Falcon	$6-$7
11/27/89	Heisman Trophy contenders	$4-$8
12/04/89	Steve McGuire, Miami	$4-$5
12/18/89	Joe Montana	$15

1990

01/08/90	Scott Erickson, Miami	$4-$5
01/15/90	Jerry Rice, 49ers	$6-$9
01/22/90	John Elway, Broncos	$6-$5
02/05/90	Joe Montana,49ers	$5-$6
04/30/90	Jeff George, Colts	$3-$4

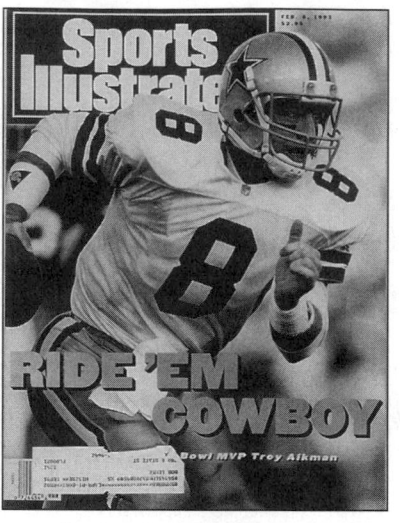

February 8, 1993

08/06/90	Joe Montana, 49ers	$6-$9
08/27/90	Troy Aikman, Cowboys	$5-$6
09/03/90	Todd Marinovich, USC	$3-$5
09/10/90	Barry Sanders, Lions (FC)	$4-$6
09/24/90	Rick Mirer, Notre Dame	$4
10/08/90	O.J. Simpson	$10
10/15/90	Burt Grossman, Chargers	$4-$5
11/12/90	William Bell, Georgia Tech	$4
11/26/90	Notre Dame vs. Penn State	$4
12/10/90	Ty Detmer, BYU	$4-$5
12/24/90	Joe Montana, 49ers (SOY)	$12

1991

12/30/90-01/07/91	K.C. Chiefs receiver	$6
01/14/91	Dan Marino, Dolphins	$8
01/28/91	Ottis Anderson, Giants	$4
02/04/91	Everson Walls, Giants	$4
02/25/91	Rocket Ismail, Notre Dame	$5
07/08/91	Lyle Alzado, Raiders	$3
08/12/91	Eric Dickerson, Colts	$5
08/26/91	David Klingler, Houston	$4
09/02/91	Bruce Smith, Bills	$4
09/23/91	Desmond Howard, Michigan	$3
10/07/91	Bobby Hebert, Saints	$3
10/14/91	Gary Clark, Redskins	$3
12/02/91	Jim McMahon, Eagles	$6
12/09/91	Desmond Howard, Michigan	$5
12/16/91	Buffalo Bills defense	$4

1992

01/20/92	Thurman Thomas, Bills	$4
02/03/92	Mark Rypien, Redskins	$3
07/27/92	Joe Montana, 49ers	$4
08/24/92	Deion Sanders, Falcons/Braves	$4
08/31/92	Miami Football player	$3
09/07/92	Jerry Rice, 49ers	$3
09/14/92	Jim Harbaugh, Bears	$3
09/28/92	Tony Mandarich, Packers	$3
10/12/92	Randall Cunningham, Eagles	$3
11/16/92	Jim Everett, Ken Norton	$3
12/07/92	Robert Blackmon, James Campen	$3

1993

01/18/93	Steve Young, 49ers (FC)	$4
01/25/93	Emmitt Smith, Cowboys (FC)	$5
02/01/93	Super Bowl Preview	$3
02/08/93	Troy Aikman	$6
03/15/93	Reggie White, free agent	$3
04/26/93	Joe Montana, 49ers	$4
08/02/93	John Elway, Dan Reeves	$4
08/30/93	Scott Bentley, FSU	$3
09/06/93	Junior Seau, Chargers	$4
09/13/93	Joe Montana, Chiefs	$5
10/04/93	Boomer Esiason, Jets	$3
10/11/93	Chuck Cecil, Cardinals	$3
10/25/93	Michael Irvin, Cowboys	$4
11/22/93	Jim Flanagan, Notre Dame	$3
11/29/93	Boston College vs. Notre Dame	$3
12/06/93	Rx for the NFL	$3
12/20/93	Don Shula, Dolphins (SOY)	$4

1994

01/10/94	PSU's #1 football team	$4
01/24/94	Joe Montana, 49ers	$5
01/31/94	Emmitt Smith, Cowboys	$5
02/07/94	Emmitt Smith, Cowboys	$5
04/25/94	Dan Wilkinson, Ohio State	$3
05/16/94	PSU's tainted title	$3
06/27/94	O.J. Simpson	$4
08/01/94	Aikman, E.Smith, Switzer	$4
08/29/94	Arizona football	$4
09/12/94	Dan Marino	$5
09/26/94	Steve McNair, Alcorn State	$4
10/03/94	Colorado vs. Michigan	$4
10/17/94	Natrone Means, Chargers	$3
10/24/94	Freddie Scott, Penn State	$3
11/21/94	Ricky Watters	$4
12/05/94	Greg Lloyd	$4
12/12/94	Dallas Cowboys	$5

July 27, 1992

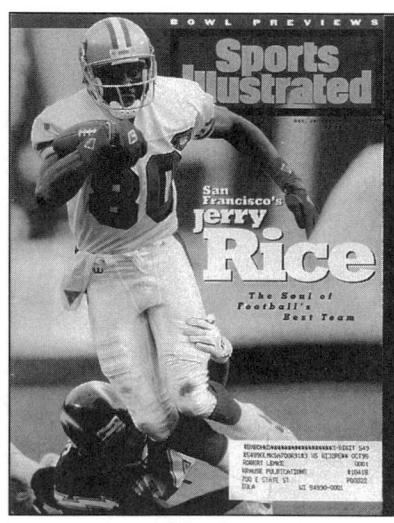

December 26, 1994

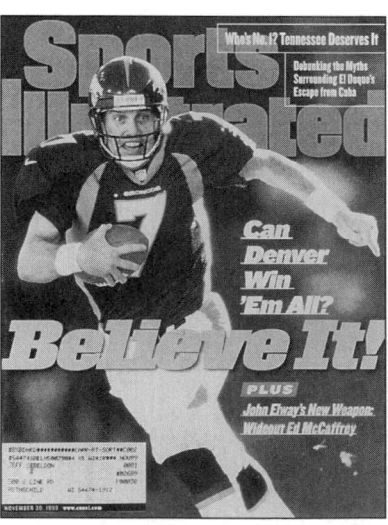

November 30, 1998

Super Bowl Programs

Early Super Bowl programs are prized collectibles. The first two programs in which the Green Bay Packers were victorious have always been in demand. The Super Bowl III program, in which the New York Jets defeated the Baltimore Colts, as Joe Namath guaranteed, has also increased in value recently.

Another program which is always high in demand is from Super Bowl V. Plenty of programs were printed for the game; however, a few days prior to the game, a truck that was delivering the programs ran off an icy highway and most of the programs were destroyed. Vendors ran out of programs before the game even started.

Super Bowl III Program

Super Bowl I at Los Angeles, Jan. 15, 1967 (Green Bay Packers vs. Kansas City Chiefs) ....$300-$425
Super Bowl II at Miami, Jan. 14, 1968 (Green Bay Packers vs. Oakland Raiders)....$375-$425
Super Bowl III at Miami, Jan. 12, 1969 (New York Jets vs. Baltimore Colts)...........$275-$350
Super Bowl IV at New Orleans, Jan. 11, 1970 (Minnesota Vikings vs. Kansas City Chiefs) ....$200-$250
Super Bowl V at Miami, Jan. 17, 1971 (Baltimore Colts vs. Dallas Cowboys).......$425-$475
Super Bowl VI at New Orleans, Jan. 16, 1972 (Dallas Cowboys vs. Miami Dolphins) ....$125-$200
Super Bowl VII at Los Angeles, Jan. 14, 1973 (Miami Dolphins vs. Washington Redskins) $125- $200
Super Bowl VIII at Houston, Jan. 13, 1974 (Minnesota Vikings vs. Miami Dolphins) ....$125-$200
Super Bowl IX at New Orleans, Jan. 12, 1975 (Pittsburgh Steelers vs. Minnesota Vikings) ....$125-$175

Super Bowl VI Program

Super Bowl X at Miami, Jan. 18, 1976 (Dallas Cowboys vs. Pittsburgh Steelers)......$125-$195
Super Bowl XI at Pasadena, Jan. 9, 1977 (Oakland Raiders vs. Minnesota Vikings) ....$75-$100
Super Bowl XII at New Orleans, Jan. 15, 1978 (Dallas Cowboys vs. Denver Broncos).$65-$95
Super Bowl XIII at Miami, Jan. 21, 1979 (Pittsburgh Steelers vs. Dallas Cowboys) ....$65-$95
Super Bowl XIV at Pasadena, Jan. 20, 1980 (Los Angeles Rams vs. Pittsburgh Steelers) ....$35-$70
Super Bowl XV at New Orleans, Jan. 25, 1981 (Oakland Raiders vs. Philadelphia Eagles) ....$30-$50
Super Bowl XVI at Pontiac, Jan. 24, 1982 (San Francisco 49ers vs. Cincinnati Bengals)$25-$40
Super Bowl XVII at Pasadena, Jan. 30, 1983 (Miami Dolphins vs. Washington Redskins) ....$25-$40
Super Bowl XVIII at Tampa, Jan. 22, 1984 (Washington Redskins vs. Los Angeles Raiders) ....$30-$40

Super Bowl X Program

Super Bowl XIX at Palo Alto, Jan. 20, 1985 (Miami Dolphins vs. San Francisco 49ers) ....$20-$30
Super Bowl XX at New Orleans, Jan. 26, 1986 (Chicago Bears vs. New England Patriots) ....$20-$30
Super Bowl XXI at Pasadena, Jan. 25, 1987 (Denver Broncos vs. New York Giants)$20-$30
Super Bowl XXII at San Diego, Jan. 31, 1988 (Washington Redskins vs. Denver Broncos) ....$15-$25
Super Bowl XXIII at Miami, Jan. 22, 1989 (Cincinnati Bengals vs. San Francisco 49ers) ....$15-$25
Super Bowl XXIV at New Orleans, Jan. 28, 1990 (San Francisco 49ers vs. Denver Broncos) ....$15-$25
Super Bowl XXV at Tampa, Jan. 27, 1991 (Buffalo Bills vs. New York Giants) .... $20-$30
Super Bowl XXVI at Minneapolis, Jan. 26,1992 (Washington Redskins vs. Buffalo Bills) ....$15-$25
Super Bowl XXVII at Pasadena, Jan. 31, 1993 (Buffalo Bills vs. Dallas Cowboys) .....$15-$25
Super Bowl XXVIII at Atlanta, Jan. 30, 1994 (Dallas Cowboys vs. Buffalo Bills).........$15-25
Super Bowl XXIX at Miami, Jan. 29, 1995 (San Francisco 49ers vs. San Diego Chargers) ....$15-$20
Super Bowl XXX at Phoenix, Jan. 28, 1996 (Dallas Cowboys vs. Pittsburgh Steelers) ....$15-$20
Super Bowl XXXI at New Orleans, Jan. 26, 1997 (Green Bay Packers vs. New England Patriots)..$15-$25
Super Bowl XXXII at San Diego, Jan. 25, 1998 (Denver Broncos vs. Green Bay Packers) ....$15-$20
Super Bowl XXXIII at Miami, Jan. 31, 1999 (Denver Broncos vs. Atlanta Falcons) ..$12-$15
Super Bowl XXXIV at Atlanta, Jan. 30, 2000 (St. Louis Rams vs. Tennessee Titans)..$12-$15
Super Bowl XXXV at Tampa, Jan. 28, 2001, (Baltimore Ravens vs. New York Giants) ....$12-$15

Super Bowl XX Program

1962 Rose Bowl Program

College Football Bowl Game Programs

Rose Bowl

1929 Georgia Tech vs. California	$850
1930 Pitt vs. USC	$485
1931 Alabama vs. Washington State	$950
1932 Tulane vs. USC	$395
1933 Pitt vs. USC	$395
1934 Columbia vs. Stanford	$495
1935 Alabama vs. California	$395
1936 SMU vs. Stanford	$275
1937 Pitt vs. Washington	$225
1938 Alabama vs. California	$250
1939 Duke vs. USC	$250
1940 Tennessee vs. USC	$225
1941 Nebraska vs. Stanford	$195
1942 Duke vs. Oregon State	$1,000
1943 Georgia vs. UCLA	$135
1944 Washington vs. USC	$135
1945 Tennessee vs. USC	$135
1946 Alabama vs. Stanford	$125
1947 Illinois vs. UCLA	$125
1948 Michigan vs. USC	$125
1949 Northwestern vs. California	$125
1950 Ohio State vs. California	$95
1951 Michigan vs. California	$95
1952 Illinois vs. Stanford	$85
1953 Wisconsin vs. USC	$85
1954 Michigan State vs. UCLA	$75
1955 Ohio State vs. USC	$75
1956 Michigan State vs. UCLA	$65
1957 Iowa vs. Oregon State	$65
1958 Ohio State vs. Oregon	$65
1959 Iowa vs. California	$65
1960 Wisconsin vs. Washington	$65
1961 Minnesota vs. Washington	$65
1962 Minnesota vs. UCLA	$65
1963 Wisconsin vs. USC	$75
1964 Illinois vs. Washington	$65
1965 Michigan vs. Oregon State	$65
1966 Michigan State vs. UCLA	$65
1967 Purdue vs. USC	$65
1968 Indiana vs. USC	$65
1969 Ohio State vs. USC	$65
1970 Michigan vs. USC	$60
1971 Ohio State vs. USC	$60
1972 Michigan vs. Stanford	$60
1973 Ohio State vs. USC	$60
1974 Ohio State vs. USC	$60
1975 Ohio State vs. USC	$60
1976 Ohio State vs. UCLA	$50
1977 Michigan vs. USC	$45
1978 Michigan vs. Washington	$45
1979 Michigan vs. USC	$45
1980 Ohio State vs. USC	$35
1981 Michigan vs. Washington	$30
1982 Iowa vs. Washington	$30
1983 Michigan vs. UCLA	$30
1984 Illinois vs. UCLA	$30
1985 Ohio State vs. USC	$30
1986 Iowa vs. UCLA	$25
1987 Michigan vs. Arizona State	$25
1988 Michigan State vs. USC	$20
1989 Michigan vs. USC	$20
1990 Michigan vs. USC	$20
1991 Iowa vs. Washington	$15
1992 Michigan vs. Washington	$15
1993 Michigan vs. Washington	$15
1994 Wisconsin vs. UCLA	$15
1995 Oregon vs. Penn State	$15
1996 USC vs. Northwestern	$15
1997 Ohio State vs. Arizona State	$15
1998 Michigan vs. Washington State	$15
1999 Wisconsin vs. UCLA	$15
2000 Wisconsin vs. Stanford	$15
2001 Washington vs. Purdue	$12

1986 Sugar Bowl Program

Sugar Bowl

1935 Temple vs. Tulane	$850
1936 TCU vs. LSU	$500
1937 Santa Clara vs. LSU	$350
1938 Santa Clara vs. LSU	$350
1939 Carnegie Tech vs. TCU	$400
1940 Texas A&M vs. Tulane	$300
1941 Boston College vs. Tennessee	$200
1942 Fordham vs. Missouri	$200
1943 Tulsa vs. Tennessee	$175
1944 Georgia Tech vs. Tulsa	$175
1945 Alabama vs. Duke	$165
1946 St. Marys vs. Oklahoma	$160
1947 North Carolina vs. Georgia	$150
1948 Alabama vs. Texas	$145
1949 N. Carolina vs. Ohio University	$125
1950 Oklahoma vs. LSU	$110
1951 Oklahoma vs. Kentucky	$95
1952 Maryland vs. Tennessee	$95
1953 Georgia Tech vs. Mississippi	$95
1954 Georgia Tech vs. West Virginia	$95
1955 Navy vs. Mississippi	$85
1956 Georgia Tech vs. Pittsburgh	$85
1957 Baylor vs. Tennessee	$85
1958 Texas vs. Mississippi	$85
1959 Clemson vs. LSU	$85
1960 Mississippi vs. LSU	$75
1961 Mississippi vs. Rice	$75
1962 Alabama vs. Arkansas	$75
1963 Mississippi vs. Arkansas	$75
1964 Alabama vs. Mississippi	$75

Cotton Bowl (continued)

1965 LSU vs. Syracuse	$65
1966 Florida vs. Missouri	$65
1967 Alabama vs. Nebraska	$65
1968 LSU vs. Wyoming	$65
1969 Georgia vs. Arkansas	$65
1970 Mississippi vs. Arkansas	$60
1971 Tennessee vs. Air Force	$60
1972 Auburn vs. Ohio University	$60
1973 Ohio University vs. Penn State	$60
1974 Alabama vs. Notre Dame	$60
1975 Florida vs. Nebraska	$60
1976 Alabama vs. Penn State	$60
1977 Georgia vs. Pittsburgh	$50
1978 Alabama vs. Ohio State	$50
1979 Alabama vs. Penn State	$50
1980 Alabama vs. Arkansas	$50
1981 Georgia vs. Notre Dame	$45
1982 Georgia vs. Pittsburgh	$45
1983 Georgia vs. Penn State	$45
1984 Michigan vs. Auburn	$40
1985 LSU vs. Nebraska	$35
1986 Miami vs. Tennessee	$30
1987 LSU vs. Nebraska	$30
1988 Auburn vs. Syracuse	$25
1989 FSU vs. Auburn	$20
1990 Miami vs. Alabama	$20
1991 Virginia vs. Tennessee	$20
1992 Florida vs. Notre Dame	$15
1993 Alabama vs. Miami	$15
1994 Florida vs. West Virginia	$15
1995 Florida vs. Florida State	$15
1996 Texas vs. Virginia	$15
1997 Florida vs. Florida State	$12
1998 Florida State vs. Ohio State	$12
1999 Ohio State vs. Texas A&M	$12
2000 Florida State vs. Virginia Tech	$12
2001 Miami vs. Florida	$12

1996 Cotton Bowl Program

Cotton Bowl

1945 Oklahoma A&M vs. TCU	$195
1946 Missouri vs. Texas	$175
1947 Arkansas vs. LSU	$200
1948 Penn State vs. SMU	$150
1949 Oregon vs. SMU	$135
1950 North Carolina vs. Rice	$125
1951 Tennessee vs. Texas	$115
1952 Kentucky vs. TCU	$95
1953 Tennessee vs. Texas	$85
1954 Alabama vs. Rice	$95
1955 Georgia Tech vs. Arkansas	$85
1956 Mississippi vs. TCU	$85
1957 Syracuse vs. TCU	$85
1958 Navy vs. Rice	$75

1959 Air Force vs. TCU $75
1960 Syracuse vs. Texas $70
1961 Duke vs. Arkansas $70
1962 Mississippi vs. Texas $70
1963 LSU vs. Texas $70
1964 Navy vs. Texas $70
1965 Arkansas vs. Nebraska $65
1966 LSU vs. Arkansas $65
1967 Georgia vs. Wyoming $65
1968 Alabama vs. Texas A&M $65
1969 Tennessee vs. Texas $65
1970 Notre Dame vs. Texas $125
1971 Notre Dame vs. Texas $125
1972 Penn State vs. Texas $60
1973 Texas vs. Alabama $60
1974 Nebraska vs. Texas $60
1975 Penn State vs. Baylor $60
1976 Georgia vs. Arkansas $50
1977 Maryland vs. Houston $50
1978 Notre Dame vs. Texas $75
1979 Notre Dame vs. Houston $75
1980 Nebraska vs. Houston $45
1981 Alabama vs. Baylor $45
1982 Alabama vs. Texas $45
1983 Pittsburgh vs. SMU $45
1984 Georgia vs. Texas $40
1985 Boston College vs. Houston $40
1986 Auburn vs. Texas A&M $35
1987 Ohio State vs. Texas A&M $30
1988 Notre Dame vs. Texas A&M $25
1989 UCLA vs. Arkansas $20
1990 Tennessee vs. Arkansas $20
1991 Miami vs. Texas $20
1992 FSU vs. Texas A&M $15
1993 Notre Dame vs. Texas A&M $15
1994 Notre Dame vs. Texas A&M $15
1995 USC vs. Texas Tech $15
1996 Colorado vs. Oregon $15
1997 BYU vs. Kansas State $15
1998 UCLA vs. Texas A&M $12
1999 Texas vs. Mississippi State $12
2000 Arkansas vs. Texas $10
2001 Kansas State vs. Tennessee $10

1948 Georgia Tech vs. Kansas $150
1949 Texas vs. Georgia $100
1950 Santa Clara vs. Kentucky $100
1951 Clemson vs. Miami $125
1952 Georgia Tech vs. Baylor $100
1953 Alabama vs. Syracuse $100
1954 Oklahoma vs. Maryland $95
1955 Duke vs. Nebraska $125
1956 Maryland vs. Oklahoma $95
1957 Clemson vs. Colorado $95
1958 Duke vs. Oklahoma $95
1959 Syracuse vs. Oklahoma $95
1960 Georgia vs. Missouri $85
1961 Navy vs. Missouri $85
1962 LSU vs. Colorado $85
1963 Alabama vs. Oklahoma $85
1964 Auburn vs. Nebraska $75
1965 Texas vs. Alabama $125
1966 Alabama vs. Nebraska $75
1967 Georgia Tech vs. Florida $75
1968 Oklahoma vs. Tennessee $75
1969 Penn State vs. Kansas $75
1970 Penn State vs. Missouri $60
1971 LSU vs. Nebraska $60
1972 Alabama vs. Nebraska $60
1973 Notre Dame vs. Nebraska $60
1974 Penn State vs. LSU $60
1975 Notre Dame vs. Alabama $60
1976 Michigan vs. Oklahoma $60
1977 Ohio State vs. Colorado $50
1978 Arkansas vs. Oklahoma $50
1979 Nebraska vs. Oklahoma $50
1980 FSU vs. Oklahoma $45
1981 FSU vs. Oklahoma $45
1982 Clemson vs. Nebraska $45
1983 LSU vs. Nebraska $45
1984 Miami vs. Nebraska $40
1985 Washington vs. Oklahoma $35
1986 Penn State vs. Oklahoma $35
1987 Arkansas vs. Oklahoma $30
1988 Miami vs. Oklahoma $25
1989 Miami vs. Nebraska $25
1990 Notre Dame vs. Colorado $15
1991 Colorado vs. Notre Dame $15
1992 Miami vs. Nebraska $10
1993 Nebraska vs. Florida State $20
1994 Florida State vs. Nebraska $20
1995 Nebraska vs. Miami (Florida) $15
1996 Florida State vs. Notre Dame $15
1997 Nebraska vs. Virginia Tech $15
1998 Nebraska vs. Tennessee $15
1999 Florida vs. Syracuse $15
2000 Michigan vs. Alabama $12
2001 Oklahoma vs. Florida State $12

Liberty Bowl

1959 Penn State vs. Alabama $95
1960 Penn State vs. Oregon $75
1961 Syracuse vs. Miami $65
1962 Oregon State vs. Villanova $65
1963 Mississippi State vs. N.C. State $65
1964 Utah vs. West Virginia $65
1965 Mississippi vs. Auburn $60
1967 N.C. State vs. Georgia $60
1968 Mississippi vs. Virginia Tech $50
1969 Colorado vs. Alabama $60
1970 Tulane vs. Colorado $50
1971 Tennessee vs. Arkansas $50
1972 Georgia Tech vs. Iowa State $50
1973 N.C. State vs. Kansas $50
1974 Tennessee vs. Maryland $50
1975 USC vs. Texas A&M $50
1976 Alabama vs. UCLA $50
1977 North Carolina vs. Nebraska $75
1978 LSU vs. Missouri $45
1979 Penn State vs. Tulane $45
1980 Purdue vs. Missouri $45
1981 Ohio State vs. Navy $45
1982 Alabama vs. Illinois $45
1983 Notre Dame vs. Boston College $45
1984 Auburn vs. Arkansas $40
1985 LSU vs. Baylor $40
1986 Tennessee vs. Minnesota $35
1987 Georgia vs. Arkansas $30
1988 South Carolina vs. Indiana $25
1989 Mississippi vs. Air Force $25
1990 Air Force vs. Ohio State $20
1991 Air Force vs. Mississippi State $20
1992 Air Force vs. Mississippi $20
1993 Louisville vs. Michigan State $15
1994 Illinois vs. E. Carolina $15
1995 E. Carolina vs. Stanford $12
1996 Syracuse vs. Houston $12
1997 So. Mississippi vs. Pittsburgh $12
1998 Tulane vs. BYU $12
1999 BYU vs. Tulane $12
2000 So. Mississippi vs. Colorado State . .$10
2001 Colorado State vs. Louisville $10

1959 Orange Bowl Program

Orange Bowl

1940 Georgia Tech vs. Missouri $275
1941 Mississippi vs. Georgetown $250
1942 TCU vs. Georgia $250
1943 Alabama vs. Boston College $250
1944 LSU vs. Texas $225
1945 Georgia Tech vs. Tulsa $200
1946 Holy Cross vs. Miami $175
1947 Tennessee vs. Rice $175

1973 Liberty Bowl Program

1996 Fiesta Bowl Program

Fiesta Bowl

1971 Arizona State vs. Florida State $50
1972 Arizona State vs. Missouri $45
1973 Arizona State vs. Pittsburgh $45
1974 Oklahoma State vs. BYU $45
1975 Arizona State vs. Nebraska $45
1976 Oklahoma vs. Wyoming $45
1977 Penn State vs. Arizona State $45
1978 Arkansas vs. UCLA $45

1979 Pittsburgh vs. Arizona $45
1980 Penn State vs. Ohio State $45
1982 Penn State vs. USC $40
1983 Arizona State vs. Oklahoma $35
1984 Pittsburgh vs. Ohio State $35
1985 Miami vs. UCLA $35
1986 Michigan vs. Nebraska $35
1987 Penn State vs. Miami $30
1988 Florida State vs. Nebraska $25
1989 Notre Dame vs. West Virginia $20
1990 Florida State vs. Nebraska $15
1991 Louisville vs. Alabama $15
1992 Penn State vs. Tennessee $15
1993 Syracuse vs. Colorado $15
1994 Miami vs. Arizona $15
1995 Nebraska vs. Florida $15
1996 Penn State vs. Texas $15
1997 Kansas State vs. Syracuse $15
1998 Kansas State vs. Texas $12
1999 Tennessee vs. Florida State $12
2000 Nebraska vs. Tennessee $12
2001 Oregon State vs. Notre Dame $12

Hall of Fame/Outback Bowl

1977 Maryland vs. Minnesota $45
1978 Texas A&M vs. Iowa State $35
1979 South Carolina vs. Missouri $30
1980 Tulane vs. Arkansas $25
1981 Mississippi State vs. Kansas $25
1982 Air Force vs. Vanderbilt $25
1984 Wisconsin vs. Kentucky $25
1986 Georgia vs. Boston College $20
1988 Alabama vs. Michigan $20
1989 Syracuse vs. LSU $20
1990 Ohio State vs. Auburn $15
1991 Clemson vs. Illinois $15
1992 Ohio State vs. Syracuse $15
1993 Tennessee vs. Boston College $15
1994 Michigan vs. North Carolina State $15
1995 Wisconsin vs. Duke $15
1996 Auburn vs. Penn State $15
1997 Michigan vs. Alabama $15
1998 Georgia vs. Wisconsin $15
1999 Penn State vs. Kentucky $12
2000 Georgia vs. Purdue $10
2001 South Carolina vs. Ohio State $10

Aloha Bowl

1982 Washington vs. Maryland $35
1983 Washington vs. Penn State $30
1984 Notre Dame vs. SMU $30
1985 Alabama vs. USC $25
1986 North Carolina vs. Arizona $20
1987 Florida vs. UCLA $20
1988 Washington State vs. Hawaii $20
1989 Michigan State vs. Hawaii $20
1990 Syracuse vs. Arizona $15
1991 Georgia Tech vs. Stanford $15
1992 Kansas vs. BYU $15
1993 Colorado vs. Fresno State $15
1994 Boston College vs. Kansas State $15
1995 UCLA vs. Kansas $15
1996 Navy vs. California $15
1997 Washington vs. Michigan State $12
1998 Colorado vs. Oregon $12
1999 Wake Forest vs. Arizona State $10
2000 Boston College vs. Arizona State . . . $10

Peach Bowl

1968 LSU vs. Florida State $85
1969 South Carolina vs. West Virginia . . . $65
1970 North Carolina vs. Arizona State $65
1971 Georgia Tech vs. Mississippi $55
1972 N.C. State vs. West Virginia $50
1973 Georgia vs. Maryland $50
1974 Vanderbilt vs. Texas Tech $50
1975 N.C. State vs. West Virginia $50
1976 North Carolina vs. Kentucky $50
1977 N.C. State vs. Iowa State $45
1978 Georgia Tech vs. Purdue $45

1979 Clemson vs. Baylor $45
1980 Virginia Tech vs. Miami $65
1981 Florida State vs. North Carolina . . . $40
1982 Tennessee vs. Iowa $45
1983 Florida State vs. N.C. State $40
1984 Virginia vs. Purdue $40
1985 Army vs. Illinois $35
1986 Virginia Tech vs. N.C. State $30
1987 Indiana vs. Tennessee $30
1988 Iowa vs. N.C. State $25
1989 Syracuse vs. Georgia $20
1990 Auburn vs. Indiana $20
1992 East Carolina vs. N.C. State $20
1993 North Carolina vs. Miss. State $20
1994 Fresno State vs. Ohio State $20
1995 Virginia vs. Georgia $20
1996 LSU vs. Clemson $15
1997 Clemson vs. Auburn $15
1998 Auburn vs. Clemson $15
1999 Virginia vs. Georgia $15
2000 Mississippi State vs. Clemson $12
2001 LSU vs. Georgia Tech $12

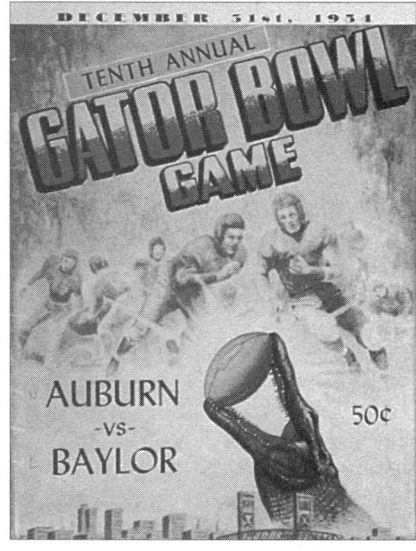

1954 Gator Bowl Program

Gator Bowl

1954 Auburn vs. Baylor $100
1960 Florida vs. Baylor $100
1961 Penn State vs. Georgia Tech $90
1962 Florida vs. Penn State $90
1963 North Carolina vs. Air Force $90
1964 Florida State vs. Oklahoma $90
1965 Georgia Tech vs. Texas Tech $90
1966 Tennessee vs. Syracuse $90
1967 Penn State vs. Florida State $75
1968 Alabama vs. Missouri $75
1969 Florida vs. Tennessee $75
1970 Mississippi vs. Auburn $65
1971 North Carolina vs. Georgia $65
1972 Auburn vs. Colorado $65
1973 Tennessee vs. Texas Tech $60
1974 Texas vs. Auburn $60
1975 Florida vs. Maryland $60
1976 Notre Dame vs. Penn State $60
1977 Clemson vs. Pitt $50
1978 Ohio State vs. Clemson $65
1979 Michigan vs. North Carolina $50
1980 South Carolina vs. Pitt $45
1981 North Carolina vs. Arkansas $40
1982 Florida State vs. West Virginia $40
1983 Florida vs. Iowa $40
1984 South Carolina vs. Okla. State $35
1985 Florida State vs. Oklahoma $35

1986 Stanford vs. Clemson $35
1987 South Carolina vs. LSU $30
1988 Georgia vs. Michigan State $25
1989 West Virginia vs. Clemson $20
1990 Michigan vs. Mississippi $20
1991 Oklahoma vs. Virginia $15
1992 North Carolina State vs. Florida $15
1993 Alabama vs. North Carolina $15
1994 Tennessee vs. Virginia Tech $15
1996 Clemson vs. Syracuse $15
1997 North Carolina vs. West Virginia . . . $15
1998 North Carolina vs. Virginia $15
1999 Georgia Tech vs. Notre Dame $15
2000 Miami vs. Georgia Tech $12
2001 Virginia Tech vs. Clemson $10

1976 Sun Bowl Program

Sun Bowl

1965 TCU vs. UTEP $65
1966 Wyoming vs. Florida State $65
1967 Mississippi vs. UTEP $65
1968 Auburn vs. Arizona $65
1969 Nebraska vs. Georgia $65
1970 Georgia Tech vs. Texas Tech $60
1971 Iowa State vs. LSU $60
1972 North Carolina vs. Texas Tech $60
1973 Auburn vs. Missouri $60
1974 N. Carolina vs. Mississippi State . . . $50
1975 Pitt vs. Kansas $50
1976 Texas A&M vs. Florida $50
1977 Stanford vs. LSU $50
1978 Texas vs. Maryland $45
1979 Texas vs. Washington $45
1980 Mississippi State vs. Nebraska $40
1981 Oklahoma vs. Houston $40
1982 Texas vs. North Carolina $40
1983 Alabama vs. SMU $40
1984 Tennessee vs. Maryland $35
1985 Georgia vs. Arizona $30
1986 Alabama vs. Washington $30
1987 West Virginia vs. Oklahoma State . . . $25
1988 Army vs. Vanderbilt $25
1989 Texas A&M vs. Pitt $20
1990 Michigan State vs. USC $20
1991 Illinois vs. UCLA $15
1992 Baylor vs. Arizona $15
1993 Oklahoma vs. Texas Tech $15
1994 Texas vs. North Carolina $15
1995 Washington vs. Iowa $15
1996 Stanford vs. Michigan State $15
1997 Iowa vs. Arizona State $15
1998 TCU vs. Southern California $12
1999 Oregon vs. Minnesota $10
2000 Wisconsin vs. UCLA $10

Football Books

Selected Hard Covers

About Three Bricks Shy of a Load, by Roy Blount Jr. (1974), HC, with dust jacket $12

Against the Grain, by Eugene "Mercury" Morris and Steve Fiffer (1988), HC 278 pages, with dust jacket $18

Always on the Run, by Larry Csonka and Jim Kiick with Dave Anderson (1973), HC 225 pages, with dust jacket $20

A Matter of Style, by Joe Namath with Bob Oates Jr. (1973) HC 196 pages, with dust jacket . .$35

The Art of Quarterbacking, by Kenny Anderson with Jack Clancy (1984), HC 220 pages, dust jacket of Anderson $18

Audibles, by Joe Montana and Bob Raissman (1986), HC 205 pages, with dust jacket . . .$18

The Best of the Athletic Boys - The White Man's Impact on Jim Thorpe, by Jack Newcombe, HC 250 pages, with dust jacket of Jim Thorpe . .$25

Best Plays of the Year, by Robert Riger (1962), HC, dust jacket of Jim Taylor $25

Blanda: Alive and Kicking, by Wells Twombley, HC 305 pages, with dust jacket $12.95

Bo Knows Bo, Bo Jackson and Dick Schaap (1990), HC 218 pages, with dust jacket $15

Bootlegger's Boy, by Barry Switzer (1990), HC 416 pages, with dust jacket $7.95

Born to Referee, My Life on the Gridiron, by Jerry Markbreit with Alan Steinberg (1988), HC 272 pages, with dust jacket $18

Born to Run, the O.J. Simpson Story, by Larry Fox, HC 173 pages, with dust jacket $25

The Boz: Confessions of a Modern Anti-Hero, by Brian Bosworth with Rick Reilly (1988), HC 252 pages, with dust jacket $12.50

Brian Piccolo: A Short Season, by Jeannie Morris (1971), HC 159 pages, basis for the movie "Brian's Song" $10

Broadway Joe and his Super Jets, by Larry Fox (1969), HC 255 pages, 1968-69 New York Jets season $20

Broken Patterns, the Education of a Quarterback, by Fran Tarkenton and Brock Yates (1971), HC 191 pages, with dust jacket $12.50

Bud: The Other Side of the Glacier, by Bill McGrane (1986), HC 175 pages, with dust jacket, Bud Grant $30

Building a Champion, by Bill Walsh with Glenn Dickey (1990), HC 272 pages, with dust jacket $20

Calling the Shots, by Mike Singletary with Armen Keteyian (1984), HC 231 pages, with dust jacket $25

Coach: A Season With Lombardi, by Tom Dowling (1970), HC 333 pages, with dust jacket .$25

Coaching: The Way of A Winner, by Knute Rockne (1929), HC $65

Dennis Byrd, Rise and Walk, by Dennis Byrd with Michael D'Orso (1993), HC 258 pages, with dust jacket $20

Distant Replay, by Jerry Kramer with Dick Schaap (1985), HC 236 pages, with dust jacket $15

Ditka, An Autobiography, by Mike Ditka with Don Pierson (1986), HC 271 pages, with dust jacket $15

Ditka: Monster of the Midway, by Armen Keteyian (1992), HC 346 pages, with dust jacket $20

Earl Campbell: The Driving Force, by Sam Blair (1980), HC 175 pages, with dust jacket $8

The End of Autumn, by Michael Oriard (1982), HC, former Kansas City Chiefs/Notre Dame player reflects on his football career $15

Even Big Guys Cry, by Alex Karras with Herb Gluck (1977), HC 246 pages, with dust jacket$25

Fatso, Football When Men Were Really Men, Arthur J. Donovan Jr. and Bob Drury (1987), HC 228 pages, with dust jacket $14

Fighting Back, by Rocky Bleier with Terry O'Neil (1975), HC 224 pages, with dust jacket of Bleier $25

Football and the Single Man, by Paul Hornung (1965), HC 252 pages, with dust jacket $15

Frank Gifford: The Golden Year 1956, by William Wallace, HC 130 pages, with dust jacket . . .$20

Great Pass Receivers of the NFL, by Dave Anderson (1966), HC $20

The Green Bay Packers, by Arch Ward (1946), HC 240 pages, with dust jacket $18.95

The Green Bay Packers: Pro Football's Pioneer Team, by Chuck Johnson (1961), HC 170 pages, with dust jacket $17.95

Halas on Halas, by George Halas (1979), HC 351 pages, with dust jacket $45

Happy To Be Alive, by Darryl Stingley with Mark Mulvoy (1983), HC 237 pages, with dust jacket $25

Hard Nose: The 1986 New York Giants, by Jim Burt (1987), HC, with dust jacket $25

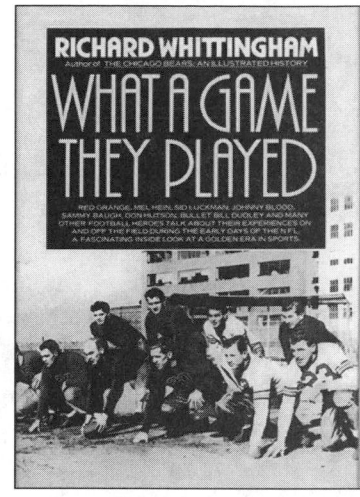

Hard Knox: The Life of an NFL Coach, by Chuck Knox and Bill Plaschke (1988), HC 274 pages $25

Hearing the Noise: My Life in the NFL, by Preston Pearson (1985), HC 303 pages, with dust jacket $30

Heart of a Lion, the Wild and Woolly Life of Bobby Layne, by Bob St. John (1991), HC 207 pages, with dust jacket $20

Hey! Wait a Minute (I Wrote a Book), by John Madden with Dave Anderson (1984), HC 241 pages, with dust jacket $35

The Hundred Yard Lie: The Corruption of College Football, by Rick Telander (1989), HC 223 pages, with dust jacket $9

I Can't Wait Until Tomorrow Cause I Get Better Looking Every Day, by Joe Namath with Dick Schaap (1969), HC 280 pages $30

I Am Third, by Gale Sayers with Al Silverman (1970), HC 238 pages, with dust jacket $15

I'm Still Scrambling, by Randall Cunningham with Steve Wartenberg (1993), HC 231 pages, with dust jacket $20

Inside Football, by George Allen (1970), HC 452 pages, with dust jacket $15.95

Inside Pro Football, by J. King (1958), HC 216 pages $10.95

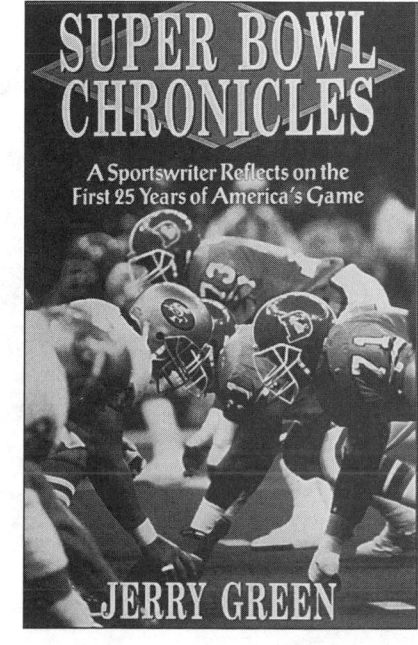

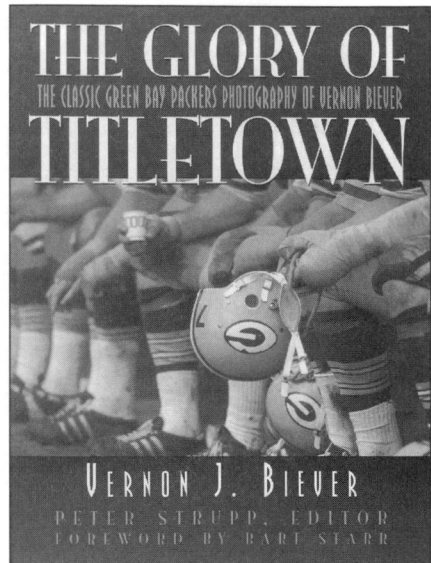

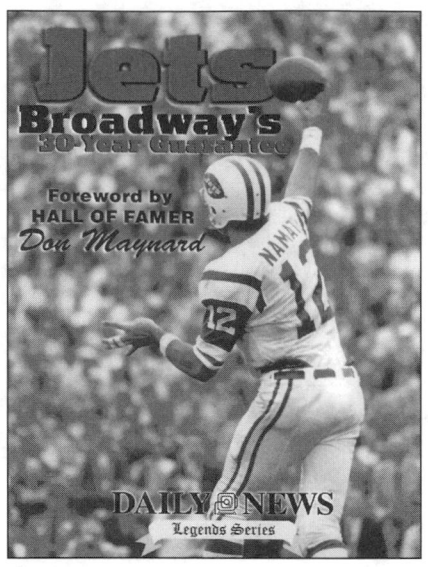

Inside the Pressure Cooker, by Gilman (1974), HC, with dust jacket, about the New York Jets $30

Instant Replay: The Green Bay Diary of Jerry Kramer, by Dick Schaap (1968), HC 287 pages, with dust jacket of Kramer $25

In the Pocket: My Life As A QB: Earl Morrall (1969), HC, with dust jacket $30

Iron Men: Bucko, Crazylegs and the Boys Recall the Golden Days of Pro Football, by Stuart Leuthner (1988), HC 324 pages, with dust jacket $8.95

Jerry Kramer's Farewell to Football, by Dick Schaap (1969), HC 200 pages , with dust jacket of Kramer $25

The Jim Plunkett Story, by Jim Plunkett and Dave Newhouse (1981), HC 256 pages, with dust jacket $30

Knute Rockne: Man Builder, by Harry Stuhldreher (1931), HC 335 pages, with dust jacket $60

The Last Season of Weeb Ewbank, by Paul Zimmerman (1974), HC 326 pages, with dust jacket $25

Little Men of the NFL, by Bob Rubin (1974), HC, Fran Tarkenton cover $20

Lombardi: Winning Is the Only Thing, by Jerry Kramer (1971), HC 177 pages, with dust jacket $35

Looking Deep, by Terry Bradshaw with Buddy Martin (1989), HC 204 pages $35

LT, Living on the Edge, by Lawrence Taylor with David Falkner, HC 225 pages, with dust jacket, autographed $125

The Man Inside, (Tom) Landry, by Bob St. John (1979), HC 250 pages, with dust jacket $11

McMahon!, by Jim McMahon and Bob Verdi (1986), HC 223 pages, with dust jacket $35

Mean Joe Greene and the Steelers Front Four, by Larry Fox (1975), HC 241 pages, with dust jacket $30

Mean on Sunday, the Autobiography of Ray Nitschke, with Robert W. Wells (1973), HC 302 pages, with dust jacket $15

The Miami Dolphins, by Morris McLemore (1972), HC 344 pages, with dust jacket $20

My Greatest Day in Football, by Murray Goodman and Leonard Lewin, HC 210 pages $10

My Life with the Redskins, by Corinne Griffith, HC 238 pages, with dust jacket $11.95

My Story (And I'm Sticking to It), by Alex Hawkins (1989), HC 264 pages, with dust jacket $18.95

My Sunday Best, by J. Fleischer, HC 202 pages $10

The New York Giants, by Al Derogatis (1964), HC $25

Nose to Nose: Survival in the Trenches of the NFL, by Joe Klecko and Joe Fields with Greg Logan (1989), HC 287 pages, with dust jacket $25

Nothing to Kick About: The Autobiography of a Modern Immigrant, by Pete Gogolack with Joseph Carter (1973), HC 274 pages, with dust jacket $7.95

Off My Chest, by Jimmy Brown with Myron Cope (1964), HC 230 pages, with dust jacket $17.95

The $1 League, by Jim Byrne (1986), HC 352 pages, history of the USFL $12.50

One Giant League, by Jeff Hostetler with Ed Fitzgerald (1991), HC 236 pages, with dust jacket $25

Once a Cowboy, by Walt Garrison with John Tullius (1988), HC 212 pages, with dust jacket $35

One Knee Equals Two Feet, by John Madden and Dave Anderson (1986), HC 227 pages, with dust jacket $14

Open Field, by John Brodie with James D. Houston (1974), HC 230 pages, with dust jacket .$14

Out of Control, by Thomas "Hollywood" Henderson and Peter Knobler (1987), HC 304 pages $10

Over the Hill to the Super Bowl, by Owens (1973), HC, with dust jacket, about the 1973 Redskins $35

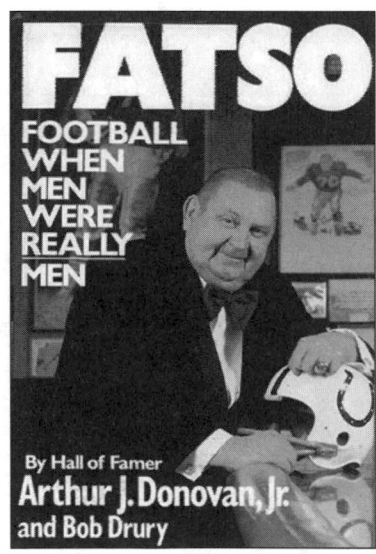

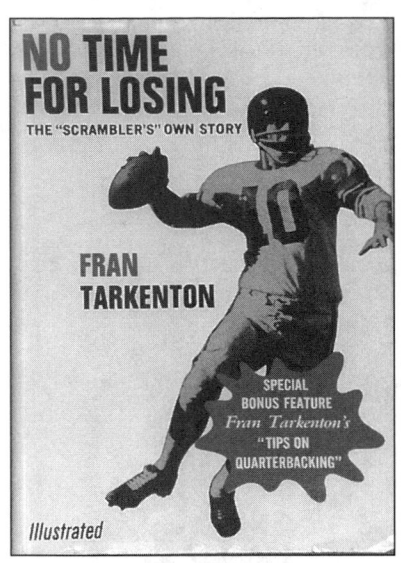

Packer Dynasty; Phil Bengston with Todd Hunt (1968), HC 278 pages, with dust jacket $35

Paper Lion, by George Plimpton (1966), HC 362 pages, with dust jacket $45

Pittsburgh Steelers - Great Teams, Great Years, by Ray Didinger (1974), dust jacket of Terry Bradshaw $20

The Players, by Tex Maule (1967), HC 238 pages $20

Quarterbacks Have all the Fun, by Dick Schaap (1974), HC 260 pages, with dust jacket $18

The Red Grange Story, by Red Grange (1953), HC 178 pages, with dust jacket $20

Roger Craig: Strictly Business, by Garry Niver (1992), HC 209 pages, with dust jacket $35

Roger Staubach: A Special Kind of QB, by Sullivan (1974, 3rd ed.), HC $25

Rosey: The Gentle Giant, by Rosey Grier with Dennis Baker (1986), HC 301 pages, with dust jacket $30

Running Tough: Memoirs of a Football Maverick, by Tony Dorsett and Harvey Frommer (1989), HC 225 pages, with dust jacket $8

Seven Days to Sunday, by Asinoff (1968), HC, with dust jacket $35

Simms To McConkey: Blood, Sweat and *Gatorade*, by Phil McConkey and Phil Simms (1987), HC 243 pages, with dust jacket $7

Singletary on Singletary, by Mike Singletary and Jerry Jenkins (1991), HC 220 pages $30

Starr - My Life in Football, by Bart Starr with Murray Olderman (1987), HC 224 pages, with dust jacket $13

Steelers, Team of the Decade, by Lou Sahadi (1979), HC, with dust jacket $45

Super Bowl: Of Men, Myths and Moments, by Marty Ralbovsky (1971), HC 208 pages, with dust jacket $12.95

Tarkenton, by Jim Klobuchar and Fran Tarkenton (1976), HC 274 pages, with dust jacket $15

Terry Bradshaw, Man of Steel, by Terry Bradshaw with David Diles (1979), HC (303 pages), with dust jacket $30

The Whole Ten Yards, by Frank Gifford and Harry Waters (1993), HC 285 pages $7.50

The Winning Edge, by Don Shula (1973), HC, with dust jacket $30

They Call It A Game, by Bernie Parrish (1971), HC 317 pages $10

They Call Me Assassin, by Jack Tatum with Bill Kushner (1979), HC 251 pages $15

They Call Me Dirty, by Conrad Dobler and Vic Carucci (1988), HC 288 pages, with dust jacket $15

They're Playing My Game, by Hank Stram with Lou Sahadi (1986), HC 166 pages, with dust jacket $4.95

Tom Landry, by Tom Landry and Gregg Lewis (1990), HC 302 pages $7.50

Total Impact, Straight Talk from Football's Hardest Hitter, by Ronnie Lott with Jill Lieber (1991), HC 305 pages, with dust jacket $20

Vikes, Mikes and Something on the Backside, by Ahmad Rashad with Peter Bodo (1988), HC, (278 pages) with dust jacket $25

Vince, A Personal Biography of Vince Lombardi, by Michael O'Brien (1987), HC 457 pages, with dust jacket $22

Weeb Ewbank's The Football Way, by Lud Duroska (1967), HC, with dust jacket of Joe Namath $20

When the Grass was Real (Ten Best Years of Pro Football), by Bob Carroll (1993), HC 303 pages, with dust jacket $27.50

Y.A. Tittle: I Pass, by Don Smith (1964), HC 300 pages, with dust jacket $35

Selected Soft Covers

1975 All-Pro Football Stars, by J. Brondfield (1975), SC, Ken Stabler cover $7

1976 All-Pro Football Stars, by J. Brondfield (1976), SC, Fran Tarkenton cover $7

The Cincinnati Bengals and the Magic of Paul Brown, by D. Forbes (1973)SC $15

1975 Complete Handbook of Pro Football, by Zander Hollander (1975), SC, Joe Greene cover $9

1979 Complete Handbook of Pro Football, by Zander Hollander (1979), SC $7

Football Stars of 1964, by Barry Goetthrer (1964), SC $10

Football Stars of 1968, by Barry Stainback (1968), SC $7

Football Stars of 1973, by Hal Bock and Ben Olan (1973), SC $6

Gifford on Courage, by C. Mangel (Frank Gifford), SC $12

I Can't Wait Until Tomorrow Cause I Get Better Looking Every Day, by Joe Namath with Dick Schaap (1969), SC $15

Instant Replay: The Green Bay Diary of Jerry Kramer, by Dick Schaap (1969), SC $12

Joe Namath, by John Devaney (1972), SC . .$12

Len Dawson: Super Bowl Quarterback, by Larry Bortstein (1970), SC $12

The Miami Dolphins: Football's Greatest Team, by A. Levine (1973), SC $10

1967 Official Pro Football Record Book, by Complete Sports Publications (1967), SC, Bart Starr cover $10

1968 Official Pro Football Record Book, by Complete Sports Publications (1968), SC, Joe Namath cover $10

O.J. Simpson: Football's Greatest Runner, by John Devaney (1974), SC $6

Pro Football 1967, by Jack Zanger (1967), SC $10

Pro Football 1971, by Jack Zanger (1971), SC$8

Sports Focus Football New York Giants, 1975, SC $12

Sports Focus Football Washington Redskins, 1975, SC $12

Super Bowl: Pro Football's Greatest Games, by S. Gelman (1975), SC, Terry Bradshaw cover $6

Super Joe: The Joe Namath Story, by Larry Bortstein (1969), SC $10

Winning Football, by Bart Starr (1968), SC .$10

•••

Super Bowl I

Super Bowl III

Super Bowl IV

Super Bowl Ticket Stubs

All the added attention on Super Bowl memorabilia from both collectors and fans has made it especially hard on dealers to find the collectibles. Super Bowl attendees aren't willing to unload their ticket stubs for a song.

Dealers have had to dig deeper into their pockets to get their hands on ticket stubs. It's tougher for dealers to buy ticket stubs from people after the game.

On the flipside, it is now easier to find ticket stubs in better condition because fans are making sure they put their ticket stubs in plastic holders.

They tell ticket tearers to be very careful and, after the stub is torn off, they put it in a protective holder.

One example where collectors would be hard-pressed to find a ticket stub in very good shape is Super Bowl IV, which was played at Tulane Stadium in New Orleans.

It seems the college students who were hired as ticket rippers for that game weren't too concerned with tearing them on the perforation.

They were more concerned with getting people in as fast as possible and just ripping the tickets right in half. It's estimated that 95 percent of all those stubs were torn in half, which makes a clean tear for that stub all that much more collectible.

Tickets and stubs from Super Bowl III, the game in which Joe Namath predicted

the underdog New York Jets' victory over the Baltimore Colts, are also highly prized by collectors.

Note: All values based on the ticket stubs in EX or better condition.

Ticket Stubs

Super Bowl I	$400-$600
Super Bowl II	$500-$700
Super Bowl III	$500-$550
Super Bowl IV	$300-$475
Super Bowl V	$250-$350
Super Bowl VI	$150-$250
Super Bowl VII	$200-$275
Super Bowl VIII	$150-$200
Super Bowl IX	$175-$225
Super Bowl X	$150-$175
Super Bowl XI	$100-$150
Super Bowl XII	$200-$275
Super Bowl XIII	$125-$175
Super Bowl XIV	$75-$125
Super Bowl XV	$75-$125
Super Bowl XVI	$100-$150
Super Bowl XVII	$100-$150
Super Bowl XVIII	$100-$150
Super Bowl XIX	$100-$150
Super Bowl XX	$100-$150
Super Bowl XXI	$100-$150
Super Bowl XXII	$50-$100
Super Bowl XXIII	$50-$100
Super Bowl XXIV	$50-$100
Super Bowl XXV	$100-$150
Super Bowl XXVI	$75-$125
Super Bowl XXVII	$50-$100
Super Bowl XXVIII	$60-$110

Super Bowl XXIX	$50-$100
Super Bowl XXX	$50-$100
Super Bowl XXXI	$75-125
Super Bowl XXXII	$75-125
Super Bowl XXXIII	$50-100
Super Bowl XXXIV	$50-100
Super Bowl XXXV	$50-100

Super Bowl XXX Stub

Football Games

Selected Football Games

ABC Monday Night Football, Aurora 1972
. . . .$8-$40

ABC Monday Night Football, Aurora,1973, Roger Staubach edition . . . .$10-$50

All-American Foot Ball Game, Parker Bros.1925
. . . .$100-$165

All-American Football Game, National Games, 1935 . . . .$35-$55

All-American Football, Cadaco, 1969 . .$35-$90

Alpha Football Game, Replica Mfg. Co., 1940s
. . . .$75-$100

All-Star Electric Baseball and Football, Harrett-Gilmar, 1955 . . . .$35-$90

All-Star Football, Gardner & Co. 1950 $55-135

American Football GameAce Leather Goods Co., 1930 . . . .$70-$115

American Football Game American News Co. 1930s . . . .$60-$100

American Football Game, Intercollegiate Football Inc., 1935 . . . .$50-$75

America's Football,Trojan Games,1939 $55-$90

APBA Pro League Football, APBA 1964
. . . .$50-$75

APBA 1970s . . . .$35-$50

APBA 1980s . . . .$12-$30

Art Lewis Football GameMorgantown Game Co. 1955 . . . .$70-$175

Bart Starr Quarterback Game,1960s .$175-$450

Baseball, Football & Checkers, Parker Bros., 1957 . . . .$35-$90

The Benson Football Game, Benson, 1930s
. . . .$85-$145

Big League Manager Football, BLM, 1965
. . . .$20-$50

Big Payoff, Payoff Enterprises Co., 1984 $6-$15

Big Ten Football Game, Wheaties' Jack Armstrong Presents,1936 . . . .$55

Big Time Colorado Football, B.J. Tall, 1983
. . . .$6-$15

Bo McMillan's Indoor Football, Indiana Game Co., 1939 . . . .$75

Booth's Pro Conference Football, Sher-Co., 1977
. . . .$10-$25

Bowl Bound!, Sports Illustrated,1973 . .$15-$40

Bowl Bound!, Avalon Hill-Sports Illustrated, 1978 . . . .$7-$15

Boys Own Football Game, McLoughlin Bros., 1901 . . . .$325-$750

Challenge Football, Avalon Hill . . . .$10-$20

Chex Ches Football, Chex Ches Games, 1971
. . . .$15-$40

College Football, Milton Bradley, 1945
. . . .$85-$125

Dan Kersteter's Classic Football, Big League Co.
. . . .$10-$20

Electric Football, Electric Game Co., 1930s
. . . .$55-$90

Elmer Layden's Scientific Football, Cadaco-Ellis, 1936 . . . .$40-$80

F/11 Armchair Quarterback, James R. Hock,1964
. . . .$10-$20

First Down, TGP Games, 1970 . . . . . .$50-$125

Fobaga, American Football Co., 1942 . .$50-$75

Fooba-Roo Football Game, Memphis Plastic Ent., 1955 . . . .$25-$65

Football, J. Pressman & Co.,1940s . . . .$30-$45

Football, All-Fair, 1946 . . . .$55-$80

Football, Samuel Lowe, 1942, with baseball, basketball and hockey . . . .$50-$75

Football, Knapp Electro Game Set, Knapp Co.,1929 . . . .$125-$205

Football, Wilder, 1930s . . . .$50-$80

Football, Parker Bros., 1898 . . . . . .$295-$495

Football-As-You-Like-It, Wayne W. Light, 1940
. . . .$85-$145

Football, Baseball & Checkers, Parker Bros., 1948 . . . .$15-$65

Football Fever, Hansen, 1985 . . . .$20-$50

Football Game, Parker Bros., 1910, Princeton vs. Yale $350

Football Strategy, Avalon Hill, 1962 . . . .$8-$45

Football Strategy, Avalon Hill, Sports Illustrated, 1972 . . . .$3-$15

Foto-Electric Football, Cadaco-Ellis, 1950
. . . .$50-$75

Frank Cavanaugh's American Football, F. Cavanaugh Assoc.,1955 . . . .$25-$60

Fut-Bal, The Fut-Bal Co., 1940s . . . . . .$35-$60

The Game of Football, George A. Childs, 1895
. . . .$350

The Game of Football, Parker Bros., 1892 .$400

Game of Touchdown or Parlor Football Union, Mutual Life Insurance Premium, 1897 .$125

Goal Line Stand, Game Shop Inc., 1980
. . . .$12-$30

Gregg Football Game, Albert A. Gregg, 1924
. . . .$175-$285

Half-Time Football, Lakeside, 1979 . . . .$5-$15

Hit That Line, The All-American Football Game, La Rue Sales, 1930s . . . .$100-$165

Howard H. Jones, Collegiate Football Municipal Service, 1932 . . . .$40-$100

Huddle All-American Football Game, 1931
. . . .$100-$165

Indoor Football, Underwood, 1919 . .$145-$250

Instant Replay, Parker Bros., 1987 . . . . . .$8-$20

Intercollegiate Football, Hustler-Frantz, 1923
. . . .$125-$245

Jerry Kramer's Instant Replay, Emd Enterprises, 1970 . . . .$15-$40

Jimmy the Greek Oddsmaker Football, Aurora, 1974 . . . .$15-$35

Jim Prentice Electric Football, Electric Game Co., 1940 . . . .$50-$75

The Johnny Unitas Football Game, Play-Rite 1960 . . . .$125-$150

Johnny Unitas' Football, Pro Mentor, 1970
. . . .$25-$65

J.R. Quarterback Football, Built Rite, 1950s
. . . .$30-$45

Kellogg's Football Game, Kellogg's Premium 1936 . . . .$25-$40

Knute Rockne Football, Radio Sports, 1940
. . . .$300

Linebacker Football, Linebacker Inc.,1990
. . . .$12-$30

Los Angeles Rams Football Game, Zondine, Game Co.,1930s . . . .$175-$295

Monday Morning Quarterback, A.B. Zbinden 1963 . . . .$20-$50

NBC Pro Playoff, NBC-Hasbro, 1969 . .$25-$65

The New Game, Touchdown, Hartford Mfg.Co., 1920 . . . .$100

NFL All-Pro Football, Ideal, 1967 . . . . .$20-$50

NFL Armchair Quarterback Trade Wind Inc., 1986 . . . .$8-$20

NFL Franchise, Rohwood, 1982 . . . . .$10-$25

NFL Game Plan, Tudor Games, 1980 . .$6-$15

NFL Play Action, Tudor, 1979 . . . .$7-$15

NFL Quarterback, Tudor, 1977 . . . . . .$14-$35

NFL Strategy, Tudor Games, 1935 . . . .$45-$70

NFL Strategy ,Tudor, 1976 . . . .$5-$25

NFL Strategy, Tudor, 1986 . . . .$6-$15

Official Knute Rockne Football Game, Radio Sports,1930 . . . .$250-$400

Official National Football League Quarterback, Toy Craft, 1965 . . . .$50-$75

Official NFL Football Game, Ideal, 1968
. . . .$20-$50

Official Radio Football, Toy Creations, 1939
. . . .$45-$75

Ot-O-Win Football, Ot-O-Win Toys and Games, 1920s . . . .$55-$90

Parlor Football Game, McLoughlin Bros., 1890s
. . . .$525-$875

Paul Brown's Football Game,Trikilis, 1947
. . . .$110-$275

Paydirt!, Sports Illustrated, 1973 . . . . . .$10-$25

Paydirt!, Avalon Hill, 1979 . . . .$10-$30

Pigskin, Parker Bros.,1940 . . . .$75-$100

Parker Bros.,1956 . . . .$30-$40

Parker Bros.,1960 . . . .$20-$30

Pigskin, Parker Bros., 1946, Tom Hamilton's Football . . . .$50-$75

Pigskin, Tom Hamilton's Football Game, Parker Bros., 1934, stadium cover $75 . . . .$100

Play Football, Whitman, 1934 . . . .$55-$90

Playoff Football, Crestline Mfg. Co., 1970s
. . . .$20-$50

Pocket Football, Toy Creations, 1940 . . . . . .$35

Pocket Football, AMV Publishing . . . . . .$5-$10

Pro Bowl Live Action Football, Marx, 1960s
. . . .$35-$95

Pro Coach Football, Mastermind Sports
. . . .$30-$40

Pro Draft, Parker Bros.,1974 . . . .$15--$40

Pro Football, Milton Bradley, 1964 . . . .$25-$35

Pro Draft Football Game by Parker Brothers.

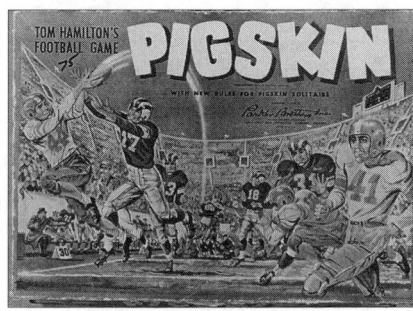

Tom Hamilton's Pigskin Football Game by Parker Bros.

Strat-O-Matic Pro Football Game.

Vince Lombardi's Game by Research Games, Inc.

Pro Football, 3M, 1964 . . . .$15-$20
Pro Football Franchise, Ron Wood., 1987
. . . .$10-$16
Pro Football, Strat-O-Matic,1968 . . . . .$25-$35
1960s cards . . . .$15-$30
1970s cards . . . .$10-$20
1980s cards . . . .$6-$15
Pro-Foto-Football, Cadaco, 1977 . . . . .$25-$60
Pro-Foto-Football, Cadaco, 1986 . . . . . .$8-$18
Pro Franchise Football, Rohrwood Inc., 1987
. . . .$10-$25
Pro Quarterback, Tod Lansing, 1964 . . .$20-$60
Pro Quarterback, Championship Games, 1965
. . . .$75
Pro Replay Football, Pro Replay . . . . . .$15-$20
Quarterback, Littlefield Mfg. Co., 1914
. . . .$100-$165
Quarterback, Olympia Games, 1914 . . . . . .$50
Quarterback Football Game, Transogram 1969
. . . .$25-$65
Radio Football Game, Toy Creations, 1939
. . . .$50-$125
Razzle Dazzle Football Game, Texantics Unlim-
ited, 1954 . . . .$50-$125
Razz-O Dazz-O Six Man Football, Gruhn &
Melton, 1938 . . . .$60-$100
Realistic Football, Match Play, 1976 . . .$15-$35
Replay Pro Football, Replay Games . . . .$30-$45
Roll-O Football, Supply Sales Co., 1923
. . . .$35-$60
Rose Bowl Championship Football Game, E.S.
Lowe Co., 1940s . . . .$40-$100
Rummy Football, Milton Bradley, 1944
. . . .$35-$60

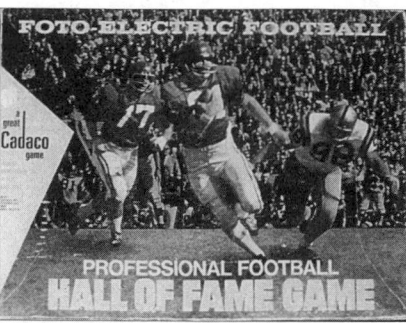

Foto Electric Football Hall of Fame Game by Cadaco.

Samsonite Football, Samsonite, 1969 . .$20-$50
Scrimmage, SPI, 1973 . . . .$15-$35
Scrimmage, Scrimmage Inc., 1978 . . . . .$5-$12
Sod Buster, D. Santee, 1980 . . . .$10-$25
Sports Illustrated College Football, Time, 1971
. . . .$8-$40
Sports Illustrated Pro Football, Time, 1970
. . . .$15-$40
Stars on Stripes Football Game, Stars & Stripes
Games Co., 1941 . . . .$55-$90
Statis-Pro Football, Statis-Pro, 1970s . .$25-$65
Statis-Pro Football, Avalon Hill-Sports Illustrated
. . . .$5-$15
Strat-O-Matic College Football, Strat-O-Matic
1976 . . . .$25-$60
Super Coach TV Football, Coleco, 1974 . . . . . .
. . . .$25-$65
Tackle, Tackle Game Co., 1933 . . . . .$75-$115
Tackle-Lite, Saxon Toy Corp., 1940s . .$50-$75
Talking Football, Mattel, 1971 . . . . . .$12-$30
Talking Monday Night Football, Mattel, 1977
. . . .$8-$20
T.H.E. Pro Football, T.H.E. Game Co., .$15-$35
Thinking Man's Football, 3M, 1969 . . .$15-$30
3M, 1973 . . . .$10-$20
Thrilling Indoor Football Game Cronston Co.
1933 . . . .$70-$115
Top Pro Football Quiz Game, Ed-U-Cards, 1970
. . . .$15-$40
Touchdown, Cadaco, 1937 . . . .$65-$110
Touchdown, Milton Bradley., 1930s . .$150-$250
Touchdown Football Game, Wilder Mfg. Co.,
1920s . . . .$100-$165

Monopoly Super Bowl XXXII board game by Parker Brothers.

21st Century Football, Kerger Co., 1930
. . . .$55-$90
Va-Lo Football Card Game, 1930s $125
Varsitee Football Playing Cards, Kerger Co.,
1938 . . . .$100
Varsity Football, PB, Kerger Co., 1925 . . . . .$75
Varsity Football Game, Cadaco-Ellis, 1942
. . . .$45-$75
Cadaco-Ellis, 1955 . . . .$25-$35
The VCR Quarterback Game, Interactive VCR
Games, 1986 . . . .$8-$20
Vince Lombardi's Game, Research Games
Inc.,1970 . . . .$20-$75
Ward Cuff's Football Game, Continental Sales,
1938 . . . .$125-$200
Whiz Football, Electric Game Co., 1945
. . . .$50-$75
Wilder's Football Game, Wilder Mfg. Co., 1930s
. . . .$50-$75
Wiry Dan's Electric Football Game, Harett-
Gilmar, 1953 . . . .$25-$65
Yale Harvard Game, McLoughlin Bros., 1890
. . . .$1,050-$1,775
Yale-Harvard Football Game, La Velle Mfg. Co.,
1922 . . . .$200-$300
Yale and Princeton Football Game, McLoughlin
Bros., 1895 . . . .$575-$950
The VCR Basketball Game, Interactive VCR
Games, 1987 . . . .$6-$15

Jostens salesman's sample of William "Refrigerator" Perry's size 23 Super Bowl ring and a size 10 ring

Football Awards/Rings/Trophies

Selected Rings/Pendants

Troy Aikman's 1992 Dallas Cowboys Super Bowl Champions ring, 14k gold-plated, salesman's sample, has a star diamond in the center . .$4,195
George Allen's 1972 Washington Redskins Super Bowl VII/NFC Championship ring, salesman's sample $1,995
Lyle Alzado's 1979 Denver Broncos team ring, salesman's sample $1,250
Terry Bradshaw's 1975 Pittsburgh Steelers Super Bowl X Championship ring, 10k yellow/gold, salesman's sample, has Bradshaw's name on the side, with two sparkling diamonds mounted on the top between the Vince Lombardi trophy $2,950
Terry Bradshaw's 1979 Pittsburgh Steelers Super Bowl Championship ring, 10k, four diamonds inside represent four Super Bowl wins, salesman's sample $3,695
Joe Greene's 1974 Pittsburgh Steelers Super Bowl Championship ring, with diamond set in an antique black onyx stone, salesman's sample $2,000
Bob Griese's 1971 Miami Dolphins Super Bowl VI/AFC Championship ring, 10k white/gold, salesman's sample, has a diamond mounted in a grayish blue stone on top, Griese's name on the shank $2,950
Jeff Hostetler's 1990 New York Giants Super Bowl Championship ring, 14k gold-plated, salesman's sample, has two football-shaped diamonds in the center $4,250
Jack Kemp's 1984 Buffalo Bills Honor Roll ring, 10k salesman's sample with a diamond set in a blue stone, given to Bills players who were inducted into the Hall of Fame $1,295

Dallas Cowboys Super Bowl Championship ring

1970 Baltimore Colts championship ring

Joe Montana's 1981 San Francisco 49ers Super Bowl XVI Championship ring, 10k yellow/gold salesman's sample, 16 diamonds surround a diamond mounted in a huge football-shaped bezel, Montana's name is on the side $3,750
Joe Montana's 1988 San Francisco 49ers Super Bowl ring, 10k, salesman's sample $4,250
Craig Morton's 1977 Denver Broncos AFC Champions ring, 10k, salesman's sample .$2,250
William Perry's 1985 Chicago Bears Super Bowl XXIII Championship ring, 10k, salesman's sample, size 22 . . . .$4,500
Jim Plunkett's 1980 Oakland Raiders Super Bowl XV Championship ring, 14k white gold, with 34 diamonds mounted on the top, salesman's sample $3,500
John Riggins' 1983 Washington Redskins NFC Champions ring, 14k gold-plated, salesman's sample, features a diamond-studded football with a ruby red stone in the center $1,595
Joe Robbie's 1972 Miami Dolphins Super Bowl Championship ring, 10k, salesman's sample, diamond set inside aquamarine stone . . .$3,595
O.J. Simpson's NFL Players Alumni ring, 10k gold, salesman's sample, has a large, gold detailed football mounted on a huge football-shaped tiger's eye stone $2,100
O.J. Simpson's 1980 Buffalo Bills Hall of Fame ring, 10k yellow gold salesman's sample, with a diamond mounted in a midnight blue stone on top $1,850
Bart Starr's Green Bay Packers Super Bowl I Championship ring, salesman's sample . .$2,750
Hank Stram's 1969 Kansas City Chiefs Super Bowl IV Championship ring, 10k yellow/gold, salesman's sample, has a football filled with sparkling diamonds mounted on a large burgundy stone $3,500
Roger Staubach's 1977 Dallas Cowboys Super Bowl Champions ring, 10k white/gold, salesman's sample, with diamonds set inside blue stars surrounded by 22 diamonds $3,500
1974 Minnesota Vikings NFC Champions ring, 10k $4,250

1991 New York Giants World Championship ring

1983 Miami Dolphins World Championship ring

1975 Pittsburgh Steelers Super Bowl World Champions player's ring, 10k by Balfour .$9,500
1981 Cincinnati Bengals AFC Championship ring, 10k, salesman's sample $2,250
1983 Oakland Raiders Super Bowl XVIII Championship player's ring, 14k $13,500
1983 Washington Redskins NFC Champs player's ring, 14k $6,500
1984 San Francisco 49ers Super Bowl XIX Championship ring, 10k yellow/gold, salesman's sample, two diamonds as big as the footballs in the Vince Lombardi trophies, which are surrounded by other diamonds $3,500
1984 Philadelphia Stars USFL Championship ring, 14k gold-plated, has the team logo with a diamond set inside it, all set on a ruby stone $1,695
1987 Washington Redskins Super Bowl XXII Championship ring, a real player's ring, it includes its original presentation box, and a lady's ring, too; made for Dennis Woodberry, #46, whose name is on the inside of the 10k gold/yellow ring, which has 42 diamonds and 30 rubies; lady's ring has 16 diamonds $15,500
1989 San Francisco 49ers Super Bowl XXIV Championship ring, 10k yellow/gold salesman's sample, with 41 diamonds $3,850

Selected Awards/Trophies

1982 St. Louis Cardinals Super Bowl tournament jewelry; sets were given to players and coaches, contains a tournament pendant, cuff links, tie bar, stick pin, in original sterling box $795
Dan Marino's 1984 Professional Athlete of the Year award, presented to him by the Florida Sports Writers Association and Florida Sportscasters Association, with letter from Marino $2,250
Super Bowl XI Oakland Raiders, city of Oakland Super Bowl trophy, given to the players; given to Skip Thomas; autographed $2,495
1988 Heisman Trophy made for Barry Sanders; one of probably three to six which were produced $29,995
O.J. Simpson, USC Heisman Trophy; one of probably three to six produced $34,995
Joe Montana Super Bowl XIX MVP Award, 18x24, has image of Montana's face and is engraved on the bottom "Joe Montana, San Francisco 49ers, MVP Super Bowl XIX, San Francisco 38 – Miami 16" given by owner Eddie DeBartolo to Montana, says "Joe - With all my Thanks, Best wishes and Friendship, Eddie," autographed by Montana $7,500
1966 Kansas City Chiefs AFL Champs 10k pendant, with diamond $1,250

Football Cereal Boxes

Kellogg's Corn Flakes

1983 Danny White $40.00
1995 J. Montana/D. Marino/D. Bledsoe Upper
Deck cards (Spanish version) 25.00

1998 Flutie Flakes

Famous Fixins

1999 Peyton's O's $6.00

PLB Sports Promotions

1998 Doug Flutie (Red) $12
1999 Doug Flutie (Blue) 12
1999 Flutie Flakes (Bilingual) 10
1999 Ed's Endzone O's 12
1999 Chrebet Chrunch 10
1999 Alstott's A-Train Express 10
1999 Warner's Crunch Time 10
2000 Virginia Tech Hokies Toasties 8
2000 Doug Flutie 10

Post
Post Toasties

1960s Football cards on back . . . .$40-$80

1960s Post Toasties

1988 Wheaties Steve Largent

Wheaties

1986 Walter Payton com. (12) $50
1986 Walter Payton pointing FB (8) 65
1986 Walter Payton point FB (23/18/24) 50
1986 Chris Spielman (AAU) R 150
1988 Steve Largent 45
1989 Redskins '88 champs R 30
1989 Broncos '88 champ (phantom) 50
1990 Boomer Esiason/Jim Kelly ProSet 30
1991 Joe Montana R 40
1991 Giants '90 champs R 30
1991 SEC Football R 90
1992 Barry Sanders R 40
1992 Redskins '91 champs R 30
1993 John Elway 45
1993 John Elway poster 60
1993 Jim Kelly poster 40
1993 Warren Moon poster 30
1993 Steve Young poster 30
1993 Bills '92 champs R 30
1993 Cowboys '92 champs R 20
1993 Steelers '92 champs R 35
1993 Vikings '92 champs R 40

1994 Jerry Rice R 20
1994 Cowboys '93 champs R 20
1994 NFL 75th Ann. (Silver) 10
1995 Dan Marino 15
1995 49ers '94 champs R 18
1995 Jacksonville Jaguars R 15
1995 Carolina Panthers R 18
1995 Oakland Raiders R 20
1995 St. Louis Rams R 15
1995 Nebraska Nat'l Champs R 25
1996 Deion Sanders (HF) 8
1996 Steve Young (CW) 10
1996 QBs: Aikman/Elway/Marino 15
1996 RBs: Allen/Sanders/Thomas 12
1996 WRs: Brown/Reed/Rice 10
1996 49ers 50th Ann. R 18
1996 Starr/Bradshaw/Aikman SB 30th A. . . .18
1996 Cowboys '95 champs R 18
1996 Baltimore Ravens R 15
1996 Steelers '95 AFC champs R 20
1996 SB XXX (three-pack) 25
1996 Neb. Nat'l Champs R 20
1996 Northwestern Wildcats R 15
1997 SB 30 Troy Aikman (HF) 8
1997 SB 30 Marcus Allen (Error) 10
1997 SB 30 Marcus Allen (Correct) 8
1997 SB 30 Joe Namath 8
1997 SB 30 Roger Staubach 8
1997 SB 30 Steve Young (CW) 8
1997 Franco Harris 25th Anniversary 12
1997 Packers NFC '96 champs 20
1997 Patriots AFC '96 champs R 18
1997 Marc & Nick Buoniconti 10
1997 Lambeau Field 12
1997 Tom Osborne: Nebraska 18
1997 Walter Payton 8
1997 Ronnie Lott (HFW) 8
1997 Roger Staubach 8
1997 Johnny Unitas 8
1997 Mean Joe Greene (CWR) 8
1998 Broncos '97 champs 12
1998 Brett Favre 3-time MVP R 10
1998 M. Holmgren/V. Lombardi R 10
1998 Walter Payton Leg. 5
1998 Walter Payton Leg. (CWR) 5
1998 Walter Payton Leg. (HW) 5
1999 Barry Sanders (RUN) 5
1999 Barry Sanders (RISK) 5
2000 St. Louis Rams SBXXXIV Champs . . .10
2000 Walter Payton Tribute 6

*1989 Wheaties
Denver Broncos (phantom)*

2001 Baltimore Ravens

Golf Collectibles

Collecting old golf memorabilia — clubs, balls, tees, etc. — is not a fad. It was first recognized in the late 1970s with reference materials and, since the mid-1980s, thousands of new collectors have entered the hobby. An additional tens of thousands putter around the edges of the field, expressing interest in the long-nose woods, feather balls, art and pottery that tell the story of the evolution of golf.

Approximately 500 years ago, golf was played along the eastern coast of Scotland, where the land called links land was non-arable and mostly sandy; its primary purpose was for grazing sheep.

Early golfers used long, whippy, shafted wooden-headed clubs to propel a leather-jacketed ball filled with goose feathers. The delicate wooden headed clubs, usually made by bow makers—Play Club (Driver), Brassie, Long and Short Spoons—were used to sweep the ball from sheep-mown grass lies. The Baffie was used to loft the ball over an obstacle or stream from a grass lie.

As a misplayed stroke would damage the delicate feather ball, few iron head clubs were used. Clubs with deep, broad concave faces were forged by the local blacksmith for playing the ball from the sandy lies and were called Bunker or Sand clubs. A small, rounded, cupped-face club was made to extract the ball from the deep hoof and cart tracks and accordingly called a Rut or Track club. A long shallow blade club with very little loft was used to hit the ball from bare hard ground or to hit a low running shot in windy weather. An Approaching Putter and/or Holing Out Putter, usually made from wood, rounded out the set.

Many collectors enjoy actually using the vintage golf items in their collections. This makes for a whole different type of collector, interested in the usability of the piece in addition to its condition and display potential. Beyond the world of wood-shaft clubs and gutta-percha balls, collectors look for vintage clothes, shoes and tees; also popular are books, instructional aids and advertisements.

Wooden-shaft Golf Clubs

Clubs during the featherball era were usually made by carpenters, bow makers, barrel makers, wheelwrights and other craftsmen with woodworking backgrounds. The irons were forged by the local armor maker or blacksmith.

A "play club" was used from the tee; a "brassie" was used to strike long, low shots from the fairway; and the "long spoon" and "mid-spoons" were used to hit moderately long-lofted shots. The "short spoon" (sometimes also called a baffie) was used to hit short-lofted shots around the green or over trouble.

Value is based on condition, rarity, availability, competition and desirability. Fewer than five percent of all wood-shafted clubs are truly valuable. Metal shafted clubs that have been painted or "wood-grained" to look like wood have no collectible value to the "wood shaft collector." Likewise, a club that has been restored or cleaned, is warped or cracked, has heavy rusting and pitting or bad or missing grips will drop substantially in value.

Tens of millions of low-grade clubs were made and sold from 1915 to 1935. Spalding, MacGregor, Burke, Kroydon, Hillerich & Bradsby, Wilson, Wright & Ditson and scores of others made clubs with line, dot, hyphen and other face markings. Most of these are common and only have value as conversation pieces, decorations or for their playability.

Vintage Golf Balls

While golf clubs were generally affordable prior to 1850, only the very wealthy could afford the feather balls of the era. A skilled maker could produce no more than three or four balls a day, which resulted in the very high cost. In the late 1840s, gutta-percha—a rubbery compound commonly used to line wooden shipping boxes containing fragile items—was molded into golf balls. The guttapercha balls were far less expensive and, as a result, golf became more affordable.

As more people took up the game of golf, the courses, clubs and balls were refined. During the late 1800s, many patents were taken out on all forms of golfing artifacts. One of the most significant was the Haskell patent. Working for Goodyear Rubber Co., Coburn Haskell and Bertram Works developed a process of winding thin rubber strips around a central core, then covered these windings with gutta-percha. The "Haskell" ball was the leading factor in the development and refinement of golf clubs and the game as we know it today.

As with clubs, pre-1800s balls are scarce. Pre-1860 gutta-percha balls are scarcer than "featheries." Balls with markings on them from this period are among the rarest. There are also a few balls painted for winter play that are highly sought after. While most are red or orange, there have been blue, yellow and black balls noted.

Many collectors cannot afford top-quality examples of odd-pattern balls, gutta-perchas, brambles and wrapped balls. For those who want to collect balls in top quality, signature balls may be the answer.

1927 Churchman's Cigarettes Who's Who in Sports W. Hagen card.

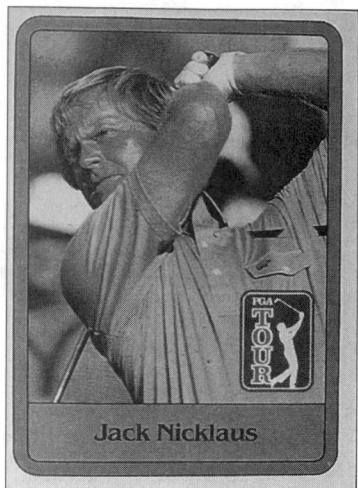

Jack Nicklaus

Signature balls are golf balls that were imprinted, at the time of manufacturing, with a professional's name. At present they are plentiful. Most are priced under $50 and can be acquired in top condition.

Common mesh pattern golf balls — circa 1930 from Worthington, Dunlop or Spalding — in above average condition sell for about $75. An identical ball, but with a cover cut or other damage, will bring only $10 to $15.

Faroid or Park Royal balls are so rare and seldom offered, even damaged examples are highly sought after and bring premium prices.

Tees

The earliest tees were not tees at all, but small mounds of sand formed into cones. Shortly before the turn of the century, metal cone-shaped molds, mostly made of brass, were in vogue. Many golf courses provided a "Sand Box" with a pail of water at each tee. The player or his caddy used the mold to shape the wet sand for a tee.

During the 1920s, the wooden tee was introduced, along with some wire, plastic, rubber and zinc tees. Tees have been made of aluminum, paper, plastic, steel, wire, zinc, rubber—anything that would raise the ball from the turf. Shapes and forms were stars, triangles, domes, tethers, spinners, molds and just about anything else imaginable.

In the early 1900s, packaging to promote the merchandising of tees became an industry in itself. Tees were packaged in large and small boxes with very ornate designs. Another packaging concept was cloth tee bags, similar to a tobacco pouch, which held 50 or 100 tees. Paper bags were also used to hold 15 to 25 tees. Most bags were white with the printed advertisement of the tee companies.

Bags or boxes of tees are less valuable if they are only partially full. Tee packets similar to matchbooks are also collectibles and have been produced since the early 1920s. A large variety of brand-name tees were produced, along with tee-holders and advertisements, which are also collectible.

Autographs

The autograph hobby dates back about 1,000 years, and with the first British Open Championship in 1860, golf began to establish itself as a sport. As a result, autographs of golf's greatest players did not escape interest of collectors. Autographed photographs, trading cards, books, golf balls, letters and other items are highly sought after by collectors.

Modern signatures should be accompanied by a certificate of authenticity or purchased from a reputable dealer. Many of today's golfers will provide a signature if it is solicited by mail, or can be visited at shows or tournaments, where a signature can be obtained in person.

Books

Golf books cover many categories including instruction, architecture, history, rules, anthologies and fiction. Some reference books generally acquired for information and pricing are highly collectible as well.

In 1457, Scotland's King James II issued a decree outlawing golf because his soldiers were golfing more than practicing their archery skills. This decree became the first printed reference to the game of golf. It wasn't until the golf boom of the 1890s that books on golf were published in great quantities. The most prominent one of this period was *Golf: The Badminton Library* by Horace Hutchinson (1890).

Richard E. Donovan and Joseph S. F. Murdoch collaborated to publish *The Game of Golf and the Printed Word* (1988) which is a bibliography of golf literature in the English language. This is a highly regarded and collectible reference book.

Prices of books are determined by condition, edition, scarcity and desirability. First printings of first editions command higher prices than later printings.

Books in poor condition (missing pages, broken cover or contents damaged, badly soiled or stained) or library books are generally useful for information only. Underlining, margin notes, repair or rebinding all reduce the value of a book.

Miscellaneous Golf Collectibles

The wealthy golfer from 1875 to 1930 spared no expense when it came to displaying the game he loved. Collectibles came in the form of trophies, tees, medals, dining utensils, jewelry, smoking paraphernalia, whiskey flasks, music boxes, watches, ink wells and more.

Trophies were made of gold and silver. There were sterling silver toast racks, teapots, knives, forks, and especially spoons with golf motifs, as well as any other dining table items. Whiskey flasks were also made of sterling silver. The businessman had in his den or on his office desk golf-affiliated paperweights, ink wells, pens, clocks, humi-dors, ashtrays, letter openers and scores of other knickknacks.

Smoking had not yet been demonized and pipe, cigar and cigarette cases, match safes, humidors, ashtrays and other tobacco related items were made of gold, silver and bronze.

An extensive amount of pottery was made with a golf theme, from some of the most well-known makers—Royal Doulton, Lenox, Copeland, Wedgewood, Kingsware, etc. While earlier pieces were hand-painted, the later pieces contain printed decorations and were produced in larger quantities.

Most glass golf items were produced in England and the United States. A popular glass design involves a sterling silver golfer overlay that was attached to a glass bottle, goblet or pitcher. It is seen in many sizes, as are etched and engraved items.

Prices are for the selected items in Excellent condition.

Clubs

Aluminum head woods, Braddell, Belfast, Ireland, 1890s, leather face insert . .$650
Beech head, many have leather face inserts
. . . .$2,250
Diamond back irons, 1910-1915, "Rampant Lion" mark at the toe $70
Gold Medal series putter, 1906-1908, brass blade "Spalding Gold Medal" $65
Gutta-percha face iron, Nicoll, patented 1892, "G. Nicoll, Leven Fife" $2,500
Holing out putter, blacksmith-made, circa 1850, thick long hosel $3,000
Large head brassie, Spalding, 1915, marked "A.G. Spalding Bros" $100
Long-nose putter, 1890s, spliced neck, beech head stamped "D. Anderson"
. . . .$1,000
Long-nose woods, McEwan, Musselburgh, 1870s, play club or brassie, long head, large lead back weight. "McEwan" mark
. . . .$2,750
Long-nose woods, Philp, Hugh, St. Andrews, 1850s, "H Philp" in block letters, thorn head $10,000
Pretty face woods, various makers, circa 1920s, various pretty face inserts . .$125
Irons, Winton, W & Co., Ltd., circa 1905, The Major, seven-pointed tines . . .$6,000
Rut iron, blacksmith-made, 1840-1860, small cupped face, long thick hosel with heavy nicking $3,500
Smooth-face putting cleek, Spalding, circa 1905, "Made in Great Britain." $60
Spalding series putter, 1898-1902, deep smooth-faced steel-blade putter $225
Ted Ray signature irons, circa 1925-1930, each $50
Wry-neck putter, Spalding, circa 1920-25, hyphen-scored, offset hosel, "thistle" marks $65

Golf Balls

Bramble, rubber core, Goodrich, B F, 1899-1905, "Haskell" and "Pat. Apr. 1, 1899" at poles $325

Bramble, rubber core, Goodrich, B F, 1910, "Haskell Royal" with celluloid cover $800

Bramble, rubber core, Goodyear Rubber Co., 1905, "The Pneumatic" at equator $600

Bramble, rubber core, Goodyear Rubber Co., 1905, "The Pneumatic" at poles $1,250

Bramble, rubber core, various makers, 1905-1920, celluloid or rubber cover $275

Bramble, rubber core, various makers, 1900, gutta-percha cover $325

Bramble, rubber core, Haskell, 1900, "Haskell Bramble" at one pole, "Pat. Apr. 11, 99" at other pole $500

Diamond cover, Spalding USA, 1920-1930, entire cover with diamonds. "Spalding" at poles $150

Dimple cover, Spalding USA, 1908-1920, Baby Dimple, Domino, Dot, Glory Dimple, and others $125

Dimple cover, Spalding USA, 1920-1940, "P.G.A" $30

Feather ball, no maker's name, 1840-1860 . . . .$5,000

Feather ball, Gourlay, John Musselburgh, 1840-1860, "J Gourlay" and size number $9,000

Feather ball, Morris, Tom, St. Andrews, 1840-1860, "T Morris" and size number $15,000

Gutta-percha, smooth, no maker's name, 1850-1860, white, brown or black usually with a "test" mark $3,000

Gutta-percha, hand-hammered, no maker's name, 1850-1880 . . . .$2,000

Gutta-percha, hand-hammered, Forgan, Robert, St. Andrews, 1865-1880, stamped "R Forgan," usually with size number 2,500

Gutta-percha, line cut, remade, no name, 1880-1905 . . . .$300

Gutta-percha, line cut, various makers, 1880-1905 . . . .$500

Gutta-percha, bramble, various makers, 1895-1905 . . . .$450

Gutta-percha, bramble, Spalding, Vardon Flyer, circa 1900, "Vardon Flyer" at both poles $950

Line cut rubber core, Goodrich, BF, Akron, Ohio, 1902, "Haskell" and "Pat. Apr. 1, 1899" in rectangular panels, gutta-percha cover $3,500

Mesh cover, various makers, 1910-1940, square markings $75

Warwick, Dunlop, Birmingham, Eng., 1925-1935, alternating rows of square and dimple markings $175

Tees

Prices shown are for full boxes or bags, unless otherwise noted.

All-My-Tee, various makers, 1930, circular Handi-Pack of nine tees $75

Bobby Tees, various makers, late 1920s, red wooden goblet-style tees $60

Cruickshank steel tees, various makers, 1930, red wire tees with circular top .$90

Just Perfect tees, various makers, early 1930s, 18 wooden tees in pale green box $60

K-D sand tee mold, K-D Mfg., Lancaster, PA, 1920s, polished aluminum with spring plunger $475

Keystone sand tee mold, 1920-1930, bakelite plastic with spring plunger $350

No-Looz-Tee, various makers, 1950s-1960s, weighted end, made of rubber $60

Novel-tees, Spurgin Mfg., Chicago, late 1920s, book of 18 paper tees $75

Perfect Golf Tee, patented 1927, molded rubber tee secured in the ground by a nail $100

Rex zinc tees, The Rex Co., Chicago, 1930, red box, zinc tees $100

Rite Pencil Tee, WIMO Specialty Co Inc., 1927, long tee with pencil lead at tip, single tee $10

Rubber Manhattan tee, 1920, five-inch-long rubber tee with round weight at one end, tee at other $100

Sand tee mold, 1890-1920, brass with spring plunger. $650

Tether tees, various makers, 1900-1930s, "tether" or colorful thistle and the tee $75

The Reddy Tee, Nieblo Mfg. Co., 1930, wooden tees in green, white and red box $70

The Scot-tee, late 1920s, box of 18 wood tees . . . .$100.

Tees in bags, various makers, 1930s-40s, draw string bags of fifty and one hundred wooden tees $50

Top Not Tee, various makers, late 1920s, made of both wood and steel, orange and white. $60

Autographed Items

Harry Vardon signed photo, 1910-1920. . . . .$650

Tom Morris signed photo, 1900 . . .$1,500

Ben Hogan signed photo, 1960-1980 .$300

Ben Hogan signed photo, 1940-1950 .$450

Robert T. Jones, Jr. signed photo, 1955-1970 shaky ballpoint pen signature .$650

Robert T. Jones, Jr. signed photo, 1930-1950, black fountain pen signature $2,250

Arnold Palmer signed photo, 1975. . . .$40

Byron Nelson signed photo, 1960-1990s $40

Byron Nelson signed photo, 1935-1950, fountain pen, vintage signature $100

Gene Sarazen signed photo, 1960s-1980s $40

Gene Sarazen signed photo, 1925-1950, fountain pen, vintage signature $90

Jack Nicklaus signed photo, 1980 . . . .$75

Books

Golf Course Mystery by C.K. Steel, 1919 . . . .$125

History of Golf in Britain by Bernard Darwin, 1952 . . . .$300

Golf, Badminton Library by Horace Hutchinson, 1890 . . . .$325

Scotland's Gift; Golf by C. B. MacDonald, 1928 (reprints $35). $700

This Game of Golf by Henry Cotton, 1948 . . . .$60

The Bobby Jones Story by G. Rice and O.B. Keeler, 1953 . . . .$65

Life of Tom Morris by W.W. Tulloch, 1908 . . . .$1,200

Power Golf by Ben Hogan, 1948 . . . . .$30

Walter Hagen Story by Hagen and M. Heck, 1956 . . . .$125

Encyclopedia of Golf by Steel, Ryde and Wind, 1975 . . . .$35

Golf in the Making by Henderson and Stirk, 1979 . . . .$150

Miscellaneous Collectibles

Ashtray, H. Hoffman, 1920s, glass, intaglio cut $300

Cigarette case, sterling, 1900-1920, golfing scene on cover. $575

Creamer, Doulton, early 1900s, Lambeth, England, Uncle Toby series $900

Creamer, Royal Doulton, 1930s, Bunnykins $600

Creamer, Wedgewood (England), early 1900s, golfers in white relief $650

Crystal decanter, Waterford, 1920, sterling silver hallmarked neck, hand-painted golfing scene $2,000

Cuff links, gold golf balls, Dunlop, New York, 1920, nickel size 10k gold mesh $175

Etched glasses, Heissey, circa 1920s, etched golfers. $650

Figurine, porcelain, Lladro, 1900s . . .$500

Jardiniere, stoneware, Copeland Spode, 1900, golfers in relief, white on blue or green background. $650

Match safe, sterling, Unger, Newark, N.J., 1900-1910, caddy with bag. $650

Plate, "The Nineteenth Hole," Royal Doulton, porcelain $600

Silver plate ink well, Birmingham, England, 1900, two golf ball inkwells $500

Sterling silver spoons, 1900-1920s, golfers on handle $80

Stoneware ewer, Copeland Spode, 1900, golfers in relief, white on green or blue background $1,000

Stoneware pitcher, Copeland Spode, 1900, golfers in relief, white on green or blue background $900

Tankard, silver-rimmed, Lenox, 1905, golfers on green background $1,500

Whiskey flask, sterling, Kerr & Co., 1920s, pint size, knickered golfers on front $800

●●●

Golf Autographs

Tommy Aaron
Photo $20
Ball $25

Amy Alcott
Photo $15
Ball $20

George Archer
Photo $20
Ball $25

Paul Azinger
Photo $20
Ball $25

Seve Ballesteros
Photo $25
Ball $30

Butch Baird
Photo $15
Ball $20

Miller Barber
Photo $20
Ball $25

Andy Bean
Photo $15
Ball $20

Chip Beck
Photo $15
Ball $20

Patti Berg
Photo $25
Ball $30

Tommy Bolt
Photo $20
Ball $25

Julius Boros
Photo $30
Ball $40

Jack Burke
Photo $15
Ball $20

Gay Brewer
Photo $15
Ball $20

Billy Casper
Photo $20
Ball $25

Jim Colbert
Photo $15
Ball $20

Fred Couples
Photo $25
Ball $30

Ben Crenshaw
Photo $25
Ball $30

John Daly
Photo $25
Ball $30

Jimmy Demaret
Photo $30
Ball $50

David Duval
Photo $30
Ball $50

Lee Elder
Photo $15
Ball $20

Steve Elkington
Photo $15
Ball $20

Ernie Els
Photo $25
Ball $30

Nick Faldo
Photo $30
Ball $40

Ray Floyd
Photo $25
Ball $30

Sergio Garcia
Photo $15
Ball $20

Hubert Green
Photo $15
Ball $20

Jay Hebert
Photo $15
Ball $20

Ben Hogan *
Photo $200
Ball $250

Julie Inkster
Photo $15
Ball $20

Hale Irwin
Photo $20
Ball $25

Lee Janzen
Photo $20
Ball $25

Tony Jacklin
Photo $15
Ball $20

Don January
Photo $25
Ball $30

Bobby Jones *
Photo $2,000
Ball $2,500

Betsy King
Photo $30
Ball $50

Tom Kite
Photo $20
Ball $25

Bernard Langer
Photo $20
Ball $25

Tom Lehman
Photo $20
Ball $25

Justin Leonard
Photo $20
Ball $25

Gene Littler
Photo $25
Ball $30

Nancy Lopez
Photo $20
Ball $25

Davis Love III
Photo $25
Ball $30

Casey Martin
Photo $15
Ball $20

Phil Mickelson
Photo $25
Ball $30

Johnny Miller
Photo $20
Ball $25

Larry Mize
Photo $15
Ball $20

Colin Montgomerie
Photo $20
Ball $25

Orville Moody
Photo $15
Ball $20

Bob Murphy
Photo $20
Ball $25

Byron Nelson
Photo $35
Ball $40

Larry Nelson
Photo $15
Ball $20

Jack Nicklaus
Photo $75
Ball $100

Greg Norman
Photo $30
Ball $40

Mark O'Meara
Photo $25
Ball $30

(Arnold Palmer signature)

Arnold Palmer
Photo $75
Ball $100

Se Ri Pak
Photo $25
Ball $30

Jesper Parnevik
Photo $15
Ball $20

Steve Pate
Photo $15
Ball $20

Corey Pavin
Photo $20
Ball $25

Gary Player
Photo $25
Ball $30

Nick Price
Photo $25
Ball $30

Betsy Rawls
Photo $20
Ball $25

Chi Chi Rodriguez
Photo $25
Ball $30

(Gene Sarazen signature)

Gene Sarazen *
Photo $30
Ball $35

Scott Simpson
Photo $15
Ball $20

Charles Sifford
Photo $25
Ball $30

(Vijay Singh signature)

Vijay Singh
Photo $20
Ball $25

J.C. Snead
Photo $20
Ball $25

(Sam Snead signature)

Sam Snead
Photo $30
Ball $35

Annika Sorenstam
Photo $15
Ball $20

Craig Stadler
Photo $25
Ball $30

Payne Stewart *
Photo $50
Ball $70

Dave Stockton
Photo $15
Ball $20

Curtis Strange
Photo $25
Ball $30

Hal Sutton
Photo $20
Ball $25

Lee Trevino
Photo $30
Ball $35

Ken Venturi
Photo $25
Ball $30

Lanny Wadkins
Photo $20
Ball $25

Tom Watson
Photo $25
Ball $30

Tom Weiskopf
Photo $20
Ball $25

Lee Westwood
Photo $15
Ball $20

Tiger Woods
Photo . . . .$150-$175
Ball . . . .$450-$500

Babe Didrikson Zaharias *
Photo $150
Ball $200

Larry Ziegler
Photo $15
Ball $20

Fuzzy Zoeller
Photo $25
Ball $30

Hockey Collectibles

It has always been cool to collect ice hockey memorabilia. Just ask the handful of hobbyists who did.

And those fans have, in recent years, been joined by many thousands more as trading cards, game jerseys, sticks, pucks and a variety of special promotions dealing with the National Hockey League have drawn enthusiastic response from serious and casual collectors alike.

As with collecting memorabilia of the three other major team sports, there is no single way to go about it. Some collectors pour their energy into acquiring items associated with a specific player such as Gordie Howe, Bobby Orr, Patrick Roy, Bobby Hull or Wayne Gretzky. Other collectors go for team-related items in order to build a collection that helps tell some of the history of their favorite franchise. Still others focus on post-season play, and seek items related solely to the Stanley Cup playoffs.

Your interests and your disposable income will determine what you will pursue. But one thing is certain: Collecting NHL-related memorabilia is a great hobby that often leads to lasting friendships with people on both sides of the U.S.-Canada border.

Hockey mementos, like the game they celebrate, enjoy a fascinating history. Knowing a little of that history will offer newcomers to the hobby a greater appreciation of what they're in store for when they visit their local hobby shop or attend a sports memorabilia show in their area.

North of the Border, We're Talkin' Hockey

At center ice for the hobby is the trading card. It's easier to come by than most other hockey collectibles, it's less expensive than most other hockey collectibles and, because of its long but sporadic history, it still has a strong emotional hold on the hobby itself.

It's little surprise that hockey cards were made in Canada well before the trading cards of baseball, football and basketball entered the market there. Although there were a few cards issued regionally a hundred years ago, most hobbyists generally point to the "tobacco cards" of 1910-13 as the birth of hockey card sets.

These trading cards, like their brethren associated with big-league baseball in the United States, came packaged with cigarettes. Measuring 1fi by 2fi inches, these cards sported the player's team affiliation history on the backs. Three sets were issued

during that period. The third, featuring black and white player photos, is the rarest.

Card production ceased with the advent of World War I. Although global hostilities ended by 1918, tobacco cards made only a brief appearance after the war. The Ontario-based Hamilton's Cigarettes issued a set featuring players from the six NHL teams for the 1924-25 season.

Candy companies somewhat filled the void during the Roaring Twenties by issuing hockey cards on a regional basis. Gum companies skated onto the hobby ice for the 1930s, and, while some of their sets and individual cards are slightly easier to find than those of the 1920s, collectors still find it a challenge to locate cards in mint condition.

History repeats itself in more ways than one, and when Canada joined its allies at the outbreak of World War II to fight the Axis powers, card production once again ceased. No hockey cards were issued between the 1940-41 season and the 1951-52 season. When Parkhurst Products debuted its hockey card set in 1951, it began a three-year "solo" run until O-Pee-Chee entered the scene for the 1954-55 season. Neither company issued hockey sets for the next two seasons, then both resumed their efforts for the 1957-58 season.

Although Parkhurst was there before O-Pee-Chee and Topps, it dropped out of the hockey card market after the 1963-64 season. That was due in part to the ability of

Parkhurst's two rivals to distribute their respective cards throughout Canada while Parkhurst remained more regional in its distribution. Topps and O-Pee-Chee formed an alliance in 1968 that resulted in the former issuing their cards Stateside and the latter issuing their cards in Canada. That business relationship lasted for more than 25 years.

By the 1990s, the hockey card market was flourishing, and throughout that decade firms such as Donruss, Fleer, Pro Set, Score and Upper Deck became synonymous with hockey cards in North America. The Parkhurst name was even revived for several years.

Today, hockey cards enjoy the same accolades enjoyed by baseball, football and basketball cards. They sport vibrant colors, computer-generated graphics and excellent photography. Their manufacturers also use numerous marketing ploys such as insert cards and parallel versions of regular sets to increase collector interest and generate greater retail sales.

Say, Dad, Are All Those Hats Thrown Onto the Ice Collectible?

Most every collector of hockey memorabilia is fascinated with the trading cards that populate the hobby landscape. The majority of these collectors will stick with at least one annual set of cards as either the foundation of their collections or as their lone pursuit.

But the scope of hockey memorabilia is so great currently that collectors can pretty much name a category and find a wealth of stuff to choose from.

At the high end of the hockey collectibles spectrum is game-used equipment. The trick here, other than a willingness to open your billfold wide, is to deal with reputable dealers in such rarities.

June 1977 Hockey Digest

You'll need to take the time to search the hobby publications to find them.

It's best not to seek out a dealer who is a "friend of a friend of a friend"—especially if the asking price for what you want sounds too good to be true. It could be a fake. Worse, the item could have been stolen or obtained illegally. There's no pride in ownership if that beautiful jersey or handsome autographed hockey stick you just bought is "hot."

Look for dealers whose inventories feature the jerseys and/or equipment of the minor stars as well as the superstars. Also, learn the terminology associated with collecting uniforms and equipment. Study the market. The phrase, "Knowledge is power," pertains to collecting just as much as it does to any endeavor.

If jerseys, sticks, masks and the like are beyond your financial means, there are plenty of other popular hockey collectibles well within most collectors' range:

● Media guides typically are priced in the $7 to $15 range, though a team's overall popularity/history, combined with the age/scarcity of a given guide, will push the price tag to $40, $50, even $100. Yet guides remain among the hobby's most desirable collectibles.

● Keeping with the theme of print matter, you might wish to consider back issues of *Hockey Digest*. Currently, the most expensive one listed in price guides is the November 1972 issue with Bobby Orr on the cover—$45 to $60 in top condition. Otherwise, expect to find most back issues at $3 to $12. Those articles are a great way to immerse yourself in NHL history.

● Figurines of NHL players are available, particularly those made by Starting Lineup. Be aware that there are several variations to consider when collecting them. First, there were distinct American and Canadian sets for the years 1993 through 1996. Second, there were two complete Canadian sets released in 1994 — a 20-player set and a 13-player set. Third, the company issued a small set (seven boxed collectibles in all) in 1997 called "Hockey One on One." Each box contained two NFL players going head to head in an action pose (for example, Jaromir Jagr vs. Patrick Roy).

Skating on Thin Ice? Not If You Do Your Homework

The current hockey collectibles market is as wide open as the opposition's net after they've pulled their goalie late in the game.

Mario Lemieux Game-Used Jersey.

That means collectors will find much to select from as they scan the hobby periodicals, visit their local retailers, attend an area hobby show and surf the Internet.

Mini jerseys are popular. These 7-inch by 7-inch fabric replicas of jerseys from various pro sports, including hockey, make them perfect for the collector who wishes to put together a nifty, colorful wall display.

There is a ton of game-used stuff being advertised, particularly on the Internet. Auction sites; buy, sell and trade sites; memorabilia sites — they're all there. Be sure to learn about the sellers before you buy.

Once your research has taken you to your personal comfort level, have fun. Choose from used sticks, gloves and skates to jerseys, helmets and elbow pads.

Some collectors seek collectibles and memorabilia associated with a single player or two. Again, check the ads in the various hobby publications and run a search or two on the Internet. If you can't find that Wayne Gretzky item you desire, you're not looking hard enough. Go with authorized dealers.

If you've received a sports gifts catalog in the mail, checked out a hobby shop or attended a sports memorabilia show, you know that items unrelated to a given sport can boast team logos of that sport. You can find golf balls and golf club head covers, watches and jewelry, mugs and glasses, and sweatshirts and T-shirts emblazoned with your favorite hockey team's logo.

Hockey just may be the coolest sport around.

Hockey items just may be the hottest sports collectibles to own.

●●●

Selected Hockey Cards
(1951-1990)

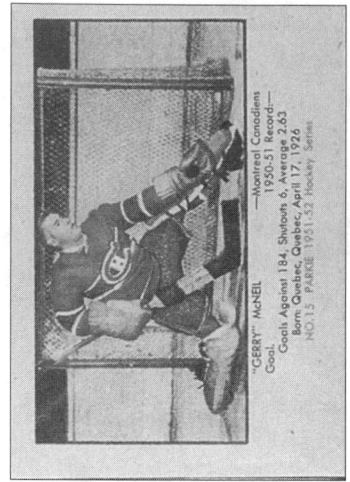

1951-52 PARKHURST

	NM
Complete Set (105):	$10,000.00
Common Player:	35.00

		NM
1	Elmer Lach	325.00
4	Maurice Richard	1,500.00
10	Doug Harvey	350.00
14	Bernie Geoffrion	400.00
52	Bill Barilko, McNeil	175.00
55	Red Kelly	250.00
56	Ted Lindsay	250.00
61	Terry Sawchuck	1,000.00
63	Alex Delvecchio	225.00
66	Gordie Howe	3,000.00
72	Howie Meeker	125.00
75	Turk Broda	125.00
86	Ted Kennedy	130.00
94	Allan Stanley	120.00
105	Jim Conacher	125.00

1952-53 PARKHURST

	NM
Complete Set (105):	$6,200.00
Common Player:	25.00

		NM
1	Maurice Richard	1,000.00
3	Boom Boom Geoffrion	200.00
10	Dickie Moore	150.00
14	Doug Harvey	150.00
51	George Armstrong	140.00
58	Tim Horton	450.00
86	Terry Sawchuk	500.00
88	Gordie Howe	1,400.00

1953-54 PARKHURST

	NM
Complete Set (100):	$4,000.00
Common Player:	20.00

		NM
1	Harry Lumley	125.00
13	Tim Horton	200.00
24	Maurice Richard	450.00
27	Jean Beliveau	600.00
28	Dickie Moore	100.00
29	B.B. Geoffrion	120.00
30	Elmer Lach, Maurice Richard	170.00
46	Terry Sawchuk	225.00
50	Gordie Howe	800.00
53	Gump Worsley	300.00
56	Andy Bathgate	115.00
57	Harry Howell	115.00

1954-55 PARKHURST

	NM
Complete Set (100):	$4,000.00
Common Player:	16.00

		NM
3	Jean Beliveau	310.00
7	Maurice Richard	400.00
31	Tim Horton	125.00
33	Terry Sawchuk	200.00
41	Gordie Howe	700.00
65	Johnny Bower	250.00
100	Sawchuk stops Boom Boom Terry Sawchuk, Bernie Geoffrion	125.00

1954-55 TOPPS

	NM
Complete Set (66):	$4,400.00
Common Player:	32.00

		NM
1	Dick Gamble	100.00
3	Harry Howell	100.00
5	Red Kelly	110.00
8	Gordie Howe	2,200.00
10	Gump Worsley	200.00
39	Alex Delvecchio	125.00
51	Ted Lindsay	120.00
58	Terry Sawchuk	600.00
60	Milt Schmidt	180.00

1955-56 PARKHURST

	NM
Complete Set (79):	$3,000.00
Common Player:	18.00
Old Time Greats:	18.00

		NM
1	Harry Lumley	.80.00
3	Tim Horton	.125.00
37	Maurice Richard	.375.00
43	B.B. Geoffrion	.100.00
44	Jean Beliveau	.250.00
45	Doug Harvey	.80.00
50	Jacques Plante	.700.00
56	Georges Vezina	.75.00
57	Howie Morenz	.75.00
72	Rocket roars through Maurice Richard	80.00
73	Richard test Lumley Maurice Richard, Harry Lumley	.80.00
78	The Montreal Forum	.150.00
79	Maple Leaf Gardens	.180.00

1957-58 PARKHURST

	NM
Complete Sets (50):	.$2,000.00
Common Players:	.16.00

		NM
2	B.B. Geoffrion	.90.00
3	Jean Beliveau	.200.00
4	Henri Richard	.350.00
5	Maurice Richard	.350.00
15	Jacques Plante	.350.00
(17)	Frank Mahovlich	.400.00

1957-58 TOPPS

	NM
Complete Set (66):	.$1,900.00
Common Player:	.15.00

		NM
10	Johnny Bucyk	.175.00
20	Glenn Hall	.275.00
22	Pierre Pilote	.125.00
35	Terry Sawchuk	.200.00
42	Gordie Howe	.600.00
46	Norm Ullman	.175.00
53	Gump Worsley	.100.00

1958-59 PARKHURST

	NM
Complete Set (50):	.$1,500.00
Common Player:	.15.00

		NM
2	Henri Richard	.140.00
22	Jacques Plante	.250.00

28	Boom Boom Geoffrion	.75.00
33	Frank Mahovlich	.200.00
34	Jean Beliveau	.125.00
38	Maurice Richard	.300.00
42	Tim Horton	.80.00
46	Johnny Bower	.85.00

1958-59 TOPPS

	NM
Complete Set (66):	.$4,200.00
Common Player:	.14.00

		NM
2	Terry Sawchuk	.150.00
8	Gordie Howe	.525.00
13	Glenn Hall	.130.00
30	Eddie Shack	.135.00
40	Johnny Bucyk	.100.00
65	Norm Ullman	.90.00
66	Bobby Hull	.3000.00

1959-60 PARKHURST

	NM
Complete Set (50):	.$1,200.00
Common Player:	.14.00

		NM
1	Canadians on Guard	.50.00
2	Maurice Richard	.250.00
6	Jean Beliveau	.100.00
23	Tim Horton	.60.00
24	Frank Mahovich	.125.00
32	Johnny Bower	.50.00

33	Boom Boom Geoffrion	.60.00
39	Henri Richard	.80.00
41	Jacques Plante	.160.00
50	King Clancy	.60.00

1959-60 TOPPS

	NM
Complete Set (66):	.$1,900.00
Common Player:	.15.00

		NM
42	Terry Sawchuk	.125.00
47	Bobby Hull	.600.00
48	Gordie Howe, Jack Evans	.90.00
63	Gordie Howe	.450.00

1960-61 PARKHURST

	NM
Complete Set (61):	.$1,700.00
Common Player:	.12.00

		NM
1	Tim Horton	.85.00
2	Frank Mahovich	.100.00
20	Gordie Howe	.400.00
31	Terry Sawchuk	.120.00
45	Maurice Richard	.200.00
46	Boom Boom Geoffrion	.60.00
47	Henri Richard	.70.00
49	Jean Beliveau	.90.00
53	Jacques Plante	.125.00
59	Linemates (Geoffrion/Beliveau, Marshall	.75.00
61	Jim Morrison	.60.00

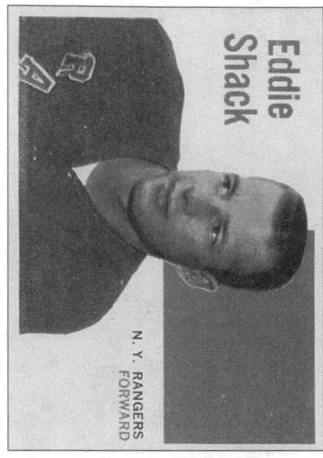

1960-61 TOPPS

	NM
Complete Set (66):	$1,900.00
Common Player:	12.00

		NM
1	Lester Patrick	50.00
14	Stan Mikita	425.00
19	George Vezina	50.00
20	Eddie Shore	60.00
25	Glenn Hall	65.00
58	Bobby Hull	400.00
59	Howie Morenz	50.00

1961-62 PARKHURST

	NM
Complete Set (51):	$1,200.00
Common Player:	10.00

		NM
1	Tim Horton	70.00
2	Frank Mahovlich	70.00
5	Dave Keon	200.00
31	Terry Sawchuk	100.00
35	Boom Boom Geoffrion	50.00
43	Henri Richard	50.00
45	Jean Beliveau	75.00
49	Jacques Plante	100.00
(55)	Unnumbered Checklist	125.00
(56)	Contest card	225.00

1961-62 TOPPS

	NM
Complete Set (66):	$1,550.00
Common Player:	12.00

		NM
29	Bobby Hull	350.00
36	Stan Mikita	180.00
60	Jean Ratelle	135.00
62	Rod Gilbert	135.00
66	Checklist	200.00

1962-63 PARKHURST

	NM
Complete Set (54):	$1,400.00
Common Player:	10.00
Checklist:	250.00
Game Card:	100.00

		NM
4	Frank Mahovich	70.00
15	Dave Keon	80.00
18	Frank Mahovlich	60.00
30	Gordie Howe	300.00
31	Gordie Howe	300.00
39	Jean Beliveau	70.00
49	Jacques Plante	90.00

1962-63 TOPPS

	NM
Complete Sets (66):	$1,250.00
Common Player:	12.00

		NM
33	Bobby Hull	300.00
34	Stan Mikita	125.00
58	Jean Ratelle	50.00
59	Rod Gilbert	50.00
66	Checklist	200.00

1963-64 PARKHURST

	NM
Complete Set (99):	$2,000.00
Common Player:	12.00

		NM
30	Jean Beliveau	75.00
53	Terry Sawchuk	100.00
55	Gordie Howe	350.00
75	Dave Keon	75.00
77	Frank Mahovlich	70.00
89	Jean Beliveau	70.00

1963-64 TOPPS

	NM
Complete Set (66):	$950.00
Common Player:	8.00

		NM
33	Bobby Hull	220.00
45	Jacques Plante	100.00
66	Checklist	125.00

1964-65 TOPPS

		NM
Complete Set (110):		$6,300.00
Common Player (1-55):		17.00
Common Player (56-110):		45.00

		NM
6	Terry Sawchuk	100.00
20	Bobby Hull	275.00
31	Stan Mikita	120.00
33	Jean Beliveau	120.00
54	1st Checklist	100.00
55	2nd Checklist	150.00
58	Tom Williams	200.00
59	Pierre Pilote	240.00
68	Jacques Plante	150.00
71	Eddie Shack	70.00
72	Gary Dornhoefer	220.00
73	Chico Maki	200.00
74	Gilles Villemure	220.00
80	Bobby Rosseau	200.00
82	Red Lindsay	75.00
85	Frank Mahovlich	135.00
89	Gordie Howe	500.00
91	Eric Nesterenko	200.00
92	Marcel Paille	300.00
94	Dave Keon	90.00
98	Bill Hicke	200.00
100	Johnny Bucyk	75.00
102	Tim Horton	125.00

105	Tim Horton	280.00
106	Stan Mikita	275.00
107	Bobby Hull	190.00
110	Glenn Hall	115.00

1965-66 TOPPS

		NM
Complete Set (128):		$2,500.00
Common Player:		7.50

		NM
12	Terry Sawchuk	60.00
21	Ed Giacomin	120.00
31	Gerry Cheevers	120.00
59	Bobby Hull	175.00
60	Stan Mikita	60.00
66	Checklist	100.00
76	Yvan Cournoyer	100.00
108	Gordie Howe	175.00
116	Phil Esposito	400.00
121	Checklist	170.00
122	Gordie Howe	350.00
123	Toronto Maple Leafs team	75.00
124	Chicago Black Hawks	75.00
125	Detroit Red Wings team	80.00
126	Montreal Canadiens team	65.00
127	New York Rangers team	80.00
128	Boston Bruins Team	175.00

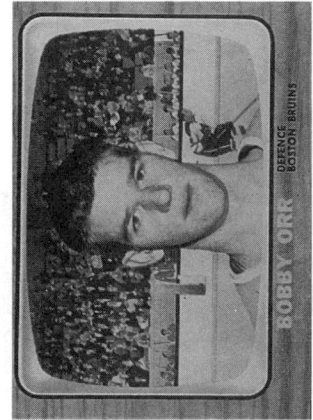

1966-67 TOPPS

		NM
Complete Sets (132):		$4,200.00
Common Player:		6.00
Checklists (66/120):		125.00

		NM
35	Bobby Orr	1750.00
63	Phil Esposito	125.00

64	Bobby Hull	75.00
66	Checklist	95.00
109	Gordie Howe	200.00
112	Bobby Hull	150.00
120	Checklist	125.00
121	Gordie Howe	110.00
125	Bobby Hull	80.00

1967-68 TOPPS

		NM
Complete Set (132):		$2,500.00
Common Player:		6.50
Checklists (66/120):		125.00

		NM
32	Phil Esposito	75.00
33	Derek Sanderson	60.00
43	Gordie Howe	160.00
66	Checklist	125.00
75	Rogatien Vachon	75.00
92	Bobby Orr	800.00
113	Bobby Hull	120.00
118	Calder Trophy Bobby Orr	250.00
120	Checklist	125.00
124	Bobby Hull	70.00
128	Bobby Orr	250.00
131	Gordie Howe	100.00

1968-69 O-PEE-CHEE

		NM
Complete Set (216):		$1,500.00
Common Player:		4.00
All-Stars (199-210):		4.00
Trophy Winners (211-216):		8.00
CL (61/121):		4.00

		NM
2	Bobby Orr	375.00
16	Bobby Hull	90.00
29	Gordie Howe	110.00
89	Bernie Parent	100.00
200	Bobby Orr	160.00
203	Gordie Howe	60.00
204	Bobby Hull	50.00
214	Bobby Orr	160.00

1968-69 TOPPS

		NM
Complete Set (132):		$625.00
Common Player:		2.50
Checklist (121):		40.00

		NM
2	Bobby Orr	200.00
7	Phil Esposito	30.00

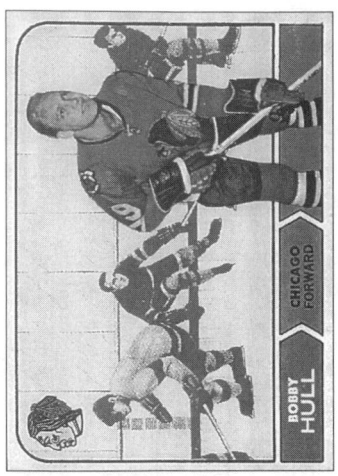

16	Bobby Hull	.60.00
29	Gordie Howe	.75.00
34	Terry Sawchuk	.30.00
89	Bernie Parent	.70.00
121	Checklist	.50.00

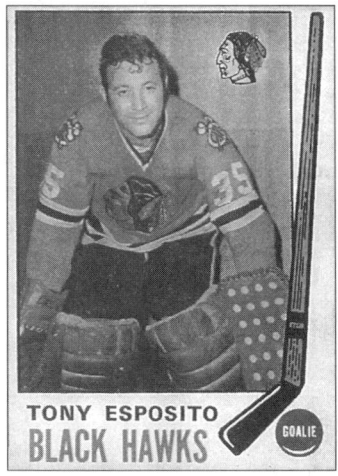

1969-70 O-PEE-CHEE

	NM
Complete Set (231):	.$1,200.00
Common Player:	.3.00
Award Winners (206-231):	.4.00
CL (31/132):	.70.00

		NM
24	Bobby Orr	.175.00
31	Checklist 2	.75.00
61	Gordie Howe	.80.00
70	Bobby Hull	.75.00
138	Tony Esposito	.135.00
193	Gordie Howe	.170.00
209	Bobby Orr	.80.00
212	Bobby Orr	.75.00
215	Gordie Howe	.50.00

1969-70 TOPPS

	NM
Complete Set (132):	.$475.00
Common Player:	.1.75
Checklist:	.50.00

		NM
24	Bobby Orr	.125.00
61	Gordie Howe	.60.00
70	Bobby Hull	.45.00

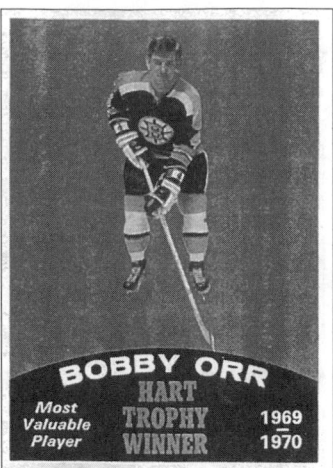

1970-71 O-PEE-CHEE

	NM
Complete Set (264):	.$1,200.00
Common Player:.	.2.50

		NM
3	Bobby Orr	.130.00
15	Bobby Hull	.50.00
29	Gordie Howe	.70.00
67	Brad Park	.50.00
131	Gilbert Perreault	.75.00
153	Tony Esposito	.50.00
195	Bobby Clarke	.130.00
218	Darryl Sittler	.120.00
231	Terry Sawchuk	.50.00
236	Bobby Orr	.55.00
246	Bobby Orr	.60.00
248	Bobby Orr	.55.00
249	Bobby Orr	.55.00
252	Bobby Orr	.50.00

1970-71 TOPPS

	NM
Complete Set (132):	.$425.00
Common Player:	.1.75

		NM
3	Bobby Orr	.75.00
29	Gordie Howe	.50.00
131	Gilbert Perreault	.50.00

1971-72 O-PEE-CHEE

	NM
Complete Set (264):	.$1,400.00
Common Player:	.2.00

45	Ken Dryden	.300.00
111	Checklist	.200.00
133	Marcel Dionne	.150.00
148	Guy Lafleur	.200.00
264	Checklist	.100.00

1971-72 TOPPS

	NM
Complete Set (132):	.$350.00
Common Player:	.1.25
League Leaders:	.1.75
Checklist (111):	.20.00

		NM
45	Ken Dryden	.100.00
70	Gordie Howe	.55.00
100	Bobby Orr	.50.00

1972-73 O-PEE-CHEE

	NM
Complete Set (341):	.$1,200.00
Common Player (1-209):	.1.50
Common Player (210-289):	.4.00
Common Player (290-341):	.7.00
CL (6/19/190):	.30.00
CL (334):	.50.00

		NM
59	Guy Lafleur	.50.00
129	Bobby Orr	.55.00
334	Checklist 3	.50.00
336	Bobby Hull	.55.00

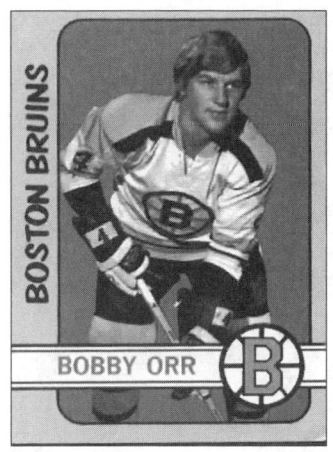

1972-73 TOPPS

	NM
Complete Set (176):	$300.00
Common Player:	1.00
Playoffs (2-7):	2.50
League Leaders (61-65):	1.00
Trophy Cards (170-176):	2.50
Checklist (94):	20.00

	NM
79 Guy Lafleur	22.00
94 Checklist 1-176	20.00
100 Bobby Orr	30.00
122 Bobby Orr	20.00
160 Ken Dryden	30.00

1973-74 O-PEE-CHEE

	NM
Complete Set (264):	$400.00
Common Player:	1.00
Teams (92-107):	2.00
LL (133-138):	2.50
CL (116/129/263):	25.00

	NM
30 Bobby Orr	42.00
142 Billy Smith	40.00
237 Larry Robinson	50.00

1973-74 TOPPS

	NM
Complete Set (198):	$200.00
Common Player:	60
League Leaders (1-4):	1.00
Team Photos (92-107):	2.00
Playoffs (191-198):	2.00

	NM
10 Ken Dryden	33.00
150 Bobby Orr	30.00
162 Billy Smith	25.00

1974-75 O-PEE-CHEE

	NM
Complete Set (396):	$475.00
Common Player:	1.00
Teams:	1.50
CL (54/162/311):	20.00

	NM
54 Checklist 1-132	20.00
100 Bobby Orr	40.00
130 Bobby Orr	25.00
155 Ken Dryden	20.00
161 Don Cherry	25.00
162 Checklist 133-264	20.00
168 Lanny McDonald	27.00
195 Denis Potvin	45.00
232 Guy Lefleur	20.00
248 Bobby Orr	20.00
280 Larry Robinson	20.00
304 Rick Middleton	20.00
316 Steve Shutt	20.00
388 Bob Gainey	20.00

1974-75 O-PEE-CHEE WHA

	NM
Complete Set (66):	$170.00
Common Player:	2.25
CL (53):	20.00

	NM
1 The Howes (Gordie/Mark /Marty)	75.00
50 Bobby Hull	35.00
64 Jacques Plante	35.00

1974-75 TOPPS

	NM
Complete Set (264):	$200.00
Common Player:	35
League Leaders (1-7):	30
All-Stars (127-138):	1.00
Team Leaders:	30
Playoffs (209-216):	1.25
Coach Cards:	30
Team Emblems:	1.00
Checklists (54/162):	8.00

	NM
100 Bobby Orr	25.00
195 Denis Potvin	27.00

1975-76 O-PEE-CHEE

	NM
Complete Set (396):	$265.00
Common Player:	50
CL (99/171):	10.00
CL (267):	15.00

	NM
35 Ken Dryden	$20.00
100 Bobby Orr	40.00
396 Harold Snepsts	20.00

1975-76 O-PEE-CHEE WHA

	NM
Complete Set (132):	$425.00
Common Player:	2.50
All-Stars (62-72):	3.00
CL (131):	20.00

	NM
1 Bobby Hull	$60.00
7 Mark Howe	33.00
34 Jacques Plante	35.00
66 Gordie Howe	30.00
100 Gordie Howe	50.00
132 Checklist	30.00

1975-76 TOPPS

	NM
Complete Set (330):	$170.00
Common Player:	25
Playoffs (1-7):	1.00
Team photos (81-98):	1.50
League Leaders (208-213):	75
All-Stars (286-297):	75

Team Leaders (313-330): 75
Checklists (99/171/267): 7.00

	NM
35 Ken Dryden	12.00
100 Bobby Orr	20.00
126 Guy Lafleur	10.00
288 Bobby Orr	10.00

1976-77 O-PEE-CHEE

	NM
Complete Set (396):	$200.00
Common Player:	.45
Teams (132-149):	1.00
CL (116/258/377):	8.00

	NM
115 Bryan Trottier	50.00
163 Guy Lafleur	12.00
200 Ken Dryden	15.00
213 Bobby Orr	30.00

1976-77 O-PEE-CHEE WHA

	NM
Complete Set (132):	$180.00
Common Player:	1.25
League Leaders (1-6):	1.50
All-Star (61-72):	1.50
Playoffs (130-132):	1.50
CL (117):	8.00

	NM
50 Gordie Howe	35.00
65 Bobby Hull	25.00
72 Gordie Howe	25.00
100 Bobby Hull	30.00

1976-77 TOPPS

	NM
Complete Set (264):	$125.00
Common Player:	.20
League Leaders (1-6):	.20
Record Breakers (65-68):	.20
Team Photos (132-149):	1.25
Checklists (116/258):	5.00

	NM
115 Bryan Trottier	28.00
213 Bobby Orr	18.00

1977-78 O-PEE-CHEE

	NM
Complete Set (396):	140.00
Common Player:	..25

Team Photos (71-88): 50
Playoff (262-264): 50
Team Emblems (322-339): 50
Record Breakers (214-218): 50
Checklists: 5.00

	NM
105 Bryan Trottier	22.00
251 Bobby Orr	30.00

1977-78 O-PEE-CHEE WHA

	NM
Complete Set (66):	$85.00
Common Player:	..75

	NM
1 Gordie Howe	35.00
50 Bobby Hull	20.00

1977-78 TOPPS

	NM
Complete Set (264):	$90.00
Common Player:	.15
League Leaders (1-8):	.15
Record Breakers (214-218):	.15
Playoffs (262-264):	.75
Team Leaders:	.75
Checklists (68/249):	4.00

	NM
100 Ken Dryden	7.00
105 Bryan Trottier	10.00
251 Bobby Orr	15.00

1978-79 O-PEE-CHEE

	NM
Complete Set (396):	$175.00
Common Player:	.35
Checklists:	4.00

	NM
115 Mike Bossy	45.00

1978-79 TOPPS

	NM
Complete Sets (264):	$75.00
Common Player:	.15
Highlights (1-5):	.15
League Leaders (63-70):	.35
Team Photos (192-208):	.75
Playoffs (262-264):	.60
Checklists (24/259):	3.00

	NM
115 Mike Bossy	28.00

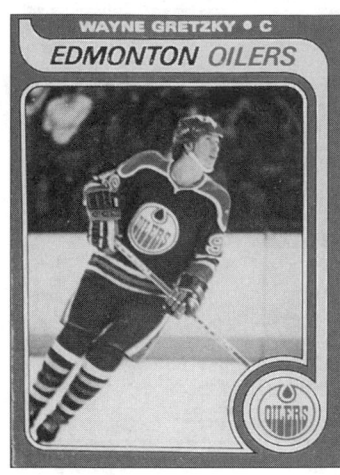

1979-80 O-PEE-CHEE

	NM
Complete Set (396):	$900.00
Commons Player:	.30
Team Photos:	1.00
Checklists:	5.00

	NM
18 Wayne Gretzky	850.00
175 Gordie Howe	30.00
185 Bobby Hull	25.00

1979-80 TOPPS

	NM
Complete Sets (264):	$575.00
Common Player:	.25
League Leaders (1-8):	.35
Playoffs (81-83):	.40
Record Breakers (161-165):	.30
Team Photos (244-260):	..65
Checklists (131/237):	3.00

	NM
18 Wayne Gretzky	400.00
175 Gordie Howe	20.00
185 Bobby Hull	15.00

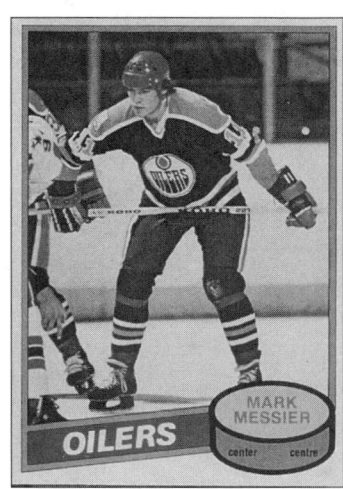

1980-81 O-PEE-CHEE

	NM
Complete Set (396):	$625.00
Common Player:	.35

	NM
87 Wayne Gretzky	45.00
140 Ray Bourque	140.00

250 Wayne Gretzky 125.00
289 Mark Messier 150.00

1980-81 TOPPS

	NM
Complete Set (264):	280.00
Common Player:	.20
Record Breakers (1-5):	.20
Team Leaders:	.25
League Leaders: (161-168):	.25
Playoff (262-264):	.50
Checklists (123/257):	2.00

	NM
140 Ray Bourque	80.00
195 Mike Gartner	18.00
250 Wayne Gretzky	90.00

1981-82 O-PEE-CHEE

	MT
Complete Set (396):	$450.00
Common Player:	.30
Checklists:	4.00
Wax Box:	1250.00

		MT
1	Ray Bourque	30.00
63	Denis Savard	20.00
106	Wayne Gretzky	60.00
107	Jari Kurri	40.00
108	Glenn Anderson	20.00
111	Paul Coffey	85.00
118	Mark Messier	50.00
120	Andy Moog	25.00
125	Wayne Gretzky	25.00
126	Wayne Gretzky	12.00
148	Larry Murphy	15.00
161	Dino Ciccarelli	20.00
269	Peter Stastny	18.00
277	Dale Hunter	10.00
339	Pat Ribble	20.00
347	Mike Gartner	20.00
383	Wayne Gretzky	10.00
384	Wayne Gretzky	10.00
392	Wayne Gretzky	10.00

1981-82 TOPPS

	MT
Complete Set (198):	$80.00
Common Player:	.10
Super Action:	.20
Team Leaders (44-66):	.20
Wax Box:	.90.00

		MT
16	Wayne Gretzky	12.00
75	Denis Savard	12.00
105	Dino Ciccarelli	10.00

1982-83 O-PEE-CHEE

	MT
Complete Set (396):	$130.00
Common Player:	.20
In Action:	.20
Highlights (1-5):	.20
Leaders (235-243):	.20
Team Leaders:	.20
Checklists:	2.50
Wax Box:	225.00

		MT
105	Grant Fuhr	25.00
106	Wayne Gretzky	40.00

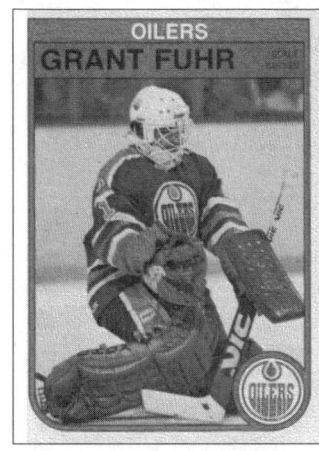

1983-84 O-PEE-CHEE

	MT
Complete Set (396):	$140
Common Player:	.15
Checklists:	2.50
Wax Box:	225.00

		MT
23	Mark Messier, Wayne Gretzky	$25.00
29	Wayne Gretzky	35.00

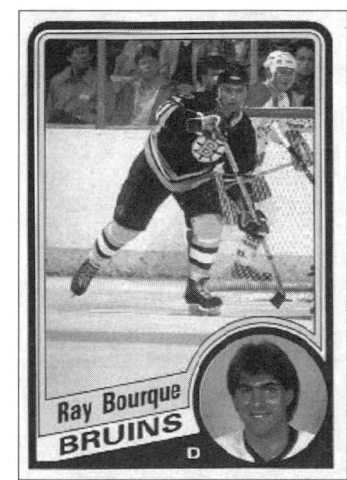

1984-85 O-PEE-CHEE

	MT
Complete Set (396):	$230.00
Common Player:	.15
Team Leaders (352-372):	.20
League Leaders (373-378):	.20
Record Breakers (388-393):	.15
Checklists:	1.00
Wax Box:	600.00

		MT
17	Dave Andreychuk	10.00
18	Tom Barasso	10.00
67	Steve Yzerman	100.00
129	Pat LeFontaine	15.00
185	Doug Gilmour	30.00
243	Wayne Gretzky	18.00
259	Chris Chelios	30.00
327	Cam Neely	10.00

1984-85 TOPPS

	MT
Complete Set (165):	$40.00
Common Player:	.05

Common (Single-print): 20
All-Stars (153-165): 15
Wax Box: 80.00

		MT
49	Steve Yzerman	25.00
51	Wayne Gretzky	8.00

1985-86 O-PEE-CHEE

	MT
Complete Set (264):	$625.00
Common Player:	.25
League Leaders:	.25
Checklists:	2.50
Wax Box:	1200.00

		MT
9	Mario Lemieux	$250.00
29	Steve Yzerman	40.00
120	Wayne Gretzky	25.00
237	Al MacInnis	25.00
262	Mario Lemieux	40.00

1985-86 TOPPS

	MT
Complete Set (165):	$250.00
Common Player:	.15
Common (Single-print):	.25
Wax Box:	550.00

		MT
9	Mario Lemieux	120.00
29	Steve Yzerman	20.00
120	Wayne Gretzky	20.00

1986-87 O-PEE-CHEE

	MT
Complete Set (264):	$325.00
Common Player:	.15
League Leaders:	.15
Checklists:	1.75
Wax Box:	900.00

		MT
3	Wayne Gretzky	20.00
9	John Vanbiesbrouck	20.00
11	Steve Yzerman	20.00
53	Patrick Roy	220.00
122	Mario Lemieux	50.00
149	Wendel Clark	9.00

1986-87 TOPPS

	MT
Complete Set (198):	$160.00
Common Player:	.10

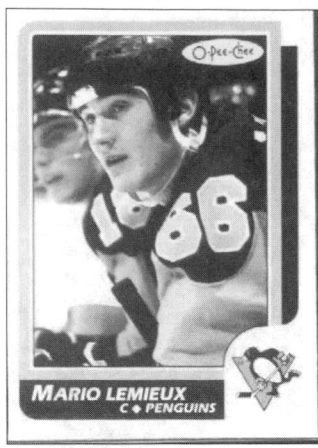

Common (Double-print): 07
Checklists: 25
Wax Box: 325.00

		MT
3	Wayne Gretzky	15.00
9	John Vanbiesbrouck	18.00
11	Steve Yzerman	15.00
53	Patrick Roy	100.00
122	Mario Lemieux	35.00
149	Wendel Clark	15.00

1987-88 O-PEE-CHEE

		MT
Complete Set (264):		$230.00
Common Player:		12
Checklists:		75
Wax Box:		425.00

		MT
2	Rick Tocchet	10.00
13	Bill Ranford	12.00

		MT
15	Mario Lemieux	25.00
36	John Vanbiesbrouck	10.00
42	Luc Robitaille	25.00
53	Wayne Gretzky	20.00
56	Steve Yzerman	10.00
123	Adam Oates	20.00
163	Patrick Roy	50.00
169	Ron Hextall	10.00
215	Mike Vernon	15.00
227	Claude Lemieux	10.00
243	Vincent Damphousse	10.00

1987-88 TOPPS

		MT
Complete Set (198):		$110.00
Common Player:		08
Common (Double-print):		04
Checklists:		25
Wax Box:		200.00

		MT
15	Mario Lemieux	20.00
42	Luc Robitaille	15.00
53	Wayne Gretzky	15.00
163	Patrick Roy	20.00

1988-89 O-PEE-CHEE

		MT
Complete Set (264):		$175.00
Common Player:		15
Checklists:		1.00
Wax Box:		290.00

		MT
66	Brett Hull	55.00
116	Patrick Roy	15.00
120	Wayne Gretzky	18.00
122	Brendan Sanahan	50.00
194	Pierre Turgeon	25.00

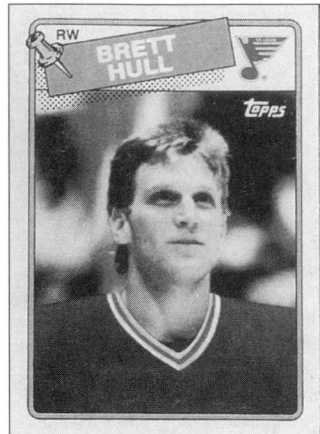

1988-89 TOPPS

		MT
Complete Set (198):		$100.00
Common Player:		07
Common Player (DP):		03
Checklists:		20
Wax Box:		150.00

		MT
66	Brett Hull	25.00
120	Wayne Gretzky	35.00
122	Brendan Shanahan	25.00

1989-90 O-PEE-CHEE

		MT
Complete Set (330):		$20.00
Common Player:		07
Checklists:		12
Team Cards (298-319):		20
Trophy Cards (319-324):		10
Highlights (325-328):		07
Wax Box:		32.00

		MT
113	Joe Sakic	6.00
136	Brian Leetch	3.00
147	Brendan Shanahan	3.00
186	Brett Hull	3.00
232	Theoren Fleury	5.00

1989-90 TOPPS

		MT
Complete Set (198):		$35.00
Common Player:		05
Checklists:		10
Wax Box:		50.00

		MT
89	Trevor Linden	3.50
113	Joe Sakic	12.00
136	Brian Leetch	5.00
147	Brendan Shanahan	5.00
156	Wayne Gretzky	3.50
186	Brett Hull	4.00

Hockey
Hall of Famer Autographs

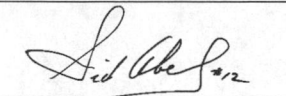

Sid Abel (1918-) 1969
Puck $30
1965-66 Topps card $15
Cut signature . . . .$5-$7
8x10 photograph . . . .$15-$20

Jack Adams (1895-1968) 1959
Puck $35
Hockey card . . . . .Unlikely
Cut signature . . . .$12-$15
8x10 photograph . . . .$35-$50

Syl Apps (1915-1998) 1961
Puck $70
1955-56 Parkhurst card $20
Cut signature . . . .$5-$7
8x10 photograph $70

George Armstrong (1930-) 1975
Puck $35
1970-71 Topps card $15
Cut signature . . . .$5-$7
8x10 photograph $25

Ace Bailey (1903-1992) 1975
Puck $60
1955-56 Parkhurst card $30
Cut signature $10
8x10 photograph $50

Don Bain (1974-1962) 1945
Puck $75
Hockey card . . . . .Unlikely
Cut signature . . . .$15-$20
8x10 photograph . . . .$50-$60

Hobey Baker (1892-1918) 1945
Puck . . . .$60-$70
Hockey card . . . . .Unlikely
Cut signature $15
8x10 photograph $45

Bill Barber (1952-) 1990
Puck $25
1974-75 Topps card $15

Cut signature . . . .$7-$10
8x10 photograph . . . .$15-$20

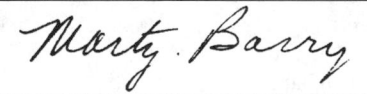

Marty Barry (1905-1969) 1965
Puck $45
Hockey card . . . . .Unlikely
Cut signature . . . .$12-$15
8x10 photograph $35

Andy Bathgate (1932-) 1978
Puck . . . .$25-$30
1968-69 Topps card $15
Cut signature . . . .$6-$11
8x10 photograph . . . .$20-$25

Jean Beliveau (1931-) 1972
Puck . . . .$30-$35
1970-71 Topps card $15
Cut signature . . . .$6-$12
8x10 photograph . . . .$25-$30

Clint Benedict (1894-1976) 1965
Puck . . . .$60-$75
Hockey card . . . . .Unlikely
Cut signature . . . .$15-$18
8x10 photograph . . . .$35-$45

Doug Bentley (1916-1972) 1964
Puck . . . .$45-$50
Hockey card . . . . .Unlikely
Cut signature $15
8x10 photograph . . . .$35-$40

Max Bentley (1920-1984) 1966
Puck . . . .$50-$60
1953-54 Parkhurst card $25
Cut signature . . . .$16-$18
8x10 photograph . . . .$45-$50

Toe Blake (1912-1995) 1966
Puck $45
1966-67 Topps card $15
Cut signature . . . .$12-$15
8x10 photograph $35

Leo Boivin (1932-) 1986
Puck . . . .$30-$35
1964-65 Topps card $15

Cut signature . . . .$5-$10
8x10 photograph . . . .$25-$30

Dickie Boon (1878-1961) 1952
Puck $60
Hockey card . . . . .Unlikely
Cut signature $18
8x10 photograph . . . .$45-$50

Mike Bossy (1957-) 1991
Puck . . . .$35-$40
1980-81 Topps card $20
Cut signature $5
8x10 photograph . . . .$30-$40

Butch Bouchard (1920-) 1966
Puck $25
1955-56 Parkhurst card $9
Cut signature $6
8x10 photograph $20

Frank Boucher (1901-1977) 1958
Puck $50
Hockey card . . . . .Unlikely
Cut signature $15
8x10 photograph . . . .$40-$45

George Boucher (1896-1960) 1960
Puck $65
Hockey card . . . . .Unlikely
Cut signature $18
8x10 photograph $50

John Bower (1924-) 1976
Puck . . . .$25-$30
1968-69 Topps card $12
Cut signature $8
8x10 photograph . . . .$20-$25

Dubbie Bowie (1880-1959) 1945
Puck $60
Hockey card . . . . .Unlikely
Cut signature $18
8x10 photograph $50

Frank Brimsek (1915-) 1966
Puck $25
Hockey card . . . . .Unlikely
Cut signature $7
8x10 photograph . . . .$18-$20

Punch Broadbent (1892-1971) 1962
Puck $45
Hockey card . . . . .Unlikely

Cut signature $17
8x10 photograph . . . .$35-$40

Turk Broda (1914-1972) 1967
Puck $45
Hockey card . . . . .Unlikely
Cut signature . . . .$22-$30
8x10 photograph . . . .$35-$50

John Bucyk (1935-) 1981
Puck . . . .$25-$35
1970-71 Topps card $12
Cut signature $6
8x10 photograph . . . .$20-$25

Billy Burch (1900-1950) 1974
Puck $35
Hockey card . . . . .Unlikely
Cut signature $5
8x10 photograph $20

Harry Cameron (1890-1953) 1962
Puck . . . .$60-$70
Hockey card . . . . .Unlikely
Cut signature $20
8x10 photograph . . . .$50-$60

Gerry Cheevers (1940-) 1985
Puck $40
1971-72 Topps card $12
Cut signature $7
8x10 photograph . . . .$25-$30

King Clancy (1903-1986) 1958
Puck $40
Hockey card . . . . .Unlikely
Cut signature $12
8x10 photograph . . . .$30-$35

Dit Clapper (1907-1978) 1947
Puck . . . .$45-$50
Hockey card . . . . .Unlikely
Cut signature $6
8x10 photograph . . . .$40-$45

Bobby Clarke (1949-) 1987
Puck . . . .$35-$45
1974-75 Topps card $12
Cut signature $6
8x10 photograph . . . .$30-$35

Sprague Cleghorn (1890-1956) 1958
Puck $65
Hockey card . . . . .Unlikely

Cut signature $18
8x10 photograph . . . .$55-$60

Neil Colville (1914-1987) 1967
Puck . . . .$25-$30
Hockey card . . . . .Unlikely
Cut signature $5
8x10 photograph . . . .$20-$25

Charlie Conacher (1909-1967) 1961
Puck . . . .$35-$40
Hockey card . . . . .Unlikely
Cut signature . . . .$6-$8
8x10 photograph . . . .$25-$30

Lionel Conacher (1900-1954) 1994
Puck $55
Hockey card . . . . .Unlikely
Cut signature . . . .$10-$20
8x10 photograph . . . .$35-$45

Roy Gordon Conacher (1916-1984) 1998
Puck . . . .$35-$40
Hockey card . . . . .Unlikely
Cut signature . . . .$6-$8
8x10 photograph . . . .$25-$30

Alex Connell (1902-1958) 1958
Puck $60
Hockey card . . . . .Unlikely
Cut signature $18
8x10 photograph . . . .$45-$50

Bun Cook (1903-1988) 1995
Puck $40
Hockey card . . . . .Unlikely
Cut signature $16
8x10 photograph . . . .$30-$35

William Cook (1896-1986) 1952
Puck $75
Hockey card . . . . .Unlikely
Cut signature $25
8x10 photograph . . . .$55-$60

Art Coulter (1909-) 1974
Puck . . . .$30-$35
Hockey card . . . . .Unlikely
Cut signature $6
8x10 photograph . . . .$25-$30

Yvan Cournoyer (1943-) 1982
Puck $35
1970-71 Topps card $10
Cut signature $5
8x10 photograph . . . .$25-$30

Bill Cowley (1912-) 1968
Puck $50
Hockey card . . . . .Unlikely

Cut signature $7
8x10 photograph . . . .$40-$45

Rusty Crawford (1885-1971) 1962
Puck . . . .$45-$50
Hockey card . . . . .Unlikely
Cut signature $16
8x10 photograph . . . .$40-$45

Jack Darragh (1890-1924) 1962
Puck . . . .$55-$60
Hockey card . . . . .Unlikely
Cut signature $20
8x10 photograph . . . .$45-$50

Scotty Davidson (1890-1915) 1950
Puck $75
Hockey card . . . . .Unlikely
Cut signature $25
8x10 photograph . . . .$50-$60

Hap Day (1901-1990) 1961
Puck . . . .$25-$30
Hockey card . . . . .Unlikely
Cut signature $5
8x10 photograph . . . .$20-$25

Alex Delvecchio (1931-) 1977
Puck . . . .$30-$35
1973-74 Topps card $10
Cut signature $6
8x10 photograph $25

Cy Denneny (1897-1970) 1959
Puck $60
Hockey card . . . . .Unlikely
Cut signature $19
8x10 photograph . . . .$45-$50

Marcel Dionne (1951-) 1992
Puck . . . .$25-$30
Hockey card . . . .$12-$15
Cut signature $7
8x10 photograph . . . .$20-$25

Gordie Drillon (1914-1986) 1975
Puck $60
Hockey card . . . . .Unlikely
Cut signature . . . .$25-$30
8x10 photograph . . . .$45-$50

Graham Drinkwater (1875-1946) 1950
Puck . . . .$75-$80
Hockey card . . . . .Unlikely
Cut signature $25
8x10 photograph . . . .$65-$70

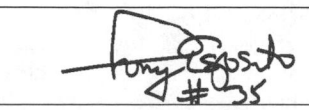

Ken Dryden (1947-) 1983
Puck $65
1972-73 Topps card $40
Cut signature $8
8x10 photograph . . . .$50-$60

Woody Dumart (1916-) 1992
Puck $65
Hockey card . . . . .Unlikely
Cut signature $15
8x10 photograph . . . .$50-$60

Thomas Dunderdale (1887-1960) 1974
Puck . . . .$75-$80
Hockey card . . . . .Unlikely
Cut signature . . . .$25-$30
8x10 photograph . . . .$65-$70

Bill Durnan (1916-1972) 1964
Puck $65
Hockey card . . . . .Unlikely
Cut signature $18
8x10 photograph . . . .$55-$60

Red Dutton (1898-1987) 1958
Puck . . . .$40-$45
Hockey card . . . . .Unlikely
Cut signature $12
8x10 photograph . . . .$30-$35

Babe Dye (1898-1962) 1970
Puck . . . .$70-$80
Hockey card . . . . .Unlikely
Cut signature $18
8x10 photograph . . . .$65-$70

Phil Esposito (1942-) 1984
Puck . . . .$40-$50
1973-74 Topps card $18
Cut signature $6
8x10 photograph . . . .$35-$40

Tony Esposito (1943-) 1988
Puck . . . .$30-$35
1973-74 Topps card $15
Cut signature $6
8x10 photograph . . . .$25-$30

Arthur Farrel (1877-1909) 1965
Puck . . . .$60-$65
Hockey card . . . . .Unlikely
Cut signature . . . .$20-$25
8x10 photograph . . . .$55-$60

Fern Flaman (1927-) 1990
Puck . . . .$25-$30
1990-91 Score card $12
Cut signature $6
8x10 photograph . . . .$20-$25

Frank Foyston (1891-1966) 1958
Puck . . . .$65-$70
Hockey card . . . . .Unlikely
Cut signature $25
8x10 photograph . . . .$55-$60

Frank Frederickson (1895-1979) 1958
Puck $65
Hockey card . . . . .Unlikely
Cut signature . . . .$22-$25
8x10 photograph . . . .$50-$55

Bill Gadsby (1927-) 1970
Puck $25
1965-66 Topps card $12
Cut signature $6
8x10 photograph . . . .$20-$25

Bob Gainey (1953-) 1992
Puck $25
1979-80 Topps card $10
Cut signature $5
8x10 photograph . . . .$20-$25

Chuck Gardiner (1904-1934) 1945
Puck $75
Hockey card . . . . .Unlikely
Cut signature $25
8x10 photograph . . . .$65-$70

Herb Gardiner (1891-1972) 1958
Puck . . . .$50-$60
Hockey card . . . . .Unlikely
Cut signature $18
8x10 photograph . . . .$45-$50

Jimmy Gardner (1881-1940) 1962
Puck . . . .$65-$70
Hockey card . . . . .Unlikely
Cut signature $15
8x10 photograph . . . .$50-$55

Bernie "Boom Boom" Geoffrion (1931-)
1972
Puck . . . .$25-$30
1967-68 Topps card $12
Cut signature $7
8x10 photograph . . . .$20-$25

Eddie Gerard (1890-1937) 1945
Puck . . . .$80-$90
Hockey card . . . . .Unlikely
Cut signature $35
8x10 photograph . . . .$75-$80

Eddie Giacomin (1939-) 1987
Puck . . . .$25-$30
1971-72 Topps card $12
Cut signature $7
8x10 photograph . . . .$20-$25

Rod Gilbert (1941-) 1982
Puck . . . .$25-$30
1971-72 Topps card $12
Cut signature $7
8x10 photograph $25

Billy Gilmour (1885-1959) 1962
Puck . . . .$70-$75
Hockey card . . . . .Unlikely
Cut signature $18
8x10 photograph . . . .$55-$60

Moose Goheen (1894-1979) 1952
Puck . . . .$60-$65
Hockey card . . . . Unlikely
Cut signature $25
8x10 photograph . . . .$50-$55

Michel Goulet (1960-) 1998
Puck . . . .$25-$30
Hockey card . . . .$12-$18
Cut signature . . . .$7-$9
8x10 photograph $25

Ebbie Goodfellow (1907-1985) 1963
Puck $40
Hockey card . . . . Unlikely
Cut signature $15
8x10 photograph . . . .$35-$40

Mike Grant (1874-1955) 1950
Puck . . . .$50-$60
Hockey card . . . . Unlikely
Cut signature $17
8x10 photograph . . . .$45-$50

Wilf Green (1896-1960) 1962
Puck $35
Hockey card . . . . Unlikely
Cut signature $7
8x10 photograph . . . .$25-$30

Wayne Gretzky (1961-) 1999
Puck . . . .$75-$80
Hockey card $35
Cut signature $25
8x10 photograph . . . .$60-$70

Si Griffis (1883-1950) 1950
Puck $90
Hockey card . . . . Unlikely
Cut signature $35
8x10 photograph $65

George Hainsworth (1895-1950) 1961
Puck . . . .$60-$65
Hockey card . . . . Unlikely
Cut signature $18
8x10 photograph . . . .$50-$60

Glenn Hall (1931-) 1975
Puck . . . .$30-$35
1969-70 Topps card $12
Cut signature $7
8x10 photograph . . . .$20-$30

Joe Hall (1882-1919) 1961
Puck $60
Hockey card . . . . Unlikely
Cut signature $8
8x10 photograph . . . .$45-$55

Doug Harvey (1924-1989) 1973
Puck . . . .$55-$60
1952-53 Parkhurst card $15
Cut signature $25
8x10 photograph . . . .$40-$45

George Hay (1898-1975) 1958
Puck . . . .$75-$80
Hockey card . . . . Unlikely
Cut signature $20
8x10 photograph . . . .$65-$70

Riley Hern (1880-1929) 1962
Puck . . . .$60-$70
Hockey card . . . . Unlikely
Cut signature $18
8x10 photograph . . . .$55-$60

Bryan Hextall (1913-1984) 1969
Puck . . . .$60-$70
Hockey card . . . . Unlikely
Cut signature $18
8x10 photograph . . . .$55-$60

Hap Holmes (1889-1940) 1972
Puck $55
Hockey card . . . . Unlikely
Cut signature $15
8x10 photograph . . . .$40-$50

Tom Hooper (1883-1960) 1962
Puck $65
Hockey card . . . . Unlikely
Cut signature $18
8x10 photograph . . . .$50-$55

Red Horner (1909-) 1965
Puck . . . .$25-$30
Hockey card . . . . Unlikely
Cut signature $6
8x10 photograph . . . .$20-$25

Tim Horton (1930-1974) 1977
Puck $300
1954-55 Parkhurst card $150
Cut signature $15
8x10 photograph $300

Gordie Howe (1928-) 1972
Puck . . . .$40-$50
1979-80 Topps card $20
Cut signature $8
8x10 photograph . . . .$35-$40

Sydney Howe (1911-1976) 1965
Puck . . . .$65-$70
Hockey card . . . . Unlikely
Cut signature $20
8x10 photograph . . . .$60-$65

Harry Howell (1932-) 1979
Puck . . . .$25-$30
1970-71 Topps card $10
Cut signature $6
8x10 photograph . . . .$20-$25

Bobby Hull (1939-) 1983
Puck . . . .$35-$40
1979-80 Topps card $15
Cut signature $7
8x10 photograph . . . .$25-$30

J.B. Hutton (1877-1962) 1962
Puck . . . .$50-$60
Hockey card . . . . Unlikely
Cut signature $18
8x10 photograph . . . .$45-$50

Harry Hyland (1889-1969) 1962
Puck . . . .$55-$60
Hockey card . . . . Unlikely
Cut signature $20
8x10 photograph . . . .$50-$55

Dick Irvin (1892-1957) 1958
Puck . . . .$60-$70
Hockey card . . . . Unlikely
Cut signature $25
8x10 photograph . . . .$55-$60

Busher Jackson (1911-1966) 1971
Puck $50
Hockey card . . . . Unlikely

Cut signature $22
8x10 photograph . . . .$45-$50

Ching Johnson (1898-1979) 1958
Puck . . . .$40-$45
Hockey card . . . . .Unlikely
Cut signature $12
8x10 photograph . . . .$35-$40

Ernie Johnson (1886-1963) 1952
Puck . . . .$40-$45
Hockey card . . . . .Unlikely
Cut signature $14
8x10 photograph . . . .$35-$40

Tom Johnson (1928-) 1970
Puck $45
1962-63 Parkhurst card $20
Cut signature $15
8x10 photograph . . . .$40-$45

Aurel Joliat (1901-1986) 1947
Puck $95
Hockey card . . . . .Unlikely
Cut signature $35
8x10 photograph . . . .$85-$90

Duke Keats (1895-1972) 1958
Puck . . . .$60-$65
Hockey card . . . . .Unlikely
Cut signature $25
8x10 photograph . . . .$55-$60

Red Kelly (1927-) 1969
Puck . . . .$25-$30
1967-68 Topps card $12
Cut signature $6
8x10 photograph . . . .$20-$25

Teeder Kennedy (1925-) 1966
Puck $25
1955-56 Parkhurst card $12
Cut signature $6
8x10 photograph . . . .$20-$25

Dave Keon (1940-) 1986
Puck . . . .$25-$30
1969-70 Topps card $12
Cut signature $7
8x10 photograph . . . .$20-$25

Elmer Lach (1918-) 1966
Puck . . . .$25-$30
Hockey card . . . . .Unlikely
Cut signature $6
8x10 photograph . . . .$20-$25

Guy Lafleur (1951) 1988
Puck . . . .$45-$50
1976-77 Topps card $18
Cut signature $6
8x10 photograph . . . .$30-$35

Newsy Lalonde (1887-1971) 1950
Puck . . . .$75-$80
Hockey card . . . . .Unlikely
Cut signature $30
8x10 photograph . . . .$70-$75

Jacques Laperriere (1941-) 1987
Puck $25
1967-68 Topps card $10
Cut signature $5
8x10 photograph . . . .$20-$25

Guy LaPointe (1948-) 1993
Puck $25
Hockey card . . . .$10-$12
Cut signature $5
8x10 photograph . . . .$20-$25

Edgar LaPrade (1919-) 1993
Puck $25
Hockey card $10
Cut signature $5
8x10 photograph $20

Jack Laviolette (1879-1960) 1962
Puck . . . .$40-$50
Hockey card . . . . .Unlikely
Cut signature $12
8x10 photograph . . . .$35-$40

Hugh Lehman (1885-1961) 1958
Puck . . . .$70-$75
Hockey card . . . . .Unlikely
Cut signature $22
8x10 photograph . . . .$55-$60

Jacques Lemaire (1945-) 1984
Puck . . . .$25-$30
1969-70 Topps card $15
Cut signature $5
8x10 photograph . . . .$20-$25

Mario Lemieux (1965-) 1997
Puck . . . .$45-$50
Hockey card . . . .$20-$25
Cut signature $15
8x10 photograph . . . .$35-$40

Percy LeSueur (1881-1962) 1961
Puck . . . .$55-$60
Hockey card . . . . .Unlikely
Cut signature $20
8x10 photograph . . . .$50-$55

Herb Lewis (1907-) 1989
Puck . . . .$50-$55
Hockey card . . . . .Unlikely
Cut signature $20
8x10 photograph . . . .$45-$50

Ted Lindsay (1925-) 1966
Puck . . . .$25-$30
1959-60 Topps card $25
Cut signature $6
8x10 photograph . . . .$20-$25

Harry Lumley (1926-1998) 1980
Puck $30
Hockey card . . . . .Unlikely

Cut signature $10
8x10 photograph . . . .$25-$30

Mickey MacKay (1894-1940) 1952
Puck . . . .$70-$75
Hockey card . . . . .Unlikely
Cut signature $20
8x10 photograph . . . .$55-$60

Frank Mahovlich (1938-) 1981
Puck . . . .$40-$50
1972-73 Topps card $10
Cut signature $7
8x10 photograph . . . .$25-$30

Joe Malone (1890-1969) 1950
Puck $75
Hockey card . . . . .Unlikely
Cut signature $30
8x10 photograph . . . .$65-$70

Sylvio Mantha (1902-1974) 1960
Puck . . . .$35-$40
Hockey card . . . . .Unlikely
Cut signature $12
8x10 photograph . . . .$30-$35

Jack Marshall (1877-1965) 1965
Puck $50
Hockey card . . . . .Unlikely
Cut signature $18
8x10 photograph . . . .$40-$45

Fred Maxwell (1890-1975) 1962
Puck . . . .$55-$60
Hockey card . . . . .Unlikely
Cut signature $20
8x10 photograph . . . .$50-$55

Lanny McDonald (1953-) 1992
Puck $35
1975-76 Topps card $10
Cut signature $5
8x10 photograph . . . .$30-$35

Frank McGee (? -1916) 1945
Puck $100
Hockey card . . . . .Unlikely
Cut signature $40
8x10 photograph . . . .$85-$90

Billy McGimsie (1880-1968) 1962
Puck $70
Hockey card . . . . .Unlikely
Cut signature $20
8x10 photograph . . . .$65-$70

George McNamara (1886-1952) 1958
Puck $60
Hockey card . . . . .Unlikely
Cut signature $15
8x10 photograph $45

Stan Mikita (1940-) 1983
Puck . . . .$25-$30
1972-73 Topps card $10
Cut signature $7
8x10 photograph . . . .$20-$25

Dickie Moore (1931-) 1974
Puck $25
1962-63 Parkhurst card $10
Cut signature $5
8x10 photograph . . . .$20-$25

Paddy Moran (1877-1966) 1958
Puck $65
Hockey card . . . . .Unlikely
Cut signature $18
8x10 photograph . . . .$55-$60

Howie Morenz (1902-1937) 1945
Puck $450
Hockey card . . . . .Unlikely
Cut signature $200
8x10 photograph $450

Bill Mosienko (1921-1994) 1965
Puck . . . .$35-$40
Hockey card . . . . .Unlikely
Cut signature $10
8x10 photograph . . . .$30-$35

Frank Nighbor (1893-1966) 1947
Puck $85
Hockey card . . . . .Unlikely
Cut signature $30
8x10 photograph . . . .$75-$80

Reg Noble (1895-1962) 1962
Puck $65
Hockey card . . . . .Unlikely
Cut signature $18
8x10 photograph . . . .$55-$60

Buddy O'Connor (1916-1977) 1988
Puck $50
Hockey card . . . . .Unlikely
Cut signature $18
8x10 photograph $45

Harry Oliver ((1898-1985) 1967
Puck $55
Hockey card . . . . .Unlikely
Cut signature $20
8x10 photograph . . . .$45-$50

Bert Olmstead (1926-) 1985
Puck . . . .$20-$25
1961-62 Parkhurst card $10
Cut signature $5
8x10 photograph . . . .$20-$25

Bobby Orr (1948-) 1979
Puck . . . .$75-$80
1973-74 Topps card $35
Cut signature $25
8x10 photograph $60

Bernie Parent (1945-) 1984
Puck . . . .$25-$30
1973-74 Topps card $12
Cut signature $6
8x10 photograph . . . .$20-$25

Brad Park (1948-) 1988
Puck . . . .$25-$35
1972-73 Topps card $12
Cut signature $6
8x10 photograph . . . .$20-$25

Lester Patrick (1883-1960) 1947
Puck . . . .$95-$100
Hockey card . . . . .Unlikely
Cut signature $35
8x10 photograph . . . .$85-$90

Lynn Patrick (1912-1980) 1980
Puck . . . .$95-$100
Hockey card . . . . .Unlikely
Cut signature $35
8x10 photograph . . . .$85-$90

Gil Perreault (1950-) 1990
Puck . . . .$25-$35
1973-74 Topps card $10

Cut signature $6
8x10 photograph . . . .$20-$25

Tommy Phillips (1880-1923) 1945
Puck . . . .$75-$80
Hockey card . . . . .Unlikely
Cut signature $30
8x10 photograph . . . .$70-$75

Pierre Pilote (1931-) 1975
Puck . . . .$25-$30
1968-69 Topps card $10
Cut signature $6
8x10 photograph . . . .$20-$25

Didier Pitre (1883-1934) 1962
Puck $75
Hockey card . . . . .Unlikely
Cut signature $20
8x10 photograph . . . .$60-$70

Jacques Plante (1929-1986) 1978
Puck $175
1958-59 Topps card $250
Cut signature $25
8x10 photograph $300

Denis Potvin (1953-) 1991
Puck . . . .$25-$30
1975-76 Topps card $15
Cut signature $5
8x10 photograph . . . .$20-$25

Babe Pratt (1916-1988) 1966
Puck $35
Hockey card . . . . .Unlikely
Cut signature $15
8x10 photograph $35

Joe Primeau (1906-1989) 1963
Puck $50
Hockey card . . . . .Unlikely
Cut signature $25
8x10 photograph $50

Marcel Pronovost (1930-) 1978
Puck $25
1967-68 Topps card $10
Cut signature $6
8x10 photograph . . . .$20-$25

Bob Pulford (1936-) 1991
Puck $50
1960-61 Parkhurst card $30

Cut signature $20
8x10 photograph $45

Harvey Pulford (1875-1940) 1945
Puck $65
Hockey card . . . . .Unlikely
Cut signature $20
8x10 photograph . . . .$55-$60

Bill Quackenbush (1922-1999) 1976
Puck . . . .$30-$35
Hockey card . . . . .Unlikely
Cut signature $5
8x10 photograph . . . .$20-$25

Frank Rankin (1889-1932) 1961
Puck . . . .$70-$80
Hockey card . . . . .Unlikely
Cut signature $18
8x10 photograph $65

Jean Ratelle (1940-) 1985
Puck . . . .$25-$35
1969-70 Topps card $10
Cut signature $5
8x10 photograph . . . .$20-$25

Chuck Rayner (1920-) 1973
Puck . . . .$25-$30
Hockey card . . . . .Unlikely
Cut signature $6
8x10 photograph . . . .$20-$25

Ken Reardon (1921-) 1966
Puck . . . .$35-$40
Hockey card . . . . .Unlikely
Cut signature $5
8x10 photograph . . . .$25-$30

Henri Richard (1936-) 1979
Puck $25
1969-70 Topps card $10
Cut signature $6
8x10 photograph . . . .$20-$25

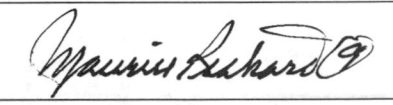

Maurice Richard (1921-2000) 1961
Puck . . . .$35-$40
1955-56 Parkhurst $75
Cut signature $8
8x10 photograph . . . .$30-$35

George Richardson (1887-1916) 1950
Puck . . . .$95-$100
Hockey card . . . . .Unlikely
Cut signature $35
8x10 photograph . . . .$85-$90

Gordie Roberts (1891-1966) 1971
Puck $70
Hockey card . . . . .Unlikely
Cut signature $18
8x10 photograph . . . .$65-$70

Larry Robinson (1951-) 1995
Puck . . . .$25-$30
Hockey card $10
Cut signature $5
8x10 photograph . . . .$20-$25

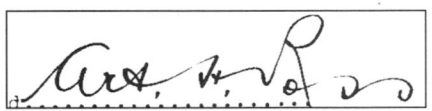

Art Ross (1886-1964) 1945
Puck . . . .$70-$75
Hockey card . . . . .Unlikely
Cut signature $25
8x10 photograph . . . .$55-$60

Blair Russel (1880-1961) 1965
Puck . . . .$40-$45
Hockey card . . . . .Unlikely
Cut signature $15
8x10 photograph . . . .$35-$40

Ernie Russell (1883-1963) 1965
Puck $65
Hockey card . . . . .Unlikely
Cut signature $18
8x10 photograph . . . .$55-$60

Jack Ruttan (1889-1973) 1962
Puck $70
Hockey card . . . . .Unlikely
Cut signature $25
8x10 photograph $65

Borje Salming (1951-) 1996
Puck $25
Hockey card $10
Cut signature $5
8x10 photograph . . . .$20-$25

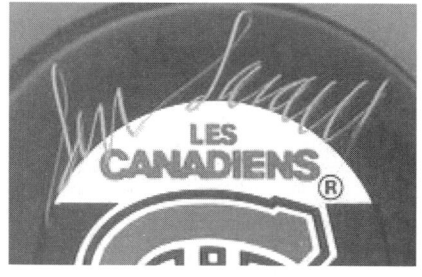

Serge Savard (1946-) 1986
Puck . . . .$25-$30
1970-71 Topps card $10
Cut signature $5
8x10 photograph . . . .$20-$25

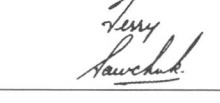

Terry Sawchuck (1929-1970) 1971
Puck $300
1953-54 Parkhurst card $250
Cut signature $30
8x10 photograph $300

Fred Scanlan (? - ?) 1965
Puck $65
Hockey card . . . . .Unlikely
Cut signature $18
8x10 photograph . . . .$50-$60

Milt Schmidt (1918-) 1961
Puck $25
1965-66 Topps card $10

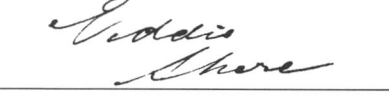

Cut signature $6
8x10 photograph . . . .$20-$25

Sweeney Schriner (1911-1990) 1962
Puck $65
Hockey card . . . . .Unlikely
Cut signature $20
8x10 photograph . . . .$55-$60

Earl Seibert (1911-1990) 1963
Puck $25
Hockey card . . . . .Unlikely
Cut signature $6
8x10 photograph . . . .$20-$25

Oliver Seibert (1881-1944) 1961
Puck . . . .$90-$100
Hockey card . . . . .Unlikely
Cut signature $30
8x10 photograph . . . .$70-$75

Eddie Shore (1902-1985) 1947
Puck $200
Hockey card . . . . .Unlikely
Cut signature $25
8x10 photograph $65

Steve Shutt (1952-) 1993
Puck $25
1975-76 Topps card $10
Cut signature $5
8x10 photograph . . . .$20-$25

Babe Siebert (1904-1939) 1964
Puck $65
Hockey card . . . . .Unlikely
Cut signature $20
8x10 photograph . . . .$55-$60

Joe Simpson (1893-1973) 1962
Puck . . . .$60-$70
Hockey card . . . . .Unlikely
Cut signature $20
8x10 photograph . . . .$55-$60

Darryl Sittler (1950) 1989
Puck $25
1974-75 Topps card $10
Cut signature $5
8x10 photograph . . . .$20-$25

Alfred Smith (1873-1953) 1962
Puck $65
Hockey card . . . . .Unlikely
Cut signature $20
8x10 photograph . . . .$55-$60

Billy Smith (1950-) 1993
Puck . . . .$25-$30
1974-75 Topps card $10
Cut signature $5
8x10 photograph . . . .$22-$25

Clint Smith (1913-) 1991
Puck $25
Hockey card . . . . .Unlikely
Cut signature $5
8x10 photograph . . . .$15-$20

Hooley Smith (1903-1963) 1972
Puck $50
Hockey card . . . . .Unlikely
Cut signature $18
8x10 photograph . . . .$45-$50

Tommy Smith (1885-1966) 1973
Puck $50
Hockey card . . . . .Unlikely
Cut signature $15
8x10 photograph . . . .$45-$50

Allan Stanley (1926-) 1981
Puck $25
1967-68 Topps card $10
Cut signature $5
8x10 photograph . . . .$20-$25

Barney Stanley (1893-1971) 1962
Puck . . . .$35-$40
Hockey card . . . . .Unlikely
Cut signature $15
8x10 photograph . . . .$30-$35

Peter Stastny (1956-) 1998
Puck . . . .$20-$25
Hockey card $10
Cut signature $6
8x10 photograph $20

Jack Stewart (1917-1983) 1964
Puck $40
Hockey card . . . . .Unlikely
Cut signature $15
8x10 photograph . . . .$35-$40

Nels Stewart (1902-1957) 1962
Puck . . . .$70-$75
Hockey card . . . . .Unlikely
Cut signature $22
8x10 photograph . . . .$55-$60

Bruce Stuart (1882-1961) 1961
Puck $65
Hockey card . . . . .Unlikely
Cut signature $20
8x10 photograph . . . .$50-$60

Cyclone Taylor (1883-1979) 1947
Puck $60
Hockey card . . . . .Unlikely
Cut signature $18
8x10 photograph . . . .$50-$55

Fred Taylor (? - 1907) 1947
Puck $65
Hockey card . . . . .Unlikely
Cut signature $18
8x10 photograph . . . .$50-$60

Tiny Thompson (1905-1981) 1959
Puck . . . .$70-$75
Hockey card . . . . .Unlikely
Cut signature $20
8x10 photograph . . . .$65-$70

Vladislav Tretiak (1952-) 1989
Puck . . . .$65-$75
Hockey card . . . . .Unlikely

Cut signature $22
8x10 photograph . . . .$60-$70

Harry Trihey (1877-1942) 1950
Puck $75
Hockey card . . . . .Unlikely
Cut signature $30
8x10 photograph . . . .$65-$70

Bryan John Trottier (1956-) 1997
Puck $25
Hockey card . . . .$10-$12
Cut signature $6
8x10 phoptograph . . . .$20-$25

Norm Ullman (1935-) 1982
Puck $25
1968-69 Topps card $10
Cut signature $6
8x10 photograph . . . .$20-$25

Georges Vezina (1887-1926) 1945
Puck $250
Hockey card . . . . .Unlikely
Cut signature $100
8x10 photograph $250

Jack Walker (1888-1950) 1960
Puck . . . .$65-$70
Hockey card . . . . .Unlikely
Cut signature $20
8x10 photograph . . . .$60-$65

Marty Walsh (1883-1915) 1962
Puck $75
Hockey card . . . . .Unlikely
Cut signature $25
8x10 photograph . . . .$65-$70

Harry Watson (1898-1957) 1962
Puck $75
Hockey card . . . . .Unlikely
Cut signature $25
8x10 photograph $65

Cooney Weiland (1904-1985) 1971
Puck . . . .$60-$65
Hockey card . . . . .Unlikely
Cut signature $22
8x10 photograph $55

Harry Westwick (1876-1957) 1962
Puck $75
Hockey card . . . . .Unlikely
Cut signature $25
8x10 photograph $65

Fred Whitcroft (1882-1931) 1962
Puck $75
Hockey card . . . . .Unlikely
Cut signature $25
8x10 photograph $65

Gordon Wilson (1895-1970) 1962
Puck . . . .$55-$60
Hockey card . . . . .Unlikely
Cut signature $15
8x10 photograph . . . .$50-$55

Gump Worsley (1929-)1980
Puck $30
1968-69 Topps card $15
Cut signature $10
8x10 photograph . . . .$25-$30

Roy Worters (1900-1957) 1969
Puck . . . .$60-$70
Hockey card . . . . .Unlikely
Cut signature $18
8x10 photograph . . . .$50-$60

Hockey Equipment

Hall of Fame Goaltenders

Goaltender	Stick	Jersey
Johnny Bower	$350	$3,000
Gerry Cheevers	300	2,500
Ken Dryden	325	2,850
Tony Esposito	300	2,750
Eddie Giacomin	300	2,600
Glenn Hall	350	3,200
Bernie Parent	300	2,500
Jacques Plante (Mont.)	425	5,500
Jacques Plante (others)	400	4,500

Hall of Fame Players

Player	Skates	Stick	Jersey
Bill Barber	$350	$200	$1,750
Andy Bathgate	500	225	2,250
Jean Beliveau	1,500	275	3,250
Leo Bolvin	800	200	2,250
Mike Bossy	625	200	2,250
John Bucyk	525	200	2,000
Bobby Clarke	600	300	2,500
Yvan Cournoyer	600	300	2,400
Alex Delvecchio	1,200	325	2,250
Marcel Dionne	1,400	250	2,300
Phil Esposito	2,550	400	4,500
Fern Flaman	1,400	275	3,000
Bill Gadsby	500	225	2,250
Boom Boom Geoffrion	950	300	3,500
Rod Gilbert	725	250	2,400
Wayne Gretzky	2,500	650	9,000
Doug Harvey	800	225	2,450
Bryan Hextall	1,200	350	3,500
Tim Horton	800	225	2,300
Gordie Howe (Detroit)	2,000	850	8,500
Gordie Howe (Hartford)	1,600	425	6,500
Harry Howell	550	225	2,200
Bobby Hull	1,850	600	8,000
Red Kelly	900	225	2,350
Dave Keon	650	225	2,200
Guy Lafleur	725	325	2,650
Jacques Laperriere	500	180	2,200
Mario Lemieux	1,500	375	5,500
Jacques Lemaire	550	200	2,300
Ted Lindsay	1,200	325	3,500
Frank Mahovlich	850	250	2,300
Stan Mikita	1,400	375	4,500
Dickie Moore	600	250	2,250
Buddy O'Connor	950	325	3,250
Bert Olmstead	850	250	3,000
Bobby Orr	1,200	700	7,500
Brad Park	575	210	2,250
Gil Perreault	650	250	2,300
Pierre Pilote	550	225	2,250
Denis Potvin	600	200	2,200
Marcel Pronovost	525	225	2,250
Bob Pulford	500	200	2,200
Bill Quackenbush	850	275	3,100
Jean Ratelle	750	250	2,400
Henri Richard	750	250	2,600
Maurice Richard	1,600	575	6,500
Larry Robinson	350	200	1,750
Borje Salming	400	225	1,950

Wayne Gretzky skates

Player	Skates	Stick	Jersey
Serge Savard	550	100	1,350
Darryl Sittler	550	125	1,250
Clint Smith	775	225	2,250
Allan Stanley	400	225	1,950
Peter Stastny	550	225	2,250
Bryan Trottier	600	225	2,450
Norm Ullman	500	225	2,250
Gump Worsley	360	225	1,850

Inactive Players

Player	Skates	Stick	Jersey
Glenn Anderson	$300	$180	$825
Brian Bellows	350	185	625
Pat Falloon	275	160	475
Johan Garpenlov	275	140	450
Mike Gartner	375	190	675
Dale Hawerchuk	325	180	850
Ken Hodge Jr.	300	165	625
Craig Janney	300	160	600
Petr Klima	300	175	675
Jari Kurri	625	225	1,900
Pat LaFontaine	450	200	1,200
Steve Larmer	400	185	900
Stephan Lebeau	250	140	425
Sergei Makarov	250	140	450
Cam Neely	625	250	1,675
Brian Propp	300	175	675
Robert Reichel	290	160	625
Tomas Sandstrom	425	185	1,000
Denis Savard	380	180	825
Peter Stastny	325	175	800
Esa Tikkanen	325	180	725
Darren Turcotte	280	150	475

Active Players

Player	Skates	Stick	Jersey
Tony Amonte	$325	$175	$650
Peter Bondra	280	150	450
Ray Bourque	800	325	2,200
Pavel Bure	325	185	850
Chris Chelios	375	185	1,200
Paul Coffey	800	250	2,400
Ulf Dahlen	400	275	900
Vin Damphousse	300	175	650
Ted Donato	300	175	675
Sergei Fedorov	375	200	1,525
Theoren Fleury	325	175	660
Peter Forsberg	300	175	675
Ron Francis	325	200	1,000
Martin Gelinas	250	140	425
Doug Gilmour	325	175	700
Alexei Gusarov	250	145	450
Dominek Hasek	650	300	1,750
Bobby Holik	300	170	650
Phil Housley	325	180	800
Brett Hull	1,500	375	2,500

Player	Skates	Stick	Jersey
Jaromir Jagr	350	185	825
Joe Juneau	325	175	700
Valeri Kamensky	300	170	675
Paul Kariya	700	350	1,850
Dimitri Khristich	300	165	625
Trevor Kidd	275	150	450
Robert Kron	250	140	450
Brian Leetch	290	300	975
Nicklas Lidstrom	325	175	650
Trevor Linden	300	175	650
Al Macinnis	700	250	1,800
Stephane Matteau	250	145	460
Mark Messier	900	350	2,500
Kip Miller	260	145	470
Mike Modano	265	150	475
Alex Mogilny	265	145	470
Kirk Muller	375	180	825
Petr Nedved	280	150	485
Sergei Nemchinov	275	145	450
Scott Niedermayer	290	165	600
Joe Nieuwendyk	450	190	1,000
Owen Nolan	325	165	1,050
Adam Oates	600	240	1,650
Chris Osgood	280	150	500
Oleg Petrov	300	175	450
Derek Plante	225	125	400
Felix Potvin	250	175	500
Keith Primeau	265	145	450
Bob Probert	325	175	950
Chris Pronger	250	160	550
Mark Recchi	300	160	650
Mike Ricci	300	160	640
Luc Robitaille	625	250	1,675
Jeremy Roenick	325	180	675
Joe Sakic	450	195	1,050
Sergei Samsonov	300	225	950
Teemu Selanne	425	200	1,500
Brendan Shanahan	325	190	750
Peter Skudra	300	175	500
Kevin Stevens	350	180	425
Scott Stevens	300	175	675
Mats Sundin	290	160	500
Jocelyn Thibault	250	165	450
Keith Tkachuk	225	160	400
Rick Tocchet	250	170	450
Ron Tugnutt	235	175	550
Pierre Turgeon	325	175	675
Pat Verbeek	250	170	575
Doug Weight	280	145	460
Eric Weinrich	250	140	550
Alexei Yashin	240	150	450
Steve Yzerman	775	250	1,925

Active Goaltenders

Goaltender	Stick	Jersey
Ed Belfour	$250	$1,450
Martin Brodeur	200	1,000
Bob Essensa	150	800
Kirk McLean	145	625
Mike Richter	175	1,050
Patrick Roy	250	1,900
Chris Terreri	145	675
John Vanbiesbrouck	140	625
Mike Vernon	145	800

Hockey Media Guides

Anaheim Mighty Ducks
1993-94 Inaugural season $12
1994-95 Guy Hebert goalie mask $8
1995-96 O. Tverdovsky/P. Kaiya $8
1996-97 P. Kariya/T. Selanne $8
1997-98 Crowd scenes/players celebrating $8
1998-99 P. Kariya/T. Selanne $8

Boston Bruins
1946-47 . . . .$150
1947-48 . . . .$125
1948-49 . . . .$100
1949-50 . . . .$75
1950-51 . . . .$50
1951-52 Team logo and year $50
1952-53 Bear's head artwork $50
1953-54 Bear's head artwork $50
1954-55 Bear's head artwork $50
1955-56 Bruins name and year $50
1956-57 Bruins name and year $50
1957-58 Bruins name and year $50
1958-59 Bruins name and year $50
1959-60 Bear cartoon $40
1960-61 Bruin cartoon $30
1961-62 Bruins mascot and year $30
1962-63 Wayne Connelly $30
1963-64 John Bucyk $75
1964-65 Gary Dornhofer, Bobby Leiter $50
1965-66 Ed Johnston $50
1966-67 Murray Oliver $45
1967-68 Bobby Orr $60
1968-69 Bruins action vs. Montreal $45
1969-70 Esposito/ Hodge vs. Blackhawks $45
1970-71 Bruins vs. Blackhawks $45
1971-72 Pregame anthems with Montreal $40
1972-73 Stanley Cup trophy $40
1973-74 50th Anniversary w/ Esposito, Orr $30
1974-75 John Bucyk $30
1975-76 Terry O'Reilly $25
1976-77 Don Cherry/ Park/ Ratelle $25
1977-78 Gerry Cheevers $25
1978-79 Bob Schmautz $15
1979-80 Rick Middleton $15
1980-81 Ray Bourque $12
1981-82 Wayne Cashman $12
1982-83 Steve Kasper with Selke Trophy $9
1983-84 60th Anniversary, Peter Peeters
    with Vezina Trophy $9
1984-85 Barry Pederson $9

1985-86 Bruins hockey pucks $9
1986-87 Gord Kluzak $9
1987-88 Ray Bourque with Norris Trophy . . .$9
1988-89 Cam Neely $9
1989-90 Rejean Lemelin, Andy Moog $9
1990-91 Team artwork $9
1991-92 Ray Bourque $9
1992-93 Fred Cusick $9
1993-94 Adam Oates $9
1994-95 "Thanks for the Memories" $8
1995-96 M. Czerkawski/J. Rohloff/B. Lacher . .$7
1996-97 T. Donato/R. Bourque/others $7
1997-98 Ray Bourque $7
1998-99 Bruins' Calder Trophy winners $7

Buffalo Sabres
1970-71 Team logo and year $85
1971-72 Action photo $30
1972-73 Roger Crozier $25
1973-74 Gil Perreault $25
1974-75 Richard Martin $20
1975-76 Rene Robert $20
1976-77 Danny Gare $15
1977-78 Gerry Desjardins $15
1978-79 Don Edwards $10
1979-80 Craig Ramsay $9
1980-81 Danny Gare $9
1981-82 Danny Gare, others $9
1982-83 Gil Perreault $9
1983-84 Mike Ramsey $9
1984-85 Tom Barrasso $9
1985-86 Tom Barrasso, Bob Sauve $9
1986-87 Sabres in action $9
1987-88 Team logo and bench $9
1988-89 Tom Barrasso $9
1989-90 Phil Housley $9
1990-91 Pierre Turgeon $9
1991-92 Dave Andreychuk $9
1992-93 Pat LaFontaine $9
1993-94 LaFontaine/Hasek/Mogilny/May . . .$9
1994-95 25th Anniversary logo $7
1995-96 Memorabilia collage $7
1996-97 Sabres logo on jersey $7
1997-98 M. Barnaby/D. Audette/D. Hasek . . .$7
1998-99 Dominick Hasek $7

Calgary/Atlanta Flames
Atlanta Flames
1972-73 Team logo $45
1973-74 Team logo, Phil Myre $35
1974-75 Flames and Flyers fighting $30
1975-76 Team logo, photos $20
1976-77 Daniel Bouchard $20
1977-78 Tom Lysiak, Willi Plett, Eric Vail $20
1978-79 Team uniform, puck, equipment $20
1979-80 Guy Chouinard $20

Calgary Flames
1980-81 Team logo $20
1981-82 Kent Nilsson $12
1982-83 Team logo $6
1983-84 Lanny McDonald $10
1984-85 Lanny McDonald $10
1985-86 Goalie gloves a puck $8
1986-87 Campbell Conference trophy $9
1987-88 Joe Mullen $9
1988-89 Hakan Loob, Joe Nieuwendyk $9
1989-90 Stanley Cup trophy $9
1990-91 Al MacInnis, Sergei Makarov $9
1991-92 . . . .$9
1992-93 Gary Roberts $9
1993-94 Art of Flames celebrating $9
1994-95 Olympic Saddledome $8
1995-96 Trevor Kidd action photo $6
1996-97 G. Roberts with Masterton Trophy $6
1997-98 Collage of "Young Guns" $6
1998-99 V. Bure, J. Wiemer, others $6

Carolina Hurricanes

1997-98 . . . .$7
1998-99 Trevor Kidd $6

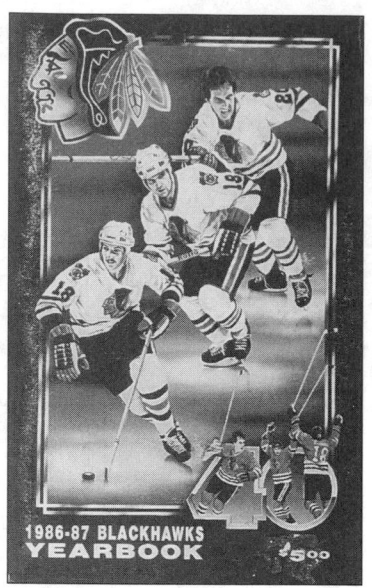

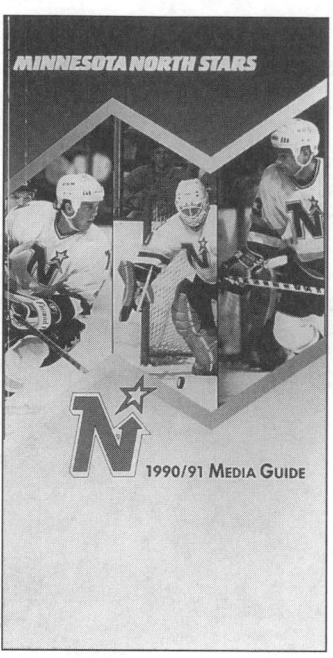

Chicago Blackhawks

1960-61 . . . .$75
1961-62 . . . .$50
1962-63 . . . .$45
1963-64 Team logo and year $45
1964-65 . . . .$45
1965-66 Team logo and year $45
1966-67 . . . .$45
1967-68 B. Hull, S. Mikita, A. Wirtz $45
1968-69 B. Hull, S. Mikita, W. Wirtz $45
1969-70 Team logo and year $30
1970-71 Team mascot, Wales Trophy $30
1971-72 Team logo and year, Western Division
Champions $30
1972-73 Team mascot $25
1973-74 Team logo, artwork $25
1974-75 Team artwork $25
1975-76 50th Anniversary artwork $25
1976-77 Team logo and year $15
1977-78 Team logo, artwork $15
1978-79 Team logo and crossed sticks $15
1979-80 Team logo $15
1980-81 Tony Esposito, others $12
1981-82 Denis Savard, Darryl Sutter $12
1982-83 Doug Wilson and Norris Trophy . . .$4
1983-84 Celebration photos $9
1984-85 Denis Savard, Al Secord, others . . .$9
1985-86 Chicago has Fans slogan $9
1986-87 R. Murray, D. Savard, Al Secord . . .$9
1987-88 Bob Murdock/ other coaches $9
1988-89 Denis Savard photos and locker $9
1989-90 Celebration photos $9
1990-91 All-Star Game logo $9
1991-92 J. Roenick/C. Chelios/others $9
1992-93 Action photos $9
1993-94 Chicago Stadium art $6
1994-95 Logo from draped uniform $6
1995-96 Logo and "Cold Steel on Ice" $6
1996-97 Chris Chelios $6
1997-98 Tony Amonte $6
1998-99 Blackhawks logo $6

Colorado Avalanche

1995-96 Avalanche logos $7
1996-97 Stanley Cup, Denver skyline $7
1997-98 Closeup of team logo on jersey $7
1998-99 Mountain scene with avalanche . . .$7

Colorado Rockies

1976-77 Team logo $40
1977-78 Mountains photo, team logo $35
1978-79 Mountains, stream, team logo $25
1979-80 Don Cherry $25
1980-81 Lanny McDonald $30
1981-82 Action photos, team logo $40
Became New Jersey Devils in 1982-83

Dallas Stars

As Minnesota North Stars
1967-68 Team logo $35
1968-69 Cesare Maniago $35
1969-70 Danny Grant, Calder Trophy $35
1970-71 Danny O'Shea $25
1971-72 North Stars vs. Boston Bruins $25
1972-73 Cesare Maniago/G. Worsley $25
1973-74 Dennis Hextall $25
1974-75 Bill Goldsworthy $20
1975-76 North Stars in action $15
1976-77 North Stars vs. Calgary Flames . . .$15
1977-78 R. Eriksson, S. Jensen, A. Pirus, ...
 G. Sharpley $15
1978-79 North Stars uniforms $15
1979-80 Action artwork $12
1980-81 Al MacAdam, Steve Payne $12
1981-82 Don Beaupre, others $12

1982-83 Celebrating vs. St. Louis Blues $9
1983-84 John Mariucci artwork $9
1984-85 Neal Broten $9
1985-86 A. Shaver, action photos $9
1986-87 Neal Broten with trophies $9
1987-88 Dino Ciccarelli $9
1988-89 Celebration photo $9
1989-90 Player in action $9
1990-91 B. Bellows, N. Broten, J. Casey $9
1991-92 Memorabilia $9
1992-93 . . . .$9

As Dallas Stars
1993-94 Artwork of Dallas city skyline $12
1994-95 Mike Modano illustration $8
1995-96 Andy Moog $6
1996-97 J. Nieuwendyk, M. Modano $6
1997-98 Spotlighted logo, action photos $6
1998-99 President's Trophy $6

Detroit Red Wings

1960-61 Cartoon $125
1961-62 . . . .$100
1962-63 Team logos $100
1963-64 . . . .$100
1964-65 . . . .$75
1965-66 . . . .$75
1966-67 R. Crozier, A. Delvecchio, G. Howe . .$75
1967-68 . . . .$65
1968-69 Gordie Howe $65
1969-70 . . . .$50
1970-71 Gordie Howe $50
1971-72 Alex Delvecchio $30
1972-73 Alex Delvecchio $30
1973-74 A. Delvecchio, M. Redmond $30
1974-75 Alex Delvecchio $20
1975-76 Goalie mask $20
1976-77 50th Anniversary photos $15
1977-78 Goalie mask, logos $15
1978-79 Action photos with headlines $15
1979-80 Olympia Stadium, Joe Louis Arena . .$15
1980-81 Red Wings in action $15
1981-82 Reed Larson $15
1982-83 Team artwork $9
1983-84 Goalie net, team jersey $9
1984-85 Team logo, action photos $9
1985-86 John Ogrodnick $9
1986-87 J. Demers, P. Klima, S. Yzerman . . .$9
1987-88 J. Demers, celebration photos $9

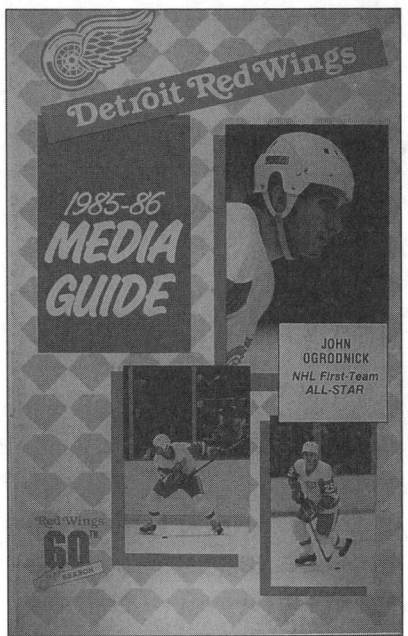

1988-89 J. Demers, G. Gallant, S. Yzerman $9
1989-90 Team logo and management $9
1990-91 Shawn Burr, Steve Yzerman $9
1991-92 S. Fedorov, M. Ilitch $9
1992-93 Y. Racine, P. Ysebaert, others $9
1993-94 Yzerman, Fedorov, Bowman $9
1994-95 Sergei Fedorov w/trophies $8
1995-96 Team celebration, 70th Anniv. $8
1996-97 "Hockeytown" winged wheel logo ...$8
1997-98 "Hockeytown" winged wheel logo ...$8
1998-99 Stanley Cup, "Hockeytown" $8

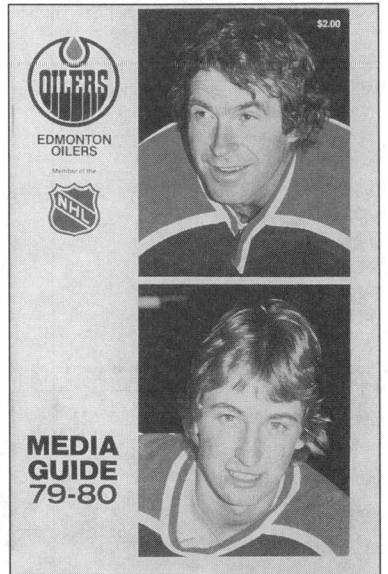

Edmonton Oilers
1975-76 Fight vs. Cleveland $50
1976-77 Oilers in action $40
1977-78 ....$40
1978-79 Dave Dryden, Hamilton $40
1979-80 Dave Dryden, Wayne Gretzky $40
1980-81 Wayne Gretzky, Blair McDonald $35
1981-82 Wayne Gretzky, Andy Moog $35
1982-83 Oilers puck $20
1983-84 Mark Messier, Andy Moog $20
1984-85 Team uniforms, Stanley Cup $20
1985-86 Wayne Gretzky with trophies $25

1986-87 P. Coffey, W. Gretzky with trophies ...$12
1987-88 Gretzky, Stanley Cup celebration $12
1988-89 10th Anniversary logo $12
1989-90 Team logo $12
1990-91 Mark Messier, trophy $12
1991-92 T. Green, coaching staff $12
1992-93 Stanley Cup memorabilia $12
1993-94 Oilers road jersey $12
1994-95 Jason Arnott $6
1995-96 Oilers logo $5
1996-97 Oil pipeline with team logo $5
1997-98 Oilers logo/goaltenders mask $5
1998-99 Art collage, 20th Anniversary logo $5

Florida Panthers
1993-94 Logo, player on beach $9
1994-95 Awards nominees $8
1995-96 Collage of Florida postcards $6
1996-97 Prince of Wales Trophy $6
1997-98 Panthers memorabilia $6
1998-99 Five original Panthers $6

New England/Hartford Whalers
1972-73 ....$45
1973-74 Ted Green with WHA trophy $40
1974-75 Al Smith, Hartford Civic Center ...$40

Hartford Whalers
1975-76 Number 5 with Whaler photos $35
1976-77 Rick Ley, Webster, others $35
1977-78 ....$30
1978-79 Gordie Howe $25
1979-80 Rick Ley $25
1980-81 Dave Keon $10
1981-82 Larry Pleau $10
1982-83 Whalers pucks $10
1983-84 R. Francis, Johnson, B. Stoughton $10
1984-85 Team logo, Greg Millen $10
1985-86 Ron Francis $10
1986-87 K. Dineen, R. Francis, M. Liut $10
1987-88 Mike Liut $10
1988-89 Ulf Samuelsson, Dave Tippett $10
1989-90 Kevin Dineen $10
1990-91 Ron Francis $10
1991-92 ....$10
1992-93 Team jersey $10
1993-94 ....$8
1994-95 C. Pronger/S. Burke/G. Sanderson $8
1995-96 ....$6
Become Carolina Hurricanes

Los Angeles Kings
1966-67 ....$75
1967-68 ....$75
1968-69 Kings artwork $50
1969-70 Gerry Desjardins $40
1970-71 Team logo $35
1971-72 Bob Pulford $25
1972-73 Butch Goring $25
1973-74 Go Kings artwork $20
1974-75 Butch Goring $15
1975-76 M. Dionne, B. Pulford, R. Vachon $15
1976-77 Butch Goring $15
1977-78 M. Dionne, B. Goring, R. Vachon $15
1978-79 Marcel Dionne $15
1979-80 M. Dionne, B. Goring, D. Taylor,
   R. Vachon $15
1980-81 M. Dionne, C. Simmer, D. Taylor ..$15
1981-82 Mario Lessard $9
1982-83 Steve Bozek $9
1983-84 Marcel Dionne jersey, photos $9
1984-85 Pat Quinn, Rogie Vachon $9
1985-86 M. Dionne, B. Nicholls, D. Taylor, others ..$9
1986-87 20th Anniversary logo $9
1987-88 B. Nicholls, L. Robitaille, others ...$9
1988-89 Wayne Gretzky, Luc Robitaille $9
1989-90 Team logo $9
1990-91 Fan photos, team logo $9
1991-92 Silver season hologram $9
1992-93 B. Melrose, N. Beverley $9
1993-94 Gretzky, Robitaille, others $9
1994-95 Illustration of unidentified player ...$8
1995-96 Wayne Gretzky $6
1996-97 Kings logo and 1996-97 ....$6
1997-98 Kings logo and 1997-98 ....$6
1998-99 Logo, player at faceoff $6

Montreal Canadiens
1953-54 Team logo $150
1954-55 Team logo $125
1955-56 Team logo $75
1956-57 ....$40
1957-58 ....$30
1958-59 ....$25
1959-60 ....$25
1960-61 ....$25
1961-62 ....$125
1962-63 Claude Provost, Henri Richard $100
1963-64 Jean Beliveau $45
1964-65 ....$45

1963-64 • 60¢
L'ANNUAIRE DES
CANADIENS
YEARBOOK

1993-94 Stanley Cup celebration $12
1994-95 Patrick Roy $9
1995-96 Montreal Forum $9
1996-97 Collage of action photos $9
1997-98 V. Damphousse/M. Recchi/S. Koivu . . .$9
1998-99 Photo of goalie and net $9

NASHVILLE PREDATORS
1998-99 INAUGURAL SEASON
MEDIA GUIDE

$6.00 NEW JERSEY
Official
1990-91
Yearbook

1998-99 Scott Stevens/M. Brodeur $10

1965-66 . . . .$45	
1966-67 . . . .$45	
1967-68 . . . .$45	
1968-69 . . . .$45	
1969-70 . . . .$45	

1970-71 Team artwork $30
1971-72 Team logo $30
1972-73 Team logo $30
1973-74 Team artwork $30
1974-75 50th Anniversary artwork $15
1975-76 S. Bowman, G. Lafleur, Pollock . . .$15
1976-77 Y. Cournoyer, K. Dryden, G. Lafleur . .$15
1977-78 Serge Savard $15
1978-79 Yvan Cournoyer $15
1979-80 Serge Savard $15
1980-81 Guy Lafleur, Pierre Larouche $15
1981-82 Bob Gainey $12
1982-83 Guy Lafleur, others $12
1983-84 Mario Tremblay $12
1984-85 Guy Carbonneau $12
1985-86 Steve Penney $12
1986-87 Stanley Cup celebration $12
1987-88 Mats Naslund $12
1988-89 M. Nasland, S. Richer, P. Roy, others . . .$12
1989-90 Stanley Cup celebration $12
1990-91 Stephane Richer, Patrick Roy $12
1991-92 . . . .$12
1992-93 Patrick Roy $12

Nashville Predators
1998-99 Memorabilia collage $8

New Jersey Devils
1982-83 Devils artwork $20
1983-84 Team in tuxes $12
1984-85 Mel Bridgman $12
1985-86 G. Adams, T. Higgins, D. Sulliman . . .$12
1986-87 Kirk Muller $12
1987-88 Devils' kids' artwork $12
1988-89 Aaron Broten, Kirk Muller $12
1989-90 Sean Burke $12
1990-91 John MacLean $12
1991-92 10th Anniversary/action photos $10
1992-93 Scott Stevens $10
1993-94 Jacques LeMaire $10
1994-95 Devils' award winners $10
1995-96 . . . .$10
1996-97 15th Anniversary/J. MacLean $10
1997-98 M. Brodeur/others $10

New York Islanders
1972-73 Team logo $45
1973-74 Billy Harris $30
1974-75 Syl Apps, Denis Potvin $30
1975-76 Playoff action vs. N.Y. Rangers . . .$30
1976-77 Denis Potvin, Chico Resch $30
1977-78 Ed Westfall $25
1978-79 Mike Bossy $25
1979-80 Bryan Trottier $25
1980-81 Stanley Cup Champions $20
1981-82 Stanley Cup Champions $15
1982-83 B. Trottier with the Stanley Cup . . .$12
1983-84 D. Potvin, B. Smith, J. Tonelli, B. Trottier
. . . .$12
1984-85 Mike Bossy 400th goal $12
1985-86 M. Bossy, B. Sutter, J. Tonelli, B. Trottier
. . . .$12
1986-87 Al Arbour, Terry Simpson $12
1987-88 . . . .$12
1988-89 P. LaFontaine, B. Trottier, others $12
1989-90 David Volek $12
1990-91 Pat LaFontaine $12
1991-92 M. Bossy, D. Potvin $12
1992-93 The New Ice Age $9
1993-94 Pierre Turgeon $9

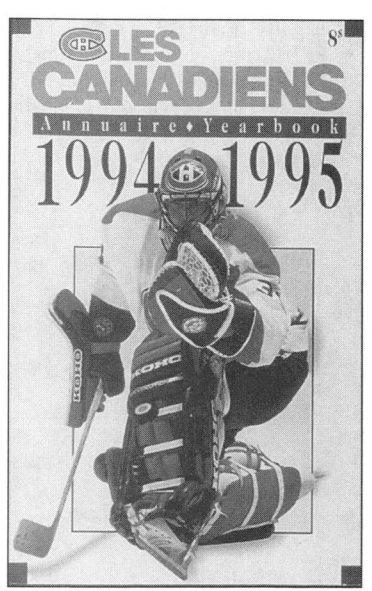

LES CANADIENS
Annuaire • Yearbook
1994 1995

PREMIERE EDITION $4.00
NEW JERSEY DEVILS
1982-83 MEDIA GUIDE/YEARBOOK

FACT BOOK
1973-1974
N.Y. ISLANDERS

1994-95 Lorne Henning $8
1995-96 Islanders jerseys, M. Milbury $6
1996-97 25th anniversary, player photos $6
1997-98 Berard, Palffy, McCabe $6
1998-99 Kenny Johnson $6

New York Rangers

1947-48 Inside the Blue Shirt $200
1948-49 Buddy O'Connor $175
1949-50 Edgar Laprade $125
1950-51 C. Rayner, 25th Anniversary $125
1951-52 Don Raleigh $75
1952-53 . . . .$50
1953-54 . . . .$50
1954-55 Muzz Patrick, Ivan Irwin $50
1955-56 . . . .$40
1956 57 . . . .$40
1957-58 . . . .$40
1958-59 . . . .$40
1959-60 . . . .$40
1960-61 . . . .$40
1961-62 . . . .$40
1962-63 . . . .$40
1963-64 Jacques Plante $40
1964-65 Rod Gilbert $40
1965-66 Harry Howell vs. Stan Mikita $40
1966-67 Bob Nevin $40
1967-68 Ed Giacomin $40
1968-69 Jean Ratelle $40
1969-70 Arnie Brown vs. Bobby Hull $35
1970-71 Ed Giacomin, Brad Park $35
1971-72 Ed Giacomin, Gilles Villemure . . .$30
1972-73 Vic Hadfield 50th goal $30
1973-74 Ed Giacomin $30
1974-75 Ted Irvine, Brad Park $25
1975-76 50th Anniversary logo $25
1976-77 Rangers jersey artwork $20
1977-78 Phil Esposito, others $20
1978-79 Fred Shero $20
1979-80 John Davidson $15
1980-81 Rangers in action $15
1981-82 Rangers in action $10
1982-83 Rangers in action $6
1983-84 Madison Square Garden $10
1984-85 Team jersey $6
1985-86 Empire State Building $10
1986-87 Statue of Liberty $10
1987-88 J. Bergeron, P. Esposito $10
1988-89 Rangers in action $10
1989-90 Tony Granato, Brian Leetch $10

1990-91 M. Gartner, B. Leetch, B. Nicholls $9
1991-92 B. Leetch, M. Richter $9
1992-93 . . . .$9
1993-94 B. Leetch/M. Messier $9
1994-95 M. Messier holding Stanley Cup . . .$8
1995-96 70th anniversary memorabilia collage
. . . .$8
1996-97 W. Gretzky/M. Messier $10
1997-98 Brian Leetch $8
1998-99 Statue of Liberty/illustration $8

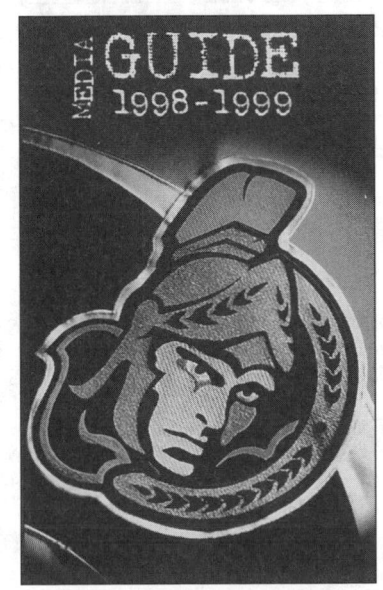

Oakland/California Golden Seals

Oakland Seals
1968-69 Seals in action $35
1969-70 Seals artwork $25
1970-71 Team artwork $20

California Golden Seals
1971-72 Seals artwork $15
1972-73 Seals artwork $10
1973-74 Goaltender artwork $10
1974-75 Closeup of Goalie mask $10
1975-76 Seals in action $10

Ottawa Senators

1992-93 Artwork collage $9
1993-94 A. Daigle, A. Yashin $7

1994-95 Overhead photo of Senator players $7
1995-96 . . . .$7
1996-97 Daniel Alfredsson $7
1997-98 Photographic slides of action $7
1998-99 Senators patch on jersey $7

Philadelphia Flyers

1967-68 Team artwork $35
1968-69 Campbell Trophy $35
1969-70 Flyers artwork $35
1970-71 Team logo, NHL pucks $30
1971-72 TV camera $30
1972-73 Dan Earle, G. Hart $30
1973-74 Flyers artwork $25
1974-75 Stanley Cup artwork $25
1975-76 Trophies $20
1976 77 B. Barber, B. Clarke, R. Leach $20
1977-78 Flyers equipment $20
1978-79 Flyers artwork $20
1979-80 Action photos $6
1980-81 Team logo, photos $15
1981-82 Players' faces $15
1982-83 Action photos $6
1983-84 Bobby Clarke $10
1984-85 Brian Propp $10
1985-86 Pelle Lindbergh $10
1986-87 Mark Howe $10
1987-88 Ron Hextall $10
1988-89 Flyers artwork $10
1989-90 Flyers artwork $10
1990-91 Team equipment $9
1991-92 Player illustrations $9
1992-93 Eric Lindros, others $10
1993-94 Eric Lindros/three others $9
1994-95 Eight player photos $8
1995-96 M. Renberg/E. Desjardins/others $8
1996-97 Action scenes, 30th Anniv. logo $9
1997-98 Lindros, Brind'Amor, Leclair, Coffey . .$8
1998-99 E. Lindros, R. Brind'Amor, others . . .$8

Phoenix Coyotes

1996-97 Coyotes new logo $7
1997-98 Coyotes head logo $7
1998-99 Tkachuk, Roenick, Tocchet, others $7

Pittsburgh Penguins

1968-69 Les Binkley $40
1969-70 Team artwork $40
1970-71 Red Kelly $40
1971-72 Team logo $35

1972-73 Team logo $35
1973-74 Ken Schinkel $20
1974-75 Syl Apps $15
1975-76 Ron Schock $20
1976-77 S. Apps, J. Pronovost, P. Larouche $20
1977-78 Syl Apps $20
1978-79 Orest Kindrachuk $20
1979-80 Randy Carlyle, George Ferguson $6
1980-81 Rick Kehoe $15
1981-82 Randy Carlyle, Rick Kehoe $15
1982-83 Michael Dion $6
1983-84 Goal celebration $10
1984-85 Mike Bullard $10
1985-86 Mario Lemieux $10
1986-87 Team memorabilia $10
1987-88 Mario Lemieux $10
1988-89 Mario Lemieux $10
1989-90 T. Barrasso, R. Brown, P. Coffey,
   M. Lemieux $10
1990-91 S. Bowman, B. Johnson, C. Patrick $9
1991-92 Stanley Cup celebration $9
1992-93 Lemieux, 1991 Stanley Cup $9
1993-94 Lemieux, Barrasso, others $9
1994-95 Jagr, Barrasso, Francis $10
1995-96 R. Francis, J. Jagr. $8
1996-97 30th anniv., Jagr, Lemieux $8
1997-98 R. Constantine, Jagr, Lemieux $8
1998-99 Jaromir Jagr $8

Quebec Nordiques
1974-75 . . . .$30
1975-76 . . . .$25
1976-77 Nordiques fleur-de-lis logo $25
1977-78 . . . .$25
1978-79 . . . .$25
1979-80 Nordiques art $20
1980-81 Nordiques art $15
1981-82 Anton and Peter Stastny $15
1982-83 Nordiques art $12
1983-84 M. Goulet, D. Hunter, others $12
1984-85 Nordiques memorabilia $10
1985-86 Nordiques art $10
1986-87 Team logo $10
1987-88 Nordiques in action $10
1988-89 Goal celebration $10
1989-90 Media equipment $10
1990-91 G. Lafleur, M.Petit, J. Sakic $10
1991-92 J. Sakic/ celebrating $10
1992-93 O. Nolan, J. Sakic, M. Sundin $10
1993-94 Artwork of generic player $10
1994-95 Quebec skyline/action scenes $8
Became Colorado Avalanche

San Jose Sharks
1991-92 Sharks memorabilia $15
1992-93 Die cut shark fin $15
1993-94 Shark fin cutting through land $12
1994-95 Hockey equipment $8
1995-96 Puck and ticket stubs $8
1996-97 Blurred battle on ice $7
1997-98 V. Kozlov/O. Nolan/J. Friesen $7
1998-99 D. Sutter/O. Nolan/others $7

St. Louis Blues
1967-68 Keenan, Martin, Schock, others . . .$40
1968-69 Glenn Hall $35
1969-70 Vezina and Campbell trophies $35
1970-71 Campbell Trophy $35
1971-72 Team action photos $35
1972-73 St. Louis Arena $35
1973-74 Action photos $30
1974-75 Andy Hebenton, Garry Unger $25
1975-76 Gratton, G. Hall, E. Johnston, others . . .$25
1976-77 Emile Francis $20
1977-78 Team artwork $15
1978-79 Team artwork $15
1979-80 Ed Staniowski $10
1980-81 Team art $15
1981-82 Mike Liut $9

1982-83 Emile Francis $9
1983-84 Brian Sutter $9
1984-85 Team jersey $9
1985-86 Team logo $9
1986-87 Team memorabilia $9
1987-88 Team artwork $9
1988-89 Berry, Micheletti, Brian Sutter $9
1989-90 Dan Kelly $9
1990-91 Brett Hull, Rick Meagher $9
1991-92 Artwork of Blues greats $9
1992-93 Brett Hull $9
1993-94 Curtis Joseph $9
1994-95 Mike Keenan $8
1995-96 Blues team logo $7
1996-97 B. Hull/A. MacInnis/G. Fuhr $7
1997-98 Blues memorabilia $7
1998-99 P. Turgeon/C. Pronger/C. Conroy $7

Tampa Bay Lightning
1992-93 Logo, small photos $15
1993-94 Terry Crisp, others $10
1994-95 C. Gratton, D. Puppa, R. Hamrlik . . .$8
1995-96 Roman Hamrlik $7
1996-97 Three players celebrating a goal $7
1997-98 Jason Wiemer, others $10
1998-99 Lightning bolt design, jerseys $8

Toronto Maple Leafs

1962-63 George Armstrong $75
1963-64 Frank Mahovlich $75
1964-65 Action photos $75
1965-66 Johnny Bower $75
1966-67 Dave Keon $60
1967-68 Dave Keon $60
1968-69 . . . .$50
1969-70 Maple Leafs in action $50
1970-71 Maple Leafs artwork $45
1971-72 Maple Leafs artwork $20
1972-73 Maple Leafs Garden, team logo $20
1973-74 . . . .$20
1974-75 Team logo $15
1975-76 Team logo $15
1976-77 B. Salming, D. Sittler, others $15
1977-78 T. Horton, B. Salming, D. Sittler, others . .$15
1978-79 Darryl Sittler $15
1979-80 Borje Salming $15
1980-81 Borje Salming $15
1981-82 50th Anniversary photos $9
1982-83 Rick Vaive 50th goal $9
1983-84 G. Gingras, R. Vaive, W. Poddubny,
    others $9
1984-85 Allen Bester, Rick Vaive $9
1985-86 Maple Leafs in action $9
1986-87 Goal celebration $9
1987-88 Wendell Clark $9
1988-89 Team logo $9
1989-90 Vincent Damphousse $9
1990-91 V. Damphousse, G. Leeman, E Olczyk
    . . . .$6
1991-92 Collage of Maple Leafs greats $9
1992-93 . . . .$9
1993-94 Newspaper clippings, souvenirs $9
1994-95 Logo, goal celebration $8
1995-96 Maple Leafs sweaters $6
1996-97 . . . .$6
1997-98 . . . .$6
1998-99 Maple Leaf greats $6

Vancouver Canucks

1970-71 Team logo, action photo $60
1971-72 Team logo, action artwork $50
1972-73 Team logo $45
1973-74 Team puck, stick $25
1974-75 Celebration vs. Blackhawks $20
1975-76 Team artwork $20
1976-77 Action photos $20
1977-78 Don Lever, others $15
1978-79 New team logo $15

1979-80 Glen Hanlon $15
1980-81 Canucks vs. North Stars $9
1981-82 Darcy Rota vs. Capitals $9
1982-83 Fans celebrating $9
1983-84 Action photos $9
1984-85 Team logo $9
1985-86 Canucks new uniform artwork $9
1986-87 Action photos $9
1987-88 B. Burke, B. McCammon, P. Quinn . . .$9
1988-89 Stan Smyl $9
1989-90 Trevor Linden $9
1990-91 Team jerseys, equipment $9
1991-92 Painting of Trevor Linden $9
1992-93 P. Bure, K. McLean, P. Quinn $10
1993-94 P. Bure/city in background $9
1994-95 Photo montage $8
1995-96 P. Bure, K. McLean, P. Quinn $8
1996-97 Lumme, Linden, Bure, Mogilny $8
1997-98 New logo on a jersey $8
1998-99 M. Messier, T. Bertuzzi, others $8

Washington Capitals

1974-75 Team locker room $60
1975-76 Ron Low $50
1976-77 Tony White $25

1977-78 Team artwork $25
1978-79 Guy Charron $25
1979-80 Ryan Walter $9
1980-81 M. Gartner, D. Maruk, others $20
1981-82 Mike Palmateer $20
1982-83 Dennis Maruk $9
1983-84 Rod Langway $12
1984-85 Rod Langway, others $9
1985-86 Bobby Carpenter, Mike Gartner $9
1986-87 Capital building, team puck $9
1987-88 Bobby Gould, Larry Murphy $9
1988-89 15th Anniversary, Scott Stevens $9
1989-90 D. Ciccarelli, R. Courtnall, M. Ridley . . .$9
1990-91 John Druce, Rod Langway $9
1991-92 Silhoutte of Capitol building $9
1992-93 Dale Hunter $9
1993-94 Kevin Hatcher $9
1994-95 Player drawing/Joe Juneau $8

1995-96 Bondra/Schoenfeld/Carey $7
1996-97 Bondra/Hunter/Carey/others $7
1997-98 Map of downtown DC $7
1998-99 Eastern Conference trophy $7

Winnipeg Jets

1972-73 Logo, action artwork $35
1973-74 . . . .$25
1974-75 . . . .$25
1975-76 Jets team photos $25
1976-77 . . . .$25
1977-78 . . . .$25
1978-79 WHA Championship trophy $25
1979-80 Lars-Erik Sjoberg with WHA trophy . . .$20
1980-81 Dave Christian $20
1981-82 Dave Babych $15
1982-83 Dale Hawerchuk, Calder Trophy . . .$9
1983-84 Dale Hawerchuk, others $15
1984-85 L. Boschman, R. Carlyle, D. Hawerchuk
    . . . .$9
1985-86 Dale Hawerchuk, Jets puck $10
1986-87 Action photos $10
1987-88 Lightning on Ice $10
1988-89 Winnipeg skyline $10
1989-90 B. Ashton, P. Elynuik, others $10
1990-91 Winnipeg Style $10
1991-92 Phil Housley, Shawn Cronin $9
1992-93 Troy Murray, Bob Essensa $9
1993-94 Tie Domi $9
1994-95 Goal celebration $7
1995-96 T. Steen/Jets farewell $7
Became Phoenix Coyotes

Sports Illustrated
Hockey Covers

1956
01/23/56 Jean Beliveau, Canadiens (FC)
. . . .$25

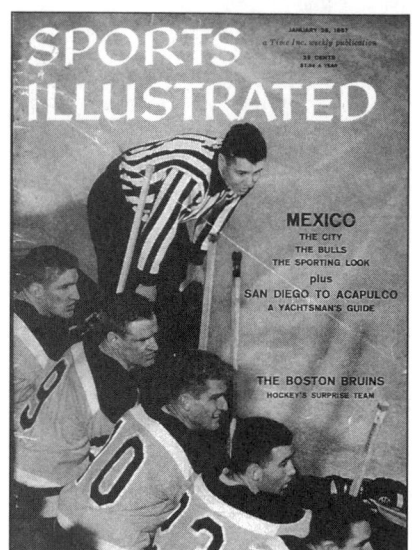

January 28, 1957

1957
01/28/57 Boston Bruins . . . .$15-$20

1958
02/17/58 Jacques Plante, Canadiens (FC)
. . . .$15

1959
01/12/59 Andy Bathgate, Rangers $20

1960
01/25/60 USSR Hockey . . . .$5-$8
03/21/60 Maurice Richard $20
11/14/60 Bobby Hull, Blackhawks (FC)
. . . .$30

1962
01/15/62 Don Head, Bruins $10

1963
01/28/63 Howie Young, Red Wings . . .$12

1964
02/03/64 Bobby Hull, Blackhawks
. . . .$20-$25
03/16/64 Gordie Howe, Red Wings
. . . .$40-$50

1965
01/25/65 Bobby Hull, Blackhawks
. . . .$30-$35

1966
01/31/66 Stan Mikita, Blackhawks (FC)
. . . .$20-$25

2/25/66 Chicago vs. Detroit Stanley Cup
. . . .$15

1967
01/30/67 Rod Gilbert, Rangers . . .$15-$20
03/20/67 Mikita/Mohns/Wharram, Black-
hawks $20
12/11/67 Bobby Orr, Bruins (FC) .$20-$25

1968
02/12/68 Bobby Hull, Blackhawks
. . . .$20-$25
04/08/68 Stanley Cup $8

1969
02/03/69 Bobby Orr, Bruins $20
04/07/69 Red Berenson, Blues . . . . .$6-$8

1970
03/02/70 Eddie Giacomin, Rangers $8
04/06/70 Keith Magnuson, Blackhawks
. . . .$10
05/04/70 Bobby Orr, Bruins $20
12/21/70 Bobby Orr, Bruins (SOY) . . .$25

1971
03/29/71 Phil and Tony Esposito $10
04/26/71 Montreal vs. Boston $8

February 14, 1972

1972
02/14/72 Ken Dryden, Canadiens (FC) .$8
06/19/72 Bobby Hull, Blackhawks
. . . .$15-$20

1973
02/26/73 Gilbert Perreault, Sabres . .$6-$8
04/02/73 Henri Richard, Canadiens $9
11/19/73 Phil Esposito, Bruins $10

1974
03/11/74 Gordie Howe, Aeros . . . .$10-$15
05/06/74 Bobby Clarke (FC),
Pete Stemkowski $10
11/25/74 Ken Dryden, Canadiens $6

1975
11/17/75 Violence in Pro Hockey $7

1976
02/23/76 Bobby Clarke, Flyers $7
05/24/76 Stanley Cup Playoffs $8

1977
02/07/77 Guy Lafleur, Canadiens $7
05/09/77 Gerry Cheevers, Brad Park . .$6
12/12/77 Bryan Trottier, Islanders $6

1978
05/29/78 Larry Robinson, Ken Dryden .$6

1979
04/16/79 Denis Potvin, Islanders $8

1980
01/21/80 Gordie Howe, Whalers . . .$8-$10
03/03/80 U.S. Olympic hockey team
. . . .$15-$20
03/10/80 Jim Craig, Flames $6
12/22/80 U.S. Olympic hockey team (SOY)
. . . .$15

1981
02/23/81 Bobby Carpenter, high school .$5
10/12/81 Wayne Gretzky, Oilers (FC)
. . . .$30-$35

1982
12/27/82 Wayne Gretzky, Oilers (SOY)
. . . .$20

1983
05/23/83 Billy Smith, Islanders $5

1984
01/23/84 Wayne Gretzky, Oilers $15
05/14/84 Mike Bossy, Islanders . . . .$6-$7

1985
02/18/85 Wayne Gretzky, Oilers $20

1986
06/02/86 Canadiens win the Stanley Cup
. . . .$6-$8

1987
06/01/87 Wayne Gretzy, Oilers $8

1988
05/30/88 Wayne Gretzky, Oilers $10
08/22/88 Wayne Gretzky, Magic Johnson
. . . .$10-$15

1989
02/06/89 Mario Lemieux, Penguins (FC)
. . . .$9-$12
12/18/89 Wayne Gretzky, Magic Johnson,
Joe Montana $15

1990
04/23/90 Tomas Sandstrom, Kings $4

1991
03/18/91 Brett Hull, Blues $9

1992
06/08/92 Mario Lemieux, Penguins $5

1993
04/19/93 Mario Lemieux, Penguins $4
06/14/93 Los Angeles/Montreal Stanley
Cup $3

1994
06/13/94 Mark Messier, Rangers . . .$5-$6
06/20/94 Mark Richter . . . .$4-$5

1996
10/07/96 Gretzky, Messier . . . .$6-$7

Hockey Books

Selected Books

Andy Bathgate's Hockey Secrets, by Andy Bathgate (1964), HC 158 pages, with dust jacket $4.95

A Spin of the Wheel: Birth of the Buffalo Sabres, by R. Brewitt (1975), HC 197 pages, with dust jacket $22.95

Bernie! Bernie! Bernie!, by Bernie Parent with Bill Fleischman and Sonny Schwartz (1975), HC 272 pages, with dust jacket $19.95

Bobby Clarke, by Edward Dolan and Richard Lyttle (1977), HC 94 pages $17

Bobby Clarke and the Ferocious Flyers, by Stan Fischler (1974), HC 213 pages, with dust jacket $35

Bobby Orr and the Big Bad Bruins, by Stan Fischler (1969), HC 273 pages, with dust jacket $18

Bobby Orr: Lightning On Ice, by Howard Liss (1975), HC 96 pages, with dust jacket ...$17.50

Bobby Orr: My Game, by Bobby Orr and Mark Mulvoy (1974), HC 235 pages, with dust jacket $20

Cowboy on Ice, by Phil Lorange (1975), HC, biography of Howie Young, autographed ...$30

Cyclone Taylor: A Hockey Legend, by Eric Whitehead (1977), HC 205 pages, with dust jacket $10

Eddie: A Goalie's Story, by H. Delano (1976), biography of Eddie Giacomin, HC 319 pages, with dust jacket $18

Face-Off at the Summit, by Ken Dryden (1973), HC 207 pages, with dust jacket $15

The Fastest Sport, by Gerald Eskenazi (1974), HC $15

The Flying Frenchmen, Hockey's Greatest Dynasty, by Maurice "Rocket" Richard and Stan Fischler (1971), HC 340 pages, with dust jacket $20

The Game, by Ken Dryden (1983), HC 248 pages $12.50

Garry Unger and the battling Blues, by Stan Fischler (1976), HC 213 pages $15

Goaltender, by Gerry Cheevers (1971), HC 211 pages, with dust jacket $18

Gordie Howe, by Stan Fischler (1967), HC .$15

Gordie Howe: Number 9, by Jim Vipond (1968), HC 157 pages, with dust jacket, autographed $125

Great Upsets of Stanley Cup Hockey, by John Devaney (1976), HC 96 pages, Bobby Orr on dust jacket $10

Gretzky, An Autobiography, by Wayne Gretzky with Rick Reilly (1990), HC, 258 pages $25

The Hammer, by Dave Schultz with Stan Fischler (1981), HC 208 pages $10

High Stick, by Ted Green (1971), HC 211 pages, with dust jacket $18

Hockey In My Blood, by Johnny Bucyk with Russ Conway (1972), HC 197 pages, with dust jacket $18

Hockey Is A Battle, by Punch Imlach (1969), HC 203 pages, with dust jacket $17

Hockey Is My Game, by Bobby Hull (1967), HC 212 pages, with dust jacket $25

Hockey Is My Life, by Phil Esposito with Gerald Eskenazi (1972), HC 207 pages, with dust jacket $14.95

I Play to Win, by Stan Mikita (1969), HC 223 pages $20

Larinov, by Igor Larinov, Jim Taylor and Leonid Reizer (1990), HC, saga of Russian player pursuing NHL career $10

The Men in the Nets, by J. Hunt (1967), HC 133 pages, with dust jacket $12

Mr. Hockey: The World of Gordie Howe (1975), HC 197 pages, with dust jacket $19

My Three Hockey Players, by Colleen Howe (1972), HC 192 pages, with dust jacket $15

None Against! by Keith Magnuson (1973), HC 179 pages, with dust jacket $12.95

Orr on Ice, by Bobby Orr (1970) with Dick Grace, HC 176 pages, with dust jacket, autographed $45

Play the Man, by Brad Park with Stan Fischler (1971), HC 211 pages, with dust jacket ..$17.95

Power Play: The Story of the Toronto Maple Leafs, by Stan Fischler (1972), HC 272 pages, with dust jacket $19

Rocket Richard, by Andy O'Brien (1969), HC 134 pages, with dust jacket $18

Strength Down Centre, by Hugh Hood (1970), HC 192 pages, biography of Jean Beliveau $27.50

They Call Me Gump, by Lorne "Gump" Worsley with Tim Moriarity (1975), HC 176 pages, with dust jacket $20

Those Were the Days, by Stan Fischler (1976), HC 337 pages, with dust jacket $15

We Love You Bruins: Boston's Gashouse Gang from Eddie Shore to Bobby Orr, by John Devaney, HC 183 pages, Bobby Orr cover ..$20

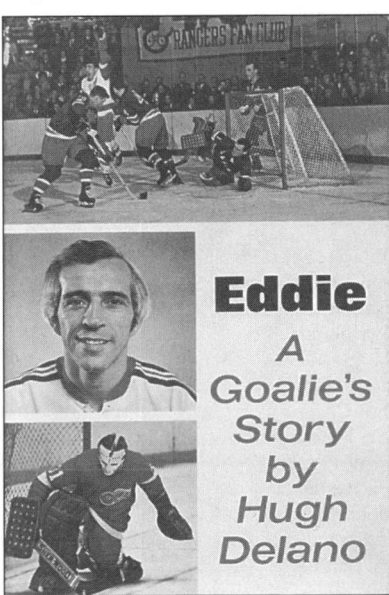

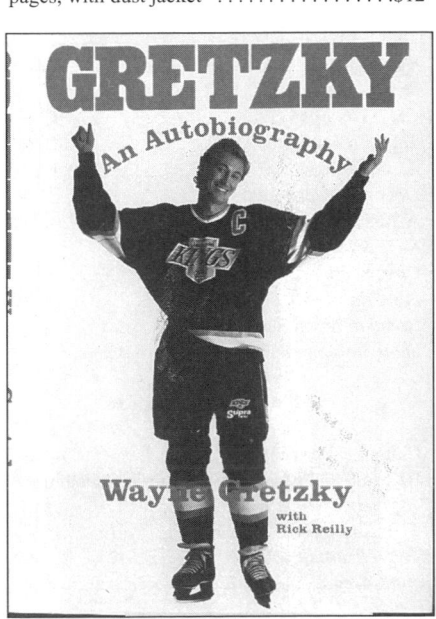

Hockey Starting Lineup Figurines

1993 American

Complete Set (12): $475.00
Ed Belfour 130.00
Ray Bourque .20.00
Grant Fuhr 175.00
Brett Hull 12.00
Jaromir Jagr .25.00
Pat LaFontaine 80.00
Mario Lemieux 20.00
Eric Lindros .40.00
Mark Messier 35.00
Jeremy Roenick 20.00
Patrick Roy 80.00
Steve Yzerman 25.00

1993 Canadian

Complete Set (11): $260.00
Ed Belfour 60.00
Ray Bourque .20.00
Brett Hull 12.00
Jaromir Jagr .25.00
Pat LaFontaine 40.00
Mario Lemieux 20.00
Eric Lindros .30.00
Mark Messier 25.00
Jeremy Roenick 20.00
Patrick Roy 70.00
Steve Yzerman 20.00

1994 American

Complete Set (20): $375.00
Tom Barrasso *35.00*
Ray Bourque .30.00
Pavel Bure *20.00*
Sergei Fedorov *17.00*
Doug Gilmour *15.00*
Brett Hull 12.00
Arturs Irbe *40.00*
Jaromir Jagr .20.00
Pat LaFontaine 16.00
Brian Leetch *20.00*
Mario Lemieux 15.00
Eric Lindros .25.00
Mark Messier 50.00
Alexander Mogilny *20.00*
Adam Oates *15.00*
Mike Richter *25.00*
Luc Robitaille *25.00*
Jeremy Roenick 20.00
Teemu Selanne *25.00*
Steve Yzerman 15.00

1994 Canadian

Complete Set (20): $375.00
Tom Barrasso *35.00*
Ray Bourque .30.00
Pavel Bure *20.00*
Sergei Fedorov *17.00*
Doug Gilmour 15.00
Brett Hull 12.00
Arturs Irbe *40.00*
Jaromir Jagr .20.00
Pat LaFontaine 16.00
Brian Leetch *20.00*
Mario Lemieux 15.00
Eric Lindros .25.00
Mark Messier 50.00
Alexander Mogilny *20.00*

Adam Oates *15.00*
Mike Richter .25.00
Luc Robitaille *25.00*
Jeremy Roenick 20.00
Teemu Selanne *25.00*
Steve Yzerman 15.00

1994 Canadian

Complete Set (13): $250.00
Pavel Bure *15.00*
Sergei Fedorov *15.00*
Grant Fuhr 75.00
Doug Gilmour *15.00*
Brian Leetch .20.00
Mario Lemieux 15.00
Eric Lindros .20.00
Alexander Mogilny *15.00*
Adam Oates .15.00
Mike Richter .30.00
Luc Robitaille *20.00*
Teemu Selanne 20.00
Steve Yzerman 15.00

1995 American

Complete Set (19): $200.00
Rob Blake *12.00*
Martin Brodeur *30.00*
Pavel Bure 15.00
Chris Chelios *10.00*
Bob Corkum *10.00*
Sergei Fedorov 10.00
Theo Fleury *10.00*
Adam Graves *10.00*
Dominik Hasek *25.00*
Brett Hull 12.00
Mike Modano *10.00*
Kirk Muller *10.00*
Cam Neely 12.00
Sandis Ozolinsh *12.00*
Felix Potvin *25.00*
Luc Robitaille 12.00
Brendan Shanahan *15.00*
Scott Stevens *10.00*
Pierre Turgeon 10.00

1995 Canadian

Complete Set (13): $180.00
Tom Barrasso 25.00
Bob Blake 12.00
Martin Brodeur *25.00*
Chris Chelios *12.00*
Theo Fleury *12.00*
Adam Graves *12.00*
Dominik Hasek *25.00*
Arturs Irbe 30.00
Mike Modano *12.00*
Cam Neely *12.00*
Felix Potvin *25.00*
Brendan Shanahan *15.00*
Scott Stevens *12.00*

1996 Hockey American

Complete Set (22): $300.00
Barrasso and LaFontaine are not included in set
    price.
T. Barrasso (Hills special) 20.00
Brian Bradley *12.00*
Jim Carey *30.00*

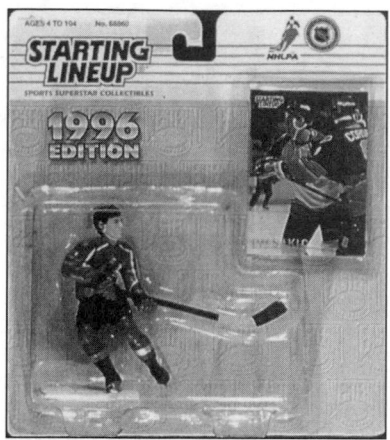

Paul Coffey *15.00*
Sergei Fedorov 12.00
Ron Francis *12.00*
Dominik Hasek 30.00
Paul Kariya 25.00
John LeClair *15.00*
Brian Leetch .12.00
Eric Lindros .15.00
Al MacInnis *12.00*
Scott Mellanby *12.00*
Mark Messier 16.00
Mike Modano 12.00
Adam Oates .12.00
Mikael Renberg *15.00*
Stephane Richer *12.00*
Jeremy Roenick 14.00
Patrick Roy 45.00
Joe Sakic *20.00*
Brendan Shanahan 15.00
Mats Sundin *14.00*

1996 Canadian

Complete Set (15): $225.00
Brian Bradley *12.00*
Jim Carey *30.00*
Sergei Fedorov 12.00
Ron Francis *12.00*
Paul Kariya *25.00*
John LeClair *15.00*
Brian Leetch .12.00
Eric Lindros .15.00
Al Macinnis *12.00*
Scott Mellanby *12.00*
Mark Messier 18.00
Mikael Renberg *15.00*
Patrick Roy *45.00*
Joe Sakic *20.00*
Mats Sundin *14.00*

1997 American

Complete Set (21): $250.00
Daniel Alfredsson 15.00
Jason Arnott .10.00
Peter Bondra .15.00
Martin Brodeur 20.00
Paul Coffey 18.00
Chris Chelios .10.00
Peter Forsberg 18.00
Wayne Gretzky 35.00
Ron Hextall 18.00
Jaromir Jagr .15.00
Patrick LaLime 20.00
Eric Lindros .15.00

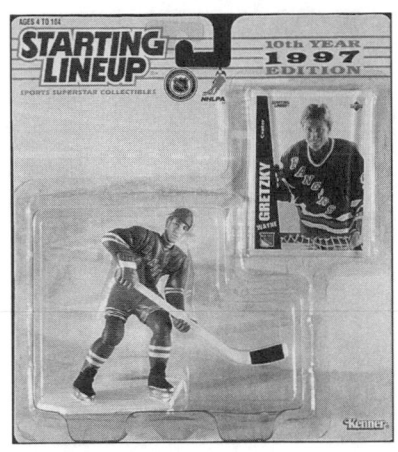

Mark Messier 15.00
Chris Osgood 20.00
Sandis Ozolinsh 10.00
Zigmund Palffy 10.00
Daren Puppa 20.00
Mark Recchi 15.00
Teemu Selanne 10.00
Keith Tkachuk 15.00
John Vanbiesbrouck 20.00

1997 One on One

Complete Set (7): $200.00
Eric Lindros, P. Kariya 30.00
Jaromir Jagr, P. Roy 30.00
Roenick, Yzerman 30.00
Joe Sakic, Mike Richter 30.00
Sundin, Bourque 30.00
Nolan, Osgood 30.00
Gretzky, Hasek 70.00

1998 Hockey

Complete Set (24) $275.00
Tony Amonte 12.00
Ed Belfour 15.00
Bryan Berard 12.00
Martin Brodeur 16.00
Jim Campbell 10.00
Vincent Damphousse 10.00
Wayne Gretzky (regular) 16.00
  (Stanley Cup) 25.00
Dominik Hasek 16.00
Jaromir Jagr .14.00
Paul Kariya .14.00
Brian Leetch 10.00
Eric Lindros .12.00
McLean, Kirk 12.00
Mark Messier 12.00
Rob Neidermayer 12.00
Chris Osgood 16.00
Felix Potvin .12.00
Jeremy Roenick 12.00
Patrick Roy .15.00
Joe Sakic 14.00
Joe Thornton 20.00
Alexi Yashin .12.00
Steve Yzerman 12.00

1998 Extended

Complete Set (10) $100.00
Peter Bondra 10.00
Theo Fleury .10.00
Grant Fuhr 10.00
Doug Gilmour 10.00
Nicolai Khabibulin 10.00
Olaf Kolzig 10.00
Tevor Kidd 10.00
Darren Puppa 10.00
Brendan Shanahan 10.00
John Vanbiesbrouck 10.00

1998 12" Figures

Complete Set (3) $60.00
Wayne Gretzky 20.00
Mario Lemieux 20.00
Bobby Orr 20.00

1998 Classic Doubles

Complete Set (6) $125.00
Gretzky/Messier. 28.00
Jagr/Barrasso. 24.00
Roy /LeClair .24.00
Fedorov/Vernon. 24.00
Brodeur/Stevens. 24.00
Clarke/Schultz 20.00

1998 One-On-One

Complete Set (6) $125.00
M. Modano/M.Vernon 30.00
K.Tkachuk /J. LeClair 20.00
B. Shanahan /J. Hackett 20.00
W. Gretzky/P. Bure 30.00
M. Messier /S. Ozolinsh 25.00
E. Lindros/A. Moog 30.00

1999

Complete Set (17) $225.00
Mike Dunham *10.00*

Peter Forsberg 10.00
Wayne Gretzky 12.00
Jeff Hackett *12.00*
Dominik Hasek 12.00
Jaromir Jagr .12.00
Curtis Joseph *16.00*
Paul Kariya .12.00
Nicolai Khabibulin 12.00
Olaf Kolzig 12.00
Nicholas Lidstrom *17.00*
Eric Lindros .10.00
Mike Modano 10.00
Keith Primeau *12.00*
Chris Pronger *15.00*
Sergei Samsonov *20.00*
Steve Yzerman 10.00

1999 12" Figures

Complete Set (7) $150.00
Wayne Gretzky
Regular 35.00
KayBee 30.00
Dominik Hasek 25.00
Jaromir Jagr .25.00
Mark Messier 20.00
Chris Osgood 20.00
Patrick Roy .20.00

1999 Classic Doubles

Complete Set (4) $70.00
G. Fuhr/W. Gretzky 25.00
M. Messier/M. Richter 20.00
J. Sakic/P. Roy 20.00
S. Yzerman/C. Osgood 20.00

1999 One-On-One

Complete Set (3) $50.00
B. Hull/W. Gretzky 25.00
C. Joseph/C. Chelios 20.00
O. Kolzig/A. Yashin 20.00

2000 Classic Doubles

Complete Set (4) $40.00
O. Kolzig/P. Roy 15.00
J. Jagr/P. Bure 15.00
P. Forsberg/S. Fedorov 15.00
P. Kariya/M. Satan 15.00

Hockey Cereal Boxes

Cheerios
Canadian
1998 Brendan Shanahan (HHC) $15

HWR Productions
1999 Fedorov Crunch $10
1999 Steve's Stars 10

Kellogg's Corn Flakes
Canadian
1992 Wendel Clark $20
1993 Montreal Canadiens 25
1996 Wendel Clark 15
1996 Gordie Howe 20
1996 Mario Lemieux 25
1996 Maurice "Rocket" Richard 20
1996 Felix Potvin (Al) 20

Kellogg's Corn Pops
Canadian
1996 Mario Lemieux $20
1996 Maurice "Rocket" Richard 15

Kellogg's Frosted Flakes
1992 JaromirJagr/Mario Lemieux $35
1933 Wayne Gretzky 40
1933 Montreal Canadiens 25
1933 L.A. Kings 35
1994 Brett Hull (Canada) 20
1994 Brett Hull w/Tony Tiger (Can.) 20
1994 N.Y. Rangers champs 30
1996 Brett Hull (Canada) 20
1997 Felix Potvin (Canada) 18

Kellogg's Frosted Mini-Wheats
Canadian
1996 Mario Lemieux $20
1996 Lanny McDonald 15

Kellogg's Raisin Bran
Canadian
1996 Brett Hull $15
1996 Mario Lemieux 20
1996 Lanny McDonald 15
1997 Curtis Joseph 15
1997 Felix Potvin 12

Kellogg's Sugar Pops
Canadian
1995 Mario Lemieux $20

Post Alpha-Bits
Canadian
1982 Mike Bossy $35
1996 Brendan Shanahan 15
1997 Joe Sakic 15
1998 Eric Lindros 20

Post Honeycomb
Canadian
1995 Tony Amonte $15
1995 Jason Arnott 15
1995 Ray Bourque 12
1995 Pavel Bure 12
1995 Chris Chelios 15
1995 Geoff Courtnall 12
1995 Russ Courtnall 12
1995 Steve Duchesne 12
1995 Doug Gilmour 15
1995 Wayne Gretzky 25
1995 Eric Lindros 20
1995 Marty McSorley 12
1995 Kirk Muller 15
1995 Rob Niedermayer 12
1995 Felix Potvin 12
1995 Luc Robitaille 12
1995 Teemu Selanne 20
1996 Doug Gilmour 15
1996 Wayne Gretzky 20
1997 Curtis Joseph 15
1997 Paul Kariya 20
1997 Eric Lindros 20

Post Sugar Crisp
Canadian
1995 Martin Brodeur $15
1997 Chris Chelios 12
1995 Sergei Fedorov 20
1995 Theo Fleury 12
1995 Doug Gilmour 15
1995 Jarri Kurri 15
1995 Alexander Mogilny 15
1995 Felix Potvin 12
1995 Joc Sakic 15
1995 Alexei Yashin 15
1996 Wayne Gretzky (2) 20
1997 Theo Fleury 12
1997 Eric Lindros 20

Pro Stars
Canadian
1984 Wayne Gretzky $100
1985 Wayne Gretzky 100
1986 Wayne Gretzky 75
1988 Wayne Gretzky 60
1989 Wayne Gretzky 50
1990 Wayne Gretzky (4) 40
1991 Wayne Gretzky (3) 30
1992 Wayne Gretzky 20
1992 Wayne Gretzky 25

Shreddies
Canadian
1996 Vincent Damphousse (GHS) $12
1997 Vincent Damphousse 12
1997 Doug Gilmour 12
1997 Eric Lindros 20
1997 Eric Lindros (GHS) 20

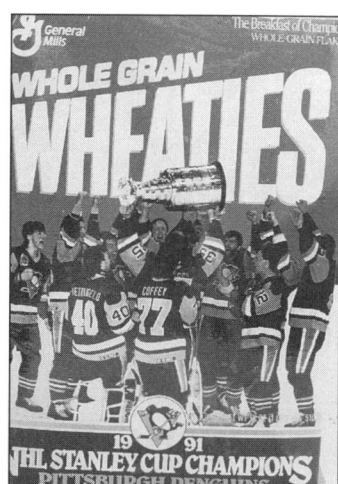

General Mills
Wheaties
1991 Pittsburgh Penguins Champs $25
1992 J. Jagr/M. Lemieux no logo R 35
1992 J. Jagr/W. Lemieux logo R 60
1998 Camp./Shan.(MFW Canada) 15
1998 Canadian Womens Team 15
1998 Desja/Drolet (MFW Can.) 15
1998 Legends 1980 Team USA 10

Horse Racing

The first Kentucky Derby was run on May 17, 1875, at Churchill Downs track in Louisville, Ky. Although not the oldest, it's the only one of the three Triple Crown races that has run continuously.

The Kentucky Derby was considered a local race until 1915, when Harry Payne Whitney sent his undefeated filly Regret from the East to win the race. This started the trend of other big eastern stables sending their top three-year-olds every year to compete.

The oldest known Derby program to have changed hands in recent years is one from 1899, which sold for $1,250. Derby program prices listed in this book prior to 1899 are a general consensus by dealers and collectors of what they would sell for if they were available.

The Preakness Stakes was first run on May 27, 1873, at the Maryland Jockey Club (now known as Pimlico Race Course) in Baltimore, Md. Although two years older than the Kentucky Derby, the Preakness was not run from 1891 to 1893. It was first run at New York's Morris Park in 1890, and then at Gravesend from 1894 to 1908. The Preakness Stakes was named for the horse Preakness that won the 1870 Dinner Party Stakes, the first stakes race ever run at Pimlico. In some years, the Preakness was run before the Derby, as in 1930, when Gallant Fox won the Preakness on May 9 and won the Derby on May 17. Some years the Derby and Preakness were run on the same day, as in 1917, when both races were run on May 12. Until recent years Preakness programs were not sought after by collectors as much as Derby programs. For various reasons, most Preakness programs, even those as recent as the late 1980s, are in short supply and in great demand, explaining their higher values over corresponding Derby programs.

The Belmont Stakes, the oldest of the Triple Crown races, was first run in 1867, at New York's Jerome Park. The race was named for August Belmont I, the first President of Jerome Park, and a monarch of the American turf. It continued to be run at Jerome Park until 1890, when it was switched to Morris Park in New York and ran there until 1904. Since 1904, it has been run at Belmont Park with the exception of 1963 to 1967, when it was run at Aqueduct while Belmont Park was being reconstructed. The Belmont Stakes was not run in 1911 and 1912.

Belmont programs, like Preakness programs, have become much more popular in recent years, and are also in short supply and great demand.

The Breeders' Cup is a championship event like the World Series or Super Bowl and is moved to a different location each year. The idea of the Breeders' Cup was first conceived in 1982 by Lexington, Ky., breeder John R. Gaines, who formed a committee to cultivate the idea. This committee was spearheaded by John Nerud, president of Tartan Farm, Ocala, Fla., and former trainer of Dr. Fager, considered by many the greatest horse of this century.

The first Breeders' Cup was run on Nov. 10, 1984, at Hollywood Park in California. The Breeders' Cup is a series of seven races run in different divisions on the same afternoon that attract the best horses in the world.

The popularity and prestige of this event in its short nine-year history has increased so dramatically that it overshadows the Triple Crown races.

Breeders' Cup programs did not really start to gain interest with collectors until after the 1988 running. Although all Breeders' Cup programs are still available through dealers in mint condition, the 1986 and 1987 programs bring a premium price. In 1986 the crowd was much smaller than expected, and although there were plenty of programs left over, the host track Santa Anita mistakenly threw them away. In 1987 the host track, Hollywood Park, anticipated a small crowd as in 1986, but the opposite occurred and it ran out.

Besides the Kentucky Derby, Preakness, Belmont and Breeders' Cup, many other thoroughbred racing programs are collected to a lesser degree (programs of a particular horse, a certain race, Triple Crown winners, and match race programs which are prized collectibles). Some programs are extremely valuable, such as any Man O' War program that would be worth at least $2,000 in decent condition.

OFFICIAL PROGRAMME
SATURDAY, JUNE 5, 1937
BELMONT PARK
GRANVILLE
WINNER 1936 BELMONT
BELMONT DAY
JUNE 5, 1937

Belmont Stakes Programs

Year	Winning Horse	Jockey	Value
1867	Ruthless	J. Kilpatrick	$2,000
1868	General Duke	Bobby Swim	1,200
1869	Fenian	C. Miller	1,000
1870	Kingfisher	W. Dick	1,000
1871	Harry Bassett	W. Miller	1,000
1872	Joe Daniels	James Roe	1,000
1873	Springbok	James Roe	1,000
1874	Saxon	G. Barbee	1,000
1875	Calvin	Bobby Swim	1,000
1876	Algerine	Billy Donohue	1,000
1877	Cloverbrook	C. Holloway	1,000
1878	Duke of Magenta	L. Hughes	1,000
1879	Spendthrift	George Evans	1,000
1880	Grenada	L. Hughes	1,000
1881	Saunterer	T. Costello	1,000
1882	Forester	Jim McLaughlin	1,000
1883	George Kinney	Jim McLaughlin	1,000
1884	Panique	Jim McLaughlin	950
1885	Tyrant	Paul Duffy	950
1886	Inspector B	Jim McLaughlin	950
1887	Hanover	Jim McLaughlin	900
1888	Sir Dixon	Jim McLaughlin	900
1889	Eric	W. Hayward	900
1890	Burlington	Pike Barnes	850
1891	Foxford	Ed Garrison	850
1892	Patron	W. Hayward	850
1893	Comanche	Willie Simms	800
1894	Henry of Navarre	Willie Simms	900
1895	Belmar	Fred Taral	800
1896	Hastings	H. Griffin	800
1897	Scottish Chieftain	J. Scherrer	800
1898	Bowling Brook	F. Littlefield	800
1899	Jean Bereaud	R. Clawson	800
1900	Ildrim	Nash Turner	750
1901	Commando	H. Spencer	750
1902	Masterman	John Bullman	750
1903	Africander	John Bullman	750
1904	Delhi	George Odom	750
1905	Tanya	E. Hilderbrand	750
1906	Burgomaster	Lucien Lyne	700
1907	Peter Pan	G. Mountain	750
1908	Colin	Joe Notter	950
1909	Joe Madden	E. Dugan	700
1910	Sweep	James Butwell	700
1911-12		Not held	
1913	Prince Eugene	Roscoe Troxler	650
1914	Luke McLuke	Merritt Buxton	650
1915	The Finn	George Byrne	650
1916	Friar Rock	E. Haynes	600
1917	Hourless	James Butwell	600
1918	Johren	Frank Robinson	550
1919	Sir Barton	John Loftus	1,100
1920	Man O' War	Clarence Kummer	1,750

Year	Winning Horse	Jockey	Value
1921	Grey Lag	Earl Sande	550
1922	Pillory	C.H. Miller	450
1923	Zev	Earl Sande	500
1924	Mad Play	Earl Sande	450
1925	American Flag	Albert Johnson	450
1926	Crusader	Albert Johnson	450
1927	Chance Shot	Earle Sande	450
1928	Vito	Clarence Kummer	450
1929	Blue Larkspur	Mack Garner	450
1930	Gallant Fox	Earl Sande	600
1931	Twenty Fox	Charles Kurtsinger	500
1932	Faireno	Tom Mally	400
1933	Hurryoff	Mack Garner	400
1934	Peace Chance	W.D. Wright	375
1935	Omaha	Willie Saunders	550
1936	Granville	James Stout	325
1937	War Admiral	Charles Kurtsinger	500
1938	Pasteurized	James Stout	350
1939	Johnstown	James Stout	375
1940	Bimelech	Fred Smith	350
1941	Whirlaway	Eddie Arcaro	500
1942	Shout Out	Eddie Arcaro	325
1943	Count Fleet	Johnny Longden	475
1944	Bounding Home	G.L. Smith	300
1945	Pavot	Eddie Arcaro	300
1946	Assault	Warren Mehrtens	450
1947	Phalanx	R. Donosco	275
1948	Citation	Eddie Arcaro	500
1949	Capot	Ted Atkinson	250
1950	Middleground	William Boland	275
1951	Counterpoint	David Gorman	250
1952	One County	Eddie Arcaro	250
1953	Native Dancer	Eric Guerin	300
1954	High Gun	Eric Guerin	225
1955	Nashua	Eddie Arcaro	250
1956	Needles	David Erb	250
1957	Gallant Man	Bill Shoemaker	300
1958	Cavan	Pete Anderson	175
1959	Sword Dancer	Bill Shoemaker	200
1960	Celtic Ash	Bill Hartack	175
1961	Sherluck	Braulio Baeza	175
1962	Jaipur	Bill Shoemaker	150
1963	Chateaugay	Braulio Baea	150
1964	Quadrangle	Manuel Ycaza	150
1965	Hail to All	John Sellers	125
1966	Amberoid	William Boland	125
1967	Damascus	Bill Shoemaker	150
1968	Stage Door Johnny	Gus Gustines	125
1969	Arts and Letters	Braulio Baeza	125
1970	High Echelon	John Rotz	100
1971	Pass Catcher	Walter Blum	100
1972	Riva Ridge	Ron Turcotte	100
1973	Secretariat	Ron Turcotte	115
1974	Little Current	Miguel Rivera	65
1975	Avatar	Bill Shoemaker	75
1976	Bold Forbes	Angel Cordero Jr.	75
1977	Seattle Slew	Jean Cruget	75
1978	Affirmed	Steve Cauthen	135
1979	Costal	Ruben Hernandez	50
1980	Temperence Hill	Eddie Maple	35
1981	Summing	George Martens	30
1982	Conquistador Cielo	Laffit Pincay Jr.	35
1983	Caveat	Laffit Pincay Jr.	35
1984	Swale	Laffit Pincay Jr.	40
1985	Crème Fraiche	Eddie Maple	30
1986	Danzig Connection	C. McCarron	25
1987	Bet Twice	Craig Perret	20
1988	Risen Star	Eddie Delahoussaye	20
1989	Easy Goer	Pat Day	15
1990	Go and Go	Michael Kinane	10

Year	Winning Horse	Jockey	Value
1991	Hansel	Jerry Bailey	6
1992	A.P. Indy	Eddie Delahoussaye	5
1993	Colonial Affair	J. Krone	5
1994	Tabasco Cat	P. Day	5
1995	Thunder Gulch	G. Stevens	5
1996	Editor's Note	R. Douglas	5
1997	Touch Gold	C. McCarron	5
1998	Victory Gallop	G. Stevens	5
1999	Lemon Drop Kid	J. Santos	5
2000	Commendable	P. Day	5

Breeders Cup Programs

Year	Value
1984	$20
1985	15
1986	35
1987	30
1988	6
1989	7
1990	6
1991-2000 (each)	5

Kentucky Derby Programs

Year	Winning Horse	Jockey	Value
1875	Aristides	Oliver Lewis	$4,000
1876	Vagrant	Bobby Swim	2,500
1877	Baden Baden	Billy Walker	2,250
1878	Day Star	Jimmy Carter	2,250
1879	Lord Murphy	Charlie Shauer	2,100
1880	Fonso	George Lewis	2,000
1881	Apollo	Babe Hurd	1,950
1883	Leontaus	Billy Bonohue	1,950
1884	Buchanan	Isaac Murphy	1,800
1885	Joe Cotton	Babe Henderson	1,750
1886	Ben All	Paul Duffy	1,750
1887	Montrose	Isaac Lewis	1,700
1888	Macbeth II	G. Covington	1,700
1889	Spokane	Thomas Kiley	1,600
1890	Riley	Isaac Murphy	1,600
1891	Kingman	Isaac Murphy	1,500
1892	Azra	Lonnie Clayton	1,400
1893	Lookout	Eddie Kunze	1,450
1894	Chant	Frank Goodale	1,400
1895	Halma	Soup Pekins	1,400
1896	Ben Brush	Willie Simms	1,400
1897	Typhoon II	Buttons Garner	1,300
1898	Plaudet	Willie Simms	1,300
1899	Manuel	Fred Taral	1,350
1900	Lieut. Gibson	Jimmy Boland	1,150
1901	His Eminence	Jimmy Winkfield	1,000
1902	Alan-a-Dale	Jimmy Winkfield	975
1903	Judge Himes	Hal Booker	950
1904	Agile	Jack Martin	900
1906	Sir Huon	Roscoe Troxler	900
1907	Pink Star	Andy Minder	875
1908	Stone Street	Arthur Pickens	875
1909	Wintergreen	Vincent Power	850
1910	Donau	Fred Herbert	800
1911	Meridian	George Archibald	775
1912	Worth	C. H. Shilling	650
1913	Donerail	Roscoe Goose	750
1914	Old Rosebud	John McCabe	650
1915	Regret	Joe Notter	900
1916	George Smith	Johnny Loftus	700
1917	Omar Khayyam	Charles Borel	700
1918	Exterminator	William Knapp	800
1919	Sir Barton	Johnny Loftus	1,250
1920	Paul Jones	Ted Rice	600
1921	Behave Yourself	Charles Thompson	575
1922	Morvich	Albert Johnson	600
1923	Zev	Earl Sande	625
1924	Black Gold	John Mooney	650
1925	Flying Ebony	Earl Sande	575
1926	Bubbling Overt	Albert Johnson	550
1927	Whiskery	Linus McAtee	525
1928	Reign County	Chick Lang	475
1929	Clyde Van Dusen	Linus McAtee	475
1930	Gallant Fox	Earl Sande	525
1931	Twenty Grand	Charles Kurtsinger	500
1932	Burgoo King	Eugene James	450
1933	Broken Tip	Don Meade	425
1934	Cavalcade	Mack Garner	425
1935	Omaha	Willie Saunders	475
1936	Bold Venture	Ira Hanford	400
1937	War Admiral	C. Kurtsinger	475
1938	Lawrin	Eddie Arcaro	375
1939	Johnstown	James Stout	350
1940	Gallahadion	Carroll Bierman	325
1941	Whirlaway	Eddie Arcaro	375
1942	Count Fleet	Johnny Longden	375
1944	Pensive	Conn McCreary	275
1945	Hoop Jr.	Eddie Arcaro	250
1946	Assault	Warren Mehrtens	275
1947	Jet Pilot	Eric Guerin	225
1948	Citation	Eddie Arcaro	350
1949	Ponder	Steve Brooks	225

1950 Middleground ...William Boland ..200
1951 County Turf .....Conn McCreary ..150
1952 Hill Gail ....Eddie Arcaro 125
1953 Dark Star ....Hank Moreno 125
1954 Determine ......Raymond York ...95
1955 Swaps ....Bill Shoemaker ..135
1956 Needles ....David Erb 100
1957 Iron Liege .....Bill Hartack 150
1958 Tim Tam ....I. Valenzuela 125
1959 Tommy Lee ....Bill Shoemaker ..125
1960 Venetian Way ...Bill Hartack 85
1961 Carry Back .....John Sellers 125
1962 Decidedly ......Bill Hartack 85
1963 Chateaugay .....Braulio Baeza 75
1964 Northern Dancer .Bill Hartack 95
1965 Lucky Debonair .Bill Shoemaker ..75
1966 Kauai King .....Don Brumfield ..65
1967 Proud Clarion ...Bobby Ussery ...65
1968 Forward Pass ....I. Valenzuela 60
1969 Majestic Prince ..Bill Hartack 60
1970 Dust Commander M. Manganello ..55
1971 Canonero II .....Gustavo Avila 40
1972 Riva Ridge ......Ron Turcotte 35
1973 Secretariat ......Ron Turcotta 95
1974 Cannonade ......Angel Cordero Jr. .30
1975 Foolish Pleasure .Jacinto Vasquez ..35
1976 Bold Forbes ....Angel Cordero Jr. .30
1977 Seattle Slew ....Jean Cruguet 30
1978 Affirmed ....Steve Cauthen ...30
1979 Spectacular Bid .Ron Franklin 30
1980 Genuine Risk ...Jacinto Vasquez ...28
1981 Pleasant Colony .Jorge Velasquez ...15
1982 Gato Del Sol ....Eddie Delahoussaye 10
1983 Sunny's Halo ....Eddie Delahoussaye 10
1984 Swale ....Laffitt Pincay Jr. ..11
1985 Spend A Buck ...Angel Cordero Jr. ..8
1986 Ferdinand ......Bill Shoemaker ...9
1987 Alysheba ......Chris McCarron ...7
1988 Winning Colors .Gary Stevens 7
1989 Sunday Silence ..Pat Valenzuela ...7
1990 Unbridled ......Craig Perret 6
1991 Strike the Gold ..Chris Antley 6
1992 Lil E. Tee ......Pat Day 5
1993 Sea Hero ......Jerry Bailey 6
1994 Go for Gin .....Chris McCarron ...5
1995 Thunder Gulch ...Gary Stevens 5
1996 Grindstone .....Jerry Bailey 5
1997 Silver Charm ...Gary Stevens 5
1998 Real Quiet .....Kent Desormeaux ..5

Preakness Stakes Programs

Year	Winning Horse	Jockey	Value
1873	Survivor	G. Barbee	$3,000
1874	Culpepper	W. Donohue	2,250
1875	Tom Ochiltree	L. Hughes	1,750
1876	Shirley	G. Barbee	1,200
1877	Cloverbrook	C. Holloway	1,200
1878	Duke of Magenta	C. Holloway	1,200
1879	Harold	L. Hughes	1,200
1880	Grenada	L. Hughes	1,050
1881	Saunterer	T. Costello	1,050
1882	Vanguard	T. Costello	1,050
1893	Jacobus	G. Barbee	1,950
1884	Knight of Ellerslie	S. Fisher	1,950
1885	Tecumseh	Jim McLaughlin	1,000
1886	The Bard	S. Fisher	1,000
1887	Dunboyne	W. Donohue	1,000
1888	Refund	F. Littlefield	1,000
1889	Buddhist	W. Anderson	1,050

The Preakness

The 104th Running
1873–1979

PREAKNESS DAY
MAY 19, 1979
PIMLICO

Official Souvenir Program
50c incl Tax

1890 Mintague ....W. Martin 1,050
1891-93 Not held
1894 Assignee ......Fred Taral 900
1895 Belmar ....Fred Taral 900
1896 Margrave ......H. Griffin 900
1897 Paul Kauvar ....T. Thorpe 900
1898 Sly Fox ....W. Simms 900
1899 Half Time .....R. Clawson 900
1900 Hindus ....H. Spencer 850
1901 The Parader .....F. Landry 850
1902 Old England ....L. Jackson 850
1903 Flocarline ......W. Gannon 850
1904 Bryn Mawr .....E. Hildebrand ..850
1905 Cairngorm .....W. Davis 850
1906 Whimsical .....Walter Miller ...850
1907 Don Enrique ....G. Mountain ...850
1908 Royal Tourist ...Eddie Dugan ...850
1909 Effendi ....Willie Doyle ...800
1910 Layminster .....R. Estep 800
1911 Watervale ......Eddie Dugan ...800
1912 Colonel Holloway C. Turner 800
1913 Buskin ....James Butwell ..800
1914 Holiday ....A. Schuttinger ...750
1915 Rhine Maiden ...Douglas Hoffman 750
1916 Damrosch ......Linus McAtee ...700
1917 Kalitan ....E. Haynes 700
1918 War Cloud .....Johnny Loftus ..650
     Jack Hare ......Charles Peak
1919 Sir Barton .....Johnny Loftus ..1,400
1920 Man O'War .....Clarence Kummer 2,250
1921 Broomspun ....John Maiben ...600
1922 Pillory ....Whitey Abel 600
1923 Virgil ....B. Marinelli 600
1924 Nellie Morse ...John Merimee ..700
1925 Conventry .....Clarence Kummer 550
1926 Display ....John Maiben ...600
1927 Bostonian .....Whitey Abel ...550
1928 Victorian ......Sonny Workman .550
1929 Dr. Freeland ...Louis Schaefer ..550
1930 Gallant Fox ....Earl Sande 750
1931 Mate ....George Ellis ...500

1932 Burgoo King ....John Maiben 500
1933 Head Play .....Charles Kurtsinger 500
1934 High Quest .....Robert Jones ...500
1935 Omaha ....Willie Saunders ..500
1936 Bold Venture ...George Woolf ...475
1937 War Admiral ....Charles Kurtsinger 600
1938 Dauber ....Maurice Peters ..475
1939 Challedon ......George Seabo ..450
1940 Bimelech ......F.A. Smith 450
1941 Whilaway ......Eddie Arcaro ...575
1942 Alsab ....Basil James 450
1943 Count Fleet ....Johnny Longden .575
9144 Pensive ....Conn McCreary .425
1945 Polynesian .....W.D. Wright 450
1946 Assault ....Warren Mehrtens .525
1947 Faultless ....Doug Dobson 400
1948 Citation ....Eddie Arcaro 650
1949 Capot ....Red Atkinson ...350
1950 Hill Prince .....Eddie Arcato ...350
1951 Bold ....Eddie Arcaro ...350
1952 Blue Man ......Conn McCreary ..350
1953 Native Dancer ...Eric Guerin 400
1954 Hasty Road .....Johnny Adams ..325
1955 Nashua ....Eddie Arcaro ...350
1956 Fabius ....Bill Hartack ...325
1957 Bold Ruler .....Eddie Arcaro ...325
1958 Tim Tam ....Ismael Valenzuela 250
1959 Royal Orbit ....William Harmatz .250
1960 Bally Ache .....Bobby Ussery ...195
1961 Carry Back ....Johnny Sellers ...250
1961 Greek Money ...John Rotz 175
1963 Candy Spots ....Bill Shoemaker ..175
1964 Northern Dancer .Bill Hartack 225
1965 Tom Rolfe .....Ron Turcotte ...140
1966 Kauai King .....Don Brumfield ...130
1967 Damascus ......Bill Shoemaker ..160
1968 Forward Pass ....Ismael Valenzuela 135
1969 Majestic Prince ..Bill Hartack 145
1970 Personality .....Eddie Belmonte ..135
1971 Canonero II .....Gustavo Avila ...125
1972 Bee Bee Bee ...Eldon Nelson ...110
1973 Secretariat ......Ron Turcotta 120
1974 Little Current ....Miguel Rivera 75
1975 Master Deby ....Darrel McHargue ..85
1976 Elocutionist .....John Lively 95
1977 Seattle Slew ....Jean Cruguet 85
1978 Affirmed ....Steve Cauthen ...135
1979 Spectacular Bid .Ron Franklin 60
1980 Codex ....Angel Cordero Jr. .45
1981 Pleasant Colony .Jorge Velasquez ...35
1982 Aloma's Ruler ...Jack Kaenel 35
1983 Deputed Testamenty Donald Miller 35
1984 Gate Dancer .....Angel Cordero Jr. .30
1985 Tank's Prospect ..Pat Day 30
1986 Snow Chief ....Alex Solis 32
1987 Alysheba ....Chris McCarron ...25
1988 Risen Star .....Eddie Delahoussaye 22
1989 Sunday Silence ..Pat Valenzuela 24
1990 Summer Squall ..Pat Day 18
1991 Hansell ....Jerry Bailey 10
1992 Pine Bluff .....Chris McCarron ...8
1993 Prairie Bayou ...M. E. Smith 8
1994 Tabasco Cat ....P. Day 7
1995 Timber Country ..P. Day 7
1996 Louis Quatorze ..P. Day 7
1997 Silver Charm ...G. Stevens 7
1998 Real Quiet .....Kent Desormeaux .6
1999 Charismatic ....Chris Antley 6
2000 Red Bullet .....Jerry Bailey 6

Horse Racing Glasses

Among the most collectible of all horse racing memorabilia are commemorative glasses. The first Kentucky Derby glass was issued in 1938. The 1938 and 1939 glasses were made of glass, while in 1940 there were two variations, one made of glass with a similar design to the 1939 glass, and one made of aluminum. Aluminum was also used in 1941. There was another aluminum version made in 1940 and 1941 issued by the French Lick Hotel Resort. Their version was identical except for the hotel's name appearing on the cup. The Bakelite (a.k.a. Beetleware) cup was also introduced in 1941. An early version of plastic, Bakelite was used through 1944 and, although the cups came in a variety of colors, there is no way to distinguish one year from another, since they all featured the same horsehead logo and phrase "Kentucky Derby, Churchill Downs."

In 1945 there were three different Kentucky Derby glasses: A "short," which is similar in size to the present day glasses; a "tall" narrow zombie-type glass; and a "jigger," sometimes referred to as a shot glass despite its closer resemblance in size to a juice glass.

In 1946, there was an undecorated glass distributed that was similar to the 1945 tall. This practice was continued in 1947 with an undecorated tall and short version. Some collectors consider these undecorated glasses as part of the set, whereas others consider them meaningless.

From 1948 to the present, all the glasses have been made of glass and are basically the same size, although some years have variations. The 1956 glass pictures three horses running and has a star at the beginning and end of the words "Churchill Downs." Some of the glasses have a missing star and/or a missing tail from one of the horses, so four variations are possible.

There were two variations of the 1958 glass, one being a recycled 1957 with the 1958 winner added on the upper part of the glass, known as the 1958 Iron Leige. The other 1958 version (known as the 1958 Gold Bar) has a large gold bar on each side.

The first Preakness glass, made in 1973, was produced in a very limited quantity and is the most sought after and valuable of the Preakness glasses. In 1974, the number of glasses produced almost doubled that of 1973, but 1974 still proves to be a difficult glass to find. In conjunction with the 100th running of the Preakness, the amount made in 1975 was again significantly increased. In 1976 and 1977, the number of glasses produced again increased substantially, while in 1978, production decreased to the level of 1975. From 1979 through 1984, the number of glasses made increased fraction-ally. Overproduced in 1985, production levels decreased from 1986 through 1989, but remained steady. In 1990, it was massively overproduced, and the seesaw pattern struck again in 1991 and 1992 as significantly fewer glasses were made. In comparison, the amounts made of Preakness glasses versus Kentucky Derby glasses of corresponding years has always been fractional. Even in 1990, when an all-time high of approximately 40,000 Preakness glasses were made, there were 600,000 Derby glasses made that year.

Belmont glasses, like Preakness glasses, were made in very small quantities compared to Kentucky Derby glasses. In some years, production was even smaller than that of corresponding Preakness glasses.

The first Belmont glass was made in 1976, and it is believed that in 1977, 1981, 1982, 1983 and 1988 there were less than 2,300 glasses produced each year. The amount made every year was always under 7,000 until 1991, when a record 14,400 were made.

Although the first Breeders' Cup was run in 1984, the first glass was not produced until 1985. This glass was produced in a very limited quantity, which explains its high value even though the glass is only 14 years old. The glass has a unique stemmed design that is a break from the traditional shape of the Triple Crown glasses. There were no Breeders' Cup glasses made in 1986 or 1987. Since 1988, they have been continually made in the same shape and size as Triple Crown glasses, but in relatively small quantities.

Belmont Stakes Glasses

Year	Description	Value
1976 "The Big Apple of Racing"		$95
1977 Black lettering & stable		350
1978 Brown horse shoe & winners listed		125
1979 Black horse shoe		75
1980 "112th Running," brown racing horses		135
1981 "113th Running," color racing horses		325
1982 "114th Running," color racing horses		275
1983 "115th Running," color racing horses		325
1984 "116th Running," color racing horses		200
1985 "117th Running," color racing horses		150
1986 "110th Running," color racing horses		95
1987 Brown & green horse, winners listed		75
1988 Brown & green horse, winners listed		85
1989 Brown & green horse, winners listed		30
1989 "121" graphic, w/ date		30
1990 Brown & green horse, winners listed		15
1991 Brown & green horse, winners listed		5

Breeders Cup Glasses

Year	Description	Value
1985 Pedestal-style glass, red & blue design		375
1986		Not issued
1987		Not issued
1988 Churchill Downs, date		15
1989 Gulfstream Park, yellow graphic		130
1990 Belmont Park, NYC graphic.		15
1991 Churchill Downs, date black graphic French Glory Error		45

Kentucky Derby Glasses

Officially Licensed Kentucky Derby Shot Glasses have been manufactured since 1987 ....$5-$10
One other licensed shot glass was available in 1945 and is valued at ......$750-$800

Year	Description	Value
1938.		$3,500
1939 Horses in black racing around base of glass		4,800
1940 (Glass) Horses in blue racing around base of glass		5,500
1940-41 (Aluminum) "Kentucky Derby Churchill Downs"		550

1941-44 (Bakelite) Reddish-brown, Derby Emblem Multicolored, Derby Emblem same
1945 Jigger: "I Have Been to the Kentucky Derby" 1,050
   Tall, Derby Emblem 455
   Short, Derby Emblem 975
1946 Undecorated 100
1947 Short-undecorated 100
   Tall-undecorated 75
1948 Clear bottom 150
   Frosted bottom. 165
1949 Matt Winn He has seen the All . .150
1950 Green, horses rounding turn 330
1951 "Where Turf Champions Are Crowned" 360
1952 Kentucky Derby Gold Cup 155
1953 Derby Emblem. "The Run for the Roses" 130
1954 Churchill Downs, winners randomly listed 165
1955 Yellow & green. Five fastest runnings 130
Yellow lettering, winners listed
   1 star, 2 tails. 180
   1 star, 3 tails. 300
   2 stars, 2 tails. 190
   2 stars, 3 tails. 200
1957 Gold horse & jockey, winners listed 100
1958 Iron Liege: gold horse & jockey graphic, winners listed. 150
   Gold Bar: same as above, w/ gold bar 180
1959 Horse & jockey dot portrait, winners listed in gold.. 75
1960 Gold horses, jockeys black. Winners listed in black 90

1961 Diagonal plot. horse & jockey, winners in gold 100
1962 Winning horse & jockey w/roses. 75
1963 Black & brown horse & jockey . .60
1964 Horse head, gold lettering.. 50
1965 Churchill Downs, Run for the Roses in red 75
1966 Gold lettering, 4 fastest runnings .70
1967 Several sm. pics., winners in black 55
1968 Red & blue coat of arms, gold lettering 50
1969 Jockey #3, horseshoe, horse racers in red 50
1970 Green coat of arms, winners listed 80
1971 Greens steeples and racers, red lettering 45
1972 Two horses in stretch, orange lettering 40
1973 Sign with steeples, red, green lettering 40
1974 100th anniversary, gold horse. . . .18
   w/ Federal Trademark 130
1975 Black & yellow lettering, year in red 6
1976 Red, white, blue, stars & stripes base 9
1977 Brown & cream colored horse & jockey 5
1978 Churchill Downs in brown, red lettering 10
1979 Grandstands, horses rounding bend 12
1980 Two horses neck & neck, b&w lettering 20
1981 Winning horse in yellow shield, green and yellow banner 7
1982 Trophy, rose garland, blue banner 7
1983 Air brush plot of Churchill Downs 7
1984 Two racers head in, lettering in red, green on back 6
1985 Post Parade Song, orange lettering 7
1986 Red roses, lettering, winners in green 8
1987 Brown horse & roses in center, winners listed in black 7
1988 Two horses head on, red roses.. 7
1989 "115 years," graphic w/ horse, steeple.. 7
1990 Horse w/steeple in back, one red rose.. 6
1991 Derby 117 graphic, one rose 6

Preakness Glasses

Year	Description	Value
1973	Black steeple, black & yellow daisies	$600
1974	Winners pictured in black	150
1975	100th Preakness in black & yellow daisies.	125
1976	Red, white, blue "Preakness of 76"	85
1977	Horse w/ daisies garland..	85
1978	Horse & jockey, 2 large daisies	125
1979	Black & yellow steeple, daisies around rim	65
1980	Horses running in front of steeple	65
1981	Horses running in front of grandstand	60
1982	Jockey w/"P" silks, daisies garland	55
1983	Horse in front of steeple, jockey head	50
1984	"Painting the Colors"	40
1985	Brown & green horse & jockey graphic	25
1986	Steeple, daisies, black bands around base	35
1987	Winners list, horses, daisies around glass	25
1988	Winners list, large daisies around base	25
1989	Large red "114," racing horse, steeple	20
1990	Horse head-on, steeple, daisies	5
1991	Horse graphic large daisies	10

●●●

Olympic Collectibles

The 27th Summer Olympiad was held in Sydney, Australia, 104 years after the modern Games were started in Athens, Greece in 1896.

While collecting Olympic memorabilia has been going on in Europe for decades, it was not until the 1980 Winter Games in Lake Placid, N.Y., that pin collecting became popular in the United States. When Atlanta hosted the 26th Summer Games in 1996, the number of collectors increased dramatically. Olympic pin collecting is one of the fastest growing hobbies in the world.

What is the appeal of collecting memorabilia from the Olympic Games? Most likely it is tied to the worldwide appeal of the Games themselves. Most people who have attended the Super Bowl, World Series, Final Four and the Olympics say the first three don't come close to the excitement and emotion experienced at the Olympics. Where else can you go and meet people like yourself, with the same dreams and aspirations, who are citizens of nations from all over the world? Dozens of different languages are spoken, yet the language barrier hardly matters when you meet on the street and exchange greetings, and maybe an Olympic pin.

Olympic pin collecting is not at all like sports card collecting. Most Olympic memorabilia was never made for collectors; it was made to identify athletes, officials and press members, or was provided in limited quantities for those working in the Olympic movement. It's often said the thrill of collecting is in the hunt. This is especially true in collecting memorabilia of the Olympics.

It is recommended that those who want to collect Olympic memorabilia, from pins to medals, should understand the history of the Olympics to give their collection meaning. It usually happens that those who get into Olympic collecting find themselves drawn to the Olympic movement and can't help but learn about this great international phenomenon. Many of today's most knowledgeable Olympic people started out as collectors, and then learned about the organization and history of the Olympics.

So one of the benefits of collecting from the Olympic Games is the knowledge gained about the movement itself. It can also pique interest in world history and geography. It's been recounted by teachers how the Olympics (and pin collecting) has helped motivate children to learn about the world we live in, and the people we share this world with.

Once someone gets involved in Olympic pin collecting, they find out there are many facets to this hobby. There are no boundaries to Olympic memorabilia collecting. A collector can take the hobby as far as he/she wishes. For example, pin collecting categories are numerous. One can dabble in the hobby, collecting from only one category or sampling several categories. Or he/she can take their collecting goals much further, trying for many types of Olympic pins.

Pins are only a part of the action. People can focus on other collectibles including books, beer mugs, coins, patches, posters and stamps. These are usually inexpensive, as they were made as souvenirs in large quantity. There are also more expensive items, produced in limited quantity because they were made for official use, or as awards. These include badges, medals, programs, reports, tickets and torches. Most of these items are costly and could be museum pieces. There are other items such as ash trays, official credentials, correspondence, statues, trophies, uniforms, etc.

So, not only do collectors have many options to select from as far as pin collecting goes, but they can look forward to infinite possibilities if he/she decides to expand from pins into other types of Olympic collectibles.

It's important to realize that Olympic memorabilia can be as common as readily available souvenirs, or so rare that only a handful of a certain item exists. This brings us to the collectors who are at opposite ends of the spectrum. For those inclined to find quick success, with little difficulty in growing their collection, many types of pins and certain types of other memorabilia are available. Commemorative pins, patches, key rings, coins, etc. are usually available to meet public demand, especially if one is fortunate enough to go to, or live near, a host city. It becomes more difficult if the

collector decides to try to fill out his/her collection with souvenirs of the past.

Badges, medals, programs, reports, tickets and torches are limited in quantity to meet the needs of the Games themselves. Imagine how much more scarce these items can be when they are from older Olympiads, when the Games were a fraction of the size they are today.

Pins

Lapel pins are far and away the most collected of all Olympic memorabilia.

The concept of Olympic pin collecting began with the birth of the modern Games. Beginning in Athens (1896), badges were given to athletes, officials, judges, dignitaries and press members to identify participants for the purpose of admittance. These badges were large, ornate pins, usually with ribbons attached.

As the Games continued, athletes from different nations brought their own identifying pins, and gradually began exchanging with each other as a form of good will. This practice occurred as early as the 1908 London Olympics. In 1928, at the Amsterdam Olympiad, several designs of souvenir pins were sold to the public. These pins were made in quantities that are insignificant compared to the souvenir pins of the 1980s and 1990s.

Around 1960, a few corporations made up their own lapel pins. In 1964, several organizations did likewise. Some pin trading involving non-athletes had begun. The pins were made not so much to identify someone, but as an advertising tool. By the 1970s, more Olympic teams made pins for their athletes to exchange. The organizers of the Olympics began producing logo pins for their Games as a fund-raising tool.

At Lake Placid in 1980, pin trading got its first major recognition. While covering the Olympics, ABC showed some of the frenzied trading between athletes, workers and fans. Suddenly the average sports fan was part of the Olympics. When the Games reached Los Angeles in 1984, the hobby

mushroomed. Merchants were loaded with commemorative pins and corporations had made thousands of their sponsor pins to trade. The athletes were ready too, having brought their Olympic team pins to trade with spectators. The hobby received worldwide attention on television.

At the last eight Olympic celebrations, the hobby continued to grow, and almost everyone got involved in the craze. Coca-Cola erected giant tents at all four sites and promoted the hobby as the "spectator sport."

There are three basic types of Olympic pins. These can be broken down further, allowing for many diverse types of Olympic pin collections. The three main categories are:

(1) Commemorative Pins. These are the pins authorized by the Organizing Committee to be made and sold in stores as souvenirs. These are generally the most plentiful and usually consist of mascots and logos depicting the various sports, and locations of the venues. One way to get such pins (in a limited quantity) is through the purchase of limited edition framed pin sets.

Otherwise, the pins are usually made to satisfy demand and never seem to grow much in value.

(2) Corporate Sponsor Pins. These pins are made by the various sponsors, suppliers and supporters, usually incorporating the Olympic logo with the corporate name and/or logo. Big business has found that pins are a marvelous means of advertising. The pins in this category are usually not for sale, but are given to employees and VIPs. Many collectors have enjoyed great success in getting corporate pins by writing the companies directly. The most coveted pins from this category are those related to the news media, i.e.: ABC, NBC, CBS and *Sports Illustrated*.

(3) National Olympic Team Pins. These pins are gradually becoming the hottest collectible among Olympic pin collectors. Their allure is more than the simple supply and demand principle. The NOC (National Olympic Committee) pins are made in different countries around the world, and are sometimes hand painted. Most NOC pins are made in small quantities, compared to commemorative and sponsor pins. There is no greater thrill for an NOC pin collector than to get a letter from a remote country with its Olympic Team pin enclosed.

As you may have suspected from the above pin categories, there are many diverse areas for an Olympic pin collector to pursue. Not everyone is looking for the same pins. What one person has for trade may be the very item another collector would cherish.

Usually, beginning collectors look for all pins with the Olympic rings on them and gradually narrow their field as they become more involved. Sometimes, it takes a long time before one decides which type of pin a collector will specialize in.

Pins can be expensive. The best advice is to shop around, whether you're buying or trading. Many pins can be obtained for free. New collectors could spend a lot of time at their local library searching for Olympic organizations' addresses, or for a corporation's public relations location because they advertised on television that they are an Olympic sponsor. Sometimes a great deal of work is required to chase down the thinnest of leads, and not all are successful. When all that effort results in adding a rare pin to a collection, there is a great deal of personal satisfaction.

Medals

There are three types of medals from the Olympic Games. The easiest to find, and therefore the least valuable, of the three are commemorative medals. These were usually struck to raise funds for some Olympic organization. They can be as cheap as $10 or $20, but can go quite a bit higher. Participation medals are given to every athlete who takes part in the Games. These medals are quite meaningful, and can be very scarce and valuable. For instance, a 1904 St. Louis Participation Medal is rarely found and can be worth in excess of $4,000.

Then there are the winner's medals. Since 1904 at St. Louis, there have been awards for each event; Gold (first), Silver (second) and Bronze (third). It is important to know that generally Gold Medals are silver, gilded with gold; Silver Medals are bronze, gilded with silver; and Bronze medals are bronze. They have great variations of availability, considering there were only 44 events at the first Olympics (Athens 1896), compared to 241 at Seoul in 1988. If those numbers seem small, consider that at the first Winter Olympics at Chamonix, France there were 14 events. At Calgary, Canada (1988), there were 46 medal events. A winner's medal from Barcelona could bring around $2,500, while a Gold medal from 1956 Stockholm (equestrian events were held in Sweden due to an animal quarantine in Australia during the year when Melbourne hosted the Summer Olympics) would be worth around $15,000-$18,000.

On the other hand, badges, medals, programs, reports, tickets and torches are limited in quantity to meet the needs of the Games themselves. Imagine how much the scarcity increases for these items when they are from older Olympiads. (The Games were a fraction of the size they are today.)

Badges

This category is the one most closely related to pin collecting. In fact, it was the official badges (made to designate athletes, officials, judges, dignitaries and media members) that caused pins to become part of the Olympic program. This background will be addressed later under "Pins." It is noteworthy that most European collectors call pins "Badges." For the purposes of this article, when we say "badges" we mean the official medal designators made in limited quantity by the host Organizing Committee.

The first badges were made for the 1896 Athens Olympiad and were fashioned out of cardboard with a thin blue ribbon tied at top. These were made in three colors: blue for athletes, pink for judges and red for officials. These are worth about $2,000 each.

As the Olympics grew and became more established, the badges were made of metal and were usually engraved to identify the type of person who wore it. Generally, colored ribbons hung from the badges, indicating which sport the wearer was involved with. The existence of badges at the 1900 Paris Olympics is debatable. They were made for the 1904 St. Louis Games (similar to the Participation Medal) and had a loop attached in order to hang from a ribbon. In 1908 in London, several variations were made as identifiers or credentials. At Stockholm in 1912, only two variations were made: competitor and press.

No metal badges of this sort have ever been found from the 1920 Antwerp Olympics. But they were made again in 1924 at Paris and continued to be produced in various styles up through the Montreal Games in 1976. Unexplainably, no badges for the Olympic Games have been made since 1976. Prices for these badges vary greatly, with older ones usually more valuable, particularly Winter Olympic badges. Just for an idea of the price variation, a 1976 Montreal badge sells for about $150, while a 1924 Chamonix Winter Games badge would garner from $1,500 to $2,000.

Although the Olympic organizing committees ceased to provide badges after Montreal in 1976, there are official badges of one type still made today. These are made for IOC (International Olympic Committee) Sessions, which are held once a year to plot the future of the Olympic movement. The first IOC Session was held in 1894 in Paris. The 99th IOC Session was held for the three days preceding the Barcelona Olympics in Spain.

The 100th Session was held in Lausanne, Switzerland, the home of the IOC headquarters.

Interestingly, at the same time (June 1993), the new IOC Olympic Museum was officially opened. It seemed for years that the IOC, as well as National Olympic Committees, was indifferent to the collector world. That is changing now, with possible IOC involvement to organize an international organization for all collectors.

The badges made for IOC sessions are usually metal with up to 15 different colored ribbons each attached, designating participants, such as IOC member (white) and press (yellow). Even the most recent badges command a value of about $150, with older session badges escalating in value rapidly.

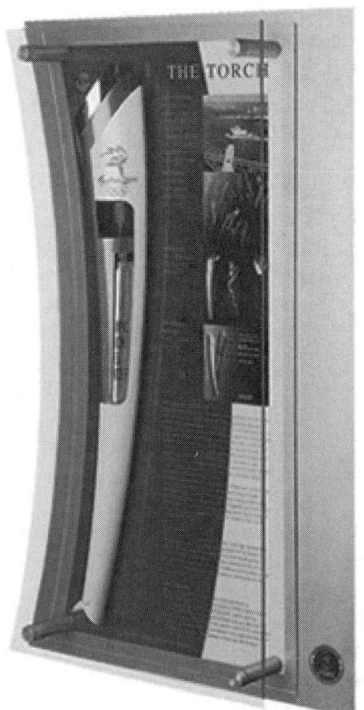

Torches

Among the elite Olympic collectibles, torches can be as rare as winners' medals, or more easily available than one might imagine. The first collectible torch used for lighting the modern Olympic flame was from the Berlin games in 1936. The torch is fairly plain, except it has engraved on the handle the major cities it passed through from Athens to Berlin. (The Olympic flame burns continuously at a site near the stadium that held the first modern Olympiad. For each Olympics, the flame is used to light a torch that is carried to the host city, where it lights a giant cauldron that burns at the main stadium throughout the competition.) The Berlin torches were given to each runner, and many are still obtainable for less than $2,000.

In 1984, the Los Angeles Organizing Committee came up with a cross-country torch run that took the flame through almost every state in America. About 3,000 segments were sold for $3,000 each to raise money for youth sports programs. In most cases, the segments were paid for as tax-deductible donations by large corporations who then awarded the torch to honored employees. The runners got to keep their torches.

Several Olympic hosts have followed with a similar plan. Thus a 1984 L.A. torch can be found for about $1,000. But, at Calgary in 1988, instead of awarding torches, the runners were given their uniforms. All but 150 of the torches were destroyed, and most of those remaining went to dignitaries, making a Calgary torch tough to obtain.

The value of an Olympic torch is not proportional to how old it is. The determining factor is supply and demand. Since many torches (especially from the Winter Games) were made in small quantity, they are hard to obtain.

Programs

Program collectors are much more plentiful than medal, badge and torch collectors. There are a lot more of these items out there. For example, if 10,000 seats were available for a soccer match, thousands of

that day's program could exist. It's not always as clear cut as that, because each Olympiad sets up its own plans for program distribution. It should be noted that the programs usually sought by these hard-core collectors are those given daily at the games, not a souvenir program which can be ordered by mail.

At some Olympics, especially the Winter Games, it seems one daily program was produced to cover all sports on a given day. If the Games covered 12 days, there would be 12 different programs to complete the set. At other Games, there were programs each day for each sport. More recently, there are only one-page handouts given as spectators enter the venue. At Barcelona, the sponsors did not even provide these!

Each collector has to decide what depth to go into the programs. One suggestion: try to get one program from every Olympics, although it's very difficult and not cheap. A 1896 Athens program has an estimated value of $5,000. Programs from the early Games up to 1924 can go as low as $150. Programs for more recent games generally are valued lower. For example, 1976 Montreal programs (there's one for each sport) are only about $10 each. Don't forget, Winter Games programs are less plentiful, and therefore generally more valuable.

Some collectors have decided rather than collect all programs, or even one from each Olympics, they will specialize and try to get every program from certain Games. This can be a big project, especially if you choose 1928 Amsterdam, 1932 Los Angeles, 1952 Helsinki or 1956 Melbourne. As with most Olympic collectibles, you have all sorts of possibilities if you do opt to collect programs.

Olympic program values are for official daily programs or common event-specific programs.

Summer Olympics Programs

1896 Athens, Greece	$10,000
1904 St. Louis, Missouri	6,000
1908 London, England	400
1912 Stockholm, Sweden	400
1920 Antwerp, Belgium	250
1924 Paris, France	150
1928 Amsterdam, Holland	75
1932 Los Angeles, California	50
1936 Berlin, Germany	75
1948 London, England	40
1952 Helsinki, Finland	35
1956 Melbourne, Australia	35
1956 Stockholm, Sweden	75
1960 Rome, Italy	35
1964 Tokyo, Japan	35
1968 Mexico City, Mexico	35

1972 Munich, Germany 20
1976 Montreal, Quebec 15
1980 Moscow, Soviet Union 25
1984 Los Angeles, California 15
1988 Seoul, South Korea 15
1992 Barcelona, Spain 10
1996 Atlanta, Georgia U.S.A. 7
2000 Sydney, Australia 7

Winter Olympics Programs

1932 Lake Placid, New York $125
1936 Garmisch-Partenkirchen, Germany
. 200
1948 St. Moritz, Switzerland 95
1952 Oslo, Norway 80
1956 Cortina d'Ampezzo, Italy 80
1960 Squaw Valley, California 75
1964 Innsbruck, Austria 75
1968 Grenoble, France 50
1972 Sapporo, Japan 50
1976 Innsbruck, Austria 30
1980 Lake Placid, New York 15
1984 Sarajevo, Yugoslavia 15
1988 Calgary, Alberta 10
1992 Albertville, France 7
1994 Lillehammer, Norway 6
1998 Nagano, Japan 5

Tickets

Ticket collecting is not as popular as program collecting. There are probably two reasons for this: (1) Many program collectors use the programs as source documents to find out who competed at an event, what the venues look like, etc., and (2) people tend to leave their tickets, or throw them away after the event. On the plus side, as opposed to varying program distribution at each Olympics, tickets have always been used at each event to the present day. So a collection can be built that encompasses more Olympiads than would be possible for a program collector.

As with programs, sometimes there were tickets that covered all events on a given day, or certain events on all days, or all events on all days. Sometimes there was a single laminated ticket (1932 Lake Placid) or a booklet issued with a packet of tickets to be used (1932 Los Angeles). These types of tickets are rarer and more valuable.

Again, ticket collectors have various options from which to choose what they will collect. One ticket from each Olympics? All tickets from one Olympics? Generally, prices are a little less than programs. Tickets, or ticket stubs, from the last 10 years usually are worth $2 to $10. The prices again climb steeply with age, especially before the 1920s. Of course, Winter Games tickets are usually higher.

Tips on Olympic Collecting

Whatever you choose to collect from the Olympics, here are some basic guidelines or suggestions. First, try to decide as early as possible what your goals are. If you find yourself getting really serious (the Olympics have a way of becoming addictive), it's best to funnel your time, effort and money into the area that most interests you. Try to get past the "anything with five rings" concept early on.

Whatever you collect should be displayed for you to look at and enjoy. Believe it or not, many pin collectors put their pins in boxes, and often can't remember if they have certain ones or not. There is no standard way to display Olympic pins or other memorabilia. You'll have to use your own ingenuity to make your collection accessible. Besides being able to quickly determine what you have, displaying your treasures allows you the luxury of remembering how you got things. There can be a wonderful story behind each and every pin.

Do not collect Olympic memorabilia in an attempt to make money. It's true that some items appreciate, but many items don't. Pins can be re-made in Taiwan after they have become scarce, thus reducing their salability. If you decide to get into Olympic collecting, you'll find many benefits besides value. Pin collecting should be a hobby that will not only give you great satisfaction in building your collection, but will enlighten you about the world and the people in it.

With any collecting hobby, patience is very important. The more you learn about the hobby and the Games, the better you will be able to control your collecting by not making impulsive purchases. Don't try to do your collecting in a vacuum. The more people you meet and know in your hobby, the easier it is to decide what you want to collect, find ways to display your collection and exhibit patience in acquiring new material.

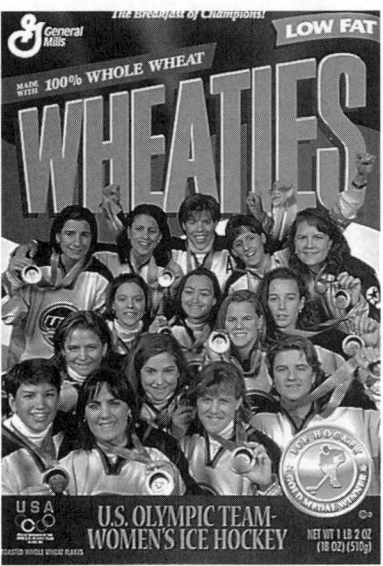

Olympics Cereal Boxes

Kellogg's Corn Flakes

1992 Bonnie Blair speedskating $15
1992 Dan Jansen speedskating 15
1994 Bonnie Blair speedskating 15
1996 D. Bailey track (Canada) 10
1996 D. Bailey (Canada w/metal) 20

Kellogg's Special K

1991 Kristi Yamaguchi '92 GM 40

Wheaties Boxes

1984 Mary Lou Retton arms raised (10) . .100
1984 Mary Lou Retton arms raised (12/18) .90
1984 Mary Lou Retton on one foot (24) . .12
1993 J. Faman Special Olympics (R) . .12
1994 H. McGee Special Olympics (R)
. 12
1995 M. Bedard mountain bike (Can.) . . .15
1995 S. Galloway Special Olympics (R)
. 12
1995 Elvis Stoiko skating (Can.) 30
1996 Tom Dolan swimming 5
1995 T. Ferguson Special Olympics (R)
. 12
1996 Michael Johnson Track & field . . .6
1996 Dan O'Brien decathlon 5
1996 Toffin/Stillings Spec. Oly. (R) . . .10
1996 Amy Van Dykan swimming 5
1996 USA Women's Gymnastics Team . .7
1996 100 Years of Olympics 8
1997 J. Finzel Special Olympics (R) 7
1998 Michigan Special Olympics 7
1998 N.Y. Special Olympics 7
1998 Texas Special Olympics 7
1998 USA Women's Hockey 7

(R) = Regionally distributed box

●●●

Soccer Collectibles

Outside of the United States, soccer is *The Sport*. Or should we say football, as it's known around the world. Football in America is the Chicago Bears and Dallas Cowboys, among others in the National Football League (NFL). Football to the rest of the world is Manchester United, Liverpool, Tottenham Hotspur and all others who play *The Game*. Whatever term you use, the sport of Pelé fame clearly is The Sport, complete with its own international governing body, FIFA (Federation Internationale de Football Association). It's a sport that, played anywhere but America, always has major political, social and economic implications. Sold-out stadiums with wild and crazy fans (hooligans, as they are often dubbed) are commonplace, from South America to Europe, Asia and Australia. America is just slow to catch the soccer bug, though popularity definitely has increased over the past few decades as seen by the millions of amateur leagues and youth organizations across America, not to mention the formation of Major League Soccer (MLS).

To find the origin of the sport, one must travel to the British Isles in 1863. Quickly, the sport moved to other areas, other regions, other countries. The first official international soccer match was between Scotland and England in late 1872. In the early 1900s, there were recorded international matches outside of the United Kingdom. The success of soccer in those areas was just as strong, and still is. The popularity of soccer in the United States didn't really come around, believe it or not, until the 1990s, though the sport was played in the U.S. long before that.

Numerous leagues and pro players came to America, such as Pelé and Georgio Chinalgia and the New York Cosmos, Chicago Sting and others, in the NASL.

So what can you collect soccer-related? Balls, jerseys, cleats and goals? Well, at first glance that might appear to be all that's out there because, well, let's face it, you don't need much to start a soccer game. But how wrong that could be. There's a ton more to collect, with new items joining the list of soccer collectibles about as quickly as a Pelé shot found the upper corner of the goal. Let's see:

Caps

We're not talking baseball hats here. We're talking an important honor given top-level players representing their country in a national game. For instance, goalie

MLS All-Star Pennant

Tony Meola played for America against, say, Japan … and Meola received a cap. Over a career, players may receive 100 or more, depending on their career, how good they are and how long they play.

The term cap (yes, it is is a soft, colorful hat) comes from the fact that players wore a cap as part of their uniform during the sport's formative years. Plus, the cap was the main method of identifying the two teams on the field. Caps were important in the pre-numbers-on-the-back-of-jersey days.

International caps are highly sought-after by collectors. The first official England international caps were awarded in 1886.

Caps changed in style throughout the 1900s, at times including tassels, patches and/or years.

Though difficult to find in America in the new millennium, caps clearly have a significant place in soccer collecting history.

Medals and Trophies

The team gets the trophy, the players get the medals. In simple terms, that's the way it's been since the late-1800s. Dating back to about 1876, winning pro-level players often received picturesque golden discs to showcase their personal accomplishments. Throughout the 1900s, the medals changed in look and design, but always for the better—maybe a bit bigger or a bit smaller,

maybe with more color or detail, or maybe with more inscriptions.

Uniforms

Hey, that isn't just a T-shirt. That's a game-used jersey and clearly one of the most collectible souvenirs from the sport. Uniforms are rich in tradition and heritage, often with an advertisement emblazed across the front of it for a sportswear manufacturer or for the team's main sponsor.

Some uniforms were short-sleeved, while others were long-sleeved; some had stripes, while others were solid. Almost all had, and still have, patches depicting the team.

Jerseys in the early days were made from a thick wool, often with thick cuffs and maybe even button-up collars. That's anything but the case now; today they're loose-fitting polyester shirts.

Since 1913, goalies have been different—in jerseys, that is. The goalies' jersey must be different from the players, it was written at the time. And so was born one of the greatest traditions: colorful, non-traditional-looking, long-sleeved uniforms.

Numbers on the back of the jersey, obviously, set players aside. But that wasn't an instant thing. That took time. Now, though, it's commonplace, along with a player's last name.

A player's shorts, though nice and attractive, have never been as collectible as the jersey.

Full size autograph of soccer legend Pelé.

Shoes

Footwear has long been collectible, too. Who wouldn't want to display the shoes worn by, say, American hero (1990s) Alexi Lalas from a major game? Or, better yet, why not collect the footwear of a player from the late 1880s, when players wore brown leather boots and had boot-studs at their disposal? (Interestingly, players' boots and boot-studs have been administered far more closely than other aspects of dress in the laws of the game due to the inherent dangers.) That explains why metal spikes were banned back in the 1800s. Early on, soccer shoes actually were soccer boots, but that changed in about 1950 when most players instead chose the Continental-style boot, designed more like a shoe.

Balls

Hands down—or should we say, hands-off—soccer balls are among the most collectible item from the sport, mostly because they are the most visible aspect of the sport. Most balls in the early days were made of hand-stitched leather and stuffed with horsehair. They could be stitched in four sections, with two vertical and two horizontal seams. Eventually, the ball became uniform, though color and shape slightly varied. Always, though, the circumference of the ball was no less than 27 inches and no more than 28 inches. Weight varies from 12 to 16 ounces. The American football-style stitching was quickly replaced due to injuries; now there are valves for air.

Pictures, Artwork, Cards, Stickers, Coins, Pins

From the miscellaneous soccer file, the sport has more than its share of collectibles. Ceramics, for instance, have a strong tradition. You've got plates, cups, mugs and teapots to start with. Then there are pictures, posters, pins, programs, books (by the thousands), illustrations, stamps, statues, player contracts, coins and the like. There even are soccer board games.

California-based Upper Deck produced soccer cards in the 1990s, which never really took off. European-made soccer cards from the mid-1900s are hard to find in America, but commonplace overseas. And some are quite pricey, too.

World Cup

Jules Rimet assumed the presidency of FIFA in 1921. Five years later, he proclaimed the need for organizing, within a period of no more than four years, the first World Tournament involving all the federations without distinction between pros and amateurs. "Soccer could reinforce the ideals of a permanent and real peace," he said at the time.

1994 World Cup Program

In 1930, the World Cup was born, with its debut in Uruguay due to that country's record in the Olympics. So started the greatest soccer event of all time, a tournament held in different countries every four years.

And, yes, anything and everything World Cup-related is collectible, especially World-Cup related relics from countries like Brazil, Germany, Italy, Argentina and England—some of the best countries in the annual extravaganza on a regular basis. So many others have participated, from South Africa to Jamaica to Zaire to Greece to Iran to Kuwait to Israel to Turkey. Everyone plays, so few succeed. Abel Laflour was hired to design the trophy: a Winged Victory made of 1,800 grams of gold.

In 1991, women joined the World Cup scene, with their own version of the tournament. And it, too, was a hit immediately, especially in America where Mia Hamm, Brandi Chastain and the rest of the Americans triumphed. *Sports Illustrated* even put Chastain on its famous cover.

1999 Columbus Crew Media Guide

2000 Mia Hamm Wheaties Box

Names, Teams and Leagues

Pelé is, without question, the biggest name ever produced by the sport. He's a goodwill ambassador for soccer and sports in general. Other superstars have captured the hearts of fans worldwide, such as Bobby Charlton, Franz Beckenbauer, David Beckham, Tatu, Sissi and literally thousands of others, from every corner of the world.

The now-defunct NASL (North American Soccer League, 1967-84) left a lasting impression on the sport. It was, without question, the most successful professional soccer league in United States history, also expanding into Canada.

Two rival leagues started in 1967, the FIFA-Sponsored United Soccer Association and the renegade National Professional Soccer League. In 1968, they merged to form the North American Soccer League. The league flourished for many years, attracting top stars and posting impressive performances and attendance figures. But overspending eventually forced the league into oblivion.

The NASL legacy includes such teams as the Seattle Sounders, Vancouver Whitecaps, Los Angeles Aztecs and Washington Diplomats. Star players included Gordon Banks, Johan Cruyff, Kyle Rote Jr., Willy Roy, Steve Zungel, Shep Messing and others.

Today's MLS features the Chicago Fire, Kansas City Wizards, Columbus (Ohio) Crew and such stars as Brian McBride.

You can also find relics nowadays from such "minor" leagues as the indoor NPSL (National Professional Soccer League), with teams such as the Milwaukee Wave and others. The NPSL once included teams in Chicago and Denver, among other cities, and many of today's top outdoor-playing stars.

Tennis Collectibles

The game is the same worldwide. Only the name differs.

In Great Britain, it is called Tennis or, to distinguish it from Lawn Tennis, "Real Tennis" or "Royal Tennis." In America, it is called "Court Tennis." In France, it's "Jeu de Paume" (hand ball). In Australia, it's simply "Royal Tennis." Why the name game? That's because of the development of the sport.

Tennis originated in France in the 11th century, historians say. The appearance of a tennis court is influenced by its origins. The first courts were to be found in court-yards immediately adjacent to a castle or in cloistered monastery quadrangles. Originally, players used their hands (hence the French name), but that progressed into gloves (used to protect the hand) then short bats to hit the balls. By the 13th century, there were, reportedly, as many as 1,800 courts in France.

Rackets came into vogue in the 16th century and, in 1750, the present configuration of lopsided head, thick gut and longer handle was introduced. And, yes, the design was done with a purpose: to help players scoop the balls out of the corners and also to put "cut" or "spin" on the ball.

Tennis long has been a noble sport, with French kings and Stuart kings playing with glee. Other noteworthy historical tennis players included Henry VIII, George IV, Prince Albert, Edward VII and George V.

Balls of the early years were made of leather, stuffed with wool or hair—and yes, they often caused serious injury, even death. That, obviously, changed over time. Starting in the 18th century, strips of wool were wound tightly around a nucleus made by rolling a number of strips into a little ball. String was then tied in many directions around the ball and a white cloth covering sewn around the ball. Today it's a rubbery ball with a soft-to-the-touch outer covering.

"Lawn Tennis," derived from "Real Tennis" in the late-1870s, is played on a marked-out surface without side or end walls. "Court Tennis," to use the American name for tennis, indicates that tennis is played in a specialty court with walls on four sides.

Whatever the type of tennis you play, there's a collectible for your gameroom. Maybe it's just a simple color, 8x10-inch photo of one of today's top players, such as Andre Agassi, Boris Becker and Pete Sampras; those go for about $40. Maybe you prefer tennis books. Well, there are

1933 Sport Kings Gum card of tennis great Bill Tilden.

countless editions, ideal for an afternoon read or an autograph party of players. Here are a few to consider:
● *American Tennis: The Story of a Game* (Little Brown, 1957).
● *Complete Book of Tennis: A New York Times Scrapbook History* (Arno/Bobbs-Merrill, 1980).
● *Fireside Book of Tennis* (Simon & Schuster, 1972).
● *Tales From The Tennis Court* (Sidgwick & Jackson, 1983); and
● *Ultimate Tennis Book: 500 Years of the Sport* (Follett, 1975).

The history of tennis is on display in picturesque fashion at The International Tennis Hall of Fame in Newport, R.I. A non-profit institution, it is dedicated to preserving the rich history of the sport, inspiring and encouraging junior tennis development, enshrining tennis heroes and heroines, and providing a landmark for tennis fans worldwide.

*March 4, 1974 issue of **Sports Illustrated** featuring Jimmy Connors.*

The facility's museum features more than 7,000 objects and includes historic tennis equipment, period clothing and a terrific tennis library. There also are exhibit galleries focusing on court tennis, the birth of lawn tennis, tennis throughout the 1900s, the Grand Slam International Federation, and the Billie Jean King WTA Tour Gallery.

The Hall of Fame is something more than a lovely physical property. It is an inspiration for the young, showing them a goal that can be attained through the sacrifice, perseverance and strength of character that won a place for those already enshrined there. Sport still has its ideals. None are loftier than those represented by The Tennis Hall of Fame, once said Allison Danzig (1955 inductee). There are more than 150 inductees, including players, writers, coaches and administrators.

All of the sport's legends now enshrined in the Hall of Fame are hits with collectors, including those card collectors who want to take a swing at tennis cards. NETPRO's Legends cards include such greats as Don Budge, Dennis Ralston, Roy Emerson, Tracy Austin, Tony Trabert, Stan Smith, Pam Shriver and Fred Stolle, among others. There also were NETPRO Tour Star Player Cards, with such men's players as Andre Agassi, Brad Gilbert, Jim Courier, Pat Cash, Robbie Weiss, Pete Sampras, Mats Wilander, Ivan Lendl and Michael Stich. Plus, there are cards of such women's players as Anne Smith, Debbie Graham, Ann Grossman, Kathy Jordan, Gigi Fernandez, Helena Sukova, Peanut Louie, Mary Lou Daniels and others.

Autographed tennis balls are, naturally, the most logical item to be signed, not to mention the easiest and most accessible. But, they rarely turn out well, due to their soft texture. Still, signed balls from any of the greats, such as Bjorn Borg or Jimmy Connors, are highly sought-after. Most major card shows in America have at least one or two dealers hawking hand-signed tennis balls. A ball signed by Sampras, for instance, sells for about $60, while Agassi is at $50.

Tennis rackets are valuable collectibles, but authentics are hard to obtain, especially match-used. They do, though, make great conversation pieces when signed.

Match-used shoes and shirts also are sought-after on the collecting front, as are signed magazines like *Sports Illustrated*.

Due to the international scope and upper-end financial flavor of the sport, obtaining autographs from the game's greats can be difficult, but not impossible. Practice rounds always are ideal autograph opportunities.

● ● ●

Tennis Autographs

Andre Agassi
Photo $50
Ball $50
3x5 index card $12

Arthur Ashe*
Photo . . . .$90-$100
Ball . . . .$100-$120
3x5 index card . . . .$15-$18

Boris Becker
Photo $25
Ball $30
3x5 index card $6

Jonas Bjorkman
Photo $15
Ball $20
3x5 index card $5

Bjorn Borg
Photo $20
Ball $25
3x5 index card $6

Sergi Bruguera
Photo $15
Ball $20
3x5 index card $5

Jennifer Capriati
Photo $20
Ball $25
3x5 index card $6

Michael Chang
Photo $25
Ball $30
3x5 index card $6

Amanda Coetzer
Photo $15
Ball $20
3x5 index card $5

Jimmy Connors
Photo $30
Ball $35
3x5 index card $7

Jim Courier
Photo $30
Ball $35
3x5 index card $7

Margaret Court
Photo $20
Ball $25
3x5 index card $6

Lindsay Davenport
Photo $25
Ball $30
3x5 index card $7

Stefan Edberg
Photo $25
Ball $30
3x5 index card $7

Chris Evert
Photo $20
Ball $25
3x5 index card $6

Mary Joe Fernandez
Photo $15
Ball $20
3x5 index card $5

Vitas Gerulaitis*
Photo $75
Ball $90
3x5 index card $15

Pancho Gonzalez *
Photo $60
Ball $80
3x5 index card . . . .$12-$14

Steffi Graf
Photo $35
Ball $45
3x5 index card . . . .$7-$8

Martina Hingis
Photo $30
Ball $40
3x5 index card $10

Goran Ivanisevic
Photo $25
Ball $30
3x5 index card $7

Yevgeny Kafelnikov
Photo $15
Ball $20
3x5 index card $5

Billie Jean King
Photo $20
Ball $25
3x5 index card $6

Petr Korda
Photo $20
Ball $25
3x5 index card $6

Anna Kournikova
Photo $30
Ball $40
3x5 index card $10

Richard Krajicek
Photo $15
Ball $20
3x5 index card $5

Rod Laver
Photo $20
Ball $25
3x5 index card $6

Ivan Lendl
Photo $20
Ball $25
3x5 index card $6

Conchita Martinez
Photo $15
Ball $20
3x5 index card $5

John McEnroe
Photo $60
Ball $80
3x5 index card . . . .$15-$18

Thomas Muster
Photo $20
Ball $25
3x5 index card $6

Ilie Nastase
Photo $35
Ball $40
3x5 index card . . . .$10-$12

Martina Navratilova
Photo $30
Ball $40
3x5 index card $8

John Newcombe
Photo $20
Ball $25
3x5 index card $6

Jana Novotna
Photo $15
Ball $20
3x5 index card $5

Mary Pierce
Photo $20
Ball $25
3x5 index card $6

Patrick Rafter
Photo $15
Ball $20
3x5 index card $5

Bobby Riggs*
Photo $50
Ball $60
3x5 index card $10

Carlos Rios
Photo $20
Ball $25
3x5 index card $6

Gabriela Sabatini
Photo $20
Ball $25
3x5 index card $6

Pete Sampras
Photo $60
Ball $70
3x5 index card $10

Vicario A. Sanchez
Photo $15
Ball $20
3x5 index card $5

Monica Seles
Photo $25
Ball $30
3x5 index card $6

Pam Shriver
Photo $15
Ball $20
3x5 index card $5

Michael Stich
Photo $15
Ball $20
3x5 index card $5

Bill Tilden*
Photo $250
Ball $300
3x5 index card . . . .$90-$100

Malivai Washington
Photo $20
Ball $25
3x5 index card $6

Mats Wilander
Photo $20
Ball $25
3x5 index card $6

Venus Williams
Photo $25
Ball $30
3x5 index card $7

Serena Williams
Photo $25
Ball $30
3x5 index card $7

Helen Wills-Moody
Photo $20
Ball $25
3x5 index card $6

Wrestling

One market that has tremendous potential is pro wrestling collectibles. Wrestling is unique in that it has the enviable position of combining the best of the so-called "traditional sports" market, as well as the television-collectibles market phenomenon. Wrestling shows have been part of a recent boom in popularity and has seriously competed for the dollars of fans from traditional sports areas. The television shows like the ones staged by the World Wrestling Federation and World Championship Wrestling rank as the top-rated cable programs and now it is difficult to keep up with the never-ending line of new merchandise that is generated. Increasingly, collectibles shops have added wrestling memorabilia out of fear for losing out on this pop-culture craze.

Hardcore wrestling fans are aware, however, that the sport has seen more than 50 years of popularity. The fact that wrestling is getting mainstream media attention is new, but wrestling has always been a popular spectator sport. Wrestling memorabilia has been bought, sold and talked about in underground circles for years. Wrestlers have appeared in advertising and movies, have had figures made of them, and have been cover stories in thousands of magazines around the globe. That, truly, just scratches the surface of the appeal wrestling has to millions of fans. Even today, with the wrestling-collectibles market at record levels of popularity, the sport has not been officially recognized as a viable part of the memorabilia marketplace.

Without question, the history of the sport is long and storied.

A lot can be learned about where wrestling is today by looking at our past. Every fan has reason to believe his favorite is a legend.

Wrestling cards are a special part of the wrestling-collectibles market. For many fans, it is their first foray into the sport. That's because wrestling cards are perhaps the one area that connects the wrestling world to the rest of sports-memorabilia collecting.

Nowadays, fans can go to any local comic book store or tobacco shop and find the latest issue of wrestling collector cards—full color, glossy and embossed cards that are true artifacts that should be kept and cherished for many years to come. But the truth is, wrestling cards are not new. In fact, the history of wrestling cards dates

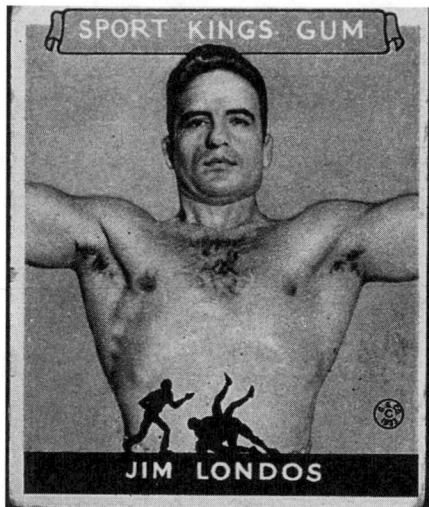

1933 Sport King Gum card of wrestler Jim Londos.

back to when the very first sports cards were made.

In the late 1800s, it was common for wrestling to be featured on classic tobacco cards. In 1887, the Allen & Ginters Tobacco Company released a set of seven wrestlers as part of a sportscard set. This, by most accounts, was the very first sports card set ever produced. Who would have thought that alongside the greats of baseball and boxing of the day would stand professional wrestlers? Today, it's hard to imagine Stone Cold Steve Austin being offered in a set with the likes of Shaquille O'Neal or Peyton Manning. But in the latter part of the 19th century, wrestling stars were considered the cream of the crop of pro athletes.

Through much of the early 1900s, many cigarette cards, which displayed pictures of oldtime grapplers, were produced in the United States and abroad. But it wasn't until the 1950s that the first all-wrestling set of collector cards was produced. In 1948, the Topps Co. issued a 25-card set called the "Magic Photo Cards." These postage stamp-sized cards had one blank side that "developed" a picture when it was moistened.

Then, from 1954 to 1956, the Parkhurst Co. in Canada issued two complete sets of

Sportscaster Card of Bruno Sammartino.

wrestling's first superstars. With stars like Beautiful Buddy Rogers, Lou Thesz and Gorgeous George, this set, complete and in superior condition, can fetch as much as $1,000 on the current market.

Fans had to wait nearly 30 years before the next full set of wrestling cards became available. In 1982, Norman Kietzer's Pro Wrestling Enterprises issued four sets of his wrestling superstars line that included stars from the regional territories like the American Wrestling Association and the National Wrestling Alliance. For new fans, this set is sentimental for many reasons, the most important being these are the stars who got them interested in wrestling to begin with. Whole sets of this type are rare, but are still floating around. No one can dispute the quality, as the card backs were loaded with information.

When the World Wrestling Federation took its promotional efforts national in 1984 and exposed pro wrestling to a mass audience, it issued the first set of WWF cards, which is one of the most popular for fans today.

In 1985, the O-Pee-Chee company released a combination French-American set of cards that is widely considered the most rare to find. Released in Canada, the cards are written in both English and French. Collectors clamor over this set because of one card: No. 70. That card is the very first WWF-released Jesse "The Body" Ventura card (his first card is No. 20 of the 1982 Pro Wrestling Enterprises line). That same year, Topps released an English set in the United States. Ventura is included in this set as well, and his card has skyrocketed in value since he became governor of Minnesota and an XFL announcer.

In 1986, Monty Gum produced a wrestling superstars line that is a mixture of old NWA and WWF grapplers. Then in 1987, Topps produced its second WWF card set and it is considered a superior-quality set when compared with the earlier release.

Three years passed before Classic Cards produced a WWF set that includes wrestlers such as the Ultimate Warrior and Shawn Michaels. In 1988, the NWA put out a line from Wonderama, and WCW's first venture into collector cards came in 1991 when Championship Marketing released a widely available set.

Through the years, especially since wrestling's boom period in the mid-'80s, fans have been treated to food cards. These are the cards that were included with ice cream bars or cookies and snacks. Though they are hard to find, fans are always on the lookout, trying to recapture their enthusiasm for wrestling they had as a youth.

1999 Topps Nitro Girls Chae

1999 Topps Nitro Girls Whisper

1987 SuperK/Coca-Cola card of Randy "Macho Man" Savage.

Wrestling Card Sets

1948 Topps Magic Photo $250
1954 Parkhurst Wrestling $900
1955 Parkhurst Wrestling $1,200
1982 Pro Wrestling Enterprises $45
1983 Pro Wrestling Enterprises $45
1985 WWF Topps Pro Wrestling Stars $30
1985 WWF O-Pee-Chee Pro Wrestling Stars $30
1986 Monty Gum Super Wrestling Stars $75
1987 WWF Topps Wrestling Stars $20
1987 WWF Topps Stickers $10
1988 NWA Wonderama Wrestling Super cards $125
1990 WWF Classic Wrestling $60
1991 WWF Euro Flash Superstars Stickers $45
1991 WWF Merlin $50
1991 WCW Championship Marketing .$45
1991 Imagine Wrestling Legends $45
1991 WWF Classic Superstars $45
1991 WCW Impel Wrestling. $30
1992 WWF Merlin Gold Series $25
1994 WWF Action Packed $35
1995 WCW Cardz Main Event $25
1995 WWF Action Packed $30
1997 Japanese Pro Wrestling $25
1998 WCW/NWO Topps $15

Main Event Eric Bischoff and Sting

1998 WWF DuoCards $15
1998 WWF DuoCards Autographs . . .$300
1998 WWF DuoCards Stone Cold's Greatest Hits $30
1998 WWF Comic Images Superstarz .$25
1998 WCW/NWO Panini Photocard . .$50
1998 WCW/NWO Authentic Signatures $900
1998 WCW/NWO Chrome $40
1998 WCW/NWO Topps Retail Stickers $8
1999 WCW/NWO Topps Nitro $15
1999 WCW/NWO Topps Authentic Signatures $1,000
1999 WWF Duo Cards WrestleMania Live $16
1999 WWF Lenticular Action Card . . .$50
1999 WWF Smackdown! Collector Card $30
1999 WWF Artbox $20

Premium Cards

1991 WCW Luchadores Card Game . .$35
1992 WCW Magazine Trading Card . .$15
1993 WWF Coliseum 3-D Trading Card $40
1993 WWF Coliseum Wrestlemania Collector Card $15
1995 WWF Magazine Trading Card . .$10
1996 WWF Magazine Trading Card . .$10
1997 WWF Magazine Trading Card . .$10
1997 WCW Chromium Card $30
1997 WWF Trivia Card Game $15
1998 WWF Magazine Trading Card . .$10
1998 WWF Trivia Card Game $10
1998 WCW/NWO Up Front Sports Pop Up Card $20

Food Cards

1986 Carnation Major League Wrestling $50
1987 WWF Hostess $40
1987 WWF Stuart Wrestling $50
1987 WWF Circle-K/Coca-Cola Super match $35

1988 WWF Hostess $25
1988 WWF Ice Cream Bar Collector Cards (Series 1) $60
1989 WWF Ice Cream Bar Collector Cards (Series 2) $30
1990 WWF Ice Cream Bar Collector Cards (Series 3) $30
1991 WWF Ice Cream Bar Collector Cards (Series 4) $30
1992 WWF Ice Cream Bar Collector Cards (Series 5) $30
1993 WWF Ice Cream Bar Collector Cards (Series 6) $30
1994 WWF Ice Cream Bar Collector Cards (Series 7) $30
1995 WWF Ice Cream Bar Collector Cards (Series 8) $30
1996 WWF Ice Cream Bar Collector Cards (Series 9) $30
1997 WWF Ice Cream Bar Collector Cards (Series 10) $30
1998 WWF Ice Cream Bar Collector Cards (Series 11) $30
1999 WWF Ice Cream Bar Collector Cards (Series 12) $30
1999 WCW/NWO Little Caesar's $15
1999 WWF Poster Puzzle $10

Selected Wrestling Collectibles

Comic Images, WWF Mini Beanie Bears, 1998

Series 1: Steve Austin, Undertaker, Godfather, Kane, Mankind, Sable, Ken Shamrock, New Age Outlaws, the set $75

Racing Champions WCW/NWO Beanie Bears, 1998

Kevin Nash, Four Horsemen, Sting, Diamond Dallas Page, Hollywood Hogan, Goldberg, Nitro Girls, Wolfpack, Konnan, the set $70

Rocky Balboa and Hollywood Hulk Hogan bears.

Toy Island, WWF Attitude Racers 1999

Series 1, 1/64: Steve Austin, Undertaker, Triple H, Ken Shamrock, Nation of Domination, The Rock, each $10

Grudge Packs, Series 1, 1/64: The Rock vs. Triple H, Mankind vs Kane, Steve Austin vs. Undertaker, each $10

Series 1, 1/24: Chyna, Triple H, Nation of Domination, each $10

Talking Monster Trucks, International Promotions, 1999

Series 1: Steve Austin, Undertaker, Legion of Doom, each $20

Mini Monster Trucks

Series 1: Steve Austin, The Rock, Undertaker, each $20

Remote Control Monster Trucks

Series 1: Steve Austin, Undertaker, The Rock, each $20

Danbury Mint
WWF 24K Trading Cards 1998 . . . .$25

DIC Animations, Hulk Hogan Rock & Wrestling Videos, 1985

Hulk Hogan All-Time Champ, Ghost Wrestlers, Four-Legged Pickpocket, The Last Resort, each $15

WWF Bean Bag Bangers, 1999
Series 1

Triple H, Undertaker, Dude Love, Undertaker, each $10
Series 2
The Rock, Kane, Sable, Steve Austin, Road Dogg, Billy Gunn, each $10

WWF Punching Bags, 1999

Steve Austin, Kane, each $10

WWF Squirt Heads, 1992

Hulk Hogan, Hawk, Animal, Shawn Michaels, Marty Janetty, Million Dollar Man, Big Bossman, Butch, Luke, Jake Roberts, Ultimate Warrior, Randy Savage, each $8

Advanced Graphics WWF Stone Cold Steve Austin life-size Standup.

ToyBiz, WCW Bobbing Heads, 1998

Sting, Goldberg, Diamond Dallas Page, Hollywood Hogan, each $15

WWF Attitude Beanie Bears, Comic Images 1999
Series 1

Val Venis (Hello Ladies) $10
Sable (Hands Down Winner) $10
Stone Cold Steve Austin (That's the bottom line) $18
Stone Cold Steve Austin (100% Pure Whoop Ass) $18
The Rock (Smell what the Rock is Cooking) $10
D-Generation X (Suck It) $10
Kane (No Kane, No Pain) $10
Undertaker (The Lord of Darkness) . . .$10

Series 2

Stone Cold Steve Austin (SCU) $18
Steve Austin (Class 3:16) $18
V. McMahon (Don't Cross the Boss) . .$10
Al Snow with Head (J.O.B Squad) $10
Mankind with Socko (Have a Nice Day) $10
The Rock (Know Your Role) $10
Road Dogg Jesse James (Roll the Dogg a Bone) $10

Cesar Inc., WWF Full Head Masks, 1997

Stone Cold Steve Austin $25
Kane $35
Kane (mask only) $8
Bret Hart $35
Shane Michaels $35
Sycho Sid $25
Goldust $35
Undertaker $35
Mankind $35
Rock $25
Vince McMahon $25
Sable $35

WCW postage stamps from St. Vincent in the Caribbean, 1999 . . . .$30

Advanced Graphics, WWF Life-size Standups, 1997

Austin, Rock, Undertaker, Shawn Michaels $30

Classic Collectible Products, WCW Commemorative Tickets 1998

Kevin Nash, Goldberg $25

Future Toys (Mexico), CMLL Wrestling Buddies 1993

Vampario Canadiense $25
Atlantis $25
Tinieblas $25

Ace Novelty Company, WWF Stuffed Dolls 1991

Hulk Hogan (2-foot) $25
Hulk Hogan (3-foot) $50

Diamond Publishing, WWF Hulk Hogan's Rock & Wrestling Sticker Album, 1986 . . . .$10

Ultimate Creations, Ultimate Warrior Comic Book, 1996 Issues 1 through 5. . . . .$10

Checkerboard Press, WWF Poster Books, 1991 . . . .$10.
Marvel Comics, WCW Comic Books, 1992 Issues 1-12 . . . .$10

CHAOS Comics, Steve Austin, Mankind, Undertaker Comic Books, 1998-99 . . .$5

BBM, Japanese Pro Wrestling Cards, 1997

8 cards in set $20

Jakks, WWF Vince McMahon Microphone, 1998 . . . .$15

Jakks, WWF title belt, Stone Cold Skullbelt, 1998 . . . .$15

Wrestling Autographs
* Indicates wrestler is deceased

Adrian Adonis *
Cut signature $10
Photo $25

Captain Lou Albano
Cut signature $6
Photo $15

Andre The Giant *
Cut signature $45
Photo $120

Tony Atlas
Cut signature $5
Photo $12

"Stone Cold" Steve Austin
Cut signature $10
Photo $40

Bob Backlund
Cut signature $8
Photo $20

Buff Bagwell
Cut signature $8
Photo $20

Paul Bearer
Cut signature $5
Photo $10

Brutus Beefcake
Cut signature $8
Photo $20

Chris Benoit
Cut signature $8
Photo $20

Bam Bam Bigelow
Cut signature $7
Photo $15

Eric Bischoff
Cut signature $8
Photo $20

Steve Blackman
Cut signature $5
Photo $12

Jerry Blackwell
Cut signature $6
Photo $15

Tully Blanchard
Cut signature $6
Photo $15

The Blue Meanie
Cut signature $5
Photo $12

Nick Bockwinkel
Cut signature $8
Photo $20

Booker T. (G.I. Bro)
Cut signature $8
Photo $20

Boss Man
Cut signature $6
Photo $15

D 'Lo Brown
Cut signature $6
Photo $15

King Kong Bundy
Cut signature $6
Photo $15

Jumpin' Jim Brunsell
Cut signature $4
Photo $10

Christian
Cut signature $5
Photo $10

Brian Christopher
Cut signature ....$10-$15
Photo $25

The Crusher
Cut signature $12
Photo $25

Chyna
Cut signature $8
Photo $20

Debra
Cut signature $10-15
Photo $25

Ted Dibiase
Cut signature $6
Photo $15

Dick the Bruiser *
Cut signature $12-15
Photo $35-40

Disco Inferno
Cut signature $6
Photo $15

Droz
Cut signature $5
Photo $12

Hacksaw Jim Duggan
Cut signature $5
Photo $11

Edge
Cut signature $6
Photo $15

Miss Elizabeth
Cut signature $10
Photo $25

Ric Flair
Cut signature $12
Photo $35

Mick Foley
(Mankind/Dude Love/Cactus Jack)
Cut signature $10
Photo $25
Terry Funk
Cut signature $6
Photo $15

Greg Gagne
Cut signature $4-6
Photo $10-12

Verne Gagne
Cut signature $10
Photo $25

Gangrel
Cut signature $5
Photo $10

Gorgeous George
Cut signature $25
Photo $60

The Godfather
Cut signature $6
Photo $15

Bill Goldberg
Cut signature $12
Photo $35

Goldust
Cut signature $6
Photo $15

Eddy Guerrero
Cut signature $8
Photo $20

Bart Gunn
Cut signature $5
Photo $10

B.A. Billy Gunn
Cut signature $8
Photo $20

Scott Hall
Cut signature $12
Photo $30

Hardcore Holly
Cut signature $5
Photo $10

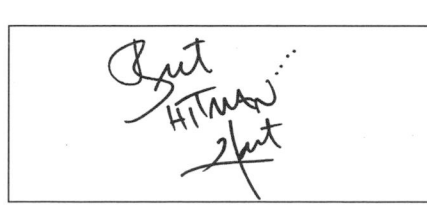

Bret Hart
Cut signature $10
Photo $25

Jimmy Hart
Cut signature $6
Photo $15

Owen Hart *
Cut signature $15
Photo $30

Curt Hennig
Cut signature $10
Photo $25

Larry "The Axe" Hennig
Cut signature $6
Photo $15

Bobby Heenan
Cut signature $8
Photo $20

Mark Henry
Cut signature $6
Photo $15

Hunter Hearst Hemsley
Cut signature $10
Photo $25

Hulk Hogan
Cut signature $15
Photo $40

Iron Sheik
Cut signature $8
Photo $20

"Road Dog" Jesse James
Cut signature $8
Photo $20

Jeff Jarrett
Cut signature $8
Photo $20

Chris Jericho
Cut signature $8
Photo $20

Kamala
Cut signature $12
Photo $30

Kane
Cut signature $10
Photo $25

Konnan
Cut signature $6
Photo $15

Kurrgan
Cut signature $5
Photo $10

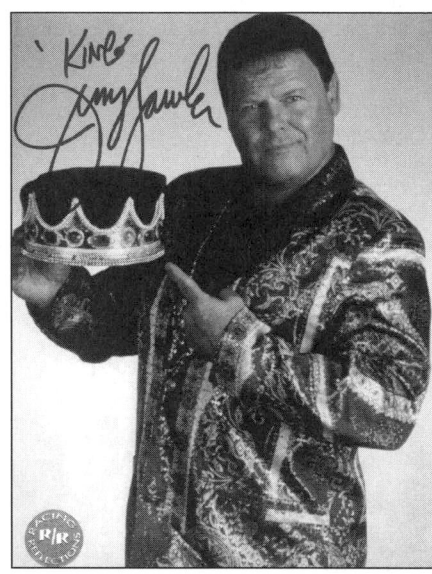

Jerry "The King" Lawler
Cut signature $10
Photo $25

Lex Luger
Cut signature $10
Photo $25

Rocky Maivia
Cut signature $12
Photo $30

Dean Malenko
Cut signature $8
Photo $20

Vince McMahon
Cut signature $8
Photo $20

Shawn Michaels
Cut signature $12
Photo $30

Midian
Cut signature $5
Photo $12

Gorilla Monsoon *
Cut signature $15
Photo $40

Rey Mysterio Jr.
Cut signature $7
Photo $17

Kevin Nash
Cut signature $15
Photo $40

Mean Gene Okerlund
Cut signature $4
Photo $10

Diamond Dallas Page
Cut signature $12
Photo $30

Ken Patera
Cut signature $8
Photo $20

"Rowdy" Roddy Piper
Cut signature $10
Photo $25

"Leaping Lanny" Poffo
Cut signature $7
Photo $18

Ivan Putski
Cut signature $8
Photo $20

Raven
Cut signature $8
Photo $20

Harley Race
Cut signature $10
Photo $25

Stevie Ray
Cut signature $8
Photo $20

Dustin Rhodes
Cut signature $7
Photo $18

Dusty Rhodes
Cut signature $8
Photo $20

Billy Robinson
Cut signature $15
Photo $40

Jake "The Snake" Roberts
Cut signature $8
Photo $20

Jim Ross
Cut signature $5
Photo $10

Ravashing Rick Rude *
Cut signature $20
Photo $60

Terri Runnels
Cut signature $6
Photo $15

Sable (Rena Mero)
Cut signature $15
Photo $40

Bruno Samartino
Cut signature $10
Photo $25

Tito Santana
Cut signature $6
Photo $15

Saturn
Cut signature $5
Photo $10

Randy "Macho Man" Savage
Cut signature $14
Photo $30

Scotty 2 Hotty
Cut signature $8
Photo $20

Ken Shamrock
Cut signature $8
Photo $20

Tiger Ali Singh
Cut signature $6
Photo $15

Sergeant Slaughter
Cut signature $10
Photo $25

Al Snow
Cut signature $6
Photo $15

Jimmy "Superfly" Snuka
Cut signature $8
Photo $20

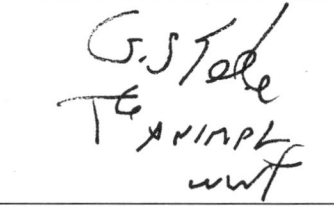

George "The Animal" Steele
Cut signature $6
Photo $15

Rick Steiner
Cut signature $8
Photo $20

Scott Steiner
Cut signature $8
Photo $20

Sting
Cut signature $12
Photo $30

Big John Studd *
Cut signature $20
Photo $50

Sunny
Cut signature $8
Photo $20

Test
Cut signature $6
Photo $15

The Undertaker
Cut signature $10
Photo $25

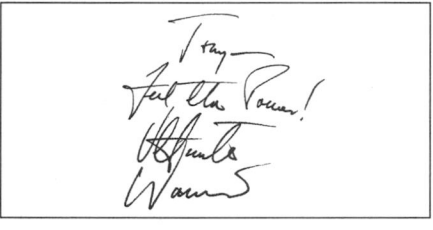

Ultimate Warrior
Cut signature $10
Photo $25

Val Venis
Cut signature $10
Photo $25

Jesse Ventura
Cut signature $20-25
Photo $40-45

Kerry Von Erich *
Cut signature $10
Photo $25

Baron Von Raschke
Cut signature $10
Photo $25

Paul Wight
Cut signature $8
Photo $20

X-Pac
Cut signature $8
Photo $20

Larry Zbyzsko
Cut signature $9
Photo $24

Wrestling Figurines

One of the more popular items in wrestling collecting is the action-figure market. The action-figure market is seeing great success, as the market has exploded in popularity. Jakks Pacific, makers of the WWF line of merchandise, recently announced reaching nearly $100 million in sales in 1999. And not too long ago, collectible maker heavy-hitter Marvel Comics took over the rights to make the WCW line of toys.

One intriguing aspect to the figure market is how much premium fans are currently placing on these figurines. Even older figures, which have discontinued production, are bringing hundreds of dollars on the open market. While most fans have been introduced to the current realistic lines of WWF and WCW figures, the market actually began with a much more conservative American Wrestling Association line produced by Remco.

In its heyday, Remco produced many different lines of all types of figures, such as superheroes and TV stars. In the early 1980s, in an attempt to save a struggling company, Remco approached Verne Gagne's AWA after seeing the immense popularity of TV wrestling. The AWA, while not the most widely seen product, was a solid choice with its catalog of major wrestling stars like the Road Warriors and Freebirds. In 1984, Remco released the first-ever mass-produced line of wrestling figures. In actuality, there were a few names, like Ric Flair, who were not AWA property but were major names in the wrestling industry nonetheless.

The first line produced such classics as Greg Gagne, Larry Zbyszko, Curt Hennig and the Fabulous Ones. Action figures were very different then, when compared to today's products. The detail of the figures left a little bit to be desired, and the AWA line was no exception. The running joke was that all the bodies were from the same mold and only the heads of the different figures were different from character to character. The Remco line was met with a lukewarm reception. But today, these dolls are very rare and are fetching high prices by sellers. While both the AWA and Remco went out of business in later years, the wheels for future wrestling figures were set in motion.

The Remco line would be the trendsetter in an industry filled with products. Just a few years later, when the WWF was taking its show national and into the homes of millions of fans around the world, it summoned the company LJN to produce an exclusive line of WWF figures. Still, today, this line is widely considered the most popular line ever produced because these characters are the ones many fans grew up watching. All the WWF regulars, and not-so-regulars, were part of the production line. Standbys like Hulk Hogan, Andre the Giant and The Iron Sheik were produced alongside classics like Bruno Sammartino and Terry Funk. The all-rubber, nonarticulating bodies of the LJN line are classics. They are a style which we will probably never see again. Included in this line was the very first, and only, Jesse Ventura figure. The Minnesota governor/XFL announcer is valued at almost $50 for a mint, in-package doll.

Since the LJN line was released, the major wrestling companies have churned out a steady stream of wrestling figures. Several lines were produced in the 1990s to little notice. Different companies have taken over the publishing rights through the years, which have seen some mediocre lines, as well as big-time money producers. A Hasbro line of WWF dolls, which closely resembled Weebells, showcased 100 different WWF characters. With no moving body parts and a very cartoonish look, most fans were turned off from the size of the doll. Most are about 4fi inches tall, although the color is superb. Galoob put out a WCW line of dolls that are also short, but rather realistic looking. Today, the Hasbro line is supported by several big hitters on the market, topped by the Dusty Rhodes doll. Meanwhile, the WCW line fetches only a little more than the original asking price.

WCW, WWF and, of late, ECW, are producing lines of their current superstars. Without question, the king of all figures makers is Jakks Pacific. Since 1996, it has been making WWF figures exclusively and fans have flocked to the stores looking for their favorites. The volume of figures being produced by Jakks has been overwhelming. The newer lines are more poseable and the latest lines are being packaged with lots of bonus toys.

Wrestling figures are as popular as, if not more, than mainstream superheroes. Sales in 1998 were topped only by the Star Wars Line.

Toy Biz/Marvel has closed the gap somewhat on Jakks with its recent lines of WCW figures. The detail has been improving greatly, but the different lines are hit and miss. Some, like the Ring Masters' line, are excellent. Others, like the Chris Benoit doll, could pass as a homemade doll. And no company can seem to perfect the likeness of Lex Luger. Even still, collectors are buying them at a record pace. Resale value has proved to be a worthwhile investment.

Other figures that have value are ones that are specialty items. The Phoenix Toys' "Thunderlips" figure, based on the character that Hulk Hogan played in the movie "Rocky III," is getting about $40. And just last year, Ventura introduced his own line of action figures to capitalize on his new life as a politician. His dolls have been extremely hot. As of October 1999, Ventura had sold more than $800,000 worth in figures. A percentage of sales goes to charity. So far, there are three renditions of Ventura: the governor, football announcer and Navy SEAL. If you're looking for a new Jesse Ventura "wrestling" doll, don't hold your breath.

In 2000, three new Ventura figures hit the market, including a buckskin-jacketed Ventura, Ventura in lightercolored fatigues from his Navy days, and another one as governor. Other future plans include a Ventura in a complete Navy SEAL outfit, with goggles, fins and all.

The Remco and LJN lines were produced in a time when no one, not company nor wrestler, knew wrestling dolls would become such a hot-selling market. After the success of LJN, the WWF and WCW have nearly made it company policy to continue churning out new products every year. With new products being cranked out about every month, it's hard to keep up pace with it all. But, no doubt, that's what is driving the dollars up on a lot of these items and it doesn't appear the market will cool off in the near future.

Series 4
Remco, AWA All-Star Wrestling, 1985
2-Packs
Series 1
Fabulous Ones, Steve Keirn & Stan Lane
. . . .$70
High Flyers, Greg Gagne & Jim Brunzell
. . . .$70
Road Warriors, Hawk & Animal $50
Grudge Match, Ric Flair vs. Larry Zbyszko
. . . .$50
Grudge Match, Rick Martel vs. Baron
Von Raschke $50

Series 2
Gagne's Raiders, Greg Gagne &
Curt Henning $60
Long Riders, Bill & Scott Irwin $60

Managers
Michael Hayes, Terry Gordy,
Buddy Roberts $80
Jimmy Garvin, Steve Regal, Precious .$80
Road Warrior Hawk & Animal,
Paul Ellering $70

Series 3
Abdullah the Butcher vs. Carlos Colon
. . . .$90

Scott Hall vs. Jimmy Garvin $80
Nick Bockwinkel vs. Larry Zbyszko ..$80
Jerry Blackwell vs. Stan Hansen $90

Series 4
Boris Zuchov $130
Buddy Rose $100
Doug Somers $100
Nord the Barbarian $120
Referee $100
Sheik Adnan Al-Kaissey $130
Midnight Rocker Shawn Michaels ...$120
Midnight Rocker Marty Janetty $100

Remco AWA Thumb Wrestlers
Ric Flair vs. Larry Zbyszko $20
Greg Gagne vs. Hawk $20
Rick Martel vs. Animal $20

Remco AWA Mini Mashers
8-Pack
Scott Hall, Curt Hennig, Boris Zukoff, Nord the Barbarian, Larry Zbyszko, Nick Bockwinkel, Ric Flair, Stan Hansen ..$30

12-Pack
Hawk, Animal, Larry Zbyszko, Nick Bockwinkel, Ric Flair, Stan Hansen, Boris Zukoff, John Nord, Shawn Michaels, Marty Janetty, Scott Hall, Curt Hennig $35

LJN, World Wrestling Federation, 1985-1987
Adrian Adonis $50
Andre the Giant (long hair) $60

(short hair) $60
(strap) $200
Ax of Demolition $100
Bam Bam Bigelow $100
Big Boss Man (night stick) $150
Big John Stud $30
Billy Jack Haynes $60
Bobby Heenan (brown hair w/design on shoulders) $30
(blonde hair w/o design on shoulders) ..$30
Bob Orton Jr $40
Bruno Sammartino $50

Brutus Beefcake $50
Cpt. Lou Albano (pic on shirt, has red vest and cumberbund) $35
(pic on shirt, has white vest/cumberbund) $35
Classy Freddy Blassie $30
Cpl. Kirschner (cleanly shaven) $20
(stubble) $20
(beard) $20
Elizabeth (gold skirt) $75
(purple skirt) $75
George the Animal Steele (clear chest hair) $30
(colored chest hair) $30
Greg the Hammer Valentine (light blonde hair) $40
(dark blonde hair) $40
Hacksaw Jim Duggan $50
Haku. $75
Hercules Hernandez $30
Hillbilly Jim $25
Honky Tonk Man $60
Hulk Hogan (yellow trunks, light blonde hair) $50
(yellow trunks, dark blonde hair) $50
(white shirt) $250
(red shirt). $50
Iron Sheik (orange design on tights) ..$30
(yellow design on tights) $30
Jake Roberts $75
Jesse Ventura (blonde hair) $40
(brown hair, same color as mustache) .$40
Jimmy Hart (Mega w/no hearts) $30
(Red Mega w/pink hearts) $30
Jimmy Superfly Snuka $60
Johnny Valiant $40
Junkyard Dog (w/silver chain) $40
(w/black chain) $40
(w/red chain) $40
Kamala $100
Ken Patera $50
King Harley Race $200
King Kong Bundy $50
Koko B. Ware $100
Magnificent Muraco $25
Gene Okerlund (logo on mic) $30
(no logo on mic) $30
Mr. Fuji $30
Paul Orndorff $30
Nikolai Volkoff $25
One Man Gang $80
Outback Jack $40
Randy Savage $60
Referee (blue shirt) $100
(white shirt) $100
Rick Rude $110
Rick Martel $125
Ricky The Dragon Steamboat $35
Rowdy Roddy Piper (red boots) $35
(brown boots) $35
Slick $55
S.D. Jones (red shirt) $30
(Hawaiian shirt) $30
Ted Arcidi $50

Ted DiBiase $50
Terry Funk $35
Tito Santana (purple trunks) $50
(white trunks) $50

Ultimate Warrior $150
Vince McMahon $40
Warlord $100
Sgt. Slaughter (Made by Hasbro for LJN) $100

Tag Teams
British Bulldogs $200
Hart Foundation $600
Killer Bees $200
Strike Force $400

LJN, WWF 14 inch, 1985
Roddy Piper. $50
Hulk Hogan. $75

LJN, WWF Bendies, 1986
Cpt. Lou Albano $20
Hulk Hogan $20
Hillbilly Jim $20
Big John Studd $20
Randy Savage $20
Junkyard Dog $20
Paul Orndorff $20
Roddy Piper $20
Iron Sheik $20
Cpl Kirschner $20
Ricky Steamboat $20
Andre the Giant $20
George Steele $20
Bobby Heenan $30
Nikolai Volkoff $20
Brutus Beefcake $20
Jesse Ventura $20
King Kong Bundy $20

LJN, WWF Thumbwrestlers, 1985
Jake Roberts $15
Iron Sheik $15
Hulk Hogan $15
Ricky Steamboat $15
Nikolai Volkoff $15
Roddy Piper $15

Hillbilly Jim $15
Randy Savage $15
Big John Studd $15
Junkyard Dog $15
Paul Orndorf $15
King Kong Bundy $15

Hasbro, WWF 1990-1994
Series 1
Akeem $100
Andre The Giant $150
Ax $50
Big Boss Man $25
Brutus Beefcake $30
Hulk Hogan $25
Jake Roberts $25
Macho Man $30
Million Dollar Man $25
Rick Rude $50
Smash $30
Ultimate Warrior $30

Hasbro Dusty Rhodes

Series 2
Dusty Rhodes $300
Hacksaw Duggan $20
Honky Tonk Man $30

Hulk Hogan $25
Mr. Perfect $15
Undertaker $20
Yokozuna $20
Macho Man $20

Million Dollar Man $20
Rowdy Roddy Piper $20
Superfly Jimmy Snuka $20
Ultimate Warrior. $50

Series 3
Big Boss Man $15
Brutus Beefcake $75
Earthquake $30
Greg Valentine $25
Hulk Hogan $20
Koko B. Ware $75
Macho Man $50
Mr. Perfect $50
Sgt. Slaughter $30
Texas Tornado $30
Typhoon $30
Ultimate Warrior $50

Series 4
Bret Hart $25
British Bulldog $30
Ricky Steamboat $20
Undertaker $25

Series 5
Hulk Hogan $20
I.R.S $20
Macho Man $30
Rick Martel $20
Skinner $20
Sid Justice $20
The Mountie $20
Virgil $20
Warlord $20

Series 6
Berzerker $20
El Matador $20
Jim Neidhart $20
Papa Shango $20
Repo Man $20
Ric Flair $20
Tatanka $20

Series 7
Crush $20
Kamala $20
Nailz $20
Owen Hart $20

Razor Ramon $20
Shawn Michaels $20

Series 8
Bam Bam Bigelow $15
Bret Hart $15
Lex Luger $20

Series 9
Doink the Clown. $12
Hacksaw Jim Duggan $12
Million Dollar Man $15
Rick Steiner $12
Scott Steiner $12
Tatanka (re-release) $10

Series 10
Butch #2 . . . .$10
Fatu $12
Giant Gonzalez $12
Marty Jannety $12
Luke $10
Razor Ramon (re-release) $20
(purple) $20
Samu $12
Shawn Michaels (black) $25
(re-release) $20

Series 11
1-2-3 Kid $45

Adam Bomb $30
Bart Gunn $20
Billy Gunn $25
Crush $30
Ludvig Borga $30
Yokozuna $20

Tag Teams
Bushwackers $20
Demolition $40
Legion of Doom $50
Nasty Boys $50
Rockers $20

Mail-Away
Bret Hart $75
Hulk Hogan $60
Undertaker $80

Hasbro, WWF 12-inch Talking Figures
Hulk Hogan $40
Ultimate Warrior $40

Hasbro, WWF Royal Rumble Mini Ring
Hulk Hogan, Big Boss Man, Jake Roberts,
Sgt. Slaughter, Million Dollar Man . . .$80

Hasbro, WWF Royal Rumble Mini 4-Pack
Roddy Piper, Texas Tornado, Mr. Perfect &
Jim Duggan $20
LOD, Typhoon and Earthquake $20
Beefcake, Valentine, Bushwackers $20

JusToys WWF Bendables
1994-current
Series 1
Diesel $10
Doink $15
Razor Ramon $10
Bret Hart (purple) $8
(pink) $20
Lex Luger $15

Series 2
1-2-3 Kid $4
Mable $4
Undertaker $6
Bulldog $4

Series 3
Shawn Michaels $4
Yokozuna $4
Goldust $4
Amhed Johnson $4

Series 4
Marc Mero $4
Sid $4
Sunny $4
Vader $4

Series 5
Farooq $4
Rocky Maivia $6
Mankind $4
Steve Austin $4

Series 6
Hawk $4
Animal $4
Triple H $4
Undertaker $4

Series 7
Owen Hart $4
The Patriot $4
Crush $4
Ken Shamrock $4

Series 8
Chyna $4
Kane $4

Double J $4
Taka Michinoku $4

Series 9
Brian Christopher $4
X-Pac $4
Cactus Jack $4
Sable $4

Series 10
Billy Gunn $4
Road Dogg $4
Steve Blackman $4
Edge $4

Series 11
Vince McMahon $4
The Godfather $4
Val Venis $4
Al Snow $4

Star Toys (Spain), WWF 1990
12-inch w/hair
Ultimate Warrior $125
Hulk Hogan $125
Jake Roberts $125
Hacksaw $125
Big Boss Man $125

JAKKS, WWF 1997-current
Superstars Series
Series 1
Bret Hart $15
Diesel $45
Goldust $25

Razor Ramon $55
Shawn Michaels $20
Undertaker $20

Series 2
Bret Hart $8
Owen Hart $20
Shawn Michaels $8
Ultimate Warrior $30
Undertaker $8
Vader $8

Series 3
Ahmed Johnson $6
Bret Hart $6
British Bulldog $6
Diesel $50
Goldust $10
Mankind $6
Shawn Michaels $6
Sycho Sid $6

Series 4
Farooq $6
Triple H $6
Jerry Lawler $6
Justin Hawk Bradshaw $6
Steve Austin $12
Vader $6

Series 5
Flash Funk $6
The Rock $6

Steve Austin $12
Savio Vega $6
Sycho Sid $6
Ken Shamrock $6

Series 6
Steve Blackman $6
Mark Henry $6
Triple H $6
Jeff Jarrett $6
Marc Mero $6

Series 7
Steve Austin $6
Steve Williams $6
Edge $6
Undertaker $6
Val Venis $6
X-Pac $12

Series 8
Kane $6
The Rock $6
Ken Shamrock $6
Shawn Michaels $6
Shane McMahon $6
Big Boss Man $6

Series 9

Gangrel $6
Christian $6
Big Show $6
Vince McMahon $6
Hardcore Holly $6
Undertaker. $6

2-Tuff Series
Series 1
Triple H/Chyna $12
Truth Commission $12
Chainz/8-Ball $12
Marlena/Goldust $12

Series 2
New Age Outlaws $20
Brian Christopher/Jerry Lawler $12
Kama/D-Lo Brown $12
Kurrgan/Jackyl $12

Series 3
Austin/Undertaker $20
Legion of Doom 2000 . . . .$12
Kane/Mankind $12
Rock/Owen Hart $12

Series 4
Austin/Boss Man $12
Kane/Undertaker $12
Rock/Mankind $12
Bad Ass/Val Venis $12

Series 5
Undertaker/Viscera $12
Bad Ass/Road Dogg $12
Austin/The Rock $12
Debra/Jeff Jarrett $12
Undertaker/Viscera $12

STOMP Series
Series 1
Steve Austin $12
Crush $6
Ahmed Johnson $6
Brian Pillman $6
Ken Shamrock $6
Undertaker $6

Series 2
Chyna $6
The Rock $6
Steve Austin $12
Owen Hart $6
Mosh $6
Thrasher $6

Series 3
Animal $6
Sable $6
Kane $10
Hawk $6
Marc Mero $6
Undertaker $10

Series 4
Steve Austin $6
Bad Ass $6
Chyna $6
Triple H $6
Road Dogg $6
X-Pac $6

Signature Series
Series 1
Goldust $6
Triple H $6
LOD Animal $6
LOD Hawk $6
Mankind $6
Steve Austin $12

Series 2
Billy Gunn $6
Road Dogg $6
Kane $6
Undertaker $6
Shawn Michaels $6
Dude Love $6

Series 3
Steve Austin $10
The Rock $8
Edge $6
Triple H $8
Undertaker $8
Jackie $6

Slammers
Series 1
Steve Austin $12
Bret Hart $6
Goldust $6
Mankind $6
Undertaker $6
Farooq $6

Series 2
Taka Michinoku $6
Brian Pillman $6
Shawn Michaels $6
Dude Love $6
Kane $10
Patriot $10

Ringside
Series 1
Sable $10
Sunny $10
Referee $25
Vince McMahon $10

Series 2
Vince McMahon $12
Referee $12
Jim Ross $8
Jim Cornette $8
Honky Tonk Man $10
Sgt. Slaughter $8

Tag Teams
Legion of Doom $12
Godwinn's $12
New Blackjacks $12
Headbangers $12

Manager 2-Packs
Series 1
Bob Backlund/Sultan $10
Clarence Mason/Crush $10
Paul Bearer/Mankind $10
Sable/Marc Mero. $10

Special Edition Tag Teams
Al Snow/Mankind $12
D-Lo Brown/Mark Henry $12
Headbangers $12

KB Special Edition
Series 1
Ahmed Johnson $8
British Bulldog $8
Sunny $10
The Rock $10
Undertaker $10
Vader $8
Yokozuna $25

Series 2
Farooq $8
Goldust $8
Triple H $8
Sable $8
Savio Vega $8
Steve Austin $12
Yokozuna $25

Series 3
LOD Hawk $8
LOD Animal $8
Dan Severn $8
Triple H $8
Ken Shamrock $8
Marc Mero $8

Series 4
Steve Austin $16
Mankind $8
Chyna $8
Road Dogg $8
Bad Ass Billy Gunn $8
Undertaker $8

Series 5
Edge $8
Al Snow $8
Ken Shamrock $8
Mark Henry $8
Val Venis $8
X-Pac $8

Don't Trust Anybody
Series 1
Kane $8
Dude Love $8
Shawn Michaels $8
Farooq $8
Chainz $8
8-Ball $8
Vader $8
Triple H $8

Series 2
Al Snow $10
Blue Blazer $30
Edge $10
Jeff Jarrett $8
Steve Blackman $8
Undertaker $12

Wrestlemania 14
Mosh $6
Trasher $6
Triple H $6
Shawn Michaels $10
Steve Austin $20
The Rock $10

Livewire
Series 1
Undertaker $6
Chyna $10
Ken Shamrock $6
Steve Austin $30
Mankind $6
Vader $6

Series 2
Shawn Michaels $8
Marc Mero $6
Mark Henry $6
The Rock $12
Val Venis $8
X-Pac $12

Shotgun Saturday Night
Series 1
Steve Austin $20
Hawk $6
Animal $6
The Rock $8
Henry Godwinn $6
Phineas Godwinn $6
Undertaker $12
Savio Vega $6

Series 2
Shawn Michaels $6
Jeff Jarrett $6
Sable $10
Kane $6
Road Dogg. $6
Billy Gunn. $6

Fully Loaded
Series 1
Al Snow $6
Triple H $8
Road Dogg $6
Billy Gunn $6
Kane $6
The Rock $6

Series 2
Steve Austin $6
The Rock $6
Shane McMahon $6
Test $6
Road Dogg $6
X-Pac $6

Maximum Sweat
Series 1
Steve Austin $10
Triple H $10
Shawn Michaels $10
The Rock $10
Kane $10
Undertaker $10

Series 2
Steve Austin $10
Undertaker $10
Road Dogg $10
Mr. Ass $10
Edge $10
Ken Shamrock $10

Series 3
Big Show $10
Gangrel $10
The Rock $10
Steve Austin $10
Big Bossman $10
Mankind $10

Series 4
Kane $10
Steve Austin $10
Mr. Ass $10
Road Dogg $10
Droz $10

Best of 1997
Series 1
Ahmed Johnson $6
Bret Hart $10
British Bulldog $8
Owen Hart $10
Steve Austin $12
Undertaker $10

Series 2
Crush $6
Goldust $6
Triple H $10
Ken Shamrock $6
Marc Mero $10
Shawn Michaels $6

Series 1 (continued)
The Rock $6
Undertaker $6

Best of 1998
Series 1
Steve Austin $10
Shawn Michaels $10
Brian Christopher $10
Chyna $10
Vader $10
Bradshaw $6

Series 2
Dan Severn $8
Dude Love $8
Triple H $8
Jeff Jarrett $8
Ken Shamrock $8
Mark Henry $8
Steve Austin $10
Undertaker $8

Tag Teams
New Age Outlaws $12
Headbangers $12
Legion of Doom $12

2-Packs
Bret Hart vs. Owen Hart $30
British Bulldog vs. Sid $12
Triple H vs. Owen Hart $12
Ken Shamrock vs. Dan Severn. $12
Luna vs. Sable $12
Mark Henry vs. Vader $12
Razor Ramon vs. Diesel. $100
Road Dogg vs. Al Snow $12
Shawn Michaels vs. Triple H $12
Shawn Michaels vs. Vader $12
Steve Blackman vs. Marc Mero $12
Steve Austin vs. Shawn Michaels $12
Steve Austin vs. Vince McMahon $12
Taka Michinoku vs. Brian Christopher $12
Undertaker vs. Kane $12
X-Pac vs. Jeff Jarrett $12

Sunday Night Heat
Bad Ass Billy Gunn $6
Road Dogg $6
Sable $6
Undertaker $6

Raw is War
Steve Austin $6
Mankind $6
Undertaker $6
The Rock $6

Deadly Games
Steve Austin $6
Droz $6
Road Dogg $6
Kurrgan $6
Triple H $6
Edge $6

Breakdown
Steve Austin $8
Droz $8
D-Lo Brown $6
Goldust $8
Mankind $10
X-Pac $8

Road Rage
Godfather $8
Hardcore Holly $6
The Rock $6
Mankind $6
Test $6
Al Snow $6

Jakk'd Up
Steve Austin $6
Undertaker $6
Kane $6
Sable $6

Federation Fighters 12" Figures
The Rock $15
Kane $15
Steve Austin No. 1 . . . .$15
Steve Austin No. 2 . . . .$15
Undertaker $15

Back Talkin' Crushers 9" Figures
Series 1
Steve Austin $15
The Rock $15
The Undertaker $15
The Big Show $15

Rumble Gear
Series 1
Austin (Camo Gear) $8
Undertaker (Lord of Darkness & Survivor
Series Versions) $8
Referee $8

Multi-Packs Survivor Series
Ahmed Johnson, Shawn Michaels, Ultimate
Warrior, Goldust $60

King of the Ring
Ahmed Johnson, Referee, Bret Hart, Steve
Austin $40
Buried Alive Mankind, Paul Bearer, The
Executioner, Undertaker $65

Raw is War
Bret Hart, Sunny, Vince McMahon, Sid
. . . .$30

Triple Threat
Ahmed Johnson, Marc Mero, Yokozuna
. . . .$35

Nation of Domination
Clarence Mason, Crush, Farooq, Savio Vega

$25

Wrestlemania 14
Triple H, Shawn Michaels, Steve Austin,
Undertaker $30

Faces of Foley
Cactus Jack, Dude Love, Mankind $25

Attitude
LOD 2000, Steve Austin, Shawn Michaels .
. . . .$25

No Holds Barred
Cactus Jack, Kane, Steve Austin $25

Degeneration X
Road Dogg, Triple H, Chyna, Billy Gunn
. . . .$25

Badd Blood
Kane, Paul Bearer, Steve Austin, Under-
taker $40

Off The Mat
Billy Gunn, Road Dogg, Steve Austin,
Undertaker $25

Shotgun Saturday Night
Kane, Shawn Michaels, Steve Austin, The
Rock $25

Go Mental
Dude Love, Triple H, Steve Austin, Under-
taker $25

Fully Loaded
Billy Gunn, Road Dogg, Steve Austin,
Undertaker $25

Legends Past & Present
Andre the Giant, Steve Austin, Undertaker
. . . .$25

Over The Edge
Triple H, Kane, Steve Austin, The Rock
. . . .$25

Judgment Day
Steve Austin, Undertaker, Vince McMahon
. . . .$25

3-Pack Special Collections
Steve Austin $25
Undertaker $25

Bad To the Bonz 3-Pack
Steve Austin $25

Titan Tron Live 3-Pack
Austin, Kane, X-Pac $25

Survivor Series 4-Pack
Austin, Rock, Kane, Undertaker $25

Championship Title
Austin, Rock, X-Pac, Kane $25

Perfect 10
Big Show, Kane, Rock, Steve Austin,
Undertaker, Billy Gunn, Mankind, X-Pac,
Triple H, Road Dogg $75

Survivor Series 3-Pack
Steve Austin, Rock, Billy Gunn $25

Camo Carnage
Steve Austin, Triple H, Billy Gunn $25

Last Man Standing
Steve Austin, The Rock, Shane McMahon,
Vince McMahon $30

Raw is War No. 2
Mankind, Austin, Rock, Undertaker . . .$30

No Chance
Austin, Vince McMahon, Paul Wight . .$25

Hardcore Match
Al Snow, Mankind, Bob Holly, Boss Man
. . . .$30

Misc.
K-Mart Steve Austin (gift set No. 1) . .$15
K-Mart Steve Austin (gift set No. 2) . .$15
K-Mart The Rock (gift set No. 1) $15
KB Toys Steve Austin $15
Toyfare Undertaker $20
Toyfare Steve Austin $20
Whites Guide Sable $20
Whites Guide Undertaker $20
Jakks Steve Austin 1-in-40 Contest . . .$25
KR Toys Austin Signature belt w/fig. . .$25

Wrestlemania 3-Packs
Triple H, Shawn Michaels, Thrasher . .$25
Steve Austin, Mosh, Undertaker $25

Fantasy Warfare
Steve Austin vs. Andre the Giant $20
Mankind vs. Undertaker $15

Jakks Ripped & Ruthless
Series 1
Goldust $10
Mankind $10
Steve Austin $15
Undertaker $10

Series 2
Triple H $10
Kane $40
Sable $10
Shawn Michaels $10

Legends
Andre the Giant $15

Capt. Lou Albano. $10
Freddie Blassie $10
Jimmy Snuka $10

Jakks Mini Figures
Wrestlemania $30
Raw is War $25
Royal Rumble $25
King of the Ring $25
No Mercy $20
Sudden Threat $20

Playmates Heroes of Wrestling
Undertaker (14 inch) $40
Undertaker (9 inch) $10
Sid (9 inch) $10

Playmates Ringmasters
Bret Hart $8
Goldust $5
Shawn Michaels $5
Sid $5
Undertaker $5
Yokozuna $8

Playmates Grudge Match
Mini Figures 2-Packs
Steve Austin vs. Bret Hart $15
Ahmed Johnson vs. Yokozuna $15
Owen Hart vs. Shawn Michaels $15
Sid vs. Vader $15
Mankind vs. Undertaker $15
Savio Vega vs. Goldust $15

Playmates Stretch'ums
Bret Hart $10
Sid $10
Undertaker $10
Shawn Michaels $10

Playmates, WWF Thumb Wrestlers 1997
Owen Hart vs. Steve Austin $10
Undertaker vs. Shawn Michaels $10
Mankind vs. Triple H $10
British Bulldog vs. Ken Shamrock $10

Galoob, WCW 1993
Ric Flair $20
Arn Anderson $20
Barry Windham $20
Sid Vicious $20
Sting $20
Lex Luger $20
Ron Simmons $20
Butch Reed $20
Rick Steiner $20
Scott Steiner $20
Brian Pillman $20
Tom Zenk $20
United Kingdom releases
Ric Flair (red) $25

Arn Anderson (red). $25
Barry Windham (blue) $25
Sid Vicious (pink) $25
Lex Luger (green) $25
Lex Luger (robe) $85
Ron Simmons (blue/striped) $60
Rick Steiner (green) $30
Scott Steiner (pink) $25
Brian Pillman (blue) $25
Sting (coat) $85
Dustin Rhodes $100
Michael Hayes $60
Jimmy Garvin $60

Big Josh $100
El Gigante $75

Galoob, WCW 14-inch
Sid $100
Sting $100
Ric Flair $100
Lex Luger $100

JusToys, WCW Bendies 1992
Ric Flair $15
Arn Anderson $20
Barry Windham $15
Sid Vicious $15
Sting $15
Lex Luger $15
Ron Simmons $20
Butch Reed $20
Rick Steiner $20
Scott Steiner $20
Brian Pillman $15
Tom Zenk $15

Original San Francisco Toymakers,
WCW 1994-1998
Series 1
Ric Flair $8
Vader $8
Johnny B. Badd $8
Hulk Hogan. $12
Sting $8
Jimmy Hart $8
Brian Knobs $8
Jerry Sags $8
Kevin Sullivan $8

Series 2
Ric Flair $15
Vader (re-release) $15
Johnny B. Badd $15
Hulk Hogan (re-release) $15
Sting (pink) $15
Sting (green) $15
Jimmy Hart $15
Kevin Sullivan $15
Macho Man $20

Tag Teams
Nasty Boys $20
Hulk Hogan & Sting $20
Booker T. & Stevie Ray $20

Series 3
Ric Flair $12
Hulk Hogan $12
Sting $12
Macho Man $12
Alex Wright $12
Big Bubba Rogers $12
Craig Pittman $12
The Giant $12
Booker T. $12
Stevie Ray $12

Figures Inc. Exclusive TagTeams
Blue Bloods $30
Hulk Hogan & Macho Man $25
Harlem Heat $25
Nasty Boys $25
Nitro (vibrating) Kevin Nash $8
Scott Hall $8
Chris Benoit $8
The Giant $8
Hollywood Hogan $8
Sting $8
Kevin Sullivan $8
Lex Luger $8

Tag Team Two Packs
Sting & Lex Luger $30
Scott Hall & Kevin Nash $30

Nitro (non-vibrating)
The Giant $8
Booker T. $6
Stevie Ray $6
Hollywood Hogan $8
Ric Flair $8
Brian Knobs $6
Jerry Sags $6
Kevin Sullivan $6
Macho Man $8
Lex Luger $10
Sting $10
Sting (2 Pack) $20

WCW/NWO Hard Plastic
Series 1
Kevin Nash $8
Sting (White) $8

The Giant $8
Ric Flair $8
Raven (Black) $8
Diamond Dallas Page $8

PPV Match-Ups
Scott Hall vs. Lex Luger $25
Hulk Hogan vs. Sting $30.00
Kevin Nash vs. The Giant. $25
Kevin Nash vs. DDP. $25

Series 2
Hulk Hogan $8
Scott Hall $8
Randy Savage $8
Curt Hennig $8
Lex Luger $8
Bret Hart (wings) $8

Series 3
Goldberg $8
Sting (Red) $8
Rey Mysterio Jr $8
Buff Bagwell $8
Scott Steiner $8
Chris Benoit $8

K-Mart Exclusive Ring
With Sting and jacket $30

4-Packs
Thunder Champions Goldberg, Bret Hart,
Scott Hall, The Giant (w/belts) $25

Fearsome Foursome
Ric Flair, Chris Beniot, Dallas Page, Goldberg $25

NWO Hollywood
Buff Bagwell, Hollywood Hogan, Scott
Steiner, The Giant. $25

NWO Wolfpack
Sting, Kevin Nash, Randy Savage, Lex
Luger $25

4.5" Mini Figures
Hollywood Hogan $6
Macho Man $6
Scott Hall $6
Scott Steiner $10
Kevin Nash $6
Rick Steiner $6
The Giant $6
Lex Lugar $6
Sting $6
Ric Flair $6
Goldberg $10

12" Figures
Goldberg $30
Hollywood Hogan $25
Macho Man $25
Sting (white) $25
Sting (red) $25

Belt Buckle 1/2" Figures
Hulk Hogan & Sting $15
Outsiders vs. Nasty Boys $15

2-Pack
Hollywood Hogan/Dennis Rodman . . .$20

ToyBiz, WCW 1997-current
Slam 'N Crunch
Series 1
Buff Bagwell $10
Konnan $10
Kevin Nash $10
Sting $10

Smash 'N Slam
Series 1
Diamond Dallas Page $10
Sting $10
The Giant w/Rey Mysterio Jr. $13
Lex Luger $10

Series 2
Hollywood Hogan $10
Kevin Nash $10
Macho Man $8
Scott Hall $10
Goldberg w/masked wrestler $12

Ring Fighters
Bret Hart $8
Chris Benoit $8
Booker T $8
Big Poppa Pump $8

Ring Masters
Series 1
Chris Jericho $12
Goldberg $10
Lex Luger $10
Bret Hart $10

Collector Twin Packs
Series 1
Macho Man & Elizabeth $15
Sting & Hollywood Hogan $15
Giant & Kevin Nash $15

Grip & Flip
Series 1
Raven vs. Diamond Dallas Page $15
Goldberg vs. Hollywood Hogan $15
Chris Jericho vs. Dean Malenko $15

Series 2
Sting vs. Lex Luger $15
Kevin Nash vs. Bret Hart $15
Scott Steiner vs. Rick Steiner $15

Road Wild Wrestlers
Series 1
Goldberg $10
Sting $10
Kevin Nash $10

Brawlin' Bikers
Diamond Dallas Page $10
Goldberg $10
Sting $10

Bend 'N' Flex 5" Wrestlers
Series 1
Goldberg $7
Sting $7
Scott Hall $7
Kevin Nash $7

Series 2
Diamond Dallas Page $7
Bret Hart $7
Booker T $7
Scott Steiner $7

IV Horsemen Set
Ric Flair, Chris Benoit, Dean Malenko,
Steve McMichael $25

Tuff Talkin' 12" Figures
Series 1
Diamond Dallas Page & Sting $20
Goldberg & Kevin Nash $20

Series 2
Konnan $15
Buff Bagwell $15
Randy Savage $15
Scott Steiner $15

Rumble 'N' Roar Wrestlers
Goldberg $15
Sting $15

Bruisers
Series 1
Kidman $10
Rey Mysterio Jr $10
Disco Inferno $8
Raven $8
Stevie Ray $8

PowerSlam
Series 1
Goldberg $8
Hak $10
Sid Vicious $8
Hollywood Hogan. $8
Dennis Rodman $10

Series 2
Roddy Piper $7
Buff Bagwell $7
Kevin Nash $7
Sting $7

Thunderslam 2-Packs
Sting vs. Bret Hart $15
Kevin Nash vs. Scott Hall $15
Goldberg vs. Bam Bam Bigelow. $15

Evolution of Sting
Six-pack $45

Original San Francisco Toymakers, ECW 1999
Series 1
Taz $6
Rob Van Dam $6
Sabu $6
Shane Douglas $6
Chris Candido $6
Justin Credible $6

Series 2
Tommy Dreamer $6
Lance Storm $6
New Jack $6
D-Von Dudley. $6
Bubba Ray Dudley $6

Hyper Heroes, New Japan Pro Wrestling 1998-current
Masa Chono $25
Riki Chosyu $25
Shinya Hashimoto $25
Kensuke Sasaki $25
The Great Muta 1 (black) $25
The Great Muta 2 (red) $25
The Great Muta 3 (nWo) $25
Hiroyoshi Tenzan $25
Antonio Inoki (red) $25
Antonio Inoki (blue) $25
Jushin Thunder Liger $25
Tatsumi Fujinami $25
Manabu Nakanishi $25
Kendoh Ka-Shin $25
Kazuo Yamazaki $25

El Samurai $25
Masa Saito $25
Satoshi Kojima $25
Koji Kanemoto $25
Shinjiro Ohanti $25

Special releases
Great Muta & Masa Chono $60
Special Antonio Inoki (red) $40
Keiji Muto & Masa Chono (nWo) $60
Atsushi Onita & Akira Maeda $45

All Japan Pro Wrestling, 1998
Jun Akiyama $20
Mitsuhara Misawa $20
Kenta Kobashi $20
Giant Baba $20
Takashi Kawada $20
Akira Taue $20

Original San Francisco Toy Makers, CMLL 1992
Satanico $10
Atlantis $10
Brazo de Plata $10
Vampario Canadiense $10
Blue Demon $10
Lizmark $10
Sangre Chicana $10
Pierroth $10
El Brazo $10
Ultimo Dragon $10
Brazo de Oro $10
Rayo de Jalisco $10

Kelian (Mexico), AAA
Octagon $20
Blue Panther $20
Hijo Del Santo $20

Fuerza Guerrera $20
Cien Caras $20
Konnan $20
La Parka $20
Mascara Sagrada $20
Psicosis $20
Heavy Metal $20
Perro Aguayo $20
Rey Mysterio Jr $20

Special Issues
Jesse Ventura, 1998-current
Governor $20
Navy SEAL $30
Football Coach $20

Sideshow Toys, Jesse Ventura 3.5" Dolls, 1999
Governor $15
Coach $15
Navy SEAL $15

Hasbro, G.I. Joe 1989
Sgt. Slaughter $35

Phoenix Toys, Rocky III 1983
Thunderlips (Hulk Hogan) $25

Figures Inc., Heroes of Wrestling, 1999
Series 1
King Kong Bundy $8
King Kong Bundy (bloody) $8

Series 2
Abdullah the Butcher $8
Abdullah the Butcher (bloody) $8

Series 3
Killer Kowalski $8

Glossary of Hobby Terms

Airbrushing: The touching up of a photo by an artist, sometimes done to avoid licensing fees.

ALS: A letter that has been signed.

Ask Price: The price a dealer, investor or collector offers to sell his items for.

Autograph guest: A current or former player or other celebrity who attends a sports convention to sign autographs for fans. A fee, which can range from a few dollars to more than $75 for an athlete such as Muhammad Ali, is usually charged for the autograph.

Autopen: A mechanical device that is programmed to duplicate a precise signature. Autopens are often used by celebrities who receive numerous requests for their autographs.

Base brand: Basic set of sports cards produced by a card maker, usually the lowest priced.

Bid price: The price an investor, dealer, etc., offers to buy items.

Blank back: A card with no printing on the back, usually because of a printing error.

Blanket: An early 20th-century collectible consisting of a square piece of felt or other fabric which came wrapped around a package of cigarettes. Baseball players were one of the several subjects found on blankets. Most popular are the 5″ x 5″ B18 blankets from 1914, so-called because they were sometimes sewn together to form a blanket.

Bobbin' Heads: A series of fragile hand-painted ceramic sports dolls that first came over from Japan in 1960. Sports, Accessories & Memorabilia (S.A.M.) reintroduced new dolls in the 1990s.

Book price: The retail selling price which appears in a price guide.

Buy price: The price which a dealer is willing to pay for cards or memorabilia. A dealer's buy price is usually quite a bit lower than that item's catalog or retail price.

Cachet: A specifically designed and produced envelope to commemorate a specific historical or sporting event that is usually postmarked on the anniversary or actual day of the event.

Centering: Refers to the positioning of a photo on a card. With all other things the same, the better the centering, the more valuable the card.

Certificate of Authenticity: A piece of paper, usually of minimal value, that guarantees that the signature or piece of memorabilia is authentic and legitimate.

Checklist: A list of every item in a particular set. A checklist can appear on a card, in a book or elsewhere.

Coin: A metal or plastic coin-sized disc which depicts a player. It can also refer to an actual coin which depicts a player. It can also refer to an actual coin or a coin-sized silver piece which commemorates an actual event.

Condition: One of the major factors in determining the value of memorabilia, this term applies to the wear and tear on an item.

Convention: Also known as a trading card show. A gathering of anywhere from one to 600 or more card dealers at a single location (convention center, hotel, school auditoriums or gymnasiums) for the purpose of buying, selling or trading memorabilia. A convention is open to the public, and oftentimes a fee is required to attend the show. Many conventions feature a player or several players to sign autographs.

Counterfeit: A card or collectible made to look like a real item. Counterfeits have no collectible value.

Cut: A signature that has been literally "cut" away from a check, card, letter or notebook on which it was originally signed.

Dealer: A person who buys, sells and trades sports cards and other memorabilia for profit. A dealer may be full-time, part-time, own a shop, operate a mail-order business from his home, deal at baseball card shows on weekends or do any combination of the above.

Distributor: Persons or organizations which buy cards and memorabilia directly from the manufacturers or from other dealers and resells them on a large scale. Sometimes distributors receive exclusive products, and thus are the only source of distribution for the product.

eBay: The huge Internet trading source in which thousands of items are offered for auction daily.

Facsimile autograph: A reproduced autograph. Facsimile autographs are often found on bats, gloves and other equipment.

F.D.C.: An envelope or cachet that is designed to be postmarked to celebrate a specific event on the day or anniversary of the event. F.D.C. stands for "first-day cover."

Felt: A baseball item consisting of a felt pennant, usually with a photograph or likeness of the player attached. Felts were made in 1916 and again from 1936-37.

Find: A "find" normally happens because of a chance encounter or casual comment that results in the purchase of an item of exceptional quality or rarity, usually at a favorable and economical price. What makes a find possible is that people look at souvenirs in a special way and tend to keep scorecards, autographs and other odd pieces of memorabilia to accumulate over the years that eventually turn up as a treasure for someone else. The belief that most "finds" have already been found is not true. There are still "finds" out there waiting to be discovered.

Flannel: A jersey made of a cotton or wool material. Most flannels were discontinued and replaced by knit jerseys in the early 1970s.

Flat: A term used at autograph shows to describe a picture, poster, magazine, postcard or card. Usually "flats" have a different pricing structure than equipment, uniforms or balls.

Fixtures: Any non-seat items that came out of a stadium, such as turnstiles, aisle signs, restroom signs, etc.

Fleer: The Pennsylvania-based maker of baseball, basketball and football cards.

Foil Pack: A tamperproof card packaging widely used since 1989.

Game: A uniform, cap, helmet or piece of equipment manufactured and designed for use in a college or professional game or sporting event. A "game" bat was ordered by the player to be used but is not "game-used" until it actually makes its way into an actual game.

Game-used or game-worn: A uniform, hat or piece of equipment actually used or worn in a professional or college sporting event.

Grade: The state of preservation of a piece of memorabilia. An item's value is based in large part on its grade (condition).

GPC: The initials GPC stand for "government postcard." These pre-stamped postcards were especially popular for obtaining autographs by mail from outside stadiums. That way, a fan could hand a player a self-addressed stamped postcard that the player could sign and return at a more convenient time.

Grading service: A company that charges a fee to grade cards or memorabilia. Most grading services work like this: After a card is graded, it is placed in a tamper-proof plastic holder. A network of member-dealers then agrees to buy that card sight-unseen at that grade. Grading services are a recent innovation, patterned after similar services in the coin collecting hobby.

Hall of Famer (HOFer): a member of a sports hall of fame. Hall of Famer items often command a premium over non-Hall of Famer items.

Hall of Fame plaque: A postcard that is sold at the Baseball Hall of Fame gift shop in Cooperstown, N.Y. The postcard is a photo of each individual's plaque honored as a member of the Hall of Fame.

Hartland: A statue produced by a Wisconsin plastics company in the late 1950s and early 1960s. Eighteen major league baseball players were models for Hartlands. The company also produced football player statues and a long line of Western and historical figures, horses and farm animals. Hartland baseball figures were reissued in in the late 1980s and early 1990s.

Headliners: A series of sports figurines produced by Corinthian Marketing, beginning in 1997.

Hobby: Folksy term used by veteran collectors that refers to the sports collectibles business/industry.

Hologram: The silvery, laser-etched trademark printed as an anti-counterfeiting device on Upper Deck cards and Upper Deck Authenticated memorabilia.

Kellogg's: The Battle Creek, Mich., cereal company which packaged three-dimensional baseball and football cards in its cereal from 1970-83. The company has also produced cereal boxes picturing famous athletes.

Knits: The modern, polyester-based fabrics

used in modern sports uniforms.

Letter of authenticity (LOA): A letter stating that a certain piece of memorabilia, such as a uniform, is authentic.

Limited edition: A term often used by makers of cards and memorabilia to indicate scarcity. A limited edition means just that — production of the item in question will be limited to a certain number. However, that number may be large or small.

Lithograph: An art print made by a specific process that results in a print of outstanding clarity. Most lithographs are limited editions — though, as always, some lithographs are more limited than others.

Mail-bid auction: A form of auction where all bids are sent in through the mail. The person who sends in the highest bid gets the merchandise.

Manufacturer's tag: A tag sewn or attached into a jersey identifying it as from a particular company, such as Rawlings or Russell.

Matted out: A term used in the framing process to describe the covering of something not wanted in the finished product. For example, if a 3 x 5 card is personalized to "William" and the owner of the autograph is named "Bob," the owner would probably want to have the name "William" matted out.

Memorabilia: Usually referred to as items other than cards which mark or commemorate a player and his career, a team or an event.

Minimum Bid: The lowest acceptable offer that an auction company or individual will take for a particular item to begin the auction.

Mylar: Type of plastic from which many card holders, plastic sheets and other protection devices are made.

National: A sports memorabilia show held annually in different parts of the United States that draws hundreds of dealers and thousands of collectors.

Obverse: The front of the card displaying the picture. Opposite of reverse.

Oddball: A catchall category of sports collectibles other than cards, autographs and game-worn uniforms. Examples include beer and soda cans, cereal boxes, ticket stubs, publications and sports movie posters.

O-Pee-Chee: Longtime Canadian licensee of Topps that produced bilingual (French/English) baseball and hockey cards.

Paint pen: Gold or silver markers with opaque ink that can be difficult to use because of inconsistent ink flow.

Parkhurst: A Canadian manufacturer of hockey cards in the 1950s and 1960s. In recent years, the name was licensed to major manufacturers of hockey cards.

Perez-Steele: Line of popular Baseball Hall of Fame art postcards that are ideal for autographs that have been produced by artist Dick Perez and his late business partner, Franklin Steele.

Phantom: A ticket or press pin produced in anticipation of a team making the playoffs, but not used when the team failed to make it.

Phone auction: An auction where bids for memorabilia are taken over the phone. The highest bidder gets the merchandise.

Post: A cereal company which made baseball and football cards from 1960-63 and put them on the backs of its cereal boxes. Today the most valuable Post cards are uncut panels found on boxes. The company has also pictured athletes on its cereal boxes.

PPD: Postage paid.

Premium: An extra. Something inserted in a package of some other product. "Premium" can also refer to the extra money a star's item commands.

Price guide: A periodical or book which contains checklists of cards, sets and other memorabilia and their values in varying conditions.

Price on request (P.O.R.): A dealer will advertise an item P.O.R. if he believes the price will fluctuate from the time he places his ad until the time the ad is seen by the public.

Private signing: An autograph signing event where a dealer employs a celebrity to sign a number of items or "pieces" that have been mailed in or ordered by collectors. A private signing is not a public event.

Provenance: The history of ownership of a particular item. It allows the buyer to secure additional insight as to the origin of the item.

Puzzle piece, poster piece: The back of a card containing a partial design which, when pieced together with corresponding pieces, forms a large picture or poster.

Rare: Difficult to obtain and limited in number.

ROY: Rookie of the Year.

Salesman's Sample: An example of a commemorative championship ring or a jersey produced by companies for players and team officials to preview. Not as collectible, but often mistaken for the real thing.

SASE: A term used in hobby advertisements and elsewhere to indicate "self-addressed, stamped envelope."

SCD: The weekly magazine known as *Sports Collectors Digest* that is published in Iola, Wis.

Sell price: The price at which a dealer will sell cards. Generally much higher than his buy price.

Sepia: A dark reddish-brown coloration used in some photos instead of traditional black and white.

Series: A group of items that is part of a set and was issued at one time.

Set: A complete run of items.

Sharpie: A permanent marker made by Sanford in a variety of colors and pen points for use on paper, cloth or leather. It is not advisable to use for autographs on baseballs because the ink has a tendency to bleed.

Single-signed: An item (often a ball) with only one signature on it.

Slabbing: Process of independent, professional grading on a scale of 1-10 or 1-100 and placing cards in hard plastic casings.

Stamp: An adhesive-backed paper which depicts a player. When the stamp, which can be an individual or a sheet of many stamps, is moistened, it can be attached to another surface or corresponding stamp album.

Stamped: An autograph applied to a photo, card or other item with a rubber stamp, not hand signed.

Starting Lineup: A line of plastic figures with accompanying cards produced by Kenner/Hasbro since 1988. Also, the trademark for a computer-based baseball game with cards produced by Parker Brothers.

Stub: A portion of a ticket left over from attending a game. Not as valuable as an untorn ticket, but usually still collectible.

Sweet spot or manager's spot: The section of a baseball reserved for the team manager on baseballs. It is usually the most desirable spot for an autograph on single-signed baseballs.

Tobacco cards: Baseball cards packaged with tobacco products in the late 1800s and early 1900s.

Topps: The oldest existing sports card manufacturer. Based in New York, the company has produced baseball cards continuously since 1951 and has also produced basketball, football and hockey cards.

Upper Deck: The Carlsbad, Calif., manufacturer of baseball, basketball, football and hockey cards.

Upper Deck Authenticated (UDA): The sister company of The Upper Deck Co., which produces authentic autographed memorabilia items under contracts with star athletes including Michael Jordan.

Uncut sheet: A full press sheet of cards that was never cut and collated into individual cards.

UV: A glossy coating applied to sports cards.

3 x 5 (lined or unlined): A 3-inch by 5-inch card that may have a lined side and a blank side. Autograph collectors prefer that signatures be on the unlined side of the card.

Variation: A card printed in more than one manner, usually to correct an error or printing mistake.

Want list: A collector's or dealer's list of items he is wishing to buy. Often, a collector will send a dealer a "want list," and the dealer will try to locate the items on the list.

Wax: Type of card packaging (for example, wax pack) widely used until the late 1980s. Wax-sealed wrappers could be easily removed and the contents tampered with.

Wheaties: The breakfast cereal by General Mills that often pictures sports personalities and championship teams on the fronts of boxes.

●●●

Sports Addresses

Baseball

MAJOR LEAGUE BASEBALL
350 Park Ave., New York, NY 10022
(212) 931-7800
Web site: www.majorleaguebaseball.com

AMERICAN LEAGUE
Anaheim Angels, 2000 Gene Autry Way,
Anaheim, CA 92806, (714) 940-7200
Baltimore Orioles, 333 W. Camden St.,
Baltimore, MD 21201, (410) 685-9800
Boston Red Sox, 4 Yawkey Way,
Boston, MA 02215, (617) 267-9440
Chicago White Sox, 333 W. 35th St.,
Chicago, IL 60616, (312) 674-1000
Cleveland Indians, 2401 Ontario St.,
Cleveland, OH 44114-40003, (216) 420-4200
Detroit Tigers, 2100 Woodward Ave.,
Detroit, MI 48201, (313) 962-4000
Kansas City Royals, P.O. Box 419969
Kansas City, MO 64141-6969,
(816) 921-2200
Minnesota Twins, 34 Kirby Puckett Place,
Minneapolis, MN 55415, (612) 375-1366
New York Yankees, Yankee Stadium, Bronx,
NY 10451, (718) 293-4300
Oakland Athletics, 7677 Oakport, Suite 200,
Oakland, CA 94621, (510) 638-4900
Seattle Mariners, P.O. Box 4100,
Seattle, WA 98104, (206) 346-4000
Tampa Bay Devil Rays, One Stadium Drive,
St. Petersburg, FL 33705, (813) 825-3137
Texas Rangers, 1000 Ballpark Way,
Arlington, TX 76011, (817) 273-5222
Toronto Blue Jays, SkyDome, 1 Blue Jays Way,
Suite 3200, Toronto, Ontario, Canada M5V 1J1,
(416) 341-1000

NATIONAL LEAGUE
Arizona Diamondbacks, P.O. Box 2095,
Phoenix, AZ 85001, (602) 514-8500
Atlanta Braves, P.O. Box 4064,
Atlanta, GA 30302, (404) 522-7630,
Chicago Cubs, 1060 W. Addison St.,
Chicago, IL 60613, (773) 404-2827
Cincinnati Reds, 100 Cinergy Ave.,
Cincinnati, OH 45202, (513) 421-4510
Colorado Rockies, Coors Field,
2001 Blake St., Denver, CO 80205-2000
(303) 292-0200
Florida Marlins, 2267 N.W. 199th St.,
Miami, FL 33056, (305) 626-7400
Houston Astros, 501 Crawford St.,
Houston, TX 77002, (713) 799-9500
Los Angeles Dodgers,
1000 Elysian Park Ave., Los Angeles, CA
90012, (213) 224-1500
Milwaukee Brewers, One Brewers Way,
Milwaukee, WI 53214-0888
(414) 933-4114
Montreal Expos, P.O. Box 500, Station M,
Montreal, Quebec, Canada H1V 3N7
(514) 253-3434

New York Mets, Shea Stadium,
Flushing, NY 11368, (718) 507-6387
Philadelphia Phillies, P.O. Box 7575,
Philadelphia, PA 19101, (215) 463-6000
Pittsburgh Pirates, Box 7000, Pittsburgh, PA
15212, (412) 323-5000
St. Louis Cardinals, 250 Stadium Plaza,
St. Louis, MO 63102, (314) 421-3060
San Diego Padres, P.O. Box 2000,
San Diego, CA 92112, (619) 283-4494
San Francisco Giants, 24 Willie Mays Plaza,
San Francisco, CA 94107, (415) 468-3700

Basketball

NATIONAL BASKETBALL
ASSOCIATION
Olympic Tower, 645 Fifth Ave.,
New York, NY 10022, (212) 826-7000
Web site: www.nba.com

For team pages add: /team name
(Ex. www.nba.com/hawks)

EASTERN CONFERENCE
Atlanta Hawks, One CNN Center, Suite 405,
Atlanta, GA 30303, (404) 827-3800
Boston Celtics, 151 Merrimac St.,
Boston, MA 02114, (617) 523-6050
Charlotte Hornets, 100 Hive Dr.,
Charlotte, NC 28217, (704) 357-0252
Chicago Bulls, 1901 W. Madison St.,
Chicago, IL 60612, (312) 455-4000
Cleveland Cavaliers, 1 Center Court,
Cleveland, OH 44115-4001, (216) 420-2000
Detroit Pistons, Palace of Auburn Hills,
Two Championship Drive, Auburn Hills,
MI 48326, (248) 377-0100
Indiana Pacers, 125 S. Pennsylvania St.,
Indianapolis, IN 46204, (317) 263-2100
Miami Heat, American Airlines Arena,
1 SE Third Avenue, Suite 2300,
Miami, FL 33131, (305) 577-4328
Milwaukee Bucks, 1001 N. Fourth St.,
Milwaukee, WI 53203-1312
(414) 227-0500
New Jersey Nets, Nets Champion Center, 390
Murray Hill Pkwy., East Rutherford, NJ 07073
(201) 935-8888
New York Knickerbockers, Two Pennsylvania
Plaza, New York, NY 10121
(212) 465-6000
Orlando Magic, P.O. Box 76,
Orlando, FL 32802, (407) 649-3200
Philadelphia 76ers, First Union Center, 3601
Broad St., Philadelphia, PA 19148
(215) 339-7600
Toronto Raptors, 40 Bay St., Suite 400,
Toronto, Ontario, Canada M5J 2X2
(416) 815-5600
Washington Wizards, 601 F. St. NW,
Washington, D.C. 20071, (202) 661-5000

WESTERN CONFERENCE
Dallas Mavericks, Reunion Arena,
777 Sports St., Dallas, TX 75207
(214) 748-1808

Denver Nuggets, Pepsi Center, 1000 Chopper
Place, Denver, CO 80204, (303) 405-1100
Golden State Warriors, 1011 Broadway, 20th
Floor, Oakland, CA 94607, (510) 986-2200
Houston Rockets, 2 Greenway Plaza,
Houston, TX 77046, (713) 627-3865
Los Angeles Clippers, Staples Center, 1111
Figueroa St., Los Angeles, CA 90015
(213) 745-0400
Los Angeles Lakers, 555 N. Nash St.,
El Segundo, CA 90245, (310) 426-6001
Minnesota Timberwolves, 600 First Ave.
North, Minneapolis, MN 55403
(612) 673-1600
Phoenix Suns, 201 E. Jefferson St.,
Phoenix, AZ 85001, (602) 379-7867
Portland Trail Blazers,
One Center Court, Suite 200,
Portland, OR 97227, (503) 224-4400
Sacramento Kings, One Sports Parkway,
Sacramento, CA 95834, (916) 928-6900
San Antonio Spurs, 100 Montana St.,
San Antonio, TX 78203, (210) 554-7700
Seattle SuperSonics, 190 Queen Anne Avenue
N. #200, Seattle, WA 98109, (206) 281-5800
Utah Jazz, Delta Center, 301 W. South Temple,
Salt Lake City, UT 84101
(801) 325-2500
Vancouver Grizzlies, General Motors Place,
800 Griffiths Way, Vancouver, B.C. V6B 6G1
(604) 899-4667

WOMEN'S NATIONAL
BASKETBALL ASSOCIATION
645 Fifth Ave., 10th Floor,
New York, NY 10022, (212) 688-9622
Web site: www.wnba.com

For team pages add:/team name
(Ex. www.wnba.com/sting)

EASTERN CONFERENCE
Charlotte Sting, 3308 Oak Lake Blvd., #B,
Charlotte, NC 28208, (704) 424-9622
Cleveland Rockers, Gund Arena,
One Center Court, Cleveland, OH 44115
(216) 263-7625
Detroit Shock, Two Championship Dr.,
Auburn Hills, MI 48326, (248) 377-0100
Indiana Fever, 125 S. Pennsylvania St.,
Indianapolis, IN 46204
Miami Sol, American Airlines Arena, 1 SE
Third Avenue, Suite 2300, Miami, FL 33131
New York Liberty, 2 Penn Plaza,
New York, NY 10121, (212) 564-9622
Orlando Miracle, P.O. Box 4000, Orlando, FL
32802-4000, (407) 916-9622
Washington Mystics, MCI Center, 601 F St.
NW, Washington, DC 20001
(202) 661-5050

WESTERN CONFERENCE
Houston Comets, 2 Greenway Plaza, Suite 400,
Houston, TX 77046-9622,
(713) 627-9622

Los Angeles Sparks, Great Western Forum, 3900 W. Manchester Blvd., Inglewood, CA 90306, (800) 978-9622

Minnesota Lynx, Target Center, 600 First Ave. N., Minneapolis, MN 55403 (612) 673-8400

Phoenix Mercury, 201 East Jefferson St., Phoenix, AZ 85004, (602) 252-9622

Portland Fire, One Center Court, Suite 200, Portland, OR 97227, (503) 224-4400

Sacramento Monarchs, One Sports Parkway, Sacramento, CA 95834 (916) 928-3650

Seattle Storm, 190 Queen Anne Avenue N. #200, Seattle, WA 98109

Utah Starzz, Delta Center, 301 West South Temple, Salt Lake City, UT 84101, (801) 325-2500

Football

NATIONAL FOOTBALL LEAGUE
280 Park Ave., New York, NY 10017
(212) 450-2000; Web site: www.nfl.com

AMERICAN FOOTBALL
CONFERENCE

Baltimore Ravens, 11001 Owings Mills Blvd., Owings Mills, MD 21117, (410) 654-6200

Buffalo Bills, One Bills Drive, Orchard Park, NY 14127, (716) 648-1800

Cincinnati Bengals, 1 Bengals Drive, Cincinnati, OH 45204, (513) 621-3550

Cleveland Browns, 76 Lou Groza Blvd., Berea, Ohio 44017, (440) 891-5000

Denver Broncos, 13655 Broncos Parkway, Englewood, CO 80112, (303) 649-9000

Indianapolis Colts, 7001 W. 56th St., Indianapolis, IN 46224-0100 (317) 297-2658

Jacksonville Jaguars, One Stadium Place, Jacksonville, FL 32202, (904) 633-6000

Kansas City Chiefs, One Arrowhead Dr., Kansas City, MO 64129, (816) 924-9300

Miami Dolphins, 7500 SW 30th Street, Davie, FL 33314, (954) 452-7000

New England Patriots, Foxboro Stadium, 60 Washington St., Foxboro, MA 02035, (508) 543-8200

New York Jets, 1000 Fulton Ave., Hempstead, NY 11550, (516) 560-8100

Oakland Raiders, 1220 Harbor Bay Parkway, Alameda, CA 94502, (510) 864-5000

Pittsburgh Steelers, 300 Stadium Circle, Pittsburgh, PA 15212, (412) 323-1200

San Diego Chargers, 4020 Murphy Canyon Rd, San Diego, CA 92123, (619) 874-4500

Seattle Seahawks, 11220 N.E. 53rd St., Kirkland, WA 98033, (425) 827-9777

Tennessee Titans, 7640 Hwy. 70 South, Nashville, TN 37221, (615) 565-4000

NATIONAL FOOTBALL
CONFERENCE

Arizona Cardinals, 8701 S. Hardy Dr., Tempe, AZ 85284, (602) 379-0101

Atlanta Falcons, 1 Falcon Place, Suwanee, GA 30024-2198, (770) 945-1111

Carolina Panthers, 800 S. Mint St., Charlotte, NC 28202, (704) 358-7000

Chicago Bears, Halas Hall at Conway Park, 1000 Football Drive, Lake Forest, IL 60045 (847) 295-6600

Dallas Cowboys, Cowboys Center, 1 Cowboys Parkway, Irving, TX 75063-4727, (972) 556-9900

Detroit Lions, 1200 Featherstone Rd., Pontiac, MI 48342, (248) 335-4131

Green Bay Packers, 1265 Lombardi Ave., Green Bay, WI 54304, (920) 496-5700

Minnesota Vikings, 9520 Viking Dr., Eden Prairie, MN 55344, (612) 828-6500

New Orleans Saints, 5800 Airline Dr., Metairie, LA 70003, (504) 733-0255

New York Giants, Giants Stadium, East Rutherford, NJ 07073 (201) 935-8111

Philadelphia Eagles, Veterans Stadium, 3501 S. Broad St., Philadelphia, PA 19148 (215) 463-2500

San Francisco 49ers, 4949 Centennial Blvd., Santa Clara, CA 95054-1229 (408) 562-4949

St. Louis Rams, 1 Rams Way, St. Louis, MO 63045, (314) 982-7267

Tampa Bay Buccaneers, One Buccaneer Place, Tampa, FL 33607, (813) 870-2700

Washington Redskins, 21300 Redskin Park Dr., Ashburn, VA 22011, (703) 478-8900

Hockey

NATIONAL HOCKEY LEAGUE
75 International Blvd., Suite 300, Rexdale, Ontario, Canada M9W 6L9, (416) 981-2777
Web site: www.nhl.com

EASTERN CONFERENCE
ATLANTIC DIVISION

Philadelphia Flyers, First Union Center, 3601 S. Broad St., Philadelphia, PA 19148 (215) 465-4500

Pittsburgh Penguins, 66 Mario Lemieux Place, Pittsburgh, PA 15219, (412) 642-1800

New Jersey Devils, Continental Airlines Arena, P.O. Box 504, East Rutherford, NJ 07073 (201) 935-6050

New York Islanders, Nassau Coliseum, Uniondale, NY 11553, (516) 794-4100

New York Rangers, Madison Square Garden, 4 Pennsylvania Plaza, New York, NY 10001, (212) 465-6000

NORTHEAST DIVISION

Boston Bruins, 1 FleetCenter, Suite 250, Boston, MA 02114, (617) 624-1050

Buffalo Sabres, Marine Midland Arena, 1 Seymour H. Knox III Plaza, Buffalo, NY 14203, (716) 856-7300

Montreal Canadiens, Molson Center, 1260 Rue de la Gauchetiere W., Montreal, Quebec, Canada H3B 5E8, (514) 932-2582

Ottawa Senators, 1000 Palladium Drive, Kanata, Ontario, Canada, K2V 1A5 (613) 599-0250

Toronto Maple Leafs, 40 Bay St., Suite 400, Toronto, Ontario, Canada M5J 2X2 (416) 815-5700

SOUTHEAST DIVISION

Atlanta Thrashers, 1 CNN Center, 13th S. Tower, Atlanta, GA 30303, 404-827-5212

Carolina Hurricanes, 1400 Edwards Mill Road, Raleigh, NC 27607, (910) 852-6170

Florida Panthers, One Panther Parkway, Sunrise, FL 33323, (954) 835-7000

Tampa Bay Lightning, Ice Palace, 401 Channelside Dr., Tampa, FL 33602 (813) 229-2658

Washington Capitals, MCI Center, 601 F Street NW, Washington, DC 20004 (202) 661-5000

WESTERN CONFERENCE
CENTRAL DIVISION

Chicago Blackhawks, 1901 W. Madison, Chicago, IL 60612, (312) 455-7000

Columbus Blue Jackets, 150 E. Wilson Bridge Road, #239, Worthington, OH 43085 614-436-2112

Detroit Red Wings, Joe Louis Arena, 600 Civic Center Drive, Detroit, MI 48226 (313) 396-7538

Nashville Predators, 501 Broadway, Nashville, TN 37203, (615) 770-2300

St. Louis Blues, 1401 Clark Ave., St. Louis, MO 63103, (314) 622-2500

NORTHWEST DIVISION

Calgary Flames, Olympic Saddledome, P.O. Box 1540, Station "M," Calgary, Alberta, Canada T2P 3B9, (403) 777-2177

Colorado Avalanche, Pepsi Center, 1000 Chopper Place, Denver, CO 80204, (303) 405-1100

Edmonton Oilers, 11230 110th St., Edmonton, Alberta, Canada T5G 3H7, (780) 414-4000

Minnesota Wild, 444 Cedar St. Suite 2000, St. Paul, MN 55101, 612-333-7825

Vancouver Canucks, 800 Griffiths Way, Vancouver, B.C., Canada V6B 6G (604) 899-4600

PACIFIC DIVISION

Anaheim Mighty Ducks, Arrowhead Pond of Anaheim, 2695 Katella Ave., Anaheim, CA 92806, (714) 704-2700

Dallas Stars, 211 Cowboys Parkway, Irving, TX 75063, (972) 868-2890

Los Angeles Kings, 555 North Nash St., El Segundo, CA 90245, (310) 535-4500

Phoenix Coyotes, 9375 E. Bell Rd., Scottsdale, AZ 85260, (602) 473-5600;

San Jose Sharks, San Jose Arena, 525 W. Santa Clara St., San Jose, CA 95113 (408) 287-7070

NASCAR

NASCAR
1801 West Speedway Blvd.,
Daytona Beach, FL 32114-1234
(904) 253-0611
Web site: www.nascar.com

NASCAR FAN CLUB
4707 E. Baseline Rd., Phoenix, AZ 85040
(888) 533-1200

NASCAR WINSTON CUP SERIES
Sports Marketing Enterprises
P.O. Box 484, 401 North Main St.,
Winston-Salem, NC 27102
(910) 741-6472

WINSTON CUP FAN CLUBS

Jeff Burton
Jeff Burton Fan Club, P.O. Box 1160,
Halifax, VA 24558

Dale Earnhardt
Club E, 4707 E. Baseline Rd.,
Phoenix, AZ 85040, (888) 332-5823
Web site: www.earnhardtfan.com

Dale Earnhardt Jr.
Club E Jr., 4707 E. Baseline Rd.,
Phoenix, AZ 85040, (877) 258-2357
Web site: www.dalejr.com

Bill Elliot
Bill Elliott Fan Club, P.O. Box 248,
Dawsonville, GA 30534

Jeff Gordon
Jeff Gordon National Fan Club, P.O. Box 515,
Williams, AZ 86046-0515,
(520) 635-JEFF

Dale Jarrett
Dale Jarrett Fan Club, 4707 E. Baseline Rd.,
Phoenix, AZ 85040, (888) 325-3527

Bobby Labonte
Bobby Labonte Fan Club, 4707 E. Baseline Rd.,
Phoenix, AZ 85040, (877) 426-2295

Mark Martin
Mark Martin Fan Club, P.O. Box 68,
Ash Flat, AR 72513

Rusty Wallace
Rusty Wallace Fan Club,
4707 E. Baseline Rd., Phoenix, AZ 85040,(
877) 787-8992

Halls of Fame and Museums

Alabama Sports Hall of Fame and Museum,
2150 Civic Center Blvd.,
Birmingham, AL 35203, (205) 323-6665
Web site: www.tech-comm.com/ashof

The American Sportscasters Association Hall of Fame, 5 Beekman St., Suite 814,
New York, NY 10038, (212) 227-8080
Web site: www.americansportscasters.com

Arena Football Hall of Fame, 319 7th St.,
Des Moines, IA 50318, (515) 362-5955

The Babe Ruth Museum, 216 Emory St.,
Baltimore, MD 21230, (410)727-1539
Web site: www.baberuthmuseum.com

Bob Feller Hometown Exhibit, 310 Mill St.,
P. O. Box 95, Van Meter, IA 50261,
(515) 996-2806,
Web site: www.bobfellermuseum.org

Canadian Football Hall of Fame,
58 Jackson St. W., Hamilton, Ontario,
Canada L8P 1L4, (905) 528-7566

Canadian Golf Hall of Fame, 1333 Dorval Dr.,
Oakville, Ontario L6J 4Z3, (905) 849-9700,
Web site: www.cghf.org

College Football Hall of Fame, 111 South St.,
South Bend, IN, 46601, (219) 235-9999
Web site: hof@CollegeFootball.org

Georgia Golf Hall of Fame, One 10th St.,
Suite 745, Augusta, GA 30901, (706) 724-4443
Web site: www.gghf.org

Green Bay Packer Hall of Fame,
855 Lombardi Ave., Green Bay, WI 54307,
(920) 499-4281,
Web site: www.packershalloffame.com

Hockey Hall of Fame, BCE Place,
30 Yonge St., Toronto,
Ontario, Canada M5E 1X8, (416) 360-7765
Web site: www.hhof.com

Indiana Football Hall of Fame,
815 North A St., Richmond, IN 47374
(765) 966-2235

International Bowling Museum and Hall of Fame, 111 Stadium Plaza,
St. Louis, MO 63102, (314) 231-6340
Web site: www.bowlingmuseum.com

International Boxing Hall of Fame,
1 Hall of Fame Drive, P.O. Box 425,
Canastota, NY 13032, (315) 697-7095
Web site: www.ibhof.com

International Hockey Hall of Fame and Museum, P.O. Box 82, York & Alfred Streets,
Kingston, Ontario, Canada K7L 4V6
(613) 544-2355.

International Tennis Hall of Fame,
194 Bellevue Ave., Newport, RI 02840
(401) 849-3990,
Web site: www.tennisfame.org

Ivan Allen Jr. Braves Museum and Hall of Fame, 755 Hank Aaron Dr.,
Atlanta, GA 30315, (404) 614-2310

Kansas Sports Hall of Fame,
213 N. Broadway, P. O. Box 35,
Abiline, KS, 67410, (785) 262-7403,
Web site: www.kshof.org

Kentucky Derby Museum, 704 Central Ave.,
Louisville, KY 40208, (502) 637-7097
Web site: www.derbymuseum.org

Louisiana Sports Hall of Fame, 6007 Financial
Plaza, Suite 401, Shreveport, LA 71129, Web
site: www.lasportshof.com

Louisville Slugger Museum, 800 West Main
St., Louisville, KY 40202, (502) 588-7228, Web
site: www.slugger.com/museum

MCI National Sports Gallery, 601 F. St., N.W.,
Washington, DC 20001, (202) 661-5133, Web
site: www.mcicenter.com

Michigan Sports Hall of Fame, 32985 Hamilton Court, Suite 218, Farmington Hills, MI
48334, (248) 848-0252

Naismith Memorial Basketball Hall of Fame,
Box 179, 150 W. Columbus Ave., Springfield,
MA 01101, (413) 781-6500, Web site:
www.hoophall.com

National Baseball Hall of Fame and Museum, P.O. Box 590 Cooperstown,
NY 13326, (607) 547-7200
Web site: www.baseballhalloffame.org

National Football Foundation and Hall of Fame, 1865 Palmer Ave., Suite 103, Larchmont,
NY 10538, (973) 829-1933

National Soccer Hall of Fame, Wright Soccer
Campus, 18 Stadium Circle, Oneonta, NY
13820 (607) 432-3351, Web site: www.soccer-hall.org

Negro League Baseball Museum,
1601 E. 18th St., Suite 260,
Kansas City, MO 64108, (816) 221-1920

Oklahoma Sports Museum, 315 W. Oklahoma
Ave., Guthrie, OK 73044, (405) 260-1342, Web
site: www.oksports.qpg.com

Paul W. Bryant Museum, 300 Bryant Dr.,
Tuscaloosa, AL,35487-0385 (205) 348-4668,
Web site: ua.edu/bryant.htm

Pennsylvania Sports Hall of Fame, P.O. Box
2034, Cleona, PA 17042, (717) 274-3644,
Web site: www.pasportshalloffame.com

Pro Football Hall of Fame,*
2121 George Halas Dr. N.W.,
Canton, OH 44708, (330) 456-8207
Web site: www.canton-ohio.com/hof

Rose Bowl Hall of Fame, 391 South Orange
Grove Blvd., Pasadena, CA 91184, (626) 449-4100, Web site:
www.tournamentofroses.com/rbhalloffame.htm

St. Louis Cardinals Hall of Fame Museum,
111 Stadium Plaza, St. Louis, MO 63102 (314)
231-6340, website: www.stlcardinals.com

Sports Museum of Champions, 700 Clyde
Fant Pkwy., Shreveport, LA (318) 221-0712,
Web site: www.independencebowl.org/museum.

Ted Williams Museum and Hitters Hall of Fame, 2455 N. Citrus Hills Blvd., Hernando,
FL 34442-5349, (352) 527-4163, Web site: http:
twmuseum.com

Ty Cobb Museum, 461 Cook St., Royston, GA
30662, (706) 245-1825, Web site: www.tycobb-museum.org

United States Hockey Hall of Fame,
801 Hat Trick Ave., Eveleth,
MN 55734, (218) 744-5167
Web site: www.ushockeyhall.co

Autograph Organizations

**International Autograph Collectors Club
(IACC) and Dealers Alliance (IADA),** 4575
Sheridan St. Suite #111, Hollywood, FL 33021,
(561) 736-8409

Sports Web sites

Auction Companies

All American Collectibles
www.aacauction.com
Amazon
www.amazon.com
American Memorabilia
www.Ami21.com
AcuBid.com
www.acubid.com
Andalé
www.andale.com
Auction Anything.com
www.auctionanything.com
AuctionBytes.com
www.auctionbytes.com
The Auction Channel
www.theauctionchannel.com
Auction Helper.com
www.auctionhelper.com
AuctionInvoice.com
www.auctioninvoice.com
Auction Rover (aka GoTo Auctions)
www.auctionrover.com
auctions.goto.com
Auction Watch
www.auctionwatch.com
Auction Works
www.auctionworks.com
Baseball Planet
www.baseballplanet.com
Beckett.com
www.beckett.com
Bidhop.com
www.bidhop.com
Boxlot.com
www.boxlot.com
Card Hobby
www.cardhobby.com
Clean Sweep Auctions
www.csauctions.com
Coach's Corner Sports Auctions
www.ccsauction.com
Collectit.net
www.collectit.net
Collectors Universe
www.collectors.com
Compares.com
www.compares.com
eBay
www.ebay.com
eWanted
www.ewanted.com
Gavel Net
www.gavelnet.com
GoTo Auctions
auctions.goto.com
Grey Flannel Collectibles
www.greyflannel.com
Hunt Auctions Inc.
www.huntauctions.com

InterNet's Baseball Card Store
www.baseball-cards.com
Leland's
www.lelands.com
Greg Manning Auctions Inc.
www.gregmanning.amazon.com
Mastro Fine Sports Auctions
www.mastronet.com
MintXpress
www.mintxpress.com
M.S. Auctions
www.msauctions.com
PSA Auctions
www.psaauctions.com
Price Radar
www.PriceRadar.com
Ron Oser Enterprises
www.ronoserent.com
Rotman Auctions
www.rotmanauction.com
www.wwcd.com/rotman
R&R Enterprises
www.rrauction.com
Sotheby's
www.sothebys.amazon.com
Sports Auction.com
www.sportsauction.com
Sports Collective Network
www.sportscollective.net
Sports Investments International
www.air23.com
Superior Galleries
www.superiorgalleries.com
Superior Sports Auctions
www.collectors.com
Teletrade Sports Auctions
www.teletrade.com
Todays Sports
www.todayssports.com
Triple Threat Cards
www.ttcards.com
Yahoo Auctions
www.auctions.yahoo.com

Autograph Collectors

Autographs.com
www.autographs.com
The Autograph Zone
www.autographzone.com
Baseball Autographs
www.expage.com/page/autographsbymail
BD's Autograph Shack
*www.members.aol.com/cb4sports/index.
html*
Celebrity Address Emporium
www.springrose.com/celebrity/b.html
JD's Baseball Autographs
*www.geocities.com/Colosseum/Base/2-
611/index.html*
Mac Maroon's Sports Autographs
www.geocities.com/Colosseum/Bench/2126/
Mark's Signing Bonus
www.angelfire.com/mb/markssigningbonus/

NBO Baseball
www.nbobaseball.com
Net's Best Autograph Collecting Links
*www.rightguide.com/topics/hobby/
autograph.htm*
Signatures of Success
www.signaturesofsuccess.com
Signings Hotline
www.signingshotline.com
The Star Archive
www.stararchive.com
Stu's Super Autograph Page
www.stu-man.com

Card Graders/Authentication Services

Action Figure Authority
toygrader.com
Advanced Grading Specialists
www.advancedgrading.com
ASA Accugrade
www.asa-accugrade.com
Authentic Autographs Unlimited
www.aaunlimited.com
Beckett Grading Services
www.beckett.com
Certified Sports Authentication Inc.
www.csacards.com
www.certifiedsports.com
CTA Grading Experts, Inc.
www.ctagradingexperts.com
Certified Express
www.certifiedexpress.com
Forensic Autograph Authenticators
www.authenticators.net
Grey Flannel
www.greyflannel.com
Online Authentics
www.onlineauthentics.com
Professional Grading Service
www.prograding.com
Pro Sports Grading Inc.
www.prograding.net
PSA
www.collectors.com/psa
www.psacard.com
PSA/DNA Authentication Services
www.collectors.com/psadna
Sportscard Guaranty Corp.
www.SGCcard.com
Ultimate Sportscard Authority
www.usasportscards.com

Card Manufacturers

Collector's Edge
www.edgefootball.com
Donruss
www.donruss.com
Fleer
www.fleerskybox.com
Goal Line Art
www.goallineart.com

Just Minors
www.justminors.com
Pacific Trading Cards
www.pacifictradingcards.com
Playoff
www.playoffinc.com
Press Pass/Racing Champions
www.racingchampions.com
Ron Mix's Football HOF Signature Series
www.halloffamecards.com
Roox Sports
www.roox.com
SA-GE
www.SA-GE.com
Score
www.scoreonline.net
Starting Lineup Authenticated
www.sluauthenticated.com
Team Best
www.teambest.com
Topps
www.topps.com
Upper Deck
www.upperdeck.com
Warning Track Cards
www.warningtrackcards.com

Collectors Web Sites

Card Links
www.cardlinks.com
The Card Mall
www.cardmall.com
Collect.com
www.collect.com
Collectibles.com
www.collectibles.com
Collecting Channel
www.collectingchannel.com
Collectors Universe
www.collectors.com
Collector Link
www.collector-link.com
Dick Butkus.com
www.dickbutkus.com
Graded Sports Cards.net
www.gradedsportscards.net
Krause Publications
www.krause.com
Oddball Mall
www.oddball-mall.com
Old Links Golf Collectibles
www.oldlinks.com
Pack Ripper
www.packripper.com
Philadelphia A's Historical
www.philadelphiaathletics.org
PriceIs.com
www.priceis.com
Seth Swirsky
www.sethsroom.com
Sports Investments Network
www.sinetwork.com
Network Top 50 sites
www.top50network.com

T206 Museum
www.t206museum.com
Top Prospect Alert
www.topprospectalert.com
Trading Card Central
www.tradingcardcentral.com
Trading Card Source
www.tradingcardsource.com
World-Wide Collectors Digest
www.wwcd.com
Worth Guide
www.worthguide.com

Dealers

Adelson Sports
www.adelsonsports.com
A.J. Sports Cards
www.ajcards.com
A&K Sports Collectibles
www.wwcd.com/a_k
All American Collectibles
www.allamericancollectible.com
All Star Cards
www.allstar-cards.com
Rich Altman Hollywood Collectibles
www.hollywoodcollectibles.com
American Card Management
www.americancardmgmt.homestead.com
American Memorabilia
www.ami21.com
America's Memories
www.americasmemories.com
Anaconda Sports
www.anacondasports.com
Antiquities of the Prize Ring
www.antekprizering.com
Thomas Appleby
www.applebyarchives.com
AU Sports
www.ausports.com
Authentics Handsigned Collectibles
www.hometown.aol.com/handsigned
Autographs For Sale.com
www.autographsforsale.com
B2 Sports Art
www.b2sportsart.com
Jeremy Bachman
www.spectatorsportcards.com
Ballpark Legends
www.ballparklegends.net
Bammerland.com
www.bammerland.com
The Baseball Card Kid
www.bbckid.com
Baseball Cards Unlimited
www.baseballcardsunlimited.com
Baseball Fanatic Superstore
www.members.aol.com/baseball
Baseball Tapes.com
www.baseballtapes.com
BB Cards 4 U.com
www.bbcards4u.com
B&J Collectibles

www.b-j.com
Big Al "The Collector's Pal"
www.sportsillustratedmags.com
Blue Chip Sports
www.bc-sports.com
Bob's Archives
www.bobsarchives.com
The Bobbinator
www.bobbinator.com
Boca Cards and Investments
www.bocacards.com
Broadway Rick's Strike Zone
www.strikezone.net
Byron's Hockeyland
www.byronshockeyland.com
California Sports Investments
www.californiasportsinv.com
Capital Cards
www.capitalcards.com
Card Collectors' Co.
www.wwcd.com/cardhaven
Cards 'n Stars
www.americasmemories.com
Steve Ciniglio
www.sportsautograph.com
Clarks Trading Stores
www.ctagradingexperts.com
Classic Collectibles
classiccollect.com
Kevin Cloutier's Hartland Figurines and Sports Memorabilia
www.hartlands.com
Joe Colabella
www.joecolabella.com
Collect Baseball.com
www.collectbaseball.com
The Collectible Closet
www.ccplayball.com
Collectibles.com
www.collectibles.com
Consolidated Sports
www.consolidatedsports.com
Creative Sports Enterprises Inc.
www.creativesportsonline.com
Danrick Enterprises
www.baseballtapes.com
Dan's Dugout
www.dansdugout.com
Dave's Vintage Baseball Cards
www.gfg.com/baseball
Dedicated Fan
www.dedicatedfan.com
Ed Dolan Jr.'s Baseball Fanatic Super Store
www.eddolan.com
Dot and Lou's Collectibles
www.dotandloucollectibles.com
The Edge-Man
www.edgeman.com
Empire State Sports Memorabilia and Collectibles
www.empirestatesports@beckett.com
The Endzone
members.aol.com/endzone494

Epic Sports and Collectibles
www.epicsportsonline.com
Everlasting Images
www.everlastingimages.com
Ewaxpax.com
www.ewaxpax.com
Doak Ewing Rare Sports Films
www.raresportsfilms.com
Fat Stacks
www.fatstacks.com
Field of Dreams
www.field-of-dreams.com
Terrence Fogarty Studio
www.terrencefogarty.com
Larry Fritsch Cards
www.fritschcards.com
Frozen Pond
www.frozenpond.com
Georgetown Card Exchange
www.gcxonline.com
Good As Gold Investments
www.goodasgold-inv.com
Grad, Ink. Autographs
www.autographs.gradink.com
Graf Baseball Card Co.
www.grafcard.com
Grandstand Sports and Memorabilia
www.grandstandsports.com
Great Traditions
www.greattraditions.com
Grosnor Sportscards Inc.
www.grosnor.com
Halsports
www.halsports.com
Bill Hendersons Cards
www.azww.com/hendo
High End Sports Cards
www.UDAautos.com
Ira Hirshhorn and Co.
www.irahirshhornandcompany.com
Hobby Store 4U
www.hobbystore4u.com
Neil Hoppenworth Cards
www.hoppenworthcards.com
Hot Rookies.com
www.hotrookies.com
Howard's Sports Collectibles
www.howardsauction.com
Robert Hurst
www.adamnfineartist.com
InterNet's Baseball Card Store
www.baseball-cards.com
Jake's Toy Chest
www.jakestoys.com
Norman James
www.normanjames.com
J. Paul Sports Promotions Inc.
www.jpaulsports.com
Jeff's Baseball Corner
www.members.aol.com/jbcorner
J&J Distributing
www.forcomm.net/jjdistributing
J&J Sports Section
www.jjsports1.com

Johnson & Johnson Sportcards
www.johnsonsportscards.com
Dennis A. Jose "Mr. Mint Tix"
www.chicagotix.com
JM Sports
www.footballhelmets.com
J.T. Sports
www.gameusedbats.com
Kaiser Cards
www.kaisercards.com
Bob "The Card" Kauffman
www.voicenet.com/~vintbase
Kings
www.dking-gallery.com
Kruk Cards Inc.
www.krukcards.com
Lake Country Minor League Prospects
www.members.xoom.com/lake_country
Carl and Maryanne Laron
www.laronsports.com
LCG Signatures
www.lcgsignatures.com
Left Field Collectibles
www.leftfieldcollectibles.com
Legends Sports
www.legendsports.com
Leisure Time Industries
www.LTIsports.com
Lew Lipset
www.oldjudge.com
Lost in Sports
www.lostinsports.com
Andy Madec Sportscards Inc.
www.andymadecsportscards.com
Greg Manning Sports
www.gregmanning.com
McAvoy Sportcards
www.mcavoysportscards.com
MeiGray Group
www.meigray.com
Mencik's Sportscards
www.mencik.com
Mile High Card Co.
www.milehighcardco.com
Minfords Minors
www.minfordsminors.com
Minnesota Connection
www.mnconn.com
Monicore Inc.
www.wheatiestrophy.com
MOS Sports Inc.
www.mos-sports.com
MVP Autographs
www.mvpautographs.com
Adam Nemeth
www.adamnemeth.com
Leroy Neiman
www.leroyneiman.com
No Bull Sports
www.nobullsports.com
Steve Novella
www.megalink.net/~damone/home.html
Official Stuff
www.officialstuff.com

Ondeck Sports
www.ondecksports.com
Oriole's Trading Post
www.geocities.com/Colosseum/5115
Osports
www.osports.com
Bob Pace's Boxing Memorabilia
www.bobpaceboxing.com
Paladins
www.paladins.com
Pastime Portfolio Collection Inc.
www.pastime-portfolio.com
Past Time Sports
www.coachhelp.com/ptsports.htm
PC Sports Inc.
www.pcsportsinc.com
Perfect Image
www.wwcd.com/pimage
Phil's Collectibles
www.sportsillustrateds.com
Port Sports
www.portsports.net
Quality Autographs and
Memorabilia of Virginia Inc.
www.qualityautographs.com
Rainbow Card Co.
www.rainbowcardco.com
Real Deal Memorabilia
www.realdealmemorabilia.com
Real Legends.com
www.reallegends.com
Recollectics
www.presspins.com
James J. Reeves
www.jamesjreeves.com
Retro-Sports
www.retro-sports.com
Rick's Coin Shop
www.rickscoinshop.com
Riverwood Gallery
www.riverwoodgallery.com
Romito Enterprises
www.romito.com
Alan Rosen
www.mrmint.com
R&R Collectibles
www.joedimaggioestate.com
707 Sportscards
www.707sportscards.com
SLS Sports
www.slssports.com
Spectator Sportcards
www.spectatorsportscards.com
James Spence Vintage Autographs
www.jspence.com
Sportan Direct
www.sportandirect.com
Sport Card Heaven Inc.
www.sportcardheaven.com
Sport Collectibles and Supplies
www.sportcollectibles.com
SportsCards Plus
www.sportscardsplus.com

Sports Center Collectibles
www.sccol.com
Sports Collectibles Inc.
www.spcollect.com
Sportsend
www.sportsend.com
The Sports Gallery
www.sports-gallery.com
Sports Investments International
www.air23.com
Sportsman's Park
www.members.spree.com/sip/sportspark/
home.htm
Sports Pages International
www.headlineclassics.com
SportsPro Marketing Inc.
www.sportspromarketing.com
Sportstop
www.sportstop.net
Stan the Man Inc.
www.stan-the-man.com
Stan "The Man" Sportscards
www.stanthemansportscards.com
Star Box
www.starbox.com
Steiner Sports Memorabilia
www.steinersports.com
Jim Stinson Sports
www.stinsonsports.com
Strictly Mint
www.smcci.com
Superstar Greetings
www.superstargreetings.net
Supercards
www.supercards.net
Ed Taylor's Baseball Dreams
www.petemaravich.com
T.C. Card Co.
www.tccardco.com
Team Wear Athletic
www.teamwearathletic.com
Texas Sportcard Co.
www.txsportcard.com
Trademark Sportscards
www.trademarksportscards.com
Trendco Inc.
www.trendco.com
TNT Collectibles
www.nb.net/~tntcoll
Trading Card Source
www.tradingcardsource.com
T-Rex Collectibles
www.trexcard.com
Triple Threat Cards
www.ttcards.com
Truly Unique Collectibles
www.uniquecollectibles.com
Trumpets East
www.calltrumpets.com
V & J Cards
www.psafootball.com
Vintage Baseball Cards
vintagebbcards.tripod.com
Visionary Art Inc./James Fiorentino
www.jamesfiorentino.com

VP Sport
www.vpsport.com
Wall of Fame
www.walloffame.com
Wallos.com
www.wallos.com
Gary Walter Baseball Cards
www.garywalterbaseballcards.com
Scott Welkowsky
www.scottwelkowsky.com
Mike Wheat Cards
www.mikewheatcards.com/index.htm
Les Wolff
members.aol.com/lwolff1823
When It Was A Game
www.wiwag.com
Wright Plaque
www.wrightplaque.com
Yankee Doodle Sports Products
www.yddsp.com
Kit Young Cards
www.kityoung.com
Zindler's Baseball Card Co.
www.zindlers.com

Halls of Fame/Sports Museums

Alabama Sports Hall of Fame
www.tech-comm.com/ashof
American Sportscasters Association
Hall of Fame
www.americansportscasters.com
Paul W. Bryant Museum
www.ua.edu/bryant.htm
Canadian Golf Hall of Fame
www.cghf.org
Ty Cobb Museum
www.tycobbmuseum.org
College Football Hall of Fame
hof@CollegeFootball.org
Bob Feller Museum
www.bobfellermuseum.org
Georgia Golf Hall of Fame
www.gghf.org
Green Bay Packers Hall of Fame
www.packershalloffame.com
Hockey Hall of Fame
www.hhof.com
International Bowling Hall of Fame
www.bowlingmuseum.com
International Boxing Hall of Fame
www.ibhof.com
International Tennis Hall of Fame
www.tennisfame.org
Kansas Sports Hall of Fame
www.kshof.org
Kentucky Derby Museum
www.derbymuseum.org
Louisiana Sports Hall of Fame
www.lasportshof.com
Louisville Slugger Museum
www.slugger.com/museum
MCI National Sports Gallery
www.mcicenter.com

Naismith Memorial Basketball Hall
of Fame
www.hoophall.com
National Baseball Hall of Fame
www.baseballhalloffame.org
National Soccer Hall of Fame
www.soccerhall.org
Oklahoma Sports Museum
www.oksports.qpg.com
Pennsylvania Sports Hall of Fame
www.pasportshalloffame.com
Pro Football Hall of Fame
www.profootballhof.com
Cal Ripken Museum
www.ripkenmuseum.com
Rose Bowl Hall of Fame
www.tournamentofroses.com/rbhallof-
fame.htm
Babe Ruth Museum
www.baberuthmuseum.com
St. Louis Cardinals Hall of Fame
www.stlcardinals.com
Sports Museum of Champions
www.independencebowl.org/museum
United States Hockey Hall of Fame
www.ushockeyhall.com
Ted Williams Museum and Hitters
Hall of Fame
www.twmuseum.com

Hobby Supplies/Software

Absolute Best Acrylics
www.acrylics.com
All Sports Labels
www.allsportslabels.com
APBA Card Collector 6.0
www.APBAgames.com
A Pro Image Sports Supply
www.aproimagess.com
Atfab
www.atfabcompany.com
BCW Supplies
www.bcwsupplies.com
Lin Terry
www.linterry.com
LK2 Card Collecting Software
www.lk2.com
Memories on Display
www.memoriesondisplay.qpg.com
Pennzoni Display Co.
www.displayco.com
Pick-N-Click Software
www.cardsoftware.com
Rembrandt/Ultra Pro
www.ultra-pro.com
Showcase Your Collectibles
www.showcaseshowplace.com
Sportan Direct
www.sportandirect.com
Sports Fulfillment
www.sportsfulfillment.com

Memorabilia Manufacturers

APBA
www.apbastadium.com
www.apbagames.com
Classic Collectible Products
www.ccpweb.com
Cooperstown Bat Co.
www.cooperstownbat.com
Crown Pro
www.crownpro.com
Enviromint
www.enviromint.com
Equity Marketing/Headliners
www.headliners.com
Famous Fixins
www.famousfixins.com
www.celebrityfixins.com
Fotoball USA
www.fotoball.com
Bill Goff/Good Sports Art
www.goodsportsart.com
Hasbro
www.hasbrocollectors.com
Harris Management Group
www.reggiejackson.com
Limited Treasures
www.limitedtreasures.com
Mattel
www.mattelhoops.com
Nikco Sports
www.nikcosports.com
Photo File
www.photofile.com
PLB Sports
www.plbsports.com
www.vpsport.com
Revolving Rainbow
www.bobbinbobbers.com
Romito Inc.
www.romito.com
Salvino's Bammers
www.salvinos.com
SAMAC
www.bobbing.com
Sierra Sun Editions
www.sierrasuneditions.com
Silk Road Gifts
www.silkroadgifts.com
Southland Art Castings
www.southlandartcastings.com
Southland Plastics
www.southlandplastics.com
Sport Collectors Guild
www.replicastadiums.com
White Rose Collectibles
www.whterose.com
Upper Deck Authenticated
www.udauthenticated.com
USAopoly
www.usaopoly.com

Players/Coaches

Auto Racing
John Andretti
www.pettyracing.com/andretti/index.html
Johnny Benson
www.johnnybenson-fanclub.com
Brett Bodine
www.brettbodine.com
Geoffrey Bodine
www.GeoffBodineFanClub.com
Jeff Burton
www.jeffburton.com
Derrike Cope
www.derrikecope.com
Wally Dallenbach
www.wallydallenbach.net
Bill Elliott
www.billelliottracing.com
Scott Gaylord
www2.privatei.com/~gaylord/
Jeff Gordon
www.jeffgordon.com
David Green
www.lhms.com
Chad Little
www.chadlittle.com
Dave Marcis
www.marcisracing.com
Sterling Marlin
www.sterlingmarlin.net
Mark Martin
www.jmarexpress.com
Steve Park
www.steve-park.com
Kyle Petty
www.kylepetty.com
Robert Pressley
www.robertpressley77.com
Ricky Rudd
www.rickyrudd.com
Elliott Sadler
www.sadlerfanclub.com/Elliott
Tony Stewart
www.tonystewart.com
Rusty Wallace
www.rustywallace.net
Darrell Waltrip
www.dw17.com
Jimmy Vasser
www.vasser.com

Baseball
Dusty Baker
www.dustybaker.com
Derek Bell
www.hit14.com
Johnny Bench
www.johnnybench.com
Yogi Berra/LTD Enterprises
www.yogi-berra.com
Tom Candiotti
www.tomcandiotti.com

Steve Carlton
www.carlton32.com
Roger Clemens
www.rocketroger.com
Roberto Clemente
www.robertoclemente21.com
Ty Cobb
www.cmgww.com/baseball/cobb/cobb.html
Rollie Fingers
www.fingers34.com
Whitey Ford – Whitey's
www.whitey-ford.com
Dwight Gooden
www.dwightgooden.com
"Shoeless" Joe Jackson
www.cmgww.com/baseball/jackson/jackson.html
Reggie Jackson
www.reggiejackson.com
Geoff Jenkins
www.geoffjenkins.com
Mike Lieberthal
www.lieberthal.com
Roger Maris
www.rogermaris.com
Don Mattingly
www.don-mattingly.com
Willie McGee
www.williemcgee.com
Stan Musial
www.stan-the-man.com
C.J. Nitkowski
www.cjbaseball.com
Paul O'Neill
www.pauloneill21.com
Chan Ho Park
www.chanhopark61.com
Cal Ripken Jr.
www.2131.com
Rick Reed
www.vvm.com/~dthacker/reed.html
Robin Roberts
www.robinrobertswhizkid.com
Alex Rodriguez
www.arod.com
Pete Rose
www.peterose.com
Babe Ruth
www.baberuth.com
Nolan Ryan
www.nolanryan34.com
Ozzie Smith
www.ozziesmith.com
Darryl Strawberry
www.dstrawberry.com
Jim Thome
www.teamthome.com
Omar Vizquel
www.omarvizquel.com/ov.html
Honus Wagner
www.cmgww.com/baseball/honus/honus.html
Ted Williams
www.tedwilliams.com

Steve Woodard
www.stevewoodard.com
Carl Yastrzemski
www.yaz8.com

Basketball
Vince Carter
www.vincecarter15.com
Tim Duncan
www.slamduncan.com
Brian Grant
www.briangrant44.com
A.C. Green
www.acgreen.com
Grant Hill
www.granthill.com
Michael Jordan
www.jordan.sportsline.com
Bobby Knight
www.coachbobknight.com
Shaquille O'Neal
www.shaq.com
David Robinson
www.theadmiral.com
Dennis Rodman
www.lonestar.texas.net/~pmagal/rodman.html
Damon Stoudamire
www.stoudamire.com
Rasheed Wallace
www.rasheedwallace.com
Bill Walton
www.billwalton.com

Biking
Lance Armstrong
www.lancearmstrong.com

Boxing
Oscar De La Hoya
www.oscardelahoya.com
Lennox Lewis
www.lennoxlewis.com

Figure Skating
Tara Lipinski
www.taralipinski.com
Kristi Yamaguchi
www.promotions.yahoo.com/promotions/kristi/

Football
Darren Bennett
www.nflaussie.com
Derrick Brooks
www.hit55.com
Robert Brooks
www.robertbrooks.com
Gilbert Brown
www.sackcity.com/index.htm
Mark Brunell
www.mark-brunell.com
Dick Butkus
www.dickbutkus.com

Santana Dotson
www.santanadotson.com
Marshall Faulk
www.marshallfaulk.rivals.com
Darrell Green
www.darrellgreen.com
Charlie Jones
www.82mph.com
Jim Kelly
www.jimkelly.com
Vince Lombardi
www.cmgww.com/football/lombardi
Joe Montana
www.joemontanafanclub.com
Joe Namath
www.sportsline.com/u/fans/celebrity/namath/index.html
Warren Sapp
www.big99.com
Junior Seau
www.juniorseau.org
Jason Sehorn
www.sehorn.com

Golf
Craig Barlow
www.craigbarlow.com
Fred Couples
www.lisinc.net/fred/
Ben Crenshaw
www.bencrenshaw.com
John Daly
www.gripitandripit.com
Ernie Els
www.ernieels.com
Raymond Floyd
www.rayfloyd.com
Lisa Ann Horst
www.horstnet.com/lisa_ann/
Jeff Maggert
www.teamgolf.com/
Casey Martin
www.thehartford.com/corporate/special/casey.html
Spike McRoy
www.spikeweb.com
Phil Mickelson
www.phil-mickelson.com/main.nsf
Greg Norman
www.shark.com/
Jack Nicklaus
www.nicklaus.com/index1.shtml
Arnold Palmer
www.arnoldpalmer.com/default2.htm
Gary Player
www.garyplayer.com/
Chi Chi Rodriguez
www.chichi.org
Jean Van de Velde
www.allezjean.com
Tiger Woods
www.tigerwoods.com

Gymnasts
Vanessa Atler
www.atler.com
Katie Lynn McFarland
www.geocities.com/Colosseum/Track/1966/
Alexandra Marinescu
www.asterisk.simplenet.com/marinescu/
Lavinia Milosovici
www.milosovici.com

Hockey
Ray Bourque
www.raybourque.com
Martin Brodeur
www.mbrodeur.com
Gordie Howe
www.mrhockey.com

Multiple Player
Athletes Direct.com
www.athletesdirect.com
MLB Players Choice
www.bigleaguers.com
NHL Players Association
www.nhlpa.com
NFL Players Inc
www.nflplayers.com
Rivals.com
www.rivals.com

Soccer
Michelle Akers
www.michelleakers.com
Mia Hamm
www.miahamm.com

Tennis
Michael Chang
www.mchang.com
Martina Hingis
www.geocities.com/Colosseum/Field/8888/martina.html
Venus and Serena Williams
www.thewilliamssisters.com

Track
Donovan Bailey
www.donovanbailey.com
Suzy Favor Hamilton
www.suzyfavorhamilton.com

Professional Leagues

American Basketball Association
www.remembertheABA.com
Major League Baseball
www.majorleaguebaseball.com
Major League Soccer
www.mlsnet.com
NASCAR
www.nascar.com
National Basketball Association
www.nba.com

National Football League
www.nfl.com
National Hockey League
www.nhl.com
United States Football League
www.geocities.com/Colosseum/Field/8520
Women's National Basketball Association
www.wnba.com
World Football League Hall of Fame
www.welcome.to/wflhalloffame

Sports Collectors Magazines

Krause Publications
www.fantasysportsmag.com
www.sportscollectorsdigest.com
www.tuffstuffonline.com

Beckett
www.beckett.com
Boxing Collectors' News
www.boxingcollectors.com

Show Promoters/Shows

A Gloria Rothstein Show Inc.
www.grshows.com
Atlantique City
www.atlantiquecity.com
The Autograph Zone
www.autographzone.com
B&L Sports Memorabilia
www.b-n-lsports.com
Central New York Promotions
www.cnypromotions.com
Collectors' Showcase of America
www.csashows.com
Gibraltar Trade Center Inc.
www.gibraltartrade.com
International Collectibles Exposition
www.collectibleshow.com
J.Paul Sports Promotions Inc.
www.jpaulsports.com
Krause Publications
www.krause.com/shows
National Sports Collectors Convention
www.thenational.net
Signings Hotline
www.signingshotline.com
Sport Card and Memorabilia Expo
www.sportcardexpo.com
SportsFest
www.sportsfestshow.com
St. Louis Sports Collectors Inc.
www.stlsportscollectors.com
Sports Collectibles of Houston
www.ghg.net/spocoho
Star Shows.com
www.starshows.com
Toronto Sportscard/Memorabilia Expo
www.sportcardexpo.com
Tri-Star Productions Inc.
www.tristarproductions.com
World Wide Show.com
www.worldwideshow.com

Sports Memorabilia Insurance

Cornell and Finkelmeier Inc.
www.cf-insurance.com
Jireh
www.jireh.com

Internet Consulting

Right Click Solutions Inc
www.sportscardswww.com

Just For Fun

Baseball
The Baseball Archive
www.baseball1.com
Baseball Heckle Depot
www.heckledepot.com
Negro Leagues
www.blackbaseball.com
Total Baseball
www.totalsports.com/baseball
Wiffle Ball
www.wiffleball.com

Basketball
Kobe Bryant Central
www.geocities.com/kbcentral2000
Los Chucks OnHoops
www.onhoops.com
Net Guide
www.netguide.com/guide/sports/nba.html
All the NBA Links in the World
www.clayvision.net/nbalinks/

Football
The Huddle
www.thehuddle.com
NFL Fans
www.nflfans.com
NFL Talk
www.nfltalk.com
Pro Football Weekly
www.profootballweekly.com
Super Bowl
www.superbowl.com

Golf
The Golf Channel
www.thegolfchannel.com
Golf.com
www.golf.com
LPGA
www.lpga.com
The Masters
www.masters.org
PGA
www.pga.com
Virtual Golfer
www.golfball.com

Hockey
In the Crease
www.inthecrease.com
Total Hockey
www.totalhockey.com

Wrestlers
Steve Austin
http://www.stonecold.com
King Kong Bundy
http://www.kingkongbundy.com/
Ted DiBiase
http://www.milliondollarman.com/
Verne Gagne
http://www.awawrestling.com
Goldberg
http://www.jackhammer.net
Bret Hart
http://www.brethart.net/
Bobby "The Brain" Heenan
http://www.bobbythebrain.com/
The Honky Tonk Man
http://www.wrestlingnation.com/honky/
Jerry Lawler
http://www.kinglawler.com/
Rena Mero
http://www.RenaMero.com
Kevin Nash
http://www.kevinbigsexynash.com/
Diamond Dallas Page
http://www.thediamondmine.com/
Ken Patera
http://www.tcguide.com/kenpatera/
Harley Race
http://www.harleyrace.com/
Jake "The Snake" Roberts
http://www.jakethesnakeroberts.com
The Rock
http://www.TheRock.com
Macho Man Randy Savage
http://www.machoman.com
The Original Sheik
http://www.primenet.com/-ferante
Jimmy Superfly Snuka
http://www.superflysnuka.com
Ricky "The Dragon" Steamboat
http://www.ricksteamboat.com/
George "The Animal" Steele
http://www.georgesteele.com
The Undertaker (comic book)
http://www.theundertaker.net/
Jesse Ventura
http://www.jesseventura.com/
The Ultimate Warrior
http://www.ultimatewarrior.com/
Torrie Wilson
http://www.torriewilson.com

Wrestling Organizations

WWF
www.wwf.com
WCW
www.wcw.com

Let The Experts Guide The Way

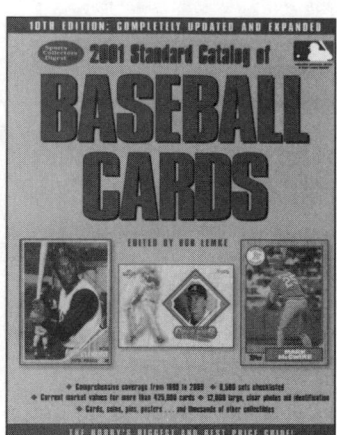

2001 Standard Catalog of® Baseball Cards
10th Edition
edited by Bob Lemke
Loaded with more than 425,000 cards from 1869 through early 2000 releases, the Standard Catalog can take your collecting skills to new levels. You'll depend on the more than 600,000 accurate, real-world prices when making crucial buying and selling decisions (each individually reviewed, updated and reverified for accuracy). And the more than 12,000 large clear photos of card fronts and backs will help you identify and grade your own cards.
Softcover • 8-1/2 x 11 • 1,664 pages
12,000+ b&w photos
Item# SB10 • $39.95

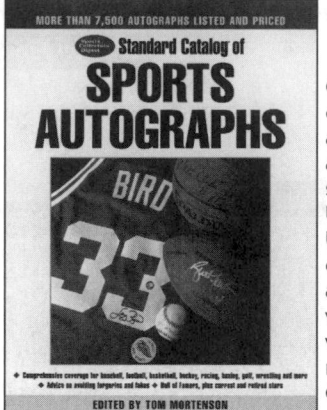

Standard Catalog of® Sports Autographs
edited by Tom Mortenson
Confidence is everything when it comes to buying and selling autographs. Now you can buy and sell autographs from current and retired stars, plus hall-of-famers from football, basketball, baseball, hockey, racing, boxing, golf, wrestling and more with complete confidence. More than 7,500 autographs, each individually priced with more than 700 large, clear photos will aid you in identification and determining authenticity. Includes listings for Official Major League, World Series and commemorative baseballs.
Softcover • 8-1/2 x 11 • 160 pages
700+ b&w photos
Item# SPAU1 • $21.95

2001 Standard Catalog of® Basketball Cards
4th Edition
From the Price Guide Editors of *Sports Collectors Digest*
More than 125,000 cards from 1948 to 2000 are checklisted and priced to help you collect smarter and faster. More than 900 sets from all the top manufacturers are listed including Topps, Fleer, Score, Pacific, Upper Deck, SkyBox, Hoops and more. NBA, WNBA, CBA, college, regional, Olympic, food sets and more are completely covered. This edition includes a certified card price guide, autograph price guide and complete pricing for Kenner Starting Lineup and other figurines.
Softcover • 8-1/2 x 11 • 368 pages • 1,500+ b&w photos
Item# SCBC4 • $21.95

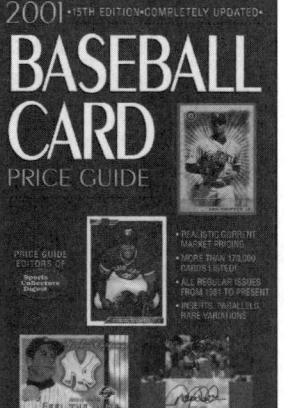

Standard Catalog of® Minor League Baseball Cards
edited by Bob Lemke
Trace the careers of your favorite stars from before Ty Cobb to today's starters in the most complete source for Minor League baseball cards ever published. Information on card quantities and rare issues are only found in this volume. Included are more than 40,000 players and 3,200 team sets, some going back to the 1880s. Listings are priced in up to three different grades. Special sections list all minor league cards for 50 of today's top major league stars. A great guide for baseball fans of all ages.
Softcover • 8-1/2 x 11 • 432 pages
400 b&w photos
Item# SG02 • $24.95

2001 Standard Catalog of® Football Cards
4th Edition
From the Price Guide Editors of *Sports Collectors Digest*
More than 325,000 cards from 2,300 sets put you in the red zone for collecting success. NFL, CFL, USFL, WLAF, college and food issues are all here. Plus you'll get a certified card price guide, an autograph price guide and a complete listing with prices for Kenner Starting Lineup and other popular figurines. Cards from 1894 to present from Topps, Fleer, SkyBox, Upper Deck, Pinnacle, Score, Pacific, Press Pass, Bowman, Sage and many more.
Softcover • 8-1/2 x 11 • 528 pages • 2,200+ b&w photos
Item# SCFC4 • $22.95

2001 Baseball Card Price Guide
15th Edition
by the Price Guide Editors of *Sports Collectors Digest*
With so many new cards, inserts and new sets, it's almost impossible to keep up with it all! Until now. Let the new edition of the 2001 Baseball Card Price Guide take control of your collection with more than 175,000 cards checklisted and priced! That's every card, insert and base card from 1981 through 2001. Plus, you'll have more than 2,000 large, clear photos at your fingertips to help you identify your favorite cards and players. Every price has been evaluated by staff members of Sports Collectors Digest, the industry's leading experts.
Softcover • 6 x 9 • 888 pages • 2,000+ b&w photos
Item# BP15 • $16.95

To place a credit card order or for a FREE all-product catalog call
800-258-0929 Offer SPB1
M-F 7am - 8pm • Sat 8am - 2pm, CST

Krause Publications, Offer SPB1
P.O. Box 5009, Iola WI 54945-5009
www.krausebooks.com

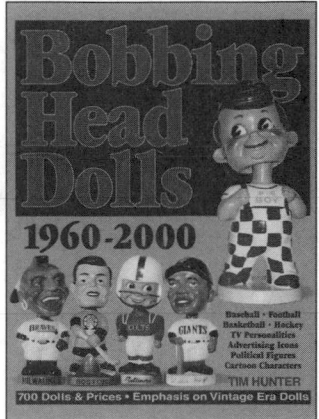

Bobbing Head Dolls
1960-2000
by Tim Hunter

This first-ever price and identification guide features hundreds of dolls, including: baseball, football, basketball, hockey, TV stars, advertising icons, political figures and cartoon characters. You'll learn how to identify which series a doll is from, if it's a rare variation, and how much it's worth. Do you have the common Houston Astros doll worth $80 or the scarce Astros version with the shooting star decal priced at $700? With over 250 photos and 700 individual listings, you're sure to find values for the dolls in your collection.

Softcover • 8-1/2 x 11 • 160 pages
250+ b&w photos • 30+ color photos
Item# BOBHD • $19.95

Antique Golf Collectibles
A Price and Reference Guide, 2nd Edition
by Chuck Furjanic

Everything you need to know about golf and golf collectibles is in this photo-packed, information-filled book. Updated with hundreds of additional items and new chapters on golf bags and tips on buying and selling golf collectibles. Includes thousands of listings, including three different value grades and historical backgrounds on products and manufacturers.

Softcover • 8-1/2 x 11
408 pages
500 b&w photos • 50 color photos
Item# GOLF3 • $29.95

The Encyclopedia of Professional Wrestling
100 Years of the Good, the Bad and the Collectible
by Kristian Pope and Ray Whebbe Jr.

Professional wrestling remains one of the hottest forms of entertainment in the world and this book covers the most notable events in the sport's history and features the greatest stars of the ring. This all-color book includes 400 photos, along with history, interviews, a listing of every professional wrestler (including ring name, when they wrestled and crowns won), commentary on title changes, sold-out arenas, fans and behind-the-scenes drama, and a "collector's corner" in each chapter that highlights the top wrestling collectibles available on the market.

Softcover • 8-1/4 x 10-7/8
176 pages • 400 color photos
Item# EPWRE • $21.95

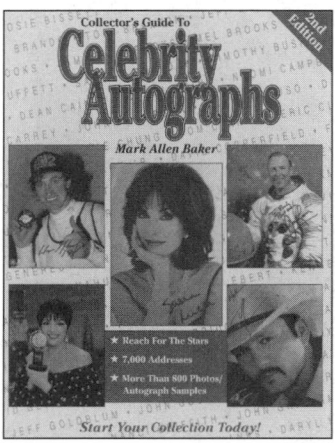

Collector's Guide to Celebrity Autographs
2nd Edition
by Mark Allen Baker

Flood your mailbox with autographs...or obtain them in person. Mark Allen Baker packs more than 30 years of autograph collecting experience into the second edition of this bestselling guide. With more than 7,000 listings and updated addresses, this new edition features a reader-friendly checklist and an author's choice symbol to guide you to great responders. Addresses include stars of the screen, stage and TV, heads of state, sports stars and other people of cultural significance.

Softcover • 8-1/2 x 11 • 352 pages
900+ b&w photos
Item# CAU2 • $24.95

Professional Wrestling Collectibles
by Kristian Pope & Ray Whebbe Jr.

Packed with 400 color photos and hundreds of wrestling-related items including dolls and figures, autographs, photographs, games, videos, and more-all identified and valued for the first time in one book. Along with the major stars of the World Wrestling Federation and World Championship Wrestling-Goldberg, "Stone Cold" Steve Austin, Kevin Nash and Hulk Hogan-the book also features international stars of the ring.

Softcover • 8-1/4 x 10-7/8
160 pages • 400+ color photos
Item# PWRES • $21.95

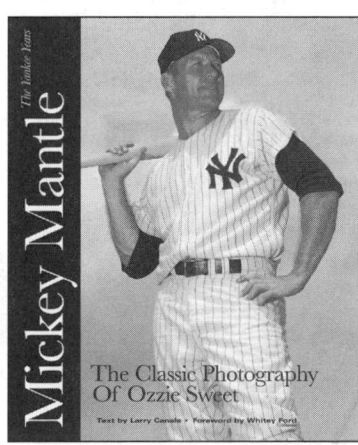

Mickey Mantle, The Yankee Years
The Classic Photography of Ozzie Sweet
Text by Larry Canale, Foreword by Whitey Ford

Nearly covering "The Mick's" entire career as a Yankee, the portraits, taken by Ozzie Sweet, appear in chronological order along with short anecdotes an summaries of Mantle's achievements. Includes photos of Yankee cohorts like Joe DiMaggio, Roger Maris and Yogi Berra.

Hardcover • 10 x 12
224 pages
20 b&w photos • 100 color photos
Item# AT5218 • $39.95